lonely planet

Malaysia, Singapore & Brunei

Chris Rowthorn
David Andrew
Paul Hellander
Clem Lindenmayer

Malaysia, Singapore & Brunei

7th edition

Published by
Lonely Planet Publications
Head Office: PO Box 617, Hawthorn, Vic 3122, Australia
Branches: 150 Linden Street, Oakland CA 94607, USA
10a Spring Place, London NW5 3BH, UK
1 rue du Dahomey, 75011 Paris, France

Printed by SNP Printing Pte Ltd
Printed in Singapore

Photographs by

David Andrew
Glenn Beanland
Mary Ann Hemphill
Clem Lindenmayer
Arasu Ramasamy
Susan Storm
Tony Wheeler
Michael Aw
Paul Beinssen
Patrick Horton
Richard Nebesky
Simon Rowe
Sue Tan
Ross Barnett
Paul Hellander
Richard I'Anson
Raffles Hotel
Chris Rowthorn
Tourism Malaysia

Many of the images in this guide are available for licensing from Lonely Planet Images.
email: lpi@lonelyplanet.com.au

Front cover: Roof detail, Chang See Shu Yuen Temple, Kuala Lumpur. (Chris Rowthorn)

First Published
May 1982

This Edition
February 1999

ISBN 0 86442 618 6

Chris Rowthorn

Chris was born in England and grew up in the USA. After graduation, he dabbled in several fields before moving to Japan on a whim. Upon finding that teaching English was not his dream job, he picked up the pen and started writing, first for the *Japan Times* and then for Lonely Planet. Before working on this book as coordinating author, he contributed to Lonely Planet's *Japan* and *Tokyo*. He has travelled extensively in South-East Asia, Europe and North America. When he's not travelling, he spends his time doing in-depth research on Kyoto's nightlife.

David Andrew

After stints as a public servant, restaurant manager and research assistant, David decided there are few things in life more fun than birdwatching and travelling. He started *Wingspan*, Australia's first magazine for birdwatchers; edited *Wildlife Australia* for a time; started another bird magazine, *Australian Birding*; then started work at Lonely Planet as an editor. In his spare time he travels around the world looking for rare wildlife and attempting to paint it. David updated the Flora & Fauna section and the East Malaysia and Brunei chapters for this edition.

Paul Hellander

Paul has never really stopped travelling since he was born in England to a Norwegian father and English mother. He arrived in Australia in 1977, via Greece and 30 other countries. He then taught Modern Greek and trained interpreters and translators for thirteen years before throwing it all away for a life as a travel writer. Paul joined Lonely Planet in 1994 and wrote our *Greek phrasebook* before being assigned to *Greece* and *Eastern Europe*. Paul's first assignment in Asia was to update the information on Singapore for *South-East Asia, Singapore city guide* and *Malaysia, Singapore & Brunei*, and was last heard of heading for Israel. He can be reached at paul@planetmail.net.

Clem Lindenmayer

Clem helped update the Peninsular Malaysia section of this book. Clem's strong interest in languages led him to study Asian studies with a major in Mandarin, interrupted by repeated bouts of lengthy travel. A keen mountain-goer, Clem researched and authored Lonely Planet's *Trekking in the Patagonian Andes* and *Walking in Switzerland*, and will be a coauthor of our forthcoming *Hiking in the USA*. He has previously also worked on the *China*, *Western Europe* and *Scandanavian Europe* guidebooks.

From the Authors

Chris Rowthorn

I would like to thank Chiori Matsunaga, Florence Gusti, Ben Soo, Zurina Susan Binti Abdullah, Chan Mun Onn, Helena Thomas, Omar Bentris, Chandra Sehgaran, Razaleigh Zainal, Alex Lee YP, Dr Jeevan Sellappah, Nurul Huda Rahim, Roselan Hanafiah, Shariff Abdullah, Zub Noor, Bruno Fehrenbach, Thomas of Mersing, John Carlson, Anna Astrom and Stefan Bjorn.

David Andrew

I am indebted to many people for their willing help in updating the Sarawak, Sabah and Brunei chapters of this book. In particular Mr Sim of Hornbill's Corner Cafe, Kuching, for his fine draught beer and candid views on life in Sarawak; Guy Pilcher-Clayton, Dave Bennet and Dina for helping me investigate the night life of Miri; John and Karen Tarawe for their hospitality in Bario; Ann Otigil of Innoprise Corporation, Sabah; Haji Ahmad Bin Datuk Haji Mohd Kassim of the Australian consulate in KK; and, for allowing me to tap into their 1st class information networks, Hilda Benidip-Chong of Tourism Malaysia and Molly HJ Johar of the Sarawak Tourist Association. Thanks also to all the travellers I met along the way for their comments, complaints and tips that helped to make this a better book. And back in Australia, special thanks are owed to Jim Truscott of SASR for providing maps of the Kelabit Highlands; Doug Laing of the Department of Foreign Affairs and Trade, Canberra; and to my partner, Robyn, for putting up with me during the long weeks of writing.

Paul Hellander

During a frenetic and more often than not hot and sticky five weeks of wandering the streets of Singapore and the near neighbours of Malaysia and the Riau Islands in Indonesia, several people come to mind who should be thanked: Elaine Lim of the Singapore Tourism Board and the Sydney office of the STB for a wealth of printed material; Véronique le Petit for her constant stream of tips and advice on eating places and homey hospitality; Evan Jones of Batam for a very helpful lowdown on the Riaus; the efficient and public-spirited people of Singapore for their interest in and assistance with my research while in their country; my wife, Stella, for her continuing support and willingness to hold the fort; and finally Hup Yick for inspiration. My work, as ever, is dedicated to my sons, Marcus and Byron, who may one day take inspiration from their father's wanderings.

Clem Lindenmayer

I would like to thank the staff at tourist offices in the cities I researched for their help.

This Book

The 1st edition of this guide was written by Geoff Crowther and Tony and Maureen Wheeler. Research for the 2nd edition was handled by Mark Lightbody. The 3rd edition was the joint effort of Sue Tan and Joe Cummings. Hugh Finlay and Peter Turner updated the 4th and 5th editions. For the 6th edition, Peter Turner covered Singapore and most of Peninsular Malaysia and Chris Taylor covered Sabah, Sarawak and Brunei, as well as the east coast of the peninsula.

From the Publisher

This 7th edition of *Malaysia, Singapore & Brunei* was produced in Lonely Planet's Melbourne office. Brigitte Ellemor coordinated the editing, with assistance from Michelle Coxall, Tony Davidson, Paul Harding and Kristin Odijk. Anna Judd was responsible for the mapping and design, with cartographic assistance from Tim Fitzgerald. Anna and Trudi Canavan provided the illustrations, and Jamieson Gross designed the cover. Thanks to Leonie Mugavin for verifying flight and embassy details; Tim Fitzgerald for hands-on Quark supervision; Tim Uden for Quark expertise; Quentin Frayne for the Language chapter; Richard Gregg for cycling knowledge; and Greg Alford for keeping up with political and economic developments.

Warning & Request

Things change – prices go up, schedules change, good places go bad and bad places go bankrupt – nothing stays the same. So, if you find things better or worse, recently opened or long since closed, please tell us and help make the next edition even more accurate and useful.

We value all of the feedback we receive from travellers. Julie Young coordinates a small team who read and acknowledge every letter, postcard and email, and ensure every morsel of information finds its way to the appropriate authors, editors and publishers.

Everyone who writes to us will find their name in the next edition of the appropriate guide and will also receive a free subscription to our quarterly newsletter, *Planet Talk*. The very best contributions will be rewarded with a free Lonely Planet guide.

Excerpts from your correspondence may appear in new editions of this guide; in our newsletter, *Planet Talk*; or in updates on our Web site – so please let us know if you don't want your letter published or your name acknowledged.

Thanks

Thanks to the many travellers who wrote in with helpful hints, useful advice and interesting anecdotes.

Albert & Sara, Shirley Abdullah, Sarah Anderson, Mark Anderson, Alice Aruthan, Jorg Ausfelt

David Bachmann, Joy Barlow, Shibu Basheer, Jocelyn Bateman, Peter Beglin, John Beilinski, Walter Berry, JP Bingham, Andre Barneveld Binkhuysen, A Birsa, Steve Black, Blinky, Alastair Blois-Brooke, M Blyth, Oliver Boedeker, Andy Bolas, Harry & Cisca Bos, Martin Bottenberg, Sarah Bowen, MJ Branch, Paul Brinkhof, Ian & Leslie Brodie, Naomi Brown, Colin Brown, Kevin Browning, Susan Bucciero, Tara Buckley, Leila Buijs, Rebecca Burdon, Lachlan Burnet, Michelle Butt, Joshua Button

Lea Campbell, Fernando Campos, Alberto Fontanillo Carrascal, Xavier Cazauran, Kym Channell, Sara & Charlotta, Tanei Chea, Nam Whue Chin, Joelynn Chin, Chris Chin, D Chong, Francis Chu, Ken Chye, Basil Condos, Grace Conrad, Bruce Cook, Stuart Cooke, Linda Cooper, David Cozy, Steve Crocker, Kevin Cunningham, Lee Ann Cunningham, Susan Curry

Ake Dahllof, Tamatha Darcey, Paisley Davidson, Isobel Davie, Belinda Davis, J Dawson, Jean & Mike Day, Derham Daymond, A Decalande, CB Denning, Peter Derrick, Naomi & Allan Dickinson, Mvan Dijk, Francis Dix, Matjaz Dolenc, Suzanne Donnelly, Ailsa J Donnelly, Tg Dora, Roger Doswell, Uta Dressen, Kirsten Dreyer, Milly Dudley-Owen, Duffy, GE Duffy, Dr RA Duncan, Pat Duncan, Jennifer Dunkley, K Duss, RJ Dyer

Matt Ebiner, Gijs Edelbroek, Sigi Edwards, Bob Ennis, Svend Erik Hansen, Patrik Eriksson, Sheila Eustace, Lisa Evans

Michael Fastenberg, Bruno Fehrenbach, Alan & Pam Fey, Stephen Fine, David Fitzmaurice, Zoe Fletcher, Ed Fogden, Joseph Fonte, Paul Fowler, Michael Fox, Sister Frances Hayes, Philippe Le Francios, Alban Franckhauser, Mary Fraser, J Arthur Freed

Tony Gerber, Gerhard, Boyd Gilchrist, Dave Gile, Deepak Gill, Cath Gillespie, Katrina Gillespie, Tony Goring, Nicola Green, Ros Green, Cathryn Gregory, Scot Guenter Guy

Martin Hadley, Jenny & Richard Hall, Russell Hall, Rowena Harding, Robert Harrison, Hisham Hashim, Tom Haslam, Gaye Haworth, Mike Hemingway, Beverley Herbert, Peter Ho, Alicia Hock, Jo'an Hoh, Carol Holmes, Nigel Hoult, Hilary Hunt, Nazlina Hussin, Hutch, Laura & Ingrid

Gams Jager, Jessy, Paul Jefferson, Johan de Jong, Kari Jussila

Rachel Kahn, Robert Kalman, Bev & Paul Karlik, George E Kavanagh, Jens Kayser, T Keeper, M Kempinga, Alan Kendall, Herb Kieklak, Sarah Kilter, Pauline King, Azman King, L Kitter, Debra A Klein, Jurgen Kock, Jeff Kok, Lena Korsnes, Peter Kosin, Lee Ann Kosternik, M Kotvas, Geoff Kricker, Ann Krumboltz, Leong Pui Kun, Hew KW

Tim & Fleur Langmead, Paul Lawlor, Lynne Layton, Isabel Leader, Alan Lee, KP Lee, S Leitners, Robert Leverton, Therese Lillieskold, Charles Lim, Ruth Littlejohn, R Liyanapathirana, Eloise Lockhart, Ian Loftus, M Loo, Lee Choong Loong, Gabriel Loos, Peter Lowe, David Ludwig, JK Lumley-Holmes, David Luxon, Mercedes Luzan

Shan Lyn Ma, Hugh MacIndoe, Vicki Mackay, Sean MacPherson, Roland Magre, Stephen Malone, Nils Marchant, Steve Marcus, Lisa Martin, Melanie Martinez, LJ & KP Mazok, Bob McAuscand, Meira McBride, Amy McDonald, Stephen McElhinney, Dudley Mcfadden, Hilary McLeod, Craig McMillan, Bronwyn Mc-

Naughton, Chris Mead, Maureen Mecozzi, Robvan Megan, Tan Meng Chwen, Tony Messanger, Heidi Meyer, Julie Miller, Phil Miller, Jon Miller, Embong Mohamad, John Moline, Zsolt Molnar, Gary Moore, Bruce & Lorraine Moss, S Mubayi, Doug Muir, Cristin Murphy, Simon Kwag Myongjin

Terry Nakazono, Rowena Narding, Debby Neiuwenhuizen, Jerome & Pauline Netter, Anita Nogarotto, BJ Norden, Margaret Norman, Massimo Nuvina, Mimmo Nuvina

Stephan Oetiker, Hakan Olofsson, Deanna Ony, Cristina Osta

Patric Paccu, Dennis Paradine, Sharon Parsonson, Lamarque Paule, Ben Peacock, Rev & Mrs JC Pearson, Jon Pearson, BR Pearson, Paul D Pelczar, NG Phoon, Guy & Janet Pinneo, Ricky Pinto, Erik Plugge, Jens Poulsen, Anna Povey, Dale Power, Sree Prekash, WP Putter

Bob Radke, Thomas Ran, Petra Rautenberg, Nor Razab, MD Reardon, J Rebecca, Ralf Reinecke, Miro Reverby, Douglas Reynolds, Jennifer Rizzo, Murray Robbins, RE Roberts, Annette Rodley, Carlos Rodriguez, Andrea Rogge, Carolyn Rubens, Frances P Ryan

Wendy S, Isabel Sabugueiro, Haavard Saksvikronning, Nicci Salmon, Agus Sarta, Jade Saunders, Frederick Schneider, Herman Scholz, John Sclater, Kevin Scott, John Sharman, Denniss N Sharp, Julie Sheard, Norman Shepherd, Alan Sheridan, Nancy Shilepsky, Julie Simkins, Lene Simonsen, Amerjeet Singh, B Skiles, Sleemy, Tom de Smet, Henny Smit, Robyn Smith, Martin Smith, L Smith, George Smith, Hans Sondern, Marlijn Sonne, Gary Spinks, David Steinke, Eric Stenson, Jennifer Stepanik, Stephane, Inge Sterk, Karen Stevenson, Debs Stockwell, Janis Strom, Sheila Su-Borstelmann, A Sulkowski, Selvi Supramaniam, Kate Swinburn

BG Tan, Victor Teo, Steve & Anne Thew, Dr William L Thomas, Nicole Thomas, Arleen Thomas, Lisette Thresh, L Tombalakian, Hanni & Tony, Jim Truscott

Paul G Unterberg

Maureen & Roger Vanstone, Eddy van der Ven, Monty Vierra, Vincent, Pedro Vilata, Hans Visser, Glen Voice

Janet Walker, Wai Lun Wan, Ian Ward, Steven Wassall, S Watts, Natisha Weissig, Paul Wellington, Jennifer West, Yvonne Wester, Roger Wicks, Peter Williams, Sean D Williams, L Williams, George S Wilson, Gardiner J Wilson, Simon Wood, Victor Wood, F Wood, SD Woodhouse, Helen Woodward, Joyce Wu, Rob Wubben, Paul Wyatt

Contents

EAST MALAYSIA

SINGAPORE

BRUNEI

Map Legend

BOUNDARIES

- International Boundary
- Provincial Boundary
- Disputed Boundary

ROUTES

- A25 Freeway, with Route Number
- Major Road
- Minor Road
- Minor Road - Unsealed
- City Road
- City Street
- City Lane
- Train Route, with Station
- MRT Route, with Station
- Cable Car or Chairlift
- Ferry Route
- Walking Track

AREA FEATURES

- Building
- Cemetery
- Beach
- Market
- Park, Gardens
- Pedestrian Mall
- Reef
- Urban Area

HYDROGRAPHIC FEATURES

- Canal
- Coastline
- Creek, River
- Lake, Intermittent Lake
- Rapids, Waterfalls
- Salt Lake
- Swamp

SYMBOLS

- CAPITAL National Capital
- CAPITAL Provincial Capital
- CITY City
- Town Town
- Village Village

- Place to Stay
- Camping Ground
- Caravan Park
- Hut or Chalet

- Place to Eat
- Pub or Bar

- Airport
- Bank
- Beach
- Castle or Fort
- Cathedral or Church
- Cave
- Cliff or Escarpment
- Dive Site, Snorkelling
- Embassy
- Hospital
- Lighthouse
- Lookout
- Monument
- Mosque
- Mountain or Hill
- Museum
- National Park

- One Way Street
- Point of Interest
- Police Station
- Post Office
- Shopping Centre
- Spring
- Stately Home
- Swimming Pool
- Telephone
- Temple
- Temple (Hindu)
- Temple (Sikh)
- Temple (Taoist)
- Tomb
- Tourist Information
- Transport
- Zoo

Note: not all symbols displayed above appear in this book

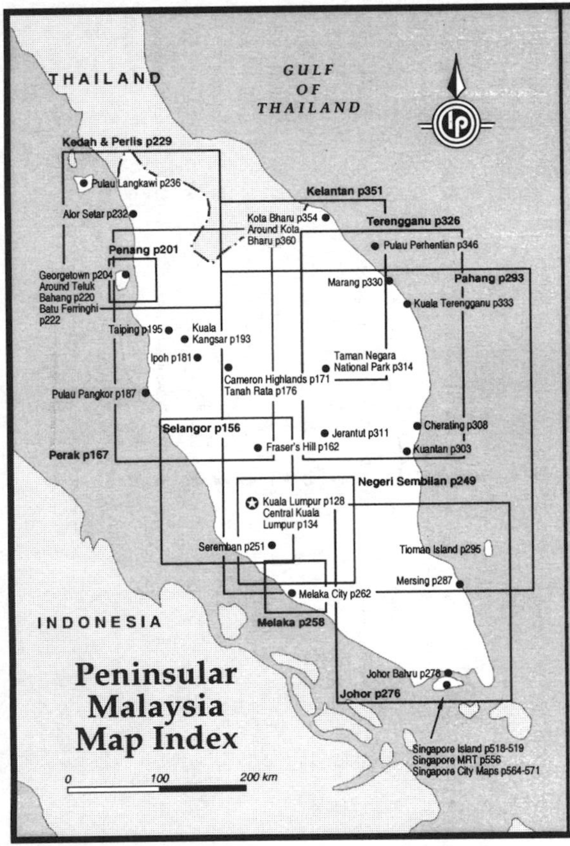

Peninsular Malaysia Map Index
0 100 200 km
THAILAND
GULF OF THAILAND
INDONESIA
Kedah & Perlis p229
Pulau Langkawi p236
Alor Setar p232
Penang p201
Georgetown p204
Around Teluk Bahang p220
Batu Ferringhi p222
Taiping p195
Kuala Kangsar p193
Ipoh p181
Pulau Pangkor p187
Perak p167
Kelantan p351
Kota Bharu p354
Around Kota Bharu p360
Terengganu p326
Pulau Perhentian p346
Marang p330
Kuala Terengganu p333
Pahang p293
Cameron Highlands p171
Tanah Rata p176
Taman Negara National Park p314
Selangor p156
Fraser's Hill p162
Jerantut p311
Cherating p308
Kuantan p303
Negeri Sembilan p249
Kuala Lumpur p128
Central Kuala Lumpur p134
Seremban p251
Tioman Island p295
Mersing p287
Melaka City p262
Melaka p258
Johor Bahru p278
Johor p276
Singapore Island p518-519
Singapore MRT p556
Singapore City Maps p564-571

East Malaysia Map Index
0 150 300 km
SOUTH CHINA SEA
PHILIPPINES
INDONESIA
Sabah p445
Kota Belud p477
Mt Kinabalu (Summit Trail) p489
Kinabalu Park HQ & Trail p485
Kota Kinabalu p450
Sandakan p499
Bandar Labuan p472
Beaufort p468
Tenom p466
Tawau p513
Bandar Seri Begawan p644
Brunei Darussalam p629
Sarawak p365
Miri p421
Gunung Mulu National Park between pp432-433
Kelabit Highlands between pp432-433
Niah Caves Area p416
Bintulu p412
Sibu p402
Kapit p407
Around Kuching p386
Bako National Park p388
Kuching p372
Other Maps
Peninsular Malaysia Colour Map between pp16-17
East Malaysia & Brunei Colour Map between pp16-17
Malaysian Airfares p115

Introduction

Malaysia, Singapore and Brunei are three independent South-East Asian nations offering the visitor a taste of Asia at its most accessible. These countries are among the richest in Asia, so they are relatively prosperous and forward-looking. Transport facilities are good, accommodation standards are high and there are few problems for visitors.

Yet, despite these high standards, these are not expensive countries to visit. Singapore may be able to offer all the air-conditioned comforts your credit cards can handle, and East Malaysia may at times be a little pricey due to its jungle-frontier situation, but in Peninsular Malaysia costs can be very cheap.

More important than simple ease of travel, this region offers amazing variety – both geographically and culturally. If you want beaches and tropical islands, it's hard to beat the east coast of the peninsula. If you want mountains, parks and wildlife, you can climb Mt Kinabalu, explore the rivers of Sarawak or trek the trails of the huge Taman Negara National Park on the peninsula. If you want city life, you can try the historic old port of Melaka, the easy-going backstreets of Georgetown in Penang or the modern-as-tomorrow city of Singapore.

When it comes to people, you've got Malays, Chinese, Indians and a host of indigenous tribes in Sabah and Sarawak. Last, but not least, there's a choice of food which brings people back to the region again and again; for many people there's no question that Singapore is the food capital of Asia.

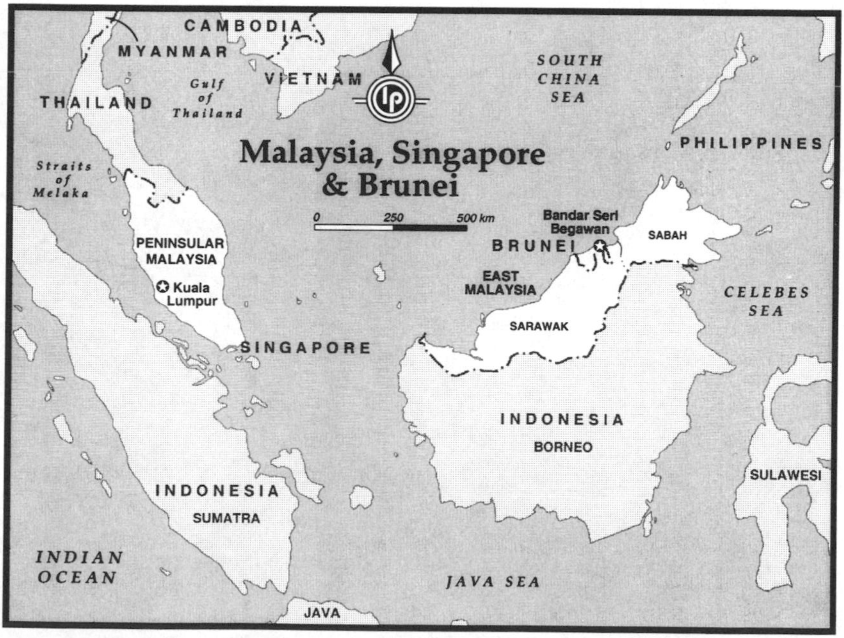

MALAYSIA

RICHARD I'ANSON

Facts about Malaysia

HISTORY

It is only since WWII that Malaysia, Singapore and Brunei have emerged as three separate, independent countries. Prior to that they were all loosely amalgamated as a British colony, Sarawak excepted, and earlier still they might have been independent Malay kingdoms or part of the greater Majapahit or Sriwijaya empires of what is now Indonesia. In the dim mists of time it's possible that Malaysia was actually the home of the earliest known Homo sapiens in Asia. Discoveries have been made in the gigantic Niah Caves of Sarawak which indicate that the Stone Age human was present there, and in other caves of north Borneo and the Malay Peninsula, as long ago as 40,000 years.

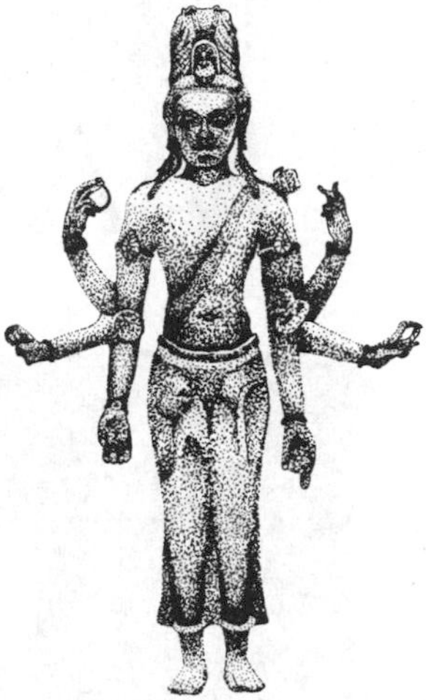

This bronze statue of a Bodhisattva is a relic of the Sriwijaya Empire.

Early Trade & Empires

Little is known about the Stone Age Malaysians, but around 10,000 years ago the aboriginal Malays – the Orang Asli – began to move down the peninsula from a probable starting point in South-West China. Remote settlements of Orang Asli can still be found in parts of Malaysia, but 4000 years ago they were already being supplanted by the Proto-Malays, ancestors of today's Malays, who at first settled the coastal regions, then moved inland. In the early centuries of the Christian era, Malaya was known as far away as Europe. Ptolemy showed it on his early map with the label 'Golden Chersonese'. It spelt gold not only to the Romans but also to the Indians and Chinese, whose traders arrived not long after in search of that most valuable metal. Hindu mini-states now began to spring up along the great Malay rivers.

The Malay people were basically similar ethnically to the people of Sumatra, Java and even the Philippines, and from time to time various South-East Asian empires extended their control over all or part of the Malay Peninsula. Funan, a kingdom based in modern-day Cambodia, at one time controlled the northern part of the peninsula. From the 7th century the great Sumatran-based Sriwijaya Empire, with its capital in Palembang, held the whole area and even extended its rule into Thailand. A significant Malay trading kingdom, under the suzerainty of Sriwijaya, became established at the Bujang Valley in today's Perak state. Its Hindu temples remain the most significant reminder of the Hindu-Buddhist period that held sway over much of the peninsula for nearly a millennium.

Sriwijaya eventually fell to the Java-based Majapahit Empire, and then in 1403 Parameswara, a Sumatran prince, established himself at Melaka, which soon became the most powerful city-state in the region. At this time the spice trade from the Moluccas was beginning to develop and Melaka, with its strategic position on the

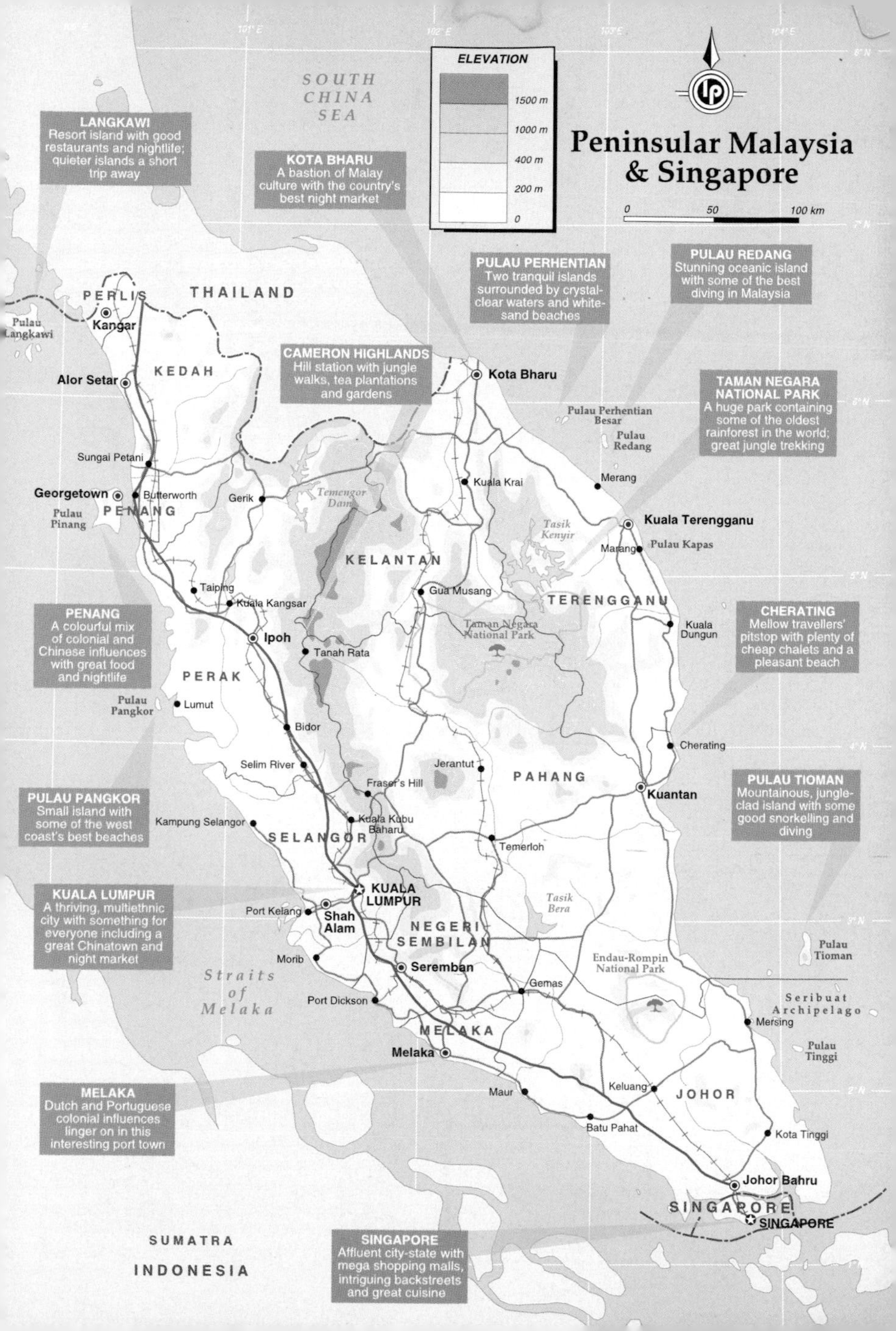
Peninsular Malaysia & Singapore
ELEVATION
1500 m
1000 m
400 m
200 m
0
0
50
100 km
SOUTH CHINA SEA
LANGKAWI
Resort island with good restaurants and nightlife; quieter islands a short trip away
KOTA BHARU
A bastion of Malay culture with the country's best night market
PULAU PERHENTIAN
Two tranquil islands surrounded by crystal-clear waters and white-sand beaches
PULAU REDANG
Stunning oceanic island with some of the best diving in Malaysia
CAMERON HIGHLANDS
Hill station with jungle walks, tea plantations and gardens
TAMAN NEGARA NATIONAL PARK
A huge park containing some of the oldest rainforest in the world; great jungle trekking
PENANG
A colourful mix of colonial and Chinese influences with great food and nightlife
CHERATING
Mellow travellers' pitstop with plenty of cheap chalets and a pleasant beach
PULAU PANGKOR
Small island with some of the west coast's best beaches
PULAU TIOMAN
Mountainous, jungle-clad island with some good snorkelling and diving
KUALA LUMPUR
A thriving, multiethnic city with something for everyone including a great Chinatown and night market
MELAKA
Dutch and Portuguese colonial influences linger on in this interesting port town
SINGAPORE
Affluent city-state with mega shopping malls, intriguing backstreets and great cuisine
THAILAND
PERLIS
Kangar
Pulau Langkawi
KEDAH
Alor Setar
Kota Bharu
Pulau Perhentian Besar
Pulau Redang
Sungai Petani
Merang
Kuala Krai
Georgetown
Butterworth
Gerik
Pulau Pinang
PENANG
Temengor Dam
Tasik Kenyir
Kuala Terengganu
Marang
Pulau Kapas
KELANTAN
Taiping
Kuala Kangsar
Gua Musang
TERENGGANU
Kuala Dungun
Taman Negara National Park
Ipoh
Tanah Rata
PERAK
Pulau Pangkor
Lumut
Bidor
Cherating
Selim River
Jerantut
PAHANG
Fraser's Hill
Kuantan
Kampung Selangor
Kuala Kubu Baharu
SELANGOR
Temerloh
KUALA LUMPUR
Port Kelang
Shah Alam
Tasik Bera
NEGERI SEMBILAN
Pulau Tioman
Morib
Seremban
Endau-Rompin National Park
Straits of Melaka
Gemas
Port Dickson
Seribuat Archipelago
Mersing
MELAKA
Melaka
Pulau Tinggi
Keluang
Maur
JOHOR
Batu Pahat
Kota Tinggi
Johor Bahru
SINGAPORE
SINGAPORE
SUMATRA
INDONESIA

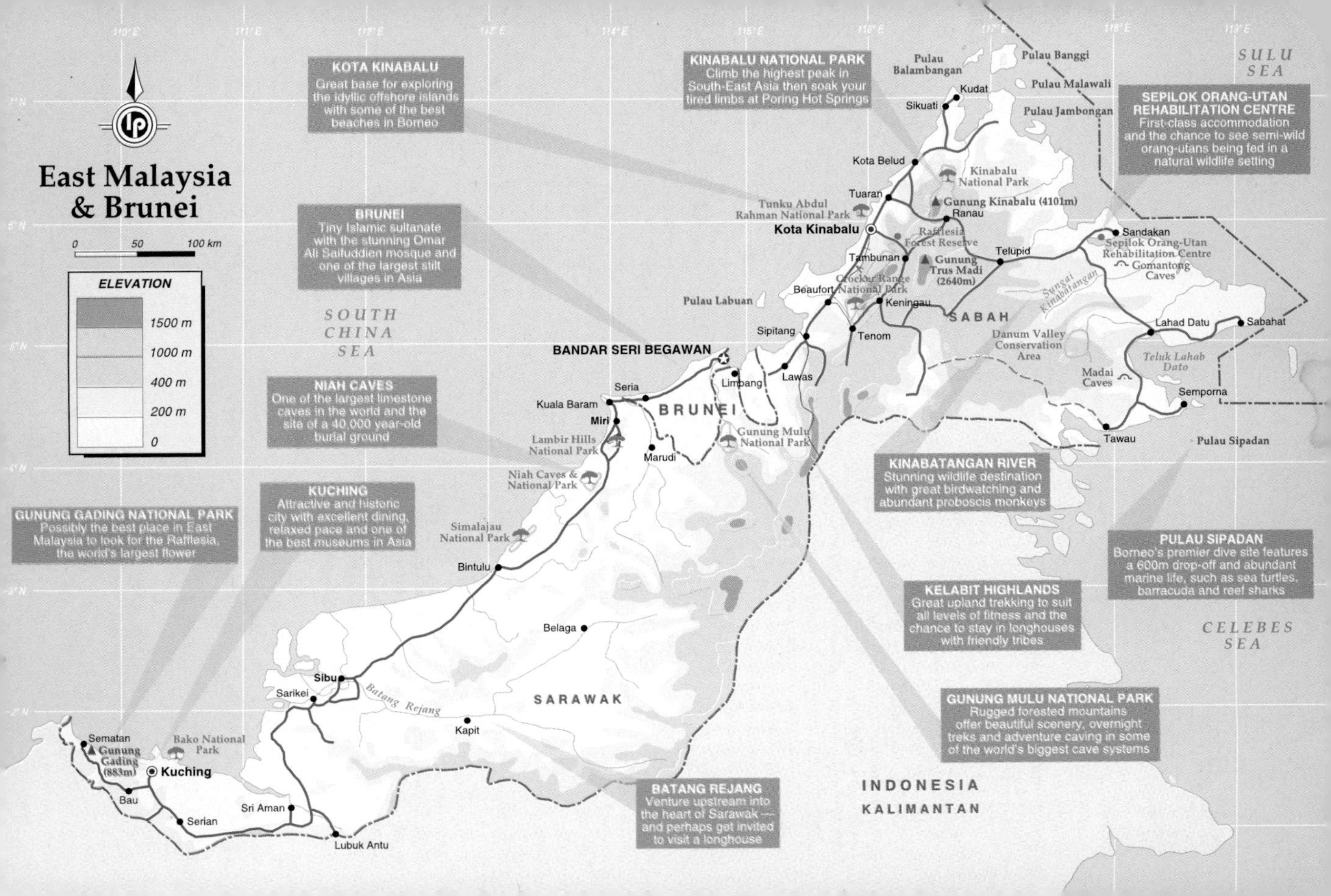
East Malaysia & Brunei
0
50
100 km
ELEVATION
1500 m
1000 m
400 m
200 m
0
KOTA KINABALU
Great base for exploring the idyllic offshore islands with some of the best beaches in Borneo
BRUNEI
Tiny Islamic sultanate with the stunning Omar Ali Saifuddien mosque and one of the largest stilt villages in Asia
NIAH CAVES
One of the largest limestone caves in the world and the site of a 40,000 year-old burial ground
KUCHING
Attractive and historic city with excellent dining, relaxed pace and one of the best museums in Asia
GUNUNG GADING NATIONAL PARK
Possibly the best place in East Malaysia to look for the Rafflesia, the world's largest flower
KINABALU NATIONAL PARK
Climb the highest peak in South-East Asia then soak your tired limbs at Poring Hot Springs
SEPILOK ORANG-UTAN REHABILITATION CENTRE
First-class accommodation and the chance to see semi-wild orang-utans being fed in a natural wildlife setting
KINABATANGAN RIVER
Stunning wildlife destination with great birdwatching and abundant proboscis monkeys
PULAU SIPADAN
Borneo's premier dive site features a 600m drop-off and abundant marine life, such as sea turtles, barracuda and reef sharks
KELABIT HIGHLANDS
Great upland trekking to suit all levels of fitness and the chance to stay in longhouses with friendly tribes
GUNUNG MULU NATIONAL PARK
Rugged forested mountains offer beautiful scenery, overnight treks and adventure caving in some of the world's biggest cave systems
BATANG REJANG
Venture upstream into the heart of Sarawak — and perhaps get invited to visit a longhouse
SULU SEA
SOUTH CHINA SEA
CELEBES SEA
INDONESIA
KALIMANTAN
SABAH
SARAWAK
BRUNEI
BANDAR SERI BEGAWAN
Kota Kinabalu
Kuching
Pulau Balambangan
Pulau Banggi
Pulau Malawali
Pulau Jambongan
Kudat
Sikuati
Kota Belud
Kinabalu National Park
Gunung Kinabalu (4101m)
Tuaran
Ranau
Tunku Abdul Rahman National Park
Rafflesia Forest Reserve
Tambunan
Telupid
Gunung Trus Madi (2640m)
Crocker Range National Park
Beaufort
Keningau
Pulau Labuan
Sipitang
Tenom
Lawas
Limbang
Sandakan
Sepilok Orang-Utan Rehabilitation Centre
Gomantong Caves
Sungai Kinabatangan
Danum Valley Conservation Area
Lahad Datu
Sabahat
Teluk Lahab Dato
Madai Caves
Semporna
Tawau
Pulau Sipadan
Seria
Kuala Baram
Miri
Marudi
Lambir Hills National Park
Gunung Mulu National Park
Niah Caves & National Park
Simalajau National Park
Bintulu
Belaga
Sibu
Sarikei
Batang Rejang
Kapit
Sematan
Gunung Gading (883m)
Bako National Park
Bau
Serian
Sri Aman
Lubuk Antu

straits which separate Sumatra from the Malay Peninsula, was a familiar port for ships from the east and west.

In 1405 the Chinese admiral Cheng Ho arrived in Melaka with greetings from the 'Son of Heaven' and, more importantly, the promise of protection from the encroaching Siamese to the north. With this support from China, the power of Melaka extended to include most of the Malay Peninsula. At about the same time, Islam arrived in Melaka and soon spread through Malaya.

Portuguese Period

For the next century Melaka's power and wealth expanded to such an extent that the city became one of the wealthiest in the east – so wealthy, in fact, that the Portuguese began to take an active interest in the place. After a preliminary skirmish in 1509, Alfonso de Albuquerque arrived in 1511 with a fleet of 18 ships and overpowered Melaka's 20,000 defenders and their war elephants. The sultan of Melaka fled south with his court to Johor, where the Portuguese were unable to dislodge him. Thus Melaka came to be the centre of European power in the region, while Johor grew to be the main Malay city-state, along with other Malay centres at Brunei in north Borneo and Aceh in the north of Sumatra.

The Portuguese were to hold Melaka for over 100 years, although they were never able to capitalise on the city's fabulous wealth and superb position. Portuguese trading power and strength was never great enough to take full advantage of the volume of trade that used to flow through Melaka, but, more importantly, the Portuguese did not develop the complex pattern of influence and patronage upon which Melaka had based its power and control. Worse, the Portuguese reputation for narrow-mindedness and cruelty had preceded them, and they gained few converts to Christianity and little support for their rule.

Thus the other Malay states were able to grow into the vacuum created by the Portuguese takeover of Melaka, and while they squabbled and fought among themselves, they also had the strength to make attacks on Melaka. Gradually Portuguese power declined, and after long skirmishes with the Dutch, who supported the rulers of Johor, Melaka eventually fell to the Dutch, after a long and bitter siege, in 1641.

Dutch Period

Like the Portuguese, the Dutch were to rule Melaka for over a century but, also like the Portuguese, the Dutch failed to recognise that Melaka's greatest importance was as a centre for entrepôt trade. To an even greater extent than their predecessors, the Dutch tried to keep Melaka's trade totally to themselves, and as a result Melaka continued to decline. Also, the greatest Dutch interest was reserved for Batavia, modern-day Jakarta, so Melaka was always the poor sister to the more important Javan port.

Arrival of the British

By the late 18th century the British began to eye Malaysia, having previously been tied up with their Indian possessions. In 1786 Captain Francis Light docked at Penang and occupied it. Light followed a free-trade policy at Penang, a clear contrast to the monopolistic intentions of the Portuguese and then the Dutch in Melaka. Penang soon became a thriving port, and by 1800 the population of the island, virtually uninhabited when Light took over, had reached 10,000.

Meanwhile, events far away in Europe were conspiring to consolidate British influence on the Malay Peninsula. When Napoleon overran the Netherlands in 1795, the British East India Company took over the administration of Melaka and other Dutch possessions in the region. In 1814, with Napoleon defeated, an agreement was reached on the return of these possessions, and by 1818 Melaka and Java had been returned to Dutch control.

Nevertheless, Britain's brief spell at the helm prompted some British figures to argue for more influence on the peninsula, particularly given that Malaysian ports of call made access to major trading destinations such as China easier. The calls of Sir

Thomas Stamford Raffles to supplant the Dutch in Malaya had largely fallen on deaf ears. But in 1818, with the re-establishment of Dutch control in the region, Raffles was told to go ahead and establish a second British base further south than Penang. In early 1819 Raffles decided on Singapore as a British base. In 1826 Singapore became part of the British Straits Settlements, governed from Bengal in India along with Melaka and Penang; by then its population was already approaching 100,000.

British Period

Despite local cultural traditions, the Malaysia of today came into being during the period of British rule. Initially in 1824 the British and the Dutch signed a treaty that divided the peninsula into 'spheres of influence'. The kingdom of Johor was split into the Dutch-administered Riau Lingga Islands and British administration on the peninsula. In 1826 the formation of the Straits Settlements under the British brought together Singapore, Melaka, Penang and Province Wellesley (the mainland opposite Penang). In 1874 the Pangkor Treaty brought the Malay state of Perak into the ambit of British rule via a British Resident, who was to be consulted on all matters 'other than those touching upon Malay religion and custom'.

As was the case in India, the British Residential system allowed colonial influence to prosper without ever having to go to war. The system preserved the prestige of local rulers while at the same time providing the British with indirect control over matters – chiefly economic – that interested them most. In 1896 the states of Perak, Selangor, Negeri Sembilan and Pahang became the Federated Malay States (FMS), each governed indirectly by a British Resident. Johor held out until 1913, while Kelantan, Terengganu, Perlis and Kedah were controlled by the Thais until 1909, when they became known as the Unfederated Malay States (UMS), again under the British Residential system.

British influence in Malaya brought enormous economic and social changes. A communications infrastructure was established to allow the smooth transport of the produce of rubber estates and tin mines to ports. A colonial legal and administrative system was put in place, providing an environment in which free enterprise could flourish. But it was on the social front that the British administration was to have the greatest long-term effects.

Raffles, and later other British administrators, argued in favour of an ethnic division of labour. A British-educated Malay elite should have a place in the administration system, while ordinary Malays should continue fishing and farming. Immigrants from China's coastal provinces of Fujian (Hokkien) and Guangdong were imported as traders and workers in tin mines. Later, Indians were brought over to work in the bureaucracy, on the rubber estates and as labourers in public works. By the turn of the 19th century, Malaya's economy had been revolutionised, but so had its social make-up. The once predominantly Malay Peninsula was emerging as an ethnic melting pot.

Meanwhile in Borneo

Across the South China Sea, in the steamy jungles of North Borneo, events were unfolding with the implausibility of high Victorian melodrama. In 1838 James Brooke, a British adventurer, arrived in Borneo with his armed sloop to find the Brunei aristocracy facing rebellion from dissatisfied inland tribes. He quelled the rebellion and in gratitude was given power over part of what is today Sarawak. Appointing himself 'Raja Brooke', he successfully tamed the fractious tribes, suppressed head-hunting, eliminated the dreaded Borneo pirates and founded a personal dynasty that was to last for over 100 years. The Brooke family of 'white rajas' were still empire building, bringing more and more of Borneo under their power, when the Japanese arrived during WWII.

The extension of British influence into Sabah took a less romantic complexion. In 1865 the American consul to Brunei managed to acquire a lease for most of what is now Sabah. He sold it in Hong Kong, after which it was sold again to the Austrian consul there, Count Von Overbeck. Overbeck had no success interesting his government in a new territory, and finally Sabah ended up in the hands of Alfred Dent, an Englishman. Dent established the British North Borneo Company, and from 1881 the land the company governed became British North Borneo.

WWII Period

By 1913 all of Peninsular Malaysia and north-west Borneo was united in a loose federation known as British Malaya. The colony prospered, though overwhelmingly the economy was dependent on tin and rubber – by the time WWII broke out in Europe, Malaya supplied nearly 40% of the world's rubber and 60% of its tin.

At the same time, Chinese and Indian immigrants arrived in such numbers that they eventually outnumbered indigenous Malays. A 1931 census revealed that the Chinese alone numbered over 1.7 million as opposed to 1.6 million Malays.

The arrival of WWII, however, was sudden and devastating. A few hours before the first Japanese aircraft was sighted over Pearl Harbor, the Japanese landed at Kota Bharu in the north of Malaya and started their lightning dash down the peninsula. British confidence that they were more than a match for the Japanese soon proved to be sadly misplaced, and it took the Japanese little over a month to take Kuala Lumpur and a month more to reach the doorstep of Singapore. North Borneo had fallen to the Japanese with even greater speed.

The Japanese were unable to form a cohesive policy in Malaya, since there was not a well-organised Malay independence movement which they could harness to secure their goals. Furthermore, many Chinese were bitterly opposed to the Japanese, who had invaded China in the 1930s. Remnants of the British forces continued a guerrilla struggle against the Japanese throughout the war, and the Communist Malayan People's Anti-Japanese Army (predominantly Chinese) also continued the struggle against the Japanese.

Meanwhile, resistance in Borneo was organised in a different fashion, as there was a much smaller Chinese population on hand. Since the Japanese only had control of the coastal areas, the vast inner regions of Borneo were ripe for the planning and resourcing of armed resistance. However, the problem of supplying and organising such resistance was almost insurmountable until the allies were able to capture islands close enough to Borneo to permit airdrops into the interior.

After securing an airstrip on the island of Moratai in 1944, a primarily Australian force known as Z Special Unit parachuted into the Kelabit highlands and succeeded in winning over the Kelabit to their cause. Armed mostly with traditional blowpipes, the Kelabit, led by the Australian commandos, scored a number of daring victories over the Japanese. (For more information on Borneo history, see the Sabah and Sarawak chapters.)

Postwar & the Emergency

When the Japanese surrendered on 15 August 1945, the British inherited a troubled country. The ethnic divide between indigenous Malays and the Chinese had polarised around the issues of Japanese resistance and the future of Malaya. The mainly Chinese Malayan Communist Party (MCP) maintained that many Malays and their leaders had capitulated to and cooperated with the Japanese occupation, and in some cases the MCP meted out punishment to the guilty parties.

The British response was a plan to form a Malayan Union under the sovereignty of the British crown, in which citizenship was to be extended to all with equal rights. There was an outcry from native Malays, and in March 1946 the United Malays National Organisation (UMNO) formed to fight the proposal. The British backed off, and in February 1948 they formed the Federation of Malaya. The sultans maintained their sovereignty and Malays were granted special privileges denied to the non-native inhabitants of Malaya – the Indians and Chinese.

Meanwhile the MCP, which had fought against the Japanese throughout the war, launched a guerrilla struggle to end British colonial rule. In 1950 the British declared the Emergency and put the country on a war footing. The Communist threat was eventually declared over in 1960, although there were sporadic outbreaks of violence until 1989. The Communists never enjoyed a broad spectrum of support. They were always predominantly a Chinese grouping, and while the Malays might have wanted independence from Britain they certainly did not want rule by the Chinese. Nor were all Chinese in favour of the party; it was mainly an uprising of the peasantry and lower classes.

Despite the diminished threat of Communist takeover, guerrillas were still resident in the jungle around the Thai border until the last remaining faithful accepted the government's long-standing amnesty in 1989.

Independence

In 1955 Britain agreed that Malaya would become fully independent within two years. Elections held in 1955 swept the Alliance Party, a union of the Malayan Indian Congress (MIC), UMNO and the Malayan Chinese Association (MCA), into power. Nevertheless, when Malaya achieved *merdeka* (independence) on 15 August 1957, the resulting Merdeka Constitution enshrined special privileges for the indigenous Malays, while at the same time offering citizenship to all. Conflicting interpretations of these twin aims were to bedevil the country in years to come. Tunku Abdul Rahman was the leader of the new nation, which came into existence with remarkably few problems.

In Singapore things went nowhere near as smoothly and politics became increasingly radical. The election in 1959 swept Lee Kuan Yew's People's Action Party (PAP) into power, but it faced a whole series of major problems. When the Federation of Malaya was formed in 1948, the Malay leaders were strongly opposed to including Singapore because this would have tipped the racial balance from Malay dominance to a Chinese majority. Furthermore, while politics in Malaya was orderly, upper class and gentlemanly, in Singapore it was anything but controlled.

Nevertheless, to Singapore, merger with Malaya seemed to be the only answer to high unemployment, a soaring birth rate and the loss of its traditional trading role with the growth of independent South-East Asian nations. Malaya was none too keen to inherit this little parcel of problems, but when it seemed possible that the moderate PAP might be toppled by its own left wing, the thought of a moderate Singapore within Malaysia became less off-putting than the thought of a Communist Singapore outside outside the country. Accordingly, in 1961 Tunku Abdul Rahman agreed to work towards the creation of a Malaysia which would include Singapore. To balance the addition of Singapore, discussion also commenced on adding Sarawak, Sabah and Brunei to the union, a move welcomed by Britain, which faced the problem of what to do with its North Borneo possessions.

Malays, Malaya & Malaysia

Malays are the indigenous people of Malaysia, although they are not the original inhabitants. Malaya is the old name for the country which, prior to 1963, consisted only of the states on the peninsula. With the amalgamation of Malaya, Sarawak and Sabah, the title Malaysia was coined for the new nation, and the peninsula is now referred to as Peninsular Malaysia, while Sarawak and Sabah are referred to as East Malaysia.

Confrontation

Accordingly, in 1963 Malaysia came into existence, although at the last moment Brunei, afraid of losing its oil wealth, refused to join.

No sooner had Malaysia been created than problems arose. First of all the Philippines laid claim to Sabah, which had been known as North Borneo prior to the union. More seriously, Indonesia laid claim to the whole island. Sukarno, the Indonesian autocrat who seized power in 1957, in an effort to oust the Malaysians, began his ill-starred 'Confrontation'. Indonesian guerrilla forces crossed the borders from Kalimantan (Indonesian Borneo) into Sabah and Sarawak, and landings were also made in Peninsular Malaysia and even in Singapore. British troops, having finally quelled the Emergency only four years earlier, now found themselves back in the jungle once again. While it took three years to quell the threat, the Malaysian states on the island of Borneo were never seriously threatened.

Singapore Departs

At the same time, relations between Malaya and Singapore soured almost as soon as Malaysia was formed. The main stumbling block to a happy union lay in Singapore's refusal to extend constitutional Malay privileges to Malays in Singapore. In August 1965, exactly two years after Malaysia was created, Singapore was kicked out.

Racial Problems

With Singapore and Brunei out of the union, Malaysia was now an independent country. One niggling problem that remained, however, was that the country was far from integrated. Naturally, the Alliance Party looked to education and language as the cornerstones of national identity. But what it had not counted on was the fierce opposition of other ethnic groups to what many saw as the extension of Malay privileges into the education system.

Privileges or no, Malays had a very weak hold on the economy. In 1969 only 1.5% of company assets in Malaysia were owned by Malays, and per capita income among Malays was less than 50% of that of others. But attempts to make Bahasa Malaysia the one national language, along with the privileges Malays had in land ownership, business licences, educational opportunities and government positions, resulted in resentment from non-Malays. Their opposition to such moves resulted in the Alliance Party losing its two-thirds majority in the May 1969 federal elections. Victorious opposition parties took to the streets in celebration. The next day, on 13 May, a UMNO rally took to the streets in Kuala Lumpur and interracial riots broke out. Hundreds of people were killed.

Following these riots the government moved to improve the position of Malays in Malaysia with greater speed. The title *bumiputra*, or sons of the soil, was created to denote the indigenous Malay people: this meant not only Malays but also the aboriginal inhabitants and the indigenous peoples of Sarawak and Sabah. New guidelines were instituted stipulating how much of a company's share must be held by bumiputras and in other ways enforcing a Malay share in the nation's wealth.

Although many Chinese realised that Malaysia could never attain real stability without an equitable distribution of the country's wealth, there was also much resentment, and many talented people either left the country or simply withdrew their abilities and capital. Fortunately, Malaysia's natural wealth enabled it to absorb this flight of talent and wealth, but the problem of bringing the Malays to an equal position in the nation, economically as well as politically, is one that is still not fully resolved.

After 1969, government policy aimed to integrate economic development and ethnic policy. A series of five-year plans have been undertaken, with the ultimate objective of transforming Malaysia into a developed country in which race no longer has any bearing on economic function. On the political front, the Alliance Party expanded, drawing in other parties, to become the National Front, though this party is dominated by the UMNO.

Malaysia & Islam

While promotion of Bahasa Malaysia has been the main focus of the drive to forge a

Asian Values

If you have not heard of Asian Values it is probably because you are an illiterate product of western degeneracy, no doubt reared in a single-parent family, most likely gay, possibly a victim (or perpetrator) of incest and an odds-on favourite for alcohol and drug addiction. As Dr Mahathir puts it in his recent book *The Voice of Asia:* 'Western societies are riddled with single-parent families, which foster incest, with homosexuality, with cohabitation, with unrestrained avarice, with disrespect for others and, of course, rejection of religious teachings and values.'

Overall this is slightly depressing news for those of us unfortunate enough to have grown up in the west. But then the pundits of Asian Values are not ones to pull their punches. The west, they maintain, has had its day and the new, 21st century will belong to Asia.

Dr Mahathir, head of an Islamic Malay state and very much an Asian Values man, is uncomfortable about equating Asian Values with neo-Confucianism, even if it *is* neo-Confucian Chinese who are making most of his money. Lee Kuan Yew, on the other hand, a pioneer of Asian Values and former head of a Chinese state, has no problems with neo-Confucianism.

However, now that the entire Asian region is mired in an intractable recession, the worth of these much-ballyhooed Asian Values has been called into question. Indeed, countries like Japan are quickly rushing in the opposite direction and adopting American business practices. Likewise, countries like Korea and Indonesia didn't mind accepting an IMF bailout when Asian Values alone were not enough to boost their sagging economies.

Still, despite the recent problems faced by Asian countries, leaders like Dr Mahathir are reluctant to give up the idea of Asian Values, especially when they make such a good foundation from which to criticise the decadence of the west.

Chris Taylor

national identity, Islam has also been an important rallying point. The Malaysian Islamic Youth Movement was formed in 1971 with the aim of promoting Islamic values and even implementing Islamic law *(syharia)* in Malaysia. In November 1993 the most Islamic of Malaysia's states, Kelantan, attempted to do just that. The new laws would have required federal constitutional changes, and among other things required that thieves have their right hands amputated and that adulterers be stoned to death.

Islam presents the national government with a prickly problem. On the one hand, UMNO is bound to represent Malay and Islamic interests. On the other, a full-blown Islamic revival would run counter to the government's economic aims. Kelantan, for example, remains a poor state, a quarter of its population lives below the poverty line, and local policies have caused foreign investment to dwindle.

The other issue to consider is that an Islamic resurgence is potentially even more destabilising to ethnic unity than the problems associated with promotion of Bahasa Malaysia and with Malay domination of politics. Efforts by Islamic groups to outlaw alcohol, lotteries, unisex hairdressers and even to enforce conservative Islamic dress standards go down badly with Malaysia's pork-eating, gambling-mad ethnic Chinese.

Malaysia Today

Ethnic problems aside, Malaysia's economy was one of the great success stories of the postwar period. This was largely due to the government's centralised economic planning and diversification of an economy that was once almost entirely reliant on rubber, tin and logging.

Riding the wave of economic success, UMNO, by far the majority faction of the National Front coalition, steadily consolidated its power in the decades that followed independence. Much of UMNO's success can be attributed directly to Datuk Seri Mahathir Mohamad, Malaysia's charismatic and occasionally controversial prime minister. Since coming to power in 1981, Dr

Mahathir has become the country's longest serving prime minister and has guided the country to prosperity.

Dr Mahathir, a man of strong opinions and near-visionary ambitions on Malaysia's part, has also been keen to raise his stature on the world stage as a pan-Asia leader. He fulminates regularly on the subject of western colonialist attitudes and decadence, and promotes 'Asian Values' as the ethical basis of Asian economic success (see the boxed text 'Asian Values'). He advocates an East Asian Economic Caucus (EAEC), an Asia-only counterpart to the Asia-Pacific Economic Cooperation (APEC), which he claims to be controlled by US and Australian interests.

In the mid-1990s, the picture looked very bright indeed for Malaysia and the country looked right on track to becoming

Battle of the Titans

In September 1998, after months of rumours about the shaky job security of Malaysia's number two, Anwar Ibrahim, Prime Minister Mahathir Mohamad did the seemingly unthinkable and sacked his deputy. As pundits saw it, Anwar had gone too far in his and his supporters' criticism of corruption and cronyism in Malaysia, which the prime minister seemed to feel was thinly veiled criticism of himself. In the preceding months, two influential Anwar supporters, editors of daily newspapers, were forced to resign, and a purge of Anwar supporters began in UMNO. In addition, since Anwar was finance minister and was seen as more sympathetic to IMF-style globalisation policies in order to restore Malaysia's economy, Mahathir made his colleague Daim Zainuddin special minister in charge of the economy, in a clear signal that he wished to dilute Anwar's influence.

Normally, the sacking would have spelt the end of any hope Anwar had of playing a significant role in Malaysia's future, and it seemed extraordinary that the country's second-in-charge, groomed for years to take over from Mahathir when the prime minister decided to retire, should have had his career ended so abruptly. However, Anwar, perhaps emboldened by the precipitate fall of Soeharto in Indonesia, declined to go quietly. Within a few days, he was making fiery speeches, railing at Mahathir's paranoia, questioning an alleged witchhunt against members of his family, and denouncing his sacking and the draconian internal security laws under which he expected to be charged. (Of course, given his former lofty position, critics might ask why he hadn't been that concerned about the supposed injustice of Malaysia's legal system previously.) In a worrying sign for Mahathir, crowds of people flocked to listen to his speeches, and many seemed to approve of what he had to say. Anwar was allowed to continue for a time but on the final day of the Commonwealth Games in KL, Mahathir cracked down on protesters and his former deputy was arrested.

Mahathir initially declined to give specific reasons for Anwar's downfall but after a few days, Mahathir finally said he had seen a report on Anwar's alleged misbehaviour, and said it confirmed Anwar's unsuitability to hold high office. (Of course, critics might again ask how it was that the undoubtedly intelligent and crafty Mr Mahathir had failed to notice Anwar's supposed failings through all the years they stood side by side.)

But the protests continued and crowds of up to 30,000 gathered. Held under the feared Internal Security Act, Anwar appeared in court with a bruised face; injuries which had been self-inflicted according to Mahathir. Supporters rallied around Anwar's wife, Wan Azizah Ismail, and Mahathir was condemned by neighbours and international heavies, including the World Bank and the United Nations.

In 1999, after months of legal argument, Anwar was sentenced to 6 years imprisonment for corruption. While UMNO officials tend to dismiss support for Anwar, the whole affair has undoubtedly caused deep divisions to appear in Malaysian society, especially among the Malays.

Greg Alford

a fully industrialised nation by the year 2020. However, starting in August of 1997, everything seemed to fall apart. A currency crisis which started in Thailand quickly spread to the entire South-East Asia region, dragging down currency values and effectively plunging the area into a recession, with Malaysia among one of the hardest hit. See the Economy section, later in this chapter, for more details on the economic crisis and its ramifications for Malaysia.

As if to add to the gloom, another shadow fell over the country in the last half of 1997: smoke from wildfires burning out of control in the Indonesian states of Kalimantan and Sumatra drifted over both east and Peninsular Malaysia, blotting out the sun and making the air all but unbreathable in some of the worst-hit areas. What came to be known as 'the haze' did little to warm relations between Malaysia and Indonesia, but hostilities never rose above angry recriminations in newspaper editorial columns.

By late December of 1997 the smoke from the fires had cleared and some economists, both inside the country and out, were starting to talk about an economic recovery. The first stirrings of recovery, however, were threatened by deep political and economic instability in neighbouring Indonesia. The Malaysian economy is still floundering compared to its pre-crisis record, and many of the country's vaunted mega-projects remain on hold.

The Commonwealth Games, held for the first time in Asia in Kuala Lumpur (KL) in September 1998, vied for attention with unfolding political developments (see the boxed text 'Battle of the Titans'). More than RM560 million was spent on infrastructure for the games, including the Bukit Jalil National Sports Complex, which has seating for 100,000 people, and 21 other sports venues. The Games earned KL international publicity and were a proud moment for Malaysia.

GEOGRAPHY

Malaysia consists of two distinct parts. Peninsular Malaysia is the long finger of land extending south from Asia as if pointing towards Indonesia and Australia. Much of the peninsula is covered by dense jungle, particularly its mountainous, thinly populated northern half. On the western side of the peninsula there is a long fertile plain running down to the sea, while on the eastern side the mountains descend more steeply and the coast is fringed with sandy beaches.

The other part of the country, comprising more than 50% of its area, is East Malaysia – the northern part of the island of Borneo (the larger, southern part is the Indonesian state of Kalimantan). East Malaysia is divided between Sarawak and Sabah, with Brunei a small enclave between them. Both states are covered by dense jungle with many large river systems, particularly in Sarawak. Mt Kinabalu (4101m) in Sabah is the highest mountain in South-East Asia between the Himalayas and New Guinea.

CLIMATE

Malaysia has a typically tropical climate – it's hot and humid year-round. The temperature rarely drops below 20°C even at night and usually climbs to 30°C or more during the day. The tropics can take some adjusting to. Take it easy when you first arrive and try to avoid running around in the heat of the midday sun.

Rain tends to arrive in brief torrential downpours and is soon replaced by more of that everpresent sunshine. At certain times of the year it may rain every day, but it rarely rains all day. Although the region is monsoonal, it's only the east coast of Peninsular Malaysia that has a real rainy season – elsewhere it's just a time of year when the average rainfall is heavier than at other times of year.

Throughout the region the humidity tends to hover around the 90% mark, but on the peninsula you can always escape from heat and humidity by retreating to the delightfully cool hill stations.

Peninsular Malaysia

The peninsula is affected by the monsoon winds blowing from the north-east between

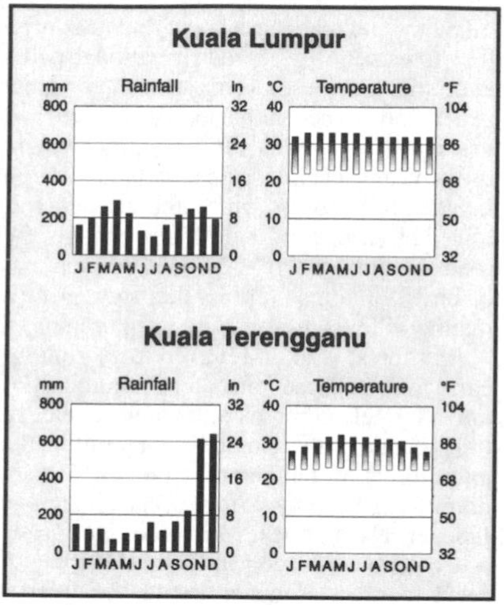

October and April, and from the south-west the rest of the year.

The October-April monsoon brings rain to most of the peninsula, but the east coast bears the full brunt, with the heaviest rain falling from November to January. For the rest of the year the east coast is relatively dry.

Rainfall on the west coast is much more variable and comes throughout the year. Much of the west coast is sheltered from the worst of the October to April rains by the central mountains, but it also gets some rain from the less pronounced May to October monsoon.

The flat south of the peninsula around Johor and Singapore gets rainfall all year, slightly more from November to February. Further north, rainfall is fairly even all year-round, with January and February and especially June and July being the drier months. The north-west around Alor Setar and Langkawi receives less rainfall and has a more distinct wet season from April to October, and the rest of the year is quite dry. Penang seasons are similar but not as pronounced and it gets high rainfall in September and October.

East Malaysia

East Malaysia also gets the north-east and south-west monsoons. Sarawak has high rainfall year-round, especially around Kuching, with October to March being the wettest months, peaking in December and January. Sabah also gets high rainfall on the north-east coast at this time, while the west coast of Sabah gets most of its rainfall from May to November. Sabah receives less rainfall than Sarawak.

ECOLOGY & ENVIRONMENT

Malaysia attracts more than its fair share of criticism on the environmental front, and it is an issue that the government is particularly sensitive about. Dr Mahathir, Malaysia's long-serving prime minister, and his government, maintain the line that western concern about environmental issues in developing countries is a form of hypocrisy. And there is some truth in this. After all, logging (and this is where foreign criticism is loudest) was started in earnest in Sabah and Sarawak during the 1930s by the British Borneo Timber Company.

Nonetheless, preserving something of Malaysia's environmental heritage before it is all shipped overseas as logs is of utmost importance. Probably more than 60% of Peninsular Malaysia's rainforests have been logged, and similar figures apply to East Malaysia. Government initiatives and the formation of national parks has slowed down logging on the peninsula, but it continues at heavy rates in Sabah and Sarawak despite international and domestic pressure.

In addition to logging, Malaysia has been attacked for undertaking several large dam construction projects, which critics claim are both economically and environmentally unsound. The most controversial of these is the Bakun Dam project in Sarawak. As well as drowning hundreds of square kilometres of virgin rainforest, construction of the dam will also force thousands of indigenous peoples from their homes. Fortunately, the current economic slowdown has put this and some of the other projects on an indefinite hold.

More recently, Malaysia's environment has been threatened by a force completely beyond its control: the so-called 'haze' from fires burning in the Indonesian states of Kalimantan and Sumatra. While this problem occurs to some extent every year, the last half of 1997 saw unprecedented levels of air pollution – at times the smoke was so thick that aeroplanes couldn't land at airports in Sabah and Sarawak.

The causes of the haze are widely debated, but most agree that fires ignited to clear the jungle for agricultural purposes are the main culprit. While the fires were burning, Malaysian officials made repeated pleas to Indonesian authorities to enforce laws governing slash and burn farming, but it was a case of too little, too late. As the fires smouldered on through October and November, tempers rose in both countries but, perhaps preoccupied by their growing economic problems, civil relations were maintained through it all.

By the end of 1997, most of the smoke had cleared, but experts say that lax enforcement of environmental laws and another dry season could bring a repeat of those smoky months.

FLORA & FAUNA

Malaysia is home to some of the most diverse systems of flora and fauna in the world. Its ancient rainforests have, in some cases, remained virtually unchanged for many millions of years. The area's climatic stability, plentiful rainfall and tropical greenhouse heat have endowed Malaysia with a cornucopia of bizarre life forms. In fact, scientists are still far from knowing even a significant percentage of the mysteries concealed in Malaysia's forests.

Flora

Malaysia's vegetation boasts a staggering range of trees, plants and flowers. The tropical climate and high rainfall promote the growth of dense rainforests and both the peninsula and Borneo once had extensive stands. Much of this forest cover has been cleared to make way for vast plantations of oil palms and other cash crops, but near-pristine forests are preserved in national parks and other reserves. Even where the original vegetation has been replaced by concrete and bricks, the climate favours quick plant growth; any cleared patch of land will be invaded by creepers, vines and grasses, followed by shrubs and, if left long enough, the seeds of rainforest trees dropped by monkeys or birds. Buildings left derelict soon grow a mantle of ferns, mosses and even orchids.

Rainforest is often referred to as dipterocarp forest. These rainforest communities are extremely complex and many species of trees can grow in a single hectare, unlike the great forests of temperate regions which are dominated by only a few species, such as pine, eucalypt or oak. Malaysian rainforests are categorised according to the type of seeds the trees produce: despite the diversity of species, most produce a similar seed structure and dipterocarp roughly translates from Latin as 'five seeds'. Dominated by tall trees, these forests nonetheless support a vast diversity of other plants, including many thousands of species of orchids, fungi, ferns and mosses.

Another term used in reference to rainforest plant communities is epiphyte, which simply means any plant growing on another, for example a cluster of ferns growing high in the fork of a tree. Epiphytes use their hosts for support only, and themselves often provide shelter to other organisms, such as insects and tree frogs.

Other important vegetation types include mangroves, which fringe coasts and estuaries, and provide nurseries for fish and crustaceans; the stunted rhododendron forests of Borneo's high peaks, which also support epiphytic communities of orchids and hanging lichens ('beard mosses'); and the kerangas of Sarawak, which grows on dry, sandy soil and can support many types of pitcher plants.

Rafflesia Probably the most famous of Malaysia's plants, the rafflesia produces the largest flower in the world; large specimens can measure up to 1m across. There are about 12 species of rafflesia, all confined to the rainforests of Sumatra, Peninsular Malaysia and Borneo. The rafflesia lives most of its life as an underground parasite, living off the root systems of select plants.

There is no apparent flowering season and rafflesias are extremely difficult to locate until they flower. The bud starts as a nondescript, brown growth; within a few days it swells to the size of a football, then gradually opens to reveal bright red petals. The flower continues to mature over a few days but gradually loses colour and withers. Rafflesias are probably most easily seen at Gunung Gading National Park, near Kuching in Sarawak, but they are reasonably common in Sabah.

Pitcher Plants Growing as unobtrusive vines in poor, often well-drained soils, these unusual plants feature a modified leaf type that forms a well filled with liquid. Insects attracted to the plants may fall into the well and drown, then are digested as part of the plant's nutrient intake. There are many species, whose pitchers can range from pipe to pint-mug sized. They reach their greatest diversity in Borneo; several species are unique to the Mt Kinabalu and Gunung Mulu regions, and at least four are common in Bako National Park.

Fauna

An incredibly diverse and unusual array of mammals, birds, reptiles and insects can be found in the region. Although vast areas of forests have been cleared, some magnificent stands remain and the range of life forms that can still be seen with a bit of patience is astonishing. For information on the mammals and the best places to spot them, see the 'Mammals of Malaysia' boxed text.

Birds Birdwatchers are drawn from all over the world in search of Malaysia's hundreds of unusual, colourful and unique bird species. Most towns and villages host at least a few species, and you won't have to go far into the countryside to see a whole lot more. Even in large cities a few species can usually be seen in parks and gardens, including bulbuls, starlings and, wheeling overhead in endless movement, house swifts.

On Peninsular Malaysia, excellent birdwatching can be had within a day's reach of Kuala Lumpur; prime locations include:

Taman Negara Malaysia's most famous national park hosts a great variety of species, sometimes in abundance; those particularly sought here include various hornbills and pheasants. Walk along the jungle trails in the early morning and wait for 'bird waves' – noisy, frenetic parties of mixed species (sometimes a dozen or more) moving through the forest.

Fraser's Hill A short trip from KL, Fraser's Hill features a great selection of lowland and highland species, including many migrants. Those particularly sought by birdwatchers include brown bullfinch, rusty-naped pitta and the rare Malaysian peacock-pheasant. One of the best strategies is to walk down the access road in the early morning (be careful of traffic), birdwatching as you go, and catch a lift back up by late morning when it gets hot and bird activity slows down.

Kuala Selangor Nature Park About 60km from KL, this pleasant little park is home to a variety of migratory wading birds – such as sandpipers, stints and shanks – from about September to March every year. Other birds seen year-round include herons, the secretive mangrove pitta, the stately crested serpent-eagle and various species of kingfishers.

The great island of Borneo hosts a slightly different range of birds to the peninsula, including some 38 species found nowhere else, and is well worth a visit. Both Sabah and Sarawak have great birdwatching, although sites in Sabah are probably slightly better and easier to reach. Good birdwatching locations include:

Gunung Mulu National Park This park in Sarawak features near pristine forest with well-marked trails along which can be seen trogons, jungle-flycatchers and several species of bulbuls and babblers. Birds of prey are another attraction here, and include the bat hawk, which picks off bats emerging from the park's great caves at dusk.

continued on page 32

Mammals of Malaysia

Wildlife and wildlife watching is one of the highlights of a visit to Malaysia, and is fast becoming a well-organised industry in East Malaysia. Most of the best wildlife viewing is to be had in an excellent system of reserves and national parks – see the relevant chapters for details. The Malay name for these mammals is in brackets after the English name.

Orang-Utan (*orang hutan*) The Malay name for this great, fiery-red haired ape means 'man of the forest' and the orang-utan is probably Malaysia's most famous animal. It is Asia's only representative of the great ape family and the only one that spends most of its life in the trees. The orang-utan is rare and found only on the islands of Sumatra and Borneo. It was once said that an orang-utan could swing from one end of Borneo to the other without touching the ground; sadly, this is no longer true as this inoffensive creature and its habitat are disappearing fast. Unlike many other primates, orang-utans are generally solitary animals; they are also unusual because they build a nest of sticks and branches in which to sleep each night. Young orang-utans are appealing and amusing animals that show all the mischievous traits of their human counterparts; they stay with their mother for up to the first five years of life. An adult male is massive: he can weigh up to 100kg, stand up to 1.5m tall and can have an armspan of nearly 3m. In contrast, the female is of far more delicate build and seldom weighs more than 50kg.

Orang-utans

Gibbons (*ungka*) More closely related to apes than monkeys, gibbons dwell strictly in the trees, where they feed on fruits such as figs. Gibbons are superbly adapted to their lifestyle: they have small, slender bodies and like other apes have no tail, but they have incredibly long arms for swinging effortlessly through the trees; their short legs dangle as they swing. Gibbons make an appalling racket in the predawn hour – a far-carrying, raucous hooting that is one of the most distinctive sounds of the Malaysian jungle. The calls help gibbons establish territories and find a mate. Several species inhabit large stands of forest on Peninsular Malaysia and in Borneo, but they are generally shy of people.

Monkeys (*monyet*) Malaysia has 10 species of monkeys, divided by biologists into two groups: langurs and macaques. The langurs (or leaf monkeys) are mostly tree-dwelling, and generally have black palms and soles and grey faces; macaques have pale palms and soles, and brown or red faces; they spend a great deal of time on the ground, although they are also agile climbers. Monkeys usually live in loose groups comprising one or more families; a large group can number up to 50 individuals.

The long-tailed macaque (*kera*) is the most common and widespread of Malaysia's monkeys, and can even be a nuisance when troupes raid orchards and plantations. It is small, and greyish-brown in colour with a long, slender tail. Family groups, usually with a dominant male in attendance, forage on the forest floor and in trees for fruit, leaves and insects. This species occasionally feeds on crabs along the shoreline.

The pig-tailed macaque (*beruk*) is slightly bigger, with golden brown fur; its tail is reduced to a dangling stump. This species is sometimes trained to pick coconuts.

The various species of langurs are far more retiring than macaques and some are very attractively marked. The silvered leaf monkey's black fur is frosted with grey tips; this beautiful monkey can be seen at Kuala Selangor Nature Park in Peninsular Malaysia and at Bako National Park in Sarawak. The banded langur (*cenaka*) is usually black or dark grey above; the spectacled langur (*cenkung*) has white rings around its eyes; and the maroon langur of East Malaysia has reddish fur like the orang-utan.

The fantastic proboscis monkey (*orang blander*) is another type of langur and probably Malaysia's second most famous animal after the orang-utan. The male is an improbable creature with a pendulous nose and bulbous belly; females and youngsters are more daintily built with quaint, upturned noses. When European traders reached the region locals saw a resemblance and the Malay name for this monkey literally means 'Dutchman'. Proboscis monkeys inhabit only the forests of Borneo, where they live almost entirely on leaves. Nowhere are they common, but they are usually encountered in forests near water, including mangroves. Proboscis monkeys occasionally enter the water and have even been seen to swim. The Sungai (River) Kinabatangan in Sabah is the best place to look for these monkeys, although colonies also exist in Bako National Park in Sarawak and in Brunei.

Proboscis monkey

The slow loris (*kongkang*) is thought to be related to the monkeys and apes, although its main similarities are its grasping hands and long toes, with which it moves about in trees. Otherwise, the slow loris is a bizarre creature: it is small (about 30cm in length), has no tail and has enormous, bulbous eyes which help it locate and catch insects and other small animals at night. The slow loris is a solitary, inoffensive creature, found in forests, plantations and even gardens. As its name suggests, it moves with painful deliberation.

Cats Malaysia has many species of wild cats, including the largest and some of the smallest. Several species are no longer common because of the pressures of hunting and, more recently, the trade in body parts for their supposed medicinal qualities.

The magnificent tiger (*harimau*), largest of the great cats, was once widespread in South-East Asia and common in Peninsular Malaysia. Hunting and habitat destruction have taken their toll, and they are now rarely encountered, although one is occasionally seen in Taman Negara. Tigers are generally nocturnal and solitary, feeding on wild pigs and other small animals such as frogs and fish. An adult tiger can measure 3m from nose to tail tip and a fully grown male can weigh up to 200kg. The leopard (*harimau bintang*) is still occasionally reported from the peninsula, although it is a secretive animal and may actually be relatively common. The black form of the leopard – often called black panther – is more common in Malaysia than the spotted variety. Neither leopard not tiger has been recorded in Borneo.

Several smaller species of cats hunt birds and small mammals in forests and adjoining plantations, although one – the bay cat (*kucing hutan*) – is a specialised fish eater. The leopard cat (*kucing batu*) is a widespread species a bit larger than a domestic cat; as its name suggests, it has spotted fur. The marbled cat (*kucing dahan*) is similar in size, with less distinct markings. The clouded leopard (*harimau dahan*) is

Clouded leopard

Borneo's biggest cat, although it is also found on the peninsula. This beautiful predator measures only 1.5m from head to tail; its spots are blurred in subtle shades of yellow and fawn. Danum Valley in Sabah is probably the best place to look for wild cats, although the bay cat is seen regularly along Sabah's Sungai Kinabatangan at night.

Civets (*musang*) Members of this diverse, sometimes attractive group of mainly carnivorous animals bear a superficial resemblance to cats. However, they differ in usually having long, pointed snouts, and move about at night with an ambling gait as they sniff out prey such as frogs, insects, nestlings and fruit. The common palm civet (*musang pulut*) is found throughout Malaysia, even straying into the outskirts of urban areas (including Singapore); it measures about 1m from its nose to the end of its tail. The Malay civet (*tangalung*) is slightly larger and attractively patterned with a ringed tail and spotted or striped coat. The binturong is the largest of the civets; it has a shaggy black or dark brown coat which helps keep it dry in its damp forest habitat. Also known as bearcat, the binturong can measure almost 2m in length and is equally at home in trees or on the ground.

Masked palm civet

Sun Bear (*beruang*) Malaysia's only bear is found throughout the South-East Asian region, including Peninsular Malaysia and Borneo. As bears go this is a small one, measuring only up to 1.5m in length and weighing 50 to 60kg. It is black with pale white or yellow chest markings, and feeds on fruit, vegetation and small animals. Sun bears also raid bee hives for honey and grubs. Sun bears are rarely encountered and are generally inoffensive to humans. However, they can behave unpredictably – especially females with young – and should be treated with caution.

Sun bear

Asian Elephant (*gajah*) Although the Asian elephant is a familiar beast of burden that has been domesticated for thousands of years, wild elephants still roam the forests of Malaysia. Borneo's elephants are believed to have been introduced by traders hundreds of years ago because no fossil records have been found. An adult male elephant can grow to 2.5m tall and weigh up to 3000kg, with tusks up to 1.5m in length; females are smaller and usually have small tusks or none at all. Adult males tend to be solitary; females and young usually form small groups, but small groups may join to form groups of 50 to 100 animals. When these groups invade plantations or crops they can be very destructive. Wild elephants can be dangerous and should not be approached.

Sumatran Rhinoceros (*badak berendam*) The two-horned rhino was once common in South-East Asia, but its numbers have declined dramatically and it is now extremely rare. In Malaysia they are known to exist only in Endau-Rompin National Park on the peninsula and in remote parts of Sabah, such as Danum Valley. An adult rhino can be up to 2.5m in length and weigh up to 900kg. Rhinos eat only plants, and are inoffensive and extremely shy; the chances of seeing one in the wild are virtually nil.

Tapir (*tapir* or *tenuk*) An extraordinary animal like a cross between a wild pig and a hippo, the Malaysian tapir's only living relative inhabits the jungles of Amazonian South America. A tapir can grow up to 2m in length and weigh some 300kg; they are vegetarian and can sometimes be seen at the salt licks in the farther reaches of Taman Negara. Adult tapirs have a two-toned colour scheme, almost black in the foreparts, changing to a white hindquarters. Young tapirs are striped and look somewhat like animated watermelons.

Squirrels (*tupai*) Malaysia has more than 20 species of squirrels, of which several are common; most are active during the day and are readily seen in parks, gardens and patches of forest. Squirrels climb and jump with agility, and generally feed on fruits and leaves. Palm squirrels are small, brown or greyish with cream stripes down their back; they are common in plantations. One of the most attractive species is Prevost's squirrel (*tupai gading*), which is variable in colour, but generally has bright chestnut belly fur, grey or silver haunches and a black body. The giant squirrel (*kerawak*) is most easily distinguished by its enormous size – it reaches almost 1m in length and has a very bushy tail. Flying squirrels (*tupai terbang*) are also large; some measure nearly 1m of which about half is tail. They don't literally fly – they glide from tree to tree by extending a flap of loose skin that stretches between each front and back leg. Flying squirrels are generally active at night and can be difficult to observe because they tend to feed high in the canopy.

Pangolin (*tenggiling*) Also known as the scaly anteater, the pangolin feeds entirely on ants and termites. It is a small, inoffensive animal, measuring only 1m in length, and covered in broad scales like a pine cone. With its powerful claws it digs open ant and termite mounds. Its own method of self defence is to roll up into a ball to protect itself. Pangolins are found throughout Peninsular Malaysia and Borneo, often straying into gardens and plantations.

Pangolin

Bats (*kelawar*) Malaysia has more than 100 species of bats, most of which are tiny, insect-eating (insectivorous) species that live in caves, and under eaves and bark. All bats are nocturnal; most insectivorous bats have poor eyesight and navigate by emitting a constant stream of high-pitched squeaks that bounce off objects like radar. This extraordinary adaptation is sensitive enough to locate small insects in flight. The fruit bats or flying foxes are only distantly related to the insectivorous bats; unlike them they have well developed eyes and do not navigate by echolocation. Fruit bats roost in great, noisy colonies and sally forth at dusk in search of fruiting trees such as figs; they also raid orchards and can become a pest to farmers. Fruit bats can be seen at Taman Negara; the great cave systems of Borneo host a famous bat spectacle: the best place to witness this is at Deer Cave in Mulu National Park in Sarawak, where several million insectivorous bats stream out at dusk in wave after chittering wave.

continued from page 27

Mt Kinabalu Sabah's most popular attraction also has great birdwatching. Follow any of the jungle trails that radiate from the park accommodation complex, or simply walk around the gardens in the early morning to see laughingthrushes, drongoes, bulbuls, Bornean treepie, green magpies and various flycatchers. The climb to the summit features several species not seen around park HQ, including the dainty mountain black-eye, mountain blackbird and mountain serpent-eagle.

Sungai (River) Kinabatangan A narrow corridor of forest along Sabah's longest river hosts all eight of Borneo's hornbill species, at least three pittas (including the endemic blue-headed and black-and-crimson pittas), rarities such as Storm's stork, and blue and paradise-flycatchers.

Danum Valley Superb, towering and untouched, the rainforest of Danum Valley in Sabah is famous for its wildlife, although some work may be required to search it out. Pheasants and hornbills are still relatively common, and a bizarre endemic species, the Bornean bristlehead, is often seen in this area.

Waterbirds you may see include various herons and storks. One of the best ways to see them is to visit Kuala Selangor Nature Park near Kuala Lumpur, although a good variety of herons and egrets can usually be seen near rice paddies and estuaries around the region.

Both Peninsular Malaysia and Borneo are home to a number of beautiful pheasants, although they are more often heard than seen. The most spectacular of these is the argus pheasant; the striking male has a long showy train that trails 1m or more behind him. Silvery-grey in colour, its tail has numerous eye-shaped markings which it raises in courtship displays.

Kingfishers usually live near waterways, where they hunt for fish, crabs and other small animals. The stork-billed kingfisher is a large, common species found along rivers and mangroves. It is coloured blue and fawn, and has a massive red bill from which it takes its name.

Hornbills are one of the bird attractions of Malaysia; nine species have been recorded and various species are important in the folklore of Bornean tribes. Hornbills are large – up to 1m in length – and generally patterned black and white. All have large, downward-curving bills, and some have a bushy crest, colourful face and bill markings or other adornments. Despite their great size, they can be difficult to spot in the rainforest canopy and are best seen when they fly. The great hornbill is the largest species in the region and is found only on the peninsula. The rhinoceros hornbill is one of the most spectacular species, because of its huge red and yellow bill with a casque on top.

Pittas are the jewels of the forest. These medium-sized birds of the rainforest are brilliantly coloured and seem to glow in the gloom of the forest floor, where they hunt insects and spiders. No fewer than eight species inhabit the rainforests of Borneo, of which two – the blue-headed and the black-and-crimson pittas – are particularly beautiful and found nowhere else. Others are also found on the peninsula – the rusty-naped pitta is found at Fraser's Hill and the rare mangrove pitta can sometimes be seen at Kuala Selangor.

The broadbills are related to pittas, and like them can be brightly coloured. Unlike pittas, they spend much time in the forest canopy, where they often perch then sally forth after insects. The aptly-named black-and-red broadbill has a bulbous, bright blue bill to offset its already colourful livery; it makes untidy nests of dried grass and is usually seen along rivers – look for it at Taman Negara or the Sungai Kinabatangan in Sabah.

The many species of babblers and bulbuls can pose a perplexing identification problem – most are rather drab in colouration and many species look very similar to each other. Babblers in particular may skulk in the undergrowth and be difficult to see – if not hear. Bulbuls are among the most common birds seen by visitors and at least one or two species usually inhabit parks or gardens.

Other small birds that may be seen in gardens and patches of forest include the

DAVID ANDREW

SIMON ROWE

RICHARD I'ANSON

Top: Rafflesia – the world's largest flower – is a carrion plant which preys on insects, Gunung Gading National Park, Sarawak.
Bottom Left: The slippery ridge of the carnivorous pitcher plant enables insects to slide down into a pool of liquid where it is digested.
Bottom Right: Heliconia at Kota Kinabalu, Sabah.

GLENN BEANLAND

PAUL HELLANDER

SUSAN STORM

SUE TAN

TOURISM MALAYSIA

TONY WHEELER

Top: Rhododendron (left); orchid in Singapore's Botanic Gardens (right).
Middle: Heliconia (False Banana) at Kota Kinabalu, Sabah (left); berries in Kinabalu National Park, Sabah (right).
Bottom: Hibiscus, Malaysia's national flower (left); orchid in the Cameron Highlands, Perak (right).

iridescent sunbirds, whose sharp, downward-curving bills are used for extracting nectar; leafbirds, which are all active little insect-hunters with bright green colouration; and a bewildering array of flycatchers – including monarchs, jungle-flycatchers and the blue-flycatcher. The Asian paradise-flycatcher is one of the most attractive examples of the latter: the female is a rich chestnut colour but the male is mainly white and sports two trailing tail streamers which are many times its own body length.

Other Animals There are far too many forms and species to name here, but a few groups stand out for their interest, beauty or – too often – for their ubiquity. Some 250 species of reptiles have been recorded, including 100 of snakes, 14 of tortoises and turtles, and three of crocodiles.

Most snakes are inoffensive, but all should be treated with caution because if you are bitten by a dangerous one you may find yourself far from help. Cobras and vipers are the most dangerous, although the chances of encountering one are low. Pythons are sometimes seen in national parks and one, the reticulated python, is reputed to grow to 10m in length. Several species of flying snakes inhabit the rainforests; they don't literally fly, but glide from trees by extending a flap of loose skin along either side of their body. There are also flying lizards and frogs. Sea turtles may be seen near offshore islands, particularly Pulau Sipadan in Borneo.

Insects are abundant, to say the least, and number upwards of 150,000 species in Malaysia. Most spectacular and beautiful are the many hundreds of species of butterflies, including the large birdwings, which may have a wingspan of 20cm. The moon moth is a large, attractive green moth with long tail streamers.

National Parks

The British established the first national park in Malaysia in 1938 and it is now included in Taman Negara, Malaysia's major national park which crosses the borders of Terengganu, Kelantan and Pahang on the peninsula. East Malaysia has several national parks which form a valuable and growing network.

For those who wish to experience the primeval world of the ancient rainforests, Taman Negara offers a spectacular introduction. However there are other places in Peninsular Malaysia which can be visited, and a trip to East Malaysia is recommended, if only to see (and perhaps climb) Mt Kinabalu.

Accommodation is not a problem when visiting most national parks. Various categories are available, from hostel to chalet. Transport and accommodation operations are increasingly being handled by private tour companies, and you have to book in advance and pay a deposit. The best times to visit are June to September (east coast, including Taman Negara), October through March (west coast) or April to September for East Malaysia. See the 'National Parks of Malaysia' table in this chapter for more information.

Marine Parks

Malaysia's marine parks range from inaccessible islands with no tourist facilities to tourist meccas like Pulau Tioman. In order to protect their fragile underwater environments, no potentially destructive activities like fishing or motorised watersports are allowed. This makes these parks ideal for activities such as snorkelling, diving or just lazing around on the beach.

Some of the more accessible marine parks are Pulau Payar (Kedah), Pulau Tioman (Pahang), the Seribuat Archipelago (Johor), Pulau Kapas (Terengganu), Pulau Redang (Terengganu), Pulau Perhentian (Terengganu) in Peninsular Malaysia and Tunku Abdul Rahman and Turtle Island national parks in Sabah in East Malaysia. Some of the parks have also been gazetted as national parks. See the relevant chapters and the special Diving & Snorkelling section in the Terengganu chapter for details of these parks, their facilities and features.

NATIONAL PARKS OF MALAYSIA

Park	Location	Features
Peninsular Malaysia		
Taman Negara	Pahang, Kelantan, Terengganu	one of the oldest tropical jungles in the world, excellent jungle trekking, large mammals, riverboat rides
Kenong Rimba (State Park)	Pahang	tropical jungle similar to Taman Negara's, good jungle trekking, some waterfalls, the possibility of spotting rare mammals and birds
Endau-Rompin	Johor, Pahang	a lowland tropical jungle, waterfalls, jungle trekking, some rare wildlife
East Malaysia		
Gunung Mulu	Sarawak	perhaps Malaysia's most spectacular park, thick tropical jungle, spectacular caves, high mountains, good trekking, fantastic plants and birds
Lambir Hills	Sarawak	small park with good short jungle trails, nice swimming hole, canopy viewing tower
Niah Caves	Sarawak	fascinating caves filled with bats and swallows, jungle walks, wildlife including monkeys, tropical birds, butterflies and crocodiles
Bako	Sarawak	beautiful coastal park with a variety of vegetation including pitcher plants and mangrove swamps, monkeys, good walking trails
Gunung Gading	Sarawak	one of the best places in Borneo to see the rafflesia, good walking trails, pleasant forest
Kubah	Sarawak	small park with good hiking trails across forested sandstone hills, waterfalls
Batang Ai	Sarawak	tropical jungle around a huge reservoir, lots of wildlife
Loagan	Sarawak	little-visited park with a large lake, home to a wide variety of aquatic birds
Similajau	Sarawak	pleasant coastal park with good beaches, walking trails, green turtles and 230 species of bird
Tanjung Datu	Sarawak	remote rainforest, excellent beaches, new park, not yet open to public
Kinabalu	Sabah	4101m Mt Kinabalu, the highest mountain in South-East Asia, great hiking, a huge variety of plant life and birds
Tunku Abdul Rahman	Sabah	five lovely islands with clear water, some coral reefs and a few hiking trails
Turtle Islands	Sabah	three small islands with white-sand beaches, nesting place of green and hawksbill sea turtles
Crocker Range	Sabah	a vast region of undisturbed tropical jungle, mountainous terrain, rare plants and wildlife

Facilities	Accommodation	Access
extensive tourist facilities both inside the park and nearby	resorts at all price levels, jungle chalets, nearby village, camping	easy access by boat or car from Jerantut
limited tourist facilities	one resort, camping	boat or train from Kuala Lipis, then a short hike
very limited facilities	some huts, camping	access is difficult, usually by boat and jeep from Endau
well-developed facilities at park HQ, limited elsewhere	privatised resort with dorms and chalets, camping	plane from Miri, Marudi, Limbang, riverboat from Miri
limited facilities, one canteen	bunkhouse and chalets	bus from Miri
well-developed tourist facilities including a visitors' centre	dorm and chalets in the park, hotels nearby	bus from Miri or Bintulu
well-developed facilities	range of options at the park HQ, camping	bus then boat from Kuching
well-developed facilities	dorm and chalet at park HQ	bus from Kuching via Lundu
limited facilities	dorm and chalet at park HQ	bus from Kuching
no facilities	none outside expensive resort	private tours from Kuching
no facilities	one hostel in the park	difficult access; bus from Miri then chartered boat or 4WD
good facilities	dorm and chalet at park HQ	car or taxi from Bintulu
no facilities	none	boat from Semetan
well-developed tourist facilities	resort with all levels at the peak's base, huts on climb	bus or taxi from Kota Kinabalu
facilities vary from island to island	camping and chalets	boats from Kota Kinabalu
nothing outside the resort	private resort	boats from Sandakan
no facilities	none	not yet accessible to public

OTHER PARKS & RESERVES

Park	Location
Templer Park	22km north of Kuala Lumpur
Sungei Buloh	15km north-west of Kuala Lumpur
Taman Alam Kuala Selangor	Selangor
Sepilok Orang-Utan Rehabilitation Centre	Sabah
Danum Valley Conservation Area	Sabah
Semenggok Wildlife Rehabilitation Centre	Sarawak

GOVERNMENT & POLITICS

Malaysia is a confederation of 13 states and the federal districts of Kuala Lumpur and Pulau Labuan (Labuan Island). It is a constitutional monarchy and the head of state is the *yang di-pertuan agong*, or 'king', elected every five years by the sultans who head nine of the peninsular states.

The country has two houses of parliament. The lower house is the Dewan Rakyat (People's Council), consisting of 180 members elected every five years, and it is this house that forms the government and holds the real power. The senate, or Dewan Negara (States' Council), consists of 70 members, 40 of whom are appointed by the yang di-pertuan agong on the basis of their experience or wisdom or to represent interest groups or minorities. The remaining 30 are elected by the state legislatures.

Each state has its own government, and members are elected to the unicameral state legislatures every five years. States have wide powers to pass laws. Each state also has a head of state, and in the case of the peninsula the hereditary sultans, who exist in all states except Melaka and Penang, are appointed. The states of Sabah and Sarawak in East Malaysia are rather different from the Peninsular Malaysian states, since they were separate colonies, not parts of Malaya, prior to independence. The four states without sultans have a *yang di-pertuan negeri*, or governor, appointed by the federal government for four years.

The judiciary is composed of the Supreme Court, High Courts and magistrates courts. Penghulus courts were set up to hear cases at a village level, but they can only try disputes worth no more than RM50, so cases are very rarely heard. The *penghulu* (village chief) acts on an informal level. In Sabah and Sarawak native courts exist to try breaches of native law or custom, acting in much the same way as Islamic courts, which are there to try breaches of Islamic *syariah* law among Muslims.

Sultans

The sultans' positions are enshrined in the constitution, but their power is largely ceremonial. The yang di-pertuan agong must approve all acts of parliament and can refuse the appointment of a prime minister, but he acts on the advice of parliament and the cabinet. Sultans, who are heads of their respective states, have the same powers and responsibilities.

The political process is very similar to the institutions of governors and governors-general as found in British Commonwealth countries.

The first great sultanate was that of Melaka, which rose to prominence in the 15th century. It began life as a Hindu kingdom, but with the conversion to Islam the raja, or

Features	Accommodation
protected forest area	none
Forestry Research Institute of Malaysia jungle park	none
mangroves, secondary forest, birdlife	simple
lowland forest and orang-utans	none
jungle trails, many species of birdlife, and mammals	luxury resort
injured wildlife, worth a visit if you can't make it to Sepilok	none

king, took on the title of sultan. Hindu traditions and court customs continued in the courts of the sultans despite the rise of Islam and are still evident today. After European intervention and the defeat of Melaka, the peninsula fragmented into several small sultanates and by the 19th century the Malay sultanates were in disarray, many of them involved in internal wars, while the Siamese controlled the north of the peninsula.

The British stepped in, using military force to resolve some disputes and appointing Residents to the sultans as 'advisers'. The British exerted their influence by shoring up the sultanates, which may well have disappeared otherwise. The British increasingly assumed power from the traditional monarchs. But the sultanate system was maintained along with the rights and privileges of the sultans, which were enshrined in the constitution after independence from the British was gained.

For Malays, the sultans are the upholders of Malay tradition and the symbolic heads of Islam. They command great respect, especially in rural areas and the more traditional east-coast states. The royal families have emerged as a modern elite and are very active in government and business. Scandals involving assault, abuse of privilege and corruption have helped to undermine their position, but they still exert a great deal of influence in modern Malaysia.

ECONOMY

Malaysia is one of the economic success stories of the postwar period. Since independence it has moved away from its reliance on tin and rubber and diversified its economy by aggressively attracting investment, both foreign and domestic. After Singapore and Brunei, it is the most developed country in South-East Asia, with the highest standard of living.

Malaysia's push to become a manufacturing centre has seen it become a major supplier of electronic components and equipment, and along with other products such as textiles and footwear, manufactured goods now account for over half of all exports. Important primary exports are petroleum and petroleum products, logs and timber, and palm oil. Rubber now accounts for less than 2% of exports, tin barely half of 1%. Major imports are machinery and equipment, chemicals, food and petroleum products. Major trading partners are Japan, the USA and Singapore.

Malaysia's rapid increase in manufacturing has been achieved by modernising the country's transport, communications and energy infrastructure, developing industrial zones and offering substantial tax breaks for investors in export-oriented industries.

The government has promoted a relatively open, market-oriented economy and has instituted significant reforms by dismantling

Sultans, Fast Cars & the Law

Like England, Malaysia has royalty and nobility – but there are nine royal families, not just one. Like Britain's House of Windsor, they come in for plenty of criticism – but you don't hear it, because criticising Malaysia's royalty can put you in prison on a charge of sedition. In part this relates back to Malaysia's early history as an independent state, when politicians often had royal connections, notably the first prime minister, Tunku Abdul Rahman.

Nine of the states of Malaysia are ruled by sultans, who are totally exempt from the law. They take it in turn to assume the title of yang di-pertuan agong, effectively the 'king' of Malaysia. Although they're not inclined towards prancing around half-naked or indulging in anguished marital separations, the Malaysian nobility does produce its own colourful scandals.

The funniest in recent years has been that concerning the sultan of Kelantan and his penchant for expensive toys. Each sultan is allowed to own seven imported cars without paying import duties and taxes. This rule has customarily been treated with some flexibility – 10 is near enough to seven if your maths isn't too good. Unfortunately for the sultan of Kelantan, it was finally decided that 20 was definitely more than seven, and when a brand new Lamborghini Diablo arrived in an air-freight consignment at Kuala Lumpur airport the sultan was informed he would have to pay import duties before he was allowed to take it home. 'Let me at least sit in my new toy', implored the sultan, who then proceeded to screech out of the hangar and burn rubber all the way back to the palace in Kelantan!

More serious than mere evasion of customs duty are outright cases of law breaking. In 1976 one member of the Johor royal family was actually convicted of manslaughter, then pardoned by his father, the sultan at the time. The Malaysian parliament was informed that the sultan of Johor and his son had been involved in 23 cases of assault.

Although the Malaysian government would quite like to bring the sultans to heel, their popularity in rural areas and their image as protectors of Malay culture and history make the government reluctant to meddle with the status quo. The Malaysian constitution also makes it difficult to institute changes, as it specifically states that no alteration can be made to the sultans' 'privileges, position, honours or dignities' without their agreement!

Tony Wheeler

many state-run enterprises and encouraging private enterprise to undertake many of the country's development projects. Though promoting a free market in some areas, the government is also an investor in the economy (usually as a minority partner) and controls prices on some key commodities such as fuel and rice.

Until August 1997, it seemed as though the Malaysian economy could do no wrong. In the 11 years from 1985 to 1996 the country enjoyed an average annual growth rate of more than 8%. Exports were booming, the nation's infrastructure was rapidly developing and standards of living were approaching those of more developed nations. Indeed, the economy was growing so fast that the nation couldn't keep up with its labour demands and had to import a substantial amount of its workforce from such countries as Indonesia, Thailand, the Philippines, Bangladesh and elsewhere.

Emboldened by success after success, the Mahathir government embarked on the construction of several well-publicised megaprojects. Intended to stimulate the economy and to guarantee future competitiveness, these were heralded as proof of the country's entry onto the world stage as a major player. The projects included the new high-tech capital city of Putrajaya (US$8 billion), the Bakun Dam (US$6 billion), a new airport and freeway links (US$7.6 billion), the city of Gelang Patah in Johor

(US$12.8 billion), Kuala Lumpur's Light Rail Transit (LRT; US$2 billion), power plants (US$4.8) ... the list goes on.

Then, in July 1997, a currency crisis in nearby Thailand quickly spread to the neighbouring countries of South-East Asia and the region was plunged into a recession. The ringgit, which had been one of the region's strongest and most stable currencies, plunged in value from RM2.5 to the US dollar to almost RM5 to the dollar, before the government fixed it at RM3.8 in September 1998.

Prime Minister Mahathir, never one to pull punches, quickly blamed international currency speculators for the disaster, singling out in particular American billionaire George Soros. Soros, he maintained, was trying to punish the member countries of ASEAN for its inclusion of Myanmar, with its record of human rights abuses. It was also whispered by some that religious prejudices were at work, since Soros is Jewish and the majority of Malaysians are Muslim.

Needless to say, these claims were coldly received in the west, and many commentators both inside and outside the country observed that Malaysia was to blame for a lot of its economic woes. Economists were quick to point out that many of the problems which threatened to destroy the Thai economy were also at work in Malaysia. These include an inefficient government bureaucracy, preferential awarding of government contracts and a rush of easily available capital which was carelessly invested in dubious projects, putting the nation's banks at risk.

Unlike Indonesia, Malaysia did not accept an IMF tendered bailout programme and many domestic critics pointed out that this was because it would have forced the country to do away with its discriminatory hiring policies which favour Malaysian bumiputra over other ethnic groups.

Without outside help, the Malaysian economy began to claw its way back and the ringgit regained some of its lost value. While most of the mega-projects have been put on hold, the new Kuala Lumpur international airport is open and progress is being made on KL's urban light rail lines. The setbacks of 1997 have, however, raised doubts about whether Malaysia can achieve the national goals of Prime Minister Mahathir's Wawasan 2020 programme, which aims for developed-nation status by 2020.

While Malaysians are suffering from the effects of a slow economy, the crisis has been a boon for tourists – favourable exchange rates have almost doubled the buying power of most major foreign currencies. Better still, prices have not risen to take advantage of the increased buying power, making travel in Malaysia one of the best bargains it's been in years.

POPULATION & PEOPLE

Malaysia's population is currently around 19.48 million, but the Wawasan 2020 programme, which is the government's plan for taking Malaysia into the next century, gives a target population of 70 million by 2020!

The people of Malaysia come from a number of different ethnic groups – Malay, Chinese, Indian, indigenous Orang Asli and the various tribes of Sarawak and Sabah. Approximately 85% of the population lives in Peninsular Malaysia and the remaining 15% in the much more lightly populated states of Sabah and Sarawak.

It's reasonable to say that political power is controlled by the Malays, while the Chinese control the economic sphere. The old images of Malays being a rural, traditional people and Chinese being an urban, capitalist class can still be applied, but the stereotypes are slowly breaking down. Malays dominate the countryside, but the number of urban Malays is growing, attracted by the new wealth and jobs of the cities.

The Indians, the next largest group, are less easy to categorise and are divided by religion and linguistic background. A small, English-educated Indian elite has always played a prominent role in Malaysian society, and a significant merchant class exists, but a large percentage of Indians, imported as indentured labourers by the British, remain a disadvantaged labouring class.

Malaysia is very much a multiracial society, something that has figured prominently and not always happily in its development. From the ashes of the communal riots of 1969, when distrust between the Malays and Chinese peaked, the country has managed to forge a much more tolerant, multicultural society. Though communal loyalties remain strong, the emergence of a single 'Malaysian' identity is now a much discussed and lauded concept, even if not yet really embraced.

Much of the improvement in race relations is due, paradoxically, to the government's bumiputra policy. This policy of positive discrimination in favour of the Malays, largely responsible for events in 1969, was accelerated after the riots to concentrate on Malay economic advancement. Through awarding government contracts to bumiputra groups, requiring bumiputra involvement in economic projects and targeting Malay areas for economic development, the government has increased Malay involvement in the economy, albeit largely for an elite, and helped defuse Malay fears and resentment of Chinese economic dominance.

A widespread backlash from the Chinese community has not emerged, because the government has given the country a booming economy, benefiting Chinese entrepreneurs and delivering jobs to Chinese and Malays alike. Dr Mahathir's government is also careful to show even-handedness in cultural issues and keep the Chinese community on side. Though Dr Mahathir expresses Asian chauvinism in his anti-west speeches, in itself a unifying populist issue at home, his government is keen to avoid Malay chauvinism. The Chinese remain excluded from political control, and are disadvantaged by bumiputra policies, but the government has indicated that the races will compete on an equal footing when the development goals of Wawasan 2020 are achieved.

The once bitter issue of the promotion of Bahasa Malaysia, the national language, has also ultimately helped unify the country as the proficiency and use of the language has spread among all races. The government has also allayed Chinese and Indian concerns at attempts to introduce it as the sole language of instruction in all levels of education and is again promoting English, for business as well as communal reasons.

Malaysia has made enormous strides in promoting racial harmony, but old divisions exist. Moves such as those by the Kelantan government to introduce Islamic law applying to all its citizens, including the Chinese, has the potential to open old wounds, but the federal government is keen to put a lid on any threats to the largely peaceful multicultural balance in today's Malaysia.

Peninsular Malaysia

Malays The Malays are the majority indigenous people of the region, although they were preceded by aboriginal people, small pockets of whom still survive. The Malays are Muslim and, despite major changes in recent decades, are still to some extent 'country' rather than 'city' people.

Despite the fact that they account for only 55% of the population of Peninsular Malaysia (much less in Borneo), they are largely responsible for the political fortunes of the country.

Chinese The Chinese were later arrivals. Although some have been here since the time of Admiral Cheng Ho's visit to Melaka in 1405, the vast majority of the region's Chinese settlers have arrived since the beginning of the 19th century.

Most arrived from southern provinces of China but belong to different dialect groups, the major ones being Hakkas, Hokkiens, Teochews, Cantonese and Hainanese. Although all Chinese use the same written language, the dialects are not mutually comprehensible. Most Malaysian Chinese nowadays speak Mandarin; if they don't, a Hokkien and a Hakka speaker may well have to resort to English or Malay to communicate.

The Baba Chinese, or Peranakans, of Melaka speak a Malay dialect but are still culturally Chinese.

The Chinese comprise about 35% of the population in Peninsular Malaysia, 30% in Sarawak and 16% in Sabah. They are generally traders and merchants.

Indians The region's Indian population arrived later still and in a more organised fashion. Whereas the Chinese flooded in of their own volition, the Indians were mainly brought in to provide plantation labour for the British colonists. Usually landless labourers, they were enticed under indentured labour schemes of three to five years, though later arrivals were free labourers who paid their own passage. Most of the Indian population is made up of Tamils, while the rest are mainly Malayalis from the other southern Indian state of Kerala, with a smattering of Punjabis, Gujeratis, Telugus and Bengalis. They account for 10% of the population on the peninsula, and are mainly concentrated in the west coast's larger towns.

Orang Asli There are still small scattered groups of Orang Asli, 'Original People', in Peninsular Malaysia. They number over 80,000 according to the latest census, and are the descendants of the people who inhabited the peninsula before the Malays arrived. Although most have given up their nomadic or shifting-agriculture techniques and some have been absorbed into modern Malaysian society, there are still a number of Orang Asli settlements in the forests and rural areas of the interior. There are many Orang Asli tribes, but the three main racial groups are the Negritos, the Senoi and the Proto-Malays.

The Negritos are thought to be the oldest inhabitants of the Malay Peninsula and are the smallest group of Orang Asli people, numbering less than 3000. They resemble Melanesians but are small in stature and have intermarried with other Orang Asli such as the Senoi. Some suggest they are more closely related to the tribal people of India and the Andaman Islands. Traditionally nomadic hunters, the Negritos inhabit the inland forest areas of the peninsula, primarily in Kelantan and Perak. The largest tribes are the Jahai and the Batek.

The Senoi are the most numerous Orang Asli (46,000), and were the second wave of immigrants to inhabit Peninsular Malaysia. Their language is related to the Mon-Khmer hill tribes of Cambodia, and for the most part they resemble Malays. Traditionally they are shifting agriculturists, forming permanent settlements, but today many Senoi have integrated into modern Malaysian society. Senoi villages are found mostly in Perak, Pahang and Kelantan, and the largest tribes are the Semai and the Temiar.

The Proto-Malays (population 35,000) are the third group of immigrants to the peninsula. It is thought that they came from Sumatra and the Riau Archipelago of Indonesia; they closely resemble the Malays and nowadays speak Malay. Proto-Malays are most numerous in Pahang, but are found

Minangkabaus

The Minangkabau people from Sumatra migrated to Peninsular Malaysia in quite large numbers from the 17th century. They were attracted by the rich tin mines of the peninsula, and many also became successful merchants and farmers, particularly in the sparsely settled interior. The Malay sultans had no objections to the large numbers of Minangkabau immigrants, as they brought Islam with them to the interior and also went a long way towards off-setting the large influxes of Chinese.

Although the Minangkabau people were related ethnically and linguistically to Malays on the peninsula, there was a marked difference in their social organisation in that it was matrilineal – descent and inheritance are traced through the female line.

While property is vested in the clan, or *suku*, ownership of it passes from mother to daughter. On marriage the husband enters his new wife's suku. Traditionally, the husband would continue to live with his mother after marriage and only visit his wife in her suku!

throughout Johor, Negeri Sembilan and Selangor. The largest tribes are the Jakun, who can be visited at Tasik Cini; the Temuan; and the Semelai, centred mostly on Tasik Bera in Pahang.

Although some Orang Asli are Muslim (most notably the Proto-Malay Orang Laut of south-west coastal Johor), the majority have resisted conversion and retain their animist religions. Orang Asli are classified as bumiputra and therefore are eligible for the same economic advantages as the Malays, but they are still the most economically disadvantaged group. While wage-earners do contribute to village economies, many Orang Asli communities still rely on traditional crops and hunting, and some still live a traditional, nomadic life in the jungles. The government is keen to promote development but also to foster Islam in some areas.

East Malaysia

The population make-up of the east Malaysian states of Sabah and Sarawak is far more complex than in Peninsular Malaysia, with around 25 different ethnic groups in the two states.

Malays The indigenous Malays, who make up around 20% of the population, are descended from local people who converted to Islam and adopted Malay customs around 400 years ago.

The Melanie, who number approximately 100,000 in Sarawak, are also native Malays but are ethnically different from the Malays – they have different physical characteristics and speak different dialects. Most of the Melanie are followers of Islam, while the rest have converted to Christianity.

Chinese The Chinese minority in the east Malaysian states is less significant than on the mainland but is no less important, as they are basically the merchants and have a large influence on the economy.

Dayaks Dayak is the term used to cover the non-Muslim people of Borneo. These people migrated to Borneo at times and along routes which are not clearly defined. It is estimated that there are more than 200 Dayak tribes in Borneo.

Ethnic Groups in Sarawak The most important ethnic group in Sarawak is the Iban, numbering around 395,000. The early Europeans in the area named them Sea Dayaks, as they used to make forays down the rivers and out to sea. They were fierce head-hunters and gave the Europeans a bad time along the coasts. Today the Iban are largely longhouse dwellers who live along the Rejang and Baram rivers in Sarawak.

Another important group is the Bidayuh people, numbering about 107,000 in Sarawak. These people live along the rivers in Sarawak's First Division, which is the area around Kuching including the Sungai (River) Skrang.

The other, much smaller, tribes, including the Kenyah, Kayan, Kelabit, Lun Bawang, Kajang, Kedayan, Bisaya and Punan, make up around 5% of Sarawak's total population. It's these small tribal communities of Sarawak that are worst hit by the logging which is currently destroying the rainforests at an incredible rate. The Penan (Punan) are particularly hard hit, as they lead a purely hunter-gatherer existence, relying totally on the forest for food and shelter. The other communities practise the much-maligned (by the government) slash-and-burn agriculture and so, while they are less devastated by the loss of forest, still find their land, lifestyle and customs under siege from the disruption.

Ethnic Groups in Sabah The people of Sabah are different again. While there are significant minorities of Chinese (16%) and Bajaus (10%), the major ethnic group is the Kadazans, who account for around 25%. Other smaller groups include the Murut (5%), Malays, Orang Sungai (river people), Sulu, Tidong and Bisaya. There are also significant numbers of refugees/immigrants from both the Philippines and Indonesia, residing mostly in the eastern towns of Sandakan, Lahad Datu and Tawau.

The Kadazans are traditionally agriculturists and longhouse dwellers who live mainly in the west of the state. These days there have been large-scale conversions to Christianity and Islam, and many Kadazans have moved to the cities.

The Bajau live mainly in the north-west of the state, and around Semporna in the south-east. They were originally Sulu Sea pirates but these days pursue the much more prosaic practices of agriculture and animal husbandry.

The only other group of any size is the Murut, who number around 40,000 and live in the south-west in the Tenom area. They are agriculturists who used to occupy a much larger area of Sabah but were pushed south by the migrating Kadazans.

EDUCATION

The Ministry of Education runs most schools in Malaysia, and has Chinese and Malay schools. However, the quality of education in cities is generally higher than in rural areas, and the best teachers and students are funnelled into top schools. English is taught from the first year of primary school, but standards of English education have dropped due to a lack of good teachers. According to the *Economist*, the adult literacy rate is 80%.

ARTS

It's along the east coast of Peninsular Malaysia, the predominantly Malay part of Malaysia, that you'll find Malay arts and crafts, culture and games at their liveliest and most widely practised. However, the Kelantan government has sought to ban dancing and other un-Islamic folk performances in its push for religious purity.

Dance

There are a variety of dances and dance dramas performed in Malaysia. Though disco dancing is the most popular dance form these days, traditional dance troupes perform for special occasions.

Menora is a dance drama of Thai origin performed by an all-male cast dressed in grotesque masks.

Mak yong is a similar traditional form of theatre, but the participants are all females. These performances often take place at Puja Keteks, Buddhist festivals held at temples in Kelantan, near the Thai border.

The *joget* is an upbeat dance with Portuguese origins. It is danced by couples who have to move quickly although they never touch. It is the most popular traditional dance in Malaysia today and is often performed at Malay weddings by professional dancers. In Melaka it is better known as *chakunchak*.

Rebana kercing is a dance performed by young men to the accompaniment of tambourines. Other dances, not all of which are from the east coast, include the *tari piring, hadrah* and *zapin*.

The *rodat* is a dance from Terengganu and is accompanied by the *tar* drum.

Berdikir barat is a comparatively recent activity – a sort of poetic debating contest where two teams have to ridicule and argue with each other in instantaneously composed verse!

Music

Musical Instruments Traditional Malay music is based largely on the *gendang* (drum), of which there are more than a dozen types. The four most commonly used are:

rebana besar – used at major festivals and on religious occasions

Kelantan men perform traditional Malay music on the rebana ubi long drums.

rebana ubi – the long drums of Kelantan, made from hollowed-out logs
kompang or rebana kercing – used widely at official functions
tar – used as an accompaniment to the rodat dance

Other percussion instruments include the gong, cerucap (made of shells), raurau (coconut shells), kertuk and pertuang (both made from bamboo), and the wooden celampang.

Wind instruments include a number of types of flute (such as the *seruling* and *serunai*) and the trumpet-like *nafiri*.

Stringed instruments are also an important component of a traditional ensemble. Instruments include the *biola, gambus* and *sundatang*.

The *nobat* is an exclusive royal orchestra of four or five players using drums, flute, trumpet and gong. They play only on ceremonial occasions and are only found these days in the states of Kedah, Terengganu, Johor and Perak.

The *gamelan*, a traditional Indonesian gong orchestra, is also found in the state of Kelantan, where a typical ensemble will comprise four different gongs, two xylophones and a large drum.

Wayang kulit is a dying art due to the advent of TV.

Music Types Much Malay music has heavy Islamic and Chinese influences and takes different forms. The major types include:

hadrah – Islamic chants, sometimes accompanied by dance and music
ghazal – female singers with orchestra, mainly in Johor
dondang sayang – Chinese-influenced romantic songs accompanied by an orchestra, mainly in Melaka
zikir – a type of religious singing

Silat

Also known as *bersilat*, this is the Malay martial art which originated in Melaka in the 15th century. Today it is a highly refined and stylised activity. Demonstrations are often performed at ceremonies and weddings, accompanied by music from drums and gongs.

Wayang Kulit

Similar to the shadow-puppet performances of other South-East Asian countries, in particular Java in Indonesia, the *wayang kulit* (shadow play) retells tales from the Hindu epic the *Ramayana*.

The Tok Dalang, or 'Father of the Mysteries', sits behind a semi-transparent screen and manipulates the buffalo-hide puppets whose images are thrown onto the screen. Characters include heroes, demons, kings, animals and, ever favourites, clowns.

Performances can last for many hours and throughout that time the puppeteer has to move the figures, sing all the voice parts and conduct the orchestra – it's a feat of some endurance. There are two forms of wayang kulit – the *wayang siam* and *wayang melayu*. Performances often take place at weddings or after the harvest.

The wayang kulit used to be an immensely popular form of entertainment, but it was all but killed off with the advent of TV. Fifty years ago there were well over 100 wayang kulit masters; these days there are less than half a dozen. The tourist industry has been something of a saviour for the wayang kulit performers, and the art form is unlikely to disappear completely.

Crafts

Batik Originally an Indonesian craft, batik has made itself equally at home in Malaysia. You'll find it in Penang on the west coast, but Kelantan is its true home.

Batik cloth is produced by drawing out a pattern with wax and then dyeing the material. The wax is then melted away by boiling the cloth, and a second wax design is drawn in. After repeated waxing, dyeing and boiling processes, an intricate and beautifully coloured design is produced.

Batik can be found as clothes, cushion covers, tablecloths, placemats or simply as works of art. Malay designs are usually less traditional than those found in neighbouring Indonesia. The wax designs can either be drawn on a one-off basis or printed with a stencil.

Kain Songket & Other Weaving A speciality of Kelantan and Terengganu, *kain songket* is a handwoven fabric with gold and silver threads through the material. Clothes made from this beautiful fabric are usually reserved for the most important festivals and occasions. *Mengkuang* is a far more prosaic form of weaving using *pandanus* leaves and strips of bamboo to make baskets, bags and mats.

Silver & Brasswork Kelantan is famed for its silversmiths, who work in a variety of ways and specialise in filigree and repoussé work. In the latter, designs are hammered through the silver from the underside. Kampung Sireh at Kota Bharu is a centre for silverwork. Brasswork is an equally traditional skill in Kuala Terengganu.

Arts & Crafts of East Malaysia The indigenous peoples of East Malaysia have a rich legacy of arts and crafts. Perhaps the most famous East Malaysian art is *pua kumbu*, a colourful weaving technique used to produce both everyday and ceremonial items decorated with a wide range of patterns. A special dyeing process known as *ikat* is used to produce the colours or pua kumbu. Ikat dyeing is performed while the threads of the pattern are already in place on the loom, giving rise to its English name 'warp tie-dyeing'.

Woodcarving is another prized art among the peoples of East Malaysia, and the most skilled carvers of all are held to be the Kenyah and Kayan peoples. In these societies, enormous burial columns carved from tree trunks were used to bury the remains of their headmen. These columns, known as *kelirieng* sometimes reached 2m in diameter and 10m high and were covered with detailed carvings from top to bottom. Decaying remnants of kelirieng are still uncovered in the rainforest of Sarawak, and an example can be seen in Kuching Municipal Park. Less formidable, but equally beautiful, the Kenyah and Kayan also produced smaller wooden hunting charms and ornate wooden knife hilts known as *parang ilang*.

Basket making is another of Borneo's more famous crafts, and those of the Iban, Kayan, Kenyah and Penan are among the most highly regarded. The most common material for basket building is rattan, but bamboo, swamp *nipah* grass and *pandanus* palms are also used. In addition to baskets, sleeping mats, seats and materials for shelters were all produced by related techniques. While each ethnic group has certain distinctive patterns, hundreds, or even thousands or years of trade and interaction has led to an intermixing of patterns. Some ethnic groups still produce baskets and other goods in the traditional way and these can be found in some of the markets of East Malaysia. Others may be offered for sale upon a visit to a longhouse.

SOCIETY & CONDUCT

Malay Customs

That Malays are Muslim is a tautology. Most follow Islam devoutly, and Islam provides the social fabric of Malay society. When Islam came to Malaysia it supplanted existing spiritual beliefs and systems of social law, or *adat*; however, conversion to Islam did not mean a total abolition of existing customs and beliefs. Many aspects of adat are still a part of everyday life in the *kampung* (village), or indeed in the suburbs of the cities. Though Islam and modern life have seen the passing of many older beliefs and customs, they have shaped Malay society.

Adat, with its roots in the Hindu period and earlier, is customary law that places great emphasis on collective rather than individual responsibility. It is very much a village-based social system and its principles still affect everyday life for many Malays. *Adat temenggong* defines the authoritarian, patriarchal system of the sultans and still influences court ritual in some areas. It owes its existence to the Hindu state, with ultimate power placed in the hands of the raja, or king.

The kampung and its obligations of kinship are at the heart of the Malay world. It is mutually supportive and places great emphasis on maintaining harmony. In principle, villagers are of equal status, though a headman is appointed on the basis of his wealth, greater experience or spiritual knowledge. Traditionally the founder of the village was appointed village leader (*ketua kampung* or penghulu), and often members of the same family would also become leaders. A penghulu is usually a *haji*, one who has made the pilgrimage to Mecca – a position of great importance.

As a religious leader, the *imam* as the keeper of Islamic knowledge and the leader of prayer also holds a position of great importance in the community. The *pawang* and the *bomoh* are keepers of a spiritual knowledge that is part of an older tradition. A pawang possesses skills and esoteric knowledge about such things as the rice harvest, rain making and fishing and knows the rituals needed to ensure their success and appease the necessary spirits. The bomoh is a spiritual healer who has not only learned the knowledge of curative plants but can contact the spirit world and harness its power. The bomoh's chants, or *mantra*, may contain Sanskrit words but will more often contain passages from the Koran and invoke the power of Allah. The bomohs, or at least their imitators, can still occasionally be seen in the markets as they put on their magic shows and then bring out their cure-all medicines for sale. Though the bomoh is a dying tradition that flies in the face of orthodox Islam, it is widely held that prominent members of UMNO (the ruling government party) consult bomohs for political guidance.

Islamic fundamentalism and western rationalism have both helped to undermine the role of the pawang and the bomoh, but spirits, magic and such things as *keramat* (saint) worship still survive in the village despite such ideas being at odds with Islamic teachings. Many traditional beliefs and adat customs have adapted to Islam, rather than having been destroyed by it.

Ceremonies Adat is most noticeable in the important ceremonies of birth, circumcision and marriage. Customs of everyday life are known as *adat resam*, while customs and traditions relating to the courts of the sultans are known as *adat istiadat diraja*.

Traditionally in a birth attended by the midwife, the baby is spat on to protect it from the spirits of disease and the Muslim call to prayer is whispered in the baby's ear. On the seventh day the baby's first haircutting *(bercukur)* is performed and the baby is named. If it is later decided that the name doesn't suit the baby or is hampering its development, the name can be changed.

The Malay wedding tradition is quite involved and there are a number of rituals to be observed. The prospective husband despatches an uncle or aunt to his wife-to-be's house to get the family's permission to marry *(hantar tanda)*. Once this is given, the couple are engaged *(bertunang)*, and then the ceremony *(akad nikah)* takes place.

The bride and groom, dressed in traditional kain songket – silk with gold thread – have henna applied to their palms and fingertips *(berinai)* and then, in a ceremony with significant Hindu influence *(bersand-*

ing), they 'sit in state' on a dais and are surrounded by both modern gifts and traditional offerings, such as a bouquet of folded paper flowers in a vase made of bath towels, ringed by quail eggs in satin ribbons. The couple are showered with *bunga rampai* (flower petals and thinly shredded *pandanus* leaves) and sprinkled with *air mawar* (rose water).

Important ceremonies in family life are accompanied by a feast known as *kenduri*. Guests can number in the hundreds and preparations take days, as many traditional dishes such as *nasi minyak* (spicy rice) and *pulut kuning* (sticky saffron rice) have to be prepared. The cost of these feasts can be a burden on poorer families.

The most important festival is Hari Raya Puasa, the end of the fasting month. New clothes are bought, families are reunited and, of course, there is much feasting in the style of the kenduri when an 'open house' is offered for family, friends and neighbours and everyone goes visiting.

Traditional Pastimes Top spinning (*main gasing*) may not seem like an activity for grown-ups to engage in, but *gasing*, Malaysian tops, are not child's play. A top can weigh up to 7kg and it takes a good deal of strength to whip the 5m cord back and spin the top competitively. The top is hurled on to a polished mud slab, then scooped up with a thin wooden bat and placed to spin on a small, metal-tipped wooden post.

Top-spinning contests are held in east-coast villages during the slack time of year while the rice is ripening. Contests are usually between teams of fighting tops, where the attackers attempt to dislodge the defenders from a prearranged pattern, or there are contests for length of spin. The record spinning time approaches two hours!

Flying kites is another child's game that takes on adult-size proportions on the east coast. Kite-flying contests include events for greatest height reached and also competitions between fighting kites.

The kites, which can be up to 2.5m wide, are real works of art. There are cat kites, bird kites and, most popular, the *wau bulan*, or moon kite. An attachment to the front of the kite makes a humming noise and in favourable conditions a kite may be left flying, humming pleasantly, all night. Kites are popular souvenirs of Malaysia, and a stylised Kelantan kite is the symbol of Malaysia Airlines.

Kites flown in Peninsular Malaysia are ornately decorated and can be 2.5m wide.

Sepak raga is one of the most popular kampung games. The equipment needed to play the game is simplicity itself – a lightweight ball made of strips of rattan. Drawn up in a circle, the opposing teams must keep the ball continuously in the air, using legs, head and shoulders. Points are scored for each time a team member hits the ball.

Sepak takraw is a version of the same game where the players hit the ball back and forth over a net, as in volleyball – but again without using hands. It's a popular sport in a number of South-East Asian countries and the Thais are the champions.

Bird-singing competitions are a popular pastime, particularly on the east coast. The *merbuk* and *tekukur* dove birds are suspended in highly decorative cages from 8m-high poles, supposedly because this is the height at which the birds feel most relaxed. Apparently each bird has its own unique song.

It's all taken very seriously and competition is fierce – at a large contest there may be as many as 300 birds, and champion tweeters can be worth anything up to RM50,000! Kota Bharu is one of the best places to see a bird-singing contest as they take place fairly regularly. Larger local and national competitions are also held annually.

Chinese Customs

The Chinese are born into a very different cultural tradition from that of the Malays. Chinese culture has evolved over 3000 years, and for much of that time it was the centre of Asia; indeed, as far as the Chinese themselves were concerned, the whole world. It's not surprising that the Chinese are proud of such a distinguished past, and most Malaysian Chinese can tell you the village, town or at least province in China from which their ancestors emigrated.

At the heart of the Chinese sense of cultural continuity is the family. Most Chinese families and family businesses have a small family shrine adorned with photographs of grandparents and usually plaques engraved with the names of ancestors stretching as far back as it is possible to trace them. Even distant ancestors, long removed from the petty troubles of everyday life, take a keen interest in their family's daily tribulations. It is important to pay respect to them by lighting incense and bowing with the hands clasped in prayer *(bai-bai)* at least once a day, and particularly when making decisions that may affect family fortunes.

Chinese families are patrilineal. Only male children are able to continue the family name – and it is the name that is all important in one's connection with one's ancestors. Women traditionally had very low status in the Chinese familial scheme of things. Married off at a young age, girls were considered a drain on family resources. Such attitudes are much less common nowadays, though boys are still coveted by Chinese parents.

The theoretical and ethical backbone of Chinese family relationships can be found in the teachings of China's most famous sage, Confucius. Confucianism provides a hierarchical structure of respect within the family that extends into society as a whole. It also places great emphasis on scholarship. Most Chinese parents will spare nothing to ensure their children get a good education.

Many Chinese customs are undergoing great changes these days. Marriages, for example, are now rarely arranged by matchmakers or by agreements between families, as they were in the past. An astrologer may be consulted, however, to determine an auspicious date for the wedding.

Funerals remain much more traditional, elaborate affairs. The body is dressed in best clothes and sealed in the coffin along with a few valuables. The coffin is placed in front of the ancestral altar in the house, and joss-sticks and candles are burnt. Mourning and prayers may go on for three days before the funeral, which is an expensive affair involving the hire of professional mourners and musicians who clash cymbals and gongs to drive away the evil spirits.

Chinese New Year is the major festival, and even Chinese who profess no religion will celebrate it with gusto. It is a time for clearing out the old and bringing in the new. The house is given a spring clean and all business affairs and debts brought up to date before the new year. It is a time for family, friends and feasting, and *ang pow*, red envelopes of money, are given to children. Chap Goh Meh is the last day of the Chinese New Year and is the peak of celebrations.

Indian Customs

Most Malaysian Indians are Hindus and come from southern India; so the customs and festivals that are important in the south of India, especially Chennai (Madras), are the most popular in Malaysia.

Traditionally, the *namakarana*, or name-giving ceremony, is held about 10 days after the birth of a baby. An astrologer will be called upon to give an auspicious name, often the name of a god. Boys are very much favoured, as only males can perform certain family rituals and the dowry system in India can mean financial ruin for a family with too many daughters.

continued on page 54

PLACES OF WORSHIP

PAUL HELLANDER

RICHARD I'ANSON

CLEM LINDENMAYER

Title Page: Buddha statue opposite the Kuan Yin Chinese temple, Singapore. (Richard I'Anson)
Top Left: Approaching the main entrance to the Sultan Mosque, Singapore.
Top Right: The modern Masjid Sultan Ahmed Kuantan, Pahang, Malaysia.
Bottom: Magnificent onion-domed Ubadiah Mosque, Kuala Kangsar, Perak, Malaysia.

RICHARD I'ANSON

DAVID ANDREW

PAUL BEINSSEN

PATRICK HORTON

Top Left: Lanterns glow in the New Year evening, Singapore.
Top Right: Incense burns outside a Chinese temple, Jalan Carpenter, Kuching, Sarawak, Malaysia.
Bottom Left: Lanterns decorate the courtyard of a Chinese temple, Kuala Lumpur, Malaysia.
Bottom Right: Decorative incense candles prepared for the Festival of the Hungry Ghosts, Singapore.

RICHARD NEBESKY

PATRICK HORTON

RICHARD I'ANSON

RICHARD I'ANSON

Top Left: The Sri Mahamariamman temple is a key focus of the Thaipusam festival, Kuala Lumpur.
Top Right: The part-elephant god Ganesh watches over the Sri Mariamman temple, Singapore.
Bottom Left: A *kavadi* carrier makes his pilgrimage during the Thaipusam festival, Singapore.
Bottom Right: Visitors climb the 272 steps to the Batu Caves near Kuala Lumpur, Malaysia.

Mosques

While much of the region's public architecture and many older mosques follow Indian styles with one minaret (rather than Middle Eastern designs), some newer mosques are modern showpieces of extraordinary design.

DESIGN & FUNCTION

The community gathers for prayer on Friday (Islam's holy day) at the Masjid Jamek (Friday Mosque). Smaller, local mosques are used for prayer on other days of the week.

Despite their sometimes astounding beauty and the great variety of designs, mosques are essentially simple buildings which provide a large space for communal prayer. Many mosques have domes because they are the best architectural devices for enclosing a large space without columns. Larger mosques may have a school attached.

ETIQUETTE FOR VISITORS

Remove your shoes before entering a mosque and make sure you dress appropriately. Men and women must cover their arms and legs, and a few larger mosques have robes for visitors who are not appropriately dressed. Some mosques don't admit women visitors and prayer times are often off-limits for sightseers.

EXAMPLES OF MOSQUES

One of the oldest surviving mosques in Kuala Lumpur is the picturesque Masjid Jamek overlooking Merdeka Square. In contrast, Kuala Lumpur's enormous Masjid Negara (National Mosque) is an example of modernistic design. Singapore's large Sultan Mosque is the focus for the Muslim community, and Brunei's Omar Ali Saifuddin Mosque is a stunning modern structure.

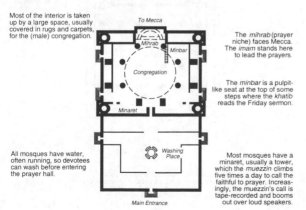

Most of the interior is taken up by a large space, usually covered in rugs and carpets, for the (male) congregation.

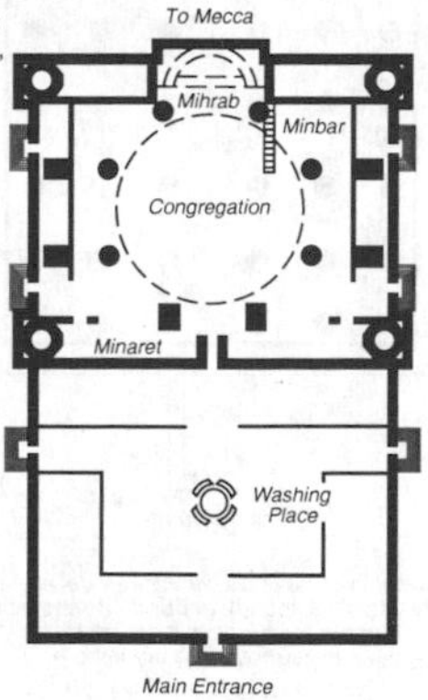

The *mihrab* (prayer niche) faces Mecca. The *imam* stands here to lead the prayers.

The *minbar* is a pulpit-like seat at the top of some steps where the *khatib* reads the Friday sermon.

All mosques have water, often running, so devotees can wash before entering the prayer hall.

Most mosques have a minaret, usually a tower, which the *muezzin* climbs five times a day to call the faithful to prayer. Increasingly, the muezzin's call is tape-recorded and booms out over loud speakers.

Hindu Temples

Most of the region's Hindus originally came from South India, so Hindu temples in Malaysia and Singapore adopt design elements from that area.

DESIGN & FUNCTION

For Hindus, the square is the perfect shape (a circle isn't perfect because it implies motion), so temples are always based on a square ground plan. Extremely complex rules based on numerology, astronomy, astrology and religious law govern the location, design and construction of each temple. These are so complicated and so important that it's customary for each temple to harbour its own set of calculations as though they were religious texts.

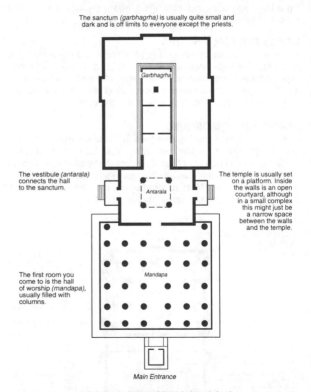

The sanctum *(garbhagrha)* is usually quite small and dark and is off limits to everyone except the priests.

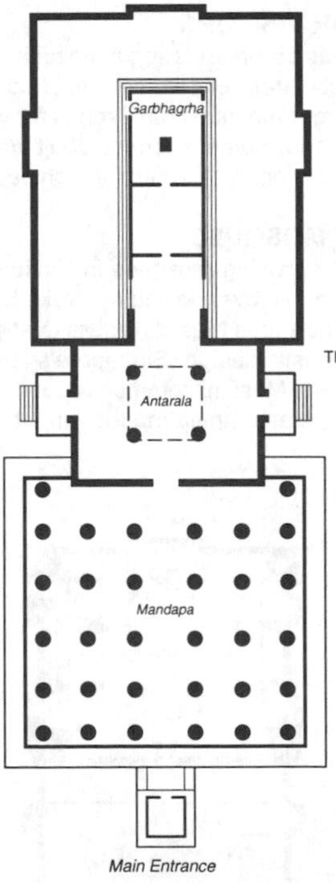

The vestibule *(antarala)* connects the hall to the sanctum.

The temple is usually set on a platform. Inside the walls is an open courtyard, although in a small complex this might just be a narrow space between the walls and the temple.

The first room you come to is the hall of worship *(mandapa)*, usually filled with columns.

Hindu temples have an elaborately decorated and usually brightly coloured *gopuram* (tower) above the street. A gopuram surmounts the gateway(s) in the walls surrounding the temple.

Thaipusam

Each year in the Hindu month of Thai (January/February), when the constellation of Pusam is in its ascendancy, up to a million devotees and onlookers flock to the Batu Caves to honour Lord Muruga. His chariot takes pride of place and is attended by thousands of devotees as it makes its way from the Sri Mahamariamman Temple in Chinatown to the Batu Caves.

The greatest spectacle is the *kavadi* carriers, the devotees who subject themselves to masochistic acts as fulfilment for answered prayers. Many of the devotees carry offerings of milk in *paal kudam*, or milk pots, often connected to the skin by hooks. Others pierce their tongues and cheeks with hooks, skewers and tridents. Couples whose prayers for children had been answered carry their babies on their shoulders in saffron cradles made of sugar cane stalks.

Most spectacular are the *vel kavadis*, great cages of spikes that pierce the skin of the carrier and are decorated with peacock feathers, pictures of deities and flowers. To the beating of drums and chants of 'Vel, Vel' the devotees form a constant procession through the caves and up the 272 steps to the main shrine, beginning their journey as early as 3 am.

Originating in Tamil Nadu and now banned in India, this is the most spectacular Hindu festival in Malaysia, celebrated with the greatest gusto in Kuala Lumpur. It is also celebrated in Penang at the Nattukottai Chettiar Temple and the Arulmigu Balathandayuthapani hilltop temple, and in Johor Bahru at the Sri Thandayuthabani Temple. Ipoh also attracts a large number of devotees, who follow the procession from the Sri Mariamar Temple in Buntong to the Sri Subramaniar Temple in Gunung Cheroh.

Each temple is dedicated to a particular god in the vast Hindu pantheon. The temple is used exclusively for religious rites. However, because Hinduism has so many rites and festivals, there's always something happening and the temple is a defacto community centre.

ETIQUETTE FOR VISITORS

Dress conservatively, remove your shoes before entering and do not attempt to enter the sanctum.

EXAMPLES OF HINDU TEMPLES

The Sri Mahamariamman Temple in Kuala Lumpur dates from 1873 and is large and ornate. Two Sri Mariamman temples, one in Singapore and the other in Georgetown on Penang Island, are also elaborately sculptured and painted.

Chinese Temples

Taoism, Buddhism and Confucianism have blended in Chinese religion, and although many temples are theoretically Buddhist or Taoist, it takes a sharp eye to tell the difference. You'll often find statues of Buddha next to Taoist deities. You may also see a statue of Confucius, but a temple devoted entirely to Confucius will be quieter and less colourful than the usual Chinese temple.

There is sometimes a separate room where the funerary tablets (small blocks of wood inscribed with characters) of deceased members of the community are displayed. Offerings are left for the spirits. The local community's 'dragon' may be stored in the temple.

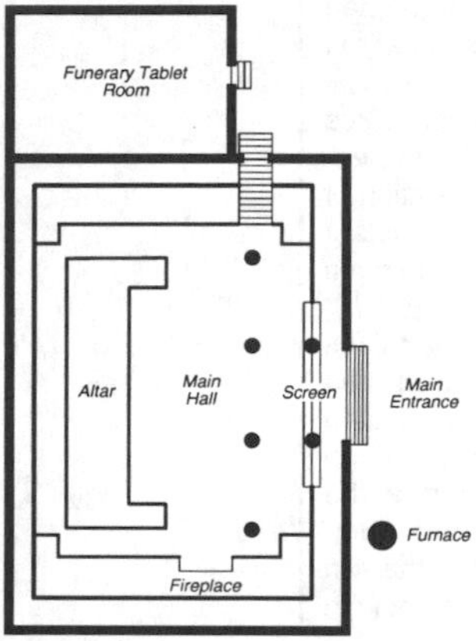

At the back of the hall there is a large and elaborately decorated altar, usually containing an image of the deity (or person) to whom the temple is dedicated. In front of the altar is a bench or table where devotees light their incense and pray.

DESIGN & FUNCTION

An elaborate 'Chinese'-style roof distinguishes most Chinese temples. Some temples are built to a multistorey pagoda design, but many are simpler single-storey buildings.

A screen often separates the entrance from the main hall, which is a riot of carved and gilded wood, bright cloth and various antiquities such as ceremonial chairs and swords. The lighting of joss sticks (incense) accompanies all prayer. People burn prayers written on paper for good fortune, or 'ghost money' to appease evil spirits. Food is offered to ghosts and later shared.

There are priests, but religious life is an individual's responsibility. There are no set times for prayers and no communal services except funerals, but the community gathers for popular holidays. In Malaysia, many Chinese participate in Buddhist and Taoist festivals, and visit a temple on days such as Wesak.

ETIQUETTE FOR VISITORS

It is customary to remove your shoes before entering a temple, although it might not be mandatory at some temples. Because people are constantly coming and going, often praying for deceased relatives, you should not treat temples as the superb art galleries they often are.

EXAMPLES OF CHINESE TEMPLES

In Kuala Lumpur, you'll find many Chinese temples, including the ornate Chan See Shu Yuen Temple. The Kuan Yin Teng Temple in Georgetown in Penang and Singapore's Kuan Yin Temple are especially popular among devotees.

In the north of Peninsular Malaysia there are some Buddhist temples (such as Wat Chayamangkalaram in Penang) which are Thai-style temples devoted to Theravada Buddhism. The Temple of 1000 Lights in Singapore is a Thai-style temple, but features technicolour Chinese decorations.

Sikh Temples

Sikhism doesn't recognise caste or class, so everyone becomes involved in ceremonies. As communal meals are a feature of temple activities, every temple has a large and colourful kitchen.

DESIGN & FUNCTION

A Sikh temple is called a *gurdwara*. Outside, a flagpole, called a *nishan sahib*, flies a triangular flag with the Sikh insignia. There is no special requirement for the building's design, but most use some elements from Punjabi gurdwaras. Sikhs worship only one god and are opposed to idol worship. You'll probably see pictures of the Gurus (the spiritual leaders who founded Sikhism), especially the first, the fifth and the 10th (last) Gurus. The wisdom of the Gurus is contained in the *Guru Granth Sahib*, a book written by Arjun, the fifth Guru, in the early 17th century. It has become an object of veneration and is regarded as the 'living' Guru. This holy book, the centrepiece of ceremonies, is 'woken' in the morning and 'draped' in robes. In the evening it is put to bed.

Food prepared in the temple kitchen is eaten as a communal meal in the dining hall.

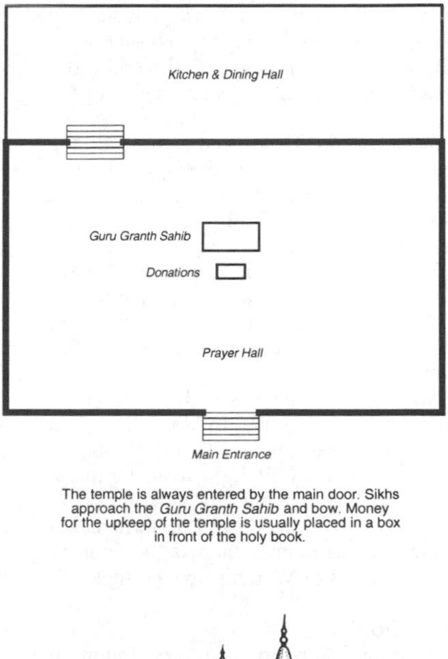

The temple is always entered by the main door. Sikhs approach the *Guru Granth Sahib* and bow. Money for the upkeep of the temple is usually placed in a box in front of the holy book.

ETIQUETTE FOR VISITORS

Sikhism is an egalitarian religion and everyone is welcome to enter the temple. However, remove your shoes and cover your head.

EXAMPLES OF SIKH TEMPLES

Sikh temples in this region have generally been quite modest buildings, such as the Sri Guru Singh Sabha on Wilkie Rd in Singapore. Unlike almost all other religions, there was little attempt to reproduce the architectural styles of the religion's birthplace. However, the increasing wealth of the Sikh community has seen some impressive new temples built recently, such as the Gurdwara Sahib Yishun, also in Singapore.

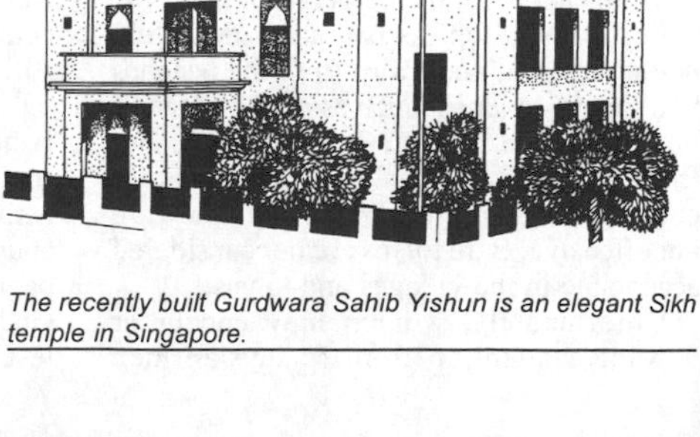

The recently built Gurdwara Sahib Yishun is an elegant Sikh temple in Singapore.

continued from page 48

The major ceremony in the life of a boy of higher caste, especially for the highest caste Brahmins, is the initiation involving receiving the sacred threads. The boy is bathed, blessed by priests and showered with rice by guests. Then three strands of thread, representing Brahma, Vishnu and Shiva, are draped around the boy's left shoulder and knotted underneath the right arm, and the boy has officially been initiated into his caste.

Arranged marriages are still common, though the bride and groom have an increasing say in the choice of their intended partner. The day, hour and minute of the wedding are also the preserve of the astrologer. The marriage is usually held at the house of the bride's family. The couple are seated on a dais and a sacred flame is placed in the centre of the room. The final ceremony involves the bridegroom placing the *thali* necklace around the bride's neck, and then the couple proceeds around the fire seven times.

Deepavali, or the Festival of Lights, is the major Indian festival in Malaysia, when homes are decorated with oil lamps to signify the victory of light over darkness. The spectacular Thaipusam is the most exciting festival, when pilgrims perform masochistic feats at temples across the country (see the Places of Worship special section).

Dos & Don'ts

As in many Muslim countries, Islam in Malaysia has seen a significant revival over the past 10 years or so. It's wise for visitors to be appropriately discreet in dress and behaviour, particularly on the more strictly Muslim east coast of the peninsula.

For women, topless bathing is definitely not acceptable, and away from the beaches you should cover as much as possible. Don't take your cue from fellow travellers but from Malaysian women. For men, shorts are considered odd attire for adults but they are not offensive. Bare torsos are not considered acceptable in the villages and towns.

Unfortunately, women may encounter unwanted attention from Malaysian men who consider western women to be of loose morals. Dressing conservatively will help to alleviate any problems.

As in most Asian countries, it is very impolite to use the left hand to give or receive something, as the left hand is used for washing after going to the toilet. Pointing or beckoning with the forefinger is considered rude, and Malaysians will motion towards something with the thumb atop a loose fist, while hailing someone will be done by waving the fingers downwards from an open hand. Shoes must be removed before entering a mosque and are also usually removed before entering someone's house.

For advice on correct etiquette in a Dayak longhouse, see the Batang Rejang section in the Sarawak chapter.

RELIGION

The variety of religions found in Malaysia is a direct reflection of the diversity of races living there. Although Islam is the state religion of Malaysia, freedom of religion is guaranteed. Hinduism has been practised in Malaysia for at least 1500 years, Islam became dominant in the mid-14th century but Hinduism has increased this century since the arrival of Indian contract labourers.

The Malays are almost all Muslims. The Chinese embrace an eclectic brew of Taoism, Buddhism and ancestor worship, though some are Christians. The majority of the region's Indian population come from south India and are mainly Hindu, though some are Muslims or Sikhs.

Although Christianity has made no great inroads into Peninsular Malaysia it has had a much greater impact upon East Malaysia, where many of the indigenous people have converted to Christianity, although others still follow their animist traditions.

Islam

In the early 7th century in Mecca, Mohammed received the word of Allah (God) and called on the people to turn away from pagan worship and submit to the one true God. His teachings appealed to the poorer levels of society and angered the wealthy merchant class. By 622 life had become sufficiently unpleasant to force Mohammed and his followers to migrate to Medina, an oasis town some 300km to the north. This migration – the *hijrah* – marks the beginning of the Islamic calendar, year 1 AH, or 622 AD. By 630 AD Mohammed had gained a sufficient following to return and take Mecca.

With boundless zeal the followers of Mohammed spread the word, using force where necessary, and by 644 the Islamic state covered Syria, Persia, Mesopotamia, Egypt and North Africa; in following decades its influence would extend from the Atlantic to the Indian Ocean.

Islam is the Arabic word for submission, and it is the duty of all Muslims to submit themselves to Allah. This profession of faith (the *Shahada*) is the first of the Five Pillars of Islam, the five tenets in the Koran which guide Muslims in their daily life:

Shahada 'There is no God but Allah and Mohammed is his prophet.' This profession of faith is the fundamental tenet of Islam. It is to Islam what the Lord's Prayer is to Christianity, and it is often quoted (eg to greet the newborn and farewell the dead).

Salah The call to prayer. Five times a day – at dawn, noon, mid-afternoon, sunset and nightfall – Muslims must face Mecca and recite the prescribed prayer. *Kiblat*, the Malay word for the direction of Mecca, accompanies an arrow in many hotel rooms.

Zakat This was originally the act of giving alms to the poor and needy. The amount was fixed at 5% of one's income. It has been developed by some modern states into an obligatory land tax which goes to help the poor.

Ramadan This is the ninth month of the Muslim calendar, when all Muslims must abstain from eating, drinking, smoking and sex from dawn to dusk. It commemorates the month when Mohammed had the Koran revealed to him; the purpose of the physical deprivation is to strengthen the will and forfeit the body to the spirit.

Hajj The pilgrimage to Mecca, the holiest place in Islam. It is the duty of every Muslim who is fit and can afford it to make the pilgrimage at least once in their life. On the pilgrimage, the pilgrim *(haji)* wears two plain white sheets and walks around the *kabbah*, the black stone in the centre of the mosque, seven times. Other ceremonies, such as sacrificing an animal and shaving the pilgrim's head, also take place.

According to Muslim belief, Allah is the same as the God worshipped by Christians and Jews. Adam, Abraham, Noah, Moses, David, Jacob, Joseph, Job and Jesus are all recognised as prophets by Islam. Jesus is not, however, recognised as the son of God. According to Islam, all these prophets partly received the word of God but only Mohammed received the complete revelation.

In its early days Islam suffered a major schism that divided the faith into two streams: the Sunnis (or Sunnites) and the Shi'ites. The Prophet's son-in-law, Ali, became the fourth caliph following the murder of Mohammed's third successor, and he in turn was assassinated in 661 by the governor of Syria, who set himself up as caliph. The Sunnis, who comprise the majority of Muslims today, including the Malays, are followers of the succession from this caliph, while the Shi'ites follow the descendants of Ali. The Shi'ites are mostly distributed in Iran, Iraq, Syria, India and Yemen. The Malaysian government actively discourages Shi'ite sects, which it regards as extremist.

Islam in Malaysia Islam came to Malaysia with the Indian traders from South India and was not of the more orthodox Islamic tradition of Arabia. Islam was adopted peacefully by the coastal trading ports of Malaysia and Indonesia, absorbing rather than conquering existing beliefs.

Islam was established in northern Sumatra by the end of the 13th century, but didn't become dominant until the third ruler of Melaka adopted it in the mid-14th century. Melaka's political dominance in the region saw the religion spread throughout Malaysia and Indonesia. By the time the Portuguese arrived in the 16th century, Islam was firmly established and conversion to Christianity was difficult.

Islamic sultanates replaced Hindu kingdoms, though the Hindu idea of kings remained. The traditions of adat (customary law) continued, but Islamic law dominated, while the caste system, never as entrenched as in India, had no place in the more egalitarian Islamic society. Women exerted a great deal of influence in pre-Islamic Malay society. There were examples of women leaders in Malay societies, and the descendants of the Sumatran Mnangkabau in Negeri Sembilan have a matriarchal society. The arrival of Islam weakened the position of women. Nonetheless, women were not cloistered or forced to wear full purdah as in the Middle East, and Malay women today still enjoy more freedom than in many other Muslim societies.

Malay ceremonies and beliefs still exhibit pre-Islamic traditions, but most Malays are ardent Muslims and to suggest otherwise to a Malay would cause great offence. With the rise of Islamic fundamentalism, the calls to introduce Islamic law and purify the practices of Islam have increased, but while the government is keen to espouse Muslim ideals, it is wary of religious extremism. Islamic law (syariah) is the preserve of state governments, as is the establishment of Muslim courts, which since 1988 cannot be overruled by secular courts. Only Muslims are tried in Islamic courts. Kelantan state is the country's hotbed of Islamic fervour, and the state government is keen to apply syariah to all of its citizens, as it has shown by outlawing alcohol in restaurants and nightclubs and banning snooker halls. The government there has also renamed the Beach of Passionate Love (Pantai Cinta Berahi) Moonlight Beach (Pantai Cahaya Bulan).

The Koran is the main source of religious law for Malays, and though few are proficient in Arabic, all Malay children are sent to learn to read the Koran. Malaysia has an annual Koran-reading competition, and passages of the Koran are read in Arabic at many Malay ceremonies. However, the main medium of religious instruction is Jawi, the Malay language written in the Arabic script. Kitab Jawi (Jawi books written by Malay religious scholars) are widely read in the mosques and *pondok* (religious schools). For centuries these books have been the main source of Islamic thought for Malays, and while they express the same beliefs and tenets held by Muslims worldwide, they do so with a Malay perspective.

There is no Malaysia-wide head of Islam. The sultans of the various states are also the Islamic heads of their respective states, while the yang di-pertuan agong is head of Islam in his own state and in Melaka, Penang, Sabah and Sarawak.

Chinese Religion

The Chinese religion is a mix of Taoism, Confucianism and Buddhism. Taoism combines with old animistic beliefs to teach people how to maintain harmony with the universe. Confucianism takes care of the political and moral aspects of life, while Buddhism takes care of the afterlife. But to say that the Chinese have three religions – Taoism, Confucianism and Buddhism – is too simple a view of their traditional religious life. At the first level Chinese religion is animistic, with a belief in the innate vital energy in rocks, trees, rivers and springs. At the second level people from the distant past, both real and mythological, are worshipped as gods. Overlaid on this are popular Taoist, Mahayana Buddhist and Confucian beliefs.

On a day-to-day level the Chinese are much less concerned with the high-minded philosophies and asceticism of Buddha, Confucius or Lao Zi than they are with the pursuit of worldly success, the appeasement of the dead and the spirits, and the seeking of hidden knowledge about the future. Chinese religion incorporates the west's idea of superstition; if you want your fortune told, for instance, you go to a temple. The other important thing to remember is that Chinese religion is polytheistic. Apart from Buddha, Lao Zi and Confucius there are many divinities, such as house gods and gods and goddesses for particular professions.

The most popular gods and local deities, or *shen*, are Kuan Yin, the goddess of mercy, and Toh Peh Kong, a local deity representing the spirit of the pioneers and found only outside China. Kuan Ti, the god of war, is also very popular and is nowadays regarded as the god of wealth. Sam Po Shan, the spirit of the Chinese Admiral Cheng Ho, who visited Melaka in the 15th century, is worshipped as the patron saint of travellers.

Joss sticks and fruit are offered at temples but most homes also have their own altars.

Integral parts of Chinese religion are death, the afterlife and ancestor worship. At least as far back as China's Shang Dynasty, funerals were lavish ceremonies involving the interment of horses, carriages, wives and slaves. The more important the person, the more possessions and people had to be buried with them since they would require them in the next world. The deceased had to be kept happy because people's powers to inflict punishments or to grant favours greatly increased after their death. Even today, a traditional Chinese funeral can be an extravagant event (see Chinese Customs under Society & Conduct earlier in this chapter).

While ancestor worship plays an important role, it is not as extensive as in China, where many generations of ancestors may be worshipped. Malaysian Chinese generally only honour the ancestors of two or three generations, that is, going as far back as their immigrant forefathers.

The most important word in the Chinese popular religious vocabulary is *joss* (luck), and the Chinese are too astute not to utilise it. Gods have to be appeased, bad spirits blown away and sleeping dragons soothed to keep joss on one's side. *Feng shui* (literally 'wind-water') is the Chinese technique of manipulating or judging the environment. Feng shui uses unseen currents that swirl around the surface of the earth and are caused by dragons which sleep beneath the ground.

If you want to build a house, high-rise hotel or find a suitable site for a grave, then you call in a feng shui expert; the wrath of a dragon which wakes to find a house on his tail can easily be imagined!

Hinduism

On first appearances, Hinduism is a complex religion. Its basic premise is simple enough though: we all go through a series of rebirths and reincarnations that eventually lead to *moksha*, the spiritual salvation which frees one from the cycle of rebirths. With each rebirth you can move closer to or further from eventual moksha; the deciding factor is your *karma*, which is literally a law of cause and effect. Bad actions during your life result in bad karma, which ends in lower reincarnation. Conversely, if your deeds and actions have been good you will reincarnate on a higher level and be a step closer to eventual freedom from rebirth. *Dharma*, or the natural law, defines the total social, ethical and spiritual harmony of your life.

Hinduism has three basic practices: *puja*, or worship; the cremation of the dead; and the rules and regulations of the caste system. Although still very strong in India, the caste system was never significant in Malaysia, mainly because the labourers brought here from India were generally from the lower classes.

Westerners often have trouble understanding Hinduism, principally because of its vast pantheon of gods. In fact, you can look upon all these different gods simply as pictorial representations of the many attributes of a god. The one omnipresent god usually has three physical representations: Brahma, the creator; Vishnu, the preserver; and Shiva, the destroyer or reproducer. All three gods are usually shown with four arms, but Brahma has the added advantage of four heads to represent his all-seeing presence. The four *Vedas*, the books of 'divine knowledge' which are the foundation of Hindu philosophy, are supposed to have emanated from his mouths.

Hinduism is not a proselytising religion, since you cannot be converted. You're either born a Hindu or you are not; you can never become one.

Hinduism in Malaysia dates back at least 1500 years and there are Hindu influences in cultural traditions, such as the wayang kulit (see Arts in the previous section) and the wedding ceremony (see the Society & Conduct section). However, it is only in the last 100 or so years, following the influx of

Indian contract labourers and settlers, that it has again become widely practised.

Religions of Indigenous Peoples

The religions of Malaysia's indigenous peoples, both on the peninsula and on the island of Borneo, are as diverse as the peoples themselves. Despite their differences, they can generally be grouped together under the term animism. While animism does not have a rigid system of tenets or codified beliefs, it can be said of animist peoples that they perceive natural phenomena to be animated by various spirits or deities, and a complex system of practices are used to propitiate these spirits.

Ancestor worship is also a common feature of animist societies and departed souls are often considered to be intermediaries between this world and the next. Some examples of elaborate burial rituals can still be found in some parts of Sarawak in East Malaysia, where the remains of monolithic burial markers and funery objects still dot the jungle around Kelabit longhouses. However, most of these are no longer maintained and they're being rapidly swallowed up by the fast-growing jungle.

The religions of the indigenous peoples of Malaysia are disappearing as fast as the rainforest in which they live. A major cause of the decline of these religions is evangelical Christianity, which is being spread through large areas of Sabah and Sarawak by competing denominations of the Christian faith. In addition to Christianity, some of the peoples of Borneo have accepted the Muslim faith, and scandals have erupted when cash bonuses were offered for those willing to convert to Islam.

However, it is clear that even without the influence of proselytising world religions, the animist religions of Malaysia would slowly disappear, as more and more indigenous peoples abandon their ancient ways and join modern technological society.

LANGUAGE

The official language of the region is Bahasa Malaysia, an Austronesian language also referred to as Bahasa Melayu (language of the Malays) or simply Malay. English is widely understood throughout Malaysia and, although it isn't the official language, it's often the common language between the various ethnic groups, especially among the middle classes. When a Tamil wants to speak to a Chinese or a Chinese to a Malay, it's likely they'll speak English.

Other languages of the region include the Chinese dialects like Cantonese, Hakka and Hokkien. The majority of the region's Indians speak Tamil, although there are also groups who speak Malayalam, Hindi or another Indian language. Many different dialects are spoken by the Dayak peoples of Sabah and Sarawak in East Malaysia (see the Batang Rejang section in the Sarawak chapter for Iban words and phrases).

For a guide to Malay and a list of useful words and phrases, see the Language chapter at the back of this book. For a more comprehensive guide to the language get a copy of Lonely Planet's *Malay phrasebook*.

Facts for the Visitor

SUGGESTED ITINERARIES

Travel in Malaysia is easily divided between the peninsula and the Borneo states of Sabah and Sarawak. To get a good look at both halves of Malaysia will take at least a couple of months, but most visitors only go to the peninsula. Borneo is almost another country, for Malaysians as well as foreign tourists.

Travel around Peninsular Malaysia is easy, so you can see a lot in a relatively short time without being hampered or exhausted by transport connections. Travel in Sarawak and Sabah is more time-consuming and requires more planning but can be more rewarding in terms of exotic vistas and off-the-beaten-track destinations.

A personal itinerary depends very much on personal interests and budget. The following outlines the major routes and main destinations to help in planning, but you'll find many more places of interest in the book. Also see the Highlights of Malaysia list.

Peninsular Malaysia

Travel on the peninsula is often divided into west and east coasts, and you can do a tour down one side and up the other for an overall look. The mountainous jungle area of the centre, containing Taman Negara National Park, is usually included in the east coast but many visit it as a diversion from the west coast.

If time is limited to a week or two, it is best to concentrate on just one coast. The west coast has the main historical and cultural attractions, while the east coast is mainly for beaches. In three or four weeks you can sample both sides, and in two months you can explore all the peninsula in depth.

The well-worn tourist route, starting from Singapore, is up the west coast via Melaka, Kuala Lumpur (KL) and the Cameron Highlands to Penang. Then over to Kota Bharu and down the east coast via Kuala Terengganu and Kuantan to the beach resorts of the Pulau Perhentian (Perhentian Islands), Pulau Tioman and others in between. Then it's back to Taman Negara and KL or Singapore. Of course there are numerous variations and a number of other places to visit, but surprisingly few visitors venture away from this route.

The main travel routes for each coast are listed below.

West Coast The west coast is the dominant half of the peninsula, containing the major cities and industry of Malaysia. Historically it is the most interesting and has the greatest colonial influence. Culturally the west coast is also the more diverse, and the cities are a vibrant Chinese/Malay/Indian mix. The west coast is more modern than the east, both in terms of economic development and people's attitudes.

The main highlights of the west coast, included in almost everyone's itinerary, are the cities of Kuala Lumpur, Penang and historic Melaka, and the hill station and tea plantations of the Cameron Highlands. The west also has a couple of decent beach resorts, as well as other hill stations and interesting cities.

Melaka-KL-Cameron Highlands-Penang in one week is possible but rushed, unless you drop one destination or just transit through KL. Two weeks is more comfortable and you could also include another destination or three: the islands and beaches of Pulau Pangkor and Langkawi, historic Taiping, Kuala Kangsar, the hill stations Fraser's Hill or Maxwell Hill. Fraser's Hill or Maxwell Hill could be substituted for the Cameron Highlands if you prefer a less developed hill station. In three weeks you could conceivably do the lot, though a month allows a more relaxing pace.

East Coast The less-developed states of Kelantan, Terengganu and Pahang are a Malay stronghold, with much less Chinese and Indian influence. The cities are bustling but

HIGHLIGHTS OF MALAYSIA

Beaches & Islands

Pulau Perhentian (Terengganu) – Deservedly popular, the white-sand beaches and crystal-clear waters of the Perhentians make these perhaps the most beautiful islands in Malaysia. Plenty of cheap accommodation and easy access from Kota Bharu.

Pulau Sipadan (Sabah) – World-class diving on the coral reefs and steep walls on this beautiful island make Sipadan Malaysia's most famous diving site.

Seribuat Archipelago (Johor) – A collection of small islands surrounded by the clear waters of the South China Sea. Easy access from Mersing and good snorkelling and diving make these a good alternative to nearby Pulau Tioman.

Pulau Tioman (Pahang) – Long the most popular island on the east coast, Tioman still holds wonders for those who choose to seek them out. Good snorkelling, diving and mountainous jungle trekking.

Pulau Langkawi (Kedah) – Decent beaches and plenty of nightlife make Langkawi a popular spot on the west coast. Those who don't like crowds can sample some of the smaller nearby islands.

Cherating (Pahang) – An oasis of laid-back tolerance on the east coast, Cherating boasts a pleasant beach, cheap bungalows, good food and some lively bars.

Cities & Kampungs

Kuala Lumpur – A modern, multiethnic city with loads of good food and nightlilfe. Take a stroll through the bustling night market of Chinatown or marvel at the world's tallest skyscrapers, the new Petronas Towers.

Penang (Penang) – Colonial neighbourhoods, colourful Chinese temples, and good food and bars make Penang one of the most interesting sights of the west coast.

Kota Bharu (Kelantan) – The best place to sample Malay cooking and culture in Malaysia with a night market second to none.

Kuching (Sarawak) – Considered by many to be the most pleasant city in Malaysia, a fine colonial district and good museums make this a popular stop in Borneo.

Melaka (Melaka) – An interesting port town where hints of the Dutch and Portuguese and their architecture remain.

Longhouses (East Malaysia) – Age old ways meet modern technology under one very long roof. If you can wrangle an invite, a stay in a longhouse is the experience of a lifetime – just watch the tuak (rice wine).

Journeys

The Jungle Railway (Kelantan, Pahang) – From Tumpat to Gemas, the Jungle Railway snakes through the peninsula's mountainous jungle – be prepared to share your seat with chickens and who knows what else.

Batang Rejang (Sarawak) – Sarawak's longest river and route for the state's trade into the jungle interior.

Beaufort–Tenom Railway (Sabah) – The only rail line in East Malaysia, this is a great way to see the jungle without sweating.

Regional Attractions

Danum Valley (Sabah) – An opportunity to sample the rainforest up close. Danum Valley offers luxury amid a teeming jungle.

Bario (Sarawak) – Excellent trekking and friendly longhouse dwellers reward travellers in these remote highlands.

Natural Wonders

Rafflesia (East Malaysia) – The largest flower in the world, this elusive plant can be glimpsed in several East Malaysian parks if your timing is right – start at Gunung Gading.

Sepilok Orang-Utan Rehabilitation Centre (Sabah) – Almost impossible to find in the wild, this is the chance to see these 'men of the forest' in fairly natural surroundings.

Poring Hot Springs (Sabah) – If you've made the ascent of nearby Mt Kinabalu, you owe yourself a soak in these hotsprings, developed by the Japanese in WWII.

National Parks

From the heights of Mt Kinabalu to the depths of Gunung Mulu's cave system, Malaysia's national parks offer great chances for energetic trekking or relaxing day trips and spotting spectacular flora and fauna. The best of the parks include Taman Negara, Gunung Mulu, Bako, Kinabalu, Tunku Abdul Rahman and Turtle Islands. See the National Parks table in the Facts about Malaysia chapter for details.

small, and it is still primarily a rural area. The east coast provides an insight into Malay culture, and Kota Bharu promotes itself as a sort of Malay culturefest, but the main attractions are the beach resorts found right along the coast. The waters on the east coast are clearer than on the west and the offshore islands have the best beaches in Malaysia.

Inland in Pahang state is the Taman Negara National Park, Malaysia's most visited and extensive area of protected rainforest.

In a week you could take in a couple of beaches, though with limited time many people prefer to choose just one and take it easy. Tioman – off Johor state, the southern gateway to Peninsular Malaysia – is a popular destination if coming from KL or Singapore. From Thailand, you could head to Kota Bharu for a couple of days and then the Perhentian Islands. In a couple of weeks you can go right along the coast, though three weeks or more is preferable if you want to take in all the beaches and relax.

Taman Negara requires at least four or five days. You really need three days in the park to do it justice, and from KL or Kuantan getting in and out of the park will take the best part of a day's travel in each direction, usually with an overnight stop in Jerantut. To do one of the longer walks, count on at least a week, closer to two if you tackle Gunung Tahan.

East Malaysia

Sarawak Sarawak is one of the least visited parts of Malaysia, and this is a pity. The longhouse experience is off limits to all but the most determined (or affluent) travellers nowadays, but Kuching is a real treat. Sarawak also has some of the best national parks in Malaysia.

In a week you could fly in to Kuching, one of the most pleasant cities in Malaysia; make a day trip to Kubah to see the world's largest flower, the rafflesia; spend two or three days on Bako National Park's jungle trails or take a longhouse tour out of Kuching for two or three days.

From Kuching, Niah Caves, some of the largest in the world, is at least a three day excursion on the way through to Sabah. Even if you fly into Mulu, at least four or five days should be allowed. A trip up the Batang Rejang to visit upriver longhouses requires a week or more to make it worthwhile.

All the highlights could be visited in three weeks, but a month is preferable.

Sabah The chief attractions of Sabah are Mt Kinabalu and the Turtle Islands National Park.

In a week, undoubtedly the place to go is Mt Kinabalu, the highest mountain between the Himalayas and the peaks of New Guinea. Though the climb is only overnight, it is easy to spend a few more days at the park itself and visit nearby Poring Hot Springs. Access is via Kota Kinabalu, from where nearby Tunku Abdul Rahman National Park's islands and beaches can be visited as a day trip, or longer if your budget allows. In two weeks, you can cover all of western Sabah, also taking in the Rafflesia Forest Reserve to see the largest flower in the world, and perhaps the Tenom-Beaufort jungle train.

Eastern Sabah has the Sepilok Orang-Utan Rehabilitation Centre, which is a day trip from Sandakan, and Turtle Islands National Park, usually a three day trip. So the main highlights of Sabah, west and east, can be seen comfortably in three weeks. The other attractions of note in eastern Sabah are Danum Valley, and Pulau Sipadan for diving, both expensive destinations – count on another week or more for these two.

PLANNING

When to Go

Rain occurs fairly evenly throughout the year in Malaysia and the differences between the main October to April rainy season and the rest of the year are not that marked, so travel is possible year-round. The exception is the east coast of the peninsula, which receives heavy rain from November to January. During these months many east-coast resorts close and the number of boat services reduce or stop altogether. Travel through the west coast is not affected. The states of Sabah and Sarawak receive high rainfall throughout the year, but it is heaviest from October to March.

Malaysia has many colourful festivals, including Thaipusam around January or February, and with such a wide ethnic diversity celebrations of one kind or another are held throughout the year. Public holidays in Malaysia are not a good time to travel. Malaysians like to get away at these times, so transport is crowded and hotel prices rise in the resorts. The peak times are Chinese New Year, Hari Raya and Christmas. If you're in the country at these times, it's best to wait until the holiday rush is over. The main beach and hill resorts also get crowded on weekends but are often deserted during the week.

The Muslim fasting month of Ramadan is generally not a problem for travel. Some services may be cut back, especially in the east-coast states of Kelantan and Terengganu, but transport, hotels, restaurants and many businesses function as normal.

Maps

Malaysia still suffers from an Emergency hangover when it comes to maps, a product of the days when detailed maps of Malaysia were unavailable because of fears that they would fall into Communist hands. The situation has barely improved and the standard of mapping in the country is one of the worst in Asia. Tourist office maps are available for the main destinations but are usually little more than sketch maps. In smaller cities and towns maps are simply unavailable unless you have government contacts. The other problem is that with so much development, maps date very quickly and new roads and buildings are not shown.

Good maps can be found for Kuala Lumpur, Penang, Melaka and some other cities. The best are foreign produced. The most useful overall map for Peninsular Malaysia is the *West Malaysia* map produced by Nelles Verlag. It has most of the major and minor roads and shows some topographical features. Nelles also produces a Malaysia all-country map which is quite good. Periplus produces an excellent series of city and regional maps, including maps of Malaysia, Johor, Kuala Lumpur, Melaka, Penang, Sabah and Sarawak. Both Periplus and Nelles maps are available in Malaysia and abroad.

A few map atlases are available in Malaysia but these are generally poor. One exception is the *Heritage Mapbook of Peninsular Malaysia* produced by Petronas – excellent if touring the peninsula by car. It has strip maps, simple town maps and descriptions of numerous points of interest.

Kuala Lumpur is the place to buy maps. (See the Bookshops entry in the Kuala Lumpur section for more information.)

What to Bring

There's really very little you need to worry about forgetting when you come to Malaysia or Singapore. There are none of those problems of finding your favourite brand of toothpaste or even common medicines. But as is the case anywhere, you will only find a good selection of products in the bigger cities, and the peninsula is a little ahead of East Malaysia in terms of availability of goods.

As for film, print film is usually not a problem, but you may want to bring slide film from your home country, as the selection in Malaysia is not very good and storage techniques are often inadequate. If it's camera equipment you want, again, it's best to bring what you need as the selection in even the biggest cities is fairly limited. Quality video film is available in major centres but hard to find in other places.

Clothes are readily available and very reasonably priced. The best advice is to bring as little with you as possible; travelling light is the only way to go. In any case, you don't need too much to start with, as the weather is perpetually of the short-sleeve variety. However, if you're planning to head up to the hill stations, you may appreciate a sweater or light jacket in the evenings. More importantly, if you're planning to climb Mt Kinabalu, it is essential to bring some warm waterproof outerwear, a pair of gloves, and a hat. A headlamp will also come in handy and is useful for those planning to explore the caves of Gunung Mulu National Park.

Dress is casual throughout the region – budget travellers may find a set of 'dress up' gear sensible for dealing with officialdom, but you're highly unlikely to need formal clothing too often. If you've forgotten something, you can easily buy it at a market and larger sizes are usually available.

Sensible accessories include sunglasses, a hat, a water bottle/canteen, a pocket knife, a day pack, a basic first-aid kit and a money belt or pouch.

If you're going to be staying primarily in budget accommodation, you should consider bringing an insect net as many of the cheaper places do not have netting on the windows.

TOURIST OFFICES

Malaysia has an efficient national tourist body, Tourism Malaysia, which has a World Wide Web site at www.tourism.gov.my and an email address tourism@tourism.gov.my. It produces several glossy brochures and other literature, most of it useful.

There are also a number of state tourist promotion organisations, such as the Penang Tourist Association, which will often have more detailed information on the area, while Tourism Malaysia can provide brochures and information for all parts of Malaysia.

Tourism Malaysia and state tourism offices are listed under the cities where there are representatives. The head office of Tourism Malaysia (☎ 03-293 5188; fax 03-293 5884) is on the 24th to 27th floors, Menara Dato Onn, Putra World Trade Centre, 45 Jalan Tun Ismail 50480, Kuala Lumpur.

Tourist Offices Abroad

Tourism Malaysia also maintains the following offices overseas. They are good places to look for information before you leave.

Australia
(☎ 02-9299 4441) Ground floor, 65 York St, Sydney 2000, NSW; (☎ 08-9481 0400) 56 William St, Perth 6000, WA

Canada
(☎ 604-689 8899) 830 Burrard St, Vancouver, BC V6Z 2K4

China
(☎ 2528 5810) Ground floor, Malaysia building, 47-50 Gloucester Rd, Hong Kong

France
(☎ 01-42 97 41 71) 29 rue des Pyramides, 75001 Paris

Germany
(☎ 069-28 37 82) Rossmarkt 11, 60311 Frankfurt-am-Main

Japan
(☎ 03-3501 8691) 5F Chiyoda Biru, 1-6-4 Yurakucho, Chiyoda-ku, Tokyo 100

Singapore
(☎ 02-532 6321) 10 Collyer Quay, 01-06 Ocean Building, Singapore 0104

South Africa
(☎ 011-327 0400) 1st floor, Hutton Court, corner of Jan Smuts Ave & Summit Rd, 2196 Johannesburg

Sweden
(☎ 08-824 99 00) Sveagen 18, Box 7062, 10386 Stockholm

Thailand
(☎ 02-631 1994), 9F Liberty Square, 287 Silom Rd, Bangkok 10500

UK
(☎ 0171-930 7932) 57 Trafalgar Square, London WC2N 5DU

USA
(☎ 213-689 9702) 818 West 7th St, Suite 804, Los Angeles, CA 90017; (☎ 212-754 1113) 595 Madison Ave, Suite 1800, New York, NY 10022

VISAS & DOCUMENTS

Passport

Visitors must possess a valid passport or internationally recognised travel document valid for at least six months beyond the date of entry into Malaysia.

Visas

Malaysian Commonwealth citizens (except those from India, Bangladesh, Sri Lanka and Pakistan), citizens of the Republic of Ireland, Switzerland, the Netherlands, San Marino and Liechtenstein do not require a visa to visit Malaysia.

Citizens of Austria, Belgium, Czech Republic, Denmark, Finland, Hungary, Germany, Iceland, Italy, Japan, Luxembourg,

Norway, Slovak Republic, South Korea, Sweden, the USA and most Arab countries do not require a visa for a visit not exceeding three months.

Citizens of France, Greece, Poland, South Africa and many South American and African countries do not require a visa for a visit not exceeding one month. Most other nationalities are given a shorter stay period or require a visa. Citizens of Israel cannot enter Malaysia.

Nationalities of most countries are given a 30 or 60 day visa on arrival, depending on the expected length of stay. As a general rule, if you arrive by air you will be given 60 days automatically, though coming overland you may be given 30 days unless you specifically ask for a 60 day permit. It's then possible to get an extension at an immigration office in the country for a total stay of up to three months. This is a straightforward procedure which can be easily done in major Malaysian cities.

Sabah and Sarawak are treated in some ways like separate countries. Your passport will be checked again on arrival in each state and a new stay permit issued. You are usually issued with a 30 day permit on arrival in Sarawak or Sabah. Travelling directly from either Sabah or Sarawak back to Peninsular Malaysia, however, there are no formalities and you do not start a new entry period, so your 30 day permit from Sabah or Sarawak remains valid. You can then extend your initial 30 day permit, though it can be difficult to get an extension in Sarawak.

Note that holders of dual citizenship should use only one passport for entering and leaving Malaysia. Declaration of dual citizenship will probably result in refusal of entry as holding two passports is technically illegal in Malaysia.

Lastly, when you go through Malaysian passport control, make sure your passport has been properly stamped. Some travellers have reported that they did not get a stamp on their way into Malaysia and then had to pay heavy fines for illegal entry into the country.

Thai You can get Thai visas from the embassies in Singapore and Kuala Lumpur or the consulates in Penang and Kota Bharu. The consulates are quick and convenient.

There are two main types of Thai visa: if you have an onward air ticket and will not be staying in Thailand for more than four weeks, you do not need to prearrange a visa and can get a free entry permit (which cannot be extended) on arrival by air or land; otherwise a two month tourist visa from a Thai consulate or embassy costs RM33. Two photos are required.

Indonesian For most western nationalities no visa is required on arrival in Indonesia, as long as you have a ticket out (not always rigidly enforced) and do not intend to stay more than 60 days. The only catch is that the 'no visa' entry only applies if you enter and leave Indonesia through certain recognised gateways. These entry and exit points include all the usual airports and seaports, but there are some places, such as Jayapura in Irian Jaya, not on the list. If you intend to arrive or leave Indonesia through one of the oddball places, then you have to get a visa in advance.

Travel Insurance

A travel insurance policy to cover theft, loss and medical problems is strongly recommended. Though Malaysia is generally a healthy and safe country to travel in, sickness, accidents and theft do happen. There are a wide variety of policies, and travel agents have recommendations. Check the small print to see if it covers potentially dangerous sporting activities, such as diving or trekking, and make sure that it adequately covers your valuables. A few credit cards offer limited, sometimes full, travel insurance to the holder.

Other Documents

Major Malaysian car hire agencies will rent a car on the production of a valid home licence with a photo and don't require an International Driving Permit. Though not required, an International Driving Permit is good to have if stopped by overly officious police looking for any dubious reason to extract 'fines' – a rare occurrence but it happens. International Driving Permits can be obtained through motoring associations in your home country. Bring your home driver's licence even if you don't intend to drive – you might decide to use it, and it can occasionally be good for identification purposes.

A Hostelling International (HI) card is of limited use in Malaysia, as only KL, Melaka and Port Dickson have HI hostels, though it can also be used to waive the small initial membership fee at some YMCAs and YWCAs. Bring it if you have one.

An ISIC international student card is worth bringing. Many student discounts, such as on the trains, are only available for Malaysian students, but some places do offer discounts for international students.

An International Health Card is not necessary to enter Malaysia except to show vaccination against yellow fever if travelling from South America. If you do get vaccinations, though, it is a good idea to have them recorded on an International Health Card, for your own record if nothing else (see the Health section for more information).

Photocopies

All important documents (passport data page and visa page, credit cards, travel insurance policy, air/bus/train tickets, driving licence etc) should be photocopied before you leave home. Leave one copy with someone at home and keep another with you, separate from the originals.

EMBASSIES & CONSULATES

Malaysian Embassies

Visas can be obtained at Malaysian diplomatic missions overseas, including:

Australia
(☎ 02-6273 1543) 7 Perth Ave, Yarralumla, Canberra ACT 2600

Brunei
(☎ 02-345652) 27 & 29 Simpeng 396-39 Kampung Sungai Akar, Jalan Kebangsaan, BC 4115, Bandar Seri Begawan

Canada
(☎ 613-241 5182; fax 613-241 5214) 360 Boteler St, Ottawa, Ontario K1N 8Y7

China
(☎ 010-6532 2531) 13 Dhongzhimenwai Dajie, Sanlitun, Beijing (☎ 2527 0921), 24th floor, Malaysia building, 50 Gloucester Rd, Wanchai, Hong Kong

France
(☎ 01-45 53 11 85) 2, bis rue Benouville, Paris 75116

Germany
(☎ 0228-38 80 30) Mittelstrasse 43, 53175 Bonn

India
(☎ 011-601 291) 50M Satya Marg, Chanakyapuri, New Delhi 110021;
Consulate: (☎ 04-434 3048) 287 TTK Rd, Chennai (Madras) 600018

Indonesia
(☎ 021-522 4947) Jalan HR Rasuna Said Kav X/6, Kuningan, Jakarta Selatan
Consulates: (☎ 061-531342) 11 Jalan Diponegoro, Medan; (☎ 761-25944) Jalan Diponegoro, No 59, Pekanbaru, Riau; (☎ 561-36060/1) 42 Jalan A Yani, Pontianak, Kalimantan

Japan
(☎ 03-3476 3840) 20-16, Nanpeidai-cho, Shibuya-ku, Tokyo 150 0036

Netherlands
(☎ 070-350 6506) Rustenburgweg, 22517 KE, The Hague

New Zealand
(☎ 04-385 2439) 10 Washington Ave, Brooklyn, Wellington

Philippines
(☎ 02-817 4581) 107 Tordesillas St, Salcedo Village, Makati, Metro Manila

Singapore
(☎ 02-235 0111) 301 Jervois Rd, Singapore 249077

Sri Lanka
(☎ 01-502 858) No 92 Kynsey Rd, Colombo 7

Thailand
(☎ 02-248 8350) 35 South Sathorn Rd, Bangkok 10120
Consulate: (☎ 74-311 072) 4 Sukhom Rd, Songkhla

UK
(☎ 0171-235 8033) 45 Belgrave Square, London SW1X 8QT

USA
(☎ 202-328 2700; fax 202-483 7661) 2401 Massachusetts Ave NW, Washington DC 20008

Vietnam
(☎ 04-846 2131) Block A-3 Van Phuc, Hanoi

Foreign Embassies in Malaysia

The following countries are among nations with diplomatic representation in Malaysia. These are in Kuala Lumpur unless noted:

Australia
 (☎ 03-242 3122) 6 Jalan Yap Kwan Sweng
Brunei
 (☎ 03-261 2800) MBF Plaza, 172 Jalan Ampang
Canada
 (☎ 03-261 2000) MBF Plaza, 172 Jalan Ampang
China
 (☎ 03-242 8495) 229 Jalan Ampang
France
 (☎ 03-249 4122) 192 Jalan Ampang
 Consulate: (☎ 04-262 8816), Wisma Rajab, 82 Bishop St, Georgetown, Penang
Germany
 (☎ 03-242 9666) 3 Jalan U Thant
Indonesia
 (☎ 03-242 1151) 233 Jalan Tun Razak
 Consulates: (☎ 04-282 4686) 467 Jalan Burma, Georgetown, Penang; (☎ 082-241734) 5A Pisang Rd, Kuching, Sarawak; (☎ 088-219110) Jalan Karamunsing, Kota Kinabalu, Sabah; (☎ 089-772052) Jalan Apas, Tawau, Sabah
Japan
 (☎ 03-242 7044) 11 Pertiaran Stonor
 Consulates: (☎ 04-229 8222) 2 Jalan Biggs, Georgetown, Penang; (☎ 088-254695), Wisma Yakin, Jalan Datuk Salleh Sulong, Kota Kinabalu, Sabah
New Zealand
 (☎ 03-238 2533) Level 21 Menara IMC, Jalan Sultan Ismail
Philippines
 (☎ 03-248 4233) 1 Jalan Changkat Kia Peng
Singapore
 (☎ 03-261 6277) 209 Jalan Tun Razak
Thailand
 (☎ 03-248 8222) 206 Jalan Ampang
 Consulates: (☎ 04-282 8029) 1 Jalan Tunku Abdul Rahman, Georgetown, Penang; (☎ 09-744 0867) 4426 Jalan Pengkalan Chepa, Kota Bharu
UK
 (☎ 03-248 2122) 185 Jalan Ampang
USA
 (☎ 03-248 9011) 376 Jalan Tun Razak
Vietnam
 (☎ 03-248 4036) Vietnam House, 4 Persiaran Stonor

Your Own Embassy

As a tourist, it's important to realise what your own embassy – the embassy of the country of which you are a citizen – can and can't do.

Generally speaking, it won't be much help in emergencies if the trouble you're in is remotely your own fault. Remember that you are bound by the laws of the country you are in. Your embassy won't be sympathetic if you end up in jail after committing a crime locally, even if such actions are legal in your own country.

In genuine emergencies you might get some assistance, but only if other channels have been exhausted. For example, if you need to get home urgently, a free ticket home is exceedingly unlikely – the embassy would expect you to have insurance. If you have all your money and documents stolen, it might assist with getting a new passport, but a loan for onward travel is out of the question.

Embassies used to keep letters for travellers or have a small reading room with home newspapers, but these days the mail holding service has been stopped and even newspapers tend to be out of date.

CUSTOMS

The following dutiable items can be brought into Malaysia free of duty: one litre of alcohol, 225g of tobacco (200 cigarettes) and souvenirs and gifts not exceeding RM200. Cameras, portable radios, perfume, cosmetics and watches do not attract duty.

The list of prohibited items includes: counterfeit currency, weapons (including imitations), 'obscene and prejudicial articles', fireworks and drugs.

Visitors can carry only RM1000 in ringgit in and out of Malaysia. There is no limit on foreign currency, but it must be declared.

MONEY

Currency

The local currency is the Malaysian ringgit (RM), which is divided into 100 sen. It lost value in the recent South-East Asian currency crisis but is starting to recover. It is fairly stable and fully transferable.

Notes in circulation are RM2, RM5, RM10, RM20, RM50, RM100, RM500 and RM1000; the coins in use are 1, 5, 10, 20 and 50 sen, and RM1. Old RM1 notes are occasionally seen.

Banks are efficient and there are also plenty of moneychangers. Banks usually charge commission, typically around RM5 per transaction, whereas the moneychangers have no charges but their rates vary more – so know what the current rate is before dealing with moneychangers. For cash you'll generally get a better rate at a moneychanger than in a bank – it's usually quicker too. Away from the tourist centres, moneychangers' rates are often poorer and they may not change travellers cheques.

Exchange Rates

The following table shows exchange rates:

Australia	A$1	=	RM2.31
Brunei	B$1	=	RM2.26
Canada	C$1	=	RM2.36
European Union	€1	=	RM4.43
France	FF10	=	RM6.70
Germany	DM1	=	RM2.25
Hong Kong	HK$10	=	RM4.70
Indonesia	Rp1000	=	RM0.46
Japan	¥100	=	RM3.18
New Zealand	NZ$1	=	RM1.95
Singapore	S$1	=	RM2.25
Thailand	100B	=	RM9.59
UK	UK£1	=	RM6.21
USA	US$1	=	RM3.65

Exchanging Money

Travellers Cheques & Cash Travellers cheques are always the safest way to carry money, though it doesn't hurt to have some cash (say US$100 to US$200) carried separately from your travellers cheques for emergencies. You'll need it if your cheques are stolen or you have to change money after hours at a moneychanger or large hotel.

All major brands of travellers cheques are acceptable in Malaysia. Cash in major currencies is also readily exchanged, though like everywhere else in the world the US$ has a slight edge.

Credit Cards & ATMs Credit cards are also a viable and very convenient way to carry money if you use them correctly. They are readily accepted for purchases in many establishments – airline offices, car hire agencies, major hotels, better restaurants, large shops etc. MasterCard and Visa are widely accepted and the best to carry.

Banks all over the country also accept credit cards for over-the-counter cash advances, or through automatic teller machines (ATMs) if your card has a personal identification number attached.

Maybank, Malaysia's biggest bank with branches everywhere, accepts both Visa and MasterCard at its ATMs. The Hongkong Bank accepts Visa and the Standard Chartered Bank accepts MasterCard through ATMs. Other bank ATMs that accept credit cards display the relevant symbols. Some banks in Malaysia are also linked to international banking networks such as Cirrus (the most common), Maestro and Plus, allowing withdrawals from overseas savings accounts. Check with your bank at home to see if you can use this facility in Malaysia.

Changes to the Ringgit

In September 1998 Malaysia fixed the ringgit at RM3.8 to the US dollar and recalled foreign holdings of ringgit in an attempt to protect the economy from currency speculators.

US dollars can still be exchanged for ringgit at banks and moneychangers in Malaysia. The rate for other currencies remains variable.

If you're travelling to Malaysia from Thailand for example, you may save money by doing some of your own speculating. Work out whether changing money into baht there, then changing baht into ringgit in Malaysia will earn you more for your dollar. You could also calculate whether exchanging another currency for ringgit would be more profitable than the US dollar.

Costs

Though one of the more expensive countries in South-East Asia, Malaysia is still cheap by world standards and caters well to all budgets. The recent South-East Asian currency crisis almost halved the value of the ringgit in late 1997, but it has since regained some of its value. At the time of writing, it is still well below pre-crisis levels meaning that travel in Malaysia is a good bargain (at least until the ringgit regains its full value).

As for accommodation, you can easily find a spartan double room in an old hotel for as little as US$5, but if you want to spend US$100 a night that's no problem either. Though still plentiful, the older cheap hotels are diminishing in number, but new travellers' guesthouses are springing up in the tourist centres and offer dormitory beds for around US$2.50, as well as cheap rooms. The mid-range is well catered for and hotel rooms with air-con and attached bathroom start at around US$12.

Food is quite cheap. There's a good variety in the cities and you can usually get away for between US$1 and US$2 for a simple meal. A full meal at a food centre with a couple of drinks and dessert will come closer to US$3. At the other end of the scale, the fancy hotels and restaurants in the main cities offer French cuisine at Parisian prices.

Alcoholic drinks are usually quite expensive, particularly in the conservative areas of the east coast or on islands. Beer costs about US$2 a can, almost double in isolated areas. As a rule, spirits cost about 50% more than beer.

It's the same story when it comes to getting around. If you want to travel by chauffeur-driven air-conditioned car you can, but there are lots of cheaper and quite comfortable means of getting around. There are plenty of reasonably priced trishaws and taxis for local travel – the drivers are reasonably honest, so there's no need to get into the frantic bargaining sessions or fear the subsequent arguments that taxi travel in some Asian countries entails. For long distances, Malaysia has excellent buses, trains and taxis, all at very reasonable prices.

On top of these travel essentials – accommodation, food and transport – you'll also find nonessentials and luxuries are moderately priced, even downright cheap.

Tipping & Bargaining

Tipping is not normally done in Malaysia. The more expensive hotels and restaurants have a 10% service charge, while at the cheaper places tipping is not expected. Taxi and rickshaw drivers will naturally not refuse a tip should you decide to give one but it's not expected as a matter of course.

Bargaining is not usually required for everyday goods, unlike in some Asian countries. Always bargain for souvenirs, antiques and other tourist items, even if prices are displayed. Prices are rarely fixed in tourist outlets and can be grossly inflated. Other major purchases, such as cameras and electronics, also usually require bargaining except in department stores. In outdoor markets, bargaining is standard procedure, especially for durable goods (as opposed to food products). Bargaining should be conducted with equanimity – aggression will only force both parties to lose face, and will push prices up.

Transport prices are fixed but negotiation is required for trishaws and unmetered taxis around town or for charter. Hotels may be willing to bend their prices, especially if business is slack. Expensive hotels are most likely to drop prices, and you should always inquire about the discount rates, which will often bring an immediate reduction.

POST & COMMUNICATIONS

Post

Malaysia has an efficient postal system with good poste restantes at the major post offices. Post offices are open daily from 8 am to 5 pm and closed on Sunday and public holidays (closed on Friday and public holidays in Kedah, Kelantan and Terengganu). The main post office in Kuala Lumpur is also open Sunday morning.

Aerograms and postcards cost 50 sen to send to any destination. Letters to Australia cost 55 sen per 10g, letters to the UK and Europe cost 90 sen and letters to the USA cost RM1.10.

It's easy to send parcels from any major post office although the rates are fairly high, from around RM20 to RM35 for a 1kg parcel, depending on the destination.

Main post offices in larger cities have POS2020 stores which sell packaging materials and stationary.

Telephone

Local Calls There are good telephone communications throughout the country. You can direct-dial long-distance calls between all major towns in Malaysia. Local calls cost 10 sen for three minutes.

All over the country you'll come across card telephones operated by Telekom Malaysia and a private communications company, Uniphone. These telephones take coins or plastic cards and are convenient, except you need different cards for each company. Telekom cardphones are usually more reliable and are better for calling overseas. In the larger cities, you'll also find Cityphone card telephones, but since these are only found in the cities it makes little sense for the traveller to buy one of these cards.

Uniphone cards can be bought from 7-Eleven outlets and some other shops. They come in denominations of RM3, RM5, RM10, RM30 and RM50 (international calls only). Telekom cards are available from Telekom offices, post offices and some shops (news sellers in particular).

Phone calls to Singapore are STD (long-distance) rather than international calls. Area codes for Malaysia include:

Town	*Area Code*
Cameron Highlands	☎ 05
Ipoh	☎ 05
Johor Bahru	☎ 07
Kota Bharu	☎ 09
Kota Kinabalu	☎ 088
Kuala Lumpur	☎ 03
Kuala Terengganu	☎ 09
Kuantan	☎ 09
Kuching	☎ 082
Labuan	☎ 087
Langkawi	☎ 04
Melaka	☎ 06
Miri	☎ 085
Penang	☎ 04
Sandakan	☎ 089
Singapore	☎ 02

Dial ☎ 999 to call the police or ambulance.

International Calls International calls can be direct-dialled from private phones, from some public phone booths using a phone card, and from Telekom offices. International calls can be made from most Telekom cardphones. They can also be made at Uniphone booths that accept international calls; these are orange (rather than yellow) booths. There are also phones in most major towns – usually at the Telekom office, the airport or a major hotel – which accept credit cards for international calls. These are the Malaysia Telekom phones where you have to swipe your card down a slot on the right-hand side of the phone. Some Uniphone phones also accept credit cards.

The access code for making international calls from Malaysia is ☎ 007. For information on international calls dial ☎ 103.

For calls via the operator, go to a Telekom office (found in all major cities), or ring ☎ 108 from a private phone. A minimum charge of around RM1 applies for the connection, even if the connection is busy.

For calls to a number of countries, it's possible to make collect (reverse charge) calls from any phone in the country. If you are at a public phone it's the same cost as a local

Home Country Direct Access Codes

Country	*Number*
Australia	
Telstra	☎ 1 800 80 0061
Optus	☎ 1 800 80 0068
Canada	☎ 1 800 80 0017
Hong Kong	☎ 1 800 80 0085
Italy	☎ 1 800 80 0039
Japan	☎ 1 800 80 0081
Netherlands	☎ 1 800 80 0031
New Zealand	☎ 1 800 80 0064
South Korea	☎ 1 800 80 0082
Taiwan	☎ 1 800 80 0088
UK	
BT	☎ 1 800 80 0044
Mercury	☎ 1 800 80 0048
USA	
AT & T	☎ 1 800 80 0011
MCI	☎ 1 800 80 0012
Sprint	☎ 1 800 80 0016

call (10 sen for three minutes); from private phones there is no charge. You'll be connected directly to the operator in the home country. For information on Home Country Direct in Malaysia dial ☎ 102. The Home Country Direct table on page 69 lists the countries hooked up to this service and the numbers to call.

If you're making a call to Malaysia from outside the country, dial ☎ 60, drop the 0 before the Malaysian area code, then dial the number you want. The list on page 69 has area codes for Malaysia's major cities and destinations.

Fax

Fax facilities are available at Telekom offices in larger cities and at some main post offices. You can also send and receive faxes at travel agencies, but the rates are usually pretty steep. Large hotels also have fax machines but these are generally only for the use of guests.

Email & Internet Access

Malaysia is just starting to get online. You will find internet cafes in some of the big cities which charge from RM7.50 to RM15 per hour of use.

INTERNET RESOURCES

The World Wide Web is a rich resource for travellers. You can research your trip, hunt down bargain air fares, book hotels, check on weather conditions or chat with locals and other travellers about the best places to visit (or avoid!).

There's no better place to start your Web explorations than the Lonely Planet Web site (www.lonelyplanet.com). Here you'll find succinct summaries on travelling to most places on earth, postcards from other travellers and the Thorn Tree bulletin board, where you can ask questions before you go or dispense advice when you get back. You can also find travel news and updates to many of our most popular guidebooks, and the subWWWay section links you to the most useful travel resources elsewhere on the Web.

For help with pre-trip planning, helpful sites on the World Wide Web include Tourism Malaysia (www.tourism.gov.my; email: tourism@tourism.gov.my) or the national rail service KTM (www.ktmb.com.my; email: passenger@ktmb.com.my).

BOOKS

A wide variety of books are available in Malaysia, and there are a number of good bookshops in which to find them (mostly in the larger cities like KL).

Most books are published in different editions by different publishers in different countries. As a result, a book might be a hardcover rarity in one country while it's readily available in paperback in another. Fortunately, bookshops and libraries search by title or author, so your local bookshop or library is best placed to advise you on the availability of the following recommendations.

Lonely Planet

South-East Asia on a shoestring is our overall guidebook to the region. For those travelling further afield, there are other LP guides to most South-East and North-East Asian countries. Lonely Planet's *Singapore* is available for travellers just going to Singapore. LP also publishes the *Malay phrasebook*, an introduction to the Malay language.

Travel

Mountains of Malaysia – A Practical Guide and Manual by John Briggs is essential reading for anyone intending to do a lot of mountain walking in Malaysia. The coverage ranges from fairly easy walks to technical climbs, mostly in Sabah and Sarawak, but Peninsular Malaysia is not forgotten and Taman Negara, the Cameron Highlands, Gunung Jerai and others are included. By the same author, *Parks of Malaysia* is a slightly dated but still useful guide to the trails of Malaysia's many national parks.

Tales from the South China Seas, edited by Charles Allen, is the South-East Asian version of *Plain Tales from the Raj*. It recounts the stories of the British colonial experience, mostly in Malaya.

A Malaysian Journey (1993) by Rehman Rashad is an excellent introduction to Malaysia. Written by an expatriate Malaysian journalist who returns to travel right around his home country, it is peppered with affectionate and critical insights and touches on Malaysia's history and current issues.

History & Politics

A Short History of Malaysia, Singapore & Brunei by C Mary Turnbull is straightforward and a good introductory volume on Malaysia's long history, from early civilisation to modern politics. *A History of Malaya* by R Winstedt is a standard history with a colonial perspective.

A History of Malaysia by Barbara Andaya & Leonard Watson is one of the best histories with a post-independence slant.

A number of books deal with the fall of Malaysia and Singapore and the subsequent Japanese occupation, and the internal and external struggles of the 1950s and 1960s. *The Jungle is Neutral* by F Spencer Chapman tells of the hardships and adventures of a British guerrilla force that fought on in the jungles of Malaya for the rest of the war. Noel Barber's *The War of the Running Dogs – Malaya 1948-1960* recounts the events of the long-running Communist insurrection in the country.

The Undeclared War – The Story of the Indonesian Confrontation by Harold James & Denis Sheil-Small tells the story of the strange and disorganised confrontation with Indonesia which arose immediately after the Communist struggle.

People & Society

Kampong Boy by Lat (Straits Times Publishing) provides a delightful introduction to Malay life. It's a humorous autobiographical cartoon series on growing up in a *kampung* (village) and then moving to the town of Ipoh. Lat has many other excellent cartoon collections in print.

Culture Shock Malaysia (1994) by JoAnn Craig explains the customs, cultures and lifestyles of Malaysia's polyglot population to expatriates working there.

An Analysis of Malay Magic (1991) by KM Endicott is a scholarly look at Malay folk religion and the importance of spirits and magic in the world view of Malays.

Chinese Beliefs & Practices in South-East Asia edited by Cheu Hock Tong is an excellent introduction to Chinese religion and society, with special reference to variations from mainland Chinese customs.

The Prime Minister, Dr Mahathir Mohamad, is a prolific writer and has written a number of books interesting for their insight into his thinking. What they lack in scholarship is made up for by Dr Mahathir's lively, controversial style. *The Malay Dilemma* (1970), written before he became prime minister, is an interesting polemic of racial stereotyping and calls for the Malays to take control of their own destiny. It was banned for a number of years. His latest offering, *The Voice of Asia* (1995), co-authored with Japan's Ishihara Shintaro, outlines his notions of Asian Values, stressing the need for Asia to assert its own identity in the face of western arrogance and decadence.

Jomo KS's *Malaysia's Political Economy – Politics, Patronage & Profits* is a critical account of the Malaysian government which was banned inside the country until very recently.

Ian Buruma's *God's Dust* looks critically at the 'westernisation' of Asia, and in a long chapter on Malaysia and Singapore searchingly examines the idea of Asian Values. It is a fascinating read by the writer of *Japanese Mirror*, already established as something of a classic.

Fiction

Singapore and Malaysia have always provided a fertile setting for novelists, and Joseph Conrad's *The Shadow Line* and *Lord Jim* use the region as a location. Somerset Maugham also set many of his classic short stories in Malaya – look for the *Borneo Stories*.

The Long Day Wanes is a reissue in one volume of Anthony Burgess' classic *Malayan*

Trilogy. It's well worth picking up a copy – it has some of the finest English-language fiction set in South-East Asia. Burgess' depiction of a variously alcoholic, set-upon, bewildered and valiant collection of Brits attempting to carry the flickering torch of empire against a backdrop of Malay nationalism bristles with superbly realised characters and fascinating insights.

The Consul's File by Paul Theroux is a very readable collection of short stories situated in, of all places, Ayer Hitam near Kuala Lumpur. Theroux's *Saint Jack* is set in Singapore.

Turtle Beach by Blanche d'Alpuget (1981) is set in Australia and Malaysia during the racial tensions of 1969 and focuses on the plight of Vietnamese boat people. The subsequent film, and its portrayal of Malay racial hatred, outraged Malaysia, and both the book and the film have been banned.

Borneo

Nineteenth Century Borneo – A Study in Diplomatic Rivalry by Graham Irwin is a good book on the fascinating history of Sarawak, Sabah and Brunei.

Rajah Charles Brooke – Monarch of all He Surveyed by Colin N Criswell tells more about the white rajas, as does *The White Rajahs of Sarawak* by Robert Payne.

In Borneo Jungles by William Krohn is a fascinating account of the author's experiences with Dayak head-hunters in the 1920s.

Vanishing World, the Ibans of Borneo by Leigh Wright has some beautiful colour photographs.

A Stroll Through Borneo by James Barclay (1980) is a delightful tale of a long walk and river trip through Sarawak, Sabah and Indonesian Kalimantan. The contrasts between Malaysian bureaucracy and the Indonesian variety are enlightening, with the Malaysians coming off distinctly second best.

Into the Heart of Borneo by Redmond O'Hanlon (1984) is the humorous, classic adventure of two foreigners as they journey by foot and boat into Borneo.

Another good read is *Stranger in the Forest* by Eric Hansen, about the author's experiences trekking right across Sarawak and Kalimantan. Or try *The Day Nothing Happened* by Terence Clarke, an entertaining novel about an American engineer who comes to Sarawak to build a road through the jungle.

Sarawak Crafts: Methods, Material and Motifs by Heidi Munan is a good introduction, but if you can afford it, buy *Hornbill and Dragon* by Bernard Sellato, a superbly illustrated large-format bible of Borneo crafts.

In addition to the books listed here, see the Further Reading section of the Sarawak chapter.

Nature

Periplus Editions puts out a great series of field guides to the plants and animals of Malaysia. Titles include: *Tropical Marine Life of Malaysia & Singapore*, *Tropical Birds of Malaysia & Singapore*, *Tropical Fruits of Malaysia & Singapore* and *Tropical Plants of Malaysia & Singapore*.

For those travelling to Borneo, *A Field Guide to the Mammals of Borneo* by Junaidi Payne, Charles M Francis & Karen Phillipps is a must. The illustrations are excellent. The definitive guide to birds is Smythies' *Birds of Borneo*, but the World Wide Fund for Nature (WWF) and the Sabah Foundation have condensed this weighty volume into the *Pocket Guide to the Birds of Borneo*, which is brilliantly illustrated and ideal for the field.

Bookshops

The best bookshop chains are MPH, Times and Berita. Only in the big cities like KL will you find an adequate selection of books, maps and periodicals, so it makes sense to stock up before heading out into remoter areas. For details on bookshops, see the Bookshops sections of each chapter.

NEWSPAPERS & MAGAZINES

Malaysia has newspapers in Malay, English, Chinese and Tamil. Malay newspapers account for just over 50% of all newspaper sales, English just under 30%, Chinese around 20% and Tamil about 3%. The *New Straits Times* is the main offering in English.

It is a broadsheet paper with good coverage of local and overseas events. Other English-language papers include the *The Star* and the *Malay Mail*, while in East Malaysia there are locals such as the *Borneo Post* and the *Sarawak Tribune*.

In Bahasa Malaysia the main paper, and the one with the highest circulation of any paper, is the *Berita Harian*, while a second-string paper is the *Utusan Malaysia*.

Newspapers tend to follow the government line, but criticism of the government is tolerated to a degree and the press is much less strictly controlled than in Singapore. Strict laws to control the press are in force but are rarely invoked.

Though 'anti-Malaysian' stories in the foreign press occasionally provoke the ire of the government, Asian and western magazines are readily available in Malaysia.

RADIO & TV

Radio and TV are equally cosmopolitan in their languages and programming. Malaysia has two government TV channels, TV1 and TV2, and three commercial stations. Programmes range from local productions in the various languages to imports from the USA and UK. TV censorship is strict. Kissing and other western decadence that threatens to undermine Asian Values is cut, though commercial stations are somewhat more liberal. Check the *New Straits Times* for details on upcoming programmes.

Radio Malaysia runs six domestic channels broadcasting in all the major languages and there are a number of commercial stations. The three main ones are HITZ FM (92.9 FM; top 40), MIX FM (94.5 FM; adult contemporary) and Light & Easy FM (105.7 FM; easy listening). Note that the frequencies given are for the KL area and may differ in other parts of Malaysia. These stations are not available in East Malaysia. For details on the latest programming, check the *New Straits Times*.

PHOTOGRAPHY & VIDEO

Photography

Malaysia is a delightful country to photograph. There's a lot of natural colour and activity and the people usually have no antipathy to being photographed. However, it is, of course, polite to ask permission before photographing people or taking pictures in mosques or temples. There is usually no objection to taking photographs in places of worship: in Chinese temples, virtually anything goes.

The usual rules for tropical photography apply: try to take photographs early in the morning or late in the afternoon. By 10 am the sun will already be high in the sky and colours are easily washed out. A polarising filter can help to keep down the tropical haze. Try to keep your camera and film in a good environment – don't leave your camera out in direct sunlight, try to keep film as cool as possible and have it developed as soon as possible after use.

Colour film can be developed quickly, cheaply and competently, but Kodachrome colour slides are usually sent to Australia for developing. Ektachrome, however, can be developed locally.

Print film is commonly available at good prices, but some slide films can be hard to come by – if you're a serious photographer, you may want to bring slide film from your own country. Processing is reasonably priced, as are cameras and accessories (if you can find what you want – not always easy in Malaysia).

Video

Properly used, a video camera can give a fascinating record of your holiday. As well as videoing the obvious things – sunsets, spectacular views – remember to record some of the ordinary everyday details of life in the country. Often the most interesting things occur when you're actually intent on filming something else. Remember too that, unlike still photography, video 'flows' – so, for example, you can shoot scenes of countryside rolling past the train window.

Video cameras these days have amazingly sensitive microphones, and you might be surprised how much sound will be picked up. This can also be a problem if there is a lot of ambient noise – filming by the side of a busy road might seem OK when you do it, but viewing it back home might simply give you a deafening cacophony of traffic noise. One good rule to follow for beginners is to try to film in long takes, and don't move the camera around too much. Otherwise, your video could well make your viewers seasick! If your camera has a stabiliser, you can use it to obtain good footage while travelling on various means of transport, even on bumpy roads.

Finally, remember to follow the same rules regarding people's sensitivities as for still photography – having a video camera shoved in their face is probably even more annoying and offensive for locals than a still camera. Always ask permission first.

TIME

Malaysia is 16 hours ahead of US Pacific Standard Time (San Francisco and Los Angeles), 13 hours ahead of US Eastern Standard Time (New York), eight hours ahead of GMT/UTC (London) and two hours behind Australian Eastern Standard Time (Sydney and Melbourne). Thus, when it is noon in Kuala Lumpur, it is 8 pm in Los Angeles and 11 pm in New York (the previous day), 4 am in London and 2 pm in Sydney and Melbourne.

ELECTRICITY

Electricity supplies are reliable throughout Malaysia. Supply is 220-240V, 50 cycles. Power sockets are almost always of the three-square-pin type found in the UK, although some older places have the three-round-pin sockets, also as in the UK.

WEIGHTS & MEASURES

Malaysia uses the metric system. For readers more familiar with the imperial system, there's a conversion table at the back of this book.

Some addresses refer to *batu* (literally stone), the mileposts that are still found on a few roads. So an address might be 'Batu 10, Jalan Ipoh', which means at the 10 mile mark on the Ipoh road, even though the 10 mile marker may have long been replaced by a 16 km post. You may come across other ancient measurements such as the *kati* (about 600g), but these are rare.

Fruit may be sold by the *biji*, eg 'three biji RM1', but the biji is not a unit of weight, as one bewildered reader thought, but a classifier for fruit and roughly translates as 'piece'. In Malay, it is poor usage to say 'tiga rambutan' (three rambutan) and the proper usage is 'tiga biji rambutan' (three 'pieces' of rambutan), just as in English 'three pieces of paper' is correct, not 'three papers'.

TOILETS

Malaysian toilets are not nearly as horrifying as those in other South-East Asian countries. You will find both western-style and Asian squat-style toilets, the former rapidly replacing the latter. In places with squat-style toilets, toilet paper is not usually provided. Instead, you will find a hose which you are supposed to use as a bidet, or in more budget places, a bucket of water and a tap. If you do not find this to your liking, make a point of taking packets of tissues or toilet paper wherever you go.

HEALTH

Travel health depends on your predeparture preparations, your daily health care while travelling and how you handle any medical problem that does develop. While the potential dangers can seem quite frightening, in reality few travellers experience anything more than an upset stomach.

Malaysia enjoys a good standard of health and cleanliness. It is one of the healthiest countries in South-East Asia, but the usual rules for healthy living in a tropical environment apply. Ensure that you do not become dehydrated, particularly before you have become acclimatised, by keeping your liquid intake up. Wear cool, lightweight clothes and avoid prolonged exposure to the sun. Treat cuts and scratches with care, since they can easily become infected.

Predeparture Planning

Immunisations Plan ahead for getting your vaccinations: some of them require more than

Medical Kit Check List

Consider taking a basic medical kit including:

- ☐ **Aspirin** or **paracetamol** (acetaminophen in the US) – for pain or fever.
- ☐ **Antihistamine** (such as Benadryl) – a decongestant for colds and allergies, eases the itch from insect bites or stings and helps prevent motion sickness. Antihistamines may cause sedation and interact with alcohol, so care should be taken when using them; take one you know and have used before, if possible.
- ☐ **Antibiotics** – useful if you're travelling well off the beaten track, but they must be prescribed; carry the prescription.
- ☐ **Lomotil** or **Imodium** – to treat diarrhoea; prochlorperazine (eg Stemetil) or metaclopramide (eg Maxalon) is good for nausea and vomiting.
- ☐ **Rehydration mixture** – to treat severe diarrhoea; particularly important when travelling with children.
- ☐ **Antiseptic**, such as povidone-iodine (eg Betadine) – for cuts and grazes.
- ☐ **Multivitamins** – especially useful for long trips when dietary vitamin intake may be inadequate.
- ☐ **Calamine lotion** or **aluminium sulphate spray** (eg Stingose) – to ease irritation from bites or stings.
- ☐ **Bandages** and **Band-aids**
- ☐ **Scissors**, **tweezers** and a **thermometer** – (note that mercury thermometers are prohibited by airlines).
- ☐ **Cold and flu tablets** and **throat lozenges** – Pseudoephedrine hydrochloride (Sudafed) may be useful if flying with a cold to avoid ear damage.
- ☐ **Insect repellent**, **sunscreen**, **Chapstick** and **water purification tablets**
- ☐ A couple of **syringes** – in case you need injections in a country with medical hygiene problems. Ask your doctor for a note explaining why they have been prescribed.

one injection, while some vaccinations should not be given together. Note that some vaccinations should not be given during pregnancy or to people with allergies – discuss with your doctor.

It is recommended you seek medical advice at least six weeks before travel. Be aware that there is often a greater risk of disease with children and in pregnancy.

Record all vaccinations on an International Certificate of Vaccination, available from your doctor or government health department.

The only vaccination required to enter Malaysia is yellow fever if coming from an infected area (parts of Africa and South America). Discuss other requirements with your doctor, but vaccinations you should consider for this trip include the following (for more details about the diseases themselves, see the individual disease entries later in this section).

Diphtheria & Tetanus Vaccinations for these two diseases are usually combined and are recommended for everyone. After an initial course of three injections (usually given in childhood), boosters are necessary every 10 years.

Polio Everyone should keep up to date with this vaccination, which is normally given in childhood. A booster every 10 years maintains immunity.

Hepatitis A Hepatitis A vaccine (eg Avaxim, Havrix 1440 or VAQTA) provides long-term immunity (possibly more than 10 years) after an initial injection and a booster at six to 12 months. Alternatively, an injection of gamma globulin can provide short-term protection against hepatitis A – two to six months, depending on the dose given. It is not a vaccine, but is a ready-made antibody collected from blood donations. It is reasonably effective and, unlike the vaccine, it is protective immediately but because it is a blood product, there are current concerns about its long-term safety. Hepatitis A vaccine is also available in a combined form, Twinrix, with hepatitis B vaccine. Three injections over a six month period are required, the first two providing substantial protection against hepatitis A.

Typhoid Vaccination against typhoid may be required if you are travelling for more than a couple of weeks in most parts of Asia, Africa, Central and South America and Central and Eastern Europe. It is now available either as an injection or as capsules to be taken orally.

Hepatitis B Travellers on a long trip to Malaysia should consider vaccination against hepatitis B, although there is not a high rate of infection. It is also advisable to be vaccinated for travel to countries where blood transfusions may not be adequately screened or where sexual contact or needle sharing is a possibility. Vaccination involves three injections, with a booster at 12 months. More rapid courses are available if necessary.

Rabies Vaccination should be considered by those who will spend a month or longer in Malaysia, especially if cycling, handling animals, caving or travelling to remote areas, and for children (who may not report a bite). Pretravel rabies vaccination involves having three injections over 21 to 28 days. If someone who has been vaccinated is bitten or scratched by an animal they will require two booster injections of vaccine, those not vaccinated require more.

Japanese B Encephalitis Consider vaccination against this disease if spending a month or longer in a high risk area (parts of Asia), making repeated trips to a risk area or visiting during an epidemic. It involves three injections over 30 days.

Tuberculosis TB risk to travellers is usually very low, unless you will be living with or closely associated with local people in high risk areas such as Asia, Africa and some parts of the Americas and Pacific. Vaccination with the BCG vaccine (against TB) is recommended for children and young adults living in these areas for three months or more.

Malaria Medication Antimalarial drugs do not prevent you from being infected but kill the malaria parasites during a stage in their development and significantly reduce the risk of becoming very ill or dying. Expert advice on medication should be sought, as there are many factors to consider including the area to be visited, the risk of exposure to malaria-carrying mosquitoes, the side effects of medication, your medical history and whether you are a child or adult or pregnant. Travellers to isolated areas in high risk countries may like to carry a treatment dose of medication for use if symptoms occur.

Health Insurance Make sure that you have adequate health insurance. See Travel Insurance under Documents in the Facts for the Visitor chapter for details.

Travel Health Guides If you are planning to be away or travelling in remote areas for a long period of time, you may like to consider taking a more detailed health guide. The following books would be useful.

Staying Healthy in Asia, Africa & Latin America, Dirk Schroeder, Moon Publications, 1994. Probably the best all-round guide to carry; it's compact, detailed and well organised.

Travellers' Health, Dr Richard Dawood, Oxford University Press, 1995. Comprehensive, easy to read, authoritative and highly recommended, although it's rather large to lug around.

Where There is No Doctor, David Werner, Macmillan, 1994. A very detailed guide intended for someone, such as a long-term volunteer worker, going to live in an underdeveloped country.

CDC's Complete Guide to Healthy Travel, Open Road Publishing, 1997. The US Centers for Disease Control & Prevention recommendations for international travel.

Travel with Children, Maureen Wheeler, Lonely Planet Publications, 1995. Includes advice on travel health for younger children.

There are also many excellent travel health sites on the Internet. From the Lonely Planet home page there are links at www.lonelyplanet.com/weblinks/wlprep.htm#heal to the World Health Organisation and the US Centers for Disease Control & Prevention.

Other Preparations Make sure you're healthy before you start travelling. If you are going on a long trip make sure your teeth are OK. If you wear glasses take a spare pair and your prescription. Losing your glasses can be a real problem, however in Malaysia it is relatively easy and cheap to get replacement glasses.

If you require a particular medication take an adequate supply, as it may not be locally available. It will be easier to find replacements if you take part of the packaging showing the generic name, rather than just the brand name. It is a good idea to have a legible prescription or a letter from your doctor to confirm that the medication is used for legal purposes. This should ensure you avoid any problems.

Basic Rules

Food Standards of food preparation in Malaysia are high and subject to government health controls, but that doesn't mean that standards of hygiene are always acceptable. Food stalls are generally safe places to eat but some are definitely on the grotty side. If a place looks clean and well run and the vendor also looks clean and healthy, then the food is probably safe. In general, places that are packed with travellers or locals will be fine, while empty restaurants are questionable. The food in busy restaurants is cooked and eaten quite quickly with little standing around and is probably not reheated.

Be particularly careful with some food. Shellfish such as mussels, oysters and clams should be avoided as well as undercooked meat, particularly in the form of mince. Steaming does not make shellfish safe for eating. Vegetables and fruit should be washed with purified water or peeled where possible. Beware of ice cream which is sold in the street or anywhere it might have been melted and refrozen; if there's any doubt (for example a power cut in the last day or two) steer well clear.

Water In the major towns and cities in Malaysia you can drink tap water, but it is still wise to ensure that water has been boiled if you're in kampungs or off the beaten track. If you don't know for certain that the water is safe, always assume the worst. A wide variety of bottled water is available in Malaysia, even though a health survey a few years ago revealed that many brands were prepared in unhygienic conditions and not purified. Don't let this worry you – at least they do check and attempt to enforce health standards in Malaysia. Reputable brands of bottled water or soft drinks are generally fine, although in some places bottles may be refilled with tap water. Only use water from containers with a serrated seal – not tops or corks.

Take care with fruit juice, particularly if water may have been added. Milk should be treated with suspicion as it is often unpasteurised, though boiled milk is fine if it is kept hygienically. Tea or coffee should also be OK, since the water should have been boiled.

If you will be going on extended walks in remote areas, you will have to rely on stream water and this should be purified.

Water Purification The simplest way of purifying water is to boil it thoroughly. Vigorous boiling should be satisfactory; but at high altitude water boils at a lower temperature, so germs are less likely to be killed. Boil it for longer in these environments.

Nutrition

If your food is poor or limited in availability, if you're travelling hard and fast and therefore missing meals or if you simply lose your appetite, you can soon start to lose weight and place your health at risk.

Finding good food in Malaysia is not a problem; the problem is deciding what to eat from all the delicious varieties. Make sure your diet is well balanced. Cooked eggs, tofu, beans, lentils and nuts are all safe ways to get protein. Fruit you can peel (bananas, oranges or mandarins for example) is usually safe (melons can harbour bacteria in their flesh and are best avoided) and a good source of vitamins. Try to eat plenty of grains (including rice) and bread. Remember that although food is generally safer if it is cooked well, overcooked food loses much of its nutritional value. If your diet isn't well balanced or if your food intake is insufficient, it's a good idea to take vitamin and iron pills.

Make sure you drink enough in Malaysia's hot climate – don't rely on feeling thirsty to indicate when you should drink. Not needing to urinate or having small amounts of very dark yellow urine is a danger sign. Always carry a water bottle with you on long trips. Excessive sweating can lead to loss of salt and therefore muscle cramping. Salt tablets are not a good idea as a preventative, but in places where salt is not used much, adding salt to food can help.

Consider purchasing a water filter for a long trip. There are two main kinds of filter. Total filters take out all parasites, bacteria and viruses, and make water safe to drink. They are often expensive, but they can be more cost effective than buying bottled water. Simple filters (which can even be a nylon mesh bag) take out dirt and larger foreign bodies from the water so that chemical solutions work much more effectively; if water is dirty, chemical solutions may not work at all. It's very important when buying a filter to read the specifications, so that you know exactly what it removes from the water and what it doesn't. Simple filtering will not remove all dangerous organisms, so if you cannot boil water it should be treated chemically.

Chlorine tablets (Puritabs, Steritabs or other brand names) will kill many pathogens, but not some parasites like giardia and amoebic cysts. Iodine is more effective in purifying water and is available in tablet form (such as Potable Aqua). Follow the directions carefully and remember that too much iodine can be harmful.

Medical Problems & Treatment

Self-diagnosis and treatment can be risky, so you should always seek medical help. Although we do give drug dosages in this section, they are for emergency use only. Correct diagnosis is vital.

In Malaysia, government hospitals are free or make a nominal charge. Medical staff and most of the senior nursing staff speak good English. In the cities queues can be long, but you usually won't have to wait long in smaller towns. Private clinics also exist, especially in KL, and there are many private practitioners, who invariably speak English. An embassy, consulate or five star hotel can usually recommend a doctor or clinic.

Antibiotics should ideally be administered only under medical supervision. Take only the recommended dose at the prescribed intervals and use the whole course, even if the illness seems to be cured earlier. Stop immediately if there are any serious reactions and don't use the antibiotic at all if you are unsure that you have the correct one. Some people are allergic to commonly prescribed antibiotics such as penicillin or sulpha drugs; carry this information (eg on a bracelet) when travelling.

Environmental Hazards

Altitude Sickness Lack of oxygen at high altitudes (over 2500m) affects most people to some extent. In Malaysia the only place you're likely to get it is on Mt Kinabalu in Sabah. The effect may be mild or severe and occurs because less oxygen reaches the muscles and the brain at high altitude, requiring the heart and lungs to compensate by working harder. Symptoms of acute mountain sickness (AMS) usually develop during the first 24 hours at altitude but may be delayed up to three weeks. Mild symptoms include headache, lethargy, dizziness, difficulty sleeping and loss of appetite. AMS may become more severe without warning and can be fatal. Severe symptoms include breathlessness, a dry, irritative cough (which may progress to the production of pink, frothy sputum), severe headache, lack of coordination and balance, confusion, irrational behaviour, vomiting, drowsiness and unconsciousness. There is no hard-and-fast rule as to what is too high: AMS has been fatal at 3000m, although 3500 to 4500m is the usual range.

It is compulsory to take a guide up Mt Kinabalu. If you develop symptoms, you should tell your guide. Treat mild symptoms by resting at the same altitude until recovery, usually a day or two. Paracetamol or aspirin can be taken for headaches. If symptoms persist or become worse, however, *immediate descent is necessary*; even 500m can help. Drug treatments should never be used to avoid descent or to enable further ascent.

The drugs acetazolamide (Diamox) and dexamethasone are recommended by some doctors for the prevention of AMS, however their use is controversial. They can reduce the symptoms, but they may also mask warning signs; severe and fatal AMS has occurred in people taking these drugs. In general we do not recommend them for travellers.

To prevent acute mountain sickness:

- Ascend slowly – have frequent rest days, spending two to three nights at each rise of 1000m. If you reach a high altitude by trekking, acclimatisation takes place gradually and you are less likely to be affected than if you fly directly to high altitude.
- It is always wise to sleep at a lower altitude than the greatest height reached during the day if possible. Also, once above 3000m, care should be taken not to increase the sleeping altitude by more than 300m per day.
- Drink extra fluids. The mountain air is dry and cold and moisture is lost as you breathe. Evaporation of sweat may occur unnoticed and result in dehydration.
- Eat light, high-carbohydrate meals for more energy.
- Avoid alcohol as it may increase the risk of dehydration.
- Avoid sedatives.

Heat Exhaustion Dehydration and salt deficiency can cause heat exhaustion. Take time to acclimatise to high temperatures, drink sufficient liquids and do not do anything too physically demanding.

Salt deficiency is characterised by fatigue, lethargy, headaches, giddiness and muscle cramps; salt tablets may help, but adding extra salt to your food is better.

Anhidrotic heat exhaustion is a rare form of heat exhaustion which is caused by an inability to sweat. It tends to strike people who have been in a hot climate for some time, rather than newcomers. It can progress to heatstroke. Treatment involves removal to a cooler climate.

Heatstroke This serious, occasionally fatal, condition can occur if the heat-regulating mechanism in the body breaks down and the body temperature rises to dangerous levels. Long, continuous periods of exposure to high temperatures and insufficient fluids can leave you vulnerable to heatstroke.

The symptoms are feeling unwell, not sweating very much (or at all) and a high body temperature (39°C to 41°C or 102°F to 106°F). Where sweating has ceased the skin becomes flushed and red. Severe, throbbing headaches and lack of coordination will also occur, and the sufferer may be confused or aggressive. Eventually the victim will become delirious or convulse. Hospitalisation is essential, but in the interim get victims out of the sun, remove their clothing, cover them with a wet sheet or towel and then fan continually. Give fluids if they are conscious.

Hypothermia Too much cold can be just as dangerous as too much heat. If you are trekking at high altitudes or simply taking a long bus trip over mountains, particularly at night, be prepared. Sarawak's Kelabit Highlands is the only place in Malaysia where there may be a risk of hypothermia.

Hypothermia occurs when the body loses heat faster than it can produce it and the core temperature of the body falls. It is surprisingly easy to progress from very cold to dangerously cold due to a combination of wind, wet clothing, fatigue and hunger, even if the air temperature is above freezing. It is best to dress in layers; silk, wool and some of the new artificial fibres are all good insulating materials. A hat is important, as a lot of heat is lost through the head. A strong, waterproof outer layer (and a 'space' blanket for emergencies) are essential. Carry basic supplies, including food containing simple sugars to generate heat quickly and fluid to drink.

Symptoms of hypothermia are exhaustion, numb skin (particularly toes and fingers), shivering, slurred speech, irrational or violent behaviour, lethargy, stumbling, dizzy spells, muscle cramps and violent bursts of energy. Irrationality may take the form of sufferers claiming they are warm and trying to take off their clothes.

To treat mild hypothermia, first get the person out of the wind and/or rain, remove their clothing if it's wet and replace it with dry, warm clothing. Give them hot liquids – not alcohol – and some high-kilojoule, easily digestible food. Do not rub victims, instead allow them to slowly warm themselves. This should be enough to treat the early stages of hypothermia. The early recognition and treatment of mild hypothermia is the only way to prevent severe hypothermia, which is a critical condition.

Jet Lag Jet lag is experienced when a person travels by air across more than three time zones (each time zone usually represents a one hour time difference). It occurs because many of the functions of the human body (such as temperature, pulse rate and emptying of the bladder and bowels) are regulated by internal 24-hour cycles. When we travel long distances rapidly, our bodies take time to adjust to the 'new time' of our destination, and we may experience fatigue, disorientation, insomnia, anxiety, impaired concentration and loss of appetite. These effects will usually be gone within three days of arrival, but to minimise the impact of jet lag:

- Rest for a couple of days prior to departure.
- Try to select flight schedules that minimise sleep deprivation; arriving late in the day means you can go to sleep soon after you arrive. For very long flights, try to organise a stopover.
- Avoid excessive eating (which bloats the stomach) and alcohol (which causes dehydration) during the flight. Instead, drink plenty of non-carbonated, non-alcoholic drinks such as fruit juice or water.
- Avoid smoking.
- Make yourself comfortable by wearing loose-fitting clothes and perhaps bringing an eye mask and ear plugs to help you sleep.
- Try to sleep at the appropriate time for the time zone you are travelling to.

Motion Sickness Eating lightly before and during a trip will reduce the chances of motion sickness. If you are prone to motion sickness try to find a place that minimises movement – near the wing on aircraft, close to midships on boats, near the centre on buses. Fresh air usually helps; reading and cigarette smoke don't. Commercial motion-sickness preparations, which can cause drowsiness, have to be taken before the trip commences. Ginger (available in capsule form) and peppermint (including mint-flavoured sweets) are natural preventatives.

Everyday Health

Normal body temperature is up to 37°C (98.6°F); more than 2°C (4°F) higher indicates a high fever. The normal adult pulse rate is 60 to 100 per minute (children 80 to 100, babies 100 to 140). As a general rule the pulse increases about 20 beats per minute for each 1°C (2°F) rise in fever.

Respiration (breathing) rate is also an indicator of illness. Count the number of breaths per minute: between 12 and 20 is normal for adults and older children (up to 30 for younger children, 40 for babies). People with a high fever or serious respiratory illness breathe more quickly than normal. More than 40 shallow breaths a minute may indicate pneumonia.

Prickly Heat Prickly heat is an itchy rash caused by excessive perspiration trapped under the skin. It usually strikes people who have just arrived in a hot climate. Keeping cool, bathing often, drying the skin and using a mild talcum or prickly heat powder or resorting to air-conditioning may help.

Sunburn In Malaysia's tropics and high altitudes you can get sunburnt surprisingly quickly, even through cloud. Use a sunscreen, hat, and barrier cream for your nose and lips. Calamine lotion or Stingose are good for mild sunburn. Protect your eyes with good quality sunglasses, particularly if you will be near water, sand or snow.

Infectious Diseases

Diarrhoea Malaysia is one of the healthiest countries in Asia to travel in, but diarrhoea is always a potential problem. Simple things like a change of water, food or climate can all cause a mild bout of diarrhoea, but a few rushed toilet trips with no other symptoms is not indicative of a major problem.

Dehydration is the main danger with any diarrhoea, particularly in children or the elderly as dehydration can occur quite quickly. Under all circumstances *fluid replacement* (at least equal to the volume being lost) is the most important thing to remember. Weak black tea with a little sugar, soda water, or soft drinks allowed to go flat and diluted 50% with clean water are all good. With severe diarrhoea a rehydrating solution is preferable to replace minerals and salts lost. Commercially available oral rehydration salts (ORS) are very useful; add them to boiled or bottled water. In an emergency you can make up a solution of six teaspoons of sugar and a half teaspoon of salt to a litre of boiled or bottled water. You need to drink at least the same volume of fluid that you are losing in bowel movements and vomiting. Urine is the best guide to the adequacy of replacement – if you have small amounts of concentrated urine, you need to drink more. Keep drinking small amounts often. Stick to a bland diet as you recover.

Gut-paralysing drugs such as Lomotil or Imodium can be used to bring relief from the symptoms, although they do not actually cure the problem. Only use these drugs if you do not have access to toilets, eg if you *must* travel. For children under 12 years Lomotil and Imodium are not recommended. Do not use these drugs if the person has a high fever or is severely dehydrated.

In certain situations antibiotics may be required: diarrhoea with blood or mucus (dysentery), any diarrhoea with fever, profuse watery diarrhoea, persistent diarrhoea not improving after 48 hours, and severe diarrhoea. These suggest a more serious cause of diarrhoea and in these situations gut-paralysing drugs should be avoided.

In these situations, a stool test may be necessary to diagnose what bug is causing your diarrhoea, so you should seek medical help urgently. Where this is not possible the recommended drugs for bacterial diarrhoea (the most likely cause of severe diarrhoea in travellers) are norfloxacin 400mg twice daily for three days or ciprofloxacin 500mg twice daily for five days, or one of their related drugs. These are not recommended for children or pregnant women. The drug of choice for children would be co-trimoxazole (Bactrim, Septrin, Resprim) with dosage dependent on weight. A five day course is given. Ampicillin or amoxycillin may be given in pregnancy, but medical care is necessary.

Two other causes of persistent diarrhoea in travellers are giardiasis and amoebic dysentery.

Giardiasis is caused by a common parasite, *Giardia lamblia*. Symptoms include stomach cramps, nausea, a bloated stomach, watery, foul-smelling diarrhoea and frequent gas. Giardiasis can appear several weeks after you have been exposed to the parasite. The symptoms may disappear for a few days and then return; this can go on for several weeks.

Caused by the protozoon *Entamoeba histolytica*, the main symptom of **amoebic dysentery**, is the gradual onset of low-grade diarrhoea, often with blood and mucus. Cramping abdominal pain and vomiting is less likely than in other types of diarrhoea, and fever may not be present. It will persist until treated and can recur and cause other health problems.

You should seek medical advice if you think you may have giardiasis or amoebic dysentery, but where this is not possible, tinidazole (Fasigyn), or metronidazole (Flagyl) are the recommended drugs. Treatment is a 2g single dose of Fasigyn or 250mg of Flagyl three times daily for five to 10 days.

Fungal Infections Fungal infections occur more commonly in hot weather and are usually found on the scalp, between the toes (athlete's foot) or fingers, in the groin and on the body (ringworm). You get ringworm (which is a fungal infection, not a worm) from infected animals or other people. Moisture encourages these infections.

To prevent fungal infections wear loose, comfortable clothes, avoid artificial fibres, wash frequently and dry yourself carefully. If you do get an infection, wash the infected area at least daily with a disinfectant or medicated soap and water, and rinse and dry well. Apply an antifungal cream or powder like tolnaftate (Tinaderm). Try to expose the infected area to air or sunlight as much as possible and wash all towels and underwear in hot water, change them often and let them dry in the sun.

Hepatitis Hepatitis is a general term for inflammation of the liver. It is a common disease worldwide. There are several different viruses that cause hepatitis, and they differ in the way that they are transmitted. The symptoms are similar in all forms of the illness and include fever, chills, headache, fatigue, feelings of weakness and aches and pains, followed by loss of appetite, nausea, vomiting, abdominal pain, dark urine, light-coloured faeces, jaundiced (yellow) skin and yellowing of the whites of the eyes. People who have had hepatitis should avoid alcohol for some time after the illness, as the liver needs time to recover.

Hepatitis A is transmitted by contaminated food and drinking water. You should seek medical advice, but there is not much you can do apart from resting, drinking lots of fluids, eating lightly and avoiding fatty foods. Hepatitis E is transmitted in the same way as hepatitis A and can be particularly serious in pregnant women.

There are almost 300 million chronic carriers of **hepatitis B** in the world. It is spread through contact with infected blood, blood products or body fluids, for example through sexual contact, unsterilised needles and blood transfusions, or contact with blood via small breaks in the skin. Other risk situations include having a shave, tattoo, or body pierced with contaminated equipment. The symptoms of hepatitis B may be more severe than type A and the disease can lead to long-term problems such as chronic liver damage, liver cancer or a long-term carrier state. Hepatitis C and D are spread in the same way as hepatitis B, and can also lead to long-term complications.

There are vaccines against hepatitis A and B, but there are currently no vaccines available against the other types of hepatitis. Following the basic rules about food and water (hepatitis A and E) and avoiding risk situations (hepatitis B, C and D) are important preventative measures.

HIV & AIDS Infection with the human immunodeficiency virus (HIV) can develop into the acquired immune deficiency syndrome (AIDS), which is a fatal disease for which there is no cure. Any exposure to blood, blood products or body fluids may put the individual at risk. The disease is often transmitted through sexual contact or dirty needles – vaccinations, acupuncture, tattooing and body piercing can be potentially as dangerous as intravenous drug use. HIV/AIDS can also be spread through infected blood transfusions; some developing countries cannot afford to screen blood used for transfusions.

If you do need an injection, ask to see the syringe unwrapped in front of you, or take a needle and syringe pack with you. Fear of HIV infection should never preclude treatment for serious medical conditions.

To avoid infection through sexual contact, make sure you practise safe sex. Condoms are available throughout Malaysia, but they are of varying quality and may be hard to find in rural areas – take your own to be safe.

According to government figures from 1996 there were 448 cases of AIDS in Malaysia, 16,439 people were infected with HIV with 300 new cases being detected each month. However, the government said these figures may be low due to the non-reporting of new cases.

Intestinal Worms These parasites are most common in rural, tropical areas. The different worms have different ways of infecting people. Some may be ingested on food such as undercooked meat (eg tapeworms) and some enter through your skin (eg hookworms). Infestations may not show up for some time, and although they are generally not serious, if left untreated some can cause severe health problems later. Consider having a stool test when you return home to check for these and determine the appropriate treatment.

Sexually Transmitted Diseases Gonorrhoea, herpes and syphilis are among these diseases; sores, blisters or rashes around the genitals, discharges or pain when urinating are common symptoms. In some STDs, such as wart virus or chlamydia, symptoms may be less marked or not observed at all, especially in women. Syphilis symptoms eventually disappear completely but the disease continues and can cause severe problems in later years. While abstinence from sexual contact is the only 100% effective prevention, using condoms is also effective. The treatment of gonorrhoea and syphilis is with antibiotics. Different sexually transmitted diseases each require specific antibiotics. There is no cure for herpes.

Typhoid Typhoid fever is a dangerous gut infection spread through contaminated water and food. Medical help must be sought.

In its early stages sufferers may feel they have a bad cold or flu on the way, as early symptoms are a headache, body aches and a fever which rises a little each day until it is around 40°C (104°F) or more. The victim's pulse is often slow in relation to the degree of fever present – unlike a normal fever where the pulse increases. There may also be vomiting, abdominal pain, diarrhoea or constipation.

In the second week the high fever and slow pulse continue and a few pink spots may appear on the body; trembling, delirium, weakness, weight loss and dehydration may occur. Complications such as pneumonia, perforated bowel or meningitis may occur.

Insect-Borne Diseases

Filariasis, Lyme disease and typhus are all insect-borne diseases, but they do not pose a great risk to travellers. For more information on them see Less Common Diseases at the end of the health section.

Malaria This serious and potentially fatal disease is spread by mosquito bites. It is endemic in East Malaysia, but apart from occasional, isolated outbreaks, it is not found in Peninsular Malaysia. It crops up every now and then in the Cameron Highlands, but the risk is low. Unless you are planning on spending extended periods in the Cameron Highlands, malarial prophylactics are unnecessary. For Sabah and Sarawak, they are recommended – malaria is prevalent throughout Sabah.

If you are travelling in endemic areas it is extremely important to avoid mosquito bites and to take tablets to prevent this disease. Symptoms range from fever, chills and sweating, headache, diarrhoea and abdominal pains to a vague feeling of ill-health. Seek medical help immediately if malaria is suspected. Without treatment malaria can rapidly become more serious and can be fatal.

If medical care is not available, malaria tablets can be used for treatment. You need to use a malaria tablet which is different to the one you were taking when you contracted malaria. The standard treatment dose of mefloquine is three 250mg tablets and a further two six hours later. For Fansidar, it's a single dose of three tablets. If you were previously taking mefloquine and cannot obtain Fansidar, then other alternatives are Malarone (atovaquone-proguanil; four tablets once daily for three days), halofantrine (three doses of two 250mg tablets every six hours) or quinine sulphate (600mg every six hours). There is a greater risk of side effects with these dosages than in normal use if used with mefloquine, so medical advice is preferable. Be aware that halofantrine is no longer recommended by the WHO as emergency standby treatment, because of side effects, and should only be used if no other drugs are available.

Travellers are advised to prevent mosquito bites at all times. The main messages are:

- wear light-coloured clothing
- wear long trousers and long-sleeved shirts
- use mosquito repellents containing the compound DEET on exposed areas (prolonged overuse of DEET may be harmful, especially to children, but its use is considered preferable to being bitten by disease-transmitting mosquitoes)
- avoid wearing perfume or aftershave
- use a mosquito net impregnated with mosquito repellent (permethrin) – it may be worth taking your own
- impregnating clothes with permethrin effectively deters mosquitoes and other insects

Dengue Fever This viral disease is transmitted by mosquitoes and occurs mainly in tropical and subtropical areas of the world, including Malaysia. Generally, there is a small risk to travellers except during epidemics, which are usually seasonal (during and just after the rainy season). With unstable weather patterns thought to be responsible for large outbreaks in the Pacific, South-East Asia and Brazil, travellers to these areas may be especially at risk of infection.

The Aedes aegypti mosquito which transmits the dengue virus is most active during the day, unlike the malaria mosquito, and is found mainly in urban areas, in and around human dwellings.

Signs and symptoms of dengue fever include a sudden onset of high fever, headache, joint and muscle pains (hence its old name, 'breakbone fever') and nausea and vomiting. A rash of small red spots appears three to four days after the onset of fever. Dengue is commonly mistaken for other infectious diseases, including influenza.

You should seek medical attention if you think you may be infected. Infection can be diagnosed by a blood test. There is no specific treatment for dengue. Aspirin should be avoided, as it increases the risk of haemorrhaging. Recovery may be prolonged, with tiredness lasting for several weeks. Severe complications are rare in travellers, but include dengue haemorrhagic fever (DHF), which can be fatal without prompt medical treatment. DHF is thought to be a result of second infection due to a different strain (there are four major strains), and usually affects residents rather than travellers.

There is no vaccine against dengue fever. The best prevention is to avoid mosquito bites at all times – see the malaria section earlier for more details.

Japanese B Encephalitis This viral infection of the brain is transmitted by mosquitoes. Most cases occur in rural areas as the virus exists in pigs and wading birds. Symptoms include fever, headache and alteration in consciousness. Hospitalisation is needed for correct diagnosis and treatment. There is a high mortality rate among those who have symptoms; of those that survive many are intellectually disabled.

Cuts, Bites & Stings

Rabies is passed through animal bites. For details see Less Common Diseases later in this section.

Bedbugs & Lice Bedbugs live in various places, but particularly in dirty mattresses and bedding, evidenced by spots of blood on bedclothes or on the wall. Bedbugs leave itchy bites in neat rows. Calamine lotion or Stingose spray may help.

All lice cause itching and discomfort. They make themselves at home in your hair (head lice), your clothing (body lice) or in your pubic hair (crabs). You catch lice through direct contact with infected people or by sharing combs and clothing. Powder or shampoo treatment will kill the lice and infected clothing should then be washed in very hot, soapy water and left in the sun to dry.

Bites & Stings Bee and wasp stings are usually painful rather than dangerous. However in people who are allergic to them severe breathing difficulties may occur and require urgent medical care. Calamine lotion or Stingose spray will give relief and ice packs will reduce the pain and swelling. There are some spiders with dangerous bites but antivenenes are usually available. Scorpion stings are notoriously painful and in some parts of Asia, the Middle East and Central America can be fatal. Scorpions often shelter in shoes or clothing.

There are various fish and other sea creatures which have poisonous stings or bites or which are dangerous to eat. Seek local advice if you fall victim to one of these.

Cuts & Scratches Wash well and treat any cut with an antiseptic such as povidone-iodine. Where possible avoid bandages and Band-Aids, which can keep wounds wet. Coral cuts are notoriously slow to heal and if they are not adequately cleaned, small pieces of coral can become embedded in the wound.

Jellyfish Avoid contact with these sea creatures, which have stinging tentacles – seek local advice. The box jellyfish found in some inshore waters around Sabah can be potentially fatal, but stings from most jellyfish are simply rather painful. Dousing in vinegar will deactivate any stingers which have not 'fired'. Calamine lotion, antihistamines and analgesics may reduce the reaction and relieve the pain.

Leeches & Ticks Leeches may be present in damp rainforest conditions; they attach themselves to your skin to suck your blood. Trekkers often get them on their legs or in their boots. Salt or a lighted cigarette end will make them fall off. Do not pull them off, as the bite is then more likely to become infected. Clean and apply pressure if the point of attachment is bleeding. An insect repellent may keep them away.

You should always check all over your body if you have been walking through a potentially tick-infested area as ticks can cause skin infections and other more serious diseases. If a tick is found attached, press down around the tick's head with tweezers, grab the head and gently pull upwards. Avoid pulling the rear of the body as this may squeeze the tick's gut contents through the attached mouth parts into the skin, increasing the risk of infection and disease. Smearing chemicals on the tick will not make it let go and is not recommended. See the Trekking in Sarawak section for more information on leeches in Malaysia.

Snakes To minimise your chances of being bitten always wear boots, socks and long trousers when walking through undergrowth where snakes may be present. Don't put your hands into holes and crevices, and be careful when collecting firewood.

Snake bites do not cause instantaneous death and antivenenes are usually available. Immediately wrap the bitten limb tightly, as you would for a sprained ankle, and then attach a splint to immobilise it. Keep the victim still and seek medical help, if possible with the dead snake for identification. Don't attempt to catch the snake if there is a possibility of being bitten again. Tourniquets and sucking out the poison are now comprehensively discredited.

Women's Health

Gynaecological Problems Antibiotic use, synthetic underwear, sweating and taking contraceptive pills can lead to fungal vaginal infections, especially when travelling in hot climates. Fungal infections are characterised by rash, itch and discharge, and can be treated with a vinegar or lemon-juice douche, or with yoghurt. Nystatin, miconazole or clotrimazole pessaries or vaginal cream are the usual treatment. Maintaining good personal hygiene, and wearing loose-fitting clothes and cotton underwear may help to prevent these infections.

Sexually transmitted diseases are a major cause of vaginal problems. Symptoms include a smelly discharge, painful intercourse and sometimes a burning sensation when urinating. Medical attention should be sought. Male sexual partners must also be treated. Remember that, in addition to these diseases, HIV or hepatitis B may also be acquired during exposure. Besides abstinence, the best thing is to practise safe sex using condoms.

Pregnancy It is not advisable to travel to some places while pregnant as some vaccinations normally used to prevent serious diseases are not advisable in pregnancy (eg yellow fever). In addition, some diseases, such as malaria, are much more serious for the mother (and may increase the risk of a stillborn child) in pregnancy.

Most miscarriages occur during the first three months of pregnancy. Miscarriage is not uncommon, and can occasionally lead to severe bleeding. The last three months should also be spent within reasonable distance of good medical care. A baby born as early as 24 weeks stands a chance of survival, but only in a good modern hospital. Pregnant women should avoid all unnecessary medication; vaccinations and malarial prophylactics should still be taken where needed. Additional care should be taken to prevent illness and particular attention should be paid to diet and nutrition. Alcohol and nicotine, for example, should be avoided.

Less Common Diseases

The following diseases pose a small risk to travellers, and so are only mentioned in passing. Seek medical advice if you think you may have any of these diseases.

Cholera This is the worst of the watery diarrhoeas and medical help should be sought. Outbreaks of cholera are generally widely reported, so you can avoid such problem areas. *Fluid replacement is the most vital treatment* – the risk of dehydration is severe as you may lose up to 20L a day. If there is a delay in getting to hospital then begin taking tetracycline. The adult dose is 250mg four times daily. It is not recommended for children under nine years or for pregnant women. Tetracycline may help shorten the illness, but adequate fluids are required to save lives.

Filariasis This is a mosquito-transmitted parasitic infection found in many parts of Africa, Asia (including Malaysia), Central and South America and the Pacific. Possible symptoms include fever, pain and swelling of the lymph glands; inflammation of lymph drainage areas; swelling of a limb or the scrotum; skin rashes and blindness. Treatment is available to eliminate the parasites from the body, but some of the damage already caused may not be reversible. Medical advice should be obtained promptly if the infection is suspected.

Lyme Disease This is a tick-transmitted infection which may be acquired throughout North America, Europe and Asia, including Malaysia. The illness usually begins with a spreading rash at the site of the bite and is accompanied by fever, headache, extreme fatigue, aching joints and muscles and mild neck stiffness. If untreated, these symptoms usually resolve over several weeks but during subsequent weeks or months disorders of the nervous system, heart and joints may develop. Treatment is best early, seek medical help.

Rabies This fatal viral infection is found in many countries, including Malaysia. Many animals can be infected (such as dogs, cats, bats and monkeys) and it is their saliva which is infectious. Any bite, scratch or even lick from an animal should be cleaned immediately and thoroughly. Scrub with soap and running water, and then apply alcohol or iodine solution. Medical help should be sought promptly to receive a course of injections to prevent the onset of symptoms and death.

Tetanus This disease is caused by a germ which lives in soil and in the faeces of horses and other animals. It enters the body through breaks in the skin. The first symptom may be experiencing discomfort in swallowing, or stiffening of the jaw and neck. This is followed by painful convulsions of the whole body. The disease may be fatal but can be prevented by vaccination.

Tuberculosis (TB) This bacterial infection is usually transmitted from person to person by coughing but may be transmitted through consumption of unpasteurised milk. Milk that has been boiled is safe to drink, and the souring of milk to make yoghurt or cheese also kills the bacilli. Travellers are usually not at great risk as close household contact with the infected person is usually required before the disease is passed on. You may need to have a TB test before you travel as this can help diagnose the disease later if you become ill.

Typhus This disease is spread by ticks, mites or lice. It begins with fever, chills, headache and muscle pains followed a few days later by a body rash. There is often a large painful sore at the site of the bite and nearby lymph nodes are swollen and painful. Typhus can be treated under medical supervision. Seek local advice on areas where ticks pose a danger and always check your skin carefully for ticks after walking in a risk area such as a tropical forest. An insect repellent can help, and walkers in tick-infested areas should consider having their boots and trousers impregnated with benzyl benzoate and dibutylphthalate.

WOMEN TRAVELLERS

Foreign women travelling in Malaysia have reported receiving unwanted attention from Malaysian men in the form of come-ons, cat-calls, groping and various other forms of harassment. This can be particularly bad in some resort areas where the local men have inaccurate images of western women.

When travelling in Malaysia it is important to bear in mind that it is a Muslim country and modesty in dress is important. While many female travellers wear fairly skimpy clothes without a hassle, it would be prudent to keep the shoulders and thighs covered. At the beach, Malaysian women and families would be embarrassed to find women bathing topless – cover up.

Other precautions apply as much to men as to women. Though Malaysia is generally a very safe country, don't walk alone at night on empty beaches or poorly lit streets.

Many travellers – not just women – have reported the existence of small peep-holes in the walls and doors of cheap hotels. Plug them up with tissue paper, ask for another room or move to another hotel. Remember that in some places cheap hotels are in fact brothels.

Tampons can be found in supermarkets in the main cities if you hunt around, but pads are more commonly available, so if you use tampons stock up in the big cities.

It also pays to treat overly friendly strangers, both male and female, with a good deal of caution.

GAY & LESBIAN TRAVELLERS

Gay issues are swept under the carpet in Malaysia. The official attitude seems to be that, as a strongly Muslim country steeped in Asian Values, homosexuality in Malaysia doesn't exist and it is a western aberration. This is of course nonsense and Malaysia has always had a substantial gay community. Indeed it tends to celebrate its transvestite community, much as in Singapore's Bugis St of old, and government and public attitudes are best defined as disinterested tolerance rather than hostility. However, resurgent Islamic fundamentalist movements, particularly in the conservative states of Kelantan and Terengganu, do occasionally call for crackdowns on homosexuals.

The Utopia Website (www.utopia-asia.com) has country-by-country details on gay organisations and venues. Gay groups and venues are thin on the ground, with the exception of the more cosmopolitan and liberal-minded KL. Pink Triangle Malaysia (☎03-444 4611; email isham@pop7.jaring.my), based in Kuala Lumpur, has regular meetings for gay men and does community based work on sexuality and AIDS.

DISABLED TRAVELLERS

For the mobility impaired, Malaysia can be a nightmare. In most cities and towns there are often no footpaths, kerbs are very high, construction sites are everywhere, and crossings are few and far between. On the upside, the modern urban rail lines being built in KL are at least reasonably accessible.

Both Malaysia Airlines and KTM (the national rail service) offer 50% discounts on travel for disabled travellers.

Three travel-information sources for the mobility-impaired are Mobility USA (☎ 1-541 343 1284), PO Box 1076, Eugene, OR 97440, USA; Holiday Care Service (☎ 01293-774535; fax 01293-784647), Imperial Buildings, Victoria Road, Horley, Surrey, RH6 7PZ; and a World Wide Web site for and by disabled travellers at www.travelhealth.com/disab.htm

SENIOR TRAVELLERS

Senior travellers get a variety of discounts on admission at most cultural attractions. The usual eligible age for seniors is 65 years. Malaysia Airlines does not offer discounts for foreign seniors, but KTM does offer a 50% discount on all travel for foreign seniors over 65 years of age.

TRAVELLING WITH CHILDREN

Like many places in South-East Asia, travelling with children in Malaysia can be a lot of fun as long as you come with the right attitudes and the usual parental patience. *Travel with Children* by Maureen Wheeler and others contains useful advice on how to cope with kids on the road and what to bring along to make things go more smoothly, with special attention paid to travel in developing countries.

There are discounts for children for most attractions and transport and Chinese hotels charge for the room rather than the number of people. However cots are not widely available in cheap accommodation. Public transport is comfortable and relatively well organised.

For the most part parents needn't worry too much about health concerns, though it pays to lay down a few ground rules – such as regular hand-washing – to head off potential problems. All the usual health precautions apply (see the Health section earlier for details); children should especially be warned not to play with animals as rabies occurs in Malaysia.

DANGERS & ANNOYANCES

Theft

Malaysia is not a theft-prone country – in fact, compared with Indonesia or Thailand it is extremely safe. Nevertheless, it pays to keep a close eye on your belongings, especially your travel documents (passport, travellers cheques etc). These items should be kept with you at all times.

A small, sturdy padlock is well worth carrying, especially if you are going to be staying at any of the cheap chalets found on Malaysia's beaches, where flimsy padlocks (with God knows how many duplicate keys) are the norm.

LEGAL MATTERS

Drugs

In Malaysia, the answer is simple – don't. Drug trafficking carries a mandatory death penalty. In almost every village in Malaysia you will see anti-*dadah* (drugs) signs portraying a skull and crossbones and a noose. No one can say they haven't been warned!

Under Malaysian law all drug offenders are considered equal, and being a foreigner will not save you from the gallows. A number of foreigners have been executed in Malaysia, some of them for possession of amazingly small quantities of heroin.

Drugs in Malaysia

Visitors to Malaysia are greeted by skull and crossbones emblems and warnings that the penalty for trafficking drugs is death. It's a sobering start to a holiday and a good reason to leave your stash at home.

The penalty imposed on local drug users is less final but also fairly sobering. Anyone suspected of using drugs in Malaysia can be stopped and required to provide a urine sample for testing. If drugs are detected – any drug, including marijuana – it's off to a 'rehabilitation centre' for one to three years.

As you might expect, Malaysian drug rehabilitation centres are not pleasant places. According to *The Economist*, there are 21 of them scattered around the country, housing around 10,000 drug users. Inmates first spend some time in a 'detoxification cell' before graduating to a regime of exercise and religious education. For good behaviour they are hired out to local factories for a very minimum wage. Anyone not keen on the idea of one to three years of detoxification and hard labour is advised to give drugs a miss while in Malaysia.

Chris Taylor

The penalties are severe and the authorities seem to catch a steady stream of unsuccessful peddlers, smugglers and users. Mere possession can bring down a lengthy jail sentence and a beating with the rotan.

Warnings

When in KL beware of scammers. One of the more common scams involves getting travellers to visit private homes where they are lured into card games – after winning a few rounds, they soon find themselves losing, and wind up cashing travellers cheques to pay off their debt. Travellers are often lured into these houses on the pretense of meeting the scam artist's mother (who is invariably worried about a daughter who is soon going abroad to study, surprisingly enough, in the home country of the hapless traveller).

The scam-of-the-day may have changed

by the time this book is published, but if you use common sense and avoid deals which seem too good to be true, then you should be all right.

BUSINESS HOURS

Government offices are usually open Monday to Friday from 8 am to 4.15 pm. Most close for lunch from 12.45 to 2 pm, and on Friday the lunch break is from 12.15 to 2.45 pm for Friday prayers at the mosque. On Saturday the offices are open from 8 am to 12.45 pm.

Bank hours are generally 10 am to 3 pm on weekdays and 9.30 to 11.30 am on Saturday. Shop hours are variable, although a good rule of thumb for small shops is that they're open from Monday to Saturday from 9 am to 6 pm. Major department stores, shopping malls, Chinese emporiums and some large stores are open from around 10 am until 9 or 10 pm seven days a week.

Most of Malaysia follows this working week – Monday to Friday with Saturday a half-day. But in the more Islamic-minded states of Kedah, Perlis, Kelantan and Terengganu, government offices, banks and many shops are closed on Friday and on Saturday afternoon. They have declared Friday the holiday, and their working week is from Sunday to Thursday with Saturday a half-day. However, federal government offices follow the same hours as the rest of the country. Kelantan has announced a five day week from Sunday to Thursday but the federal government is trying to block it.

PUBLIC HOLIDAYS & SPECIAL EVENTS

With so many cultures and religions in Malaysia, there is quite an amazing number of occasions to celebrate. Although some of them have a fixed date each year, the Hindus, Muslims and Chinese all follow a lunar calendar, so the dates for many events vary each year. Tourism Malaysia puts out bi-annual *Calendar of Events* sheets with specific dates and venues of various festivals and parades, but state tourist offices have more detailed listings.

Public Holidays

In addition to the national public holidays, each state has its own holidays, usually associated with the sultan's birthday or a Muslim celebration. Muslim holidays move back 10 or 11 days each year. Dates are given for 1999, but may vary by one day. Hindu and Chinese holiday dates also vary but stay roughly within the designated months. Malaysia's mind-boggling number of public holidays are:

January-February

New Year's Day
  1 January (National except Johor, Kedah, Kelantan, Perlis, Terengganu)
Nuzul Al-Quran
  Variable (5 January 1999; Kelantan, Pahang, Perak, Perlis, Selangor, Terengganu)
**Hari Raya Puasa*
  Variable (19 & 20 January 1999)
Thaipusam
  Variable (31 January 1999; Johor, Negeri Sembilan, Perak, Penang, Selangor)
Federal Territory Day
  1 February (KL, Labuan)
Sultan of Kedah's Birthday
  7 February 1999 (Kedah)
**Chinese New Year*
  Variable, two days (16 and 17 February 1999; one day only in Kelantan, Terengganu)

March

Sultan of Selangor's Birthday
  2nd Saturday of March (Selangor)
Anniversary of Installation of Sultan of Terengganu
  21 March (Terengganu)
**Hari Raya Haji*
  Variable (28 March 1999; the following day is also a holiday in Kedah, Kelantan, Perlis and Terengganu)
Sultan of Kelantan's Birthday
  30 & 31 March (Kelantan)

April

Good Friday
  Variable (2 April 1999; Sarawak, Sabah)
Sultan of Johor's Birthday
  8 April (Johor)
Melaka Historical City Day
  15 April (Melaka)
**Awal Muharram (Muslim New Year)*
  Variable (17 April 1999)

Sultan of Perak's Birthday
19 April (Perak)
Sultan of Terengganu's Birthday
29 April (Terengganu)

May
**Worker's Day*
1 May
Hol Day
7 May (Pahang)
Raja of Perlis' Birthday
Variable (18 May 1999; Perlis)
**Wesak Day*
Variable (29 May 1999)
Harvest Festival
30 & 31 May (Sabah, Labuan)

June
**Yang di-Pertuan Agong's (King's) Birthday*
1st Saturday in June
Dayak Festival
1 & 2 June (Sarawak)
**Prophet's Birthday*
Variable (26 June 1999)

July
Governor of Penang's Birthday
2nd Saturday in July (Penang)
Governor of Negeri Sembilan's Birthday
19 July (Negeri Sembilan)

August
**National Day*
31 August

September
Malaysia Day
16 September (Sabah)

October-November
Governor of Melaka's Birthday
2nd Saturday in October (Melaka)
Hol Day (Sultan Ismail)
Variable (16 October 1999; Johor)
Sultan of Pahang's Birthday
24 October (Pahang)
Israk & Mikraj
Variable (6 November 1999; Kedah, Negeri Sembilan)
Deepavali
Variable (7 November 1999; National except Sarawak & Labuan)

December
Awal Ramadan (Beginning of Ramadan)
Variable (9 December 1999; Johor, Melaka)
**Christmas Day*
25 December

* National Holiday

Festivals & Events
The public holidays mark many of the major festivals, but numerous other events are celebrated with temple offerings or chanting from the Koran.

The major Islamic events each year are connected with Ramadan, the month during which Muslims cannot eat or drink from sunrise to sunset.

Fifteen days before the start of Ramadan the souls of the dead are supposed to visit their homes on Nisfu Night. During Ramadan Lailatul Qadar, the 'Night of Grandeur', Muslims celebrate the arrival of the Koran on earth from heaven before its revelation by Mohammed. A Koran-reading competition is held in Kuala Lumpur (and extensively televised) during Ramadan.

Hari Raya Puasa marks the end of the month-long fast with two days of joyful celebration. This is the major holiday of the Muslim calendar and it can be difficult to find accommodation in Malaysia, particularly on the east coast. During this time everyone wears new clothes, homes are cleaned and redecorated and everyone seems to visit everyone else.

Hari Raya Haji is the day when pilgrims mark the successful completion of the *hajj* (pilgrimage to Mecca). It is a two day holiday in many of the peninsula states and is marked by the consumption of large amounts of cakes and sweets.

The major Chinese event is Chinese New Year, and the major Indian celebration is Deepavali, though Thaipusam is the most spectacular, celebrated with masochistic spectacle in some states of the peninsula.

Other special events are held, ranging from fun runs and Grand Prix events to kite flying and fishing competitions. Tourism Malaysia publishes pamphlets.

January-February
Thai Pongal A Hindu harvest festival marking the beginning of the Hindu month of Thai,

Malaysia – the Holiday Country

With so many religions that require ritual celebration, and strong state loyalties that also need appeasement, Malaysia has a mind-boggling 44 days of public holidays each year, not including any special holidays proclaimed from time to time. That, however, is in a good year. Most holidays are based on the Muslim lunar calendar (which is 10 or 11 days shorter than the Gregorian calendar), or the Hindu and Chinese calendars (based on lunar and solar cycles), so holiday dates vary each year and a few usually overlap, reducing the number.

A major combination of holidays occurred in 1996 and 1997, when Hari Raya, the most important Muslim celebration, and Chinese New Year, the most important Chinese celebration, coincided. The combination produced chaos across the nation as everyone went on holiday and there was plenty of self-congratulatory reflection on how the races get along so well in today's multicultural Malaysia.

Malaysia's massive number of holidays are not celebrated nationwide, because holidays vary from state to state. No one gets all those holidays, except perhaps a crafty travelling salesperson who can carefully arrange their itinerary. So which state is the big winner of all those days off?

Every state gets at least 11 national holidays and most get another five or six state holidays, but Sabah is the party state, topping the rankings with 18 holidays per year. And who is the big loser? Well, you – if you happen to hit Malaysia when the calendars align and inadvertently cross borders just in time to catch a few sultans' birthdays. Then you may find yourself constantly looking around for a bank that isn't closed, a bus that isn't full and a hotel that hasn't raised its prices. The compensation is that you may see some spectacular events and street parades or be invited to an 'open house', for hospitable Malaysians will always entertain family, friends, neighbours and perhaps even passers-by at the times of major celebrations.

considered the luckiest month of the year. Celebrated among Tamils.

Chinese New Year Dragon dances and pedestrian parades mark the start of the new year. Families hold open house, unmarried relatives (especially children) receive *ang pows* (money in red packets), businesses traditionally clear their debts and everybody wishes you a Kong Hee Fatt Choy (a happy and prosperous New Year).

Birthday of the Jade Emperor Nine days after New Year, a Chinese festival honours Yu Huang, the supreme ruler of heaven, with offerings at temples.

Ban Hood Huat Hoay A 12 day celebration for the Day of Ten Thousand Buddhas is held at the Kek Lok Si Temple in Penang.

Chap Goh Meh On the 15th day after Chinese New Year, the celebrations officially end.

Chingay In Johor Bahru, processions of Chinese flagbearers balancing bamboo flagpoles six to 12m long can be seen on the 22nd day after New Year.

Thaipusam One of the most dramatic Hindu festivals (now banned in India), in which devotees honour Lord Subramaniam with acts of amazing masochism. In Kuala Lumpur they march in a procession to the Batu Caves carrying *kavadis*, heavy metal frames decorated with peacock feathers, fruit and flowers. The kavadis are hung from their bodies with metal hooks and spikes driven into the flesh. Other devotees pierce their cheeks and tongues with metal skewers, or walk on sandals of nails. Along the procession route, the kavadi carriers dance to the drum beat while spectators urge them on with shouts of 'Vel, Vel'. In the evening the procession continues with an image of Subramaniam in a temple car. On Penang, Thaipusam is celebrated at the Waterfall Temple. See the information on Thaipusam in the special Places of Worship section after the Facts about Malaysia section.

Kwong Teck Sun Ong's Birthday Celebration of the birthday of a child deity at the Chinese temple in Kuching in late February.

March-April

Tua Peck Kong Paper money and paper models of useful things to have with you in the afterlife are burnt at the Sia Sen Temple in Kuching.

Easter On Palm Sunday a candlelight procession is held at St Peter's in Melaka. Good Friday and Easter Monday also provide colourful celebrations at St Peter's and other Melaka churches.

Panguni Uttiram On the full moon day of the Tamil month of Panguni, the marriage of Shiva to Shakti and of Lord Subramaniam to Theivani is celebrated.

Birthday of the Goddess of Mercy Offerings are made to the very popular Kuan Yin at her temples in Penang and Kuala Lumpur.

Cheng Ming On Cheng Ming, Chinese traditionally visit the tombs of their ancestors to clean and repair them and make offerings.

Sri Rama Navami A nine day festival held by the Brahmin caste to honour the Hindu hero of the *Ramayana*, Sri Rama.

Birthday of the Monkey God The birthday of T'se Tien Tai Seng Yeh is celebrated twice a year. Mediums pierce their cheeks and tongues with skewers and go into trances during which they write special charms in blood.

April-May

Songkran Festival A traditional Thai Buddhist New Year in which Buddha images are bathed.

Chithirai Vishu Start of the Hindu New Year.

Puja Pantai A large three day Hindu-inspired Malay festival held 5km south of Kuala Terengganu.

Birthday of the Queen of Heaven Ma Cho Po, the queen of heaven and goddess of the sea, is honoured at her temples.

Wesak Day Buddha's birth, enlightenment and death are celebrated by various events, including the release of caged birds to symbolise the setting free of captive souls.

Turtle season From May until September giant turtles come ashore each night to lay their eggs along the beach at Rantau Abang on the east coast of the peninsula.

June

Gawai Dayak Annual Sarawak Dayak Festival on 1 and 2 June to mark the end of the rice season. War dances, cockfights and blowpipe events all take place.

Festa de San Pedro Christian celebration in honour of the patron saint of the fishing community on 29 June, particularly celebrated by the Eurasian-Portuguese community of Melaka.

Birthday of the God of War Kuan Ti, who has the ability to avert war and to protect people during war, is honoured on his birthday.

Dragon Boat Festival Commemorating the death of a Chinese saint who drowned himself. In an attempt to save him, the local fishing community paddled out to sea, beating drums to scare away any fish that might attack him. To mark the anniversary, this festival is celebrated from June to August with boat races in Penang and other places.

July

Birthday of Kuan Yin The goddess of mercy has another birthday!

Feast of St Anne A Roman Catholic festival celebrated at St Anne's Church in Penang.

Prophet Mohammed's Birthday Muslims pray and religious leaders recite verses from the Koran.

July-August

Sri Krishna Jayanti A 10 day Hindu festival celebrating popular events in Krishna's life is highlighted on day eight by celebrations of his birthday. The Laxmi Narayan Temple in Kuala Lumpur is a particular focus.

Lumut Sea Carnival At Lumut, the port for Pulau Pangkor, boat races, swimming races and many other events are held.

August

Festival of the Seven Sisters Chinese girls pray to the weaving maid for good husbands.

Festival of the Hungry Ghosts The souls of the dead are released for one day of feasting and entertainment on earth. Chinese operas and other events are laid on for them and food is put out. The ghosts eat the spirit of the food, but thoughtfully leave the substance for mortal celebrants. Mainly in Penang.

National Day (Hari Kebangsaan) Malaysia celebrates Malaysia's independence on 31 August with events all over the country, but particularly in Kuala Lumpur, where there are parades and a variety of performances in the Lake Gardens.

Vinayagar Chathuri During the Tamil month of Avani (around August and September), prayers are offered to Vinayagar, another name for the popular elephant-headed god Ganesh.

September

Feast of Santa Cruz A month-long pilgrimage season in September at the Church of Santa Cruz at Malim, Melaka.

Papar Tamu Besar This annual market festival is held from 15 to 20 September in an area of Sabah renowned for its beautiful Kadazan girls.

Moon Cake Festival The overthrow of the Mongol warlords in ancient China is celebrated by eating moon cakes and lighting colourful paper lanterns. Moon cakes are made with bean paste, lotus seeds and sometimes a duck egg.

September-October

Thimithi (Fire-Walking Ceremony) Hindu devotees prove their faith by walking across glowing coals at the Gajah Berang Temple in Melaka.

Navarathri In the Tamil month of Purattasi the Hindu festival of 'Nine Nights' is dedicated to the wives of Shiva, Vishnu and Brahma. Young girls are dressed as the goddess Kali.

Festival of the Nine Emperor Gods Nine days of Chinese operas, processions and other events honour the nine emperor gods. At the Kau Ong Yah Temples in Kuala Lumpur and Penang fire-walking ceremonies are held on the evening of the ninth day.

Puja Ketek Offerings are brought to Buddhist shrines, or *keteks*, in the state of Kelantan during this festival in October. Traditional dances are often performed.

October-November

Kantha Shashithi Subramaniam, a great fighter against the forces of evil, is honoured during the Hindu month of Aipasi.

Deepavali Later in the month of Aipasi, Rama's victory over the demon king Ravana is celebrated with the 'Festival of Lights', when tiny oil-lamps are lit outside the homes of Hindu people, as it's believed that Lakshmi, the goddess of wealth, will not enter an unlit home. For business people, this is the time to start a new financial year, and for the family a pre-dawn oil bath, new clothes and lots of sweets is the order of the day. It's bad luck to sweep the house, as this would sweep away good fortune, and it is also bad luck to break anything on this day.

Birthday of Kuan Yin The birthday of the popular goddess of mercy is celebrated yet again.

Kartikai Deepam Huge bonfires are lit to commemorate Shiva's appearance as a pillar of fire following an argument with Vishnu and Brahma. The Thandayuthapani Temple in Muar is a major site for this festival.

Guru Nanak's Birthday The birthday of Guru Nanak, founder of the Sikh religion, is celebrated on 22 November.

December

Pesta Pulau Penang Two month carnival on Penang in November and December featuring many water events, including dragon-boat races towards the end of the festival.

Winter Solstice Festival Chinese festival to offer thanks for a good harvest.

Christmas Day On 25 December Christians celebrate the birth of Jesus Christ.

ACTIVITIES

The following is a brief list of some of Malaysia's more popular activities. For details on the locations listed, please see the individual entries later in this book.

Diving & Snorkelling

With its tropical location and wealth of islands, it's not surprising that Malaysia has some great snorkelling and diving. The main centres include Pulau Perhentian, Pulau Redang, Pulau Tioman, the Seribuat Archipelago and Pulau Sipadan. See the colour Diving & Snorkelling section in the Terengganu chapter for more information.

Mountain Climbing

Mt Kinabalu, the highest mountain in South-East Asia, is an obvious choice for those interested in mountain climbing. See the special section, Climbing Kinabalu, for details. However, this is not the only mountain worth climbing in Malaysia. Gunung Mulu, in Sarawak's Gunung Mulu National Park, is a challenging four day climb. On the peninsula, there are several good climbs in Taman Negara National Park. There are also a few lesser peaks scattered around that make pleasant day outings.

Jungle Trekking

Despite the pressures of logging, Malaysia is still home to some of the world's most impressive stands of virgin tropical jungle. Almost all of Malaysia's national parks offer excellent jungle trekking, including Taman Negara on the peninsula and Gunung Mulu in East Malaysia. There are treks to suit all ability levels, from 20-minute jaunts to 10-day expeditions. The special section, Trekking in Sarawak, has more information on routes in this area.

Caving

Malaysia's limestone hills are riddled with caves to lure the spelunker. Some of these are easily accessible and can be visited without any special equipment or preparation while others are strictly the terrain of the experienced caver. There are caves both on the peninsula (Gua Charas, Gua Musang and Taman Negara) and dotted around East Malaysia, including one of the world's premier caving destinations: Gunung Mulu National Park.

Bicycle Touring

Malaysia is one of the best places in South-East Asia for bike touring. Perhaps the most popular route is the one up the east coast of Peninsular Malaysia, with its relatively quiet roads. However, if you're fit and energetic, you may prefer the hillier regions of the peninsula's interior or East Malaysia. Refer to the boxed text, 'By Bicycle – Peninsula Malaysia and Singapore' in the Getting Around chapter, for details of routes.

Traditional Crafts

Several of Malaysia's cultural centres offer classes in traditional Malaysian handicrafts. Kota Bharu and Cherating are perhaps the best places to get a hands-on feel for batik, puppet making and kite making.

Birdwatching

Malaysia's tropical jungles and islands are home to a tremendous variety of bird species. On the peninsula, Taman Negara, Kenong Rimba and Endau-Rompin national parks all offer excellent birdwatching. In East Malaysia, Kinabalu, Gunung Mulu, Simalajau and Gunung Gading are similarly rich in bird species. See the relevant chapters for more details.

ACCOMMODATION

Malaysia has a very wide range of accommodation possibilities – you can still find places to stay for US$4 per person per night, while at the other end of the scale more luxurious 'international standard' hotels can be well over US$100 a night for a room. Note that most hotels quote similar prices for single and double rooms (sometimes even triples) so that it is a lot cheaper to travel with another person or two. Sometimes both standard and deluxe rooms are availalble. Accommodation possibilities include the following options.

International Hotels

There are modern, multistorey, air-con, swimming pool, all mod-cons hotels of the major international chains (Hyatt, Holiday Inn, Hilton) and of many local chains such as the Merlin hotels, all over Malaysia. In these hotels, nightly costs are generally from RM200 and up for a double. Malaysia has not suffered the price hikes of neighbouring Singapore, but Kuala Lumpur and Penang have seen climbing occupancy rates and higher prices.

Traditional Chinese Hotels

At the other end of the price scale are the traditional Chinese hotels found in great numbers all over Malaysia. They're the mainstay of budget travellers and backpackers, and in Malaysia you can generally find a good room for RM12 to RM25. Chinese hotels are generally fairly spartan – bare floors and just a bed, a couple of chairs and a table, a wardrobe and a sink. The showers and toilets (which will sometimes be Asian squat style) will generally be down the corridor. A point to watch for: couples can sometimes economise by asking for a single, since in Chinese hotel language single means one double bed, while double means two beds. Don't think this is being tight; in Chinese hotels you can pack as many into one room as you wish.

The main catch with these hotels is that they can sometimes be terribly noisy. They're often on main streets, and the bottom rung of the Chinese hotel ladder has a serious design problem – the walls rarely reach the ceiling. The top is simply meshed or barred in. This is great for ventilation but terrible for acoustics. Every noise carries throughout the hotel and Chinese hotels all awake to a terrible dawn chorus of hawking, coughing and spitting.

There are also many older-style Chinese places a notch up from the most basic places, where RM12 to RM25 will get you a fan-cooled room with common facilities. For RM25 to RM40 you can often find air-conditioned rooms with attached bathroom – but still basically Chinese in their spartan style.

Resthouses

Some of the old British-developed resthouses are still operating. These were set up during the colonial era to provide accommodation for travelling officials, and later provided excellent shelter for all types of travellers. Many of the resthouses are still government owned but are now privately operated. Some have been turned into mid-range resorts, but many retain traditional style. The average price for a room in a resthouse is RM50, and this usually includes air-con and attached bathroom.

Guesthouses

At beach centres and in the major tourist cities you will find a variety of cheap accommodation which can be grouped together under the term 'guesthouses'. These may be huts on the beach or private homes or rented houses divided by partition walls into a number of rooms. Dormitory accommodation is available. Rooms are usually spartan, but this is the cheapest accommodation around and often the nicest, with a real family atmosphere. These places often cater only to foreign travellers and offer their customers lots of little extras to outdo the competition, such as free tea and coffee, bicycles, transport and even haircuts. A dorm bed will cost RM6 to RM8, and rooms will cost from RM12 up to RM40 for a hotel-style room with air-con.

Homestays

A homestay is a private home with a few rooms set aside for travellers. They are not nearly as common as they once were, but you can still find them in KL, Kota Bharu and Johor Bahru. Some of the bigger homestays offer both dorm rooms (RM5 to RM15 per bed) and private rooms (from RM12 to RM20 per double room). Many homestays also serve breakfast and/or dinner and this is often a good chance to sample authentic Malaysian food.

It's a good idea to take a good look at a homestay before deciding to stay as some places have squalid rooms and constantly arguing owners.

Longhouses in East Malaysia

Longhouses are the traditional dwellings of the indigenous peoples of Borneo. These communal dwellings may contain up to 100 individual family 'apartments' built under one long roof. The most important area of a longhouse is the common veranda which serves as a social area. These days there are two main types of longhouse: 'tourist longhouses' and 'authentic longhouses'. While a visit to a tourist longhouse is easily enough arranged it is unlikely to be of much interest. A visit to an authentic, living longhouse can be a magical experience, but it is easier said than done – one does not merely show up on the veranda with a carton of cigarettes and expect to be welcomed inside. Indeed, there is a very specific etiquette to visiting a longhouse. For details, see the Visiting a Longhouse section of the Sarawak chapter.

Camping

Camping is another good, cheap option in Malaysia. Many of the national parks have official campgrounds and will permit camping in non-designated sites once you are into the back country. There are also many lonely stretches of beach, particularly on the east coast of the peninsula, which are ideal for camping. Likewise, it is possible to camp on uninhabited bays on many of Malaysia's islands. If you do decide to camp in Malaysia, a two season tent with mosquito netting is ideal. As for sleeping bags, a summer-weight bag is good, but the best choice is a lightweight bag liner, since even the nights can be quite warm in Malaysia.

Taxes & Service Charges

In Malaysia there's a 5% government tax that applies to all hotel rooms. On top of this there's a 10% service charge in the more expensive places. You are not expected to tip in addition to this. Expensive places almost always quote prices exclusive of tax and service charge – this is represented as ++ (called plus-plus), for example $120++ for a double. Nett means that tax and service charges are included. Tax and service charges are also applied to food, drinks and services in the more expensive hotels and restaurants.

Cheap Malaysian hotels, however, generally quote a price inclusive of the 5% government tax.

FOOD & DRINKS

While travelling around some parts of Asia is as good as a session with Weight Watchers, Singapore and Malaysia are quite the opposite. The food is simply terrific, the variety unbeatable and the costs pleasantly low. Whether you're looking for Chinese food, Malay food, Indian food, Indonesian food or even a Big Mac, you'll find happiness! There's also a good range of nonalcoholic and alcoholic drinks. For a complete description, see the illustrated section Food & Drinks in Singapore & Malaysia in this chapter and the Food section in the Glossary at the end of this book.

ENTERTAINMENT

Entertainment in Malaysia is much the same as in western countries, though Asian Values apply. The traditional pastimes of wayang puppet theatre and traditional dance have all but disappeared, except for special occasions or tourist recreations. The main cities have discos, clubs, pubs and bars, usually fairly tame with high bar prices. KL has a very lively and extensive nightlife scene – if you are looking for a place to rage, this is it. Almost every town has a karaoke bar if you are desperate for something to do, and large hotels usually have something happening.

Cinemas generally show B-grade adventure movies and Hong Kong kungfu flicks, either dubbed or with multiple subtitles covering all the major languages. The latest Hollywood blockbusters are occasionally shown, though movies are heavily censored. The various cultural organisations in KL and Penang, such as Alliance Française and the Goethe Institut, have regular screenings of their foreign-language films.

SPECTATOR SPORT

The main spectator sports in Malaysia are football, badminton, squash and track and field. In the smaller kampungs you may also be able to observe *sepak takraw*, a game similar to volleyball in which players use only their head and feet to propel a ball over a net. To find out about upcoming sporting events look in the *New Straits Times* or check with Tourism Malaysia.

Some of Kuala Lumpur's larger sports venues are:

Bangsar Sports Kompleks
  Jalan Terasek 3, 59100 Kuala Lumpur
National Sports Kompleks
  Jalan Duta, 50480 Kuala Lumpur
Stadium Merdeka
  Jalan Stadium, 50150 Kuala Lumpur
Stadium Negara
  Jalan Hang Jebat, 50150 Kuala Lumpur

SHOPPING

Every tourist centre has a selection of shops and stalls selling souvenirs but because of high wages handicrafts are not a big item in Malaysia. Many of the 'Malay' handicrafts on sale are imported from Indonesia and elsewhere. Nevertheless, many attractive souvenirs and handicrafts can be found, but bargain hard for tourist-oriented items.

Malaysian kites *(wau)* are readily available and are a colourful and typical souvenir from Malaysia – Kota Bharu is a good place to find them. The distinctive Kedah pottery – hand-painted, bulb-shaped pots with long necks – is another Malaysian craft, as is pewterware, most of which comes from Selangor, and wavy-bladed *kris* knives, many of which come from Indonesia. Some fine Dayak weavings and woodcarvings can be found in Sarawak, but prices are very high. The east coast of the peninsula has attractive *songket* (weaving with gold thread) and Malaysia also produces batik, usually with floral motifs though the work is not always that fine.

Antiques are readily available in Melaka and to a lesser extent Penang. Everything from lion-head door knockers to marble-topped tables are on sale, but prices are often very high and hard bargaining is required. Chinese pottery and jewellery is available everywhere.

Malaysia is reasonably priced for electronics, though the range is not great and prices are slightly higher than in Singapore, which has a much better range. Portable radios and cameras are duty-free in Malaysia. Cameras and accessories in particular are a good buy.

Copies of brand-name goods can be found – you can outfit yourself with Nike, Lacoste and Rolex for a fraction of the cost of the real thing – or the real thing is also on sale in many places.

Depending on your country of origin you may find clothes and shoes a reasonable buy. The range and styles are good, and larger sizes are available. Cheap cotton beachwear can be found at the beach centres.

TASTES OF MALAYSIA, SINGAPORE & BRUNEI

Food

Malaysia, Singapore and Brunei are renowned for their diverse cuisines and great food. The ethnically mixed countries mean you can eat Malay food for breakfast, Chinese for lunch and Indian for dinner! And you can snack on deliciously fresh tropical fruit between meals. Many types of Chinese food are available, particularly in Singapore, and don't forget to try the Peranakan cuisine of the Straits Chinese or Peranakan (Baba-Nyonya) people. There's good quality food to fit all budgets and tastes, ranging from the popular hawker centres and coffee shops to fine dining at exclusive restaurants. This section will help you negotiate your way around the array of culinary options in the three countries, identify the variety of tasty tropical fruits and know which alcoholic drinks to watch out for! See also the separate Food section in the Glossary at the end of this book.

WHERE TO EAT

In Malaysia you'll probably wind up eating a lot of your meals in *kedai kopi* (coffee shops), which generally serve a few noodle and rice dishes plus a variety of beverages such as coffee and tea, soda and occasionally juice. Light meals and snacks are also available; usually a *nasi kampur* buffet and dishes such as *nasi goreng* and *mee goreng*. Chinese or Indian-run kedai kopi serve more varied ethnic cuisine reflective of their ownership. Coffee shops are called *kopi tiam* in Singapore (tiam is Hokkien for shop). These range from spartan restaurants with open fronts and two or three stalls to restaurant-like shops offering a greater range of dishes.

You'll also find a variety of hawker stalls in Malaysia and Brunei, particularly in the night markets of the bigger cities. While some of these are generalist, serving the standard noodle and rice favourites, you will also find specialist stalls selling dishes like Thai *tom yam kum* soup, Indian *murtabak*, Chinese *chicken-rice* as well as various seafood specialities. Some carts also specialise only in drinks. Most travellers find that the food from hawker stalls is superior to that served by kedai kopi. These two types of places to eat are often the only options outside large cities.

The real Singaporean dining experience is a meal at a more modern hawker centre, where you can choose from stalls in a large food court area, all for under S$5.

In Malaysia's cities and in Singapore and Brunei, you will also find a range of ethnic restaurants. These will primarily serve Chinese and Indian food. Ironically, Malay restaurants are the hardest to find. Complementing these places, the big cities also have the

The Hawkers' Variety

Singapore's popular hawker stalls offer a huge variety of the cheapest meals in town. Eating at these huge food centres is part of a visit to Singapore, and you'll be experiencing life and meal times as they are for the average Singaporean.

Some typical hawker food you may come across includes carrot cake, or *chye tow kway*, usually sold for S$2 to S$3. Also known as radish cake, it's a vegetable and egg dish, which tastes something like a potato omelette, and totally unlike the western health-food idea of carrot cake.

Indian *biryanis* cost around S$3 or you can buy a *murtabak* for around S$2. Naturally, chicken-rice and *char siew*, or roast pork, will always be available in food centres (S$2 to S$3). All the usual Cantonese dishes like fried rice (S$1.50 to S$3), fried vegetables (S$3), beef and vegetables (S$5), and sweet and sour pork (S$3 to S$5) are available, plus other dishes like fish heads with black beans and chilli from S$3 to S$5.

There will often be Malay or Indonesian stalls with satay from 30c to 35c a stick, *mee rebus* for S$2 and *mee soto* at similar prices. *Won ton mee*, a substantial soup dish with shredded chicken or braised beef, costs from S$2 to S$3. You could try a *chee chong fun*, a type of stuffed noodle, which costs from S$2 to S$4 or more, depending on whether you want the noodles with prawns, mushrooms, chicken or pork. *Hokkien fried prawn mee* costs around S$2 to S$4, as does *prawn mee soup*. *Popiah* (spring rolls) and *laksa* (a spicy coconut-based soup) are other regulars, but there's also a whole variety of other dishes and soups. You can even opt for western food like sausages, egg and chips, burgers or fish and chips.

Drinks include a large bottle of beer for S$8, soft drinks from 80c, *ais kacang* for 80c or sugar cane juice from 50c to S$1, depending on the size. Fruit juices such as melon, papaya, pineapple, apple, orange or starfruit range from 80c to S$2. To finish up you might try a fruit salad for S$2 or a *pisang goreng* (fried banana) for S$0.50.

inevitable fast-food restaurants, with KFC leading the way. Those who want to self-cater will find supermarkets in the cities and outdoor markets in the smaller towns.

CUISINES

The three most prominent cuisines in Malaysia and Singapore are Chinese and Indian food, in all their regional variations, and Malay food. You'll also find Indonesian and Peranakan dishes, so make the most of the range of eating options.

Chinese

Chinese or Cantonese? When people in the west speak of Chinese food, they probably mean Cantonese food. It's the best known and most popular variety of Chinese cooking – even in Singapore, where the majority of Chinese are not Cantonese. Cantonese food is noted for the variety and freshness of its ingredients. The food is usually stir-fried with just a touch of oil to ensure that the result is crisp and fresh. All those best known 'western Chinese' dishes fit into this category – sweet and sour dishes, won ton soup, chow mein, spring rolls.

With Cantonese food, the more people you can muster for the meal the better, because dishes are traditionally shared so that everyone manages to sample the greatest variety. A corollary of this is that Cantonese food should be balanced: traditionally, all foods are said to be either *yin* (cooling), like vegetables, most fruits and clear soups, or *yang* (heating) like starchy foods and meat. A 'cooling' dish should be balanced by a 'heating' dish: too much of one or the other is not good for you.

Ginger is used in its fresh and preserved forms in Chinese cooking.

Another Cantonese speciality is *dim sum*, or 'little heart'. Dim sum is usually eaten at lunchtime or as a Sunday brunch. Dim sum restaurants are often large, noisy affairs and the dim sum – little snacks that come in small bowls – are whisked around the tables on individual trolleys or carts. As they come by, you simply ask for a plate of this or a bowl of that. At the end of the meal your bill is toted up from the number of empty containers on your table.

Cantonese cuisine can also offer real extremes – shark's-fin soup or bird's-nest soup are expensive delicacies from one end of the scale; *mee* (noodles) or *congee* (rice porridge) are cheap basics from the other end.

Hokkien It is quite easy to find a number of regional styles of Chinese food – particularly since so many of the region's Chinese are Hokkiens or Hakkas. One of the best known of these southern dishes comes from the island of Hainan. Around Malaysia one of the most widespread and economical meals is Hainanese chicken-rice, known in Singapore and Malaysia as *nasi ayam* or *nasi ayam Hainan*. It's one of those dishes whose very simplicity ensures its quality. Chicken-rice is simply steamed chicken, rice boiled or steamed in the chicken stock, a clear soup and slices of cucumber. You can flavour this delicate dish with soy or chilli sauce for a delicious meal costing around RM3. The Hainanese also produce steamboat, a sort of Oriental variation of a Swiss fondue, where you have a boiling stockpot in the middle of the table, into which you dip pieces of meat, seafood or vegetables.

Star anise features in Chinese five spice powder.

The Hokkiens come from the Fujian Province in China and make up the largest dialect group in Singapore. Although Hokkien food is rated way down the Chinese gastronomic scale, it has provided the unofficial national dish of Singapore – Hokkien fried mee, or Singapore noodles. It's made of thick egg noodles cooked with pork, seafood and vegetables and a rich sauce. Hokkien popiah spring rolls are also delicious.

Szechuan The fiery food of China, peppers really get into the act in Szechuan (or Sichuan) food. Whereas the tastes of Cantonese food are delicate and understated, in Sichuan food the flavours are strong and dramatic – garlic and chillies play their part in dishes like diced chicken or hot and sour soup.

Beijing The famous Beijing duck is the best known dish in this cuisine. The specially fattened ducks are basted in syrup and roasted on a revolving spit and the skin is served as a separate first course. Like the other northern cuisines, Beijing food is less subtle than Cantonese food. Although Beijing food is usually eaten with noodles or steamed buns in China, because rice does not grow in the cold northern Beijing region, in Singapore and Malaysia it's equally likely to come with rice.

Teochew From the area around Swatow in China, Teochew is another style noted for its delicacy and natural flavours. Teochew cuisine is also famous for seafood, and a popular food-centre dish is *char kway teow* – broad noodles, clams and eggs fried in chilli and black bean sauce.

Hakka Simple ingredients are a feature of Hakka food. The best known Hakka dish, again easily found in food centres, is *yong tau foo* – bean curd stuffed with minced meat.

Shanghai Food from Shanghai is to some extent a cross between northern and Cantonese cuisines – combining the strong flavours of the north with the ingredients of Canton. It is not easy to find, however, in Singapore and Malaysia.

Indian

Indian food is one of the region's greatest delights. Indeed, some people say it's easier to find really good Indian food in Singapore or Malaysia than in India! Very approximately, you can divide Indian food into southern, Muslim and northern styles.

Common to all Indian food are the spices, or *masala*, the lentil soup known as *dhal*, the yoghurt and water drink known as *lassi* and the sauces or condiments called chutneys.

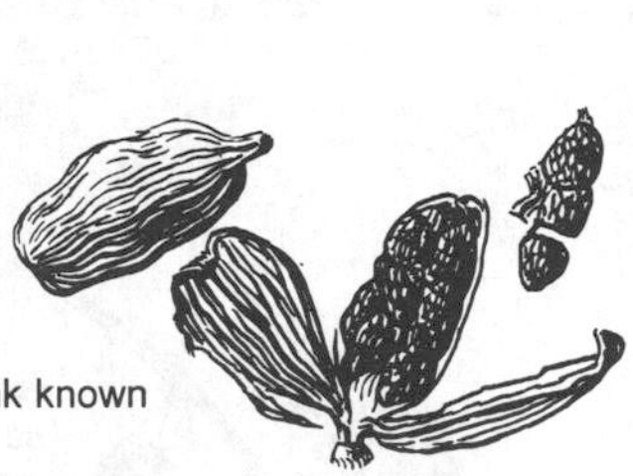

Cardamom is an important flavour in Indian food.

South India Food from southern India tends to be hot, with the emphasis on vegetarian food. The typical South Indian dish is a *thali* (rice plate), but if you ask for one in a vegetarian restaurant you won't get a plate at all but a large *daun pisang* (banana leaf). On this a large mound of rice is placed, then scoops of a variety of vegetable curries and a couple of pappadams are tossed in for good measure. With your right hand (South Indian vegetarian food is never eaten with utensils), you then knead the curries into the

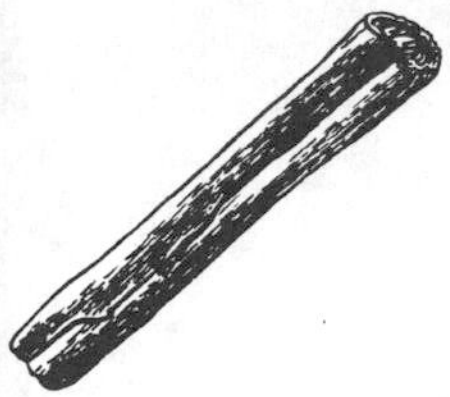

Cinnamon tree bark is ground and used in curry powders.

rice and eat away. Use the tips of your fingers, without the food passing your middle knuckles. When your banana leaf starts to get empty you'll suddenly find it refilled – for the rice plate is always an 'as much as you can eat' meal. When you've finished, fold the banana leaf in two, with the fold towards you, to indicate that you've had enough.

Other vegetarian dishes include the popular *masala dosa*, a thin pancake which, when rolled around the masala (spiced vegetables) with some *rasam* (spicy soup) on the side, provides about the cheapest light meal you could ask for. An equivalent snack meal in Indian Muslim restaurants is *murtabak*, made from paper-thin dough filled with egg and minced mutton and lightly grilled with oil. A *roti canai* – made from murtabak dough – which you dip into a bowl of dhal or curry, is a very popular and filling breakfast eaten throughout the region. A *samosa* is a vegetable or meat-filled pastry.

Muslim India Muslim food tends to be more subtly spiced and uses more meat than cuisines from the south of India. It is a mixture of southern and northern Indian influences and has developed a distinctly Malaysian style. A favourite Indian Muslim dish, and one which is cheap, easy to find and of excellent standard, is *biryani*. Served with a chicken or mutton curry, the dish takes its name from the saffron-coloured rice it is usually served with.

North India A particular favourite is the north Indian *tandoori* food, which takes its name from the clay tandoor oven in which meat is cooked after an overnight marinade in a complex yoghurt and spice mixture. Tandoori chicken is the best known tandoori dish.

Although rice is also eaten in north India, it is not the ubiquitous staple it is in the south. North Indian food makes wide use of the delicious Indian breads like *naan*, *chapatis*, *parathas* and *rotis*. The rich Mogul dishes of northern India are not so common and are generally only found in more expensive restaurants.

Chillies add spice to many Malay dishes.

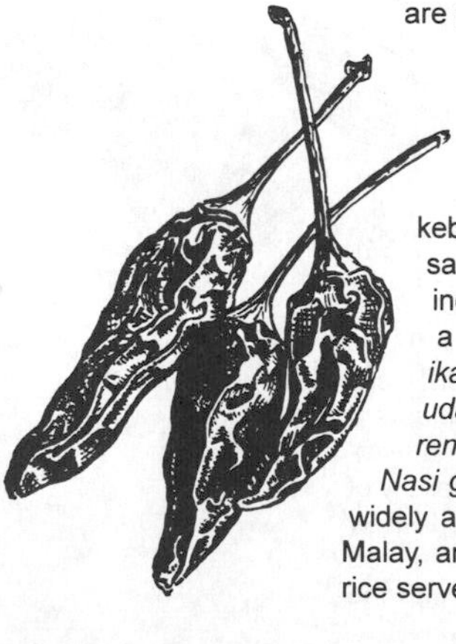

Malay

Surprisingly, Malay food is not as easily found in Malaysia as Chinese or Indian food, although many Malay dishes, like *satay*, are everywhere. Satay is delicious tiny kebabs of chicken, mutton or beef dipped in a spicy peanut sauce. Some Malay dishes you may have a chance to try include *tahu goreng* – fried soybean curd and bean sprouts in a peanut sauce; *ikan bilis* (anchovies) – tiny fish fried whole; *ikan assam* – fried fish in a sour tamarind curry; and *sambal udang* – fiery curry prawns. *Ayam goreng* is fried chicken and *rendang* is a sort of spiced curried meat in coconut marinade.

Nasi goreng (or fried rice – 'nasi' is rice and 'goreng' is fried) is widely available, but it is as much a Chinese and Indian dish as Malay, and each style has its own flavours. *Nasi lemak* is coconut rice served with fried ikan bilis, peanuts and a curry dish.

Indonesian
Indonesian food is very similar to Malay, and you'll find Malaysian regional dishes that have been influenced by Indonesian cuisine, as well as a number of Indonesian restaurants scattered around. In Sumatra the Indonesian food bends much more towards curries and chillies. The popular Sumatran food is *nasi padang*, from the Minangkabau region of West Sumatra, and consists of a wide variety of hot curries served with rice. The Malaysian equivalent is found in the state of Negeri Sembilan which was originally peopled by Minangkabau settlers from Sumatra. *Mee rebus,* noodles in a rich soya-based sauce, is a Javanese dish that has been adopted as a local favourite in Johor.

Nyonya
Nyonya or Peranakan cooking is a local variation on Chinese and Malay food – it uses Chinese ingredients but with local spices like lemon grass and coconut cream. This cuisine evolved from the intermarriage of Chinese and Malay people, now known as Baba-Nyonya or Straits Chinese.

Nyonya cooking is essentially a home skill rather than a restaurant one, but a number of Nyonya restaurants can be found. *Laksa lemak*, a spicy coconut-based noodle soup, is a classic Nyonya dish that has been adopted by all Malaysians and found everywhere. *Laksa Penang* is the more sour variety from Penang that uses fish paste for the stock.

DESSERTS
Although desserts are not a really big deal in the region, you can find some interesting after-dinner snacks, such as *pisang goreng* (banana fritters) or *ais kacang* and *cendol*. Halfway between a drink and a dessert, ais kacang is rather like an old-fashioned 'snow-cone', but the shaved ice is topped with syrups and condensed milk and it's all piled on top of a foundation of beans and jellies. It sounds gross and looks lurid but tastes terrific! Cendol is similar – it consists of coconut milk with brown sugar syrup and greenish noodle-like things topped with shaved ice (it also tastes terrific).

TROPICAL FRUIT
Once you've tried rambutans, mangosteens, jackfruit and durians, how can you ever go back to boring old apples and oranges? If you're already addicted to tropical fruit, Singapore and Malaysia are great places to indulge the passion. If you've not yet been initiated, there could hardly be a better place in the world to develop a taste for these exotic flavours.

For an easy introduction, head for the fruit stalls, which you'll find in food centres or even just on the streets. Slices of a whole variety of fruits (including those dull old apples and oranges) are laid out on ice in a colourful and mouth-watering display from which you

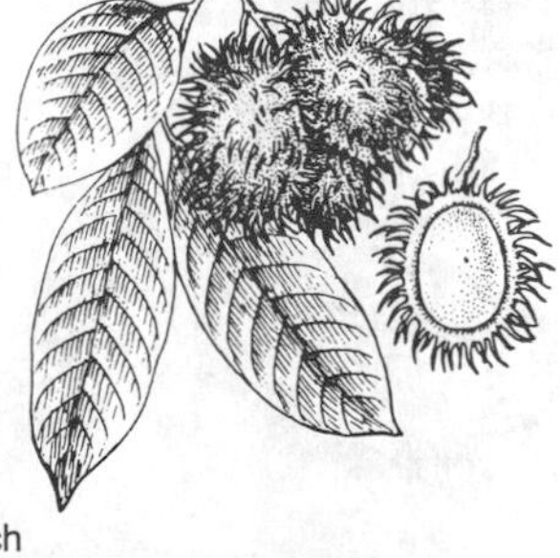

Rambutan should be nibbled carefully so you don't bite into the seed.

can make a selection for just 30 sen and up. You can also have a fruit salad made up on the spot from as many fruits as you care to choose. Some tastes to sample include:

Rambutan *(Nephelium lappaceum)*
The Malay name means 'spiny' and that's just what they are. Rambutans are the size of a large walnut or small tangerine and they're covered in soft red spines. You peel the skin away to reveal a very close cousin to the lychee, with cool and mouth-watering flesh around a central stone. The main rambutan season is from June to September.

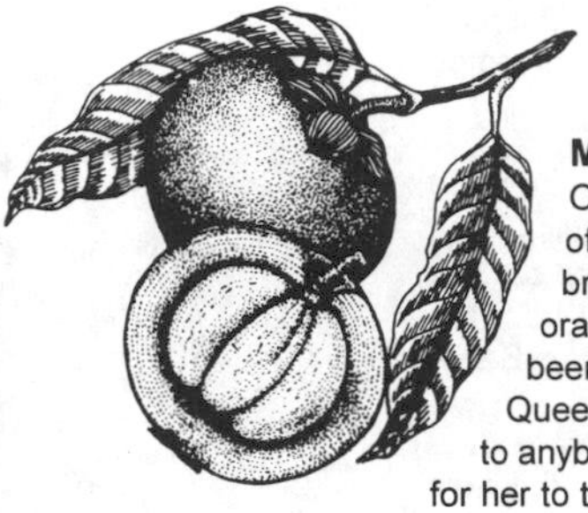

Mangosteen are best eaten when they're shiny and a deep purple colour.

Mangosteen *(Garcinia mangostana)*
One of the finest tropical fruits, the mangosteen is the size of a small orange or apple. The dark purple outer skin breaks open to reveal pure white segments shaped like orange segments – but with a sweet-sour flavour which has been compared to a combination of strawberries and grapes. Queen Victoria, so the story goes, offered a considerable prize to anybody able to bring a mangosteen back intact from the east for her to try. The main season is from June to September.

Durian *(Durio zibethinus)*
The region's most infamous fruit, the durian is a large oval fruit about 20 to 25cm long, although it may often grow much larger. The durian is renowned for its phenomenal smell, a stink so powerful that first-timers are often forced to hold their noses while they taste. In fact durians emanate a stench so redolent of open sewers that in season you'll see signs in hotels all over Malaysia warning that durians are expressly forbidden entry. It's definitely an acquired taste – the nearest approximation is onion-flavoured ice cream.

When the hardy, spiny shell is cracked open, pale white-green segments are revealed with a taste as distinctive as their smell. Durians are so highly esteemed that great care is taken over their selection and you'll see gourmets feeling them carefully, sniffing them reverently and finally demanding a preliminary taste before purchasing.

Durians are also expensive and, unlike other fruits which are generally yin (cooling), durians are yang (heating) – so much so that the durian is said to be a powerful aphrodisiac. It's no wonder that durians are reputed to be the only fruit which a tiger craves!

There are two seasons: from June to August and November to February.

Durian is ripe and ready to eat when it splits around the seam.

Jackfruit *(nangka; Artocarpus hetero-phyllus)*
This enormous watermelon-sized fruit hangs from trees and, when opened, breaks up into a large number of bright orange-yellow segments with a slightly rubbery texture. The nangka is covered by a green pimply skin, but it's too big and too messy

to clean to make buying a whole one worthwhile. From street fruit stalls you can often buy several nangka segments skewered on a stick. Nangka is available year-round, but is most prolific from June to December.

Papaya *(Carica papaya)*
The papaya, or pawpaw, originated in Central America but is now quite common throughout South-East Asia and is very popular at breakfast time: a slice of papaya served with a dash of lemon juice is the perfect way to start the day. The papaya is about 30cm or so in length and the bright orange flesh is somewhat similar in texture and appearance to pumpkin but related in taste to a melon. The numerous black seeds in the centre of a papaya are said to have a contraceptive effect if eaten by women. The fruit is available year-round.

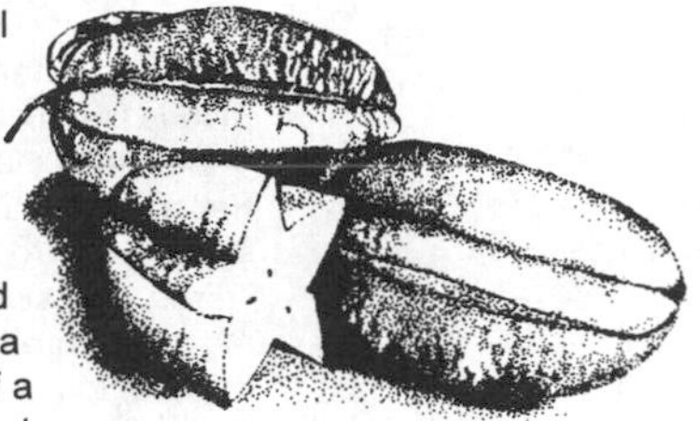

Starfruit is often eaten half-ripe and sprinkled with salt.

Starfruit *(carambola, belembing; Averrhoa carambola)*
The starfruit takes its name from its cross-sectional star shape. A translucent green-yellow in colour, starfruit has a crisp, cool, watery taste. It is available year-round.

Custard Apple *(Annona muricata)*
Sometimes known as soursop or white mango, the custard apple has a warty green outer covering and is ripe and ready to eat when it begins to look slightly off – the fresh green skin begins to look blackish and the feel becomes slightly squishy. Inside, the creamy white flesh has a deliciously thirst-quenching flavour with a hint of lemon. This is another fruit you can often find at fruit stalls.

Pomelo *(Citrus grandis)*
The pomelo looks like a huge orange or grapefruit, although the skin is generally more green than yellow. The flesh often has a purplish tinge, and the flavour is similar to a grapefruit, although the texture is tougher and drier. A single fruit can weigh as much as 1.5kg.

Mango *(Mangifera indica)*
There are many types of mango found in Malaysia; some are specifically for cooking while others are for eating. Ask before you buy.

Other Fruit
Coconuts, lychees, *jambus* (guavas), *dukus*, *chikus*, *jeruks*, and even strawberries up in the Cameron Highlands, are among the other fruits available. There are also temperate climate fruits imported from Australia, New Zealand and further afield.

Malaysia is a major producer of bananas (*pisang; Musa*) and more than 40 varieties are grown here. Some, such as the *pisang embun* and *pisang mas*, are eaten raw, while others, such as the *pisang abu* (or plantain) and *pisang awak*, must be cooked.

Drinks

NONALCOHOLIC DRINKS

Life can be thirsty in the tropics so you'll be relieved to hear that drinks are excellent, economical and readily available. For a start, water can be drunk straight from the taps in Singapore and most larger Malaysian cities (which is a far cry from many other Asian countries, where drinking water without elaborate sterilising preparations is foolhardy).

Secondly there is a wide variety of soft drinks, from Coca-Cola, Pepsi, 7-Up and Fanta to a variety of more unusual flavours like sarsaparilla (for root beer fans). Soft drinks generally cost around RM1.

You can also find those fruit-juice-in-a-box drinks all over the region in both normal fruit flavours and also oddities like chrysanthemum tea.

Sipping a coffee or tea in a Chinese coffee shop or restaurant is a time-honoured pursuit at any time of day or night. If you want your tea, which the Chinese and Malays make very well, without the added thickening of condensed milk, then ask for *teh-o*. Shout it out – it's one of those words which cannot be said quietly. If you don't want sugar either, you have to ask for *teh kosong*, but you're unlikely not to get it – they simply cannot believe anyone would drink their tea that way!

Fruit juices are very popular and very good. With the aid of a blender and crushed ice, delicious concoctions like watermelon juice can be whipped up in seconds. Old-fashioned sugar cane crushers, which look like grandma's old washing mangle, are still used.

The milky white drink in clear plastic bins at street drink stalls is soybean milk, which is also sold in a yoghurty form. Soya bean milk is also available in soft drink bottles. Medicinal teas are very popular with the health-minded Chinese.

ALCOHOLIC DRINKS

Beer drinkers will probably find Anchor, Tiger or Carlsberg beer to their taste, although the minimum price for a large bottle of beer in Malaysia is at least RM8, and its hard to find in some states. Irish travellers may be surprised to find that Guinness has a considerable following in Malaysia – in part because the Chinese believe that it has a strong medicinal value. ABC Stout is a cheaper local equivalent of the dark black brew. Singapore is known for its cocktail, the 'Singapore Sling' (see the boxed text opposite).

Beware of the only really cheap alcohol in Malaysia, the dreaded *samsu*. Sold in small bottles of around 150ml and costing only RM2, this firewater has an alcohol content from 20% to 70%. Some claim tonic properties, curing everything from rheumatism to indigestion, but make no mistake: this is cheap, deadly booze.

Or at least it used to be deadly, especially in the Indian plantation areas where contaminated, home-distilled samsu regularly killed half a village. Though illegal distilling still goes on, many brands of samsu are legally manufactured under brand names

The Singapore Sling

A visit to Singapore is considered by many as incomplete without sampling Singapore's famous cocktail the 'Singapore Sling'. This colourful and refreshing drink was created at Raffles Hotel in 1915 by a Hainanese-Chinese bartender Ngiam Tong Boon.

Originally, the Singapore Sling was meant to be a woman's drink, hence the attractive pink colour. Today it is very definitely a drink enjoyed by all, without which any visit to Singapore is incomplete. Raffles Hotel makes a killing by selling rather overpriced and commercially prepared versions of the cocktail in the Bar & Billiard Room. However, if you can't make it to the Raffles Hotel to enjoy this national cocktail, you can make your own.

Ingredients

½ measure gin
¼ cherry brandy
¼ mixed fruit juices (orange, lime or lemon, pineapple)
a few drops of Cointreau & Benedictine
a dash of Angostura Bitters
top with a cherry and a slice of pineapple

Method

Mix all the ingredients in the proportions listed above, pour into a long glass, find a comfy cane chair on a sunny verandah, grab a Somerset Maugham novel and sip away and make believe that you're in the tropics under a swishing ceiling fan back in the heydays of Singapore's colonial past.

such as Three Snakes, Horse Brand, Tiger and other descriptive labels. Many are also named after Indian warriors, for samsu is typically a product of the South Indian brewing tradition, where villages produce a variety of 'toddy' from fermented coconut and stronger rice-wine brews.

Samsu drinking is a problem not just among the poor, rural Indian community but also in the cities and among Malays and foreign workers. Though only licensed outlets are allowed to sell it, most of it is sold under the counter through general shops and private houses.

Getting There & Away

AIR

Kuala Lumpur (KL) is the major gateway to Malaysia, handling almost all international flights except for a few regional flights from Asia, which come via Penang, Kota Kinabalu and a few other cities. Many airlines service Malaysia, but the country's international carrier, Malaysia Airlines, is the major carrier.

KL and Penang (and Singapore) are good places to buy tickets for onward travel, though prices fluctuate and good deals available one year may not be available the next. In the past, many shady fly-by-night travel agents operated here. Though they aren't such a problem now, it pays to be wary and deal with the more established agents.

The air fares quoted here give an indication of deals available at the time of research, but air fares can vary substantially from season to season, even month to month. They reflect the cheapest fares on offer, which may rise, but keep an eye out for special promotional offers.

Warning

The information in this chapter is particularly vulnerable to change: international travel prices are volatile, routes are introduced and cancelled, schedules change, special deals come and go, and regulations and visa requirements are amended. Governments and airlines seem to take a perverse pleasure in making price structures and rules as complicated as possible. You should check directly with the airline or a travel agent to make sure you understand how a fare (and ticket you may buy) works. In addition, the travel industry is highly competitive and there are many lurks and perks.

The upshot of this is that you should get opinions, quotes and advice from as many airlines and travel agents as possible before you part with your hard-earned cash. The details given in this chapter should be regarded as pointers and are not a substitute for your own careful, up-to-date research.

The USA

It's possible to find fares from the US west coast to Malaysia for around US$830 return, with Malaysia Airlines being one of the cheapest. Both Virgin and Singapore Airlines have route-sharing deals with Malaysia Airlines and offer cheap fares. It is only marginally more expensive to fly to KL than to Singapore. From New York, fares start at US$1050. Some cheap fares may include a stopover in Hong Kong. There are also budget and Super Apex fares available from the west coast. Similar deals from the east coast can be found in the Sunday papers there.

The *New York Times*, the *Los Angeles Times*, the *Chicago Tribune* and the *San Francisco Examiner* all produce weekly travel sections in which you'll find many travel agents' ads. Council Travel and STA Travel have offices in major cities nationwide.

Australia

Malaysia Airlines is the main carrier between Australia and Kuala Lumpur. Qantas and Ansett also fly to KL. Malaysia Airlines used to offer good deals to KL but prices have risen. Fares are usually lower from Australia to Singapore as there is more competition on this route.

Discounted fares from Melbourne/Sydney to Kuala Lumpur cost around A$899 return in the low season, rising to A$1100 in the high season (December to February). Flying from Brisbane is about A$100 cheaper, from Perth A$200 cheaper.

STA Travel and Flight Centres International are major dealers in cheap air fares. Also check the travel agents' ads in the travel sections of newspapers and ring around to find the best deal.

New Zealand

Malaysia Airlines and Qantas fly between Auckland and Kuala Lumpur. Discounted economy fares start at around NZ$1735 for return tickets, but flights to Singapore are considerably cheaper. STA Travel and Flight Centre are large air ticket discounters with offices around the country.

The UK

London has the best deals for flights to Malaysia and Singapore. You can take your pick of a wide range of carriers, but the cheapest (book as far ahead as possible) are Aeroflot, Pakistan International Airlines and Air Lanka. Low season discount tickets start from UK£400.

Other airlines such as Lufthansa, Virgin and Malaysia Airlines have return prices from around UK£550, but there are seasonal fluctuations of around UK£100. One-way flights start at around UK£235. Bear in mind that all flights out of the UK now carry a UK£10 departure tax and this is added to the cost of your ticket.

For information on travel agents and special deals, check the Sunday papers and weekly listings magazines such as *Time Out*. London's 'bucket' shops can offer some great deals, but some of these places are fly-by-night operations. Most British agents are registered with the Association of British Travel Agents (ABTA), which guarantees tickets booked with member agents.

Popular and reliable British agents include Campus Travel (☎ 0171-730 3402), with 41 branches nationwide; STA Travel (☎ 0171-361 6123); Trailfinders (☎ 0171-938 3366), with branches in London, Birmingham, Bristol, Glasgow and Manchester; and Crusader Travel (☎ 0181-744 0474).

Continental Europe

Prices for return tickets from Belgium start at around FB27,400 (low season) to FB29,600 (high season). In France, return tickets from Paris to KL cost from FF3600/4500. Also, check with Nouvelles Frontières to see if it is offering its spring/autumn specials on Gulf Air.

Return flights from Frankfurt to KL start at around DM1460/1665 low/high season. Prices for return tickets from Switzerland start at around FS1250/FS1450. Return flights from Amsterdam to KL start at around G1768/2380 low/high season.

Asia

Hong Kong Hong Kong is no longer the discount centre it once was. The cheapest one-way flights to Malaysia cost around US$200. It may work out to be cheaper to fly to Singapore rather than KL. In addition to KL, it is also possible to fly from Hong Kong to Penang, Langkawi and Kota Kinabalu.

Tsim Sha Tsui is Hong Kong's budget travel agency centre. Most of the operators nowadays are reliable. One of the best around is Phoenix Services (☎ 2722 7378) at 6F, Milton Mansion, 96 Nathan Rd, Tsim Sha Tsui.

Japan Return flights from Japan to Singapore and Kuala Lumpur or Penang cost between ¥50,000 and ¥70,000. One-way tickets are expensive, averaging around ¥50,000. The best agency to deal with is STA Travel, which has branches in Tokyo (☎ 03-5485 8380) and in Osaka (☎ 06-262 7066). A'Cross Travel is another reliable agency that is used to dealing with foreigners; it has branches in Tokyo (☎ 03-3340 6741), Osaka (☎ 06-345 0150) and Kyoto (☎ 075-255 3559).

For information on the latest discount prices Tokyo residents should pick up a copy of *Tokyo Journal*, while residents of the Kansai region should get hold of *Kansai Time Out*. The four English-language newspapers also run advertisements from the major travel agents.

Thailand The place to buy tickets to Malaysia and Singapore in Bangkok is Khao San Rd. The agents here deal in discounted tickets; rip-offs do occur from time to time, so take care. A reliable agent on Khao San Rd is GM Tour & Travel (☎ 282 3979) at 273 Khao San Rd. Flights from Bangkok to KL cost from B4800/6500 one way/return

Air Travel Glossary

Baggage Allowance This will be written on your ticket and usually includes one 20kg item to go in the hold, plus one item of hand luggage.

Bucket Shops These are unbonded travel agencies specialising in discounted airline tickets.

Bumped Just because you have a confirmed seat doesn't mean you're going to get on the plane (see Overbooking).

Cancellation Penalties If you have to cancel or change a discounted ticket, there are often heavy penalties involved; insurance can sometimes be taken out against these penalties. Some airlines impose penalties on regular tickets as well, particularly against 'no-show' passengers.

Check-In Airlines ask you to check in a certain time ahead of the flight departure (usually one to two hours on international flights). If you fail to check in on time and the flight is overbooked, the airline can cancel your booking and give your seat to somebody else.

Confirmation Having a ticket written out with the flight and date you want doesn't mean you have a seat until the agent has checked with the airline that your status is 'OK' or confirmed. Meanwhile you could just be 'on request'.

Courier Fares Businesses often need to send urgent documents or freight securely and quickly. Courier companies hire people to accompany the package through customs and, in return, offer a discount ticket which is sometimes a phenomenal bargain. In effect, what the companies do is ship their freight as your luggage on regular commercial flights. This is a legitimate operation, but there are two shortcomings – the short turnaround time of the ticket (usually not longer than a month) and the limitation on your luggage allowance. You may have to surrender all your allowance and take only carry-on luggage.

Full Fares Airlines traditionally offer 1st class (coded F), business class (coded J) and economy class (coded Y) tickets. These days there are so many promotional and discounted fares available that few passengers pay full economy fare.

ITX An ITX, or 'independent inclusive tour excursion', is often available on tickets to popular holiday destinations. Officially it's a package deal combined with hotel accommodation, but many agents will sell you one of these for the flight only and give you phoney hotel vouchers in the unlikely event that you're challenged at the airport.

Lost Tickets If you lose your airline ticket an airline will usually treat it like a travellers cheque and, after inquiries, issue you with another one. Legally, however, an airline is entitled to treat it like cash and if you lose it then it's gone forever. Take good care of your tickets.

MCO An MCO, or 'miscellaneous charge order', is a voucher that looks like an airline ticket but carries no destination or date. It can be exchanged through any International Association of Travel Agents (IATA) airline for a ticket on a specific flight. It's a useful alternative to an onward ticket in those countries that demand one, and is more flexible than an ordinary ticket if you're unsure of your route.

No-Shows No-shows are passengers who fail to show up for their flight. Full-fare passengers who fail to turn up are sometimes entitled to travel on a later flight. The rest are penalised (see Cancellation Penalties).

and flights from Bangkok to Penang cost from B3600/6800.

Indonesia There are several interesting variations to travel from Indonesia to Malaysia.

The short hop from Medan in Sumatra to Penang costs around US$74; from Penang it's RM185. There are also weekly flights between Kuching in Sarawak and Pontianak in Kalimantan, the Indonesian part of the island of Borneo, for RM276. Similarly, at the eastern end of Borneo there is a weekly connection between Tawau in Sabah and Tarakan in Kalimantan.

On Request This is an unconfirmed booking for a flight.
Onward Tickets An entry requirement for many countries is that you have a ticket out of the country. If you're unsure of your next move, the easiest solution is to buy the cheapest onward ticket to a neighbouring country or a ticket from a reliable airline which can later be refunded if you do not use it.
Open Jaw Tickets These are return tickets where you fly out to one place but return from another. If available, this can save you backtracking to your arrival point.
Overbooking Airlines hate to fly empty seats and since every flight has some passengers who fail to show up, airlines often book more passengers than they have seats. Usually excess passengers make up for the no-shows, but occasionally somebody gets bumped. Guess who it is most likely to be? The passengers who check in late.
Point-to-Point Tickets These are discount tickets that can be bought on some routes in return for passengers waiving their rights to a stopover.
Promotional Fares These are officially discounted fares, available from travel agencies or direct from the airline.
Reconfirmation At least 72 hours prior to departure time of an onward or return flight, you must contact the airline and 'reconfirm' that you intend to be on the flight. If you don't do this the airline can delete your name from the passenger list and you could lose your seat.
Restrictions Discounted tickets often have various restrictions on them – such as needing to be paid for in advance and incurring a penalty to be altered. There are other restrictions on the minimum and maximum period you must be away, these may be a minimum of 14 days or a maximum of one year.
Round-the-World Tickets RTW tickets give you a limited period (usually a year) in which to circumnavigate the globe. You can go anywhere the carrying airlines go, as long as you don't backtrack. The number of stopovers or total number of separate flights is decided before you set off and they usually cost a bit more than a basic return flight.
Stand-by This is a discounted ticket where you only fly if there is a seat free at the last moment. Stand-by fares are usually available only on domestic routes.
Travel Agencies Travel agencies vary widely and you should choose one that suits your needs. Some simply handle tours, while full-services agencies handle everything from tours and tickets to car rental and hotel bookings. If all you want is a ticket at the lowest possible price, then go to an agency specialising in discounted tickets.
Transferred Tickets Airline tickets cannot be transferred from one person to another. Travellers sometimes try to sell the return half of their ticket, but officials can ask you to prove that you are the person named on the ticket. This is less likely to happen on domestic flights, but on an international flight tickets are compared with passports.
Travel Periods Ticket prices vary with the time of year. There is a low (off-peak) season and a high (peak) season, and often a low-shoulder season and a high-shoulder season as well. Usually the fare depends on your outward flight – if you depart in the high season and return in the low season, you pay the high-season fare.

To get to Java, the cheapest connections are from Singapore for as little as US$70. However it's worth remembering that Malaysia Airlines also has competitively priced flights from Johor Bahru to Jakarta. (Note that the prices mentioned above are for one-way tickets.)

India & Other Places in Asia Although Indonesia and Thailand are the two usual places to travel to or from, there are plenty of other possibilities, including India, Sri Lanka, Myanmar (Burma) and the Philippines. Check prices in Singapore and Penang – the two airline ticket centres.

Departure Tax
Malaysia levies airport taxes on all flights. The fee is RM40 on international departures and RM20 for flights to Singapore and Brunei. If you buy your tickets in Malaysia, the departure tax is included in the price.

LAND

Thailand

You can cross the border by land at Padang Besar (road or rail), Bukit Kayu Hitam (road) or Keroh-Betong (road) in the west, or at Rantau Panjang-Sungai Golok or Pengkalan Kubor in the east. For information on Thai visas, refer to the Visas & Documents section in the Malaysia – Facts for the Visitor chapter.

West Coast Road Although there are border points at Padang Besar and Keroh, most travellers cross by road at Bukit Kayu Hitam on the Lebuh Raya (North-South Highway) for Hat Yai. The easiest way to cross here is to take a bus from Georgetown (see the Penang chapter) to Hat Yai for around RM20. Buses also run from Alor Setar to the large border post complex at Bukit Kayu Hitam, from where you walk a few hundred metres to the Thai checkpoint. On the other side buses and taxis run to Sadao and Hat Yai. Buses and trains run from Hat Yai to Phuket, Bangkok and other places.

The other alternative is to cross at Padang Besar, where it is an easy walk across. The only reason to go this way by road is if you're heading to/from Langkawi. Buses run from Kuala Perlis to Padang Besar via Kangar. The train from Alor Setar all the way to Hat Yai is the easiest way to cross this border.

East Coast Road The Thai border is at Rantau Panjang (Sungai Golok on the Thai side), 1½ hours by bus from Kota Bharu. From Rantau Panjang walk across the border, and it's about 1km to the station, from where trains go to Hat Yai, Surathani and Bangkok. Buses also take this route. See Kota Bharu in the Kelantan chapter for more details.

An alternative route into Thailand is via Pengkalan Kubor on the coast. It's more time-consuming and very few travellers go this way. See Around Kota Bharu for more details.

Train The rail route into Thailand is on the Butterworth-Alor Setar-Hat Yai route, which

International Express

Fares (2nd class):

	Singapore	Kuala Lumpur	Butterworth
Hat Yai	S$64.20	RM40.30	RM14.90
Bangkok	S$91.70	RM70.30	RM44.90

Schedule:

Train No 48
(International Express from Butterworth – runs daily)

Butterworth	12:52
Alor Setar	16:13
Hat Yai	18:10*
Bangkok	9:50*

Train No 47
(International Express from Bangkok – runs daily)

Bangkok	15:15*
Hat Yai	7:02*
Alor Setar	11:01
Butterworth	14:35

* Thai time (one hour behind Malaysian time).

In addition, there is an express surcharge on the International Express of RM13.60 for air-con and RM8.10 for non-air-con, plus RM7.20 for the Thai leg of the journey. Sleeping berths in 2nd class cost an additional RM28.50 for an upper berth and RM22.30 for a lower berth.

crosses into Thailand at Padang Besar. You can take the *International Express* from Butterworth all the way to Bangkok with connections from Singapore and Kuala Lumpur. From Hat Yai there are frequent train and bus connections to other parts of Thailand (see the International Express table for train fares and schedules). One train a day also goes from Alor Setar to Hat Yai (see Alor Setar in the Kedah & Perlis chapter for details).

A variation on the *International Express* is the *Eastern & Oriental Express*, which runs once a week and caters to the well-heeled. The train is done out in antique opulence and is South-East Asia's answer to the *Orient Express*. It takes 42 hours to do the 1943km journey from Singapore to Bangkok. Don your linen suit, sip a gin and tonic and dig deep for the fare – around US$1200 (see the Singapore Getting There & Away chapter).

Singapore

The Causeway linking Johor Bahru with Singapore handles most traffic between the countries. Trains and buses run from all over Malaysia straight through to Singapore, or you can take a bus to Johor Bahru and get a taxi or one of the frequent buses from JB to Singapore.

The JB buses drop you at the border posts and don't wait long, but you simply keep your ticket and get on the next bus that comes along. Some travellers who have taken the through express buses from elsewhere in Malaysia have reported that they have been left stranded at the border after delays at immigration. These buses should (and usually do) wait – complain to the bus company if this happens.

There is also a new causeway linking Tuas, in western Singapore, with Geyland Patah. This is known as the Second Link, but it's of little use to travellers without their own transport. If you do have a car, tolls on the Second Link are much higher than the charge on the main Causeway.

See the Singapore Getting There & Away chapter and the Johor Bahru section of the Johor chapter for more details.

Indonesia

It is easy to cross the land border between Malaysia and Indonesia, which is between Pontianak in Kalimantan and Kuching in Sarawak. A daily express bus (10 hours) runs between Pontianak and Kuching. The bus crosses at the Tebedu/Entikong border, a visa-free entry point into Indonesia. See the Kuching Getting There & Away section for details.

SEA

Thailand

Regular daily boats run between Langkawi and Satun in Thailand. There are customs and immigration posts here, so you can cross quite legally, although it's an unusual and rarely used entry/exit point. Make sure you get your passport stamped on entry.

In the main tourist season (around Christmas) yachts also operate irregularly between Langkawi and Phuket in Thailand, taking in Thai islands on the way. The trip usually takes five days and costs around US$70 per person, per day. The best way to find a boat is to ask around the travellers' bars and restaurants in either Langkawi or Phuket. Otherwise, check with the owners of the Kapas Island Resort in Terengganu (☎ 011-98 1686); they do this run once during the season.

Singapore

There are a number of possible crossings across the Straits of Johor, but most people cross on the main Causeway, either by train or by road.

The main ferry crossing is between Changi Village (Singapore) and Tanjung Belungkor (Malaysia), and exists mainly for Singaporeans holidaying in Desaru on the Malaysian coast. High-speed catamarans run between the Tanah Marah ferry terminal in Singapore and the island of Tioman in Pahang state, again, primarily for Singaporean holiday makers. Small boats also ply between Pengerang in Johor and Changi Village in Singapore.

The Singapore Getting There & Away chapter has full details.

Indonesia

The three main ferry routes between Malaysia and Indonesia are Penang-Medan and Melaka-Dumai connecting Peninsular Malaysia with Sumatra, and Tawau-Tarakan linking Sabah with Kalimantan in Borneo.

The popular crossing between Penang and Medan is handled by two companies that between them have services most days of the week. The journey takes 4½ hours and costs RM90/110 in 2nd/1st class. The boats actually land in Belawan in Sumatra, and the journey to Medan is completed by bus (included in the price). See the Penang chapter for details.

Twice daily high-speed ferries operate between Melaka and Dumai (2½ hours, RM80) in Sumatra. Dumai is now a visa-free entry port into Indonesia for citizens of most countries. This is becoming a more popular connection, but there is nothing in Dumai – take a bus out to other parts of Sumatra. See the Melaka chapter for details.

Boats also operate most days from Tawau in Sabah to Nunukan in Kalimantan and then on to Tarakan in Kalimantan (see under Tawau in the Sabah chapter for details). This is not a recognised border crossing for visa-free entry so an Indonesian visa must be obtained in advance if entering or exiting this way.

Another possibility is to take a boat from the Bebas Cukai ferry terminal in Johor Bahru. Boats go direct to Batu Ampar and Tanjung Pinang, both in Sumatra. See Johor Bahru in the Johor chapter for details on all these boats. You can also take a ferry from Kukup, in Johor, to Tanjung Balai in Sumatra. See the Kukup section in the Johor chapter for details.

Philippines

Passenger ferries now operate between Sandakan and Zamboanga in the Philippines. The trip takes 18 hours and costs from RM60.

The MV *Sampaguita* leaves Sandakan on Saturday at 1 pm, arriving in Zamboanga at 8 am the following day. It leaves the Philippines for Sandakan on Thursday at 1 pm, arriving on Friday at 8 am.

The *Lady Mary Joy* departs Sandakan on Thursday at 3 pm, arriving Friday at 9 am; the return trip is on Tuesday at 3 pm, arriving Zamboanga on Wednesday at 9 am.

Getting Around

AIR

Malaysia Airlines is the country's main domestic operator. The Malaysian Air Fares chart below details some of the main regional routes and the standard one-way fares in Malaysian ringgit. Malaysia Airlines has many other regional routes in Sarawak and Sabah. It operates Airbuses, Boeing 737s and Fokker F50s on its domestic routes, plus 12-seater Twin Otters on most of the more remote Sarawak and Sabah routes.

In East Malaysia, where many communities rely on air transport as the only quick way in or out, many local flights operate. These flights are very much dependent on the vagaries of the weather. In the wet season, places like Bario in Sarawak can be isolated for days at a time, so don't venture into this area if you have a very tight schedule. During school holidays these flights are completely booked. At other times it's easier to get a seat at a few days' notice, but always book as far in advance as possible.

Malaysia Airlines is very accommodating about changes in travel plans and will alter any ticket on the spot in any of its offices. If the value of the new ticket is less than the old one, it will issue vouchers for the difference.

The other domestic carrier is Pelangi Air. It offers far fewer flights but covers a few destinations that Malaysia Airlines doesn't, notably Pulau Tioman and some routes to Ipoh and Langkawi. Pelangi reservations should be made through Malaysia Airlines.

Malaysia Airlines Discounts & Special Flights

A variety of worthwhile discounts are available, especially for groups and for travel between Peninsular Malaysia and East Malaysia. Student discounts are only available for students enrolled in Malaysian institutions.

The following discounts apply for families or groups (a group must comprise at

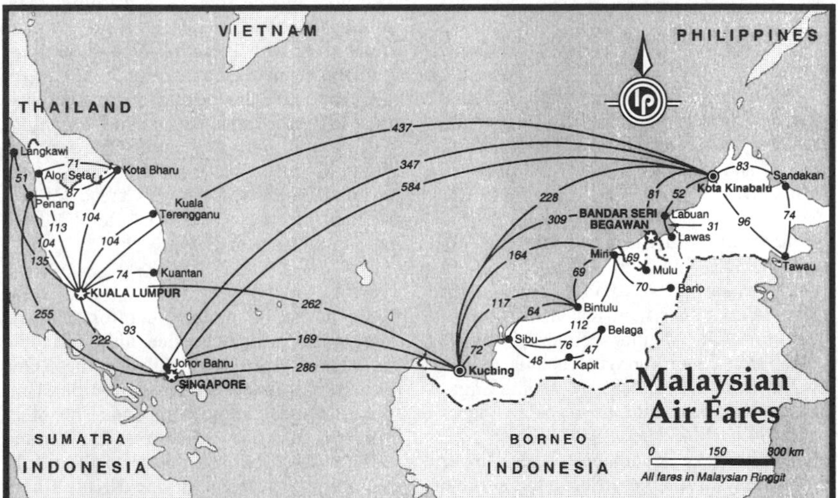

Malaysian Air Fares

least three people) on regular Malaysia Airlines return economy air fares. Maximum stay is 30 days, and tickets must be booked and paid for at least seven days in advance.

- 50% between Peninsular Malaysia and East Malaysia, and between Sabah and Sarawak
- 25% within Peninsular Malaysia, Sabah or Sarawak
- 25% anywhere in Malaysia for families (a couple with or without children), provided one spouse pays full fare. Children receive a discount on the applicable child's fare.

Other discounts include travel for groups of 10 or more between Malaysia and Singapore or Brunei, and for escorted disabled passengers (50% discount and 25% for the escort).

Malaysia Airlines also has a number of special night flights and advance purchase fares (restrictions apply). Seven-day advance purchase one-way tickets/Apex 30-day return tickets are available for the following flights from Johor Bahru or Kuala Lumpur:

Destination	Fare (RM)
JB to Kuching	144/305
JB to Kota Kinabalu	295/624
JB to Penang	150/318
KL to Kuching	227/425
KL to Kota Kinabalu	372/689
KL to Miri	359/679
KL to Labuan	372/656

There are also a few economy night flights between Kuala Lumpur and Kota Kinabalu (RM306), Kuching (RM187), Alor Setar (RM74) and Penang (RM73), and between JB and KK (RM260).

Flying from Malaysia vs Singapore

You can save quite a few ringgit if you are flying to Sarawak or Sabah by flying from Johor Bahru rather than Kuala Lumpur or Singapore. The regular economy fare is RM169 from Johor Bahru to Kuching against RM262 from KL and S$199 from Singapore. To Kota Kinabalu, the respective fares are RM347, RM437 and S$403. To persuade travellers to take advantage of these lower fares, Malaysia Airlines offers a bus service directly from its office at the Novotel Orchid Hotel in Singapore to the Johor Bahru airport for S$10.

It is worth bearing in mind that fares on flights between Singapore and Malaysia cost almost the same in ringgit/dollar terms whether bought in Malaysia or Singapore making Singapore tickets much more expensive when the exchange rate is taken into account.

BUS

Malaysia has an excellent bus system. There are public buses on local runs and a variety of privately operated buses on the longer trips, as well as the big fleet of Ekspres Nasional express buses. In larger towns there may be a number of bus stops – a main station or two, plus some of the private companies may operate directly from their own offices.

Buses are fast, economical and comfortable and seats can be reserved. There are so many buses on major runs that you can often turn up and get a seat on the next bus. On main routes most buses are air-conditioned and cost only a few ringgit more than the trip on regular buses. They make daytime travel a sweat-free activity, but you should take note of one traveller's warning: 'Malaysian air-conditioned buses are really meat lockers on wheels with just two settings: cold and suspended animation'.

Getting off the beaten track is a little more difficult. Small towns and *kampungs* (villages) all over the country are serviced by public buses, but these are usually non-air-con rattlers and services are a lot less frequent. In these cases it is often better to get a taxi rather than wait.

TRAIN

Malaysia has a modern, comfortable and economical railway service, although there are basically only two railway lines. One runs from Singapore to Kuala Lumpur, Butterworth and on into Thailand. The other branches off from this line at Gemas and runs through Kuala Lipis up to the north-east corner of the country near Kota Bharu (often referred to as the 'Jungle Train').

Other lines are just minor branches off these two routes and are not much used. Malaysia's first railway line was a 13km route from Taiping to Port Weld which was laid in 1884, but it is no longer in use. By 1903 you could travel all the way from Johor Bahru to near Butterworth, and the extension of the line to the Thai border in 1918 and across the Causeway to Singapore in 1923 meant you could travel by train from Singapore right into Thailand. In 1931 the east-coast line was completed, effectively bringing the railway system to its present state.

The privatised national railway company, Keretapi Tanah Melayu (KTM), offers a Tourist Railpass for 30 days (US$120, children US$60) or 10 days (US$55, children US$28). This pass entitles the holder to unlimited travel on any class of train but does not include sleeping berth charges. Railpasses are available only to foreigners and can be purchased at a number of main railway stations. You have to do a lot of train travel to make them worthwhile.

Another deal is the ISSA Explorer pass which is available to holders of ISSA student cards (to qualify, you must be under 30 years of age). This pass entitles the holder to unlimited 2nd class travel on all KTM trains in Malaysia, Singapore and Thailand. Seven-day passes cost US$36, 14-day passes cost US$48 and 21-day passes cost US$60. These are available from MSL Travel in Kuala Lumpur (☎ 03-442 4722) and Penang (☎ 04-227 2655).

Malaysia basically has three types of rail services – express, limited express and local trains. Express trains are air-conditioned and generally 1st and 2nd class only, and on night trains there's a choice of sleepers or seats. Limited express trains may have 2nd and 3rd class only but some have 1st, 2nd and 3rd class with overnight sleepers. Local trains are usually 3rd class only, but some have 2nd class (see the train fares and timetable listing in this chapter).

The express trains stop only at main stations. Limited express trains stop at a few more stations but still provide a quick service; however, these are being gradually phased out. These two options are much faster than the local trains, and in most respects are definitely the ones to take. The local services that operate, mostly on the Tumpat-Singapore line, are colourful experiences for short journeys. They stop everywhere, including out in the middle of the jungle, to let passengers and their goods on and off, but they take more than twice as long as the express trains and run to erratic schedules.

For more information on KTM schedules and fares call ☎ 03-273 8000 or ☎ 03-275 7269, or access KTM's Internet site at www.ktmb.com.my or email them at passenger@ktmb.com.my. Train schedules are reviewed every six months so check before you make detailed plans.

In Sabah there's also a small narrow-gauge railway line which can take you through the Sungai Pegas gorge from Tenom to Beaufort. The trip is a great experience and is well worth doing.

TAXI

Long-Distance Taxis

Long-distance taxis make Malaysian travel, already easy and convenient even by the best Asian standards, a real breeze. A long-distance taxi is usually a diesel Mercedes, Peugeot or, more recently, Japanese car. In almost every town there will be a 'teksi' stand where the cars are lined up and ready to go to their various destinations.

The taxis are ideal for groups of four, and are also available on a share basis. As soon as a full complement of four passengers turns up, off you go. Between major towns you have a reasonable chance of finding other passengers to share without having to wait too long, but otherwise you will have to charter a whole taxi, which is four times the single fare rate (quoted throughout this book). As Malaysia becomes increasingly wealthy, and people can afford to hire a whole taxi, the share system is becoming less reliable. Early in the morning is the best time to find other people to share a taxi, or you can inquire at the taxi stand the day before to see when is the best time.

Train Fares from Butterworth (RM)

Class	Express 1st	Express 2nd	Express 3rd	Local 1st	Local 2nd	Local 3rd
Padang Besar	34	20	11	25.50	11.10	6.30
Taiping	23	15	8	14.40	6.30	3.60
Ipoh	36	21	11	27.80	12.10	6.90
Tapah Road	44	24	13	36.00	15.60	8.90
Kuala Lumpur	67	34	19	58.50	25.40	14.40
Tampin	85	42	23	76.50	33.20	18.90
Johor Bahru	122	58	33	114.00	49.40	28.10
Singapore	127	60	34	118.50	51.40	29.90

Train Fares from Kuala Lumpur (RM)

Class	Express 1st	Express 2nd	Express 3rd	Local 1st	Local 2nd	Local 3rd
Padang Besar	–	–	–	81.00	35.10	20.00
Butterworth	67	34	19	58.50	25.40	14.40
Taiping	53	28	16	45.00	19.50	11.10
Ipoh	40	22	12	31.50	13.70	7.80
Tapah Road	32	19	10	23.30	10.10	5.80
Tampin	27	17	9	18.80	8.20	4.70
Johor Bahru	64	33	18	55.50	24.10	13.70
Singapore	68	34	19	60.00	26.00	14.80
Jerantut	48	35	15	–	–	–
Kuala Lipis	56	36.50	18	–	–	–
Wakaf Baharu	78	45.50	28	–	–	–
Tumpat	80	46.50	29	–	–	–

Train Fares from Singapore (S$)

Class	Express 1st	Express 2nd	Express 3rd	Local 1st	Local 2nd	Local 3rd
Padang Besar	–	–	–	139.50	60.50	34.40
Butterworth	127	60	34	118.50	51.40	29.20
Taiping	112	53	30	103.50	44.90	25.50
Ipoh	100	48	27	91.50	39.70	22.60
Tapah Road	92	45	25	84.00	36.40	20.70
Kuala Lumpur	68	34	19	60.00	26.00	14.80
Tampin	50	27	15	42.00	18.20	10.40
Johor Bahru	13	10	6	4.20	1.90	1.10
Kuala Lipis	76	31	21	–	29.30	16.70
Wakaf Baharu	119	41	32	–	48.10	27.40
Tumpat	121	57	32	–	48.80	27.70

Supplementary berth charges for these services are as follows: RM30 for 1st class lower berth; RM20 for 1st class upper berth; RM14 for 2nd class air-con lower berth; RM11.50 for 2nd class air-con upper berth.

Taxi rates are fixed by the government and are posted at the taxi stands; usually the rate for a whole taxi is listed. Some areas have taxis with and without air-conditioning; the air-conditioned taxis cost a few more ringgit. Taxi fares generally work out at about twice the comparable bus fares. If you want to charter a taxi to an obscure destination or by the hour, you'll probably have to do some negotiating.

Timetables for Main West Coast Services

Train/No	ER/1	XSP/3	EL/7	SM/9
Hat Yai	–	–	1550	–
Alor Setar	–	–	2002	–
Butterworth	0800	1515	–	2200
Taiping	0930	1647	2316	2358
Ipoh	1104	1818	0110	0206
Kuala Lumpur	1429	2150	0512	0634

Train/No	XSP/4	ER/2	EL/8	SM/10
Kuala Lumpur	0735	1425	2052	2205
Ipoh	1058	1755	0044	0215
Taiping	1242	1941	0225	0419
Butterworth	1428	2101	–	0630
Alor Setar	–	–	0545	–
Hat Yai	–	–	0900	–

Train/No	XSP/5	ER/1	SM/11
Kuala Lumpur	0740	1450	2230
Tampin	0929	1643	0034
Gemas	1013	1727	0133
Johor Bahru	1252	2016	0537
Singapore	1345	2105	0642

Train/No	ER/2	ES/62	XSP/6	ES/64	SM/12
Singapore	0815	1120	1425	1805	2230
Johor Bahru	0838	1150	1448	1833	2253
Gemas	1127	–	1732	2215	0232
Tampin	1209	–	1820	–	0345
Kuala Lumpur	1411	–	2030	–	0620

ES & SM trains are limited express services, all others express.

Timetables for Main East-Coast Service

Train/No	91	XST/15		92	XST/14
Tumpat	0600	2010	Singapore	–	2115
Wakaf Baharu	0621	2020	Johor Bahru	–	2138
Kuala Lipis	1429	0045	Gemas	0730	0015
Jerantut	1558	0140	Jerantut	1124	0329
Gemas	1955	0430	Kuala Lipis	1255	0422
Johor Bahru	–	0713	Wakaf Baharu	2018	0857
Singapore	–	0810	Tumpat	2056	0920

XST trains are express services, 91 & 92 are local trains.
For details on train types and services, see the Train section of this chapter. Train schedules may change but departure times can be checked on the KTM Web site (www.ktmb.com.my).

Taxi drivers often drive at frighteningly high speeds. They don't have as many head-on collisions as you might expect, but closing your eyes at times of high stress certainly helps! You also have the option of demanding that the driver slow down, but, this is met with varying degrees of hostility. Just be grateful that the roads aren't quite as hazardous as those in some other Asian countries.

CAR

Rental

Rent-a-car operations are well established in Malaysia. Major rental operators in Malaysia include Avis, Budget, Mayflower, Hertz, National and Thrifty, although there are many others including many local operators only found in one city. Unlimited distance rates

By Bicycle – Peninsular Malaysia & Singapore

Bicycle touring from Singapore, around Malaysia and on to Thailand is an increasingly popular activity.

Equipment A well-maintained bike with good tyres is essential. Road conditions are good enough for touring bikes.

Essential tools include: Allen keys, spoke key, tyre levers and a small Swiss army knife.

Accessories include: helmet, gloves, panniers, front pack with map-holder, rear-view mirror that attaches to the right handlebar, sunglasses, spare tube and patch kit, pump, bungee cord, two large water bottles, insect repellent and sunscreen.

Pack lightly, with everything in waterproof plastic bags. Warm weather clothes, pullover (for high altitudes) and a rain shell are recommended.

Shipping Bikes are carried free in lieu of luggage on most scheduled international flights. Charter carriers have their own rules. You can purchase a box from the airlines or supply your own. When boxes are unavailable, handlers are often more careful with the unboxed bikes. Take the pedals off (tape them to the back rack), secure the pump with tape and turn the handlebars. Place your panniers in the dead space of the shipping box to protect the gears.

Planning The Tourist Board map (scale 1:1,000,000) is adequate, but Nelles' map of *West Malaysia* (scale 1:650,000) is better. Weather and wind will hasten or slow your progress, so a flexible overall plan is best. The equatorial climate has high temperatures, and it's wet all year round. The winds are north-east from November to February and south-west from April to September. March and October are the changeover months when winds are light and variable. Due to the seasonal headwinds, ride north on the west coast from November to February and south on the east coast from April to September. There are no organised bicycle tours to Singapore/Malaysia.

Road Rules *Ride on the left.* Third world rules apply: the right of way belongs to the larger vehicle. Use a rear-view mirror.

Practical Information The main road system is well engineered with good surfaces. The secondary road system is limited. In high-traffic areas, road safety is a problem because of narrow roads with no shoulders (especially within a radius of 50km of KL).

Singapore has many bicycle shops. Throughout Malaysia minor repairs can be handled but major repairs on foreign bikes can be made in KL at Triathlon Sports Centre (☎ 03-982 6633).

A major concern when riding in a tropical climate is dehydration. Drink at least half a litre of water before riding and keep drinking fluids all day. Drink *before* you feel thirsty.

Alternative Transport In general, buses do not take bicycles, although some express buses might if their luggage compartment is empty – good luck! Trains take bikes, but they must be shipped ahead with freight. Hitching in small trucks is always an excellent option, but rides are tougher to get here than in the rest of Asia. Pick-up trucks are best. Keep the panniers on the bike to protect the gears when putting bikes in trucks.

are posted at around RM150 per day or RM900 per week, including insurance and collision damage waiver. This price is for a 1.3 litre Proton Saga, the cheapest and most popular car in Malaysia; the Proton Wira is a step up in standard and a bit more expensive. The Proton is basically a Mitsubishi assembled under licence in Malaysia. Charges for

Routes

Changi Airport to Singapore (25km) There is no way to take your bike on public transport. You must ride, but it's officially illegal on the East Coast Parkway. However, you'll have to take this road to get the East Coast Parkway Service Rd. Turn left onto the East Coast Parkway Service Rd and follow this to the 13km road marker, then turn right onto Fort Rd. Turn left onto Mountbatten Rd, pass Stadium Rd and then turn left onto Nicoll Hwy into the city.

Singapore to Johor Bahru (27km) There are multiple options on city streets through Singapore to the bridge to Johor Bahru. The most direct route is along Bukit Timah Rd to Woodlands Rd to the bridge. It is also possible to take bicycles on the ferries that leave from Changi Village, going to Pengerang for Desaru in Johor state.

West Coast Peninsular Malaysia This route is through rolling hills and flat country, with interesting cities to visit. From Johor Bahru follow the coast west to Highway 1 (four lanes with shoulder) and turn onto a secondary road to Pontian Kecil (61km) on the coast. Follow Highway 5 along the coast to Batu Pahat (73km), then Muar (53km) and Melaka (45km). There are some views of the Straits of Melaka from the road. Port Dickson is another 94km and from there to Banting it's 83km.

After Banting the traffic becomes treacherous on this narrow highway to Kelang (32km), where there is a turn-off to KL (32km). There are some designated bicycle lanes in KL.

From Kuala Lumpur to Butterworth, the best route is via the coast and inland roads to Taiping, and then secondary roads to Butterworth. From Butterworth, take the ferry to Penang (bikes are not allowed on the bridge). There is some good riding on the island along the beaches.

Cross-Peninsula Route This route has very light traffic. From Butterworth (Penang) to Baling (91km) there are multiple routes with few signposts. Ask for Baling or Gerik and note that there are hills between these towns (62km). Gerik has facilities and hotels, and you can also stay at Pulau Banding. Highway 4 is a well-engineered road with good surfaces. There are some long climbs through the interior mountains; facilities are sparse with no hotels. Gerik to Jeli is 124km, and Jeli to the crossroads of Highway 4 and 3 is 97km. Expect rain.

East Coast Peninsular Malaysia This is the most popular route for cycling through the peninsula. Although like all highways, traffic is increasing, there is less traffic on this route than on the west-coast route, and it's flat and follows the coast for long stretches.

Highway 3 from Kota Bharu (168km) south to Kuala Terengganu has light traffic but fast-moving buses and trucks. About 80km before Kuala Terengganu you can cut into the beach (14km) and enjoy a quiet ride into the city. Highway 3 runs along the coast to Kuala Dungun (78km). From Kuala Dungun to Kuantan (131km) there are many beach hotels (most are closed in the off season).

Take the passenger ferry across the river from Kuantan and follow another quiet coastal road south to Pekan (47km). Continue from Pekan to Mersing back on Highway 3 (144km). Follow Highway 3 to Kota Tinggi (92km). The busy highway is wider from here to Johor Bahru (41km).

Peter & Sally Blommer

From *Cycle Singapore/Malaysia* – Blommer

a Ford Laser are around RM200 per day or RM1200 per week.

These are the standard rates from the major car hire companies but you can often get better deals, either through smaller local companies or when the major companies offer special deals. Rates drop substantially for longer rentals and you can get a Proton Saga for as little as RM2000 per month, including unlimited kilometres and insurance, if you shop around by phone. The main advantage of dealing with a large company is that it has offices all over the country, giving better backup if something goes wrong and allowing you to pick up in one city and drop off in another (typically for a RM50 surcharge). Mayflower is one local company with offices all over and some pretty competitive rates.

KL is the best place to look for car hire and Penang is also good (see those sections for more details). In Sabah and Sarawak there is less competition and rates are higher, partly because of the condition of the roads.

A valid overseas licence is needed to rent a car. An International Driving Permit is usually not required by local car hire companies but it is recommended to bring one (see Documents in the Malaysia – Facts for the Visitor chapter). Age limits apply, and most companies require that drivers are at least 23 years old.

Driving

In many Asian countries driving is either a fraught experience (ever seen the rush hour in Bangkok or Jakarta?), full of local dangers (I'd hate to think what would happen if you collided with a cow in India), the roads are terrible, cars are unavailable, or for some reason driving yourself is not really possible. None of these drawbacks apply in Malaysia. The roads are generally of a high standard, there are plenty of new cars available and driving standards are not too hair-raising.

The Lebuh Raya, or North-South Highway, is a new six-lane expressway which runs virtually the whole length of the peninsula from the Thai border in the north to Johor Bahru in the south. There are toll charges for using the expressway, and these vary according to the distance travelled. It's not all that cheap, the result being that the normal highways remain crowded while traffic on the expressway is light. As an example, a 50km journey costs around RM5. Many other highways are in excellent condition and many are under construction.

Driving in the big cities, especially KL, is confusing, chaotic and not much fun, but once out in the countryside driving is relatively easy and a car gives you a great deal of flexibility.

Basically, driving in Malaysia follows much the same rules as in Britain or Australia – cars are right-hand drive and you drive on the left side of the road. The only additional precaution you need to take is to remain constantly aware of the possible additional road hazards of stray animals and the large number of motorcyclists. Take it easy on the back roads through the kampungs.

Although most drivers in Malaysia are relatively sane, safe and slow, there are also a fair few who specialise in overtaking on blind corners and otherwise trusting in divine intervention. Long-distance taxi drivers in paricular specialise in these dangerous activities. Malaysian drivers also operate a curious signalling system where a left flashing indicator means 'you are safe to overtake', or 'I'm about to turn off', or 'I've forgotten to turn my indicator off', or 'look out, I'm about to do something totally unpredictable'. Giving a quick blast of the horn when you're overtaking a slower vehicle is common practice and helps alert otherwise sleepy drivers of your presence.

Petrol is inexpensive at around RM1.10 a litre; diesel fuel costs RM0.65 per litre. Remember that wearing safety belts *is* compulsory, although these are fitted to the front seats only. Parking regulations are a little curious – though most cities have parking meters, in some places there is a strange human parking-meter system where your car collects a stack of little tickets under its wiper and you then have to find somebody to give the money to, at a rate of so many sen per ticket.

The Automobile Association of Malaysia will let you join its organisation if you have a letter of introduction from your own automobile association.

HITCHING

Malaysia has long had a reputation for being an excellent place for hitchhiking and it's generally still true, though with the ease of the buses most travellers don't bother.

You'll get picked up both by expats and by Malaysians and Singaporeans, but it's strictly an activity for foreigners – a hitchhiking Malaysian would probably just get left by the roadside! So the first rule of thumb in Malaysia is to look foreign. Look neat and tidy too (a worldwide rule for successful hitching), but make sure your backpack is in view and you look like someone on their way around the country.

On the west coast of Malaysia, hitching is generally quite easy but it is not possible on the main Lebuh Raya expressway. On the east coast, traffic is lighter and there may be long waits between rides. Hitching in East Malaysia also depends on the traffic, although it's quite possible.

Keep in mind that hitching is never entirely safe in any country in the world, and we don't recommend it. Travellers who decide to hitch should understand that they are taking a small but potentially serious risk. People who do choose to hitch will be safer if they travel in pairs and let someone know where they are planning to go.

BOAT

There are no services connecting the peninsula with East Malaysia. On a local level, there are boats between the peninsula and offshore islands, and along the rivers of Sabah and Sarawak – see the relevant sections for full details.

LOCAL TRANSPORT

Local transport varies widely from place to place. Large cities have city taxis (as opposed to long-distance taxis), and usually these have meters, though in some cases (notably Johor Bahru) drivers may be unwilling to use them. In major cities there are buses – in Kuala Lumpur the government buses are backed up by private operators. KL also has new commuter trains and the LRT (Light Rail Transit).

In many towns there are also bicycle rickshaws. While they have died out in Kuala Lumpur and have become principally a tourist gimmick in many Malaysian cities, they are still a viable form of transport. Indeed, in places like Georgetown, with its convoluted and narrow streets, a bicycle rickshaw is probably the best way of getting around. See the relevant city sections for more details on local transport.

In the bigger cities of East Malaysia, like Kuching and Kota Kinabalu, you will find taxis, buses and minibuses. Once you're out of the big cities, though, you're basically on your own and must either walk or hitch. If you're really in the bush, of course, riverboats and aeroplanes are the only alternative to lengthy jungle treks.

Kuala Lumpur

In 130 years, Kuala Lumpur has grown from nothing to a modern, bustling city of well over a million people. Today the city's skyline is a reflection of the (now flattened) Malaysian economic boom of the 1990s, with a host of gleaming skyscrapers.

KL (as it's almost universally known) is a federal territory, directly under the control of the central government. The city's urban sprawl extends well beyond the boundaries of the territory into surrounding Selangor state, particularly along the Kelang Valley to Petaling Jaya, Shah Alam and Kelang, where much of the city's workforce and industry is located.

Greater KL, with a population closer to two million, forms the powerhouse of the Malaysian economy. This area has many of the country's extravagant mega-projects, including the skyscraping twin Petronas Towers (the world's tallest building), slick new rapid urban transit systems and the recently opened Kuala Lumpur international airport (KLIA) at Sepang. Work is well advanced on Putrajaya, a US$8 billion capital city on Kuala Lumpur's southern periphery. Despite the economic squeeze of the late 1990s, an adjoining ultra-high-tech 'multimedia supercorridor' dubbed Cyberjaya is also taking shape, although one of Cyberjaya's major projects – the construction of the world's longest building – has been postponed.

Despite all the recent developments, KL retains plenty of character – old colonial buildings still stand out proudly right in the centre of town, and Chinatown, with its street vendors and night markets in the heart of the city, is as vibrant as any you'll encounter. To complete the cultural mix, there's a bustling Little India and the sprawling Malay-dominated Chow Kit Market north of the centre.

On first impressions, many visitors find KL to be just another busy and noisy Asian city, but it more than repays any time spent if you're prepared to delve a bit deeper. It still has the colour that has been so effectively wiped out in Singapore, yet lacks the pollution and congestion of Bangkok and in September 1998 it became the first city in Asia to host the Commonwealth Games.

HIGHLIGHTS

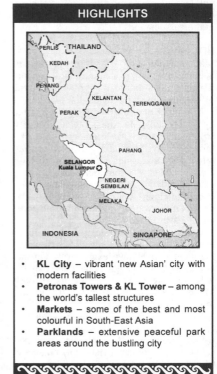

- **KL City** – vibrant 'new Asian' city with modern facilities
- **Petronas Towers & KL Tower** – among the world's tallest structures
- **Markets** – some of the best and most colourful in South-East Asia
- **Parklands** – extensive peaceful park areas around the bustling city

History

Kuala Lumpur came into being in the 1860s when a band of prospectors in search of tin landed at the meeting point of the Kelang and Gombak rivers and imaginatively named the place Kuala Lumpur – 'Muddy

Confluence'. More than half of those first arrivals were to die of malaria and other tropical diseases, but the tin they discovered in Ampang attracted more miners and KL quickly became a brawling, noisy, violent boom town.

As in other parts of Malaysia, the local sultan appointed a 'Kapitan China' to bring the unruly Chinese fortune-seekers into line – a problem which Yap Ah Loy jumped at with such ruthless relish that he became known as the founder of KL.

In the 1880s successful miners and merchants began to build fine homes along Jalan Ampang, British Resident Frank Swettenham pushed through a far-reaching new town plan, and in 1886 a railway line linked KL to Port Kelang.

The town has never looked back, and now it's not only the business and commercial capital of Malaysia, but also the political capital and the largest city in Malaysia.

The federal territory of Kuala Lumpur within Selangor state was ceded by Selangor in 1974.

Orientation

The traditional heart of KL is Merdeka Square, not far from the confluence of the two muddy rivers from which KL takes its name. The square is easily spotted because of its 95m-high flagpole – claimed to be the world's tallest – and parades and ceremonies are held here on festive occasions. Just to the south-east of this square across the river, the banking district merges into the older Chinatown, a bustling area with a wide range of accommodation.

The main post office is just south of Merdeka Square. A little further on is the national mosque (Masjid Negara) and the historic KL train station, and further west is KL's green belt, where you can find the Lake Gardens, National Museum and Monument and the Malaysian Parliament.

Heading east from the Merdeka Square area is Jalan Tun Perak, a major trunk road which leads to the long-distance transport hub of the country, the Puduraya bus station on the eastern edge of the central district.

To the east of Puduraya bus station, around Jalan Ampang and Jalan Sultan Ismail, the Golden Triangle is the modern development centre, crammed with luxury hotels, shopping centres and office towers. This is the real heart of the new KL.

Running north from Merdeka Square is Jalan Tunku Abdul Rahman (Jalan TAR). It runs one way north-south, through Little India and Chow Kit. Jalan Raja Laut runs almost parallel to Jalan TAR and takes the northbound traffic. Both roads are horrendously noisy during peak hours.

Jalan Tun Sambanthan runs south-west from the main train station through the Brickfields area. Although something of a backwater compared to other parts of inner KL, Brickfields will liven up once the city's new public transport hub of KL Sentral (Grand Central) station is completed in 1999.

KL is a relatively easy city to find your way around, although getting from place to place on foot around the city can be frustrating as the new six-lane roads and flyovers divide the area up into sections which are not connected by footpaths.

Information

Tourist Offices KL is well endowed with tourist offices.

The biggest and most useful is the Malaysia Tourist Information Complex (MATIC, ☎ 03-264 3929), 109 Jalan Ampang, north-east of the city centre. Housed in the former mansion of a Malaysian planter and tin miner (later the British and then the Japanese army headquarters), it is almost a tourist attraction in its own right. As well as a tourist information counter (open 9 am to 6 pm daily), there are national parks and express bus counters, a souvenir shop and an expensive restaurant. A 10 minute audiovisual presentation on Malaysia is shown every few hours (check at the office for times), and cultural performances, including dances (see under Entertainment), are also held here. This is the best place to come for information on other states, as there are push-button maps and video presentations on each state in the Federation.

Tourism Malaysia runs a smaller information centre (☎ 03-293 6664) located in the underground Plaza Putra on the southern side of Merdeka Square (opposite the National History Museum) which is open from 10 am to 6 pm (closed Sunday). There's also a Malaysia Tourism office at the KL train station (☎ 03-274 6063) open from 9 am to 9 pm daily, and at the new Kuala Lumpur international airport (KLIA) in Sepang.

Tourism Malaysia (☎ 03-293 5188; fax 03-293 5884; Web site www.tourism.gov.my; email tourism@tourism.gov.my) has its head office at the Putra World Trade Centre at 49 Jalan Tun Ismail in the north of KL, open Monday to Friday from 8 am to 4.15 pm. It also has a tourist information counter (☎ 03-441 1295) on level two of the same building, open Monday to Saturday from 9 am to 6 pm.

There's also the KL Visitors Centre (☎ 03-238 1832) in an old colonial building on Jalan Sultan Hishamuddin, just south of the National Art Gallery.

The widely available *Vision Kuala Lumpur* is a good tourist publication. Although produced monthly, it is not always updated. The weekly magazine *Day & Night* has tips on entertainment and other leisure activities throughout Peninsular Malaysia (especially in KL); it's available free at most better hotels, but otherwise costs RM2.

Immigration Office The immigration office (☎ 03-255 5077) for visa extensions is at Block I, Pusat Bandar Damansara, about 1km west of the Lake Gardens. Get there on bus No 18 from Chow Kit or No 21 from the Puduraya bus station.

Money Banks can be found throughout the central area of KL. The biggest concentration is on and around Jalan Silang at the northern edge of Chinatown. In this area, banks include the Hongkong Bank, Citibank and Maybank for changing cash and travellers cheques and for withdrawals through ATMs. Maybank also has a convenient branch on Jalan Bukit Bintang in the Golden Triangle district. Banks are open from 10 am to 4 pm, Monday to Friday, and 10 am to 12.30 pm on Saturday.

Moneychangers are also in plentiful supply; try Jalan Sultan near the Kelang bus station, Jalan Ampang or Jalan TAR near Little India. Most shopping centres have moneychangers.

Post & Communications The huge main post office is across the Sungai Kelang from the central district. It is open Monday to Saturday from 8 am to 6 pm, and 10 am to 12.45 pm on Sunday. Poste restante mail is held at the information desk. There's a credit-card fax machine here.

For international calls and faxes the best place to head for is the Telekom office (☎ 03-239 6025) on Jalan Raja Chulan, open daily from 8.30 am to 9.30 pm.

There's also a Home Country Direct phone at the train station on which you can make direct collect (reverse charge) calls to a number of countries.

New self-service Internet booths are being installed in some larger shopping complexes, including the Central Market and Sungei Wang Plaza. A RM5 card buys you a 15 minute log-on, but you may have a long wait before you get a turn.

Travel Agencies Ecstasy Travel (☎ 03-441 1069), 754 Jalan Sentul, organises various guided day tours of KL and surroundings.

MSL (☎ 03-442 4722), 66 Jalan Putra, is a long-running and reliable student travel agency offering some interesting deals. Another big established agent for airline tickets and tours is Mayflower (☎ 03-248 6700), which also has a branch in the Sogo department store (☎ 03-294 0933) on Jalan TAR. Also consider STA Travel (☎ 03-248 9800) in Plaza Magnum at 128 Jalan Pudu.

The Utan Bara Adventure Team (UBAT), whose office (☎ 03-422 5124) is in the Heritage Hotel, organises inexpensive jungle trips for people genuinely interested in learning about wilderness ecology.

Bookshops The two best bookstore chains, Times and MPH, are well represented in

KL. Times has branches in The Weld shopping centre on the corner of Jalan P Ramlee and Jalan Raja Chulan, at the Star Hill shopping centre on Jalan Bukit Bintang and at the Sungei Wang Plaza on Jalan Sultan Ismail. MPH has bookstores in the Metrojaya Plaza and the BB Plaza on Jalan Bukit Bintang, where the Berita Book Centre also has a good range. The Minerva Bookstore on Jalan TAR (just north of the Coliseum Hotel) stocks mainly technical literature, but it also has a good range of magazines upstairs.

Cultural Centres & Libraries The following libraries can be found in KL:

Alliance Française
(☎ 03-292 5929) 15 Lorong Gurney
Australian Information Library
(☎ 03-242 3122) Jalan Yap Kwan Seng
British Council
(☎ 03-298 7555) Jalan Bukit Aman
Goethe Institut
(☎ 03-242 2011) 1 Jalan Langgak Golf
Japan Cultural Centre
(☎ 03-230 6630) Wisma Nusantara, Jalan Puncak
Lincoln Resource Center
(☎ 03-242 0291) 376 Jalan Tun Razak
National Library
(☎ 03-294 3488) Jalan Tun Razak
New Zealand Library
(☎ 03-248 6422) 193 Jalan Tun Razak

Merdeka Square

Merdeka Square, at the heart of colonial KL, was part of the open field formerly known as the Padang. It was here during the colonial days that Malaysia's administrators engaged in that curious English rite known as cricket. In 1957 Malaysia's independence was proclaimed here, and dignitaries still gather at Merdeka Square to watch the parades on National Day.

At the northern end of the square is the **Royal Selangor Club**, which became a social centre for KL's high society in the tin-rush days of the 1890s. It's still a gathering place for the KL elite. Plaza Putra, a small underground shopping complex with a tourist office, restaurants and a theatre, is accessible from the southern side of Merdeka Square.

Across the road east of the square is the **Sultan Abdul Samad building**, a wonderful blend of Victorian and Moorish architecture, typical of the colonial buildings that give the city much of its character. Designed by the British architect AC Norman and built between 1894 and 1897, the Sultan Abdul Samad building was formerly the Secretariat building for the British administration and now houses the supreme court. It is topped by a 43m-high clock tower.

Norman was also responsible for several other buildings in this area, including **St Mary's Cathedral**, just north of the Royal Selangor Club, which dates back to 1894. St Mary's houses a fine pipe organ.

The old City Hall, just north of the Sultan Abdul Samad building, is in a similar Moorish style and now houses the **Textile Museum**. The museum has excellent demonstrative exhibits on traditional batik, weaving and embroidery methods, and there is also a good handicrafts shop.

On the south side of Merdeka Square is the **National History Museum**, in an attractive building dating back to 1909 which was one of the city's original administration offices. Although well presented, its exhibits on Malaysia's Stone Age, Buddhist, Islamic, colonial and postcolonial periods are unsatisfyingly scant. Next door is the **Kuala Lumpur Memorial Library**.

Further south along Jalan Sultan Hishamuddin, the **Dayabumi Complex** is an impressive example of modern architecture, using Islamic arches and motifs in a multisided high-rise tower.

Masjid Jamek

The most delightful of all KL's mosques, the 'Friday Mosque' is at the confluence of the Kelang and Gombak rivers and lies behind the Sultan Abdul Samad building. This was the place where KL's founders first set foot in the town and where supplies were landed for the tin mines.

Set in a grove of palm trees, the mosque is a picturesque structure with onion domes

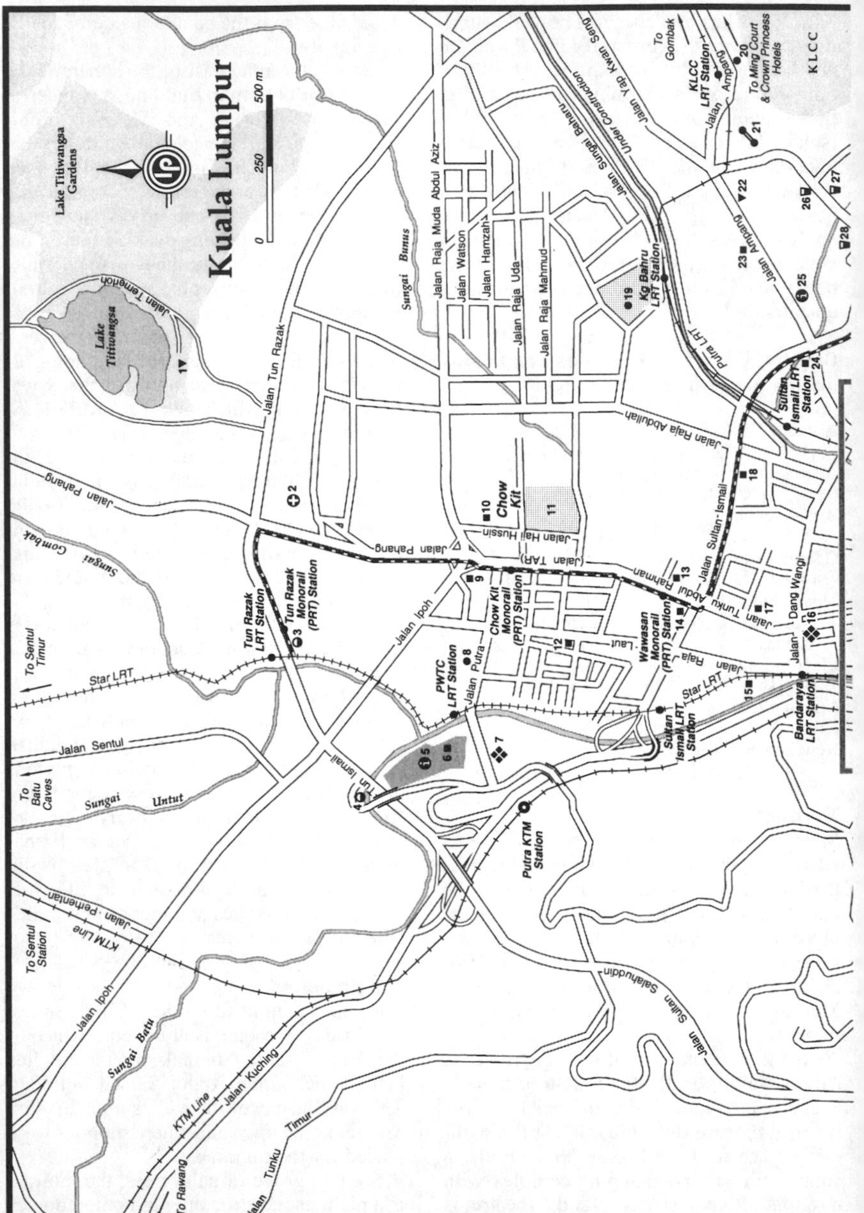
Kuala Lumpur
0
250
500 m
Lake Titiwangsa Gardens
Lake Titiwangsa
Jalan Temerloh
Sungai Bunus
Jalan Tun Razak
Jalan Raja Muda Abdul Aziz
Jalan Watson
Jalan Hamzah
Jalan Raja Uda
Jalan Raja Mahmud
Jalan Sungai Bahru
Under Construction
Jalan Yap Kwan Seng
To Gombak
KLCC LRT Station
Jalan Ampang
To Ming Court & Crown Princess Hotels
KLCC
Kg Bahru LRT Station
Putra LRT
Sultan Ismail LRT Station
Jalan Raja Abdullah
Jalan Sultan Ismail
Jalan Pahang
Sungai Gombak
Chow Kit
Jalan Haji Hussin
Jalan TAR
Jalan Tunku Abdul Rahman
Jalan Dang Wangi
Jalan Raja Laut
Wawasan Monorail (PRT) Station
Chow Kit Monorail (PRT) Station
Jalan Ipoh
Jalan Putra
PWTC LRT Station
Tun Razak LRT Station
Tun Razak Monorail (PRT) Station
To Sentul Timur
Star LRT
Jalan Sentul
To Batu Caves
Sungai Untut
Jalan Tun Ismail
Putra KTM Station
Bandaraya LRT Station
Sultan Ismail LRT Station
Jalan Perhentian
KTM Line
To Sentul Station
Jalan Ipoh
Sungai Batu
Jalan Kuching
To Rawang
Jalan Tunku Timur
Jalan Sultan Salahuddin

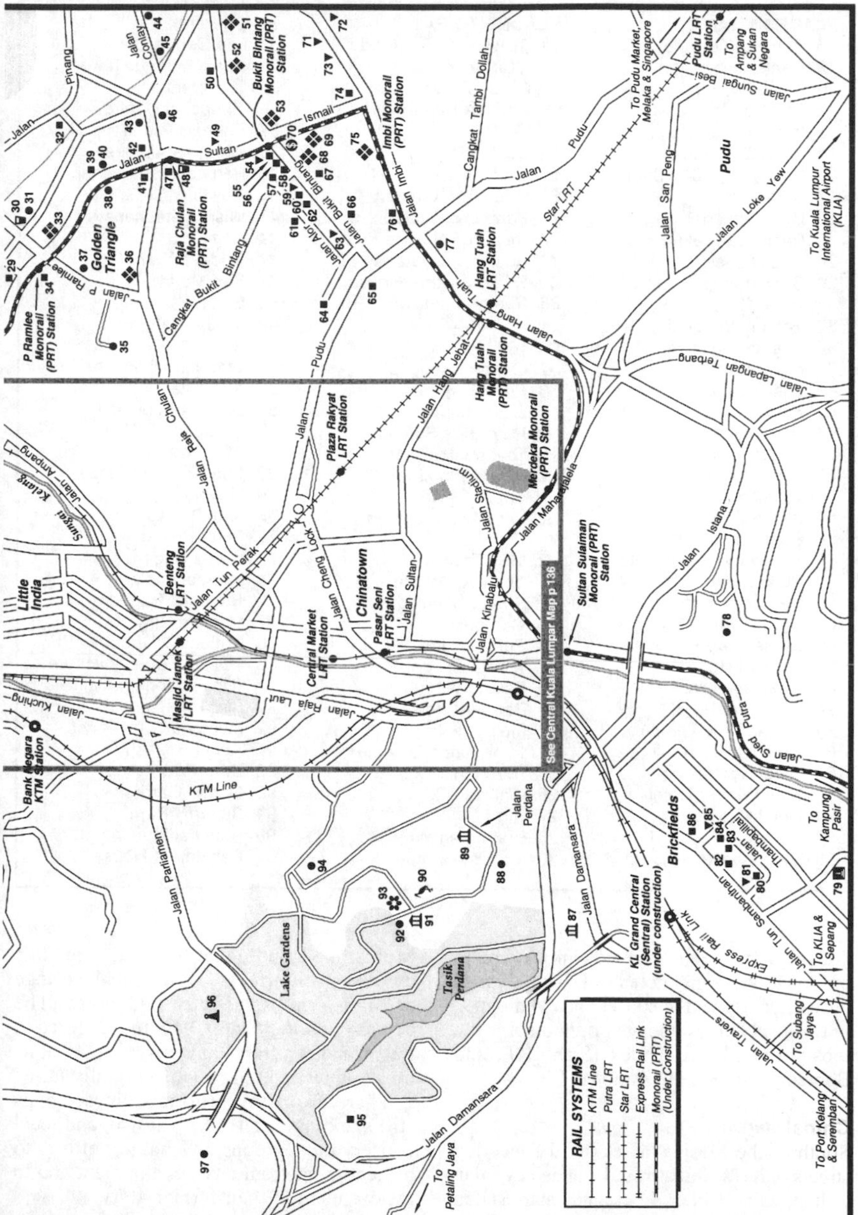

PENINSULAR MALAYSIA

PLACES TO STAY

6 Pan Pacific Hotel
9 Central Hotel
10 City Villa Hotel
12 Ben Soo Homestay
13 International Hotel
14 Hotel Centrepoint
15 Holiday Inn City Centre
17 Shiraz Hotel
18 Hotel Imperial
23 Radisson Plaza Hotel
24 Hyatt Hotel
29 Concorde Hotel; Hard Rock Cafe
32 Holiday Inn on the Park
34 Shangri-La Hotel
39 Equatorial Hotel
41 Lodge Hotel
42 Hilton Hotel
47 Hotel Istana
50 Regent Hotel
55 Agora Hotel
56 Toriman
57 Imperial Hotel
58 Bonanza Hotel
60 Bintang Warisan Hotel
61 Budget Inn
62 Cardogan Hotel
64 Corona Inn
65 Swiss Garden Hotel
66 Federal Hotel
67 Malaysia Hotel
74 Parkroyal Hotel
76 Melia Kuala Lumpur
80 Hotel La Posh Villa
82 Hotel Sentral
83 New Winner Hotel
84 Hotel Mexico
86 YMCA
95 Carcosa Seri Negara

PLACES TO EAT

1 Titiwangsa Seafood Village
22 Le Coq d'Or
49 Berjaya Roadhouse Grill
54 Sushi King
59 Tamnak Thai
63 Restoran Ramzan
71 Fong Lye Restaurant
72 Restoran Sakura
73 Restoran Overseas
81 Sri Devi Curry House
85 Restoran Intown

OTHER

2 General Hospital
3 Pekeliling Bus Station
4 Putra Bus Station
5 Tourism Malaysia (Putra World Trade Centre)
7 The Mall Shopping Complex
8 MSL Travel
11 Chow Kit Market
16 Sogo Shopping Complex
19 Sunday Market (Pasar Minggu)
20 Pelangi Air
21 Petronas Towers
25 Malaysia Tourist Information Complex (MATIC)
26 Wall $t
27 Rio
28 Brannigan's
30 Modesto's
31 Sri Perak
33 Life Centre
35 Kuala Lumpur Tower
36 The Weld Shopping Centre
37 Energy; The Wall
38 Malaysia Airlines
40 Pernas International Building
43 Wisma Stephens
44 Kompleks Budaya Kraf
45 Seri Melayu
46 Eden
48 Malibu Cafe
51 Star Hill Shopping Complex
52 KL Plaza
53 Lot 10 Shopping Complex
68 BB Plaza
69 Sungei Wang Plaza
70 Maybank
75 Imbi Plaza
77 Pudu Prison
78 Istana Negara
79 International Buddhist Pagoda
87 Muzium Negara
88 National Planetarium
89 Museum of Islamic Arts (Under Construction)
90 Bird Park
91 Memorial Tun Abdul Razak
92 Deer Park
93 Orchid Garden
94 Butterfly Park
96 National Monument
97 Parliament House

and minarets built of layered pink and cream bricks. It was constructed in 1907 and looks best when viewed at sunset and evening.

Both LRT lines intersect right outside the mosque at Masjid Jamek (Star LRT) and Benteng (Putra LRT) stations.

Chinatown

South of the Masjid Jamek are the teeming streets of KL's Chinatown. Bounded by Jalan Sultan, Jalan Cheng Lock and Jalan Sultan Mohammed and Jalan Tun HS Lee, this crowded, colourful area is the usual melange of signs, shops, activity and noise. The central section of **Jalan Petaling** is closed to traffic and is a frantically busy market, at its most colourful at night when brightly lit.

There are many historic Chinese shops still standing in KL's Chinatown, and local conservation groups are making efforts to protect them from city development and to restore them to their former glory.

Central Market Previously the city's produce market, this Art Deco building has been refurbished to become a centre for handicraft, antique and art sales. It is surrounded by pedestrian areas, providing a welcome break from Chinatown's choking traffic. There are shops on two levels, hawker centres, restaurants, fast-food outlets, bars and a cinema complex in the annexe on the northern side.

It is easy to spend an hour or more wandering around the various craft outlets, which sell everything from cheap souvenirs and jewellery to very expensive Asian artefacts and antiques. As a general rule, the higher the price the more you should bargain. Shops also stock clothes, music tapes and other goods. Various rotating exhibits are on display and cultural shows are staged in the evenings. Or get your palm read for fortune, fame and happiness from Master Chin upstairs on the 2nd level.

Temples The small **Sze Yah Temple**, hidden behind some shops at 14A Lebuh Pudu near the Central Market, is one of the oldest in KL. 'Kapitan China' Yap Ah Loy himself organised its construction, and there is a photograph of him on an altar in the back of the temple.

Built in 1906, the typically ornate **Chan See Shu Yuen Temple** stands at the end of Jalan Petaling and is one of the largest in KL.

The **Khoon Yam Temple** is a Hokkien Chinese temple dating back to the turn of the century and is just across Jalan Stadium from the Chan See Shu Yuen Temple.

Dating from 1873, the **Sri Mahamariamman Temple** is a large and ornate south Indian Hindu temple at 163 Jalan Tun HS Lee. The temple was refurbished in 1985 and houses a large silver chariot dedicated to Lord Muruga. During the Thaipusam festival this chariot is a central part of a long procession to Batu Caves.

Train Station

KL's magnificent train station, close to the national mosque, is a building full of eastern promise. Built in 1911, this delightful example of British colonial humour is a Moorish fantasy of spires, minarets, towers, cupolas and arches. It couldn't look any better if it had been built as a set for some whimsical Hollywood extravaganza.

Across from this superb train station is the equally wonderful Malayan Railway Administration building.

National Art Gallery

This art gallery (Balai Seni Lukis Negara) is housed in the former Majestic Hotel, opposite the train station. It has permanent exhibitions of modern paintings by Malaysian artists and rotating exhibitions that include art from around the world. It's not worth a special trip, but if you're in the vicinity (say, waiting for a train), you could while away half an hour or so there.

Admission is free and it's open from 10 am to 6 pm daily.

Masjid Negara

Situated in five hectares of landscaped gardens, the modernistic National Mosque is one of the largest in South-East Asia. A 73m-high minaret stands in the centre of a pool, and the main dome of the mosque is in the form of an 18-pointed star which represents the 13 states of Malaysia and the five pillars of Islam. Forty-eight smaller domes cover the courtyard; their design is said to be inspired by the Grand Mosque in Mecca. The mosque, which is close to the train station, can accommodate 8000 people.

Visitors must remove their shoes upon entry and be 'properly' attired – they'll lend you a robe if your own clothing is not suitable. It's open to non-Muslims outside of prayer times, which are around 8 to 9 am, 1 to 2 pm, 4 to 5 pm and 7 to 8 pm. Women must use a separate entrance.

Opposite the mosque is the **Islamic Centre**, and nearby (on the way up to the National Planetarium) is the new **Museum of Islamic Arts**, due to open in 1999.

Muzium Negara

At the southern end of the Lake Gardens and immediately north of the new KL Sentral

(Grand Central) station, the Muzium Negara (National Museum) was built on the site of the old Selangor Museum, which was destroyed during WWII. The museum was opened in 1963, and its design and construction is a mixture of Malay architectural styles and crafts. It houses a varied collection on Malaysia's history, economy, arts, crafts, cultures and traditions, although the exhibits are getting rather tacky and could do with a facelift.

One intriguing exhibit is an 'amok catcher', an ugly barbed device used to catch and hold a person who has run amok. Art and other exhibitions are held at the museum, and machinery such as locomotives and an aircraft are on display.

The museum is open daily from 9 am to 6 pm. Admission is RM1.

Lake Gardens

The 92 hectare gardens, established in 1888, form the green belt of KL. As in many planned colonial cities in Malaysia, the garden district lies at the edge of the central city area, typically around landscaped hills, and the British elite built their fine houses nearby, away from the hurly burly of downtown commerce and other races. The British Resident, Frank Swettenham, built his official residence overlooking the gardens, and it is now the Carcosa Seri Negara, Malaysia's most expensive hotel.

The central focus of the gardens is **Tasik Perdana**, the 'Premier Lake', which was once known as Sydney Lake. On weekends you can rent boats for a leisurely paddle around the lake.

The gardens contain a host of other attractions, open from 9 am to 6 pm. You can take a leisurely, if sweaty, stroll to them, or a shuttle bus (20/50 sen for children/adults) does a loop of the main attractions from 9 am to 7 pm daily, except Friday, when it stops from noon to 3 pm. Minibus No 18, 21, 46 or 48 from Jalan Tun Perak or Intrakota bus No 244 or 250 from the Sultan Mohammed bus stand will take you to the gardens.

One of the highlights of the gardens is the **Bird Park**, an enormous walk-in aviary with 160 (largely South-East Asian) species of birds. Entry is RM1/3 children/adults. Opposite is the **Orchid Garden**, with over 800 species of orchids, and the adjoining **Hibiscus Garden**. Entry is free except on weekends (RM1). The nearby **Memorial Tun Abdul Razak**, at the corner of Jalan Perdana and Jalan Cenderawasih, is dedicated to Malaysia's second prime minister and displays his memorabilia. On its northern side is the **Deer Park**, which has a number of tame deer including the tiny kancil.

The **Butterfly Park** claims to be the largest in South-East Asia and has a number of species in its landscaped enclosure. There is also an interesting insect museum. Entry is RM2/5 children/adults.

The massive **National Monument** overlooks the Lake Gardens from a hillside at their northern end. Sculpted in bronze in 1966 by Felix de Weldon, the creator of the Iwo Jima monument in Washington DC, the monument commemorates the successful defeat of the Communist terrorists during the Emergency.

Overlooking the Lake Gardens from the north-west, Malaysia's **Parliament House** is dominated by an 18 storey office block. Prior permission must be obtained to visit parliament.

Also at the Lake Gardens is the **National Planetarium** (closed on Monday and Tuesday), which resembles a futuristic mosque. It has a small space exhibition (children free/adults RM1), but also puts on audiovisual science shows (RM2/3) and IMAX films on a 20m domed screen (RM4/6).

Jalan Tunku Abdul Rahman (Jalan TAR)

North from the city centre, Jalan TAR leads through an old section of the city, passing Little India. The main street of **Little India** is Jalan Masjid India, crammed with Indian shops and restaurants. Here you can buy saris, batik or Muslim religious paraphernalia. Centred on the mosque, Little India has all the feel of a Middle Eastern bazaar.

Heading further north along Jalan TAR many of the buildings are modern, but one surviving colonial relic is the **Coliseum Hotel**. Enter through the saloon doors to the bar, where you can relax in a planter's chair and sip a drink; waiters in starched linen jackets serve grills in the adjoining restaurant. The Coliseum hasn't changed in decades because, in Chinese tradition it is said, the wealthy owner began his business empire here and has retained it in its original form for good luck.

Jalan TAR is good for shopping during the day, and you can browse in the Globe Silk Store for cheap clothes or in the larger Sogo department store. Further north you enter the Chow Kit area, once a famed red-light district and hang-out for transvestites, though it has largely been cleaned out now. The **Chow Kit Market** is a Malay market, with a gaggle of roadside vendors lining the main street. All manner of goods are on sale – cheap clothes, basketware and leather goods are good buys if you bargain hard. The area around the City Villa Hotel is crammed with hawker stalls, good for satay or nasi lemak. The high-rise redevelopment of Chow Kit Market, involving its temporary relocation to a site on Jalan Ipoh, is planned although widespread opposition may yet stop this project.

On Saturday night Jalan TAR is closed to traffic and hosts the liveliest night market in the city. Stalls line the street as far as the Sogo department store, and buskers play.

Golden Triangle

Crammed with numerous postmodern high-rises, including the new **Petronas Towers**, the Golden Triangle is KL's flashy business,

The Petronas Towers – The Tallest in the World

Rising some 451.9m above the flat plain of Kuala Lumpur, the Petronas Towers have quickly become a symbol of the new Malaysia. Arguably the tallest buildings in the world, they are a bold statement to the world of Malaysia's rising economic stature and intentions. Completed in 1998, they can also be considered a monument to the overreaching ambitions of an economy which is now mired deep in a recession. Some critics have even suggested that it is 'mega-projects' like the towers themselves that led to the present slowdown.

All economic considerations aside, the 88-storey towers are an arresting sight. Unique in design, their floor plan is based on an eight-sided star pattern which echoes the arabesque patterns of Islamic art. Islamic influences can also be seen in the 63m-masts which crown each tower, calling to mind both the minarets of a mosque and the star of Islam. The design of these uniquely Islamic skyscrapers is the result of lengthy dialogue between the architects, the American firm of Cesar Pelli and Associates, and the government of Malaysia, including Dr Mahathir.

It is the masts that caused so much controversy. As soon as they were installed, the government of Malaysia jubilantly announced that the Petronas Towers were the tallest buildings in the world. However, this claim was quickly disputed by critics who argued that it was unfair to count the masts in the overall measurement of the buildings.

In an effort to resolve the issue, the US-based Council on Tall Buildings and Urban Habitats announced four categories for determining the world's tallest building: height to top of building, height to tip of antenna, height to highest occupied floor and height to roof of building. According to the new standards, the Petronas Towers only qualify as the world's tallest buildings according to the first category, the World Trade Center in New York is tallest according to the second criteria and the Sears Tower in Chicago is tallest according to the last two.

Whatever the case, you shouldn't let these petty squabbles get in your way. Go out and take a look for yourself – you'll have to agree that you've never seen anything like these distinctive silver spires.

Chris Rowthorn

shopping and entertainment district. Encompassing an area of several square kilometres, it extends from its base along Jalan Imbi north to its apex at the **Petronas Towers**. The world's tallest buildings, these graceful twin skyscrapers (currently not open to the public) rise up from the spacious landscaped gardens of the **Kuala Lumpur City Centre (KLCC)**.

Jalan Sultan Ismail is the main drag, with most of the luxury hotels and nightspots spaced out along it. The most lively area, with the biggest concentration of shopping malls, is near the intersection of Jalan Sultan Ismail and Jalan Bukit Bintang.

At the western edge of the Golden Triangle is the impressive 421m **Kuala Lumpur Tower**, the fourth highest telecommunications tower in the world. Visitors can ride the lift to the viewing deck (RM3/8 children/adults) for a superb panorama of the city. Nearby on Jalan Raja Chulan is the new high-rise **Stock Exchange**, built in a curious amalgam of postmodern and neo-classical styles.

At the northern edge of the Golden Triangle, **Jalan Ampang** was built up by the early tin millionaires and is lined with impressive mansions. Today many of the fine buildings have become embassies and consulates, so the street is KL's 'Ambassador's Row'. One of these fine stately homes has been converted into a luxurious restaurant, Le Coq d'Or, while another houses the Malaysia Tourist Information Complex.

Other Attractions

Museums Museums are scattered around the city, though most visitors only bother taking in the Muzium Negara – the rest are for those with special interests.

The **Numismatic Museum** houses an interesting collection of coins and notes. It's in the Maybank building at 100 Jalan Tun Perak, near the Puduraya bus station. It is open daily from 10 am to 6 pm and admission is free. The small **Telekom Museum**, in the old Telekom building on Jalan Raja Chulan, deals with the history of telecommunications in Malaysia.

About 5km north of the city on Jalan Padang Tembak, the **Armed Forces Museum** has a display of weapons, paintings, uniforms and other military paraphernalia inside, and cannons and tanks outside. The museum is open Saturday to Thursday from 10 am to 6 pm (free). In the same area is the **Police Museum** on Jalan Semarak, which is open daily from 8 am to 3.15 pm, except Saturday and Sunday, when it closes at noon. Both of these museums can be reached on a No 20A Intrakota bus from Chow Kit and on No 19 or 20 minibus from 1 Jalan Tun HS Lee in Chinatown. At the Malaysian Air Force Base 6km from the city centre, the **Air Force Museum** is just a hangar containing a few light planes and air force memorabilia. You can reach this museum by catching a No 13 bus from Jalan Hang Jebat.

Pudu Prison KL's historic Pudu Prison is 2km south-east of the city centre on Jalan Hang Tuah. Built in 1891 by the British colonial authorities, it finally closed on 1 November 1996 and has since been opened to the public. A self-guided tour leads through the cell blocks, including a graphic video of caning with a rotan (using actors) and a rather tacky audiovisual show in death row.

Pudu Prison is on prime real estate and will eventually be demolished to make way for a planned high-rise development. For the moment, however, Malaysia's current financial crisis has given these buildings a 'stay of execution'.

Admission is RM7/12 children/adults. The prison is a few minutes' walk from Hang Tuah (Star LRT) station.

International Buddhist Pagoda This modern pagoda is in the south of Kuala Lumpur, off Jalan Tun Sambanthan in the Brickfields area. On the same site there's a Bodhi tree and a Buddhist shrine dating back to the late 1800s. The shrine was built by Sinhalese Buddhists from Sri Lanka. Bus No 12 from Kelang bus station will take you there.

Markets

KL's lively streets are host to busy **pasar malam** (night markets), where hawker food stalls set up and a variety of goods are on sale. The Saturday night market along Jalan TAR is one of the best in the city. Open day and night, Jalan Petaling in Chinatown is a bustling street market where you can have a Chinese alfresco meal or snack, seek out some cheap clothes, or pick up a kilogram of lychees or mangoes.

In the Kampung Bahru area north-east of the city centre, Jalan Raja Muda comes alive each Saturday night for KL's **Pasar Minggu (Sunday Market)** so-called because it continues through into Sunday morning. It's a food and produce market, a handicrafts market and a place to sample a wide variety of Malay foods. Also in the north of town is the **Chow Kit Market**, an incredibly busy place from early morning until late at night. During the day the stalls here sell all manner of bits and pieces, while after 6 pm the food stalls take over.

The predominantly Chinese-run **Pudu Market**, 3km south-east of the city centre, is the largest wet (produce) market in KL. It's definitely a *wet* market – it's a good idea to wear shoes rather than thongs or sandals – but very colourful and well worth a visit. At

Hash House Harriers

The internationally known Hash House Harriers was first established in KL in 1938 by a group of British colonials who found themselves drinking too much and needing exercise. 'Hash house' was the nickname for the dining room of the Selangor Club Chambers, a social centre of the times. The harrier idea of a group of runners chasing papers along trails set by an appointed member (the 'hare') was not altogether new – previous groups had existed in KL, Ipoh, Johor Bahru and Melaka in colonial Malaya. In Shanghai and Kuching the sport was carried out on horseback. However, the original Hash House Harriers (HHHs) institutionalised the chase to such a degree that it became an expat tradition all over Asia.

Until 1961 there was only the KL Hash, but in the following year a second chapter opened in Singapore, followed by others in Brunei, Kuching, Kota Kinabalu, Ipoh and Penang. Eventually the first group outside Singapore/Malaysia was opened in Perth in 1967. There are now around 500 HHHs in 70 countries and there are annual interhash meetings held at a different place each year. To mark the 60th anniversary of the Hash House Harriers, Malaysia hosted the Interhash 1998, an event which attracted thousands of participants from scores of countries.

A few hours in advance of a hash run, the hare goes to the run site – which changes with each run – and lays an irregular trail (sometimes including false trails) using paper markers. The point is to allow faster runners to scout for the next bit of trail while slower harriers catch up. The run begins with a call of 'on, on' – the slogan of all HHHs – and when looking for paper markers runners shout out 'are you?', to which runners ahead reply 'checking' to help in trail-finding. A typical run lasts one to 1½ hours and is followed by beer drinking at the end of the trail and a meal at a local restaurant. In KL the meals are usually at a Chinese restaurant and each runner contributes about RM8 to cover costs.

There are several branches in the KL area, including one for men only (the original tradition) and one for women only (the Hash House Harriettes). The rest are mixed. Most of the larger Malaysian towns have their own branches. All Malaysian hash clubs have local members.

The hash welcomes guest participants. For those so inclined, a hash run would be an interesting way to meet locals and expats while seeing a bit of the Malaysian countryside (runs tend to be held in secondary jungle areas, or on rubber or palm oil estates).

For further information, contact the Kuala Lumpur Hash House Harriers (☎ 03-282 9798; fax 03-242 9796), PO Box 13603, 50816 Kuala Lumpur.

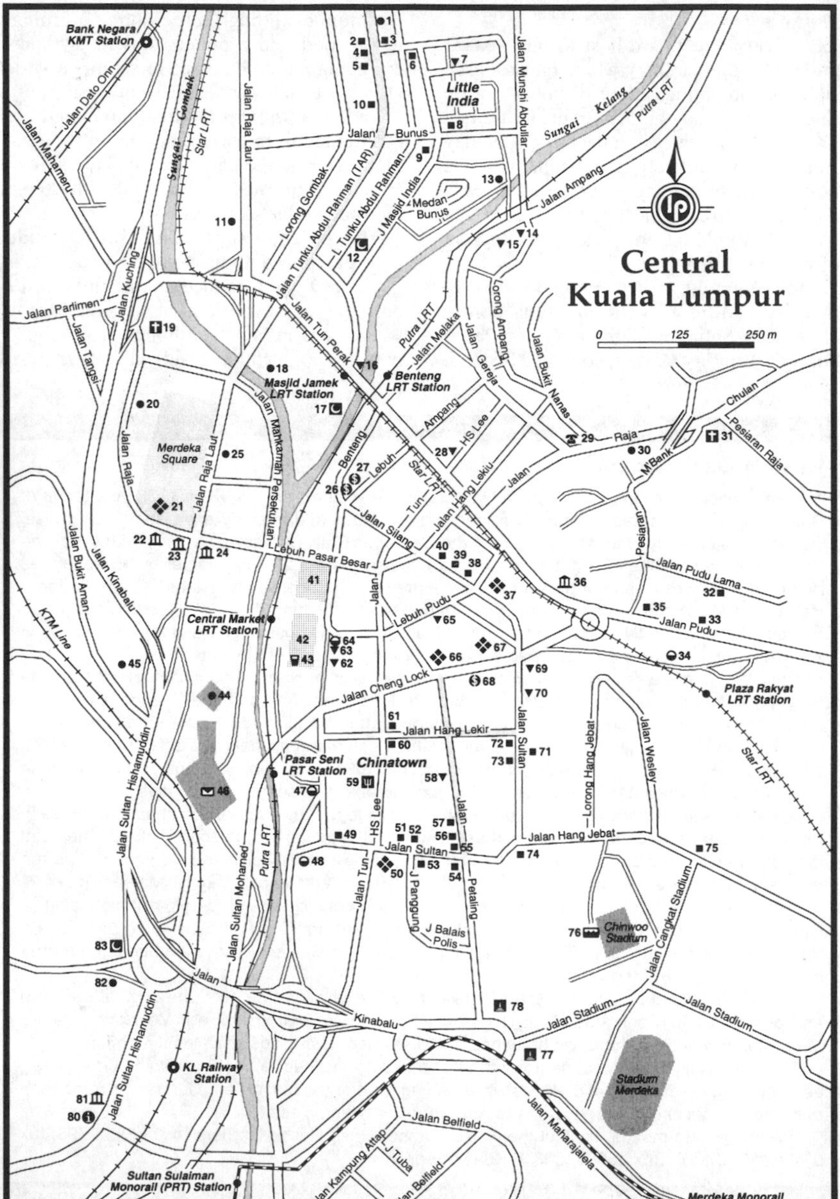
Central
Kuala Lumpur
0
125
250 m
Little India
Chinatown
Merdeka Square
Bank Negara KMT Station
Masjid Jamek LRT Station
Benteng LRT Station
Central Market LRT Station
Pasar Seni LRT Station
Plaza Rakyat LRT Station
KL Railway Station
Sultan Sulaiman Monorail (PRT) Station
Merdeka Monorail (PRT) Station
Chinwoo Stadium
Stadium Merdeka
Sungai Kelang
Sungai Gombak
Star LRT
Putra LRT
KTM Line
Jalan Dato Onn
Jalan Maharmeru
Jalan Raja Laut
Jalan Bunus
Lorong Gombak
Jalan Tunku Abdul Rahman (TAR)
L Tunku Abdul Rahman
J Masjid India
Medan Bunus
Jalan Munshi Abdullah
Jalan Ampang
Jalan Parlimen
Jalan Kuching
Jalan Tangsi
Jalan Tun Perak
Jalan Melaka
Jalan Gereja
Lorong Ampang
Jalan Bukit Nanas
Jalan Raja Chulan
Pesiaran Raja
Jalan Raja
Jalan Mahkamah Persekutuan
Benteng
Lebuh Ampang
HS Lee
Jalan Tun HS Lee
Lebuh Pasar Besar
Jalan Silang
Jalan Hang Lekiu
M'Bank
Pesiaran
Jalan Pudu Lama
Jalan Pudu
Jalan Bukit Aman
Jalan Kinabalu
Lebuh Pudu
Jalan Cheng Lock
Jalan Hang Lekir
Jalan Sultan
Jalan Hang Jebat
Lorong Hang Jebat
Jalan Wesley
Jalan Sultan Hishamuddin
Jalan Sultan Mohamed
Jalan Petaling
J Panggung
J Balais Polis
Jalan Cangkat Stadium
Jalan Stadium
Jalan Kinabalu
Jalan Maharajalela
Jalan Belfield
Jalan Kampung Attap
J Tuba

PLACES TO STAY

2 Kowloon Hotel
3 Noble Hotel
4 Tivoli Hotel
5 Rex Hotel
6 TI Lodge
8 Hotel Champagne
9 Hotel Chamtan
10 Coliseum Hotel
32 Kawana Tourist Inn
33 Hotel Katari
35 KL City Lodge
38 Twin Happiness Inn
39 Travellers' Home
40 Travellers' Moon Lodge
49 Starlight Hotel
51 Mandarin Hotel
52 Wan Kow Hotel
53 Hotel City Inn
54 Hotel Lok Ann
55 Lee Mun Travellers Inn
56 CT Guest House
57 Excel Inn
60 Hotel Malaya
61 Backpackers Travellers Lodge
71 Hotel Furama
72 Swiss Inn
73 Backpackers Travellers Inn
74 Colonial Hotel
75 YWCA
79 KL International Youth Hostel

PLACES TO EAT

7 Govinda's Vegetarian Restaurant
14 Kapitan's Club
15 Bilal
16 McDonald's
28 Baba's Curry House
58 Food Centre
62 Restoran Yusoof
63 McDonald's
65 Restoran Wilayah Baru
69 Meidi-ya
70 KFC

OTHER

1 Globe Silk Store
11 City Hall
12 Masjid Little India
13 Little India Night Market
17 Masjid Jamek
18 High Court
19 St Mary's Cathedral
20 Royal Selangor Club
21 Plaza Putra (Tourism Malaysia & Actors Studio Theatre)
22 KL Memorial Library
23 National History Museum
24 Textile Museum (Old City Hall)
25 Sultan Abdul Samad Building
26 Citibank
27 Hongkong Bank
29 Telekom Office & Telekom Museum
30 KL Stock Exchange
31 St Andrew's Church
34 Puduraya Bus Station
36 Numismatic Museum; Maybank
37 Metrojaya Department Store
41 Central Market Annexe
42 Central Market
43 Bull's Head; Riverbank
44 Dayabumi Complex
45 British Council
46 Main Post Office
47 Jalan Sultan Mohammed Bus Stand
48 Kelang Bus Station
50 UDA Ocean Plaza
59 Sri Mahamariamman Temple
64 Bus Stand
66 S&M Shopping Complex
67 Kota Raya Shopping Complex
68 Standard Chartered Bank
76 Swimming Pool
77 Chan See Shu Yuen Temple
78 Khoon Yam Temple
80 KL Visitors Centre
81 National Art Gallery
82 Islamic Centre
83 Masjid Negara

the market stalls you can get every imaginable type of fruit, vegetable, fish and meat – everything from a chicken's foot (from a chicken slaughtered and butchered on the spot) to a stingray fillet or a pig's penis. Pudu Market is five minutes walk from Pudu (Star LRT) station; go south along Jalan Pudu, left into Jalan Pasar, then right down Jalan Pasar Baharu.

Swimming Pool

There's a public swimming pool next to the Chinwoo Stadium, on the rise just off Jalan Hang Jebat, a couple of minutes' walk from Chinatown.

Places to Stay

The main area for cheap accommodation is Chinatown, near the Puduraya bus station. Chinatown is noisy, traffic-clogged and grotty, but very central, always lively and interesting to wander around. Most of KL's backpackers' guesthouses are here, and the area also has a good selection of mid- range hotels.

The Jalan TAR area also has quite a few cheap and mid-range hotels and a couple of guesthouses. Though not quite as convenient as Chinatown, it is still central and lively during the day. Since the red-light district around here has been cleaned out, it tends to be quiet at night, except Saturday night when the city's best night market is held along Jalan TAR.

The main area for mid-range and top end hotels is the Golden Triangle district, to the east of the downtown area, where you'll find most of KL's shopping malls and nightlife. Lively Jalan Bukit Bintang is a good hunting ground for mid-range hotels and a large number of luxury hotels are scattered around nearby.

Places to Stay – Budget

Bottom-end accommodation in KL consists of a variety of ever-dwindling Chinese hotels and a choice of guesthouses. Many of the cheap hotels are very seedy and run-down, and their days are numbered. As a rule, hotels with signs written only in Malay, 'Rumah Tumpangan', are long-term boarding houses or offer more than just rooms.

Guesthouses KL has quite a number of guesthouses that cater exclusively to budget travellers. Competition among the guesthouses generally keeps prices down, but don't expect much for your money. They typically consist of partitioned rooms in city buildings, so rooms with a window are rare. They all offer similar services: dorm beds as well as rooms, washing facilities and a noticeboard and they will book buses. The better places fill up quickly and it can be difficult to find a cheap room if you arrive in the evening.

Chinatown On the edge of Chinatown and only a few minutes' walk from the Puduraya bus station is the *Travellers' Moon Lodge* (☎ 03-230 6601) at 36C Jalan Silang. It is crammed with hot little plywood-walled singles/doubles for RM20/25, but the hallway dorm on the top floor next to the rooftop breakfast area is at least cooler and costs RM8. Just a few doors along at No 46C and run by the same people is the *Travellers' Home* (☎ 03-230 6601). It's smaller and quieter with larger, nicer rooms for the same price. The *Twin Happiness Inn* (☎ 03-238 7667) next door is similar.

Also in Chinatown, at 60 Jalan Sultan, is the *Backpackers Travellers Inn* (☎ 03-238 2473). This is another popular place, and though a little cramped with typically small and windowless rooms, it's clean and well run. A dorm bed costs RM8, or RM10 with air-con. A variety of singles/doubles range from RM22/25 with fan up to RM40/50 with air-con.

Its offshoot, the more spacious *Backpackers Travellers Lodge* (☎ 03-201 0889), 158 Jalan Tun HS Lee, is one of the better guesthouses. Very basic windowless doubles start at RM22, and somewhat better rooms with fan are RM25, ranging up to RM50 with air-con and shower. Dorm beds cost RM8 each. There's a good, if spartan, TV lounge and the usual variety of services are offered.

Close by at Wisma BWT, 103 Jalan Petaling, is the *CT Guest House* (☎ 03-232 0417). It's a bit scruffy and chaotic, but is on the night market in the middle of Chinatown. Dorm beds cost RM10 each in four-bed rooms, while singles/doubles are RM17/25.

The *Lee Mun Travellers Inn*, a grotty dive on the 5th floor on the corner of Jalan Sultan and Jalan Petaling in Chinatown, should be considered only if you have run out of other options. Singles/doubles are RM25/30 and the dorm costs RM15.

Puduraya The *KL City Lodge* (☎ 03-230 5275) at 16 Jalan Pudu is opposite the bus station. This is more a regular, scruffy hotel but still draws a few travellers. Air-con dorm beds cost RM12 each, while simple singles/doubles are RM20/30 with fan or RM25/35 with air-con. In the same area, the quiet *Kawana Tourist Inn* (☎ 03-238 6714) at 68 Jalan Pudu Lama is well kept but lacks atmosphere. A bed in the tiny dorm costs RM12, while singles/doubles with fan cost RM35/40, or RM45/60 with air-con and toilet.

Chow Kit Just off Jalan Raja Laut near Chow Kit at 61B Jalan Tiong Nam (opposite the Hotel Wilayah) is the very friendly, family-run *Ben Soo Homestay* (☎ 03-291 8096). It offers rare value in budget accommodation with secure, spacious, clean singles/doubles with fan for only RM25/32 including a light breakfast. For a minimal fee, the owner will pick you up from the train or bus stations.

Little India Another friendly place is the *TI Lodge* (☎ 03-293 0261), in the heart of Little India at 20 Lorong Bunus Enam. Quite good rooms cost RM39 with fan, RM46 with air-con and RM55 with air-con and bathroom. Breakfast is included.

Train Station Inside KL's historic old train station is the *Travellers Station* (☎ 03-273 5588; email station1@tm.net.my). With beds in large air-con dorms for RM15 each it's not dirt-cheap, but many backpackers favour this place for its convenience, spaciousness, good facilities (including kitchen, laundry and Internet access) and its easy-going staff. Simple air-con doubles cost RM45.

Less than 10 minutes' walk east of KL train station, the fully air-conditioned *KL International Youth Hostel* (☎ 03-273 6870) is at 21 Jalan Kampung Attap. Dorm beds cost RM15 each.

Other Areas At the top of the guesthouse range is the *Bonanza Hotel* (☎ 03-245 8457) on Jalan Bukit Bintang at No 72 next to the Bintang Warisan Hotel. This place offers a bit more space than the Chinatown guesthouses but is also more expensive because of its location. A dorm bed costs RM20, and there are simple rooms with fan for RM36, RM45 with a window, and from RM55 with air-con.

Finally, there are the Ys. Conveniently located close to KL's new Sentral (Grand Central) station at 95 Jalan Padang Belia is the *YMCA* (☎ 03-274 1439). It has simple singles/doubles with fan for RM38/50 and triples/quads for RM65/75. Better air-con rooms with bathroom cost RM68/78.

The *YWCA* (☎ 03-230 1623) is much more central at 12 Jalan Hang Jebat. It has plain but acceptable rooms for women at RM30/50 and for couples from RM50. Family rooms are also available.

Hotels Along Jalan TAR and its adjacent sidestreets there are quite a few basic but cheap hotels.

Moving up Jalan TAR from its junction with Jalan Tun Perak, there's the *Coliseum Hotel* (☎ 03-292 6270) at No 100 with its famous old planters' restaurant and bar downstairs. All rooms share bathrooms and cost RM25/28 for a single/double with fan or RM35/40 with air-con. The rooms are a little run down but large and quiet and the location is very good. It's a very good deal for KL; consequently it is often full.

The *Rex Hotel* (☎ 03-298 3895) at 132 Jalan TAR is a good Chinese cheapie charging a reasonable RM30 for basic rooms with fan and common bathroom, but the *Tivoli Hotel* (☎ 03-292 4108) a few doors up is overpriced at RM40 for dingy rooms without external window.

Further north, the *International Hotel* (☎ 03-298 6452) at No 335 has singles/doubles with fan for RM22/28, but the rooms are very noisy.

The *Central Hotel* (☎ 03-442 2981), not far north of Chow Kit at 510 Jalan TAR (although the entrance is via a short laneway off Jalan Ipoh), offers exceptional value in low-budget accommodation. Simple doubles with fan cost RM25 and air-con doubles with bathroom are just RM36.

Chinatown Cheapest of the Chinese cheapies is the well-camouflaged *Wan Kow Hotel* (☎ 03-238 2909) at 16 Jalan Sultan. Very basic rooms with fan and common bathroom cost RM27.

Also very cheap is the *Colonial Hotel* (☎ 03-238 0336) at 39 Jalan Sultan, where singles/doubles go for RM23/30, or RM37 with air-con. This hotel is more geared towards travellers, but the noisy, wire-topped rooms are run down. Check for peepholes. There are many more cheap hotels in Chinatown, most of them short-term places.

More expensive is the *Starlight Hotel* (☎ 03-238 9811) at 90 Jalan Hang Kasturi, opposite the Kelang bus station. It has air-con singles/doubles with bathroom from RM55/70. The rooms are large although sparsely furnished, and some cop the noise from the bus station across the road.

Places to Stay – Mid-Range

KL has a good selection of mid-range hotels, but prices are higher than elsewhere in Malaysia. In the past few years new mid-range hotels have cropped up and more are being built, so increased competition means that discounts are often offered, especially in the more expensive hotels. Attached bathroom, air-conditioning and TV are standard facilities at these hotels.

Brickfields The *Hotel Sentral* (☎ 03-272 3748), at 128 Jalan Tun Sambanthan opposite the new train station, has small clean air-con singles/doubles with bathroom, TV and phone from RM55/78. Ask for a discount if staying several nights.

Several good medium-range places can be found around the corner on the quiet side-street of Jalan Thambapillai. The curiously named *La Posh Villa* (☎ 03-273 6677) at No 72 charges RM57.50/75 for good standard singles/doubles. Not far north at No 11 is the *New Winner Hotel* (☎ 03-273 3766), offering freshly painted air-con rooms with bathroom for RM70. The *Hotel Mexico* (☎ 03-274 0817) at 1 Jalan Thambapillai charges RM110/130 for well-appointed singles/doubles with all mod cons.

Chinatown At 11 Jalan Sultan, near Jalan Tun HS Lee, is the quiet *Hotel City Inn* (☎ 03-238 9190). The rooms are comfortable but small. It's central and reasonable value at RM69/81 a single/double. Just a few doors along is the *Hotel Lok Ann* (☎ 03-238 9544) at 113A Jalan Petaling, which has large rooms for RM70. Unfortunately, all the rooms front the noisy Jalan Sultan, though things usually quieten down by about 11 pm. A discreet refuge on this lively market lane is the *Excel Inn* (☎ 03-201 8621), 89 Jalan Petaling, which offers windowless but clean rooms with bathroom for only RM50.

You'll find many more luxurious hotels in Chinatown in this price range. The *Hotel Malaya* (☎ 03-232 7722; fax 03-230 0980), on the corner of Jalan Tun HS Lee and Jalan Hang Lekir, has good double rooms for RM140 and RM165, before discount. There's also a 24-hour restaurant and a coffee shop here.

Another good place right in the heart of Chinatown is the *Swiss Inn* (☎ 03-232 3333; fax 03-201 6699) at 62 Jalan Sultan. Comfortable, spotless rooms cost RM130 to RM160 (plus 15% tax). The hotel has a lounge bar with live music and a good coffee shop popular for its RM6.50 buffet. Diagonally opposite is the high-rise *Hotel Furama* (☎ 03-230 1777; fax 03-230 2110), where rooms start at RM98/148 including breakfast. The *Mandarin Hotel* (☎ 03-230 3000; fax 03-230 4363), 2-8 Jalan Sultan, is a similar hotel.

The *Hotel Pudu Raya* (☎ 03-232 1000; fax 03-230 5567) is on top of the Puduraya bus station. This large high-rise is a little faded but has well-appointed singles/doubles for RM103/115. The hotel has a good coffee shop and a couple of bars. It may be ideal if you are overnighting for bus or taxi connections, but the hot and chaotic bus station downstairs does not offer a welcoming face to KL for longer stays.

Opposite the Puduraya bus station at 38 Jalan Pudu is the modern *Hotel Katari* (☎ 03-201 7777), where standard rooms cost RM120 plus 15%. There's a good cafe on the ground floor.

Jalan TAR The *Shiraz Hotel* (☎ 03-291 0035) at 1 Jalan Medan Tuanku on the corner of Jalan TAR is an unremarkable place at the bottom of this range and has singles/doubles for RM70/90.

The *Kowloon Hotel* (☎ 03-293 4246) at 142 Jalan TAR is one of the older breed of modern hotels. It has an infamous reputation because of its health club on the 2nd floor, but guests are not disturbed. Singles/doubles costing from RM80/95 could do with an upgrade but are otherwise clean, large and well appointed. The newer and much plusher *Noble Hotel* (☎ 03-925 7111) directly opposite has singles/doubles for RM130/

160 plus tax, but offers frequent 'promotion' rates with hefty discounts.

Little India, just off Jalan TAR, has quite a few mid-range options. One popular place is the *Hotel Champagne* (☎ 03-298 6333) at 141 Jalan Bunus, where air-con rooms with bathroom cost RM73.50. The nearby *Hotel Chamtan* (☎ 03-293 0144), 62 Jalan Masjid India, is only marginally more expensive.

At the top end of Jalan TAR at 69 Jalan Haji Hussein is the *Hotel City Villa* (☎ 03-292 6077), a recently renovated place with rooms for RM100/110. The hotel fronts the buzzing Chow Kit market.

The *Hotel Centrepoint* (☎ 03-293 3988) at 316 Jalan TAR offers one of the best mid-range deals in KL. Rooms well insulated from traffic noise cost RM125 including taxes and breakfast.

Jalan Bukit Bintang Jalan Bukit Bintang, just to the east of the city centre at the edge of the Golden Triangle, has a large selection of mid-range hotels and the competition means that discounts are often available. It's a lively street good for shopping, eating and nightlife.

The *Malaysia Hotel* (☎ 03-242 8033; fax 03-242 8579) at 67 Jalan Bukit Bintang is looking a little down at heel but provides comfortable accommodation. It charges RM118/128 for twin/double rooms plus 15% tax. Across the street, the *Cardogan Hotel* (☎ 03-244 4856; fax 03-244 4865) at No 64 is similar but a touch better appointed. Standard rooms are excellent value for money at RM128 including 15% tax and complementary breakfast.

At No 106, the *Agora Hotel* (☎ 03-245 8133; fax 03-242 7815) is an old hotel that has undergone a major facelift. Standard singles/doubles cost RM130/150 nett. Another of the mid-range places is the *Bintang Warisan Hotel* (☎ 03-248 8111; fax 03-248 2333) at No 68, with singles/doubles from RM130/150, plus 15%.

One street west of Jalan Bukit Bintang in buildings at No 42, 74 and 82 Jalan Alor is the *Budget Inn* (☎ 03-248 4732), where air-con rooms with bathroom are good value at RM60. At the top of Jalan Alor on Cangkat Bukit Bintang is the *Imperial Hotel* (☎ 03-248 1422), with well-appointed singles/doubles from RM62/96.

Nearby at 22 Jalan Tong Shin is the *Corona Inn* (☎ 03-244 3888; fax 03-244 0715) with rooms from RM110/130 a single/twin, including tax and breakfast. Periodic discounts are available and there's a well-known seafood restaurant downstairs.

Train Station The *Heritage Hotel* (☎ 03-273 5588; fax 03-273 5566) is housed in KL's magnificent neo-Moorish train station. This recently renovated building has some fine old touches although most rooms have modern decor. The cheapest rooms cost RM130, but grander colonial style suites are available for RM305.

Places to Stay – Top End

Kuala Lumpur has a profusion of luxury hotels catering primarily to business travellers. All of these hotels have a swimming pool and a host of restaurants and bars. Many offer discounts on the regular rates quoted here, but advance bookings through travel agents will give you a better deal. All these places add 5% tax and 10% service charge to the rates.

Most luxury hotels are found in the Golden Triangle commercial district, and Jalan Sultan Ismail has the biggest collection. Towards the top end of Jalan Sultan Ismail are the *Imperial*, one of KL's most luxurious establishments, and the *Renaissance* and *Hyatt*, two new gleaming high-rise towers opposite each other at the junction with Jalan Ampang. Further down are the ever-popular *Hilton*, the huge *Shangri-La* and the *Concorde*, which is home to the fashionable Hard Rock Cafe.

The *Istana* on the corner with Jalan Raja Chulan has one of the most impressive lobbies and is favoured by visiting dignitaries. At the bottom end of Jalan Sultan Ismail, the *Parkroyal* is next to Lot 10 and handy for other shopping plazas.

Set among the mid-range hotels on Jalan Bukit Bintang, the *Federal* was the first modern luxury hotel in KL, dating from independence. It is smaller and slightly cheaper than the new hotels. At the north-eastern end of Jalan Bukit Bintang, the impressive *Regent* is well located and in the superluxury category.

The eastern end of Jalan Ampang also has a few top end hotels, and more are being built. The *Ming Court* is close to shopping possibilities, while a few hundred metres south, *Mi Casa* is an apartment hotel with suite-style rooms.

The Holiday Inn chain has two hotels in KL. The *Holiday Inn on the Park* is on Jalan Pinang in the Golden Triangle, while the older *Holiday Inn City Centre* is indeed in the city centre, on Jalan Raja Laut. Further north is the new *Legend* in The Mall.

For colonial style, the *Carcosa Seri Negara* comprises two magnificent colonial mansions in tranquil gardens at the western edge of the Lake Gardens. Carcosa was the residence of Sir Frank Swettenham, the British Resident, and Seri Negara was the official guesthouse. They now house 14 luxury suites.

Carcosa Seri Negara (☎ 03-282 1888; fax 03-282 7888) Taman Tasik Perdana. Suites from RM950 to RM1900.

Concorde Hotel (☎ 03-244 2200; fax 03-244 1628) 2 Jalan Sultan. Rooms from RM220.

Federal Hotel (☎ 03-248 9166; fax 03-248 2877) 35 Jalan Bukit Bintang. Rooms from RM260 and RM280.

Garden Hotel (☎ 03-241 3333; fax 03-241 5555) 117 Jalan Pudu. Rooms from RM300.

Hilton Hotel (☎ 03-242 2222; fax 03-244 2157) Jalan Sultan Ismail. Rooms from RM380 and RM410.

Holiday Inn City Centre (☎ 03-293 9233; fax 03-293 9634) Jalan Raja Laut. Rooms from RM340 and RM360.

Holiday Inn on the Park (☎ 03-248 1066; fax 03-248 1930) Jalan Pinang. Rooms from RM340 and RM360.

Hotel Imperial (☎ 03-468 9900; fax 03-468 9999) Jalan Sultan Ismail. Rooms from RM600.

Hotel Istana (☎ 03-241 9988; fax 03-244 0111; email istana@histana.po.my) 73 Jalan Raja Chulan. Rooms from RM430 and RM460.

Hotel Renaissance (03-262 2233; fax 03-263 1122) Jalan Sultan Ismail. Rooms from RM235.

Legend Hotel (☎ 03-442 9888; fax 03-443 0700; email tlegend@po.jarin.my) 100 Jalan Putra. Rooms from RM340 and RM360.

Mi Casa Hotel Apartments (☎ 03-261 8833; fax 03-261 1186) 386B Jalan Tun Razak. Suites from RM320 to RM800.

Ming Court Hotel (☎ 03-261 8888; fax 03-261 2393) Jalan Ampang. Rooms from RM300 and RM330.

Parkroyal Hotel (☎ 03-242 5588; fax 03-241 5524) Jalan Sultan Ismail. Rooms from RM370 and RM400.

Regent Hotel (☎ 03-241 8000; fax 03-242 1441) 160 Jalan Bukit Bintang. Rooms from RM490.

Places to Eat

Hawker Food KL is well endowed with hawker venues, dotted all around the city.

In Chinatown, *Jalan Petaling* is closed to traffic between Jalan Cheng Lock and Jalan Sultan and tables are set up in the evenings outside the Chinese restaurants on Jalan Hang Lekir between Jalan Petaling and Jalan Sultan. The stall on the corner of Jalan Sultan and Jalan Hang Lekir does steamboat. The food on skewers is laid out on the table, so you just cook what you want and pay at the end based on the number of empty skewers you have. There are also stalls in this area selling peanut pancakes, sweets, drinks and fruit.

The *Central Market* in Chinatown also has a good selection of hawker food. Check upstairs on the 2nd level and in the covered rooftop Taman Selera where there are more food stalls.

Other night markets with good food include the *Sunday Market* out at Kampung Bahru and the *Chow Kit Market*, just off Jalan TAR. Both are good places for Malay food, and night owls head to Chow Kit for the all-night *nasi lemak stalls*.

The Saturday night market on *Jalan TAR*, between Jalan Tun Perak and Jalan Dang Wangi (although not the entire length of this street section), has a large collection of food vendors and a great atmosphere. Most stalls sell takeaway snacks, but a few also set up tables for eating there. Jalan Masjid India in Little India is good for both Indian and non-Indian food in the evenings.

Jalan Alor, one street north-west of Jalan Bukit Bintang in the Golden Triangle district, has some of the best Chinese hawker stalls and coffee shops in KL, including excellent ikan bakar (grilled fish). It starts around 7 pm and closes late. The small *Sri Perak* just back from Modesto's is one of the relatively few hawker centres in the Golden Triangle where you can get Malay food.

Most shopping malls have food courts for slightly more expensive hawker food in air-con surrounds. One of the best is in The Mall shopping complex, opposite the Putra World Trade Centre on Jalan Putra. The *Medan Hang Tuah* on the top floor is a re-creation of an old city street, complete with mock shophouses, and has an excellent selection of Malay, Chinese and Indian favourites at cheap prices.

Shopping malls in the Golden Triangle also have hawker food. For something a little different, the *Chilli Food Court* in the basement of the Isetan department store in Lot 10 has a wide range of Asian food including Korean, Vietnamese and Japanese – there's a teppanyaki bar for sizzling serves straight off the hotplate.

Indian Little India is a good hunting ground for Indian food. Plenty of coffee shops can be found in the *Jalan Masjid India/Jalan TAR* area, and food stalls also specialise in cheap Indian food such as tandoori chicken, naan, dosas and chapatis. One good tip is *Govinda's Vegetarian Restaurant*, upstairs on the right at the end of Jalan Bunus 3, which has simple vegetarian buffet food from RM5 per person.

For something more upmarket, *Bangles* (☎ 03-298 3780), upstairs at 60A Jalan TAR, is an Indian restaurant with a good reputation. Further along, the *Shiraz Hotel* on the corner of Jalan TAR and Jalan Medan Tuanku has a reasonable Pakistani restaurant. Some people prefer the similar *Omar Khayyam* next door.

The *Bilal* (☎ 03-238 0804) restaurant at 33 Jalan Ampang is a KL institution for north Indian food at reasonable prices. Tandoori chicken and breads are featured.

Facing the Central Market on the Jalan Hang Kasturi pedestrian mall, *Restoran Yusoof* at No 36 is another popular place for roti, biryani and other Indian Muslim fare. The original coffee shop restaurant is complemented by a slightly more upmarket offshoot a couple of doors along.

Baba's Curry House at 31 Jalan Tun HS Lee serves clean and simple but sound vegetarian and meat dishes.

At 44 Jalan Bukit Bintang the *Restoran Ramzan* has an excellent range of murtabak, biryani and curry at cheap prices.

For south Indian food, head to the Brickfields area, a couple of kilometres south of the city centre, where there are several daun pisang (banana leaf) restaurants serving rice with vegetarian, fish, chicken and mutton curries. Two popular places are the *Sri Devi Curry House* and *Restoran Intown*. The *Sri Devi Curry House* at 144 Jalan Tun Sambanthan, opposite the new KL Sentral (Grand Central) station, specialises in spicy, tropical Chettinad cookery. The slightly more upmarket *Restoran Intown*, nearby at 31 Jalan Thambapillai, has a bar at the back.

Chinese Chinese restaurants can be found everywhere, but particularly around Chinatown and along Jalan Bukit Bintang, which is off Jalan Pudu past the Puduraya bus station.

At the entrance to the Sungei Wang Plaza on Jalan Sultan Ismail near Jalan Bukit Bintang is the cheap and popular *Super Noodle House*. The *Mayblossom* at No 1/F inside is more upmarket, but the set meals are good value for superior Cantonese fare.

A local speciality in KL is bah kut the, which is supposed to have originated in Kelang. It's pork ribs with white rice and Chinese tea and is a very popular breakfast meal. There are stalls in the Chinatown night market selling this dish for a few ringgit.

There are some outstanding Chinese restaurants along Jalan Imbi just north-east of Jalan Sultan Ismail, with banquet-style meals for groups and all the Chinese favourites from shark's fin to belacan (prawn paste). These include the *Fong Lye Restaurant* at

No 94, the Malaysian-Chinese *Restoran Sakura* (☎ 03-248 8528) at No 163 and the popular *Restoran Overseas* (☎ 03-248 7567), 86 Jalan Imbi, which dishes up mainly Cantonese food.

Malay There are Malay *warung* (small eating stalls) and *kedai kopi* (coffee shops) throughout KL, but especially along and just off Jalan TAR. Several of those in the vicinity of the Coliseum Hotel, including two inexpensive *Insaf* restaurants at Nos 116 and 158 Jalan TAR, are excellent and cheap; look for nasi lemak in the early mornings.

The *Restoran Wilayah Baru* at 29 Lebuh Pudu in Chinatown, has excellent cheap Malay food. One of the house specialities is rojak singapura, a Malay salad served with a spicy dip-sauce.

One of Kuala Lumpur's classic old eating dens, the *Kapitan's Club* (☎ 03-201 0242) is a semi-restored shophouse at 35 Jalan Ampang specialising in Peranakan (Nyonya) cuisine. Curry Kapitan is a speciality, as are the savoury Peranakan pastries, or try the sambal (RM8) with a spicy mango salad (RM7.50).

In the BB Plaza on Jalan Bukit Bintang there are a couple of Malay restaurants – the *Rasa Utara* (☎ 03-248 8369), which specialises in food from Kedah state, and the *Nyonya Wok* (☎ 03-421 4203), which has Nyonya specialities and moderately high prices. Another restaurant serving Nyonya cuisine is the classy *Dondang Sayang* (☎ 03-261 8888) in the Life Centre on Jalan Sultan Ismail.

The *Titiwangsa Seafood Village* (☎ 03-422 8400), set in the Lake Titiwangsa Gardens in northern KL, serves daily-changing menus in amazing huts built over the water. It's one of the best 'splurge' restaurants for Malay food. The rather exclusive *Seri Angkasa* (☎ 03-208 5055), a revolving restaurant high up in the KL Tower, offers more exhilarating scenery as you dine. The *Eden Village Restaurant* (☎ 03-241 4027), a huge, elaborate Malay-style building at 260 Jalan Raja Chulan, serves western and Malay seafood.

Thai Thai food possibilities range from tom yam soup at food centres to some expensive Thai restaurants in the big hotels.

A cheaper restaurant is the *Thai Kitchen* in the Central Market on Jalan Hang Kasturi. Decor amounts to air-conditioning and not much else, but the food is tasty and reasonably priced.

The *Tamnak Thai* (☎ 03-248 8191), 74 Jalan Bukit Bintang, has a bit more atmosphere and an extensive menu of classic Thai dishes. Prices are reasonable, with most mains around RM12. An excellent meal for two without drinks should cost under RM50.

The more expensive *Barn Thai* (03-244 6699) at 370B Jalan Tun Razak is as popular for the live music as for the Thai food. The very stylish *Mekong* (☎ 03-262 5522) in the Crown Princess Intercontinental Hotel on Jalan Tun Razak serves Vietnamese as well as Thai dishes from RM16.

Japanese As usual, Japanese food is expensive, but *Sushi King* at 63 Jalan Sultan Ismail has reasonably priced self-serve sushi available from the conveyor belt bar. *Toriman* (☎ 03-248 9203), just around the corner on Jalan Bukit Bintang, is atmospheric yet affordable – you can eat for a little over RM20 per person. The *Edo Kirin* in the Regent Hotel on Jalan Bukit Bintang has excellent Japanese food, but at suitably breathtaking prices.

International KL has a surprising variety of western restaurants. Not to be missed is the restaurant in the *Coliseum Hotel* on Jalan TAR, which has excellent steaks. When they say it's served on a sizzle plate they really mean it; the waiters zip up behind you and whip a bib around your neck to protect your clothes from the sizzle. For a little over RM20 you can get a great steak and salad, and there's also roast chicken and grilled fillet of sole with chips. The place is quite a colonial experience and has scarcely changed over the years.

American fast-food outlets abound, including, *KFC* and *A&W* takeaways at the bottom of Jalan Sultan. *McDonald's* seems to be everywhere, and some of the more convenient outlets are opposite the Central Market, on Jalan Bukit Bintang and near Masjid Jamek (Star LRT) station.

In the Central Market is the *Decanter Steakhouse* serving fillet steaks from RM28, and for quiche eaters there's the *Be My Friend Deli* on the first floor of the Central Market annexe, with a terrace overlooking the river.

Le Coq d'Or (☎ 03-261 9732), a restaurant in a fine turn-of-the-century mansion at 121 Jalan Ampang, is not quite as expensive as the elegant surroundings might indicate. Western food is served in the dark, cavernous interior, which has faded touches of the raj. Expect to pay around RM80 for two at dinner, or the set lunch with a main of fish, lamb chops etc is excellent value for RM13 plus 15%. It's open daily from noon to 2.30 pm and 7 to 10 pm.

Scalini's (☎ 03-245 3211) at No 19 Jalan Sultan Ismail has authentic Italian food. Another good Italian connection is the *Ristorante Bologna* (☎ 03-241 9988) in the Istana Hotel.

American grills are easy enough to find. The *Berjaya Roadhouse Grill* (☎ 03-244 2318) at 42 Jalan Sultan Ismail has great porterhouse steaks for around RM33.

TGIF (Thank God It's Friday) in the Life Centre on Jalan Sultan Ismail is a very popular bistro, especially on Fridays. The *Bierkeller* (☎ 03-201 3313) is in the Menara Haw Par (opposite the Hard Rock Cafe). It's full of expat central Europeans savouring their bratwurst and sauerkraut (RM14.50) while they sip on imported brews (from RM10) and peruse the selection of recent German newspapers and magazines.

Bakeries & Cafes Two inexpensive sit-down bakeries in Chinatown, the *Meidi-ya*, at 121 Jalan Sultan, and the *King Coffee Shop*, under the Backpackers Travellers Inn, serve excellent pastries. Other recommended cafes where hot croissants and real coffee are available include *Four Leaves*, in the Sogo shopping complex, *La Palma* in the basement of the Lot 10 shopping complex, and the *Delifrance* branches in The Weld on Jalan Raja Chulan and the Sungei Wang Plaza and Lot 10.

Self-Catering For self-catering, you can find supermarkets in Chinatown at the S&M Shopping Arcade on Jalan Cheng Lock and at the UDA Ocean Plaza on the corner of Jalan Sultan and Jalan Tun HS Lee. On Jalan TAR, Sogo department store has a well-stocked supermarket. Many of the shopping malls and department stores in the Golden Triangle have supermarkets, including one in the basement of the Isetan department store in Lot 10 on Jalan Sultan Ismail.

Entertainment

Bars, Discos & Live Music A recent government 'morality' campaign against late-night revellers has forced most venues to close at 1 am (previously 3 am). Most of KL's nightlife is found in the Golden Triangle. Jalan Sultan Ismail is the centre of the universe for KL's middle class, while bored youth who can't afford the prices at the fashionable bars and clubs hang out in front of McDonald's on Friday and Saturday nights.

The *Hard Rock Cafe* in the Concorde Hotel on Jalan Sultan Ismail is still the hottest spot in town. It has the usual food-and-rock memorabilia blend. Bands play from 10.30 pm, interspersed with disco music for dancing. Since the government crackdown on late-night raging, the HRC is open only until 1 am every night. There is a cover charge of RM23, but this includes your first drink.

A short stroll behind the Hard Rock Cafe on Lorong Perak is *Brannigan's*, a pub with a long-held reputation as a pick-up spot, which means that it's packed with men; there are pool tables upstairs. On the corner of Jalan Perak and Jalan P Ramlee is *Modesto's*, a bar popular among trendy KL-ites where better than average Italian food is served. At 1 Jalan Pinang is *Rio* (☎ 03-241 0882). Upstairs there's an upmarket pseudo-Brazilian restaurant but the pub downstairs is OK.

Wall $t (☎ 03-466 6666) is a clubby sort of yuppie's pub with live music (often jazz) from 10 pm every night except Sunday. It's at 22 Jalan P Ramlee on the ground floor of the Menara TA-One, another Golden Triangle high-rise block dwarfed by the nearby Petronas Towers.

Around the corner from the Shangri-La in the basement of the Menara Pan Global on Lorong P Ramlee is *Energy* (☎ 03-230 0880), a lively disco. Next door, and under the same management, is *The Venue* (☎ 03-201 1594), where foreign bands play. RM25 gets you in to both venues.

The trendy *Malibu Cafe* on Sultan Ismail near the Hotel Istana is open 24 hours. It serves some interesting east-meets-west culinary combinations like spaghetti Siamese and beef ginger fettucini, but the free live bands in the basement every night (except Sunday) is what really draws the crowds.

A restaurant-come-pub, the *Blues Cafe* (☎ 03-244 4517), is at ground level in the Lot 10 shopping centre. It features anything from tropical jazz to reggae and Latin rock every night (except Monday) with no cover charge. The bar is small and the volume is cranked up high but the open-air terrace facing the street offers a respite and serves grills.

Nearby in the Parkroyal Hotel is *Delaney's* (☎ 03-241 5195), an Irish-style pub with live bands most nights. Go during evening happy hours (6 to 9 pm) when your pints of draught Guinness will only cost half the usual RM22.

The Jump (☎ 03-245 0046), in the Wisma Inai at 241 Jalan Tun Razak (next to the Indonesian Embassy) is a well-patronised American style bar-restaurant with Tex-Mex food and a late-night disco. Along the way at No 370B, *Barn Thai* (☎ 03-244 6699) is a Thai restaurant and long-running jazz/rock joint with a good atmosphere – bands play from around 10 pm to 1 am on weekends.

Liquid is a club for the gay and lesbian community in the Central Market Annexe. It's open five nights a week: Wednesday, Thursday and Sunday from 5 pm to 1 am and Friday and Saturday until 2 am.

Chinatown is quiet in the evenings, but the Central Market has a few more laid-back places for a drink. Facing the river on the western side of the market, the *Riverbank* has the occasional jazz band or guitar strummer. You can also sit outside for a break from the smoky interior. A few doors away, the *Bull's Head* is an English-style pub. Despite the decor, it's Eagles on the jukebox and Anchor on tap, but the beer is cheap, conversation is audible and you can sit outside and snack on curries and breads from a tandoori hawker.

Cultural Shows The *Malaysian Tourist Information Complex* (MATIC; ☎ 03-264 3929) on Jalan Ampang has traditional dance performances at 3.30 pm on Tuesday, Thursday, Saturday and Sunday, and other special events, usually in the evening. MATIC produces monthly brochures listing events in the city, or you can ring for details.

In the underground Plaza Putra below Merdeka Square is the large *Restoran Sri Putra* (☎ 03-294 3411) which has a buffet and cultural show every evening for RM28.

The *Central Market* (☎ 03-274 6542) has a regular program of events ranging from Indian dancing and *pencak silat* martial arts performances to Malay comedy nights. Pick up a copy of their monthly calendar from the tourist offices.

Hotels and restaurants also have dinner cultural shows. Regular venues include the *Seri Melayu* (☎ 03-245 1833), 1 Jalan Conlay, near the Kompleks Budaya Kraf (crafts complex), where traditional Malay wedding dances are staged. The *Titiwangsa Seafood Village* also has dance performances every evening except Monday.

Cinemas There are plenty of cinemas in the inner city area. Check the *New Straits Times* or other dailies for listings. Hollywood features are now widely shown (in English with Malay/Chinese subtitles), but kungfu extravaganzas, Indonesian dramas and Indian musicals also draw in the crowds.

Theatre The *Actors' Studio Theatre* (☎ 03-294 5400) in the underground Plaza Putra complex below Merdeka Square has performances (especially comedy) in English most nights. Tickets cost around RM20.

Shopping

KL promotes itself as a shopping haven, and certainly the city has plenty of shopping malls to cater to affluent Malaysians. Clothes and shoes are inexpensive, and though not as cheap as the neighbouring countries of Thailand and Indonesia, the range is better. Electronics are reasonably priced, but Singapore has a much wider range at lower prices. KL is very competitively priced for camera gear and film.

KL is the best place to buy handicrafts in Malaysia, but higher wages mean that Malaysia produces fewer handicrafts these days. Traditional Malay pottery and kites can be found, but almost everything else is imported from Indonesia, Thailand or elsewhere. However, attractive jewellery, wood carvings, lacquerware, kris knives etc are available.

Shops & Markets Housed in a cavernous Art Deco building (formerly a wet market) in Chinatown, the Central Market complex is a fun place to shop and offers a large range of souvenirs, antiques, art, clothes and more. Some of the antique shops are interesting for old bric-a-brac, and Wan Tradisi at shop M51 has a good collection of Malaysian kites. Stalls sell cheap jewellery, while the art shops can be very expensive. Bargain hard.

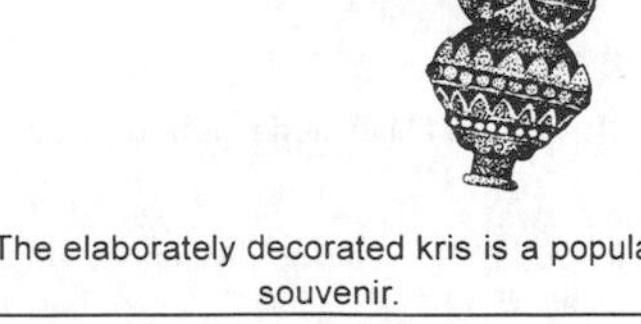

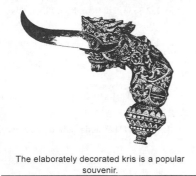

The elaborately decorated kris is a popular souvenir.

Jalan Petaling in the heart of Chinatown is one of the most colourful shopping streets in KL, particularly at night. This roadside market has some craftwork, cheap clothes and copy watches. Hard bargaining is definitely in order.

The Kompleks Budaya Kraf (☎ 03-262 7533), on Jalan Conlay (just off Jalan Raja Chulan), is a large new handicrafts complex with an impressive variety of locally produced batiks, carved wooden artefacts, pewter utensils, woven baskets, rattan furniture, glassware, glazed ceramics and more. It's open daily from 9 am to 6 pm.

The stalls along the street at the Chow Kit Market sell cheap clothes and leather goods. Shops in the lanes around the market, particularly Jalan Haji Hussin, specialise in made-to-order *songkoks*, the traditional Malay male headdress. Jalan Masjid India is the place to shop for saris, Indian silks and other textiles. Jalan Melayu has Indonesian religious goods and also local batik and other art.

Pewterware, made from high-quality Malaysian tin, is an important local craft. Royal Selangor Pewter is the main manufacturer and its pewter is available in department stores and shops around town. Its factory is at 4 Jalan Usahawan, 8km north-east of central KL. Free 15-minute tours of the factory are conducted from Monday to Saturday between 8.30 am and 4.45 pm, and 9 am and 4 pm on Sunday.

To get there take bus W12 from Jalan Ampang or ride the (Putra) LRT to Setapak Jaya station then walk 1km south-west along Jalan 2/27A.

Shopping Malls KL's many shopping malls are the places to go to buy clothes, shoes, electronics, cameras and everyday goods. The Golden Triangle has the biggest selection. Shopping malls are generally open from 10 am to 10 pm, but smaller shops in the malls start closing earlier, at around 9 pm.

Sungei Wang Plaza on Jalan Sultan Ismail and the BB Plaza on Jalan Bukit Bintang adjoin to form one of the biggest and best complexes. The Metrojaya and Parks on

Grand department stores combine with hundreds of small shops to sell just about everything, but these malls are particularly good for clothes, shoes, books and camera gear. Two other nearby shopping malls are Lot 10 and Star Hill, both on Jalan Bukit Bintang. These new, upmarket centres sell designer label goods, and Star Hill also features children's wear, toy shops and a playground on the top floor.

Imbi Plaza, around the corner on Jalan Imbi, is a small complex specialising in computers. It's a good place to pick up cheap (but possibly pirated) copies of software and CD-ROM drives.

The large Weld shopping centre, and a number of other shops in the same complex, is on Jalan Raja Chulan. On Jalan Ampang, Ampang Park includes the Hankyu department store and some jewellery shops. It is linked by a pedestrian bridge to Central Square on Jalan Tun Razak, which has clothes shops and interesting interior design and furniture stores.

On Jalan TAR, Globe Silk is a KL institution. This long-running, smaller department store has cosmetics, textiles and clothes at some of the cheapest prices in town. In contrast, Sogo, further north, is a huge, new department store for designer clothes, household goods and a few electronics.

For genuine designer-label clothes, shoes and perfume, The Mall shopping centre on Jalan Putra opposite the Pan Pacific Hotel is a good place to look. The Yaohan department store here has a reasonable selection of electronics in the basement – it's a good place to go to get an idea of prices. Most of the shopping malls have small electronics shops, where you'll probably have to bargain to get a reasonable deal.

Chinatown also has a few busy shopping centres, including the cramped S&M Shopping Arcade on Jalan Chen Lock and the more upmarket Kota Raya nearby for clothes, shoes and a reasonable selection of music tapes and CDs.

KL's newest shopping complex is the Suria KLCC, at the foot of the Petronas Towers, which opened in May 1998.

PENINSULAR MALAYSIA

Getting There & Away

Kuala Lumpur is Malaysia's principal international arrival gateway and a central crossroads for bus, train or taxi travel.

Air The colossal new Kuala Lumpur international airport (KLIA), 43km south of the city centre at Sepang, was opened to commercial air traffic in June 1998. It has state-of-the-art facilities, with two terminals linked by a 1.3km rail shuttle system. KLIA, which replaced the old airport at Subang, now takes all scheduled international flights to/from Kuala Lumpur. The old airport still handles domestic Air Asia, Berjaya Air, Pelangi Air and Transmile Air flights and Air Malaysia is considering moving some domestic services back to Subang.

In spite of the RM9 billion expense of building KLIA, airport departure taxes have – for the moment – been held at RM40 for international flights, RM20 to Singapore and Brunei and RM5 on domestic flights.

International airlines fly to/from Kuala Lumpur and Australia, Singapore, Indonesia, Thailand, India, the Philippines, Hong Kong and various destinations in Europe.

Some of the airlines with offices in KL include:

Aeroflot
(☎ 03-261 3231) Wisma Tong Ah, 1 Jalan Perak

Air India
(☎ 03-242 0166) Angkasa Raya building, Jalan Ampang

Air Lanka
(☎ 03-232 3633) 3rd floor, MUI Plaza, Jalan P Ramlee

Ansett
(☎ 03-201 9211) UBN Tower, Jalan P Ramlee

British Airways
(☎ 03-232 5797) Plaza See Hoy Chan, Jalan Raja Chulan

Cathay Pacific Airways
(☎ 03-238 3377) UBN Tower, 10 Jalan P Ramlee

China Airlines
(☎ 03-242 7344) Amoda building, 22 Jalan Imbi

Garuda Airways
(☎ 03-262 2811) 3rd floor, Menara Lion, Jalan Ampang

Japan Airlines
(☎ 03-261 1722) 20th floor, Menara Lion, Jalan Ampang
Lufthansa
(☎ 03-261 4666) 3rd floor, Pernas International Building, Jalan Sultan Ismail
Malaysia Airlines
(☎ 03-261 0555; 24-hour reservations ☎ 03-746 3000) Malaysia Airlines building, Jalan Sultan Ismail
Pakistan International Airlines
(☎ 03-242 5444) Angkasa Raya building, Jalan Ampang
Pelangi Air
(☎ 03-262 4448) 18th floor, Menara TR, 161B Jalan Ampang
Qantas
(☎ 03-238 9133) UBN Tower, 10 Jalan P Ramlee
Royal Brunei Airlines
(☎ 03-230 7166) UBN Tower, 10 Jalan P Ramlee
Royal Jordanian
(☎ 03-248 7500) MUI Plaza, Jalan P Ramlee
Singapore Airlines
(☎ 03-292 3122) Wisma SIA, 2 Jalan Dang Wangi
Thai Airways International
(☎ 03-201 1900) Wisma Gold Hill, 67 Jalan Raja Chulan

On the domestic network, KL is the hub of Malaysia Airlines services and there are nonstop flights to:

Destination	*Flights daily*	*Fare (RM)*
Alor Setar	5	113*
Ipoh	3	66
Johor Bahru	8	93
Kota Bharu	8	104*
Kota Kinabalu	6	437*
Kuala Terengganu	4	104
Kuantan	7	74
Kuching	6	262*
Labuan	2	437
Langkawi	12	135
Miri	2	422
Penang	16	104*
Singapore	16	222

* Cheaper night fares and advance purchase fares are applicable on some flights on these routes.

Malaysia Airlines and Singapore Airlines also operate a joint shuttle service between KL and Singapore. Tickets cost RM200 (including airport tax) and are sold on a stand-by basis. Simply turn up at the shuttle counter at the airport, take a number and wait for the next available flight. So many flights operate that you shouldn't have to wait more than an hour.

Pelangi Air has nonstop flights to Pulau Tioman (twice daily, RM141), Ipoh (four weekly, RM66), Johor Bahru (twice weekly, RM91) and Kerteh (twice daily, RM125).

The local discount carrier Transmile Air (☎ 03-243 2022) flies to Labuan (twice weekly RM300), Kota Kinabalu (three times weekly, RM300) and Kuching (weekdays, RM190).

Bus KL's main bus station is Puduraya, just east of Chinatown. From here buses go all over Peninsular Malaysia, including the east coast, and to Singapore and Thailand. The Pekeliling and the Putra bus stations to the north of the city handle a greater number of services to the east coast, but most visitors to KL find Puduraya more convenient. The other bus station is Kelang in Chinatown, which has buses to Shah Alam and Kelang, now virtually suburbs of KL.

The only long-distance destinations that Puduraya doesn't handle are Kuala Lipis and Jerantut, the jumping off point for Taman Negara National Park. These buses leave only from the Pekeliling bus station.

A direct shuttle minibus (RM25 one way) runs daily at 8 am from the Hotel Istana to the Kuala Tembeling jetty for the trip to Taman Negara. Most guesthouses and some hotels will also reserve bus tickets for you to Kuala Tembeling and elsewhere. Otherwise, bookings can be made directly at the bus company booths at the bus stations.

Puduraya Bus Station This hot, confusing, clamorous bus and taxi station is centrally located on Jalan Pudu. Inside there are dozens of bus company ticket windows, so it's just a matter of checking them to find one with a departure time that suits you. Right at the main entrance is a Tourist Police Office and, opposite, there's also an Information

Counter (Kaunter Pertanyaan; ☎ 03-230 0145). It pays to ask at one of these first, so the staff can direct you to the appropriate window for buying a ticket. Buses leave from the various numbered platforms in the basement, and note that you'll have to look for the name of the bus company rather than your destination.

There are departures to most places during the day, and at night to main towns. On the main runs, services are so numerous that you can sometimes just turn up and get a seat on the next bus. However, tickets should preferably be booked at least the day before, and a few days before during the peak holiday periods.

Transnasional (☎ 03-238 4670) has the largest office inside the terminal and has buses to most major destinations. Outside the station on Jalan Pudu there are at least another dozen companies that handle the buses to Thailand.

There's a left-luggage office in the Puduraya bus station. It is open daily from 8 am to 10 pm and the charge is RM1.50 per item per day.

Typical fares and journey times from KL are provided in the table. There are limited daily services to the Cameron Highlands and east coast destinations, however departures to the other destinations listed are more frequent.

Destination	*Fare (RM)*	*Duration (hrs)*
Alor Setar	25	9
Butterworth	18	7
Cameron Highlands	11	5
Ipoh	10	4
Johor Bahru	16.50	6
Kota Bharu	25	10
Kuala Terengganu	25	7
Kuantan	15	5
Lumut	12.50	4
Melaka	8	3½
Mersing	18	6½
Penang	21	7½
Singapore	23	7
Taiping	15	6

Puduraya itself can be reached by taking the Star LRT to Plaza Rakyat station.

Kelang Bus Station Buses to Kelang and Port Kelang (No 793) and Shah Alam (No 337, 338) leave from the Kelang bus station at the end of Jalan Hang Kasturi in Chinatown.

Putra Bus Station Though Puduraya handles buses to the east coast, Putra bus station (☎ 03-442 9530), opposite the Putra World Trade Centre, also has a number of the large coach services. Most buses leave in the morning around 8 to 10 am and then in the evening from 8 to 10 pm. Buses go to Kota Bharu (RM21), Kuantan and Kuala Terengganu.

Putra bus station is easily reached by KTM Komuter trains to Putra station.

Pekeliling Bus Station Buses to Jerantut (for Taman Negara) and Kuala Lipis operate only from Pekeliling bus station (☎ 03-442 1256) in the north of the city, just off Jalan Tun Razak. Transnasional has five daily departures to Kuala Lipis (RM8, four hours).

Perwira Ekspres and Nusa Ekspres each have several daily buses via Temperloh to Jerantut (RM9, 3½ hours). Alternatively, between 8.30 am and 7 pm Perkasa Ekspres has departures roughly every 1½ hours to Temerloh (RM6), from where regular buses run to Jerantut.

From Pekeliling buses also go every 30 minutes to Raub (RM5.50), and every hour to Kuantan from 8 am to 6.30 pm. Buses run every half hour to the Genting Highlands (RM2.60).

Pekeliling bus station can be reached by taking the Star LRT to Tun Razak station, or (when completed in late 1999) the monorail (PRT) to its northern terminus on Jalan Tun Razak.

Train Kuala Lumpur is also the hub of the KTM national railway system. Long-distance trains still depart from KL's historic old train station, 1km north of the new KL Sentral (Grand Central) station. The KTM information office (☎ 03-274 7435, open daily from 6.30 am to 10 pm) in the main hall can advise on schedules and check seat availability. There are daily departures for Butterworth, Wakaf Baharu (for Kota Bharu), Johor Bahru and Singapore. On most express services seats can be booked up to 30 days in advance. See the Malaysia Getting Around chapter for full fare and schedule information. City Trains also link KL with Shah Alam and Kelang in Selangor, and Seremban in Negeri Sembilan (see the Getting Around section below).

There is a KTM ticket booth (☎ 03-245 6902) on the concourse level of the Sungei Wang Plaza on Jalan Sultan Ismail, at the Parkson Grand department store entrance. It is open daily from 10 am to 6 pm.

Taxi While the buses depart from downstairs in the Puduraya bus station, the long-distance taxis are upstairs on the 1st floor. If you want to share a taxi, it is best to turn up early in the morning. Chances are reasonable of finding other passengers waiting to share on the main runs to Johor Bahru, Melaka, Ipoh and Penang. But it's always a matter of luck and sometimes there's a long wait to get a full complement of four passengers. Otherwise, you will have to charter a whole taxi, which is four times the per person rate. Taxis often do not make the journey much faster than buses.

Per person fares include Melaka (RM17), Johor Bahru (RM35), Singapore (RM40), Ipoh (RM25), Lumut (RM35), Cameron High lands (RM35), Penang (RM60), Genting Highlands (RM10), Fraser's Hill (RM20), Jerantut (RM18), Kuala Lipis (RM15), Kuantan (RM35), Kuala Terengganu (RM40) and Kota Bharu (RM45). These prices are for non-air-con – add about RM3 to RM5 per person for air-con, depending on the distance. Prices should include toll charges, but some taxi drivers, especially those on the Johor Bahru run, insist on charging extra.

Car Driving around the city has little benefit, but KL is the best place to hire a car for touring the peninsula. Rates start at around RM170 a day for a recent model small car. The best deals are for rentals of longer periods – as low as RM2250 for one month, including insurance and unlimited kilometres. As well as the major companies, dozens of small hire companies are listed in the Yellow Pages.

All the major companies have offices at the airport as well as the following city offices:

Avis
(☎ 03-241 7144) 40 Jalan Sultan Ismail
Budget
(☎ 03-262 4119) Wisma MCA, 163 Jalan Ampang
Hertz
(☎ 03-248 6433) 214A Kompleks Antarabangsa, Jalan Sultan Ismail
Mayflower
(☎ 03-622 1888) 18 Jalan Segambut Pusat, GPO Box 10179
National
(☎ 03-248 0522) G47, Wisma HLA, Jalan Sultan Ismail
Pacific
(☎ 03-262 4119) Wisma MCA, Jalan Ampang

Getting Around

In just a few years Kuala Lumpur's public transport system has gone from slow, chaotic and crowded to speedy, comfortable and uncomplicated. Efforts to ease the city's chronic traffic congestion have seen massive investment in new infrastructure, including the construction of new expressways and a sophisticated rail-based urban transport system. When completed in 1999, KL Sentral (Grand Central) station, in the Brickfields area 1km south of the historic old train station, will serve as the main hub for the network of KTM Komuter, LRT, Monorail (PRT) and ERL systems (see the entries below). Combined ticketing to facilitate passenger interchange between the various rail systems is planned.

To/From KLIA Airport Intrakota bus No 19 (90 sen) operates between downtown KL and the Hendian Duta bus station (across from the Jalan Duta Hockey Stadium on the outskirts of the city). From there, buses operate to/from KLIA. Luxury coaches (RM25; one hour 15 minutes) and semi-luxury coaches (RM 16; one hour 15 minutes) do the trip.

There may also be local buses which do the same route for RM7.70 and take one hour 45 minutes, but these seem to be irregular and may not be running in the future.

Trains operate between KL station and Nilai station (RM4.50; one hour) from where you can take a bus to/from the airport (RM2.50, 30 minutes). There are plans for a train to connect KLIA and the new KL Sentral (Grand Central) rail station being built at Brickfields, but this is years away.

Taxis from KLIA operate on a fixed-fare coupon system. Purchase a coupon from a counter at the arrival hall and use it to pay the driver. Going to the airport, take any city taxi. Standard taxis cost RM55 to the airport from KL and RM65 from the airport to KL. Luxury taxis cost RM66 and RM88, to and from the airport.

To/From Subang Airport The old airport at Subang is 20km west of the city centre. Terminal 3 still handles the domestic flights from here.

By bus, take No 47 from the Jalan Sultan Mohammed bus stand opposite the Kelang bus station. Sri Jaya is taking over the Intrakota buses, but the number will remain the same. The fare is RM1.60/1.90 for regular/air-con services. The trip takes 45 minutes, though it's a good idea to allow more time since traffic can be heavy.

Special taxis from the airport operate on a coupon system and the fare is RM22 to Chinatown and RM26 to the Golden Triangle (more from midnight to 6 am). Purchase a coupon from a booth to the right of the terminal as you leave the arrivals hall and pay the driver with it. The price does not include the freeway toll of 70 sen. Going to the airport, take any city taxi and negotiate a price of RM25 to RM30, although if you can get the driver to use the meter, the fare should be RM22 to RM26 plus a RM3 service charge.

Bus KL's chaotic pink minibuses are rapidly being phased out as most of the private buses are incorporated into two main companies, Intrakota (☎ 03-707 7771) and Cityliner (☎ 03-782 7060). Together Intrakota's (grey with blue stripes) and Cityliner's (white with red stripes) modern air-con buses now run along most key routes throughout the city, although the already baffling bus system has been further confused by the renumbering of some routes. The maximum fare is 90 sen or RM1; try to have correct change ready when you board, especially during rush hours.

Since KL's inexpensive taxis and the new LRT and monorail (PRT) systems generally offer such a good alternative, there's little point in trying to come to grips with the bus system unless you're going to be in KL for some time. You'll only really need the bus for trips to outlying areas, such as the Batu Caves or the zoo.

There are many bus terminals around the city, including the huge Puduraya bus station on Jalan Pudu, the Kelang bus station on Jalan Sultan Mohammed, the Jalan Sultan Mohammed bus stand opposite the Kelang bus station, and another stand by the Central Market.

City Trains The KTM Komuter service (☎ 03-273 8000) runs along the existing long-distance railway lines, stopping at city stations. The main north-south line runs from Sentul, just north of the city centre, to Port Kelang via Shah Alam and Kelang. The other line runs from Rawang, 20km northwest of the city centre, to Seremban, 66km south-east of KL. All KTM Komuter trains pass through the historic old train station as well as the new KL Sentral (Grand Central) station being built at Brickfields.

The service is primarily designed for those who commute to KL from the vast, outlying urban sprawl. It is of limited use to visitors since it does not connect central KL with any of the city's attractions. Trains run every hour (every half hour during peak periods) between 6 am and 11.30 pm. Ticket dispensing machines are installed at stations – select your destination and the price is displayed. To Kelang costs RM3.10, to Seremban RM5.70. A RM5 'go anywhere' day ticket allows unlimited travel on KTM Komuter trains after 9 am.

Light Rail (LRT) KL's pride and joy is the new Light Rail Transit (LRT), a fast, frequent and inexpensive 'metro'. The mostly elevated LRT network integrates two separate systems run by private consortiums, the Star LRT (System I) and Putra LRT (System II). An electronic control system checks tickets as you enter and exit the network via turnstiles. The minimum fare is 75 sen.

The Star LRT runs south from Sentul Timur in northern KL via Masjid Jamek and Pudu, after which it divides into two separate lines going east to Ampang and south to Sukan Negara (site of the 1998 Commonwealth Games village).

The newer Putra LRT runs south-east from Gombak in north-eastern KL to intersect with the Star LRT at Benteng station (near Masjid Jamek) then continues south via the new KL Sentral (Grand Central) station and the University of Malaya to Subang Jaya on the city's western outskirts.

Monorail (PRT) KL's public transport infrastructure will really come into its own once a new 16km elevated monorail, officially called the People-Mover Rapid Transit (PRT), is completed in the second half of 1999. The PRT will run south from Jalan Tun Razak near Pekeliling bus station via the Golden Triangle to terminate at Kampung Pasir on the city's south-western outskirts. It will connect with the Putra LRT at Sultan Ismail station and with the Star LRT at Hang Tuah station. In addition, a 1km monorail branch line in Brickfields will link the new KL Sentral (Grand Central) station with Tun Sambanthan PRT station.

Taxi KL has plenty of taxis and fares start at RM2 for the first 1km, with an additional 10 sen for each 200m. From midnight to 6 am there's a surcharge of 50% on the metered fare, and extra passengers (more than two) are charged 20 sen each. RM1 is charged for luggage placed in the boot.

At these rates taxis are very cheap – perhaps too cheap, as the drivers claim. With KL's traffic problems, many drivers don't want to sit in a traffic snarl for just a couple of ringgit or are unwilling to go to out-of-the-way destinations from where it is hard to get a fare back. In these cases they are sometimes unwilling to use the meter. Get out and hail another, or if you have to bargain, short fares around town will cost around RM5 and it should cost no more than RM10 to go right across the inner city area. The government is talking about reviewing the fare structure, so if the rates increase taxis may be more willing to use meters.

Taxis at bus stations don't use the meter and prey on new arrivals to the city. They will ask at least double the going rate. It is better to go to the street and hail a taxi from there. At the train station, taxis operate on a coupon system from outside platform 4 (the river side of the station). It costs RM5 to Chinatown, RM7 to the Jalan TAR/Chow Kit area, and RM8 to the Golden Triangle.

When you do finally get a taxi, it may seem to head in the opposite direction to what you'd expect, simply because in KL the quickest route between two points is not necessarily the most direct one, or the system of one-way streets makes direct travel impossible.

Around Kuala Lumpur

A number of attractions lie just outside the city boundaries in Selangor state, though they are within the urban bounds of Greater KL. The Batu Caves are the premier attraction, and the zoo also makes a pleasant escape from the city. Many of the attractions further afield in Selangor can also be visited as day trips from KL (see the following Selangor chapter).

BATU CAVES

The huge Batu Caves are the best-known attraction near KL; they're just 13km north of the capital, a short distance off the Ipoh road. The caves are in a towering limestone formation and were little known until about 100 years ago. Later a small Hindu shrine was built in the major cave, and it became a pilgrimage centre during the annual Thaipusam festival. Each year in February, thousands of pilgrims flock to the caves to engage in or watch the spectacularly masochistic feats of Thaipusam devotees (see the separate Thaipusam entry in the Places of Worship special section in the Facts for the Visitor chapter).

The main cave, a vast open space known as the Temple Cave, is reached by a straight flight of 272 steps. Beyond the stairs is the main temple. There are a number of other caves in the same formation, including a small cave at the base of the outcrop with elaborately painted figures of the various Hindu gods. Lord Subramaniam, an aspect of Shiva, takes centre stage as the dancing Shiva, and other deities such as the fearsome Durga, Shiva's female half, are on display.

Getting There & Away

The caves can be reached in about 30 minutes by taking Intrakota bus No 11D from the Central Market annexe (90 sen) or the Cityliner bus No 69 from Jalan Pudu outside the Restoran Wilaya Baru in Chinatown (RM1). During the Thaipusam festival special trains carrying devotees and onlookers also run to the caves.

NATIONAL ZOO & AQUARIUM

About 13km east of KL on the road to Ulu Kelang is the 62 hectare site of the National Zoo & Aquarium. Laid out around a central lake, the zoo collection features the wildlife found in Malaysia. There are elephant rides and other amusements for children. A shuttle bus runs around the spacious, landscaped grounds. Though a good zoo by Asian standards, some of the animal enclosures are still cramped despite all the open space.

The zoo is open daily from 9 am to 5 pm and admission is RM4/6 children/adults plus RM2/15 with your camera/video camera. To get there take a No 20 bus from Central Market, a No 170 bus from Jalan Ampang, or a No 17 bus from Jalan Raja Laut in the Chow Kit area.

FORESTRY RESEARCH INSTITUTE

The Forestry Research Institute of Malaysia (FRIM; ☎ 03-634 2633) maintains this jungle park at Sungei Buloh, 15km northwest of the city centre. This area of jungle is the centre of FRIM studies into forest regeneration. The museum outlines the work done by FRIM and explains the rainforest habitat and its renewal. Various arboretums display the flora of Malaysia's rainforests.

The main interest is the jungle trails, the closest to KL. The park is popular for picnics on weekends but also has a variety of walks, from short strolls to the more strenuous walk up to the waterfall. There is also a canopy walkway that allows closer inspection of the rainforest canopy.

To reach the park, take a Rawang-bound KTM Komuter train and get off at Sungei Buloh at the northern edge of the park.

TEMPLER PARK

Beside the Ipoh road, 22km north of KL past the Batu Caves, Templer Park was established during the colonial period by the British high commissioner Sir Gerald Templer. The 500 hectare park is a tract of primary jungle, preserved within easy reach of the city. There are a number of marked jungle paths, swimming lagoons and several waterfalls within the park boundaries.

Just north of the park is a 350m-high limestone formation known as Bukit Takun, and nearby is the smaller Anak Takun, which has many caves.

Templer Park is a one hour ride on bus No 66 from the Puduraya bus station.

Selangor

Selangor state surrounds the Federal Territory of Kuala Lumpur city. Its focus is the busy Kelang Valley, which runs from KL down to the coast at Port Kelang, the nation's busiest port. The valley is almost an urban extension of KL and contains much of Malaysia's industry. Shah Alam has modern glories, such as its huge mosque, and you can also visit the nearby agricultural park. Further towards the coast, Kelang has a few reminders of the old sultanate, but it is not until you reach Kuala Selangor, further north on the coast, that you finally leave the traffic and urban sprawl behind.

Many of the state's attractions – such as the Batu Caves, National Zoo and Templer Park on the northern outskirts of KL – are best visited on day trips from KL and are included in the KL chapter. However, further north from KL are a number of other places of interest. The main attractions are the hill stations of Genting Highlands and Fraser's Hill, which both straddle the state border with Pahang.

HIGHLIGHTS

- **Kuala Selangor** – spectacular fireflies and Taman Alam nature park
- **Genting Highlands** – ultramodern hill station favoured by KL's well-to-do where you can 'chill out' in the cooler climes
- **Fraser's Hill** – old-fashioned hill station which has retained its colonial charm

PENINSULAR MALAYSIA

History

In the 15th century, Selangor was under the control of Tun Perak, the great *bendahara* (chief minister) of Melaka. Once Melaka fell to the Portuguese, control of Selangor was hotly contested, partly because of its rich tin reserves. The Minangkabau settlers, who had started to migrate to the area from Sumatra only about 100 years earlier, were themselves displaced by Buginese immigrants from Celebes (present-day Sulawesi). The Dutch, meanwhile, made some fairly ineffective moves to establish control over the tin trade by building forts at Kuala Linggi and Kuala Selangor.

By the middle of the 18th century, the Buginese had established the current sultanate, based at Kuala Selangor, and their sphere of influence spread as far as western Sumatra and the Riau Archipelago. The 19th century saw an influx of Chinese merchants and miners, drawn by the rapidly growing and lucrative tin trade, and many attained powerful positions – in 1857 two merchants went into partnership with two Selangor chiefs to open tin mines at Ampang, out of which grew the city of Kuala Lumpur.

The success of the tin trade and the growing wealth of the Chinese communities led to conflicts among the Selangor chiefs and between the miners. The outcome was a prolonged civil war, initially only between the chiefs, but before long the Chinese miners were also dragged into the conflict. The miners fought not only against the chiefs but also among themselves, as they belonged to different secret societies and allied themselves with different chiefs. In 1872 KL, which until then had been controlled by the 'Kapitan China' Yap Ah Loy (Chinese leader appointed by the miners), was captured and razed to the ground, although it was retaken in 1873, which brought about an end to the civil war.

By this time the British were keen to impose some order on the chaos, especially as tin production had dropped to a fraction of what it had been, and this at a time when industrialisation in Europe meant high demand – and prices – for raw materials. In 1874 a British Resident was installed at Kelang, and for the next 25 years the state prospered, largely on the back of another boom in tin prices. Kuala Lumpur was resurrected from the wreckage of the 1872 attack and by the turn of the century was a well-ordered and prosperous place.

In 1896 Selangor was one of four states which formed the Federated Malay States,

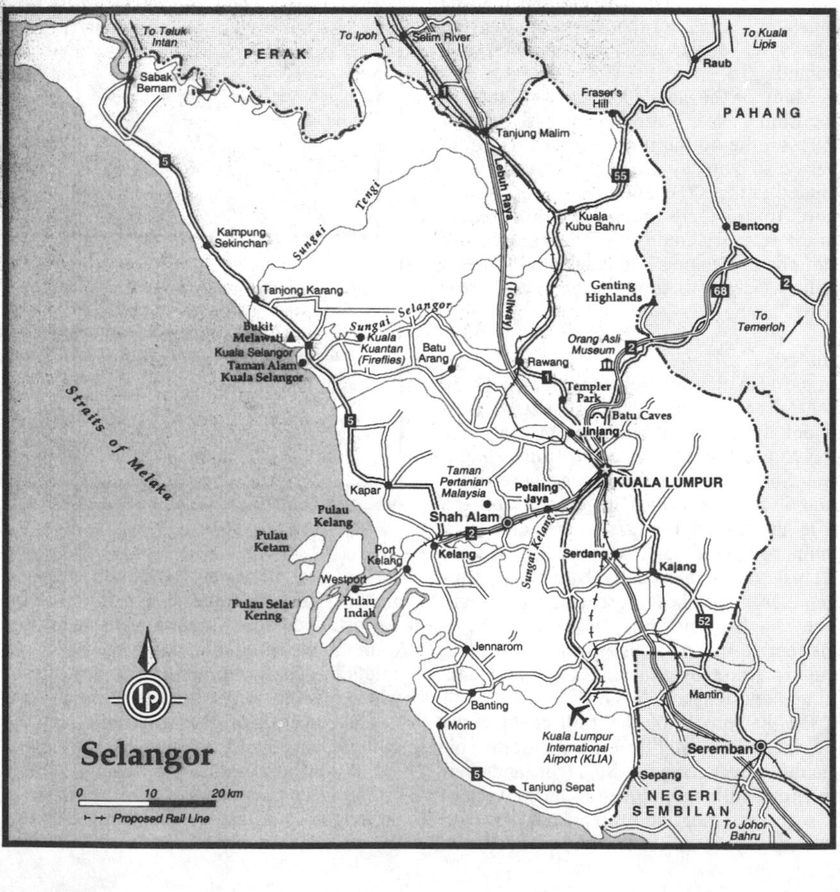

all centrally administered from Kuala Lumpur. This in turn led to the Federation of Malaya in 1948 and finally the Federation of Malaysia in 1963. In 1974 Kuala Lumpur city was ceded by the sultan of Selangor and became the Federal Territory.

KELANG VALLEY

Heading south-west of KL along the Kelang Highway, you pass under the Kota Darul Ehsan ceremonial archway marking the boundary between KL and Selangor. Apart from the archway, little else distinguishes the expanse of housing estates and industrial parks. Just over the boundary is Petaling Jaya, for all intents and purposes a suburb of KL. Petaling Jaya blends into Shah Alam, the state capital, which blends into Kelang, the old royal capital.

Petaling Jaya

Petaling Jaya is a modern suburb of KL, just 11km south-west of the city centre. Originally developed as a dormitory town to the capital, PJ has grown so successfully and rapidly that it has become a major industrial centre in its own right. Many engineering and high-tech industries, such as Motorola, have huge industrial installations here. PJ, including the surrounding districts, has a population of 500,000, and its neat, planned housing estates are favourites of the middle classes. This satellite town has grown so quickly that it now has its own satellite, Subang Jaya.

The **University of Malaya**, near the strikingly unusual Menara Telekom building in Bandaraya, is en route to Petaling Jaya. On the university grounds is the **Museum of Asian Arts**, which houses a good collection of ceramics.

PJ is well supplied with shopping malls, gourmet restaurants and good nightlife, popular with well-to-do KL residents. **Sunway Lagoon** is a huge theme park with large waterslides and the world's biggest surf-wave pool. Admission is RM15 for adults, RM10 for children (closed Tuesday).

In Petaling Jaya sections are numbered (eg SS2); SS means 'sub-section'.

Places to Stay The cheapest place is the *South Pacific Hotel* (☎ 03-756 9922) at 7 Jalan 52/16, which is off Jalan Yong Shook Lin. It has rooms from RM80. In PJ's southern industrial zone is the *Grade Hotel* (☎ 03-795 0000), 23 Jalan Petaling Utama 11, with rooms from RM98.

Next up the scale is *Shah's Village Hotel* (☎ 03-756 9322), 3 Lorong Sultan, Peti Surat 115, where rooms start at RM170. The *Hotel Armada* (☎ 03-754 6888), Lorong Utara C, Section 52, offers rooms from RM290.

The *Sunway Lagoon Resort Hotel* (☎ 03-582 8000; fax 03-582 8001) at Jalan 17, right at the watery theme park, has singles/doubles from RM275/295. The main business hotel, the *Petaling Jaya Hilton* (☎ 03-755 9122), 2 Jalan Barat, charges RM370/400 for singles/doubles.

Places to Eat Petaling Jaya's numerous restaurants are particularly good for East Asian fare, including Baba-Nyonya, Vietnamese and Thai.

At the *Restoran Sri Saigon* (☎ 03-775 3681), 53 Jalan SS2/30, you can eat out Vietnamese style for around RM50 for two. The *Suriyo Restaurant* (☎ 03-737 5491), at 13 Jalan PJS 11/28B near the Sunway Lagoon Resort, has excellent Thai food.

Out of Africa (☎ 03-755 3432), 1 Jalan Sultan, not far from the Hilton, is a very popular and moderately priced South African restaurant, serving everything from venison pie to Malay 'Cape' curries.

Kelana Seafood Centre (☎ 03-703 8118) on Jalan Perbandaran in the SS7 district is a PJ institution. In a lakeside setting west of PJ centre, it has a la carte main courses averaging RM30.

Entertainment PJ was once the centre of KL's nightlife, but with so much happening in the Golden Triangle these days it caters mainly to local residents and business travellers. The *Merchant*, an English-style pub in the Hotel Armada, has Malaysia's longest bar counter (33.5m) and live bands. The *DV8*, next door to the Out of Africa restaurant, is a popular disco.

Getting There & Away Buses to PJ run regularly from the Kelang bus station in KL for about RM1.80. A taxi from KL will cost around RM15.

Shah Alam

The new capital of Selangor state is just an hour's drive west of KL. Two decades ago it was just a rubber and palm oil plantation, but in the late 1970s a massive building programme was undertaken and the city now boasts a well-developed infrastructure, some enormous public buildings and a rapidly growing population. Shah Alam is home to many industrial complexes, including the Proton Saga plant.

Like many planned cities, Shah Alam has very wide streets, an artificial lake and great distances between parts of the city, making it very difficult to get around. It is, however, quite an attractive city, with the centrepiece being the lake and the **Sultan Salahuddin Abdul Aziz Shah Mosque**. This huge, gleaming mosque accommodates up to 24,000 worshippers and is the largest in Malaysia.

Millions of ringgit have been lavished on the **State Museum**, a short walk from the mosque around the lake. It's a very impressive structure, both inside and out, and the range of displays and the depth of labelling are creditable. After a couple of hours here you'll know everything there is to know about Selangor and the sultan. Entry is free.

Shah Alam is also the venue for the 500cc Malaysian Motorcycle Grand Prix, held in April every year.

Places to Stay & Eat The cheapest option is *7A Lodge* (☎ 03-559 9225), 7A Jalan Sukun 4/7, 1km west of the mosque, with dorm beds for RM25. The *Palma Inn* (☎ 03-542 8080), at Jalan Nelayan/15 Section 19, has well-appointed rooms from RM120.

The luxurious new *Concorde Hotel* (☎ 03-552 2200), 3 Jalan Tengku Ampuan Zabedah 9/C, offers rooms from RM320. It has a pool, a cafe and the *Raku*, and a restaurant and art gallery. The *Holiday Inn* (☎ 03-550 3696) is in the Plaza Perangsang tower near the state mosque. Rooms cost RM360/380 including breakfast and taxes.

On the ground floor of the central PKNS Plaza shopping mall are a number of fast-food places, including a *KFC* outlet. On the nearby lake is the *In Park Restaurant* (☎ 03-550 5995), an expensive 'floating' restaurant with mainly East Asian fare.

Getting There & Away From KL, take a Komuter train to Shah Alam KTM station or a Kelang bus from the Kelang bus station.

Taman Pertanian Malaysia

This 'agroforestry theme park' at Bukit Cahaya Seri Alam is a popular family escape for KL residents on weekends. It's a curious blend of landscaped gardens and forest areas, designed to emphasise ecological values along with the need for agriculture and to keep the kids amused. The park has attractive lakes, gardens and cropping fields, arboretums, animal enclosures and an aviary as well as forest walks and a canopy walkway.

The park is open from 9 am to 5 pm daily, except Monday. It is 4km north-west of the state mosque, reached by bus.

Kelang

Kelang (often spelt Klang) is the former capital of Selangor and the old royal capital where the British installed their first Resident in Selangor in 1874. The main attractions are in the old city, south of the bus station and across the river near the train station.

The **Gedung Raja Abdullah** is an old warehouse several hundred metres west (to the right) from the train station near the bridge. This is one of the oldest Malay buildings in the country, and was once used by the sultan to store tin from the rich mines in the area. It now houses a museum with displays on local history and the ore that was so important to Selangor and Malaysia.

The **Sultan Sulaiman Mosque**, 1km south of the train station along Jalan Raya Timur, blends Art Deco with Middle Eastern influences. Behind the mosque is the **Istana Alam Shah**, the main palace of the sultan before Shah Alam became the capital.

The only recommended budget hotel in Kelang is the *Kian Ping Hotel* (☎ 03-342 7498), at 2 Jalan Pos Baru near the bus station, which has simple, clean rooms for RM25 or RM35 with air-con. You can get a well spiced curry at the *Restoran Sri Nachial* on Jalan Dato Hamzah (off Jalan Stesen) on the southern side of town.

Getting There & Away Kelang's bus station is on the northern side of the river opposite the Orchard Square shopping complex. Buses go to all major destinations on the west coast, including Melaka, Johor Bahru, Ipoh and Kuala Lumpur. Air-con buses run to Kuala Selangor every 20 minutes (RM2). The taxi station is behind the bus station, one street east. Express buses from the Kelang bus station in KL to Port Kelang also stop in Kelang.

To visit Kelang on a day trip from KL, the KTM Komuter trains are more convenient as the Kelang train station is on the southern side of the river closer to the museum and mosque.

Port Kelang

Some 30km south-west of KL, 8km past Kelang, is Port Kelang (Pelabuhan Klang in Malay). Until the establishment of a major new harbour at Westport 12km away on Pulau Indah, Port Kelang was the main seaport for KL. Though not a particularly attractive place, Port Kelang is renowned for its excellent seafood, particularly chilli crabs (about RM35 per plate).

The 30 minute ferry trip to **Pulau Ketam** is a popular excursion on weekends with KL residents. The island has a stilt fishing village and Chinese seafood restaurants. Public ferries leave every couple of hours from the wharf at the end of Persiaran Raja Muda Musa.

Morib, south of Port Kelang and 64km from KL, is a popular weekend escape and beach resort, although the beach itself is nothing special.

One of the few places to stay in Port Kelang is the *Embassy Hotel* (☎ 03-368 6901), 2 Jalan Kem, off Persiaran Raja Muda Musa about 600m back from the port. Air-con doubles with bathroom cost RM52.

Getting There & Away Buses from KL's Kelang bus station run to Port Kelang, and Komuter trains also run to/from the capital. Ferries to Tanjung Balai in Sumatra leave Port Kelang daily at 11 am (RM100/190 one-way/return), but as Tanjung Balai is not a visa-free entry point you must have an Indonesian visa before boarding.

KUALA SELANGOR

This small town is on the coast where the Sungai (River) Selangor meets the sea. Though well off the beaten tourist track, it has a few notable points of interest for those venturing along this back route to Perak state and Pulau Pangkor.

Bukit Melawati

The flat coastal plain along this stretch of the coast is broken by Bukit Melawati, the hill overlooking the town. It provided an ideal site for monitoring shipping in the Straits of Melaka, first by the sultans of Selangor, then by the Dutch and British. The hill once contained two forts, though the only remains of note are some sections of wall and restored cannons under the lighthouse on top of the hill.

It is a pleasant walk through the landscaped parklands and forest to the top, with views across the mangrove coastline. Further down the hill is the **Makam Di-Raja Kuala Selangor**, the mausoleum of the local rajas, and some fine colonial bungalows, now the preserve of government officials.

The road up Bukit Melawati starts just one block behind the shops facing the bus station. The road does a clockwise loop of the hill and you can walk up and around in about an hour.

Taman Alam Kuala Selangor

This 290 hectare nature park is on the estuary of the Sungai Selangor, 2km from town below Bukit Melawati. The turn-off to the park is a few hundred metres from the bus station, at the archway over the road to

Bukit Melawati. This park of mangroves and some secondary forest is noted for its birdlife, especially waders in the mangroves. Around 150 species have been sighted, including 100 local species, the rest migratory. The definite 26 sightings of waders include the rare spoonbilled sandpiper. The park is also home to many leaf monkeys, and you may be lucky enough to spot otters, nocturnal leopard cats and civets.

To aid in birdwatching, two watchtowers and hides have been constructed, and two boardwalks lead through the mangroves to the sea. Nature trails, which take from 25 minutes to 2½ hours to complete, radiate from the visitors' centre. The main trails are dirt roads but the side trails are more interesting. Don't expect great jungle walks – the birdlife is the main attraction here. The visitors' centre at the park is open daily and rents binoculars. The park also has good accommodation. Entry costs RM2.

Fireflies

Of the 130-odd species of firefly, those of South-East Asia are the most spectacular, noted for their displays of synchronised flashing. The folded-wing fireflies *(Pteroptyx tener)* gather in particular berembang trees along the banks of the Sungai Selangor. Some of these mangrove type trees are ablaze with their flashes, while others fail to attract any. When large numbers form (sometimes in their thousands) their flashing becomes synchronised at about three flashes per second.

This natural light show can be seen at Kuala Kuantan, 10km east of Kuala Selangor. Malay-style wooden boats oar out on the river to the show trees and their dazzling display. Boats take four people at RM10 each for the 45 minute trip, and go on demand throughout the evening from around 8 until 10.30 pm. Bookings can be made on ☎ 03-889 2403. The trips are not recommended on full moon and rainy nights, when the fireflies are not at their luminous best. Take mosquito repellent.

Take the turn-off to Batang Berjuntai, 2km south of Kuala Selangor. A taxi from Kuala Selangor costs RM30 for the return trip and it will wait for you.

This is a very popular excursion for tour groups and KL residents. Various tours run from KL but these tend to cater for large groups. Some of the operators are Asean Overland (☎ 03-292 5622), Reliance Sightseeing (☎ 03-248 0111) and Ecstasy Travel (☎ 03-441 1069).

Places to Stay

Kuala Selangor is just one long block of shops next to the bus station. Directly opposite the bus station is *Hotel Kuala Selangor* (☎ 03-889 2709), 90B Jalan Stesen, with spotless rooms for RM25 with fan, RM38 with air-con and RM43 with air-con and bathroom. One street back, the *Melawati Ria Hotel* (☎ 03-889 1268), 15 Jalan Raja Jalil, is an older hotel with air-con rooms for RM40 and RM50.

The most attractive option, but a long walk from town, is right in the nature park. *Taman Alam Kuala Selangor* (☎ 03-889 2294) has small, simple A-frames for RM25, or larger four-person chalets with bathrooms for RM45. A kitchen is available for guests but cooking utensils must be hired.

Another good option is the *Bukit Melawati Rest House* (☎ 03-889 1357) on the hill. A double costs RM40, but it's best to book ahead. Meals are available.

The *De Palma Inn* (☎ 03-889 7070), about a kilometre from the town centre at the eastern foot of Bukit Melawati, has comfortable new chalets from RM120.

Getting There & Away

Buses (RM4.90, two hours) run roughly hourly between Kuala Selangor and KL's Puduraya bus and taxi station. Air-con buses also run every 20 minutes between Kuala Selangor and Kelang (RM2, air-con). Heading north from Kuala Selangor to Perak state, first take one of the old rattlers to Tanjong Karang (80 sen), where services connect to Sabak Bernam and Teluk Intan.

A chartered taxi from Kuala Selangor bus station costs: KL (RM40), Kelang (RM118) and Teluk Intan (RM45).

RICHARD I'ANSON

CLEM LINDENMAYER

RICHARD I'ANSON

Kuala Lumpur
Top Left: The busy central city of Kuala Lumpur.
Top Right: The twin spires of Petronas Towers, the highest buildings in the world.
Bottom: The drum festival fills Kuala Lumpur's streets with pounding rhythm.

ROSS BARNETT

RICHARD I'ANSON

Cameron Highlands, Malaysia
Top: View over the Sungai Palas Tea Estate on the slopes of Gunung Brinchang, Perak.
Bottom: Tea bushes cover the hills at Boh Tea Estate in the Cameron Highlands, Perak.

TANJONG KARANG

This uninspiring town on the highway 18km north of Kuala Selangor is at the heart of the state's premier rice-growing district. The only real attraction in the area is the chance to stay in a *kampung* in the rice fields at nearby Sungai Sireh.

For a good opportunity to experience kampung life, *Sungai Sireh Agrotourism/ Homestay* (☎ 03-879 8004, ☎ 010-272 3956) places visitors in family homes. Accommodation is in a simple but comfortable kampung house, and you share facilities with the family. The cost is around RM50 per day, including breakfast and lunch. The office for this programme is 5km north of the highway from Tanjong Karang, and then 8km to the end of Sungai Sireh Rd, directly opposite the large water purification plant. It is best to book, and the company can arrange transport from Tanjong Karang.

KAJANG

This town, about 20km south of KL on the KL-Seremban route, is said to have the best satay in Malaysia. If your meal time is approaching, it's worth stopping.

ORANG ASLI MUSEUM

This very informative museum is 24km north of Kuala Lumpur on the way to the Genting Highlands. Though small, it houses a large number of exhibits and gives some good insights into the life and culture of Peninsular Malaysia's 80,000 indigenous inhabitants. It's well worth a look.

It is open Saturday to Thursday from 9.30 am to 5.30 pm (free). The museum is on the Old Pahang Rd, 1km past the now-defunct Mimaland amusement park.

GENTING HIGHLANDS

While the style of other Malaysian hill stations is Old English, it's modern skyscrapers in the Genting Highlands; where the entertainment at the older stations is jungle walks, here it's nightclubs and a casino; instead of waterfalls and mountain views, Genting has an artificial lake and a cable car. If that does not sound to your taste, then leave it out, for the Genting Highlands is a thoroughly modern hill station designed to cater for the affluent citizens of KL, just 50km to the south.

The first stage of the Genting Highlands was opened in the early 70s and concrete high-rise blocks dominate the landscape. These include Malaysia's only casino, with all the usual western games of chance and eastern favourites like *keno* and *tai sai*.

Then there's the four hectare artificial lake with boating facilities, which is encircled by a miniature railway for children. Naturally there's a golf course, 700m below near the lower cable car station. Forgetting nothing, the resort also has a bowling alley and a cave temple, the Chin Swee Temple, on the road up to the resort. Of course, Genting has cooler weather like any other hill station; the main part of the resort is at a little over 1700m altitude.

Places to Stay

There are four upmarket hotels on the Highlands proper, and all are run by the Genting Highlands Resort (GHT, ☎ 03-211 1118; fax 03-211 1888). Rates vary enormously between low, shoulder, peak and super-peak seasons. The *Theme Park Hotel* has the least expensive rooms, ranging from RM88/178 in low/super-peak, while the *Resort Hotel* charges RM98/268 low/super-peak for somewhat better rooms. The *Genting Hotel* and the *Highlands Hotel* have every facility imaginable, from saunas and swimming pool to tennis courts. Rooms cost from RM138/ 298 low/super-peak.

The non-GHT *Awana Golf & Country Club* (☎ 03-211 3015), lower down at the Km 12 marker, has doubles for RM85/140 low/high season, and offers activities such as swimming, tennis, squash, golf and horse riding. The huge *Hotel Gohtong Jaya*, near the lower station of the Genting Skyway cable car, is nearing completion.

Getting There & Away

Buses from KL's Pekeliling bus station go to the Genting Highlands every 30 minutes (RM2.60, 1½ hours). From Puduraya bus and taxi station Bus Express runs less frequent air-con services to the Highlands (RM4.30). From the Genting Highlands bus station the 3.4km-long Genting Skyway cable car hums up past imaginative sculptures in the rainforest to the main resort 700 vertical metres above (RM3, 15 minutes).

A share taxi from Puduraya costs RM10, but count on having to hire a whole taxi for RM40.

FRASER'S HILL

Fraser's Hill takes its name from Louis James Fraser, a reclusive ore trader who lived here around the turn of the century. It's said he ran a remote and illegal gambling and opium den, but he was long gone when the area's potential as a hill station was recognised in 1910. The station, set at a cool 1524m altitude, is quiet and relatively undeveloped.

Of all the hill stations, Fraser's retains the most colonial charm. Despite some relatively modest hotel and infrastructure development it remains too laid back to attract the types who flock to the Genting or Cameron Highlands as there is relatively little to do besides relax in the cool and enjoy a stroll and the views. Though a family destination, it also has a reputation as a resort for illicit liaisons, but old-fashioned service prevails at Fraser's and discretion is assured.

Information

The tiny village clustered at the western end of the golf course forms the centre of Fraser's Hill. Here you'll find the post office and, under the Puncak Inn, the Fraser's Hill Development Corporation (FHDC) information office (☎ 09-362 2201). It's open daily from 8 am to 9 pm, but closes for lunch. Maps and brochures are available, and the office can book all FHDC accommodation in Fraser's Hill. Not far uphill is the FHDC headquarters, open Monday to

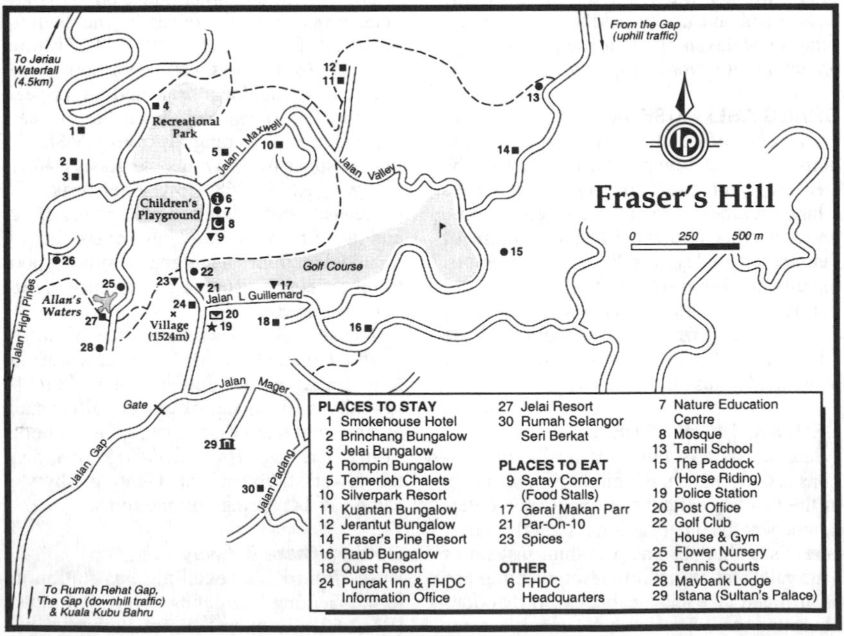

Friday from 8 am to 4.15 pm, and to 12.45 pm on Saturday.

The Nature Education Centre (☎ 09-362 2517) near the FHDC headquarters has a small museum on local flora and fauna. The knowledgeable staff can answer queries and organise guided jungle walks.

A small branch of the Maybank is at the Quest Resort, open Monday to Friday from 9.30 am to 4 pm, and Saturday from 9.30 to 11 am. Outside these hours, change money at the Quest itself. Mountain bikes can be hired for RM4 per hour through the FHDC information office or golf club and there's a Home Direct Phone near the post office for international calls.

Like the Genting Highlands, Fraser's Hill is right on the Selangor-Pahang state border. Though usually claimed by Pahang, almost all visitors come through Selangor, and the state border actually cuts right through the town.

Things to See & Do

As in the Cameron Highlands, there are many beautiful gardens around the town, and also many wild flowers. The dense jungle and towering trees are impressive, though walks are mostly limited to strolls around the paved but quiet roads. The only real trail of note is the 2½ hour walk from the children's playground to near the small Tamil school. The walk is strenuous and the trail is muddy in parts.

Fraser's Hill is a birdwatcher's delight, with 265 species sighted, included 100 resident birds. Native species include the rare cutia, mountain peacock-pheasant, rusty-naped pitta and Malaysian whistling-thrush.

At the picturesque nine hole golf course, where banded leaf monkeys wander, a game costs RM30/40 on weekdays/weekends. You can also play a spot of tennis (RM6/8 per hour on weekdays/weekends), go horse riding at the Paddock, or hire a paddle boat at Allan's Waters, a small lake next to the flower nursery.

About 5km from the information office is the Jeriau Waterfall with a swimming pool fed from the falls. It's easily reached by road.

Places to Stay

Most of the accommodation is run by the FHDC, a government-contracted *bumiputra* organisation, and there are no real budget places to stay. Rates at FHDC lodgings are slightly lower during the week, while the 'peak season' is on weekends and public holidays, when bookings are strongly recommended. All rooms have bathrooms with hot showers, but they tend to be musty due to the cool, damp climate at Fraser's. A tax of 10% is added to the rates.

Places to Stay – Mid-Range

The *Puncak Inn* (☎ 09-362 2201) is above the little shopping centre right where the bus stops. Although it's convenient and looks inviting from the outside, rooms are ordinary and expensive at RM65 to RM95, or RM58.50 to RM85.50 off-peak.

The *Temerloh Chalets*, 1km north on Jalan L Maxwell, are modern-styled octagonal chalets divided into two rooms costing RM50 each. The rooms are run-down but large with fine views. There's a simple restaurant here.

The FHDC also has bungalows – well worth the extra money. They are stone buildings with pleasant gardens, good views, large lounge areas and plenty of colonial grace. The dozens of other private bungalows scattered around Fraser's Hill are not for public use.

The FHDC bungalows are a fair way from the bus stop, but once you get your gear there it is a pleasant walk around the roads. All the bungalows cost RM89.10 (RM99 peak) for large rooms, and food is provided if there is enough demand. The bungalows are the *Jerantut*, *Kuantan*, *Rompin*, *Raub* and *Brinchang*. The Raub is the most central, while the Kuantan and Jerantut have pleasant hillside aspects but are almost 3km from the centre. The Rompin and Brinchang are only 1km or so from the centre. The Brinchang, in a secluded position with inspiring views across the mountains, is the pick of all the bungalows.

Another option is the *Rumah Selangor Seri Berkat*, the Selangor government resthouse on Jalan Pudang, across the state line on the south side of Fraser's Hill. Book through the District Office (☎ 03-804 1026) in Kuala Kubu Bahru. This two storey colonial edifice built in 1926 has large rooms with high ceilings for RM60. Even larger VIP rooms (with views over the football field towards the sultan's palace) cost RM80.

The Selangor government also runs the wonderful old-fashioned *Rumah Rehat Gap* (☎ 09-362 2227) at the Gap turn-off on the main road 8km below Fraser's Hill. This is a fine place if you get stuck. Spacious rooms cost RM60 with bathroom and they're big enough for three people with room to spare.

Places to Stay – Top End

Most of the top end hotels will give discounts of around 30% on weekdays and in the low season.

Overlooking the golf course is the *Quest Resort* (☎ 09-362 2300), a modern hotel with well-appointed rooms from RM180. The *Jelai Resort* (☎ 09-362 2600), on the south side of Allan's Waters, has spacious if slightly damp doubles overlooking the lake for RM130/180 off-peak/peak.

The *Fraser's Pine Resort* (☎ 09-362 2122) has bright, better one/two/three bedroom apartments for RM286/374/440 at peak holiday periods. Similar in style but even larger is the *Silverpark Resort* (☎ 09-362 2888), which has 140 self-contained apartments costing from RM200 for a smaller studio up to RM360 for a three bed unit. Both resorts offer major discounts in the low season and for stays of a week or more.

Fraser's classiest lodging is the *Smokehouse Hotel* (☎ 09-362 2226), a mock-Tudor building in the same style as the Smokehouse in the Cameron Highlands. With its exposed beams, log fires, wooden stained armchairs and the lingering smell of roasts, it has all the charm of a country squire. Standard doubles cost RM265/320 in low/high season, but more luxurious rooms are available.

Other privately-owned bungalows and condominiums are sometimes available for rent, but advance bookings are necessary. The FHDC can help.

Places to Eat

The small shopping centre at the Puncak Inn is the model of a multiethnic community with Malay, Chinese, and Indian restaurants all represented. At one end is the Chinese *Hill View* with simple meals and snacks, while at the other is the Malay *Arzed*. Between the two is the *Restoran Puncak*, serving roti canai for 60 sen any time of day.

Just uphill, *Spices* serves western food like fish and chips for RM11.50 and sirloin steaks for RM17.50. Across the road, the *Par-On-10* at the golf club has more varied western/Malaysian dishes at moderate prices. The restaurant terrace overlooking the golf course is a great spot for breakfast. In the evening they turn up the music and it becomes a disco/karaoke lounge.

Below the Quest Resort is the *Gerai Makan Parr*, a simple yet good and cheap Malay restaurant. The *Satay Corner*, by the mosque near the FHDC headquarters, has basic hawker fare.

The resorts and hotels all have their own restaurants. A Devonshire tea in an English garden at the *Smokehouse Hotel* is a pleasant if somewhat expensive experience at RM14.50.

Getting There & Away

Fraser's Hill is 103km north of KL and 240km from Kuantan on the east coast. The usual access is via Kuala Kubu Bahru (KKB), 62km north of KL, just off the KL-Butterworth road and the KL-Butterworth railway line.

From platform 20 or 21 of KL's Puduraya bus station, take a No 66 or 100 Tanjung Malim bus to KKB (RM3.50, 1¾ hours). These buses run roughly every 20 minutes (via the old Ipoh road, not the freeway), but to ensure connections you must take one no later than either 6.30 or 10.30 am. Otherwise, a taxi from KKB to Fraser's Hill is RM45. A direct taxi all the way from KL's Puduraya bus station costs around RM70.

From KKB buses depart for Fraser's Hill (RM2.30, 1½ hours) at 8.30 am and 12.30 pm, returning from Fraser's to KKB shortly after 10 am and 2 pm. If you plan to head east afterwards, the bus can drop you off on the main road to meet the Kuala Lipis bus at 3.30 pm. The Kuala Lipis bus travels via Raub where you can make connections to Jerantut and Kuantan.

The buses to Fraser's Hill run via the Gap, a mountain pass on the KKB-Raub road. From the Gap, two narrow one-way roads wind their way up via separate routes. The new 11km-long road is for *uphill* traffic only, and runs via the Tamil school and Fraser's Pine Resort. The old 8km-long road, which descends directly from Fraser's Hill village centre, is now used exclusively for *downhill* traffic. Before the completion of the new road, an alternating one-way system applied, with fixed times for uphill and downhill traffic.

Fraser's Hill is open to private vehicles, but drivers are warned that there's no fuel station in Fraser's; the nearest places with fuel are Raub and KKB.

Perak

Perak is one of the largest states on the peninsula and has a population of just over two million. For many years the state was famous for its rich tin deposits; in fact, it gained its name from the ore (*perak* means 'silver' in Malay). Perak also gave birth to another mainstay of the Malaysian economy – the rubber industry.

For the visitor, the main attractions of Perak are the island of Pangkor, which lies just off the southern coast; the capital city of Ipoh with its cave temples; and the historic town of Kuala Kangsar. Perak is also the access point for the Cameron Highlands, Malaysia's premier hill station and one of the country's most popular tourist destinations. Taiping and nearby Maxwell Hill also make an interesting detour.

HIGHLIGHTS

- **Cameron Highlands** – cool green rolling heights with tea plantations and strawberry fields surrounded by lush rainforest
- **Pulau Pangkor** – a small resort island with lovely beaches and rainforest walks
- **Taiping** – a gracious provincial city of fine old colonial buildings

History

The current sultanate of Perak dates back to the early 16th century, when the eldest son of the last sultan of Melaka, Sultan Muzaffar, established the dynasty on the banks of the Sungai (River) Perak. Being so rich in tin, the state was regularly threatened. Dutch efforts in the 17th century to monopolise the tin trade came to little, and remains of their forts can still be seen on Pulau Pangkor and at the mouth of the Sungai Perak.

The Bugis in the south and the Siamese in the north made concerted attempts to dominate Perak in the 18th century and, but for British assistance in the 1820s, the state would have come under Siam's influence.

The British remained reluctant to intervene in the peninsula's affairs, but growing investment from the Straits Settlements saw the government petitioned to assume control. The rich tin mines of Perak attracted British interests, especially when the canning industry boomed in Europe in the 1860s. The mines also attracted a great influx of Chinese miners, who formed rival clan groups which battled to control the mines, with Malay chiefs taking sides. British interests in the tin trade were threatened, and so in 1874 they decided to step in, marking the first real colonial incursion on the peninsula.

The Perak sultanate was in disarray, and fighting among the successors to the throne gave the British their opportunity. In 1874 the governor, Sir Andrew Clarke, convened a meeting at Pulau Pangkor in which Sultan Abdullah was installed on the throne in preference to Raja Ismail, the other main contender. The Pangkor Treaty that ensued

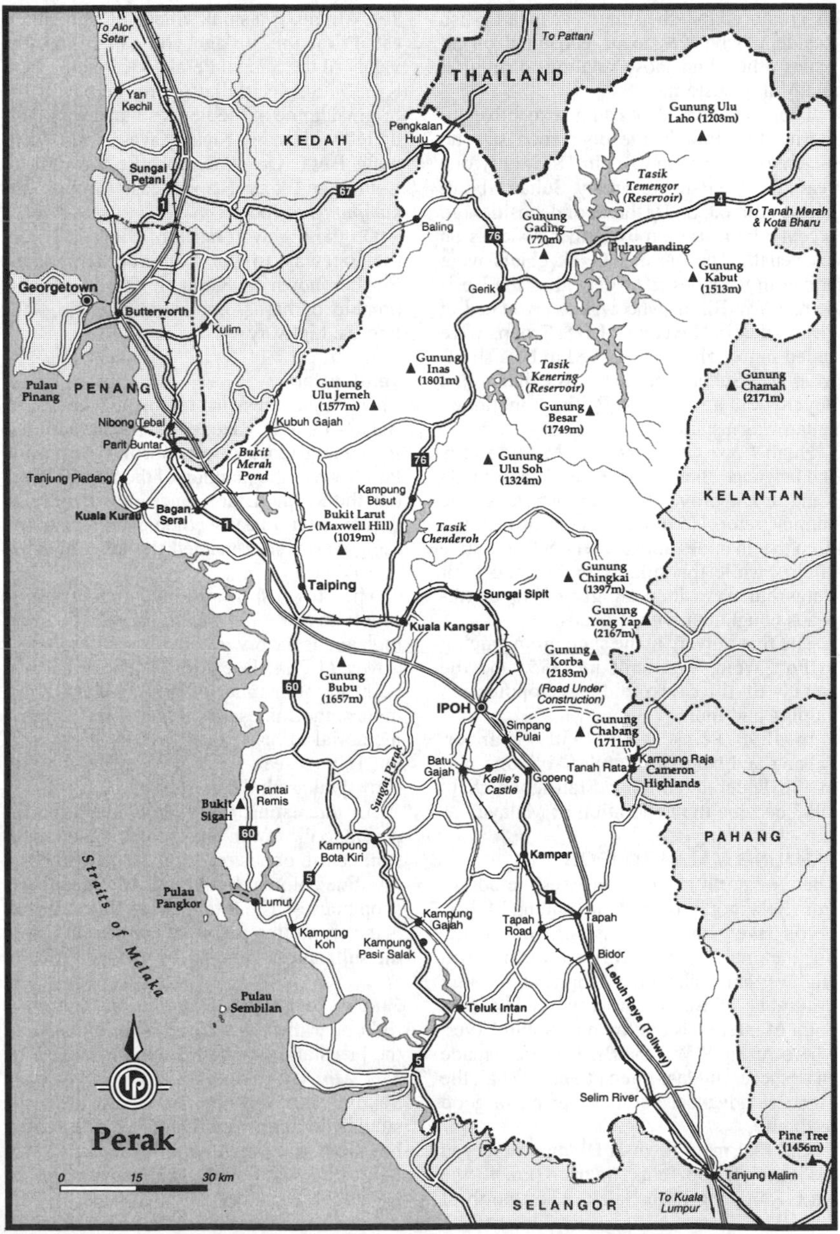
To Alor Setar
To Pattani
THAILAND
Yan Kechil
KEDAH
Pengkalan Hulu
Gunung Ulu Laho (1203m)
Tasik Temengor (Reservoir)
Sungai Petani
67
1
Baling
76
Gunung Gading (770m)
4
To Tanah Merah & Kota Bharu
Pulau Banding
Gunung Kabut (1513m)
Georgetown
Gerik
Butterworth
Kulim
Gunung Inas (1801m)
Tasik Kenering (Reservoir)
Gunung Chamah (2171m)
Pulau Pinang
PENANG
Gunung Ulu Jerneh (1577m)
Gunung Besar (1749m)
Nibong Tebal
Kubuh Gajah
Parit Buntar
Bukit Merah Pond
Gunung Ulu Soh (1324m)
Tanjung Piadang
Kampung Busut
KELANTAN
Kuala Kurau
Bagan Serai
Bukit Larut (Maxwell Hill) (1019m)
Tasik Chenderoh
Gunung Chingkai (1397m)
Taiping
Sungai Siput
Gunung Yong Yap (2167m)
Kuala Kangsar
Gunung Korba (2183m)
Gunung Bubu (1657m)
60
(Road Under Construction)
IPOH
Simpang Pulai
Gunung Chabang (1711m)
Batu Gajah
Kellie's Castle
Gopeng
Kampung Raja
Tanah Rata
Cameron Highlands
Pantai Remis
Bukit Sigari
Sungai Perak
PAHANG
Kampung Bota Kiri
Kampar
5
Pulau Pangkor
Lumut
Straits of Melaka
Kampung Gajah
Tapah Road
Tapah
Kampung Koh
Kampung Pasir Salak
Bidor
Lebuh Raya (Tollway)
Pulau Sembilan
Teluk Intan
Selim River
Perak
Pine Tree (1456m)
0
15
30 km
Tanjung Malim
SELANGOR
To Kuala Lumpur

PENINSULAR MALAYSIA

also required that the sultan accept a British Resident, who was to be consulted on all issues other than those relating to religion and Malay custom.

Though the Resident had no executive authority, this foot in the door soon saw an escalation of British rule. In 1875, only one year after the Pangkor Treaty, Sultan Abdullah was forced, under threat of deposition, to accept administration by British officials on his behalf. The various Perak chiefs were united in their desire to get rid of the Resident, JWW Birch, who was assassinated at Pasir Salak in November 1875. Troops were called in to fight what proved to be a short-lived war, Sultan Abdullah was exiled to the Seychelles, and a new British-sanctioned sultan was installed.

Hugh Low, well versed in Malay affairs and language, then became Resident in Kuala Kangsar and proved to be a much more able administrator. He assumed control of taxes from the tin mines and greater control in state affairs, while the sultans maintained their status but were increasingly effete figureheads bought out with stipends.

The first railway in the state, from Taiping to Port Weld, was built in 1885, and the wealth of tin saw rapid development in Taiping and Ipoh.

In 1896 Perak, along with Selangor, Pahang and Negeri Sembilan, became part of the Federated Malay States, which in 1948 became the Federation of Malaya.

TANJUNG MALIM TO IPOH

The road north from KL crosses the border from Selangor into Perak at Tanjung Malim. If you have your own transport, you can get off the main Lebuh Raya (North-South Highway) and take the old highway through a number of interesting towns. The first point of interest is the town of Selim River, where during WWII the British forces made an unsuccessful last-ditch attempt to halt the Japanese advance. Selim River has a good resthouse.

The first main town is Bidor, where you can turn off for Teluk Intan, 42km to the west. Kampung Pasir Salak, 25km north of Teluk Intan, is a small village of some interest. From this village you can follow the valley of the Sungai Perak to Kampung Bota Kiri. The river valley along here was the original home of the Perak sultanate and it is dotted with many royal graves. From Kampung Bota Kiri you can take the road to Lumut and travel north-east through the *kampungs* to Ipoh.

On the highway north of Bidor is Tapah, the gateway to the Cameron Highlands. Further north is Kampar, famous for its pomelo orchards, and many pomelo stalls line the highway.

Teluk Intan

There is no pressing reason to visit Teluk Intan – its only gazetted tourist attraction is its leaning clock tower, but it's a pleasant, lazy town at the junction of the Sungai Perak and the Sungai Bidor. Once known as Teluk Anson, after an early colonial administrator, the government renamed the town after independence.

The town's impressive pagoda-style **clock tower** *(jam besar)* is seven storeys high and is the town's answer to the Leaning Tower of Pisa. Local lore has it that it was built, in the manner of the Taj Mahal, by a mourning Chinese merchant in 1885 as a memorial to his wife. Officially it's closed, but if you seek out the caretaker he will show you around for a few ringgit.

An interesting, old-style covered market is next to the tower, and there is a good food-stall centre opposite. Teluk Intan also has a few fine colonial buildings and old Chinese shop houses. The **Istana Raja Muda Perak** is the crumbling palace of the next in line to the sultanate of Perak.

Places to Stay & Eat The bus station is right near the clock tower. One block from the bus station away from the tower, *Hotel Kok Min* (☎ 05-622 1529), 1605A Jalan Sekolah, is a well-kept old villa with simple singles/doubles from RM16/23. The similar but more run-down *Kum Ah Hotel* (☎ 05-622 1407) next door has singles/doubles for RM20/24.

A little further along, the *Anson Hotel* (☎ 05-622 6166) is the best in the town centre, with air-con rooms from RM60. Downstairs is the *Flora Cafe*, a good Chinese restaurant.

Getting There & Away The hourly buses running between Lumut and Kelang, in Selangor, pass through Teluk Intan. There are also frequent direct buses to/from Ipoh (RM4) and Puduraya bus station in KL (RM7.60).

Kampung Pasir Salak

This sleepy village is best known as the place where the first British Resident of Perak, James WW Birch, was slain in 1875 while bathing at a raft-house on the river. Birch is widely characterised as an intolerant man, insensitive to Malay customs and known to lecture Sultan Abdullah in public. However, his murder was as much a reaction to the colonial government's decision to assume direct control in Perak as it was to any shortcomings in Birch's personality. His executioners, Maharaja Lela, a local chief, Dato Sagar and Pandak Indut were arrested by British troops and later hanged. They have since been enshrined as national heroes, and there are plans to construct a memorial here dedicated to them.

A memorial to Birch marks the spot, but of more interest are the three restored traditional houses, *rumah kutai*, that are the main feature of the historical complex at Pasir Salak. They show the features of Perak houses, with carved eaves, shuttered windows, and walls of wood and woven bamboo to allow breezes to enter the house. One functions as a VIP guesthouse, while another, reputed to be 120 years old, is a museum which describes the events of 1875, and features a few paintings, kris and other old weapons. The third house has displays explaining traditional customs and other memorabilia.

The complex is open from 10 am to 6 pm on Saturday and Sunday, and from 9.30 am to 5 pm Monday to Friday, but closes on Friday between 12 and 12.45 pm.

Getting There & Away The frequent buses running between Lumut and Kelang, in Selangor, pass through Kampung Gajah, 4km by road from Teluk Intan across the Sungai Perak bridge. A chartered taxi from Kampung Gajah to Kampung Pasir Salak costs around RM15 return.

Tapah

The small town of Tapah has no attractions, but is the main transit point for bus connections to and from the Cameron Highlands.

Places to Stay If you get stuck, Tapah has good, cheap hotels only two minutes walk from the bus station.

There's a good choice of well-priced hotels on Jalan Stesen, easily reached by taking the street directly opposite the bus station for two short blocks. The *Hotel Utara* (☎ 05-401 2299) at 35 Jalan Stesen has doubles with fan for RM20, or RM30 with air-con and bathroom. At No 23, the *Hotel Timuran* (☎ 05-401 1092) offers fan rooms with bath for RM20 and good air-con rooms for RM35. There's also a good Chinese coffee shop downstairs. Just across the tiny lane at No 24 is the *NH Hotel* (05-401 7288), where nice air-con doubles with bathroom and TV are good value at RM50.

Getting There & Away The bus station on Jalan Raja is central and only 250m from the main road. Local buses to the Cameron Highlands leave roughly every 1½ hours from 8.15 am to 6 pm. The winding journey to Tanah Rata takes two hours and costs RM3.50. Taxis to Tanah Rata leave from the taxi station on Jalan Raja, 100m from the bus station, although some also go from the Restoran Caspian (see the following paragraphs). In the afternoon it is more difficult to get a share taxi (RM10 per person), and you may have to charter a whole taxi (RM40).

From the bus station a few departures go to KL and Penang, but most express long-distance buses leave from the Restoran Caspian (☎ 05-401 1193), 9 Main Rd. Turn right as you come out of the bus station, then left at Main Rd, and the Restoran Caspian is just four shops down from KFC. It also has a sub-agent, the Kah Mee Agency, directly opposite the bus station.

From the Restoran Caspian, air-conditioned buses go to: Hat Yai at 11.30 pm (RM35, 10 hours); Ipoh hourly until 8 pm (RM4, 1½ hours); KL about hourly until 6.20 pm (RM8.50, three hours); Kuantan at 9.30 am and 10 pm (RM22, eight hours); Lumut at 11.30 am (RM10, three hours); Melaka at 11 am (RM16, six hours); Penang at 10 and 11 am and noon (RM10, four hours); and Singapore at 8 am and 9.30 pm (RM43, eight hours). These buses can also be booked at CS Travel & Tours in Tanah Rata.

Regular buses to Ipoh also leave from the next street north. From the bus station turn right and follow Jalan Raja over Main Rd, then turn right at the next street – the depot is just around the corner.

The train station, known as Tapah Rd station, is 9km west of town. Tapah Rd buses run every half hour from the bus station between 7 am and 7 pm. To Butterworth, trains leave at 9.50 am and 4.40 pm, to KL at 11.35 am and 5.50 pm. Other services leave in the middle of the night.

CAMERON HIGHLANDS

Malaysia's most extensive hill station, about 60km off the main KL-Ipoh-Butterworth road at Tapah, is at an altitude of 1300 to 1800m. The Cameron Highlands encompasses a large area stretching along the road from the town of Ringlet, then through the main towns of Tanah Rata, Brinchang and beyond.

The Cameron Highlands takes its name from William Cameron, the surveyor who mapped the area in 1885. He was soon followed by tea planters, Chinese vegetable farmers and finally by those seeking a cool escape from the heat of the lowlands.

The temperature rarely drops below 8°C or climbs above 24°C, and the area is fairly fertile. Vegetables grow in profusion, flowers are cultivated for sale all over Malaysia, it's the centre of Malaysian tea production and wild flowers bloom everywhere.

The cool weather tempts visitors to exertions normally forgotten at sea level – there's an excellent golf course, a network of jungle trails, waterfalls and mountains, and less taxing points of interest such as a colourful Buddhist temple and a number of tea plantations where visitiors are welcome (see under Tea Plantations).

Until recently, development here was fairly limited, but construction of large apartment blocks has somewhat changed the old-fashioned, English atmosphere of the Cameron Highlands. A new road is being pushed through from Kampung Raja to link up with Simpang Pulai on the Lebuh Raya, which will make the Highlands much more accessible and speed development, but mercifully that is still a few years away. Until then, the ugly, new intrusions are relatively few and the Cameron Highlands is still a relaxing destination.

Orientation

Though the Cameron Highlands lies just over the Perak state border in Pahang state, it can be accessed only from Perak and so is included in this chapter for convenience.

From the turn-off at Tapah it's 46km up to Ringlet, the first village of the Highlands. Ringlet is primarily a Malay town and not particularly interesting. Although it has a few places to stay most visitors continue higher up.

Soon after Ringlet you skirt the lake created by Sultan Abu Bakar Dam. About 14km past Ringlet, Tanah Rata is the main town of the Highlands. As you enter, the new apartment blocks towering above give way to the busy Jalan Besar (Main Rd), lined with restaurants and old-fashioned shops. Tanah Rata has a large Indian population, descendants of the Indian workers brought here to pick tea. It is the most central town with the widest range of accommodation. Most visitors stay in Tanah Rata.

A few kilometres further up is the golf course, around which you'll find many of the Highlands' more expensive hotels. Continue beyond the golf course, and at around the Km 65 marker you reach the other main

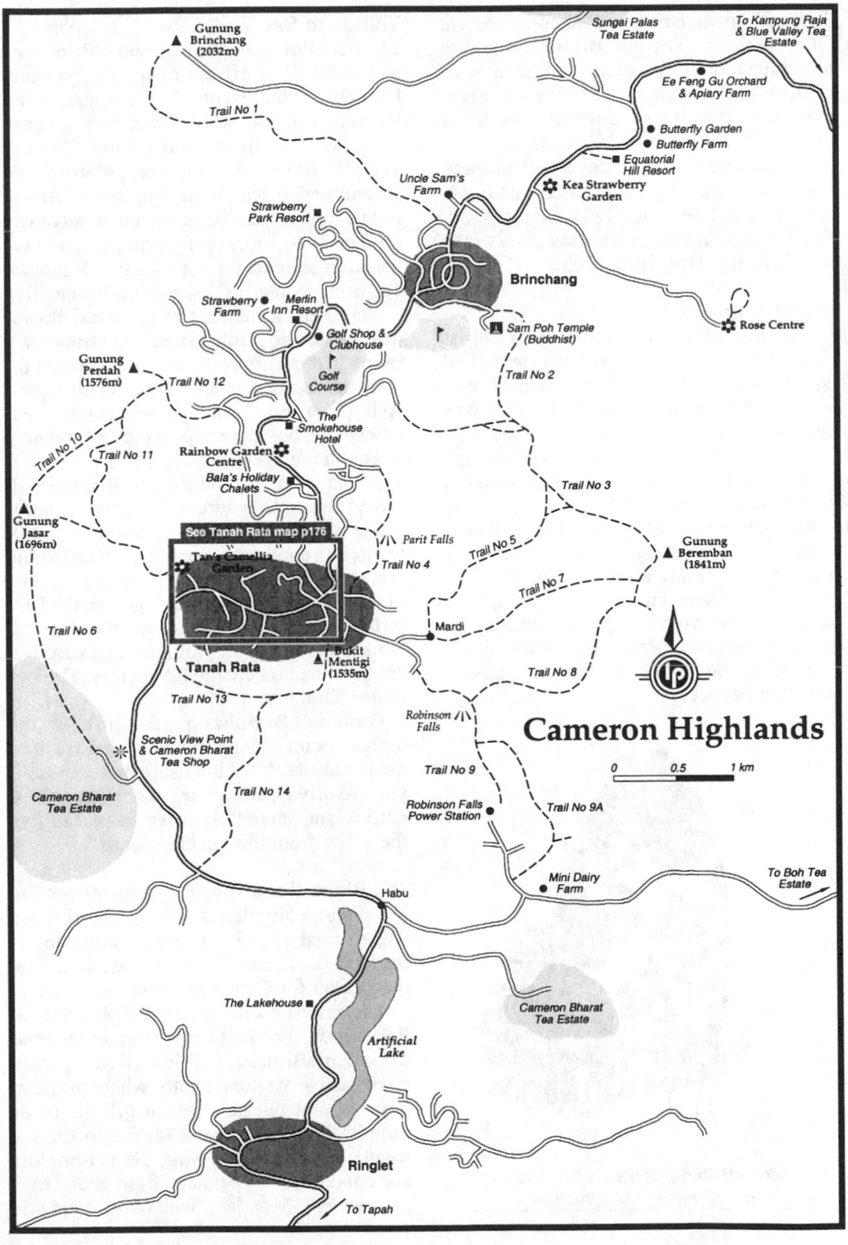
Cameron Highlands
Gunung Brinchang (2032m)
Trail No 1
Sungai Palas Tea Estate
To Kampung Raja & Blue Valley Tea Estate
Ee Feng Gu Orchard & Apiary Farm
Butterfly Garden
Butterfly Farm
Equatorial Hill Resort
Kea Strawberry Garden
Uncle Sam's Farm
Strawberry Park Resort
Brinchang
Strawberry Farm
Merlin Inn Resort
Golf Shop & Clubhouse
Sam Poh Temple (Buddhist)
Rose Centre
Gunung Perdah (1576m)
Trail No 12
Golf Course
Trail No 2
The Smokehouse Hotel
Trail No 10
Trail No 11
Rainbow Garden Centre
Bala's Holiday Chalets
Trail No 3
Gunung Jasar (1696m)
See Tanah Rata map p176
Parit Falls
Tan's Camellia Garden
Trail No 4
Trail No 5
Gunung Beremban (1841m)
Trail No 7
Trail No 6
Mardi
Tanah Rata
Bukit Mentigi (1535m)
Trail No 8
Trail No 13
Robinson Falls
Scenic View Point & Cameron Bharat Tea Shop
Trail No 9
0 0.5 1 km
Trail No 14
Cameron Bharat Tea Estate
Robinson Falls Power Station
Trail No 9A
Mini Dairy Farm
To Boh Tea Estate
Habu
The Lakehouse
Cameron Bharat Tea Estate
Artificial Lake
Ringlet
To Tapah

Highlands town, Brinchang, a more modern, Chinese town. Though Brinchang has a good range of facilities and is close enough to many of the attractions, it has less character than Tanah Rata and is more isolated if you are dependent on public transport.

The road continues up beyond Brinchang to grungy Kampung Raja, a tea estate village, and the Blue Valley Tea Estate at 90km. You can also turn north-west at 80km, to the top of Gunung Brinchang (2032m).

Information

At the time of writing, Tanah Rata tourist office, at the western end of Jalan Besar, had closed for renovation, and the Majlis Daerah (local council offices; ☎ 05-941 1455) was handling basic tourist inquiries. The souvenir shops in Tanah Rata sell useful colour maps of the Cameron Highlands, but walkers should not assume that detail shown on these maps is completely accurate, or up to date.

The post office, hospital, bus station and a Hongkong Bank are also on Jalan Besar in Tanah Rata. There's a new Maybank on the corner of Jalan Mentigi and Persiaran Camellia 4 opposite the hotel construction site.

Most of the budget backpacker places offer Internet access.

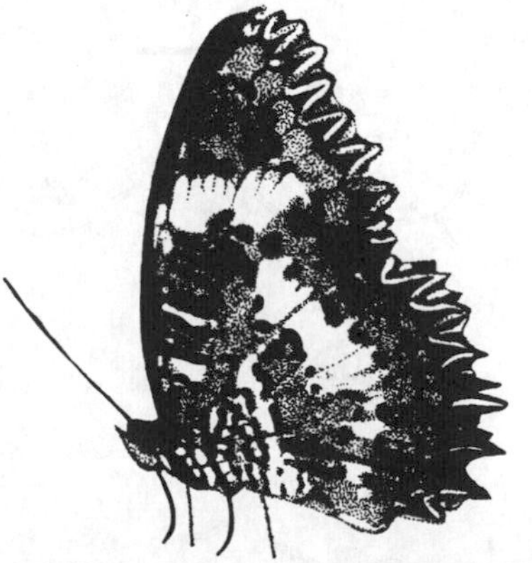

Brinchang's Butterfly Garden is home to more than 300 varieties of butterflies.

Things to See

The **Sam Poh Temple**, just below Brinchang and about 1km off the road, is a typically Chinese kaleidoscope of colours, with Buddha statues, stone lions and incense burners. It is signposted as the 'Tokong Temple' from the main road. **Mardi** is an agricultural research station east of Tanah Rata – tours must be arranged in advance. CS Travel & Tours or Titiwangsa can make the arrangements for you (see the Organised Tours entry later in this section for details).

There are a number of **apiaries**, **flower nurseries**, **vegetable farms** and **strawberry farms** in the Highlands. The main season for strawberries is January. There is an Orang Asli (aboriginal Malay) settlement near Brinchang, but there appears to be little here to attract the average traveller.

About 10km beyond Brinchang is the **Butterfly Garden**, where over 300 varieties flutter around, as well as an impressive collection of enormous rhinoceros beetles and scorpions. In true Asian style, where vendors of the same product cluster together, the **Butterfly Farm** is a virtually identical competing attraction next door. Both are open from 9 am to 6 pm, and charge RM3 entry. The bus tours call in here.

Gunung Brinchang (2032m) is the highest point reached by surfaced road on the peninsula. It's a long slog on foot, but if you are driving it's a must. The 7km road is narrow and incredibly steep in places, but the views from the top are superb.

Tea Plantations A visit to a tea plantation is a popular Highlands outing. The first tea was planted in 1926. The main company is the Boh Tea Estate, and its brands dominate the market for Cameron Highlands tea.

The easiest estate to visit is Boh's Sungai Palas Estate, north of Brinchang off the road to Gunung Brinchang. It is well set up with an attractive visitors' centre where you can buy tea and tea sets in the gift shop, or sample the brew of your choice in the tea rooms. Free tours showing the tea process are conducted on demand from 8 am to 3 pm, except Monday, when the estate is

Tea Processing

Tea bushes are plucked every seven to eight days, and though once done by hand it is now almost all mechanised in Malaysia. It takes 5kg of leaves to make 1kg of tea. The collected leaves are weighed and 'withered' – a drying process in which air is blown across troughs by fans in order to reduce the moisture content by about 50%. The dried leaves are then rolled, to twist, break and rupture the leaf cells and release the juices for fermentation. The finer leaves are then separated out and the larger ones are rolled once again.

Fermentation, which is really oxidisation of the leaf enzymes, has to be critically controlled to develop the characteristic flavour and aroma of the tea. The fermented leaves are then 'fired', a process in which excess moisture is driven off in a drying machine. It is at this time that the leaves become black. Finally, the tea is sorted into grades, and stalks and fibres are removed before it is stored in bins to mature.

closed. Sunday is the pickers' day off, but the processing factory remains open.

The tea is still cured with wood fires, which imparts flavour to the finished product. The process is almost all mechanised now, including the picking and sifting into grades from dust to choice leaf.

Most tours include the Sungai Palas Estate, but public buses running between Tanah Rata and Kampung Raja pass the plantation entrance, from where it's 15 minutes walk to the processing factory. You can also visit other tea estates, but guided tours are usually given only for organised groups.

Activities

Walks There are a variety of walks around the Highlands, many leading to waterfalls, mountain peaks and other scenic spots. The walks are sometimes difficult to follow, and no high-quality maps are available.

The start of the trails are marked with large but sometimes obscured signboards. The popular tracks are reasonably well maintained and periodically cleared with brush cutters, but it doesn't take long for them to become overgrown, especially the less popular trails. There is little or no signposting of side trails, and you occasionally come across false trails that go nowhere. The guesthouses in Tanah Rata all have books with comments from guests who have walked the trails. They are a good source of information for the latest track conditions.

You should take care not to get lost, and always carry water, some food and rain gear for the unpredictable weather. Trails 4 and 9 (as far as Robinson Falls) are easy walks taking an hour or less. Trail 14 is an easy longer walk, while a combination of Trails 11 and 12 is slightly more challenging. The rest may be 'tough going', depending on your level of fitness.

The walks are generally interesting, as they pass through relatively unspoiled jungle, and the cool weather makes walking a pleasure. Trail 12 is particularly good for wild flowers – the Cameron Highlands is famed for its orchids.

Although the walks around the Highlands are all relatively short, there is obviously great potential for longer walks from there. A glance at the Perak map will indicate what a short, steep distance it is from the Highlands down to Ipoh or the main road. For any walk outside the immediate area, however, the local authorities have to be notified and a guide is necessary.

Trail 1 This trail leads from around the side of the transmitter station on top of Gunung Brinchang down to the army camp, just north of Brinchang. It is a steep, muddy, overgrown trail and should only be tackled from the top down by experienced hikers. Take the 7km paved road to Gunung Brinchang through the tea plantations – pleasant enough to start, but dull after a while, so try hitching. The trail down takes about 1½ hours, unless you get lost and wander through the jungle for a couple of days, as two foreigners did some time ago.

Trail 2 Starting just before the Sam Poh Temple outside Brinchang, this steep, strenuous hike

Jim Thompson

The Cameron Highlands' most famous jungle walker was a man who never came back from his walk. American Jim Thompson is credited with founding the Thai silk industry after WWII. He made a fortune, and his beautiful, antique-packed house beside a *khlong* (canal) in Bangkok is now a major tourist attraction today. On 26 March 1967, while holidaying in the Highlands, Jim Thompson left his villa for a pre-dinner stroll – never to be seen again. Despite extensive searches, the mystery of his disappearance has never been explained. Kidnapped? Taken by a tiger? Or simply a planned disappearance or suicide? Nobody knows.

follows a thin, slippery track for 1½ hours before it eventually joins Trail 3.

Trail 3 This starts at Arcadia Cottage behind the golf course and climbs towards Gunung Beremban (1841m), getting steeper near the summit. It is a strenuous three hour walk all the way to the mountain, or an easier walk if you only go as far as Trail 5 and take it back to Mardi.

Trail 4 Trail 4 starts next to the river just past the New Garden Inn in Tanah Rata. It leads to the Parit Falls, but unfortunately these are more like 'sewerage falls' as all the garbage from the nearby village finds its way here. The falls can also be reached from the road around the southern end of the golf course. Both walks are less than a kilometre.

Trail 5 Trail 5 starts at Mardi. Take the road inside the complex and follow the sign around to the left. It's a 1½ hour walk though open country and forest, and an easy walk if done downhill from Trail 3.

Trail 6 One of the least popular and most overgrown routes, Trail 6 goes from the end of the road at Bharat Tea Estate and merges with Trail 10 at the summit of Gunung Jasar (1696m). It's a 2½ hour uphill walk.

Trail 7 This one also starts inside Mardi and is a steady three hour uphill hike, with a very steep final climb to the summit of Gunung Beremban. The start of Trail 7 can be hard to find.

Trail 8 This branches off Trail 9 just before Robinson Falls and is a steep approach to Gunung Beremban. Although a slightly easier walk, it's still a strenuous 2½ hours if done in reverse from the mountain, or 3 hours uphill.

Trails 9 & 9A Popular Trail 9 starts 1.5km from the main road in Tanah Rata. Take the road past Mardi and follow it all the way around to the right, where it ends at a footbridge. From here the trail leads downhill past Robinson Falls to a metal gate, about 15 minutes away. Trail 9 leads through the gate and follows the water pipeline down a very steep, sometimes slippery incline through the jungle to the power station, less than one hour away. From the power station, you can walk to the Boh Rd and back to the main road, or take the more gradual Trail 9A back up to the waterfall, a less taxing walk.

Trails 10, 11 & 12 Gunung Jasar is a fairly strenuous walk reached by Trail 10, starting behind the Oly Apartments near the digital clock in Tanah Rata. Go through Tan's Camellia Garden and uphill to the left. You can bypass the summit and take Trail 11, which joins Trail 12 and emerges at the Hilltop Bungalow, a moderately easy two hour walk. Trail 12 also leads to Gunung Perdah (1576m), a moderate one hour climb from the Hilltop Bungalow.

Trails 13 & 14 Trail 14 takes three hours and starts on Jalan Dayang Endah in Tanah Rata, just to the side of the big milk bottle at the Pusat Pengumpulan Susu. This pleasant, moderately easy trail winds gradually downhill, most of the way through thick jungle, before it reaches vegetable gardens near the main road, halfway between Tanah Rata and Ringlet. About 10 minutes from the start of the trail it forks – turn left for Trail 14, while the right fork is Trail 13, a short side trail that comes out behind the tourist office.

Golf & Tennis If you want a game of golf, you'll need to be suitably dressed, as regulations prohibit singlets and 'revealing' shorts. Green fees, payable at the clubhouse (☎ 05-491 1126), are RM42 for a whole day (RM63 on weekends), or RM32 after 4 pm. Club, shoe and ball hire will cost around RM40 more.

Across the road from the clubhouse there are a couple of tennis courts for hire. Inquire at the golf shop (☎ 05-491 4167).

Organised Tours

Titiwangsa (☎ 05-491 1142) in Brinchang and CS Travel & Tours (☎ 05-491 1200) at 57 Jalan Besar in Tanah Rata run popular half-day tours of the Highlands for RM15, leaving around 9 am and 2 pm. They also organise various other, longer tours of the area. This can be a good way of seeing all the various attractions, which are well spread out and either difficult, or impossible to reach by public transport. Places visited include a tea estate, a butterfly farm and a rose garden (entry fees are not included).

Places to Stay

The Highlands can be very busy during the school holidays, in April, August and December, when many families come here for vacations. At these times it is a good idea to book accommodation. Prices in the more expensive places vary with demand and have high-season rates in holiday periods and substantially lower rates in quiet periods. Accommodation is generally expensive.

Fortunately, Tanah Rata has a good selection of travellers' guesthouses for cheap accommodation, as well as more expensive hotels. Brinchang, the secondary Highlands town a few kilometres beyond Tanah Rata, also has a selection of hotels and prices are a bit lower than at Tanah Rata, but there is little reason to stay here, especially if you depend on public transport. There's even less reason to stay in Ringlet, 14km from Tanah Rata, which has little budget accommodation.

Many mid-range and top-end hotels are scattered around the Highlands, mostly between Tanah Rata and Brinchang.

Places to Stay – Budget

Tanah Rata A popular travellers' place is the friendly *Twin Pines Chalet* (☎ 05-491 2169), just a short walk from the town centre. The communal veranda is a good place for tuning into the travellers' grapevine. Dorm beds cost RM6 upstairs, or RM7 in roomier dorms downstairs, and doubles are RM16 to RM30.

Just behind the Twin Pines, the *Papillon Guest House* (☎ 05-491 4069) is a very congenial place in a spacious family house, with a kitchen, laundry and good common room. Rooms range from simple singles for RM20 to doubles/triples with bathroom for RM25/35. Dorm beds are RM7 each.

On the same road as the Twin Pines but in a quieter position, the *Cameronian Inn* (☎ 05-491 1327) is another converted house, complete with an expanse of lawn. Facilities are similar to those at the other guesthouses, including a small restaurant and a TV/video room. Rooms from RM16 are internal-facing and dark, but others with bathroom from RM25 are very good value. Dorm beds are available for RM6, but this place is more popular with couples.

Tanah Rata's newest budget place is *Daniel's Lodge* (☎ 05-491 5823) at 9 Lorong Perdah. It's quiet, surrounded by rainforest, yet is still very central. Dorm beds are RM7, and simple fan rooms cost RM16, rising to RM30 with bathroom and external window.

Also worthwhile is the *Hotel BB Inn* (☎ 05-491 4551) in the newer section of town at 79A Persiaran Camellia 4, where beds in a clean secure dorm cost RM9, and nice doubles are RM35, or RM45 with balcony.

A short way from the town centre (up a long flight of stone steps – a bit of a grunt with a heavy backpack) is *Father's Guest House* (☎ 05-491 2484). The old, bunker-style Nissen huts are surprisingly clean and comfortable inside. This well-run guesthouse has a restaurant, a TV area with an extensive video collection and it offers Internet access. Dorm beds cost RM6, and doubles are RM16. A few rooms for RM25 are also available in the seminary house nearby on the hill. These rooms have a small bathroom cubicle. French doors lead onto the garden.

Just 1.5km along the road to Brinchang is *Bala's Holiday Chalets* (☎ 05-491 1660), a converted old colonial era boarding school, set in a lovely hillside garden. The dorm beds for RM8 are very basic, as are the cheaper rooms for RM18 to RM25. Better doubles with bathroom are RM66, while larger family rooms cost RM80. There's a good budget restaurant, and you can call for a free pick-up.

Tanah Rata also has plenty of hotels along Jalan Besar. The unpretentious *Cameson Hotel* (☎ 05-491 1160) at No 29 has a fine old wooden interior and rooms for RM30/40 without/with bathroom, or RM35/45 in the

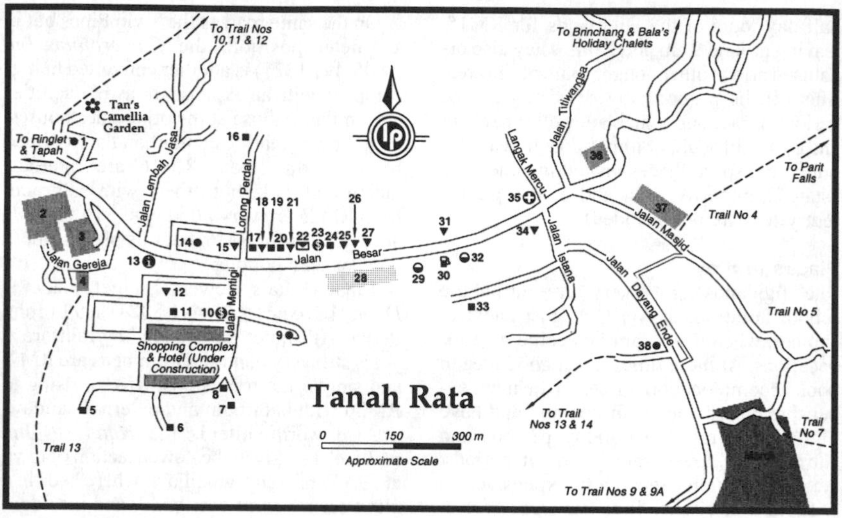

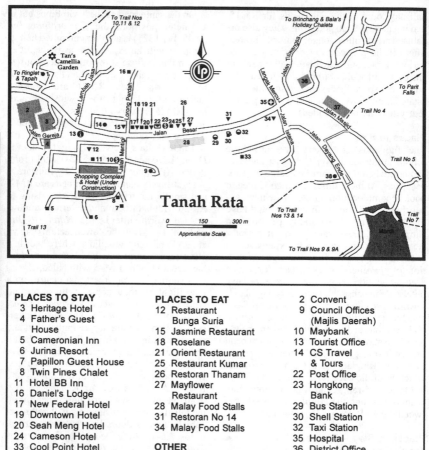

PLACES TO STAY
3 Heritage Hotel
4 Father's Guest House
5 Cameronian Inn
6 Jurina Resort
7 Papillon Guest House
8 Twin Pines Chalet
11 Hotel BB Inn
16 Daniel's Lodge
17 New Federal Hotel
19 Downtown Hotel
20 Seah Meng Hotel
24 Cameson Hotel
33 Cool Point Hotel
37 New Garden Inn

PLACES TO EAT
12 Restaurant Bunga Suria
15 Jasmine Restaurant
18 Roselane
21 Orient Restaurant
25 Restaurant Kumar
26 Restoran Thanam
27 Mayflower Restaurant
28 Malay Food Stalls
31 Restoran No 14
34 Malay Food Stalls

OTHER
1 Oly Apartments
2 Convent
9 Council Offices (Majlis Daerah)
10 Maybank
13 Tourist Office
14 CS Travel & Tours
22 Post Office
23 Hongkong Bank
29 Bus Station
30 Shell Station
32 Taxi Station
35 Hospital
36 District Office
38 'Big Milk Bottle'

high season. Another good place is the exceptionally friendly *Seah Meng Hotel* (☎ 05-491 1618) at No 39, where very clean doubles with common bathroom cost RM35, or RM50 with bathroom.

Others include the *Downtown Hotel* (☎ 05-491 2868) at No 41, with carpeted singles/doubles for RM45/60. The *New Federal Hotel* (☎ 05-491 5652 or 018-896 8740) at No 44 has large doubles for RM39, triples for RM49 and family rooms for RM80, all with bathroom. Tanah Rata's only bar, the lively Butterfly Pub, is downstairs.

Brinchang Almost all of Brinchang's hotels are on the central square. The basic *Silverstar Hotel* (☎ 05-491 1387) is the cheapest place, with rooms from RM20. The *Hotel*

Sentosa (☎ 05-491 1907) is similar. Right next door is the *New Plastro Hotel* (☎ 05-491 1009), which looks dingy from the outside but has good-sized doubles with bathroom for RM40. The *Hotel Highlands* (☎ 05-491 1588) is edging towards the mid-range, and has rooms with bathroom from RM42, rising to RM63 in the high season.

Places to Stay – Mid-Range

Tanah Rata You don't get a lot of choice in the mid-range area, and prices are higher than elsewhere in Malaysia.

The new *Jurina Resort* (☎ 05-491 5522), halfway between the Cameronian Inn and the Twin Pines, has neat doubles for RM100, or RM70 in the low season. There are communal kitchens and sitting rooms.

The *New Garden Inn* (☎ 05-491 5170) is just the other side of the kids' playground in Tanah Rata. It has blocks of modern rooms in the large grounds from RM165, but the low season rate is only RM65. The rooms in the main building have a more old-fashioned character. It is comfortable but nothing special.

The *Cool Point Hotel* (☎ 05-491 4914) is a modern hotel in the centre of town providing higher standards for a few ringgit more. Standard rooms with balcony, TV, bathroom and breakfast cost RM125, or RM90 in the low season.

Private apartments can be rented and are worth considering for longer stays. Check with the shops on Jalan Besar displaying 'apartment for rent' signs.

Brinchang Brinchang also has a few mid-range hotels. At the bottom of this range, the *Hill Garden Lodge* (☎ 05-491 2988) on the western side of the town square has neat and tidy rooms with bathroom from RM58, rising to a steep RM98 during holidays. Perhaps the best deal in Brinchang is the new *Pines & Roses Hotel* (☎ 05-491 2203), where a clean double with bathroom and TV costs RM70. It's down behind the Hotel Rosa Passadena.

The *Parkland Hotel* (☎ 05-491 1299), a four storey block on the eastern side of the central square, has better doubles for RM108, or RM68 in the low season.

Places to Stay – Top End

The 'olde worlde' *Lakehouse* (☎ 05-495 6152), overlooking the lake 2km from Ringlet, is one of the most delightful hotels in the Highlands. Doubles/singles from RM240/280 are good value, but you really need your own transport to stay here.

Tanah Rata In Tanah Rata, the *Heritage Hotel* (☎ 05-491 3888; fax 05-491 5666) is part of a large apartment complex dominating the western edge of town. It has 170 rooms from RM210, plus 15%, but substantial discounts are often on offer.

Near the golf course on the other side of Tanah Rata, *The Smokehouse Hotel* (☎ 05-491 1215) is a copy of an old English country pub, with exposed beams, low ceilings, open fireplaces and a suitably genteel atmosphere. Doubles with English breakfast start at RM180 plus tax. Overlooking the northern end of the golf course is the large *Merlin Inn Resort* (☎ 05-491 1211), where plain-looking doubles cost from RM180 on Monday to Friday, RM210 on weekends and RM300 on 'super-peak' periods (plus taxes).

About 1km past the golf course towards Brinchang, at the top of a windy side road, is the *Strawberry Park Resort* (☎ 05-491 1166). It's a huge new apartment-type set-up popular with Singaporeans on package holidays. Rates for one/two/three room apartments are RM250/270/310 (plus tax).

Brinchang In Brinchang, the large, modern *Hotel Rosa Passadena* (☎ 05-491 2288) is on the downhill side of the central square. Double rooms start at RM140 plus taxes, but there are regular out-of-season specials.

The huge *Equatorial Hill Resort* (☎ 05-496 1777; fax 05-496 1333) is currently the Highlands' highest high-rise hotel. Built on a hilltop several kilometres north of Brinchang, this huge luxury complex really is a case of over-the-top development. Doubles in the tower block cost from RM188, or from RM156 in the wing block.

Places to Eat

Tanah Rata The cheapest food in Tanah Rata is to be found at the rows of mainly Malay food stalls stretching down Jalan Besar. One stall, the *Excellent Food Centre*, has an extensive menu and good food. On Saturday night it becomes a 'sizzler' restaurant and is a cheap place to have a steak. Adjoining this stall is the *Fresh Milk Corner*, where you can enjoy dairy-fresh (and pasteurised) fruit milkshakes, yoghurts and lassis. Other stalls have Chinese food, satay and all the usual Malay dishes.

The other side of the road is Tanah Rata's lively restaurant scene. A host of cheap and moderately priced restaurants line the wide footpath perched above the street. Many of them set up tables outside so customers can dine alfresco.

Two of the most popular are the *Restaurant Kumar* and adjacent *Restoran Thanam*. Both serve Indian food and spruik for the travellers' trade. They also do western breakfasts, juices, lassis and Chinese food, including good claypot rice meals in the evening, all at low prices.

The best Indian food at even lower prices is at *Restoran No 14* on Jalan Besar. It offers big thali meals and the popular masala dosa. It is so popular that it sometimes runs out of food, so don't leave your dining here too late. Slightly more upmarket, is the *Restaurant Bunga Suria* in the new commercial block at 66A Persiaran Camellia, with delicious mee rojak, samosas and dosa (filled pancake made from crushed lentils).

Steamboat in the Highlands is a traditional taste treat. It's the Chinese equivalent of a Swiss fondue. You get plates of meat, shrimp, vegetables and eggs on skewers, and cook them yourself in a boiling stockpot over a burner on the table. You need at least two people, but the more the better. Try the set lunch or dinner at the *Orient Restaurant*, on Jalan Besar. It's a traditional steamboat meal, and is very good value at RM13 per person (minimum of two people). Further along Jalan Besar is the Chinese *Jasmine Restaurant*, with set four-course meals for RM26 that are well worthwhile.

Another Highlands tradition is (local) coffee or tea with scones and jam. Two inexpensive cafes, the *Roselane* and the *Downtown* (in the hotel of the same name), serve freshly baked pastries and do breakfasts from RM3.50. Out at *Bala's Holiday Chalets*, there is an extensive menu, including excellent scones with jam and cream.

In addition to these places, all the middle and top-end hotels have their own expensive restaurants. *The Smokehouse Hotel* is ideal for homesick Brits – you can get expensive tea and scones, sandwiches with the crusts cut off and fairly pricey meals.

Brinchang Brinchang has a good night market, which sets up in the central square in the late afternoon, where you can eat for just a couple of ringgit. A permanent food-stall centre is at the southern end of the square.

Brinchang has excellent Chinese food, and steamboat also features widely. For cheap, no-frills coffee-shop fare, the *Kwan Kee* on the western side of the square is a good bet. The mid-range *Kowloon Restaurant* on the other side of the square has a broad selection of Cantonese dishes from around RM18.

A few doors up is *Shal's Curry House*, which specialises in *roti* and dosa served on banana leaf (with imaginative strawberry, butter and coconut combinations), but also has clove and cardamom teas, fresh lassis and excellent apple strudel.

Ringlet You can have a banana leaf meal at the *Restoran Letchumy*, or try one of the Malay food stalls near the town market.

Getting There & Away

Bus It's a long, gradual and often scenic climb from Tapah in Perak state to the Highlands, with plenty of corners on the way. From the golf course down to the main road junction, one visitor reported counting 653 bends. The road passes a number of poor Orang Asli settlements and roadside shanties where the Orang Asli sell their produce.

The bus drivers on this route seem to be frustrated racing drivers, and almost everyone overtakes on blind corners. There are seven daily buses from Tapah to Tanah Rata (RM3.50, two hours) between 8.15 am and 6 pm. Most buses continue to Brinchang. In the other direction, the first and last buses are at 8 am and 5.30 pm.

Direct long-distance services from Tanah Rata bus station (☎ 05-491 2978) on Jalan Besar go to KL (RM10, five hours) at 8.30 and 10.30 am, and 1.30 and 4 pm, and to Penang (RM14, six hours) at 8.30 am and 2.30 pm. Many more services leave from Tapah and can be booked at any of the backpacker places, or at CS Travel & Tours (☎ 05-491 1200), 47 Jalan Besar, Tanah Rata. See the Getting There and Away entry under Tapah for more information on these bus services.

Taxi There are regular taxis from the taxi station (☎ 05-491 2355) on Jalan Besar in Tanah Rata. Things are much busier in the morning, so it's best to go then if you are looking for someone to share your ride. Full-taxi fares are RM40 to Tapah, RM70 to Ipoh and RM150 to KL.

Getting Around

Bus Most of the buses coming up from Tapah to Tanah Rata continue on to Brinchang, so getting between those two places is not a problem between 9 am and 6 pm.

From Tanah Rata to Kampung Raja, 25km away across the Highlands, there are five buses daily. It's quite a scenic trip, and you can use these buses to get to the butterfly farm past Brinchang.

Taxi Taxis fares from Tanah Rata are: RM12 to Ringlet, RM4 to Brinchang and RM16 to Boh Tea Estates. For touring around, a taxi costs RM15 per hour, or you can go up to Gunung Brinchang and back for RM60.

IPOH

The 'City of Millionaires' made its fortune from the rich tin mines of the Kinta Valley. The elegant mansions of Ipoh testify to the many successful Chinese miners, and some of the mines around Ipoh are still producing today. With a population of 390,000 people, and over 500,000 if the surrounding districts are included, Ipoh is Malaysia's third largest city, but development fever is less rabid in this Chinese-dominated city than in other parts of Malaysia. As a result it is not as busy as its size indicates, and has retained many of its historic buildings.

For the visitor, Ipoh is mainly a transit town, a place where you change buses if you're heading for Pulau Pangkor, or where you pause to sample what is reputed to be some of the finest Chinese food in Malaysia. It's worth a longer visit to explore the Buddhist temples cut into the limestone outcrops north and south of the town.

'Old Town' Ipoh is centred on the Sungai Kinta, between Jalan Sultan Idris Shah and Jalan Sultan Iskandar, and is worth a wander for the old Chinese and British architecture. The grand civic buildings close to, and including, the train station give some idea of just how prosperous this city must have once been. When the city expanded at the end of the 19th century, it extended east over the river to the 'New Town', which is also a repository of fine colonial shophouses, and now the more lively part of town. While the city centre remains largely preserved and free from development, it is rather dead in the evenings.

Information

The helpful Perak Tourist Information Centre (☎ 05-241 2959) is in the old city council building on Jalan Bandaraya (Jalan Tun Sambanthan), opposite the Padang. It is open Monday to Friday from 8 am to 4.15 pm, closed for lunch from 12.45 to 2 pm (12.15 to 2.45 pm on Friday), and also opens on Saturday morning from 8 am to 12.45 pm. Ask for the excellent free city map.

Banks include the Hongkong and Standard Chartered banks on Jalan Dato Maharajah Lela near the clock tower and the Maybank on Jalan Bandar Timah.

Many of Ipoh's main streets have been renamed in recent years, and while the street signs give the new (and often overly lengthy) names, the streets are often still known by the old names. The main ones include Jalan Chamberlain (now Jalan CM Yussuf), Jalan Leech (Jalan Bandar Timah), Jalan Station (Jalan Dato Maharajah Lela), Jalan Post Office (Jalan Dato Sagor) and Jalan Kelab (Jalan Panglima Bukit Gantang Wahab!).

Colonial Architecture

Ipoh's grand colonial architecture is found in the Old Town. The **train station** is a blend of Moorish and Victorian architecture, similar to the KL train station. It houses the wonderfully old-fashioned Majestic Hotel. Directly opposite, the **Dewan Bandaran** (City Hall) is a dazzling white neoclassical building of grand proportions. A short walk away on Jalan Dato Sagor, the **Birch Memorial Clock Tower** was erected to the memory of JWW Birch, Perak's first British Resident, who was murdered at Pasir Salak. The friezes on the clock tower try to show more cultural sensitivity than Birch was reputed to have, by depicting the growth of civilisation, including Asian civilisation.

The mock-Tudor **Royal Ipoh Club** overlooks the playing fields of the Padang and is still a centre of exclusivity. To the north of the Padang, **St Michael's Institution** is the most imposing of all colonial buildings, a grand three storey building with arched verandas.

The Old Town also features many rows of colonial shops, though those in the city area, east of the river are generally in better condition. They form one of the most extensive areas of later shophouse architecture in Malaysia.

Cave Temples

Ipoh is set among jungle-clad limestone hills that jut out spectacularly from the valley. The hills are riddled with caves that are a great source of mystic power, and over the years favourite meditational grottoes have became large scale temples. There are cave temples both south and north of the town – the most important being the **Perak Tong Temple** about 6km north of town and the **Sam Poh Tong Temple** a few kilometres south of town. Both are right on the main road and easy to get to. Less impressive, but the closest to town, is the **Gunung Cheroh Hindu Temple** on Jalan Raja Musa Aziz, just a short walk from the YMCA. It comes alive during the spectacularly masochistic Thaipusam festival in February. See the entry on Thaipusam in the Places of Worship section after the Facts about Malaysia chapter.

Perak Tong Temple The main feature of this large and impressive complex of caverns and grottoes is the paintings on the interior walls, done by artists from all over South-East Asia. There are various figures of the Buddha in the main chamber, as well as a huge bell which is rung every time someone makes a donation.

A winding series of 300-odd steps leads up through the cave and outside to the balconied areas above. There are good views of the surrounding countryside from here – it's just a pity that Ipoh's factories clutter the immediate area.

The temple is open daily between 9 am and 5 pm; entrance is free, but visitors are asked for donations. Take either bus No 3, 41, or 141 to Kuala Kangsar from the city bus station.

Sam Poh Tong Temple This temple to the south of town is very popular with passers by, and the main attraction seems to be the turtle pond in a small natural courtyard, created ages ago when the roof of a cave collapsed. There are literally dozens of turtles swimming in the thick green water. The turtles are 'released' into the pond by locals, as it is good luck to do so. As you enter the temple you'll be accosted by kids trying to sell you bunches of greenery to feed the turtles.

Inside the temple there's one huge cavern with a small reclining Buddha, and various smaller caverns. There's a vegetarian restaurant to the right of the temple entrance. The ornamental garden in front of the temple is quite scenic, and a popular spot to have your photo taken.

The temple is open daily from 7.30 am to 5.30 pm and can be reached by bus No 66 or 73 (55 sen).

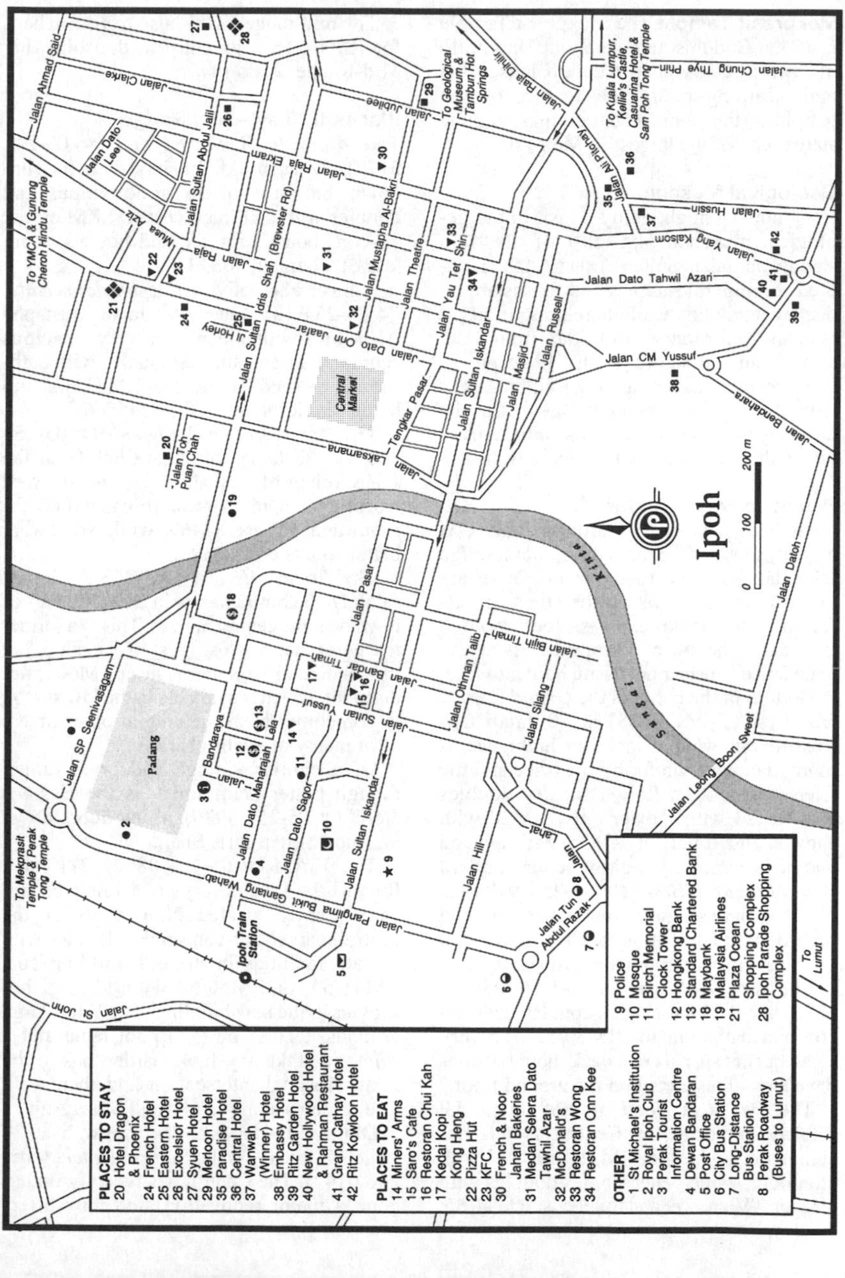
Ipoh
0 100 200 m
PLACES TO STAY
20 Hotel Dragon & Phoenix
24 French Hotel
25 Eastern Hotel
26 Excelsior Hotel
27 Syuen Hotel
29 Merloon Hotel
35 Paradise Hotel
36 Central Hotel
37 Wanwah (Winner) Hotel
38 Embassy Hotel
39 Ritz Garden Hotel
40 New Hollywood Hotel & Rahman Restaurant
41 Grand Cathay Hotel
42 Ritz Kowloon Hotel
PLACES TO EAT
14 Miners' Arms
15 Saro's Cafe
16 Restoran Chui Kah
17 Kedai Kopi Kong Heng
22 Pizza Hut
23 KFC
30 French & Noor Jahan Bakeries
31 Medan Selera Dato Tawhil Azar
32 McDonald's
33 Restoran Wong
34 Restoran Onn Kee
OTHER
1 St Michael's Institution
2 Royal Ipoh Club
3 Perak Tourist Information Centre
4 Dewan Bandaran
5 Post Office
6 City Bus Station
7 Long-Distance Bus Station
8 Perak Roadway (Buses to Lumut)
9 Police
10 Mosque
11 Birch Memorial Clock Tower
12 Hongkong Bank
13 Standard Chartered Bank
18 Maybank
19 Malaysia Airlines
21 Plaza Ocean Shopping Complex
28 Ipoh Parade Shopping Complex
To Mekprasit Temple & Perak Tong Temple
To YMCA & Gunung Cheroh Hindu Temple
To Geological Museum & Tambun Hot Springs
To Kuala Lumpur, Kellie's Castle, Casuarina Hotel & Sam Poh Tong Temple
To Lumut
Ipoh Train Station
Padang
Central Market
Sungai Kinta
Jalan St John
Jalan SP Seenivasagam
Jalan Panglima Bukit Gantang Wahab
Jalan Dato Maharajah Lela
Jalan Bandaraya
Jalan Dato Sagor
Jalan Sultan Iskandar
Jalan Sultan Yussuf
Jalan Bandar Timah
Jalan Pasar
Jalan Tun Abdul Razak
Jalan Hill
Jalan Lahat
Jalan Silang
Jalan Othman Talib
Jalan Bijih Timah
Jalan Leong Boon Sweet
Jalan Datoh
Jalan Bendahara
Jalan CM Yussuf
Jalan Dato Tahwil Azar
Jalan Yang Kalsom
Jalan Hussin
Jalan Ali Pitchay
Jalan Chung Thye Phin
Jalan Raja Dihilir
Jalan Jubilee
Jalan Raja Ekram
Jalan Mustapha Al-Bakri
Jalan Theatre
Jalan Yau Tet Shin
Jalan Sultan Iskandar
Jalan Masjid
Jalan Russell
Jalan Tengkar Pasar
Jalan Laksamana
Jalan Dato Onn Jaafar
Jalan Sultan Idris Shah (Brewster Rd)
Jl Horley
Jalan Raja Musa Aziz
Jalan Sultan Abdul Jalil
Jalan Dato Lee
Jalan Clarke
Jalan Ahmad Said
Jalan Toh Puan Chah

Mekprasit Temple The Mekprasit Temple is a Thai Buddhist temple about 3km north of town at 102A Jalan Kuala Kangsar, the main Taiping road. The feature of the temple is the 24m-long reclining Buddha statue, one of the largest in Malaysia.

Geological Museum

Rock hounds might enjoy a visit to the geological museum, 5km east of the train station on Jalan Sultan Azlan Shah. Hundreds of mineral samples and fossils are on display, including exhibits relating to tin. It is open from Monday to Friday from 8 am to 4.15 pm and Saturday until 12.45 pm.

To get there take a Tanjung Rambutan bus from the city bus station and get off at the crossing of Jalan Sultan Aslan Shah, from where the museum is a 10 minute walk.

Places to Stay – Budget

Most budget hotels are around Jalan CM Yussuf, south of the main drag, Jalan Sultan Iskandar. As most roads around here are busy, rooms overlooking the street are affected by traffic noise, so ask for a room at the back. Though mid-range hotels are in abundance, cheaper hotels are harder to find.

Bottom of the barrel is the *Grand Cathay Hotel* (☎ 05-241 9685) at 88 Jalan CM Yussuf, but what it lacks in ambience is more than made up for by the price and the friendly manager. Large, scruffy doubles cost RM23 with shower only, RM28 with shower and toilet, or RM35 with air-con and bathroom. Of a slightly better standard is the *Embassy Hotel* (☎ 05-254 9496) at No 35, where singles/doubles with fan and bathroom cost RM24/28.50 and air-con doubles with bathroom are RM38.50.

The *New Hollywood Hotel* (☎ 05-241 5322) at No 72 has singles/doubles with air-con and bathroom for RM39/53. It's very clean but not such a great deal, though it does have a good restaurant on the ground floor.

The *Paradise Hotel* at 29A Jalan Ali Pitchay, opposite the Central Hotel, has simple fan doubles for RM31, or RM33 with bathroom, while better singles/doubles with air-con, TV, shower and toilet cost RM44/55.

The mid-range *YMCA* also has dorm beds for RM15. (See its entry in the following Mid-Range section.)

Places to Stay – Mid-Range

The *Wanwah (Winner) Hotel* (☎ 05-241 5177), 32 Jalan Ali Pitchay, is a bit run-down but still offers good value. Fan doubles with bathroom cost just RM30, but air-con rooms with TV and hot water are less of a bargain at RM49.

A nicer alternative is the *Merloon Hotel* (☎ 05-254 1351) at 92-98 Jalan Mustapha Al-Bakri, with clean and very spacious economy air-con singles/doubles with bathroom, TV and phone for RM41/62, and better singles/doubles for RM55/76.

The *Hotel Dragon & Phoenix* (☎ 05-253 4661) at 23 Jalan Toh Puan Chah (near the Jalan Sultan Idris Shah bridge) is also well worthwhile. Quiet air-con rooms with bathroom and TV are RM69, while somewhat better rooms cost RM82.

The *French Hotel* (☎ 05-253 3111), 60 Jalan Dato Onn Jaafar, is in a livelier part of town near the central market. This is a former top hotel that has lost most of its shine, but its standard air-con rooms from RM60 (after discount, which is available in the low season or sometimes by bargaining at other times) have plenty of 1960s character.

Of a similar vintage and price range, though better maintained, is the *Eastern Hotel* (☎ 05-254 3936), a few doors down on Jalan Sultan Idris Shah.

The *YMCA* (☎ 05-254 0809), 211 Jalan Raja Musa Aziz, is very good value, but inconveniently located 2km north of the central market. Air-con singles/doubles with private facilities in the old building cost RM41/53, or RM56/68 with TV and hot shower in the new building. The Y has large grounds, tennis courts, a pool table and a cafeteria. Take any Ipoh Garden bus to the Jalan Hospital intersection and then walk five minutes along Jalan Raja Musa Aziz.

Diagonally opposite the Wanwah at 20 Jalan Ali Pitchay is the *Central Hotel* (☎ 05-241 0142). The Central has recently undergone a major renovation, and now offers small standard doubles with all mod-cons for RM90, while larger, superior/deluxe rooms at the front cost RM101/113. Ask about discounts.

Places to Stay – Top End

Discounts of 20% or more off the rates quoted here are readily available.

For style, but not service, the pick of Ipoh's hotels is undoubtedly the *Majestic Hotel* (☎ 05-255 5605) at the train station. Although not particularly well restored, this magnificent colonial edifice has at least maintained its character from the days when it was the preferred British hotel. Singles/doubles costing RM100/120 on the 2nd floor face a courtyard and are comfortable, but look like motel rooms. Go for the RM150 deluxe doubles on the 3rd floor, which have parquetry floors, high ceilings and planters' chairs outside on the wide, arched veranda. Discounts of up to 30% are available on all rooms.

The *Ritz Garden Hotel* (☎ 05-254 7777), 79 Jalan CM Yussuf, is a somewhat characterless hotel, but has well appointed rooms with all the trimmings for RM118. Its sister hotel, the *Ritz Kowloon Hotel* (☎ 05-254 7778), 92 Jalan Yang Kalsom, has slightly smaller but virtually identical rooms for only RM88, but discounts are also available.

Ipoh's best hotels add 15% tax to their rates, but often offer major discounts. In ascending order they are: the older *Excelsior Hotel* (☎ 05-253 6666), 43 Jalan Clarke, with singles/doubles from RM200/210; the *Casuarina Hotel* (☎ 05-255 5555) on Jalan Gopeng (the KL road), with spacious grounds and doubles from RM230; and the *Syuen Hotel* (☎ 05-252 8889), 88 Jalan Sultan Abdul Jalil, with doubles from RM230.

Places to Eat

Ipoh has numerous restaurants and is the home of the rice noodle dish known as kway teow. Ipoh's kway teow is reputed to be the best in Malaysia. The city's best known place for kway teow is *Kedai Kopi Kong Heng* on Jalan Bandar Timah, between Jalan Pasar and Jalan Dato Maharajah Lela, a bustling restaurant serving a bit of everything. The kway teow soup has tender strips of chicken and prawns. It also has good roast chicken and popiah (a type of savoury pastry). *Kong Heng* is one of the oldest Chinese restaurants in the city, but there are several others like it, on and off Jalan Bandar Timah, which bustle during the day.

In the same area, the *Restoran Chui Kah*, on the corner of Jalan Bandar Timah and Jalan Pasar, is an upmarket Chinese restaurant which specialises in steamboat.

Ipoh also has plenty of food-stall centres. On Jalan Raja Musa Aziz, the large *Medan Selera Dato Tawhil Azar*, better known as the Children's Playground, has food stalls arranged around a small square. It's a very popular place for Malay food in the evening, and is open late. During the day there's a small *food centre* next to the Birch Memorial Clock Tower, while at night the *Pusat Makanan Majestic* on Jalan Raja Musa Aziz is sometimes lively when market stalls set up on the streets out the front. Ipoh's most renowned hawker centre is *Glutton Square* at Ipoh Garden, but it is 6km north-east of the city centre.

At night, many of the restaurants in the Old Town are closed, so a good place to head for is Jalan Yau Tet Shin in the New Town. On opposite corners, the *Restoran Wong* and *Restoran Onn Kee* specialise in tauge ayam (chicken and bean sprouts) and kway teow. These very popular coffee shop restaurants set up tables on the footpath that spill over onto the street when diners flock during the evening.

For Indian food, the clean and breezy *Saro's Cafe* at 37 Jalan Pasar serves good seafood and vegetarian dishes, as well as goat's milk yoghurt. The *Rahman Restaurant* at 78 Jalan CM Yussuf in the same building as the New Hollywood Hotel, is very clean and has a wide range of dishes. It also has an air-con room upstairs.

For something more familiar, *McDonald's* is on Jalan Dato Onn Jaafar opposite the central market, and *KFC* and *Pizza Hut* have branches further north along this street, near the Plaza Ocean shopping complex. There's a well-decorated English pub at 8 Jalan Dato Maharaja; the *Miners' Arms* (☎ 05-253 5488) is a good place to eat meaty grills.

The central market is huge and has a wide range of fruit and vegies; it's a great place if you are putting your own meals together. The *French* and *Noor Jahan* bakeries on Jalan Raja Ekram sell Indian-style breads and pastries. For self-catering, there are also supermarkets on the ground floor of the *Plaza Ocean shopping complex*, on Jalan Dato Onn Jaafar, and the large *Ipoh Parade*, on Jalan Abdul Adil.

Getting There & Away

Air Pelangi Air (☎ 05-312 4770) flies four times weekly to both KL (RM66) and Medan in Sumatra (RM224), with services to each on Monday, Tuesday, Thursday and Saturday. Malaysia Airlines (☎ 05-241 4155), in the Bangunan Seri Kinta building on Jalan Sultan Idris Shah, has four departures daily to KL (RM66).

Bus Ipoh is on the main KL-Butterworth road; 219km north of the capital, 173km south of Butterworth. The long-distance bus station is in the south-west corner of the city centre, a taxi ride from the main hotel area. There are numerous companies operating from this station, with services departing at varying times.

Destinations and standard fares include Alor Setar (RM16), Butterworth (RM8), Hat Yai in Thailand (RM28), Johor Bahru (RM26), Kota Bharu (RM18), Kuala Kangsar (RM2.20), KL (RM9.50, or RM13 luxury express), Lumut (RM3.80), Melaka (RM17) and Tapah (RM4). Try to book your tickets in advance.

Ekspres Sri Perak, at the long-distance bus station, and Perak Roadways, which has a separate terminus directly across Jalan Tun Abdul Razak, both run regular buses to Lumut (RM3.70, 1¾ hours).

The city bus station also handles buses to the outlying regions close to Ipoh, such as Batu Gajah and Gopeng, and local services to Kuala Kangsar.

Train Ipoh's train station (☎ 05-254 0481) is on the main Singapore-Butterworth line and all trains stop here. Trains run to KL (RM22/40 2nd/1st class) at 12.50 am, 1.50 am, 10.50 am and 4.50 pm; the 10.50 am service continues to Singapore. Trains run to Butterworth (RM21/39 2nd/1st class) at 2.30 and 11.20 am and 4.50 pm; the 12.15 am train to Hat Yai in Thailand stops only at Bukit Mertajam train station (on the main line, 10km east of Butterworth).

Taxi Long-distance taxis leave from beside the bus station, and there is also another rank directly across the road. The per-person rate varies depending on the number of passengers. Fares for a whole (air-conditioned) taxi are: Butterworth (RM90), Cameron Highlands (RM100), Kuala Kangsar (RM35), KL (RM120), Lumut (RM50), Taiping (RM50) and Tapah (RM45).

AROUND IPOH

Kellie's Castle

This amazing leftover from colonial times is set by a small river about 30km south of Ipoh. The castle referred to is in fact an old unfinished mansion. It was to be one in the mould of great colonial houses, complete with Moorish-style windows and even a lift (elevator). A wealthy British plantation owner William Kellie Smith, who lived in a splendid mansion in this area early this century, commissioned the building of the 'castle', which was to be the home of his (as yet unborn) son. Seventy Hindu artisans were brought from Madras to work on the mansion. Smith died in Lisbon in 1926 on a trip home to England, and the house was never finished. The jungle has reclaimed some of the building, entwined with vines and massive trees, but the well-tended site is now a popular tourist spot, open daily from 8.30 am to 7.30 pm (admission 50 sen).

Close by is a **Hindu temple**, built for the artisans by Smith when a mysterious illness decimated the workforce and the remaining workers believed that a temple was needed to appease the gods. To show their gratitude to Smith, the workers placed a statue of him, complete with white suit and topee, among the Hindu deities on the temple roof. The temple is about 500m from the 'castle'.

Kellie's castle is inconvenient to reach without your own transport. From Ipoh's city bus station you can take either the frequent No 66 bus to Gopeng (RM1.20) or the less frequent No 36 bus to Batu Gajah. The No 67 bus runs approximately hourly in either direction between Batu Gajah and Gopeng, passing the front of Kellie's castle. You could also charter a taxi from Ipoh for RM30 return.

Tambun Hot Springs

The Tambun Hot Springs are 8km north-east of Ipoh beside a lake at the base of forested limestone cliffs. These natural thermal springs have long been a popular getaway for locals, with various hot pools in which to 'take the waters'. Tambun Hot Springs is currently being redeveloped, and a new luxury hotel is due to open on the site around the time of this book's publication.

The regular bus to Tanjung Rambutan from the city bus station passes the Tambun Hot Springs.

LUMUT

Lumut is the departure point for Pulau Pangkor and – despite attempts to promote Lumut as a tourist destination in its own right – has little to offer apart from souvenir shops selling shells and some reasonable beaches outside town. It's a fast developing area, and the port has been upgraded to service the nearby industrial estates.

The Malaysian Navy has its principal base just outside town, and some 25,000 sailors make up the overwhelming majority of the town's inhabitants. You'll see the huge, Singapore-like apartment complexes of the naval quarters as you go out on the Sungai Dindings to Pulau Pangkor. At the base is the **Royal Malaysian Navy Museum**, open daily except Friday.

The sailors frequent **Teluk Batik** beach, a good beach 7km from town. Teluk Batik is also the site for the Pesta Lumut sea carnival in August each year.

Information

The Tourism Malaysia office (☎ 05-683 4057) is behind the clock tower, near the jetty. Motorists on their way to Pangkor can find a 24-hour, long-term car park behind the Shell petrol station. Cars are guarded, and the charge is RM6 per day.

Places to Stay & Eat

If you get marooned on the way to Pangkor, Lumut has a reasonable choice of hotels and plenty of restaurants.

The *Phin Lum Hooi Hotel* (☎ 05-683 5641), 93 Jalan Titi Panjang, is about half a kilometre from the bus station, not far from the ferry jetty. It charges RM20 for fan rooms or RM28 with air-con; it's clean and friendly with a good cheap restaurant downstairs.

The most convenient hotels are those on the main street, Jalan Iskandar Shah, right near the ferry jetty. *Hotel Indah* (☎ 05-683 5064) at No 208 is a good mid-range hotel with spotless air-con rooms for RM45, or RM50 facing the sea with a balcony. Next door, the *Hotel Manjung Permai* (☎ 05-683 4934) at No 212 is a more upmarket high-rise with rooms from RM80. It has a good restaurant.

The *Orient Star* (☎ 05-683 4199), 1km further out along Jalan Iskandar Shah towards the navy base, is typical of the new developments. This international-class hotel is on the waterfront but has no beach and seems over the top for Lumut. Doubles start at RM240 including tax and breakfast.

Getting There & Away

Bus Lumut is 206km south of Butterworth and 101km south-west of Ipoh, the main turn-off for Lumut on the KL-Butterworth road. The bus station is near the centre of town, a five minute walk to the ferry jetty. Lumut is well connected with other destinations on the peninsula. On Pulau Pangkor, bus agents in Pangkor town, such as the Chuan Full Hotel, handle bookings for the express buses.

The easiest connection is on the new highway to/from Ipoh via Batu Gajah. Ipoh-Lumut buses run at least hourly and cost

RM3.70. Direct buses between KL and Lumut (RM13, five hours) run roughly hourly. Lumut has half a dozen direct daily buses to/from both Butterworth (RM10) and Taiping (RM4.50). Alternatively, take a bus from Butterworth to Taiping, then another bus to Lumut. Other destinations served by buses from Lumut, include Johor Bahru (RM29), Melaka (RM21) Singapore (RM33), and Tapah (RM8.50) for the Cameron Highlands.

Taxi Fares for a long-distance air-con taxi from Lumut are: RM120 to Butterworth, RM45 to Ipoh and RM40 to KL.

PULAU PANGKOR

The island of Pangkor is close to the coast off Lumut – easily accessible via Ipoh. It's a popular resort island noted for its fine beaches. These can be visited via the road running around the island, however, the jungle-clad hills of the interior are virtually untouched.

At 8 sq km, and with a population of 25,000, Pangkor is a relatively small island, but that hasn't stopped the government trying to promote and develop it as one of Malaysia's main tourist destinations. This means that Pangkor's laid-back, kampung feel is disappearing, though development is still relatively low key. Pasir Bogak is the most developed beach, consisting of a string of mid-range hotels, a few restaurants and not much else. Teluk Nipah, probably the best beach on the island, is in transition from a small kampung to another Pasir Bogak as new mid-range hotels spring up around the local guesthouses. The only other developments on Pangkor are the three mega-resorts on isolated beaches.

Pangkor is a popular local resort, only a 30 minute ferry ride from Lumut on the mainland and close to large population centres, so crowds are inevitable. It is very popular on weekends and holidays, but during the week the beaches are almost empty. A visit to the island is still principally a 'laze on the beach' operation, but there are also a few interesting things to do.

Before tourism took off, Pangkor relied on fishing. Fishing and dried fish products are still a major industry for the island, particularly on the east coast.

Pangkor was also a bit player in the battle to control trade in the Straits of Melaka. In the 17th century the Dutch built a fort on the island in their bid to monopolise the Perak tin trade, but were less than keen to defend Perak against Acehnese and Siamese incursions. They were driven out by a local ruler before returning briefly some 50 years later. In 1874 it was the setting for the signing of the Pangkor Treaty, when a contender to the Perak throne sought British backing. As a result, a British Resident, JWW Birch was installed in Perak and the colonial era on the peninsula began.

Orientation

Finding things on Pangkor is very simple. The east coast of the island, facing the mainland, is a continuous village strip comprising Sungai Pinang Kecil (SPK), Sungai Pinang Besar (SPB) and Pangkor town, the main town.

Most ferries to and from Lumut stop at SPK before reaching Pangkor town. The road that runs along the coast on this side turns west at Pangkor town and runs directly across the island, which is only 2km wide at this point, to Pasir Bogak. From there it runs north to the village of Teluk Nipah, where you'll find most of the budget accommodation clustered. It then goes to the northern end of the island, past the new airstrip to Pangkor's other flash hotels at Teluk Belanga and Teluk Dalam. The road from there back to the eastern side of the island is winding and very steep in parts, but it's paved all the way.

Information

The Maybank, in the same building as the Hotel Lin Mian, in Pangkor town is open the usual hours, and also has an ATM for credit-card withdrawals. The moneychanger in the Wonderful shop on the road to Pasir Bogak changes cash and travellers cheques at lower rates.

Beaches

The beach at **Pasir Bogak** is OK for swimming but during holidays it's crowded – at least by Malaysia's 'empty beach' standards. It's a lovely, if rather narrow, white-sand beach. **Teluk Nipah** further north is a wider, better beach.

The best beach on this side is at Coral Bay, about a 20 minute bicycle ride from Pasir Bogak. The water is a clear emerald-green colour due to the presence of limestone, and usually the beach is quite clean and pretty.

In May, June and July turtles come in to lay their eggs at night on **Teluk Ketapang** beach, only a short walk north of Pasir Bogak. There are reports that the increasing numbers of tourists going to watch the turtles are seriously impacting on them, and sightings are becoming increasingly rare. We strongly recommend that you refrain from contributing to this problem. For details see the the boxed text 'The Disapperaing Turtles of the East Coast' in the Terengganu chapter.

Teluk Belanga (Golden Sands Beach) at the northern end of the island is pleasant.

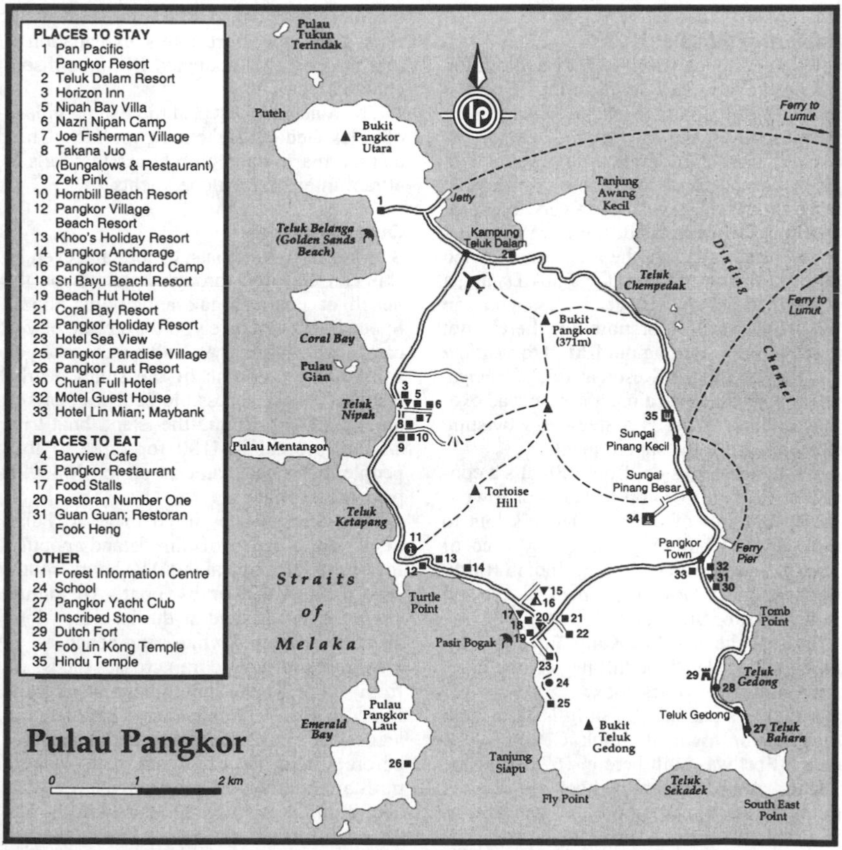

Access is restricted to Pan Pacific Pangkor Resort guests, though day-trippers can visit for a ridiculous RM40. In between there are a number of virtually deserted beaches which you can reach by boat, motorcycle or on foot.

Emerald Bay on nearby Pulau Pangkor Laut is a beautiful little horseshoe-shaped bay with clear water, fine coral and a gently sloping beach. The entire island of Pangkor Laut has been taken over by a hotel conglomerate, but some of the boat tours stop at the beach.

Pangkor sometimes suffers the usual blight of Malaysian beach resorts – litter, especially after a long weekend.

Exploring the Island

The island lends itself well to exploration by motorcycle, bicycle or on foot. Spend a day doing a loop of the island, following the paved road all the way around. By motorcycle it takes about three or four hours with stops, around six or seven hours by bicycle, or you could even walk it in a very long day.

Along the western side there are a few deserted beaches before the road heads inland past the airstrip to Kampung Teluk Dalam, a straggling fishing village. Unless you can talk your way in for nothing, there's not much point in forking out RM40 to visit the Pan Pacific Pangkor Resort at Teluk Belanga, so keep heading east along the new road over the headland. This is a steep and twisting road through some superb jungle.

On the eastern side, from SPK it's a continuous village strip on to Pangkor town – messy but full of interest. There's lots to look at: boat building, fish being dried or frozen, and a colourful South Indian **Hindu temple**. This is principally the Chinese and Indian part of the island.

In SPB the **Foo Lin Kong Temple**, situated on the side of the hill just off the main road, is worth a quick look.

Pangkor's one bit of history is 3km south of Pangkor town at Teluk Gedong. The **Dutch Fort** was built here in 1670, after the Dutch had been given the boot from Lower Perak. In 1690 they rebuilt the wooden fort in brick, but lost it soon afterwards. The Dutch retook the fort in 1693 but, despite frequent visits, did not reoccupy it until 1745; only three years later they abandoned it for good. The old fort was totally swallowed by the jungle until 1973, when it was rebuilt as far as the remaining bricks would allow.

On the waterfront 50m beyond the fort is a huge **inscribed stone**, carved with the symbol of the Dutch East India Company (Veerigde Oost-Indische Compagnie; VOC) and other ancient graffiti, including a faint carving which supposedly depicts a tiger stealing a child. This is said to relate to an incident when a child of a local European dignitary disappeared while playing near the rock. The Dutch liked the idea of the tiger story; the more likely explanation is that the boy was abducted by some disenchanted locals.

The road ends just past the fishing village of Teluk Gedong at the Pangkor Yacht Club, a small marina and club house that fails to attract interest, let alone yachts.

Other Activities

Snorkelling gear, boats, canoes and even jet skis can be hired through hotels or on the beach at Pasir Bogak and Teluk Nipah. Speed boats will take you for a blast, or you can go water skiing. A small boat to take you snorkelling on some of the small nearby islands, or less accessible beaches starts at around RM60. Round-the-island boat trips start at around RM180 for three to four people, but a boat can cost up to RM300. It pays to negotiate.

Boats can also be hired to go to Pulau Sembilan, a group of nine islands popular for sports fishing, about 1½ hours southwest from Pangkor by boat. An annual fishing event is held at the islands, which also have deserted white-sand beaches.

A four hour jungle trail crosses the island from Teluk Nipah and comes out near the Foo Lin Kong Temple, while another trail leads from Pasir Bogak to Bukit Pangkor before joining the east coast road. Walking trails are lightly used and often overgrown – take a guide and *parang* (bush knife). The Forest Information Centre (Pusat Pameran

Dan Publisiti Hutanan) at the northern end of Pasir Bogak can advise of walks on the island, but is often unstaffed.

Places to Stay

Pasir Bogak has most of the larger mid-range resorts and, while it's not the Costa Brava, it does get crowded. A number of new places have sprung up at the next bay to the north, Teluk Nipah. This has a better beach and still clings to its kampung atmosphere, having seen only modest development.

Teluk Nipah The hotels here are at the mercy of the taxi mafia, which not only get the high taxi fare but also extract a large commission from hotel owners for each guest they deliver. Consequently this is added to the hotel rates, but if you are staying more than a couple of nights you may be able to negotiate a discount.

The most popular travellers-only place is *Joe Fisherman Village* (☎ 05-685 2389). Accommodation consists of the usual A-frame 'chalets' found at beach resorts throughout the country. While very basic, most people find them quite adequate. The cost is RM25 for two, or slightly more substantial cottages cost RM35. Good basic meals are available, and there are motorbikes and bicycles for rent.

Much less cluttered than Joe's is *Nazri Nipah Camp* (☎ 05-685 2014) diagonally opposite. It's a friendly place at the edge of the rainforest with simple A-frames for RM20, and bungalows or larger A-frames with bathroom for RM30/40 in low/high season.

Closer to the beach, accommodation is mostly mid-range. *Pangkor Indah* (☎ 05-685 2017) is a small place with a good cafe. Attractive air-con chalets for RM60/95 in the low/high season are one of the best deals around. Next along is another new construction, the *Pangkor Bayview* (☎ 05-685 3540). Its comfortable rooms at RM95/120 in the low/high season are not bad value either.

The *Nipah Bay Villa* (☎ 06-685 2198) has quite luxurious air-con chalets for RM145 a double, including dinner and breakfast. The *Suria Beach Resort* (☎ 05-685 3922), a newer blue and white building on the beachward side of Teluk Nipah, offers rooms for RM80/120 in the low/high season.

Nearer the beach in a garden setting is the *Ombak Inn* (☎ 05-685 3944). It has various options, from A-frame huts for RM20 to air-con bungalows for RM70.

A few places directly opposite the beach are well worth considering. The *Horizon Inn* (☎ 05-685 3398) has nice rooms facing the sea for RM80/110 in the low/high season.

The *Hornbill Beach Resort* (☎ 05-685 2005) has an even better aspect, and its charming hosts offer high standards of accommodation and service. Attractive air-con rooms, the best in Teluk Nipah, face the beach or the jungle behind and cost RM135.

The street at the southern end of Teluk Nipah also has an increasing number of places to stay. The *Takana Juo* (☎ 05-685 3477) has basic bungalows with bathroom for RM25, right beside its popular restaurant. The *Parma Beach Resort* (☎ 05-685 3693) has quite nice wooden chalets with TV and air-con for RM95. A few steps along, the *Flora Beach Resort* (☎ 05-685 3878) and the *Zek Pink* (☎ 05-685 3529) offer a similar deal.

The *Coral Beach Camp* (☎ 05-685 2711) is a long-running budget place with tiny A-frame huts for RM20, or doubles with bathroom for RM45, but it lacks atmosphere. The *Suka Suka Beach Resort* (☎ 05-685 2494) opposite, has pleasant gardens and attractive but fairly spartan bamboo chalets with bathroom for RM40. The *Seagull Beach Resort* (☎ 05-685 2878) has simple mini huts with shared bathroom for RM30/40 single/double and good air-con doubles for RM110.

Pasir Bogak The rest of Pangkor's accommodation possibilities are grouped at each end of the beach at Pasir Bogak, where there is a mixture of top end and cheaper places to stay. Prices quoted are peak rates, but discounts are available on Monday to Friday and in the low season.

Starting at the western end, the *Pangkor Village Beach Resort* (☎ 05-685 2227), has small, air-con chalets along the beachfront for RM145 a double, or RM130 in the low season, including dinner and breakfast. Basic huts cost RM40, or RM30 in the low season, including breakfast only.

Next up is *Khoo's Holiday Resort* (☎ 05-685 1164). The main building is a rather ugly concrete conglomeration, but the simple wooden chalets with bathroom on the steep slope behind have great views across to Pulau Pangkor Laut. At RM41 with fan or RM67 with air-con these rooms offer good value for your ringgit.

The cheapest option is the *Pangkor Anchorage* (☎ 05-685 1363), a short distance along from Khoo's. Small, rustic A-frame huts with a mattress on the floor cost RM10 per person, but they are in a shady grove and remain fairly cool.

At the other end of the beach, where the road from Pangkor town crosses the island, are the other hotels. The *Hotel Sea View* (☎ 05-685 1605) has very average air-con doubles for RM115 with bathroom, and better family rooms or chalets for RM161, all including breakfast. Low-season discounts are offered.

The *Beach Hut Hotel* (☎ 05-685 1159) has ageing fan rooms with bathroom for RM57, or RM80 with air-con. Double chalets with all mod cons, in a garden setting just back from the beach, cost RM138. Discounts are also offered.

On the other side of the road behind the beach is the *Pangkor Standard Camp* (☎ 05-685 1878), a reasonable cheaper option. Cramped three person A-frame huts cost RM37.80 or RM31.50 in the low season, and two-person chalets are RM52.50 or RM42 low season. It rents bicycles and motorbikes.

Right beside the Beach Hut Hotel is the recently extended *Sri Bayu Beach Resort* (☎ 05-685 1929; email sbbr@po.jaring.my). This top-end resort boasts a swimming pool, water slides, tennis courts and a choice of eating options, though it doesn't take full advantage of the attractive beach right out the front. Rooms cost RM368 to RM1728 for the 'Maharaja suite', and all rates include taxes, breakfast and dinner.

The *Pangkor Paradise Village* (☎ 05-685 1496) is in a coconut grove at the southernmost end of Pasir Bogak, and is accessible only via a foot track leading past the school. It has rather ordinary chalets with air-con for RM60/70 single/double, but the isolated little beach here is the real attraction.

On the road to Pangkor town is the *Coral Bay Resort* (☎ 05-685 5111), a new complex with rooms from RM230 – rather overpriced since it's not even on the beach, though major discounts are usually offered. The *Pangkor Holiday Resort* (☎ 05-685 3626) right behind it has bungalows for RM147.

Pangkor Town As the whole attraction of Pangkor is the beaches, there is little point in staying in Pangkor town, but if you get stuck, there are several cheap Chinese hotels.

The *Hotel Lin Mian* (☎ 05-685 1294), right above the Maybank, is tidy but unwelcoming. Air-con rooms start at RM40. The exceptionally friendly *Chuan Full Hotel* (☎ 05-685 1123), 60 Jalan Besar, is a rickety old wooden hotel, but is immaculately kept and has a veranda at the back overlooking the waterfront. Singles/doubles cost RM15/20 with bathroom or RM35 a double with air-con. At the northern end of town is the new *Motel Guest House* (☎ 05-685 4139) offering clean doubles with bathroom for RM55.

Elsewhere on the Island Apart from Pasir Bogak, there is also the *Pan Pacific Pangkor Resort* (☎ 05-685 1399; email resvn@pprp.po.my) at the secluded Teluk Belanga (Golden Sands Beach) on the northern end of the island. Rooms start at RM320 plus 15% and go up to RM800 for a bungalow. The recreational facilities include a golf course, and the resort is on a very pleasant stretch of beach. Access is restricted to hotel guests, although for RM40 you can use the pool and beach (not the golf course) and get a lunch included.

A couple of kilometres away, the new *Teluk Dalam Resort* (☎ 05-685 5000) has individual luxury bungalows from RM230. The beach is not bad, but the resort is not as well sited as the Pan Pacific.

Pulau Pangkor Laut, the island opposite Pasir Bogak, is totally in the grasp of the *Pangkor Laut Resort* (☎ 05-699 1100; email plr@po.jaring.my). It is certainly exclusive and does its best to shun locals, day-trippers and other riff raff. There is a small swimming pool, tennis courts, two restaurants, a disco, and three or four private beaches around the island, including the picturesque Emerald Bay on the western side. Rates start at RM517 for a double, including meals, and range up to RM11,500 for a luxury yacht. There's a reservation office at Lumut on the mainland, which arranges transport to the island.

Places to Eat

Teluk Nipah Many guests tend to dine at their accommodation places, which nearly all serve food, but Teluk Nipah does have some basic *food stalls* at the beach and a couple of restaurants.

The *Bayview Cafe* is a good spot for a meal, either inside or opposite at tables overlooking the beach. The *Takana Juo* is a family-run Indonesian restaurant down the street from the Bayview Cafe. *TJ's* cooks up delicious, cheap food – often with a teasingly long wait before it arrives.

Pasir Bogak All the hotels have restaurants and there are a few other places as well. *Khoo's* has a good inexpensive restaurant and there are *food stalls* nearby. Further along the beach, near the Sri Bayu, are more *food stalls*.

Tucked away along a small dirt road which runs alongside the Pangkor Standard Camp, is the *Pangkor Restaurant*, a cheap seafood and Chinese restaurant that is popular with the locals.

More upmarket is the *Restoran Number One*, an excellent seafood restaurant where a good meal of prawns, fish or crab will cost around RM20 per person.

The restaurant in the *Hotel Sea View* is outdoors, right by the beach. Although the food is only mediocre, it's an excellent place to watch the sunset. The restaurant in the *Beach Hut Hotel* is reasonable.

Pangkor Town Pangkor town has a proliferation of cheap, Chinese *kedai kopi*, some of which serve excellent seafood. On Jalan Besar, the *Guan Guan* is an old favourite for seafood, and *Restoran Fook Heng* is also popular.

Getting There & Away

Air The Pangkor airport reopened in August 1988 after an upgrade. There are flights to/from KL (RM120) and Singapore's Seletar airport (RM204, S$190 from Singapore).

Boat In the high season the Pan Silver Ferry runs between Lumut and Pangkor town every 20 minutes from 6.30 am to 8 pm, but in the low season ferries run only every one to 1½ hours from 7.15 am to 6.45 pm, and from 6.45 am to 5.45 pm from Pangkor. The fare is RM3 each way. Most ferries also stop at Sungai Pinang Kecil.

There are also ferries every 1½ to two hours in either direction between Lumut and the jetty at the northern end of the island across the isthmus from the Pan Pacific Pangkor Resort. The first ferry to Pangkor is at 8.30 am, the last at 6.30 pm from Monday to Thursday or at 8 pm on Friday and weekends. Another ferry service connects Lumut with the Pangkor Laut Resort on Pulau Pangkor Laut, with departures several times a day.

Getting Around

Bus Buses run every hour or so from Pangkor town across the island to the far end of the beach at Pasir Bogak (RM1), and back again. Two buses a day go to Teluk Nipah, but these are for locals only, forcing you to take the taxis.

Motorcycle & Bicycle The ideal way to see the island is by motorcycle or bicycle. There are a number of places at Pangkor town, Pasir Bogak and Teluk Nipah that rent motorcycles for around RM25 to RM30 per day and bicycles for RM10 per day.

Taxi Pangkor has many minibus taxis. Standard fares from the jetty in Pangkor town are

Pasir Bogak (RM5), Teluk Nipah (RM12), Pan Pacific Pangkor Resort (RM22) or around the island (RM35).

KUALA KANGSAR

Beside the highway, north-west of Ipoh, Kuala Kangsar has been the royal town of Perak state since the sultan moved his capital here in the 18th century. It was also the first foothold for the British, as they moved to control the peninsula by installing Residents at the royal courts in the 1870s. By the 1890s the rapid growth of the tin towns of Ipoh and Taiping overshadowed Kuala Kangsar, and the town remains a quiet backwater steeped in Malay tradition.

This small town has a split personality. The small central business area bustles like any town, but to the east overlooking the Sungai Perak, the royal district is spacious and quiet, and the most attractive of all Malaysia's royal cities. Kuala Kangsar's main sights are quite impressive though few, and the whole town can easily be explored in a morning or afternoon.

PENINSULAR MALAYSIA

Things to See

Heading out on Jalan Istana beside the wide Sungai Perak, the first striking example of the wealth of the sultanate is the small but magnificent **Ubadiah Mosque**, with its superb golden onion-dome. It's probably the finest mosque in Malaysia, although it looks almost as if it's viewed through a distorting mirror, since its minarets are squeezed up tightly against the dome. It was completed in 1917 after delays due to WWI and rampant elephants that destroyed the marble tiles.

Overlooking the river, **Istana Iskandariah** is a suitably opulent palace *(istana)* built in 1933. It is best viewed from the river side to appreciate the original palace, which mixes Art Deco with Islamic motifs. The later annexe, on the southern side, dating from 1984 is less striking. Unfortunately, the palace is not open to visitors.

There is also an earlier wooden istana, **Istana Kenangan**, which was built in 1926 without the use of nails, and served as the royal quarters until the Istana Iskandariah was completed. This earlier istana houses the Royal Museum, with displays relevant to the state and the Perak royal family. The museum is open daily from 9.30 am to 5 pm, but is closed on Thursday afternoon and Friday.

Closer to town on Jalan Istana near the Ubadiah Mosque, the **Istana Hulu** is another substantial palace inspired by Victorian architecture. Built in 1903, it is now the Raja Perempuan Mazwin School.

Kuala Kangsar was the birthplace of Malaysia's great **rubber industry**. A number of rubber trees had been planted by Hugh Low in his residency gardens, from seed stock smuggled out of Brazil. However, it was not until the invention of the pneumatic tyre in 1888, and then the popularity of the motor car at the start of the 20th century, that rubber suddenly came into demand and rubber plantations sprang up across the country. All of the trees in the new plantations are descended from the original rubber trees planted in Kuala Kangsar or the Singapore Botanic Gardens. You can still see one of those first trees in the district office compound.

As in many Malaysian cities with a colonial past, the **Malay College** to the north of town is the most impressive colonial building. Established in 1905, it was the first and one of the only Malay schools to provide English education for the Malay elite destined for the civil service. It not only provided clerical workers for the British administration but also, nationalist leaders who formed the more conservative 'Malaya for Malays' faction.

Opposite the Malay College, the **Pavilion Square Tower** is a delightful folly overlooking the surrounding parkland and playing fields. Built in 1930, this small, three storey sports pavilion of Malay and colonial design allowed the royalty and VIPs to view polo matches in comfort.

Places to Stay & Eat

Kuala Kangsar has a couple of cheap hotels for an overnight stay. The most convenient is the *Double Lion Hotel* (☎ 05-776 1010), close to the bus station and above a bakery

RICHARD I'ANSON

CHRIS ROWTHORN

CLEM LINDENMAYER

RICHARD I'ANSON

RICHARD I'ANSON

Colourful street scenes greet visitors to Malaysia and Singapore. Basketware for sale at Singapore's Arab St stalls (top left), ducks prepared for the famous Beijing Duck dish in Kuala Lumpur (top right), sarungs flutter on the line at Batu Ferringhi (centre), leather goods at Arab St stalls (bottom left) and assorted vegetables neatly arranged at Kota Bharu's central market (bottom right).

SIMON ROWE

RICHARD I'ANSON

CHRIS ROWTHORN

SUSAN STORM

SIMON ROWE

SUSAN STORM

Feast your eyes and tastebuds on the delights of Malaysia, Singapore and Brunei's markets: (clockwise from top) mangosteens, jack fruit, rice cakes, cumquats, watermelon and rambutan.

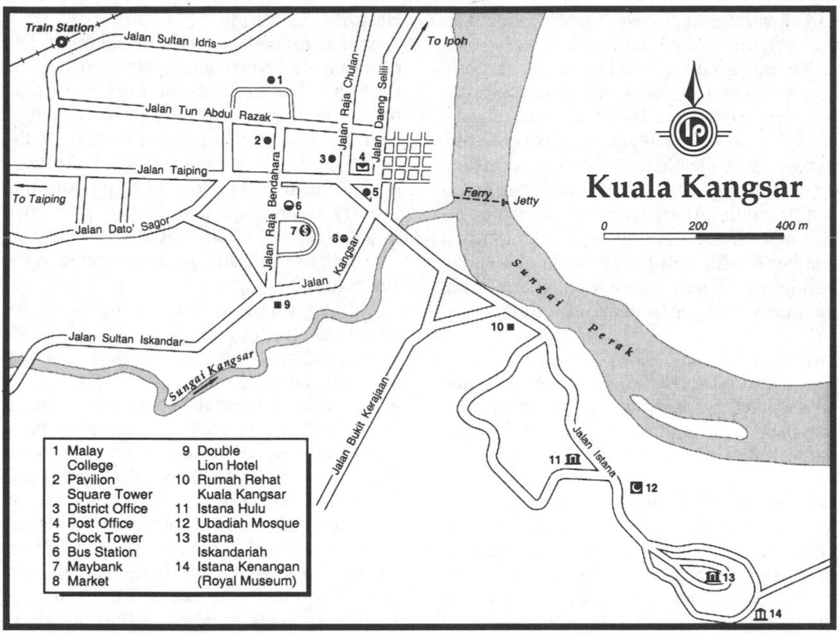

at 74 Jalan Kangsar. Large rooms with bathroom are good value at RM18/30 single/double. At the rear are newer air-con rooms with all mod cons for RM75.

The best place to stay in town is the modernised resthouse *Rumah Rehat Kuala Kangsar* (☎ 05-777 3705), just off Jalan Istana near the kris monument. Large, air-con rooms, many overlooking the river, cost RM60 to RM100. It has a reasonable Malay restaurant also overlooking the river.

Getting There & Away

Kuala Kangsar is 50km north-west of Ipoh, just off the main KL-Butterworth road. It's 123km south of Butterworth and 269km north of KL. More frequent bus connections include Butterworth (RM6), Ipoh (RM2.20), KL (RM12.50), Lumut (RM5.70) and Taiping (RM4; from the local bus station). There are less frequent services to Kota Bharu (RM14.50) and Gerik (RM15).

Taxis leave regularly from next to the bus station to Butterworth (RM60, whole car), KL (RM90), Ipoh (RM22) and Taiping (RM18).

The train station is less conveniently located to the north-west of town. All KL-Butterworth trains stop in Kuala Kangsar.

TAIPING

The 'Town of Everlasting Peace' hardly started out that way. A century ago, when it was known as Larut, the town was a raucous, rough-and-tumble tin-mining centre – the oldest one in Malaysia. Bitter feuds broke out three times between rival Chinese secret societies, with injury, torture and death taking place on all sides. When colonial administrators finally brought the bloody mayhem under control in 1874, they took the prudent step of renaming the town. Though it was then the largest and most important town in Perak, by 1890 the Kinta Valley around Ipoh had already begun to overshadow Taiping as the centre of the tin industry.

Taiping is now a low-key town, and any new developments are centred on the highway, on the outskirts. The central part of town is somewhat down-at-heel but always lively, in contrast to the old colonial district centred on the famous Lake Gardens which are green and tranquil. Apart from misty, Chinese-looking views, Taiping also has quite a number of old, well-preserved Anglo-Malay buildings. There's good food in the night market, a great museum and few tourists.

Information

The helpful Tourist Police office, on Jalan Iskandar at the taxi station, can provide a map and answer most queries. It is open daily from 9 am to 1 pm and 2 to 5 pm.

Lake Gardens (Taman Tasik)

Taiping is renowned for its beautiful Lake Gardens, built on the site of an abandoned tin mine right beside the town in 1890. The well-kept gardens owe some of their lush greenery to the fact that Taiping has one of the highest annual rainfalls in Peninsular Malaysia. In the hills that rise above the gardens is Bukit Larut (formerly Maxwell Hill), the oldest hill station in Malaysia.

The Lake Gardens also contain the small, but very pleasantly landscaped **Taiping Zoo**. It's open daily from 8 am to 6.30 pm, but you won't see many animals in the midday heat. Admission is RM1.50/3 child/adult plus a small fee for a camera.

Muzium Perak

North west of the gardens, the state museum is open from 9 am to 5 pm daily, but closed from 12.15 to 2.45 pm on Friday. Housed in a fine colonial building, it's the oldest (since 1883) and one of the best museums in Malaysia. Its contents include well-displayed exhibits on the Orang Asli, as well as craft and historical displays.

The motley collection of stuffed Malaysian animals, reptiles and birds is slightly repugnant but very educational and includes almost all native mammals and many birds.

Historic Buildings

A wander around town will reveal reminders of Taiping's former glory. The neoclassical **District Office** on Jalan Taming Sari (it's set back from the street at the edge of Taiping's central Chinatown), and at the start of the colonial district around today's Lake Gardens. Almost next door is the **Independence Library**, established in 1882. Closer to town on Jalan Kota, the **Jam Besar** (Clock Tower) was built in 1890, and once functioned as the fire station.

Taiping was also the starting point for Malaysia's first railway line; opened in 1885, it ran 13.5km to Port Weld but is now closed. The original train station is now part of the **King Edward School**, a gracious colonial building. The train station building is just to the west of the main school building. Also on Jalan Stesyen are **St George's School** and the **Town Rest House** which was built in 1885, and was once the governor's residence. Another colonial-era landmark is the white-washed **New Golf Club** building, on Jalan Bukit Larut which also dates from 1885.

Taiping has a number of fine old shophouses, such as the **Peace Hotel** on Jalan Iskandar. This magnificent example of Peranakan architecture has stucco tiles, stained glass, and beautifully carved bird and flower designs on the upper wall dividers inside. Renovation would turn it into a real showpiece, but until then don't contemplate staying here – it's a seedy dive.

Opposite Muzium Perak, the **prison**, built in 1885 to house lawless miners, was used by the Japanese during WWII, later as a rehabilitation centre for captured Communists during the Emergency and then for housing political detainees under the Internal Security Act (ISA) ruling.

Also near the museum, the **Ling Nam Temple** is the oldest Chinese temple in Perak and has a boat figure dedicated to the Chinese emperor who built the first canal in China.

Other Attractions

Taiping has an **Allied War Cemetery**, just east of the Lake Gardens, with row upon row of headstones for the British, Australian

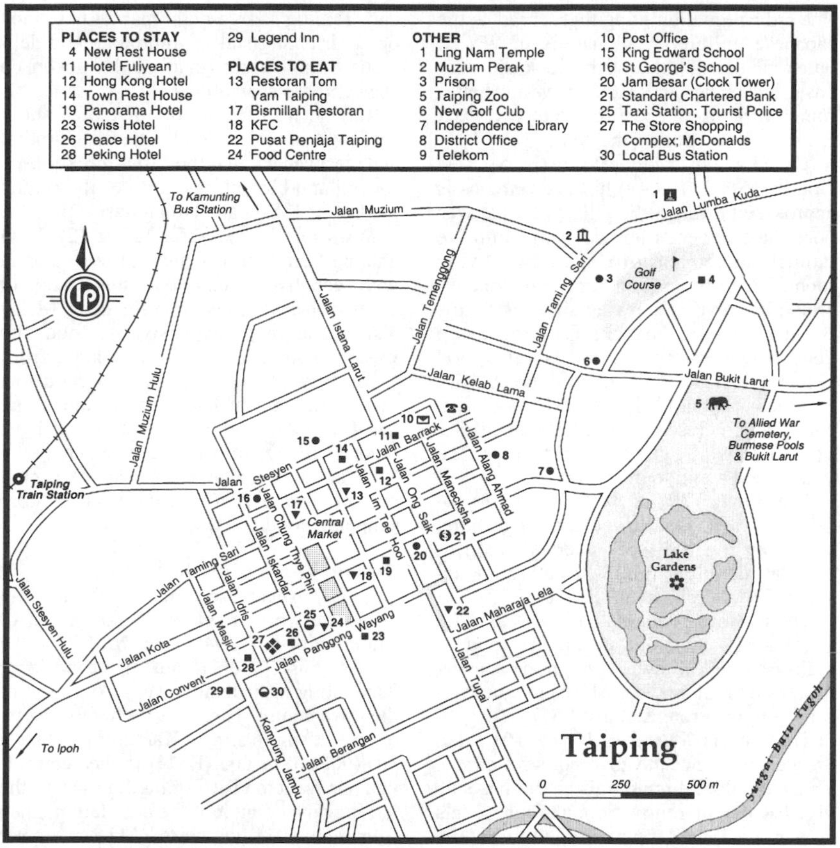

and Indian troops killed during WWII. Further past the cemetery down a side road, the **Burmese Pools** are a popular bathing spot by the river.

Places to Stay

Taiping has an excellent selection of moderately priced accommodation. Most of the cheap hotels are scattered around the central market, the liveliest but noisiest part of town. The better choices are a few streets away.

The *Hong Kong Hotel* (☎ 05-807 3824) at 79 Jalan Barrack (the entrance is on Jalan Lim Tee Hooi) is close to everything, but in a quiet side street. Its simplest fan rooms for RM22 are small and rather grubby, but the larger rooms with air-con for RM30 are a better deal.

Right in the thick of things near the central market, the *Swiss Hotel* (☎ 05-807 4899), 37 Jalan Panggong Wayang, is reasonably clean and good value, with fan rooms with bathroom for RM20, or RM38 for a larger room with air-con.

In the same area, the friendly *Peking Hotel* (☎ 05-807 2975), 2 Jalan Idris, is a fine old colonial building that served as the Japanese military headquarters in WWII. Quiet singles/doubles at the back are very basic but cheap at RM20/25, while better rooms with air-con cost RM35 or RM40. It tends to fill up during the week.

The *Rumah Rehat Baru* (New Rest House; ☎ 05-807 2044) in Lake Gardens is approached through the pillars of what was once the Resident's house – you can drive through the remains of Hugh Low's living room. The resthouse is a large, modern concrete place that is showing signs of decay, but it overlooks the Lake Gardens, has a good terrace restaurant, and is very good value at RM31.50 for huge doubles with bathroom, fan and balcony, RM35 with air-con. Though close to Taiping's main attractions it is well out of the city centre, so you'll need a taxi to get there.

The *Hotel Fuliyean* (☎ 05-806 8648), 14 Jalan Barrack, is a newer mid-range hotel with dazzling tile work everywhere. Immaculate doubles/triples with bathroom, hot water, TV and phone are RM50/55.

The six storey *Panorama Hotel* (☎ 05-808 4111) at 61 Jalan Kota was the first modern high-rise hotel in town. It might be starting to show a bit of age, but who can argue with fully equipped rooms at just RM75?

The historic *Town Rest House*, 101 Jalan Stesyen, was once the governor's residence. This old colonial building's charm has survived a recent renovation, though it has now moved well upmarket, with rooms from around RM100.

Taiping's best hotel is the *Legend Inn* (☎ 05-806 0000), a three star hotel opposite the local bus station on Jalan Masjid with rooms for RM120 and RM160, less after discount. Rooms have all the trimmings and the hotel has a good lobby coffee shop.

Places to Eat

Taiping has a good array of food centres. The one next to the taxi station is very clean and has a wide variety. The biggest, the *Pusat Penjaja Taiping*, takes up a whole block on Jalan Tupai and serves mostly Chinese food with a Malay section at one end. Taiping's large night market has many open-air eating stalls – murtabak and delicious ayam percik (marinated chicken on skewers) are specialities.

Taiping also has a host of coffee shops serving economical food. One of the oldest and most venerable is the *Bismillah Restoran* for roti and biryani; it's north of the central market, at 138 Jalan Taming Sari.

Restoran Tom Yam Taiping at 120 Jalan Taming Sari is an excellent little restaurant with seductive air-con and a huge range of cheap dishes. It offers tom yam, many Malay dishes and more expensive seafood and western dishes, such as steak or lamb grills.

The *New Rest House* makes a good stab at western food, such as chicken cutlets, and has fine views of the mountains and the Lake Gardens from the terrace. There's a *KFC* outlet on Jalan Kota near the central market, and a *McDonald's* in The Store shopping complex.

Getting There & Away

Taiping is several kilometres off the main KL-Butterworth road. It's 88km south of Butterworth and 304km north of KL. The express bus station is out in the sticks at Kamunting near the highway, 7km north of the town centre. There are no hotels nearby or any reason to stay in Kamunting – take a bus (60 sen) or taxi (RM4) to the centre. If you just want to visit Taiping for the day, the left luggage counter at the bus station, open from 9 am to 11 pm, costs RM2 per bag per day. Frequent buses go to Butterworth (RM4), Ipoh (RM4.30) and KL (RM13), with less-frequent connections to other destinations, including Lumut and Kuantan.

The local bus station in the centre of town near the central market has non-air-con buses to the surrounding towns and further afield to Kuala Kangsar, Ipoh and Gerik. You can transfer to Kamunting from the local bus station on the No 8 bus to Parit Buntar, but only every second No 8 departure runs via Kamunting.

All KL-Butterworth trains stop at Taiping's train station, half a kilometre east of the town centre.

Regular long-distance taxis operate from the taxi station near the central market. Whole-taxi fares are: RM48 to Butterworth, RM48 to Ipoh and RM20 to Kuala Kangsar.

BUKIT LARUT (MAXWELL HILL)

The oldest hill station in Malaysia is 12km from Taiping, at an altitude of 1019m. It was formerly a tea estate, and this quiet little station is simply a cool and peaceful place to visit. There are no golf courses, fancy restaurants or other hill-station trappings – let alone casinos. Few people visit Maxwell Hill, renamed Bukit Larut but still more commonly known by its original name. In fact, the bungalows there only accommodate around 70 visitors. During the school holidays all are full. Even if you don't stay, Maxwell Hill makes an excellent day trip.

Getting up to Maxwell Hill is half the fun, and once there you've got fine views down over Taiping and the Lake Gardens far below. On a clear day from the road towards the top you can see the coast all the way from Penang to Pangkor.

Exploring the Hill

Most visitors go up and back by Land Rover, though the hill is also a favourite with locals who walk up in three to four hours. The walk along the road through the jungle is pleasant but taxing. You can also take a Land Rover up and walk down.

The first stop is at the Tea Gardens checkpoint at the Batu 3.5 (Km 5.5) mark, where a ramshackle guesthouse and a few exotic trees are the only reminder of the former tea estate. Next up at Batu 6 (Km 9.5) is the main post at Maxwell Hill, where you'll find the Bukit Larut Guesthouse, Bungalow Beringin, Rumah Angkasa and a canteen for meals. The Land Rovers stop at the main administration office, where you book for the return journey – very advisable on weekends. There are some very nice strolls through the nearby gardens from here.

The Land Rovers usually continue 1km up the hill to Gunung Hijau Rest House. Nearby are the Cendana, Tempinis and Sri Kanangan bungalows. From here it is a 30 minute walk along the road, noted for its profusion of butterflies, to the Telekom transmitter station at the top of the hill.

The jungle on the hill is superb, but the only real trail for exploring it leads off the main road between the two transmission towers. It follows a water pipe to Gunung Hijau (1448m) and an abandoned guesthouse. You can follow the leech-ridden path for only about 15 minutes to an old pumping station, now curiously functioning as a small Shiva shrine, but even this short walk allows a good chance of seeing monkeys and numerous birds. Beyond the shrine, the trail is overgrown and should only be undertaken with a guide.

Walking back down the road, it takes half an hour from Gunung Hijau Rest House to the Bukit Larut Guesthouse, another hour to the Tea Gardens checkpoint, then another 1½ hours to get to the Land Rover station at the bottom of the hill, near the Taiping Lake Gardens.

Places to Stay & Eat

You can book space in one of the bungalows by ringing ☎ 05-807 7241 or by writing to the Officer in Charge, Bukit Larut Hill Resort, Taiping. If you've not booked earlier, you can ring from the Land Rover station at the bottom of the hill.

There are two resthouse bungalows, *Bukit Larut Guesthouse* and the *Gunung Hijau Rest House*; both have four doubles for RM15. The bungalows *Beringin*, *Cendana* and *Tempinis* are equipped with kitchens, so you need to bring provisions. Beringin and Cendana both accommodate up to eight people and cost RM150 and RM100 respectively. Tempinis can accommodate 10 people and costs RM100. You pay for the whole bungalow regardless of how many people are in your party. The *Rumah Angkasa* and *Sri Kayangan* are more luxurious and cost RM150 and RM200, but are normally available only for VIPs. The *Tea Gardens Guesthouse* has long been closed, but there are (vague) plans to renovate and reopen it. Meals are available at the bungalows, but should be ordered in advance.

There is also a basic camping ground near the Tempinis bungalow costing RM2 per person.

Day-trippers can get basic rice or noodle meals at the *Surau Kanteen* near the main Bukit Larut Land Rover office, or the nearby *Bukit Larut Guesthouse* is usually open for meals and has great views.

Getting There & Away

Prior to WWII, you had a choice of walking, riding a pony or being carried up in a sedan chair, as there was no road to the station. Japanese POWs were put to work building a road at the close of the war, and it was opened in 1948.

Private cars are not allowed on the road, which is only open to government Land Rovers which run a regular service from the station at the foot of the hill, just above the Taiping Lake Gardens. They operate every hour on the hour from 8 am to 6 pm (5 pm in the low season) and the trip takes about 40 minutes.

The winding road negotiates 72 hairpin bends on the steep ascent, and traffic is strictly one way. There are superb views through the trees on the way up. The up and down Land Rovers meet at the Tea Gardens, the midway point. The fare from the bottom is RM2 to the administration office and RM2.50 to Gunung Hijau Rest House. Alternatively, you can walk to the top in three or four hours.

To book a seat on a Land Rover (which is advisable), ring the station (☎ 05-807 7243) at the bottom of the hill. A taxi from central Taiping to this station, about 2km east of the Lake Gardens, should cost around RM5.

GERIK

Gerik, in the isolated north-east of Perak, was once just a logging 'cowboy town', but the Lebuh Raya and the huge Temengor Dam hydroelectric scheme have put it on the map. For WWII buffs, the area has many associations with the exploits of Force 136.

Lying at the edge of some of most extensive and untamed jungle in Malaysia, this small, grotty town still has something of a frontier feel, with a very mixed population of Chinese merchants, Malay and Indian logging workers, and a noticeable presence of negrito Orang Asli.

Places to Stay

Gerik has a number of basic hotels. A short walk downhill from the bus station along Jalan Takong Datuk, the *Friendly Park Hotel* (☎ 05-791 2378) at No 60 is one of the better choices. Clean, comfortable rooms with bathroom cost RM32 or RM40 with air-con and hot water. Further along the *Great Wall Hotel* (☎ 05-791 1211) at No 20 is the best budget option. Clean, basic rooms with shared bathroom cost RM20.

The *Rumah Rehat Gerik* (Rest House; ☎ 05-791 1454), 682 Jalan Haji Meor Yahya, is the best. It is in the only attractive part of town, surrounded by gardens, 1.5km west of the town centre. Large, modern doubles cost RM55 or RM70 with air-con.

Getting There & Away

Though it is a central point between the east and west coasts, Gerik is not well connected for buses. A morning express bus runs to Butterworth; otherwise catch a local bus to Baling first, then a bus from there to Butterworth. For Kota Bharu, first catch a bus to Tanah Merah. There are two daily buses to/from Ipoh, Kuala Kangsar and Taiping, and one to/from KL. The taxi station is opposite the bus station; fairly regular share taxis go to Butterworth (RM20), Ipoh (RM20) and Kuala Kangsar (RM15) in the morning.

A few buses each day go to Pulau Banding for RM5, or Tanah Merah buses also go via Pulau Banding. A chartered taxi to Pulau Banding costs RM20, or RM30 return.

TASIK TEMENGOR

This huge lake, formed by damming the upper reaches of the Sungai Perak, is now one of Malaysia's largest bodies of water. It is at the centre of the most undeveloped region of the peninsula, surrounded by dense jungle, and home to the negrito Orang Asli tribes of the Kintak and Jahai.

The main attraction for tourists is **Pulau Banding**, a small island in the middle of the lake, straddled by the Lebuh Raya. The highway connects the island to the shore, with bridges over the lake on either side. A few resorts cater to anglers attracted by the many fish in the lake, the largest variety being the *tomak* (giant snakefish) weighing in at up to 5kg.

The climate is appreciably cooler than on the coast and, though the dead trees poking out of the lake detract from the beauty, the expanses of water and surrounding jungle-clad hills are very scenic. Boat and fishing trips can be organised, as well as trips to Orang Asli Kintak and Jahai villages on the edge of the lake.

Places to Stay & Eat

The *Banding Island Resort* (☎ 05-791 2273) is on the western side of the island, 35km north-east of Gerik. It's an old-fashioned hotel with a good dining room and wonderful views of the lake. Comfortable and well maintained rooms cost from RM85 up to RM180 plus 10%. The hotel has a restaurant and organises various boat tours, including a day trip to a remote Orang Asli village.

Aman Resort (☎ 05-791 7549) on the eastern side of the island is better value for accommodation and tours, though somewhat dull. Accommodation is in floating chalets on the lake for RM40. The *Mohammed Shah Resort* (☎ 05-791 2885), across the bridge on the mainland, offers rather basic rooms on a floating pontoon. Both resorts have simple restaurants.

Getting There & Away

Pulau Banding can make a good overnight stop on the Lebuh Raya if you have a car, but bus connections are more difficult. Butterworth-Kota Bharu buses will drop you off if you pay for the whole trip, but they are usually full when passing through and won't pick up. The easiest access is from Gerik, or coming from Kelantan, take a Gerik bus from Tanah Merah.

Penang

Penang state, or Pulau Pinang, is made up of the island of Penang and a narrow strip of land on the mainland coast known as Sebarang Prai (or Province Wellesley). While there is little to see on the coastal strip, the island itself and the state's capital Georgetown, is a major tourist attraction and has been on the travellers' overland trail for many years.

HIGHLIGHTS

- **Georgetown** – a melting pot of cultures with some of the best-preserved colonial and Chinese architecture in South-East Asia
- **Good Beaches** – along the island's north coast
- **Penang Hill** – superb views of the Straits of Melaka after a ride on a historic funicular railway

History

In 1786 Captain Francis Light, on behalf of the East India Company, acquired possession of Penang (Betelnut) Island from the local sultan in return for protection. He renamed the island Prince of Wales Island, as the acquisition date happened to fall on the Prince's birthday. It is said that Light loaded his ship's cannons with silver dollars and fired them into the jungle in order to encourage his labourers to hack back the undergrowth.

Whatever the truth of the tale, he soon established the small town of Georgetown, named after the Prince of Wales who later became King George IV, with Lebuh Light, Chulia, Pitt and Bishop as its boundaries. Founding towns must have been a tradition for the Light family – his son is credited with the founding of Adelaide in Australia, which is today a sister city to Georgetown. Light also negotiated with the sultan for a strip of land on the mainland adjacent to the island, and this became known as Province Wellesley.

To encourage settlers, Light permitted new arrivals to claim as much land as they could clear, and this, coupled with the duty-free port which Light had declared, quickly attracted settlers from all over Asia. Although it was virtually uninhabited in 1786, by the turn of the century Penang was home to over 10,000 people.

The local economy was slow to develop, as mainly European planters set up pepper and spice plantations – slow-growing crops requiring a high initial outlay. They were also hindered by a limited labour force.

In 1805 Penang became a presidency government, on a par with the cities of Chennai (Madras) and Mumbai (Bombay) in India, and so gained a much more sophisticated administrative structure.

In 1816 the first English-language school in South-East Asia was opened in Georgetown. Penang has always been a cosmopolitan place and has attracted dreamers, artists, intellectuals and dissidents.

Sebarang Prai

BUTTERWORTH

There's not much reason to spend time in the industrial town of Butterworth; the main reason for coming here is to cross the channel to visit Penang Island. The town has a large ferry port and air force base.

The only real point of interest is the **Penang Bird Park**, 12km east of the ferry terminal across the river. This large landscaped park has more than 800 species of birds, most from South-East Asia. It is open from 9 am to 7 pm; entry is RM2/5 for children/adults. To get to the park, take bus No 65 from the Butterworth bus station, or a Transit Link bus from the Komtar Centre in Georgetown.

Most of the land transport (buses, trains, taxis) between Penang and other places in Peninsular Malaysia and Thailand leaves from Butterworth, next to the terminal for ferries going to and from Georgetown on the island.

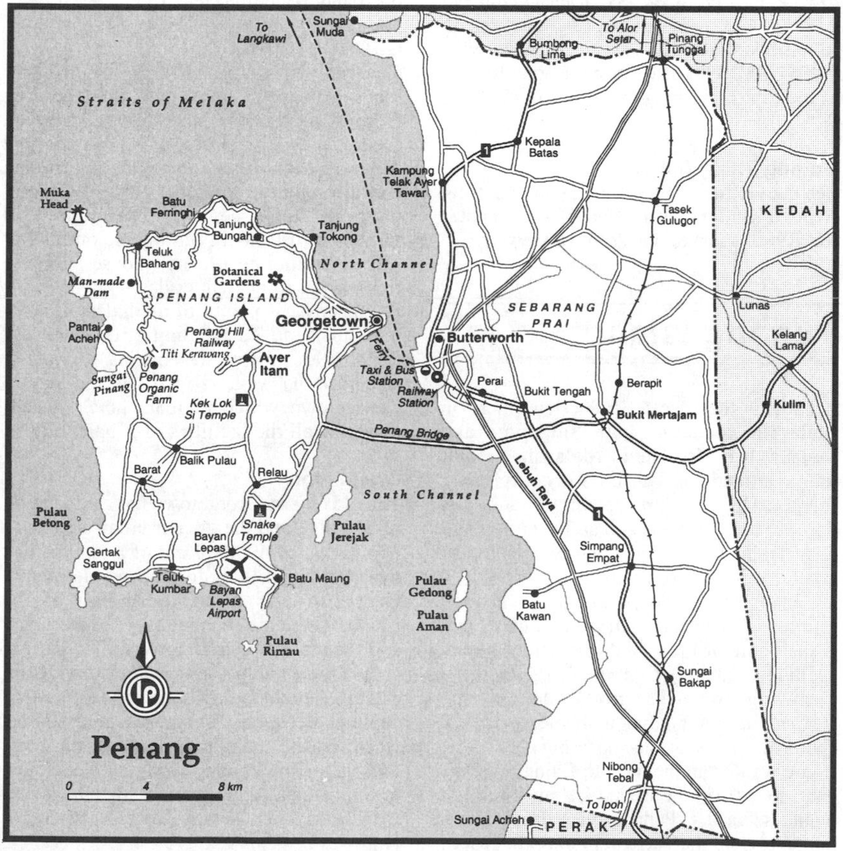

Places to Stay
Butterworth has a number of hotels, if for some reason you want to stop. *G-Seven Transit Lodge* (☎ 04-331 2662), 4832 Jalan Pantai, is only a five minute walk north from the bus station. It's a plain but clean guesthouse with partitioned singles/doubles for RM20/25; air-con rooms are RM30/35, RM45 with bathroom. A few doors down is the friendly *Beach Garden Hotel* (☎ 04-332 2845) with air-con rooms with private shower (external toilet) for RM45.

Plenty of other hotels can be found a few kilometres further north in the centre of the town. The *Ambassadress Hotel* (☎ 04-332 7788) at 4425 Jalan Bagan Luar has air-con rooms from RM52.50. The *Travel Lodge* (☎ 04-333 3399) at 1 Lorong Bagan Luar is at the top of the range and has rooms from RM120.

Getting There & Away
See the Getting There & Away and Getting Around sections at the end of this chapter for all transport to and from Butterworth.

Penang Island

Penang is the oldest British settlement in Malaysia, predating both Singapore and Melaka. It is also one of Malaysia's major tourist attractions. This is hardly surprising, for the 285 sq km Penang Island has popular beach resorts and an intriguing and historically interesting town which is also noted for its superb food.

Penang's major city, Georgetown, is often referred to as Penang, although officially that is the name of the island (the actual Malay spelling is Pinang). Central Georgetown is a sprawling, somewhat grotty Chinese city, steeped in history and with plenty of old character that is fast disappearing elsewhere. If you walk from the ferry to Chinatown, the main tourist centre around Lebuh Chulia, it would seem that Penang missed the development boom that has swept over the rest of the country. However, high-rise apartments and industrial areas crowd the outskirts of expanding Georgetown, especially south towards the bridge and airport, and west to the beaches.

Penang's beaches are touted as a big drawcard for visitors. The main resort of Batu Ferringhi has its appeal, but the beaches are not as spectacular as the tourist literature would make out. Beaches close to the city suffer to some extent from pollution. The beaches along the north coast are the most visited and easily accessible, while those around the south of the island are undeveloped and difficult to reach.

GEORGETOWN
Georgetown is a real Chinatown, with far more Chinese flavour than Singapore or Hong Kong. Those larger cities have had their Chinese characteristics submerged under a gleaming concrete, glass and chrome confusion, but in the older parts of Georgetown the clock seems to have stopped 50 years ago. It's an easy-going, colourful city full of crumbling old shophouses, bicycle rickshaws and ancient trades.

The city has plenty of reminders of colonial rule, and its winding streets and old temples are always fascinating to wander around. Most visitors to the island stay in Georgetown, which has many hotels, restaurants and all the facilities of a major city.

Orientation
The old city of Georgetown has a population of 220,000, and the greater urban area has a population of 400,000 out of a total of just over half a million for the whole island. Georgetown is in the north-east of the island, where the channel between the island and the mainland is narrowest.

A vehicle and passenger ferry service operates 24 hours a day across the 3km-wide channel between Georgetown and Butterworth on the mainland. South of the ferry crossing is the Penang Bridge – the longest in South-East Asia – which links the island with Malaysia's Lebuh Raya (North-South Highway).

Georgetown is a compact city and most places can easily be reached on foot or by bicycle rickshaw. The old colonial part of town centres on Fort Cornwallis. Lebuh Pantai is the main street of the 'city', the financial district crammed with banks and stately buildings that once housed the colonial administration.

You'll find most of Georgetown's popular cheap hotels along Lebuh Chulia in Chinatown. Jalan Penang is a main thoroughfare and a popular shopping street. In this area are a number of the top end hotels, including the venerable Eastern & Oriental (E&O) Hotel at the waterfront end of Jalan Penang.

If you follow Jalan Penang south you'll pass the modern multistorey Kompleks Tun Abdul Razak (Komtar Centre), where the Malaysia Airlines office is located, and eventually leave town and continue towards the Bayan Lepas airport. If you turn west at the waterfront end of Jalan Penang, you follow the coastline and eventually come to the northern beaches, including Batu Ferringhi. This road runs right around the island and eventually brings you back into town, via the airport.

Finding your way around Georgetown is slightly complicated by the street names. Jalan Penang may also be referred to as Jalan Pinang or as Penang Rd – but there's also a Penang St, which may also be referred to as Lebuh Pinang! Similarly, Chulia St is Lebuh Chulia, while Pitt St is sometimes called Lebuh Pitt – but shown on some maps and signposts as Jalan Masjid Kapitan Keling. The old spelling for Lebuh is Leboh and some of the street signs still use this spelling. Maps are sold at bookshops – see the separate Bookshops entry for more details.

Trishaws are the ideal way of getting around Georgetown, particularly at night when trishaw travel takes on an almost magical quality.

Information

Tourist Offices The Penang Tourist Association (☎ 04-261 6663) is on Jalan Tun Syed Sheh Barakbah, close to Fort Cornwallis in the centre of Georgetown. It is a useful source of information and the office is open from 8.30 am to 1 pm and 2 to 4.30 pm Monday to Thursday, from 8.30 am to 12.30 pm and 2.30 to 4.30 pm on Friday and from 8.30 am to 1 pm on Saturday.

The central government tourist body, Tourism Malaysia (☎ 04-262 0066), also has an office just a few doors along in the same building with all the usual Tourism Malaysia literature, although it has nothing really specific for Penang. It is open similar hours.

The best of the tourist offices is the Penang Tourist Guides Association office (☎ 04-261 4461) on the 3rd floor of the Komtar Centre on Jalan Penang. It is open daily from 10 am to 6 pm and is staffed by helpful volunteer guides who really know their stuff.

Foreign Consulates Medan, the entry point from Penang to the Indonesian island of Sumatra, is counted as one of the 'usual' entry points where most nationalities are issued an entry permit for 60 days on arrival.

For most nationalities, visas are not required for visits to Thailand of up to four weeks. For longer stays, apply for a visa at the Thai Consulate (☎ 04-226 9484), 1 Jalan Tunku Abdul Rahman, open 9 am to noon and 2 to 4 pm, Monday to Friday; take bus No 7, 136 or 137. It has a reputation for being difficult with long stayers renewing their visas, but bona fide tourists shouldn't have problems. Tourist visas cost RM33 for two months; travel agencies along Lebuh Chulia will get you the visa for an additional RM10. See the Foreign Embassies in Malaysia entry in the Malaysia Facts for the Visitor chapter for addresses of other consulates in Georgetown.

Immigration The immigration office (☎ 04-261 5122) is at 29A Lebuh Pantai in the centre of town.

Money There are branches of the major banks on Lebuh Pantai near the main post office. At the north-western end of Lebuh Chulia there are numerous moneychangers, who are open longer hours than the banks and have competitive rates.

PENINSULAR MALAYSIA

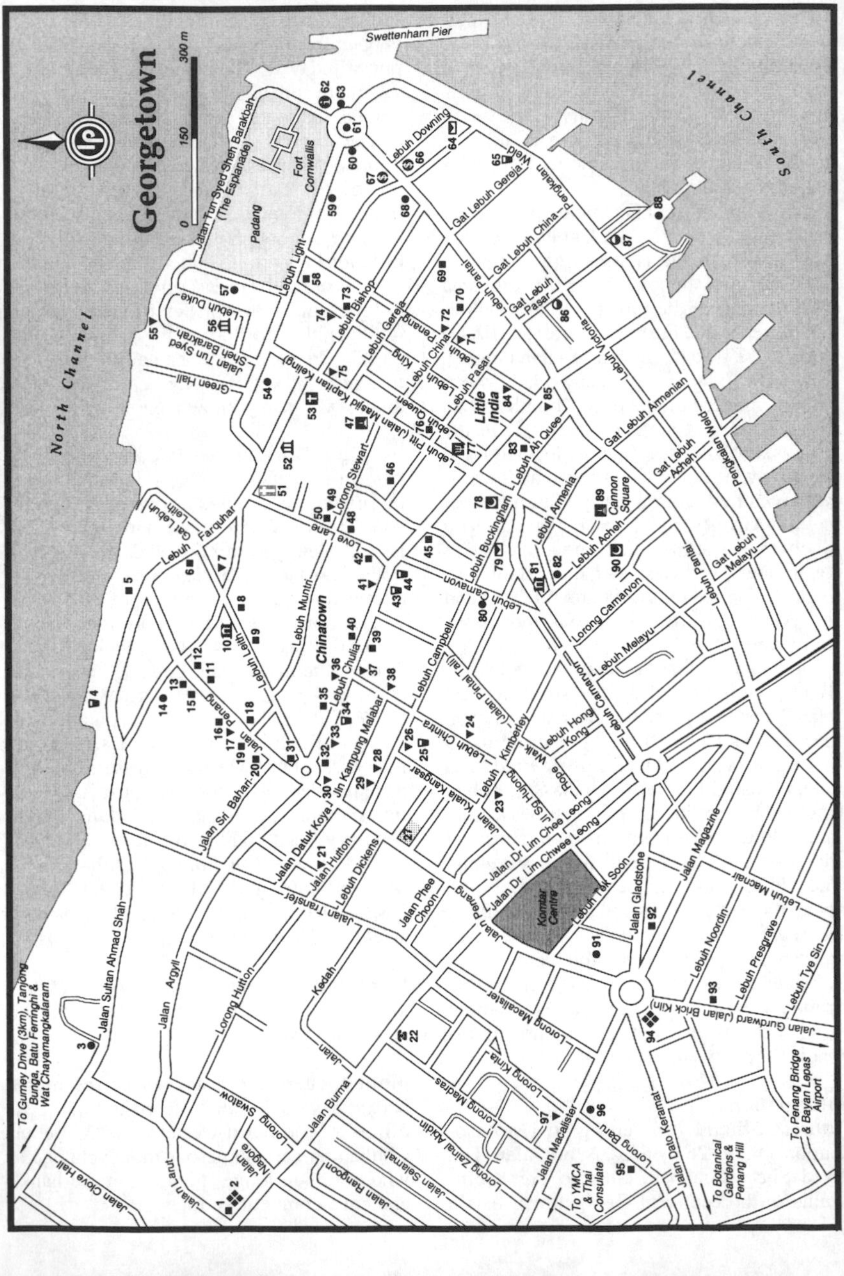

PLACES TO STAY
1 Sheraton Inn
5 Eastern & Oriental Hotel
6 City Bayview Hotel
8 Waldorf Hotel
9 Cathay Hotel
11 Malaysia Hotel
12 Hotel Continental
13 Polar Cafe
15 Peking Hotel; Soho Free House
16 Hotel Cititel
18 Merchant Hotel
19 Towne House Hotel
20 White House Hotel
31 Oriental Hotel
32 Hang Chow Hotel
35 Blue Diamond Hotel
39 Swiss Hotel
40 Eng Aun Hotel
42 Pin Seng Hotel
45 Honpin Hotel; Coco Island Cafe
46 Hotel Noble
48 Wan Hai Hotel
50 Oasis Hotel
58 Esplanade Pathe Hotel
69 D'Budget Hostel
70 GT Guest House
73 Hotel Rio
76 Broadway Hostel
83 Golden Plaza Hostel
92 Shangri-La
93 Hotel Grand Continental
95 Sunway Hotel

PLACES TO EAT
7 Jaipur Court; 20 Leith Street
17 Restoran May Garden
21 Tandoori House
23 Kedai Kopi Kimberly
24 Green Planet
26 Diner's Bakery
28 Hameediyah Restaurant
29 Taj Restaurant
30 Yasmeen Restaurant
33 Tai Wah Coffee Shop & Bar
36 Secret Garden
37 Sin Kuan Hwa Cafe
38 Hong Kong Restaurant
41 Kafe BB
49 Rainforest Cafe
55 Esplanade Food Centre
71 Shusi Banana Leaf Restaurant
72 Kaliaman Restaurant
74 10 King Street Cafe
75 Dragon King
84 Meena Cafe
85 Restoran Tomyam
97 Oriental

OTHER
2 Penang Plaza
3 Singapore Airlines
4 Latin Quarter
10 Cheong Fatt Tze Mansion
14 Christian Cemetery
22 Telekom
25 Rock World
27 Chowrasta Bazaar
34 Reggae Club
43 Hong Kong Bar
44 Hard Life Cafe
47 Kuan Yin Teng Temple
51 Cathedral of the Assumption
52 Penang Museum
53 St George's Church
54 Supreme Court
56 Penang Library; Art Gallery
57 City Hall
59 State Assembly Building
60 Immigration Office
61 Victoria Memorial Clocktower
62 Penang Tourist Association & Tourism Malaysia
63 Medan & Langkawi Ferry Offices
64 Main Post Office
65 Flint's Club
66 Hongkong Bank
67 Standard Chartered Bank
68 MS Ally
77 Sri Mariamman Temple
78 Kapitan Kling Mosque
79 Post Office
80 Market
81 Syed Alatas Mansion
82 Thieve's Market
86 City Bus Station (Transit Link)
87 Round Island Buses
88 Railway Booking Office
89 Khoo Kongsi
90 Acheen St Mosque
91 Malaysia Airlines
94 Gama Department Store
96 Thai International

Mayflower Tours (☎ 04-262 8196) at 274 Lebuh Victoria is the local American Express agent.

Post & Communications The main post office is in the centre of town on Lebuh Downing near the South Channel waterfront. It is open Monday to Saturday from 8 am to 6 pm. There are also post offices on the ground floor of the Komtar Centre, and on Lebuh Buckingham near Lebuh Pitt (Jalan Masjid Kapitan Keling).

If you need a parcel wrapped for posting, MS Ally, a stationers on Lebuh Pantai near the main post office, provides this service for around RM4.

The Telekom office (☎ 04-261 0791) is on Jalan Burma, a 15 minute walk from Lebuh Chulia. It is open 24 hours a day and calls can be made quickly and easily. There is also a phone here which you can use to connect instantly to the operator in your home country and make reverse charge (collect) calls. There's another telephone office at the main post office, open Monday to Friday from 8.45 am to 4.15 pm and Saturday to 12.30 pm. The only place where you could access email or the Internet at the time of research was the Rainforest Cafe, although there'll probably be other places by the time you read this.

Travel Agencies Penang has many travel agents, particularly at the northern end of Lebuh Chulia, offering excellent bargains in discounted airline tickets. Although most of them are fine, there are some who are not totally trustworthy.

Silver-Econ Travel (☎ 04-262 9882) at 436 Lebuh Chulia; MSL (☎ 04-227 2655) in the Agora Hotel at 202A Jalan Macalister; and Happy Holidays (☎ 04-262 9222) at 442 Lebuh Chulia are all reliable operators that many travellers use. See the Getting There & Away section at the end of this chapter for more on airline ticket discounters.

Bookshops There are several fairly good bookshops along Lebuh Pantai, as well as a good one in the E&O Hotel. The Popular Bookshop in the Komtar Centre is a large shop with cheap novels, a good travel book section and a reasonable selection of books on Malaysia and Penang. Times has the best English bookshop in town – it's in Penang Plaza and there's a smaller branch in the Yaohan department store in the Komtar Centre.

For second-hand books, check out the small shops along Lebuh Chulia between the Swiss Hotel and Jalan Penang or browse through the huge selection of second-hand books in the stalls on the 2nd floor of the Chowrasta Bazaar on Jalan Penang.

Libraries The Penang Library (☎ 04-262 2523) is on the 1st floor of the Dewan Sri Pinang building on Lebuh Duke. It has a large collection of books of local interest and is open from 9 am to 5 pm Tuesday to Saturday and from 9.30 am to 1 pm on Sunday.

The Alliance Française (☎ 04-227 6008) at 8 Jalan Yeoh Guan Seok has a library which is open every day (except Sunday) from 10 am to 1 pm then from 2.30 to 7 pm; it's only open from 2.30 pm on Monday and closes at 6 pm on Saturday. The Malaysian German Society Library (☎ 04-229 6853) at 250B Jalan Air Itam is open from 9.30 am to 1 pm and from 2.30 to 6 pm weekdays.

Medical Services Outpatient medical care is generally inexpensive in Malaysia. The following hospitals are recommended for travellers. Dial ☎ 999 for ambulance service.

General Hospital
(☎ 04-229 3333) Jalan Residensi
Penang Adventist Hospital
(☎ 04-226 1133) 465 Jalan Burma

Dangers & Annoyances Georgetown still bears traces of its seamier past, and though the opium dens have gone, heroin is a large problem. Beware of trishaw riders who offer drugs and remember that Malaysia's penalties for drug use are very severe (death for possession of more than 15g of any contraband). Prostitution is also big in Penang, and trishaw drivers will try to push women as much as drugs onto unaccompanied male travellers.

Colonial District

As the oldest British settlement in Malaysia, many grand colonial buildings can still be found in Penang. Francis Light first stepped ashore in 1786 on the site of Fort Cornwallis, which is the main attraction and a good place to start a tour of the colonial district around the waterfront. Many of the buildings in the area are marked with signs explaining their history and significance. They are included in a numbered walking tour that also includes the temples and mosques of old Chinatown further inland. This good walking tour is described in the *American Express Heritage Trail* pamphlet, which is well worth picking up at the

Penang Tourist Guides Association office (if it has a copy) and some hotels.

Opposite the south-east corner of Fort Cornwallis is the **Victoria Memorial Clocktower**, a gleaming white tower topped by a Moorish dome. Donated by a local Chinese millionaire to honour Queen Victoria's Diamond Jubilee in 1897, it stands 18m (60 feet) tall – one foot for each year of her reign.

Another typical feature of a Malaysian colonial city is the *Padang*, the open playing field that serves as a green, central square surrounded by public buildings. Georgetown's Padang stretches west from Fort Cornwallis to the **City Hall** (Dewan Bandaran), one of Penang's most imposing buildings, with fine porticos. The Public Library behind is not architecturally interesting, but it houses the city's **Art Gallery**, featuring rotating exhibits on the 3rd floor (closed Sunday).

On the southern side is the neoclassical **State Assembly building** (Dewan Undangan Negeri), and further north-west along Lebuh Light is the equally impressive **Supreme Court**.

Behind the Supreme Court, **St George's Church** on Lebuh Farquhar was built in 1818 and is the oldest Anglican church in South-East Asia. This gracefully proportioned building with its marble floor and towering spire was built by convict labour. Also on Lebuh Farquhar is the double-spired **Cathedral of the Assumption**.

Fort Cornwallis The timeworn walls of this fort in the centre of town are one of Penang's oldest sights. It was here that Captain Light first set foot on the virtually uninhabited island and established the free port where trade would, he hoped, be attracted from Britain's Dutch rivals. At first a wooden fort was built, but between 1808 and 1810 convict labour was used to replace it with the present stone structure.

Today only the outer walls of the fort stand. The area within has been made into a park, with souvenir shops and a couple of food outlets. You can walk around the battlements, liberally studded with old cannons. Many of these were retrieved from local pirates, although they were originally cast by the Dutch. Seri Rambai, the most important and largest cannon, faces the north coast and dates back to 1603. It has a chequered history, having been given by the Dutch to the sultan of Johor. There it fell into the hands of the Acehnese and was taken by pirates before ending up at the fort. It's famed for its procreative powers, and childless women are advised to place flowers in the barrel of 'the big one' and offer special prayers.

Underneath the cannon in an old gunpowder magazine is a small, interesting museum chronicling the history of the fort and Penang.

The fort area is open daily from 8.30 am to 7 pm and entry is RM1.

Penang Museum From the town's foundation site it's only a short stroll to the Penang Museum on Lebuh Farquhar, recently renovated and now one of the best presented in Malaysia. In front is a statue of Captain Light, which was removed by the Japanese during WWII but retrieved and re-erected, minus its sword, after the war. The exhibits on the ground floor introduce Penang's immigration and ethnic history, with photos, documents, costumes, furniture, the medal collection of Tunku Abdul Rahman and other displays.

On the 2nd floor is the history gallery. An interesting section recounts the bloody nine days of rioting between Chinese secret societies in 1867, attributed by bewildered British authorities to a rambutan-throwing incident. Georgetown suffered a near civil war before the administrators took a firm hand. The societies were heavily fined and the proceeds used to build police stations which subsequently kept the peace.

Also upstairs are two smaller sections with early 19th century oil paintings by Captain Robert Smith and prints showing landscape scenes of old Penang. Outside, one of the original Penang Hill funicular railcars now serves as a kiosk selling souvenirs and drinks. Entry is free but the museum is closed on Friday.

Chinatown

Inland from the former British administration centre lie the twisting streets of the old city, dotted with temples, mosques and traditional businesses. The large Chinatown stretching from Lebuh Pantai to Jalan Penang is centred on Lebuh Chulia, still the lively heart of Georgetown, but pockets of Indian and Malay areas remain within and around it.

Georgetown is a delight to wander around at any time of day. Set off in any direction and you're certain to find plenty of interest, whether it's the beautiful old Chinese shophouses, an early morning vegetable market, a temple ceremony, the crowded shops or a late *pasar malam* (night market).

Jalan Penang and Lebuh Campbell are the main shopping streets which have modern air-conditioned shops, but it's along the more old-fashioned streets like Lebuh Chulia or Rope Walk (Jalan Pintal Tali) that you'll find the unusual bargains – like a 'Beware of the Dog' sign that adds the warning in Malay ('Awas – Ada Anjing') and in Chinese characters. At the Lebuh Farquhar end of Jalan Penang there is a string of handicraft and antique shops.

All the usual Chinese events are likely to be taking place at any time: a funeral procession with what looks like a run-down Dixieland jazz band leading the mourners, colourful parades at festival times and ancient grandmas pushing out their stalls to set up for a day's business. All around you'll hear those distinctively Chinese noises – the clatter of mahjong tiles from inside houses, the trilling of caged songbirds as well as the sound of loud arguments and conversations everywhere.

Altogether, Georgetown is a place where there's always something of interest to see. For an excellent view over this whole sprawling scene, there's a viewing gallery on level 58 of the Komtar Centre. Admission costs RM5, although this can be credited towards any purchase from the (overpriced) souvenir shop on the same floor. Buy tickets from the counter of the Penang Tourist Guides Association on the 3rd floor.

Kuan Yin Teng Temple On Lebuh Pitt (Jalan Masjid Kapitan Keling), just around the corner from the museum, is the temple of Kuan Yin, the goddess of mercy. Built in the 19th century by the first Chinese settlers in Penang, Kuan Yin Teng Temple is not terribly impressive or interesting, but it's very central and popular among the Chinese community. There's often something going on: worshippers burning paper money at the furnaces in front of the temple, a night-time puppet or Chinese theatre performance, or devotees offering joss sticks inside.

Khoo Kongsi The Khoo Kongsi is in Cannon Square close to the end of Lebuh Pitt (Jalan Masjid Kapitan Keling). A *kongsi* is a clan house, a building which is partly a temple and partly a meeting hall for Chinese of the same clan or surname.

Penang has many kongsis, but this one, the clan house of the Khoo, is by far the finest. Its construction was first considered around 1853, but it was not built until 1898. The completed building was so magnificent and elaborate that nobody was surprised when the roof caught fire on the night it was completed! That misfortune was interpreted as a message from above that they had really been overdoing things, so the Khoo rebuilt it in a marginally less grandiose and extravagant style.

The present kongsi, dating from 1906 and extensively renovated in the 1950s, is also known as the 'Dragon Mountain Hall'. It is a colourful mix of dragons, statues, paintings, lamps, coloured tiles and carvings, and is one part of Penang which should not be missed. The Khoo Kongsi is open from 9 am to 5 pm daily and entrance is free.

Acheen St Mosque A short walk from the Khoo Kongsi, this Malay mosque on Lebuh Acheh is unusual because of its Egyptian-style minaret – most Malay mosques have Moorish minarets. Built in 1808 by a wealthy Arab trader, the mosque was the focal point for the Malay and Arab traders in this quarter, which is the oldest Malay *kampung* in Georgetown.

Syed Alatas Mansion This mansion, just north of the Acheen St Mosque on the corner of Lebuh Acheh and Lebuh Armenia, was the residence of Syed Mohd Alatas, a powerful Acehnese merchant of Arab descent. Syed Alatas led the local Acehnese community during the Penang riots of 1867 and organised resistance to the Dutch siege of Aceh in 1870. The building was restored in 1994 and is open daily from 9 am to 5 pm.

Cheong Fatt Tze Mansion Cheong Fatt Tze Mansion on Lebuh Leith was built in 1870 by Cheong Fatt Tze, a local merchant trader who established a vast financial empire throughout East Asia. The magnificent 38 room mansion blends eastern and western influences to conform with Chinese geomancy (or feng shui), and is one of the only two surviving examples of the grandiose architectural style of wealthy overseas Chinese. Its most interesting features include ingeniously crafted louvered shutter windows, Art Nouveau stained glass windows, elaborate wrought ironwork and a superb glazed-tile roof adorned with ceramic motifs.

Irregular tours are given several times a week; it is essential to reserve – call ☎ 04-261 6301 or ☎ 04-228 5016.

Little India
You can't miss Georgetown's other inhabitants. Tamils from the south of India cool boiled milk by nonchalantly hurling it through the air from one cup to another. Money changing is almost exclusively an Indian enterprise, and stocky Sikhs with antique-looking guns can be seen guarding many banks and jewellery shops. Little India, with its spice and sari shops, Indian temples and restaurants, is centred around Lebuh Pasar.

Sri Mariamman Temple Lebuh Queen runs parallel to Lebuh Pitt (Jalan Masjid Kapitan Keling), and about midway between the Kuan Yin Teng Temple and the Kapitan Kling Mosque you'll find this Hindu temple, another example of Penang's religious diversity.

The Sri Mariamman Temple is a typical South Indian temple with elaborately sculptured and painted *gopuram* towering above the entrance. Built in 1883, it's Georgetown's oldest Hindu temple and is testimony to the strong Indian influence you'll also find in this most Chinese of towns.

Kapitan Kling Mosque At the time when Kuan Yin's temple was being constructed, Penang's first Indian Muslim settlers (East India Company troops) built this mosque at the junction of Lebuh Buckingham and Lebuh Pitt (Jalan Masjid Kapitan Keling). The mosque is yellow, in a typically Indian-influenced Islamic style, and has a single minaret.

Wat Chayamangkalaram
At Lorong Burma just off the road to Batu Ferringhi is a major Thai temple – the Temple of the Reclining Buddha. This brightly painted temple houses a 32m-long reclining Buddha, loudly proclaimed in Penang as the third longest in the world – a dubious claim since there's one other in Malaysia that is larger and at least half a dozen more scattered around Thailand, Myanmar (Burma), China or elsewhere. Nevertheless, it's a colourful and picturesque temple and worth a visit.

The **Dhammikarama Burmese Buddhist Temple** is opposite, with two large stone elephants flanking the gates. The first Buddhist temple on Penang, it was built in 1805 and has had many later additions.

You can get to both temples on bus No 93 from Lebuh Chulia.

Penang Buddhist Association
Completed in 1931, this is a most unusual Chinese Buddhist temple. Instead of the usual gaudy and colourful design of most Chinese temples it is quiet, tasteful and refined. The Buddha statues are carved from Italian marble, and glass chandeliers, made in Penang, hang from above. Housed in a large building showing Art Deco influences, Buddhist devotees flock here on Wesak Day. It's on Jalan Anson.

Other Mosques, Churches & Temples

The **Shiva Temple** on Jalan Dato Keramat is hidden behind a high wall. The **Nattukotai Temple** on Waterfall Rd is the largest Hindu temple in Penang and is dedicated to Bala Subramaniam.

Out at Tanjung Tokong the **Tua Pek Kong Temple** is dedicated to the God of Prosperity and dates from 1837. The glossy, modern **Penang State Mosque** at Ayer Itam has good views from the 50m-high minaret.

Festivals

All the usual festivals are celebrated in Penang, but some are celebrated with extra special energy. In November and December the annual **Pesta Pulau Penang**, or Penang Islands Festival, features various cultural events, parades, carnivals and all the fun that usually accompanies such occasions.

The masochistic Hindu festival of **Thaipusam** is celebrated in Penang as fervently as it is in Singapore and KL, but without quite the same crowds. The Nattukotai Temple on Waterfall Rd is the main centre in Penang for the activities. For more information on the Thaipusam festival see the special Places of Worship section in the Facts about Malaysia chapter.

Chinese New Year is celebrated with particular gusto in Penang. The Khoo Kongsi gets done up for the event and dance troupes perform all over the city.

Pick up a copy of the annual *Penang Calendar of Events* from the tourist offices.

Organised Tours

The big hotels and travel agents all book tours. Admiral Tours & Travel (☎ 04-228 6815) is one of the larger companies offering half-day city tours for RM20. It picks up from hotels (RM5 extra from Batu Ferringhi) and offers various day and half-day tours including the Round Island Tour (RM33), Hill & Temple Tour (RM35) and Georgetown By Night Tour (RM60, including dinner).

Places to Stay – Budget

Hostels Hostels in Penang are relatively clean and are well set up for travellers, but rooms are partitioned and spartan – you usually get a bed, a fan and that's about it.

The *Golden Plaza Hostel* (☎ 04-263 2388), 32 Lebuh Ah Quee, is very popular and has an air-con lounge. Beds in the large dorm cost RM8 each, or RM10 in a small dorm. Singles/doubles start at RM16/25 and go up to RM45 for a 'suite' with air-con and balcony, all with shared bathroom. There's an excellent cheap restaurant downstairs.

Another favourite is *D'Budget Hostel* (☎ 04-263 4794), 9 Lebuh Gereja, close to the ferry terminal and buses. A dorm bed costs RM7, small singles/doubles are RM16/22, and larger rooms with air-con and shower are RM38. This hostel is big on security and the 5th floor rooftop sitting area is a winner.

The *Broadway Hostel* (☎ 04-262 8550), 35F Lebuh Pitt (Jalan Masjid Kapitan Keling), is less popular with travellers but has good singles/doubles, many with windows, for RM20/25 and up to RM40 with air-con. Dorm beds cost RM7 each.

GT Guest House (☎ 04-262 5833), 14 Lebuh China, has large dorms with beds for RM8 each and small partitioned rooms for RM15/20 a single/double. It is friendly enough but less appealing than some of the others. There's a noisy bar downstairs.

The *YMCA* (☎ 04-228 8211) at 211 Jalan Macalister is at the top of this range. Fan-cooled rooms cost RM35, or RM45 with air-con and TV, while carpeted rooms with hot water cost RM60. All rooms have showers. There's a RM2 temporary membership charge for non-members of the YMCA, but this can be waived if you're a HI member or have a student card. The YMCA also has an activities room, gym, squash courts and cafeteria. Take a No 7 bus from the Komtar Centre.

Hotels Georgetown has several cheap hotels with lots of character but some are long overdue for an overhaul. Stroll down Lebuh Chulia, Lebuh Leith or Love Lane and you'll come across them. In most places listed here two people can share a bed and just take a single room, while double often means two double beds.

Two popular travellers' places are the *Swiss Hotel* (☎ 04-262 0133) at 431F Lebuh Chulia and the *Eng Aun* (☎ 04-261 2333) opposite at No 380. Both these hotels attract lots of travellers, have travellers' cafes and are well positioned on Lebuh Chulia, but far enough back from the street with car parks in front to insulate them from street noise. The well-run, if sometimes over-run, Swiss Hotel has tidy singles/doubles with fan and shared bathroom for RM18.70/23.10. But if you're returning after the 1 am lock-out you may not get back in. The Eng Aun has an excellent cafe and simple singles/doubles for RM16/20 or RM18/22 with shower and shared toilet. Some of the rooms have had a quick paint job recently, but most are still rather decrepit and would benefit from a good scrub.

In the streets just off Lebuh Chulia there are a number of other popular places. At 35 Love Lane, the *Wan Hai Hotel* (☎ 04-261 6853) has dorm beds for RM8 each and basic rooms for RM20 with shared bath. It's a friendly, well-run place in a classic Chinese hotel. It's a little noisy but rooms have been upgraded recently.

The *Oasis Hotel* (☎ 04-261 6778), nearby at 23 Love Lane, is a typical older-style Chinese place in a very quiet area. A dorm bed costs RM8, rooms range from RM20 to RM35 with shower (but common toilet).

Also on Love Lane, at No 82 and close to Lebuh Chulia, is the friendly *Pin Seng Hotel* (☎ 04-261 9004). It's actually tucked down a little alley and so is well insulated from any street noise. Rooms vary from the crumbling to the presentable, so it pays to check a few. Rooms start at RM18, and from RM25 with shower (but no toilet).

The *White House Hotel* (☎ 04-263 2385) at 72 Jalan Penang is a definite notch up in quality, with large spotless singles/doubles for RM25/30 or RM35/40 with air-con. Those which overlook Jalan Penang are noisy – try to get one at the rear.

At 36 Lorong Pasar, just a small block north of Lebuh Chulia, the *Hotel Noble* (☎ 04-261 2372) is a quiet place with basic rooms from RM20.

Back on Lebuh Chulia near the junction with Jalan Penang, there are a few more places if none of the above appeal. At 511 Lebuh Chulia is the *Hang Chow Hotel* (☎ 04-261 0810), a rickety old wooden hotel with simple rooms from RM22, RM28 with shower, or RM38 with shower and air-con. It's well run and has an excellent coffee shop downstairs. The *Eastern Hotel* (☎ 04-261 4597) next door at 509 Lebuh Chulia has slightly better rooms, but the mosque next door may be a deterrent because of the loud calls to prayer.

The *Blue Diamond Hotel* (☎ 04-261 1089) at 422 Lebuh Chulia looks unpromising with its modern facade, but behind it you'll find a typical Chinese hotel with some magnificent woodcarvings at the back of the lobby. Beds in small dorms cost RM8 each, simple fan rooms are RM20 and RM25 with shower, or RM30 with shower and toilet. The hotel has a kitchen and sells home-made bread.

In Little India at 64-1 Lebuh Bishop, the *Hotel Rio* (☎ 04-262 5010) has singles/doubles for RM25/30 with shared bathroom. While nothing special, it is close to the ferry terminal.

The *Polar Cafe* (☎ 04-262 2054) at 48A Jalan Penang is a bed and breakfast with fairly average rooms, but it has a very social pub. Rooms with fan are RM20, or RM40 with air-con, bathroom and hot water, including breakfast.

Places to Stay – Mid-Range

The graceful old *Cathay Hotel* (☎ 04-262 6271) at 22 Lebuh Leith is one of Penang's few well-maintained grand colonial hotels. The cavernous lobby nearly equals the exterior. Prices for the huge spotless rooms with fan and bathroom are RM57, or RM69 with air-con. The hotel also has a 'health club', but patrons use the rear entrance and guests are not disturbed.

If the Cathay is full, next door at 13 Lebuh Leith is the *Waldorf Hotel* (☎ 04-262 6140). It's a characterless concrete box but has reasonable rooms (all air-con) for RM51/62.50 a single/double with bathroom, or larger doubles for RM74.

The *Honpin Hotel* (☎ 04-262 5243), 273B Lebuh Chulia, is another more modern place right in the thick of things with reasonable rooms from RM60 with air-con, TV, phone and bathroom.

On Lebuh Light there's the *Esplanade Pathe Hotel* (☎ 04-262 0195), a charmingly dilapidated old place right opposite the Padang. It has good-sized singles/doubles for RM44/55 with air-con and bathroom. It's just a pity that all the rooms have frosted glass so you can't take advantage of the view.

While Lebuh Chulia is the main street to look for cheap hotels, busy Jalan Penang around the corner has a string of mid-range hotels. They range from large three-star hotels that have seen better days to smaller, fully air-con hotels.

The cheaper options are on the western side of the street. The *Peking Hotel* (☎ 04-263 6191) at 50A Jalan Penang is good value in this range, with singles/doubles for RM52/64 with air-con, bathroom and TV. The *Towne House Hotel* (☎ 04-263 8621), 70 Penang Rd, is similar but more expensive at RM76.

If its distant location doesn't bother you, try the *Paramount Hotel* (☎ 04-227 3649), about 1.5km north of Jalan Penang at 48F Jalan Sultan Ahmed Shah. This old seaside hotel is set well back from the busy road, and although the old-style rooms with air-con and bathroom have seen better days, they're a bargain at RM57. There's a breezy seafood restaurant in front above the tiny private beach.

The bigger high-rises on the eastern side of Jalan Penang are a slightly higher standard and have coffee shops, car parking and room service. Rooms are well appointed with air-con, bathroom, TV and phone but are often a bit tired-looking. Competition is stiff so discounts are readily offered.

The newest high-rise is the *Hotel Cititel* (☎ 04-370 1188), a good if unsurprising place at No 66. Singles/doubles, all with excellent views, cost from RM150/175 at the undiscounted rate.

The *Oriental Hotel* (☎ 04-263 4211), on the corner of Jalan Penang and Lebuh Chulia, has good-sized rooms for RM115 before discount. The *Merchant Hotel* (☎ 04-263 2828) has rooms from RM150, but you can often stay here for half that price. The *Malaysia Hotel* (☎ 04-263 3311) at 7 Jalan Penang has rooms from RM136 including buffet breakfast. The adjacent *Hotel Continental* (☎ 04-263 6388) at No 5 has recently had a facelift, and now boasts a pool and health centre/gym. Standard rooms cost RM156, dropping to RM92 after a seasonal discount.

Places to Stay – Top End

Penang's biggest hotels, of the resort variety, are out at Batu Ferringhi and Tanjung Bungah, but Georgetown has an increasing number of luxury hotels. All have swimming pools and add 15% tax and service charge to the rates.

Grandest (and oldest) is the *Eastern & Oriental Hotel*, 10 Farquhar St, which reopened in late 1998 after a total renovation of the historic old wing and the construction of a new 13 storey annexe. Built in 1885, the original E&O was one of those superb, stylish old establishments designed in the Raffles manner – indeed it was built by the Sarkies brothers, who also constructed the Raffles in Singapore and the Strand in Yangon (Rangoon). The E&O has featured in several Somerset Maugham stories. It's right on the waterfront and has beautiful gardens down to the water.

Opposite the E&O at the top of Jalan Penang is the multistorey *City Bayview Hotel* (☎ 04-263 3161), 25A Farquhar St, topped by a revolving restaurant with great views over Georgetown. Rates start at RM190/210, or RM127/138 after seasonal discount, for singles/doubles with all the trimmings. Although they're comfortable, rooms are looking worn. A new hotel wing is under construction.

The *Hotel Grand Continental* (☎ 04-263 6688), 68 Jalan Gurdwara (Jalan Brick Kiln), is similar but much better value with rooms from RM148 including taxes and breakfast for two.

The *Sheraton Inn* (☎ 04-226 7888) on Jalan Burma is another of Penang's top-class places, though not quite as good as the best. Rooms start at RM400, but are normally heavily reduced.

The *Sunway Hotel* (☎ 04-229 9988), 33 Lorong Baru, off Jalan Macalister, offers well-appointed singles/doubles for RM290/310 – one of the best for the money in this range. The *Shangri-La* (☎ 04-262 2622) is next to the Komtar Centre on Jalan Magazine. It boasts a host of bars and restaurants and rooms start at RM390/425, but discounts of 40% are common.

Places to Eat

Penang offers another of the region's delightful food experiences, with a wide range of restaurants and many local specialities to tempt you.

Laksa is particularly associated with Penang. Laksa assam, or Penang laksa, is a fish soup with a sour taste from the tamarind, or assam paste; it is served with special white laksa noodles. Originally a Thai dish, laksa lemak has also been adopted by Penang. It's similar to laksa assam, except coconut milk is substituted for the tamarind.

Seafood is very popular in Penang and there are many restaurants that specialise in fresh fish, crabs and prawns – particularly along the northern beach.

Despite its Chinese character, Penang also has a strong Indian presence and there are some popular specialities to savour. Curry Kapitan is a Penang chicken curry which supposedly is said to have been named when a Dutch sea captain asked his Indonesian mess boy what was to eat that night. The answer was 'curry, Kapitan', and it's been on the menu ever since.

Murtabak (a thin roti canai pastry stuffed with egg, vegetables and meat), while not actually a Penang speciality, is done with particular flair on the island.

Hawker Food Georgetown has a big selection of street stalls, with nightly gatherings at places like the seafront *Esplanade Food Centre* behind the Penang Library. This is one of the best hawker centres, as much for the delightful sea breezes as the food. The wide range of Malay stalls are good for trying Penang specialities. The more restaurant-like Chinese section features seafood and icy cold beer.

Gurney Drive, 3km west along the coast on the way to Tanjung Bungah, is another popular seafront hawker venue. Hawker-style restaurants here, including those in the lively *New Golden Phoenix* outdoor food court and the larger group of stalls 1km further west at the end of Gurney Drive, are noted for their seafood.

Lorong Baru, just off Jalan Macalister, is another lively location where food stalls set up in the evenings. Another market good for Malay food springs up every night along Lebuh Kimberley on the corner of Lebuh Chintra, not far from the Komtar Centre. Two other hawker areas can be found northwest of the Komtar Centre just off Jalan Burma on Lorong Selamat and Lorong Swatow. Lorong Swatow is good for laksa, rojak (green fruit salad in a spicy sauce) and ais kacang, the shaved-ice dessert.

Lebuh Chulia is a great place for noodles at night. After 9 pm, small Chinese stalls set up tables underneath the shop verandas and the street is always a lively procession. Most stalls are found along the street around the Honpin Hotel at No 273.

The big pasar malam changes venue every three weeks, so check at the tourist office for its current location (usually some distance from the centre of town). It's mainly for clothes and household goods, but there are a few hawker stalls. It doesn't really get going until around 8 pm.

Chinese There are so many Chinese restaurants in Penang that it's difficult to make recommendations. Here are a few, however.

At 29 Lebuh Chintra, the *Hong Kong Restaurant* serves good, cheap and varied Cantonese food and has a menu in English. One of Georgetown's 'excellent Hainanese chicken-rice' purveyors is the *Sin Kuan Hwa Cafe*, on the corner of Lebuh Chulia and Lebuh Chintra.

The *Kafe BB* on Lebuh Chulia has Chinese fast food at downmarket prices; you can eat here for around RM6. Also very cheap is the *Kedai Kopi Kimberly* on Jalan Kimberly.

One of Lebuh Chulia's most popular outdoor Chinese places is *Hsiang Yang Cafe*. It's really a hawker centre, with a cheap and good Chinese buffet, plus noodles, satay and popiah (vegetable rice cake) vendors.

For that long-awaited splurge try the *Restoran May Garden* (☎ 04-261 6435) at 70 Jalan Penang (next to the Hotel Cititel), a large, upmarket Cantonese restaurant popular with locals.

Indian The eateries in Penang's Little India are along Lebuh Pasar between Lebuh Penang and Lebuh Pitt (Jalan Masjid Kapitan Keling) or along the side streets between. Several small restaurants and stalls in this area offer cheap north (Muslim) and south (vegetarian) Indian food.

In Chinatown on Lebuh Campbell, the *Taj Restaurant* at No 166 and the *Hameediyah Restaurant* at No 164A are two Indian Muslim coffee shops with pre-war decor, good curries, idli (steamed rice flour cakes) and murtabak at very cheap prices. The Taj also has an upstairs, air-con section, which is amazingly dowdy.

The *Yasmeen Restaurant* at 177 Jalan Penang, near the corner of Lebuh Chulia, is another place for murtabak, biryani or a quick snack of roti canai with dhal dip – an inexpensive meal at any time of the day.

A number of unpretentious south Indian restaurants serving vegetarian and meat dishes can be found along Lebuh Penang. These include the popular *Shusi Banana Leaf Restaurant*, with cheap meals served on the traditional banana-leaf base, and the small *Meena Cafe* at No 118, where you can eat good mutton or fish curries for around RM5. The air-conditioned *Kaliaman Restaurant* is a bit more upmarket and offers a broader range of subcontinental dishes.

For good north Indian curries and tandoori food in modern, air-con surroundings, try *Tandoori House* at 34 Lorong Hutton, where there are also a number of mid-range restaurants. You can eat well for around RM20 per person. The much classier *Jaipur Court* (☎ 04-263 0306), in the renovated former servants' quarters just opposite Cheong Fatt Tze Mansion at 11 Lebuh Leith, serves truly fine cuisine at reasonable prices.

Nyonya & Malay Penang, like Melaka and Singapore, was the home of the Straits-born Chinese, or Babas and Nyonyas. They combined Chinese and Malay traditions, which is evident in their cuisine. The *Dragon King* on the corner of Lebuh Bishop and Lebuh Pitt (Jalan Masjid Kapitan Keling) specialises in traditional Nyonya wedding food and although it's a bit overpriced, it is definitely worth a try. Expect to pay around RM40 for two.

The small air-conditioned *77 Restaurant* (☎ 04-227 9086) north-east of town at 77D Gurney Drive also has Nyonya food, including curried fish head.

10 King Street Cafe on Jalan King is good for very cheap Malay set-menu lunches.

Seafood Penang has a number of seafood restaurants.

The simple *Restoran Tomyam* at 21 Lebuh Chulia serves interesting spicy combinations from Islamic southern Thailand like steamed fish with garlic and sour plum for RM12.80.

Gurney Drive has a good selection of restaurants for dining by the sea. Housed in the old villas facing the foreshore are a number of very popular restaurants with outdoor tables, each with a selection of hawkers providing seafood and other fare. The *Kedai Makanan Song River* is most popular and does great seafood, but the *Carnation*, which also has live music, and the *Restoran New Zealand* are two other excellent venues here.

The *Oriental* (☎ 04-890 4500), 42 Tanjong Tokong, on the water at the north-western end of Gurney Drive, is an upmarket restaurant with excellent seafood. Their branch at 62 Jalan Macalister is cheaper and favoured by locals for reasonably priced seafood.

Breakfast & International Lebuh Chulia has some delightfully old-fashioned coffee shops where you can take a leisurely, cheap breakfast at marble-topped tables while you peruse the *New Straits Times*. As well as the coffee, tea and toast served at coffee shops everywhere, those on Lebuh Chulia have much more extensive western breakfast menus that include muesli, porridge, toast and marmalade and other favourites. Small Chinese cafes with western breakfast menus include the excellent coffee shop at the *Hang Chow Hotel* at No 511 and the very popular *Tai Wah Coffee Shop & Bar* at 487 Lebuh Chulia, which buzzes with activity until late at night. Good western breakfasts are also available at the *Eng Aun, Swiss* and *Cathay* hotels. Another travellers' hang-out is the *Secret Garden* at 414 Lebuh Chulia. It's run by a German expat who serves a range of wholesome breakfasts from RM3.50.

The *Green Planet* at 63 Lebuh Chintra is a popular but more stylish travellers' restaurant where you can read (and add to) the travel-tips logbooks they have on India, Thailand, Africa and elsewhere. It offers an exceptionally varied menu including pizza, lasagne, falafel and nachos for well under RM10, as well as a few Nyonya dishes like cinnamon meat with pickled vegetables (RM10). The *Rainforest Cafe* is at 294 Lebuh Chulia near Love Lane. It has the same management as Green Planet and is a virtual clone, but it also offers Internet access.

The Komtar Centre has a supermarket and is a good hunting ground for fast food. At street level on Jalan Dr Lim Chwee Leong at the north-western side of this centre is a *Delifrance* cafe where you can savour fresh pastries. On the 1st to 3rd floors you'll find *KFC, McDonald's, Pizza Hut* and *A&W*. On the 5th floor there's a pleasant hawker centre with all the usual Chinese and local dishes.

Diner's Bakery on Lebuh Campbell has great take-away baked goodies ranging from Black Forest cake to Chinese peanut tarts, although there are cheaper bakeries around.

For a meal with a view, there's the *Anggrik Biru Tower* (☎ 04-262 2222), on level 60 of the Komtar Centre, which has western lunch or dinner buffets for RM17.50 per person.

The *Soho Free House*, a bistro downstairs in the Peking Hotel, serves hearty Anglo-Saxon grub like fish and chips or steak-and-beer pie.

Entertainment

Lebuh Chulia is a good place to find a beer, with a good selection of street-side cafes popular with travellers. The *Reggae Club* at No 483 is a popular little bar where the music is stuck on Bob Marley and the beers are reasonably priced. The *Hard Life Cafe* at No 363 is a slightly fancier clone but less lively. A couple of doors from the Reggae Club, the *Tai Wah Coffee Shop & Bar* at No 487 is a long-running favourite that attracts patrons until the early hours. The *Coco Island Cafe* under the Honpin Hotel at No 273 has tables on the footpath and is great for taking in the street life. Last, and least, the *Hong Kong Bar* at No 371 is an air-con bar with grimy Emergency decor popular with expat armed forces personnel.

Around the corner on Lebuh Leith opposite the Cheong Fatt Tze Mansion is *20 Leith Street*, housed in the mansion's former servants' quarters. It's a favourite haunt for the more moneyed class, and has a variety of bar areas, tables out the front as well as an upmarket Japanese teriyaki bistro and restaurant.

Georgetown also has discos open until around 3 am. The *Rock World*, set back from Lebuh Campbell, gets lively on weekends and features local Chinese bands. Admission is RM25, including the first drink. A better value place is *Flint's Club* (☎ 04-261 0121), on the corner of Pengkalan Weld and Gat Lebuh Gereja, a breezier pub with deejay music, live bands or variety acts. Entry fees here start from RM18 (depending on the night and the performer) and includes your first drink.

The *Latin Quarter* (☎ 04-263 2049), 38A Lebuh Farquhar, has live bands from 11.30 pm every night except Monday; entry is free but there's a RM5 table charge.

There have been reports that women are occasionally harassed when armed services personnel are in town.

Shopping

Even though Penang lost its duty-free status to Langkawi back in the 1980s, it is still a good place to shop. Kuala Lumpur (KL) has a bigger range, but Penang has good antique and curio shops and plenty of outlets for cameras, electronics, clothes and shoes at competitive prices. Copies of brand name goods are cheap. Bargaining is usually required, except in department stores.

Jalan Penang is the best shopping street in Georgetown. Start at the Komtar Centre, where dozens of small and large shops sell everything from clothes, shoes and electronics to everyday goods. Opposite Komtar on Jalan Penang is a collection of small shops good for pewter, jewellery, basketware and other handicrafts. There are also camera specialists here, and a recommended camera repair shop is Soon Camera Clinic, around the corner at 2-04 Wisma Central, 41 Jalan Macalister. Further south on Jalan Penang, the Gama department store is good for cheap clothes and household goods. The Penang Plaza on Jalan Burma near the Sheraton is another central shopping mall.

A number of interesting shops sell arts, antiques and curios. At the top end of Jalan Penang near the E&O Hotel is a string of half a dozen art and craft shops. A wander along Lebuh Chulia will also turn up a selection, such as Oriental Arts & Antiques at No 440A. Prices range from the reasonable to the ridiculous. Bargain hard.

Also check out the second-hand shops on Pitt St (Jalan Masjid Kapitan Keling) near Lebuh Chulia, which specialise in old coins, banknotes and stamps. Lebuh Campbell is another good shopping street, and stalls on the corner at Jalan Penang have a large range of leather and rattan goods.

Shopping possibilities in Batu Ferringhi range from the large and expensive Yahong Gallery for Asian antiques and art to the night market selling all sorts of souvenirs, copy watches, etc. Cheap beachwear and light cotton clothes can be found at the souvenir centre on the beach near the guesthouse strip.

The Thieves' Market is an evening flea market outside the Syed Alatas Mansion on the corner of Lebuh Acheh and Lebuh Armenia. It has all sorts of unsorted bric-a-brac, much of which is useless junk, but there are also antique pieces for sale – even the odd genuine stolen item.

Getting There & Away

See the Getting There & Away and Getting Around sections at the end of this chapter for all transport to and from Georgetown.

AROUND GEORGETOWN

Penang Hill

Rising 830m above Georgetown, the top of Penang Hill provides a cool retreat from the sticky heat below – it's generally about 5°C cooler than at sea level. From the summit there's a spectacular view over the island and across to the mainland. There are pleasant gardens, an old-fashioned kiosk, a restaurant and a hotel, as well as a Hindu temple and a mosque at the top. Penang Hill is particularly pleasant at dusk as Georgetown, far below, starts to light up.

Penang Hill was first cleared by Francis Light soon after British settlement in order to grow strawberries; it was originally known as Strawberry Hill. A trail to the top was cleared from the Botanical Gardens waterfall and access was by foot or packhorse, or sedan chair for the wealthy. In 1890 the famous hoteliers, the Sarkies brothers, opened the Crag Hotel, which is now a Public Works Department building. The official name of the hill was Flag Hill (now translated as Bukit Bendera), but it is universally known as Penang Hill.

Efforts to make it a popular hill resort were thwarted by difficult access, and the first attempt at a mountain railway proved to be a dismal failure. In 1923 a Swiss-built **funicular railway system** was completed, and the tiny cable-pulled Penang Hill Railway cars have trundled up and down ever since. The trip takes a crawling 30 minutes with a change of train at the halfway point. On the way you pass the bungalows originally built for British officials and other wealthy citizens. A few years ago the original funicular cars were replaced by more modern ones, but the queues on weekends and public holidays can still be as long as ever.

A number of roads and **walking trails** traverse the hill. You can walk all the way to the Botanical Gardens in about three hours from the trail near the upper funicular station or via the jeep track from the top. Take water and food on longer walks. The Bellevue Hotel has a good map in the lobby showing trails. The hotel also has a small aviary garden featuring exotic birds. It's open from 9 am to 6 pm; admission is RM2.

Places to Stay On top of Penang Hill, the small *Bellevue Hotel* (☎ 04-829 9500; fax 04-829 2052) is quiet with a delightful garden, a good restaurant and the best views in town. Though a historic building, later remodelling has destroyed most of its architectural features, but the rooms retain some character and are large and comfortable. Buckminster Fuller was a regular guest here and photos and commentaries in the lobby commemorate him. A retreat here will cost RM89/120 for singles/doubles including taxes. Access is via the funicular railway and then it's a five minute walk. Alternatively, ring to arrange a 4WD pick-up (RM40) from the Botanical Gardens.

Getting There & Away Take the frequent Transit Link bus No 1 or No 101 (or Lim Seng bus No 91, or minibus No 21) from Pengkalan Weld or Lebuh Chulia to Ayer Itam. From Ayer Itam walk five minutes (or take Transit Link bus No 8) to the funicular railway station. A taxi from the ferry terminal in Georgetown to the funicular station costs RM12.

The funicular costs RM3/4 one way/return. Departures are every 15 to 30 minutes from 6.30 am to 9.15 pm, or until 11.45 pm on weekends. The queues at the bottom are often horrendous – waits of half an hour and more are not uncommon on weekends.

The energetic can get to the top by an interesting 6km hike starting from the Moon Gate at the Botanical Gardens. The hike takes nearly three hours, so bring a water bottle. The easier jeep trail to the top starts beyond the Moon Gate and is closed to private vehicles. Both routes meet near a small tea kiosk.

Kek Lok Si Temple

The largest Buddhist temple in Malaysia stands on a hilltop at Ayer Itam, close to the funicular station for Penang Hill. Construction started in 1890 and took more than 20 years to complete.

Walk through arcades of souvenir stalls to reach the entrance, past a tightly packed turtle pond and murky fish ponds until you reach the **Ban Po Thar**, or Ten Thousand Buddhas Pagoda.

A 'voluntary' contribution is the price to climb to the top of the seven-tier, 30m-high tower, whose design is said to be Burmese at the top, Chinese at the bottom and Thai in between. In the other three storey shrine there is a large Thai Buddha image that was donated by King Bhumibol of Thailand. Standing high above all the temple structures is a striking white figure of Kuan Yin, the goddess of mercy.

It's an impressive temple, though crowded with tourists as much as worshippers. You must take off your shoes to enter the temple, but beware of the 'one-shoe bandits', local pranksters who steal just one shoe.

Getting There & Away To get here from Georgetown, take a Transit Link bus No 1 or No 101 or Lim Seng bus No 91 or minibus No 21 from Lebuh Chulia to the Ayer Itam terminal.

Ayer Itam Dam

Ayer Itam Dam, 3km from Kek Lok Si, is an 18 hectare lake, one of several reservoirs on the island. Penang's largest Hindu temple, the **Nattukotai Chettiar**, is on top of a hill beyond the dam. There's a good view from the top, 233m above sea level. This is the most important site in Penang for ceremonies during the Thaipusam festival.

Botanical Gardens

The 30 hectare Botanical Gardens off Waterfall Rd, are also known as the Waterfall

Gardens after the stream that cascades through them from Penang Hill. They've also been dubbed the Monkey Gardens, due to the many monkeys that appear on the lawn for a feed early each morning and late each afternoon. Within the grounds are an orchid house, palm house, herbal garden, cactus garden and sun rookery. A path leads to the top of Penang Hill. The gardens are open daily from 5 am to 8 pm.

Getting There & Away Take a Transit Link bus No 7 from Lebuh Chulia or a Sri Negara 137 bus from Pengkalan Weld to the nearby waterfall. The No 7 bus runs every hour and the No 137 is a half-hourly service.

AROUND THE ISLAND

You can make an interesting circuit of the island by car, motorcycle, bicycle (if you're keen), public transport or on a tour. If travelling by motorcycle or car, figure on spending about five hours with plenty of sightseeing and refreshment stops. If you're on a bicycle, allow all day.

It's 70km all the way round, but only the north coast road runs right on the coast, so you're not beside the beaches all the way. The following route takes you from Georgetown around the island clockwise. The road to Bayan Lepas and the airport is congested and built up, but it is much quieter further around.

Snake Temple

At the Km 15 marker, a couple of kilometres before the airport, you reach Penang's Snake Temple, or the Temple of the Azure Cloud. The temple was built in 1850 and is dedicated to Chor Soo Kong. The several resident (venomous) Wagler's pit vipers and green tree snakes are said to be slightly 'doped' by the incense smoke drifting around the temple during the day, but at night slither down to eat the offerings. Admission is free, although 'donations' are requested.

Getting There & Away Take a Yellow Bus No 66 from Lebuh Chulia, or a No 32 minibus from the Komtar Centre.

Batu Maung

After the snake temple you soon reach a turn-off to the Chinese fishing village of Batu Maung, about 3km from the Snake Temple. There's an expensive seafood restaurant built on stilts over the water which is an excellent place for a meal at sunset.

Getting There & Away Catch a Yellow Bus No 68 from Lebuh Chulia.

Bayan Lepas

Just beyond the village of Bayan Lepas and Penang's international airport, a renovated temple has a shrine dedicated to the legendary Admiral Cheng Ho (see the Melaka chapter for more information on this historic figure). The temple sanctifies a huge 'footprint' on the rock which is said to belong to the famous eunuch.

Getting There & Away Yellow Bus No 66 goes through Bayan Lepas.

Teluk Kumbar

Back on the main road you climb up, then drop down to Teluk Kumbar, from where you can detour to the fishing village of **Gertak Sanggul**. You'll pass some beaches, including Pantai Asam, on the way. Although scenic, these beaches are not particularly good for swimming.

Balik Pulau

A little further north, Balik Pulau is the main town on the island circuit. There are a number of restaurants and cafes here, but no accommodation – circuiting the island must be a one-day operation, unless you bring camping gear. Balik Pulau is a good place to have lunch though, and the local speciality, *laksa balik pulau*, is a must. It's a tasty rice-noodle concoction with a thick fish broth, mint leaves, pineapple slivers, onions and fresh chillies.

The Holy Name of Jesus Church was built in 1854 and its twin spires stand out impressively from the jungle behind.

Between Balik Pulau and Sungai Pinang you pass through an area of Malay kampungs

– if you're on a bicycle or motorcycle (the side roads aren't quite wide enough for cars), turn off at Jalan P Pasir and tour the picture-perfect village there, with carefully-kept traditional Malay houses, flower gardens and coconut groves that look like they've been neatly swept.

Getting There & Away Balik Pulau is the terminus of the Yellow Bus No 66 from Georgetown. It can also be reached on YB bus No 85, which takes the inland route.

Sungai Pinang & Pantai Acheh

Sungai Pinang, a busy Chinese village built along a stagnant river, is the antithesis of the preceding Malay village, but worth a peek nonetheless. Further on, a road turns off to Pantai Acheh, another small fishing village with very little of special interest.

About 2km north, at the Km 14 marker on the road to Teluk Bahang, is a trail to the **Penang Organic Farm** (☎ 04-657 5591). By motorbike it is a 10 minute ride along the track, or a 30 minute walk. Interested visitors can stay in return for help on the farm (though you need to phone ahead to organise this).

Getting There & Away The infrequent Transit Link bus No 351 from the jetty in Georgetown goes to Balik Pulau, and the equally infrequent Yellow Bus Nos 75 and 76 run between Balik Pulau and Teluk Bahang.

Titi Kerawang

From the turn-off to Pantai Acheh, the road starts to climb and twist, offering glimpses of the coast and the sea far below. During durian season, there are stalls set up along the road selling the spiky orbs, and you can also see the trees themselves, with nets strung below the trees to protect the precious fruit when they fall.

The jungle becomes denser and soon you reach Titi Kerawang. Until recently a waterfall just off the road here flowed into a natural swimming pool, but water diversion for the nearby dam has left the stream gully dry. As you descend towards the north coast you pass the dam construction site – a new road is being built higher up as the old road will be submerged. Soon after you reach the **Forest Recreation Park,** several kilometres from Teluk Bahang, which has a forestry museum (closed Monday) and trails through the jungle.

A short distance closer to the coast is the **Butterfly Farm**. It has 3000 live butterflies representing over 50 species, and it also has a mounted insect display and a huge (and expensive) souvenir shop. It's open from 9 am to 5 pm daily (to 6 pm on weekends), but admission is a pricey RM5/10 for children/adults.

Nearby, you can wander around an **Orchid Farm** which also sells potted orchids. Entry is RM2.

Getting There & Away The Butterfly Farm is a 1km walk south from the bus stop in Teluk Bahang.

Teluk Bahang

Finally back at the coast at Teluk Bahang, this village marks the western end of the northern beach strip. It is a laid back, overgrown fishing village, but the huge Penang Mutiara Resort at the eastern end of the bay, and ugly multistorey tenement housing at the western end, point to the future. The effluent from the many fishing boats and refuse washed down the river make this a dirty beach, but the stretch in front of the hotel is good. The main reason to visit Teluk Bahang is for the excellent seafood and the walks around the headland.

Teluk Bahang has a couple of **batik factories** where you can see batik production and buy a wide variety of batik articles at quite high prices.

From Teluk Bahang you can also trek down the beach to **Muka Head**, the isolated rocky promontory marked by a lighthouse at the extreme north-western corner of the island. The trail passes the University of Malaysia marine research station and the privately owned Teluk Duyong, one of the best beaches on the island. South of Muka Head

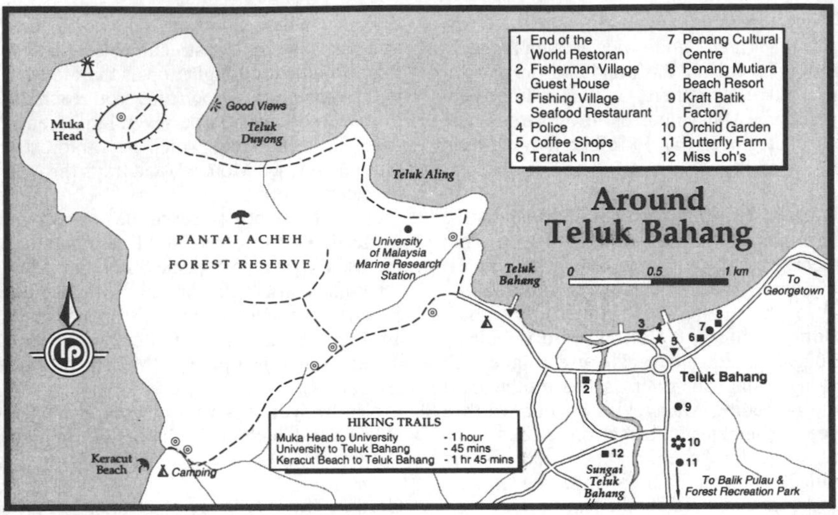

is Keracut Beach, also called Monkey Beach, where there are shelters, pit toilets and lots of bird and monkey life – camping is possible. Refer to the map for hiking trails.

The **Penang Cultural Centre** (☎ 04-885 1175) next to the Penang Mutiara Resort has a traditionally styled *balai* (meeting house) and Borneo longhouse, where there are exhibitions of local crafts and pastimes and cultural shows. The centre stages dance performances (from RM75 including buffet lunch or dinner), and also runs 2½-hour cultural tours of the island at 9.30 am and 4.30 pm (RM35).

Places to Stay Although few travellers bother staying in Teluk Bahang, it has some relaxed and cheap family homestays and a luxury resort. *Miss Loh's* is a guesthouse off the Balik Pulau road before the Butterfly Farm. Miss Loh can be contacted at the Kwong Tuck Hing shop near the roundabout on the main road. It's a comfortable place to stay, set in a large garden. Dorm beds are RM8, doubles from RM20 to RM30.

Fisherman Village Guest House (☎ 04-885 2936) is down a small lane, signposted off the road leading to the End of the World Restoran. It's in Kampong Nelayan, the Malay fishing kampung, and offers simple, tidy rooms for RM18.

The unremarkable *Teratak Inn* (☎ 04-885 2913), in the shopping area on the main street, offers motel-style rooms with fan for RM40 and with air-con and bathroom for RM60.

The *Penang Mutiara Beach Resort* (☎ 04-885 2828) is a top-class hotel, one of the best on the island. The sand on the beach is raked and sifted with a net so the beach is kept spotlessly clean, and it has a range of water sport activities. Rooms with garden view cost RM375, while rooms facing the sea are RM425 (plus taxes).

You could also camp near the beach.

Places to Eat With all those fishing boats in the harbour, excellent, fresh seafood is guaranteed. The *End of the World Restoran*, at the western end of the village by the jetty, is renowned for its reasonably priced seafood and attracts crowds of diners ordering huge prawns, whole fish and crabs in the evening. Hidden away but just as good is the

Fishing Village Seafood Restaurant, which also serves excellent, fresh seafood dishes.

The shopping area in the main street also has a few coffee shops offering Chinese dishes and seafood, and a couple of good Indian places do murtabak, south Indian dishes like dosa, and milk shakes.

Getting There & Away The Hin Bus No 93 runs from Georgetown all the way along the north coast of the island as far as Teluk Bahang. You can catch it from Lebuh Chulia.

Batu Ferringhi

East along the coast, Batu Ferringhi (Foreigner's Rock) is a resort strip stretching along the main road, Jalan Batu Ferringhi, which is lined with big hotels, tourist shops and restaurants.

The beach is quite good, though not as good as Malaysia's best, and the water is not as clear as you might expect. The beach is kept clean, even on weekends when hordes of day-trippers visit.

Though it can get crowded and much of the greenery has been replaced by concrete, Batu Ferringhi has plenty of restaurants, watering holes and recreation facilities and there is a good night market on the main road. The big hotels offer good deals sometimes and cheaper accommodation is available if you want a few days by the beach.

Although Georgetown is only half an hour away by bus, public transport from Batu Ferringhi is inconvenient if you want to explore the city in any depth. The road from Batu Ferringhi to Teluk Bahang is a picturesque stretch with small coves and more beaches.

Places to Stay – Budget Back in the 1970s when the grass was green and the living cheap and easy, Batu Ferringhi, along with Teluk Bahang, was a favourite on the budget travellers' trail. Batu Ferringhi is much more upmarket these days, so far fewer backpackers come here.

The cheaper guesthouses are all right opposite the beach. On the road down from the Guan Guan Cafe the *Baba Guest House* (☎ 04-881 1686) is the first place you reach. This very tidy family home has rooms for RM25 and average air-con rooms with bathroom for RM60.

Slightly better value is *Shalini's Guest House* (☎ 04-881 1859), an old, two storey wooden house next door. Rooms are spartan, but cheap for Batu Ferringhi at RM20/30 single/double. Air-con rooms cost RM45 or RM60 with bathroom. Meals are available.

Right next door is the long-running *Ali's Guest House* (☎ 04-881 1316), which has a shady jungle of a garden. The rooms at the back for RM30 are dank, but the new rooms with bathroom for RM45 are much better.

Next along are *ET Budget Guest House* (☎ 04-881 1553) and the *Ah Beng Guest House* (☎ 04-881 1036) two other double-storey houses with upstairs balconies, similar rates and good views out to sea. Simple singles/doubles with polished floorboards cost RM25/30 and air-con rooms with bathroom go for RM50.

The *Popular Ferringhi Motel* (☎ 04-881 3333), further north on Jalan Ferringhi, offers compact air-con doubles with bathroom and TV from RM50, but there's no direct access to the beach.

Places to Stay – Mid-Range The only place in this category is the *Lone Pine Hotel* (☎ 04-881 1511), north-east of the budget strip. It's a low-rise 1960s-motel style place with a small swimming pool, and shabby rooms at the side for RM149.50 or better rooms with sea views for RM161. It's overpriced, but you can get a hefty 50% discount outside the holiday periods.

Places to Stay – Top End Batu Ferringhi's 'international standard' hotels, almost all of which are right on the beach, are strung out along several kilometres of coastline. Although the Batu Ferringhi beach is not one of the best in Malaysia, these beachfront hotels are relaxed places for a family vacation. There are facilities along the beach for a variety of watersport activities, including boat tours, windsurfing and parasailing, offered either by the hotels or by independent

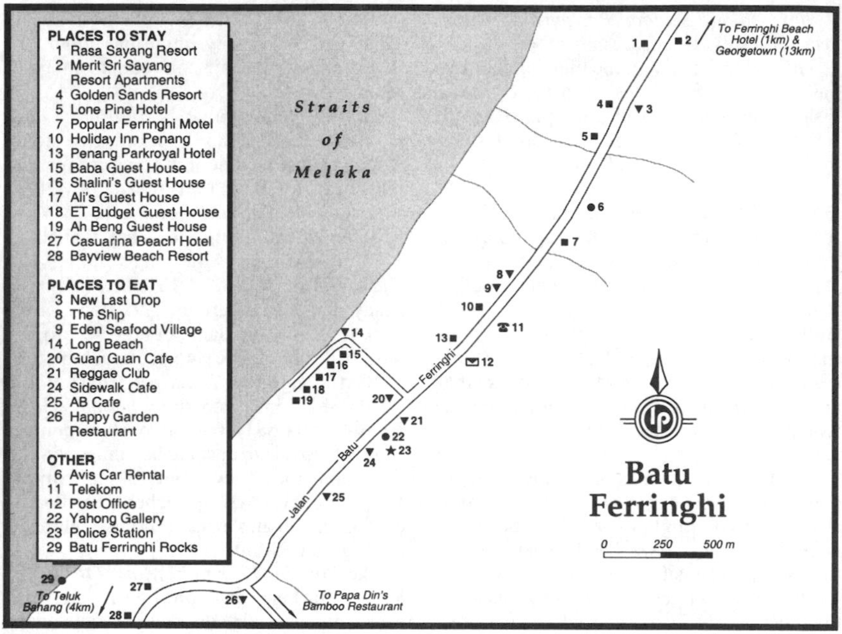

operators. Prices vary depending on whether rooms face the beach. There are major discounts outside the high season (roughly 1 December to 28 February).

At the north-eastern (Georgetown) end of the beach, on a scenic headland just a couple of kilometres east of Batu Ferringhi town, is the luxurious *Ferringhi Beach Hotel*. Access to the beach is by an overhead walkway.

At 188 Jalan Batu Ferringhi, at the beginning of the main beach area, is the *Merit Sri Sayang Resort Apartments*. It's a multistorey complex of suites with kitchenettes and balconies. There's a pool, laundry facilities, a gymnasium etc, and good mid-week discounts are available.

Opposite is the *Rasa Sayang Resort* – the largest and most expensive of them all. Its design is an exotic interpretation of traditional Malay styles and it's the one place at Batu Ferringhi with real local character. The adjoining *Golden Sands Resort* is under the same management, and if you stay at either you can use the facilities of both.

Further along are the *Holiday Inn Penang*, whose beach wing has just been renovated, the *Penang Parkroyal Hotel* and the older *Casuarina Beach Hotel*. The *Bayview Beach Resort* is at the far end of the beach. The beach slopes into the water a little more gradually here, so the swimming is better.

All these hotels have rooms and suites and add 15% tax and service charge to the rates.

Bayview Beach Resort
(☎ 04-881 2123) 400 rooms, doubles from RM320.

Casuarina Beach Hotel
(☎ 04-881 1711) 180 rooms, singles/doubles from RM260/280.

Ferringhi Beach Hotel
(☎ 04-890 5999) 350 rooms, singles/doubles from RM250/275 to RM275/300.

Golden Sands Resort
(☎ 04-881 1911) 400 rooms, singles/doubles from RM320/340 with breakfast and dinner.

Holiday Inn Penang
(☎ 04-881 1601) 350 rooms, doubles from RM270 to RM370

Merit Sri Sayang Resort Apartments
(☎ 04-881 1113) 180 one/two/three bedroom suites for RM190/320/420 (or RM88/138/198 low season)

Penang Parkroyal Hotel
(☎ 04-881 1133) 330 rooms, doubles from RM320 to RM370.

Rasa Sayang Resort
(☎ 04-881 1966) 510 rooms, singles/doubles from RM390/425.

Places to Eat & Drink The big hotels are well stocked with excellent, expensive restaurants, including *Sigi's by the Sea* bistro in the Golden Sands Resort and the Casuarina Beach Hotel's *El Ritrovo* for Italian food. The Rasa Sayang has restaurants ranging from Japanese to a 'British grill room'.

On Jalan Batu Ferringhi is the upmarket *Eden Seafood Village* (☎ 04-881 1236), which serves fresh seafood (plucked straight from the aquariums at the entrance). *The Ship* next door is a galleon-styled monstrosity with a steak restaurant (steaks from RM24) on the top deck and the Captain's Cabin bar downstairs.

The *New Last Drop*, a trendy open-air bar-restaurant opposite the Golden Sands Resort, serves Chinese, Malay, Indian and western food. Further along the road in the main group of shops, there are a couple of cheap restaurants. The lively *Reggae Club* is a popular place to chat with other travellers over a cold beer and hot nachos. The *Guan Guan Cafe* diagonally opposite has mostly Chinese food but you can also get everything from steak and chips to seafood. A good meal should cost under RM10.

At the *Long Beach*, right on the beachfront near the guesthouses, you can sit at tables by the sand while your fresh fish is fried on a large open hotplate.

Further south-west on Jalan Batu Ferringhi, the fancy *Sidewalk Cafe* has terraced dining areas and Chinese food for around RM12.50 per main course. The *AB Cafe* nearby does filling breakfasts with French toast, banana pancakes or oatmeal porridge.

A short distance towards Teluk Bahang is the very pleasant *Happy Garden Restaurant*, where western and Chinese meals are served to outdoor tables among flowering bougainvilleas.

Next to the Happy Garden there's a side road which leads to *Papa Din's Bamboo Restaurant.* It's run by an interesting and friendly old gentleman and has excellent, cheap Malay food.

Getting There & Away See the Getting Around section at the end of this chapter for details on getting to Batu Ferringhi from Georgetown.

Tanjung Bungah

Heading west from Georgetown, Tanjung Bungah (Cape of Flowers) is the first real beach, but it's not good for swimming. Although it has also experienced a building boom with big hotels and apartment blocks cropping up everywhere, Batu Ferringhi is a better option.

Places to Stay A good budget option here is *Lost Paradise* (☎ 04-890 7641), at the western end of town, just past the Mar Vista Resort. It's set on the beach and consists of Penang bungalows that are somewhat rundown but have plenty of character. A good restaurant in a garden setting overlooks the beach and Georgetown. Singles/doubles cost RM20/30 with common bathroom.

The nearby *Mar Vista Resort* (☎ 04-890 3388) is typical of the newer developments: a large high-rise with a swimming pool. Apartments with kitchenettes cost RM220/320/420 for one/two/three bedrooms. You'll need to factor in a 15% tax, though larger discounts are usually available. Other top-end places include the *Crown Prince Hotel* (☎ 04-890 4111) with rooms from RM230 and the *Novotel Penang* (☎ 04-890 3303).

GETTING THERE & AWAY

Air

International Malaysia Airlines has at least one daily flight to Medan in Sumatra, and Malaysia Airlines and Singapore Airlines fly

Typical One-way Tickets on Offer in Penang

Destination	*Fare* (RM)*	*Airline*	*Departs From*
Australia (east)	1080	Malaysia Airlines	Penang
	1215	Singapore Airlines	Penang
Australia (west)	950	Malaysia Airlines	Penang
Banda Aceh	235	Pelangi Air	Penang
Bangkok	440	THAI	Penang
Hong Kong	750	Singapore Airlines, Malaysia Airlines	Penang
Jakarta	350	Malaysia Airlines	Penang
London	980	Aeroflot	KL
Medan	185	Sempati, Malaysia Airlines	Penang
Mumbai (Bombay)	700	Air India	KL
Phuket	195	THAI	Penang
USA (west)	1240	China Airlines	KL

* quoted fares are excluding airport taxes

regularly to Singapore. Malaysia Airlines and Thai Airways International (THAI) fly between Penang and Hat Yai, Phuket and Bangkok. Other international connections include direct flights to Hong Kong with Malaysia Airlines or Cathay Pacific, to Jakarta with Air Asia, or to Chennai (Madras) in India with Malaysia Airlines.

Pelangi has direct flights to Banda Aceh in Sumatra on Monday and Friday at 9.15 am, both returning to Penang at 12.25 pm.

Although the international air fares are less competitive than they once were, Penang is a major centre for cheap airline tickets. There are fewer cut-and-run merchants at work nowadays, though it still pays to be cautious. Long-running, reliable agents are listed under the Information entry earlier in this chapter.

Domestic Penang is well served on the Malaysia Airlines/Pelangi domestic network (quoted fares are excluding airport tax):

Destination	*Frequency*	*Fare (RM)*
Johor Bahru	daily	183
Kota Bharu	daily	87
KL	17 daily	104
Langkawi	three daily	51
Singapore	four daily	255

Airline Offices Some of the airline offices or their agents in Penang include:

Air Asia
(☎ 04-262 9882) 463 Lebuh Chulia
Cathay Pacific
(☎ 04-226 0411) Menara PSCI, Jalan Sultan Ahmad Shah
Malaysia Airlines
(☎ 04-262 0011) Komtar Centre, Jalan Penang
Pelangi Air
(☎ 04-648 2107) Komtar Centre, Jalan Penang
Singapore Airlines
(☎ 04-226 3201) Wisma Penang Gardens, Jalan Sultan Ahmad Shah
Thai Airways International
(☎ 04-226 6000) Wisma Central, 41 Jalan Macalister

The Malaysia Airlines office in the Komtar Centre is open from 8.30 am to 6 pm Monday to Saturday, and from 8.30 am to 1 pm on Sunday.

Bus

The main city bus station is on the mainland beside the ferry terminal in Butterworth. Butterworth has many more buses than Penang. However a number of services also leave from the Komtar Centre in central Georgetown.

Most of the buses depart from the basement of this centre, where the bus companies have ticket offices. However, it's much easier to use the travel agents on Lebuh Chulia (there are several near the Eng Aun and Swiss hotels) and hotels also sell bus tickets. Some long-distance buses leave from other parts of Georgetown: New SIA Tours & Travel (☎ 04-262 2951), 35 Pengkalan Weld, is a major agent and buses stop at the office.

From the Komtar Centre there are several daily buses to KL, as well as two buses each to Kota Bharu and Kuala Terengganu – book well in advance. Other east coast buses leave from across the channel in Butterworth. Only two daily buses at 8 am and 3 pm leave Georgetown for the Cameron Highlands (RM15). The other option is to take a bus to Tapah.

Many of the long-distance departures are at night. Typical fares are:

Destination	*Fare (RM)*
Alor Setar	6
Cameron Highlands	15
Ipoh	8
Johor Bahru	38
Kota Bharu	20
KL	17-21
Kuala Perlis	8
Kuala Terengganu	24
Kuantan	25
Lumut	10
Melaka	24
Singapore	33-40
Taiping	4
Tapah	10

There are also bus and minibus services out of Malaysia to Hat Yai (RM20), Krabi (RM30), Phuket (RM42), Surat Thani (RM32) and Bangkok (RM75). Many hotels or travel agents can arrange tickets.

Train

The train station, like the bus and taxi stations, is across the channel from Georgetown at the ferry terminal in Butterworth.

The Malaysia Getting There & Away and Getting Around chapters have full details on fares and schedules for the Butterworth, KL and Singapore services and the train services to Hat Yai and Bangkok in Thailand.

Make reservations at Butterworth station (☎ 04-323 7962) or the train booking office (☎ 04-261 0290) at the ferry terminal on Pengkalan Weld in Georgetown. There's a good left-luggage facility at the station in Butterworth, open from 6 am to 9 pm daily.

Taxi

The long-distance taxis also operate from a depot beside the Butterworth ferry terminal on the mainland. It's also possible to book them at some of the hot-spot backpacker hotels or directly with drivers. Typical single-passenger/whole-taxi fares include:

Destination	*Fare (RM)*
Alor Setar	12.50/50
Ipoh	22/88
KL	42.50/170
Kuala Perlis	20/80
Kota Bharu	47.50/190
Lumut	22/88
Taiping	12.50/50

Car

Penang Bridge, completed in 1985, is one of the longest bridges in Asia. If you drive across, there is a RM7 toll at the toll plaza on the mainland, but there is no charge to return.

Rental Penang is a good place to rent a car. Good deals can be found at the smaller agents, especially those at Batu Ferringhi, though the main companies are also worth trying for special deals. Rates start at around RM97 per day including insurance (for a 1.3L Proton Iswara), but drop considerably for longer rentals. Two cheaper agents are Ruhanmas (☎ 04-881 1760), opposite the Penang Parkroyal Hotel in Batu Ferringhi, and Bob Rent-A-Car (☎ 04-229 1111), 11 Gottlieb Rd near the Botanical Gardens. The major companies with offices in Penang are:

Avis
(☎ 04-881 1522) Bayan Lepas airport or Batu Ferringhi

Budget
(☎ 04-643 6025) Bayan Lepas airport

Hertz
(☎ 04-263 5914) 38 Lebuh Farquhar, Georgetown
National
(☎ 04-262 9404) 1 Pengkalan Weld, Georgetown

Boat

Sumatra Two companies currently operate boats to Medan in Sumatra. These land in Belawan and the journey to Medan is completed by bus (included in the price), taking a total of 4½ hours.

The Kuala Perlis Langkawi Ferry Service Co (☎ 04-262 5630) has its office near the tourist office. Ferries leave Georgetown on Tuesday, Thursday and Saturday at 10 am. The journey costs RM90/110 in 2nd/1st class. Departures from Belawan are at 10 am on Wednesday, Friday and Sunday. The Medan office of the *Perdana Ekspres* (☎ 061-545803; fax 061-549325) is at 35C Jalan Katamso. Pacto (☎ 061-510081), next door at 35G Jalan Katamso, handles tickets for the *Bahagia Ekspres*.

The Ekspres Bahagia company (☎ 04-263 1943), has departures from Georgetown at 9 am on Monday, Tuesday, Wednesday and Friday. These boats also go to Belawan. The one-way fare is RM45/90 children/adults. Departures from Belawan are on Monday and Tuesday at 1.30 pm, Thursday and Saturday at 10 am.

A new ro-ro (roll-on, roll-off) car ferry between Belawan and Georgetown was due to begin service in mid to late 1998.

Langkawi The same two companies also run daily ferries from Georgetown to Kuah on Langkawi (4½ hours). The Kuala Perlis Langkawi Ferry Service leaves at 8 am, returning from Langkawi at 6.15 pm, and the fare is RM35/45 in 2nd/1st class. The *Bahagia Ekspres* ferry runs daily from Penang at 8 am, returning from Kuah at 5.50 pm, and costs RM35.

Another ferry to Langkawi is the ultra-modern *Star Express* (☎ 04-324 4677), which goes to Pantai Tengah at the south-western tip of Langkawi. This large, high-speed Seacat leaves from the dock terminal just south of Butterworth bus and train station, and is the only car ferry operating between Langkawi and the mainland. Departures from Butterworth are at noon and 6 pm, and from Pantai Tengah at 9 am and 3 pm. The trip takes three hours, and the one-way fare is RM50 on Monday to Thursday, and RM75 from Friday to Sunday.

GETTING AROUND

To/From the Airport

Penang's Bayan Lepas airport (☎ 04-643 0373), with its Minangkabau-style terminal, is 18km south of Georgetown. A coupon system operates for taxis from the airport. The fare to Georgetown is RM19.

Take a Yellow Bus No 83 to/from the airport (RM1.40) with stops along Pengkalan Weld and Lebuh Chulia – they operate hourly on this route from 6 am to 9 pm. Taxis take about 45 minutes from the centre of town, while the bus takes at least an hour.

Around the Island

Getting around the island by road is easiest with your own transport, particularly since the road does not run along the coast except on the northern side, and you have to leave the main road to get to the small fishing villages and isolated beaches.

Bus There are three main bus departure points in Georgetown, and half a dozen bus companies. The city (Transit Link) buses depart from the terminal at Lebuh Victoria, in front of the ferry terminal. Most Transit Link buses also go along Lebuh Chulia, so you can pick them up at stops along that street.

The other main stand is at Pengkalan Weld, next to the ferry terminal. Transit Link buses all run via Pengkalan Weld, but the other company buses – Yellow Bus, Hin Bus, Sri Negara, Lim Seng and Orient Minibus – all depart from the Pengkalan Weld stand. Fares around town vary, but are typically under RM1. Some handy routes, as well as the operators, route numbers and pick-up points, are listed in the table below.

For around RM5 you can circuit the island by public transport. Start with a Yellow Bus

No 66 and hop off at the Snake Temple. This Yellow Bus No 66 will take you all the way to Balik Pulau, from where you have to change to another Yellow Bus, No 76, for Teluk Bahang. There are only a few per day, roughly every 2¼ hours from 7.30 am to 7.15 pm, so it's wise to leave Georgetown early and check the departure times when you reach Balik Pulau. At Teluk Bahang on the northern beach strip simply take a Transit Link bus No 202 or a blue Hin Bus No 93 to Georgetown via Batu Ferringhi.

Some of the main bus routes are listed in the table below.

Destination	*Operator & Route No*	*Pick-Up*
Ayer Itam	LS 91, TL 1	Lebuh Chulia
Bayan Lepas airport	YB 83	Lebuh Chulia
Batu Ferringhi	HB 93	Lebuh Chulia
Botanical Gardens	TL 7	Lebuh Chulia
Gurney Drive	SN 136, HC 93 or 94	Lebuh Chulia
Penang Hill railway	TL 8	Ayer Itam
Snake Temple	YB 66	Lebuh Chulia
Teluk Bahang	HB 93	Lebuh Chulia
Thai Consulate	SN 136 or 137	Lebuh Chulia

(HB: Hin Bus; LS: Lim Seng; SN: Sri Negara; TL: Transit Link; YB: Yellow Bus)

Taxi Penang's taxis are all metered, but getting the drivers to use the meters is difficult, so it's usually a matter of negotiating the fare before you set off. The typical around-town fare is RM5, and some sample fares from Georgetown are: Batu Ferringhi RM18, Botanical Gardens RM10, Penang Hill/Kek Lok Si Temple RM8, Snake Temple RM15 and Bayan Lepas airport RM19.

Trishaw Bicycle rickshaws are an ideal way to negotiate Georgetown's backstreets and cost around RM1.50 per kilometre – but, as with the taxis, agree on the fare before departure.

If you come across to Penang Island from Butterworth on the ferry, take a trishaw to the cheap hotel area around Lebuh Chulia for RM4 – or you can walk there in five or 10 minutes. For touring around, the rate is about RM15 an hour.

Motorcycle & Bicycle You can hire bicycles from many places, including hotels catering to travellers and shops along Lebuh Chulia. Bicycles cost RM8, and motorcycles cost from RM25 to RM30 per day. Just remember that if you don't have a motorcycle licence your travel insurance probably won't cover you in the case of an accident.

Ferry There's a 24-hour ferry service between Georgetown and Butterworth on the mainland. Ferries take passengers and cars every eight minutes from 7 am to 9 pm, then every 20 minutes until midnight, then every 40 minutes until 7 am. Fares are charged only from Butterworth to Penang; the other direction is free. The adult fare is 60 sen; cars cost RM7 depending on the size.

Kedah & Perlis

On the north-western corner of the peninsula, the picturesque states of Kedah and Perlis are the rice bowls of Malaysia, producing over half of the country's domestic supplies. Much of this region is covered by a green sea of rice paddies. Perlis, once part of Kedah, is also the smallest state in Malaysia, with an area of 795 sq km, and both states are important gateways into Thailand.

This corner of Peninsular Malaysia sees very few tourists, although there are a number of attractions in the area worth visiting. The main feature is the island of Langkawi.

HIGHLIGHTS

- **Pulau Langkawi** – a rugged and scenic island of superb beaches and jungle-clad hills
- **Lembah Bujang** – remains of ancient temples dating back to a 5th century Hindu-Buddhist Kingdom
- **Alor Setar** – famous for the Balai Besar (Big Hall), a unique mixture of British colonial and local architecture

Kedah

Kedah is very much a Malay state. It was controlled or influenced by the Thais for much of the 19th century, and the British did not gain a foothold until well after they had established themselves in most other parts of Malaysia. With miles of flat rice-paddy plains, it still has a largely rural feel.

For travellers, the most important towns in the state are Alor Setar and the small fishing ports of Kuala Kedah and Kuala Perlis, from where ferries operate to Langkawi. The small hill station of Gunung Jerai and the archaeological remains of Lembah Bujang (the Bujang Valley) are interesting side trips for those with time to spare.

Kedah state has different business hours to most of the peninsula. Banks and government offices are closed on Friday. Saturday is a half-day and Sunday is a business day.

History

Settlement in Kedah goes right back to the Stone Age; some of the earliest archaeological sites in the country are found near Gunung Jerai. More recent finds in Lembah Bujang date back to the Hindu-Buddhist period in the 5th century AD, and the current royal family can trace its line back directly to this time. Finds in Lembah Bujang show that it was the cradle of Hindu-Buddhist civilisation on the peninsula and one of the first places to come into contact with Indian traders.

During the 7th and 8th centuries, Kedah paid tribute to the Sriwijaya Sumatran Empire, but later fell under the influence of the Thais until the 15th century, when the rise of Melaka led to the Islamisation of the area. In the 17th century Kedah was attacked by the Portuguese, after their conquest of Melaka, and by the Acehnese, who saw Kedah as a threat to their own spice production.

After the handover of Penang to the British in the late 18th century, Kedah once again came under Siam's control early in the 19th century. It remained under Siamese control, either directly or as a vassal, until early in the 20th century when Siam passed control to the British.

After WWII, during which Kedah (along with Kelantan) was the first part of Malaya to be invaded by the Japanese, Kedah became part of the Federation of Malaya in 1948.

SUNGAI PETANI

Known locally as SP, the acronym gives Sungai Petani an air of importance it doesn't deserve. The only reason to stop at this unremarkable town, on the highway between Butterworth and Alor Setar, is for transport connections to Gunung Jerai or the archaeology museum at Lembah Bujang.

If you get stuck, cheap hotels are within walking distance of the bus station. The

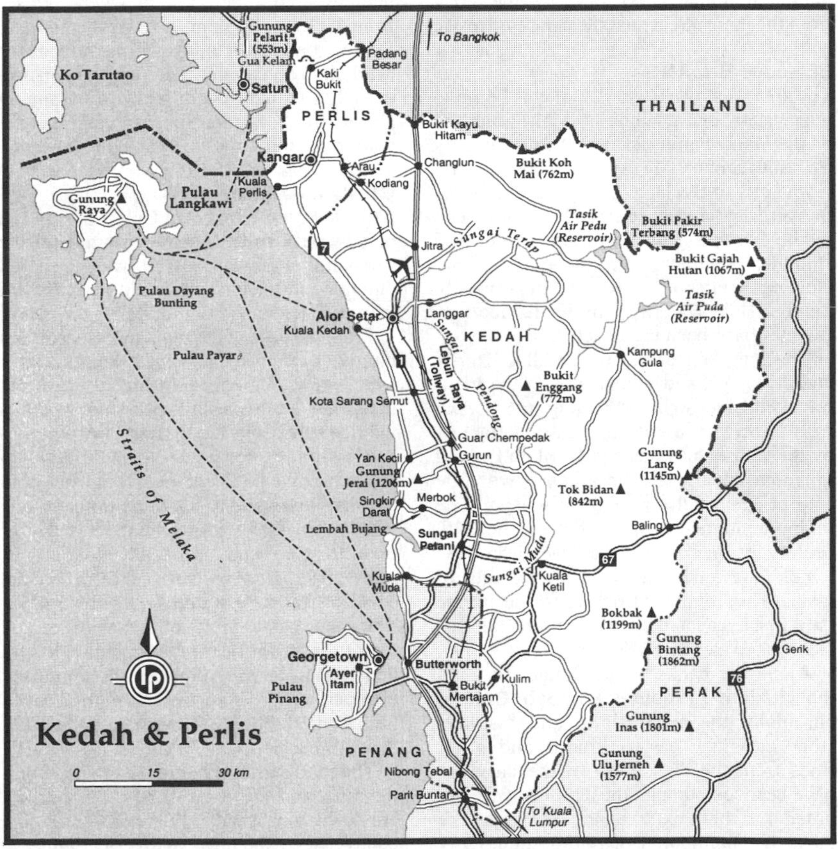

Kedah & Perlis

Hotel Duta (☎ 04-421 2040), 7 Jalan Petri, is one of the best options, with fan doubles for RM27 and air-con doubles with TV for RM52.50. Top of the heap by far is the *Sungai Petani Inn* (☎ 04-421 3411), 427 Jalan Kolam Air, which has a swimming pool and singles/doubles for RM132/149.50.

There are excellent Chinese and Malay food stalls on the lanes behind the Hongkong Bank. At 19 Jalan Tunku Ibrahim, diagonally opposite the Hongkong Bank, is the *Restoran Tajmal*, where you can get a good cheap south Indian feed.

Sungai Petani is on the main train line, and the bus station and taxi stand are one block from the main street near the centre of town.

LEMBAH BUJANG

The area west of Sungai Petani was home to the most important Hindu-Buddhist kingdom on the Malay Peninsula, dating from as early as the 5th century AD. By the 7th century AD it was part of the large Sriwijaya Empire of Sumatra, and it reached its architectural peak in the 9th and 10th centuries. Hindu and Buddhist temples were scattered from Gunung Jerai south to Kuala Muda, and in Lembah Bujang alone, some 53 archaeological sites have been excavated.

The kingdom traded with India, Khmer and Sriwijaya, and was visited by the well-travelled Chinese monk I-Tsing in 671 AD. In 1025 Sriwijaya and Bujang were attacked by the Cholas of India, and Lembah Bujang kingdom later forged an alliance with the Cholas against the waning Sriwijaya. The region continued to trade, but by the 14th century its significance had faded and the temples were deserted with the coming of Islam. They remained buried in the jungle until first excavated by British archaeologist Quatrich-Wales in 1936.

Along the banks of the Sungai Bujang, the **Muzium Arkeologi Lembah Bujang** chronicles the excavations, and displays stone carvings, pottery shards and other finds from the digs. Most of the carvings have been lost, though the temples were not noted for their extravagant carvings like those of contemporaneous Borobudur. Only a handful of carvings are on display, such as a fragment of a wall frieze and a statue of the elephant god Ganesha. Most numerous are the Shivaite *yoni* fertility stones.

Though of enormous archaeological significance, the exhibits are neither breathtaking nor well labelled – most labels are in Malay, but even they are not particularly enlightening. The main interest are the temples *(candi)* behind the museum. They are small, unadorned temples and only the bases remain. The most significant and largest is that of 1000-year-old Candi Bukit Batu Pahat.

The museum is free and open daily from 9 am to 4 pm, except Friday, when it closes from 12.15 to 2.45 pm. It is off the Tanjung Dawai road, 2km north of the village of Merbok. You can get there by taxi, or take one of the roughly hourly buses to Tanjung Dawai and Yan from Sungai Petani, get off at Merbok and walk the 2km to the museum.

GUNUNG JERAI

At 1206m, the forest clad Gunung Jerai, the highest peak in Kedah state, dominates the surrounding flat plains. It was a sacred mountain in the ancient Hindu period and a landmark for ships from India and Indonesia.

From the base of the mountain, a steep and narrow road snakes its way 13km through a forest recreation park to a hill resort. From here there are expansive views north across the rice paddies of Kedah and over to Langkawi. As hill resorts go, this is definitely a minor one, well off the tourist route, but from Monday to Thursday it's often deserted and makes a pleasant, cool retreat for a day or two. Bring a friend, or lots of books.

Roughly 2km before the resort is the small **Muzium Perhutanan**, a forestry museum that has exhibits on native trees and their uses, but little on the mountain's flora and fauna. The highlight is the fossilised elephant dung. From the museum a paved trail leads through the forest to a waterfall and bathing pools.

The road continues 3km past the resort to the peak and the remains of a 6th century Hindu bathing shrine, but the area is now controlled by the army and is off limits.

Places to Stay

Peringan Gunung Jerai (☎ 04-423 4345) is a low-key resort with an old, converted villa housing a moderately priced restaurant. Accommodation is in modern but worn chalets. Standard doubles with private balconies, hot water showers and towering ceilings cost RM92 a double; deluxe doubles are RM115, but in the low season the rate drops to RM60. Chalets sleeping six cost RM200. Camping costs RM5 per site (but tents cannot be hired).

Getting There & Away

Gunung Jerai is 60km north of Butterworth, 4km south-west of Gurun just before Guar Chempedak. From the car park on the highway at the bottom of the mountain, 10 seat minibuses run up to the resort from 8 am to 5 pm. They charge RM50 return (ie up *and* down), but bargaining is possible. Private vehicles can also use the road.

Although some buses between Butterworth and Alor Setar pass right by the car park, the express services use the Lebuh Raya (North-South Highway). From Sungai Petani take a taxi or the Guar Chempedak bus to the car park.

ALOR SETAR

The capital of Kedah state is on the mainland north of Penang, on the main road to the Thai border. Few visitors stop in Alor Setar, the turn-off point for Kuala Perlis, from where ferries run to Pulau Langkawi, but it does have a few notable points of interest.

Alor Setar's long association with Thailand is evident in the Thai temples around the city, but the main points of interest lie around the Padang, where some grand reminders of the sultanate are worth seeing, especially the Zahir Mosque and the Balai Besar audience hall.

The city came under Thai suzerainty until the 1909 Bangkok Treaty transferred rights to the British. Alor Setar and the state therefore had less colonial influence, and it is very much a Malay city, with fewer Chinese and Indians than in other west coast cities. Alor Setar's small but thriving Chinatown, situated where the Sungai Anak Butik flows into the Sungai Kedah, is nevertheless quite lively and crammed with Chinese shops, workshops, hawker stalls and a street market – there are even old Chinese ferrymen who will row you across the river for a few sen.

Alor Setar has the feel of a large village being dragged towards development, with the building of wide-paved roads, shopping plazas and the futuristic Telekom tower dominating the city. The tallest building is still the UMNO centre, not surprisingly as Alor Setar is a stronghold of the ruling Malay party, having provided the country's two longest-serving prime ministers, Tunku Abdul Rahman and Mahathir Mohamad.

Information

The state tourist office (☎ 04-730 1957) is upstairs in the State Secretariat Building on Jalan Sultan Badlishah. It has a few brochures.

The Padang

The large, open town square has a number of interesting buildings around its perimeter. The open-sided **Balai Besar**, or Big Hall, was built in 1898 and is still used by the sultan of Kedah for ceremonial functions. Supported on tall pillars topped with Victorian iron lacework, it also shows Thai influences in its decoration.

Around the side of the Balai Besar is the **Muzium Di Raja**, which served as the royal palace for the sultan and other members of the family from 1856. It has the usual royal family regalia and the Dewan Astaka room is lined with hunting trophies. Tunku Abdul Rahman, a prince of the Kedah royal family and the first prime minister of Malaysia, is honoured with his own displays. Of note is a picture of the Tunku and his wife with Queen Elizabeth and Prince Philip, who looks very chic in a stockinged outfit. The museum is open daily from 10 am to 6 pm, but closes from noon to 2.30 pm on Friday.

Housed in a fine colonial building at the southern edge of the square is the **Balai Seni Negeri**, the state art gallery, with a small collection including some fine Malaysian landscape watercolour paintings by AB Ibrahim. It is open the same hours as the Muzium Di Raja.

On the western side of the square is the **Zahir Mosque**, the state mosque completed in 1912. It is one of the largest and grandest mosques in Malaysia. Topped with domes, and medieval and Mogul spires, it looks more like an eastern potentate's castle.

Further north the **Balai Nobat**, a small octagonal building topped by an onion-shaped dome, houses the *nobat*, or royal orchestra. A nobat is principally composed of percussion instruments, and the drums in this orchestra are said to have been a gift from the sultan of Melaka in the 15th century. It is not open to the public and the instruments are only resurrected on special occasions.

The **clock tower** is another architectural whimsy of a type found in many Malaysian cities.

Muzium Negeri

The Muzium Negeri (State Museum) is on the main road, 2km north of the Padang, and

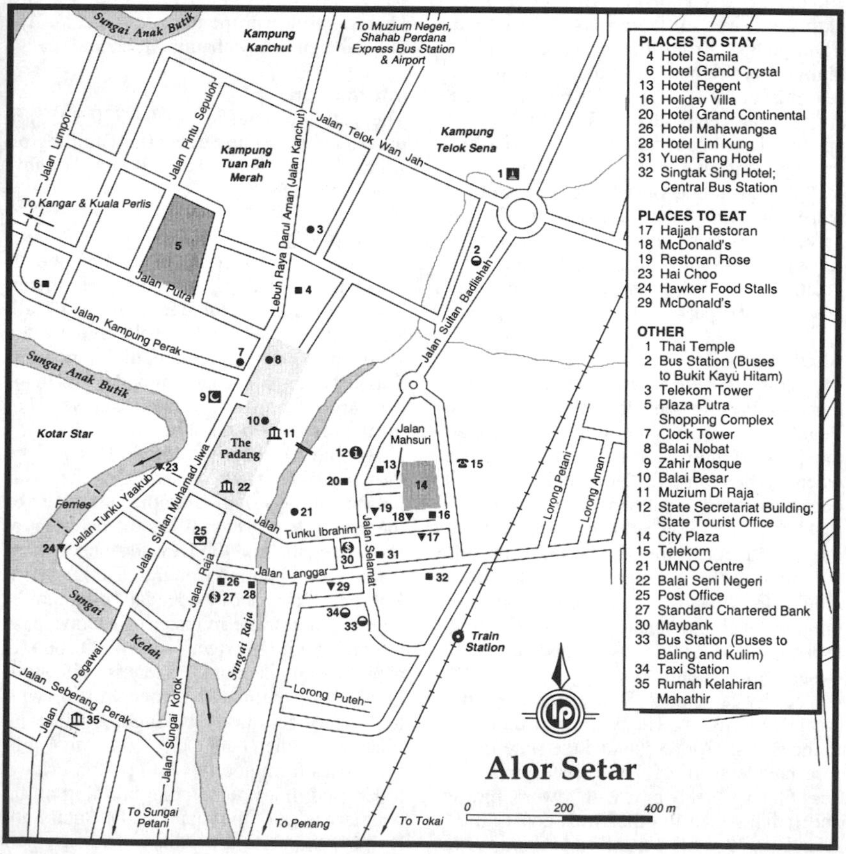

is built in a style similar to that of the Balai Besar. The collection includes early Chinese porcelain, artefacts from the archaeological excavations made at Lembah Bujang, and a fabulous 'gold tree' produced as a tribute to the Thais.

The large new block next door, built more for functionality than style and due to open around the time of this book's publication, is the royal boathouse, where royal barges and boats will be housed.

The museum is open from 10 am to 6 pm daily (closed Friday from noon to 2.30 pm).

Rumah Kelahiran Mahathir

This *kampung* house at 18 Lorong Kilang Ais, off Jalan Pegawai, is the family home and birthplace of the current prime minister. It has been turned into a museum which, though not particularly interesting, manages to avoid sycophancy. It provides a good history of Dr Mahathir, the son of a teacher, who became a doctor in Alor Setar before venturing into politics. Most interesting are his articles on Malay themes, published in the *Straits Times* in the late 1940s under a pseudonym, providing an interesting insight into Dr Mahathir's thinking and political development.

Places to Stay

Cheap hotels are scarce, but can be found along Jalan Langgar. They are noisy but OK for one night.

The *Hotel Lim Kung* (☎ 04-732 8353), in an old wooden building at 36A Jalan Langgar, is not without charm but has only very basic singles/doubles for RM14/18. The *Yuen Fang Hotel* (☎ 04-733 1736) on Jalan Langgar has comparable rooms for RM16/20. A touch better is the *Sing Tak Sing Hotel* (☎ 04-732 5482) at 74 Jalan Langgar, right above the central bus station, which offers simple singles for RM18 and doubles with bathroom for RM30.

Good mid-range hotels abound. The *Hotel Mahawangsa* (☎ 04-732 1433) at 449 Jalan Raja, diagonally opposite the post office, has air-con doubles for RM49. A step up the scale is the *Hotel Regent* (☎ 04-731 1900), 1536G Jalan Sultan Badlishah, with air-con rooms for RM55 and RM66. The *Hotel Samila* (☎ 04-731 8888) at 27 Lebuh Raya Darul Aman (Jalan Kanchut) is another 1970s hotel with doubles that have all the trimmings for RM81. It also has a good restaurant and MTV lounge.

The *Hotel Grand Continental* (☎ 04-733 5917), in the centre of town at 134 Jalan Sultan Badlishah, has single/double rooms from RM143/156, including taxes, but substantial discounts are often offered. Better value is its smaller sister hotel, the *Hotel Grand Crystal* (☎ 04-731 3333) at 40 Jalan Kampung Perak, which has doubles from RM160, including breakfast and taxes, but discounts are possible. It also has a swimming pool.

Alor Setar's newest and most luxurious hotel is the *Holiday Villa* (☎ 04-734 9999), a high-rise at 163 Jalan Tunku Ibrahim. The rate for a standard single/double is RM195/205, but big discounts are normal.

Places to Eat

At 53 Jalan Tunku Ibrahim, opposite the City Plaza, is a popular Thai Muslim place, *Hajjah Restoran*. The *Restoran Rose* around the corner on Jalan Badlishah is also popular for Indian food.

The *Hai Choo*, beside the Sungai Anak Butik on Jalan Tunku Yaakub in Alor Setar's little Chinatown, has been in business since 1862. It's so Chinese that it doesn't even have a menu in English, but the food (specialities are seafood and steamboat) is very good and moderately priced. *Food stalls* down at the nearby river confluence serve varied hawker fare until late.

Getting There & Away

Alor Setar is 91km north of Butterworth and 48km from the Thai border at Bukit Kayu Hitam. Only a few buses go from Alor Setar all the way to Hat Yai in Thailand. More frequent buses run to the border, from where Thai buses go to Hat Yai (see the Bukit Kayu Hitam entry later in this chapter for this border crossing). The train is slower but easier and more interesting.

Air The airport is 11km north of town just off the Lebuh Raya. Malaysia Airlines (☎ 04-731 1106) flies daily to KL (RM113), and Pelangi has flights most days to Kota Bharu (RM71).

Bus Alor Setar has a confusing array of bus stations.

The central bus station on Jalan Langgar handles local destinations, including at least hourly buses to Sungai Petani (RM2.85, one hour) and Kangar (RM3, one hour) as well as half-hourly buses to Butterworth (RM4.25, 1½ hours) and Kuala Kedah (RM1, 30 minutes), from where ferries run to Langkawi.

The smaller bus station, behind the nearby taxi station, mainly handles local services to Baling and Kulim (inland from Butterworth).

Another small bus station, north of the town centre on Jalan Sultan Badlishah, has a few local services to the north of the state including air-con HBR (☎ 04-733 3399) buses every hour to Bukit Kayu Hitam (RM3, one hour) on the Thai border.

Almost all long-distance buses now leave from the large modern Shahab Perdana express bus station on Jalan Mergong, 4km north of the town centre. From here there are regular coach buses to KL, Melaka, Johor Bahru, Singapore etc, as well as to the east coast destinations of Kuantan, Kuala Terengganu and Kota Bharu. Black shuttle minibuses run between the central bus station and Shahab Perdana (RM1).

Train The railway from Butterworth to Bangkok runs through Alor Setar and the border town of Padang Besar in Perlis. The *International Express* via Hat Yai to Bangkok comes through at 4.15 pm. Tickets cost from RM52.80 for a seat and up to RM87 for an air-conditioned lower berth, but book well in advance. Alternatively, take the 5.50 am train to Hat Yai (RM8, three hours), a more scenic option than the bus – seats are almost always available on the morning of departure. From Hat Yai the train departs to Alor Setar at 3.50 pm. For information call ☎ 04-733 1798.

Taxi Rates for a four passenger taxi from the taxi station include Bukit Kayu Hitam (RM22), Butterworth (RM40), Kangar (RM20), Kuala Kedah (RM10) and Padang Besar (RM28).

KUALA KEDAH

This busy fishing village 12km from Alor Setar is the southern gateway to Langkawi. The **Kota Kuala Kedah** is a fort on the opposite bank of the Sungai Kedah from the town. Built around 1770 to protect the main port of the sultanate, it fell to the Thais in 1821. The walls, cannons and gateway of this partially restored fort can be inspected.

There is little else to detain you from catching a ferry straight to Langkawi. Ferries leave approximately every 1½ hours from 8 am to 6 pm (RM15).

PULAU LANGKAWI

The 104 islands of the Langkawi group are 30km off the coast from Kuala Perlis, at the northern end of Peninsular Malaysia bordering Thailand. They're accessible by boat from Penang, Butterworth, Kuala Perlis, Kuala Kedah and Thailand; or by air from Penang and KL.

The islands, strategically situated where the Indian Ocean narrows down into the Straits of Melaka, were once a haven for pirates, and could easily have become the site for the first British foothold in Malaya instead of Penang. They were charted by Admiral Cheng Ho on his visit to Melaka in 1405, and for centuries they came under Thai suzerainty.

The only island with any real settlement is 478.5 sq km Pulau Langkawi, with jungle-clad hills in the interior and good beaches scattered around the coast. It is almost as big as Singapore Island, and like Singapore it is growing through land reclamation.

Langkawi is a go-ahead area, targeted by the government for development as the country's premier tourist resort. The island is a symbol of the new Malaysia and a showcase for advancement of the *bumiputra* (indigenous) Malays. Its development is backed enthusiastically by Prime Minister

Dr Mahathir, who worked as a doctor on Pulau Langkawi in the 1950s before entering parliament.

Tourism took off in 1986 when Chinese-dominated Penang lost its duty-free status to the then Malay backwater of Langkawi. Billions of ringgit have since poured in to develop the island, which has excellent roads, impressive resort hotels, burgeoning shopping centres and a new international airport. Recent efforts have been made to broaden Langkawi's appeal beyond beach holidays, with a host of new tourist projects, including the Langkawi International Book Village, along with major annual events such as the Tour de Langkawi cycling race held in February, and the Langkawi International Maritime and Aerospace (LIMA) exhibition around November.

Most of the development is in the main town, Kuah, and in isolated beach resorts around the coast. Away from the built-up areas, Langkawi is still a rural Malay island of small villages, rice paddies and water buffalo.

It is an island steeped in legends, and the favourite legend is of Mahsuri, who was wrongly accused of infidelity and, before being killed for her crime, put a curse on the island for seven generations. The curse seems to have expired and the island's 50,000 inhabitants are enjoying the growing wealth of the tourism developments.

Langkawi certainly has its natural attractions, though the atmosphere and beaches of Peninsular Malaysia's east coast attract more western travellers and Langkawi still caters primarily to Malaysians, Singaporeans and the east Asian tourism market. Yet it has some good beaches and excellent resorts for a luxury holiday.

The wet season in Langkawi is around April to October, and the dry is much drier than most of the peninsula.

Orientation

Kuah, in the south-east corner of the island, is the main town and the arrival point for the ferries, but the beaches are elsewhere on the island. The two main beaches, Pantai Cenang and Pantai Kok, are on Langkawi's western coast.

By far the most popular beach is Pantai Cenang, which is crammed with numerous cheap and expensive hotels and restaurants, although the water there is fairly murky at times. Pantai Tengah is almost a southerly continuation of Pantai Cenang. The beach at Pantai Kok is much better, but nowadays the only accommodation there is in four scattered luxury resorts.

The airport is on the island's central-west coast near Kuala Muda. There are also several resorts here, although the beach is one of the worst on Langkawi. A new artificial island and marina at Kuala Muda will improve the bathing conditions.

Along the north coast of the island virtually the only accommodation is in upmarket resorts, two at Teluk Datai in the west and one at Tanjung Rhu in the east. The latter has one of the better beaches on the island. In between the two is the island's cargo port, Teluk Ewa. No ferries dock here, only cargo vessels. Teluk Ewa is dominated by a huge cement factory nearby.

Information

Tourism Malaysia (☎ 04-966 7789) has an office in Kuah, on the foreshore near the mosque, 1km towards the town centre from the jetty. It's open daily from 9 am to 1 pm, and 2 to 5 pm.

Langkawi is part of Kedah state, so banks and government offices are closed on Friday and Saturday afternoon, but open Sunday. The only banks are at Kuah. Elsewhere you'll have to rely on the resort hotels, and they may not change money for non-guests.

You can make international telephone calls at the Telekom office in Kuah, and all larger resorts have phones for international calls using a phone card.

Kuah

The once small fishing village of Kuah is the island's main town. Though still not very large, it is a hive of activity and new industry, and the island taxi drivers even complain about the afternoon rush hour. In recent years, large shopping malls and new luxury hotels have been built in Kuah, although the town has no real beach.

Kuah is the main place to shop on Langkawi, but despite all the promotion as a duty-free shopping paradise, the range of goods is disappointing and the prices much the same as elsewhere in Malaysia. Banks, duty-free shops and small emporiums are found in the main centre of town, just over a kilometre from the jetty.

The **Lagenda Langkawi Dalam Taman**, a 20 hectare landscaped theme park stretching from the jetty towards town along the newly reclaimed waterfront, has various sculptures based on local folklore and history set among artificial ponds and a lagoon. Closer to town is Kuah's picturesque **Al-Hana Mosque**, with its golden dome, Moorish arches and minarets rising above the palm trees.

Several kilometres north of Kuah is **Langkawii Crystaal**, Malaysia's only glass-blowing works, and, next door, the **Kedah Marble** quarry. Both are open to visitors. At the **Langkawi Golf Club** (☎ 04-966 7195),

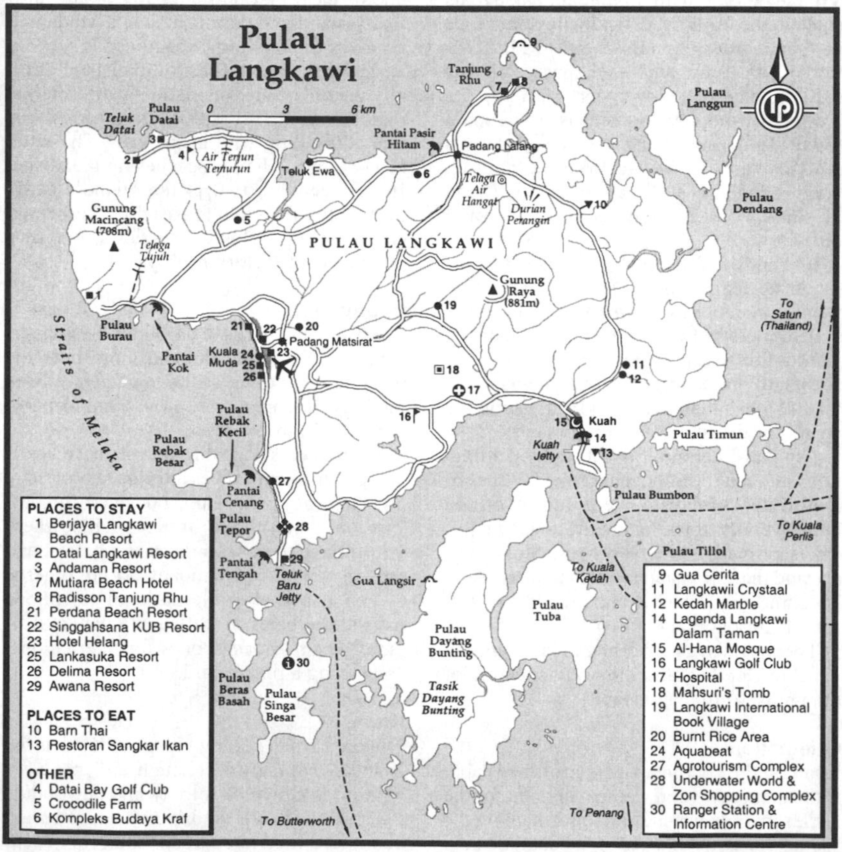

5km west of town past the new hospital, green fees are RM60 Monday to Friday, and RM80 on weekends.

Langkawi International Book Village

The book village is situated within a pleasant rainforest park at Lubuk Sembilang, roughly in the geographical centre of the island. Here, half a dozen wooden kampung-style buildings house a rather disparate collection of (mostly Bahasa Malaysia and English) books and magazines.

Mahsuri's Tomb & Padang Matsirat

These sites are a few kilometres west of Kuah, on the road leading to the west coast beaches and to the airport. Mahsuri was a legendary 10th century Malay princess, unjustly accused of adultery and sentenced to death. All attempts to execute her failed until the indignant Mahsuri *agreed* to die, but not before issuing the curse that 'there shall be no peace or prosperity on this island for a period of seven generations'.

A result of that curse can still sometimes be seen in the 'field of burnt rice' at nearby Padang Matsirat. There, villagers once burnt their rice fields rather than allow them to fall into the hands of Siamese invaders. It is said that heavy rain still sometimes brings traces of burnt rice to the surface.

Pantai Cenang

This 2km-long strip of good beach lies at the south-west corner of Langkawi, 25km from Kuah.

A sandbar appears at low tide where you can inspect the local sea life. Between November and January, you can walk across this sandbar to the nearby island of Pulau Rebak Kecil, but only for two hours around low tide. Another nearby island is Pulau Tepor, which can be reached by a hired boat from Pantai Cenang.

Pantai Cenang is where almost all of Langkawi's beach chalets are concentrated, and with its good restaurants and bars things get lively in the main tourist season. Unfortunately, because the blocks of land are long and narrow, the beach frontage is minimal so some of the chalets only have a view of the chalet in front. During the season it seems all these places fill up, but at any other time most are virtually empty, especially at the southern end of the beach and at Pantai Tengah.

At the southern end of Pantai Cenang, near Pantai Tengah, is the Zon duty-free shopping complex. It also includes **Underwater World**, a large aquarium with a walk-through tunnel to view the many fish up close. It is open daily from 10 am to 6 pm, and entry is RM10/15 for children/adults. At the northern end of Pantai Cenang is the new **Agri-Tourism Complex**, which includes a museum and landscaped gardens.

Pantai Tengah

Pantai Tengah is a smaller, quieter beach just south of Pantai Cenang over a small rocky point; it's similar to Pantai Cenang. There have been several major new resorts built here in recent years, along with a few low-key places with chalet accommodation.

Kuala Muda

Kuala Muda is the beach directly opposite the airport runway, north of Pantai Cenang. It has a reasonable stretch of sand for sunbathing, but step into the shallow water and you'll find yourself ankle deep in mud. Here you'll also find the new **Aquabeat**, a water theme park in an enormous hangar-like construction with a surf-making pool, aquarium, and waterslides.

Pantai Kok

On the western part of the island, 12km north of Pantai Cenang, Pantai Kok fronts a beautiful bay surrounded by limestone mountains and jungle. The water is a bit clearer here than at any of the other beaches, but since all of the budget accommodation was demolished to make way for a new golf course, the only places to stay are four exclusive resorts scattered around the bay. The beach itself will remain open to the public.

Telaga Tujuh

Telaga Tujuh is only a 2.5km walk inland from Pantai Kok. Water cascades nearly

100m down a hillside through a series of seven *(tujuh)* wells *(telaga)*. You can slide down from one of these shallow pools to another near the top of the falls – the stone channels are very smooth.

The only way to get there is by rented car, motorbike or taxi; drive to the end of the road, about 1km past Pantai Kok, then turn along the road to the right, away from the Burau Bay Resort, until you reach the car park. From here it's a steady 10 minute climb through the rainforest to the wells at the top of the falls.

Teluk Datai

Teluk Datai is some distance off the main road around the island. It is the site of the island's most exclusive resort and an upmarket golf course. The resort's beautiful beach is only for guests. The road continues past the resort to a headland where a short trail will take you through the jungle and down to the sea – a pleasant spot but there is no beach to speak of.

On the way to Teluk Datai is the **Crocodile Farm**, where you can view saltwater crocodiles *(Crocodilus porosus)* at various stages of their development. It's quite well run and informative, with daily shows at 11.15 am and 2.45 pm, and hourly feedings. Piped music is played to keep the crocs docile. It is open daily from 9 am to 6 pm, and entry is RM5/7 children/adults.

Air Terjun Temurun (Temurun Waterfall) is halfway between the Crocodile Farm and the resort. The high falls are worth a look and are marked by a huge concrete archway spanning the road.

Pantai Pasir Hitam

A couple of kilometres west of Tanjung Rhu, this beach is noted for its black sand, although it's not a real black-sand beach – simply streaks of black through the sand caused by a spring that deposits mineral oxides. It's really a very contrived attraction, as the beach is only a couple of metres wide and is at the foot of a 5m drop, so you can't even walk along it. The waters off Pasir Hitam are dotted with huge boulders.

The new **Kompleks Budaya Kraf** is an enormous handicrafts centre built in an extravagant neo-Islamic style. A wide range of regional and Malaysian-made goods are on sale, from batiks and ikats to pottery and wood carvings.

Tanjung Rhu

Just beyond Pasir Hitam at the village of Padang Lalang there's a roundabout with a turn-off to the north to Tanjung Rhu, while the main road continues back to Kuah.

Tanjung Rhu has one of Langkawi's better beaches. The water is shallow and at low tide you can walk across the sandbank to the neighbouring island, except during monsoon season. The water swirls across the bank as the tide comes in. There are mangrove cruises and kayaks can be hired.

Around the promontory, accessible by boat, is the **Gua Cerita** (Cave of Legends). Along the coast for a couple of kilometres before the beach, the tiny fish known as *ikan bilis* (anchovies) are spread out on mats to dry in the sun.

Gunung Raya

The tallest mountain on the island at 881m can be reached by a snaking, paved road through the jungle. It is a spectacular drive to the top with views across the island and over to Thailand. At the top is a VIP bungalow, a sort of Camp David for government ministers, which means access is restricted when it's occupied.

Telaga Air Hangat

These hot springs are towards the north of the island, not far from the turn-off to Tanjung Rhu. Like so many places in Malaysia, they are associated with an intriguing legend:

Pulau Langkawi's two most powerful families became involved in a bitter argument over a marriage proposal. A fight broke out and all the kitchen utensils were used as missiles. The gravy *(kuah)* was spilt at Kuah and seeped into the ground at Kisap (Seep). A pot landed at Belanga Perak (Broken Pot) and finally the saucepan of hot water *(air panas)* came to land here. The fathers of these two families got their comeuppance for causing all this mayhem – they are now the island's two major mountain peaks.

The hot springs themselves, although unimpressive, have become something of a tourist trap. Entry costs RM4.

Durian Perangin
Roughly 15km north of Kuah is the turn-off to these waterfalls, which are 3km off the road along a rough track. In the dry season it's not very spectacular, though the swimming pools, 10 minutes walk up through the forest, are always refreshingly cool. The falls are best seen at the end of the monsoon season – late September, early October.

Nearby Islands
The islands off Langkawi's southern shore can be easily visited as a rewarding day trip. You can either charter a boat yourself, or join one of the organised 'island hopping' tours from Pantai Cenang or Kuah jetty, costing around RM35 per person (minimum six people). The large hotels and travel agents in Kuah often organise trips.

The organised trips almost always go to Pulau Dayang Bunting and Pulau Singa Besar, which has a wildlife reserve and reasonable snorkelling. Some add a stop at the much smaller Pulau Beras Basah. However, during the monsoon season from July to mid-September, the seas are usually too rough and unpredictable for boat trips.

Pulau Dayang Bunting Tasik Dayang Bunting, or the 'Lake of the Pregnant Maiden', is located on the island of the same name. It is a freshwater lake and is good for swimming.

A legend states that a childless couple, after 19 years of unsuccessful efforts, had a baby girl after drinking from this lake. Since then it has been a popular pilgrimage centre for those hoping for children. Legend also says that the lake is inhabited by a large white crocodile.

Also on Pulau Dayang Bunting is Gua Langsir, or the 'Cave of the Banshee', which is inhabited by thousands of bats. Marble is quarried on the island and shipped to the mainland for processing.

Pulau Bumbon This island with pleasant beaches is only 10 minutes from the Kuah jetty, from where day trips can be booked for RM25. The simple resort on the island is currently closed.

Pulau Payar Marine Park This marine park, 30km south of Langkawi, incorporates a number of islands, the largest being Pulau Payar. A large floating platform is moored off the island and includes a bar/restaurant and underwater observation chamber to view the reef. From here, you can go snorkelling and diving or rent glass-bottom boats. This upmarket marine tourism venture is reached on day tours from the Kuah jetty for RM220. Hotels and travel agents take bookings, or phone Sriwani on ☎ 04-966 7318. See the special Diving & Snorkelling section for advice about safe and responsible diving.

Places to Stay
Budget accommodation is becoming increasingly rare on Langkawi, and is now only available in Kuah and on the island's south-west coast. Even then it starts at around RM35 a night for a simple room or beach chalet. The resorts range from small mid-range chalets to five-star luxury. Prices drop in the low season but some of the large resorts hold their prices. Mid-range options are expensive compared with elsewhere in Malaysia. Package deals through travel agents are usually the cheapest way to enjoy Langkawi's beaches in luxury.

Although during school holidays and at the peak time of November to February Langkawi gets very crowded, at other times of the year supply far outstrips demand.

Kuah Kuah has seen the greatest tourist development in recent years, which is hard to understand given its lack of beaches. It has a wide selection of hotels, but it is much better to head for Pantai Cenang or one of the luxury resorts elsewhere on the island.

A short ride by share taxi will take you from the pier to any of Kuah's cheaper accommodation, which is strung out along the waterfront around the bay.

Past the mosque, roughly 1km from the pier, you'll come to two vaguely budget hotels. The *Asia Hotel* (☎ 04-966 6216) has reasonable air-con doubles with bathroom from RM50. A few doors down at the *Hotel Langkawi* (☎ 04-966 6248) doubles cost RM25 for a small windowless box with fan and shared bathroom, RM50 with air-con, TV and bathroom.

Better value is the slightly grander *Region Hotel* (☎ 04-966 7719), Jalan Persiaran Putra. This three storey hotel has air-con doubles with bathroom and TV for RM50. It is back from the main road – take the street near the mosque. The *JB Motel* (☎ 04-966 8545) at 19 Jalan Pandak has similar rates.

About a kilometre north of the centre of town, in the new area, is the *Malaysia Hotel & Restaurant* (☎ 04-966 8087), 39 Pusat Mas. Small singles/doubles with air-con, TV, minibar and bathroom cost RM65/75. Dorm beds are available for RM20. Similar mid-range hotels can be found nearby.

A top end hotel is the large new *Tiara Hotel* (☎ 04-966 2566) towards the northern end of town, built in a 'medieval castle' design, complete with moat. Doubles start at RM200 before discount. The more central *City Bayview Hotel* (☎ 04-966 1818), another high-rise block set back from the waterfront, has singles/doubles for a 'published rate' of RM320/340, but offers some great discounts. The *Sheraton Perdana Resort* (☎ 04-966 2020), 2km or so south of the jetty away from town, has doubles from RM390/455 in the low/high season.

Pantai Cenang Pantai Cenang is the liveliest beach strip with accommodation from budget to international standard, though most places are mid-range. They all straggle the 2km of beach between the turn-off to Kuah at the northern end and Pantai Tengah to the south.

At the southern end of the beach, near the Zon shopping complex, the *Langkapuri Beach Resort* (☎ 04-955 1202) has small, comfortable cottages for RM95 to RM160.

Directly opposite and across the road from the beach, is *2020 Chalets* (☎ 04-955 2806), a reasonable budget place with chalets for RM35 and larger ones for RM70 with air-con.

Just past 2020 Chalets is the *Paloma Boutique Resort* (☎ 04-955 6789), a new upmarket hotel with doubles from RM280 plus 10% tax. It has a pool but no direct beach access, which means it's less attractive than other places in this upmarket range.

Next door is *Nadia's Inn Comfort* (☎ 04-955 1401), offering spotless carpeted air-con doubles, with bathroom and TV from RM100 on Friday and weekends or RM75 during the week; check for discount deals. It has a small pool.

Opposite, on the beach, is the *Samila* (☎ 04-955 1964) a rather cramped and unattractive place where chalets start at RM40 with bathroom.

Next is the *AB Motel* (☎ 04-955 1300), one of the older laid-back places facing the beach. Big chalets among palms and casuarina trees cost RM40, or RM70 with air-con, but you could do better. It has a decent restaurant.

A short way along is the popular *Sandy Beach Resort* (☎ 04-955 1308), where two person A-frame chalets with fan and bathroom cost RM50; the ones near the beach are quite good, but towards the road they are packed a bit too tightly together and it can get very crowded. In the resort's hotel section directly across the road, air-con doubles with bathroom and TV go for RM90, and more deluxe carpeted bungalows for RM105. There's a laundry next door.

Beside the Sandy Beach is a good mid-range place, the *Semarak Beach Resort* (☎ 04-955 1377), which has pleasant, roomy chalets on lawns facing the beach for RM88 with fan and bathroom, or RM120 with air-con, dropping to RM70 and RM100 in the low season. There's a nice, moderately priced restaurant.

A few paces further north you'll find the *Melati Tanjung Motel* (☎ 04-955 1099), where free-standing beachfront chalets cost RM35, or RM55 with air-con; all feature ceiling fan, polished wooden floor, shower and – luxury – western toilets.

The next place along is the *Cenang Rest House* (☎ 04-955 2061), which has reasonable air-con chalets with bathroom for RM50. Its neighbour, the *Chenang Beach Motel* (☎ 04-955 1395), also offers fair value for money, with clean air-con doubles for RM55.

A favourite of budget travellers is the *Grand Beach Hotel* (☎ 04-955 1457), where simple beachfront chalets with bathroom are an especially good deal at RM35. Larger chalets with air-con, TV and hot water cost RM100.

Near the northern end of the built-up strip is the very pleasant *Beach Garden & Bistro* (☎ 04-955 1363), run by a German couple. It has a small swimming pool and just a dozen doubles which cost RM137 with air-con and bathroom, rising to RM176 in the high season. The restaurant here is excellent.

The most northerly place on this beach, the first you reach when coming from Kuah or the airport, is the flash *Pelangi Beach Resort* (☎ 04-955 1001; email pbrl@tm.net.my), with every luxury, including island swimming pool, sports facilities, restaurant and even electric buggies to take you to your room. No expense has been spared here, and the prices reflect this – the cheapest singles/doubles are RM326/348, including breakfast, evening cocktails and tax.

Pantai Tengah Several new hotels have been built at Pantai Tengah recently, though it's still less built up than Pantai Cenang.

Just after the headland which separates the two beaches is a cluster of three budget places which all charge RM35 for basic chalets and from RM65 for air-con bungalows: *Green Hill Beach Motel* (☎ 04-955 1935); the *Sugary Sands* (☎ 04-955 3473); and the *Tanjung Malie* (☎ 04-955 1895). The Green Hill and Sugary Sands are pretty basic and little thought has gone into the location of the chalets. The Tanjung Malie is marginally better.

Next along is probably the best value place on this beach – the mid-range *Sunset Beach Resort* (☎ 04-955 1751). The brick chalets, all with bathroom and air-con, run in a line back from the beach, so they have no sea views. Small/medium/large units cost RM55/80/100. The restaurant and bar are right on the beach.

After a gap of undeveloped land there is another place right on the beach. The *Charlie Motel* (☎ 04-955 1200) has been around for some years, and has basic air-con chalets with shower and (squat) toilet for RM55, or nicer chalets facing the beach for RM85. The restaurant on the beach is good.

Finally, there are the luxury resorts. The *Langkawi Village Resort* (☎ 04-955 1511) has individual two storey chalets dotted around the main building. It has a pool and a couple of places to eat and is popular among European tour groups. Rates are from RM175 plus taxes for a semi-detached two storey chalet.

Further south is the *Langkawi Holiday Villa* (☎ 04-955 1701). This is a superb place with every imaginable facility, including a pool, a couple of restaurants and bars. Accommodation is in rooms rather than chalets, and the design is such that all rooms have sea views. Rooms start at RM215/235.

At the end of the road at the Teluk Baru jetty is the *Awana Resort* (☎ 04-955 5111), a new luxury complex built in California bungalow style. The location, opposite several tiny rock islands, is rather scenic and there's a broad promenade along the waterfront. Singles/doubles cost from RM360/380 before discount.

Pantai Kok Until recently Pantai Kok was the cheapest and most laid-back beach on the island, but now all accommodation, other than four upmarket resorts scattered around the bay, has been demolished to make way for a planned new golf course. The strip between the beach and the road is to remain public, however.

Just around the headland, at the north-western end of the beach, right by the track leading to Telaga Tujuh, is the *Burau Bay*

Resort (☎ 04-959 1061). Although owned by the same company, it's not quite as classy as the Pelangi at Pantai Cenang, but it does have good facilities, nice beaches and an impressive setting below craggy limestone peaks. Rates are from RM210/240 for a single/double, including taxes and breakfast.

Further on is the big *Berjaya Langkawi Beach Resort* (☎ 04-959 1888; email lgk@hr.berjaya.com.my), one of the best on the island. Luxury chalets cost RM280 to RM350 and suites are available. It has an excellent range of sporting facilities, which will eventually also include the new Pantai Kok golf course.

Several kilometres back towards Pantai Cenang is *Mahsuri Beach Resort* (☎ 04-955 2977), built on a forested, rocky headland with its own lovely beachlet. Spacious chalets cost from RM297 with sea view or RM350 near the water.

A little further south-east is the sparkling *Sheraton Langkawi Resort* (☎ 04-955 1901), with over 200 rooms arranged around a shady headland and a small beach. Room rates range from RM350 in the low season to RM365 in the high season. Discounts of 30% apply for stays over three days.

Teluk Datai Just past the Datai Bay Golf Club in a grandiose wooden Malay-style building within the rainforest, the *Andaman Resort* (☎ 04-959 1088) has its own private beach. Doubles start at RM530, rising to the 'presidential suite' for RM2100

Further on is the *Datai Langkawi* (☎ 04-959 2500), the island's most exclusive and isolated beach resort. Attractive chalets, many built on stilts over the water, are scattered around the large grounds and cost from RM950.

Tanjung Rhu There are two places here. The *Mutiara Beach Hotel* (☎ 04-955 6488) is small and low-key, with swimming pool and restaurant. The single/double rates are RM150/180, including taxes.

Right next door is the newly renovated multi-storey *Radisson Tanjung Rhu* (☎ 04-959 1033), in a secluded cove with a glorious golden beach opposite several tiny islands. Its buildings are arranged around a central courtyard, with poolside doubles for RM600 up to RM1400 for a luxury suite.

Kuala Muda Due to Kuala Muda's relative isolation and poor beach, rates are lower than elsewhere on the island.

The *Delima Resort* (☎ 04-955 1801) is huge with 1500 rooms, a massive swimming pool and its own shopping centre. It looks very flash from the road, but it is mostly a mid-range resort. The somewhat shabby, cheaper doubles are still good value at RM60, or RM83 with balcony, as are the more luxurious, air-con chalets from RM110 with breakfast.

Catering largely to business travellers, the *Hotel Helang* (☎ 04-962 2020), between the airport terminal and the international exhibition and convention centre, has soundproofed doubles from RM330, but offers generous low season discounts.

The *Lankasuka Resort* (☎ 04-955 6888) is just south of the huge Aquabeat water theme park. It caters largely to Korean and Japanese tourists, and has doubles from RM165. Just north along the coast from the airport, the *Singgahsana KUB Resort* (☎ 04-955 6262) offers doubles from RM120, but the isolated location is dull.

Still under construction but due for completion around the time of publication, 1km further north is the *Perdana Beach Resort*, a huge new hotel and apartment complex with a marina and artificial island.

Places to Eat

Kuah You'll find good night *food stalls* in front of the City Bayview Hotel, and on the nearby laneway of Lencongan Putra 1. In the streets behind the Sime Langkawi Duty Free are inexpensive Chinese coffee shops, including the *Sri Indah*.

The new Langkawi Fair shopping complex, nearer to the jetty, has a *McDonald's* and a large *supermarket* for self-catering. In the park opposite is the *Cafe Rahim*, a simple open-air Malay restaurant. There is also a worthwhile inexpensive outdoor Malay restaurant on the seaside promenade, in front of the Hotel Tiara.

Kuah has some good seafood restaurants, such as the recently renovated *Sari Seafood* overlooking the water in the centre of town. For Chinese-style seafood try the large *Restoran Langkawi*, near the Asia Hotel.

Roughly 2km from town, but worth the effort to get there, *Restoran Sangkar Ikan* (☎ 04-966 8888) is a restaurant on stilts at the edge of a tiny bay. Excellent seafood from the floating fish farm out the front will set you back around RM30 per person. To get there, take the main back road, Jalan Penarak (behind the mosque) south and follow the signs.

Some 10km north of Kuah on the island's east coast is the *Barn Thai*, an upmarket Thai restaurant with live jazz most nights. It's accessible via an interesting 500m-long, raised walkway through a mangrove forest reserve, which is worth experiencing even if you don't eat there.

Pantai Cenang The *Hot Wok Cafe*, opposite the Semarak Beach Resort, has very good Chinese and western food, and seafood is featured. The prices are reasonable and it's a very popular place in the evenings.

The *Backofen* next door has bratwurst and other Germanic fare. It comes alive around Christmas, the main tourist season for German speakers, but is quiet at other times of the year.

At the northern end of the beach you'll find the *Restoran Pantai*, a more upmarket restaurant serving western and Malay food.

The *Champor-Champor* (☎ 04-955 1449) is a tranquil garden restaurant which offers imaginative dishes blending western and Asian cuisine. The food is excellent, and it has a good little bar for a drink, but prices are high, with mains at around RM20.

Many of the hotels at Pantai Cenang have restaurants. The one at the *Sandy Beach Resort* is cheap and popular, and the food is quite good.

For a splurge try the *Beach Garden & Bistro*, which serves excellent western food in a lovely restaurant and beer garden right on the beach, or a sumptuous buffet meal at the *Pelangi Beach Resort*.

Pantai Tengah Pantai Tengah also has quite a few decent places to eat. The *Charlie Motel* is good for a cheap meal. The restaurant overlooks the beach and does a good job of Thai and Malaysian food.

The *Oasis Beach Pub* next door is a congenial bar for drinking, but also serves more than passable food.

Just north along the road towards Pantai Cenang is the *Eagle's Nest*, a small garden restaurant with an intimate atmosphere. The air-conditioned *Hoyas Cafe* nearby has Danish pastries and does good breakfasts from RM3.90.

At the start of the road to Teluk Baru, the *White Sand Seafood Restaurant* (☎ 04-955 3168) is a moderately priced Chinese restaurant with an extensive menu.

Pantai Kok The only restaurants are found at the resorts, which are invariably atmospheric and upmarket. The *Mahsuri Beach Resort* has a charming restaurant built right over the water.

Shopping

Despite its duty-free status, Langkawi's shopping is disappointing. Apart from cheap cigarettes and liquor, including Malaysian beer, shopping is either geared to domestic visitors, with oddities like kitchen utensils on offer, or the Japanese market with imported designer-name T-shirts and fashion accessories at inflated prices. Electronics are no bargain and the range is poor. You'll find a much bigger range of goods, and the same or lower prices, in Kuala Lumpur and Penang. Langkawii Crystaal glassware and marble souvenirs are the only significant locally made goods, and are best bought at the production sites on the road north from Kuah.

Kuah is the main shopping area with a handful of duty-free shops, which are only really worth browsing for cigarettes and alcohol; smaller shops have clothes, shoes and a few electronics, and even Harley Davidson has an outlet. Duty-free shops can also be found at the ferry terminal, the airport and the Zon shopping complex at Pantai Cenang. Some resorts also have small shopping plazas.

Getting There & Away

Air Malaysia Airlines (☎ 04-966 6622) and Air Asia have direct daily flights between Langkawi and KL (RM135). Malaysia Airlines and Silk Air fly daily to Singapore (RM333), and Malaysia Airlines also flies to Johor Bahru (RM199) and Penang (RM51).

The island's international terminal is an impressive structure with a number of shops. A few hundred metres from the terminal is the large duty-free complex and an international exhibition and convention centre, where the huge annual LIMA exhibition is held around November.

Boat Most passenger ferries to/from Langkawi operate out of Kuah.

From 8 am to 6 pm regular ferries operate roughly every hour in either direction between Kuah and the mainland ports of Kuala Perlis (RM12, one hour) and Kuala Kedah (RM15, 1½ hours).

Two companies, Kuala Perlis Langkawi Ferry Service (KPLFS, ☎ 04-966 6929) and Ekspres Bahagia (☎ 04-966 5784), run daily ferries between Kuah and Georgetown on Penang (4½ hours). The KPLFS ferry costs RM45/35 in 1st/2nd class and leaves Kuah at 6.15 pm, while the Ekspres Bahagia ferry costs RM35 and leaves at 5.50 pm. Both depart from Georgetown at 8 am.

The *Superstar Express* (☎ 04-955 7110) is a much faster ferry running twice daily between the Teluk Baru jetty, at Pantai Tengah on Langkawi's south-western tip, and the mainland port of Butterworth, directly opposite the island of Penang. This is the only car ferry operating between Pulau Langkawi and the mainland. The one way passenger-only fare is RM50 from Monday to Thursday and RM75 from Friday to Sunday. This ferry service leaves Pantai Tengah at 9 am and 3 pm, and departs from Butterworth at noon and 6 pm. The trip takes three hours.

Thailand There are up to six daily ferries to Satun (RM18) on the Thai coast from the Kuah jetty between 9 am and 5 pm. From Satun buses and taxis go to Hat Yai.

Getting Around

To/From the Airport Taxis from the airport cost RM12 to the Kuah jetty and RM10 to Pantai Kok or Pantai Cenang. Buy a coupon at the desk before leaving the airport terminal and use it to pay the driver.

Bus The bus station in Kuah is in front of the City Bayview Hotel. Apart from buses from the jetty to the centre of Kuah (RM1), the only (infrequent) service is to Pantai Cenang (RM1.70).

Taxi Taxis are the main way of getting around, but fares are high. From the Kuah jetty fares are: Kuah town (RM5), airport (RM15), Pantai Cenang/Pantai Tengah (RM12) and Pantai Kok (RM20).

Car Cars can be rented cheaply on Pulau Langkawi. Touts at the Kuah ferry terminal will assail you on arrival, or cars can be rented at any of the beach resorts. The going rate is around RM80 per day.

Motorcycle & Bicycle The easiest way to get around is to hire a motorbike (usually Honda 70cc step-thrus). You can do a very leisurely circuit of the island (70km) in a day. The roads are excellent and, though traffic is increasing, outside Kuah it's very pleasant and easy riding. Motorbikes can be hired at stands all over the island, and noone seems too fussed about whether you have a licence or not. The charge is around RM25 per day.

Most of the places with motorbikes also have bikes for rent. Mountain bikes cost RM12 per day.

BUKIT KAYU HITAM

This is the main border crossing between Malaysia and Thailand, 48km north of Alor Setar. The Lebuh Raya handles the vast majority of road traffic between the two countries, and all the buses to Hat Yai in Thailand come this way.

At the border post there are a few restaurants, private car parking facilities and a Tourism Malaysia office. The easiest way to cross the border is to take a through bus all the way to Hat Yai, or buses and taxis from Alor Setar run right up to the Malaysian customs post. From here walk a few hundred metres past the big duty-free shopping complex to the Thai checkpoint. Taxis on the other side run to Sadao (100B), from where there are buses on to Hat Yai.

If arriving from Thailand, ensure that your passport is stamped by the Malaysian border police – otherwise you may be fined for 'illegal entry' when you leave Malaysia.

A budget place to stay on the Malaysian side is the *Sri Madani* (☎ 04-922 2688), which has large, simple doubles for RM35. The only accommodation on the Thai side is the *Satit Hotel* (☎ 074-434 164) at 1/1-6 Soi Thai Ghangloon 6, with doubles for 750B.

You'll find taxis (RM30) and regular buses (RM2.60) to Alor Setar, from where frequent buses go to Kuala Kedah for Langkawi, and to Butterworth and KL. Kuala Perlis, the other departure point for Langkawi, is more difficult to reach – first take a bus to Changlun, another to Kangar and then another to Kuala Perlis.

Perlis

The tiny state of Perlis, tucked away in far north-east Malaysia on the Thai border, tends to be the forgotten state of Malaysia. Apart from a sugar refinery and cement factory, its economy is still dominated by agriculture. With few tourist attractions, Perlis is primarily a state to transit through. Kuala Perlis is one of the access ports for Langkawi, and Padang Besar is the main border town if arriving by train from Thailand.

Being a predominantly Muslim state, Perlis observes the same business hours as neighbouring Kedah.

History

Perlis was originally part of Kedah, though it variously came under Thai and Acehnese sovereignty. After the Siamese conquered Kedah in 1821, the sultan of Kedah made unsuccessful attempts to regain his territory by force until, in 1842, he agreed to accept Siamese terms. The Siamese reinstalled the sultan, but made Perlis into a separate vassal principality with its own raja.

As was the case in Kedah, power was transferred from the Thais to the British in 1909 under the Treaty of Bangkok, and the British installed a Resident at Arau. During the Japanese occupation in WWII, Perlis was returned to Thailand. After the war it became part of the Malayan Union and then the Federation of Malaysia.

KANGAR

Kangar, 56km north-west of Alor Setar, is the main town in the state of Perlis. It's a low-lying, modern town surrounded by rice paddies with little of interest for travellers. If you're stuck for something to do, you can see the state mosque on Jalan Besar out towards the Pens Travelodge.

Places to Stay

The cheapest place in town is the basic *Hotel Ban Cheong* (☎ 04-976 1184) at 76 Jalan Kangar, a typical old Chinese hotel with doubles from RM22. It's on the corner of the side street running along the eastern side of the bus station.

The *Federal Hotel* (☎ 04-976 6288) at 104 Jalan Kangar is a mid-range place with fan-cooled doubles for RM48 and air-con doubles from RM63. The hotel also has very basic doubles above a nearby cafe for RM25. Coming from the bus station head left one block when you reach the Hotel Ban Cheong, and it's on your right-hand side.

Top of the pile is the *Pens Travelodge* (☎ 04-976 7755), 135 Jalan Besar, on the road to Arau. This international hotel is about the biggest thing in Kangar, and has a swimming pool, restaurants and a bar. Doubles cost from RM200 (plus 15%), before any discount.

Getting There & Away
The bus station is central and has buses to KL (RM27), Butterworth (RM12) and Alor Setar (RM3). Regular buses run to Kuala Perlis (85 sen) and Padang Besar (RM2.05). A taxi to Kuala Perlis costs RM13.

KUALA PERLIS
This small port town in the extreme northwest of the peninsula is visited mainly as the departure point for Langkawi. It is the closest access port to the island if coming from Thailand. The landing jetty for ferries is only 700m from the town centre.

The main part of Kuala Perlis consists of a couple of streets with a bank and plenty of restaurants and shops. Kangar is only 11km away if you need access to more facilities. The older part of town has interesting houses and mosques built on stilts over the water around the mangrove swamps.

Places to Stay & Eat
On Jalan Kuala Perlis, the main street, *Pens Hotel* (☎ 04-985 4122) is a good mid-range hotel with doubles for RM75. The much more basic *Asia Hotel* (☎ 04-985 5392) is on the outskirts, 1.5km along the road directly from the jetty. Doubles cost RM25.

Near the jetty is the *Hai Thien*, a moderately priced Chinese restaurant built on stilts over the water. There are *Malay food stalls* further along this road and a big *food hall* 1km out towards Kangar.

Getting There & Away
A new bus station is being built on the road to Kangar near the jetty. Until it opens, the frequent No 56 bus to Kangar (85 sen) will leave from Jalan Pangung Wayang in the town centre. Less frequent direct buses currently go from the jetty to Butterworth, Alor Setar, KL and Padang Besar (for Thailand), but will also leave from the new bus station. Taxis to Kangar (RM13) and Padang Besar (RM42) go from the jetty.

Ferries to Kuah, on Pulau Langkawi, leave roughly hourly from 8 am to 6 pm, and cost RM12. Private car parks near the jetty will look after your vehicle for RM6 per day.

ARAU
The royal capital of Perlis is 10km east of Kangar. It has an *istana* (palace), looking almost Dutch colonial in design, though it is nowhere near as grand as those of other states. Opposite is the royal mosque.

Arau is on the train line north to Padang Besar and is connected by bus to Kangar.

PADANG BESAR
This border town to Thailand is 50km north of Kangar. The town itself is nothing special but it's a popular destination for Malaysians because of the duty-free market that operates in the neutral territory between the two countries. This area is a prime smuggling route for both Malaysians and Thais. Malaysia's Anti-Smuggling Unit occasionally makes an arrest, but the overall trade is hardly affected.

Places to Stay
There's little accommodation on the Malaysian side if you get stuck, but on the Thai side of the border there are quite a few – mostly disreputable – budget hotels. One reasonable option is the *Berlin Guest House* (☎ 074-521 901) at 24 Sukapiban 1 Thanon, which charges 300B for a room.

Getting There & Away
If arriving from Thailand ensure that your passport is stamped by the Malaysian border police – otherwise you may be fined for 'illegal entry' when you leave Malaysia.

Bus The bus station is about a kilometre from the large border crossing complex. There are regular buses to/from Kangar, and bus connections on the Thai side to/from Hat Yai and other destinations. Motorcyclists shuttle travellers back and forth for RM3 each way. There are also four daily aircon buses to and from Butterworth (RM8).

Train The train is a better bet, with connections from Padang Besar to Hat Yai at 7.30 am and 6 pm; train passengers coming from Alor Setar must disembark to clear customs before re-boarding.

GUA KELAM

Near Kaki Bukit in the extreme north-west corner of the state, this limestone cave is the state's premier tourist attraction, which says little for tourism in Perlis. The cave is interesting enough, but difficult to reach.

The cave is the only access to the village of Wang Kelian, an area of high quality tin ore, and in 1970 a suspension boardwalk was installed right through the 400m-long cavern. A river runs through the cave and emerges in a cascade, making a popular swimming spot. On the other side of the cave is a landscaped park with walks. It's a pleasant picnic spot and the tin mine is a short distance from the far end of the cavern. However, be warned that motorcycles also use the boardwalk, so you need to keep an ear open.

The cave is a 1km walk from the small village of Kaki Bukit, 35km from Kangar, but bus connections are very infrequent.

Negeri Sembilan

The small state of Negeri Sembilan (Nine States) is one of the most unusual states historically, and a centre for the Minangkabau people, who originally came from Sumatra. Negeri Sembilan's main tourist destination is the beach resort of Port Dickson, popular with Kuala Lumpur residents, but Malaysia has many other better beaches. Few international visitors include Negeri Sembilan in their itinerary, but the area around the capital, Seremban, has a few points of interest for those interested in the Minangkabau and their distinctive architecture.

HIGHLIGHTS

- **Seremban Region** – traditional Minangkabau culture and architecture
- **Port Dickson** – beaches and the romantic old lighthouse at nearby Tanjong Tuan (Cape Rachado)

History

During the Melaka sultanate of the 15th century, many Minangkabau people from Sumatra settled in the Melaka area. They lived under the protection of the Melaka rulers initially, but with the fall of Melaka to the Portuguese, the Minangkabaus sought protection from the sultans of Johor.

With the rising power of the Bugis in Selangor, the Minangkabaus felt increasingly insecure, so they sought protection from the royal house of Sumatra. Raja Melewar, a Minangkabau prince, was appointed the first *yang di-pertuan besar* (head of state) of Negeri Sembilan in 1773, by the *undang* (territorial chiefs) of the districts of Sungai Ujong, Jelebu, Johol and Rembau. Out of this initial union emerged a loose confederation of nine luaks or states, although there is some debate about its exact make-up.

The royal capital of Negeri Sembilan was established at Sri Menanti, and Raja Melewar indulged himself here. However, he had little real power.

Like Selangor to the north, Negeri Sembilan was rich in tin, and so suffered unrest and political instability in the 17th century. After Raja Melewar's death, the post of yang dipertuan was filled by a succession of Sumatran chiefs, until a series of protracted tin-related wars from 1824 to 1832 led to the severance of political ties with Sumatra.

In the second half of the 19th century the civil disturbances continued, particularly in the northern state of Sungai Ujong. There was also much interstate rivalry between the yang di-pertuan besar, the undang and the *dato klana* (the ruler of Sungai Ujong).

In the 1880s the British gradually increased their influence in the area, and the territories of Sri Menanti, Tampin, Rembau and Jelebu were united in a new confederacy controlled by a British Resident. In 1895 Sungai Ujong was added to the union, and it is this union of five districts that makes up the current state of Negeri Sembilan, with an area of 6643 sq km.

SEREMBAN

South of KL, Seremban is a modern city of 270,000 people founded during the tin boom of the late 19th century. The central area is a grid of constant traffic, a few colonial shophouses and modern shopping centres. This area is noisy and devoid of interest.

Heading east to the hills bordering the city centre, Seremban takes on a different personality. The Lake Gardens are a pleasant respite from the traffic, and further into the hills is the old colonial district, dotted with bungalows, colonial buildings and more parks favoured by joggers and tai-chi exponents.

Though not brimming over with tourist interest, Seremban is a centre for Minangkabau culture. Buffalo horn roofs adorn many of the new buildings, but the only real access to Minangkabau culture is at the Muzium Negeri on the outskirts of town.

Muzium Negeri

The Muzium Negeri (State Museum) is built in the style of a Minangkabau palace, and has good craft and historical exhibits. It covers

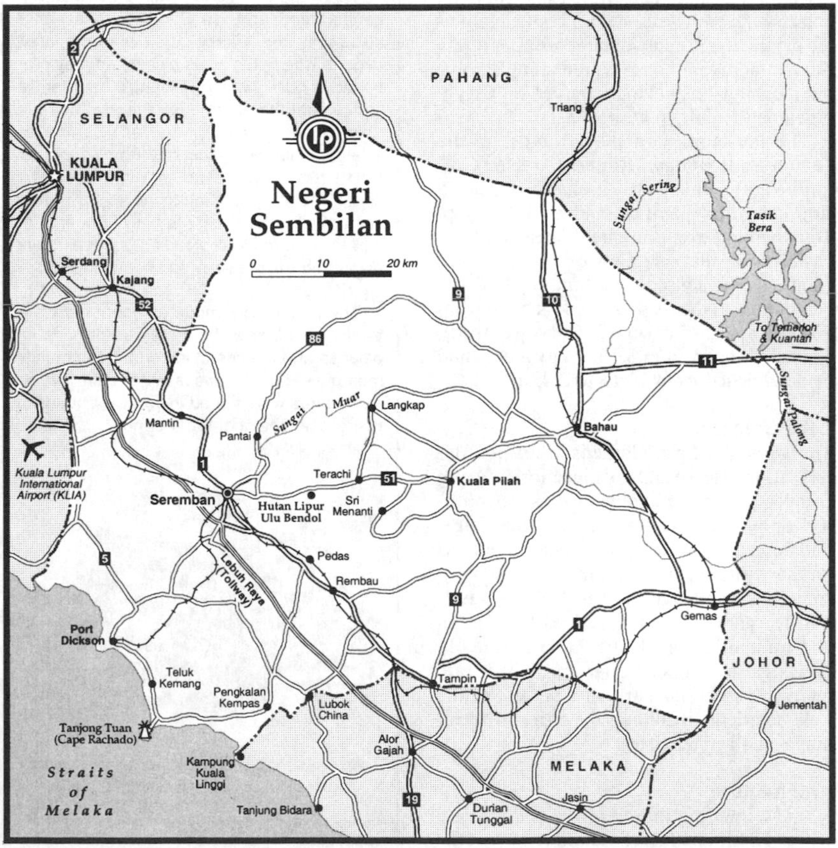

the Emergency, complete with photographs of the Communist leaders, including some gruesome post-capture portraits reminiscent of those of the bullet-ridden Che Guevara.

The main interest lies in the two traditional Minangkabau houses in the grounds next to the museum. The **Istana Ampang Tinggi** (Ampang Tinggi Palace) was originally constructed in the 1860s near Sri Menanti, a gift from the sultan to his daughter. Though small, it shows the intricate carving of palace architecture and traditional thatch roof. Minangkabau houses were built entirely without nails, though this is now a lost art it seems, for nails were used when the palace was reconstructed on this site. Next to the palace, the **Rumah Minangkabau** is a less ornate traditional house with a shingle roof, but it exhibits the hallmark curved roof style based on the buffalo horn.

The museum is in the grounds of the **Taman Seni Budaya Negeri** (Arts & Cultural Park), which also includes a *gasing* (top spinning) pavilion and a craft shop. Top-spinning events are held on special occasions but the selection of crafts is not exciting. The museum is 3km west of the bus station on the road to KL. It is open from 10 am to 6 pm, except Monday (closed), Thursday (open from 8.15 am to 1 pm) and Friday (closed from 12.15 to 2.45 pm).

Lake Gardens

The attractive Lake Gardens are a popular recreation reserve and the place for courting couples to commit khalwat ('close proximity' or public affection) in the evenings. Paddle.boats can be hired, a small aviary is on the western side and cultural events are sometimes staged at the park's open pavilion. The gardens are at the edge of the green and tranquil colonial district, now mostly housing government quarters. There are many other parkland areas to the east of the Lake Gardens, including the **Hutan Rekreasi**, a small jungle park.

Architecture

No new building in Seremban is complete without a Minangkabau curved roof, but the

The Minangkabau House

The Minangkabau house is probably the most distinctive Malay kampung house. Its most striking feature is the upswept curve of the roofline, which resembles the upward sweep of buffalo horns. The design was imported from Sumatra by the Minangkabau settlers, and is responsible for their name.

The word Minangkabau comes from *minang* (to win) and *kerbau* (water buffalo). The buffalo plays a leading role in Minangkabau tradition and is the major player in a legend surrounding their origins.

When the Javanese came to the Minangkabau homelands in Sumatra to assume suzerainty, the Minangkabau were prepared to go to war, but to avoid bloodshed they proposed a bullfight. The Minangkabau sent a calf to fight the enormous Javanese bull – a ruse which stunned the bull and onlookers. The calf had been separated from its mother for several days before the fight and, with sharp metal spears attached to its horns, went straight for the bull's belly in search of milk. The gored and bleeding bull took to its heels and the crowd shouted 'minangkabau, minangkabau!'

The houses are made of wood and were traditionally built without the use of nails. In palaces and houses of important community members, the doorways were built low so that visitors were forced to bow their heads in respect on entering, like it or not.

The curved shape of buffalo horns is reflected in Minangkabau architecture.

PENINSULAR MALAYSIA

only really fine welding of modern and traditional architecture is the **State Secretariat building**. The wonderful multiple points of the roof are a central landmark for Seremban. Opposite is the **Istana Besar**, home of the sultan of Negeri Sembilan, but it is closed to the public. Directly south is the neoclassical **State Library**, Seremban's most imposing colonial building and once the centre for the colonial administration.

Further south towards the city centre is the **State Mosque**, with its nine pillars symbolising the nine original states of Negeri Sembilan. This modern, futuristic mosque is relatively restrained compared with some other mosques erected to the glory of Islam in Malaysia.

In the central area, colonial architecture includes the **Catholic Church** (Gereja Katolik Visitation), with its Gothic spires, and the more sober **Methodist Church** built in 1920. The **King George V School** on Jalan Za'aba was the premier colonial school for Seremban's elite and still functions as a high school. It is one of the largest and most impressive colonial buildings.

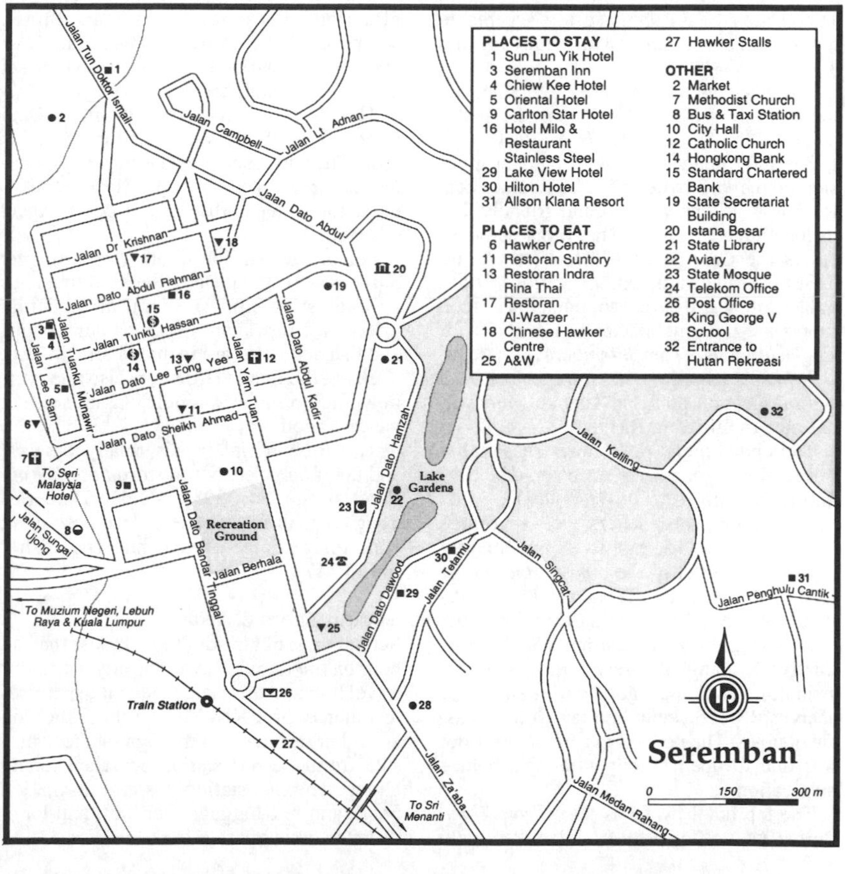

Places to Stay

Seremban has a collection of seedy and dirty hotels in the central area. Many function as boarding houses or bordellos, and the halfway decent cheap hotels are some of the most overpriced in Malaysia.

The *Oriental Hotel* (☎ 06-763 0119) at 11 Jalan Tuanku Munawir is at least a little cleaner. It has simple rooms with fan for RM23, RM30 with bathroom, or RM40 with air-con as well. The *Chiew Kee Hotel* (☎ 06-162 2095) at No 41 has rather grubby, simple doubles for RM30, but the air-con rooms with bathroom for RM50 are reasonable. The *Hotel Milo* (☎ 06-762 3451) at 22 Jalan Dato Abdul Rahman offers acceptable air-con singles/doubles with bathroom and TV for RM38/60.

The mid-range hotels are preferable, but there are few bargains. One of the better places is the *Sun Lun Yik Hotel* (☎ 06-763 5735) at 19 Jalan Tun Doktor Ismail (opposite the market), where singles/doubles cost RM50/60. It's new, clean and friendly, but its location is less than ideal. More convenient is the *Carlton Star Hotel* (☎ 06-762 5336) near the train and bus stations. It has a flash lobby and coffee shop but the air-con rooms are nothing special at RM56/70 for singles/doubles. The *Seremban Inn* (☎ 06-761 7777), a modern six storey block in a central location on Jalan Tuanku Munawir, has nice rooms from RM95.

Top-end hotels are more reasonably priced for the facilities on offer. The *Seri Malaysia Hotel* (☎ 06-764 4181), Jalan Sungai Ujong, also offers well-appointed rooms for RM115, but is inconveniently located 1km west of the bus station, on the road to the museum. The *Lake View Hotel* (☎ 06-763 0994) is on Jalan Dato Dawood, overlooking the Lake Gardens. With a distinctive Minangkabau-style roof, it has a swimming pool and a good coffee shop, and charges RM155 (including taxes) for pleasant doubles. The new *Hilton Hotel* next door was due to open shortly after this book's publication.

The top hotel by far is the *Allson Klana Resort* (☎ 06-762 9600), Jalan Penghulu Cantik, on a hill to the east of the Lake Gardens. Set in large grounds, it has all the facilities of an international-class hotel. Rooms start at RM300/320 for singles/doubles, before discount.

Places to Eat

Seremban has a good selection of hawker centres for cheap eats. Food stalls, serving mostly Malay dishes and some spicy Minangkabau fare, can be found at the train station and at the modern, upstairs *hawker centre* on Jalan Lee Sam. Jalan Lee Sam also hosts the lively Saturday *night market*, which has plenty of food stalls. The best place for Chinese favourites in an alfresco setting is on the corner of Jalan Yam Tuan and Jalan Dr Krishnan, where hawkers set up in the car park on fine evenings.

The *Restoran Al-Wazeer* on Jalan Dato Bandar Tinggal has cheap and tasty Malay food. The curiously named *Restaurant Stainless Steel*, downstairs in the Hotel Milo, is good for Chinese dishes, but don't expect silver service.

For budget air-con dining, the *Restoran Suntory* at 10 Jalan Dato Sheikh Ahmad has an extensive Chinese menu at moderate prices. Western dishes such as lamb chops and fish and chips are included for RM7.80. *A&W*, at the Lake Gardens, is also a favourite with Seremban's middle classes seeking western food.

Thai food in Malaysia is usually tom yam and not much else, but *Restoran Indra Rina Thai* (☎ 06-764 3598), 4 Jalan Dato Lee Fong Yee, is an excellent Thai restaurant with a huge range of authentic Thai dishes from RM7.

Getting There & Away

Seremban is 62km south of KL, less than an hour on the Lebuh Raya. The city is a major travel hub and there are frequent departures to Johor Bahru, KL, Melaka, Port Dickson and other destinations throughout the peninsula from the bus station on Jalan Sungai Ujong. The bus station has an information booth and left-luggage facilities, and long-distance taxis operate from upstairs.

Seremban is on the main north-south rail line. KTM Komuter trains, part of KL's city rail network, also run between Seremban and the historic main train station in KL (via the new KL Sentral (Grand Central) station now under construction) every 20 minutes. The trip takes just over one hour and costs RM5.70.

SEREMBAN TO KUALA PILAH

Heading east from Seremban the road meanders through the hills to the town of Kuala Pilah, passing points of interest on the way. This is the heartland of Minangkabau culture, centred on the old royal town of Sri Menanti.

Along the main road to Kuala Pilah are a number of **Minangkabau houses**, though the traditional thatch of the buffalo horn roofs has been replaced by more utilitarian corrugated iron. The village of Terachi, 27km from Seremban at the turn-off to Sri Menanti, has some particularly fine traditional houses, as does Sri Menanti itself. Pantai and Nilai, a short distance north-east of Seremban, also have Minangkabau houses.

Hutan Lipur Ulu Bendol

This dense forest park makes a good day trip from Seremban, only 20km away, and the primary dipterocarp rainforest has some excellent short walks. The well maintained main trail from the park headquarters (500m back from the restaurant and food stalls on the main road, where the Seremban-Kuala Pilah bus drops you off) follows Sungai Batang Terachi. The route passes small cascading waterfalls before rising more sharply to the summit of Gunung Angsi (825m), with fine views across Seremban and out to the Straits of Melaka. The steeper sections can be taxing, but this is a relatively easy 4.5km walk, taking around four hours return. Shorter self-guided trails, with plaques identifying the trees, branch out around the park headquarters. The park is very popular on weekends.

Though usually done as a day trip, the park also has accommodation in attractive but unfurnished cabins and chalets costing RM10 to RM30 per night. Bookings must be made in advance at Pejabat Hutan Daerah (the District Forest Office; ☎ 06-481 1036), about 1km out of Kuala Pilah, towards Bahau.

Sri Menanti

Sri Menanti, just off the Seremban to Kuala Pilah road, is the old royal capital, first settled over 400 years ago by the Minangkabau from Sumatra. This sleepy hamlet is nestled in a highland valley surrounded by green hills, and the manicured lawns are as much a product of the sheep that wander around the town as the royal gardeners.

Things to See The centre of town is just a row of ramshackle shops and a few houses, but just past Sri Menanti's own small Lake Gardens is the **Istana Besar**, the impressive palace of the sultan of Negeri Sembilan. Built in the 1930s, it has a new addition featuring a blue tiled Minangkabau roof. It is not open to the public.

The main interest lies just beyond the Istana Besar at the **Istana Lama** (Old Palace), now a museum. Built in 1908 as a replacement for an older palace that burnt down, the three storey palace is raised off the ground on pillars, many of them carved, and is topped by a tower which once served as the royal treasury. Though not particularly Minangkabau in style, it is a good example of court architecture typical of early 20th century palaces. It now houses the **Muzium Diraja**, dedicated to Negeri Sembilan's royalty, with costumes, weapons and preserved royal bedrooms. Memorabilia of the sultans features prominently, especially that of Tunku Abdul Rahman, the first *yang di-pertuan agong*, or king of Malaysia, at the time of independence in 1957. Both Abdul Rahman and his son, Tunku Ja'afar, who was appointed yang di-pertuan agong in 1994, were noted sports fanatics and Sri Menanti even has a royal golf course just beyond the museum.

The museum is open from 10 am to 6 pm, except Monday (closed), Thursday (open from 8 am to 12.45 pm) and Friday (closed from 12.15 to 2.45 pm). Opposite is one of the finest Minangkabau houses you'll see in Negeri Sembilan, though this former palace is falling into disrepair.

Also of note in Sri Menanti is the **Makam Diraja**, the royal graves in the compound next to the mosque. The graveyard has a Victorian/Moorish pavilion and the grave of Tuanku Abdul Rahman, immediately inside the gates, is prominent.

Places to Stay Though you can easily see all of the sights in an hour or two, Sri Menanti is a very quiet, pleasant spot for an overnight stay. The only accommodation is the *Sri Menanti Resort* (☎ 06-497 9620), right next to the Istana Lama, which has a swimming pool, restaurant and nice singles/doubles for RM75/95 or attractive chalets for RM50/60. It's often empty, so discounts may be available.

Getting There & Away From Seremban, first take a bus to Kuala Pilah from where there are several daily buses to Sri Menanti. Alternatively, charter your own taxi from Seremban or Kuala Pilah for around RM20 return.

Kuala Pilah

Kuala Pilah, 40km east of Seremban, is one of the main towns of this strongly Minangkabau region. It is mostly a place for making transport connections, though it's a pleasant valley town, and the interesting old **Sim Tong Chinese temple**, on the main street towards Bahau, is worth a look. Opposite is a Chinese-style arch dedicated to Martin Lister, the first British Resident of Negeri Sembilan. Kuala Pilah is also a good place to try Minangkabau food such as *rendang*, a fiery meat curry.

Places to Stay Kuala Pilah has several cheap Chinese hotels, including the *Hotel Hinyi* (☎ 06-481 8335), 227 Jalan Tung Yen, where good air-con rooms with bathroom cost RM38. On a hill overlooking the town, a pleasant resthouse, *Rumah Persinggahan* (☎ 06-481 4146) on Jalan Bukit has rooms for RM77 and chalets for RM148.50.

Getting There & Away From Seremban, several companies run buses to Kuala Pilah, with departures roughly hourly between 7 am and 7 pm daily. From Kuala Pilah it is also possible to get connections north to Temerloh, and east all the way to Kuantan, but usually you will first have to take another local bus to Bahau, on the highway 20km to the east.

PORT DICKSON

Port Dickson is just a small port town of no interest, but it is the gateway to the stretch of beach extending 16km south to Tanjong Tuan (Cape Rachado). This beach is very popular with KL residents on weekends, and a string of mostly upmarket hotels is spread out all the way to Tanjong Tuan. Despite their popularity, the beaches are not great. The sands vary from red to grey-white. The water, like elsewhere along the Straits of Melaka, is murky and very shallow for swimming. Occasional oil spills from passing tankers don't help. If you are desperate for a quick escape to the beach from KL, or just want to live it up in a resort, Port Dickson is OK for a couple of days, but Malaysia has better beaches.

Originally built by the Portuguese in the 16th century, the **Tanjong Tuan lighthouse** offers fine views. On a clear day you can see Sumatra, 38km away across the Straits of Melaka. The turn-off to the lighthouse is near the Km 16 marker. Head down the road for 2km and then through the forest reserve for another kilometre to the lighthouse.

Port Dickson's tourist office is on the beach, 4km from town.

Places to Stay

The attraction is the beach, so don't bother with the hotels in Port Dickson town. The best beaches start from around the Km 8 peg. Most hotels are upmarket, and new resorts and condominiums are plentiful. On weekends many hotels are fully booked, especially the cheaper places (apart from the youth hostel), but discounts often apply during the week. Unless otherwise specified the following prices are for doubles.

Just 3.5km south of town is the *Delta Paradise Lagoon Hotel* (☎ 06-647 7600; fax 06-647 7630), which charges RM242 for its standard rooms. The hotel has its own artificial beach and inlet lagoon ringed by coconut palms. Another big new resort is the *AVillion* (☎ 06-647 6688) at Km 5.5. Rooms built over the water on stilts cost from RM430, but there are cheaper options. It has two swimming pools and several restaurants.

Not far on at Km 6.5, the *Port Dickson Youth Hostel* (☎ 06-647 2188) is back from the road in spacious grounds, but it attracts few visitors. A bed in a fan cooled dorm costs RM10, or RM15 in an air-con dorm. Four-bed chalets are also available for RM50. Non-Hostelling International members pay an extra one-off fee of RM5. There are shops and *warungs* (stalls) in front of the hostel, on the main road.

Just before the youth hostel is the *Seri Malaysia Hotel* (☎ 06-647 6070), part of a chain that offers quality rooms for only RM100. It is a very popular Malay hotel.

At Km 7, the *Bayu Beach Resort* (☎ 06-647 3703) is a big hotel with a pool, bar and restaurants. Rooms and apartments range from RM200 to RM450 on weekends, with major discounts from Monday to Friday.

At Km 8 is another collection of big hotels, the best being the Minangkabau-style *Regency* (☎ 06-647 4090) with a pool, tennis and squash courts. Rooms cost from RM170 on weekdays, or RM180 on weekends.

Next along is the *Si-Rusa Inn* (☎ 06-662 5233) at Km 12. This older mid-range resort has rooms for RM80, or RM92 with hot water in the bathrooms, while chalets with fridge and TV cost RM120 and RM140. It is back from the road and right on the beach.

A selection of budget places can be found at Km 13. The *Hotel Selat* (☎ 06-662 5109) is a standard mid-range place near the main road, with air-con rooms from RM60. Past the Hotel Selat is the red sand beach, but it is well away from the main road and quiet, with water deep enough for swimming and a boat shed with canoes for hire. The friendly *Kong Ming Hotel* (☎ 06-662 5683) is right by the beach and good value at RM30 for rooms with bathroom, or without but facing the sea. Nearby, the very run-down *Lido Hotel* (☎ 06-662 5273) has doubles from RM35.

In Teluk Kemang at Km 15.5 is *The Travers* (☎ 06-662 6693), a mid-range hotel with rooms from RM170 or RM150 on weekdays. Half a kilometre further on is the more upmarket *Guoman Resort* (☎ 06-662 7878), a large new resort with a nine hole golf course and deluxe rooms from RM250 on weekends, or RM150 on weekdays.

Finally, on the turn-off road to Tanjong Tuan, 1km before the lighthouse, are a couple of upmarket apartment resorts, although the shallow beach here is no better than elsewhere. The *Rachado Point* (☎ 03-253 8116) has one, two and three-bedroom apartments for RM207, RM460 and RM575. Three and four-bedroom apartments at the *Ilham Resort* (☎ 06-662 6800) cost RM400 and RM500 respectively.

Getting There & Away

Port Dickson is 94km south-west of KL, 34km south of Seremban and 90km north of Melaka. The bus and taxi stations are next to each other in the centre of the town. By bus it's RM4.20 from Melaka, and RM5.60 from KL's Puduraya bus station. The taxi fare to KL is RM60, and to Melaka RM55.

From Port Dickson town, local buses (and buses to Melaka) will drop you off wherever you like along the beach.

PEDAS HOT SPRINGS

Heading south of Seremban along the old highway are the Pedas Hot Springs, 1km before the small town of Pedas. Here you can soak in the somewhat run-down private baths. Both buses and trains from Seremban stop in Pedas.

PENGKALAN KEMPAS

About 50km north of Melaka is the small town of Pengkalan Kempas. A short distance towards Lubok China or Melaka from here, a 'Kompleks Sejarah Pengkalan Kempas' sign indicates the **grave of Sheikh Ahmad Majnun**, about 100m off the road. This local hero died in 1467 and beside his grave, which is sheltered by a structure in the final stages of complete collapse, are three 2m-high stones standing upright in the ground.

These mysterious stones, known as the sword, the spoon and the rudder, are thought to be older than the grave. Immediately in front of the grave is another stone with a hole through it. The circular opening is said to tighten up on the arm of any liar foolish enough to thrust it through.

The buses that run along the coast between Port Dickson and Melaka travel via Pengkalan Kempas.

Melaka

The small state of Melaka (formerly Malacca), centred on the historically important port of Melaka, is one of the most interesting on the peninsula. In the 15th century Melaka became the greatest trading port in South-East Asia and attracted waves of conquering Europeans. Though Melaka's importance has long since declined, it retains reminders of its rich history and a fascinating mixture of Chinese and European culture.

History

Under the Melaka sultanates the city was a wealthy centre of trade with China, India, Siam (Thailand) and Indonesia, due to its strategic position on the Straits of Melaka. The Melaka sultanates were the beginning of what is today Malaysia, and some Malaysians say this city is where you find the soul of Malaysia.

Melaka was just another fishing village until it attracted the attention of Parameswara, a Hindu prince from Sumatra. Parameswara had thrown off allegiance to the Majapahit Empire and fled to Temasek (modern-day Singapore), where his piracy and other exploits brought Siamese attack in 1398, forcing him to flee again to Melaka, where he set up his headquarters.

Melaka under Parameswara soon became a favoured port for resupplying trading ships plying the strategic Straits of Melaka. Halfway between China and India, and with easy access to the spice islands of Indonesia, Melaka attracted merchants from all over the east.

In 1405 Admiral Cheng Ho, the 'three-jewelled eunuch prince', arrived in Melaka bearing gifts from the Ming emperor and the promise of protection from archenemies, the Siamese. Based on these early contacts with China, Chinese settlers followed and came to be known as the Babas and Nyonyas, or Straits Chinese. They are the longest-settled Chinese people in Malaysia and added many Malay customs to their Chinese heritage.

HIGHLIGHTS

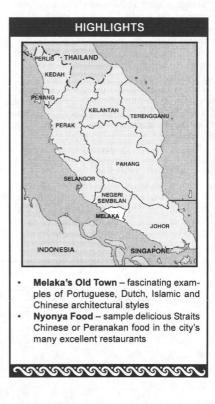

- **Melaka's Old Town** – fascinating examples of Portuguese, Dutch, Islamic and Chinese architectural styles
- **Nyonya Food** – sample delicious Straits Chinese or Peranakan food in the city's many excellent restaurants

Despite internal squabbles and intrigues, by the time of Parameswara's death in 1414, Melaka was already a powerful trading state. The cosmopolitan centre also came in contact with Islam, brought by traders from India. The third ruler of Melaka, Maharaja Mohammed Shah (1424-44), converted to Islam, and his son, Mudzaffar Shah, took the title of sultan and made Islam the state religion.

Under the banner of Islam, Melaka became the major entrepôt port in South-East Asia, attracting Muslim Indian merchants from competing Sumatran ports. Melaka became a centre for Islam, disseminating the religion throughout the Indonesian archipelago. The Melaka sultans ruled over the greatest empire in Malaysia's history, and successfully repelled Siamese attacks. The Malay language became the lingua franca of trade in the region, and Melaka produced the first major piece of Malay literature, the *Sejarah Melayu* (or *Malay Annals*), a history of the sultanate.

In 1509 the Portuguese arrived at Melaka seeking the wealth of the spice and china trades, but after an initially friendly reception, the Melakans attacked the Portuguese fleet and took a number of prisoners.

This action was the pretext for an outright assault by the Portuguese, and in 1511 Alfonso d'Albuquerque took the city and the sultan fled to Johor, where he re-established his kingdom. Under the Portuguese, the fortress of A'Famosa was constructed, and missionaries like the famous Francis Xavier strove to implant Christianity. Melaka continued to be an important trading post, but while Portuguese cannons could easily conquer Melaka, they could not force Muslim merchants from Arabia and India to trade there. Other trading ports in the area, such as Islamic Demak on Java, grew to overshadow Melaka.

The Portuguese left behind their language and Catholicism, both still practised among Melaka's Portuguese Eurasians, but the period of Portuguese strength in the east was short-lived. Melaka suffered harrying attacks from the rulers of neighbouring Johor and Negeri Sembilan, as well as from the Islamic power of Aceh in Sumatra. As Dutch influence in Indonesia grew, Batavia (modern-day Jakarta) developed as the key European port of the region and Melaka declined further. Finally, the Dutch launched an attack on the city and in 1641, after a siege which lasted eight months, it passed into their hands.

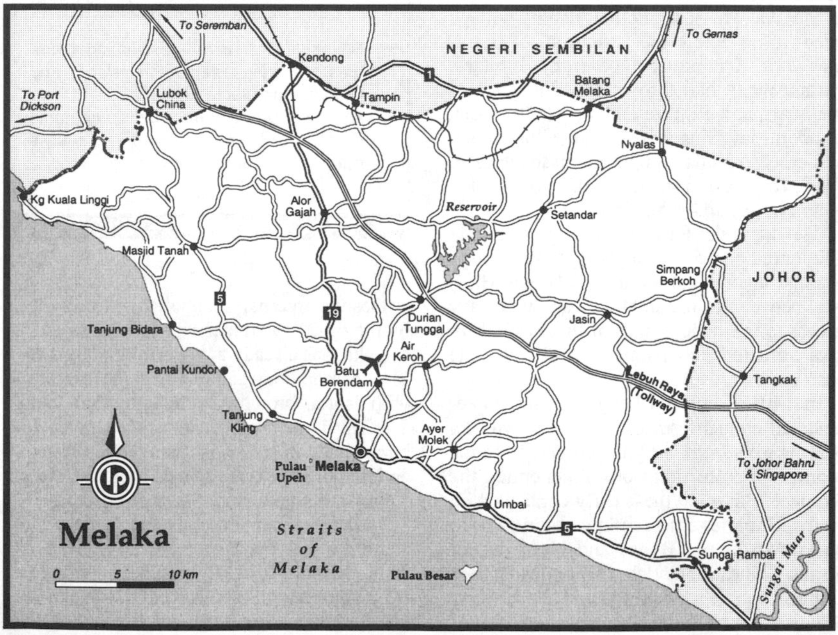

The Dutch built fine public buildings and churches, which today are the most solid reminders of the European presence in the city. Melaka became the centre for peninsular trade, but it was only a minor part of a greater empire; the Dutch directed more energy into their possessions in Indonesia. Like their Portuguese predecessors, the Dutch ruled Melaka for only about 150 years.

When the French occupied Holland in 1795, the British, allies of the Dutch, temporarily took over administration of the Dutch colonies. The British administrators, essentially traders, were opposed to the Dutch policy of trade monopoly and clearly saw that the Dutch and themselves would be bitter rivals in Malaysia when and if Melaka was returned. Accordingly, in 1807 they started to demolish the fortress and forcibly move the population to Penang, to ensure that if Melaka was restored to the Dutch it would be no rival to the British Malayan centres.

Fortunately Stamford Raffles, the far-sighted founder of Singapore, stepped in before these destructive policies went too far, and in 1824 Melaka was permanently ceded to the British in exchange for the Sumatran port of Bencoolen (Bengkulu today).

Melaka, together with Penang and Singapore, formed the Straits Settlements, the three British territories that were the centres for later expansion into the peninsula. However, under British rule Melaka was always the lesser light of the Straits Settlements, and it was soon superseded by the rapidly growing commercial importance of Singapore. Apart from a brief revival of its fortunes in the early 20th century when rubber was an important crop, Melaka once again became a quiet backwater.

MELAKA

Malaysia's most historically interesting city, Melaka was the greatest trading state in South-East Asia under the Melaka sultanates. The complete series of European incursions in Malaysia (Portuguese, Dutch and British) were played out here, and Melaka still bears testament to their presence. In the centre of town, much of the old Dutch city remains, and Medan Portugis is still home to Portuguese Eurasians. Of all Melaka's mixed traditions, perhaps the most interesting are the Babas and Nyonyas, the offspring of the original Chinese settlers who intermarried and adopted many Malay customs.

Melaka is a place of intriguing Chinese streets and antique shops, old Chinese temples and cemeteries and nostalgic reminders of the European colonial powers. The traditional Malay *kampung* house, with its distinctive colourful tiled entrance steps, can be seen along the river in east Melaka or in the Tanjung Kling district north of the city.

Melaka, for long a sleepy backwater town living on memories of past glories, is starting to experience an economic boom. Massive land reclamation has seen the historic waterfront retreat inland, and a huge shopping complex and new apartment blocks now enjoy Melaka's sea views. Despite this modernisation, Chinatown and the old city area are still delightfully old-fashioned, and Melaka remains one of Malaysia's premier tourist destinations.

Orientation

Melaka is a small town – easy to find your way around and compact enough to explore on foot, bicycle or trishaw.

The interesting and older parts of Melaka are mainly near the river and the original waterfront, particularly around the old Dutch-built Stadthuys (Town Hall), where you'll also find the tourist office, Christ Church, St Paul's Church, Porta de Santiago and the Cultural Museum. Across the river, Chinatown also has many points of interest. Further afield within the city are more historic attractions such as Bukit China, St John's Fort and Medan Portugis.

South of Melaka's old historical quarter are Taman Mahkota and Taman Melaka Raya, two completely new areas built on reclaimed land, and the large artificial island of Pulau Melaka just off the new shoreline.

Information

The tourist office (☎ 06-283 6538) in the heart of the city almost opposite Christ

Church, has very helpful staff. It's open daily from 8.45 am to 5 pm, but is closed from 12.15 to 2.45 pm on Friday. On the opposite corner, the Malacca Tourist Police (☎ 06-282 2222) has a good map of Melaka and its attractions, and can answer basic queries.

The main post office is 3km north of central Melaka on Jalan Bukit Baru at the corner of Jalan Panglima Awang. To get there, take bus No 19 from the local bus station. More convenient are the post office branches in the centre of town opposite the Karyaneka Handicrafts Emporium and on the ground floor of the Mahkota Parade shopping complex.

For visa extensions, the immigration office (☎ 06-282 4955) is at Wisma Persekutuan on Jalan Hang Tuah. There is another post at the ferry dock to handle departure and entry to/from Dumai in Indonesia.

Convenient banks for changing money include the Hongkong Bank near the Stadthuys, the Maybank opposite Robin's Nest guesthouse, and the Bank of Commerce on the main thoroughfare of Jalan Taman Melaka Raya (Jalan TMR). The Bank of Commerce and the Bank Bumiputra also have change counters on the ground floor of the Mahkota Parade shopping complex.

Town Square & Bukit St Paul

The main area of interest in Melaka is the old city on the eastern side of the river. In front of the tourist office is Town Square, also known as Dutch Square, where the Stadthuys and Christ Church are solid reminders of the Dutch presence.

Rising above Town Square is Bukit St Paul (St Paul's Hill), site of the original Portuguese fort of A'Famosa. The ruins of St Paul's Church and the Porta de Santiago are the only remains of the Portuguese presence. Nearby are the Cultural Museum and Proclamation of Independence Hall, while the Maritime Museum is back on the river.

All the historical points of interest are included on a signposted 'Heritage Trail', an excellent self-guided walking tour that also

The Melaka House

While following the standard kampung house pattern of a wooden structure on short stilts, the Melaka kampung house is easily identifiable by its tiled front stairway. This leads up to the front veranda and is the formal entrance to the house. This entrance is the one used by guests, and the front veranda itself is the formal entertainment area.

The middle *(tengah)* section is the living area, and the steps at the side of the house here are those used by the family and friends. It would be inappropriate for guests to enter here. The kitchen and eating area *(dapur)* is at the rear of the house and the steps here are used only by the women.

Typical Melaka kampung homes can be seen in the east of the state and the Tanjung Kling district.

takes in parts of Chinatown (ask for a brochure at the tourist office).

Stadthuys The most imposing relic of the Dutch period in Melaka is the massive red town hall, built between 1641 and 1660 and believed to be the oldest Dutch building in the east. It displays all the typical features of Dutch colonial architecture, including substantial solid doors and louvred windows. The other buildings around the Town Square, including the old clock tower at the Stadthuys, follow the same red theme.

Today the Stadthuys houses the excellent historical, ethnographic and literature museums, where a couple of fruitful hours can be spent. The **History Museum** gives a detailed explanation of Melaka's past through old maps, lithographs, oil paintings and photos. Unlike most museums in Malaysia that give little or no explanation, here it would take a couple of hours to read your way through the labels. The **Ethnographic Museum** has displays on many aspects of local culture and traditions, including good exhibitions of the marriage ceremonies of the various ethnic communities in Melaka. The less-interesting **Literature Museum** is housed in a separate building behind. The Stadthuys and its museums are open from 9 am to 6 pm daily, except Friday lunchtime from 12.15 to 2.45 pm; entry is RM2.

Christ Church Nearby, facing one end of the main square, is the bright red Christ Church. The pink bricks were brought from Zeeland in Holland and faced with local red laterite when the church was constructed in 1753. Under the British this Dutch Reformed church was converted for Anglican use, and the weathercock and bell tower were added, but it still has its old Dutch tombstones laid in the floor. Its massive 15m-long ceiling beams were each cut from a single tree.

St Paul's Church From the Stadthuys, steps lead to the top of Bukit St Paul, topped by the ruins of St Paul's Church. Originally built by the Portuguese in 1521 as the small

This Dutch tombstone from St Paul's Church in Melaka is a reminder of the century of Dutch rule.

'Our Lady of the Hill' chapel, it was regularly visited by Francis Xavier. Following his death in China, the saint's body was brought here and buried for nine months before being transferred to Goa in India, where it remains today. A marble statue of Francis Xavier commemorates his interment here over 400 years ago.

In 1556 the church was enlarged to two storeys and a tower was added to the front in 1590. The church was renamed following the Dutch takeover, but when the Dutch completed their own Christ Church at the base of the hill it fell into disuse. Under the British it lost the tower, although a lighthouse was built at the front, and it eventually ended up as a storehouse for gunpowder. The church has been in ruins now for more than 150 years, but the setting is beautiful, the walls are imposing and fine old Dutch tombstones stand around the interior.

Porta de Santiago There are steps from St Paul's Church down the hill to the Porta de Santiago, once the main gate – and all that

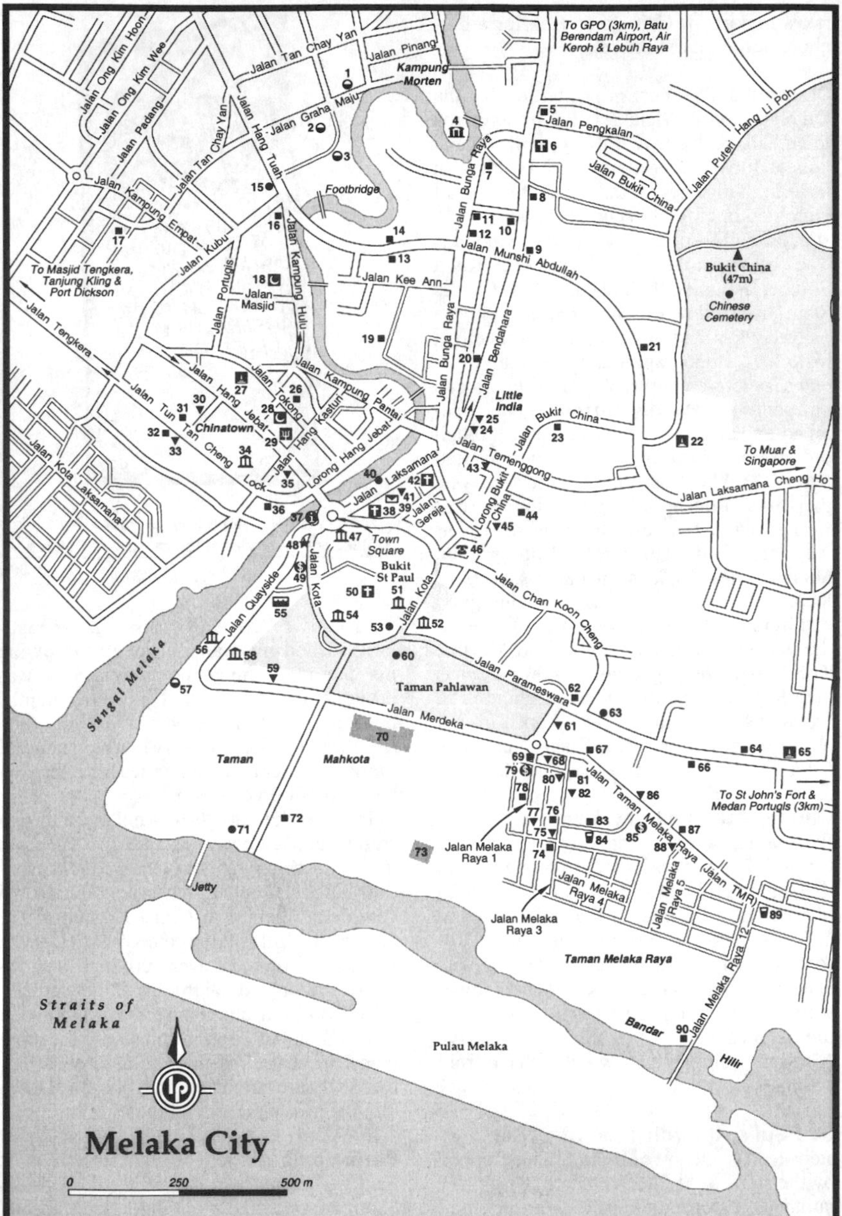
Melaka City
To GPO (3km), Batu Berendam Airport, Air Keroh & Lebuh Raya
Jalan Ong Kim Hoon
Jalan Ong Kim Wee
Jalan Padang
Jalan Tan Chay Yan
Jalan Pinang
Kampung Morten
Jalan Graha Maju
Jalan Hang Tuah
Jalan Pengkalan
Jalan Bunga Raya
Jalan Bukit China
Jalan Puteri Hang Li Poh
Jalan Kampung Empat
Footbridge
Jalan Kubu
Jalan Kampung Hulu
Jalan Munshi Abdullah
Bukit China (47m)
Chinese Cemetery
To Masjid Tengkera, Tanjung Kling & Port Dickson
Jalan Portugis
Jalan Masjid
Jalan Kee Ann
Jalan Tengkera
Jalan Bendahara
Jalan Hang Jebat
Jalan Tokong
Jalan Kampung Pantai
Little India
Jalan Tun Tan Cheng Lock
Chinatown
Jalan Hang Kasturi
Lorong Hang Jebat
Jalan Temenggong
To Muar & Singapore
Jalan Kota Laksamana
Jalan Laksamana
Jalan Gereja
Lorong Bukit China
Jalan Laksamana Cheng Ho
Town Square
Bukit St Paul
Jalan Kota
Jalan Quayside
Jalan Chan Koon Cheng
Sungai Melaka
Jalan Parameswara
Taman Pahlawan
Jalan Merdeka
Taman
Mahkota
Jalan Taman Melaka Raya (Jalan TMR)
To St John's Fort & Medan Portugis (3km)
Jalan Melaka Raya 1
Jalan Melaka Raya 4
Jalan Melaka Raya 3
Jalan Melaka Raya 5
Jetty
Taman Melaka Raya
Jalan Melaka Raya 12
Straits of Melaka
Bandar Hilir
Pulau Melaka
0
250
500 m

PLACES TO STAY

5 Hotel Grand Continental
7 Majestic Hotel
8 City Bayview Hotel
9 Hotel Accordian
10 Renaissance Hotel
11 Ng Fook
12 Hong Kong Hotel
13 Regal
14 May Chiang Hotel
16 Visma Hotel
17 Malacca Town Holiday Lodge 2
19 Gold Leaf Hotel
20 Valiant Hotel
21 Palace Hotel
23 Eastern Heritage Guest House
26 Chong Hoe Hotel
31 Hotel Puri
32 The Baba House
36 Heeren House
44 Apple Guest House
62 Hotel Equatorial
64 Kancil Guest House
66 Hinly Hotel
67 Heritage Hotel
69 Robin's Nest
72 Century Mahkota Hotel
74 Melaka Youth Hostel
76 Grand Star Hotel
78 Travellers' Lodge
81 Sunny's Inn
83 Hotel Ambassador
87 Malacca Town Holiday Lodge 1
90 Harbour Inn

PLACES TO EAT

24 Sri Lakshmi Vilas
25 Sri Krishna Bavan
30 Old China Cafe
33 Restoran Peranakan
35 Jonkers Melaka Restoran
41 Restaurant Kim Swee Huat
43 Restoran Veni
45 UE Tea House
59 Glutton's Corner
61 Malay Food Stalls
68 Mei Chong
75 Ole Rasa
77 Peppermint Cafe
80 Restoran Lim (Mee Yoke)
82 Tandoori House
86 Nyonya Makko
88 Ole Sayang

OTHER

1 Local Bus Station
2 Taxi Station
3 Express Bus Station
4 Villa Sentosa
6 Church of St Peter
15 Immigration
18 Kampung Hulu Mosque
22 Sam Po Kong Temple & Hang Li Poh Well
27 Cheng Hoon Teng Temple
28 Kampung Kling Mosque
29 Sri Pogyatha Vinoyagar Moorthi Temple
34 Baba-Nyonya Heritage Museum
37 Tourist Office
38 Christ Church
39 Post Office
40 Karyaneka Handicrafts Emporium; Dulukala
42 Church of St Francis
46 Telekom
47 Stadthuys
48 Tourist Police
49 Hongkong Bank
50 St Paul's Church
51 Cultural Museum
52 Proclamation of Independence Hall
53 Porta de Santiago
54 People's Museum
55 Swimming Pool
56 Maritime Museum
57 Ferries to Dumai
58 Royal Malaysian Navy Museum
60 Sound & Light Show
63 Jin Trading (Bicycle Hire)
65 Chinese Temple
70 Mahkota Parade Shopping Complex
71 Mahkota Seaworld (Under Construction)
73 Mahkota Medical Centre
79 Maybank
84 Jam Pub; Orchid Pub
85 Bank of Commerce
89 Jim's Cottage Pub

remains – of the Portuguese fortress A'Famosa, originally constructed by Alfonso d'Albuquerque in 1512. Stamford Raffles may have stepped in before the complete destruction of the old fortress, but it was a near thing. Curiously, this sole surviving relic of the fort bears the Dutch East India Company's coat of arms: this was part of the fort which the Dutch reconstructed in 1607, following their takeover.

Nearby is a small grandstand, used as the venue for the Sound & Light Show each evening (see under Entertainment).

People's Museum This unique museum is on Jalan Kota just west of the Porta de Santiago. On the ground floor there are displays explaining the local economy and society, however the upstairs section is much more intriguing.

The exhibits here deal with a wide variety of bizarre 'beautification' practices. These range from tattooing, piercing and scarring to body stretching, foot binding, head shaping and modern cosmetic surgery. It's fascinating, but not for the faint hearted. Entry is RM2.

Muzium Budaya Just along from the Porta de Santiago at the base of Bukit St Paul is a wooden replica of a Melaka sultan's palace which houses the Muzium Budaya (Cultural Museum). This new building is based on the original 15th century palace, supposedly from descriptions in the *Malay Annals*. Although the exhibits concentrate on traditional Melakan culture, there are also exhibits from other parts of Malaysia. Displays include apparel, games, weaponry, musical instruments, stone inscriptions and photographic exhibits, as well as a diorama of the sultan's court, with costumed mannequins representing the various positions in the hierarchy. Admission to this interesting building costs RM1.50 (children 50 sen), and it is open from 9 am to 6 pm (closed from 12.15 to 2.45 pm on Friday).

Proclamation of Independence Hall Housed in a British villa dating from 1912, this museum (Memorial Pergistiharan Kemerdekaan) is dedicated to events leading up to independence in 1957. Ironically, it was once the Melaka Club, a bastion of colonialism. The grand building features the architectural whimsies of the day and is topped by Mogul-inspired domes. Inside, the historical displays are a bit dry but are still good for an insight into the political history of Malaysia, even if the mood tends to be ultra-nationalistic and the role of the Communists is ignored. Many will find the 1957 Chevy outside, used by Tunku Abdul Rahman to tour the hustings, of equal interest.

The museum is open daily from 9 am to 6 pm, but closed from noon to 3 pm on Friday and all day Monday. Entry is free.

Maritime Museum This huge re-creation of a Portuguese ship, the *Flora de la Mar*, is next to the river near the tourist office. It houses more detailed descriptions of Melaka's history, as well as ship models, dioramas and an interesting map room featuring charts dating back to Portuguese times.

The museum is open daily from 9 am to 6 pm (closed Friday from 12.15 to 2.45 pm) and entry is RM2. The price includes entry to the **Royal Malaysian Navy Museum** across the street, which has navy memorabilia and salvaged remnants from the *Diana*, sunk off Melaka in 1817 while voyaging from Guangzhou (Canton) to Madras. A major salvage operation in 1993 recovered the ship and its cargo of tea, sugar and over 18 tons of chinaware. New technology has made salvage expeditions in the Straits of Melaka a viable business, and the waters potentially hold a trove of ancient treasures. There is concern that Melaka's land reclamation is permanently burying historical artefacts, and that any new reclamation should only proceed after detailed archaeological studies of the shoreline.

Chinatown

Melaka's Chinatown, west of the river, is a fascinating area to wander around. With twisting streets, Peranakan (Straits Chinese) shophouses, ancient temples and mosques, its history of settlement and trade is as fascinating as the reminders of colonial rule.

Although Melaka has long lost its importance as a port, ancient-looking Sumatran schooners still sail up the river and moor at the banks. Today, however, their cargo is not the varied treasures of the east, but charcoal for the cooking fires of the city or lumber from Indonesia. There's a good view of the river and boats from the bridge beside the tourist office, and you can also take a river boat tour (see Organised Tours later in this chapter).

Crossing over the bridge you enter **Jalan Hang Jebat**, formerly known as Jonkers St, or Junk St. Melaka is famed for its antique shops scattered along this street. You can easily spend an hour or more browsing, but although you may still find some of the treasures of the east, don't expect any bargains. There's an assortment of interesting shops and the occasional mosque or Chinese or Hindu temple squeezed into this intriguing old street. The most notable temple is the Cheng Hoon Teng Temple (see the following entry).

Jalan Tun Tan Cheng Lock, running parallel to Jalan Hang Jebat, is also worth a stroll. This narrow street, now a one-way thoroughfare with disturbingly fast moving traffic, was the preferred address for wealthy Baba traders who were most active during the short-lived rubber boom of the early 20th century. These typical Peranakan houses, with their intricate tiles and plasterwork, exhibit Chinese, Dutch and British influences. The Baba-Nyonya Heritage Museum (see below) is the main highlight, but also stop to look at the fine Chee Mansion set back from the street at No 117.

Other points of interest in Chinatown are the **Sri Pogyatha Vinoyagar Moorthi Temple**, dating from 1781 and dedicated to the Hindu deity Vinoyagar, and the **Kampung Kling Mosque**. This ancient mosque has a multitiered *meru* roof, which owes its inspiration to Hindu temples, and a watch-tower minaret typical of early mosques in Sumatra and Java. In the same style further north, the **Kampung Hulu Mosque** dates from 1728 and is the oldest in Malaysia.

Cheng Hoon Teng Temple This fascinating temple in the old part of the city is the oldest Chinese temple in Malaysia and has an inscription commemorating Admiral Cheng Ho's epochal visit to Melaka. The brightly coloured roof bears the usual assortment of mythical Chinese creatures. Entered through massive hardwood doors, the temple is equally colourful and ornate inside. The temple's ceremonial mast rises above the old houses in this part of Melaka.

Cheng Hoon Teng (literally 'Temple of the Evergreen Clouds') was founded in 1646 by Kapitan China Lee Wei King, a native of Amoy in China. All materials used in building the original temple were imported from China, as were the artisans who designed and built it. The temple was constructed in the southern Chinese style to pay respect to the San Y Chiao, or Three Teachings, of Buddhism, Taoism and Confucianism.

Baba-Nyonya Heritage Museum At 48-50 Jalan Tun Tan Cheng Lock is a traditional Peranakan townhouse which has been made into a small museum. The architecture of this type of house, many examples of which survive in Melaka today, has been described as Chinese Palladian and Chinese Baroque. The interiors of these houses contain open courtyards which admit sun and rain. The interior of the museum is arranged so that it looks like a typical 19th century Baba-Nyonya residence.

Furniture consists of Chinese hardwoods fashioned in a mixture of Chinese, Victorian and Dutch designs with mother-of-pearl inlay. There are also displays of 'Nyonya ware', multicoloured ceramic designs from the Jiangxi and Guangdong provinces in China, made specifically for Straits Chinese. Nyonya ceramics and tilework are usually a blend of pink, yellow, dark blue and green colours.

The museum (☎ 06-283 1273) is open daily from 10 am to 12.30 pm and 2 to 4.30 pm. Admission is RM7 (children RM4), which includes a good 45 minute tour of the house conducted by the Baba family who own the house – well worth it if you are interested in Peranakan culture.

Bukit China

In the middle of the 15th century the sultan of Melaka's ambassador to China returned with the Ming emperor's daughter to wed the sultan and thus seal relations between the two countries. She brought with her a vast retinue, including 500 handmaidens, and Bukit China (China Hill) was established as their residence. It has been a Chinese area ever since and, together with two adjoining hills, forms a Chinese cemetery covering over 25 hectares. With more than 12,000 graves, this is said to be the largest in the world outside China. Some of the ornate graves date back to the Ming Dynasty, but most of them are now in a sorry state.

Chinese graveyards are often built on hillsides because the bulk of the hill shields the graves from evil winds, while the spirits get a good view of what their descendants are up to down below. In our more space-conscious modern world, Chinese graves are gradually losing their spacious and expansive traditional design.

Sam Po Kong Temple & Hang Li Poh Well Apart from his real-life role as an admiral and ambassador, Cheng Ho is also religiously venerated, and this temple is dedicated to him. Built in 1795, it's at the foot of Bukit China.

Next to the temple is the Hang Li Poh Well, built in the 15th century by Sultan Mansor Shah for his Chinese wife, Princess Hang Li Poh. It was an important source of water for Melaka and a prime target for opposition forces wanting to take the city. Johor forces poisoned it in 1551, killing 200 Portuguese. The Dutch in 1606 and the Acehnese in 1628 subsequently employed the same tactic. The Dutch eventually built the fortifications that surround the well, but it has long since fallen into ruin. Taking a drink from the well was said to ensure a visitor's return to the city. Today the water is visibly impure, and tossing a coin into the well is the recommended way of ensuring a return trip.

Church of St Peter

This unexceptional church on Jalan Bendahara was built in 1710 by descendants of the early Portuguese settlers. It has some old tombstones and interesting stained-glass windows. It does not get much use for most of the year, but comes alive on Good Friday when Melakans flock here. Many of them make the occasion an excuse for an annual trip home from other parts of the country. The church is still associated with the Portuguese church in Macau.

Villa Sentosa

While not an official museum, this 1920s Malay kampung house, just across the river from the Majestic Hotel in Kampung Morten, is open to the public. The family still lives here and one of the family members will show you around. Though not exactly full of collectibles and history, it provides a good opportunity to poke around a kampung house and meet the family. A donation is expected after the tour. Villa Sentosa is open daily from 9 am to 1 pm and 2 to 5 pm, except Friday, when it is open from 2.45 to 5 pm. Female visitors are advised to be wary if visiting Villa Sentosa unaccompanied.

After you've finished you can wander around Kampung Morten, where there are a number of more traditional kampung houses. The one next to Villa Sentosa is typical.

Medan Portugis

About 3km east of the city centre on the coast is the area known as Medan Portugis, or Portuguese Square. In this small kampung there are about 500 descendants of marriages which took place between the colonial Portuguese and Malays 400 years ago. The kampung is centred on the square, styled after a typical Portuguese mercado, though it was built in the late 1980s in order to give the settlement a cultural focus. The kampung is unexceptional but visitors may be interested in the restaurants, live music and occasional Portuguese-Malay cultural shows.

Fort St John

Although the British demolished most of Porta de Santiago, they left the small Dutch fort of St John untouched. The fort was originally a Portuguese chapel dedicated to St John the Baptist until it was rebuilt by the Dutch in the 18th century. It stands on a hilltop to the east of town just before the turn-off to Medan Portugis – heading east along Jalan Parameswara, turn left into Jalan Bukit Senjuang. There are fine views from the top of the hill, but only a few walls and cannon emplacements of the fort remain.

Masjid Tengkera

This 150-year-old mosque, 2km towards Port Dickson, is of typical Sumatran design, featuring a square, multitiered roof. In its graveyard is the tomb of Sultan Hussein of Johor, who in 1819 signed over the island of Singapore to Stamford Raffles. The sultan later retired to Melaka, where he died in 1853. Take bus No 18 from Jalan Kubu.

Pulau Melaka

The construction of a new RM2 billion offshore island called Pulau Melaka is the culmination of a major land reclamation project that has dramatically altered Melaka's historic old town. This 90 hectare, 2km-long artificial island forms a modern marina-like resort ringed by sandy, palm-lined beaches – the only real beaches in the town area – and is separated from the mainland by a narrow, sheltered lagoon. Shops, condominiums, a 33 storey five star hotel, a theme park and public gardens are being built on Pulau Melaka, which is accessible from Jalan Melaka Raya 12 via a 300m bridge at Bandar Hilir.

Pulau Melaka is only the first of a whole 'archipelago' of artificial islands planned – ostensibly to combat erosion – for Melaka state's coastline between Kuala Linggi and Sungai Rambai.

Organised Tours

Boat Trips Daily riverboat tours of Melaka leave from the quay behind the tourist office. The trip takes 45 minutes, costs RM7 (RM3 for children) and passes through the downtown area and old godowns, riverside fish markets and on to Kampung Morten, where the Villa Sentosa is located. On the way back it takes in the wharves further downriver. Departure times are partially dependent on demand, but there are usually boat trips at 11 am, noon and 1 pm. There must be at least six passengers before the tour will operate, or you can pay RM35 for the whole boat.

Boat trips can also be made to the offshore islands in the Straits of Melaka (see the Around Melaka section).

Special Events

Major festivals in Melaka include the Good Friday and Easter Sunday processions at St Peter's, and the feast in June in honour of the patron saint of the fishing community, also held at St Peter's.

The nationwide bathing festival known as Mandi Safar is exuberantly celebrated in the Tanjung Kling district during the Muslim month of Safar.

Places to Stay – Budget

Guesthouses Melaka has some excellent traveller-oriented guesthouses. Most of them are in Taman Melaka Raya, the area just east of Taman Mahkota. They are virtually all on the 2nd and 3rd floors of some new and rather characterless blocks of buildings, but offer good facilities: common rooms with books, TVs and noticeboards, small kitchens and a variety of rooms. Though few rooms have windows, some do have skylights. The interior walls are often only plywood.

The atmosphere in all these places is generally good, and there's lots of competition so they provide good value for money. Prices are typically RM8 for a bed in a dorm, though some are still charging the 'old' RM7 price, and rooms start at RM12/15 for singles/doubles and range up to RM35 or more for larger rooms with air-con. The very cheapest rooms are in short supply and are usually full. Breakfast is often included in the price. There's also quite a turnover in the guesthouse business and some tend to move around the area in search of cheaper rents.

To get to Taman Melaka Raya, take bus No 17 from the express bus station for 40 sen and get off just past the huge Mahkota Parade shopping complex. Alternatively, a taxi or trishaw will cost RM6 from the station. Confusingly, most streets in this area are named Jalan Melaka Raya and are identified by an individual number.

On Jalan Melaka Raya 1 (the street running south off the roundabout), you'll find two of the most popular guesthouses. *Robin's Nest* (☎ 06-282 9142) at No 205B is very clean and well run with a good atmosphere. Dorm beds are RM8 each, and rooms range from RM15 to RM25. Further down at 214B is the similarly priced *Travellers' Lodge* (☎ 06-281 4793). This popular, long-running guesthouse has a large, welcoming common room and a rooftop garden.

Just east on Jalan Melaka Raya 3 is the *Melaka Youth Hostel* (Asrama Belia; ☎ 06-282 7915). This spotless, well-run hostel has a large TV/sitting/dining area with a small kitchen, but like many places it's not really set up for cooking. The dormitory rooms are larger and quieter than most and lockers are provided. A bed in the fan-cooled dorm costs RM10, or RM14 in the air-con dorm.

In the same street, the *Grand Star Hotel* (☎ 06-281 8199) at No 258B is a slightly more upmarket place, with good rooms and higher prices, but it's not as popular with travellers. A bed in the fan-cooled dorm (during peak periods only) costs RM8, simple fan rooms are RM15, while air-con rooms start at RM25.

Close by, at 270A-B Jalan Melaka Raya 3, is *Sunny's Inn* (☎ 06-283 7990), a family-run guesthouse with a variety of rooms. A bed in a dorm costs RM7, a tiny single is RM12, but most rooms range from RM15 up to RM35/55 single/double with air-con and shower (but external toilet).

On Jalan Taman Melaka Raya (Jalan TMR), this area's main thoroughfare, is the *Malacca Town Holiday Lodge 1* (☎ 06-284 8830) at 148B. Although it doesn't have a dorm or a decorated common room like most other hostels, this place is kept squeaky clean and is well run. Simple singles/doubles cost RM15/20, or RM36/50 with bathroom. Some of the rooms look onto a balcony with lots of greenery.

Away from Taman Melaka Raya there are a number of other guesthouses dotted around. One of the best is the popular *Eastern Heritage Guest House* (☎ 06-283 3026) at 8 Jalan Bukit China, well located just a short walk from the centre of town. It is housed in a superb old Melaka building dating from 1918, which has Peranakan tiling and impressive carved panelling. It has loads of character but the rooms are just typical guesthouse rooms, costing from RM15/18 a single/double, up to RM30 for more expensive rooms with balconies, or RM7 for a dorm bed. Downstairs is a common room, and a kitchen which provides meals.

Nearby, the *Apple Guest House* (☎ 017-671 1203) at 24-1 Lorong Banda Kaba, is in a newer house with quite clean rooms and a good atmosphere. There's no dorm now, but rooms are reasonably priced at RM12.50/18.

The *Kancil Guest House* (☎ 06-281 4044) at 177 Jalan Parameswara (near the Chinese temple) makes up for its slightly inconvenient location by offering spacious, secure yet laid-back lodgings. Dorm beds cost RM10, while clean, fan-cooled rooms with shared bathrooms range from RM20 to RM35. There's a quiet garden out the back.

North of the river is the *Malacca Town Holiday Lodge 2* (☎ 06-284 6905) at 52 Kampung Empat. It's run by the same people who have the Malacca Town Holiday Lodge 1. The location is inconvenient as it's a bit of a walk to the historical sites, but, like the other guesthouse, it is impeccably clean. There is a good variety of rooms (no dorms) from RM15/20. Large fan rooms with bathroom cost RM25 to RM35, or quite palatial air-con rooms with bathroom cost RM50.

Hotels Melaka is also well endowed with hotels in all price ranges.

Many cheap hotels are found along or just off Jalan Munshi Abdullah near the bus terminal. The *Majestic Hotel* (☎ 06-282 2367) at 188 Jalan Bunga Raya, is a classic old place reminiscent of the Cathay Hotel in Penang. High ceilings and swishing fans add to the cool lazy atmosphere, and there's a bar and car park. Rates range from RM27 for a small room with fan up to RM53 for a large room with air-con and bathroom.

The *Ng Fook* (☎ 06-282 8055) at 154 Jalan Bunga Raya, just north of Jalan Munshi Abdullah, is basic but OK, with simple double rooms for RM23, RM32 with bathroom, or up to RM41 with air-con and bathroom. A few doors away the somewhat cheaper *Hong Kong Hotel* (☎ 06-282 3392) costs RM18/20 for a simple single/double, RM22/26 with bathroom, and RM28/35 with bathroom and air-con.

Hidden away in a backstreet of Chinatown (opposite the old Kampung Kling Mosque) is the small *Chong Hoe Hotel* (☎ 06-282 6102) at 26 Jalan Tukang Emas. It offers good value, with simple rooms with fan for RM20 and air-con singles/doubles with TV and bathroom for RM36/46. At the *Valiant Hotel* (☎ 06-282 2323), 41A Jalan Bendahara, you'll pay RM23 for simple rooms with fan, RM30 with bathroom, or RM39 with air-con as well.

The *Heritage Hotel* (☎ 06-282 7515), 16A Jalan TMR, has small but clean singles/

doubles for RM25/40, but not all have windows. The *Hinly Hotel* (☎ 06-283 6554), in an older-style converted house set back from the street at 151 Parameswara, is very quiet despite the busy road. Air-con rooms with TV, phone and bathroom for RM40 are good value.

Places to Stay – Mid-Range

Most of the mid-range hotels are in the northern part of town and the central Chinatown area has a couple of good options.

At the bottom end of this range, the *Regal Hotel* (☎ 06-283 5959) at 66 Jalan Munshi Abdullah, just a few minutes' walk from the express bus station, has spacious if rather dim air-con singles/doubles with bathroom for RM35/40. Opposite at No 52 is the friendly *May Chiang Hotel* (☎ 06-283 9535), where comparable but nicer rooms cost RM40. The *Visma Hotel* (☎ 06-283 8799), closer to the bus station at 111 Jalan Kampung Hulu, also offers air-con, carpeted rooms with bathroom from RM40, but most have no external window.

Better value is the quiet and friendly *Gold Leaf Hotel* (☎ 06-283 6555) at 31 Jalan Kee Ann, whose clean air-con doubles with bathroom, TV and phone cost just RM45.

Further east at 114 Jalan Munshi Abdullah is the small *Hotel Accordian* (☎ 06-282 1911). Rooms are comfortable, if a bit faded, and cost from RM85 including tax. The *Palace Hotel* (☎ 06-282 5355) at No 201 Jalan Munshi Abdullah is similar and has singles/doubles for RM80/100 and larger deluxe rooms for RM120/140 plus 15% tax, but discounts are usually available.

In a recently restored row of former shophouses at 125 Jalan Tun Tan Cheng Lock is the *Baba House* (☎ 06-281 1216). With its tilework, carved panels and cool, interior courtyard downstairs, this place has loads of style. Standard rooms with bathroom are very comfortable and cost RM75/85, while deluxe rooms are RM95. Diagonally opposite at No 118 is the *Hotel Puri* (☎ 06-282 5588), another superb old renovated Peranakan manor house with an elaborate lobby decked out with beautiful old cane furniture and a glassed-over inner courtyard. Rooms with all mod-cons cost from RM100 plus tax, and are good value.

For position and style it's hard to beat *Heeren House* (☎ 06-281 4241), 1 Jalan Tun Tan Cheng Lock, in the heart of town. Immaculate rooms in this former godown all overlook the river and have polished floorboards, a few pieces of antique furniture and all mod-cons for RM119, or RM129 on weekends. This small, six-room guesthouse also has a good cafe downstairs serving Peranakan and Portuguese food.

The *Harbour Inn* (☎ 06-281 1929), at 28 Jalan Melaka Raya 12 beside the bridge to Pulau Melaka, has modern doubles for RM100, but the building design doesn't take advantage of its waterside location.

Places to Stay – Top End

Melaka has a couple of older high-rise hotels that are no longer up with the best but offer all facilities and substantial discounts. The *City Bayview Hotel* (☎ 06-283 9888; fax 06-283 6699) on Jalan Bendahara has a swimming pool, a health centre and a number of eating and drinking venues. Room rates start at RM275 plus 15%, before discount. A few blocks north at 20 Jalan Tun Sri Lanang is the *Hotel Grand Continental* (☎ 06-284 0088; fax 06-284 8125), where rooms from RM160 are excellent value.

Just off Jalan Merdeka on the reclaimed seafront behind the Mahkota Parade shopping complex is the large new *Century Mahkota Hotel* (☎ 06-281 2828; fax 06-281 2323). It has two large swimming pools, tennis and squash courts. Rooms – many looking out across the strait over Pulau Melaka – start at RM300. Nearby are two brand new high-rise hotels, the *Hotel Equatorial* on Jalan Parameswara beside the Taman Pahlawan park, and the *Hotel Ambassador* on Jalan Taman Raya 2.

On Jalan Bendahara, the *Renaissance Hotel* (☎ 06-284 8888; fax 06-284 9269) is still the most luxurious in town. Facilities include tennis and squash courts, a swimming pool and a disco. Rooms start at RM350, plus taxes.

Places to Eat

Melaka's food reflects its history. It is the home of Nyonya cuisine and Portuguese Eurasian food. The classic Nyonya dish, *laksa* soup, is the best in Malaysia – the rich coconut base makes it tastier than the sour Penang variety. Medan Portugis is the place to try Portuguese-influenced dishes – mostly seafood, though the fiery 'devil curry' is also worth a try.

One good place to find food is along Jalan Taman Merdeka, on what used to be the waterfront. The permanent stalls here, known locally as *Glutton's Corner*, serve the usual food centre specialities, though at higher prices. The land reclamation has spoilt the sea views, but the food is still good. Just walk along and see what attracts you; the *Bunga Raya* at No 39-40 has excellent – though not cheap – steamed crabs.

The *Mahkota Parade* shopping complex nearby is mostly a centre for western fast food, though the food court on the 1st floor serves the full range of Asian cuisines. You'll find a supermarket in the basement for self-catering.

In the centre of town, at 38 Jalan Laksamana, the *Restaurant Kim Swee Huat* caters to western tastes; breakfasts are particularly good, with muesli, porridge, yoghurt fruit salad and pancakes.

Good, if slightly expensive, daytime cafes for Nyonya food can be found in restored Peranakan houses in Chinatown. The *Vegetarian Corner* in the Jia Sheng Art Gallery at 88 Jalan Hang Jebat offers excellent meatless noodle dishes, while the *Old China Cafe* at 15 Jalan Hang Lekir has genuine Nyonya fare. Also good is the *Restoran Peranakan* at 107 Jalan Tun Tan Cheng Lock.

Less authentically Nyonya, yet thoroughly recommended, is *Jonkers Melaka Restoran*, another cafe in a craft shop at 17 Jalan Hang Jebat, which serves great home-made food to tables in its central courtyard. Try their green tea ice cream with ginger and lime or the truly exquisite cheesecakes. The cafe within the *Heeren House* guesthouse has a delightful atmosphere and is a good place to buy cakes and Peranakan and Portuguese food. You can also get western breakfasts here.

The *UE Tea House*, 20 Lorong Bukit China, is a simple Chinese coffee shop specialising in steamed dumplings.

For Indian food head to Little India, the area around the corner of Jalan Temenggong and Jalan Bendahara. The *Sri Lakshmi Vilas*, 2 Jalan Bendahara, has cheap Tamil meals served on a banana leaf (RM3.50) as well as excellent South Indian sweets. The *Sri Krishna Bavan* next door is very similar. Around the corner at 34 Jalan Temenggong, the *Restoran Veni* has cheap vegetarian and non-vegetarian set meals and roti canai breakfasts. A more upmarket air-con place with north Indian fare is the *Tandoori House* a few doors down from Sunny's Inn.

The lively Taman Melaka Raya area, where many of the travellers' guesthouses are located, has a good range of cheap Chinese and Malay eateries. For duck-rice, noodles and other Chinese hawker fare, the *Restoran Lim (Mee Yoke)* is a good coffee shop open until late with tables outside on the pavement. The *Ole Rasa*, just north of the youth hostel, is an excellent cheap Malay restaurant and there's a row of Malay food stalls opposite the eastern entrance to the Sound & Light Show.

For western food, the *Peppermint Cafe*, a slick new bistro at 321A Jalan Melaka Raya 1 (diagonally opposite the Traveller's Lodge), has set meals for around RM12. The *Mei Chong*, an air-con bakery and cafe at 158 Jalan TMR, serves a wide range of cakes and pastries with real coffee, and is surprisingly cheap.

For excellent Nyonya cuisine head to the *Ole Sayang* at No 198 or the *Nyonya Makko* at No 123. Both these air-conditioned restaurants serve a variety of Nyonya specialities from around RM8 per dish.

It's well worth making the trip out to Medan Portugis, where you can sample Malay-Portuguese dishes at outdoor tables facing the sea. Take bus No 17 from the local bus station, or a taxi (RM8). Inside the square, *Restoran de Lisbon* is the most popular, as much for the entertainment as the food. Bands play most nights of the week, though the big night is Saturday, when cultural shows are held. The seafood is superb – chilli crabs cost RM20, or the devil curry is RM10. There are two other restaurants in the square, *Restoran Papa Joe* and *El Chico's*. With side dishes and drinks the bill soon mounts at these places. You could try the somewhat cheaper seafood stalls fronting the sea next to the square, including the popular *De Costa's* and *J & J*. Finally, *San Pedro*, at 4 Jalan D'Aranjo, on the street immediately behind the square, is a more stylish and intimate place for Malay-Portuguese meals or a drink.

Entertainment

The *Sound & Light Show*, held near the Porta de Santiago, is Melaka's most popular form of evening entertainment. The sound system booms and the ruins are lit up to present Melaka's history from a strongly nationalistic angle. It's nevertheless quite good theatre, and the one-hour shows are held each evening at 8 pm in Malay and at 9.30 pm in English. Entry is RM5 (children RM3).

Portuguese cultural shows are held at the restaurants at Medan Portugis every Saturday night from around 8 pm. Dance groups perform Portuguese and Malay dances to traditional music and make for a lively night. Pop bands play every other night, so the Medan Portugis still makes a pleasant spot for a drink during the week.

Melaka's nightlife is otherwise unexciting. *Sparks Disco* (☎ 06-281 2567) on the top floor of Mahkota Parade shopping complex is the current favourite. The small and homey *Jim's Cottage Pub*, at 577 Jalan TMR, is a pleasant place for a pint. Danish beer is on tap and there's live music most nights. The *Orchid* and *Jam* pubs in the Taman Melaka Raya area opposite the Hotel Ambassador are other lively bars with live music.

Shopping

You can easily spend a couple of hours strolling through the many antique shops along Jalan Hang Jebat (Jonkers St) and Jalan Tun Tan Cheng Lock in the old part of town. Here you'll find Malaysia's best range of antiques, but not all of them are old and not all are from Malaysia. Prices are very high and haggling is essential.

Shops are stocked with an impressive range of antique furniture, porcelain, old lamps, coins, *songket* material, assorted bric-a-brac and crafts. Silver Galore at 27 Lorong Hang Jebat has an interesting collection of trinkets, gem stones and jewellery. For something different, Wah Aik at 92 Jalan Hang Jebat crafts doll-like shoes for bound feet, once the height of gruesome fashion for well-to-do Chinese women in Melaka. The shoes for bound feet cost RM75; or, if you can wait a few weeks, you can order some magnificent, custom-made Peranakan slippers from Mr Yeo.

Souvenir stalls selling cheap trinkets (mostly from Indonesia) can be found at the Cultural Museum, next to Christ Church near the tourist office. Across from Christ Church on Jalan Laksamana are a few galleries and upmarket shops. Karyaneka Handicrafts Emporium on Jalan Laksamana is good for traditional pottery. Dulukala at No 9 is the most interesting, with Indonesian crafts, primitive art and some fine modern pottery tea sets.

Orang Hutan, a shop at 59 Lorong Hang Jebat, sells work by a young local artist, Charles Cham, including printed T-shirts.

Getting There & Away

Melaka is 149km from KL, 216km from Johor Bahru and just 90km from Port Dickson. Melaka's local bus station, express bus terminal and taxi station are all in the same area beside Jalan Hang Tuah.

Air Melaka's airport is at Batu Berendam, 9.5km north of the centre of town. The Batang bus No 65 runs from the local bus station (80 sen). Pelangi Air (☎ 06-317 4175), based at the airport, flies to/from Pekanbaru (RM150) in Sumatra on Wednesday, Friday and Sunday. There are currently no other scheduled flights to/from Melaka, although there is a Malaysia Airlines office (☎ 06-283 5722) in the City Bayview Hotel.

Bus Most of the bus companies have their offices in the buildings near the express bus station. It pays to book the day before for any destination other than KL: there are so many buses to KL that you can usually just turn up and get on the next departure. Half a dozen companies have air-con buses to KL (2½ hours, RM6.80) throughout the day from 7 am to 7 pm.

To Singapore (four hours, RM11.50), express buses leave hourly from 8 am to 6 pm, and it's advisable to book in advance. Buses to Johor Bahru (3½ hours, RM10) leave roughly every half hour. To Muar (one hour, RM2.50) the No 2 bus departs every half hour throughout the day.

There are several evening buses to Butterworth and Penang (RM26), and to Lumut (RM21) and Ipoh (RM16). To the east coast there are direct buses at 8.30 am and noon to Kuantan (RM14) and at noon and 8 pm to Kuala Terengganu (RM21) and to Kota Bharu (RM24).

Train The nearest train station (☎ 06-341 1034) is on the main north-south line at Tampin, 38km north of Melaka. Taxis and buses run between Melaka and Tampin.

Taxi Taxis leave from just opposite the local bus station. Full-vehicle rates are: to Port Dickson (RM60), Johor Bahru (RM120), Seremban (RM70), Mersing (RM130), KL (RM100) and to KL international airport (KLIA) at Sepang (RM70).

Car If you are driving your own vehicle, Melaka's one-way traffic system will probably frustrate you at every turn.

If you want to rent a vehicle, the following companies have offices in Melaka:

Avis
(☎ 06-284 6710) 124 Jalan Bendahara
Hawk
(☎ 06-283 7878) 126 Jalan Bendahara

Boat High-speed ferries (2½ hours, RM80/150 one way/return) operate every day between Melaka and Dumai in Sumatra. Two companies, Madai Shipping (☎ 06-284 0671) and Tunas Rupat Utama (☎ 06-283 2506), run ferries daily at 10 am from Melaka, and both have ticket offices at the wharf and the express bus station. Same-day tickets are on sale after 8.30 am, but it's best to book the day before. Dumai is a visa-free entry port into Indonesia for citizens of most countries.

Getting Around

Melaka is easily explored on foot, but one useful service is the No 17 town bus which runs from the local bus station to Taman Melaka Raya and on to Medan Portugis. To get out to Tanjung Kling take Patt Hup bus No 51 from the local bus station. Bus No 19 goes to Air Keroh.

Bicycles are an ideal way to get around Melaka. They can be hired at many of the guesthouses or from Jin Trading, 53 Jalan Parameswara. This business has new, well-maintained racers and mountain bikes for RM5 per day.

A trishaw (bicycle rickshaw) is another ideal way of getting around compact and slow-moving Melaka. By the hour they should cost about RM20, or RM6 for any one-way trip within the town, but you'll have to bargain. Taxis are unmetered, and similarly charge a rather steep RM6 for a trip anywhere around town.

AROUND MELAKA

Air Keroh

About 15km north of Melaka at the Melaka turn-off on the Lebuh Raya, Air Keroh (also spelled Ayer Keroh) is home to a number of contrived tourist attractions popular with Malaysian and Singaporean families on weekends. Air Keroh can be reached in 30 minutes by a No 19 town bus (RM1) from the local bus station in Melaka, or a taxi will cost around RM15. All attractions are open from 9 am to 6 pm daily.

Things to See & Do Heading north from Melaka, the first point of interest is the lushly landscaped **Melaka Zoo**, where the small but well-fed collection includes

Sumatran rhinos, Malayan sun bears and native guar oxen. Entry is RM1/3 children/adults, and there are elephant rides for RM2/1. Behind the zoo is the Air Keroh Country Club & Golf Course and an artificial lake where paddle boats can be hired.

Nearby is the rather tacky **Taman Buaya Melaka** (Melaka Crocodile Farm), where you can inspect sluggish sauries in a series of soupy tanks. Entry is RM4 (RM2 for children). Just north is the small **Orang Asli Museum** (RM1), with worthwhile exhibits on local indigenous tribes.

A little further north along the main road you come to the **Air Keroh Recreational Forest**, a part secondary jungle and part landscaped park with paved trails, picnic areas and a forestry museum. The Orang Asli Village inside the park has a few scruffy grass huts, ostensibly to give some insight into the lifestyle of Malaysia's Orang Asli tribes. The forest is a pleasant place for a stroll and entry is free, but it certainly ain't Taman Negara.

Just a few hundred metres on, **Taman Mini Malaysia/Mini ASEAN** is the main attraction at Air Keroh. This large theme park has examples of traditional houses from all 13 Malaysian states as well as from neighbouring ASEAN countries (though several recently admitted ASEAN nations are not yet represented). Each house contains a few handicrafts and wax dummies in traditional dress representing the region. Though a lot of the houses tend to look the same, it's educational and good value at RM4 (RM2 for children). Cultural dance shows are held on weekends.

About 2km further north is the **Butterfly & Reptile Sanctuary**, which has a pleasantly landscaped enclosure with dozens of butterfly species. At least as impressive is the collection of snakes, scorpions and enormous spiders. Entry is RM5 (RM3 for children).

Places to Stay Air Keroh has some pleasant accommodation, but few visitors bother staying this far out. The *Air Keroh Recreational Forest* (☎ 06-232 8401) has camp sites for 50 sen per person, small log cabins for RM40 and more comfortable two-person chalets for RM50. It has been primarily set up for school groups.

Near Mini Malaysia, the *Air Keroh Country Resort* (☎ 06-232 5211) is an older-style resort with a swimming pool and tennis courts. Motel rooms start at RM126 and chalets at RM215. Behind the zoo near the lake, the similar *Air Keroh D'Village* (☎ 06-232 8061) has rooms from RM130 plus tax, but major discounts are available. Nearby is the more upmarket *Paradise Malacca Village Resort* (☎ 06-232 3600), where rooms cost from RM250.

Near the Butterfly & Reptile Sanctuary is the *Puteri Resort* (☎ 06-232 3333), a large new complex that caters mainly to tourists from Singapore and China.

Islands

A couple of islands off the coast of Melaka have resorts, and they make popular day trips.

Pulau Besar The small island of Pulau Besar, south-east of Melaka and 5km off the coast, is a popular weekend getaway. The island has a few historic graves and reminders of the Japanese occupation, but the main reason to come here is for the pleasant beaches. The water is a little clearer than on the mainland and the hilly island is cloaked in greenery. There is also a golf course.

There are two upmarket places to stay on Pulau Besar. The new *Pandanusa Resort* (☎ 06-281 8007) has luxury accommodation for around RM180. The *Samudera Resort* has been recently renovated and offers attractive chalets over the water for around RM150.

Pulau Besar is most easily reached by boat from Umbai, 10km south-east of Melaka. There are no scheduled times, but the return fare is RM10 (or RM80 to charter a boat).

Pulau Upeh Though less interesting, the much smaller Pulau Upeh is closer to Melaka and makes a good retreat from the city. The *Upeh Island Resort* (☎ 06-336 9999) offers comfortable chalets from RM155 to RM250, and can arrange transport to the island. Parameswara Tour (☎ 06-283 6538/018-860 3459) also runs boats to Pulau Upeh from the riverside jetty near the tourist office. These depart (if there's a minimum of six passengers) around 9 am and return at 3 pm. The return fare is RM16.

Tanjung Kling/Pantai Kundor

Tanjung Kling is 10km north-west of Melaka on the main road to Port Dickson, while Pantai Kundor is right on the water several kilometres further out. Tanjung Kling has seen much recent top-end hotel development, which is hard to understand given the rather ordinary beach. Pantai Kundor is quieter and the beach is a decent enough stretch of whitish sand, but it's certainly no tropical paradise.

Places to Stay & Eat The *Klebang Beach Resort,* 9km from Melaka, offers nice rooms for RM138 and RM155. This mid-range hotel has a pool and restaurant, but the nearby beach is just a tiny strip of sand. Several hundred metres along is the very pleasant *Shah's Beach Resort*. This Mediterranean-style resort is well set out and has a swimming pool, tennis courts, bar and restaurant. Accommodation is in chalet-type rooms which cost RM159 by the pool, RM147 by the beach and RM124 near the road, but discounts are regularly offered. The nearby high-rise *Riviera Bay Resort* (☎ 06-315 1111) is more upmarket, with doubles for RM250 including tax and buffet breakfast.

Past Tanjung Kling is the turn-off to Pantai Kundor, where the beach is better and not as heavily trafficked. The first place you come to is the *Motel Tanjung Kling* (☎ 06-351 5749), a run-down hotel 12km from Melaka with a pleasant location right by the water. The gloomy rooms with fan for RM48 are poor value; the better renovated rooms with bathroom and air-con cost RM78.

A better bet for mid-range accommodation at Pantai Kundor is the *Straits View Lodge* (☎ 06-351 4620), 2km or so further on. A variety of comfortable but quite basic chalets with air-con and bathroom cost from RM60. It's a very pleasant place with a good seafood restaurant.

Right next door, the *Mutiara Malacca Beach Resort* (☎ 06-351 8518) is a luxury high-rise hotel with a pool, gym, sauna, tennis courts and fronted by one of the best stretches of beach. Suites cost RM280 including taxes and evening meal.

Getting There & Away Catch the Patt Hup bus No 51 from the local bus station. They go every half hour or so. A share-taxi to Tanjung Kling costs around RM2.50 per person, or RM10 for the whole vehicle.

Tanjung Bidara

About 20km north-west of Melaka on the way to Port Dickson is Tanjung Bidara, one of the better beach areas along this stretch of coast. It is quiet and well away from the main road, and though the water is murky, the sandy beaches are pleasant and greenery is reasonably prolific. The main beach is at the Tanjung Bidara Beach Resort, where there is also a public beach area with food stalls.

Places to Stay The *Tanjung Bidara Beach Resort* (☎ 06-384 2990) is a quiet, relaxing resort with a swimming pool and restaurant. Comfortable rooms facing the sea are RM150, while more luxurious chalets cost from RM250 to RM350.

Good, cheaper accommodation can also be found at the beach a few kilometres away at Kampung Pasir Gembur. *Bidara Beach Lodge* (☎ 06-384 3340), 78 Lorong Haji Abdullah, has double rooms with air-con, TV and bathroom for RM94 including tax and breakfast.

Getting There & Away The No 42 and No 47 buses from Melaka run to Masjid Tanah, where a taxi to Tanjung Bidara Beach Resort or Kampung Pasir Gembur costs RM12. Infrequent No 52 buses also run to the army base at Tanjung Bidara, from where it is a short walk to the beach.

Johor

The state of Johor occupies the southernmost tip of the Malay Peninsula, and is connected to the island of Singapore by a causeway. Economically it is one of the most important states in the country, with huge rubber, palm oil and pineapple plantations, and a growing industrial base. It is also the most populated, and Johor Bahru, with a population of over 807,000 people is the second-largest city in Malaysia.

Once the most powerful and important sultanate in Malaysia, Johor now has a royal family with something of a notorious reputation. The sultan has accumulated an army of bodyguards, and after an incident in which the Johor sultan allegedly beat a hockey coach, the prime minister stepped in to curtail the powers and privileges of the sultans, which include immunity from prosecution.

Few visitors stop in Johor, although many visit Mersing on the east coast, simply because it is the access point for the island of Tioman (which is in Pahang state) and the other islands of the Seribuat Archipelago.

History

Johor's history is really a continuation of Melaka's. When the latter fell to the Portuguese in the 16th century, Johor became the pre-eminent Malay state, and its rulers (the first of whom was the son of the last sultan of Melaka) were seen as the protectors of the western Malay states. Early on the Portuguese attacked Johor on a number of occasions, but eventually were more or less content to let them rule from their capital on the Sungai (River) Johor, even though they were something of an impediment to trade in the area.

The kingdom of Aceh on the northern tip of Sumatra also had ambitions in the area, and so for the entire second half of the 16th century Johor was under constant threat. It was a period which saw a triangular struggle between the Portuguese, Johor and Aceh for control of the peninsula and the Straits of Melaka.

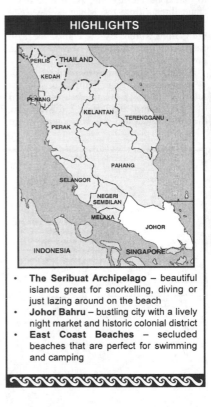

The Acehnese attacks on Johor continued well into the 17th century, and for a period from 1623 the kingdom's rulers had no fixed address, as their capital on the island of Lingga in Sungai Johor had been razed.

Johor's fortunes took a decided turn for the better with the coming of the Dutch, who allied themselves with Johor for a combined (and ultimately successful) attack against the Portuguese at Melaka in 1641. Johor was freed from virtually all the tariffs and trade

HIGHLIGHTS

- **The Seribuat Archipelago** – beautiful islands great for snorkelling, diving or just lazing around on the beach
- **Johor Bahru** – bustling city with a lively night market and historic colonial district
- **East Coast Beaches** – secluded beaches that are perfect for swimming and camping

restrictions imposed on other states by the Dutch, in return for cooperation in helping to defeat the Portuguese. Johor also overcame threats from the Minangkabaus and managed to ride out some domestic squabbling from within. By the end of the 17th century it was among the strongest Asian powers in the region.

A war with the Bugis in 1716 left Johor weakened, and further political instability followed when a Minangkabau, Raja Kecil of Siak, claimed the throne and overthrew the weak sultan in 1719. His control lasted for just two years and was never secure, and he was soon toppled by the Buginese. At this time Sulaiman, the son of the former sultan Abdul Jalil, was installed on the throne by the Buginese. His descendants were to rule the state until it eventually disappeared in the early years of the 20th century. Throughout the 18th century the Bugis influence within the state increased. However, when the Dutch East India Company wrested control of Riau-Johor in 1784, the era of Bugis domination of western Malaya came to an end.

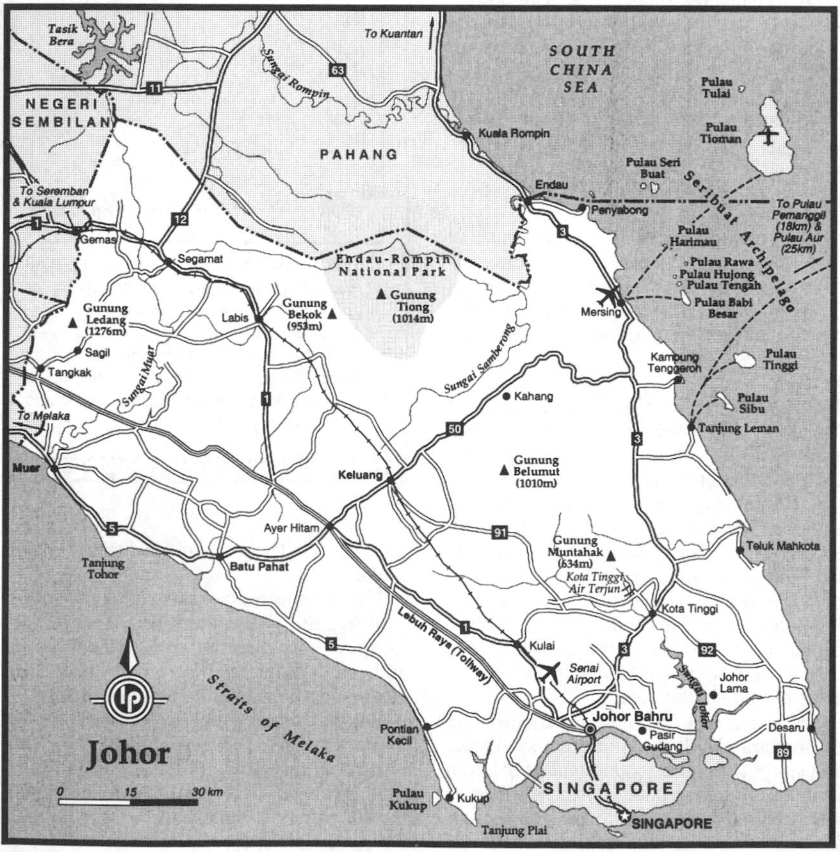

In 1819, with the court of the Johor sultan split by Malay and Bugis factions, Stamford Raffles was able to bring about the cession of Singapore to the British and the pensioning off of the sultans, while actual power went to the *temenggong* (Malay minister in charge of defence and justice). The temenggongs continued to rule the state very ably, the most notable among them being the flamboyant Abu Bakar, who elevated himself to the position of sultan of Johor in 1886. Through his contacts with people in high places in London and Singapore, he was able to resist the British desire to bring Johor closer under its control. Abu Bakar also undertook an ambitious modernisation programme for the state, while continuing to live the high life. Today he is fondly remembered as the Father of Johor.

Abu Bakar's successor and son, Ibrahim, was less powerful and in 1914 was forced by the British to accept a 'general adviser' who had powers similar to those exercised by the Residents in other states. Sultan Ibrahim was still the ruler of Johor when it became part of the Federation of Malaya, which was formed in 1948.

JOHOR BAHRU

Capital of the state of Johor, Johor Bahru is the southern gateway to Peninsular Malaysia. Connected to Singapore by road and rail across the 1038m-long Causeway, JB (as it is known throughout the country) inevitably suffers as a poor relation to its more glamorous neighbour. Despite its historical significance and various points of interest, few travellers pause in JB; it's just the place to get your passport stamped on arrival or departure in Malaysia.

On weekends and public holidays, Singaporeans flock across the Causeway for sex, shopping and excitement, and Johor Bahru puts on a show. Central JB exudes a real border-town feel, with crowds, mostly male Singaporeans, cruising the streets. Street theatre is provided by the medicine vendors dangling snakes and promising penis enlargement with their elixirs, or turbaned *bomohs* selling magical 'love oil' at astronomical prices. The *kedai gunting rambut* (barber shops) are a frequent sight, offering not haircuts but women.

Despite its reputation as a sin centre for Singaporeans, JB has closed its bawdier nightclubs in an effort to improve its image. A major centre of the Singapore-Johor-Riau (SIJORI) growth triangle, JB is a burgeoning centre of investment and construction. New roads, industrial estates, shopping centres and hotels are changing the face of the city. Despite all this, JB is still chaotic and fairly tatty. It is both a breath of fresh air and a bad aroma as you arrive from squeaky-clean and sterile Singapore.

It's possible to spend an enjoyable day or two in JB, as it has an excellent museum to visit by day and a thriving night market. In the business centre of town you still get the footpath hawkers and other colourful stalls which are so much a part of Asia – and which, to a great extent, the Singaporeans have so effectively killed off.

Orientation

The road and railway across the Causeway run straight into the middle of JB. The main area for cheap and mid-range hotels is on and around Jalan Meldrum, in the centre of town. Many of JB's fancier hotels and new shopping centres are a few kilometres north on Jalan Tebrau, the main highway leading to the north and to the east coast.

Off to the left almost as soon as you cross the Causeway is Jalan Tun Dr Ismail, leading along JB's waterfront. Along here you will find the city's colonial district, with its parkland, colonial buildings and museum. In front of the colonial district, the Johor Bahru Waterfront City sits half-finished, another giant project put on hold by the current economic slowdown. About 2km east of the Causeway is the new 'Free Zone' (Kompleks Bebas Cukai) duty-free shopping centre, which caters to bargain-hungry Singaporeans from across the channel.

The Larkin bus and taxi station is 5km north-west of the train station. Most long-distance buses and taxis operate from here. Local buses operate from several bus stops

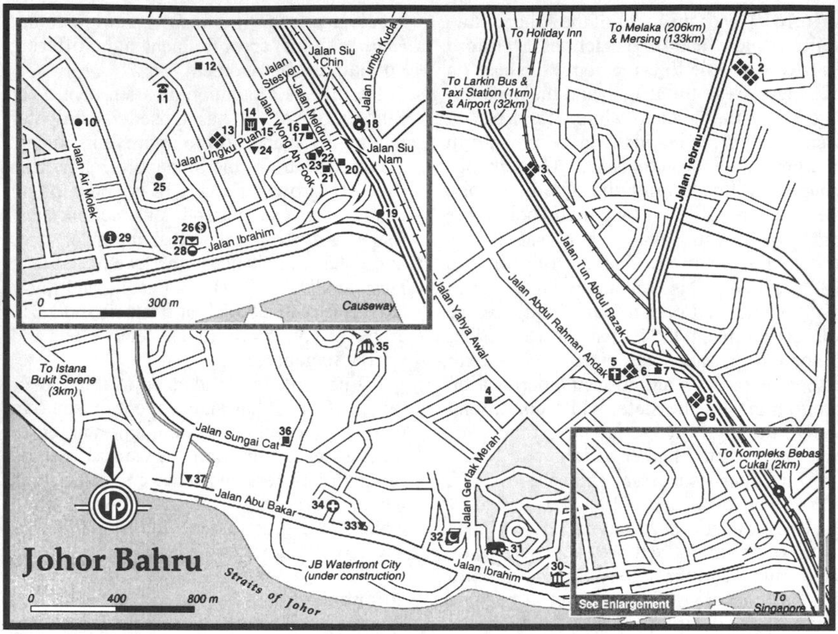

around town, the most convenient of which is the stop in front of the post office on Jalan Tun Dr Ismail. Sultan Ismail airport is 32km north-west of the city centre in Senai.

Note that street names in Johor Bahru have a habit of changing several times in the space of a few kilometres. For example, Jalan Air Molek suddenly becomes Jalan Yahya Awai as it crosses Jalan Gertak Merah. In similar fashion, the major Jalan Tun Dr Ismail undergoes several name changes as it heads away from the Causeway.

Information

The Tourism Malaysia office (☎ 07-222 3590) is on the 5th floor of the JOTIC building, on Jalan Air Molek, about 750m west of the Causeway. It's open from Monday to Friday from 9 am to 5 pm, Saturday until 1 pm and is closed on Sunday. A branch office is also located on the Causeway, just before you go through Malaysian immigration. It is open from Monday to Friday from 9 am to 5 pm and weekends and holidays until 4 pm. Also on the 5th floor of the JOTIC building, you will find the slightly less informative Johor State Tourism office (☎ 07-223 4935), which has similar hours to the JOTIC Tourism Malaysia office.

The immigration office (☎ 07-224 4253) is on the 1st floor, Blok B, Wisma Persekutuan, Jalan Air Molek.

With so many people crossing to and from Singapore every day (many Malaysians commute to work there), there are literally dozens of moneychangers in the central area and the rates are competitive.

For international calls, the Telekom building is opposite the Puteri Pan Pacific Hotel in the city centre, where it's possible to make credit-card calls at any time, or calls through the operator during business hours. There are more credit-card phones in the lobby of the Tropical Inn.

PLACES TO STAY	OTHER	
4 Footloose Homestay	1 Plaza Pelangi	19 Immigration Check Point
7 Tropical Inn	2 Menara Pelangi; Malaysian Airlines	25 Bangunan Sultan Ibrahim
12 Puteri Pan Pacific Hotel	3 Best World	26 Hongkong Bank
16 Fortuna Hotel	5 Church of the Immaculate Conception	27 Post Office
17 Hawaii Hotel	6 Wisma Landmark Tower & Shopping Mall	28 Local Bus Stop
20 Causeway Inn	8 Komtar Building	29 JOTIC; Tourism Malaysia Tourist Information Centre; Food Court
21 Top Hotel	9 Singapore Taxi Station	30 Muzium Diraja Abu Bakar (Royal Abu Bakar Museum)
23 Hotel Le Tian	10 Immigration Office	31 Zoo
36 Hyatt Regency	11 Telekom	32 Sultan Abu Bakar Mosque
PLACES TO EAT	13 Plaza Kota Raya	34 General Hospital
15 Pasar Malam	14 Sri Mariamman Temple	35 Johor Art Gallery
22 Restoran Medina	18 Johor Bahru Train Station	
24 Restoran Nilla		
33 Tepian Tebrau Food Centre		
37 Selera Sungai Chat Food Centre		

There is an Internet cafe called the *Causeway Restaurant* on the 4th floor of the JOTIC building.

Muzium Diraja Abu Bakar (Royal Abu Bakar Museum)

Overlooking the Straits of Johor, the Istana Besar was once the main palace of the Johor royal family. It was built in Victorian style by Anglophile sultan Abu Bakar in 1866, and is now open to the public as the Muzium Diraja Abu Bakar.

Every state with a sultan has a similar museum, but this is undoubtedly the finest in Malaysia, conveying the wealth and privilege of the sultans. The museum is full of the sultan's possessions, including furniture and hunting trophies, and is set out much as it was when in use as the palace. The superb exhibits include Chinese, Japanese, Indian and Malay carved wooden pieces, and an amazing full-size crystal-glass table and chairs from France. The hunting room has some bizarre exhibits from the pukka days when wildlife was there to be shot, including elephant's-foot umbrella stands and antelope-leg ashtrays.

The palace is open daily, except Friday, from 9 am to 6 pm, although there's no entry after 5 pm. Entrance for foreigners is a hefty US$7 (children US$3), payable in ringgit at lousy exchange rates. Despite the price, it's well worth a visit.

The 53 hectare palace grounds (free entry) are beautifully manicured and are a great breathing space in this fairly cramped city. There are good views across the Straits of Johor, although Singapore's industrial backside is not terribly picturesque.

Other Attractions

Further west from the museum is the most attractive part of Johor Bahru, the old colonial/royal district of greenery and fine buildings. The whole waterfront opposite is being redeveloped and may be a pleasant place to stroll when finished, but until then the high-speed traffic along the main road and the distance between sights make for a hot, dusty walk.

Behind the Muzium Diraja Abu Bakar and approached through the palace gardens is a small **zoo**, once the private zoo of the sultan. The zoo is open from 8 am to 6 pm daily, and entry is RM2 for adults and RM1 for children.

Built from 1892 to 1900, the magnificent **Sultan Abu Bakar Mosque,** is a mixture of architectural styles, principally Victorian. The minarets look like British clock towers, and this mosque is difficult to distinguish from a colonial administrative building. The large mosque can accommodate up to 2000 people.

Further north is the **Galeri Seni Johor** (Johor Art Gallery; ☎ 07-224 5488) at 144 Jalan Petri, with a collection of kris, pottery and traditional clothing. The fine building dates from 1910. It's open daily, except Tuesday, from 9 am to 6 pm.

With a 32m stone tower, **Istana Bukit Serene** is the residence of the sultan of Johor. The palace was built in 1932 and features Art Deco influences. Though not open to the public, you can glimpse it along Jalan Skudai. It is on the waterfront, 5km west of the Muzium Diraja Abu Bakar.

One building that is hard to miss is the imposing **Bangunan Sultan Ibrahim** (State Secretariat building) on Bukit Timbalan, overlooking the city centre. This city landmark has a 64m-high square tower, and looks like a medieval fortress transported from Turkey or Mogul India. It was built in the 1940s.

Places to Stay – Budget

Few visitors stay in JB; it's too close to the greater attractions of Singapore. On the other hand, Johor is an important business centre, so there are plenty of hotels, although prices are generally high for Peninsular Malaysia. With this in mind, those on a tight budget may want to head to onward destinations rather than spend a night in JB.

The only real budget accommodation in JB is the *Footloose Homestay* (☎ 07-224 2881), in a quiet suburban neighbourhood at 4H Jalan Ismail, just off Jalan Yahya Awai (the continuation of Jalan Air Molek). There's one double room for RM28, or six dorm beds for RM14 per person. Be warned, however, that conditions are extremely basic, especially in the dorm room. Footloose is a 15 minute walk from the train station, best approached via Jalan Air Molek from the seafront. After crossing Jalan Gertak Merah, take the second turn on the left after passing a Shell petrol station, and look for the small sign about 150m up the hill.

Apart from this option, even the most basic accommodation in JB is mid-budget in price.

Places to Stay – Mid-Range

JB's cheaper hotels are mostly clustered in the Jalan Meldrum neighbourhood, just west of the train station. Note that all hotels in this section raise their prices at the weekend by about 10%. Probably the best bet in terms of price and comfort is the *Hawaii Hotel* (☎ 07-224 0633) at 21 Jalan Meldrum, which has carpeted rooms with fan and bathroom for RM40. Rooms with air-con start at RM50.

Also good value is the *Top Hotel* (☎ 07-224 4755) at 12 Jalan Meldrum. All rooms have air-con and bathroom and cost RM66. Just around the corner at 2 Jalan Siew Niam, the *Hotel Le Tian* (☎ 07-224 8151), next to the Restoran Medina, costs slightly more but is actually a step down in quality, with air-con rooms for RM77. The *Fortuna Hotel* (☎ 07-223 3210) at 29A Jalan Meldrum costs as much as the Hotel Le Tian and is similarly uninspiring.

For those willing to spend a little more, the *Causeway Inn* (☎ 07-224 8811) at 6A Jalan Meldrum is good value for clean well-appointed rooms with air-con, TV and bathroom. Singles/doubles cost RM82/92.

Places to Stay – Top End

Big hotels are sprouting up everywhere in JB, primarily to cater to business travellers. The government keeps talking about a tourist boom, but hotels are often quiet and big discounts (called 'promotions') are readily available on published rates.

The older *Tropical Inn* (☎ 07-224 7888) at 15 Jalan Gereja has rooms from RM125, including breakfast. The hotel has a restaurant and coffee house, as well as a bar and health centre, but no swimming pool.

The *Holiday Inn* (☎ 07-332 3800) is a couple of kilometres north of the centre in Century Gardens on Jalan Dato Sulaiman. Rooms cost from RM204. There is a swimming pool, health club, restaurant and coffee lounge open 24 hours.

The *Puteri Pan Pacific Hotel* (☎ 07-223 3333), in the city centre and easy to spot, has an impressive range of features, including a swimming pool, fitness centre, business centre and four restaurants. Rooms start at RM320/350 standard/deluxe.

Competing with the Pan Pacific to be JB's best is the *Hyatt Regency* (☎ 07-222 1234) on Jalan Sungai Chat, 2.5km west of the city centre, past the Sultan Abu Bakar Mosque. Rooms start at RM360.

Places to Eat

Johor Bahru is a good place for food, especially seafood. JB also has good hawker venues, the best being the very active *pasar malam* (night market) outside the Hindu temple on Jalan Wong Ah Fook. Divided into three sections – Chinese, Malay and Indian – it has a great selection of dishes. Local specialities to look out for include laksa Johor, a noodle dish relying heavily on coconut, and mee rebus, noodles in a thick sauce, showing the Javanese influence in Johor.

Plaza Kota Raya, near the night market, has a selection of western fast food, a supermarket on the 2nd level and a good indoor food court on the top floor, with all the local specialities available. Another smaller indoor food court can be found in the *JOTIC building*, which also boasts a few, slightly upmarket, western-style restaurants.

JB has some good Indian restaurants, including the ever busy *Restoran Medina* on the corner of Jalan Meldrum and Jalan Siew Niam. It serves excellent murtabak, biryani and curries. Opposite the Sri Mariamman Temple, *Restoran Nilla* at 3 Jalan Ungku Puan specialises in South Indian banana leaf set meals. Most meals are vegetarian, but fish-head curry is also featured.

Singaporeans come across the Causeway in the evenings just to eat cheap seafood. The main venues are along the waterfront to the west of the city centre. The food is great, but the sea aspect is spoiled by the very busy road. The *Tepian Tebrau* food centre on Jalan Abu Bakar is famous for its excellent seafood. One kilometre further west is the *Selera Sungei Chat*, another well-patronised seafood centre specialising in ikan bakar (grilled fish).

For those who wish to self-cater, there is a good supermarket on the ground floor of *Kompleks Tun Abdul Razal*, the shopping centre beneath the Komtar building about 500m north of the train station.

Shopping

JB promotes itself as a major shopping destination, and new shopping centres are being built at a frantic pace. Singaporeans do come across to JB to do their shopping – petrol and groceries – but for most goods Singapore has better prices and a far better range. Major shopping centres in central JB are the Kompleks Tun Abdul Razal beneath the Komtar centre, or the much flasher Plaza Kota Raya. Just next to the Church of the Immaculate Conception, another giant shopping mall, the Wisma Landmark, is under construction and should be finished by the time of publication. Other large new malls to the north of the city centre include the Plaza Pelangi on Jalan Tebrau and Best World on Jalan Tun Abdul Razak.

Another shopping complex, designed specifically to cater to the Singaporean market, is the newly finished Kompleks Bebas Cukai duty-free shopping complex about 2km east of the Causeway (even locals commonly refer to it by the English name: 'Free Zone Complex'). This complex also incorporates a ferry terminal which handles a lot of ferry traffic to/from Singapore and a few destinations in Indonesia.

Getting There & Away

Air The Malaysia Airlines office (☎ 07-334 1001) is on the 1st floor of the Menara Pelangi building, on Jalan Kuning at Taman Pelangi, 2.5km north of the city centre. JB is well served by Malaysia Airlines flights and, as an incentive to fly from JB rather than Singapore, fares from here to other places in Malaysia are much lower than from Singapore. There are direct flights from JB to Kota Kinabalu (daily, RM347),

KL (nine daily, RM93), Kuching (twice daily, RM169) and Penang (daily, RM178). Malaysia Airlines also has direct international flights to Denpasar, Surabaya and Jakarta in Indonesia.

Pelangi Air (contact Malaysia Airlines above) has flights to Padang (three times weekly, RM260) and Palembang in Sumatra (four times weekly, RM280). International tickets are cheaper if purchased through a travel agent.

Bus Due to the hassles of crossing the Causeway – customs, immigration and so on – there's a wider selection of buses and long-distance taxis to other towns in Peninsular Malaysia from JB than from Singapore.

Frequent buses operate between Singapore's Ban San terminal on Queen St and JB's Larkin bus station, inconveniently located 5km north of the city (a taxi to/from central JB should cost RM6). The most convenient service is the air-con Singapore to Johor Bahru Express, which operates roughly every 15 minutes from 6.30 am until midnight, and costs RM2.10. Alternatively, regular SBS (city bus) No 170 costs RM1.20 Tickets should be bought before boarding at the relevant booths at the JB Larkin bus station. Tickets for SBS bus No 170 can also be purchased on board the bus, while for the express bus, you can buy tickets at the southernmost travel agent in the building block across the street from the train station.

Note that it is possible to board both SBS bus No 170 and the express bus at the stop just before Malaysia immigration on the Causeway. Coming from Singapore, it is also possible to walk out of Malaysian immigration and straight into central Johor Bahru. (See the Singapore Getting There & Away chapter for more information on this crossing.)

At Larkin bus station there are at least a dozen bus companies with departures throughout the day for all the major towns in Peninsular Malaysia. Destinations include: Melaka (hourly, RM10), KL (RM16.60 regular/RM22.10 'business class'), Lumut (RM29), Ipoh (RM27) and Butterworth (RM33.60). Most buses to Melaka come through from Singapore, so it pays to book in advance. To the east coast departures are to Kota Tinggi (RM2.60), Mersing (RM7), Kuantan (RM15.40), Kuala Terengganu (RM23) and Kota Bharu (RM29).

Train There are daily trains from JB to KL and Butterworth, and these can be used to get to most places on the west coast. The line passes through Tampin (for Melaka), Seremban, KL, Tapah Road (for Cameron Highlands), Ipoh and Taiping. It is also possible to change at Gemas and board the *Jungle Train* for connections to Taman Negara National Park and Kota Bharu. The train station booking office is open from 9 am to 6 pm daily. There are also trains to Singapore, but it's more convenient to take a bus or taxi. See the Malaysia Getting Around chapter for full timetable and fare information.

Taxi The long-distance taxi station is at the Larkin bus station, 5km north of the city centre. Regular taxi destinations and costs (per person) include Kota Tinggi (RM4.50), KL (RM40), Kuantan (RM45), Melaka (RM30) and Mersing (RM20).

Registered taxis to Singapore only leave from the terminal north of the city centre on Jalan Wong Ah Fook, on the 1st level of the car park next to the Komtar building. A taxi across the Causeway to the Queen St terminal in Singapore should cost RM28 for the whole vehicle. From Singapore to JB the fare is S$28. Other taxis and private cars around town will also offer their services, but bargaining is required. You can negotiate to get dropped off at a hotel in Singapore – RM40 to RM60 depending on where you want to go.

Walking It is possible to walk across the Causeway in both directions. In addition to being free of charge, this is the fastest way across when traffic clogs the roadway. The one way journey on foot takes about 25 minutes (if you don't succumb to the heat and fumes mid-crossing).

Boat Ferries leave from the Bebas Cukai duty-free shopping complex about 2km east of the Causeway. Sriwani Tours & Travel (☎ 07-221 1677), located in the complex itself, handles tickets to most destinations.

There are daily departures to Batu Ampar (RM45) and Tanjung Pinang (RM60), both on Sumatra in Indonesia; and 2 daily departures to Tanah Merah (RM20) in Singapore.

Additional boats depart from Kukup, west of JB, to Tanjung Balai, also in Sumatra (see Kukup).

Getting Around

To/From the Airport JB's Sultan Ismail airport is 32km north-west of town at Senai, on the road to Melaka and KL.

The SPS Coach Service (☎ 07-334 1001) to the airport leaves from the Puteri Pan Pacific Hotel and costs RM4. It meets all incoming and outgoing flights between 5 am and 7 pm. This is the same bus that comes through from Singapore's Novotel Orchid Hotel – it costs S$10 from Singapore to JB's Sultan Ismail airport, or RM10 from JB to Singapore. You could take local bus No 207 (RM2) from the bus stop in front of the post office, but departures are infrequent.

A taxi to the airport is RM25 per car and takes 30 to 45 minutes depending on traffic.

Taxi Taxis around town have meters, but drivers are not always willing to use them. If you bargain, you can go almost anywhere around JB for RM5, or taxis can be hired at around RM25 per hour for sightseeing.

Car The main car rental companies include:

Avis
(☎ 07-224 4824) Tropical Inn Hotel, 15 Jalan Gereja
Budget
(☎ 07-224 3951) 2nd Floor, Orchid Plaza, Jalan Wong Ah Fook
Hertz
(☎ 07-223 7520) Level 1, JOTIC building, Jalan Ayer Molek
Mayflower
(☎ 07-224 1357) 2nd Floor, Wisma Tan Chong, Jalan Tun Abdul Razak
National
(☎ 07-599 4532) Sultan Ismail airport, Senai

AROUND JOHOR BAHRU

Kukup

About 40km south-west of JB, on the Straits of Melaka, across from Sumatra, is the fishing village of Kukup. The village is famous throughout Malaysia and Singapore for its seafood, especially prawns, and for its open-air restaurants, most of which are built on stilts over the water. Singaporeans, who are obsessed with the loss of their own *kampung* (village) life, flock to this village on weekends, mostly for the seafood. While there's no denying the quality of the seafood, the availability of similar fare in JB, and the tattiness of the village make Kukup a low-priority destination for the average traveller.

Next to Kukup is **Kampung Air Masin** (Salt Water Village), renowned for its top quality *belacan* (shrimp paste). Both villages are largely inhabited by Hokkien Chinese.

Kukup is reached by taking a bus or taxi from JB to Pontian Kecil and then another to Kukup. A shared taxi from JB to Pontian Kecil costs RM6, and then another to Kukup costs RM4. A chartered taxi all the way from JB costs RM60.

Getting There & Away Ferries leave from the ferry terminal in Kukup for Tanjong Balai in Indonesia. Boats leave twice daily (three times on Friday) and cost RM30 one way.

JOHOR BAHRU TO MELAKA

The main road north from JB runs to KL and Melaka. It's a productive region of palm oil, rubber and pineapple plantations.

Ayer Hitam

Ayer Hitam, 80km north-west of JB, is an important crossroads. Here you can turn left to go to Batu Pahat, Muar and Melaka; you can continue straight on for Segamat, Seremban and KL or, alternatively, for Segamat and Temerloh; or you can turn right for Keluang and Mersing on the east coast. Ayer Hitam is a popular rest stop for buses,

Palm Oil

The oil palm *(Elaeis guineensis)* is probably the most common tree in Peninsular Malaysia today. When travelling along main roads particularly in Johor, Pahang and also Sabah, you come across seas of oil-palm trees which seem to stretch on endlessly.

The oil palm was first introduced in the 1860s from seeds brought from Sri Lanka (although the tree itself is a native of West Africa), but it was not until 1917 that the first oil-palm plantation was established. Since WWII Malaysia has been the world's top producer of palm oil, and current annual output is around 7.2 million tonnes.

The oil is extracted from the orange-coloured fruit, which grows in bunches just below the fronds. It is used primarily for cooking, although research is under way to find other uses, such as for engine fuel. Malaysia has invested heavily in palm oil, and it is one of the country's major primary industry exports. Unfavourable assessments of palm oil as an edible oil by the US Food & Drug Administration has caused an uproar in Malaysia, which blames these assessments on the US sunflower oil industry lobby.

CHRIS ROWTHORN

The oil extracted from palm fruit is a major export earner for Malaysia.

taxis and motorists, so there are lots of small restaurants. **Kampung Macap**, south of Ayer Hitam, is well known for its Aw Pottery works.

Batu Pahat

The riverine town of Batu Pahat is famed for its Chinese cuisine, although it also has a minor reputation as a 'sin city' for jaded Singaporeans. It has a few buildings of note, such as the town's Art Deco mosque and the Chinese Chamber of Commerce building.

Places to Stay Accommodation can be hard to find on weekends. The best choice is the *Rumah Persinggahan (Batu Pahat Rest House;* ☎ 07-434 1181) at 870 Jalan Tasek, which has large air-con doubles for RM52/63 a standard/deluxe room. It's just by the roundabout in the south of town, where the roads from Ayer Hitam and Kukup meet; without your own transport, a RM4 taxi from the centre of town is the best way here.

The more basic *Fairyland Hotel* (☎ 07-434 1777) at 91 Jalan Rahmat has simple rooms with fans for RM25. At the upper end of the scale, *Hotel Carnival* (☎ 07-431 5122) at 2 Jalan Fatimah, in the centre of town, has air-con doubles from RM110.

Muar

This riverside town, also known as Bandar Maharani, was once an important commercial centre. It is noted for its traditional Malay culture, including *ghazal* music and the *kuda kepang* (horse trance) dance, originally from Java.

It's a typical Malaysian town with a bustling Chinatown of restaurants and hotels, but further along the river is the graceful colonial district, with its government offices, courthouse, customs house and school. Further along Jalan Petri by the river, Masjid Jamek is a Victorian fantasy of a mosque, in much the same style as JB's Sultan Abu Bakar Mosque.

At the mouth of the river, just past the mosque, the **Tanjung Riverside Park** is a pleasant place for a picnic lunch, with creeper-festooned trees and the occasional timid monitor lizard hanging about.

Though Muar sees few tourists, it is worth a stop on the trip to or from Melaka. Between Muar and Melaka there are a number of kampungs with traditional-style Melaka houses.

Places to Stay & Eat The very good *Rumah Persinggahan Tanjong Emas (Muar Rest House;* ☎ 06-952 7744) at 2222 Jalan Sultanah has huge air-con doubles for RM60. To get there, walk along the river past the mosque, then turn left on Jalan Sultanah, following the signs for 'Rumah Persinggahan'. It's quite a way on a hot day, and those with a lot of luggage may want to spend a few ringgit to go by trishaw.

Muar also has plenty of cheaper hotels, most of which are in the central Chinatown area. The bottom of the barrel, in terms of price and comfort, is the *Hotel Lee Wa* (☎ 06-951 5995) at 75 Jalan Arab, with rooms from RM32. The much better *Kingdom Hotel* (☎ 06-952 1921) at 158 Jalan Meriam charges RM28 for rooms with fan and bathroom, and RM35 for similar rooms with air-con. The nearby *Town View Hotel* (☎ 06-951 1178) at 60 Jalan Sisi has clean, spacious air-con rooms with bathroom for RM64. To get to these three hotels, walk away from the river on Jalan Sisi, one street east of the larger Jalan Sulaiman.

For eats, there are plenty of *kedai kopi* scattered about Chinatown. Otherwise, *hawker stalls* set up nightly along the waterfront, particularly between the bus station and the bridge.

Gunung Ledang

The highest mountain in Johor, Gunung Ledang (formerly Mt Ophir; 1276m) is noted for its series of waterfalls and pools for swimming. The 'falls are a lot nicer than those at Kota Tinggi and they stretch along the mountainside for a longer way', reported one visitor, and they are a popular weekend day trip for locals. From the falls longer, rugged trails lead to the summit.

To get here, take a Muar-Segamat bus and ask to be dropped at Sagil (some buses stop at Gunung Ledang – ask when you buy your ticket). It's then a 1km-plus walk through the rubber plantation to the bottom of the falls (posted as 'Air Terjun'). From JB, Cepat Express buses run to Segamat, and can also drop you at Sagil (but be sure to request this stop when you board). A long-distance taxi from JB will cost RM150 for the whole car.

JOHOR BAHRU TO MERSING

Kota Tinggi

The small town of Kota Tinggi is 42km north-east of JB on the road to Mersing. The town is of little interest, but the waterfalls at **Lumbong**, 15km north-west of the town, are a very popular weekend retreat.

The falls, at the base of 624m **Gunung Muntahak**, leap down 36m and then flow through a series of pools which are ideal for a cooling dip. The smaller pools are shallow enough for children. Entry to the falls is RM2 per person, plus RM2.50 per car.

A couple of kilometres south-east of Kota Tinggi town is **Kampung Kelantan**, where the sultans of Johor have their mausoleums.

Places to Stay & Eat At the falls you can stay at the *Kota Tinggi Waterfall Resort* (☎ 07-833 1146), a recently renovated place where overpriced air-con chalets cost RM150 on weekends and RM110 from Monday to Friday. Bookings at weekends can be heavy, so check before you go.

It is cheaper to stay in Kota Tinggi town. One of the best options is the *Sin May Chun Hotel* (☎ 07-833 3573) at 26 Jalan Tambatan, where clean, spacious fan/air-con rooms cost RM20/32 with bathroom. The *Hotel Bunga Raya* (☎ 07-833 3023) at 12 Jalan Jaafar, opposite the bus station, is a less appealing choice, with doubles from RM30. The clean *Nasha Hotel* (☎ 07-833 8000) at 40 Jalan Tambatan has air-con singles/doubles with bathroom for RM48, and may be willing to offer discounts if business is slow. All three of these hotels are just west of the bus station.

For meals, you will find several decent *Indian* and *Chinese restaurants* in the same area as the hotels. Otherwise, try the *food stalls* near the bus station.

Getting There & Away Regular buses (No 41 and 227, RM2.60) go from JB's Larkin bus station to Kota Tinggi, as do PGBS express buses (RM3). Share taxis from JB cost about RM5 per person. From Kota Tinggi to the waterfalls, take bus No 43. If you have your own transport, take the road which heads north out of the city just east of the bridge; follow the signs marked 'Air Terjun' (waterfalls).

Johor Lama

Following the fall of Melaka to the Portuguese, the Malay kingdom was transferred to Johor Lama, about 30km down Sungai Johor from Kota Tinggi. The town was built as a fortified capital between 1547 and 1587, but was later abandoned as JB rose in prominence. There were a number of skirmishes between Malay and Portuguese fleets along Sungai Johor, and on two occasions the town was sacked and burnt.

Today the old fort of Kota Batu, overlooking the river, has been restored, but getting to Johor Lama is difficult. If you have transport, you can drive there. The turn-off is 26km from Kota Tinggi on the Desaru road (Route 92), and from there it's 13km – seven of which are along a dirt road, which becomes treacherous after rain. Once you get to the river, be prepared to stop and ask for directions frequently, as the route is unmarked and takes several twists and turns as it winds through the tiny villages scattered along the riverside. The difficulty of finding the place on your own makes sharing a taxi from JB an appealing option (RM80 per car).

Teluk Mahkota

A turn-off 13km north of Kota Tinggi leads down 24km of rather rough road to the sheltered waters of Teluk Mahkota (Jason's Bay). There are 10km of shallow, sandy beach at this isolated spot. Although secluded, the beach is not great, and those in search of white sand and turquoise water would be better advised to try the islands and beaches further up the east coast. If you do find yourself in the region, however, it's worth travelling a little further to a better beach, just beyond the point at the southern end of the bay. To get to this beach, continue 10km south from Jason's Bay Beach Resort; after crossing a bridge, the road becomes dirt, after which it's a further 2km to a smaller dirt track on the left, which leads down to the beach. This would be a good camping spot for travellers with bicycles or cars.

There are no regularly scheduled bus services out to Teluk Mahkota, and a share taxi will cost RM100 per car from JB.

Places to Stay The *Jason's Bay Beach Resort* (☎ 07-891 8077) has four-person chalets with fan and bathroom for RM80, or with air-con for RM100. It's also possible to camp here. There are two places further along the beach, both of which are overpriced. As for food, be sure to bring plenty with you, since there are no restaurants or shops in the area.

Desaru

On a 20km stretch of beach at Tanjung Penawar, 88km east of JB, and also reached via Kota Tinggi, this resort area is a popular weekend escape for Singaporeans. The beach is quite good, but access is almost entirely controlled by the giant resorts which crowd the seafront. Anyone with a backpack would look distinctly out of place here as Desaru is largely the preserve of wealthy golfers.

Places to Stay & Eat Accommodation at Desaru is provided by expensive resorts. The *Desaru Golden Beach Hotel* (☎ 07-822 1205) does, however, have a camping ground, called the Desaru Leisure Camp, which has tent sites for an inflated RM10 per person. Unless you cook your own food, you will have to eat in the resort restaurants. The resort also has top-end accommodation with the full range of amenities from S$180. Prices rise significantly on weekends.

The *Desaru View Hotel* (☎ 07-822 1221) is a similar resort with doubles for RM120 on Monday to Friday and RM198 on weekends and holidays.

Getting There & Away Buses (RM3.50) and taxis (RM80 per car) operate from Kota Tinggi. From JB, buses cost RM5 and taxis cost RM100 per car. A popular way for Singaporeans to reach Desaru is to take the ferry to Belungkur from North Changi for S$18, and from there take a taxi to Desaru for RM40 per car. Contact Ferry Fantasy (☎ 02-545 3600) for details.

MERSING

Mersing is a small fishing village on the east coast of Peninsular Malaysia. It's the departure point for the boats which travel between the mainland and the beautiful islands of the Seribuat Archipelago just off the coast in the South China Sea. The river bustles with fishing boats, and there's an impressive mosque on a hill above the town.

While most travellers rush through Mersing on their way to the islands, the town is pleasant and makes for quite a relaxing stopover. There are also some good beaches nearby, including Sri Pantai and Sekakap – six and 13km south; and Air Papan and Panyabong – 10 and 50km to the north of the town.

Orientation

From the north or south, you'll enter Mersing at the town's main roundabout on Route 3. Leading off this to the east is Jalan Abu Bakar, the main street down to the jetty. Jalan Ismail also meets the roundabout and runs roughly parallel to Jalan Abu Bakar. Most of the town's hotels, restaurants and banks are clustered on or near these two streets. A few hotels can also be found across the bridge to the north and down Jalan Nong Yahya to the south, off Jalan Ismail.

Information

The new Mersing Tourist Information Centre (METIC; ☎ 07-799 5212) is a good place to get information on ferry schedules for the islands and accommodation around town. It's about five minutes walk from the jetty.

At the Plaza R&R centre, next to the ferry jetty, the office of the Mersing Tourist Boat Hire Association (☎ 07-799 1222) is another good source of information on sailing times. There's also a credit-card phone in this shopping centre and a number of travel agents.

Travellers cheques can be changed at the Bank Bumiputra or Maybank on Jalan

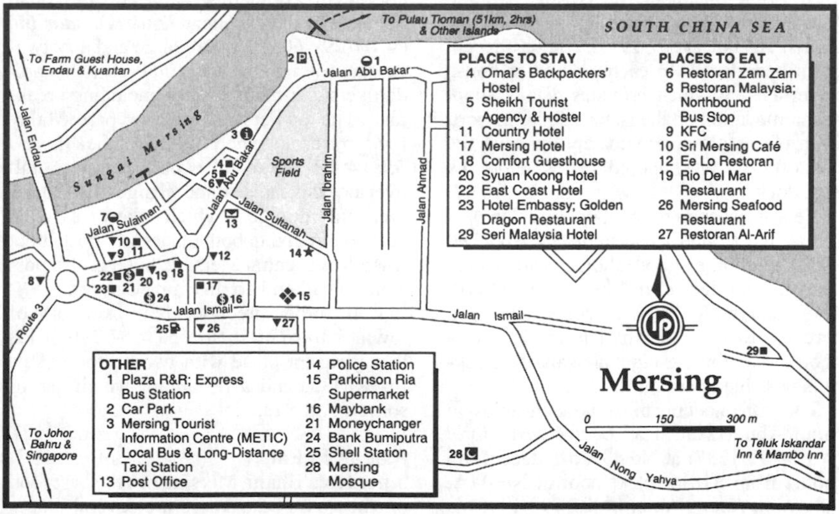

Ismail, or at the licensed moneychanger in the goldsmith shop on Jalan Abu Bakar.

Activities

The best way to sample several of the islands of the Seribuat Archipelago without spending lots of cash is to join Omar's Island Hopping tour (☎ 07-799 5096/019-774 4268). Run by the people who operate Omar's Backpackers' Hostel (see Places to Stay), this tour stops for snorkelling and swimming at up to five of the islands near Mersing in a day trip aboard a converted fishing boat. The cost is RM60 per person, and snorkelling equipment and lunch are provided. Also available is Omar's Overland Tour, which includes stops at palm-oil and rubber plantations, a batik studio, orchid farm, traditional Malay kampung, latex processing facility and a jungle walk. The one-day tour costs RM50, including lunch.

Places to Stay – Budget

Omar's Backpackers Hostel (☎ 07-799 5096/019-774 4268) on Jalan Abu Bakar is the traveller's place, with clean dorm beds for RM7 and good value doubles for RM15. The owners, Helena and Omar, are good sources of information about the islands and the Mersing area. A few doors down, the *Sheikh Tourist Agency* (☎ 07-799 3767) has decent dorm beds for RM6 each, and an in-house travel agency which provides details about accommodation on the islands and transport. Both places are approximately opposite the post office, a few hundred metres before the boat dock.

Near the second roundabout on Jalan Abu Bakar, the *Comfort Guesthouse* (☎ 07-799 6911) is another good choice, with clean, semi-partitioned dorm beds for RM10. Those starved for Internet access can log on here for RM7.50 per half hour. This is a good option for late-night arrivals, as check-in is possible at any time.

There are a couple of Chinese cheapies on Jalan Abu Bakar. The *East Coast Hotel* (☎ 07-799 1337) at No 43A has decent fan rooms from RM15. Next door at No 44A, the *Syuan Koong Hotel* (☎ 07-799 1498) is a less inspiring choice with rooms with fan for RM20, and with air-con for RM28.

The *Farm Guest House* (☎ 07-799 3767) is a rustic retreat a few kilometres from town, where dorm accommodation and all meals costs RM20. There are also two chalets with bathrooms which cost RM45 for two people, including breakfast. Ask at the Sheikh Tourist Agency (☎ 07-799 3767) or METIC for directions.

Places to Stay – Mid-Range

The best value hotel in Mersing is the popular *Hotel Embassy* (☎ 07-799 3545) on Jalan Ismail near the roundabout, where clean, comfortable rooms with bathroom, hot water and fan cost RM25, or RM35 with air-con. Another in this range is the *Mersing Hotel* (☎ 07-796 1004) between Jalan Ismail and Jalan Abu Bakar, with rooms for RM25 with fan, and RM35 with air-con, all with bathroom. If both of these places are full, try the *Country Hotel* (☎ 07-799 1799), near the local bus station, which charges RM45 for rooms of a similar standard.

Those looking for more atmospheric lodgings might want to try some of the interesting alternatives on the outskirts of town. A couple of kilometres south at 1456 Jalan Sekakap is the excellent *Teluk Iskandar Inn* (☎ 07-799 6037), where large and airy two-person rooms cost RM50/60/70 (standard/deluxe/super-deluxe/suite), including breakfast. The owners can also prepare Malay food by arrangement. Nearby, the *Mambo Inn* (☎ 07-799 6380) is built high on a hill overlooking the sea and charges RM70 for pleasant doubles which share a wide veranda. A taxi to both places will cost about RM5 from central Mersing, but it is also possible to call and arrange a pick-up.

In the other direction, about 1km north of town, *Kali's Guest House* (☎ 07-799 3613) is a pleasant place with two-person cabins for RM35, and a restaurant which serves some good fare.

Places to Eat

After Kota Bharu, Mersing has the best food on the east coast. There are several places around town for a roti canai and coffee breakfast, the best of which is the *Restoran Al-Arif*, which also serves excellent Indian food for lunch and dinner. Another place which serves decent Indian food is *Restoran Zam Zam*, next to Sheikh Tourist Agency. For inexpensive Chinese fare, including breakfast, try the *Ee Lo* restaurant near the second roundabout.

Those in search of a western-style breakfast can try the *Sri Mersing Cafe* on Jalan Sulaiman, but be warned that the service is poor. A much better choice for western-style meals at any hour is the *Rio Del Mar* restaurant on Jalan Abu Bakar. The menu includes tacos, salads, burgers, pizzas and beer. The expat owner is also a good source of information on the area.

Mersing, being a fishing port, is also a good place for seafood, and there are several Chinese restaurants which specialise in seafood dishes. The Chinese *Golden Dragon Restaurant* below the Hotel Embassy is good, and has some unusual menu items including curried wild-boar meat. Perhaps the best choice is the air-con *Mersing Seafood Restaurant*, which costs a little more than some but turns out consistently tasty fare. Try the shrimp with coconut sauce.

For Malaysian fare, the *Plaza R&R* has a small food court with hawker stalls selling the usual favourites. There's all much the same and make for a decent lunch.

Lastly, for satay in the evenings, head to the *night stalls* near the first roundabout.

Getting There & Away

Mersing is 133km north of JB and 189km south of Kuantan. Most long-distance buses start and terminate at the Plaza R&R, near the jetty. Destinations include Ipoh (RM26), Johor Bahru (RM11), Kuala Lumpur (RM16.60), Melaka (RM11.20), Penang (RM35) and Singapore (RM11). The ticket booths are at the back of the plaza, and are run by various long-distance bus companies.

Most north-bound long-distance buses stop at the Restoran Malaysia on the roundabout. You can buy tickets at the restaurant, but in peak travel periods it is sometimes difficult to get a seat. Destinations include Kota Bharu (RM25), Kuala Terengganu (RM16.10) and Kuantan (RM10.35).

The local bus and long-distance taxi station is on Jalan Sulaiman, near the river. Taxi destinations include JB (RM15), Kota Tinggi (RM10), Kuantan (RM20), Melaka (RM30) and Pekan (RM15) per person.

SERIBUAT ARCHIPELAGO

The Seribuat Archipelago off the east coast of Johor contains some of Malaysia's most beautiful islands. The largest and most popular of these, Pulau Tioman, is actually in Pahang, but is usually reached from Mersing, as are the archipelago's other islands. Unfortunately, many of the islands have been developed as high-price resorts catering only to wealthy package tourists.

Islands with regular ferry services accessible to independent travellers include Tioman, Rawa, Besar and Sibu. Of these, only Tioman has an abundance of budget accommodation. Besar has two small budget places, and Sibu one. Rawa is wholly owned by an upmarket resort, and is effectively off-limits to all but resort guests.

Two more distant islands, Pemanggil and Aur, boast some of the best diving, but are the province of wealthy package tourists.

For more information and details on safe and responsible diving, see the Pahang chapter and the Diving & Snorkelling section in the Terengganu chapters.

Pulau Tioman

The giant of the archipelago, Tioman boasts the widest variety of beaches, great diving and snorkelling, and lots of inexpensive accommodation. For details see the Pahang chapter.

Pulau Besar

Also known as Pulau Babi Besar (Big Pig Island) this is one of the closest islands to the peninsula. It has a good white-sand beach on its western side and one or two secluded beaches on its isolated eastern side. Unfortunately, most of the accommodation is in the form of expensive resorts.

Budget travellers can try the four A-frames in front of the D'Coconut Resort a little north of the jetty which rent for RM30 per night. Call D'Coconut (see the following paragraph) for details. Further north along the beach, *Pulau Besar Chalet* (☎ 010-775 8136) is a simple place with clean bungalows for RM40. If you're staying at these places, you may want to bring some food from Mersing, since outside the resorts there are only two very simple restaurants on the island.

D'Coconut (☎ 010-272 9306) is the best of the upmarket resorts on the island, with clean air-con double cabins with bathroom for RM165, including breakfast. At the northern end of the island, *Hillside* (☎ 07-799 4831) is an interesting spot with bungalows built on a rocky headland overlooking the sea. Full-board rates start at RM150 per person for double-occupancy bungalows. At low tide, it's possible to walk from the jetty in about 30 minutes.

The other places on the island are overpriced and not geared towards independent travellers.

Regular ferries to Besar leave from the main Mersing jetty daily at around 9 am and 12.30 pm, and cost RM18 one way. Return ferries leave Besar daily at around 10.30 am and 2 pm. The ride takes a little under an hour.

Pulau Sibu

Easily accessible and quiet, Sibu is a good option for those who want to escape the crowds on larger islands like Tioman. The island has some good white-sand beaches and decent coral.

Most travellers gravitate to *O&H Kampung Huts* (☎ 07-799 5096/011-354 322) in the middle of the island on the eastern side. It's a friendly place with A-frames with shared bathroom from RM27 to RM35 and chalets with bathrooms from RM55 to RM65. The restaurant serves western and Malaysian dishes, with dinners averaging about RM12.

Most of the other places on the island are resort style, selling full-board packages from their offices in JB, but walk-ins are usually welcome if there is space. The cheapest of these is *Sibu Island Cabanas* (☎ 07-331 7216) around the headland to the south of O&H. Full-board packages in its large chalets start at RM138 per person for two days.

Perhaps the nicest spot on the island is *Rimba Resort* (☎ 011-711 528) which has its own private beach at the northern end of the island. The resort has an African theme and is conducive to serious relaxation. The restaurant turns out some great food and lunch guests from other resorts are accepted. Full board packages start at RM185 per person double occupancy.

Boats to Sibu leave from Tanjung Leman, about 30km south of Mersing. Taxis from Mersing to the jetty cost about RM40 for the whole car. Alternately, you can take a bus to Tenggaroh Junction, from where you can catch a waiting taxi to the jetty for RM15. However, there are not usually taxis waiting at the jetty for the return journey, so you should ask the owner of the resort where you're staying to make arrangements for pick-up before you depart. The Sheikh Tourist Agency in Mersing can help with travel arrangements (see Mersing, Places to Stay).

Most resorts operate their own boats to the island, but for RM20 they will take non-guests. It's best to show up at the jetty around noon to be sure of catching a boat over. The trip takes about 30 minutes.

Pulau Rawa

The tiny island of Rawa, 16km from Mersing, is wholly owned by the *Rawa Safaris Island Resort* (☎ 07-799 1204). There is an excellent white-sand beach, and the waters around the island are good for snorkelling. Unfortunately, the island is closed to non-guests.

Accommodation at the resort ranges from basic but comfortable bungalows for RM110 to beachfront rooms for RM184, including taxes. The restaurant has a bar, and facilities include windsurfing, canoeing, scuba diving and snorkelling.

The resort has its own boat, and the booking office is in Mersing, next to the jetty.

Pulau Tinggi

Tinggi is probably the most impressive island when seen from a distance, as it's an extinct volcano (*tinggi* means 'tall').

Accommodation is in resorts, though some locals reportedly supply budget accommodation. The top spot on the island is *Nadias Inn* (☎ 011-333 656), where the air-con rooms cost from RM100 to RM125.

All boats to the island leave from Tanjung Leman (see Pulau Sibu for transport details). There are no regular ferries since most guests go as part of all-inclusive package tours. You may be able to hitch a ride for RM50, by prior arrangement with the resort. The ride takes two hours.

Pulau Pemanggil & Pulau Aur

Far from the mainland, these two islands were not developed until fairly recently. With crystal-clear water and excellent coral they are popular with divers, but all accommodation is resort style and there are no facilities for independent travellers, nor are there any regularly scheduled ferries.

At the time of writing, Pulau Aur was wholly owned by *Aur Samudera Resort* which sells only group diving packages in conjunction with a company called Dive Atlantis (Singapore ☎ 02-295 0377). Once on the island, chalets for up to three people cost RM60, and food is available at an extra charge.

Pemanggil is also controlled by large resorts and is basically off limits to independent travellers.

Those who aren't put off by this can charter a boat to Pemanggil or Aur for approximately RM350 from Tanjung Leman.

Other Islands

There are several more small islands within about 20km of Mersing. These uninhabited islands include (from north to south) Harimau, Mensirip, Gual, Hujung and Tengah. The most famous of these is Pulau Tengah, which was once a Vietnamese refugee camp but is now only home to the sea turtles who come in July to lay their eggs. The island has some superb coral on its northern side. The other islands also have good coral and some isolated white-sand beaches.

Since there are no resorts on these islands, there are no regularly scheduled ferries. About the only way to visit them without spending hundreds of ringgit to charter a boat, is to join Omar's Island Hopping tour described in the Mersing Activities section.

NORTH OF MERSING

There are some pleasant shallow beaches along the coast from Mersing. These see few visitors and are good for camping.

Penyabong

Fifty kilometres north of Mersing, Penyabong is the best mainland beach in the area. Several small islands of the Seribuat Archipelago lie just offshore and reward the adventurous traveller with a real deserted island experience.

Places to Stay & Eat About the only place to stay in Penyabong is *Zul's Guesthouse* (☎ 07-799 1781), a funky little place with only four rooms, each of which can hold up to three people for a total of RM25. Zul also serves breakfast for RM3 and dinner for RM7.

Zul and his partner run trips to the nearby islands of the Seribuat Archipelago with his sailing boat. In addition to day trips, he will drop campers off on an uninhabited island and pick them up again at a prearranged time. His trips cost between RM10 and RM50 per person depending on the distance sailed.

Getting There & Away The best way to get to Penyabong is to take a bus from Mersing to Endau (RM2), then take a taxi for RM15 per car. A taxi direct from Mersing costs RM25 per car. If you call ahead early enough, the above-mentioned Zul may be able to provide a pick-up in Mersing.

Pahang

By far the largest state in Peninsular Malaysia, Pahang has plenty to offer the visitor. The east coast has some beautiful beaches, and the tropical Pulau Tioman (Tioman Island) lies just off the south coast, but the interior, with its pristine rainforests is equally alluring. Taman Negara National Park, accessible only by boat, is the usual place to get right into the rainforest, and places like Kenong Rimba near Kuala Lipis are also gaining in popularity.

For those who want to get right off the beaten track, the beautiful Tasik (Lake) Chini, close to the huge Sungai (River) Pahang in the centre of the state, is worth exploring, and even more remote is the Endau-Rompin National Park, one of Malaysia's newest and least visited national parks.

HIGHLIGHTS

- **Taman Negara National Park** – one of the oldest rainforests in the world, home to several endangered species and a profusion of exotic plants
- **Pulau Tioman** – an island made famous in the film *South Pacific*, offers excellent snorkelling, diving and mountainous jungle trekking
- **Cherating** – laid-back backpackers' pit stop, with a pleasant beach, good food and the best nightlife on the east coast
- **Tasik Chini** – beautiful lotus-covered lake and home to an Orang Asli indigenous group

History

Important archaeological finds dating back to Neolithic times have been made along Pahang's Sungai Tembeling. By the 8th century the Sumatran Sriwijaya Empire held sway along the coast, until its collapse in the 14th century, after which Pahang became a Siamese dependency.

Pahang only really emerged as a separate political entity when the Melaka sultanate launched an attack against the Siamese in the middle of the 15th century and installed Muhammad, the eldest son of the Melaka sultan, as ruler.

In the 16th century the state became a pawn in the four-way struggle for ascendancy between Johor, Aceh, the Dutch and the Portuguese. In a period of 30 years it was sacked many times, its rich, mineral-based economy was ruined, its rulers were killed or abducted and much of its population was murdered or enslaved. After the decline of the Acehnese empire in the mid-17th century, Pahang was ruled by Johor for the next 200 years.

From 1858 until 1863 Pahang suffered a protracted civil war brought about by a leadership struggle between two brothers, Wan Ahmad and Mutahir, on the death of their father, the sultan. Wan Ahmad finally won, and in 1887 he became sultan. His role from then on was largely reduced to a symbolic position as the British had forced him to sign a treaty bringing Pahang under the control of a British Resident. The British were very interested in the state's commercial potential and were concerned about Ahmad's autocratic style and the way he had been dishing out large concessions to other foreign speculators.

In 1896 Pahang was one of the four states which became the Federated Malay States (the others were Perak, Selangor and Negeri Sembilan). These in turn formed the Federation of Malaya in February 1948 and finally the Federation of Malaysia, as it is today, in 1963.

Pulau Tioman

Turtle-shaped Pulau Tioman is the largest and most impressive of the east coast islands. The sheer size of the island (39km long and 12km wide) affords a variety of activities not found on most of the east coast's other islands. Visitors can choose between snorkelling and diving in the clear waters, lazing around on white-sand beaches or exploring the rugged trails of the interior.

Back in the late 1950s Hollywood got wind of Tioman and famously made it the setting for the mythical Bali Hai in the film *South Pacific*. Later, in the 1970s, *Time Magazine* proclaimed it one of the world's most beautiful islands. The crowds have been pouring in ever since for a taste of paradise; an airport has materialised, sandwiched between vertiginous mountains and the sea; and express boat services to the mainland have multiplied.

It comes as no surprise then, that Tioman today is geared almost entirely to tourism. The permanent population is low, with just a handful of small *kampungs* dotted around the coast; the mountainous jungle of the interior is home only to monkeys and other wildlife. Visitors usually outnumber villagers, and at certain times of the year Tioman can get quite crowded, especially in Salang and Air Batang (usually known as ABC).

Unfortunately, even an island the size of Tioman is not immune to the ravages of excessive tourism and heedless development. Many parts of the island are decidedly rundown and some common areas are strewn with litter. This is compounded by a noticeably hostile attitude on the part of many locals. Worse still, sandflies are endemic on many of the island's beaches and some tourists suffer badly from their bites. Check the Health section of the Malaysia Facts for the Visitor chapter for details on how to cope with bites and stings.

Thus, the visitor heading to Tioman in search of an unspoiled tropical paradise is likely to be disappointed. Those who go with an idea of what to expect, and the energy to get off the beaten track, will still find some spectacular vistas. Furthermore, the underwater world around Tioman is largely intact and the island still offers some of the best diving and snorkelling in Malaysia.

Orientation & Information

The wide southern end of the island is wilder and more mountainous than the narrow northern end. Most of the places to stay can be found on the west coast of the island, with the expensive places clustered to the south and the budget places to the north, primarily in ABC and Salang. On the east coast, there is one very quiet beach, Juara, which has a few cheap places to stay for those who really want to get away from it all. With only one short stretch of road running from Berjaya Tioman Beach Resort to the northern end of Tekek, transport around the island is still by creaky fishing boats or on foot, via rugged mountain trails.

You can cash travellers cheques at the Berjaya Tioman Beach Resort and at the moneychangers in ABC and Salang, although their rates are nothing to sing about – generally around 10% less than you'd get at a bank on the mainland.

There are numerous public phones at Tekek, ABC and at Salang, but you will find many of these in disrepair. Only Telekom cards can be used for calls and these are on sale at shops around the island – though they frequently sell out. A number of the guesthouses have mobile phones, and they will often let you make calls, usually at prohibitive rates.

Bear in mind that everything stocked in shops on Tioman is shipped over from the mainland and tends to be expensive, so stock up on essentials before you arrive.

Wildlife

Tioman is of great interest to biologists because of its relative isolation from the peninsula's similarly forested terrain. Some animals which are common on the peninsula are completely missing from the island, while others are present in unexpectedly large numbers.

Tioman has a very large mouse-deer population, for example, and also has a variety of lizards in larger than usual numbers. There's a good chance you'll see some wildlife while you're on the island, particularly bats, which come out in force each evening.

The waters around Tioman shelter the usual technicolour schools of exotic fish and a surprising number of turtles. At Nipah, Juara and Pulau Tulai (Coral Island) you have a good chance of seeing turtles come ashore to lay their eggs.

Activities

Cross-Island Walk The most popular walk is the cross-island trek from Tekek to Juara. While not too strenuous, parts of the walk are quite steep and hiking in tropical heat can be taxing – be sure to bring plenty of water. The walk starts about 1km north of the jetty in Tekek, near the convenience store. There is a sign at the start of the trail saying '4km' but the actual distance is closer to 6km.

The trail starts just after you pass the mosque on your left. At this point, it's a narrow track and a little tricky to follow; the best advice is to follow the power lines overhead. Soon after the mosque, you come to the first set of concrete steps, which continue intermittently for most of the way to the top. Halfway up the hill, you pass a small waterfall, in which swimming is prohibited.

Once over the top of the range, the trail slopes down more gradually and soon leaves the damp, dark jungle for the cooler and brighter area of a rubber plantation and then coconut palms as you reach the coast. The walk across the island to Juara takes 1½ to three hours. If you don't want to walk back,

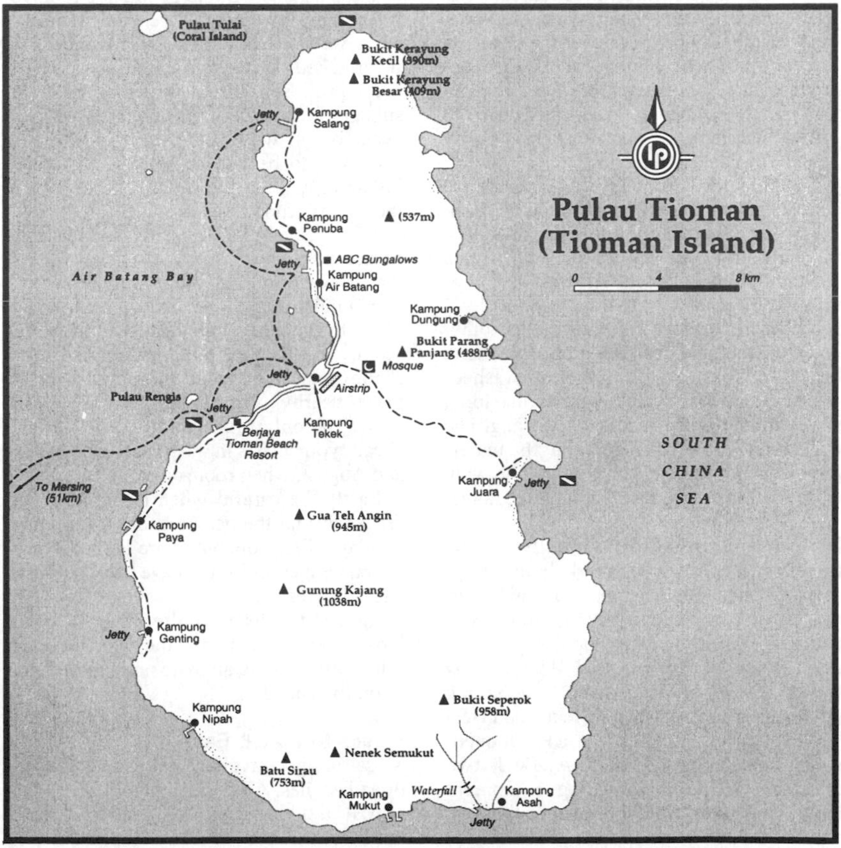

a ferry leaves Juara for Salang, ABC and Tekek (RM20) at 3 pm. If you'd like to do the journey in reverse, a boat leaves Tekek for Juara every day around 4.30 pm (RM20).

Other Walks You can also walk along much of the west coast, but the trails are often difficult to follow, and you should take water.

From Tekek you can walk south to Berjaya Tioman Beach Resort in about 30 minutes, either by the road or by rock-hopping around the headland. From there you can walk through the golf course. Just before the telecommunications tower, there is a trail to the beautiful, deserted beach of Bunut. From the end of the beach, the sometimes faint trail continues over the headland to a couple of rickety bridges across the mangroves just before Paya. From Paya you can walk south to Genting – the trail is easy to follow and there are houses along the way where you can ask directions.

Heading north from Tekek, you cross the small headland to ABC, and from ABC Bungalows at the other end of the bay it's a 10 minute climb over the headland to Penuba Bay and Monkey Beach. The trail then goes through the rainforest to a deserted yellow-sand beach, where it continues at the other end over the next headland to a white-sand beach. At the end of this is a rotten, washed-out bridge where the trail starts the long, steep climb over the headland to Salang. The trail is not well marked here, but the undergrowth is not thick if you lose it. The walk from ABC to Salang takes about three hours.

Diving & Snorkelling Virtually all the travellers' centres have snorkelling equipment for hire, and there are a number of places offering scuba diving and PADI courses. Two of the more popular are DiveAsia (☎ 09-419 5017) and B&J Diving Centre (☎ 09-419 5555), both at Salang (DiveAsia also has a shop in Tekek and B&J has one in ABC). At DiveAsia, a PADI open-water course costs RM795. At B&J, two dives cost RM160, including equipment rental, or RM130 with your own equipment, and PADI open-water courses are RM795.

There is good snorkelling off the rocky points on the west coast of the island, particularly those just north of ABC, but the best snorkelling is around the nearby island of Pulau Tulai, better known as Coral Island. Most chalet operators can arrange day trips to the island which cost about RM45, including equipment rental.

See the Diving & Snorkelling section in the Terengganu chapter for information about other dive sites and advice for safe and responsible diving.

Warning There are sandflies on most of the island's beaches. Some people are relatively immune to them, while others suffer a nasty welt, which can become an open sore if scratched. Various countermeasures have been proposed, from insect repellent to suntan lotion, to eating a course of brewer's yeast for two weeks before arrival. The only sure way to beat these insects is to avoid laying around on the beach, particularly in the late afternoon and evening.

When leaving for the island, don't take the advice of dockside touts who'll assure you that all places on the island are full (and will then kindly book you into their 'friend's' place by phone). If you fall victim to this scam, you'll find yourself staying in a shabby place for twice the price of better places nearby (which invariably have vacancies). The only time you may want to call ahead (yourself) is in the peak season of July and August, when rooms may be full.

Lastly, be careful when riding the large ferries during the peak season or on public holidays. Ferry operators are lax in observing passenger limits and have been known to pack ferries in order to make an extra ringgit. If the ferry you're about to board looks overcrowded, take the next one, even if it means staying an extra night in Mersing or on the island.

Places to Stay & Eat

Most foreign travellers gravitate to one of three beaches: ABC, Salang or Juara.

ABC is a long stretch of beach, and, while there is a range of chalet operations to choose from, they tend to keep their distance from each other, giving the beach a less 'developed' feel. Salang, on the other hand, is somewhat cluttered, though the beach is excellent, and it is also the place to be if you want a good selection of restaurants and a couple of places to enjoy late night drinks. Juara is a get-away-from-it-all destination. It has a good beach and just a few chalet outfits with restaurants, and everything winds down early. It's also the cheapest place to be based. From June to August, when the island is swarming with people, accommodation becomes tight, but either side of these months it's a buyer's market. During the heavy November to January monsoon the island is almost deserted.

Apart from the international-standard Berjaya Tioman Beach Resort, accommodation is mostly in the form of small and often ridiculously cramped wooden chalets and longhouse rooms. Chalets generally cost from RM20 to RM50, depending on facilities. For RM20 you'll get a small chalet with a double bed and bathroom. Once you start paying over RM25 you should also get a mosquito net and fan. For air-conditioning, you must pay RM50 per night and up, and these rooms are usually much nicer than fan-only rooms. Most operations now have a few larger family cabins for those with children. Wherever you stay, it's worth bargaining, especially for longer visits.

There are very few of the old A-frame, huts with *atap* (thatch) roofs left, most have been demolished to make way for new chalets. Those remaining cost from around RM10 (no bath, no fan, no net, no light) to about RM15 – bring your mosquito coils.

Resort The *Berjaya Tioman Beach Resort* (☎ 09-414 1000), a sprawling place, is the only international-class hotel on the island. It has 375 rooms priced from RM245, with discounts of up to 25% from November to February. Most rooms are chalet style with air-con. The beach here is probably the best on the island. The hotel has a very impressive range of facilities – a beautiful 18 hole golf course, tennis, horse riding, jet-skis, scuba diving etc. There's even a room full of poker machines, although Muslims are not allowed to enter.

This resort can be heavily booked, particularly during the school holidays. The four restaurants are all very good, but, as you might expect, they're by no means low-budget options.

Kampung Tekek Tekek is the island's largest village, and its administrative centre. The airport is here, and a few well-stocked shops. Tekek's beach is not among the best on the island. There is accommodation on both sides of the jetty, but most of it is in a state of advanced disrepair and we cannot recommend staying here.

ABC (Air Batang) ABC is a popular beach just over the headland, an easy walk to the north of Tekek. Along with Salang, it's the main travellers' centre, with a lazy string of chalet operations, connected by a concrete path that runs the length of the beach. ABC is a more relaxing place to be than Tekek and it has more greenery. The northern end of the beach, however, is rocky and poor for swimming; the southern end, near Nazri's, has the best white-sand beach.

Stepping off the jetty and heading north, the first place you come to is *South Pacific* (☎ 09-419 1176), a basic place offering chalets with fan for RM18 and air-con for RM65. Next along is *Johan's House* (☎ 011-664257), a slightly more attractive place with chalets with fan for RM18 and air-con for RM75. After Johan's is the *Tioman Guest House* (☎ 09-419 1196) where clean standard/deluxe chalets cost RM25/35 with fan and RM70 with air-con.

After the Tioman Guest House, *Rinda House* (☎ 09-419 1957) has simple but clean chalets with fan for RM15. Considering the price, this is one of the better deals in ABC. After Rinda is *Nazri's Beach Cabanas* (☎ 011-333486). More commonly known as Nazri's II, bungalows are large and fairly clean, ranging in price from RM30 to RM100. There is also a decent restaurant with a good view of the sea.

Just past Nazri's Beach Cabanas is the popular *ABC Bungalows* (☎ 09-419 1154), with a variety of chalets spread over pleasant, well-tended grounds. The simplest huts with fan cost RM10, while standard huts with fan and bathroom cost RM25. There's also a decent restaurant out the front.

Finally, at the far northern end of the beach are the lovely *Bamboo Hill Chalets* (☎ 09-419 1339; email bamboosu@tm.net.my). Perched on the rocks overlooking the water, these clean, well-kept chalets are by far the most pleasant place to stay on the island. With only six chalets ranging in cost from RM50 to RM100, the place is almost always full and calling ahead is a good idea. In an effort to cut down on litter, the owners will refill water bottles with filtered water for RM1 per 1.5L bottle (non-guests are welcome to bring their empties). They also produce an informative leaflet about the island and sell phone cards.

Working south from the ABC jetty, you soon come to *Mawar Resort* (☎ 09-419 1153), one of the better places on the beach, with clean standard/deluxe cabins with fan for RM25/30. The restaurant serves good food as well. Next along is *Mohktar's Place* (☎ 09-419 1148), a simple establishment with fan cabins for RM20.

The last accommodation option before the headland, *Nazri's Place* (☎ 011-349534) is popular with travellers and lays claim to the best stretch of beach in ABC. There are some dilapidated A-frames right on the beach for RM12, RM50 set back from the beach and larger cabins for RM70 near the beach. There is also a decent restaurant here.

Kampung Penuba Over the headland from ABC, the *Penuba Inn Resort* (☎ 011-952963) has 30 chalets with fan and bathroom for RM30 to RM56 and with air-con for RM60 to RM150. They're built on a hill overlooking the bay and are very attractive. It's certainly peaceful, but accommodation is limited and often taken by large dive groups, so it's worth checking to see if there's room before lugging your gear over the headland, although it's not a long walk.

Salang If you stopped at Tekek or ABC on the way, the small bay at Salang is likely to come as a surprise. The beach is beautiful, but the waterfront area is the most congested on the island. In terms of swimming and easy access to a variety of restaurants and activities, however, Salang is probably the best location on Tioman. It's also popular with divers. Two of Tioman's better dive centres are also located here (see the Diving & Snorkelling entry earlier in this section). The beach is about 700m long, and the jetty is towards the southern end.

The best places to stay are south of the jetty. *Khalid's Place* (☎ 011-953421) is a popular option. It's set back from the beach and has a nice garden, although there is some litter scattered about. Standard chalets will cost you RM35, or there are larger single/double chalets for RM60/100 with air-conditoning.

Across the small creek is another cluster of chalet outfits. Most of these are cheap but grim. An exception is *Zaid's* (☎ 09-419 5019), one of the most popular with travellers. There are chalets with fan for RM50 for two people and RM65 for three. Larger family cabins with fan go for RM80. It also has a decent library.

The *Indah Salang* (☎ 09-413 1406) is the second place north of the jetty, and it sprawls along the beach for some distance. It has a big restaurant, bar, shop and a wide variety of accommodation. Clean, basic bungalows with fan are RM30 and nicer cabins with air-con are RM80.

The *Salang Beach Resort* (☎ 07-799 3607) is another resort-style operation with pricey chalets – RM40 with fan, or RM110 and upwards with air-con. There is also a large restaurant with lots of Chinese dishes for around RM10 per serve.

Finally, near the north end of the beach there are two small, cheap bungalow operations. *Ella's Place* (☎ 09-419 5004) has simple cabins with fan for RM25. Next door, *Salang Huts* (no phone) has similar cabins for the same price. Both places have small restaurants. Check these places if the southern end of the beach doesn't suit you.

Juara The only place to stay on the east coast of the island, Juara is less developed and quieter than most beaches on the west coast. The beach is excellent, though the sea is very rough in the monsoon season. This is a place for serious relaxation, since there is little to do except swim and laze away the day under the coconut trees. Juara is also one of the cheapest beaches on the island, with bungalows ranging from RM15 to RM30.

About 150m north of the jetty, *Paradise Point* (no phone) has simple, clean chalets with fan for RM15 and a small restaurant.

Just south of the jetty, *Kejora* (no phone) is right on the beach and has clean chalets for RM20 with fan. On the headland dividing the two half-moon beaches of Juara, *Juara Bay Village Resort* (☎ 03-981 6122) is the most upmarket operation in the village, with clean new cabins for RM30 to RM40.

On the other side of the headland, *Mizani* (no phone) has a good beach-side location and pleasant, simple standard/deluxe cabins for RM15/20.

Paya Paya is a few kilometres south of the Berjaya Tioman Beach Resort. The beach is OK but nothing special. Most of the people coming to this beach are on package holidays, and costs are higher than elsewhere. The *Paya Beach Resort* (☎ 07-799 1432) has standard/deluxe air-con rooms for RM90/110. A cheaper option is the *Paya Holiday Resort* with rooms from RM35. There are other accommodation options at the *Paya Village* and the upmarket *Paya Tioman Resort*.

Genting Very few travellers make it to Genting, and with good reason. There's little transport to other parts of the island, the beach is poor and tourist developments are aimed at free-spending Singaporeans. There is some reasonably cheap accommodation about, but most of it is resort style, complete with karaoke entertainment. Boats go to Genting from Mersing.

Nipah This is the place to stay if you really want to get away from it all. The beach is superb, with good snorkelling, and, apart from a couple of longhouse blocks that are only open during the holiday periods, there's only one place to stay.

Prices at the *Nipah Beach Resort* (no phone) start at around RM30, but you may be able to bargain for something cheaper. Only the boats to and from Mersing stop here, by arrangement, and there are no trails to Nipah.

Getting There & Away

Air Pelangi Air (☎ 09-419 1301) has daily flights to/from Singapore's Seletar airport for RM151 plus RM40 airport tax. Pelangi also flies daily to/from KL (four daily, RM146) and to/from Kuantan (daily, RM84). Contact Malaysia Airlines for Pelangi bookings. Berjaya Air (☎ 09-419 1303) has two daily flights to/from KL for RM146. Both airlines have offices at the Berjaya Tioman Beach Resort, and at the airport.

Boat Mersing in Johor is the main access port for Tioman. Two companies operate large ferries to Tioman, Master and Seagull lines, both of which charge RM25 one way and RM45 return (unless you ask, you won't be given the RM5 discount on the return ticket). In theory, you must buy your tickets in advance from one of the agents near the jetty, but in practice you can buy one as you board if there is space.

Departure times vary with the tide, but are usually at around noon from Mersing and for the trip from Tioman ask at the place you're staying for the next day's sailing times. From Mersing, ferries leave from the main jetty and stop at Genting, Paya, the Resort, Tekek, ABC and Salang, in that order, picking up from those jetties in the reverse order on the return trip. Sailing time averages about two hours.

There are also several speedboat companies that do the trip between Mersing and Tioman in 1½ hours for RM30 one way. These operate from the same jetties as the big ferries and depart several times a day, making them a good option if you've missed the day's ferry sailings. Tickets are sold by ticket agents in Mersing or as you board in

Tioman. Note that there is a movement underway to ban these boats for safety reasons, so they may not be operational by the time you read this.

The Mersing jetty is five minutes walk from the town centre and you'll find the offices for boats to all the nearby islands in this area.

For the last several years, efforts have been made to establish regular ferry services to Tioman from Tanjong Gemok, 38km north of Mersing. At the time of writing these efforts had not eventuated. However, the state of Pahang is trying to revive Tanjong Gemok as a port, and has even threatened to ban ferries from Mersing. For the time being, though, the trip from Mersing is still the way to get there.

Singapore There's a daily high-speed catamaran service between Singapore and Pulau Tioman. It departs from Singapore's Tanah Merah ferry terminal daily at 7.55 am, and from the Berjaya Tioman Beach Resort jetty at 1.30 pm. The trip takes 4½ hours and costs S$79/140 one way/return. Bookings can be made at the desk in the lobby of the Berjaya Tioman Beach Resort. In Singapore the office for bookings is Kalpin Tours (☎ 02-271 4866), 02-40 World Trade Centre. There are usually no sailings in the monsoon season, from October or November to 1 March.

Getting Around

Boat The only regular boat service around the island is the Juara ferry, which leaves Tekek for Juara around 4.30 pm, stopping at ABC and Salang on the way (1½ hours, RM20). In the reverse direction, it departs from Juara daily at 3 pm, stopping at Salang and ABC on the way to Tekek.

For other journeys around the island, travellers are at the mercy of independent boat operators who generally charge usurious prices for even the shortest journeys. A boat from Salang to ABC, for example, will run to about RM20. Most chalet operations can arrange these boats.

Boat charter is expensive, costing between RM300 and RM400 per day.

The Coast

ENDAU TO KUANTAN

Endau

There's little of interest in Endau, but you can hire boats to make trips up the remote Sungai Endau to the Endau-Rompin National Park and Orang Asli settlements in the interior.

It is possible to get about 110km upriver in fair-sized boats, almost to Kampung Patah, which is the last village up the river. From there, smaller boats are required to negotiate the rapids into Orang Asli country. Smaller boats can be hired at Kampung Punan, about 100km from Endau.

Endau-Rompin National Park

At 870 sq km, Endau-Rompin is one of the largest national parks on the peninsula. It is Malaysia's last refuge of the Sumatran rhinoceros, though they only roam remote areas that are off limits to visitors. The park's lowland forests are among the few remaining in Malaysia and have been identified as harbouring unique varieties of plant life.

There has been little development of tourist facilities at Endau-Rompin, which means that visiting the park on a budget, and as an independent traveller is not easy. You will need to organise an entry permit, which costs RM20 and can be obtained from the State Security Council, 2nd floor, Bangunan Sultan Ibrahim, Bukit Timbalan, Johor Bahru. It is also worth asking staff at the tourist office in Kuantan about organising a permit in Kuantan.

Accommodation at base camp is provided by the Forestry Department. Maps are available at base camp, but officials here generally require that you hire a guide to explore the park. Fees for the park include: guide RM35 per day, tent RM12.50 per person per night, insurance RM1.50 per day and camera RM10.

The chief attractions of the park are the flora and fauna, river trips and some magnificent waterfalls. Rare animals in the forest include tigers, elephants and tapir. There are also various kinds of hornbills, as well as unique plant life such as the walking stick palm *(Phycorapis syngaporensis)* and the climbing bamboo *(Rhopa loblaste)*.

Getting There & Away There are two main routes into the park. The first involves taking the Keluang Jemaluang road (Route 50) in Johor to a turn-off 5km east of the small town of Kahang. From there it's a 56km drive over rough 4WD roads to Kampung Peta, the park's visitors' centre. Alternatively, boats can be hired in Endau to take you up the Sungai Endau as far as Kampung Peta; a journey which takes the better part of a day and costs about RM380 return.

Currently, the easiest way to see the park is to take an organised trip. There are numerous agencies in Johor Bahru offering trips here, and the tourist information office in Kuantan also has tours for RM350 for two people, for three days and two nights. The Watering Hole Bungalows in Kuala Rompin also has economical tours to Endau-Rompin. They cost RM280 per person all-inclusive for a five day trip (minimum of four people; RM380 per person for three or less). The tours leave on Thursday from the Watering Hole Bungalows, but you need to get there a few days before so staff can organise permits (photocopy of passport and three photos needed).

Kuala Rompin & Nenasi

There is nothing to see or do in Kuala Rompin, but with a 4WD vehicle you can go inland to Ibam (10km) and a further 25km to Kampung Aur, where there are Orang Asli settlements.

At Nenasi boats can be hired and you can go upriver to the Orang Asli village of Kampung Ulu Serai.

Places to Stay Three kilometres south of Kuala Rompin and 2km off the main road is the very pleasant *Watering Hole Bungalows* (☎ 011-411894). It's a very quiet and isolated place – perfect if you want to do nothing for a few days. It's run by a Swiss-Malaysian couple, and is kept very clean and neat. The beach here is nothing special but is perfectly OK for swimming. A-frame huts cost RM14 per person and there are small bungalows at RM20 per person, or with bathroom for RM30 per person. Dinner and breakfast are included in the price. The easiest way to get there is to take a taxi from the Kuala Rompin bus station.

Pekan

The royal town of Pahang state has a couple of well-built white-marble mosques and the sultan's palace, the modern and downright ugly **Istana Abu Bakar**. The *istana* is on the Kuantan edge of town.

Much more interesting is the **Museum Sultan Abu Bakar**, the state museum housed in a building constructed by the British for the local Resident. It has a wide variety of exhibits, although unfortunately much of the labelling is in Bahasa Malaysia only. Much of the museum is dedicated to the lives of the Pahang royal family, but there are also some natural history, ceramics and tin-mining displays. Set in the shady garden there's a depressing mini-zoo, the sultan's old Cadillac, a 'traditional' kampung house (complete with non-traditional items such as a wind-up gramophone and a treadle sewing machine) and a houseboat once used on the river. The museum is open daily from 9.30 am to 5 pm, except Monday (closed) and Friday (9.30 am to 12.15 pm). Entry is RM1.

Sungai Pahang, crossed at this town by a lengthy bridge, is the longest river in Malaysia and was the last east-coast river to be bridged. At the river mouth on the other side is the small fishing village of Kuala Pahang.

A road follows the Sungai Pahang to Chini, from where you can reach **Tasik Chini** (see the Around Kuantan section later in this chapter). Buses run along this road.

Places to Stay There's not much in the way of accommodation in Pekan, and most travellers visit as a day trip from Kuantan. The *Pekan Hotel* (☎ 09-422 1378), close to the bus station at 60 Jalan Tengku Arif Bendahara, is a typical Chinese hotel with spartan rooms for RM15. The *Deyza Hotel* (☎ 09-422 3690) next door is similar. A better choice is the *Pekan Rest House* (☎ 09-422 5989), on the corner of the park near the bus station, where large rooms cost RM40. Rooms at all these places have attached bathrooms.

Getting There & Away The bus station is in the centre of town and buses run regularly between Kuantan and Pekan. Bus No 31 leaves approximately every 45 minutes from the local bus station in Kuantan. The taxi station is across the road on the bank of the river. A taxi to or from Kuantan costs RM20 per car.

KUANTAN

About midway up the east coast from Singapore to Kota Bharu, Kuantan is the capital of the state of Pahang, and the start of the east-coast beach strip which extends all the way to Kota Bharu.

Kuantan is a well-organised, bustling city and a major stopover point when you are travelling north, south or across the peninsula. There's little of interest in Kuantan itself, but it's one of the more pleasant east-coast cities and there are a number of places of interest nearby.

Information

The tourist office (☎ 09-513 3026) is by the taxi station, opposite the Kompleks Teruntum, one of Kuantan's new shopping centres and office blocks. The immigration office (☎ 09-514 2155) is in the Wisma Persekutuan on Jalan Gambut.

Hamid Bros Books, on Jalan Mahkota, is a licensed moneychanger and also has some English-language books. The post office, Telekom office and most banks are on Jalan Haji Abdul Aziz (the continuation of Jalan Mahkota), near the huge and soaring Sultan Ahmed I mosque.

The long-distance bus station is about 600m north-west of the central city area. Near the bus station are the Central Market (with lots of food stalls), some cheap hotels and the giant Megamall shopping complex.

Mr Dobi is a laundromat at 128 Jalan Telok Sisek, near the Hotel New Meriah, and charges RM5 for a full-load wash and dry (staff do the work).

Things to See

Take a stroll along the riverbank and watch the activity on the wide **Sungai Kuantan**. From the jetty at the end of Jalan Masjid you can get a ferry across the river for about 50 sen, to the small fishing village of **Kampung Tanjung Lumpur**.

The Kuantan area produces some good **handicrafts**, and there is a batik factory a few kilometres from the town centre on the road to the airport. On Jalan Besar, near the Samudra River View Hotel, there are a number of shops selling local trinkets and craftwork.

Kuantan's major attraction is the beach, **Teluk Chempedak**, about 4km from town. See the Around Kuantan section for details.

Places to Stay

Kuantan has dozens of cheap Chinese hotels and a few upmarket places, but the big international hotels are a few kilometres out of town at Teluk Chempedak.

Places to Stay – Budget

On Jalan Mahkota near the taxi station, the *Min Heng Hotel* (no phone) is the cheapest in town at RM16 for rooms with shared bathroom. It should only be considered as a last resort, as the place is in pretty bad shape. Similar is the *Tong Nam Ah Hotel* (☎ 09-514 4204) on Jalan Besar, where rooms start at RM15.

The *Hotel Baru Raya* (no phone), also near the taxi station, is better with rooms for RM29 with fan and bathroom, or standard/deluxe rooms with air-con for RM39/49. The rooms are clean but the bathrooms are on the dirty side. It's open 24 hours, which is convenient if you arrive on a night bus.

For a room with bathroom, the *New Capital Hotel* (☎ 09-513 5222), 55 Jalan Bukit Ubi, is a good choice. It has clean rooms for RM22 with fan and bathroom, or RM32 with air-con and bathroom.

The *Hotel New Meriah* (☎ 09-525 433) at 142 Jalan Telok Sisek, has large but slightly dingy carpeted rooms with bathroom and occasional hot water for RM35. Rooms with air-con cost RM45.

Not far from the mosque, the *Titi Hotel* (☎ 09-552 8252) has rooms with shower for RM35. The nearby *Hotel Embassy* (no phone) is a less welcoming choice with fan rooms for RM20.

Near the central market are a few good hotels, including The *Hotel Makmur* (☎ 09-514 1363) which has rooms with shared bathroom for RM28 and with bathroom for

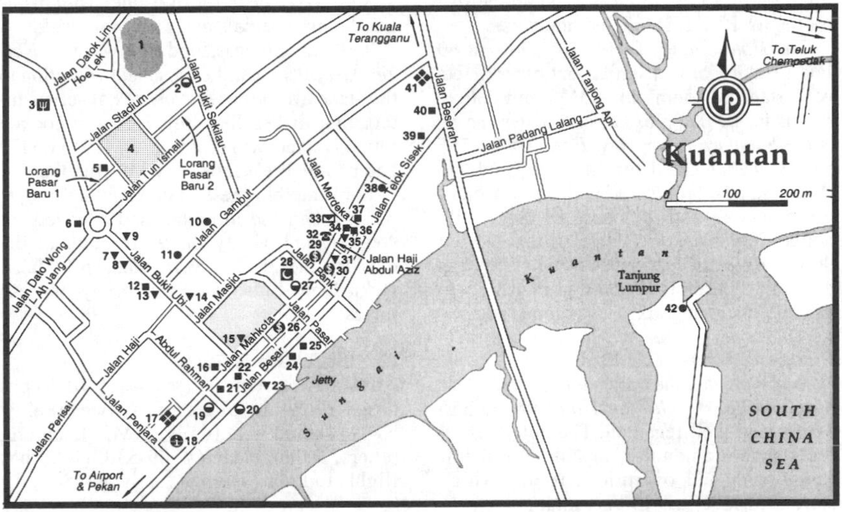

PLACES TO STAY
- 5 Hotel Makmur
- 6 Hotel Pacific
- 12 New Capital Hotel
- 16 Min Heng Hotel
- 21 Hotel Baru Raya
- 22 Tong Nam Ah Hotel
- 24 Samudra River View Hotel
- 25 Hotel Classic
- 34 Suraya Hotel
- 36 Hotel Embassy
- 37 Titi Hotel
- 39 Hotel New Meriah
- 40 MS Garden Hotel

PLACES TO EAT
- 4 Central Market
- 7 Food Stalls
- 8 Restaurant Panvathy
- 9 Restoran Biryani
- 12 Restoran Parvathy
- 13 Food Stalls
- 14 Swan Bakery Cafe
- 15 Food Stalls
- 23 Outdoor Food Stalls
- 31 Restoran Tawakkal
- 35 New Yee Mee Restaurant

OTHER
- 1 Stadium
- 2 Long-Distance Bus Station
- 3 Hindu Temple
- 10 Immigration
- 11 Malaysia Airlines
- 17 Kompleks Teruntum
- 18 Tourist Office
- 19 Taxi Station
- 20 Local Bus Station; Food Stalls
- 26 Moneychanger; Hamid Bros Books
- 27 Local Bus Stop for Northbound Buses
- 28 Mosque Sultan Ahmed I
- 29 Maybank
- 30 Standard Chartered Bank
- 32 Telekom
- 33 Post Office
- 38 Mr Dobi Laundry Service
- 41 Megamall Shopping Centre
- 42 Kampung Tanjung Lumpur

RM35; all have air-con. Most of the rooms have no windows, but the place is fairly new.

Places to Stay – Mid-Range

For three star, fully air-con western-style hotels, there are a few choices. The *Suraya Hotel* (☎ 09-555 4268) is in a busy part of the city, on the corner of Jalan Mahkota and Jalan Merdeka. It has clean standard/deluxe rooms for RM75/85, including taxes.

The *Hotel Pacific* (☎ 09-514 1980) at 60 Jalan Bukit Ubi is a similar but older place, with standard rooms for RM78 and deluxe rooms for RM88, plus taxes. A better choice is the *Samudra River View Hotel* (☎ 09-555 5333), well located by the river on Jalan Besar. Standard rooms, all with air-con, bathroom, phone and TV, cost RM80, while deluxe rooms are RM100, plus taxes. Next door, the *Hotel Classic* (☎ 09-554 4599), has pleasantly decorated rooms from RM65 to RM105, including taxes, also good value.

Places to Stay – Top End

Within Kuantan, the only international-class hotel is the *MS Garden Hotel* (☎ 09-555 4020) near the Megamall. The hotel has all the standard amenities, including a swimming pool, and overpriced rooms which start at RM200 (ask if it is running any promotional deals).

Places to Eat

Kuantan has a good selection of eating places. The small *Muslim food stalls* dotted along the riverbank, across from the Hotel Baru Raya, are a great place to sit and watch the boats pass by. The seafood is particularly good and the prawns are huge, although expensive at RM8 each for the largest ones.

There are more *food stalls* near the central market, with serve-yourself nasi padang places and good Chinese seafood hotpot – select what you want and cook it in the vats of boiling water. Food stalls can also be found on Jalan Bukit Ubi and near the local bus station.

There are indoor food courts in all of Kuantan's shopping centres, most of which have at least one fast-food outlet like *KFC*. The best indoor food court is in the giant Megamall shopping centre on Jalan Tun Ismail, near the long-distance bus station.

There are some good Indian restaurants on Jalan Bukit Ubi, past Jalan Gambut, including the *Restoran Biryani* and the *Restoran Parvathy*. Another good Indian choice is *Restoran Tawakkal* on Jalan Haji Abdul Aziz, near the mosque, which has good daily specials and tasty murtabak.

The best Chinese food in town is at *New Yee Mee*, also near the mosque. In addition to the standard Chinese favourites, it serves interesting dishes like frog legs and cooked turtle. Dinners will cost from RM10 to RM20 and noodle breakfasts for RM5 with tea.

For something resembling a western-style breakfast in the morning, and a variety of western and Malay dishes throughout the day, try the air-con *Swan Bakery* in Jalan Bukit Ubi. It also serves a variety of fresh juices.

Getting There & Away

Air Malaysia Airlines (☎ 09-515 7055) has direct flights to Singapore (twice weekly, RM244) and KL (daily, RM74), among others. Pelangi Air (☎ 09-538 1177) has flights to Pulau Tioman (daily, RM84).

Bus All the bus companies have their offices on the 2nd floor of the huge long-distance bus station on Jalan Stadium. Many operate the same routes, so it's usually simply a question of choosing a departure time that suits you. There is an information office on the 2nd floor of the building near the food court.

Buses to KL (RM12, five hours) leave at least hourly from 7.30 am until 1 am. Buses to Mersing (RM11, three hours), Johor Bahru (RM16, five hours) and Singapore (RM16.50, seven hours) leave between 9 am and 1 pm, and again at 11 pm.

Buses go throughout the day to Kuala Terengganu (RM9, four hours) and Kota Bharu (RM16, six hours), and there are a couple of late-night buses. For Taman Negara, direct buses to Jerantut (RM8.50, three hours) leave between 9 am and 3 pm. Buses to Melaka (RM14, four hours) leave around 8 am and 2 pm. For Penang (RM26, 12 hours) there are two evening departures.

For Cherating, take the No 27 Kemaman bus from the local bus station for RM2.50. The trip takes about one hour.

Car All the major car rental companies have offices in Kuantan.

Avis
(☎ 09-552 3666) 102 Jalan Telok Sisek
Budget
(☎ 09-552 6370) 59 Jalan Haji Abdul Aziz
Hertz
(☎ 09-555 5333) Samudra Riverview Hotel, Jalan Besar
Mayflower
(☎ 09-513 1866) A7348 Jalan Beserah
National
(☎ 09-552 7303) 49 Jalan Telok Sisek

Taxi The long-distance taxi stand is in the same building as the long-distance bus stop. Taxis cost RM5 to Pekan, RM80 to Mersing and RM180 to Johor Bahru. Heading north it's RM30 to Kemaman or Cherating. To Kuala Terengganu it's RM90, or RM140 to Kota Bharu. Across the peninsula it's RM60 to Temerloh, RM80 to Jerantut and RM120 to KL. Note that all the prices listed here are per taxi not per person.

Getting Around

The local bus station is near the river on Jalan Besar. Buses leave from here to such destinations as Pekan, the airport and Teluk Chempedak. Some buses also stop at a stand in front of the mosque on Jalan Mahkota, including those bound for Teluk Chempedak. While some local buses have numbers, most are identified by their final destination.

AROUND KUANTAN

Teluk Chempedak

Teluk Chempedak, Kuantan's main beach, is quite pleasant and there are a number of walking tracks in the park area on the rocky promontory at the northern end of the beach. This was a quiet little place until the early 1970s, but now sports two international-class hotels and a row of bars, clubs and restaurants. It's a popular promenade and meeting place in the evening and approaches the feeling of a European seaside resort. All in all, it makes a pleasant day trip out of Kuantan, but if you're headed to the islands or Cherating anyway, there is little reason to stop.

Places to Stay Teluk Chempedak is an upmarket accommodation alternative to Kuantan. There are no real budget hotels.

In the streets behind the outdoor food stalls, the *Sri Pantai Resort* (☎ 09-568 5250) has decent rooms with fan for RM30, or with air-con for RM60; self-contained, semi-detached apartments cost RM98, and discounts are available in the low season.

Right behind the Hyatt is the drab *Hotel Kuantan* (☎ 09-568 0026), with good fan-cooled rooms for RM44 and air-con standard/deluxe rooms for RM66/77.

The top place in town is the *Hyatt Kuantan* (☎ 09-566 1234), which takes up most of the beachfront. It's got all the amenities you'd expect and a pleasant airy feel to the common areas. Most Hyatt rooms cost from RM320 to RM525. Further down the beach, the former *Samudra Beach Resort* is being rebuilt as another international resort. If the Hyatt doesn't suit you, give it a try.

Places to Eat Apart from the *food stalls* at the end of the beach there's not much in the way of cheap eats in Teluk Chempedak. However, the beachfront restaurants are not as expensive as they look, and the food is generally quite good.

On the foreshore, *Pataya* is a pleasant, open-air restaurant specialising in seafood, though the air-con places on the main road are generally better value.

Also worth checking are *Checkers Pub* and *Country Ranch* across from the Hilton on the road coming into the beach. Both places serve reasonably priced northern Indian cuisine, draught beer and other drinks.

Getting There & Away The No 39 bus from Kuantan takes you to Teluk Chempedak for 60 sen. You can catch it at the local bus station or the more convenient local bus stop for northbound buses on the corner of Jalan Mahkota and Jalan Masjid. You may have to stand closer to Jalan Mahkota and actually wave down the bus, as it doesn't always stop right in front of the stop. A taxi out to Teluk costs RM5.

Beserah

Just 10km north of Kuantan, the small fishing village of Beserah is a Cherating that never really happened. While the beach itself is pleasant, if not a little shallow, the poverty-stricken surroundings and lack of decent accommodation are usually enough to discourage the kind of long stays that Cherating is famous for.

Places to Stay & Eat About the only functioning place to stay in Beserah is *Jaafar's Place* (no phone), a kampung house about 500m off the road on the inland side. A sign points it out, and bus drivers know it. Accommodation costs RM8 a night, or RM15 including all meals. Facilities are very basic, and it's a long walk to the beach. You're probably better off heading to Cherating.

Getting There & Away Buses to Kemaman (No 27), Balok (No 30) and Sungai Karang (No 28) all pass through Beserah. They leave from the main bus station in Kuantan and the fare is 60 sen. Taxis from Kuantan cost RM6.

Coming from the south, Beserah is poorly marked – there is a small sign marked 'Beserah Beach' but you're better off looking out for the Mobil petrol station, from which it's a 20 minute walk to the beach. From the north, look for the large 'Pantai Beserah' sign.

Air Terjun Berkelah (Berkelah Falls)

These falls are about 50km from Kuantan. The final 6km of the trip involves a jungle trek from the main road. The falls come down a hillside in a series of eight cascades. The **Marathandhavar Temple** is the venue for a major Hindu festival in March or April each year.

Getting There & Away Catch a bus to Maran from the main bus station in Kuantan for RM3.35. At Maran, you'll see a bridge by the river. This is where the walk to the falls begins (there is a sign indicating the direction). A taxi to the same spot from Kuantan should cost RM25. The jungle track is overgrown due to lack of use and maintenance. The walk takes about three hours.

Gua Charas (Charas Caves)

Twenty-six kilometres north of Kuantan at Panching, the limestone outcrop containing the Charas (also spelt Charah) caves rises sheer above the surrounding palm plantations. The caves owe their fame to a Thai Buddhist monk who came to meditate here about 50 years ago. There's a monk in residence, and the caretaker's wife can tell you about the caves.

It's a steep climb up an external stairway to the caves' entrance. In the more enclosed cave there's a 9m-long reclining Buddha carved from solid rock, and other Buddhist statuary. Once a year in July, sunlight penetrates the cave and illuminates the head of the reclining Buddha.

Admission is RM1. The caves are lit, but bring a torch to explore the side caverns, or hire one for RM2.

Three kilometres before Panching is a turn-off that leads to the airport and the Pandan waterfalls, 5km from the main road.

Getting There & Away Take the Sungai Lembing bus (No 48) from the main bus station in Kuantan and get off at the small village of Panching. From the bus stop in town it's a hot 4km walk each way, but there's usually someone visiting the caves who will offer you a lift. Traffic is heaviest on Sunday. The alternative is to hire some one in Panching to give you a lift on the back of a motorcycle for around RM2. A taxi from Kuantan to the caves should cost RM25.

Tasik Chini

Turn south off the Temerloh road 56km west of Kuantan, and 12km from the turn-off is Kampung Belimbing, the main access point for Tasik Chini. From here you can hire a boat to cross the Sungai Pahang and go through the jungle up the Sungai Chini to the lotus-covered expanse of Tasik Chini.

The lake is in fact a series of 12 lakes, and around its shores live the Jakun people, an Orang Asli tribe of Melayu Asli origin. The Jakun believe that the spirit of the lake is the serpent Naga Seri Gumum, which translates in the tourist literature as 'Loch Ness monster'.

Although getting to Tasik Chini is not that easy, it's well worth the effort. It's a beautiful area, and you can walk for miles in jungle territory. There is a very low-key resort, or you can stay at the nearby Orang Asli village of Kampung Gumum and use it as a base from which to make jungle treks.

Places to Stay & Eat The *Lake Cini Resort* (☎ 09-456 7897), on the southern shore of the lake, has good cabins with bathroom from RM77 for doubles. Some cabins are also set aside for dormitory accommodation – a bed in a 10 bed cabin costs RM18.50. Outside school holidays you may have a dormitory to yourself.

The restaurant at the resort serves simple food for RM4 to RM6 per dish. Accommodation, food and equipment rental are subject to a 10% service charge.

A much cheaper option is *Rajan Jones Guest House* in the Orang Asli settlement of Kampung Gumum, a two minute boat ride from the resort or a 30 minute walk. Rajan is of Indian descent (making him Indian Jones?), he speaks excellent English and is knowledgeable about the Orang Asli. Accommodation is extremely basic – there's no electricity or running water in the village – but it's a rare opportunity to stay near the jungle and make expeditions into it. The cost is RM15 per person, including dinner and breakfast. Rajan organises overnight jungle treks, canoeing, fishing and night hikes. There's also a chance of seeing a traditional 'healing ceremony', in which the local witch doctor does his stuff. These ceremonies are still practised – they are not just for the tourists' benefit.

Getting There & Away Tasik Chini can be reached by boat from Belimbing or by road from Pekan, but both routes are difficult by public transport.

The tourist office in Kuantan can arrange day trips to Tasik Chini for RM50 per person, but the cheapest tours are from Cherating at RM35 per person (ask at the Travel Post travel agency, among other places).

From Kuantan you can catch a bus to Maran and get off at the Tasik Chini turn-off, from where it's 12km to Kampung Belimbing. You will have to hitch, take a taxi or walk, as bus services to Belimbing no longer operate. Traffic on this road is light.

From Belimbing you can hire a boat to Tasik Chini. The cost is RM60 per boat for a two hour trip, including a tour of the lakes and a visit to an Orang Asli village. The price is the same if you just want to be dropped at the resort or Kampung Gumum. A boat carries four people.

The alternative is to take a bus to Felda Chini, south of the lake, from Kuantan or Pekan. The Mara No 121 buses marked 'Cini' leave Kuantan's bus station five times daily, cost RM5.70 and take two hours. It's 2km from Felda Chini to the palm-oil factory, and a further 11km (although the sign says 8km) from the intersection there to the resort, along a sealed road. Without a car, the only way to get to the resort or Kampung Gumum is by hiring someone with a motorcycle to take you there for about RM5, or by walking or hitching (but there's very little traffic). If you stay at the resort, staff can drop you at Kampung Chini when you leave.

For a group of four, a taxi from Kuantan is another option. The cost is RM60 to the resort or Kampung Gumum. If you want the latter, tell the taxi driver you want to go to the Tasik Chini Orang Asli kampung. A taxi from Kuala Rompin costs RM80.

BESERAH TO CHERATING

There are small resorts along this stretch of coast offering good mid-range to top-end accommodation. The sheltered beaches are quite good, but the water is very shallow when the tide is out.

Places to Stay

The *Gloria Maris Resort* (☎ 09-544 7788) is 9.5km from Kuantan, 1km past Beserah. Chalets on the beach cost from RM98/118 for a standard/deluxe, including breakfast. The rooms are large, clean and close to the beach. Further along, 14km from Kuantan, is the village of Balok and *Le Village* (☎ 09-544 7900), a new, small resort. Good chalets with bathroom and air-con start at RM160, including taxes.

Further out, 16km from Kuantan, is the large *Coral Beach Resort* (☎ 09-544 7544). It is approaching international standard and standard/deluxe rooms cost RM190/220 (internal-facing) and RM230/250 (facing the beach), all including taxes. In Pantai Balok, 17km north of Kuantan, the *Peranginan Tamukami Resort* (☎ 09-583 9090) is a pleasant new resort with tastefully designed suites and a nice swimming pool. Standard rooms start at RM150 and suites are priced from RM220.

CHERATING

Along with Tioman and the Perhentian islands, Cherating is one of the most popular stops on the east coast. A travellers' kampung, complete with budget shacks by the sea, a handful of bars, some good restaurants with banana pancake breakfasts and a reasonable beach with windsurfer breezes, Cherating is as close as the east coast gets to southern Thailand.

Many people visiting Cherating settle down and stay for weeks. While the beach can't compare with the white-sand beaches of the Perhentians, it's the mellow atmosphere of the town that keeps people around. Indeed, this is one of the few places on the east coast where you can party the night away without feeling distinctly guilty. When you do finally wake up, there are several places where you can make your own batik (the most popular of these is Matahari Chalets).

Cherating is a good base from which to explore the surrounding area. You can arrange mini-treks and river trips, and most of the places to stay and the two travel agents on the main road can arrange tours to Gua Charas; Sungai Lembing and Air Terjun Pandan (RM35); Tasik Chini (RM45); and Pulau Ular.

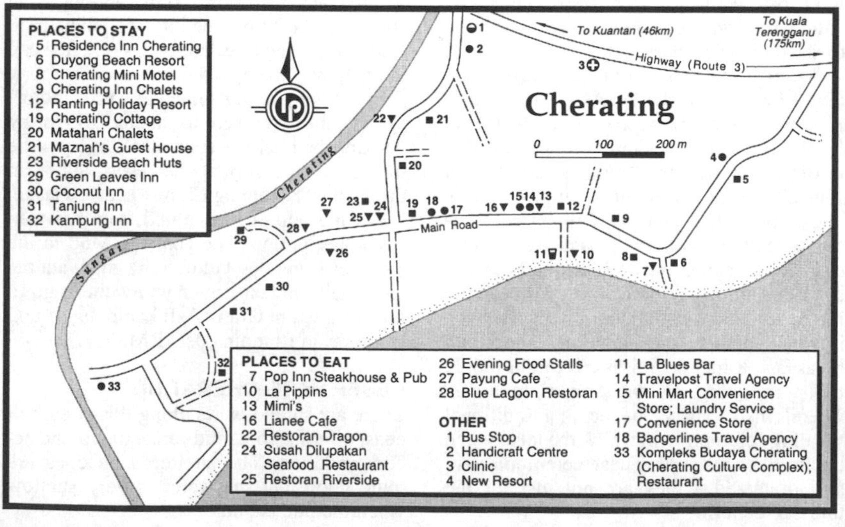

Information

There's no bank in Cherating, but you can change US cash at La Pippins restaurant on the beach. A few other places, including the two travel agents on the main road, will change travellers cheques and cash, but the rates are poor. For domestic and international phone calls, there are a few Telekom payphones on the main road. Bicycles and kayaks can be rented at the Payang Cafe and canoes at the Kompleks Budaya Cherating.

Places to Stay

Accommodation ranges from basic A-frame huts, each with a double mattress and light, but no fan, to more comfortable 'chalets' with bathrooms. Most of the A-frame huts cost around RM10 and sleep two people; the chalets range from RM15 to RM50. Most have their own restaurants and you could easily spend a few days in Cherating and not sample them all.

One of the best places for an extended stay is the *Matahari Chalets* (☎ 09-581 9126) on the road between the beachfront and the highway. Large rooms with balcony, fridge (yes, fridge), mosquito net and fan are a bargain at RM20. There's a common room with TV and a kitchen for guests' use. It's a very relaxed place and you can do batik courses here.

Between Matahari's and the highway, *Maznah's Guest House* (no phone) is a good choice for those on a tight budget. Simple A-frames cost RM12, including breakfast and a home-cooked Malaysian dinner. It's a little run down and you really have to watch your step traversing the rickety plankwalk which connects the buildings.

At the western end of the main road are three similar-looking places to consider. The *Coconut Inn* is too run-down to merit a recommendation. Next door is the attractive *Tanjung Inn* (☎ 09-581 9081). Its chalets in a pleasant lawn area cost RM45 with bathroom and fan; there are also family chalets for RM65. The third place is the *Kampung Inn* (☎ 09-581 9344), set in a pretty coconut grove, which has ageing chalets for RM20/25 a standard/deluxe.

One of the most interesting places in Cherating is the *Green Leaves Inn* (☎ 010-337 8242). Right on the banks of the river, and set among low trees, the place invites lengthy stays. The few chalets here are very small and the facilities quite basic, but the cool atmosphere and friendly owner make up for any shortcomings.

On the same side of the road is the *Payung Cafe* (☎ 012-303 3911), also on the riverbank. There are a few chalets around a large lawn; those on the river cost RM20 and those nearer the road cost RM15. Its restaurant is quite good.

Next along on the same side of the road is the *Riverside Beach Huts* (☎ 09-589 1128), an uninspiring place with chalets with fan for RM35, and with air-con for RM50.

The *Cherating Cottage* (☎ 09-581 9273) has simple rooms with fan and bathroom for RM20, and nicer air-con rooms with TV and hot water for RM50.

Towards the eastern end of the main road is the *Ranting Holiday Resort* (☎ 09-581 9068). This place is one of the better mid-budget choices with clean cottages with fan and bathroom for RM40, and with air-con for RM60. The restaurant here is decent.

Less appealing are the *Cherating Inn Chalets* near a garbage dump. Across the road the *Cherating Mini Motel* (☎ 09-581 9335) has grotty chalets. The mid-range *Duyong Beach Resort* (☎ 09-581 9189) is the last place on the main road. It's a bit of a resort affair, with chalets ranging from RM70 to RM100; prices go up 10% on weekends and holidays. The caged monkeys out the front are a deterrent to guests.

Continuing up the road toward the high way, you come to the giant *Residence Inn Cherating* (☎ 09-581 9333), which has clean, resort-style rooms starting at RM160. It's probably too sterile for most travellers.

Places to Eat

Most guesthouses have their own restaurants, but there are also a few other restaurants in Cherating, all within easy walking distance of each other. *Mimi's* does good banana roti canai for breakfast and gets good reviews for lunch and dinner as well. The *Payung Cafe* is a good spot for dinner, offering two daily specials, one Malay and one western style, for RM10 each.

The new *Kompleks Budaya Cherating* complex has a restaurant with an extensive western and Malay menu, including some vegetarian dishes. The dining area is built over the river and the views are very pleasant. This is also a decent spot for breakfast. Prices here are a little higher than at some of the other places in town.

For Chinese and Malay food, there are the *Lianee Cafe*, the *Restoran Riverside*, the *Blue Lagoon Restoran* and the *Susah Dilupakan* restaurants on the beach road, all of which offer similar dishes and prices. A similar place is the *Restoran Dragon* near Maznah's Guest House.

The *Pop Inn Steakhouse and Pub* does good steaks for around RM25 and has a few other dishes on the menu. Down by the beach, *La Pippins* does good western-style breakfasts and dinners, as well as satay. Located next to La Blues bar, this is a great spot for a late snack; it's open until 3 am.

Entertainment

Most of the Chinese-run restaurants in town serve beer. There are also a few bars scattered around the town, the most popular of which are *The Pop Inn Steakhouse and Pub* and *La Blues Bar*. The Pop Inn often has live music and is a good spot to start your evening as it also serves food. La Blues Bar, pleasantly located right on the beach, is a good place to rage until the wee hours of the morning. It starts to get crowded around midnight, and peaks around 2 am. Since La Blues Bar and the Pop Inn are nearby, it's possible to wander back and forth as the mood strikes you.

Getting There & Away

To get to Cherating, catch a bus marked 'Kemaman' from the long-distance bus station in Kuantan. Buses leave every half hour, the fare is RM1.50 and the journey takes one hour. When coming from the north, any bus going to Kuantan will drop you on the main road. From Cherating to Kuantan, wave down a bus to Kuantan from the bus stop on the highway (Route No 3).

Central Pahang

JERANTUT

The small town of Jerantut is the gateway to Taman Negara National Park. Most visitors to the park spend at least one night here, but the town has no real attractions.

Information

Nusa Camp (☎ 09-266 2369) has an office at the bus station (open from 8 am to 6 pm), for bookings at their Taman Negara camp. It also changes travellers cheques and cash, but banks have better rates (try Bank Bumiputra near the park). The travel agent at the train station has general information and can take bookings for Taman Negara Resort.

You can stock up on supplies at the Jaya Emporium or at the QMA Emporium, both on Jalan Besar; the former has a better selection. Fruit stalls line the road opposite the Jaya Emporium.

There is a good Chinese laundry on the main road a few doors north of the Hotel Jerantut. It provides quick service for the inevitably stinking trekkers coming out of Taman Negara.

Places to Stay

Jerantut has plenty of hotels, but the popular places can get very busy during the peak periods for visiting Taman Negara.

A couple of new guesthouses have sprung up in Jerantut. Perhaps the friendliest and most atmospheric is the small *Chong Heng Hotel Travellers Inn* (☎ 09-266 3693) on Jalan Besar. There are singles and doubles for RM10 with fan, wash basin and a shared bathroom, and similar triples for RM15. The place is furnished with antiques, and there are stacks of magazines on hand. The owner, Chan Mun Onn, is also very knowledgeable about the town and the park.

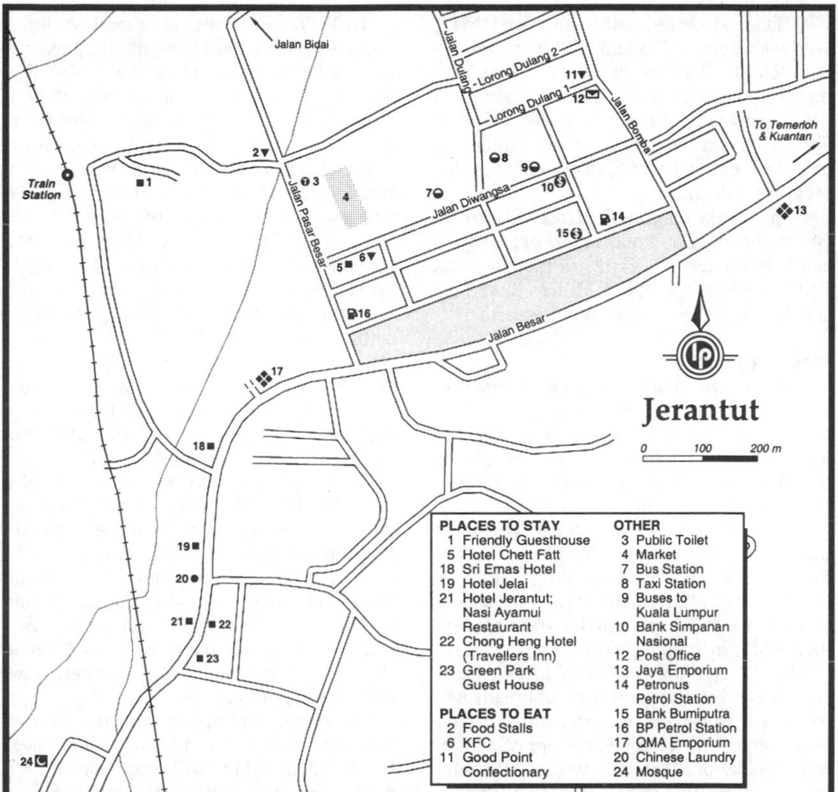

The small, friendly *Green Park Guest House* (☎ 09-266 3884) on Jalan Besar has four-bed dorms for RM8 and singles/doubles/triples for RM12/20/27. Accommodation is simple, but snacks are served and the owner, a former guide in Taman Negara, is an excellent source of information, and arranges transport to the park.

The less-inspiring *Friendly Guesthouse* (no phone) opposite the train station has large dorms for RM8, doubles and triples with fan and shared bathroom for RM15, and with attached bathroom for RM20. The rooms upstairs are much nicer than those downstairs.

The cheapest hotels can be found on Jalan Besar, south of the train station. The best of the bunch is the clean, friendly *Hotel Jelai* (☎ 09-266 7412), with air-con rooms with bathroom for RM30, and similar triples for RM40. If you have a big group, its RM60 quad rooms can sleep up to eight people.

Also on Jalan Besar, the *Hotel Jerantut* has squalid rooms. Up the street, the *Sri Emas Hotel* (☎ 09-266 4499) has grotty common areas and overpriced rooms. Rooms with fan and shared bathroom cost RM15, with bathroom RM25 and with bath and air-con RM38. The owner, Steven, gives a nightly talk about the park and operates a daily minivan all the way to Kuala Tahan in Taman Negara and the jetty in Tembeling (see the Getting There & Away entry in this section for details).

Opposite the market, the *Hotel Chett Fatt* (☎ 09-266 5805) is a reasonable place if you can't be bothered walking further. It costs RM15 for a fan room, or RM20 to RM28 for standard to deluxe rooms with air-con.

Places to Eat

The *food-stall centre* between the market and train station is surprisingly good, offering Thai dishes and seafood as well as the usual favourites. Cheap *coffee shops* can be found along Jalan Besar and in the building blocks across from the bus station.

Fast-food fans can try the *KFC* near the bus station. For a much healthier chicken dish, head to the *Nasi Ayamui* restaurant, in the Hotel Jerantut, on Jalan Besar for a tasty plate of Chinese-style chicken-rice for less than RM5, including a drink.

The closest thing you'll find to a western-style breakfast is the selection of breads and pastries at the *Good Point Confectionary* near the post office. This is more of a take-away place, but there are two small tables and a cooler filled with a variety of drinks.

For more upmarket fare, particularly good Chinese food, you'll have to hike, or take a taxi to the Chinatown area on Jalan Besar in the direction of Temerloh. Here, you'll find several large *Chinese restaurants* where good meals can be had for around RM15 per head.

Getting There & Away

Train Jerantut is on the Tumpat-Gemas railway line. The daily express train to Singapore (seven hours) leaves at 1.30 am and arrives in Singapore at 8.10 am. A local train leaves at 3.50 pm for Gemas, where you can catch another train to Singapore (nine hours in total). Express fare to Singapore is RM19 and regular fare is RM15.

To Wakaf Baharu (the nearest station to Kota Bharu on the Tumpat line) express trains take six hours and leave at 1.50 or 3.30 am; otherwise a local train leaves at 11.15 am and takes about 11 hours. All northbound trains go via Kuala Lipis and Gua Musang, and a Gua Musang-only train leaves at 4.15 pm. Express fare to Wakaf Baharu is RM17 and regular fare is RM12.60.

Note that the National Rail Service (KTM) schedule changes every six months, so it's a good idea to double-check departure times with the owner of your guesthouse before setting out.

Bus & Taxi The bus and taxi stations are in the centre of town. Buses to KL leave from the ticket offices on the other side of the taxi station from the main bus station.

At present two companies operate buses to KL's Pekeliling bus station (RM9, 3½ hours) via Temerloh. The last bus leaves around 6 pm, but schedules vary. If you miss the bus to KL, buses go every hour to Temerloh (RM3, one hour), from where there are more connections to KL and other destinations.

Two companies have buses to Kuantan (RM8.50, three hours), with three departures daily until 2.30 pm.

The buses coming through from KL continue to Kuala Lipis; otherwise first take a bus to Benta (RM3.30, hourly from 7 am to 6 pm), and then another to Kuala Lipis.

Taxis cost RM4 to Kuala Tembeling, RM6 to Temerloh, RM20 to KL and RM16 to Kuantan (per person).

Kuala Tembeling & Taman Negara Buses to Kuala Tembeling (RM3, 45 minutes), for Taman Negara, leave at 7.15 and 10 am, and 1.30 and 3.45 pm. Be warned that schedules are unreliable and the buses sometimes do not arrive in time to catch boat departures to the park. From the jetty, buses to Jerantut come by at around 12.30 and 4 pm, but don't count on it.

The best bet is to take a taxi between Jerantut and Kuala Tembeling. A whole taxi costs RM16, but chances of finding other passengers to share are good. If you can muster a full complement of four passengers, then this is the way to go, as it costs only RM1 more per person than the bus.

The Sri Emas Hotel and the Green Park Guest House arrange minibuses to Kuala Tembeling for RM4 per person. They can also arrange transport by road all the way to Kuala Tahan for RM23 per person. The minibuses depart at 8.10 am to both destinations from the respective hotels. Most visitors prefer to take the scenic river trip to the park from Tembeling, but if you're pressed for time, you can go one way by boat and one way by minibus or taxi.

Lastly, beware of touts at the train and bus stations who tell you that there are no boats running from Tembeling to the park; they're only trying to get you to take their *very expensive* alternatives.

TAMAN NEGARA NATIONAL PARK

Peninsular Malaysia's great national park covers 4343 sq km and sprawls across the states of Pahang, Kelantan and Terengganu. The part of the park most visited is in Pahang.

Taman Negara is billed, perhaps wrongly, as a wildlife park. Certainly this magnificent wilderness area is a haven for endangered species such as elephants, tigers, leopards and rhinos, but numbers are low and sightings of anything more exotic than snakes, lizards, monkeys, small deer and perhaps tapir, are rare. The birdlife is prolific, however, and chances are you'll see more insects – many at extremely close quarters – than you've ever seen in your life.

Taman Negara is not wide open savannah as in African game parks, and the jungle is so dense that you could pass within metres of an animal and never know it. Chances of spotting wildlife are greatest if you do an extended trek away from the heavily trafficked park HQ, but sightings are never guaranteed.

For this reason, many travellers come away disappointed, but the greatest reward of a visit to Taman Negara is simply the chance to get out into one of the most pristine primary rainforests still existing in the world. The jungle here is claimed to be the oldest in the world, having existed largely as is for the past 130 million years. None of the ice ages affected this part of the world, and it has also been free of volcanic activity and other geological upheavals.

The 60km boat trip from Kuala Tembeling to Kuala Tahan (park HQ) takes two to three hours, depending on the level of the river. You reach the park boundary near Kuala Atok, 35km from Kuala Tembeling.

Along the river, you'll see several Orang Asli kampungs, domestic water buffalo and the local fishing people. You might also see monkeys, otters, kingfishers and hornbills from the boat. It's a beautiful journey.

The best time to visit the park is in the dry season between February and September, though the park is now open during the rainy season, when it doesn't always rain, and the number of visitors drops dramatically. The peak season for visitors is from April to August.

Entrance to the park costs RM1, a camera permit is RM5 and a fishing licence costs RM10. You get these at the office at the Kuala Tembeling jetty. If you are driving, there's a car park at the jetty which charges RM5 per day.

Orientation & Information

The park HQ and the privately run Taman Negara Resort are at Kuala Tahan. There is an information counter at the resort's reception area capable of dealing with most queries regarding the park. The Wildlife Department is right around the corner from the reception area, and you must register with it before heading off into the park, or to other park accommodation outside the resort. Both the Wildlife Department and the resort have maps of the park which are OK for casual rambling but inadequate for any serious exploration. Unfortunately, outside the National Survey Department in Kuala Lumpur, you won't find anything better.

Facilities at Kuala Tahan include chalets, a hostel, campground, restaurant, cafeteria, and a shop selling a range of tinned foods, toiletries, batteries and snacks – all at inflated

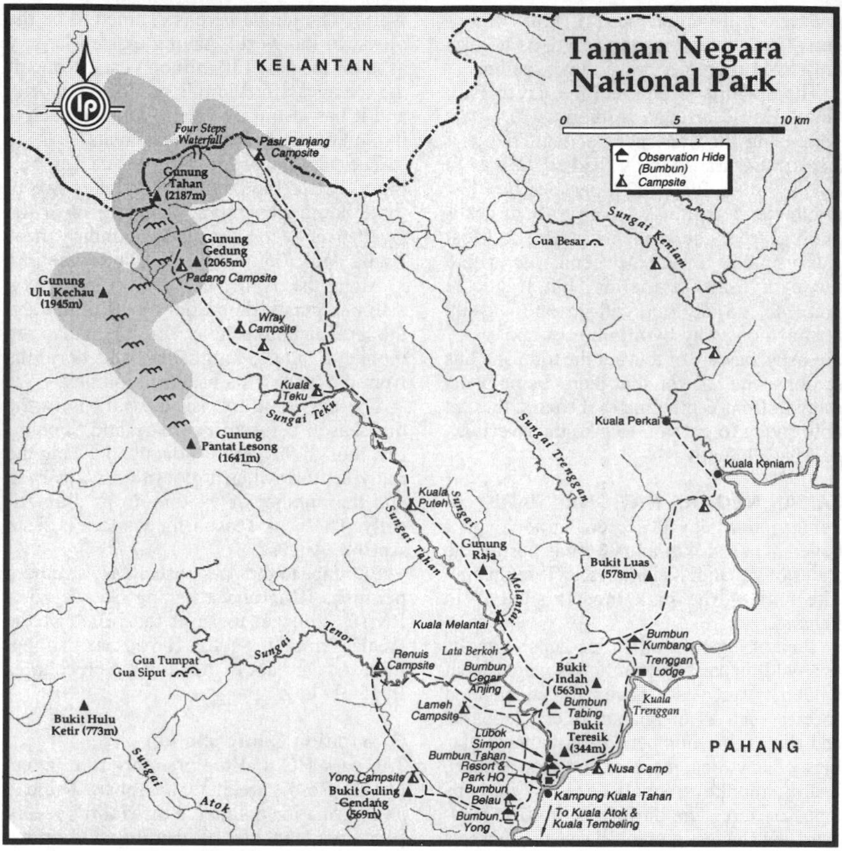

prices (stock up in Jerantut before heading to the park). Camping, hiking and fishing gear can be hired from the campground office past the shop.

Every night at 8.45 pm a free video presentation is held in the Interpretive Centre near the cafeteria. Boats or a guide for trekking can be arranged at the Wildlife Department office or at the resort, which also offers activities such as a night jungle walk (RM15), cave trip (RM35), rapids shooting (RM25) and a picnic trip to Lata Berkoh rapids (RM120 for four people). Guides cost RM100 per day, whether hired at the resort or through the Wildlife Department (one guide can lead up to 12 people). At the resort you can also change money (lousy rate) and make phone calls (expensive).

Staying in the village of Kuala Tahan, directly across the Sungai Tembeling from park HQ, is a good option for those who don't want to pay resort prices. In the village there are a couple of cheaper shops, cafes moored on the river and a selection of budget accommodation. Access to the park is no problem, just hail a boat at any one of the floating cafes and they'll take you across the river free of charge. The only other places with organised accommodation (other than the hides, see the following entry) are Nusa Camp, about 15 minutes by boat up the Sungai Tembeling from the park HQ, and lodges at Kuala Trenggan, Kuala Keniam and Kuala Perkai.

Planning Although everyday clothes are quite suitable around Kuala Tahan, be well prepared if heading further afield. Lightweight cotton clothing is ideal. Loose-fitting, long trousers are better than shorts and protect legs against scratches and insect bites. Whatever you wear, you'll soon be drenched in sweat and covered in mud. Take a water bottle, even on short walks, and on longer walks take water purifying tablets to sterilise stream water. See the basic rules on water purifying in the Health section in the Malaysia Facts for the Visitor chapter for details.

Good boots are essential. Lightweight, canvas jungle boots cost RM2.50 per day from the campground office and lace up high to help keep out leeches. Sleeping bags, tents, cooking gear and torches (flashlights) can also be hired for trekking or overnighting in a hide.

River travel in the early morning hours can be surprisingly cold. Mosquitoes can be annoying, but you can buy repellent at the park shop.

Leeches are generally not a major problem, although they can be a nuisance after heavy rain. There are many ways to keep these little blood-suckers at bay – mosquito repellent, tobacco, salt, toothpaste and soap can all be used, with varying degrees of success. A liberal coating of insect spray over shoes and socks works best. Leech-proof socks are also a good idea.

The best book about Taman Negara is John Briggs' *Parks of Malaysia*. This book contains some good trail maps and route descriptions but it's hard to find – check with the bigger bookstores in Kuala Lumpur. (See the books section in the Malaysia Facts for the Visitor chapter for other relevant titles.)

Hides & Salt Licks

Taman Negara has several readily accessible hides *(bumbun)*, many close to Kuala Tahan and Kuala Trenggan. All hides are built overlooking salt licks and grassy clearings, which attract feeding nocturnal animals. There's a chance of spotting tapir, wild boar or deer, but sightings of elephant and other large game are extremely rare. Your chances of seeing wildlife will increase if you head for the hides furthest away from the park's headquarters.

If you're staying overnight, you need to take your food and a sleeping bag. Hides are very rustic and have pit toilets. They cost RM5 per person per night and sleep seven or eight people. It pays to book at the Wildlife Department the day before. Tabing and Kumbang are the most popular hides, and these offer the best chances of seeing wildlife.

Even if you're not lucky enough to see any wildlife, the fantastic sounds of the jungle are well worth the time and effort taken to reach the hides. The 'symphony' is best at dusk and dawn.

A powerful torch (flashlight) is necessary to see any animals that wander into the salt-lick area. It's best to arrange shifts where one person stays awake, searching the clearing with a torch every 10 to 15 minutes, while everyone else sleeps until it's their turn to take over.

Rats can be a problem at some of the hides. They search for food during the night and have been known to move whole bottles of cooking oil (one of their favourite treats) from hides to their nests. Either hang food high out of reach, or, as one traveller suggested, leave some in the centre of the floor so you can see them – some of the rats are gigantic.

Bumbun Tahan This is an artificial salt lick less than five minutes walk from the reception building. It's a clearing which has been planted with pasture grass and there's a waterhole nearby. This close to the resort, there's little chance of seeing any animals apart from monkeys.

Bumbun Belau & Bumbun Yong These hides on the Sungai Yong sleep eight people and have water nearby. It takes about 1½ hours to walk to Bumbun Belau from the park HQ, and you can visit Gua Telinga along the way (see the Short Walks from Kuala Tahan entry). From Belau it's less than half an hour to Bumbun Yong. Both can also be reached by the riverboat service (RM40 per four person boat).

Bumbun Tabing The hide at this natural salt lick is about a one hour walk from Kuala Tahan, and is equipped with a toilet and *tempat mandi* (bathing area). Nearby, there's a river with fairly clean water (though it should be boiled before drinking). Going by boat costs RM45 per four person boat.

Bumbun Kumbang You can either walk to Bumbun Kumbang (about seven hours from Kuala Tahan) or take the riverboat service up the Sungai Tembeling to Kuala Trenggan. The boat journey from Kuala Tahan takes about 35 minutes, and then it's a 45 minute walk to the hide. The animals seen there most commonly are tapir, rats, monkeys and gibbons, but the odd elephant has also been spotted.

Bumbun Cegar Anjing Once an airstrip, this is now an artificial salt lick, established to attract wild cattle and deer. A clear river runs a few metres from the hide. Bumbun Cegar Anjing is 1½ hours walk from Kuala Tahan, but after rains it may only be accessible by boat. Going by boat costs RM45 per four person boat.

Mountains & Walks

The major activity at Taman Negara is walking through the magnificent jungle. There's a wide variety of walking and trekking possibilities – from an hour's stroll to nine arduous days of up and down 2187m Gunung Tahan.

The trails around the park HQ allow quick access to the jungle but are heavily trafficked. However, relatively few visitors venture far beyond the HQ, and the longer walks are far less trammelled. A long day-walk will take you away from the madding crowd. Getting well away from it all requires a few days trekking and/or expensive trips upriver by boat.

Short Walks from Kuala Tahan Trails around park HQ are easy to follow. They are signposted and have approximate walking times marked clearly along the way. If you're interested in birdlife, it's best to start walking before 8 am.

Heading out past the chalets and cafeteria, the Bukit Indah trail leads along the Sungai Tembeling to the **Canopy Walkway**, suspended 25m above the ground between massive trees and allowing closer inspection of the higher reaches of the forest. It's open from 11 am to 2.45 pm every day, except Friday when hours are from 9 am to noon. Entry is RM3/5 children/adults.

From behind the canopy walkway a trail leads to **Bukit Teresik**, from the top of which are fine views across the forest. The trail is steep and slippery in parts but quite easily negotiated and takes about an hour up and back. You can descend back along this trail to the resort or, near the Canopy Walkway, a branch trail leads across to **Lubok Simpon**, a swimming area on the Sungai Tahan. From here it is an easy stroll back to park HQ. The entire loop can easily be done in three hours.

Past the Canopy Walkway, another branch off the main trail leads to **Bukit Indah**, another steep but rewarding hill with fine views across the forest and the rapids in the Sungai Tembeling.

The well-marked main trail along the bank of the Sungai Tembeling leads 9km to **Kuala Trenggan**. This is a popular trail for those heading to the Bumbun Kumbang hide. You need to set out early and allow five hours. Though generally flat, it traverses a few small hills before reaching the Sungai Trenggan, where Trenggan Lodge lies on the other side. From the lodge boats go back to Nusa Camp and Kuala Tahan, or it's a further 2km walk to **Bumbun Kumbang**. An alternative, longer trail leads inland, back across the

The Future of Taman Negara

First established as a preservation area in 1937, Taman Negara is Malaysia's oldest and most prestigious national park. However, the largest protected area of primary rainforest on the peninsula is coming under increasing scrutiny. Promoted internationally as a wildlife haven and *the* place to experience the jungle in Malaysia, many doubt that the park can withstand the onslaught.

Since the park accommodation was privatised in 1991 and facilities upgraded, visitor numbers have more than doubled to over 40,000 per year. The effects are very noticeable. Where large animals once roamed right up to park HQ, sightings are now rare and the effective animal habitat area of the park has decreased. Trails around park HQ are up to 4m wide and suffer from erosion due to the number of walkers.

With all the increased traffic putting strains on the park, there has been much talk of how to best preserve Taman Negara and cater to increasing visitor interest.

The uneasy mix of privatisation and government control has been blamed for many of the problems, but it is only one of many factors affecting Taman Negara. Improved facilities and easier access have attracted many more visitors, but only a small percentage venture far beyond park HQ or Sungai Tembeling.

The boom in visitors is not all bad news though, as the resort also provides necessary local employment; the increased wealth from tourism, along with stiff government penalties, has helped eliminate poaching by villagers.

Poachers, attracted by the illicit trade in rare species and the high price of ivory and tiger bones, enter the park from the north. Poaching is largely blamed on Thais, but policing is difficult and few poachers are caught. The Orang Asli who live within the park are also allowed to hunt and continue their traditional nomadic lifestyle, but their impact is relatively low.

Lack of government funding and understaffing means that the more remote parts of the park are largely beyond the control of the Wildlife Department. Taman Negara is home to perhaps 600 elephants and a high percentage of Malaysia's estimated 300 tigers, which are increasingly being pushed towards the Kelantan and Terengganu borders, but no one really knows because there is little or no monitoring of wildlife numbers or movement in the park.

Problems not only exist within the park but also outside it. Once animals would roam beyond the park boundaries into neighbouring districts, but increasing settlement along the park boundaries is eliminating this buffer zone, driving the animals further into the interior.

Solutions to the park's problems are not easy to find, and even harder to implement. At a recent conference, one suggestion was to completely privatise the park, though it was probably put forward to highlight the problems facing the Wildlife Department and spur the government to allocate more resources. Restricting access, by introducing quotas or raising prices, also seems unpalatable. Taman Negara is one of Malaysia's major tourist attractions. Not only does it provide foreign income but it is an important educational resource for Malaysians, increasingly aware of the ecology and natural beauty of their own wilderness areas.

Sungai Trenggan from Bumbun Kumbang to the campsite at Lubok Lesong on the Sungai Tahan, and then back to park HQ. This trail is flat most of the way and crosses many small streams. Count on six hours from the hide. Check with park HQ for river levels – the Sungai Trenggan can only be forded when levels are low.

Gua Telinga is a cave south-west of the park HQ, and it takes about 1½ hours to walk there, after first crossing the Sungai Tahan by sampan. There is a stream through the cave and a rope to guide you for the 80m (bring a torch). It's a strenuous half-hour walk – and crawl – through the cave, and there's plenty of bat droppings which can't be avoided. You can either return to the main path through the cave, or take the path around the rocky outcrop at the far end of the cave. Once back at the main path, it's a further 15 minutes walk to the Bumbun Belau hide, where you can spend the night, or walk directly back to Kuala Tahan.

Heading north through the campground at Kuala Tahan, the trail leads all the way to Gunung Tahan, but you can do an easy day walk to **Lata Berkoh**, the cascading rapids on the Sungai Tahan. The trail passes Lubok Simpon swimming hole and Bumbun Tabing, 1¼ hours from Kuala Tahan. About 15 minutes further is the turn-off to Lata Berkoh. There is one river crossing before you reach the falls which can be treacherous if the water is high. You may be able to hitch a ride back on one of the boats which stop just below the falls, but don't count on it.

Short Walks from Nusa Camp If you are staying at Nusa Camp there are a couple of interesting walks in the vicinity, outside the park. **Air Terjun Abai** is only an hour's walk along a clear trail, and it's a great spot for a swim.

Gunung Warisan is a small peak devoid of trees a couple of hours walk from the camp. It's an excellent walk in the very early morning, but it gets hot in the afternoon as there is no shade.

Longer Treks The shortest of the longer treks is **Rentis Tenor** (Tenor Trail), which takes three days from Kuala Tahan. It's quite popular, but the trail is not always clear and a guide is needed. The first day involves getting a boat across the Sungai Tahan at park HQ, and then taking the trail to Gua Telinga and beyond for about seven hours, to Yong campsite. The second day is a six hour walk to the Renuis campsite. On the third day you have to cross the Sungai Tahan (up to waist deep) to get back to Kuala Tahan. It's about a six hour walk. Or you can stop for another night at the Lameh campsite, about half way.

Another popular walk is the trail from Kuala Trenggan to **Kuala Keniam**. It is normally done by chartering a boat to Kuala Keniam and then walking back to Kuala Trenggan. Taking at least six hours, the trail is quite taxing and hilly in parts, and passes a series of limestone caves. This walk can be combined with one of the Kuala Tahan-Kuala Trenggan trails to form a two day trip, overnighting in the Trenggan Lodge or Bumbun Kumbang. It is also possible to walk from Kuala Keniam to the lodge at Kuala Perkai, an easy two hour walk.

The trek for the really adventurous is the ascent of **Gunung Tahan** (2187m, the highest peak in Peninsular Malaysia), 55km from park HQ. It takes nine days at a steady pace, although it can be done in seven. A guide is compulsory and the Taman Negara Resort organises trips for eight people costing RM638, or RM680 for 12 people. This trek is certainly no picnic, but those who do it say it is well worth the effort. Guides and equipment can be arranged at park HQ, although it is generally better to organise this trek in advance, so you don't have to hang around park HQ for a couple of days, which is often necessary. There are no shelters along the way, so you have to be fully equipped. For camping near the summit of Tahan you'll need a lightweight sleeping bag, blanket or tracksuit to sleep in.

Fishing

Anglers will find the park a real paradise. Fish found in the park rivers include the superb fighting fish known in India as the mahseer but here as the kelasa.

Popular fishing rivers include Sungai Tahan, Sungai Keniam (above Kuala Trenggan) and the remote Sungai Sepia. The best fishing months are February, March, July and August. A fishing permit costs RM10, and hiring a rod costs RM5 per day.

Boat Trips

The easiest and least expensive way to get around the park by river is the riverbus service. There are scheduled departures to Nusa Camp, Bumbun Belau, Bumbun Yong, Kuala Trenggan and Kuala Keniam (see Getting Around later in this section for details). Otherwise boats can be chartered from park HQ or Kuala Tahan village.

Boat charter can be very expensive unless you organise a group. Book a boat at park HQ at least the day before and the staff may be able to combine individuals. Boat trips to Lata Berkoh rapids, Kuala Trenggan and Kuala Keniam are all popular and can be combined with short or long walks. Prices for four/10 seater boats include:

Kuala Keniam	RM150/180
Kuala Perkai	RM190
Kuala Trenggan	RM80/120
Lata Berkoh	RM80

Places to Stay & Eat

Kuala Tahan All accommodation at park HQ is operated by the privately run *Taman Negara Resort* (☎ 09-266 3500; fax 09-266 1500). Bookings can also be made through its Kuala Lumpur Sales Office (☎ 03-245 5585) on the 2nd floor of the Hotel Istana, 73 Jalan Raja Chulan. A 15% tax and service charge is added to all the rates quoted here.

You can camp at park HQ for RM2 per person per night. Two/four person tents can be hired for RM8/14. Other camp sites with minimal facilities are scattered throughout Taman Negara.

The resort's hostel has nine fairly clean and comfortable rooms, each with four bunk beds, overhead fans and personal lockers. Men and women share the dormitory rooms, but there are separate toilets and showers. The hostel costs RM35 per person, including breakfast.

Rooms in the brick guesthouse, the old park accommodation centre, cost RM125 for large rooms with air-con, hot water and slightly grotty bathrooms. More attractive and luxurious wooden chalets, 85 in all, cost RM175, or RM260 for larger chalet suites. Top of the range are the two-bedroom VIP bungalows for RM520.

The *Teresek Cafeteria* at the resort serves fried rice, noodles, spaghetti and the like for around RM5. The *Tahan Restaurant* has surprisingly high standards of food and service out here in the jungle. Count on around RM15 for breakfast, RM20 for lunch and at least RM30 for dinner.

Kampung Kuala Tahan The village of Kuala Tahan, directly across the river from park HQ, is slightly less convenient but much cheaper for accommodation and food. Crossing the river is easy; sampans go on demand throughout the day and evening, and are free if you eat at the restaurants or stay in the village.

First on the right as you climb the steps away from the river is the *Tembeling River Hostel & Chalets* (no phone), where a bed in the hostel costs RM12, two person chalets cost RM35 with a fan and shared bathroom, and three person chalets cost RM60 with fan and bathroom. All beds have nets and are fairly clean, and there's a good view over the river.

First on the left as you climb the steps is the *Liana Hostel* (no phone), which has a barracks-like but clean hostel with beds for RM10 each. There are fans in the rooms but no insect nets.

Fifty metres to the right from the top of the steps, the *Ekoton Chalets* (no phone) is a good mid-budget choice, with clean air-con chalets for RM80. It also has a decent dorm with beds for RM10, with a fan and fridge.

In the middle of the village, the *Agoh Chalets* (☎ 010-988 0049) are a less inviting choice with small chalets with fan and bathroom for RM30. They also have a dorm with beds for RM10 each.

Beyond Agoh Chalets, the *Teresek View Village* (☎ 09-266 3065) has large dorm beds for RM10, small A-frame huts for RM30, and newish, good-value chalets with fan and bathroom for RM50. It also has some large semi-detached triples for RM60 with fan and bath (avoid these as they stink of sewage). This is the closest thing to a tourist resort in the village; it also has a mini-mart and large restaurant overlooking the river.

Floating barge restaurants line the sandbar (more a rockbar) opposite park HQ, all selling basic noodle and rice meals for as little as RM3. The *Restaurant Terapong* is one of the most popular with a slightly more varied menu, and the *Family* and *Ria* restaurants are also good places to dine over the river. Some of these restaurants will prepare a fish dinner with fresh river fish if you order early in the day. The Family restaurant will also arrange some of the same activities as the resort for reduced prices.

Nusa Camp Quieter and away from park HQ, *Nusa Camp* is 15 minutes up the Sungai Tembeling from Kuala Tahan. It's much more of a 'jungle camp' than anything at park HQ. Dorm beds cost RM10 (with no insect nets and a grotty bathroom) and slightly run-down A-frames are RM45. Better value are the clean, spacious double cottages with fan and bathroom for RM60/80 (semi-detached/detached). The restaurant serves good but unexciting food for RM6 for breakfast, RM8 for lunch and RM8.50 for dinner.

Bookings can be made in KL at the Nusa Camp desk at the Malaysia Tourism centre (☎ 03-264 3929, ext 112) on Jalan Ampang, or at its Jerantut office (☎ 09-266 2369) at the bus station. It runs its own boat from Kuala Tembeling, and a riverbus service between Nusa Camp and Kuala Tahan (see Getting Around later in this section).

Kuala Trenggan & Kuala Keniam About 35 minutes upstream from Kuala Tahan at Kuala Trenggan is the quite luxurious *Trenggan Lodge* and further upriver is the *Keniam Lodge*. These are the places to get right away from it all, but they are both run by the resort, so creature comforts are well catered for. Each has a restaurant and 10 rooms with bathroom. Rooms cost RM80.

Kuala Perkai The Wildlife Department has a basic, isolated lodge at Kuala Perkai, two hours walk past Kuala Keniam. It costs RM10 per person, and you must take all bedding and cooking equipment with you. It is popular with fishing enthusiasts. Check for availability at park HQ.

Getting There & Away

The main way to get to Taman Negara is to take a bus or train to Jerantut, the gateway town to the park, then a bus or taxi to Kuala Tembeling. From here two boats per day go to park HQ. It is also now possible to go by road all the way to the village at Kuala Tahan, just across the river from the resort and the park HQ. But to do so is to miss the river trip, which is a big part of the Taman Negara experience.

Bus & Taxi See the Jerantut section, earlier in this chapter, for details of buses and taxis to Kuala Tembeling.

From the resort's office at the Hotel Istana in KL, Reliance Travel has a daily shuttle bus all the way to Kuala Tembeling, leaving at 8 am and costing RM35 (the return journey leaves Kuala Tembeling at 1 pm). Other small operators also offer this service. Most of the travellers' guesthouses in KL can arrange pick up and drop off at Kuala Tembeling for the same price.

Car A rough road now goes all the way from Jerantut to Kuala Tahan village. The road is unsealed much of the way and, though negotiable by car when dry, it is recommended only for 4WD vehicles. The Sri Emas Hotel and the Green Park Guest House (see the Jerantut entry earlier in this chapter) can organise transport to the park this way. Places to stay in Kuala Tahan can arrange a trip out on a local minibus (RM19, two hours) that goes to Jerantut most mornings. Though slightly quicker than the boat, the road is less interesting.

Walking You can walk into the park from Merapoh, at the Pahang/Kuantan border. The trail from Merapoh joins the Gunung Tahan trail, adding another two days to the Gunung Tahan trek. Guides are compulsory and can be hired in Kuala Lipis to take you in, but it is easier to arrange a guide at the park for the walk out. It is also possible to take a boat to the upper reaches of the park and walk out to Terengganu state.

Boat The main entry point into the park is by riverboat from Kuala Tembeling, 18km from Jerantut. Boats leave from the jetty,

CHRIS ROWTHORN

CHRIS ROWTHORN

DAVID ANDREW

RICHARD I'ANSON

GLENN BEANLAND

JOE CUMMINGS

Top: Traditional Malay house, Johor (left); canopy walk at Taman Negara National Park (right).
Centre: Boats are the main form of transport for stilt village residents on the Santubong Peninsula, Sarawak (left); fishing boats greet the sunrise, Marang, Terengganu (right).
Bottom: Pulau Sapi is Tunku Abdul Rahman National Park's most visited island, Sabah (left); the white-sand beaches of Pulau Langkawi make it a popular island resort, Kedah (right).

RICHARD I'ANSON

Fishing boats lie idle during the day at the picturesque village of Marang, Terengganu, Malaysia.

500m west of the turn-off to the small village of Kuala Tembeling.

There are two daily departures, at 9 am and 2 pm (2.30 pm on Friday). Boats are operated by the resort and Nusa Camp, whose boats also stop at park HQ before continuing to Nusa Camp, so you can take either service regardless of where you stay. You can make reservations with the resort's office in KL or the Nusa Camp offices in KL (☎ 03-264 3929) or with its office in Jerantut (☎ 03-266 2369), but bookings are not essential, except perhaps during holiday periods. At Tembeling, the resort has an office up the steps above the jetty, and Nusa Camp has one near the parking area.

It's a 2½ to three hour boat trip from Kuala Tembeling to park HQ at Kuala Tahan, depending on how swiftly the river is flowing. The trip costs RM19 one way. On the return journey boats depart at 9 am and 2 pm and take two to 2½ hours.

Getting Around

Nusa Camp has a riverboat service from Kuala Tahan to Nusa Camp (RM3 for Nusa Camp guests, RM5 for non-guests) at 10 am and 12.30 and 6 pm. In the opposite direction there are departures from Nusa Camp at 8.15 and 11.15 am and 2.15 and 3.45 pm. To Kuala Trenggan, boats from Kuala Tahan go via Nusa Camp and leave at 10 am and 3 pm, and cost RM10 from Kuala Tahan, RM5 from Nusa Camp. The return boats leave Kuala Trenggan at 11 am and 3.30 pm.

Nusa Camp also has a riverboat service from Kuala Tahan to Bumbun Belau and Bumbun Yong at 8.30 am and 5.30 pm (RM5).

The resort has a riverboat service which departs at 8.30 am and 1.30 and 2.15 pm for Kuala Trenggan and Kuala Keniam (RM10, 30 minutes to Trenggan; RM20, one hour to Keniam). In the reverse direction, boats depart from Kuala Keniam for Kuala Tahan at 10.15 am and 3.15 and 4.45 pm, stopping at Kuala Trenggan on the way.

While the riverboat services keep pretty much to schedule during peak periods, in the wet season some services are dropped or stop all together. Ask at the resort or in the village for the latest information on these boats.

The Wildlife Department can help arrange groups for those who want to share the costs of charter boats. They can also be arranged in Kuala Tahan village for the same price.

KUALA LIPIS

At the confluence of the Lipis and Jelai rivers, Kuala Lipis is a small town with a strong colonial past. The centre of town, with fine rows of shophouses down the main street, is the busy Chinese commercial district. Further south on the hilly outskirts, Kuala Lipis has a few reminders from the days when it was the most important town in Pahang.

Kuala Lipis was a gold-mining centre long before the British arrived in 1887, but its heyday dates from 1898 when it became the capital of Pahang. Grand colonial buildings date from this period, and trade increased when the railway came through in 1924.

In 1955 the capital shifted to Kuantan, and Kuala Lipis declined. It is a sleepy town, but new construction and the delights of a shopping mall are signs of new wealth. The long closed gold mines have been reopened with the help of new technology.

Kuala Lipis makes a pleasant enough overnight stop, but the main reason to visit is to make a jungle trek in the nearby Kenong Rimba State Park. Two popular budget hotel operators and two travel agents arrange these treks (see the Kenong Rimba State Park entry later in this chapter for details).

Information

The so-called Tourist Information Centre at the train station is a private travel agent that sells its own trips to Kenong Rimba, but you can get a map of the town and basic queries answered. The post office and a branch of Maybank are conveniently located near the train station.

Things to See

Colonial architecture buffs will appreciate the imposing **District Offices,** on a hill 1km south of the centre of town. The offices overlook the exclusive **Clifford School,** another grand public building that began life as the Anglo-Chinese School in 1913, before it was renamed after Sir Hugh Clifford, the second British Resident of Pahang.

The road next to the school leads up the hill to the **Pahang Club**, a sprawling wooden bungalow with wide, open verandas. With its planters' chairs and hunting trophies, it clings to its colonial club traditions in the face of decay.

The **Rest House** on another hill facing the District Offices is a large, gracious building, once the British Resident's residence. It houses a small museum in the foyer chronicling the town's history.

Places to Stay

Most of the hotels in town are on Jalan Besar (the main street) and Jalan Jelai (the street by the river), both of which are a short walk from the bus and train stations.

On Jalan Besar, on the right as you leave the train station, the *Hotel Tong Kok* (☎ 09-312 1027) has rooms for RM15 with fan and shared bathroom. The reception is in the restaurant downstairs. Down by the river, the *Hotel Jelai* (☎ 09-312 1562), at 44 Jalan Jelai, is a very clean hotel with a variety of rooms from RM18 with fan to RM40 with air-con. This is probably the best buy in town.

For something different, try *De' Rakit Chalet* (☎ 09-312 3963), a floating hotel and restaurant moored on the river on Jalan Jelai, right in the centre of town. Self-contained chalets with balconies go for RM50. The chalets are starting to show their age, but they're an interesting choice.

The *Rumah Persinggahan Kuala Lipis* (Rest House; ☎ 09-312 2599) is a fair hike from the station on a hill overlooking the town but it has loads of colonial style. Large, almost spooky standard/deluxe rooms with air-con and bathroom cost RM40/50.

The top-ranking hotel in Kuala Lipis is the three star *Lipis Inn* (☎ 09-312 5888) on Jalan Lipis Benta, which has new, clean rooms with air-con and bathroom for RM88. It is near the Rest House, at the bottom of the hill.

Places to Eat

Kuala Lipis has surprisingly good food for such a small town, most of which is Chinese, reflecting the area's largely Chinese population. The covered alley which connects Jalan Besar and Jalan Jelai, heading straight out from the train station, is filled with *small restaurants*. Many of these operate only for breakfast and lunch, but some stay open for dinner as well. The best place is the *no-name joint* in the small alley that intersects the covered alley about half-way up (parallel to Jalan Besar). This place is only open for dinner and it serves some remarkably delicious stir-fries at bargain prices. Otherwise, there are plenty of *coffee shops* on Jalan Besar.

You will also find a *KFC* in the complex on the other side of the tracks from the train station.

Getting There & Away

Six buses per day run between Kuala Lipis and Kuala Lumpur's Pekeliling bus station from 8 am to 6 pm (RM8). Two buses go daily to Kuantan (RM14), and to Gua Musang (RM8). Marzin Express has a bus to Kota Bharu for RM14.

There is an express train to Singapore (RM21, eight hours) at 12.45 am, and a local train at 7.22 am. The 2.29 pm local train to Gemas also allows you to connect to Singapore. There is also an 11 pm express to KL, which takes eight hours and costs RM18. Any Singapore, KL or Gemas-bound train will stop at Jerantut, the closest station for travellers on their way to Taman Negara National Park.

Express trains to Tumpat (five hours) leave at 2.45 and 4.25 am and stop at Wakaf Baharu, the closest station to Kota Bharu (RM16). A slow but interesting local ('jungle') train departs at 12.55 pm and takes 11 hours to Wakaf Baharu (RM16). There is also a local train up to Gua Musang which leaves at 5.20 pm.

Taxis leave from the bus station to KL (RM25), Jerantut (RM10), Gua Musang (RM12), Kota Bharu (RM40) and Kuantan (RM40); these prices are per person.

KENONG RIMBA STATE PARK

This 120 sq km forest park is a sprawling area of lowland forest rising to the limestone foothills bordering Taman Negara. The park can be explored on good three or four-day jungle treks organised out of Kuala Lipis. The loop trail through the park provides an excellent opportunity to experience the jungle at close hand, and at affordable prices. Kenong Rimba is attracting an increasing number of visitors, but the trail is still relatively untrammelled.

Despite fanciful local claims that the park is a haven for elephants, tigers and rhinos escaping from over-touristed Taman Negara, big mammals are rare. Monkeys, wild pigs, squirrels, civets and possibly nocturnal tapir are all you should expect to see.

A permit from the District Forest Office is not required, contrary to what you may be told in Kuala Lipis, but you must be accompanied by a registered guide.

Walking the Trail

Access is from Kuala Lipis on southbound local trains ('jungle trains') to Batu Sembilan (Mile 9), a 30 minute trip. These depart Kuala Lipis daily at 7.22 am and 2.29 pm. From Batu Sembilan, boats are hired for RM15 per person to Jeti Tanjung Kiara, just across the river from Kampung Kuala Kenong. From the jetty it is a 30 minute walk to the park entrance along the road through Kampung Dusun, which is just a scattering of a few houses with one small shop. Further on from the shop, past the house with the 'souvenirs' sign, a side trail to the right leads to three caves – Gua Batu Tangga, Gua Batu Tangkup and Gua Batu Telahup. A number of confusing trails go through the swampy forest here. The guided trips include an exploration of the caves. The main trail eventually rejoins the road right at the entrance to the park where there is a gate and a footbridge over a stream.

If you walk for another 30 minutes the trail brings you to Gunung Kesong, a large limestone outcrop. The forest department has a hut here, and 200m further on are the Persona Chalets. Sheltered by the hill, some of the trees here are enormous. Gunung Kesong contains a number of caves, the most impressive being Gua Hijau, the 'Bat Cave', on a side trail around to the right (east) across two bridges. It is a large cavern where hundreds of small bats hang from the ceiling.

From Gunung Kesong the trail leads north through lowland forest to the waterfall of Lata Kenong, better known as the 'Seven Steps'. It is a three to four hour walk following the Sungai Kenong and crosses small streams. About an hour before the falls is the first of two log bridges across the river that require something of a balancing act to negotiate. The less sure-footed can straddle their way across. The trail then crosses the foothills to the huts at the Kenong campsite just before the falls, a series of cascades.

From Lata Kenong, the trail continues up and down more hills with other river crossings to Gunung Putih. Though no mountain climbing is involved, this is the most strenuous part of the trek, taking about five hours and passing through some impressive forest. Gunung Putih is another rocky, cave-ridden outcrop that can be climbed via a side trail.

The main trail continues past Gunung Putih through the foothills, back to the lowland forest. Another side trail leads to a nearby Orang Asli village, home of the Batek people. The main trail leads back to Gunung Kesong, about four hours all up from Gunung Putih.

Other side trips can be made in the park, including a visit to the Lata Babi waterfall, and to Gua Batu Tinggi, across the river from Kampung Dusun.

Organised Tours

Guides are compulsory for entry to the park and can be arranged in Kuala Lipis. The two most popular tour operators are Mr Tuah at the Tourist Information Centre (☎ 09-312 3277) in the Kuala Lipis train station building, and the Persona Rimba Resort (☎ 09-312 5032) in the Stesyen building opposite the station.

Persona Rimba operates the only chalets in the park and charges RM180 for a two night, three day trip (RM120 for groups of four or more). Mr Tuah offers similar trips for RM200 but may give discounts for larger groups.

Prices for both include food, guide and all expenses in the park. These are no-frills jungle experiences – you camp in the park (when not staying in the chalets) but all equipment and cooking is provided. Trips go when enough people are interested, usually every two or three days, or you can ring ahead to make a booking.

Considering the difficulties in locating a guide not affiliated with the above two organisations and all the costs involved, you won't save many ringgit by organising the trip yourself. If, however, you would like to do so, these tour operators can put you in contact with guides and you can negotiate your own prices, itineraries and arrangments with them.

Places to Stay

The only real accommodation in the park is the *Persona Chalets* at Gunung Kesong (see the previous Organised Tours entry). These spartan but comfortable huts each have four bunk beds and cost RM40.

The *Kenong campsite* near the Lata Kenong waterfall consists of open-sided huts on stilts and a campfire for cooking. The jungle treks camp at this site, and also at caves and rock overhangs at Gunung Kesong and Gunung Putih.

Apart from these two facilities, you'll be sleeping in tents, and if you are not part of an organised tour, you must bring your own camping gear.

RAUB

You may find yourself in this large, crossroads town getting transport connections to Fraser's Hill or Kuala Lipis. From Raub (pronounced 'Rob'), frequent buses also go to KL's Pekeliling bus station.

Raub has a few cheap hotels on the main road, including the very basic *Hotel Raub*, 57 Jalan Kuala Lipis, where singles/doubles cost RM14/25. The more gracious *Rumah Persinggahan* (Rest House; ☎ 09-355 5230) has rooms for RM50.

TEMERLOH

Temerloh is an old town on the banks of the enormous Sungai Pahang. It has a hint of colonial style and a colourful Saturday market. New industrial estates on the outskirts point to the future, and Temerloh is pressing to supersede Kuantan as the state capital. As the main city of central Pahang, it is a transport hub, the only real reason to visit.

The train station is 12km away at **Mentakab**, a thriving satellite of Temerloh that has little of interest for the visitor.

Places to Stay

From the bus station head away from the river along the main street past the new shops. At the T-junction take the laneway up the steps almost opposite. This will bring you to the *Hotel Bersih* and the *Hong Fong Hotel*, both dives. On the corner opposite, the *Hotel Isis* (☎ 09-296 3136), 12 Jalan Tengku Bakar, is a bit better and has rooms with fan and shared bathroom for RM20 or RM28 with air-con and bath. Further along at No 40, the *New Ban Hin Hotel* (☎ 09-296 2331) is similar.

A kilometre from the bus station, past the mosque, the old *Rumah Rehat Temerloh* (Temerloh Rest House; ☎ 09-296 3218) on Jalan Datok Hamzah has large and well-appointed rooms with air-con, hot water and TV for RM85. Next door, the *Seri Malaysia Hotel* (☎ 03-296 5776) is a new and more luxurious hotel with rooms from RM90, including breakfast.

Getting There & Away

Temerloh's bus station is central, about 400m from the cheap-hotel area. Buses go to all parts of the peninsula, including Kota Bharu (RM22.60) at 10 pm, Melaka (RM8.50) at 9 and 10 am and 5 pm, and Penang (RM30) at 10.30 pm. Buses to Jerantut (RM3.50) leave every half-hour between 6 am and 6.45 pm. Buses to KL's Pekeliling bus station (RM6) leave at least every hour between 7 am and 6 pm, and there are frequent buses to Kuantan.

Taxis at the bus station go to Mentakab (RM1), Jerantut (RM6), Kuantan (RM10) and KL (RM15); these prices are per person.

Terengganu

The small east coast state of Terengganu is, along with Kelantan to the north, one of the states richest in Malay culture. Until the completion of the roads to Kuala Lumpur (KL) and the west coast, this part of Malaysia was fairly isolated from the rest of the country and didn't receive many Indian and Chinese migrants. Consequently, cultural influences came more from the north. Traditional activities such as kite flying, top spinning, weaving of *songket* (fabric with gold threads) and batik printing are alive and well here.

If you seek a beach to laze around on for a few days, Terengganu has some of the best in the country, including those of the Pulau Perhentian, Pulau Redang and Pulau Kapas. All of these islands are far less developed than the more famous Pulau Tioman in Pahang, and the water surrounding them is crystal-clear blue. They offer great opportunities for diving and snorkelling; see the relevant sections and the Diving & Snorkelling section in this chapter for more information. The state is also famous for the leatherback turtles which come ashore from May to September at Rantau Abang.

Like its northern neighbour, Terengganu is a very conservative Muslim state, so you should dress and behave accordingly. If knocking back a few beers in the evening is an essential part of your travel routine, it is also worth bearing in mind that alcohol – while not impossible to get hold of – is not widely available in Terengganu.

HIGHLIGHTS

- **Pulau Perhentian** – perhaps the most beautiful in Malaysia, these islands have white-sand beaches and crystal-clear aquamarine water
- **Pulau Redang** – some of the best diving in Peninsular Malaysia, great beaches and walks for the non-diver
- **Pulau Kapas** – pretty little island; a great stop on the east coast
- **Tasik Kenyir** – inland lake surrounded by thick jungle and high waterfalls

History

When the Melaka sultanate was established in the 14th century, Terengganu was already paying tribute to the Siamese in the north, although a 1303 inscription at Kuala Brang establishes that an Islamic state existed here at that time. It wasn't long before Terengganu became a vassal of Melaka, but it managed to retain a large degree of independence during the Riau-Johor ascendancy, and was trading with Siam and China.

Terengganu was formally established as a state in 1724. The first sultan was Tun Zainal Abidin, a younger brother of one of the former Johor sultans. The close association with Johor was to continue for some years, and in fact the sultan Mansur spent 15 years in the mid-18th century in Johor trying to rally anti-Bugis sentiment. After failing there, Mansur turned his attention to Kelantan to the north and, after some fighting and

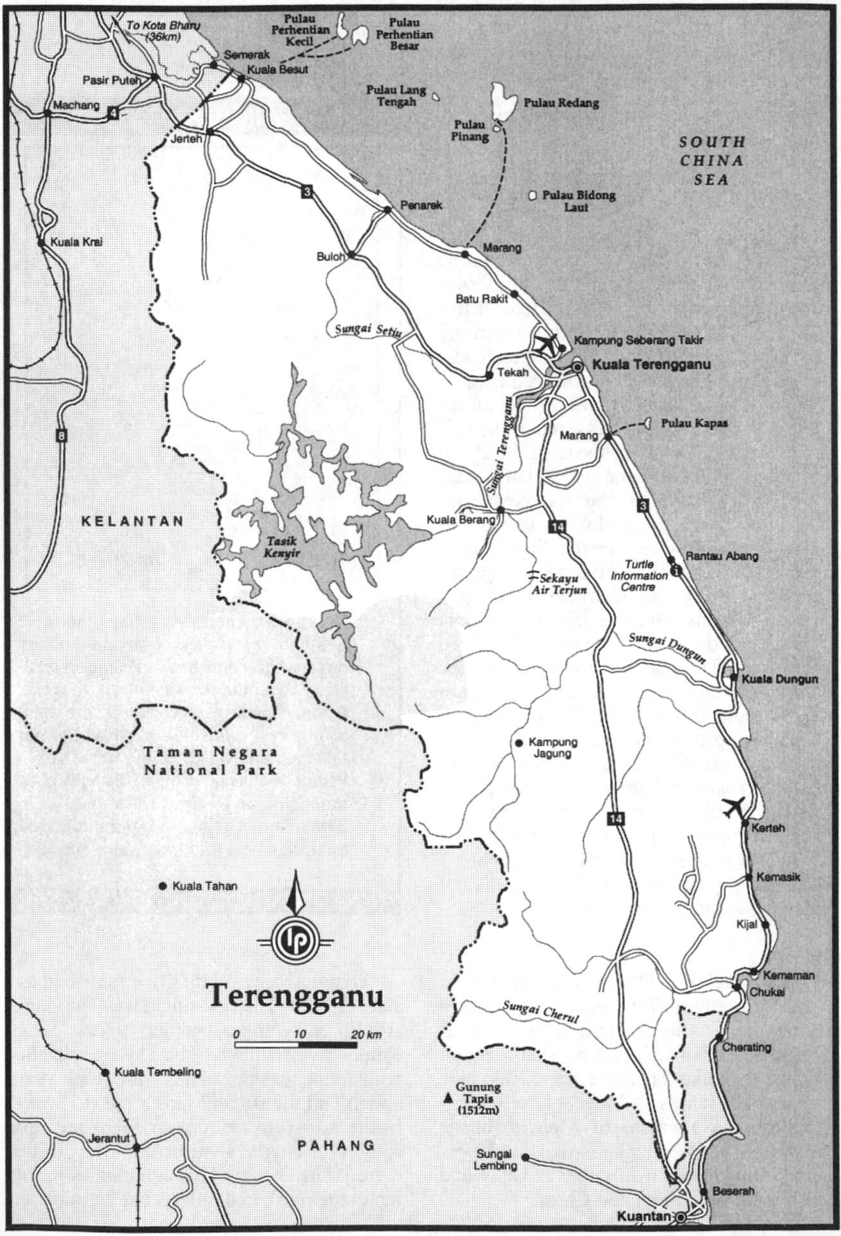
To Kota Bharu (36km)
Pulau Perhentian Kecil
Pulau Perhentian Besar
Semerak
Kuala Besut
Pasir Puteh
Machang
4
Jerteh
Pulau Lang Tengah
Pulau Redang
Pulau Pinang
SOUTH CHINA SEA
3
Penarek
Pulau Bidong Laut
Kuala Krai
Buloh
Merang
Batu Rakit
Sungai Setiu
Kampung Seberang Takir
Kuala Terengganu
Tekah
Sungai Terengganu
Marang
Pulau Kapas
8
KELANTAN
Kuala Berang
14
Tasik Kenyir
Rantau Abang
Turtle Information Centre
Sekayu Air Terjun
Sungai Dungun
Kuala Dungun
Kampung Jagung
Taman Negara National Park
Kerteh
Kemasik
Kuala Tahan
Kijal
Kemaman
Chukai
Terengganu
Sungai Cherul
0
10
20 km
Cherating
Kuala Tembeling
Gunung Tapis (1512m)
Jerantut
PAHANG
Sungai Lembing
Beserah
Kuantan

shrewd manoeuvring, had his son installed as the ruler of Kelantan. The main legacy of Mansur's reign was that Terengganu became a vassal of the Siamese.

Terengganu was controlled by the Siamese for the duration of the 19th century. However, the Terengganu sultan, Baginda Omar, a man renowned for his intelligence and energy, kept the Siamese at arm's length and the state flourished under his rule.

In 1909 an Anglo-Siamese treaty saw power pass to the British. It was an unpopular move locally, and in 1928 a peasant uprising erupted. It was quickly put down and the British went about consolidating their power in the state until the Japanese arrived in WWII. During the Japanese occupation control of the state was passed back to Thailand, but this was short-lived and Terengganu became a member of the Federation of Malaya when it was formed in 1948.

South of Kuala Terengganu

KEMAMAN/CHUKAI

About 25km north of Cherating, Kemaman and Chukai are the first towns of any size north of Kuantan and also the first towns you reach in Terengganu state when travelling up the coast. The two towns have merged into one long developed strip with little of interest to keep passing travellers.

Places to Stay

Given that accommodation is available close by in Cherating, it is unlikely you will need to overnight in Kemaman or Chukai.

A reasonable Chinese cheapie is the *Hotel Tong Juan* (☎ 09-859 1346) at K117 Jalan Sulaiman, with rooms from RM15. For something a bit better try the *Cathay Hotel* (☎ 09-859 1901) at 351 Jalan Kampung Tengah. Decent mid-range rooms are available at the *Hotel Diara* (☎ 09-859 1802) at K353-355 Jalan Kg Tengah, where costs start from RM58/66 for standard/deluxe rooms with air-con and hot shower.

Getting There & Away

Buses to Cherating cost RM1. To Marang it's RM7 by express bus, or you can catch a local bus to Kuala Dungun and then another bus from there. Taxis cost RM14 to Kuala Terengganu, RM8 south to Kuantan and RM6.50 to Kuala Dungun (per person).

KERTEH

Kerteh is a modern blot on the landscape that owes its existence to offshore oil. Esso and Petronas have their oil refineries here. The town has an airport, but public transport connections are not good.

There are some decent beaches along the stretch of coast near Kerteh, but there is no accommodation. Kemasik's palm-fringed beach has some of the clearest water on the east coast, and Kijal and Paka are picturesque fishing villages.

KUALA DUNGUN

From Kemaman there are more stretches of beach and small *kampungs* (villages) before you reach Kuala Dungun, which is actually a couple of kilometres off the main road.

The beaches, where the giant leatherbacks come in to lay their eggs, stretch north of there. The main reason to come to Kuala Dungun is to catch a bus or taxi out again, but there are plenty of hotels if you need to spend the night. Most of the hotels are in the old town, which is also home to the local bus station.

Buses run every hour to Kuantan (RM8) and Kuala Terengganu (RM4). Buses to Mersing (RM16) and Singapore (RM23) leave at 9.30 am and 9.30 pm, and buses to Kuala Lumpur (RM16.50) leave at 10.30 am and 10 pm.

RANTAU ABANG

This is the principal beach for spotting the great leatherback turtles during the laying season. The long, sandy beach is also good for long, lonely walks. Swimming is possible, but the undertow can be savage.

The Disappearing Turtles of the East Coast

Four species of turtle visit the east coast, in an area ranging from 35 to 150km north of Kuantan: the leatherback *(Dermochelys coriacea)*, the hawksbill *(Eretmochelys imbricata)*, the green turtle *(Chelonia mydas)* and the olive ridley *(Lepidochelys oliveacea)*.

The villagers believe that the giant leatherback turtles are attracted to Rantau Abang every year because of a large black stone resembling a turtle in the river. A more mundane explanation is that the sharp drop-off at the beach means that the turtles' laborious climb onto land is made considerably easier. At other times of the year the leatherbacks can wander as far away as the Atlantic Ocean, but each year between June and September they return to the Malaysian coast to lay their eggs. Or at least they used to. Sightings of leatherback turtles numbered almost 1000 back in the 1984 season; numbers have now dropped and only 30 were spotted in 1997. No one knows what has happened to the turtles, but certainly visitor interest hasn't helped. Hopefully they have found another secluded breeding ground.

If you do get to see a turtle, the egg-laying process is awesome, as the female leatherback can weigh up to 750kg and reach over 3m long. After crawling laboriously up the beach, well above the high-tide line, each female digs a deep hole in the sand for her eggs. She usually digs a decoy hole first and fills it in before digging the laying hole.

Into this cavity the turtle, with much huffing and puffing, lays between 50 and 140 eggs which look rather like large ping-pong balls. Having covered the eggs, she then heads back towards the water, leaving tracks as if a tank had just driven down the beach. It all takes an enormous effort, and the turtle will pause to catch her breath several times as 'tears' trickle down to keep sand out of her eyes.

Finally the giant turtle reaches the water and an amazing transformation takes place. The heavy, ungainly, cumbersome creature is suddenly back in its element and glides off silently into the night.

The whole process can take two or more hours from start to finish, and in each laying season an individual turtle may make several trips to the beach before disappearing until the next year.

The eggs take about 55 days to hatch. It's a fraught process, as many eggs are taken by crabs and other predators. Newly hatched young turtles weigh only about 35g and are around 6cm long. During their perilous crawl to the sea they are easy prey for birds, and for fish and other creatures when they reach the water. It's a long time before they're as large as their parents.

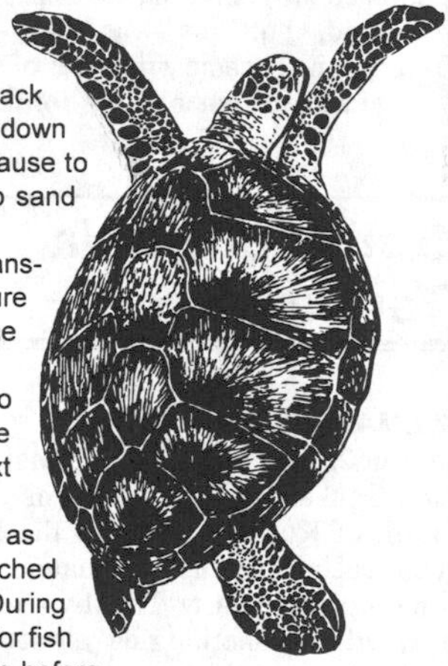

The hawksbill turtle.

There's a Turtle Information Centre (Pusat Penerangan Penyu Rantau Abang), run by the Department of Fisheries, close to most of the budget accommodation. It has a few decent displays but is missable for all but the most ardent turtle lover. The centre is open every day during the turtle-watching season (May to August), but is otherwise closed on Friday and public holidays. Note that the nearest bank is at Kuala Dungun, 22km south.

August is the peak egg-laying season, when there's a good chance of seeing turtles, but you may also be lucky in June and July. Full-moon and high-tide nights are said to be best. The villagers know the season is about to end when the smaller green turtles come to lay their eggs – a week later the leatherbacks are gone until next year.

The turtles were once the east coast's key tourist attraction, which contributed to the decline of turtle numbers. Now fewer and fewer turtles attract fewer and fewer tourists (the 1997 season saw only 30 leatherback turtles). The government has made a concerted, if not always well policed, effort to preserve the turtles and their egg-laying habitat. They introduced heavy fines and tried to stamp out the gross behaviour – pulling the turtles' flippers, shining lights in their eyes, taking eggs and even riding on their backs. Flash photography and shining torches (flashlights) on the turtles are prohibited, and you must keep a reasonable distance.

The beach is now divided into three sections during the season – prohibited, semi public (where you have to buy tickets) and free access – in an attempt to control the 'hang gang, the turtles are up' mentality.

Places to Stay & Eat

Right on the beach, just south of the Turtle Information Centre, are two travellers' places. *Awang's* (☎ 09-844 3500) is the more popular of the two. Standard/deluxe rooms with fan and bathroom go for RM10/20; there are also air-con family standard/deluxe rooms (two double beds and one single) available for RM60/80.

The *Ismail Beach Resort* (☎ 09-844 1054) next door has similar rooms for RM20 with bathroom and fan and RM80 with two double beds and air-con. It's worth having a quick look at both places before making a decision on which to stay at. Both Awang's and Ismail offer discount rates off season.

Awang's and the Ismail Beach Resort have guides and transport to bring you to see the turtles once they are spotted on the beach.

Dahimah's Guest House (☎ 09-845 2843) is about 1km south towards Kuala Dungun and is a good option. Simple rooms with fan and bathroom cost RM15. Rooms with air-con and bathroom are RM30. Larger air-con family rooms are RM100. It has a good restaurant and arranges trips in the area.

The *Merantau Inn* (☎ 09-844 1131) is a mid-range motel-style place at Kuala Abang, about 3.5km north of Rantau Abang. Chalets cost from RM42 with bathroom and fan and from RM65 with air-con. There are also family rooms for RM80 with fan and RM120 with air-con. If you have your own camping equipment, you can camp here for RM5 per tent.

Apart from the restaurants in the various hotels, there are a few food stalls next to the Turtle Information Centre.

Getting There & Away

Rantau Abang is only about 22km north of Kuala Dungun, which in turn is 80km south of Kuala Terengganu and 138km north of Kuantan. The nearest airport is at Kerteh, where there are flights to Kuantan, Kuala Terengganu and KL.

Dungun-Kuala Terengganu buses run in both directions every hour from 7 am to 6 pm and there's a bus stop near the Turtle Information Centre. Rantau Abang to Kuala Terengganu costs RM4 and to Dungun costs RM1.50. Heading south you can try to hail a long-distance bus, or take the bus to Kuala Dungun, from where hourly buses go to Kuantan, as well as to Mersing, Singapore and KL.

MARANG

Marang, a picturesque fishing village on the mouth of the Sungai (River) Marang, has long been a favourite stopover for travellers making their way along the east coast. Unfortunately, much of the town's traditional charm has fallen victim to an ill-planned modernisation programme. Now, much of the once picturesque waterfront area is occupied by characterless concrete structures.

Nonetheless, Marang is still worth a visit. The harbour is packed with colourful fishing boats, there are a few good beaches north and south of town and traditional Malay culture is still alive on the outskirts of town. Be warned, however, that Marang is a conservative village, especially across the river from the main town, and reserved dress and behaviour is recommended.

Places to Stay & Eat

Most of the travellers' places are on the lagoon to the north of the jetty, and a couple of mid-range places can be found across the bridge to the south-east.

The most popular spot with travellers is the pleasant *Green Mango Inn* (☎ 09-618 2040), on a hill near the jetty. Single rooms with fan go for RM10, doubles for RM15. Chalets with fan go for RM20. These have shared bathrooms and there's a kitchen, laundry facilities and a small library. This is the place to meet fellow travellers.

North of the jetty, *Kamal's Guest House* (☎ 09-618 2181) has rooms with fan for RM12 and for RM16 with bathroom. Check a few rooms before deciding as they are a mixed bag.

Nearby, the *Island View Resort* (☎ 09-618 2006) charges RM20 for rooms with fan and bathroom and RM40 upwards for air-con rooms. The rooms are a little run-down.

On the hill behind Kamal's is the *Marang Guesthouse* (☎ 09-618-1976). It's a notch up from the other guesthouses and has its own restaurant. Rooms with fan are RM20 and nicer air-con rooms are available from RM50.

Sandwiched between Kamal's Guesthouse and the Island View Resort is the *Hotel Seri Malaysia* (☎ 09-618 2889), an upmarket chain hotel, where excellent air-con doubles start from RM90. It often has specials, however, when standard rooms go for as little as RM65.

Across the bridge to the south-east, the *Angullia Beach House Resort* (☎ 09-618 2403) is a good mid-budget choice. It's right on a beautiful stretch of beach in a lovely garden setting, but is overpriced at RM50 for rooms with fan and RM65 upwards with air-con. The restaurant is aimed at free-spending Singaporeans and makes few concessions to budget travellers.

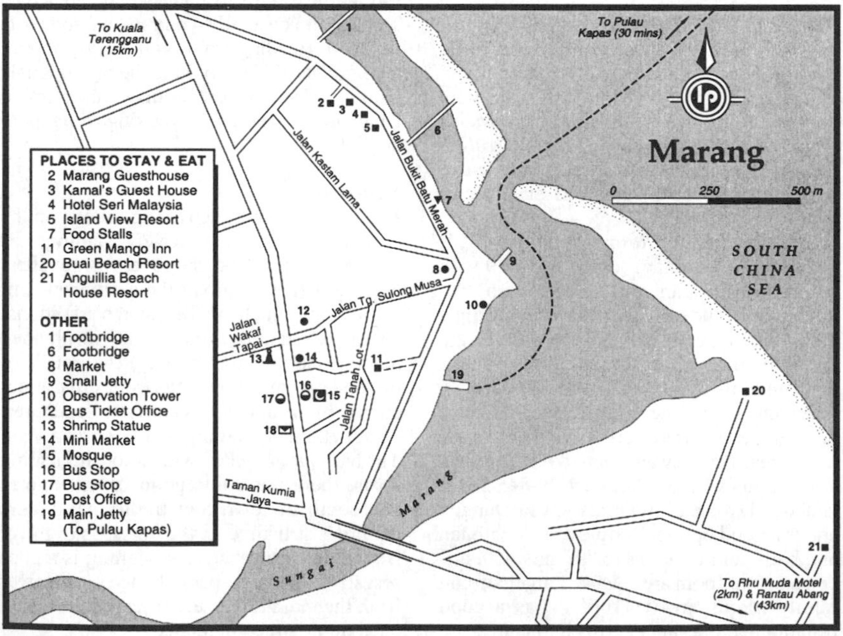

Further south are more places to stay, but they are a long way from anywhere and see very few foreign guests. The *Rhu Muda Motel* (☎ 09-618 2328), between the main road and the beach, is well kept and costs from RM80 for rooms with air-con and bathroom. The restaurant is good.

Occupying the sandy point opposite the main jetty, the *Buai Beach Resort* (☎ 09-618 3888) is an upmarket option where clean, atmospheric chalets start at RM140 with hot water and air-con. The beach here is excellent and there is a swimming pool and restaurant.

Getting There & Away

Marang is 30 minutes south of Kuala Terengganu, and regular buses run to and from Kuala Dungun and Kuala Terengganu. There is a ticket office on Jalan Tanjung Sulong Musa near the town's main intersection. There are express buses twice daily to KL (RM21.70), Johor Bahru (RM22) and Kuantan/Cherating (RM8). The local bus fare is RM1 to Kuala Terengganu.

There are four bus stops on the main road. Southbound express buses usually stop in front of the mosque and northbound services will pick you up just north of the post office. This is not a hard and fast rule, however, and it's best to ask at the ticket office or the owner of your guesthouse before taking the chance on departure.

PULAU KAPAS

Six kilometres offshore from Marang is the beautiful small island of Kapas, with clear water and beaches of powdery white sand. All the accommodation is clustered together on two small beaches in the centre of the island, but you can walk around the headlands to quieter beaches. There is also a rough track across the middle of the island to the rocky eastern shore which is good for sightseeing but dangerous for swimming.

Pulau Kapas is best avoided during holidays and long weekends, when it is overrun with day-trippers. The island also shuts down during the east coast's monsoon season from November to March.

Diving & Snorkelling

Kapas is billed as a snorkellers' paradise, though coral is scarce on the most accessible beaches facing the coast. Some of the best snorkelling can be found around the northern end of the island.

The Kapas Garden Resort has scuba gear and a boat, and charges RM90 for one dive, RM150 for two dives, including equipment.

Any of the budget places in town can organise snorkelling, and the cost is around RM25 for the day, including the return boat ride to Kapas.

Places to Stay & Eat

Most people visit Kapas on a day trip, but there are a number of places to stay and each has its own restaurant. The *Kapas Garden Resort* (☎ 011-984 1686), run by a hospitable Dutch-Malay couple, is good value with rooms for RM75 with bathroom and fan including breakfast. They also have chalets for RM50. It's located at the northern end of the island, around the corner from an excellent secluded beach.

Next door is the *Mak Cik Gemuk Beach Resort* (☎ 09-618 1221), which has lots of rooms and charges RM18 for a basic room with two beds; RM40 with bathroom, fan and mosquito nets; and RM50 with a double bed, bathroom, fan and mosquito nets. The rooms are all set well back from the beach and are somewhat cramped.

On the same beach, *Zaki Beach Chalet* (☎ 09-613 1631) is an inexpensive option, with longhouse rooms for RM20, or RM25 with bathroom. They also have A-frames with bathroom, fan and mosquito nets for RM35.

A short walk around a headland brings you to a longer beach with a few more possibilities. The first is the upmarket *Kapas Island Village Resort* (☎ 09-622 0712), complete with swimming pool, where basic but clean rooms with fan and bathroom start at RM80 and chalets with air-con and bathroom start at RM120. The restaurant here is pretty good.

Down a narrow walkway, the *Ayah Island Resort* (☎ 09-624 5088) is poorly located well back from the beach. Beds in the barracks-like dorm go for RM10 each and standard chalets with fan and bathroom cost RM45. Air-con chalets go for RM80. This is really only a last resort if all the other spots are full.

Back on the beach, the *Tuty Puri Resort* (☎ 09-624 6090) is another large resort-style place which charges RM40 for basic chalets with fan and bathroom and RM80 for deluxe chalets with fan and bathroom. Note that there are no nets on the windows here, so you may need to get some mosquito coils.

The last place, at the southern end of the beach, is *Lighthouse* (☎ 010-215 3558), a budget spot popular with backpackers. All the rooms are in one elevated longhouse. Dorm beds go for RM10 each and private rooms for RM20. The owner is interesting and knowledgeable about the island.

It is also possible to *camp* on some of the isolated beaches at the north and south ends of the island, but bring your own food and water.

Finally, those in search of something more exclusive can try the *Gem Isles Resort* (☎ 09-624 5110), the sole occupant of the small island immediately to the north of Pulau Kapas. Packages including all meals, lodging and boat transfer start at RM180 for two days. Call to make a reservation before heading out.

Getting There & Away

Boats to Pulau Kapas leave from the larger of the town's two jetties and tickets can be purchased from any of the agents near the jetty. Slow boats cost RM7.50 one way but are gradually being replaced by speedboats which charge RM25 return. Most speedboat operators will only sell return tickets and you must arrange a pick-up time when you purchase your ticket. There are usually morning departures at 8 and 9 am. Some guesthouse operators also sell tickets, but will also charge a RM5 commission. Don't believe them if they claim there aren't any other boats sailing that day – they're just after an extra RM5.

Kuala Terengganu

Standing on a promontory formed by the South China Sea on one side and the wide Sungai Terengganu on the other, Kuala Terengganu is the capital of Terengganu state and the seat of the sultan. Oil revenue has transformed Kuala Terengganu from a sprawling, oversized fishing village of stilt houses into a medium-sized modern city.

Kuala Terengganu remains a fairly conservative place and has a strong Islamic presence. There is little to see or do around town and nothing to do by night. Most travellers use it as a staging post to nearby attractions such as Tasik Kenyir, Marang or Merang and Pulau Redang.

Information

Jalan Sultan Ismail is the commercial hub of town and home to most of the banks and office blocks. The state tourist office (☎ 09-622 1553) is near the post office and is a good source of information (the office is closed on Friday). The Tourism Malaysia tourist office (☎ 09-622 1433) can give you a full range of brochures for other parts of Malaysia and can also answer questions about local attractions and accommodation. There is also an information counter at Sultan Mahmud airport.

The long-distance taxi stand and main bus station are on Jalan Masjid in the centre of town and there is an express bus station in the north of town near the Kompleks Taman Selera Tanjung.

The immigration office (☎ 09-622 1424) is at Wisma Persekutuan on Jalan Sultan Ismail. There's a good laundry service next door to the Seaview Hotel.

Things to See

Kuala Terengganu's compact **Chinatown** can be found on Jalan Bandar. It comprises the usual array of hole-in-the-wall Chinese shops, hairdressing salons and restaurants, as well as a sleepy Chinese temple and some narrow alleys leading to jetties on the waterfront.

The **central market** is a lively, colourful spot, with fruit and foods of all types on sale. When they say the fish is fresh, they really mean it – the fishing boats dock right outside. The floor above the fish section has a good collection of batik and songket.

Across the road from the market and next door to the state tourist office, look for the flight of stairs leading up to **Bukit Puteri**, a 200m hill with good views of the city. The hill is also home to the remains of a 19th century fort (the legacy of inter-sultanate warfare), some cannons and a bell. It is a minor attraction.

Continuing past the market, you come to the **Istana Maziah**, the sultan's palace, on your right. The palace is closed to the public, except for some ceremonial occasions. Nearby is the gleaming **Zainal Abidin Mosque**.

Pantai Batu Buruk is the city beach and a popular place to stroll in the evening when the food stalls open. It is a pleasant stretch of sand, but swimming can be dangerous here. Across the road, the **Cultural Centre** sometimes stages *pencak silat* and *wayang* shows on Friday between 5 and 7 pm from 1 April to 31 October. Check with the tourist office.

The **Istana Tengku Long Museum** is housed in the old sultan's palace at Losong, a few kilometres south-west of town on the riverbank. The wooden palace buildings are set in attractive gardens, and there's a boat museum. It's open from 10 am to 6 pm daily and admission is RM5. Take minibus No 60 from the main bus station (60 sen).

From the jetty take a 50 sen ferry ride to **Pulau Duyung Besar**, the largest island in the estuary. Fishing boats are built here using age-old techniques and tools; it's worth a wander.

A boat from beside the central market will take you across to **Kampung Seberang Takir**, a fishing village on the other side of the river mouth. Five kilometres upriver is

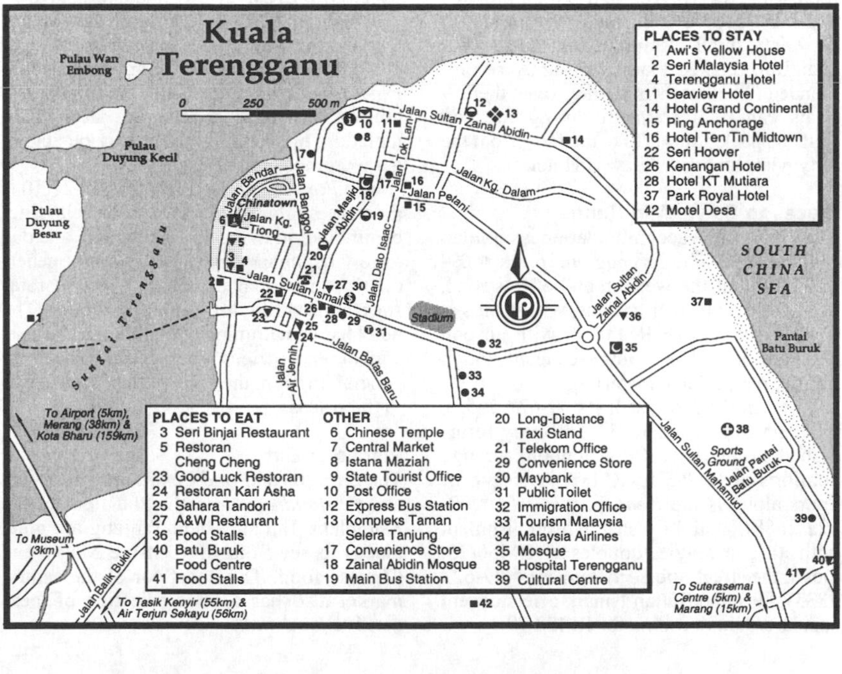

Kampung Pulau Rusa, which has a number of interesting old traditional houses. Ferries and buses come here. Take minibus No 17 (60 sen) from Kuala Terengganu or the local bus to Manir for the same price. You can also charter a boat at the Syahbandar jetty in Kuala Terengganu for RM20 per hour.

Places to Stay – Budget

Ping Anchorage (☎ 09-622 0851), upstairs at 77A Jalan Dato Isaac, is the No 1 travellers' place. It has a rooftop restaurant and bar and also organises tours to Pulau Kapas, Pulau Redang, Air Terjun Sekayu and Tasik Kenyir. Dorm beds are RM6 each and rooms are RM12 to RM15, or RM20 with bathroom. The rooms are good and the owners friendly.

Awi's Yellow House is a unique guesthouse built on stilts over the river. It's in the boat-building village on Pulau Duyung Besar, a 15 minute ferry ride across the river. A bed with mosquito net costs RM5 per night in the open dorm, or the small thatched rooms are RM16. Tea and coffee are free and most people cook their own food, but there is a small restaurant next door. It's a beautiful, relaxed place and highly recommended. The catch is getting over there – boats can be infrequent during the day (outside peak hours). Take the ferry from the jetty near the Seri Malaysia Hotel.

Places to Stay – Mid-Range

Most mid-range accommodation is on Jalan Sultan Ismail. The *Terengganu Hotel* (☎ 09-622 2900), at the western end of this road, is one of the cheaper options, with rooms at RM33 with fan or RM38.50 with air-con and bathroom. The rooms are clean enough but not particularly inspiring.

The *Hotel KT Mutiara* (☎ 09-622 2655), 67 Jalan Sultan Ismail, is a recently refurbished hotel that offers good mid-range comforts at RM55 to RM85. A couple of doors along is the *Kenangan Hotel* (☎ 09-622 2688), a slightly shabby establishment with air-con singles/doubles at RM50/75. Down the street, the *Seri Hoover* (☎ 09-623 3833), 49 Jalan Sultan Ismail, offers decent standard/deluxe rooms for RM58/79.

Another good mid-range value for money place is the *Seaview Hotel* (☎ 09-622 1911) at 18A Jalan Masjid Abidin, close to the istana. Clean rooms with fan and bathroom cost RM30, and those with air-con and bathroom cost RM45.

The *Motel Desa* (☎ 09-622 3033) is in a beautiful garden setting on the top of Bukit Pak Api, but unless you have your own transport it's a very inconvenient place to stay. Singles/doubles with air-con and bathroom go for RM65; it has a good restaurant and a swimming pool.

Places to Stay – Top End

For top-end luxury at affordable prices, the *Seri Malaysia Hotel* (☎ 09-623 6454), at the southern end of Jalan Bandar, is the best option in town. Rooms cost RM100, and spacious family rooms are RM120.

Another reasonably priced place is the *Hotel Yen Tin Midtown* (☎ 09-623 5288), where clean, new rooms with air-con and hot water go for RM90/150 (standard/deluxe).

Working hard to capture the luxury market, the new *Hotel Grand Continental* (☎ 09-625 1888) has all the amenities you'd expect at such a place including a good restaurant. Standard rooms start at RM230 including breakfast, but you may be able to get a promotional rate.

The *Park Royal Hotel* (☎ 09-622 2100) is the closest thing to international-class accommodation in Kuala Terengganu, and due to low occupancy rates often sports generous 'promotional discounts'. Posted rates start at RM220 for standard rooms. The hotel has a swimming pool, three restaurants and other services you would expect. In general, though, the level of service is not up to the prices.

Places to Eat

The *Batu Buruk Food Centre* near the beach and the *food court* on the 2nd floor of the Kompleks Taman Selera Tanjung are good places to seek out inexpensive Malay and Chinese food. The 2nd floor of the central market also has a good selection of inexpensive *food stalls*.

The *Restoran Cheng Cheng* at 224 Jalan Bandar has the standard Chinese favourites for reasonable prices and staff seem used to the occasional traveller popping in. For better Chinese fare, try the *Good Luck Restoran* on Jalan Kota Lama, which has an extensive menu and outside tables where you can sit and watch life roll by.

There are two decent Indian places on Jalan Air Jernih, *Sahara Tandori* and *Restoran Kari Asha;* both serve filling Indian meals for around RM5.

For satay, try the *Seri Binjai Restaurant* near the waterfront. The place is quite rundown, but the satay is good.

If you feel like a minor extravagance, the *Hotel Grand Continental* puts on a lunchtime buffet of Malay and international food for RM17.50.

Shopping

Kuala Terengganu is a good place to buy wicker goods, batik and songket, the intricate weaving using gold and silver threads. You can see silk weaving at the Suterasemai Centre, a few kilometres south of town on the road to Marang. The handicraft centre is 10km from town at Rhusila, not far from Marang, but the best place to buy handicrafts is upstairs at the central market. Prices at the market average RM80 to RM250 for a 1 sq metre piece of songket and RM20 to RM100 for locally made wicker baskets. Bargaining is possible here and necessary to get fair prices.

Getting There & Away

Air Malaysia Airlines (☎ 09-622 1415), 13 Jalan Sultan Omar, services Kuala Terengganu. There are direct flights daily to/from KL (RM104) and to/from Johor Bahru (RM149). A taxi to the airport costs RM15.

Bus There's a new bus station on Jalan Masjid Abidin which serves as a terminus for all local buses and most long-distance buses. The ticket counter is on the ground floor at the south end of the building.

Heading south, there are regular buses to Marang (RM1), Rantau Abang (RM3, terminates at Kuala Dungun), Kuantan (RM9), Mersing (RM18), Johor Bahru (RM22.10) and Singapore (RM23.10). To Kuala Lumpur the fare is RM21.70, and to Melaka it's RM24.

Northbound, there are buses to Merang (RM2.30) and Kuala Besut (RM6). Buses also leave for Kota Bharu (RM7.40) every 1½ to two hours from 8.30 am to 7 pm. There are also buses to Butterworth (RM24).

Note that some express buses depart from the express bus station in the north of town near the Kompleks Taman Selera Tanjung.

Taxi The main taxi stand is near the bus station. Taxis cost RM4 to Marang, RM6 to Merang, RM12 to Jerteh (for Kuala Besut), RM8 to Rantau Abang, RM14 to Kota Bharu, RM15 to Kuantan and RM40/50 (non-air-con/air-con) to KL (prices per person).

Getting Around

Bus There are regular regional buses from the main bus station. For the museum take a 'Museum/Losong' minibus (60 sen); for the handicraft and silk-weaving centres take minibus No 13 bound for Chendering (60 sen).

Taxi Taxis around town cost a minimum of RM5, but there are not many about; try for one at the long-distance taxi stand.

Trishaw Kuala Terengganu was once the trishaw capital of Malaysia, and although numbers have dropped, they are still the main form of inner-city transport. Cost is roughly RM3 per kilometre.

AROUND KUALA TERENGGANU

Air Terjun Sekayu

These waterfalls are 56km south-west of Kuala Terengganu. You can catch a bus to Kuala Berang (RM2), and from there it is about 15km to the falls where there are pleasant natural swimming pools (a taxi costs RM2.50 from Kuala Berang and you must arrange a pick-up time). A taxi to the falls from Kuala Terengganu costs RM5 per person. Ping Anchorage does day trips to the falls for RM40 (see Kuala Terengganu, Places to Stay). There is a resthouse and chalets, costing around RM40 per night. Phone the District Office in Kuala Berang (☎ 09-681 1259) for bookings.

Tasik Kenyir

Tasik Kenyir (Lake Kenyir) is being developed as a massive 'eco-tourist' destination by local tourist authorities (eco-tourism equals eco-dollars). Access roads are being laid and new accommodation options and other tourist facilities are either on the drawing board or under construction. Despite the 'eco-tourism' slogan, the lake was formed by the construction of Kenyir Dam in 1985. The lake covers over 38,000 hectares, has 340 islands and is good for watersports.

Tasik Kenyir is 15km west of Kuala Berang and 55km from Kuala Terengganu, and can be combined with a trip to Air Terjun Sekayu. The main access point is Pengkalan Gawi, a nondescript place with a tourist information office.

Waterfalls are high on the list of Kenyir's attractions. **Air Terjun Lasir**, around 16km south of Pengkalan Gawi, is the most impressive, and can be reached by boat – a resthouse, camping facilities and jungle treks are planned for the area. **Air Terjun Saok**, on the other side of the lake from Pengkalan Gawi, is a picturesque spot popular with local picnickers. **Batu Biwa** and **Batu Taat limestone caves** border the lake and are actually inside Taman Negara National Park. It takes around two hours by boat to reach them from Pengkalan Gawi.

Places to Stay Most of the accommodation is in resort chalets or longhouse-style structures built over the lake. There are no budget options, but camping facilities are being developed. The resorts generally offer packages including meals and boat transport from Pengkalan Gawi. Ping Anchorage (see Kuala Terengganu, Places to Stay) has a wide variety of packages at competitive prices.

One of the cheaper possibilities is *Kenyir Woods* (☎ 09-623 8188), across the lake from Pengkalan Gawi. Comfortable chalets built on a slope overlooking the lake cost from RM50. A two day/one night package costs RM120.

The *Primula Kenyir Lake Resort* (☎ 09-622 2100) is on Pulau Poh, just three minutes by speedboat from Pengkalan Gawi. Chalets range from RM100 to RM150 – the more expensive ones are built on stilts over the water.

South of Pengkalan Gawi (about 30 minutes by boat) is the *Muping Island Resort* (☎ 09-681 2197), a longhouse village built over the lake. Rates start at RM130 for two days and one night. Nearby is *Uncle John's Resort* (☎ 09-622 9564), where rates start at RM135 for two days and one night; access is via the main dam at Jenagor.

Getting There & Away You can reach Kuala Berang by bus or taxi from Kuala Terengganu, but from Kuala Berang to the lake you'll have to hire a taxi or private car for around RM20. You can arrange day trips or accommodation at the state tourist office in Kuala Terengganu. Ping Anchorage can also arrange transport out to the lake.

Getting Around Getting around the lake can be expensive. There are fairly regular services from Gawi jetty to the main attractions. Representative prices include (from the jetty): Air Terjun Lasir RM25, Batu Biwa and Batu Taat caves RM50 and a one day fishing trip, RM300.

North of Kuala Terengganu

North of Kuala Terengganu the main road (Route 3) leaves the coast and runs inland to Kota Bharu, 165km north, via Jerteh. The quiet coastal backroad from Kuala Terengganu to Kuala Besut runs along a beautiful stretch of coast and is quite popular with cycling travellers.

continued on page 343

DIVING & SNORKELLING

Title page: Colourful sea stars search for food as they crawl across coral reefs. (photograph by Michael Aw)

MICHAEL AW

MICHAEL AW

TOURISM MALAYSIA

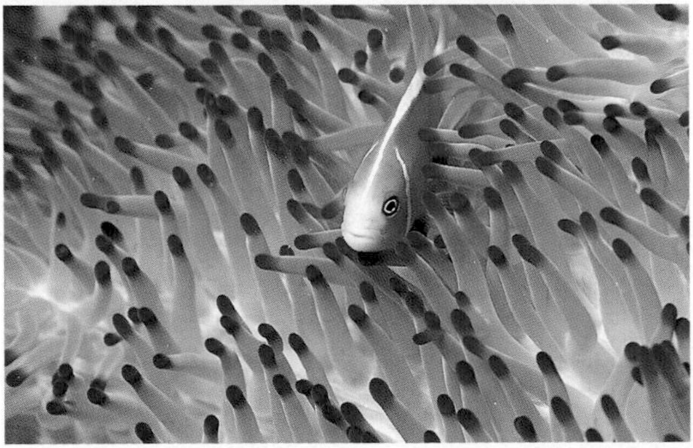

MICHAEL AW

Top: The predatorial Crown of Thorns starfish threaten some areas of coral.
Middle Left: The Pink Nudibranch, or sea slug, often attaches itself to a sea squirt.
Middle Right: Red Feather Star climbs over the seabed on short-jointed legs.
Bottom: Pink Anemonefish seeking food and camouflage in anemones.

Diving & Snorkelling

Surrounded by the waters of the Celebes Sea and the South China Sea to the east and the Straits of Melaka to the west, Malaysia has some of the best diving in South-East Asia. While not as cheap as Thailand nor as spectacular as Indonesia, the combination of reasonable prices, good variety and easy access makes Malaysia a good choice for first-time divers and old hands.

Located in a series of marine parks established in the 1970s and 80s, most of Malaysia's dive sites are protected from the destructive activities which wreaked havoc on coral reefs in the past, such as dynamite fishing, collection of rare species and pollution from motorboat engines. Reefs are regenerating and the diving industry is booming.

Island-based boat dives are the most common, but a few areas, like Sabah's Pulau Sipadan, have some great sites right off the beach. Recent years have also seen an increase in the number of live-aboards that take divers to previously inaccessible spots. Most sites are over fairly shallow reefs, but there are also a couple of islands with deep drop-offs and even a few wreck dives in East Malaysia.

The standards of diving facilities in Malaysia are generally quite high and equipment rental is widely available. Most places offer instruction leading to Professional Association of Diving linstructors (PADI) certification (which will then allow you to dive) and this certification is almost universally recognised. While it is possible simply to show up and dive at some of the larger dive centres like Pulau Tioman, it is usually a good idea to make some arrangements in advance, if only to avoid waiting a day or two before starting.

EQUIPMENT

Although you can hire equipment through dive operators, most divers prefer to bring their own mask, snorkel and fins at the very least. They may also carry their own regulator, depth gauge and buoyancy control device (BCD). You don't really need a wetsuit in tropical waters to keep you at a comfortable temperature, but it will also protect you from cuts, grazes and stings. Coral cuts are particularly prone to infection so taking steps to prevent them is always better than treating the problem. A 4mm wetsuit is considered ideal for the tropics and a lycra skin is also suitable in the right water conditions. Check what equipment you'll need with the boat operator when you book your dive.

PRICES

Most dive centres charge around RM160 for two dives, including equipment rental (RM130 without rental). PADI open-water courses average around RM800. Many resorts and dive operators also offer all-inclusive dive packages which vary widely in price.

BOOKS

Jack Jackson's *The Dive Sites of Malaysia and Singapore* (Passport Books, 1997) has detailed information on preparation for diving and snorkelling, and the individual sites in this region.

DIVE SEASONS

The north-east monsoon brings strong winds and rain to the east coast of Peninsular Malaysia from early November to late February, during which time most dive centres simply shut down. Visibility improves after the monsoon, peaking in August and September. On the west coast things are reversed, and the best diving is from September to March.

In East Malaysia the monsoons are less pronounced and rain falls more evenly throughout the year. However, the same general seasons apply, with the best diving on the east coast from May to November and on the west from October to March.

SNORKELLING

Snorkelling is possible at all the places listed in this section. However, some places are more snorkel-friendly than others. Places like the Perhentians, Kapas and Tioman are inexpensive

Pre-Dive Safety Guidelines

Before embarking on a scuba diving, skin diving or snorkelling trip, careful consideration to the following should be given to ensure a safe as well as enjoyable experience. You should:

- Possess a current diving certification card from a recognised scuba diving instructional agency (if you are scuba diving).
- Be sure you are healthy and feel comfortable diving.
- Obtain reliable information about physical and environmental conditions at the dive site, for example from a reputable local dive operation.
- Be aware of local laws, regulations, and etiquette about marine life and environment.
- Dive at sites within your experience level; if available, engage the services of a competent, professionally trained dive instructor or dive master.

Underwater conditions vary significantly from one region, or even site, to another. Seasonal changes can significantly alter any site and dive conditions. These differences influence the way divers dress for a dive and what diving techniques they use.

Regardless of location, there are special requirements for diving in that area. Before your dive, ask about the environmental characteristics that can affect your diving and how local, trained divers deal with these considerations.

and popular options. Others, like Redang and Sipadan, are more dive-oriented. Indeed, it makes little sense to pay the high prices involved in getting to these dive meccas if you are not going to dive.

Rental equipment is almost universally available, but the quality varies. Serious snorkellers are advised to bring their own equipment, at least mask and snorkel. Rental fees average around RM10 per day. As with diving, snorkelling can be a dangerous activity and you are advised to take the same precautions you would if you were diving (see the boxed text 'Pre-Dive Safety Guidelines' in this section). The preservation of the reef is also important and snorkellers are urged to read the Responsible Diving section on page 341.

DIVE SITES

Most of Peninsular Malaysia's dive sites are on the east coast. These include, working north to south, Pulau Perhentian, Pulau Redang, Pulau Kapas, Pulau Tioman and the many smaller islands of the Seribuat Archipelago. On the west coast of the peninsula, Pulau Payar, 30km south of Langkawi, offers decent diving for those who can't make it to the east coast.

In East Malaysia, off Sabah, you'll find the islands of Tunku Abdul Rahman National Park, Pulau Labuan and the famous oceanic island of Pulau Sipadan. Those with more money and time can also try Pulau Layang Layang, 300km north of Kota Kinabalu, in the disputed Spratley chain. In Sarawak, diving is limited to a few shallow sites off Miri.

Peninsular Malaysia

East Coast Dive sites off the east coast of Peninsular Malaysia include the following:

Pulau Perhentian Twenty-one kilometres off the coast of northern Terengganu, the two islands of the Perhentian group offer some of the most accessible diving in Malaysia. Shallow coral gardens in clear water typify the diving, with some of the best sites around the Susu Dara group a few kilometres north-west of the main islands. With several dive centres and very competitive prices, this is a good place to get certified or take a few casual dives. You're likely to see schools of colourful reef fish, sea turtles, the occasional manta and perhaps a blacktip reef shark or two. For more information, see the Pulau Perhentian Diving & Snorkelling section in the Terengganu chapter.

Pulau Redang One of Malaysia's most spectacular dive sites, Terengganu's Pulau Redang is actually a group of nine islands surrounded by fine coral reefs and very clear water. In addition to small reef fish, you may also see groupers, mantas, sea turtles, some reef sharks, and perhaps even a whale or tiger shark. Most of the resorts on the island have their own dive centres and sell all-inclusive packages (see Redang's Places to Stay section in the Terengganu chapter), but you can also arrange independent dive trips (contact Ping Anchorage; see the Kuala Terengganu Places to Stay section in the Terengganu chapter).

Pulau Kapas Pulau Kapas is a small sandy island 6km off the coast of Marang in Terengganu. There are some decent coral gardens in the shallow waters around the island. While it is not particularly interesting for the experienced diver, the convenient location and shallow waters make Kapas a good place to learn. Most of the resorts on Kapas have their own dive centres but the best is at the Pulau Kapas Garden Resort (see Pulau Kapas' Places to Stay section in the Terengganu chapter).

Pulau Tioman The largest east coast island, Pahang's Pulau Tioman has something for everyone, diver and non-diver alike. With lots of dive centres and low prices, Tioman is a great place to get your certification. Off Tioman and some of the smaller islands nearby, you'll find lots of shallow coral gardens, rocky points and deeper coral gardens. There is an excellent variety of fish, everything from colourful reef fish to large mantas and sharks. See the Tioman Diving & Snorkelling section in the Pahang chapter for more details.

The Seribuat Archipelago While not as famous as Tioman, the other islands of Johor's Seribuat Archipelago offer some of the same conditions without the crowds. Diving is typically over shallow coral gardens and water clarity ranges from good to excellent. The most accessible islands include Besar, Sibu and Rawa, while some of the best diving is around Pemangill and Aur (both of which are unfortunately expensive and hard to get to). Most of the resorts on the islands have their own dive centres (see the Seribuat Archipelago section in the Johor chapter) or you can visit their offices in Mersing near the jetty.

West Coast Kedah's ***Pulau Payar***, 30km south of Langkawi, has a good variety of coral, lots of reef fish and decent visibility. The construction of an artificial reef at the southern tip of the island has increased the number of fish species visible. Prices are higher here than on the east coast and access is a little inconvenient, with most boats leaving from Kuah on Langkawi.

East Malaysia

Sabah Sabah has some of the best dive sites in Malaysia, including the spectacular Pulau Sipadan.

Tunku Abdul Rahman National Park The five islands that make up Tunku Abdul Rahman National Park, just off Kota Kinabalu's coast, offer decent diving in a convenient location. The coral gardens in the shallow waters surrounding the islands are home to several varieties of reef fish, with the occasional reef shark swimming by to keep things lively. This is a good place to learn but would probably bore the more experienced diver. Contact Borneo Divers & Sea

Sports (☎ 088-222226), 4th floor, Wisma Sabah, in Kota Kinabalu, or some of the travel agents listed in the Kota Kinabalu Travel Agencies entry in the Sabah chapter for more details.

Pulau Labuan Pulau Labuan offers some of the only wreck diving in Malaysia with two WWII and two more-modern wrecks lying off the coast. There are also some coral reefs around, but much of the coral has been destroyed by dynamite fishing. Soon to be gazetted as a marine park, the situation around Pulau Labuan will hopefully improve in the near future. Contact some of the agents listed in the Kota Kinabalu section in the Sabah chapter for more details.

Pulau Sipadan Malaysia's only world-class dive site, Pulau Sipadan is a five hectare island which sits atop a 600m limestone pinnacle 36km off the east coast of Sabah. With beautiful coral gardens ending in abrupt drop-offs, the diving around Sipadan is likely to thrill even the experienced diver. Highlights include sea turtles, leopard sharks, huge varieties of reef fish and the occasional school of hammerhead sharks. Due to the island's small size, the number of visitors is strictly limited, and all guests must stay in resorts owned by five dive companies. Needless to say, this drives prices up, and Sipadan is one of Malaysia's most expensive dive destinations. Contact Borneo Divers & Sea Sports (☎ 088-222226), 4th floor, Wisma Sabah, in Kota Kinabalu, or some of the travel agents listed in the Kota Kinabalu Travel Agencies section for more details.

Pulau Layang Layang Three hundred kilometres north-west of Kota Kinabalu, Layang Layang, part of the famous Borneo Banks, is a six hectare island surrounded by a large coral atoll. The diving here is excellent, with both shallow reef dives and impressive drop-offs. Count on seeing large pelagics, tuna, barracuda and the usual schools of reef fish. There is only one resort on the island but you can also dive the area from live-aboards operating from Sabah. See the Layang Layang section in the Sabah chapter for more details.

Sarawak Diving in Sarawak is basically limited to a few shallow spots off the coast of Miri, including one decent wreck dive. With better spots to the north around Labuan and on Sipadan, it is unlikely that experienced divers will want to make this a high-priority destination. For more details on diving around Miri, contact Scuba Sarawak (☎ 085-421121), Ground floor, RIHGA Royal Hotel, Miri.

CONSIDERATIONS FOR RESPONSIBLE DIVING

The popularity of diving is placing immense pressure on many sites in Malaysia. Please consider the following tips when diving and help preserve the ecology and beauty of reefs:

- Do not use anchors on the reef, and take care not to ground boats on coral. Encourage dive operators and regulatory bodies to establish permanent moorings at popular dive sites.

- Avoid touching living marine organisms with your body or dragging equipment across the reef. Polyps can be damaged by even the gentlest contact. Never stand on corals, even if they look solid and robust. If you must hold on to the reef, only touch exposed rock or dead coral.
- Be conscious of your fins. Even without contact the surge from heavy fin strokes near the reef can damage delicate organisms. When treading water in shallow reef areas, take care not to kick up clouds of sand. Settling sand can easily smother the delicate organisms of the reef.
- Practise and maintain proper buoyancy control. Major damage can be done by divers descending too fast and colliding with the reef. Make sure you are correctly weighted and that your weight belt is positioned so that you stay horizontal. If you have not dived for a while, have a practice dive in a pool before taking to the reef. Be aware that buoyancy can change over the period of an extended trip: initially you may breathe harder and need more weight; a few days later you may breathe more easily and need less weight.
- Take great care in underwater caves. Spend as little time within them as possible as your air bubbles may be caught within the roof and thereby leave previously submerged organisms high and dry. Taking turns to inspect the interior of a small cave will lessen the chances of damaging contact.
- Resist the temptation to collect or buy corals or shells. Apart from the ecological damage, taking home marine souvenirs depletes the beauty of a site and spoils the enjoyment of others. The same goes for marine archaeological sites (mainly shipwrecks). Respect their integrity; some sites are even protected from looting by law.
- Ensure that you take home all your rubbish and any litter you may find as well. Plastics in particular are a serious threat to marine life. Turtles can mistake plastic for jellyfish and eat it.
- Resist the temptation to feed fish. You may disturb their normal eating habits, encourage aggressive behaviour or feed them food that is detrimental to their health.
- Minimise your disturbance of marine animals. In particular, do not ride on the backs of turtles as this causes them great anxiety.

continued from page 336

The final stretch into Kota Bharu runs through fertile rice-growing areas, mirroring the area in Kedah and Perlis at the northern end of the peninsula on the western side.

MERANG

Gateway to Pulau Redang, the sleepy little fishing village of Merang (not to be confused with Marang) is 38km north of Batu Rakit. It is one of the few remaining villages of its kind where development hasn't gone ahead in leaps and bounds. There is little of interest in the village, but the beach is pleasant if you have to spend some time waiting for ferry connections to Redang.

Places to Stay & Eat

The best place to stay is the *Kembara Resort* (☎ 09-653 1770), about 500m south of the village (follow the signs from the main road). Dorm beds go for RM7 and pleasant chalets with fan and bathroom cost RM25. There are larger family chalets for RM35. A common kitchen is available for those who bring their own food.

In the centre of the village, the *Merang Inn* (☎ 09-653 1435) is another decent choice with semi-detached chalets for RM35 with fan and bathroom and RM60 with air-con. It also has one of the village's only restaurants.

Another option is *Razak's Kampung House* (no phone), also in the centre of the village. Rooms here cost RM15 per person.

Up on the hill behind the jetty, the *Merang Resthouse* (☎ 09-653 2018) has slightly shabby single/double rooms with air-con and bathroom for RM60. The management also owns a few nearby A-frames with fan and bathroom which cost RM50.

At present, the only place to eat in town is the restaurant at the Merang Inn. Anyone planning to spend a few days in the village would be wise to stock up on food supplies before coming.

Getting There & Away

There are daily buses from the main bus station in Kuala Terengganu to Merang (RM2.30). Taxis from Kuala Terengganu costs RM6 per person. Coming from the north is more difficult and it is easiest to go south as far as Kuala Terengganu and then backtrack. Otherwise, taxis from Kota Bharu cost RM12 per person.

PULAU REDANG

One of the largest and most inaccessible of the east coast islands, Redang is also one of the most beautiful. Unfortunately, the island has been targeted by big developers and there are few options for the independent traveller. Considering the island's beauty, it may be worth paying the money for a package at one of the resorts, particularly now that Tioman is falling into a state of disrepair.

Redang is one of nine islands that form a protected marine park, and it offers excellent diving and snorkelling. Siltation from resort construction is said to have resulted in some coral damage, but concerted efforts are being made to prevent further damage – even snorkelling is restricted to certain areas.

A small village is located in a bay at the southern end of the island and the huge Berjaya Island Resort and golf course are hidden on the north shore. Of most interest to travellers are the beautiful bays on the east side of the island including Teluk Dalam, Teluk Kalong and Pasir Panjang.

Note that the island basically shuts down from 1 November to 1 March and the best season to visit is from mid-April to mid-September.

Nearby Islands

Pulau Lang Tengah is an uninhabited island about 10km from Redang and has excellent snorkelling. **Pulau Pinang** is the small island opposite the fishing village, and other nearby islands include Pulau Tenggol, Pulau Ekor Tebu and Pulau Ling. **Pulau Lima**, a group of five islands two hours by boat from Redang, also has good snorkelling.

Places to Stay

Accommodation on Pulau Redang is best organised as a package in Kuala Terengganu. Ping Anchorage (see Kuala Terengganu, Places to Stay) has the cheapest deal at

RM240 for two nights/three days with camping equipment and meals provided. It also sells packages for all the resorts listed below at competitive prices.

Other than the camping plan, most of the accommodation is in small resorts built on a beautiful stretch of white-sand beach known as Pasir Panjang, on the east coast of the island. Starting at the northern end of the beach, the *Redang Holiday Villa* (☎ 09-622 3932) is well situated and has clean rooms contained in one large building. Two night/three day packages including boat transfer and meals start at RM280.

Next along is the *Coral Redang Island Resort* (☎ 09-623 6200), a full-blown resort affair with overpriced but pleasant double rooms for RM276 per night including meals. If the turquoise water in the bay doesn't suit you, there's a swimming pool here as well.

Next door is the *Redang Pelangi Resort* (☎ 09-623 5202), which is a slightly more casual resort-style affair with two-night/three-day packages in air-con rooms for RM400 per person. A cheaper alternative is its two night/three day camping package which includes meals and boat transfer for RM260 per person.

At the southern end of the beach, the *Redang Bay Resort* (☎ 09-620 3200) has a commanding location, clean rooms and a good dive centre. Its two-night/three-day packages start at RM390.

In the bay directly south of Pasir Panjang you will find several more accommodation options strung out along an excellent white-sand beach. The cheapest of these is *Redang Lagoon Chalet* (☎ 09-827 2116), where two-night/three-day packages start at RM330. This is one of the few places on the island which will take walk-ins at a rate of RM50 per night if there's space.

Getting There & Away

Most visitors to Redang purchase packages which include boat transfer to the island. If you choose to go independently, the private ferries to Redang operated by the Berjaya Island Resort leave Merang daily at 10 am, 2 and 6 pm and cost RM40 (return ferries leave Redang daily at 8 am, noon and 4 pm). Tickets can be purchased at the Merang Inn. Note that priority is given to guests of the Berjaya Island Resort and if its boat is full you will have to try to squeeze onto one of the other resorts' boats. Alternatively, you can charter your own speed boat at the Merang Inn for RM240.

If you go over on the ferry, you'll be dropped in the village where there is no accommodation for travellers. In order to get to the beaches of the island's east coast you will have to hire a taxi boat for RM20 (note that these can't land in rough weather).

KUALA BESUT

Kuala Besut, on the coast south of Kota Bharu, has a reasonably pleasant beach and is an interesting, though grubby, fishing village. A visit to this town is usually just a preliminary to a trip to the Pulau Perhentian.

Orientation & Information

Taxis and local buses operate to/from the taxi stand in the centre of town, very near the seafront. Around the square formed by the taxi and bus stand you will find a few simple shops and restaurants. On the east side of the square, Perhentian Ferry Travel & Tours (☎ 09-691 9679) is a reliable travel agent which can arrange transport to and accommodation on the Perhentians.

Places to Stay

There aren't many places to choose from in Kuala Besut. The cheapest option around is *Yaodin Guesthouse* (☎ 09-697 0887), which has basic rooms with fan for RM10/20 a single/double and air-con rooms for RM30. It's above Yaodin Holidays & Tours travel agency, a minute's walk from the town square (taxi stand). Close by, *Coco Hut Chalet* (☎ 09-697 2085) has very basic rooms for RM20 with fan. It's just north of the town's main square on the right. All rooms have shared bathroom.

If you want a little more comfort, the *Nan Hotel* (☎ 010-985 3414) is just down the road from the Pulau Perhentian ferry pier and has rooms with bathroom and ceiling fan for RM40 and air-con doubles for RM60. All rooms are clean and can accommodate three people.

Getting There & Away

From the north or south, take a bus to Jerteh on the main highway (Route 3), from where buses go hourly to Kuala Besut from 8 am to 4.30 pm (RM1). A share taxi from Jerteh to Kuala Besut costs RM2. Since a share taxi from Kota Bharu all the way to Kuala Besut costs only RM5 per person it seems hardly worth the trouble of going by bus. Most guesthouses in Kota Bharu can arrange share taxis. Likewise, a share taxi from Kuala Terengganu costs only RM10.

PULAU PERHENTIAN

A 1½ hour boat trip from Kuala Besut will take you to the beautiful islands of Perhentian Besar and Perhentian Kecil, just 20km off the coast. These are arguably the most beautiful islands in Malaysia, with crystal-clear aquamarine water and white-sand beaches.

Activities on the islands include snorkelling and diving, jungle walks or just hanging around on the beach waiting for the coconuts to drop. Be warned that there is very little alcohol available on these relatively conservative islands – a Perhentian evening generally involves nothing more decadent than a decent meal and a good book.

Note that these islands basically shut down during the monsoon (usually from mid-November to early-March).

Orientation

A narrow strait separates 'besar', or big island, from 'kecil', or small island. While both islands have their strong points, most travellers tend to gravitate to Kecil, where there is an abundance of cheap accommodation. Some avoid the island precisely for this reason and head to Besar, where budget chalets can still be found. For the undecided, it's possible to cross the strait from island to island for only RM7, a journey which takes about 20 minutes.

On Perhentian Kecil, the most popular spot is Long Beach (Pasir Panjang), an excellent white sandy beach with a string of economical bungalow operations. Perhentian Kecil is also the administrative centre and has a fair-sized village with a few *kedai kopi* (coffee shops) and shops. Across the narrow waist of the island, Coral Bay is another popular choice with a decent stretch of beach and the best sunsets on the islands.

Over on Besar, most of the accommodation is clustered on the west side of the island along a series of beaches divided by rocky headlands. For those looking to get away from it all, a brief walk through the jungle leads to the isolated bay of Teluk Dalam, which has a wide beach and decent snorkelling.

Information

The only place to change money is at the Perhentian Island Resort on Perhentian Besar, but the rate is about 10% less than you'll get in a bank. You can also make telephone calls from here – again, at exorbitant rates. A couple of the chalet operations around the islands also offer telephone services on their mobiles.

Diving & Snorkelling

There are excellent coral reefs off both islands and around nearby uninhabited islands, Pulau Susu Dara in particular. For land-based snorkelling the best bets are the northern end of Long Beach on Kecil and the point in front of the Perhentian Island Resort on Besar. Most of the chalets organise boating trips for snorkelling, and these are well worth the RM15 or so per person. All places also rent out mask, snorkel and flippers for RM10 per day.

For scuba divers there are several operations on Perhentian Besar. Steffen Sea Sports (☎ 09-691 0943), at the Coral View Island Resort, is the cheapest, with two dives including equipment costing RM100 and PADI open-water courses for RM500. Nearby, Watercolours (☎ 018-893 1852) is a competent outfit in front of Paradise Resort on the main beach. It offers two dives for

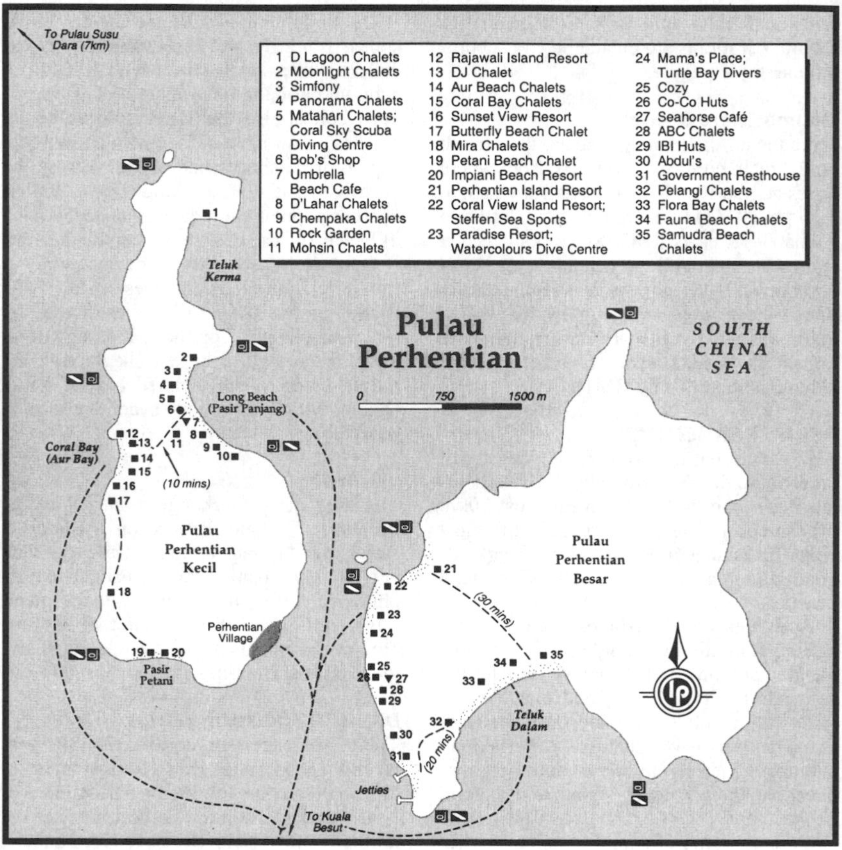

RM140 and PADI courses for RM750. Further down the same beach, Turtle Bay Divers (☎ 010-331 9624) sells two-dive packages for RM140 and PADI courses for RM750. At the Perhentian Island Resort (☎ 09-691 0946), two dives cost RM165 and PADI courses cost RM700.

Over on Kecil, the diving scene is dominated by Coral Sky Scuba Diving Centre (☎ 010-910 1963), at Matahari chalets in the middle of Long Beach. Here, two dives will cost you RM140 and PADI courses go for RM750.

Whoever you choose to dive with, there's a good chance of seeing sea turtles, stingrays, a wide variety of colourful reef fish and the occasional reef shark.

Places to Stay & Eat

Accommodation on Besar is more upscale than on Kecil and generally includes a fan and attached bathroom. As far as eating, no one would call the Perhentians a gourmet paradise – you'll most likely have to put up with lots of mee and nasi dishes, with the occasional fish dinner. Almost all chalet operations have their own restaurant, and there are one or two separate restaurants on the main beach on Besar and on Long Beach on Kecil. Those with special dietary requirements should consider bringing supplies over on the ferry.

Pulau Perhentian Besar There are three main choices on Besar: the Resort, the main beach on the west side of the island, and Teluk Dalam, on the island's southern coast.

The *Perhentian Island Resort* (☎ 010-903 0100) overlooks perhaps the best beach in the islands – a beautiful half-moon bay with good coral around the points on either side. The resort is comfortable and attractive but not of international standard. The cheapest accommodation is in roomy fan-cooled bungalows with bathroom, which cost RM120. Standard air-con bungalows range from RM230. Everything is subject to a 10% service charge and 5% government tax. The restaurant is expensive but does a reasonably good job and at least serves drinks – unlike anywhere else on the island. The resort also hires windsurfers for RM15 per hour, sailboats for RM30 per hour and kayaks for RM7 per hour.

Besar's main beach is a 10 minute clamber over a headland from the resort. This beach stretches all the way to the southern tip of the island, interrupted by several rocky headlands – at low tide you can walk around them on the sand, otherwise you'll have to go up and over on wooded trails. As a rule, the further south you go, the cheaper the accommodation gets.

At the northern end of the beach, the *Coral View Island Resort* (☎ 09-691 0943) is a fairly upscale place with A-frames with fan and bathroom for RM80 and with air-con for RM140. It has a good restaurant and a great location. Next door, *Paradise Resort* (☎ 010-981 0930) has clean chalets with fan and bathroom for RM60/80 (standard/deluxe). Next along, *Mama's Place* (☎ 010-981 3359) is a good mid-budget option with standard rooms with fan and bathroom for RM30 and nicer chalets with fan and bathroom for RM55. It also has family rooms for RM80. The restaurant here does a good Malay-style fish dinner with all the trimmings for RM12 if you request early in the day.

Over the headland, the first place you come to is *Cozy* (no phone), a group of chalets built on the rocks overlooking the water. Slightly tatty chalets here with fan and bathroom are RM35. Down on the beach, *Co-Co Huts* (no phone) are a bargain choice with simple but clean A-frames for RM15 with shared bathroom. Behind Co-Co, the *Seahorse Café* manages some decent western and Malay-style food for around RM5 per order. Next along, *ABC Chalets* (no phone) has A-frames for RM50, and no visible front desk – if you're lucky you may find someone to show you a room. The next spot on the beach, *IBI Huts* (no phone), has huts with fan and bathroom for RM35/50 (standard/deluxe) and a good location.

Clambering over the next headland brings you to another nice stretch of beach where you'll find the popular *Abdul's* (☎ 010-983 7303). Options range from longhouse rooms for RM15 to chalets with fan and bathroom for RM40. Down the beach from Abdul's, you'll find the *Government Resthouse*, the last place on the main beach, which is reserved for Malaysian politicos and their friends.

It is possible to *camp* on the beach beyond the government resthouse, although this area is far from quiet on long weekends (notably the end of April, when the Sultan's Birthday and Worker's Day coincide), when the place is packed with Malaysian families enjoying the break by camping out.

An easily missed track leads from behind the second jetty over the hill to Teluk Dalam, a secluded bay on the south side of the island with a long stretch of shallow beach. The first spot you come to is *Pelangi Chalets* (no phone), a rather ramshackle operation with A-frames for RM25 and bungalows for RM40. Next door, *Flora Bay Chalets* (☎ 09-697 7266) has a variety of slightly run-down accommodation priced from RM30 to RM100. Next along, *Fauna Beach Chalets* (☎ 09-691 8919) is a better choice offering clean chalets with fan and bathroom for RM45 and family rooms for RM70. Last on the beach, *Samudra Beach Chalets* (☎ 010-983 4929) is a pleasantly isolated operation with bungalows with fan and bathroom for RM50 and A-frames with fan and bathroom for RM30.

Pulau Perhentian Kecil Accommodation over on Kecil is more basic and prices are generally lower – most places hover at around RM20 for a chalet with two beds, a mosquito net and a well or common shower.

With a great strip of white sand out front and good swimming and snorkelling, Long Beach is the most popular place on Kecil. On the rocks at the southern end of the beach, *Rock Garden* (no phone) has an interesting location and some of the cheapest bungalows around at RM10 for rugged bare-bones huts. Down the hill, *Chempaka Chalets* (no phone), run by the ever-helpful Musky, has a string of simple A-frames for RM18. Next door, *D'Lahar Chalets* (no phone) has standard/deluxe chalets with shower for RM60/80. Set back from the beach, *Mohsin Chalets* (☎ 010-333 8897) are a cut above the rest of the offerings at Long Beach. Built on the hillside overlooking the bay, clean and relatively new chalets with fan and bathroom start at RM60.

Back on the beach, the *Umbrella Beach Café* has a decent range of western and Malay choices for around RM5 per dish. The restaurant and the nearby *Bob's Shop* have phones, rent snorkelling equipment and can arrange boat trips around the island or to Besar.

In the middle of the beach, set back a bit, *Matahari Chalets* (no phone) is a popular choice with a range of accommodation. Simple chalets with fan are RM30 and A-frames with fan and bathroom are RM55. This is one of the better choices on Long Beach and the restaurant gets good reviews. Nearby, *Panorama Chalets* (☎ 010-912 2518) has basic chalets for RM12 and chalets with fan and bathroom for RM25. Next along, *Simfony* (☎ 010-910 8683) has basic A-frames with shared bathroom for RM15 which aren't bad for the price.

At the northern end of the beach, *Moonlight Chalets* (☎ 010-985 8222) is another popular spot with a range of accommodation. Rooms in the longhouse start at RM10 and simple chalets with shared bathroom go for RM20. Nicer chalets with bathroom are RM35 and family rooms are RM40. The place also has one of the better restaurants on the island with a pleasant veranda.

A trail over the narrow waist of the island leads from Long Beach to the quieter Coral Bay (sometimes known as Teluk Aur, or Aur Bay) on the west side of the island. The beach is decent and gets good sunsets. The southernmost spot is *Butterfly Beach Chalet* (☎ 010-985 8603), which has chalets built over the rocks at the end of the beach for RM30/45 (standard/deluxe). Next door, *Sunset View Resort* (☎ 09-697 7703) has a good location but slightly tatty rooms and chalets which range from RM45 to RM80.

Central *Coral Bay Chalets* (☎ 010-984 7636) has some of the nicest chalets and A-frames on the beach which rent for RM50. Its restaurant, the *Iguana Bistro*, turns out some of the best food on this side of the island. Set back a little from the water, *Aur Beach Chalets* (☎ 010-895 6486) is the budget choice, with simple chalets for RM20 and dorm beds for RM15. Nearby, *DJ Chalet* (☎ 010-985 6155) is also set back from the beach and has rooms for RM20, and RM35 with bathroom. This is a friendly place set back in the forest that might appeal to some.

Built on the rocks at the northern end of the bay, *Rajawali Island Resort* (☎ 010-985 9807) has chalets with shared bathroom for RM15. The chalets are a mixed bag here and it's a good idea to look at a few before deciding.

As well as Long Beach and Coral Bay, there are a number of small bays around the island, each with one set of chalets, and often only accessed by boat. *D Lagoon Chalets* (☎ 010-976 0631) is on Teluk Kerma, a small bay on the north-western side of the island. The beach here has quite a bit of dead coral but the tranquillity of the spot more than makes up for it. There are longhouse rooms and chalets which range from RM10 to RM40. There's a small restaurant, and tracks lead to a couple of very remote beaches in the north-west corner of the island. This is one of the few places on Pulau Perhentian Kecil which has chalets with attached bathrooms.

On the south-western coast is *Mira Chalets* (no phone). This is on another beautiful little beach and there are only a few chalets which cost RM15/20 (standard/deluxe). The elevated restaurant has great views over the water and is a popular place. Walking tracks lead through the rainforest to Pasir Petani (30 minutes) or north to Coral Bay (one hour).

On the south coast at the lovely isolated beach of Pasir Petani, there are a couple of choices. The cheaper of the two is *Petani Beach Chalet* (☎ 019-313 3887), which has just a few chalets by the beach ranging in price from RM15 to RM45.

Next door is the more upmarket *Impiani Beach Resort* (no phone), where nice chalets with air-con and bathroom cost a healthy RM170. While you can get here on foot from Mira Chalets or Perhentian Village, it's much easier to get dropped off by a boat, especially when you first arrive with all your luggage.

Getting There & Away

Both speedboats and regular boats run between Kuala Besut and the Perhentians. Speedboats depart Kuala Besut at 9.30 and 10.30 am, and 2.30 pm daily (30 minutes, RM30 one way, RM60 return) while slowboats depart approximately every hour from 9.30 am to 4.30 pm daily (about 1½ hours, RM25 one way, RM40 return). The boats will drop you off at any of the beaches. In the other direction, speedboats depart from the islands daily at around noon and 4 pm, and slowboats hourly from 8 am to 2 pm. When you want to leave it's a good idea to let the owner of your chalet know the day before. Tickets are sold by several travel agents around town, the best of which is Perhentian Ferry Travel & Tours (see the Kuala Besut Orientation & Information entry).

Getting Around

While there are some trails around the island (see the Perhentian map), the easiest way to go from beach to beach or island to island is by boat. Most resort and chalet owners can arrange for a boat and driver. From island to island, the trip costs RM7 per boat, and a jaunt from one beach to another on the same island usually runs to about RM5, though some friendly chalet owners don't charge.

Kelantan

Kelantan is Malaysia at its most Malayan – a centre for Malay culture, crafts and religion. It's the place to watch batik being made, see kite-flying contests, admire traditional woodcarving techniques, photograph colourful marketplaces and marvel at the skills of *songket* (fabric woven with gold thread) weavers and silversmiths.

The capital, Kota Bharu, is a good place to sample traditional Malay culture, and makes a good base from which to explore the surrounding countryside, but the true Malay spirit is found in the villages of Kelantan.

The most conservative state in Peninsular Malaysia and a last bastion of opposition rule, Kelantan's government is an alliance of the dominant Islamic party of Malaysia (PAS) and the National Front (BN). The government has tried for years without success to impose Islamic law on its citizens. It's still a poor state and is a world apart from the go-go western states of Peninsular Malaysia.

The Kelantan state economy is driven by the production of rice, based mainly on the fertile plain of the Sungai (River) Kelantan, which flows due north through the state, finding the sea just north of Kota Bharu. Fishing and tobacco growing are other important activities.

HIGHLIGHTS

- **Kota Bharu** – bastion of traditional Malay culture, with the best night market in the country
- **The 'Jungle Railway'** – from Tumpat down into Pahang state; it's a great way to see Malaysia's mountainous interior without breaking a sweat
- **The Tumpat Region** – area of strong Thai influence, with several unusual wats scattered between pleasant farming kampungs

History

Archaeological finds at Gua Musang and Gua Cha have turned up evidence of human settlements dating back to prehistoric times.

In later times (early Christian era), Kelantan was influenced by the Indianised Funan kingdom on the Mekong River. Farming methods used in Kelantan are based on Funan practices, and the *wayang kulit* shadow play and weaving methods are also thought to have come from Funan.

After being a vassal of first the Sumatran Sriwijaya Empire, and then the Siamese, Kelantan came under the sway of the new Melaka sultanate in the 15th century. On the demise of that sultanate in the 17th century, Kelantan was ruled by Johor and then, the following century, by Terengganu.

By the 1820s Kelantan was the most populous and one of the most prosperous states on the peninsula. As was the case in Terengganu, Kelantan escaped the ravages of the disputes that plagued the west coast states, and so experienced largely unimpeded development. Also like Terengganu, Kelantan had strong ties with Siam throughout the 19th century,

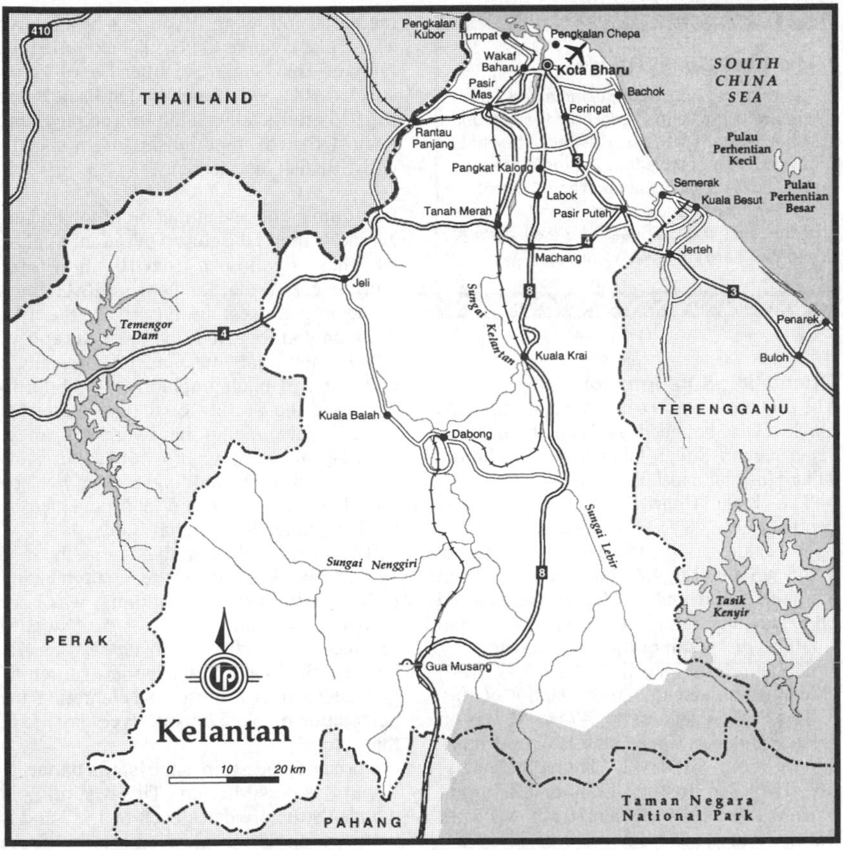

before control was passed to the British following the signing of an Anglo-Siamese treaty in 1909. The biggest upheaval for the state came in the late 18th century, when it was hit by a spate of natural disasters – hurricanes, famine and cattle plagues – and many of its residents migrated to Kedah.

During WWII, Kelantan was the first place in Malaya to be invaded by Japanese troops. During the Japanese occupation, control of the state was passed to Thailand, but in 1948 Kelantan became a member of the Federation of Malaya.

KOTA BHARU

In the north-east corner of the peninsula, Kota Bharu is the termination of the east coast road, and a gateway to Thailand.

At first glance, Kota Bharu is much like the other east coast cities – a modern, architecturally uninspired town, set on the banks of a wide river. But if you scratch the surface, Kota Bharu has a number of attractions and is a good base for exploring the surrounding region. Many travellers plan an overnight stop here en route to or from Thailand. Many end up staying much longer.

The East Coast House

The kampung houses of Kelantan and Terengganu differ quite markedly from those found in the western peninsula states. The most obvious difference is that the roofs are tiled and show a Thai or Cambodian influence.

As in Thai houses, the walls and columns of the east coast houses are well carved, and there are far fewer windows.

Orientation & Information

The centre of town is a busy area, north of the clock tower, bounded by Jalan Pintu Pong, Jalan Kebun Sultan/Jalan Sultan Mahmud, Jalan Hospital and Jalan Temenggong.

The Kota Bharu tourist information centre (☎ 09-748 5534) is a useful outfit. It's open Sunday to Wednesday from 8 am to 12.45 pm and 2 to 4.45 pm, Thursday from 8 am to 1.15 pm and 2 to 4.30 pm and closed on Friday and Saturday. It's on Jalan Sultan Ibrahim, just south of the clock tower.

The immigration office (☎ 09-748 2120) is at Wisma Persekutuan on Jalan Bayam.

The Thai consulate (☎ 09-744 0867) is on Jalan Pengkalan Chepa, and is open from 9 am to 4 pm Sunday to Thursday, but is usually closed between 12.30 and 2.30 pm.

Banks are open between 10 am and 3 pm Saturday to Wednesday, 9.30 to 11.30 am Thursday and closed on Friday. You'll find a number of banks on Jalan Tok Hakim and Jalan Padang Garong.

There are several Internet cafes scattered around town, including the ITA Pro Multimedia Café on Jalan Kebun Sultan. You can also log on at KB Backpacker's Lodge (see Places to Stay in this section).

In Kelantan, state offices are closed Thursday afternoon and Friday, but open on Saturday and Sunday.

Padang Merdeka

Padang Merdeka (Independence Square) is a strip of grass that was established as a memorial following WWI. It is best known as the place where the British exhibited the body of Tok Janggut, 'Father Beard', a respected elder who was killed at Pasir Puteh in 1915 after leading a 2000 strong uprising against British imperialism (more specifically, British land taxes).

Museums The real attraction of the Padang Merdeka area is the cluster of museums close by. They are all open from 10 am to 6 pm daily, except Friday, and charge RM3 entry.

Starting closest to the river, the first museum you come to is the **Bank Kerapu**, or WWII Memorial Museum. It's basically a collection of photographic memorabilia illustrating the perfidy of the Japanese, but there is also some hardware (Japanese swords) on display. It's housed in Kota Bharu's first stone building, built in 1912 by the Mercantile Bank and later occupied by the Hongkong & Shanghai Bank.

The mosque-like building across the road from the Bank Kerapu is the **Muzium Islam**, (Islamic Museum). The building was once known as Serambi Mekah, or the 'Veranda to Mecca' – a reference to its days as Kelantan's first school of Islamic instruction. Nowadays it is a museum celebrating the percolation of Islam into the everyday life of the state.

Further along again is the **Istana Jahar**, or Royal Customs Museum. This beautiful old wooden structure dates back to 1887 and is worth a look. The displays on courtly life are tastefully presented, even if the English captions could do with a bit of editing – in one instance we are told it was customary for the sultan to offer his 'brid' a 'goft' after which there was no more 'wailing' for invitations. Inside, take note of the wrought-iron staircases on either side of the room – they lead upstairs to a glorious wooden veranda.

From the Istana Jahar, turn left (north) and look for the sky-blue building that houses the **Istana Batu**, or the Royal Museum. The building was constructed in 1939 and served as the palace of the crown prince from 1969, until it was donated to the state. It now houses a royal dining room, an opulent living room, replicas of the crown jewels and other royal bric-a-brac.

Finally, across the road is the **Kampung Kraftangan**, or the Handicraft Village. This is a touristy *kampung* (village) idyll (all arts and crafts, no toiling in the fields), featuring a museum with displays of silversmithing, batik making and other cultural activities.

Opposite the Istana Batu, surrounded by walls and closed to the public, is the **Istana Balai Besar**, or the Palace of the Large Audience Hall.

State Museum

The State Museum is opposite the clock tower, next to the tourist information centre. It brings together an eclectic array of artefacts, crafts, paintings and photographic displays, all connected in some way or another with Kelantan state. There's some excellent Ming and Qing dynasty porcelain downstairs and kites upstairs. The downstairs local art exhibit is given over to nostalgic exhibits celebrating kampung life. It is open daily from 10.30 am to 4.45 pm, except Friday; entry is RM3.

Markets

The **central market** is one of the most colourful and active in Malaysia. It is in a modern octagonal building with traders selling fresh produce on the ground floor, and stalls on the floors above selling spices, basketware and other goods. Near the market is the **Bazaar Buluh Kubu**, a good place to buy handicrafts.

The **old central market** consists of a complete block of food stalls on the ground floor, and a good selection of batik, songket and clothes on the 1st floor.

Gelanggang Seni (Cultural Centre)

Kota Bharu provides an opportunity to see top spinning, traditional dance dramas, wayang kulit and other traditional activities. The place to go is Gelanggang Seni, across the road from the Hotel Perdana on Jalan Sultan Mahmud. Free afternoon and evening sessions are held on Saturday, Monday and Wednesday from 2 March to 31 October, except during Ramadan. Check with the tourist information centre for more details.

Special Events

Each year around August, Kota Bharu has a bird-singing contest when you can see Malay songbirds perform. On Friday morning there's also a bird-singing contest out near Johnty's Guest House. Here the locals hang their decorative bird cages up on long poles, then sit back and listen. It happens to a lesser extent on other days of the week as well. Ask at the tourist information centre for details.

The spectacular kite festival is usually held in May, the drum festival in July and the top-spinning contest in September. The Sultan's Birthday celebration involves a week of cultural events. The dates vary, so check with the tourist information centre or get hold of Tourism Malaysia's *Calendar of Events* brochure.

Malay songbirds perform in Kota Bharu's annual bird-singing contest.

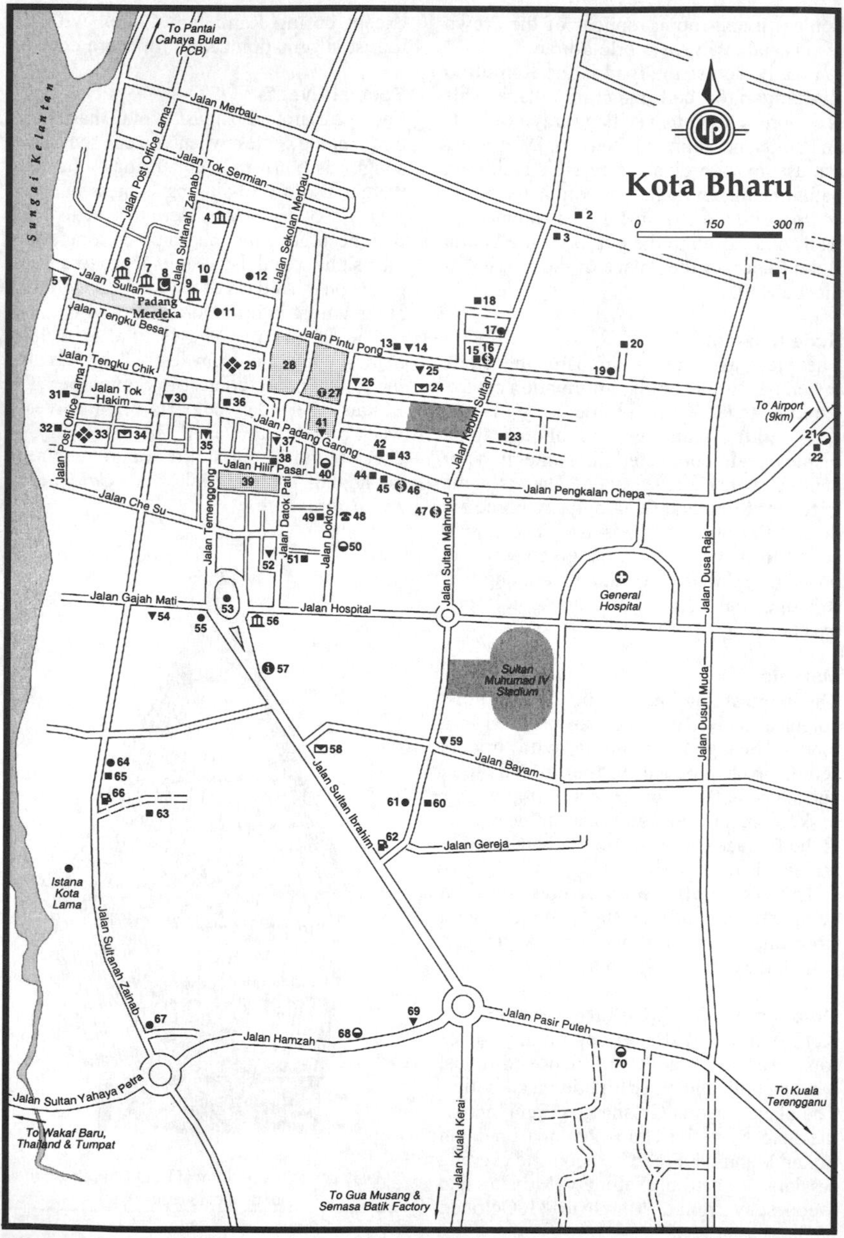
Kota Bharu
0
150
300 m
To Pantai Cahaya Bulan (PCB)
Sungai Kelantan
Jalan Merbau
Jalan Tok Sermian
Jalan Post Office Lama
Jalan Sultanah Zainab
Jalan Sekolah Merbau
Jalan Sultan
Padang Merdeka
Jalan Tengku Besar
Jalan Tengku Chik
Jalan Tok Hakim
Jalan Pintu Pong
Jalan Padang Garong
Jalan Hilir Pasar
Jalan Che Su
Jalan Temenggong
Jalan Datok Pati
Jalan Doktor
Jalan Kebun Sultan
Jalan Pengkalan Chepa
Jalan Sultan Mahmud
Jalan Dusa Raja
To Airport (9km)
General Hospital
Jalan Gajah Mati
Jalan Hospital
Sultan Muhumad IV Stadium
Jalan Bayam
Jalan Dusun Muda
Jalan Sultan Ibrahim
Jalan Gereja
Istana Kota Lama
Jalan Sultanah Zainab
Jalan Hamzah
Jalan Pasir Puteh
Jalan Sultan Yahaya Petra
To Wakaf Baru, Thailand & Tumpat
Jalan Kuala Kerai
To Gua Musang & Semasa Batik Factory
To Kuala Terengganu

PLACES TO STAY
1 Johnty's Guest House
2 KB Garden Hostel
3 Star Hostel
10 Safar Inn
13 City Guest House
15 Juita Inn
18 Ideal Travellers' Guest House
20 Zeck Traveller's Inn
22 Rainbow Inn
23 Friendly Guest House
31 Hotel New North Malaysia; Restoran Donald Duck
32 Diamond Puteri Hotel
36 Temenggong Hotel
38 Thye Ann Hotel
42 KB Backpackers Lodge
43 Kencana Inn
44 KB Inn
45 Yee Guest House
49 Kencana Inn City Centre
51 Hotel Ansar
60 Hotel Perdana; Aris
63 Rebana House
65 Menora Guest House

PLACES TO EAT
5 Food Stalls
14 KFC
25 Muhibah Vegetarian Restaurant
26 McDonald's
30 McDonald's
35 Sun Too Restaurant
37 Restoran Razak
41 Night Market Food Stalls
52 Family Restaurant
54 Meena Curry House
59 Food Stalls
69 Outdoor Market; Food Stalls

OTHER
4 Istana Batu (Royal Museum)
6 Bank Kerapu (WWII Memorial Museum)
7 Muzium Islam
8 State Mosque
9 Istana Jahar (Royal Customs Museum)
11 Istana Balai Besar
12 Kampung Kraftagan (Handicraft Village)
16 Maybank Finance
17 ITA Pro Multimedia Café
19 Bird-Singing Place
21 Thai Consulate
24 Post Office
27 Public Toilet
28 Central Market
29 Bazaar Buluh Kubu
33 Hankyu Jaya Department Store; KFC
34 Post Office
39 Old Central Market
40 Central Bus & Taxi Station
46 Hongkong Bank
47 Maybank
48 Telekom
50 Taxi Station
53 Clock Tower
55 Malaysia Airlines
56 State Museum
57 Tourist Information Centre
58 Post Office
61 Gelanggang Seni (Cultural Centre)
62 Petrol Station
64 Silver Shops
66 Caltex Petrol Station
67 Silversmith
68 External (Jalan Hamzah) Bus Station
70 Langgar Bus Station

Organised Tours

The tourist information centre has expensive but rewarding tours: a river safari and jungle-trekking tour (RM80), a three day 'kampung experience' (RM100 for two days and one night) and a 'homestay' programme (RM225 all inclusive), where you stay with a family and get the opportunity to learn local crafts. The latter is very popular. It also has a one day Malay craft workshop (RM125, including lunch) which gives you an opportunity to try your hand at kite making, batik and puppetry. Lastly, it offers a morning course in Malay cooking for RM55. Note that none of these are available during Ramadan.

Some of the guesthouses around town also run tours. Johnty's Guesthouse has a two night/three day package to the Jelawang Jungle for RM130 which gets good reviews from travellers. Other travel agents around town provide the same service at higher rates.

Places to Stay – Budget

Locals count upwards of 60 guesthouse outfits in Kota Bharu, and there will probably be more by the time you have this book in your hands. Prices vary only marginally, hovering around RM6 for a dorm bed, RM10/12 for a single/double and RM15 to RM20 for a room with bathroom. Many have bicycles and cooking facilities.

For anyone spending more than a couple of days in Kota Bharu, the best places to be based in are the 'homestays' on the outskirts of town. The guesthouses in the centre of town are generally noisy and slightly claustrophobic (coffin-size rooms divided by paper-thin wooden panelling), though few of them lack smiles or useful travelling tips.

Zeck Travellers' Inn (☎ 09-743 1613) is a popular spot with a friendly, informative owner. It's your standard-issue guesthouse and the rooms are clean, if a little cramped. It's around 15 minutes walk from the centre of town and is very quiet. Five minutes walk away, *Johnty's Guest House* (no phone) is a laid back place with the air of a 1960s crash pad, which might appeal to some. Back down on Jalan Pengkalan Chepa is the *Rainbow Inn* (☎ 09-743 4936). This house has a pleasant garden, free bikes and some great artwork on the walls, courtesy of inspired travellers – the drawback is the noise from the traffic on the main road.

If you want to be more centrally located yet insulated from the traffic noise, the *Ideal Travellers' Guest House* (☎ 09-744 2246), in a private house down an alley off Jalan Pintu Pong, is a decent choice. It's quiet and has a pleasant garden, but it's often full. It also runs the *Friendly Guest House*, a few hundred metres away, just off Jalan Kebun Sultan. It's not as attractive, but is also quiet and has good rooms, some with bathroom, for RM15.

One of the best places in the centre of town, the *KB Backpackers Lodge* (☎ 09-743 2125), on Jalan Padang Garong, is a friendly and popular choice. It has both dorm and private rooms, a pleasant common area and cooking facilities. The owners can also help with local and ongoing travel arrangements, and have Internet and fax facilities. Nearby, the *KB Inn* (no phone) and *Yee Guest House* (☎ 09-744 1944) are less-inspiring options. In particular, the Yee Guest House has had bad reports from single female travellers who complain of harassment by staff and other guests. A little further north, on Jalan Pintu Pong, the *City Guest House* (☎ 09-743 5343) is a clean but rather characterless choice, with both dorm and private rooms.

At 3338D Jalan Sultanah Zainab is the *Menora Guest House* (☎ 09-748 1669), which has a variety of accommodation, from dorm beds for RM5 to large doubles for RM22. It also has air-con rooms for RM38. This place is cleaner than many other guesthouses in town. Although on a busy road, it's fairly quiet, and the rooftop terrace is popular.

Not far south of the Menora is *Rebana House* (no phone) – look for the faded sign pointing up an alley next to the Caltex petrol station. It's a lovely house, decorated Malay style with lots of artwork around. There's a variety of rooms available, from the RM6 dorm and poky RM8 singles to some beautiful old rooms and chalets in the garden for RM10 to RM15.

Another option, if you are desperate, is one of the old Chinese hotels – they are usually noisy and seedy, but relatively inexpensive, with rooms at around RM15. Possibilities include the *Thye Ann Hotel*, near the bus station, and the *Hotel New North Malaysia*, by the river.

If you're willing to pay slightly more, there are two good value, but characterless, places out on Jalan Merbau. The *Star Hotel* (☎ 09-748 6115) has clean air-con rooms for RM35. Across the street, the *KB Garden Hostel* (☎ 09-748 5696) is really a hotel masquerading as a guesthouse. Air-con singles/doubles are RM30/35.

Places to Stay – Mid-Range

Kota Bharu's mid-range accommodation has been steadily improving in recent years, and there are now a number of good value options to choose from. All offer air-con rooms, 24 hour hot water, TV and all the other services you'd expect.

The *Kencana Inn* (☎ 09-744 7994), Jalan Padang Garong, is fully air-conditioned and conveniently located, with rooms for RM53 and upwards. The same organisation also has a cheaper place on Jalan Doktor, the *Kencana Inn City Centre* (☎ 09-744 0944), which is a few steps down in quality, and charges RM49 for standard rooms.

Nestled away in a quiet part of town between the Royal Customs Museum and the Royal Museum is the *Safar Inn* (☎ 09-747 8000; fax 09-747 9000), where excellent air-con rooms start at RM75. This is probably the best mid-budget choice in town. The *Hotel Ansar* (☎ 09-747 4000; fax 09-746 1150) offers very similar standards at slightly higher rates – RM70 for a standard single and RM105 for a double.

The *Temenggong Hotel* (☎ 09-744 1481) on Jalan Tok Hakim is a nondescript mid-range hotel, with rates starting at RM68 for rooms in the old wing and RM75 in the new one. This hotel doesn't quite measure up to the above-mentioned competition.

The *Juita Inn* (☎ 09-744 6888; fax 09-744 5777) is priced higher than most in this range at RM95/110 for singles/doubles. The rooms are, in fact, something of a step down in quality.

Places to Stay – Top End

The top hotel is undoubtedly the new *Diamond Puteri Hotel* (☎ 09-743 9988). Located near the waterfront, this sprawling international-class hotel has all the amenities you'd expect. Standard rooms start at RM220, and deluxe rooms and suites are also available.

The 136 room *Hotel Perdana* (☎ 09-748 5000) on Jalan Sultan Mahmud is the other contender in the luxury market. Superior singles/doubles cost RM190/210 and deluxe rooms are also available. It's fully air-conditioned, with swimming pool, bowling alley, and squash and tennis courts.

Places to Eat

The best and cheapest Malay food in Kota Bharu is found at the *night market*, opposite the central bus station. The food stalls are set up in the evening and there's a wide variety of delicious, cheap Malay food. Just bear in mind the whole thing closes down for evening prayers between 7 and 7.45 pm and Muslims and non-Muslims alike are forced to vacate the premises.

Most of the stalls at the night market deal in variations on the nasi goreng theme, but Thai-style tom yam soups and Indian murtabak are also popular dishes. More unusual possibilities include blue rice, hard-boiled quail eggs or that old favourite, barbecued stingray.

It's also a good place to snack-track and then buy rice wrapped in banana leaf from one of the rice stalls. You can then sit at any of the tables, eat your meal and order a drink (nothing alcoholic). Traditionally you eat with the right hand – each table has a jug of water and a roll of tissue paper to clean your fingers – but forks and spoons are readily available. Local specialities include: ayam percik (marinated chicken on bamboo skewers) and nasi kerabu (rice with coconut, fish and spices). Some locals reckon that the best ayam percik comes from the *Yati* stall, in the south-east corner of the market.

It's easy to write off the rest of Kota Bharu after the night market, but there's a surprising amount of good food around town. More *food stalls* can be found next to the river opposite the Padang Merdeka, by the Jalan Hamzah bus station and at the Sultan Muhamad IV stadium.

The *Restoran Razak*, on the corner of Jalan Datok Pati and Jalan Padang Garong, is cheap and has good Indian Muslim food. For an excellent lunch of Malay curry on a banana leaf, try the *Meena Curry House* on Jalan Gajah Mati.

There are also plenty of Chinese restaurants around town, including good chicken-rice places on Jalan Padang Garong near the Kencana Inn. The *Restoran Donald Duck*, on the ground floor in the Hotel New North Malaysia, cooks up a very good Cantonese-style duck and rice, and the beer comes in chilled glasses so cold that a block of ice forms in the glass before you finish.

Nearby at the *Family Restaurant* you can get something approaching a western-style breakfast. The *Sun Too Restaurant* also turns out western dishes, as well as Thai and Malay favourites. It also serves beer.

Vegetarians can try the *Muhibah Vegetarian Restaurant* on Jalan Pintu Pong, which serves meatless Malay, western and Chinese dishes. Also note that some of the stalls in the night market serve tasty tofu satay.

Shopping

Kota Bharu is a centre for Malay crafts. Batik, songket, silverware, woodcarving and kite-making factories and shops are dotted around town.

One of the best places to see handicrafts is on the road north to Pantai Cahaya Bulan (PCB). There are a number of workshops representing most crafts stretched out along the road all the way to the beach.

There are silversmiths on Jalan Sultanah Zainab, and the Semasa Batik Factory is on the road to Gua Musang, down the road beside Lee's garage, which you reach on bus No 5.

The markets are as good a place as any to buy handicrafts, if you know the prices and bargain hard. Figure on RM5 to RM100 for decorative kites and RM30 to RM200 for real flying kites, RM7 to RM50 for batik pieces and at least RM100 for one square metre of batik.

For batik, you can also try Wisma Batik on Jalan Che Su, just around the corner from the Hotel Murni, and the outdoor stalls near the night market.

Getting There & Away

Air The Malaysia Airlines office (☎ 09-744 7000) is opposite the clock tower on Jalan Gajah Mati. Direct flights go to Penang (RM87), Alor Setar (RM71) and KL (RM104).

Bus The state-run SKMK is the largest bus company, and runs all the city and regional buses, as well as most of the long-distance buses. It operates from the central bus station (city and regional buses) and the Langgar bus station (long-distance buses). All the other long-distance bus companies operate from the Jalan Hamzah external bus station. On arrival in Kota Bharu some of the buses will drop you at the central bus station, but they don't depart from there.

SKMK is the easiest to deal with, as it has ticket offices at all the bus stations. Long-distance departures are from the Langgar bus station but, just to make things confusing, a few evening, long-distance buses also go from the central bus station. Ask which station your bus departs from when you buy your ticket, and book as far ahead as possible, especially for the Butterworth and Penang buses.

SKMK has regular buses from the central bus station to Kuala Terengganu (three hours, RM7.40) and Kuantan (six hours, RM16). Other SKMK buses leave from Langgar bus station in the south of the city. Buses to Johor Bahru (10, hours, RM29 air-con), Singapore (12 hours, RM30) and KL (10 hours, RM25) leave at 8 pm (also 9 pm to KL). The buses to Butterworth (eight hours, RM20) and Penang (RM19.50) leave at 10 am and 10 pm. There is a bus to Jerantut (RM18) at 8.30 am. Other destinations are Alor Setar, Gerik, Kuala Dungun, Kuala Lipis, Melaka, Mersing and Temerloh.

The other companies cover many of the same routes and are worth trying if the SKMK buses are full. Buy your tickets at the Jalan Hamzah external bus station, or some of the companies have agents at the Bazaar Buluh Kubu. Bumi Express is the only company with buses to Melaka.

All regional buses leave from the central bus station. Destinations include: Wakaf Baharu (Nos 19, 27, 27A, 43); Rantau Panjang (Nos 29, 29A, 36); Tumpat (No 19); Bachok (Nos 2, 23, 29); Pasir Puteh (Nos 3, 3A); Jerteh (No 3A); Kuala Krai (Nos 5, 57); and Gua Musang (No 57).

Train The jungle railway starts at Tumpat and goes through Kuala Krai, Gua Musang, Kuala Lipis and Jerantut (for Taman Negara National Park), and eventually meets the Singapore-KL line at Gemas. There are express and local trains on this line. The nearest station to Kota Bharu is at Wakaf Baharu, a RM1 trip on bus No 19 or 27. Times listed here are for Wakaf Baharu.

There is a daily express train all the way to KL at 6.40 pm. It stops at Kuala Lipis, Jerantut and Gemas before arriving in KL at 6.30 am the following morning. There is also a daily express to Singapore at 8.20 pm making the same stops en route before arriving at 8.10 am the following morning. Note that as both of these trains leave in the evening, you'll miss out on most of the jungle scenery.

A local train leaves daily at 6.21 am and stops at almost every station before arriving at Gemas at 7.55 pm. There are also two local trains daily that only go as far as Gua Musang, one at 3.50 am and one at 1.55 pm. From there, you can catch an ongoing express train the same day to KL or Singapore, or wait until the following day and continue south on a local train.

Note that the national railway company, Keretapi Tana Melayu (KTM), has a ticket office (counter 5) at the Jalan Hamzah bus station in Kota Bharu. Refer to the introductory Getting Around chapter for the train timetable and fare details on express trains.

Taxi The taxi station is on the southern side of the central bus station, and there is an overflow station during the day at site of the night market.

Main taxi destinations and costs per person are: Butterworth (RM40); KL (RM35/45 for non-air-con/air-con); Kuala Terengganu (RM12); Kuala Lipis (RM35); and Kuantan (RM25).

Car Avis has an office (☎ 09-748 4457) in the Hotel Perdana on Jalan Sultan Mahmud.

Thailand The Thai border is at Rantau Panjang (Sungai Golok on the Thai side), 1½ hours by bus from Kota Bharu. Bus No 29B departs on the hour from the central bus station, and costs RM2.70. From Rantau Panjang walk across the border; it's about 1km to the station – a trishaw costs RM3. Malaysian currency is accepted in Sungai Golok. Share taxis from Kota Bharu to Rantau Panjang cost RM14 per car and take 45 minutes.

From Sungai Golok there is a train to Surathani at 6 am, to Bangkok at 10.05 am and an express train to Bangkok at 10.55 am. All stop at Hat Yai and Surathani. Buses to Hat Yai leave from the Valentine Hotel in Sungai Golok until 3 pm, and there are taxis to Yala and Narathiwat town.

An alternative route into Thailand is via Pengkalan Kubor, on the coast. It's more time consuming and very few travellers go this way. See the following Around Kota Bharu section for more details.

Getting Around

Kota Bharu itself is fairly compact, and it is possible to get almost everywhere on foot.

To/From the Airport The airport is 8km from town. You can take bus No 9 from the old central market, or a taxi costs RM12.

Bus Most of the city buses leave from the middle of the old central market, on the Jalan Hilir Pasar side, or from opposite the Bazaar Buluh Kubu. To Pantai Cahaya Bulan (PCB) take bus No 10. It leaves from the Bazaar Buluh Kubu or you can catch it at the bus stand in front of the Kencana Inn.

Trishaw Trishaws still linger on, though most people nowadays get around on motorbikes. A short journey of up to a kilometre costs RM3.

AROUND KOTA BHARU

Masjid Kampung Laut

Reputed to be the oldest in Peninsular Malaysia, this mosque was built about 300 years ago by Javanese Muslims as thanks for a narrow escape from pirates.

It originally stood at Kampung Laut, just across the river from Kota Bharu, but each year the monsoon floods (November to January) caused considerable damage to the wooden mosque, and in 1968 it was moved to a safer location. It now stands about 10km inland at Kampung Nilam Puri, a local centre for religious study. Note that entry is forbidden to non-Muslims. To get there, take bus No 44 from Kota Bharu's central bus station.

Pantai Cahaya Bulan (PCB)

PCB is a Malay acronym that sounds far more appealing translated into English – the 'Beach of Passionate Love'. At least that is what it was once called. Pantai Cinta Berahi is now known as Pantai Cahaya Bulan – 'Moonlight Beach' – in keeping with Islamic sensitivities. Fortunately the same acronym applies and everyone refers to it as PCB.

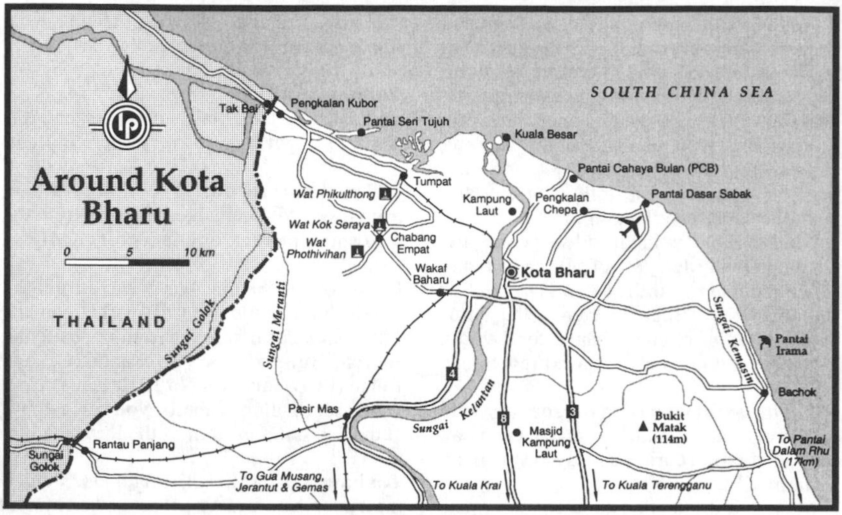

PCB is 10km north of the town, only 30 minutes by bus from Kota Bharu. It's a good day trip option on a sunny day, but hardly the kind of place you'd want to retire to. Accommodation is provided by shabby resorts, and even the beach looks a little tired.

Places to Stay & Eat Near the beach the *Resort Pantai Cinta Berahi* (☎ 09-774 2020) has a number of run-down cottages dotted among the trees. Room rates start at RM138 for a double, including taxes. It also has a swimming pool.

About 1km off the main road, the *Perdana Resort* (☎ 09-773 3000) has a restaurant, swimming pool, tennis courts, and even a five hole golf course. Bungalows cost RM150 to RM210, including taxes.

Getting There & Away The No 10 bus from Kota Bharu stops at the Perdana Resort and terminates close to the main beach. A taxi from Kota Bharu costs RM12.

Pantai Irama

Pantai Irama (Beach of Melody) at Bachok has landscaped gardens along the foreshore and is popular with day-trippers. Like most of the beaches around Kota Bharu, it's pleasant but nothing special. Bus Nos 2A and 2B run out to the beach.

Places to Stay The *Motel Bachok* (☎ 09-778 8462) has mid-range accommodation.

Other Beaches

Thirteen kilometres from Kota Bharu and 3km beyond the Pengkalan Chepa airport, **Pantai Dasar Sabak** is a beach with a history. On 7 December 1941, the Pacific Theatre of WWII commenced on the beach there when Japanese troops stormed ashore, a full hour and a half before the rising sun rose over Pearl Harbor.

Other beaches close to Kota Bharu include **Pantai Dalam Rhu,** near the fishing village of Semerak, 19km from Pasir Puteh, not far from the Terengganu state border. It's sometimes known as Pantai Bisikan Bayu, the 'Beach of Whispering Breeze'. North of Kota Bharu there's **Pantai Kuda** (Horse Beach), 25km away in the Tumpat area, and **Pantai Seri Tujuh** (see the following Tumpat District section).

Tumpat District

Tumpat district is a major agricultural area bordering Thailand, and the Thai influence is very noticeable. Small villages are scattered among the picturesque rice fields, and there are a number of interesting Thai Buddhist temples, such as Wat Phothivihan. Other places of interest include the beach resort at Pantai Seri Tujuh, and Pengkalan Kubor is an exit point for Thailand. Tumpat town is at the end of the railway line, but it has no hotels.

Temples Claimed to be one of the largest temples in South-East Asia, **Wat Phothivihan** is a Buddhist temple with a 40m-long reclining Buddha statue. It was built in 1973. The Buddha statue itself is unremarkable, but the novelty of finding a wat in strongly Muslim Kelantan is enough to add some interest. There is a resthouse available for use by sincere devotees, for a donation.

To get to Wat Phothivihan, take bus No 19 or 27 to Chabang Empat. Get off at the crossroads and turn left (south-west). Walk 3.5km along this road, through interesting villages and paddy fields, until you reach Kampung Jambu and the reclining Buddha, it takes about one hour. A taxi from Chabang Empat, if you can find one, costs RM4 to the wat.

The region is dotted with Thai-influenced temples, or wats, and the Wesak Festival (usually held in April or May) is a particularly good time to visit them. At Chabang Empat, if you take the turn to the right (north) at the light in front of the police station, you will come to **Wat Kok Seraya** after about 1km. This wat houses a modest standing Buddha. Continuing north about 4km in the direction of Tumpat, you will come to **Wat Phikulthong**. This wat houses an impressive gold, standing Buddha and has pleasant grounds for strolling. You can get to these wats on bus No 19; continue past Chabang Empat and ask the driver to let you off in front of these temples.

Pantai Seri Tujuh Resort This downmarket beach resort is on a long spit of land, with a sweeping stretch of beach facing the sea and a quiet bay behind. It is popular during holidays, but otherwise very quiet. The surrounding villages are still very traditional and you can see Malay fishing boats being built at a few shipyards. The government-run *Chalet Pantai Seri Tujah* (☎ 09-721 1753) has air-con chalets from RM60.

Pengkalan Kubor Right on the Thai border, Pengkalan Kubor is the immigration checkpoint for this little-used back route into Thailand. During the day a large car ferry (50 sen for pedestrians) crosses the river over to busy Tak Bai in Thailand. From Kota Bharu, take bus No 27, 27A or 43 from the central bus station.

Don't take the small long-propeller boats that cross in the evening. These cater to Malaysians looking for Thai girls.

Waterfalls

There are a number of waterfalls in the Pasir Puteh area. **Jeram Pasu** is the most popular; to reach it you have to follow an 8km path from Kampung Padang Pak Amat, about 35km south of Kota Bharu en route to Pasir Puteh. Bus No 3 from Kota Bharu's central bus station will take you as far as Padang Pak Amat. Other falls in this area include **Jeram Tapeh**, **Cherang Tuli** and **Jeram Lenang**.

JUNGLE RAILWAY

The central railway line goes largely through aboriginal territory. It's an area of dense jungle offering magnificent views.

Commencing near Kota Bharu, the line runs to Kuala Krai, Gua Musang, Kuala Lipis and Jerantut (access point for the Taman Negara National Park), and eventually meets the Singapore-KL railway line at Gemas. While express trains make the journey by night, those who want to see the jungle are advised to take a daytime local train. If you do you'll probably find yourself sharing a seat with vast quantities of agricultural produce and babies. The local trains stop almost everywhere and don't strictly adhere to posted schedules – allow for at least a couple of hours delay.

While it's possible to make a similar journey by bus from Kota Bharu to Kuala Lipis and onward, the train is more interesting and gives a better picture of local life.

See the Kota Bharu Getting There & Away section earlier in this chapter for timetable and fares on the jungle train.

Kuala Krai

Kuala Krai, 65km south of Kota Bharu, is not an attraction in itself, and about the only thing to do is to visit the small zoo specialising in local wildlife, including native bears and musang (civet cats). It's open daily, except Friday, from 9 am to 6.30 pm, closed from 12.30 to 2 pm.

Places to Stay The only place to stay in town is the *Hotel Seri Maju* (no phone). It's your standard Chinese cheapie with rooms with fan for RM17. To get to the hotel, take a right out of the station, then the next left; it's above the Wang Fu Emporium one street north of the main road.

Gua Musang

This former logging camp is now rapidly expanding, and planners see it as the centre of a huge new development area carved from the jungle. Logging is still a major industry, and the town has a frontier feel to it, but the massive new administrative buildings on the outskirts of town point to its future.

Gua Musang is named after the caves in the limestone outcrop towering above the train station. The musang is a native civet cat that looks like a cross between a large cat and a possum, with long fur and a long curling tail. Unfortunately hunters have killed most of these cave dwellers.

It is possible to explore the caves, but it is a very steep, hazardous climb to the entrance, which is above the kampung next to the railway line, a few hundred metres from the train station. Take a torch (flashlight). A guide is recommended and can be arranged by the hotels in town or by asking around the village at the base of the cliffs (expect to pay RM20 to RM30 for a two hour tour).

Places to Stay There are several hotels on the main road which leads away from the train station. The best of these is the *Evergreen Hotel* (☎ 09-912 2273), on the left just before the bend in the road. Clean rooms with air-con cost RM32. On the right side of the same road, closer to the station, the *Hotel Gunung Emas* (no phone) is a standard Chinese cheapie with rooms from RM15. Further down this road, the *Hotel Usaha* (☎ 09-912 4003) is a newish place with decent rooms from RM40 with air-con.

The *Kesedar Inn* (☎ 09-912 1229), just outside town, is the only mid-range place in town with clean singles/doubles for RM35/42 with fan, RM50/57 with air-con.

Sarawak

Approximately the same size as Peninsular Malaysia, yet with only around 10% of its population, Sarawak is possibly the best kept secret in South-East Asia. It is probably the least visited of all Malaysia's states and receives fewer visitors than neighbouring Sabah, but it has excellent national parks, one of the most pleasant cities in Asia and a diverse tribal culture whose hospitality to strangers is a byword. Independent travel is easy and cheap in Sarawak and the excellent state tourist information service is helpful.

Many of the tribes living upstream of the major rivers of Sarawak (the Rejang, Balleh, Belaga, Balui, Baram and Skrang) live in longhouses – 'villages' where the entire population lives under one roof with separate rooms leading on to one long communal veranda. Hospitality to visitors is a way of life in the longhouses, and some travellers in Sarawak will stay overnight at one during their travels. Sarawak has a good system of national parks: Bako, Niah, Lambir Hills and Gunung Mulu are popular destinations that offer visitors a good chance to explore the jungle.

HIGHLIGHTS

- **Kuching** – a quiet, picturesque town dotted with historic buildings, fine museums and good dining venues
- **Gunung Mulu National Park** – Sarawak's biggest and most impressive national park; a pristine rainforest with limestone pinnacles and massive caves
- **Bario** – clear mountain air in the Kelabit Highlands and great walks to longhouses
- **Bako National Park** – close to the capital yet unspoilt, with pitcher plants and easy-to-see wildlife including proboscis monkeys
- **Gunung Gading National Park** – a good place to look for rafflesia, the world's biggest flower
- **Similajau National Park** – a bit off the beaten track, but features some of Sarawak's best beaches, backing onto rainforest
- **Batang Rejang** – the state's longest river and the main thoroughfare for commerce between the hinterland and the coast
- **Bidayuh Longhouses** – a traditional way of life little changed despite the advent of TV and mobile phones; longhouse hospitality is legendary

History

From the 15th until the early 19th century Sarawak was under the loose control of the sultanate of Brunei. It was only with the arrival of Sir James Brooke, the first of the 'white rajas', that it became a separate political region.

James Brooke, invalided from the British East India Company, set off on a journey of discovery armed with a sizeable inheritance and a well-armed ship. He arrived in Sarawak in 1839 only to find the local viceroy, Prince Makota, under siege from rebellious Bidayuh and Malays of the Sungai (River) Sarawak. Brooke's fortuitous arrival put him in the perfect position to ingratiate himself with the local leaders. He put down the rebellion, and by way of reward was installed as Raja of Sarawak on 18 September 1842.

When James Brooke died in 1868 he was succeeded by his nephew, Charles Brooke. Through a policy of divide-and-rule among the local tribes, and sometimes ruthless punishment of those challenging his authority, he extended his control and the borders of his kingdom during his long reign until his death in 1917.

The third white raja was Charles Vyner Brooke, second son of Charles Brooke, who was to be last in this Boy's Own dynasty of white potentates.

Sarawak's period as the personal kingdom of the Brooke family ended with the arrival of the Japanese in WWII. When the Japanese forces capitulated in August 1945, Sarawak was placed under an Australian military administration until April 1946, when Charles Vyner Brooke, who had fled to Sydney during the war, made it known that he wanted to cede Sarawak to the British. The Bill of Cession was debated in the State Council (Council Negeri) and was finally passed in May 1946. On 1 July Sarawak officially became a British Crown Colony, thus putting Britain in the curious position of acquiring a new colony at a time when it was shedding others. Cession was followed by a brief but bloody anti-cession movement supported chiefly by Anthony Brooke, Charles Vyner Brooke's nephew and heir apparent to the white raja title, and about 300 government officers who had resigned in protest at being excluded from the political process. The conflict climaxed in late 1949 when the governor of Sarawak, Duncan Stewart, was murdered by a Malay student. By 1951 the movement had lost its momentum and Anthony Brooke urged its supporters to give it up.

Along with Sabah (then North Borneo) and Brunei, Sarawak remained under British control when Malaya gained its independence in 1957. In 1962 a British inquiry concluded that the people of the Borneo territories wished to become part of the Malay Federation. At the last minute Brunei pulled out, as it didn't want to see the revenue from its vast oil reserves channelled to the peninsula. At the same time Malaya also had to convince the UN that Filipino claims to North Borneo were unfounded, as were Indonesia's claims that the formation of Malaysia was a British neocolonialist plot. The agreement was finally hammered out in July 1963, and in September of the same year the Federation of Malaysia was born. The so-called Confrontation with Indonesia continued until 1966 and at its height 50,000 British, Australian and New Zealand forces were deployed in the Malaysian-Indonesian border area.

Although the Emergency over the Communist insurgency on the peninsula was declared over in 1960, things were still on the boil in Sarawak. The state had a large population of impoverished Chinese peasant farmers and labourers, and it was these people who found appeal in the North Kalimantan Communist Party, which supported guerrilla activity. Communist aspirations in Borneo were killed off, however, after the collapse of the Indonesian Communist Party in 1965, after which time the Indonesians and Malaysians combined forces to drive them out of their bases in Sarawak.

Today, Sarawak is doing better than its neighbour Sabah. Kuching has an air of easy affluence, and the state economy is growing at over 10% annually. Oil and timber are the mainstays of the economy, though the state gets a mere 5% of oil revenues – the rest goes to the federal government.

Logging in Sarawak

Sarawak has long been a favourite target of conservationists' ire, and with good reason. Extensive logging has done irreparable damage to the rainforests and displaced the indigenous peoples who lived there. Nevertheless, before leaping to the moral high ground and indulging in a tirade against greedy developers and unscrupulous authorities, it is also worth considering the record of other countries in the region, or those in the west for that matter. Most authorities on the subject agree that the Sarawak state government has done a better job of restraining loggers than neighbouring countries such as Indonesia, Thailand and the Philippines.

Sarawak still has about 60% forest cover, although much of this forest has been selectively logged at least once in the past 20

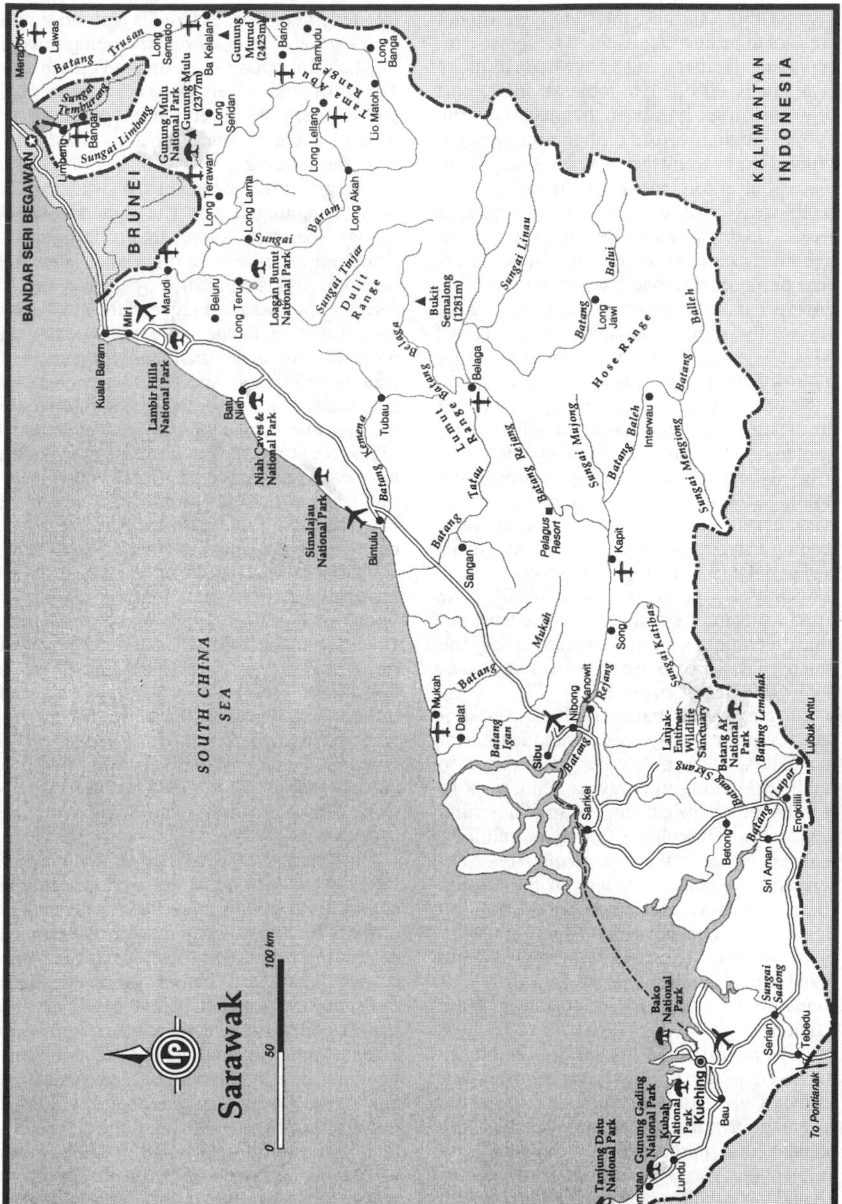

EAST MALAYSIA

years. On the surface, the state government appears to be keeping its word on forest conservation. Timber quotas have been reduced (making 30,000 people jobless), the export of whole logs has been banned, and the current slump in world timber prices has cut production even further. The laws may be in place, but enforcement, particularly in remote areas (that is, most of Sarawak), is weak. Unemployed timber workers return to shifting cultivation, putting further pressure on the forest. Meanwhile, new jobs in downstream timber-processing plants are reserved for Indonesian migrant labourers, who are prepared to work for wages the poorest Sarawakian would deem an insult.

Selective logging and helicopter logging are being portrayed as eco-friendly, but no matter how much care is taken they still involve the construction of logging roads and holding areas. These roads, bulldozed across bare earth, cause massive soil erosion, leading to river silting and the destruction of fish populations, an important protein source for Sarawak's population. The World Wide Fund for Nature estimates that the 'sustainable' techniques of the selective logging practised in Sarawak led to the destruction of 46% of the forest cover.

Logging roads have another disadvantage; they allow easy access into the interior to hunters, Sarawak's other great threat to wildlife. Hunting in Sarawak is not a sport. It is the indiscriminate massacre of anything that moves, regardless of rarity or edibility. A recent report in the *New Straits Times* described how native wardens in the Lanjuk Entimau Total Conservation Zone attempted to arrest a group of people shooting orang-utans for fun. The poachers were able to avoid arrest, as they included a number of (unnamed) senior police officers from Kuching!

The greatest threat to Sarawak's forests, however, is the political system. Sarawak enjoys a great deal of autonomy from the federal government, a situation which is both popular and appropriate. Yet the state government has very few sources of revenue as oil and gas royalties and taxation go straight into federal coffers. A famous cartoon shows a cow grazing in Sarawak and being milked in Kuala Lumpur. Given that the only major source of state revenues is the royalty paid on logs, the state government is naturally reluctant to cut its own throat by drastically reducing logging.

The greatest injustice of the system is the area of logging rights. The right to extract timber does not belong to the indigenous communities on whose traditional lands the trees stand. It is controlled by the director of forests, a political appointee of the chief minister. Logging licences are used to reward political allies and enrich family members of leading politicians and the chief minister's own family has one of the largest interests in the industry. Applications by native communities to extract timber from their own land have been flatly rejected. Finally, compensation is never paid to communities who have had their Native Customary Rights land damaged by logging activities.

This marginalisation of longhouse communities led to several logging blockades throughout the late 1980s and early 1990s. However mass arrests and a heavy-handed response by the police (including beatings and rapes while in custody) have caused these to slowly fade from view. The people who have suffered most are the semi-nomadic Penan, whose situation was first brought to light in the 1980s by the Swiss activist Bruno Manser, who lived with the tribespeople.

Unfortunately the state government's attitude to the plight of indigenous people seems to be to turn them from independent farmers to coolies on palm-oil plantations, destroying traditional lifestyles in the name of development. Whether Sarawak's rainforest and the people who live in and around it will end up winners or losers in Vision 2020 (Prime Minister Mahathir's ambitious plan for a fully developed Malaysia) remains to be seen. But with projects like the Bakun Dam going ahead, Dr Mahathir's race to the future may well leave Sarawak, its natural heritage and indigenous peoples worse off as a result.

Further Reading For a deeper insight into the problems of logging and its effects on the tribal people in Sarawak, there are a few booklets which deal with the problem admirably. Surprisingly, these booklets are on sale around Malaysia. The best are:

The Battle for Sarawak's Forests (SAM, Penang). A large-format paperback chronicling the events in the struggle until early 1989.

Logging against the Natives of Sarawak (INSAN, Petaling Jaya). A case study of the effect of logging on longhouse communities in the Belaga district, as well as some accounts of the shocking injuries and paltry compensation paid to some local logging workers.

Pirates, Squatters & Poachers (Survival International, London). An excellent introduction to the subject, this book has good background material.

Solving Sarawak's Forest & Native Problem (Sahabat Alam Malaysia, Penang). As the title suggests, some proposals for a solution to the problems in Sarawak, including a draft of the UN Universal Declaration on Rights of Indigenous Peoples, which is to be presented to the UN General Assembly for discussion and, hopefully, adoption.

Visas & Permits

Even though Sarawak is part of Malaysia it has its own immigration controls. These are designed to protect indigenous people from being swamped by migrants from the peninsula and elsewhere. They also attempt to restrict the access of foreigners to the same tribal people – the last thing the government wants is another Bruno Manser alerting the world to the shoddy treatment these people are receiving as logging continues. You will have to clear immigration every time you cross a border – from the peninsula or Sabah, and of course Brunei or Indonesia.

On arrival, most nationalities will be granted a one month stay. Since you could easily spend a month exploring Sarawak, you may have to extend. (It's puzzling that nearby Sabah will automatically give you a two month visa.) Extensions can be granted at immigration offices in Kuching or Miri – just say how much you love the place and want to see the national parks. The Sarawak state government is touchy about researchers, journalists, photographers and the like arriving unannounced, so remember, you're a tourist, nothing more.

For travel into some parts of the interior, foreigners are supposed to obtain permits from the nearest District Office (these offices are mentioned in the appropriate sections). Many travellers don't bother and just go where they want. It is very rare to be asked to show a permit, except when travelling in the Batang Baram headwaters, but getting one is painless and it'll save you a headache should you be challenged. The government has stated that it wants to cut down on logging and promote tourism as an alternative source of income.

National park permits are also required but these are largely a formality. They are generally issued as a matter of course when you check in at the park HQ, so there's little point in trying to get one in advance. The penalty for visiting national parks without a permit is a fine of RM1000 *and* six months in prison (at least it's not death), so always check in at the park HQ before going any further.

If you plan to visit any of the longhouses above Kapit on the Rejang or Balleh rivers you will need a permit, which can be obtained in Kapit without fuss or fee. It can be trickier getting a permit for travel in the interior of the north-east. This is the scene of most logging and where the Dayaks are most active against the government. Permits are required from the District Office in Miri or Marudi for travel to Bario and the upper reaches of the Batang Baram. You will only be grilled if you are travelling into the Baram area; you will be interviewed to determine your real reason for travelling to the interior, but most travellers don't have any problems as long as they have absolutely nothing to do with journalism. Tell them you are a carpenter if you think your profession may be a problem.

National Parks

The Malaysian jungles contain some of the world's oldest undisturbed areas of rainforest. It's estimated that they've existed for about 100 million years, since they remained largely unaffected by the far-reaching climatic changes brought on elsewhere by the Ice Ages.

Fortunately, quite large areas of some of the best and most spectacular of these rainforests have been made into national parks, in which all commercial activities are banned. These parks are, in effect, the essence of a trip to Borneo, other than visits to longhouses. A lot of effort goes into maintaining them and making them accessible to visitors, and you cannot help but be captivated by the astonishing variety of plant and animal life.

There are 10 national parks in Sarawak:

Bako National Park – north of Kuching (27 sq km)
Batang Ai National Park – 250km east of Kuching (240 sq km)
Gunung Gading National Park – on Sarawak's extreme western tip near Sematan (54 sq km)
Gunung Mulu National Park – east of Marudi near the Brunei border (529 sq km)
Kubah National Park – just 20km west of Kuching (22 sq km)
Lambir Hills National Park – 32km south of Miri (69 sq km)
Loagan Bunut National Park – protects Sarawak's largest freshwater lake, in the Miri hinterland (10.7 sq km)
Niah Caves National Park – massive caves and source of the raw ingredient for bird's-nest soup; about halfway between Bintulu and Miri (31 sq km)
Similajau National Park – on the coast, northeast of Bintulu (75 sq km)
Tanjung Datu National Park – near Gunung Gading National Park; recently gazetted and not yet open to the public (13 sq km)

Batang Ai, Loagan Bunut and Tanjung Datu do not have accommodation and visitor facilities, but these are planned and may open in the near future.

Costs Charges and accommodation for national parks have been standardised for all of Sarawak. Most of the incidental charges are small, but they can mount up. First of all, there is a 10% non-refundable reservation charge for accommodation bookings, or the full amount if the total is less than RM10 – in other words, if you book a room in a chalet for one night at RM120, you will end up spending RM132. Secondly, all national parks have a park entrance fee of RM3, RM1 if you are under 18. There are also fees for cameras and video cameras brought into the parks: RM5 per camera; RM10 per video camera. Professional filming of the parks will cost RM200.

Getting There & Away

For information on getting to Sarawak, see the individual Getting There & Away sections throughout this chapter, especially the entry under Kuching.

Getting Around

Air Malaysia Airlines has a comprehensive network of domestic flights served by its fleet of 18 seater Twin Otter aircraft. The Malaysian government subsidises domestic flights and can be a real bargain. This is just as well, because flying is sometimes the only means of reaching remote areas, apart from walking. If you plan to visit places such as Bario and Long Lellang in the highlands, then chances are you'll be going at least one way by plane. Kuching and Miri are connected to each other and to Sabah by regular flights on 120 seater Boeing 737s, while Sibu and Bintulu are served by 50 seater Fokker F50s.

Places in Sarawak served by Malaysia Airlines flights are Ba Kelalan, Bario, Belaga, Bintulu, Kapit, Kuching, Lawas, Limbang, Long Lellang, Long Semado, Long Seridan, Marudi, Miri, Mukah, Mulu and Sibu.

The hassle with taking the Twin Otter flights in the interior is that they are subject to the vagaries of the weather. In the dry season (April to September) this is usually not a problem, but in the wet season, especially in Bario, it can rain continuously for a few days. If you are relying on these flights, make sure you have some time up your sleeve to allow for delays. Overbooking is another problem, and during school holidays (mid-May to mid-June, late October to early December) it is virtually impossible to get a seat on *any* Twin Otter flight into the interior at short notice. The only hope is to turn up at the airport and hope for a cancellation.

The free baggage allowance on the Twin Otters is only 10kg per person, but excess baggage only costs from 40 sen to RM1.30 per kilogram, depending on the distance flown.

With the cost of accommodation in Brunei so high, many people fly straight over that country, although it is possible to transit overland in a day without having to stay overnight. The cheapest and most convenient option is the flight from Miri to Labuan (RM66), a duty-free island off the coast of Sabah, from where there are plane and boat connections to the mainland and Kota Kinabalu. It's also possible to fly from Miri to Sandakan (RM152), Tawau (RM167) or direct to Kota Kinabalu (RM104).

Road Travel by road in Sarawak is improving rapidly, as the trunk road from Kuching to the Brunei border is surfaced all the way. Between Sibu, Bintulu and Miri there are plenty of buses daily in each direction – an estimated 70 companies operate on these routes. At the moment Sibu to Bintulu takes three hours, Bintulu to Niah Caves takes two hours, Niah Caves to Miri is two hours and Miri to Kuala Baram (the Brunei border) is one hour. The road between Kuching and Sibu is completed, but the high-speed passenger launches, which do the trip in a very smart 3½ hours, are still the best way to travel. Buses take around seven hours and are not much cheaper.

There are also buses heading west from Kuching to Bau, Lundu and Sematan, and north to Bako (for Bako National Park).

Hitchhiking is possible in Sarawak, although traffic is usually light. In this chapter we've indicated where hitching is feasible. However, hitching is never entirely safe and travellers who decide to hitch should understand that they are taking a small but potentially serious risk. People who do choose to hitch will be safer if they travel in pairs and let someone know where they are planning to go.

Boat War parties and traders used to rely on oars to get them up and down Sarawak's rivers; these days river travel is accomplished in fast passenger launches known by the generic term *ekspres*. These long, narrow boats carry approximately 100 people in air-conditioned comfort with aircraft-type seats – they look a bit like jumbo jets with the wings removed. Powered by turbo-charged V12 diesel engines, they can travel up to 60km/h and create a powerful wake that has motorised canoes scattering for calmer waters.

River travel used to be measured in bends, that is a certain longhouse would be so many bends up a river. Today it is measured in violent videos – all the launches show very loud, and often very bad, kungfu movies on video discs. With the air-con turned up full blast (as it usually is) and the noise of the engines and videos, these river trips can be something of an endurance test.

The riverboats provide regular connections between Sibu and Kapit (two to three hours, RM15), and Kuala Baram and Marudi (two hours, RM18). In the wet season, when there is more water in the rivers, there are also services from Kapit to Belaga (six hours, RM25), Marudi to Kuala Apoh (two hours, RM10) and from Kuala Apoh to Long Terawan (RM8).

As well as the river ekspres boats, there are sea/river services between Kuching and Sibu (3½ to four hours, RM35). These are larger, ocean-going versions of the river ekspres boats – with the same aircraft seats, air-con and violent videos.

Kuching

Kuching is without a doubt the most pleasant and interesting city in Borneo, and one of the most attractive cities in South-East Asia. It's an ideal base from which to start exploring Sarawak, and there's plenty in and around Kuching to keep you busy for a few days. Nearby there are longhouses, caves and a number of good national parks, including Bako and Gunung Gading (where you have a good chance of seeing the rafflesia, the world's largest flower).

Built principally on the south bank of the Sungai Sarawak, Kuching was known as Sarawak in the 19th century. Before James Brooke settled here, the capital had been variously at Lidah Tanah and Santubong. Kuching was given its name in 1872 by Charles Brooke, the second white raja. The name means 'cat' in Malay and there is much speculation as to how the city got its name. Two of the more likely theories are that it was named after the Sungai Kuching which in turn was named after a common tree whose fruit resemble cat's eyes *(mata kuching)*, or that it was so called because of the many wild cats found along its banks in the time of the white rajas.

Although Kuching is quite a large city, the centre is very compact and seems isolated from the suburbs by the river and parks. Its landscaped parks and gardens make it as green a city as you'll find in South-East Asia. The usual frenetic commerce is conducted in busy streets lined with historic buildings, but within a short walk is one of Asia's best museums, a collection of Chinese temples and the striking State Mosque. The south bank of the river has been paved and landscaped and a peaceful promenade links the main attractions.

Orientation

The main sights – and most of the city – are on the south bank of the Sungai Sarawak and few people live north of the river. Almost all sights and places of importance to travellers are within easy walking distance of each other. Although parts of town are obscured by low hills, everything is deceptively close. The west end is overlooked by the green and white Masjid Negeri (State Mosque), and includes markets, local bus stations and museums. All hotels, places to eat, banks, the main post office and airline offices are between the mosque and the Great Cat of Kuching, 2km east. The waterfront is a quiet thoroughfare between the east and west parts of town.

Looking across the river, on the left opposite the markets is the *istana* (palace); Fort Margherita occupies a low hill and is visible from most points along the waterfront; and the Ministerial Complex is the ugly multistorey building in the background.

You should only need to use public buses or taxis to reach the Cat and Timber museums in Petra Jaya (north of the river), the airport (about 12km), the long-distance bus station (5km) or the wharf at Pending for boats to Sibu (6km).

Maps Periplus produces *Sarawak & Kuching* as part of its Malaysia Regional Maps series. This excellent folding colour production is regularly updated and has detailed maps of Kuching, Bintulu, Miri, Sibu, Kapit and Gunung Mulu National Park. It is readily available in bookshops in Kuching. (The *Sabah* map in the same series is far easier to find in Kuching than in Kota Kinabalu – you may want to pick up a copy here if you're heading north after Sarawak.)

For good topographic maps try the Lands & Survey Department (Jabatan Tanah dan Ukar) on the 7th floor of the state government offices, near the end of Jalan Simpang Tiga. Large-scale maps (1:1,000,000 and 1:500,000) of Sarawak are readily available, but to obtain the more detailed 1:50,000 maps of various parts of the state you need security clearance from the police HQ in the centre of town.

Information

Tourist Offices Kuching has two excellent tourist information offices which distribute leaflets on accommodation, sights, national parks and transport. The staff are helpful and either office can answer most questions.

The Sarawak Tourist Association (STA) office (☎ 082-240620), Main Bazaar, is in an octagonal building on the waterfront. It is open Monday to Thursday from 8 am to 12.45 pm and 2 to 4.15 pm, Friday from 8 to 11.30 am and 2.30 to 4.15 pm, and Saturday from 8 am to 12.45 pm. The staff have the latest bus and boat schedules. Disabled people can hire wheelchairs from this office. There is also an STA office at the airport that has a limited range of brochures.

The Visitors' Information Centre Kuching (☎ 082-410944) is on Padang Merdeka, near the new wing of the Sarawak Museum. It is open Monday to Thursday from 8 am to 4.15 pm, Friday from 8 am to 4.45 pm, and Saturday from 8 am to 12.45 pm. In the same building is the National Parks & Wildlife booking office (☎ 082-248088), which can arrange permits and accommodation for Bako, Gunung Gading and Kubah national parks, and for Matang and Semenggok wildlife rehabilitation centres.

The Sarawak Tourism Association has a Web site at www.sarawak.gov.my/stb.

For information on Sabah and the peninsula, Tourism Malaysia (☎ 082-246775) has an office in the Rugayah building on Jalan Song Thian Cheok. The ground floor office is often unattended, but you can help yourself to leaflets; for specific inquiries walk up to the 2nd floor.

Look out for the *Official Kuching Guide*, an excellent locally produced publication with information on Kuching and surrounding sights. It is available in the arrivals hall at the airport, at tourist offices and at some hotel desks.

Visas The immigration office for visa extensions (☎ 082-245661) is on the 2nd floor of the state government offices on Jalan Simpang Tiga, about 3km south of the centre on the way to the airport. To get there, catch a CLL bus No 8, 8A, 8B, 14, 14A, 14B, 17 or 19 from near the State Mosque; the fare is 60 sen.

For Indonesian visas, take a CLL bus No 8, 8A, 8B, 14, 14A or 14B from near the State Mosque to the Indonesian Consulate (☎ 082-241734) at 5A Jalan Pisang. It is open Monday to Friday from 8 am to noon and from 2 to 4 pm. At the time of writing visas were not required for most nationalities to enter Indonesia by air at Pontianak or by land at Entikong, where two-month entry permits are issued. A visa is required if entering Indonesia through a nonrecognised crossing. Visas cost RM10; four colour photos are required and if you drop off your passport before 9.30 am you can collect it in the afternoon on the same day.

Money The Hongkong Bank, on Jalan Tun Haji Openg, and the Standard Chartered Bank, near the Holiday Inn, are the best places to change travellers cheques and cash. Banking hours are Monday to Friday from 9.30 am to 3.30 pm and Saturday from 9.30 to 11.30 am. The Hongkong Bank charges less commission, but gets very crowded and can be slow. Another bank with exchange services is the Bank of Commerce.

Mohamed Yahia & Sons, the bookshop in the basement of the Sarawak Plaza, is a licensed moneychanger; it is open longer hours than the banks, but does not change travellers cheques. It is open every day from 10 am to 9 pm, but closed on Friday from noon to 2 pm. The branch in the Holiday Inn does not offer this service.

American Express (☎ 082-252600) has an office on the 3rd floor of the Malaysia Airlines building on Jalan Song Thian Cheok.

Post & Communications The main post office is in the centre of town on Jalan Tun Haji Openg. It is open Monday to Friday from 8 am to 4 pm, Saturday from 8 am to 6.30 pm and Sunday from 9 am to 4 pm; it gets very crowded on weekends. Next door there's a POS2020 office which sells stationery, sticky tape, packaging etc. It's open Monday to Friday from 9 am to 5 pm and Saturday from 9 am to 4 pm. The post office and many mid-range and top-end hotels have fax facilities.

Rasa Belissini Restaurant/Cyber Cafeteria, in the Sarawak Steamship building on the waterfront, charges RM11.50 per hour for terminal use.

There's another cyber cafe in the downstairs restaurant at the Kuching Hilton; terminals are available between 6 am and 1 am for RM15 per hour.

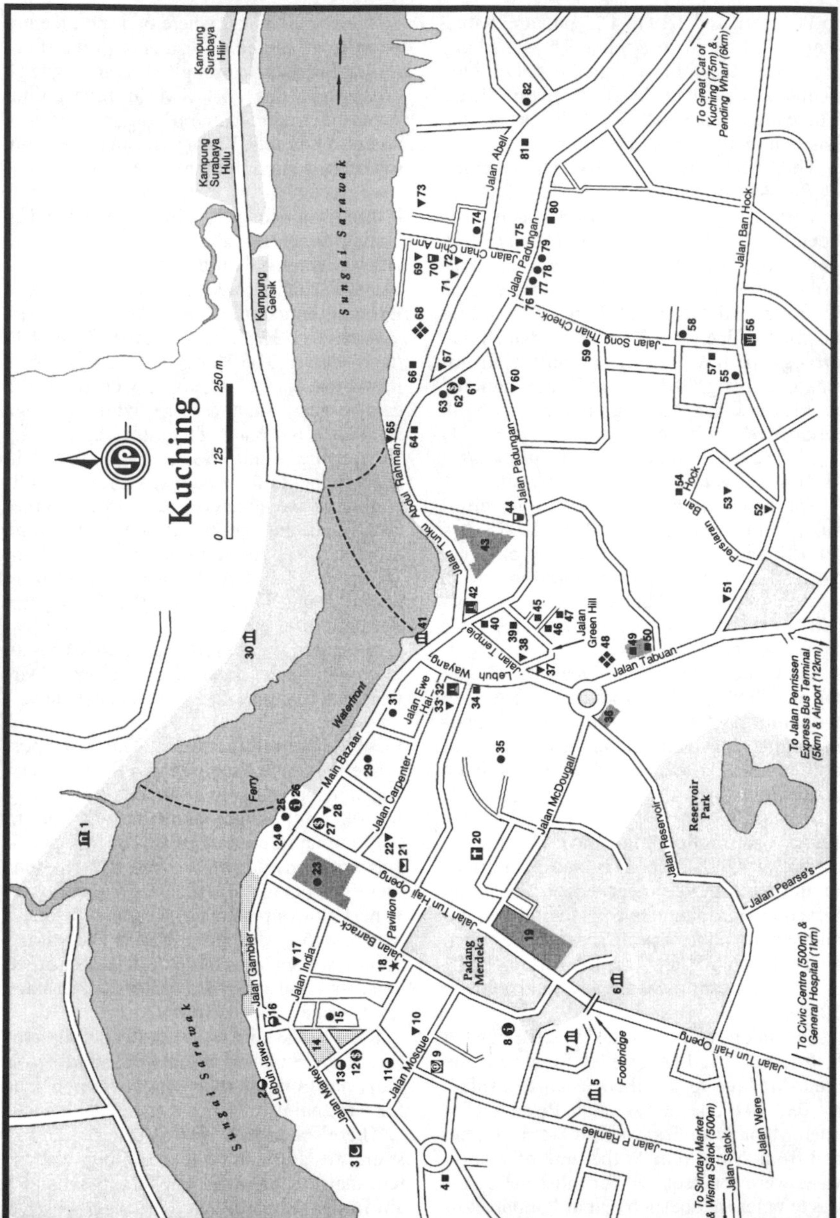
Kuching
0
125
250 m
Sungai Sarawak
Kampung Surabaya Hilir
Kampung Surabaya Hulu
Kampung Gersik
To Great Cat of Kuching (75m) & Pending Wharf (6km)
Jalan Abell
Jalan Chan Chin Ann
Jalan Padungan
Jalan Song Thian Cheok
Jalan Ban Hock
Persiaran Ban Hock
Jalan Tunku Abdul Rahman
Jalan Tabuan
Jalan Temple
Lebuh Wayang
Jalan Green Hill
Waterfront
Main Bazaar
Jalan Ewe Hai
Jalan Carpenter
Ferry
Jalan McDougall
Jalan Reservoir
Reservoir Park
To Jalan Penrissen Express Bus Terminal (5km) & Airport (12km)
Jalan Pearse's
To Civic Centre (500m) & General Hospital (1km)
Jalan Tun Haji Openg
Padang Merdeka
Pavilion
Jalan Barrack
Jalan India
Jalan Gambier
Lebuh Jawa
Jalan Market
Jalan Mosque
Footbridge
Jalan P Ramlee
To Sunday Market & Wisma Satok (500m)
Jalan Satok
Jalan Were

PLACES TO STAY
4 Arif Hotel
19 Merdeka Palace Hotel
34 Anglican Diocesan Rest House
36 Fata Hotel
39 River View Inn
40 Kuching Hotel
43 Kuching Hilton Hotel
45 Goodwood Inn
46 Mandarin Hotel
47 Orchid Inn
49 Borneo Hotel
50 B&B Inn
54 Telang Usan Hotel
57 Liwah Hotel
64 Riverside Majestic; Riverside Shopping Complex
66 Holiday Inn
75 Kapit Hotel
76 Ban Hua Hin Hotel
80 Chung Hin Hotel
81 Hotel Longhouse

PLACES TO EAT
10 Saujana Food Centre
14 Open Air Market
17 Jubilee Restaurant
22 National Islamic Cafe
28 Green Vegetarian Restaurant
33 Life Cafe
37 Tiger Garden
38 Green Hill Corner
51 San Francisco Grill
52 Hornbill's Corner Cafe
53 See Good Food Centre
60 Top Spot Food Court
65 Beijing Riverbank Restaurant
67 McDonald's
69 Kuching Food Centre
71 Suan Chicken Rice
72 Pizza Hut
73 Benson's Seafood Centre

OTHER
1 Istana
2 STC Buses
3 Masjid Negeri (State Mosque)
5 Muzium Islam Sarawak
6 Sarawak Museum (Old Building)
7 Sarawak Museum (New Building)
8 Visitors' Information Centre Kuching; National Parks Office
9 Sikh Temple
11 CLL Buses
12 Bank of Commerce
13 Petra Jaya Buses
15 Electra House
16 Taxi Stand
18 Central Police Station
20 Anglican Cathedral
21 Post Office
23 Court House & Brooke Memorial
24 Square Tower
25 Sarawak Steamship Building
26 Sarawak Tourist Association Office
27 Hongkong Bank
29 Star Bookshop
30 Fort Margherita
31 Borneo Adventure
32 Hong San Temple
35 Bishop's House
41 Chinese History Museum
42 Tua Pek Kong Temple
44 De Tavern; The Royalist
48 Ting & Ting Supermarket
55 Easy-Wash
56 Hindu Temple
58 Tourism Malaysia; Royal Brunei
59 Malaysia Airlines
61 Dragonair
62 Standard Chartered Bank
63 Singapore Airlines
68 Sarawak Plaza
70 Cat City
74 Mr Dobi
77 Tan & Sons Souvenir & Handicraft Shop
78 Ekspes Bahagia Office
79 CPH Travel
82 British Council

Bookshops Kuching has the best bookshops in Borneo, and there is a huge range of books on every topic to do with Sarawak and Sabah, including history, culture, headhunting, wildlife, horticulture, arts and crafts. Most also stock good maps of Sarawak.

The best range of books on Borneo and Malaysia is at Mohamed Yahia & Sons, which has branches in the basement of the Sarawak Plaza and the Holiday Inn's lobby. The Sarawak Plaza branch has a large stock of the scholarly *Sarawak Museum Journal* and the Holiday Inn branch has good maps. On the 2nd floor of the Sarawak Plaza, Belle's Bookshop, has a good range on every topic, including paperbacks. The Star Bookshop, 30 Main Bazaar, and the bookshop at the Sarawak Museum also have good books on Borneo. For novels and general reading the best selection is at Times Books, downstairs in the Riverside Shopping Complex.

Laundry Mr Dobi, 175 Jalan Chan Chin Ann, is close to the big hotels; Easy-Wash, 282 Jalan Ban Hock, is between the Telang Usan and Liwah hotels.

Medical Services Sarawak General Hospital (☎ 082-257555) is on Jalan Ong Kee Hui and the Timberland Medical Centre

(☎ 082-234991) is further out of the centre on Jalan Rock. Both have English-speaking doctors. There's a female doctor at Klinik Kotaraya (☎ 082-232177), Lot 177, Bangunan Haji Abdul Rasit, Jalan Satok, near Wisma Satok.

The well stocked Apex Pharmacy on the 1st floor of Sarawak Plaza is open till 9 pm.

Waterfront

The south bank of the Sungai Sarawak between the Beijing Riverbank restaurant and the markets at the west end has been tastefully developed with a paved walkway, lawns and flowerbeds, a children's playground, cafes and food stalls. It's a quiet, pleasant place to walk or sit and watch the river traffic; in the evening an endless stream of people promenade, or take their children for a walk. There's a relief map of historic Kuching and fountains are lit up at night.

Tambangs (ferries) ply back and forth across the river all day until late; the jetty near the istana services Fort Margherita; downstream past the fort the jetties service the Malay *kampungs* (villages) north of the river. To cross the river costs 30 sen and it's a local custom to leave the exact change on the seat as you leave the boat. If you want to hire a tambang for a cruise up or down the river, negotiate the fare but expect to pay RM15 for 1½ hours.

Istana

This shingle-roofed white palace, set amid rolling lawns on the north bank of the river, was built by Charles Brooke in 1870. During the Japanese occupation prisoners were detained in the basement. It's the Governor of Sarawak's residence now and no longer open to the public, but it looks very grand, especially when lit up at night. It's in plain view from the western end of the waterfront.

Fort Margherita

Built by Charles Brooke in 1879 and named after his wife, the Ranee Margaret, Fort Margherita guarded the approach to Kuching against pirates. Sitting on a knoll opposite the waterfront, this little white fort, complete with battlements, is starting to look its age and is now almost obscured by trees.

It is now a police museum (Muzium Polis), tracing the history of the Malaysian Police Force, and housing memorabilia of the Japanese occupation and the Communist insurgency. The museum features uniforms, photographs, captured weapons and drug-taking paraphernalia, as well as gruesome re-enactments of executions using life-size dummies. There's a good view along the river from the top of the wall.

Fort Margherita is well worth a visit and is open every day, except Monday and public holidays, from 10 am to 6 pm. There's no entry charge but you have to show your passport at the guard's room at the entrance.

To get there take a tambang from the landing stage behind the Square Tower to the bus stop below the fort. The fare is 30 sen each way.

Sarawak Museum

This is one of the best museums in Asia and consists of two sections, old and new, connected by a footbridge over Jalan Tun Haji Openg. Both are worth a visit.

Built in the style of a Normandy townhouse, the old wing was opened in 1891 under the direction of the noted anthropologist Alfred Wallace, a contemporary of Darwin, who spent two years in Kuching at the invitation of Charles Brooke. This is a museum of the old style, with stuffed and mounted animals in glass cabinets that look like they've been there since 1891. Upstairs there's a display of longhouse and tribal artefacts.

The new wing is air-conditioned and features the culture and lifestyle of Sarawak's many tribal peoples. There are displays on longhouse life with artefacts, including skull trophies, and photographs of tribal people from the beginning of the century. Arts on display include ceramics, brassware, Chinese jars and furniture, and there's a replica cave and a description of harvesting birds' nests for soup. The foyer has temporary exhibitions and during the day slide shows and videos on a range of topics are presented.

There's also a souvenir and gift shop with a good range of postcards.

Together, the two wings house a fascinating collection. The museum is open every day from 9 am to 6 pm; entry is free.

Muzium Islam

Islam has far less hold on Sarawak than on the rest of Malaysia, but this excellent museum is one of Kuching's surprises. Seven galleries exhibiting aspects of the Malay Islamic heritage face onto a courtyard garden. Among the various displays are ceramics, costumes and jewellery, weaponry, science and technology and Islamic art.

The Muzium Islam Sarawak is adjacent to the new wing of the Sarawak Museum. It is open every day except Friday from 9 am to 6 pm and entry is free.

Chinese History Museum

Housed in one of the few original waterfront warehouses to survive the redevelopment of Kuching, this small museum records the Chinese influence on Sarawak. It's a mixed bag; historical notes and photos document the Chinese diaspora and the formation of trading associations, and examples of traditional furniture, musical instruments and costumes are on display.

The Chinese History Museum is on the waterfront opposite the Tua Pek Kong temple. The museum is open every day except Monday from 10 am to 6 pm; entry is free.

Cat Museum

Billed as the only one of its kind in the world, Kuching's Cat Museum will delight cat lovers. It's filled with interesting titbits of information about cats; you probably didn't know that Victor Hugo had a throne constructed for his cat and Albert Schweitzer, who normally wrote with his left hand, wrote right handed when his cat fell asleep on his left arm.

Several small galleries feature, among other things, cats through history, domestic breeds, cats in superstition, cat behaviour and the benefits cats have bestowed on their owners. There are cat stamps, statues, photos and every movie poster you can think of with a cat in it. It's a bit over the top, but strangely fascinating and good fun.

The Cat Museum is in the UFO-shaped DBKU building north of the river. It is open Tuesday to Sunday from 9 am to 5 pm; entry is free, although there is a camera/video charge of RM3/5. It's too far to walk so take Petra Jaya bus No 2B or 2C, or MTC bus No 2; the fare is 60 sen.

Timber Museum

This is the timber industry's answer to all the criticism about logging. There's much justfication of the industry with facts and figures, and well-presented displays on the philosophy and techniques of forestry, botany and the uses of wood, and a walk-through rainforest diorama.

It's a bit boring really, but if you want a different perspective on the often hysterical logging debate you might think it worthwhile.

Opening hours are Monday to Thursday from 8.30 am to 4 pm, Friday from 8.30 to 11.30 am and 2.30 to 4.30 pm, and Saturday from 8.30 to 12.30 pm. Entry is free.

The Timber Museum is inconveniently located across the river in Wisma Sumber Alam, Petra Jaya. To get there take the Kuching Matang Transport bus No 8 from near the market; the fare is 90 sen. A taxi costs about RM15 each way.

Court House & Brooke Memorial

The court house was opened in 1874 and is still in use today. It was the third to be built on this site, and was previously the centre of government operations. The clock tower at the front was added in 1883 and there's also a memorial to Charles Brooke. State magistrate councils were held in the court house until 1973, when the government complex on Jalan Tun Haji Openg opened.

The court house is at the north end of Jalan Tun Haji Openg opposite the Square Tower. It's a quiet corner of town, with shady benches under massive fig trees, but there's nothing much to see.

Temples, Mosques & Churches

Kuching's Chinese temples are modest affairs, although there are a few colourful examples around town. Historically, the most important is the **Tua Pek Kong**, just along from the Hilton Hotel. Officially it is dated at 1876, but written sources mention it as long ago as 1846, which would make it the oldest building in Kuching.

The **Hong San Temple**, at the junction of Jalan Carpenter and Jalan Wayang, dates back to 1897 and is also worth a look. There's a massive Chinese-style gate over the eastern end of Jalan Padungan at the other end of town, and if you look up near the intersection of Jalan Padungan and Jalan Chan Chin Ann, you'll see another temple on a rooftop several storeys high.

Other colourful religious buildings include a **Hindu temple** on Jalan Ban Hock and a Sikh temple off **Jalan Mosque**. An **Indian mosque** dating back to the 1850s can be found down a passageway between Nos 37 and 39 Jalan India.

Completed in 1968, the **Masjid Negeri** (State Mosque), looks impressive particularly from across the river, but is otherwise uninteresting. There's no admission for non-Muslims from Thursday 3 pm to Friday 3 pm, Saturday from 4 to 6 pm and Sunday from 2 to 5 pm.

Of the Christian churches in Kuching, perhaps the most interesting is the **Roman Catholic cathedral**, 500m south past the Sarawak Museum on Jalan Tun Haji Openg.

Civiç Centre

About 1km south of the city centre along Jalan Tun Haji Openg, a huge white tower looking like an upside down, half furled umbrella on stilts dominates the skyline. This is Kuching's Civic Centre and on a clear day it offers a panoramic view. There's also a planetarium, with shows in English at 3 pm daily, a restaurant and a public library.

To get to the Civic Centre walk down Jalan Tun Haji Openg and turn left at Jalan Budaya; most buses going past the main post office will get you there. Entry to the viewing platform costs RM2.

Other Interesting Buildings

There are many historic **godowns** (river warehouses), dwellings and other buildings of note in the blocks around the waterfront and markets. Their often decaying facades are part of Kuching's distinctive character.

The **Square Tower**, on the waterfront opposite the istana, was built in 1879 as a prison; it is currently closed to the public. On Jalan Tun Haji Openg opposite the main post office there is a curious three storey building known as the **Pavilion**. Built in 1907, it has been home to various government bodies and at the time of writing was being renovated as a textile museum. The **main post office** itself is a grandiose structure fronted by Corinthian columns.

Behind the Anglican cathedral, the **Bishop's House**, is the oldest dwelling in the state. It was built in 1849 and was occupied by the first Anglican bishop of Borneo. You can wander around the cathedral grounds but the Bishop's House is not open for public visits.

Cat Statues

A perfect counterpoint to Kuching's tastefully preserved historic buildings and Iban artwork, these wonderfully kitsch and photogenic statues could have come straight from the studio of Jeff Koons, the New York artist famous for his larger-than-life creations of animals.

The huge white, blue-eyed pussycat at the eastern end of Jalan Padungan is known as the **Great Cat of Kuching**. Other cat statues can be seen opposite the Holiday Inn, at the intersection of Jalan Padungan and Jalan Central and also on the waterfront. Just in case you forgot, Kuching means 'Cat' in Malay.

Markets

Kuching's best market – and one of the best in Sarawak – is the Sunday morning market along Jalan Satok. It is sometimes very busy and can be well worth the walk. The market actually begins late on Saturday afternoon, when villagers bring in their produce and livestock and start trading. They sleep at their stalls and resume trading around 5 am on Sunday.

The air is heady with the smell of fresh coriander, ginger and herbs you've never seen before among piles of bananas, mangoes, custard apples and obscure jungle fruits. Fresh fish and other seafood takes up one section, while elsewhere wild boars and goats are butchered to hang with turtles and other free-range meat. Other stalls sell beautiful orchids, live fish hanging in plastic bags of water, birds in cages and pets – you name it, it's for sale. There are also plastic toys, clothes and other odds and ends usually reserved for Woolworth's. Food stalls set up near the pedestrian overpass.

To reach the Sunday market walk up Jalan Tun Haji Openg from the museum and turn right at Jalan Satok; the market is on your left about 500m along.

The open-air market at the west end of the waterfront, on Jalan Gambier, is small and not particularly interesting unless you hit a day when some villagers are in town. At the waterfront there is an outdoor area, and a clothes and hawker centre in a large white building. Along Jalan Gambier there are open-air food stalls where fresh vegetables and foodstuffs can also be bought.

Bamboo nose flutes are used by many of Sabah's ethnic groups.

Jalan Carpenter

This narrow street, lined with old Chinese shophouses, is signposted as Jalan Ewe Hai at its eastern end. Jalan Carpenter exists on two levels: on the street there are busy little shops and coffee shops, and above, the families who run them live cheek by jowl behind whitewashed walls and painted shutters.

Jalan Carpenter burned down in the Great Fire of Kuching in 1884 and rows of brick terraces replaced the old thatched buildings. It is picturesque and interesting to wander along and take pictures, particularly on Sunday morning when it's a bit quieter.

Kampung Kuching

Across the river from the waterfront you'll see traditional Malay houses and mosques stretching away to the east. It's a world away from the commerce and tourism of central Kuching, but you can take a tambang across the river and walk around. Children are generally unaccustomed to visitors and you may hear cries of '*orang putih*' (white people). You may even be invited in for a cup of tea by a friendly family.

Organised Tours

There is an incredible array of travel agents and tour operators in town, and most of the hotels listed in Places to Stay offer tours or have links with an operator. Ask the tourist offices to recommend one; if you want to visit a longhouse they can find out when a tour is going and can help find an agent. All the agents offer city tours, longhouse tours, and tours to national parks and other points of interest around Sarawak; some can cater for special interests, such as photography, natural history and textiles or crafts.

Besides day trips in and around Kuching town, many travel agents offer longer trips to national parks or longhouses along the Skrang and Rejang rivers. Half-day city tours are around RM40; day trips to longhouses at Annah Rais are around RM120 per person; and expect to pay at least RM220 each for a two day/one night longhouse trip for a minimum of four people on the Skrang. Longer trips to more remote longhouses around Batang Ai will cost much more, but you're guaranteed a far less touristy experience.

The jury's out on these tours; they're beyond the price range for most budget travellers, and cheaper tours are definitely a bit commercialised. However, travellers with limited time who wanted to see an authentic jungle lifestyle have given enthusiastic reports.

The MV *Equatorial* cruises up and down the Sungai Sarawak in the evenings if there is sufficient demand. A two hour sunset cruise costs RM25. Departures are from the wharf behind Sarawak Plaza at 5.30 pm, but contact Leisure Holidays (☎ 082-240566), 37 Jalan Padungan, to see if one is going.

A few of the well-established operators are listed here.

Borneo Adventure
(☎ 082-245175) 55 Main Bazaar. An award-winning company specialising in eco-tourist projects involving the indigenous peoples of Sarawak.

Borneo Excursion Travel
(☎ 082-418318) A65 Level 2, Sarawak Mall. Good for booking longhouse tours.

Borneo Interland Travel
(☎ 082-413595) 1st floor, 63 Main Bazaar. A general agency offering a wide variety of tours.

CPH Travel
(☎ 082-243708) 70 Jalan Padungan. Offers a huge range of tours, including boat cruises on the Sungai Sarawak, and longhouse trips on the Skrang and Lemanak rivers.

Interworld Travel
(☎ 082-252344) 85 Jalan Rambutan. Day trips to longhouses and longer overnight trips to the Batang Skrang.

EAST MALAYSIA

Places to Stay – Budget

Kuching's only backpackers' hostel is the *B&B Inn* (☎ 082-237366), at 30 Jalan Tabuan, next to the Borneo Hotel. It's close to all attractions, clean and friendly, has left-luggage facilities and can help with travel information. A bed in a six-bed dorm costs RM15. Fan-cooled and air-con rooms are also available starting at RM23 for a single or RM29 for a double/twin.

The *Anglican Diocesan Rest House* (☎ 082-414027), at the back of the Anglican cathedral, is normally reserved for those on church business, but if they're not full they'll probably let you stay. Rooms with fan and shared bathroom cost RM18 to RM25, while larger, fan-cooled flats with bathroom cost RM30 to RM35. The easiest access is up the steps from the road linking Lebuh Wayang and Jalan Tun Haji Openg, next to the Hong San Temple, but if the gate is locked you'll have to walk around to the driveway off Jalan McDougall.

In general, hotel prices start at around RM25 to RM30 for a single, but there are a couple of cheaper options around town. The *Kuching Hotel* (☎ 082-413985), Jalan Temple, has simple rooms fitted with fan and sink that cost from RM21/22 a single/double to RM26/27 for twin/triple rooms. The communal bathrooms and toilets are clean, and the manager and staff are very helpful. The *Ban Hua Hin Hotel* (☎ 082-242351), 36 Jalan Padungan, has fan-cooled rooms with shared bathroom for RM22. It's clean enough but noisy and dilapidated.

The *Arif Hotel* (☎ 082-241211), not far from the State Mosque, has friendly owners but the rooms are a bit tatty. Reasonable fan-cooled rooms with a sink and shared bathroom cost RM25; air-con rooms with bathroom start at RM50. It's in a handy location for buses, but the mid-range places offer better value.

Places to Stay – Mid-Range

Kuching has dozens of mid-range hotels that compete keenly for business, so most are reasonably priced. Discounts are usually available out of tourist season, and it's worth asking for one at any time. All of these hotels have air-conditioning, attached bathrooms, carpet, TV and IDD phones in the rooms. Extras may include a minibar and in-house video.

On Jalan Green Hill there's a cluster of mid-range 'lodging houses', many of which cater to long-term residents. There's little difference between them – they are all quite acceptable, if a bit stark, and cost roughly the same; none has a lift and the climb upstairs can get tedious. Rooms at the *Green Mountain Lodging House* (☎ 082-232828) at No 1 start at RM42, and the *Mandarin Hotel* (☎ 082-418269) at No 6 has rooms from RM40 to RM45. The *Orchid Inn* (☎ 082-411417) at No 2 has singles from RM28 and bigger rooms from RM35 to RM45. The *Goodwood Inn* (☎ 082-244862) at No 16 has dark, bare singles/doubles from RM40/45.

Also on Jalan Green Hill is the *River View Inn* (☎ 082-412551) at No 22 – a much larger hotel, with a lift, where airy rooms range from RM45 to RM65. At the end of Jalan McDougall, the *Fata Hotel* (☎ 082-248111) has an old and a new wing. Small rooms in the old part cost RM42; some at the back of the building are quiet and look out over parkland. Better, more modern rooms in the new wing cost RM60 and up.

On the other side of town, the *Hotel Longhouse* (☎ 082-419333), 101 Jalan Abell, offers similar standards from RM40 for an economy single, to RM50 for a standard double and RM65 for deluxe rooms. The *Kapit Hotel* (☎ 082-244179), upstairs at 59 Jalan Padungan, has dark, poky rooms for RM40/50 a single/double. You could squeeze three into a double room, but you'll get more for your money elsewhere. Over the road at 74 Jalan Padungan, the *Chung Hin Hotel* (☎ 082-441678) is better and charges the same for larger, brighter rooms.

The *Liwah Hotel* (☎ 082-429222) on Jalan Song Thian Cheok looks impressive from the lobby, but even at a substantial discount it is overpriced. Singles/doubles start at RM120/135 and suites start at RM240.

Some of the good upper mid-range places to stay in Kuching provide reasonably priced alternatives to the top-end hotels. Top of the list in this category is the *Telang Usan Hotel* (☎ 082-415588), Jalan Ban Hock. It is Sarawak's only Orang Ulu owned and managed hotel, and the Kenyah decor inside is just one of the touches that make it stand out. Spacious, comfortable rooms range from RM90 to RM200, but discounts are sometimes available upon polite request.

The *Borneo Hotel* (☎ 082-244122), 30 Jalan Tabuan, is another good choice. Kuching's longest-running hotel, it has very large rooms from RM110/125, though again discounts are often available. The Borneo boasts in-house videos, minibar and a business centre.

Places to Stay – Top End

During quieter periods, many of Kuching's top-end hotels offer dramatically discounted rates, sometimes by as much as 40%. All these hotels have pools, restaurants, bars and night spots, but add 10% service charge and 5% tax to all prices for the privilege.

Pick of the bunch, and the best hotel in Sarawak, is the brand new, five star *Merdeka Palace Hotel* (☎ 082-258000) on Jalan Tun Haji Openg next to the Padang (town square). This gleaming white tower is tastefully fitted out and, apart from the mandatory pool and gymnasium, there's a coffee shop, cigar bar and two excellent restaurants. Spacious rooms with a view start at RM380, although good weekend deals are available, and suites start at RM800.

The *Kuching Hilton Hotel* (☎ 082-248200) provides the full complement of services, plus a good handicrafts shop. Standard rooms start at RM350/380 and suites cost from RM720. It's a popular hotel and bookings are advised.

On Jalan Tunku Abdul Rahman, the *Holiday Inn* (☎ 082-423111) is central and right next to the river. Rooms range from RM270 to RM350, but are overpriced unless you get one with a view over the river. Suites cost from RM550 to RM2000.

The *Riverside Majestic* (☎ 082-247777) is across from the Holiday Inn and has better rooms ranging from RM330 to RM370; suites cost RM410 to RM3300. The Riverside complex also houses a modern shopping centre, cinemas and a bowling alley.

Places to Eat

Kuching has the best selection of food in Sarawak, arguably in all of Borneo, and the choice ranges from hawker stalls through good seafood to 1st class Italian. At the cheaper end expect to pay RM3 to RM4 for standard rice and noodle dishes at most stalls and restaurants, a bit more for beef or murtabaks. Seafood varies according to demand and availability – check prices before ordering; for good and even excellent western fare look into the upmarket hotels, where prices are reasonable by western standards.

Food Centres The so-called *Open Air Market* (it's covered) on Jalan Market next to the taxi stand is one of the largest and most popular food centres. One section serves mostly Muslim food and the other has mostly Chinese.

On the 5th floor of the Saujana car park the *Saujana Food Centre* is a Muslim food centre where most of the 40 stalls serve standard rice and noodle dishes, though some have good rotis and murtabaks. There's also a *Pizza Ria* where pizzas cost RM10 to RM14.

The *Top Spot Food Court*, off Jalan Padungan behind the Malaysia Airlines building, is another popular food stall centre on top of a car park. It is cleaner and more salubrious than the Saujana and specialises in fresh seafood.

Chinese The *Beijing Riverbank* is the round, thatched building opposite the Riverside Majestic Hotel. Downstairs is a 24 hour open-air restaurant serving tasty Chinese and Malay food, with a view, for RM6 to RM8. It's a pleasant place to catch the breeze in the evening and watch the people on the riverfront. Upstairs is a Chinese Muslim restaurant.

For something cheaper, there are two decent restaurants opposite the Rex Cinema near Jalan Green Hill: the *Green Hill Corner*, which has a good selection of Malaysian Chinese standards, and the *Tiger Garden*, which has outdoor seating, and is a good place to down a beer and enjoy a leisurely meal.

Hornbill's Corner Cafe, on Jalan Ban Hock near the Telang Usan Hotel, is a popular steamboat restaurant where you select your own seafood and meats then cook them at the table. It's a lively place with good draught beer and great for a group of people.

Malay Jalan India has three long-running restaurants: the *Jubilee*, at No 49, *Madinah*, next door, and the *Malaya*, at No 53. All serve inexpensive (RM2 to RM4) Malay curries. Not far away on Jalan Carpenter is the *National Islamic Cafe*, which serves tasty, cheap Malay food, and has excellent rotis and murtabak.

Rasa Belissini Restaurant/Cyber Cafeteria, in the Sarawak Steamship building on the waterfront, has good Malay regional and western dishes, including tom yam (RM4), gorengs (RM4.50), laksa (RM4.50), fish fillets (RM14) and steak (RM17.50).

Seafood Kuching has a good variety of seafood. Local specialities include steamed pomfret fish and sambal prawns. *See Good Food Centre* is a Chinese seafood restaurant near the Telang Usan Hotel where English is spoken. Here you can try local Sarawak specialities like lobster in pepper sauce, midin (crispy jungle fern) or ambol (finger clam), which looks like a fleshy worm. It's delicious steamed with ginger and lemongrass, but is also known locally as monyet punya – literally 'monkey's got one' – and you'll never look at a monkey the same way again. The friendly staff will help you choose.

Benson's Seafood Centre is an open-air restaurant that sets up tables and chairs on the waterfront in the evening. It's expensive but has some of the best seafood in town.

Vegetarian There are no exclusively vegetarian places in Kuching, but the *Life Cafe*, 108 Jalan Ewe Hai (next to the Hong San temple), is a spotless cafe serving delicious Chinese vegetable dumplings and rice dishes for RM3 to RM4. There's also an excellent range of Chinese teas and the best coffee in Kuching. It's closed on Sunday.

The *Green Vegetarian Cafe*, 16 Main Bazaar, has a variety of vegetable dishes as well as Indian curries and rotis. You can stuff your face at lunchtime on the vegetarian platter for RM4.50.

International The best western cuisine is provided by the international hotels, although they're expensive by local standards and alcohol will probably double your bill. Setting the pace is the Merdeka Palace Hotel, where the outstanding *Ristorante Beccari* has superb pasta dishes and pizza costing RM18 to RM28; a glass of house wine is RM16.

The *Steak House* at the Hilton offers a fixed price three course dinner for RM39 plus drinks; it is good value for a special night out, but it should change its butcher. For something more economical, the *Dulit Coffee House* at the Telang Usan Hotel has a good range of Malay and western dishes at reasonable prices. The *San Francisco Grill*, just south-east of the Borneo Hotel, tries hard with its steaks and is popular with expats; most dishes are RM14 to RM24.

Fast Food For fast food, check out the area around the Holiday Inn, particularly Sarawak Plaza, where there are branches of *KFC*, *McDonald's*, *Pizza Hut* and local permutations like *SugarBun* and *Hertz Chicken* in the Sarawak Plaza.

Self-Catering The *Ting & Ting Supermarket* is just a few doors down from the Borneo Hotel; there's another well-stocked supermarket in the basement of the Riverside Shopping Complex.

Entertainment

Sarawak has a strong endemic drinking culture and Kuching has a large number of bars, karaoke lounges and nightclubs. It's worth getting out in the evening at least once – you are much more likely to meet people, and possibly get some useful upriver contacts, in a bar than you are at a cheap hawker stall or a restaurant. Established bars are packed at weekends with everyone from logging barons to transvestites. There's usually a convivial atmosphere so be prepared for a late night.

Opposite the Hilton car park, look out for *De Tavern*. This extremely friendly place is Kayan-run and frequented by an interesting mix of Malays, Chinese, Indians, Ibans, Kayans and expats – a couple of nights in here and you'll be on a first-name basis with half of Kuching. First-time visitors are usually treated to a free tipple of tuak, the Iban rice wine. Next to De Tavern is *The Royalist*, an English-style pub named after James Brooke's sloop and fitted out with a nautical theme.

For late night action, there are a number of venues. *Cat City* has live music, but doesn't really get going until around 11 pm. *Peppers*, in the Hilton, is probably the most popular club in town, particularly on ladies nights – Wednesday and Friday.

The newest place in town is the *London Pub* in the Merdeka Palace Hotel, which has authentic English pub decor, pool table, soccer telecasts and live bands some nights. There's a cover charge for non-hotel guests. *Hornbill's Corner Cafe* (see Places to Eat) is a great open-air pub/restaurant that gets packed on Saturday nights with football-mad Sarawakians watching telecasts on the TV.

Shopping

Kuching is the best place in Borneo to buy tribal artefacts. There are dozens of shops selling arts and crafts scattered around the city, particularly along Main Bazaar. Don't expect any bargains, but don't be afraid to negotiate either – there's plenty to choose from.

Apart from the Iban, whose intricate paintings and carvings you'll see decorating everything from tourist leaflets to buildings, most Sarawakian tribes don't have a strong craft tradition. Genuine pieces may be very old, venerated or functional; these will set you back hundreds of ringgit, but they will be good quality. The bulk of what's on offer is made for tourists, and although a piece may actually come from a longhouse, it will probably have no traditional significance. Many of the more garish and polished pieces are actually mass produced outside Sarawak and even Borneo.

As a rough guide, hog charm sticks are RM35 to RM100; larger, crudely carved totems range from RM400 to RM1000; intricately patterned baskets can be anything up to RM800, depending on quality, source and age; and necklaces should be RM110 and up for a string, or RM3 per bead. Masks

Traditional heritage beads are among the popular purchases in Kuching.

start at about RM100 and range beyond RM200; good hornbill carvings will be RM200 and up; and burial vases can be anything from RM700 to RM2500. You may need special permission from the Sarawak Museum to take certain antiques out of the country – inquire before you buy.

Some of the textiles are very fine, especially the Iban weaving *pua kumbu*, which start at around RM200.

It's best to spend some time browsing to familiarise yourself with prices and range before committing yourself to a purchase. Sibu is a cheaper place to buy artefacts, but the range there is far smaller and the quality is generally inferior.

The best area to start browsing is along Main Bazaar, where every second shop seems to be a gallery-style craft centre. Even if you are not thinking of buying it is well worth ducking into some of these places. Some are piled with all manner of bric-a-brac, others are presented like studios – most make for fascinating browsing and the shopkeepers are generally very laid back.

The following are recommended for a good selection and at least some genuine Bornean pieces:

Arts of Dayak
: 19 Main Bazaar. An excellent range of masks, beads and carvings.

Atelier Gallery
: 104 Main Bazaar. A fascinating selection of antiques and furniture.

Fabrito
: 56 Main Bazaar. Beautiful, authentic textiles such as hangings and clothing; also cheaper but good Indonesian imitations.

Galeri M
: In the lobby of the Kuching Hilton. Guarantees authenticity and has a small range of antique pieces, including textiles.

Sarakraf
: 14 Main Bazaar. Set up by the Sarawak Economic Development Corporation, a good place for smaller and cheaper items.

Sarawak House
: 67 Main Bazaar. A small range of superb pieces.

Tan & Sons Souvenirs & Handicraft Shop
: 54 Jalan Padungan. A very good range of cheaper souvenirs and artefacts at reasonable prices. The place to go for mounted scorpions, spiders and butterflies.

Some outlets can organise fumigation of wooden artefacts and shipping, these services are generally reliable and fairly priced. Check the customs restrictions in your country; many western nations have restrictions on the import of animal products and of course protected species are a no-no.

There are numerous shops around town which sell gold jewellery, particularly clustered near the Hongkong Bank. Outlets for dried Chinese delicacies, such as birds' nests and sharks' fins are along Main Bazaar.

Getting There & Away

Air The Malaysia Airlines office (☎ 082-244144) is on Jalan Song Thian Cheok and is open Monday to Friday from 8 am to 5 pm, and Saturday from 8 am to 4.30 pm. Singapore Airlines (☎ 082-240266) is in the Ang Chang building on Jalan Tunku Abdul Rahman. Royal Brunei Airlines (☎ 082-243344) has an office on Jalan Song Thian Cheok and Silkair (☎ 082-233322) is next to the Standard Chartered Bank.

Singapore & Peninsular Malaysia The regular Malaysia Airlines fare between KL and Kuching is RM262. There are early-morning flights for RM187 (economy fare). Charter flights between KL and Kuching are also operated five times weekly by Transmile Air (TA) for RM173 one way, RM298 return. Tickets can be booked in Kuching (☎ 082-231033) or in KL (☎ 03-243 2022).

From Singapore to Kuching the fare is S$199, and in the opposite direction it's RM451. Singapore Airlines does this route twice weekly for the same price.

Skipping over to Johor Bahru from Singapore drops the fare to Kuching to RM169, or RM144 if you take a special night excursion fare. You can buy the ticket in Singapore at the Malaysia Airlines office for the Singapore dollar equivalent. To encourage people to fly from Johor Bahru, Malaysia Airlines has a direct bus service from its office at the Novotel Orchid Hotel to the Johor Bahru airport for S$10. The absurd aspect of this arrangement is that you have to go through Malaysian immigration when entering from Singapore, and again a couple of hours later when entering Sarawak from the peninsula! Malaysia Airlines also has a 14 day (sometimes more) advance purchase fare which can lower prices even further.

Malaysia Airlines' economy fare from Kuching to Bandar Seri Begawan is RM250.

Indonesia Malaysia Airlines operates three flights per week, on Monday, Wednesday and Friday, from Kuching to Pontianak (Kalimantan). The cost is RM276 plus RM20 departure tax. Pontianak is a 'visa free' entry point to Indonesia, and most nationalities do not require a visa – but check with your embassy first.

Around Sarawak & Sabah Although Malaysia Airlines has an extensive provincial network, none of the flights to the interior operates from Kuching – you must go to Sibu or Miri. From Kuching there are several daily flights to Sibu (at least 10 daily, RM72), Bintulu (at least six daily, RM117), Miri (at least five daily, RM164), Kota Kinabalu (at least seven daily, RM228), and Labuan (daily, RM199). There's also a daily Twin Otter service to Mukah (RM76).

Bus Long-distance buses leave from the regional express bus station on Jalan Penrissen, 5km south-east of the city centre. Buses for Sri Aman, Sarikei, Sibu, Bintulu and Miri leave from here and several bus companies have daily services to all these places; some also have a regular service to Pontianak in Kalimantan.

Very few travellers bother with buses through to Bintulu and Miri because it is faster to travel by boat via Sibu. Sarikei is the main interchange for points further north-east, but buses to Bintulu and Miri can also be caught from Sibu. Daily buses from Kuching to all centres stop at Sarikei.

Except at weekends and public holidays, there's usually no need to book – just roll up, buy a ticket and hop on. Most of the long-distance bus companies have ticket offices at or near the Petra Jaya bus station on Jalan Khoo Hun Yeang. Check the daily papers for times and fares, or ask at the tourist office to see if there are changes to the schedules. Long-distance buses are modern with air-con and kungfu movies.

The main long-distance companies are Biaramas Express (☎ 082-452139), Borneo Highway Express (☎ 082-427035) and PB Ekspress (☎ 082-461277).

Sarikei The trip to Sarikei takes about five hours and costs RM28. Biaramas Express departs at 6.30 and 8.30 am, 12.30 and 10 pm; Borneo Highway Express has services at 6.30 and 8.30 am, and 12.30, 5 and 10 pm; and PB Ekspres leaves at 6.30 and 8.30 am, and 12.30 and 9 pm.

Sibu, Bintulu & Miri Most services to Sarikei continue to Sibu – check with the bus company. The trip to Sibu takes about seven hours and costs RM32. From Sibu take connections to Bintulu and Miri – see the relevant sections for details.

Borneo Highway Express has five services daily between 6.30 am and 10 pm all the way to Bintulu; the fare is RM52 and the trip takes 11 to 12 hours. There are also several services every day through to Miri between 6.30 am and 10 pm; the fare is RM70 for the 15 to 16 hour trip – but you'd be mad to do it all by bus.

South-West Sarawak Companies servicing Kuching and nearby towns are Chin Lian

Long (CLL), Matang Transport Company, Petra Jaya Transport (☎ 082-429418), Regas Transport and Sarawak Transport Company (STC; ☎ 082-242967). These services depart from the bus stands near the markets at the west end of the Kuching waterfront.

Generally there is no need to book, but tickets can be bought at the Biaramas Express booking office (☎ 082-429418) on Jalan Khoo Hun Yeang, near Electra House. Buses, departure times, journey durations and fares to some popular destinations are listed here.

Annah Rais (Longhouse): STC bus No 9A; 9, 10.20 and 11.30 am (two hours, RM5.10)
Bako National Park: STC bus No 12A to Kampung Bako; first departure at 6.40 am, last 6 pm (45 minutes, RM2.10). See the Bako section for details of boat charter to the national park.
Bau: STC bus No 2; approximately every 40 minutes between 6 am and 6 pm (one hour, RM3)
Kubah National Park: Matang Transport Co bus No 11; between 6.30 am and 4.50 pm (about 40 minutes, RM1.65)
Lundu (for Gunung Gading National Park): STC bus No 2B; departures at 8 and 11 am, and 12.45, 2.15 and 4 pm (about two hours, RM7.80)
Sematan: STC bus No 2B to Lundu then a connecting bus.
Semenggok: STC bus No 6; approximately every hour (about 45 minutes, RM1.50)
Serian: STC Express bus No 3 or 3A; approximately every 35 minutes between 6.30 am and 5.50 pm (about one hour, RM5)

EAST MALAYSIA

See the relevant sections for more information and the following Getting Around section for details of buses around the city.

Sri Aman The trip to Sri Aman takes about three hours and costs RM15. STC buses depart at 7.30 and 9.30 am, and 12, 3 and 7.30 pm; Biaramas Express does the same leg at 1 pm.

Indonesia Several companies have a daily service to Pontianak in Kalimantan. The price for most is RM34.50, although the plush SJS 'Super Executive' costs RM70 including meals; the trip takes between eight and 10 hours and departs at 11 am. Kirata Express departs at 7.30 am, Sapphire Pacific leaves at 11 am, and Biaramas Express has buses at 7, 8 and 10.30 am and 12.30 pm.

The buses cross at the Tebedu/Entikong border. This is now a visa-free entry point into Indonesia for most nationalities, but check with the Indonesian Consulate in Kuching first. (See the Visas entry in the Kuching section for more information.) It is a slow haul from Serian to Tebedu on the Sarawak side, but there's a good highway from Entikong to Pontianak.

Boat Two companies operate daily express boats between Kuching and Sibu. They are far quicker than the express buses and cost about the same. The trip takes around four hours; a change from a sea-going boat to a smaller river boat is sometimes necessary at Sarikei. These boats have freezing air-con and violent videos for your entertainment.

Coastal Union Express
(☎ 082-335516) 177 Jalan Chan Chin Ann. Departs at 8.30 am daily; RM33/35 for economy/1st class.
Ekspres Bahagia
(☎ 082-421948) 50 Jalan Padungan. Direct service to Sibu at 12.45 pm daily for RM33/38. An additional service via Sarikei leaves on Monday, Wednesday and Friday at 8.30 am.

Borneo Interland (☎ 082-413595), 63 Main Bazaar, sells tickets for both services. The Coastal Union Express boat is perhaps better because you can sit outside on the ocean leg of the trip. All boats should be booked at least a day in advance to be on the safe side.

All boats leave from one of the wharves in the suburb of Pending, about 6km east of the city centre. Catch CLL bus No 17 or 19 from outside the market on Main Bazaar and tell the driver which boat you are catching; the fare is 60 sen. A taxi costs RM10.

Getting Around

To/From the Airport STC (green and cream) buses run between the airport and the centre of town. Bus No 12A runs approximately every 50 minutes between 6.30 am and 7.10 pm; six No 12C buses also leave at irregular intervals between 7 am and 6 pm; the fare is RM1 and you can catch the buses either at the waterfront at the western end of the Main Bazaar or outside the main post office.

A taxi between Kuching airport and the city centre costs RM16.50; there's a booth to the right as you leave the terminal where you can buy a fixed price coupon.

Bus Most points of interest around the city and nearby towns are covered by a good local bus network. At first the system may seem chaotic because there's no central terminal, but the five local companies congregate near the markets at the west end of the waterfront. Check with either of the tourist offices for changes to schedules and fares. The five bus companies are recognisable by their colour schemes; routes and fares are listed here.

Cat Museum – Petra Jaya Transport (yellow, red and black stripes) bus No 2B or 6 (air-con); 60 sen
Express Bus Terminal – STC (green and cream) bus Nos 3, 3A, 4, 4A, 5, 6, 6A, 6B, 6C, 8, 8D and 12A; 50 sen
Immigration Office – CLL (blue and white) bus Nos 8, 8A, 8B, 14, 14A and 14B; 60 sen
Indonesian Consulate – CLL (blue and white) bus Nos 8, 8A, 8B, 14, 14A and 14B; 60 sen
Jong's Crocodile Farm – STC (green and cream) bus No 3; RM2.50
Pending Express Wharf (for boats to Sibu) – CLL (blue and white) bus Nos 17 and 19; also Regas Transport Co (cream) bus No 1C; 60 sen
Timber Museum – Kuching Matang Transport (yellow and orange) bus No 8; 90 sen

Taxi Kuching's taxis are unmetered but usually have air-con; check the fare before getting in. They can be found waiting at the market, at the long-distance bus station and outside major hotels. There is usually no problem flagging down a taxi on main streets, even late at night. Most short trips around town cost RM5.

Car Car rental costs in Sarawak start at around RM140 per day for a Proton Saga. The main rental companies are listed below, but if they can't help ask at the reception desk of major hotels – there's bound to be a jobber around who can organise a car for you.

Happy Rent A Car
(☎ 082-234964) Lot 1727, Ground floor, Laman Bong Chin, Batu 2½, Jalan Rock
Mayflower Acme Tours
(☎ 082-410110) 4.24A, 4th floor, Bangunan Satok, Jalan Satok; the branch at the airport (☎ 082-575233) is easier to find
Pronto Car Rental
(☎ 082-237889) 1st floor, 98 Jalan Padungan; has a large fleet of vehicles

Boat Small boats and express boats ply the Sungai Sarawak, connecting the small villages around Kuching. The standard fare across the river is 30 sen, but you can also charter boats for RM15 to RM20 per hour. Make sure you agree on the fare before you take the ride.

Around Kuching

BAKO NATIONAL PARK

Bako is Sarawak's oldest national park and protects 2728 hectares of an unspoilt promontory between the mouths of the Sarawak and Bako rivers. It's a beautiful spot, where mangroves fringe the coasts and the rocky headlands are indented with clean beaches. The park features seven of the state's main vegetation types. These include rainforest and *kerangas*, a distinctive plant community that grows on the sandstone plateau forming the backbone of the national park.

Bako is most famous for its wildlife and is the best place in Sarawak to see the rare proboscis monkey. Macaque monkeys are common and fun to watch as they forage along the beach in the evening. And botanically Bako is a fascinating place where you can easily see four species of pitcher plants

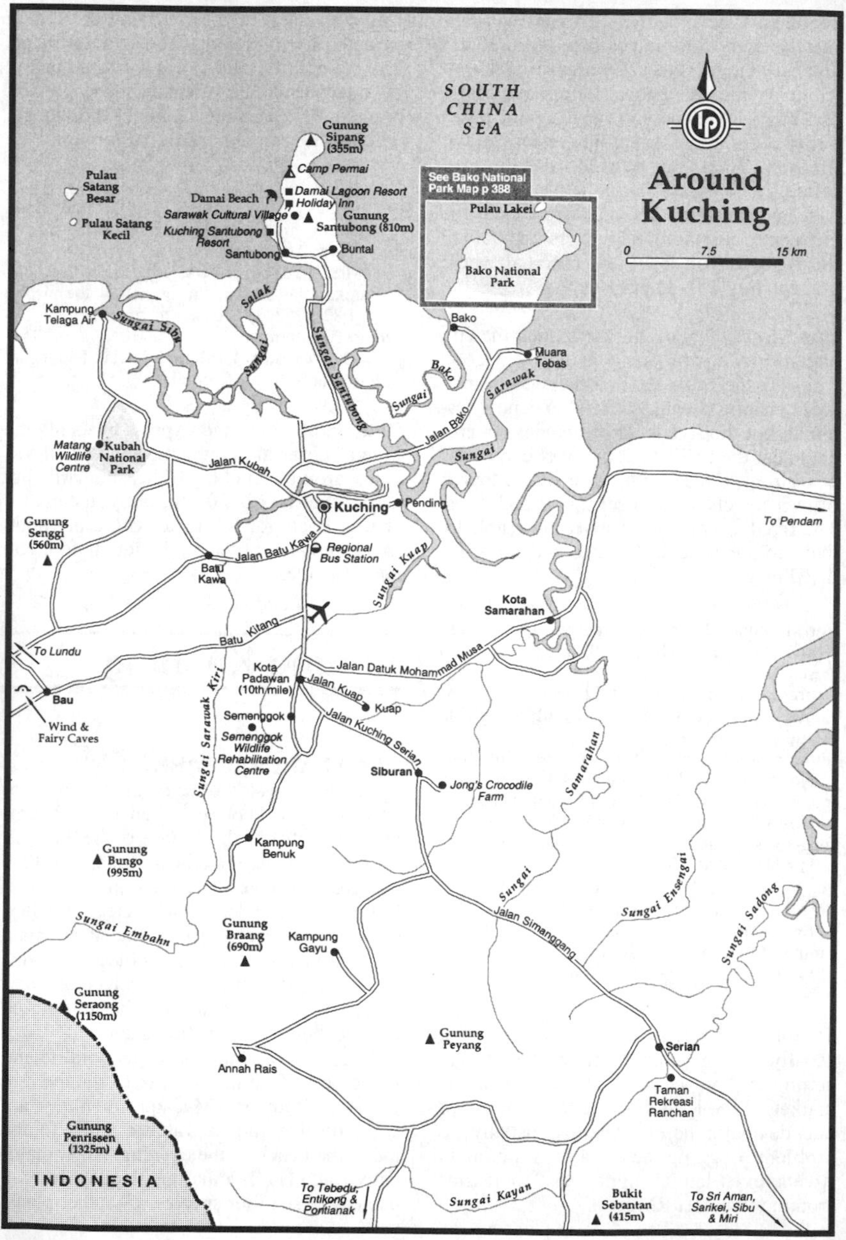

Around Kuching
0
7.5
15 km
SOUTH CHINA SEA
See Bako National Park Map p 388
Pulau Lakei
Bako National Park
Gunung Sipang (355m)
Camp Permai
Damai Lagoon Resort
Holiday Inn
Damai Beach
Sarawak Cultural Village
Gunung Santubong (810m)
Kuching Santubong Resort
Santubong
Buntal
Pulau Satang Besar
Pulau Satang Kecil
Kampung Telaga Air
Sungai Sibu
Sungai Salak
Sungai Santubong
Sungai Bako
Bako
Muara Tebas
Sungai Sarawak
Jalan Bako
Matang Wildlife Centre
Kubah National Park
Jalan Kubah
Kuching
Pending
To Pendam
Gunung Senggi (560m)
Jalan Batu Kawa
Regional Bus Station
Batu Kawa
Sungai Kuap
Kota Samarahan
Batu Kitang
To Lundu
Jalan Datuk Mohammad Musa
Kota Padawan (10th mile)
Jalan Kuap
Kuap
Bau
Wind & Fairy Caves
Semenggok
Semenggok Wildlife Rehabilitation Centre
Jalan Kuching Serian
Sungai Sarawak Kiri
Siburan
Jong's Crocodile Farm
Samarahan
Kampung Benuk
Gunung Bungo (995m)
Sungai Ensengai
Sungai Sadong
Sungai
Jalan Simanggang
Sungai Embahn
Gunung Braang (690m)
Kampung Gayu
Gunung Seraong (1150m)
Gunung Peyang
Serian
Annah Rais
Taman Rekreasi Ranchan
Gunung Penrissen (1325m)
INDONESIA
To Tebedu, Entikong & Pontianak
Sungai Kayan
Bukit Sebantan (415m)
To Sri Aman, Sarikei, Sibu & Miri

EAST MALAYSIA

within an hour's walk of park HQ (see the Flora & Fauna section in the Facts about Malaysia chapter for more details).

It's well worth a visit, but being only 37km north of Kuching it is popular with day-trippers – bookings are essential at weekends and during school holidays.

Fees & Permits

A permit is needed if you intend to stay at Bako, but is not necessary for a day trip. Permits and accommodation can be organised at the National Parks & Wildlife booking office (☎ 082-248088) in Kuching. Telephone bookings are accepted, but must be confirmed and paid for at least three days before your intended departure. It's a good idea to avoid weekends because the park can get very crowded.

The park HQ area is called Telok Assam, and you'll find accommodation, a cafeteria and the park office here. The office is about 100m along the shore from the landing dock. You must register upon arrival and pay the RM3 park entry fee, plus RM5 per camera and RM10 per video camera. Staff will show you to your quarters and can answer any questions about trails. There's a large trail map outside the office and a free copy is given out at the office.

Next to the park office there's a very good information centre with photos and displays on various aspects of the park's ecology. An entertaining video on proboscis monkeys is shown at regular times or on request – ask at the office.

Walking

Bako has more than 30km of well-marked trails, ranging from short walks around park HQ to strenuous day walks to the end of the peninsula. Although you may be told that a guide is necessary, it's easy to find your way around because all trails are colour coded with paint on trees or rocks next to the path. You don't have to go far to see some wildlife and there are walks to suit all levels of fitness and motivation. You should plan your route before starting the longer walks, and aim to be back at Telok Assam before dark at about 6.45 pm. Some trails are closed for maintenance after the wet season – check at the park office before setting out.

If you have only one day in Bako, try to get there early and attempt the **Jalan Lintang**: it traverses a wide range of vegetation and climbs the sandstone escarpment up to the kerangas, where you'll find many pitcher plants.

The longest trail, **Jalan Telok Limau**, is a 10km walk that's impossible to do as a return trip on foot in one day. You will either need to carry camping equipment or arrange to be collected by boat. Arrange a pick-up with the park warden, but expect to be charged about RM100. Listed in the 'Walking Trails' table below are the main trails in the park, and the times given are those recommended by the national park (fast walkers could almost halve them).

Take adequate water on all hikes; it gets particularly hot in the kerangas and there's no shade for long stretches.

Walking Trails – Bako National Park

Name of Path	*Destination*	*Time Required*
Jalan Bukit Keruing/Jalan Bukit Gondol	Mountain Path	7 hours
Jalan Lintang	Circular Path	3-4 hours
Jalan Serait	Park Boundary	1½ hours
Jalan Tanjor	Waterfalls	2 hours
Jalan Tanjung Rhu	Cliffs/Viewpoint	2½ hours
Jalan Tanjung Sapi	Cliffs/Viewpoint	½ hour
Jalan Telok Delima	Mangroves	¾ hour
Jalan Telok Paku	Cove Beach	¾ hour
Jalan Telok Pandan	Cove Beaches	1½ hours
Jalan Ulu Serait/Jalan Telok Limau	Pulau Lakei (Island)	8 hours

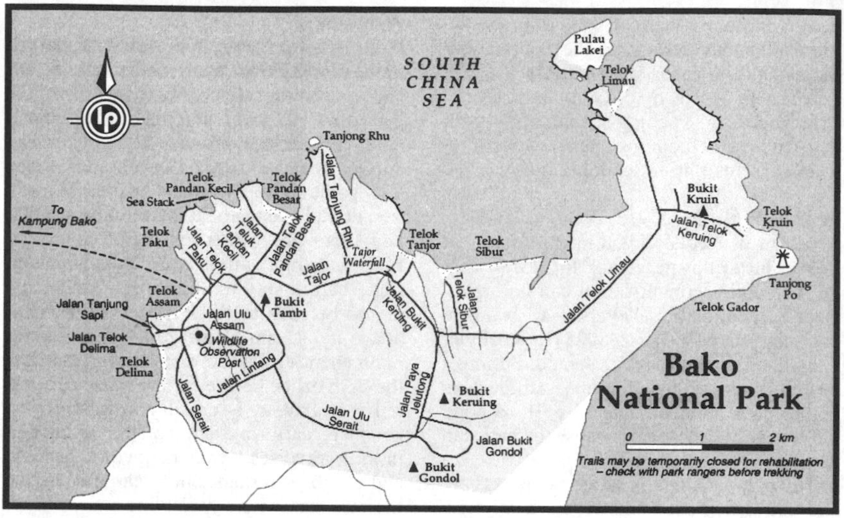

Wildlife

Walking trails pass through peat swamp, rainforest and, on the low sandstone plateau behind Telok Assam, kerangas. The latter is a fascinating ecosystem where pitcher plants are common, especially near the intersection of the Jalan Lintang and Jalan Ulu Serait trails. This kerangas is the spitting image of some parts of the Australian east coast, even though it is botanically very different.

Common animals include the long-tailed macaque and silvered leaf monkey, large monitor lizards, palm squirrels and, at night, bearded pigs, mouse deer and the culago or flying lemur. The best places to look for proboscis monkeys are along the Telok Paku and Telok Delima walking trails, a short distance from the park HQ: walk very quietly and listen for them crashing through the trees – they will see you long before you see them.

Bird-watching is best near the park HQ, especially in and around the mangroves at Telok Assam. Although there are about 150 species on the park list, many of these are migrants that are only present during the wet season.

Warning Don't feed the monkeys! The long-tailed macaques that hang about park HQ are great to watch but they are cunning and mischievous. Do not leave valuables, food or drink unattended, especially on the beaches, at the canteen or on verandas. Lock all doors and close all bags – they are quick opportunists and will make running leaps at anything they think they can carry off – including drink bottles, food, laundry, sunglasses and hats. Under no circumstances should you feed them – the males can be aggressive and put up some impressive threatening displays. If you get bailed up, yell for the park staff. Monkeys are not a problem after dark.

Places to Stay & Eat

There is plenty of accommodation at Bako, including two-room lodges, hostels and a camping ground, but it is well used and some facilities are in desperate need of repair.

Hostel rooms with shared kitchen and bathrooms sleep four and cost RM10 per person. Linen, cooking utensils and a few cups and plates are provided. The facilities in some hostels are looking pretty shabby, and you may opt to use the shower block nearby – if nothing else it's better lit.

Fan-cooled *lodges* with various sizes of rooms are also available; a double room costs RM40 and bigger rooms sleeping three or five people cost RM80. Bathrooms and kitchens are shared and facilities include fridges, gas burners, all utensils and bed linen. Bookings are essential for the lodges and advisable for the hostel rooms, though you should be able to get a bed if you just front up during the week.

Camping costs RM4 per site; there's a shower block and lockers can be hired for RM3 per day. Bring your own utensils and sheets or sleeping bags. The monkeys are a particular nuisance near the camping ground and will steal anything that is not firmly secured.

The park *cafeteria* is open from 8 am to 9 pm, and sells cheap noodle and rice meals. The adjoining shop sells a good variety of reasonably priced tinned and dried food, film, chocolate, biscuits and toiletries, although fresh bread and vegetables are not always available.

Getting There & Away

To get to Bako you must first take a bus to Kampung Bako then charter a boat to the park. Petra Jaya bus No 6 (air-con) leaves from near the market in Kuching approximately every 40 minutes from 6.40 am to 4 pm. The last bus back to Kuching departs at 5 pm. The trip to Kampung Bako takes about 45 minutes; the fare is RM2.10 one way (RM3.80 for a return ticket, valid for a week).

From Kampung Bako, you must charter a private boat to the national park. A boat costs RM30 for up to 10 people, or RM3 per person if there are more than 10. The chances are that someone on the bus will be looking to share a boat, especially on a weekend.

When you're ready to leave Bako, make sure you ask around to see who's heading back – the boatmen will happily let you charter a whole boat without telling you six people are about to leave. It's a pleasant 30 minute boat trip past coastal scenery, fishing boats and people duck-diving for finger clams in the bay. From November to February the sea is often rough, and at times it may not be possible for boats to approach or leave Telok Assam. Take a waterproof jacket to protect against spray in the open boats.

SANTUBONG & DAMAI

The Santubong Peninsula is an exclusive tourist area 32km north of Kuching near the mouth of the Sungai Santubong. It's a picturesque setting with jungle trekking on nearby Gunung Santubong and good seafood at two small fishing villages, Santubong and Buntal. The peninsula has the nearest beach to Kuching, other than those in Bako National Park, and is very popular with local people on the weekends. At Sungai Jaong, about 1.5km upriver from the coast, primitive rock carvings can be seen.

The peninsula also has the Sarawak Cultural Village – a photogenic ethnic theme park – but the only accommodation is in expensive resorts and the area is difficult to get to as an independent traveller.

The Official Damai Guide is an excellent colour guide to all activities and accommodation on the peninsula. It is available at the tourist offices in Kuching.

Sarawak Cultural Village

Surrounding an artificial lake at the foot of Gunung Santubong, the Sarawak Cultural Village is a living museum with examples of traditional dwellings built by different peoples of Sarawak – in this case Orang Ulu, Bidayuh, Iban and Melanau – as well as Malay and Chinese houses. There are six buildings in all, plus a shelter of the type the nomadic Penan periodically inhabit. The dwellings are inhabited by tribespeople who demonstrate local arts and crafts, including basketry and weaving, top spinning, blowpipe shooting and sago processing.

All the tribespeople are paid to take part in the daily activities, and sell their products or handicrafts. Great pains are taken to make it authentic and just to prove the point, the nomadic Penan occasionally go AWOL.

A visit is capped by a choreographed one hour dance performance at 11.30 am and

4.30 pm. It is all very touristy, as you would expect, but tasteful and if nothing else could help you get your head around the sometimes complicated ethnic diversity of Sarawak.

The village has a morning programme (9 am to 12.30 pm) and an afternoon programme (2 to 5.15 pm). Be sure to get there at 9 am or 2 pm to get your money's worth, as entry is a hefty RM45 (RM22.50 for children). For more information phone ☎ 082-422411.

There's a restaurant and souvenir shop at the Sarawak Cultural Village.

Getting There & Away There is no public transport to Sarawak Cultural Village, but a shuttle bus runs to and from the Holiday Inn in Kuching. Departures from Kuching are at 9 am and 12.30 pm. Going back, the bus leaves at 1.45 and 5.30 pm. The fare is RM10 each way.

The Cultural Village is a five minute walk from the Damai Lagoon Resort and Holiday Inn Resort Damai Beach, and from Camp Permai.

Jungle Walks

The Santubong Peninsula offers good jungle trekking within easy reach of Kuching, and the more adventurous could attempt the ascent of 810m Gunung Santubong.

An easy to moderate circular walk starts near the Holiday Inn resort and ends near the Cultural Village, passing a pretty waterfall on the way. There's a cafe at the beginning where you can pick up a map, but the trail is marked with splashes of paint so it's very hard to get lost.

The ascent of Gunung Santubong leads off this trail. This is a serious trek, taking six to seven hours there and back, and involves scaling near-vertical rock faces via rope ladders. A guide is not essential, but fitness and stamina are. If you are attempting this climb take plenty of water.

Places to Stay & Eat

Accommodation in Santubong and Damai is resort style and definitely not for budget travellers. The *Holiday Inn Resort Damai Beach* (☎ 082-846999) has standard rooms from RM190 to RM290, although discounts are sometimes offered. It has a small beach created from imported sand.

The *Damai Lagoon Resort* (☎ 082-846900) is twinned with the Riverside Majestic Hotel in Kuching. Standard rooms cost RM276 to RM330, and suites are RM600 to RM2250.

The *Santubong Kuching Resort* (☎ 082-846888) is the least expensive of the resorts, and provides a wide range of services and activities (such as tennis and basketball courts, watersports, golf and mountain biking) at RM150 for standard rooms and RM220 to RM250 for suites.

Camp Permai (☎ 082-255393) caters mostly for school groups, but independent travellers are welcome. There's a variety of accommodation, from air-con tree houses and log cabins to camping; substantially discounted rates may be available for tree-top cabins on weekdays. Tree-top accommodation starts at RM80 per night and campers can stay for RM6.

There are seafood restaurants at Santubong and Buntal. *Lim Hock Ann Seafood* in Kampung Buntal has a wooden deck on stilts overlooking the South China Sea; it's a perfect place to sink a few beers and watch the moon rise over Bako Peninsula. The food is fresh but prices are subject to seasonal variation – expect to pay around RM10 for some dishes. From restaurants at Santubong, on the other side of the peninsula, you can watch the sunset while enjoying your dinner.

There are sterile *restaurants* at the resorts where you can enjoy international cuisine at international prices.

Getting There & Away

For Buntal and Santubong take Petra Jaya bus No 2B from near the market; the fare is RM2.30. The last bus leaves the peninsula at 6 pm so if you want to stay for a meal the only option is to fork out for a taxi for the 45 minute ride back.

There's no bus to the resorts, but the shuttle bus from the Holiday Inn, Kuching, goes to both Damai resorts for RM10 each way; departures from Kuching are at 9 am, and 12.30, 3.15, 6.30 and 8.45 pm. The shuttle returns at 1.45, 5.30 and 7.15 pm.

A taxi to the resorts costs RM25 to RM30; if you want to be picked up after dinner expect to pay RM60 for the return trip. Taxis can also be hired from the resorts out to Buntal and Santubong.

KUBAH NATIONAL PARK

Just 20km west of Kuching, Kubah National Park is the nearest national park to the city and makes an easy day trip. Its 2230 hectares protect a range of forested sandstone hills which rise dramatically from the surrounding plain to a height of 450m. There are waterfalls, walking trails through rainforest and lookouts. Kubah's forest features a wide variety of palms and orchids, but there is less chance of encountering animals than in Bako National Park.

The area was used for a forgettable film called *Farewell to the King* starring Nick Nolte and Nigel Havers; one of the sets stands behind a locked gate next to the entrance road and if you ask at the park office they may let you look around.

Walking trails include the paved entrance road, which runs right up to the summit of Kubah's highest peak, **Gunung Serapi**; it's a two or three hour walk and often shrouded in mist, but there are lookouts along the way. You could probably cadge a lift up then walk down. Most of the other trails run off this road: the **Rayu Trail** links Kubah with the Matang Wildlife Centre, 5km from the turn-off, and takes about three hours; and the **Waterfall Trail** takes about 45 minutes from the turn-off and ends at a natural swimming pool.

There's a RM3 park entrance fee plus a RM5 camera fee payable at the gate. A hand-drawn map is available at the park office and a sign and the map shows the trails.

Places to Stay

Accommodation at the park is in a comfortable, clean hostel or chalets. Rooms in the *hostel* rooms sleep two, four or six people and have pillows, linen and ceiling fan; a bed costs RM10 or rooms are RM20, RM40 or RM60, respectively. There's a kitchen with all facilities including a fridge.

Air-conditioned chalets with all facilities sleeping six people cost RM180; less swanky *chalets* sleeping 12 cost RM120. It's entirely self-catering at Kubah; if you have transport you could get supplies in the local kampungs or even dine back in Kuching, but otherwise you'll have to bring all you require. You should book this accommodation for weekends, but at other times you can just turn up.

Getting There & Away

Matang Transport Co (yellow and orange) bus No 11 leaves approximately every hour between 6.30 am and 4.50 pm from Kuching. The ride to Kubah costs RM1.65 and takes around 40 minutes. The bus will drop you at Sungai Cina, from where it's a 300m uphill walk to the park entrance.

Otherwise it's a taxi from town, which will cost about RM50 return; arrange a time to be picked up with the driver. Another option is to drive yourself, but the park is not well signposted: follow the signs to Matang then turn left at the crossroads 200m past the Red Bridge; the park entrance is about 3.5km further on.

MATANG WILDLIFE CENTRE

Adjacent to Kubah National Park and on the other side of the same plateau, the Matang Wildlife Centre is scheduled to replace Semenggok as a wildlife rehabilitation centre. It is open to the public, but at the time of writing the rehabilitation programme had not started and there wasn't much to see. Enclosures and facilities were being built to house and feed injured and orphaned animals, and an orang-utan enclosure and walk-through aviaries were almost complete. There are rainforest walking trails – including one that links up with Kubah National Park – and other developments on the drawing board include a butterfly farm.

The Matang centre is open to visitors and is popular among locals, who come to swim in the nearby river at weekends.

There's accommodation, a cafeteria and a very good information centre. Park entry costs RM3 plus a RM5 camera fee.

Places to Stay & Eat

A bed in Matang's *hostel* costs RM10 or four people can rent a room for RM40; *chalets* sleeping six cost RM120 and, if you're self-sufficient, a *camp site* costs RM4. A *longhouse* is under construction and would probably be a fun way to spend the night at Matang.

Getting There & Away

The Matang Bus Company has discontinued the service to Matang because of insufficient demand. This situation may improve when Semenggok closes and Matang is fully operational, so check with the National Parks office or either of the tourist offices in Kuching for an update. For the time being the only options are taxi (about RM70 return) or hitching; from the Kubah National Park turn-off it's another 12km to Matang.

SEMENGGOK WILDLIFE REHABILITATION CENTRE

This is Sarawak's equivalent to the orang-utan sanctuary at Sepilok in Sabah. It's a low-key place, 32km south of Kuching, that tries to rehabilitate orang-utans, monkeys, honey bears and other unfortunate creatures which have been orphaned or illegally caged. You're not guaranteed to see wild orang-utans, because they're set free at Semenggok and only return when they're hungry. The centre was scheduled to close sometime late in 1998 so check with the National Parks office or tourist offices in Kuching before jumping on a bus.

There's a vet station and a few cramped cages, but Semenggok is a working field-station and is not really set up for tourism. The semi-wild orang-utans are fed at 8.30 to 9 am and again at 3 to 3.15 pm, so it's best to time your visit to coincide with one of these sessions. The centre is open every day from 8 am to 12.45 pm and from 2 to 4.15 pm.

A permit is required to visit the centre and can be arranged, free of charge, at the National Parks office near the Sarawak Museum. There is no accommodation or cafeteria at Semenggok.

Getting There & Away

To get to Semenggok take STC bus No 6 from Kuching; there are departures at 8.20 and 10.30 am, and 12 and 1.30 pm. The trip takes about 40 minutes and costs RM1.50. Tell the driver you wish to get off at the Forest Department Nursery, then follow a plankwalk through the forest to get to the centre; the walk takes about 30 minutes. The last bus back passes Semenggok at 2 pm.

BIDAYUH LONGHOUSES

The most interesting and unspoilt longhouses in Sarawak are those furthest from large settlements, particularly along the upper reaches of the Skrang, Lemanak, Rejang, Balleh, Belaga, Balui and Baram rivers.

If you're not planning on going that far, or would like a preview, then the nearest examples to Kuching are the Bidayuh longhouses south of the city. All of them have been on the tour operators' circuit for years and are used to tourists. You'll experience none of the hospitality Sarawak's longhouses are famed for – polite indifference will be about the extent of it.

Kampung Benuk is a 35km bus ride south, followed by a short walk. It is only a few kilometres past Semenggok on the same road. **Kampung Annah Rais** is one of the best known of the 'tourist' longhouses. It's an impressive structure, with over 100 doors, and has preserved its traditional look, largely because the deal with the tour agencies doesn't allow the use of non-traditional materials (corrugated iron is bad for tourism). The villagers also keep the tour operators informed of any special festivities happening in the village. **Kampung Gayu** is another village visited by tour groups, and there are many others in this area.

If you arrive late in the day and bring gifts such as sweets and cigarettes, you may be invited to stay at one of these longhouses. However, remember that these are people's homes and you are a guest; there may not be

The Beauty of the Bidayuh

Life can get a little difficult when you're heavily outnumbered by warlike Ibans who want your head and your farmland. That Sarawak's 90,000 Bidayuh survived at all is tribute to their legendary toughness, adaptability and good humour.

The Bidayuh responded to the Iban threat by building fortified longhouses far inland, leading early European travellers to call them 'Land Dayaks', to distinguish them from the Iban 'Sea Dayaks'. They also built imposing octagonal skull houses *(baruk)* to house their enemies' heads.

In their remote hill farms, the Bidayuh grow hill rice, maize and sugar cane as staples, and pepper, cocoa and rubber for cash. They have developed superb handicrafts: their basketry is every bit as fine as that of the Penan, although subtly different, and they are splendid craftsmen in bamboo – whole longhouses are built of this tough, durable material, and water supplies are delivered from remote mountain springs through complex systems of bamboo plumbing.

The Bidayuhs were James and Charles Brooke's favourite people. This may have something to do with their legendary honesty, their love of music and dance and their physical beauty.

Aesthetics aside, one of the best reasons to spend time with the Bidayuh is because they are Borneo's master wine makers. Their *tuak*, or rice wine, is comparable to that of the Iban, and they produce liquid masterpieces from anything that contains carbohydrates. *Tuak tebu* (sugar cane wine), *tuak tampui* (mangosteen tuak) and *tuak appel* (cider) can enliven an evening spent in a kampung or longhouse beyond your wildest expectations.

Don't bother learning the language, though. When Bidayuhs are introduced they speak in Malay or English, because if they're not from the same village they probably can't understand each other's dialect. Maybe that's why they became such good brewers – to overcome the language barrier.

Mike Reed

anyone in the longhouse who speaks English and you will have to do without creature comforts.

Getting There & Away

STC bus No 9A goes to Annah Rais at 9, 10.20 and 11.30 am; it's a two hour trip and the fare is RM5.10. For Kampung Benuk take STC bus No 6 and ask the driver to let you off; departure times are at 7.15, 8.10, 10.20, 11.20 and 11.50 am, and 1.20 pm; buses return at 7.55, 8.50 and 11 am, and at 12, 12.30 and 2 pm. The fare is RM1.50. For other longhouses you'll have to walk, hitch or hire a car.

GUNUNG PENRISSEN

Gunung Penrissen is a 1325m-high mountain just over the border in Kalimantan. Experienced, well-equipped climbers can climb the mountain, but it's a strenuous two to three day trek. There are no regular treks up the mountain, although one of the adventure tour companies in Kuching should be able to put together a package for you. It would be cheaper for a group to attempt the climb because, apart from transport costs, guides need to be hired in Kampung Annah Rais or nearby Kampung Padawan.

JONG'S CROCODILE FARM

As these places go, Jong's is relatively inoffensive. There are impressive specimens kept safely behind bars, cute baby crocs and gruesome photos of a famous man-eater and its last victim. But when crocodiles aren't eating they don't do much, and the other displays, including monkeys, hornbills and beautiful leopard cats, are probably more interesting.

Jong's is open from 9 am to 5 pm daily, and entry is RM8 for adults and RM2 for children. Feeding times on Sunday are 11 am and 3 pm.

The croc farm is 29km south of Kuching at Siburan; STC bus No 3, 3A, 9A or 9B will drop you at the turn-off along the highway, from where it is a short walk. The fare is RM2.50 and the trip takes about 40 minutes.

FAIRY & WIND CAVES

A few kilometres from the little town of Bau, south of Kuching, two very different cave systems in a range of steep limestone hills make an interesting day trip. Bau is an old gold-mining town, though there's nothing to see there and most travellers give it a miss. Take a picnic lunch, drinks and a good torch (flashlight) for exploring the caves, although torches can be hired at the entrance to both.

Wind Cave

About 3km south-west of Bau, the Wind Cave is a network of underground streams on the bank of the Batang Kayan. It's easy to walk through the caves on elevated boardwalks (though it isn't lit), or walk around the jungle-clad perimeter of the park. You can walk right through the caves to the river, where there are barbecues, food and drink stalls and changing facilities. The river is usually quite shallow and safe to swim in; it's a popular spot with locals on weekends.

Fairy Cave

About 5km further south, Fairy Cave is an extraordinary elevated cave: a massive concrete walkway leads up to the entrance, 30m above the ground in the side of a cliff. After a steep, slippery climb, you enter a grotto formed by the collapse of the cave roof. For generations this area has been used as a shrine by Chinese, who offer incense and other goods to various anthropomorphic cave formations. It's quite large and you could easily spend an hour exploring.

Getting There & Away

Direct transport to Bau is via STC bus No 2. The journey takes around one hour and costs RM3. Buses leave every 20 minutes between 6 am and 6 pm.

To get to the caves, take a bus from Bau bazaar and ask the driver to let you off; from the road to Wind Cave is about 700m and to Fairy Cave 1.3km. You could walk to the Wind Cave from Bau in about an hour, but Fairy Cave is much further away – you would have to hitch.

LUNDU

This quiet little town sits between the forested bulk of Gunung Gading National Park and the Sungai Kayan (see the Sarawak map). To most travellers it's just the transport node for the national park, but there are far worse places to get stranded. Lundu was established by Datuk Sulaiman and his followers, who arrived from Kuching and opened up the area. One day they were attacked by 2100 pirates in 70 vessels. Datuk Sulaiman killed 2070 of them (he just could not manage the last 30) before he was beheaded. The pirates fled, leaving Lundu in peace for ever more. That's the word on the street, anyway.

Lundu has a fish market along the riverfront and a hawker centre at the west end of town. The town centre is a square bounded by old godowns, and brightly painted houses line the quiet country lanes. Check out the garish rafflesia monument near the bus station.

The road north out of town leads to two beaches – **Pandan** (10km) and **Siar** (8.5km). They're both OK but strewn with flotsam and hardly worth a special trip.

Places to Stay & Eat

Lundu has a couple of hotels which are quite acceptable if the national park is full. The *Cheng Hak Boarding House* (☎ 082-735018), 51 Lundu Bazaar, has simple fan-cooled rooms with shared bathroom for RM22, or RM28 with air-con. The office is at the Goh Joo Hok shop, a few doors down from the *Lundu Gading Hotel* (☎ 082-735199), which has air-con rooms with bathroom for RM58.

There are Chinese *kedai kopi* around the square and a *hawker centre* cranks up in the evening over on the west side of town.

EAST MALAYSIA

Getting There & Away

To get to Lundu from Kuching take STC bus No 2B. There are departures every day at 8 and 10.45 am and 1.45 and 3.45 pm. Back the other way, buses leave Lundu at 10 am, and at 1, 2.45 and 4.15 pm. The trip takes about two hours and the fare is RM7.80.

GUNUNG GADING NATIONAL PARK

The chief attraction at Gunung Gading is the rafflesia, the world's largest flower, and this is one of the best places in Borneo to see this rarity. The rafflesia blooms all year round, but at unpredictable times and places, and a measure of luck is necessary to see it. It's a good idea to check whether any are in bloom before heading out to the park. Ring the park HQ (☎ 082-735714) or the National Parks booking office (☎ 082-248088) in Kuching. Rafflesias bloom for only a few days so if one is out, get to Gunung Gading as soon as you can. If it's off the trail, you may need a guide to find it – this should cost only RM5 per hour – but quiz the park staff first and don't just automatically hire a guide. After all, it's hard to miss a flower nearly 1m in diameter!

Even if you don't see the flower, this is a pleasant and often deserted national park with well-marked walking trails, a swimming hole and good accommodation. A large colour-coded map outside the park office indicates the walking trails and times needed to complete each. One of the easiest is to a lookout point near the park HQ (1½ hours), and there's a natural swimming pool a few minutes from the office that's popular with locals.

The energetic could climb to the summit of 906m Gunung Gading (three hours each way), but wildlife is not easy to see because much of the walking is under the canopy. There's a good information centre with displays and photos on the rafflesia, the park's wildlife and local culture.

Remember to get a permit from the National Parks booking office in Kuching before heading out to Gunung Gading, and the usual RM3 entry fee and RM5 camera fee can be paid at the gate.

Places to Stay & Eat

There's good, clean accommodation at the park HQ, although there's no shop so you'll have to bring supplies from nearby Lundu or all the way from Kuching.

The hostel has fan-cooled rooms with pillows and blankets for RM10 per bed or RM40 for a four-bunk room. There's a shared bathroom and fully equipped kitchen with fridge and gas stove. Air-conditioned chalets with cooking facilities, fridge and TV sleep six people and cost RM120. It's a good idea to book ahead, especially during busy weekends and school holidays. Book can be made at the parks office in Kuching (☎ 082-248088).

If the park accommodation is full, there are two places to stay in Lundu (see the earlier Lundu section for details).

Getting There & Away

See the Lundu Getting There & Away entry for information on getting there from Kuching. The park entrance is 2km north of Lundu on the road to Pantai Pandan. Take bus No 17C (50 sen) and ask to be dropped off at the park, or hitch. It's probably as quick to walk from Lundu if you miss a bus, as the park entrance is another 500m from where the bus drops you. The last bus is supposed to leave Lundu for Kuching at 4 pm, but it occasionally doesn't show up. If you get stranded you will have to overnight in the park or in Lundu, so it may be a good idea to put a toothbrush in your day pack.

SEMATAN

Sematan is a coastal village near the far western end of Sarawak. The beach is clean, deserted and lined with coconut palms, but the water is very shallow and only good for paddling. All things considered, it is a long way to go for a so-so beach, but it is popular with well-to-do Kuching residents who have beach bungalows.

Sematan's importance may grow when visitors' facilities at Tanjung Datu National Park are improved, but at present Lundu is a more pleasant town and its beaches more accessible.

Places to Stay & Eat

The *Thomas Lai Bungalows* are wooden bungalows in a coconut palm grove beside the beach. They are very run-down and rather spartan, with mandi, basic kitchen facilities and veranda. At RM80 to RM120, depending on quality and proximity to the beach, they are way overpriced, though you could try bargaining for mid-week specials; telephone ☎ 082-332098 in Kuching, or ask around for the caretaker in Sematan.

A few hundred metres out of town on the road to Lundu, the *Sematan Hotel* (☎ 082-711162) has reasonable fan rooms with shared bathroom for RM22 to RM30, and better air-con rooms from RM50 with bathroom.

Sematan has a couple of Chinese *kedai kopi* and *food stalls* at the small market.

Getting There & Away

To get to Sematan, first take a bus to Lundu (see the Lundu section). From Lundu STC bus No 17 leaves regularly for Sematan; it takes about an hour and costs RM2.

The beach is within walking distance, about 1km west of town.

TANJUNG DATU NATIONAL PARK

This is the newest and smallest of Sarawak's national parks. It is in the far-flung west of the state, abutting the border with Kalimantan, and its 1379 hectares protect rainforest, unpolluted rivers and near-pristine beaches. There are no facilities for visitors, although their construction is probably not far off. Access is only possible by boat from Sematan; ask around in the kampungs, but negotiate a price before you set out. If you visit Gunung Gading on the way, someone at the park office may be able to organise a boat for you, or you could try the District Office in Sematan.

SERIAN

Serian is a very small town 65km south-east of Kuching. On weekends it's a popular destination for Kuching residents, who come to picnic at Taman Danu, a landscaped park with a small lake, a short walk from the town centre. Taman Rekreasi Ranchan, about 5km from town, is another popular weekend spot where there are small waterfalls. Serian's other attraction is a bustling market, where people from nearby longhouses come to sell unusual produce, such as jungle fruits and herbs, snake meat and sago worms.

Places to Stay

If you want to stay overnight, the *Kota Semarahan Serian Hotel* (☎ 082-874118), 47 Serian Bazaar, has fan-cooled rooms with shared bathroom for RM20 and larger rooms with bathroom for RM35.

Getting There & Away

Serian's bus station is in the centre of town near the market. From Kuching take an STC express bus from the long-distance bus station on Jalan Penrissen. There are 10 buses every day between 6.55 am and 5.45 pm; the journey takes about an hour and the fare is RM5. Buses back to Kuching leave between 6.30 am and 5 pm.

Taman Rekreasi Ranchan is further up a side road off the road to Sri Aman. There's lots of traffic if you go on a weekend so you could try hitching; otherwise you'll have to take a taxi.

SRI AMAN

Originally known as Simangangg, Sri Aman is a sleepy town on the muddy Batang Lupar, halfway between Kuching and Sarikei. The name Sri Aman means 'Abode of Peace' and this is where the treaty ending the Confrontation was signed; there's a commemorative park in the centre of town. Sri Aman's other claim to fame is a tidal bore that periodically sweeps up the river, scattering all craft in its path. It's hard to predict the occurrence of this phenomenon, but it nearly took the life of W Somerset Maugham, an event he recorded in a short story called *The Yellow Streak*. There's not much to see or do, but some travellers use Sri Aman as a base to explore the surrounding area and its longhouses.

There's a Chinese temple on the waterfront, and a little downstream is one of Raja Brooke's old forts, Fort Alice, which dates from 1864; it isn't open to the public. The Skrang, Lemanak and Ai rivers flow into the Lupar, and many of the tours organised out of Kuching bring their groups to the longhouses along these tributaries. Several tour operators have built their own accommodation facilities next to the longhouses.

There isn't a lot of river traffic at Sri Aman itself, and while it is close to the confluence of the Batang Skrang, most boats to the longhouses go from Kampung Skrang, further north, where the highway crosses the Batang Skrang. Similarly, most boats to the Lemanak and Ai rivers leave from Engkilili, or on the highway outside town where the road crosses the Batang Lupar.

Places to Stay

The basic *Sun Sun Hotel* (☎ 083-322191), Jalan Club opposite the market, has large, clean singles/doubles with fans for RM20/33. It is spartan but quite acceptable.

The newer *Alishan Hotel* (☎ 083-322578), 4 Jalan Council, is a better bet for a cheap room. It has air-con rooms with bathroom for RM30, and small fan-cooled rooms for RM20 that are better than those at the Sun Sun. A few doors along, the *Taiwan Hotel* (☎ 083-322494) has newly renovated air-con double rooms from RM32 to RM45; three people can fit into the larger rooms.

The mid-range *Hoover Hotel* (☎ 083-321985), 139 Jalan Club, is the best place in town and has rooms with air-con, bathroom and TV from RM53 to RM80 plus tax; a junior suite costs RM115. The Hoover occupies the 2nd, 3rd and 4th floors above a supermarket on the corner – take the lift next to the supermarket entrance.

Getting There & Away

STC (☎ 083-322081) has five buses a day between 7.45 am and 7.45 pm from Kuching to Sri Aman; the trip takes about three hours and costs RM15 (RM26 return). Buses to Kuching leave between 7.30 am and 3.30 pm.

Six buses a day run between Sri Aman and Sarikei at 6.30, 6.50, 8.10, 10.15 and 11.30 am and 1 pm (about three hours, RM13.50). From Sarikei you can get connections to Bintulu and Miri, and boats up the Rejang to Sibu.

From Sri Aman STC buses go to the surrounding villages of Skrang (RM3.80), Batu Lintang (RM2.80), Engkilili (RM2.80) and Lubok Antu (RM5.50).

BATANG AI NATIONAL PARK

Batang Ai covers 24 sq km and protects the catchment of the Batang Ai reservoir, which was formed by a hydro-electric scheme 250km east of Kuching. The park's rainforest features wildlife such as orang-utans, gibbons and hornbills, but there is no visitors' centre and no accommodation. Access is possible by chartering a boat from Batang Ai, but it is difficult and expensive. Until facilities are developed – likely in the near future – the park is best visited as part of a longhouse tour. Some travel agencies in Kuching can arrange for longhouse accommodation nearby and treks into the park – see the Kuching section for details.

One expensive option is the *Hilton Batang Ai Longhouse Resort* (☎ 083-584338), a luxury longhouse resort on the shores of the reservoir. Longhouse tours and jungle treks can be arranged from here, and there are also watersports such as kayaking. All rooms have air-con, and the hotel has a swimming pool, bar and restaurant with cultural performances. Standard rooms cost from RM170 to RM190, and suites cost from RM230 – plus tax. A transfer from Kuching is RM45 each way, but as the trip takes around four hours it's hardly worth it for an overnight trip.

Up the Batang Rejang

The mighty Batang Rejang is the main artery of trade with the interior for all of central and southern Sarawak. Scattered along its banks, and those of its tributaries, particularly in the upper reaches, are the longhouses of the Iban and other tribes. Staying at a longhouse is one of the highlights of a trip to Sarawak.

The Iban Greet the New Century

TOURISM MALAYSIA

The Iban longhouse is now an interesting mix of traditional architecture and modern conveniences.

The Iban are likely to come as a shock to anyone who imagines them to be happy natives marooned from the 20th century deep in the jungles of Borneo. Sarawak's most adaptable and resourceful ethnic group are far too savvy to ignore the convenience of a Land Cruiser or the pleasure afforded by satellite TV. However, those who shake their heads in disappointment should look again. The Iban manage to maintain a tribal culture that is every bit as rich in a Kuching housing estate as it is in the rural longhouse tradition.

For most Ibans, however, the longhouse is still their first choice of dwelling, even when it's built of concrete. Urban Ibans in housing estates buy terraced houses adjacent to each other, so that a semblance of longhouse life is maintained in the city. They enjoy close friendships with their Chinese and Malay neighbours across the street, but they generally prefer to have an Iban family living either side of them, as they would in their grandparents' longhouse.

But the majority of Sarawak's 550,000 Ibans (the largest single ethnic group) still live in the countryside, growing hill rice, breeding pigs and chickens, and supplementing their income with pepper, rubber, palm oil and cocoa. Most longhouses are still built of ironwood, with ancient skulls still hanging from the ceiling. Women still weave the fabulous *pua kumbu* blankets, although lighting is supplied nowadays by a generator rather than a paraffin lamp. Cooking is usually done with gas instead of charcoal. The children all go to school, but they can still perform the Ngajat dance to alarming effect. And although most Ibans are nowadays Christian, impressive feasts are still held for the dead (Gawai Antu), and for the great bird of omen, the hornbill (Gawai Kenyalang). And the rice wine *(tuak)* is as potent as it ever was.

Economic development has not dragged the Iban reluctantly into the late 20th century. Rather, the Iban have seized the 20th century by the scruff of the neck and dragged it kicking and screaming into the longhouse.

Mike Reed

EAST MALAYSIA

However, travellers who view the Rejang as a ticket to longhouse retreats and tribal innocence are likely to be disappointed.

For a start, the Rejang is the main conduit for felled logs from the forests in the upper reaches of the river and its tributaries – the Balleh, Belaga and Balui. The number of log-laden barges on the river is astounding. Before the loggers arrived, the river was a clear green; these days it's a muddy brown from all the topsoil which has washed out of the forests. What's more, a massive hydroelectric dam project to the north of Belaga at Bakun has brought roads, labourers and far-reaching change to the area.

The best time for a trip up the Rejang is in late May and early June. This is the time of Gawai, the Dayak harvest festival, when there is plenty of movement on the rivers and the longhouses welcome visitors. There are also plenty of celebrations, which usually involve the consumption of copious quantities of arrack and tuak.

On the river the only hotel accommodation available is in Song, Kanowit, Kapit and Belaga.

Visiting a Longhouse

Most people head off up the river with the intention of visiting a longhouse. This is certainly worth doing but there is no guarantee of success. The hospitality of the longhouse tribes is famous, but cannot be relied on for unannounced visits. It's not just a matter of rolling up on the doorstep and expecting to be welcomed with open arms. Without an introduction, the Orang Ulu are not going to invite you into their homes – turning up unannounced is not just bad manners, in certain circumstances it can be a minor catastrophe, particularly if there has been a recent death or certain rituals are under way. Without an invitation, there's not much point making this often expensive and time-consuming journey upriver.

Longhouses can be found all the way along the Rejang. While most visitors head for Kapit and beyond, there are plenty of longhouses further downriver around Kanowit and Song. As you go further upriver, the longhouses will not necessarily be more traditional. Most are made from modern building materials and in fact many longhouse communities are moving towards individual houses, which fare much better if there is a fire (fire can destroy a longhouse in as little as 30 minutes).

Similarly, amulets and head feathers are reserved for ceremonial occasions; jeans, shorts and T-shirts are the preferred everyday longhouse attire. Traditional customs, beliefs and festivals are still practised, but the jungle *is* part of the 21st century – you may spend days getting to a longhouse only to find everyone sitting around watching CNN on satellite TV.

To arrange a visit, the most important commodity you need is time. If you are short of it, take a tour. Most travellers head for Kapit, a small administrative town upriver. It's the last big settlement on the river, and it's here that the longhouse people come in for supplies. The best strategy for finding someone to take you to a longhouse is to make yourself known around the town – sit in the cafes and get talking to people. If you are not the sociable type, it's unlikely that anyone is going to want to invite you to their home – unless you have a couple of bottles of Hennessy XO.

Before heading upriver from Kapit, you need to get a permit from the state office (see Permits under Kapit for details). This only takes a few minutes, but permits are not available on Saturday afternoon or Sunday. The permit is merely a formality, and you'll probably never be asked for it.

Many travellers head for the stretch of the Batang Rejang between Kapit and Belaga. This area is easily accessible as there are express boats operating between the two towns, in the wet season at least. Perhaps a more interesting river is the Balleh, which branches off to the east a short distance upstream from Kapit. Both these rivers have dozens of small tributaries, and it's up these that you really want to go. At Belaga the Balui and Belaga rivers merge and become the Batang Rejang. To travel up either of these rivers from Belaga requires permission from the Resident in Belaga; this is usually not granted, although it seems there's little to stop you if you are determined. The Katibas, which joins the Rejang at Song (between Sibu and Kapit), is also a good river to explore and no permits are required.

Some people have reported that some of the longhouse inhabitants between Kapit and Belaga are unfriendly towards visitors. No doubt they're sick to death of strangers turning up out of the blue and expecting to be welcomed with open arms, fed and entertained. One traveller was stuck for words when an old Iban lady asked: 'Where in Europe can I go and be welcomed into a stranger's house?'. Don't let this put you off, as generally the Iban are very friendly, hospitable people who welcome foreigners and are pleased to invite you into their homes.

Having found someone to take you, you'll need to stock up with gifts with which to 'pay' for your visit. Forget any qualms you may have about giving people things that might be bad for them – cigarettes and alcohol are the most-appreciated gifts. A carton of cigarettes and a few bottles of whisky will go down well. Sweets are always popular too, and not just with the kids. Of course if you can give something original, especially from your own country, it will be well received.

On arrival at the longhouse ask for the *tuai rumah* (chief). You'll then probably be offered a place to stay for the night and be invited to join them for a meal.

Longhouse Etiquette Longhouse etiquette is fairly formal, and there are a number of important customs you need to be aware of so you don't make a fool of yourself or cause offence. Firstly, never enter a longhouse without permission; always wait to be invited. If there is a *pemali* (ritual prohibition) in force (usually after a death or some misfortune), indicated by a bunch of branches tied to the rail at the bottom of the ladder or by a white flag near the entrance, you won't be invited in – find another longhouse.

Once inside, always remove your shoes; it's extremely bad form to wear footwear inside a longhouse. Chances are you'll be given a welcome drink of tuak; drink it, or at least some of it. Accept food and drinks with both hands rather than just one.

Meals are usually taken with the tuai rumah and are served on the floor and eaten with both hands. Don't stretch your legs when sitting on the mat; this applies at any time, not just during meals. Don't spit or blow your nose during a meal. Chances are the food will be fairly bland and uninteresting but, again, eat some of it, or at the very least touch the food and then touch your mouth. Vegetarians may find it difficult because meat is usually used in local cooking. It's not a bad idea to take along some food of your own, but you should offer to share it.

When washing or bathing in the river, men are expected to wear at least underpants while women should stay covered with a sarung. Nudity is not on – this is not Europe.

In the evenings there'll probably be a lot of tuak drinking, and you may well be expected to sing and dance. Join in and don't be afraid to make an idiot of yourself – the locals will love it! Tuak usually tastes weak but it is pretty potent stuff, and although it

Some Iban Words & Phrases

Good morning.	*Salamat pagi.*
Good afternoon.	*Salamat tengah-hari.*
Good night.	*Salamat malam.*
Goodbye.	*Salamat tinggal.*
Thank you.	*Terima kasih.*
How are you?	*Gerai nuan?*
Pleased to meet you.	*Rindu amat betemu enggau nuan.*
See you again.	*Arap ke betemu baru.*
Who is the chief?	*Sapa tuai rumah kita ditu?*
What's your name?	*Sapa nama nuan?*
Where do we bathe/wash?	*Dini endor kitai mandi?*
Can I take a photograph of you?	*Tau aku ngambi gambar nuan?*
I'm sorry.	*Aku minta ampun.*
Where?	*Dini?*
What?	*Nama?*

I	*aku*
you	*nuan*
today	*saharitu*
tomorrow	*pegilah*
day	*hari*
night	*malam*
good	*manah*
not good	*jai also enda manah*
eat	*makai*
drink	*ngirup*
go	*bejalai*

DAVID ANDREW

The tree of life design is common in Iban art and architecture.

doesn't usually result in a hangover it is a fairly safe bet that you'll find yourself going to the toilet frequently the following day. The accepted way to drink it is from the glass in a single shot.

Make an effort to speak at least a few words of Iban (see the boxed text 'Some Iban Words & Phrases'). Although there's always someone who speaks Malay, any attempt at communication in the local lingo is warmly appreciated. Your conversations will be limited if you speak only English.

What to Take Apart from gifts, other indispensable items include a torch (flashlight), mosquito repellent and a medical kit with plenty of aspirin or Panadol and Lomotil, Imodium or other anti-diarrhoeal.

SIBU

The busy port of Sibu is Sarawak's second biggest city and the main centre for trade between the coast and the vast hinterland. Situated 60km upstream from the sea, it's here that the interior's raw materials – logs, gravel, minerals and agricultural produce – are brought for transhipment and export. Sibu's bustling waterfront hosts all manner of craft from motorised dugouts to ocean-going container ships. Along the muddy river there's a constant procession of colourful double-decker cargo boats, seemingly endless barges laden with timber, tugs, fishing boats and speedboats skipping across the wash of bigger traffic.

For a time Sibu was known as New Foochow, named after the Chinese migrants who came from Foochow in the early years of the 20th century. The city owes much of its prosperity to these settlers and today Chinese make up more than 60% of Sibu's population.

Sibu will probably be your first stop on the Batang Rejang. There's not a great deal to do in the city itself unless you like hanging around on waterfronts or at vegetable markets. Although both of these can be quite entertaining, most travellers just stay overnight then head off up the Rejang the following day.

Orientation & Information

Sibu lies on the north bank of the Rejang near its confluence with the Batang Igan. The town's frantic commerce belies the fact that all places to stay and eat, express boat wharves and banks, are within an easy walk of the centre. A seven storey Chinese pagoda marks the western edge of the waterfront and the clock tower the eastern; and the enormous two storey Lembangan Market is in between.

The wharf for express boats to Kuching is right in the centre of town, just near the Chinese temple, and local buses also terminate on the waterfront. Boats upriver to Kapit and other centres leave 200m west of the local bus station. The long-distance bus terminal is at Sungai Antu, 3km west of town and the airport is 20km to the east.

The helpful Visitors' Information Centre (☎ 084-340980), 32 Jalan Cross, stocks a good free tourist map and can help with inquiries about travel up the river or elsewhere. The centre is open Monday to Thursday from 8 am to 4.15 pm, Friday from 8 am to 4.45 pm, and Saturday from 8 am to 12.45 pm.

There's also a tourist information office at the airport. All major banks have branches in Sibu.

Things to See & Do

Most people use Sibu as a transit point to catch boats upriver, or to await one on their return, and few would find reason to stay more than one night. The most outstanding sight on the waterfront is the 100 year old **Tua Pek Kong Temple** above the Kuching wharf – or rather its adjoining seven tiered pagoda. This colourful temple is guarded by two gilt lions outside and a host of curling dragons on the eaves, and by a caretaker whom you'll have to get past if you want to climb to the top. He'll probably want to give you a crash course in Taoism, but if you make it past him there's a great view of the river and town awaiting; it's particularly good at sunset, when hundreds of swifts wheel around the tower at eye level.

At the other end of the waterfront, just past the bus station, there is a **clock tower**,

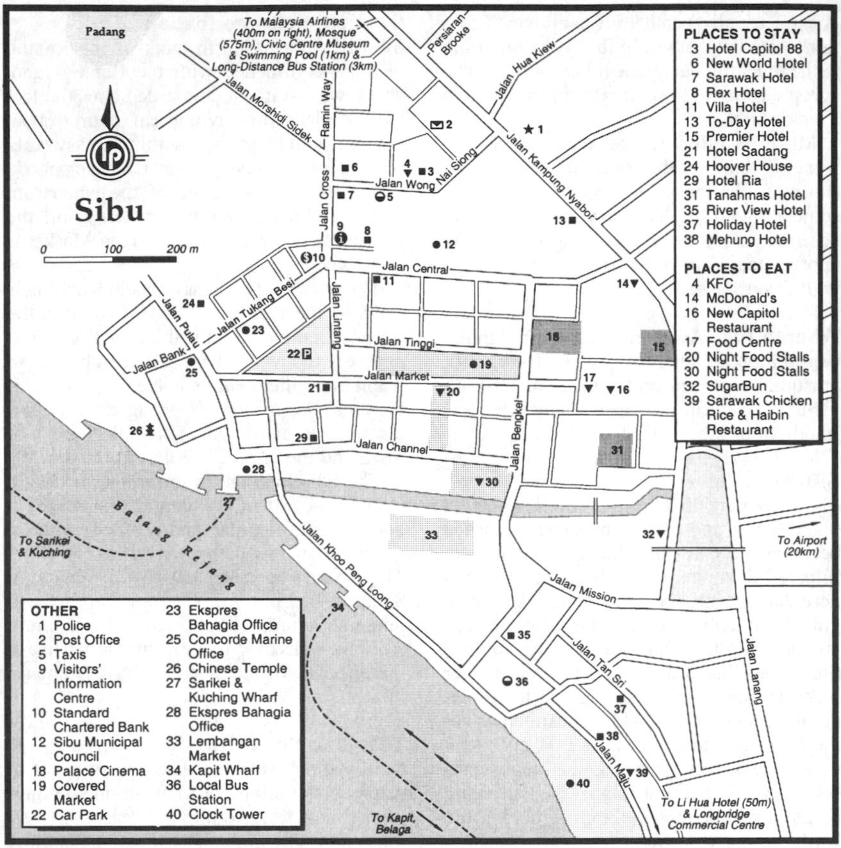

donated by the Orient Clock Co, with a clock playing different tunes on the hour.

The **Civic Centre Museum** tells the story of settlement on the Rejang, with antiques, artefacts and photos in displays about the Chinese settlers, and the endemic Iban and Melanau cultures. The museum is open every day except Monday and public holidays from 10.30 am to 5.30 pm. To get there take Sungei Merah bus No 1, 1A or 4 from the local bus station; the fare is 40 sen.

One thing Sibu has in abundance is market space, from the massive **Lembangan Market** – which has some 700 stalls – to the older **covered market** on Jalan Market, and the tiny hawkers' barrows and street vendors that seem to appear from nowhere at nightfall. It's a fascinating, sometimes colourful world of bartering and selling.

There is a good swimming pool about 30 minutes bus ride from the centre. To get there take bus No 10 from the local bus station. The pool is open every day, but hours are sporadic – check with the Visitors' Information Centre. The entry fee is RM1.

Places to Stay – Budget

Sibu has dozens of budget hotels although many are dark, dingy and often seedy. Those displaying signs saying *bilik untuk sewa* (or variations), which means 'rooms for rent', house long-term residents, but can be a cheap option.

The best place to stay is the Methodist guesthouse, *Hoover House* (☎ 084-332973), next to the church on Jalan Pulau. It's excellent value at RM12 per person for clean, well-kept rooms with fans and attached bathrooms. Unfortunately, it is hard to get a room here because it is usually full; check with the caretaker around the back.

If you can't get into Hoover House, there are several budget hotels around the local bus station. It's a grotty part of town, but despite appearances it's safe. The *Mehung Hotel* (☎ 084-324852), 17 Jalan Maju, has small rooms with fan and shared bathroom for RM15, and better rooms with fan and a tiny bathroom from RM20 (RM30 with air-con). On the street behind, the *Holiday Hotel* (☎ 084-317440), 16 Jalan Tan Sri, is a clean boarding house where simple fan-cooled rooms cost RM15/20, and air-con rooms with shower and toilet go for RM30.

The town centre has better hotels, though naturally prices are higher. The *To-Day Hotel* (☎ 084-336499), upstairs at 40 Jalan Kampung Nyabor, is a friendly, well-run place that welcomes travellers. Clean air-con rooms with bathroom and TV cost RM25/30.

Places to Stay – Mid-Range

Sibu's mid-range hotels can be good value; all have air-con rooms with phone, TV and attached bathroom, and are usually carpeted. There are plenty in the centre of town.

The *River View Hotel* (☎ 084-325241), 65 Jalan Mission, overlooks the local bus station and is handy for the wharves, but there is a noisy karaoke parlour next door. Slightly tattered but clean and comfortable rooms cost from RM30/36 for singles/doubles up to RM50 for large rooms with two beds.

The *Sarawak Hotel 1992* (☎ 084-333455), at 34 Jalan Cross on the corner of Jalan Wong Nai Siong, is recommended. Bright and clean rooms start at RM35 a single and doubles cost from RM45 to RM55. Opposite is the *New World Hotel* (☎ 084-310311), 1 Jalan Wong Nai Siong, which has rooms from RM33/35; the Sarawak is slightly better value. *Hotel Capitol 88* (☎ 084-336444), 19 Jalan Wong Nai Siong, has good rooms for RM35/40, but the Hideaway Pub, on the 1st floor, can get a bit noisy.

The *Rex Hotel* (☎ 084-330625), next to the Visitors' Information Centre, has air-con rooms with bathroom for RM35/40. The *Hotel Ria* (☎ 084-326622), 21 Jalan Channel, has good, clean rooms with big beds and bathroom for RM33/40. It is also handy for the markets and wharves. If the Ria is full, they'll try and squeeze you into the *Villa Hotel* (☎ 084-337833), 2 Jalan Central, which is of a similar standard.

The *Li Hua Hotel* (☎ 084-324000) at the Longbridge Commercial Centre, about 300m east along the river from the bus station, overlooks the river and is popular with local businesspeople. It is one of the top mid-range places and has a rooftop swimming pool. Singles/doubles cost from RM66/105 to RM88/120 and suites are available.

Places to Stay – Top End

Two of the best hotels are very close to the centre of town – and each other – on Jalan Kampung Nyabor. Add 10% service charge and 5% tax to the prices, but you can normally get a discount of around 20%. Apart from their height and price, the main difference between these places and the better mid-range choices is the size of their rooms.

The *Premier Hotel* (☎ 084-323222) charges from RM160/180 to RM180/200 for singles/doubles; suites cost between RM270 and RM570. If you get a discount (very likely) it's not a bad deal because these rates include a decent buffet breakfast. All rooms have a minibar, IDD phone, cable TV and in-house movies.

The *Tanahmas Hotel* (☎ 084-333188) is newer but offers much the same standard as the Premier at higher rates. Singles/doubles start at RM165/190 – those facing the river cost RM185/210 – and suites are RM350 to RM850.

Places to Eat

The best cheap food in Sibu can be found at various *hawker centres* and *food stalls*. There's a small two storey *food centre* at the end of Jalan Market, at the rear of the Palace Cinema, where stalls sell Malay curries, roti and laksa as well as Chinese food and ais kacang. There are also food stalls on the 2nd floor of the Lembangan Market.

In the late afternoon a host of *stalls* set up near the covered market selling delicious snacks such as pau (steamed dumplings), barbecued chicken wings and all manner of sweets. This is a fun way to sample local fare at a pittance and the food is usually very fresh.

The riverfront area near the Mehung Hotel has a number of *Chinese restaurants*. One of the best for an inexpensive chicken and rice plate is *Sarawak Chicken Rice*; close by is the more upmarket *Haibin Restaurant*. If you're taking an early boat, the Chinese *kedai kopi* along the waterfront are open for breakfast well before dawn. There's also a small *supermarket* where you can get snacks, drinks and a paper for the trip upriver.

For a sit-down Chinese meal at an upmarket air-con restaurant, the *New Capitol Restaurant,* diagonally opposite the Premier Hotel, is supposed to have the best food in town. There are some expensive dishes on the menu, but if you choose carefully you'll only need to spend a few ringgit on a pretty good feed.

The *Premier Hotel* has one of the best restaurants in town, and it's a good deal better than that at the Tanahmas Hotel, but tax will add to the bill. An all-you-can-eat buffet dinner costs RM16, and there's a good a la carte selection of western and local dishes. The *Li Hua Hotel* has good and moderately priced food in its coffee shop/restaurant.

For western fast food, *SugarBun* and *McDonald's* are on Jalan Kampung Nyabor, and there's a *KFC* outlet on Jalan Wong Nai Siong.

Getting There & Away

Air The Malaysia Airlines office (☎ 083-326166) is at 61 Jalan Tunku Osman, a few minutes walk from the town centre. It is open Monday to Friday from 8 am to 5 pm, and Saturday from 8 am to 4 pm.

Regular Malaysia Airlines flights go to main centres around Sarawak and in the interior, including Kuching (10 daily, RM72) and Bintulu (four daily, RM64). Some of the Bintulu flights go on to Miri (RM112) and five daily flights go direct. You can also fly to Kota Kinabalu (two daily, RM180) via Bintulu or Miri.

If you're travelling by boat from Sibu to Kapit and Belaga and want to fly back, book as far in advance as possible because the Sibu-Kapit-Belaga (and return) sector is only covered once a week, on Sunday. The fare is RM48 to Kapit and RM76 to Belaga. Malaysia Airlines also has Twin Otter flights to Marudi three times a week (RM100).

Bus The main bus lines have ticket stalls at the long-distance bus station, west of town at Sungai Antu. There should be no problem getting a seat if you arrive 15 minutes before departure, but it may pay to book ahead for weekends and school holidays.

The main bus companies running services from Sibu are Biaramas Express (☎ 084-313139), Borneo Express Bus (☎ 084-319773), Borneo Highway Express (☎ 084-319533), Lanang Road Bus Co (☎ 084-314527), PB Express (☎ 084-332873) and Suria Express (☎ 084-319773). Most have ticketing agencies around the local bus station on the waterfront.

Bintulu The 220km trip to Bintulu takes around four hours and costs RM16.50. There are services virtually every hour between 6 am and 8 pm, although they are more frequent in the morning; some continue to Miri. The main companies plying this route are Suria Express, Biaramas, Lanang Road and PB Express.

Kanowit Lanang Road buses leave from the local bus station for Kanowit at 6, 8 and 10 am, and at noon, 2 and 4.30 pm. The fare is RM5.70 and the trip takes about an hour.

Kuching There are regular express buses to Kuching, most of which change at Sarikei, but the trip takes about seven hours and boats do the trip in a bit over half the time for around the same price. The fare to Kuching is RM32.

Lanang Road buses leave at 9.30 am and 1.30 and 8 pm; Biaramas has daily runs at 9.30 am and 2, 8 and 10 pm; and Borneo Highway Express buses leave at 6.30 and 9.15 am, and 1, 5 and 8.15 pm.

You could also take a bus from Sibu to Sarikei then take a ferry. Biaramas leaves for Sarikei at 9.15 am and 1.30, 8 and 10 pm. The fare is RM6.

Miri The 418km trip to Miri takes about 7½ hours and costs RM34. Ideally, tickets should be bought half a day or more in advance, though turning up an hour or so before departure is usually fairly safe. Suria Express buses leave at 7 and 9 am, and 1 and 5.30 pm; and Biaramas Express buses leave at 5.45, 10 and 11.15 am, 2 and 8 pm.

Mukah Lanang Road buses leave for Mukah at 6.30 am, 12.30 and 2.30 pm daily; the fare is RM13.85 (RM12.80 in non-air-con buses) and the trip takes 3½ hours.

Pontianak (Indonesia) The PB Express service to Pontianak in Indonesia costs RM72 and departs at 3 and 8 am. See the Kuching Getting There & Away section for details of the crossing.

Boat Streamlined passenger express boats travel between Sibu and Kuching via Sarikei, and up the Rejang to Kanowit, Song and Kapit. Boats from Sibu travel beyond Kapit only when there is sufficient water. To get to Belaga you should expect to overnight in Kapit as the first express boat from Sibu doesn't always connect with the last regular service to Belaga.

Services to Sarikei and Kuching leave from the wharf below the Chinese pagoda; all upriver services leave from the wharf near the market. All boats are very fast with airline seats, ultra-violent videos and freezing air-con (take a blanket or warm clothing for the trip). Although there's plenty of river traffic to look at, the longer trips are something of an endurance trip – take a good book or a loud Walkman.

Sarikei & Kuching The express boat trip to Kuching takes around four hours and costs a standard RM35/38 for economy/1st class. A change from riverboats to larger sea-going vessels is sometimes necessary at Sarikei.

Although it's best to buy tickets in advance, especially during holiday periods, you should have no difficulty getting one on the boat. Ticket outlets and departure times from Sibu are as follows.

Concorde Marine
(☎ 084-331593) 1 Jalan Bank; 8.15 am
Ekspres Bahagia
(☎ 084-319228) 20 Jalan Tukang Besi; 11.30 am

Kapit & Belaga Getting to Kapit is the first leg of the journey up the Batang Rejang. Ekspres launches cover the 130km or so from Sibu to Kapit in just 2½ hours (that's one and a bit kungfu movies).

The first launch from Sibu leaves at approximately 5.45 am. When there's enough water in the river this boat goes on to Belaga – if not, you'll have to change boats at Kapit (see the Kapit section for details). Other launches leave approximately hourly until about 2.30 pm. Just go down to the Kapit wharf and ask which is the next boat. People are very helpful and the boats usually have a 'clock' showing intended departure time. The fare to Kapit is RM15/20 for economy/1st class.

All boats to Kapit pass Kanowit and Song, and may stop at smaller settlements and logging camps en route. Scheduled services that stop at Song leave Sibu at 7.30 am and 12.15 and 1 pm; the Sibu-Song leg takes about two hours/one video and costs RM10.

Some services also call at Kanowit (about one hour, RM6). If you want to get off tell the driver or ticket seller, but it can be hard to flag down a boat when you want to leave.

Getting Around

To/From the Airport Sibu's airport is inconveniently situated 20km east of town. Bus No 3A leaves from the local terminal hourly between 7 am and 6 pm; the fare is RM2 and the trip takes about 30 minutes. The bus stops at the end of the airport access road (about a 500m walk from the terminal). Going into Sibu, you could also try flagging down any of the rural buses that pass by. The taxi fare is RM20.

There's an air-conditioned cafeteria upstairs at the airport.

Bus The local bus station is on the waterfront. To get to the long-distance bus station take Lanang Road bus No 7 from the local bus station. It leaves every 15 minutes between 6 am and 9 pm and costs 60 sen. A taxi costs RM7.

If you arrive in Sibu by boat you will dock at either the Sarikei or the Kapit wharf, both of which are only a few minutes walk from all the main hotels and restaurants.

KANOWIT

This small riverside settlement is the last stop on the Rejang that's connected to the coast by road – it's boat only from here upstream. Fort Emma, one of the white rajas' fortifications, sits to the right of the wharf; it's not open to the public. There's also a colourful clock tower decorated in Iban 'tree of life' style and a brightly painted Chinese temple.

If you get stuck here, the *Kanowit Hotel* (☎ 084-752155), in a shophouse on the waterfront above the Dung Fang Coffee Shop, has fan-cooled rooms for RM30 and 'air conditional' rooms costing RM40 to RM50; all rooms are clean with attached bathroom. Virtually next door is the *Harbour View Inn* (☎ 084-753188), which has similar air-con rooms for RM40.

Getting There & Away

Buses to Kanowit leave Sibu at 6, 9 and 10 am, and 2 and 4.30 pm; buses back to Sibu leave at 6, 8 and 10 am, and at noon, 2 and 5 pm. The fare is RM5.70 and the trip takes about an hour. Buy your ticket at the Hock Sing Guan Cafe (☎ 084-752632) on the main street of Kanowit.

Some ekspres boats from Sibu have a scheduled stop at Kanowit, but they are few and far between. The fare is RM6 and the trip takes about an hour.

KAPIT

Kapit is another river town on the Rejang dating from the days of the white rajas; Fort Sylvia still stands on the riverbank. To travellers it's just a sleepy riverside town perched above the river, but Kapit is the biggest settlement for 100km in any direction. To people upriver it's the 'big city', where they come to buy, sell and exchange goods, and to enjoy the diversions of urban life, such as pool halls and video movies.

The bank of the river here is steep and in the dry season, when the water level falls, it's quite a drop to the river. For an idea of how high the water can get in times of flood, check out the markers on the walls of the old fort.

Kapit is a small place and everything is within an easy stroll. There's nothing much to do, but there is some surprisingly good accommodation. If you are looking for a lift and an introduction to a longhouse, ask at the Petronas or Shell fuel barges.

There are two longhouses about 7km from town along Jalan Selerik, but they're thoroughly urbanised.

Information

If you need to change travellers cheques there are three banks in town. The MBF is in the same block as the Kapit Longhouse Hotel; there's a Maybank next door to the Hotel Meligai; and Bank Simpanan Nasional has a branch on the riverfront at the west end of town. There's a licensed moneychanger a few doors up from the Ark Hill Hotel.

Permits A permit is not required to get to Kapit or to the luxury Pelagus Resort further up the Batang Rejang. If you want to travel beyond the Pelagus Rapids to Belaga, or anywhere up the Balleh, you must get a permit in Kapit.

Go to the Pejabat Am office on the 1st floor of the State Government Complex. Fill in the necessary form then take it next door to the Resident's Office, where the permit will be issued in a few minutes. It's quite painless – one question in the form asks when your cholera vaccination expires, but this is not checked. The permit is valid for either five or 10 days, depending on which you specify, and is valid for travel up the Rejang as far as Belaga, and up the Batang Balleh for an unspecified distance.

Whether or not your permit will be checked is another matter; it depends on the political climate and how much criticism the government is getting over logging or the controversial Bakun Dam at the time. In general there is no problem going upriver, as long as you come back again, but you will not be allowed to go near the dam construction site. Upon arrival in Belaga, you are supposed to report to the police, who can issue another permit to go even further upriver.

The government offices in Kapit are only open normal office hours, so if you arrive after lunch on a Saturday you'll have to wait until Monday morning to get a permit for the the rest of trip.

Things to See & Do

For a bit of outdoor action combined with visits to longhouses, the **Balleh-Kapit Raft Safari** is an annual two day event that's open to all comers. Participants in teams of six to eight race traditional wooden rafts down the Sungai Sut, a river near Kapit, stopping overnight at a longhouse. There are various categories of competition, including men's and women's; the cost of hiring a raft is US$100 and there's an entry fee of US$50 per team. The safari is usually held in April, but dates change so contact the Ministry of Tourism in Kuching (☎ 082-441957) for details.

During the day the Kapit **waterfront** is always packed with ferries, barges, and people coming and going. It's fascinating to watch the activity on the water and the people shouldering incredible loads of every description up from the wharf.

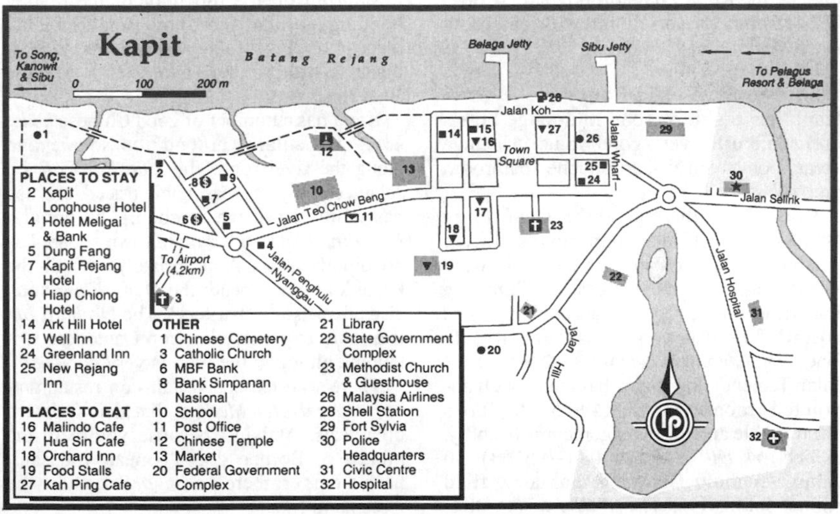

The yellow and red **Chinese temple** works up a sweat on the big drums some evenings and **Fort Sylvia** is probably the most photogenic of Raja Brooke's fortifications. Built in 1880, it's just along to the left as you climb the jetty steps, but isn't open to the public.

Also worth a look is the small **museum** in the lavish civic centre (RM2.5 million was spent on this), which is open every day, except Friday and Sunday, from 9 am to noon and 2 to 4 pm. There is a relief map showing all the longhouses in the area, and a couple of cultural displays.

Places to Stay – Budget

It's worth checking at the *Methodist Guesthouse* to see if there are any vacancies. It is normally reserved for those on church business, but if it's not full they may let you stay. Most travellers head for the *Kapit Rejang Hotel* (☎ 084-796709), on Jalan Temenggong Jugah, which has good, cheap singles/doubles on the top floor for RM15/18 with fan and shared bathroom, or air-con rooms with bathroom for RM20/24 on the lower floors. The management here is helpful and welcomes travellers. If there's no other choice, the *Kapit Longhouse Hotel* (☎ 084-796415) has air-con rooms with bathroom for RM30.

Places to Stay – Mid-Range

Kapit has a glut of good mid-range hotels and some offer very good value. All have clean rooms with air-con, attached bathroom and TV.

Cheapest in this range, the *Dung Fang* (☎ 084-797779), Jalan Temenggong Jugah, has an unfortunate name (in case you were wondering, dung means 'east' in Chinese), but some bright rooms. Fan-cooled rooms cost RM30 and air-con rooms start at RM40. The *Hiap Chiong Hotel* (☎ 084-796314), 33 Jalan Temenggong Jugah, has clean, well appointed rooms for RM40/45. It looks comfortable and the management is friendly.

The *Ark Hill Hotel* (☎ 084-796168), 10 Jalan Penghulu Geridang, has airy, tiled rooms for RM45. The *Well Inn* (☎ 084-796009), 40 Jalan Court, costs RM45/50 for singles/doubles. These two are a few years older than most of the other hotels but both are good.

The *New Rejang Inn* (☎ 084-796600), 104 Jalan Teo Chow Beng, has comfortable singles/doubles with phone and fridge starting at RM45/50.

The pick of the bunch is the *Greenland Inn* (☎ 084-796388), where immaculate rooms start at RM65. If you want a bit of luxury at a bargain price, this is the place to find it.

Places to Stay – Top End

The *Hotel Meligai* (☎ 084-796611), Jalan Teo Chow Beng, has a grand entrance and uniformed staff, but it doesn't live up to its pretensions and the mid-range hotels offer better value. Uncarpeted air-con rooms are RM50; better singles/doubles on the upper floors start at RM70/80 and range up to RM180 for a suite.

Places to Eat

Food stalls set up in the evening at the night market along the riverbank at the western end of town. The *River View (Ming Hock) Restaurant* on the top floor of the market building on Jalan Teo Chow Beng is a good place to try. For Malay Muslim food including rotis, head for the *Malindo Cafe* near the Well Inn.

Kapit has a number of good Chinese *kedai kopi*, particularly around the square and along the riverfront. The *Hua Sin Cafe* on Jalan Teo Chow is reasonably priced, but also has more expensive seafood. The popular *Kah Ping Cafe* on the main town square has good pork dishes. Appropriately enough, the kedai kopi underneath the *Dung Fang* hotel also advertises a 'barkery'. The *Orchard Inn* is a more expensive, air-con Cantonese restaurant, although the food is very good.

There's an expensive, air-con restaurant/bar at the *Hotel Meligai* that does western breakfasts. And just because you're in the middle of Borneo doesn't mean you can't have a burger: there's a *SugarBun* under the Greenland Inn.

Getting There & Away

Air The Malaysia Airlines agent is Hua Chiong Co (☎ 084-796344), 6 Jalan Temenggong Koh, a block from the river.

When the river is really low you will not be able to get a launch or boat to Belaga, and the only way to get there is to fly. Malaysia Airlines flies Sibu-Kapit-Belaga and back on Sunday only; this flight is usually booked well ahead. The fare from Kapit is RM47 to Belaga and RM48 to Sibu.

Boat Boat services from Kapit include the following:

Sibu Ekspres launch departures to Sibu are from about 7.30 am until around 3 pm. Just go down to the jetty when you're ready and hop on. The Kapit to Sibu fare is RM15 and the journey takes from 2½ to three hours, depending on the number of stops made.

Belaga Ekspres launches leave for Belaga daily at 8 and 9 am; the trip takes up to six hours and costs RM25. The first ekspres from Sibu doesn't always reach Kapit in time to connect with the Belaga service. Rather than spend a whole day in Kapit, you'd be better off catching a later boat from Sibu and overnighting.

When the river is low, ekspres boats can't get past the Pelagus Rapids, about an hour upstream of Kapit. Small cargo boats do the run, but they are uncomfortable, take around eight hours and charge RM50. If you catch one of these boats, wear clothes that protect you from the sun, as there may be no shade.

If you don't want to pay RM50 to get to the Pelagus Resort, a boat leaves Kapit every day for various points upriver at 11.30 am for RM10. There are also boats heading up the Batang Balleh every day as far as Interwau – ask at the fuel barges in Kapit.

If you want to charter a longboat to take you upriver you're looking at around RM200 per day, excluding fuel – so the final charge for the trip will be around RM250. This includes the services of the operator and someone who keeps an eye out for obstructions when the river is low.

Getting Around

You can walk from one end of Kapit to the other in 10 minutes. The only local road transport is by taxi and there are very few of these, but then there's hardly anywhere to go by road. Share taxis meet the plane on Sunday for the 2km trip into town.

PELAGUS RESORT

Around 45 minutes upriver from Kapit is the *Pelagus Resort* (☎ 082-238033). For those with the money, Pelagus offers an opportunity to visit nearby Iban and other Orang Ulu longhouses, as well as the rainforest in a part of Sarawak that would otherwise be inaccessible. There is a 4km walking trail that follows the rapids for part of the way.

The resort was modelled on an Iban longhouse and rooms overlook the Pelagus Rapids; there's a restaurant and swimming pool, and tours can be organised to nearby longhouses. Standard singles/doubles with ceiling fan cost RM85/105; air-con rooms cost RM110/130 plus taxes. A longhouse tour costs RM100 per person.

You can arrange to be picked up from Kapit in the resort's launch for a whopping RM50 per person, or you can hop on one of the motorboats that head up the Batang Belaga every day at 8 and 9 am for RM10.

BELAGA

Belaga is just a small village and government administration centre on the upper reaches of the Rejang, where it divides into the Belaga and Balui rivers. It is a good base to explore the interior of Sarawak and there are many Kayan and Kenyah longhouses along the rivers. If you start talking to a friendly local on the boat you might be invited to stay at their longhouse. Don't forget to offer food, cigarettes or some small gift as a contribution towards your keep. Otherwise, the chances are you will find someone in Belaga (or they will find you) with suggestions of longhouses to visit, or offers to guide you. A few operators have jungle treks at reasonable rates, costing from about RM150 for three days/two nights; longer treks are available.

Travel beyond Belaga requires police and District Office clearance. It is usually not a problem to get a permit, though it may be restricted to travel as far as the Bakun Rapids, an hour upstream from Belaga on the Batang Rejang. This may well be because of the dangers of upriver travel during the dry season, or because the Penan people live beyond the Bakun Rapids. The reports are mixed: some travellers have been issued permits for unrestricted travel with no fuss at all, while others have simply gone ahead without permits. If you do this it might be an idea to let someone else know where you are heading, in case any problems arise. Permits are not required to use the logging road to Tubau.

Upriver from Belaga

The easiest way to head upriver is to take the ekspres boat that goes up the Batang Balui as far as Long Pangai, a Lahanan longhouse past the Sungai Linau.

The nearest longhouses to Belaga, such as Uma Aging and Uma Kahei, are mostly Kayan, but Uma Neh is a Kejaman longhouse and Long Semiang is a Lahanan longhouse within a 30 minute boat trip. The Kenyah also live along the Balui, such as at Uma Baudang before the Bakun Rapids, and much further up the river beyond Long Panai at Long Bulan, Long Jawi and Long Busang. Other peoples along the upper reaches of the Balui include the Punan at Long Belangan and the Ukit at Uma Ukit.

Do not turn up unannounced. Get an invitation to a longhouse from someone in town.

Places to Stay & Eat

Belaga's accommodation is cheap and quite good considering its isolation. The *Belaga Hotel* (☎ 084-461244) is good value and the

Spend a Memorable Night with the Orang Ulu

If you don't fancy the idea of having your face smeared with greasy soot and being dumped unceremoniously in the river, then perhaps you should steer well clear of the Kayan and Kenyah tribes. But if you do you'll miss out on one of the best travel experiences in Borneo.

The two tribes are numbered among the Orang Ulu (a general term, literally meaning 'upriver people', which covers a host of different inland tribes). The Kayan and Kenyah tribes are the people you're most likely to meet when travelling on the Upper Rejang or Upper Baram rivers.

Both are originally from Central Kalimantan, and have been moving downriver into Sarawak for centuries, fighting fierce territorial wars with the Iban that ended as recently as 1923. They have different languages but similar cultures, based on settled dry rice farming. Sarawak's most artistic peoples, the Kayan and Kenyah, build imposing longhouses, with exquisite woodcarvings and 'tree of life' paintings. And like all Sarawakians, they take hospitality very seriously.

If you visit a longhouse around Belaga or the Upper Baram, you won't find a boisterous Iban-style welcome, but appearances can be deceptive. The Kayan and Kenyah are more reserved and refined than the Iban, but if you spend a day or two with them they will start to let their hair down. At sunset, huge glasses of *borak* (sour, very potent rice wine) are handed out and downed to a chorus of '*duiiiii ...*', the local drinking song. Cigarettes made from fierce local tobacco are passed around. Sape players weave complex and haunting melodies on their mandolin-like instrument, and long-eared, tattooed ladies sing praise songs to the guests between chews of betel nut.

You may be treated to warrior dances from the men and fan dances from the young women, and even a display of traditional wrestling. And if you're lucky, the festivities will last to sun-up, when the soot-smearing and dunking take place. It's the traditional Orang Ulu sense-of-humour test, given only to true friends. After such a memorable night you probably need a bath anyway.

Mike Reed

most popular place with travellers. A double room with bathroom is RM18 with fan or RM25 to RM40 with air-con. Next door, the *Bee Lian Hotel* (☎ 084-461416) is a little newer but otherwise the same standard. Air-con rooms cost RM25. There's also the *Sing Soon Huat Lodging House* (☎ 084-461257), a basic hotel with cheap fan-cooled rooms for RM15, but the Belaga is preferable.

There's a good *kedai kopi* downstairs at the Belaga Hotel and others around the main street.

Getting There & Away

See the Kapit section for details of boats as far as Belaga. Going the other way, boats to Kapit leave at roughly 8 and 9 am; the fare is the same (RM25) but the trip downstream can sometimes be faster than six hours.

From Belaga, ekspres boats go upriver as far as Long Pangai.

In the dry season it's possible to travel overland between Belaga and Bintulu. The journey is neither easy nor cheap, and travellers are usually advised not to try it in case they get stranded – this is logging country and there are no facilities for visitors. It is possible to do the journey in one day, but allow two in case you get stuck along the way. Ask around at Belaga for advice on local conditions, but when logging camps are abandoned there may be no traffic on some of the backroads.

North-East Sarawak

BINTULU

Bintulu is a modern boom town at the mouth of the Batang Kemena. It is a dull commercial centre servicing offshore oil and gas installations and upriver logging; industrial estates virtually surround the town. Bintulu came under James Brooke's sway in 1861 and an ugly monument near the town centre commemorates Sarawak's first Council Negeri (National Council) in 1867. There's a colourful Chinese temple near the waterfront, but otherwise the town has no attractions.

Travellers heading north to Niah Caves and Miri, and south to Sibu, the Rejang and Kuching, may need to use Bintulu's bus station as a staging post. Unless you're going to the nearby Similajau National Park it's best to pass through as quickly as possible.

Similajau National Park, 20km north-east of Bintulu, is worth visiting. It has sandy beaches, walking trails and good wildlife; there is accommodation at the park and with any luck you won't have to stay in Bintulu itself. If you are self-catering at Niah Caves, Bintulu is a good place to stock up with provisions, although both Niah and Similajau have good, cheap cafeterias.

Orientation

Bintulu lies along the east bank of the Batang Kemena within walking distance of the mouth. The airport bisects the town (Bintulu's one claim to fame is that it's listed in the *Guinness Book of Records* as the town closest to an airport in the world) and marks the northern edge of the centre. Within a grid of shophouses a short walk from each other and the airport you'll find all the places to stay and eat, banks and other services. The waterfront has markets and the Li Hua shopping plaza. The long-distance bus station is 5km north of town at Medan Jaya, so take a local bus or taxi to get to the centre.

Information

There is no tourist information centre, though Similajau Adventure Tours (☎ 086-331552), in the lobby of the Plaza Hotel, can supply basic information about the town.

The Bintulu Welcome Centre (☎ 086-332277) is designed to welcome business opportunities rather than travellers and is inconveniently located at the BDA building, about 5km out of town.

Places to Stay – Budget

If you're unlucky enough to get stuck Bintulu has plenty of mid-range hotels but there are a couple of cheap options.

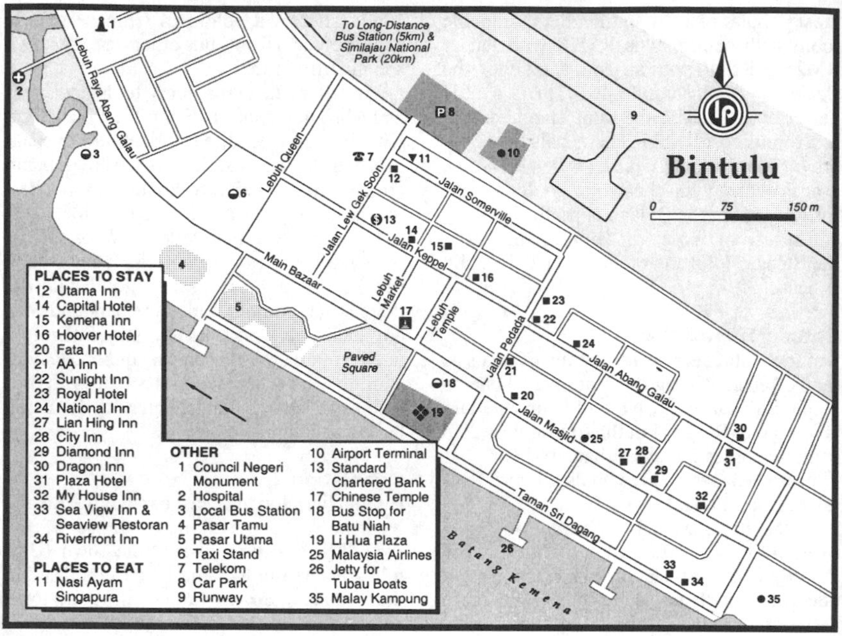

The *Capital Hotel* (☎ 086-331167) on Jalan Keppel has a few scruffy fan-cooled rooms with shared toilet and mandi for RM15, and air-con rooms with private toilet and mandi costing from RM30 to RM35. The *Dragon Inn* (☎ 086-315150), 1 New Commercial Centre, is opposite the Plaza Hotel. It's brighter and more pleasant than the Capital; basic fan rooms with shower/toilet cost RM20, and air-con rooms with bathroom and TV cost RM30. The *AA Inn* (☎ 086-335733), 107 Taman Sri Dagang, has air-con rooms for RM32.

Places to Stay – Mid-Range

Most of the hotels in Bintulu are fairly new, air-con, mid-range places whose rooms have TV, IDD phone and attached bathroom. They are all of a similar standard and there is little difference between them.

The *Sea View Inn* (☎ 086-339118), 254 Jalan Masjid, has the best location – on the waterfront – and is probably the most pleasant in this price range. Perfectly good rooms overlooking the river start at RM40 for a single, and doubles are RM45 to RM50. Ask for a river view.

The next best option is the *Lian Hing Inn* (☎ 086-316663), 143 Jalan Masjid, which has clean, tile-floor singles/doubles for RM50/55. Among the cluster of hotels at this end of Jalan Masjid there's the *City Inn* (☎ 086-337711), at No 149, where rooms are RM40. Going down a step, the *Diamond Inn* (☎ 086-338911), No 151, is OK for RM42/50 a single/double, but *My House Inn* (☎ 086-336399), at No 161, is better value for RM40/45.

The *National Inn* (☎ 086-337222), upstairs at 47 Jalan Abang Galau, has grotty air-con rooms with TV and bathroom for a ridiculous RM40. The *Utama Inn* (☎ 086-334539), 40 Jalan Somerville, is close to the airport and is reasonable value for RM43/47.

Fata Inn (☎ 086-332998), 113 Jalan Masjid, is no better though a little more expensive at RM42/48 for singles/doubles. The *Kemena Inn* (☎ 086-333378), at the back of 78 Jalan Keppel, is on a quiet street and has good refurbished rooms for RM55/58.

For slightly upmarket mid-range accommodation, the *Sunlight Inn* (☎ 086-332577), on the corner of Jalan Abang Galau and Jalan Pedada, is overpriced at RM50/55 a single/double plus service charge and tax. It's much the same as the *Royal Hotel* (☎ 086-332166) next door at 10 Jalan Pedada. The Royal charges RM69 a room, but it does provide a phone (next to the toilet). For this money you may as well spend a few more dollars and stay at the Riverfront Inn (see the next section).

Places to Stay – Top End

Bintulu has only three top-end hotels; all have restaurants and bars, spacious rooms with minibar and usually a view, but for the money they aren't really much better than the better mid-range accommodation. Add 10% service charge and 5% tax to these prices.

Head straight for the *Riverfront Inn* (☎ 086-333111), 256 Taman Sri Dagang. It's a pleasant, new hotel on the riverside where singles/doubles with a view start at RM75/85, and cheaper rooms without windows start at RM55.

The *Plaza Hotel* (☎ 086-335111), 116 Jalan Abang Galau, is the swankiest hotel in town, but it has all the charm of a suburban shopping mall. There's a rooftop swimming pool. Prices range from RM173/197 for a standard single/double, or RM220/245 for a deluxe. Discounts are usually available on weekends and during the low season.

The *Hoover Hotel* (☎ 086-337166), 92 Jalan Keppel, is a less desirable multistorey hotel. Stuffy singles/doubles with mosquitoes and vinyl curtains are way overpriced at RM125/145, though a substantial discount is often available.

Places to Eat

The top floor of the *pasar utama* (new market) is the place to go for hawker food. It has dozens of *food stalls*, and you can sit and look out over the river. The stalls at the *pasar tamu* (night market), near the local bus station, are good for take-away satay, grilled chicken and fish. By the waterfront, the *Seaview Restoran* is a kedai kopi with standard Chinese food that also does toasted sandwiches and coffee at breakfast. There are literally dozens of Chinese *kedai kopi* on Jalan Masjid, all offering very similar fare.

For western fast food there's a *SugarBun* in Li Hua Plaza and a *KFC* outlet near the council memorial. A good western breakfast can be had downstairs at the *Riverfront Inn*, where you can also try the Melanau speciality, umai (raw fish marinated and served with onions). The *Plaza Hotel* has expensive western food.

Near the airport, *Nasi Ayam Singapura* is a good, air-con stop for lunch, and a Chinese/Indian *kedai kopi* further down Jalan Somerville does good rotis and murtabaks. There are *kedai kopi* and other shops opposite the long-distance bus station that stay open well into the night.

Entertainment

There is no shortage of places to drink in Bintulu. However, with the exception of the bar in the *Plaza Hotel*, which has live bands on the weekend, entertainment is for the most part restricted to karaoke bars. The disco next door to the City Inn is popular, but will probably be empty before midnight. If you need a night on the town, save your energy for Miri or Kuching.

Getting There & Away

Air The Malaysia Airlines office (☎ 086-331554) is on Jalan Masjid and is open Monday to Friday from 8.30 am to 4.30 pm and Saturday from 8.30 am to 3.30 pm. Malaysia Airlines has regular flights to Sibu (four daily, RM64), Kuching (at least six daily, RM117), Miri (three daily, RM69) and Kota Kinabalu (two daily, RM127). A weekly Twin Otter service flies to Mukah (RM40).

The runway bisects the town and the terminal is about 100m from the main street.

Taxis meet the flights and a ride to any hotel shouldn't cost more than RM5.

Bus Bus services to Miri, Batu Niah, Sibu, Sarikei and Kuching and other destinations leave from Bintulu's long-distance bus station, about 5km from town at Medan Jaya. To get there from town take local bus No 29 (70 sen) from the local bus station or a taxi for RM8. Various bus companies occupy the ticket booths, and display departure times and fares in the window. Normally you can just buy a ticket and get on the next bus.

The main companies servicing Miri, Batu Niah, Sibu, Sarikei and Kuching are: Borneo Highway Express (☎ 086-339855), Freesia Express (☎ 086-314898), Lanang Express (☎ 086-338518), Syarikat Bas Suria (☎ 086-334914), Hornbill Bas Ekspres (for Batu Niah) and Biaramas (☎ 086-339821). Several other companies service small towns in the area. There is no bus service to Similajau National Park – see the Similajau Getting There & Away section.

Miri There are numerous departures between 6 am and 11.30 pm every day; bookings shouldn't be necessary. The trip to Miri takes about four hours and the fare is RM18. Express buses to Miri pass the turn-off to Batu Niah, but don't go there; late in the afternoon you may find it hard to get to the caves from the highway – see the Batu Niah section for more information.

Batu Niah (Niah Caves) Hornbill Bas Ekspres services the Bintulu-Batu Niah route. Catch buses at the long-distance terminal or outside the Li Hua Plaza on the Bintulu waterfront. Departures are at 6, 7, 9 and 10.30 am, and at noon, 1, 3 and 4.30 pm. The trip takes about two hours and the fare to Batu Niah is RM10.

Sibu, Sarikei & Kuching For Sibu there are dozens of departures every day between 6 am and 11.30 pm. All major companies ply this route although departures are more frequent in the morning. The trip costs RM16.50.

Rejang Transport (☎ 086-338518) has air-con buses to Kanowit, on the Batang Rejang upstream from Sibu, at 6, 8 and 10.30 am, and noon; the fare is RM22.30.

Many of the services to Sibu continue via Sarikei to Kuching. It's a long haul which can be speeded up by taking the bus to Sibu then the fast passenger ferry to Kuching (see the Sibu section for details). However, this will depend on what time you leave Bintulu – if you have to overnight in Sibu to catch a ferry the next day it will be cheaper to stay on the bus to Kuching. The fare to Sarikei is RM24 and to Kuching it's RM52.

Five Borneo Highway Express buses leave for Kuching between 6 am and 11.30 pm every day, stopping at Sibu and Sarikei. Freesia Express buses leave for Sarikei at 12.30 and 11.30 pm, the latter continuing to Kuching. The Lanang Express buses to Sarikei at 6, 7.30 and 10 am and 3 pm continue to Kuching; and PB Express has four services between 7 am and 11.30 pm through to Kuching. Biaramas has departures for Kuching at 6 and 10.30 am, and at 5 and 6.30 pm.

Boat If you're trying to get to Belaga there are ekspres launches that go up the Batang Kemena as far as Tubau. The journey takes about 3½ hours and costs RM18. Boats leave from the jetty approximately every hour between 9 am and noon.

Getting Around

Everything in the town centre is a short walk south of the airport terminal. Taxis meet all flights.

Local buses for the long-distance bus station leave from near the markets. Taxis congregate at the Chinese temple, the airport and at the big taxi stand near the markets. Most taxi fares around town are RM5; further afield to the long-distance bus station costs RM8 and to Similajau costs RM30. See the Similajau National Park section for details on getting there.

Super Nova Auto (☎ 086-336301) is a car rental firm with a desk in the lobby of the Plaza Hotel.

SIMILAJAU NATIONAL PARK

Similajau National Park is a beautiful spot 20km north-east of Bintulu whose deserted sandy beaches are among the best in Sarawak. Access is not easy, and you must pass through Bintulu to get there, but it is relatively untouristed and worth the effort.

Similajau occupies a narrow coastal strip 30km long but only a few kilometres wide. Green turtles sometimes come ashore to lay their eggs on the park's remoter beaches and because Similajau is flanked by logged forest it acts as a haven for wildlife: a recent survey recorded 230 bird species, making it one of the most diverse in Sarawak. The forest is also home to 24 species of mammals; there are a few shy macaques around the park HQ.

There are pavilions along the casuarina-lined beach as well as good accommodation, a cafeteria and an information centre at park HQ. It would be easy to spend a day or two walking in the coastal rainforest or lazing on the beach. In fact, it's a minor miracle that this beautiful spot hasn't been bulldozed to make way for a resort and golf course.

Permits to visit the park and bookings for accommodation are obtained from the National Parks office (☎ 085-331117) on the Bintulu-Sibu road, about 2km north of Bintulu town centre. It's inconvenient to get there; take local bus No 29 and ask to be dropped off at the National Parks office. During the week you could take pot luck and head straight out to Similajau – chances are it won't be full. There's an RM3 entrance fee and RM5 camera fee payable at the park gate.

Walking Trails

The park HQ occupies the south bank of the mouth of the Sungai Likau, but most of the park sits north of the river and to get to the walking trails it is necessary to take a boat. The boatman is generally around from 8 am until 5 pm, unless he goes fishing, in which case you'll have to get one of the park staff to row you across; the trip costs RM1 each way. To get back just ring the bell and wait at the landing stage. Whatever you do, don't swim – crocodiles occasionally hang around the river mouth.

Similajau's trail network is still being developed and will probably be more extensive by the time you read this. After crossing the river, head left off the plankwalk towards the headland. It's about half an hour's walk to a pavilion from where you can enjoy the view back along the coast towards Bintulu.

Further along the coast, the main trail leads to **Turtle Beach** (12km/2½ hours) and **Golden Beach** (three hours), two beautiful deserted spots where turtles come ashore to lay their eggs. Other trails forge into the low hills behind the coast to **Selunsur Rapid** (2½ hours) and **Kolam Sebubong**, which is reached only by boat then a 15 minute walk.

It's a long, hot walk to any of these sights – take lots of water. To get to Kolam Sebubong you'll have to organise a boat, which should cost about RM75; you could also be dropped off at the beaches and walk back. The boatman will also take you up the mangrove-lined Sungai Likau for RM50 per hour (an hour should be enough); if you go in the early morning you'll see a range of birds (including hornbills) and maybe mammals or even crocodiles.

Places to Stay & Eat

Accommodation at Similajau is good and comfortable. A bed in the four room, fan-cooled *hostel* costs RM10, including pillow and linen, and RM40 for the whole room. The air-con *chalets* have two rooms sleeping four people; a room costs RM60. A new dormitory-style *astana* was being built at the time of writing.

There's a *cafeteria* serving basic rice and noodle dishes, and drinks; a small range of dried and tinned foods is also available. The hostels are equipped with fridge and stove, but you'll have to ask at the park office for utensils.

Getting There & Away

For the moment access to Similajau is possible only by car or taxi from Bintulu, although it's close enough for a day trip. The restaurant (☎ 086-333019) at the park can organise a lift and charges RM7 per person each way from Bintulu. If you can't contact it a taxi will cost about RM30 each way – negotiate with the driver and arrange a time to be picked up. You may be able to talk a boat operator into taking you from Bintulu, but expect to pay hundreds of ringgit and this would only be economical for a group.

NIAH NATIONAL PARK

This small national park near the coast between Miri and Bintulu protects one of Sarawak's most famous attractions, the Niah Caves. A visit to the caves will probably be one of your most memorable experiences in East Malaysia, although at certain times of year smoke haze can severely reduce visibility around the park. We recommend that you get information from other travellers on the current situation. Niah is easier to get to than Mulu, but Mulu's caves are bigger, pristine and more interesting.

The Niah National Park is about 110km south of Miri and centres on the Great Cave, one of the largest in the world. The park is dominated by a 394m-high limestone massif, Gunung Subis, that's normally visible from far away, although when it's hazy you may not see it at all.

In 1958 archaeologists discovered evidence that humans have been living in and around the caves for some 40,000 years. Rock paintings were found in what became known as the Painted Cave and several small canoe-like coffins indicated that this site had been used as a burial ground. A reconstruction of the cave and some of the artefacts found here can be seen in the Sarawak Museum in Kuching. Unfortunately, the Painted Cave is no longer open to visitors.

Niah Caves are also home to vast numbers of bats, and an important nesting site for swiftlets that supply the vital ingredient for the famous bird's-nest soup. During the harvesting season collectors live in the caves. The tools of their trade can be seen inside: massive bamboo poles lashed together and wedged against the cave roof above.

Fees & Permits

A permit is needed to visit Niah Caves and can be issued at the National Parks office in Bintulu (☎ 085-331117) or the Visitors' Information Centre in Miri (☎ 085-434180). Accommodation at the park can also be booked at these offices. It's better to book

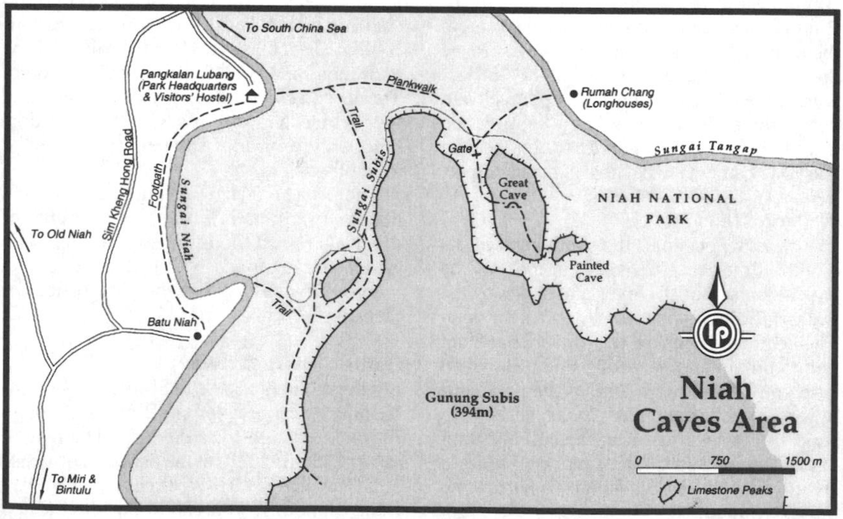

ahead, but a permit can be issued without fuss when you check in at the park HQ at Pangkalan Lubang. You could also book accommodation at the National Parks office in Kuching, but make sure you get a receipt because the information isn't necessarily passed on to the park office at Niah. Upon arrival you must register at the office and pay the RM3 park entrance fee and RM5 camera fee.

Bookings are advisable for accommodation at Pangkalan Lubang, particularly for the resthouses. If you're staying at the hostel it's usually not a problem to just turn up without a booking, especially during the week. If it's busy and there's no accommodation, the worst you'll have to do is head back 4km to Batu Niah, where there are three hotels.

The park visitors' centre has some interesting displays on the geology, archaeology and ecology of the caves.

The Caves

To get to the caves from park HQ you must first take a boat across the Sungai Niah; the jetty is down the path between the office building and the cafeteria. It's not very far to the opposite bank, but crocodiles are sometimes seen in the river so it's as well to fork out the 50 sen fee. Once across the river follow the 3km-long raised plankwalk to the caves – you can't get lost. The plankwalk can get very slippery when it's raining.

The plankwalk passes through primary rainforest, but most visitors are so intent on reaching the caves that they miss the wildlife along the way. Unfortunately, the boards are loose in places and make a lot of noise if you walk quickly. If you stop for a while along the way you'll hear lots of birds and may be lucky enough to see macaques. Other wildlife (apart from the hundreds of beautiful butterflies) includes squirrels and lizards such as flying lizards and a striking emerald green species that sometimes sits on the plankwalk.

As you approach the caves the trail skirts jagged limestone outcrops which appear like ancient ramparts festooned with giant vines and creepers. Shortly before the cave entrance the plankwalk forks; head right for the caves – the left fork goes to the village of Rumah Chang, where there are a couple of longhouses. Villagers usually sit at the junction selling cold beer and soft drinks. The trail goes under a massive overhang with stout stalactites, then rounds a corner to enter the vast **Great Cave**.

The sheer size of this cavern is awe inspiring – it measures 250m across at the mouth and 60m at its greatest height. According to the park information centre, 470,000 bats roost and four million swiftlets nest here, although these estimates were made more than 20 years ago and are well out of date. There are no current figures, but the walls of the caves are no longer thick with bats and the more valuable birds' nests have long been depleted. Between them these creatures deposited a tonne of guano on the cave floor every day; harvesting guano was once another important industry at Niah Caves.

Several species of swiftlets nest on the cave walls. The most common by far is the glossy swiftlet, whose nest contains vegetation and is not harvested. The edible species are far less abundant, for obvious reasons, and can only be seen at the remotest corners of the cavern. Several species of bats also roost in the cave, but they are not in dense colonies and must be picked out in the gloom among the birds' nests – take a powerful light. The best time to see the cave wildlife is at dusk, during the 'changeover', when the swiftlets all return to their nests for the night and the bats, sometimes in vast flocks, come hurtling out for the night's feeding.

Inside, the plankwalk continues down to the right but you'll need a torch (flashlight) to explore any distance. Steep stairs lead deep into the bowels of Gunung Subis and in the harvesting season you'll probably see nest collectors going about their business, although they tend to shun tourists. The stairs and handrails are usually covered with dirt or guano, and can get slippery in places. Allow a good hour to explore the Great Cave; the trail branches around a massive central pillar but both branches finish at the same point and it's impossible to get lost if you stick to the plankwalk. There's no need to hire a guide, although you can hire torches at the river crossing for RM5.

Outside the cave, trails through the jungle will take you to the summit of Gunung Subis if you feel like some more walking.

Places to Stay & Eat

Pangkalan Lubang The park accommodation is next to the Sungai Niah at Pangkalan Lubang, about 4km from Batu Niah.

The *hostel* has comfortable four-bed dorms with fan costing RM10 per bed, or RM40 for the room. Also available are four-bed rooms in *chalets* for RM60, and air-con two-bed *VIP chalets* at RM200. On checking in you are issued with a sheet and a blanket, and eating utensils are provided if you want to cook. You can also camp for RM4 per night and hire a fly for RM8.

The park has a *canteen* with quite a good range of noodle and rice meals, and you can buy a limited range of provisions here. In the dry season the rainwater tanks may run out, so the water is drawn from the river and must be boiled before drinking.

Batu Niah There are three hotels in Batu Niah if you arrive outside park office hours, or don't want to stay at the park.

The *Niah Caves Hotel* (☎ 085-737726), near the river, is the cheapest and a good option. Simple but clean air-con rooms with shared bathroom cost RM22/26 for a single/double. There's a *restaurant* downstairs and it's handy for the jetty if you want to take a boat down the river to the caves.

The *Park View Hotel* (☎ 085-737021), around the main square, is a jump up in price, but offers more salubrious air-con rooms with bathroom and TV for RM45. The unfortunately named *Niah Cave Inn* (☎ 085-737333) is the big hotel on the corner as you arrive in Batu Niah. It's the best hotel in town, with air-con, TV and fridge; rooms are advertised at RM80/100, plus tax, but a good discount should be readily available.

EAST MALAYSIA

Getting There & Away

Bus Access to Batu Niah – the town nearest the caves – is by road only. Batu Niah is 11km west of the Miri-Bintulu Highway; the turn-off is 102km south of Miri.

There are services to Batu Niah from both Bintulu and Miri, but check times at the park office or Visitors' Information Centre in Miri in case of changes. Express buses also pass the turn-off, but if you take one of these you'll have to make your own way to Batu Niah.

Bintulu There are seven direct Hornbill Bas Ekspres buses to Batu Niah every day from the long-distance terminal at Bintulu, although they also stop outside the Li Hua Plaza on the waterfront. Services leave at 6, 7, 9 and 10.30 am, and noon, 1, 3 and 4.30 pm; the fare is RM10 and the journey takes about two hours.

From Batu Niah to Bintulu, buses leave at 6, 7, 10 and 11 am, and noon, 1.30 and 3 pm. Buses leave from the bus stand in the centre of town, and there is no ticket agency – pay as you board.

Miri There are 10 buses every day from Miri to Batu Niah. Departures are at 6.45, 7.30, 8.30, 9.30 and 10.30 am, then hourly from noon to 4 pm. The fare is RM8.50 and the trip takes about two hours. The bus can be caught at the stop opposite the local bus station in Miri.

From Batu Niah to Miri there are departures at 6.45, 7.10, 8, 9 and 10.30 am, then hourly from 11 am to 3.30 pm. Catch these same buses for Lambir Hills National Park, 32km from Miri (RM2).

Getting Around

Transport to the park HQ from Batu Niah is by taxi or boat. The boat trip costs RM2 per person for five or more people, or RM10 per boat. Taxis also cost RM10. Boats do most of their business in the morning; after noon it is usually less time consuming to get a taxi, a few of which are always waiting next to the bus stand. The boat trip takes an exhilarating few minutes past jungle-clad limestone cliffs.

Lastly, you can walk along the track by the river, but this takes about an hour. Whichever way you do it, check in at the park office on arrival.

LAMBIR HILLS NATIONAL PARK

Although mainly a regional attraction and a popular weekend retreat for Miri residents, Lambir Hills has pleasant rainforest walking trails and a picturesque natural swimming pool. At its closest point the park is only 20km from Miri, and city residents come by the carload to take the 15 minute walk to the pretty waterfalls near park HQ. The waterfall cascades into a good swimming hole and there are picnic shelters along the river.

The national park covers 6952 hectares and protects a range of low sandstone hills which reach a height of 465m at Bukit Lambir. Much of the forest was logged before the park was declared, but the secondary forest is beautiful in its own right and Lambir Hills boasts a good range of wildlife.

The trails are officially open from 8 am to 4 pm Monday to Friday, and 8 am to 5 pm on weekends and public holidays, but if you are seriously interested in wildlife watching you would have to get an earlier start. Wildlife which has been recorded here includes gibbons, tarsiers, pangolins and barking deer, though you are unlikely to see any close to park HQ. Lambir Hills is also home to many species of birds.

Lambir Hills makes an easy day trip from Miri, and since accommodation has been built, visitors can now spend a few days enjoying the forest and exploring some of the longer walks without having to hurry. While it doesn't have the spectacular scenery of Niah and Mulu, or the diversity of Bako, Lambir Hills is an excellent park for short jungle walks.

The park HQ is 32km from Miri next to the highway. Here you'll find the park office and information centre, a canteen and accommodation. Permits and accommodation bookings can be arranged at the Visitors' Information Centre Miri (☎ 085-434181). The RM3 park entrance fee and RM5 camera fee are payable at the park office.

Walks

Walking times given here are as posted at park HQ; you could halve them if you are fit and in a hurry. The most popular walk is to **Latak Waterfall** – it is an easy 15 minute stroll from the park HQ. The trail passes two insignificant falls before reaching the main waterfall, where there are picnic shelters, a changing shed and a large clear pool, ideal for swimming. This walk is much quieter on weekdays.

From Latak Falls the main trail heads off to **Bukit Pantu** (one hour 35 minutes) and Bukit Lambir. Just above the falls at the start of the trail is a 40m tree tower. If you have a head for heights the view of the forest canopy from the top is magnificent, although the tower sways a bit in the breeze.

The main trail goes all the way to **Bukit Lambir** (3½ hours), from where there are fine views. Off the main trail there are many worthwhile diversions. Nibong (about two hours), Pantu (70 minutes), Pancur (2½ hours), Dinding (about 2½ hours) and Tengkorong (two hours) waterfalls can be visited, and Bukit Pantu is the nearest peak to the park HQ. The trail is steep and slippery in places, but the walks are not overly strenuous. Bukit Pantu is a straightforward climb, though the stretch to Bukit Lambir can be tiring.

It is possible to arrive at the park in the morning, walk to Bukit Lambir and back, then be on your way to Miri or Niah National Park, but this doesn't leave much time to appreciate the forest or look for wildlife. Register your name at the booth at the start of the trail before you head off.

Places to Stay & Eat

The accommodation at the park is comfortable, but it's only a few hundred metres from the main highway and you won't feel like you're in the middle of the jungle. You should book in advance, particularly on weekends, though you are unlikely to be turned away if you don't have a reservation. Bookings can be made at the Visitors' Information Centre in Miri, or at the office at Niah National Park.

Accommodation at the park is limited. Rooms in a *lodge* sleeping either two or three people cost RM40, although if they're not full you could probably talk them into letting you have a bed for less.

The park has a *canteen* which sells rice and noodle dishes, drinks and basic provisions if you intend to cook. Opening hours depend on demand, but are generally from 8 am to about 7 pm. The hostel and resthouses have their own cooking facilities.

Getting There & Away

Lambir Hills is on the main highway and easily reached by bus from Miri. Take any Batu Niah bus for RM2.40 (see the Batu Niah section for times), or any non-express bus going to Bintulu. The fare to Bintulu is RM16.50. Going the other way, buses from Batu Niah to Miri pass Lambir Hills and cost RM6.

From the park you must stand out the front to hail the buses. The national park staff can tell you when they pass. Heading south, the last buses to Batu Niah and Bintulu pass at around 3.15 pm. Heading north to Miri, the last buses leave at around 4.30 pm. The express buses might stop for you, but don't count on it.

MIRI

Miri is Sarawak's most northerly city, a major commercial centre and an R&R retreat for expat oil workers. It is a pleasant enough place, but there are no sights nearby and there is little to hold the average traveller. Most just overnight in Miri en route to Brunei, Niah Caves, Gunung Mulu or Bario. But if you are yearning for the bright lights, Miri has plenty of good restaurants and probably the most lively nightlife in Borneo.

Miri is changing fast: big, shiny new shopping plazas outshine those that were new just a few years ago, and the town has grand plans for even more shopping plazas, resorts and a marina.

Orientation & Information

Miri lies on a narrow plain between the east bank of the Sungai Miri and low, scrubby hills that were once covered in oil wells and the source of the city's wealth. All places to stay and eat are within walking distance of everywhere else, but you'll need a bus or taxi to get to the long-distance bus station or airport. A few blocks north of the town centre there are a few modern shopping malls with fast food outlets.

The Visitors' Information Centre (☎ 085-434181) is on Jalan Melayu near the local bus station, at the southern end of the town centre. This is where you organise permits and accommodation for Gunung Mulu, Niah Caves and Lambir Hills national parks. The helpful staff can also provide bus times, and information on places to stay and tours. The local bus station and stop for Lambir Hills and Niah Caves is next door. The centre is open Monday to Thursday from 8 am to 4.15 pm, Friday from 8 am to 4.45 pm, and Saturday from 8 am to 12.45 pm.

The post office is about 10 minutes walk north of the centre along Jalan Sylvia.

National Parks Office There is a National Parks office (☎ 085-436637) in the government office complex opposite Wisma Pelita Tunku, but they'll probably just refer you to the Visitors' Information Centre over the road. Opening hours are Monday to Friday from 8 am to 12.45 pm and 2 to 4.15 pm, and Saturday from 8 am to 12.45 pm.

Permits The only travel permits you'll need are to get to Bario for trekking in the Kelabit Highlands, and for visiting longhouses upriver on the Baram and its tributaries (see the Marudi section for details).

For Bario, just front up with your passport at the Resident's Office on Jalan Kingsway. You'll have to fill in a form with details of your intended visit; they'll photocopy your passport then the Resident will sign the permit. It appears to be a formality, but when you fill in the form keep the details simple – you're a tourist, right? There's no charge and stays of up to 10 days are usually permitted.

It's probably OK just to head off into the blue without a permit, but it's painless

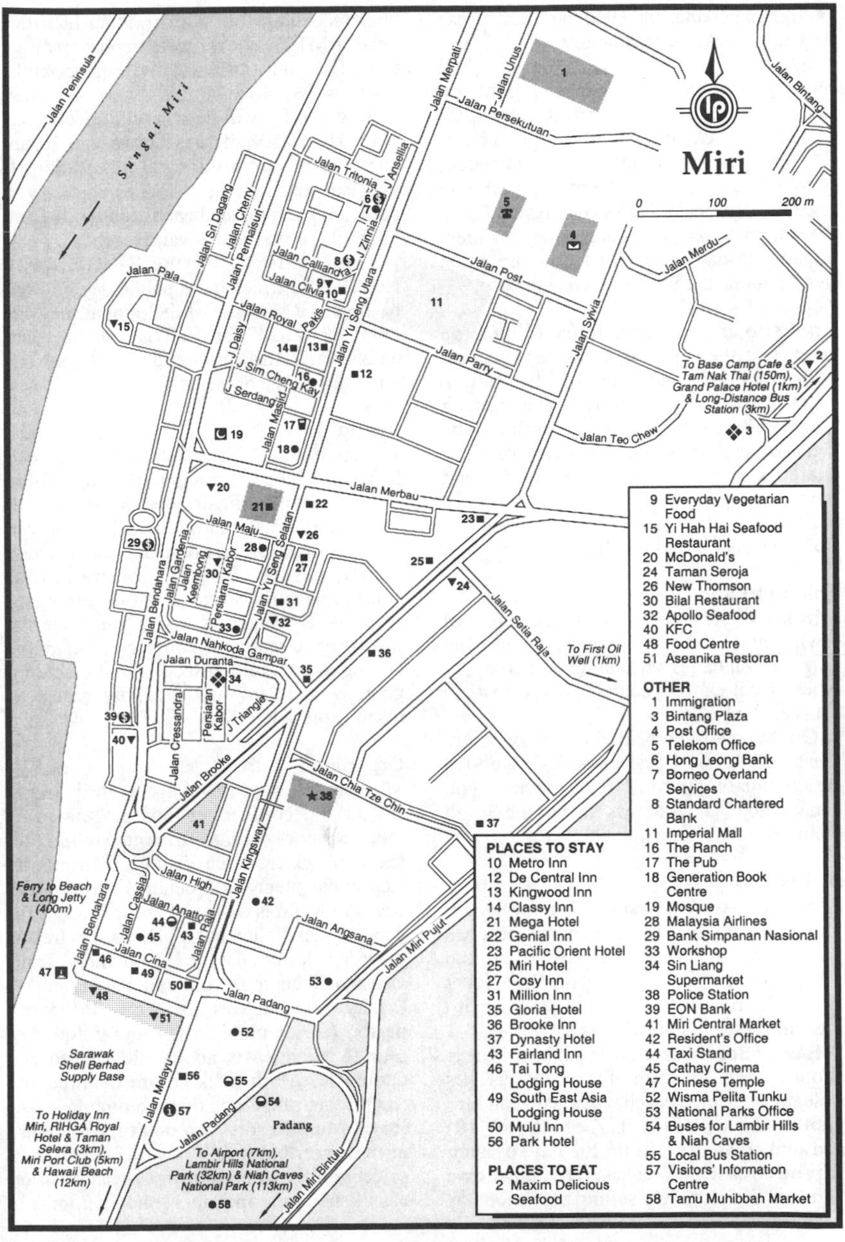
Miri
0
100
200 m
Jalan Peninsula
Sungai Miri
Jalan Merpati
Jalan Unus
Jalan Persekutuan
Jalan Bintang
Jalan Tritonia
J Ansellia
J Zinnia
Jalan Sri Dagang
Jalan Cherry
Jalan Permaisuri
Jalan Calliandra
Jalan Clivia
Jalan Pala
Jalan Royal
Pakis
Jalan Yu Seng Ultara
J Daisy
J Sim Cheng Kay
J Serdang
Jalan Masjid
Jalan Post
Jalan Merdu
Jalan Sylvia
Jalan Parry
Jalan Teo Chew
To Base Camp Cafe & Tam Nak Thai (150m), Grand Palace Hotel (1km) & Long-Distance Bus Station (3km)
Jalan Merbau
Jalan Maju
Jalan Bendahara
Jalan Gardenia
Jalan Keembong
Persiaran Kabor
Jalan Yu Seng Selatan
Jalan Setia Raja
To First Oil Well (1km)
Jalan Nahkoda Gampar
Jalan Duranta
Jalan Cressandra
Persiaran Kabor
J Triangle
Jalan Brooke
Jalan Chia Tze Chin
Jalan Kingsway
Jalan High
Jalan Cassia
Jalan Anatto
Jalan Raja
Jalan Angsana
Jalan Miri Pujut
Jalan Cina
Jalan Padang
Ferry to Beach & Long Jetty (400m)
Sarawak Shell Berhad Supply Base
Jalan Melayu
Padang
To Holiday Inn Miri, RIHGA Royal Hotel & Taman Selera (3km), Miri Port Club (5km) & Hawaii Beach (12km)
To Airport (7km), Lambir Hills National Park (32km) & Niah Caves National Park (113km)
Jalan Miri Bintulu
PLACES TO STAY
10 Metro Inn
12 De Central Inn
13 Kingwood Inn
14 Classy Inn
21 Mega Hotel
22 Genial Inn
23 Pacific Orient Hotel
25 Miri Hotel
27 Cosy Inn
31 Million Inn
35 Gloria Hotel
36 Brooke Inn
37 Dynasty Hotel
43 Fairland Inn
46 Tai Tong Lodging House
49 South East Asia Lodging House
50 Mulu Inn
56 Park Hotel
PLACES TO EAT
2 Maxim Delicious Seafood
9 Everyday Vegetarian Food
15 Yi Hah Hai Seafood Restaurant
20 McDonald's
24 Taman Seroja
26 New Thomson
30 Bilal Restaurant
32 Apollo Seafood
40 KFC
48 Food Centre
51 Aseanika Restoran
OTHER
1 Immigration
3 Bintang Plaza
4 Post Office
5 Telekom Office
6 Hong Leong Bank
7 Borneo Overland Services
8 Standard Chartered Bank
11 Imperial Mall
16 The Ranch
17 The Pub
18 Generation Book Centre
19 Mosque
28 Malaysia Airlines
29 Bank Simpanan Nasional
33 Workshop
34 Sin Liang Supermarket
38 Police Station
39 EON Bank
41 Miri Central Market
42 Resident's Office
44 Taxi Stand
45 Cathay Cinema
47 Chinese Temple
52 Wisma Pelita Tunku
53 National Parks Office
54 Buses for Lambir Hills & Niah Caves
55 Local Bus Station
57 Visitors' Information Centre
58 Tamu Muhibbah Market

enough to get one, and even in remote areas they are checked occasionally.

Money The Standard Chartered Bank on Jalan Calliandra is best equipped for changing travellers cheques, but it charges a hefty RM20 per transaction and 15 sen per cheque, so you'd best change as much as possible in one go. Other major banks are clustered near the Imperial Mall. There are moneychangers on and around Jalan Cina that are open longer hours, but they only change cash.

Bookshops The Pelita Book Centre, on level 3 of the Imperial Mall, has the best range of books and maps on the region. Popular is a huge bookstore in the Bintang Plaza with a more general selection. The Generation Book Centre on Jalan Yu Seng Utara has a good range of paperbacks, and the bookshop in the RIHGA Royal Hotel, on the beach south of Miri, has glossy books on Borneo's people and wildlife.

Things to See

Miri's **markets** are lively and the old part of town is home to various market blocks. The Tamu Muhibbah is a newer market complex where local Dayaks come down to Miri to sell vegetables.

On the low ridge behind the town centre there's Malaysia's first **oil well**, a wooden structure dating from 1910, from where you can get good views across Miri to the South China Sea.

Swimming

Miri has a passable **beach** at Taman Selera, 3km south of town. There are closer beaches on the spit next to the long jetty, where the oil-rig boats pull in – take the free ferry across the river – but they are strewn with logs and rusting industrial debris.

Hawaii Beach, the best beach near Miri is about 15 minutes south of town by bus. It's a clean palm-lined beach where you can hire picnic tables (RM10), barbecues (RM10) and umbrellas (RM10) for the day; a patch of sand costs RM3. You can rent bungalows here and there's a shop selling provisions. A chalet sleeping four with cooking facilities costs RM150; the proprietor can arrange fresh fish and lobsters daily. For bookings phone ☎ 085-482346.

To get to Hawaii Beach, take Bakam bus No 5 (RM1.50); it runs between 6.30 am and 6.30 pm from the local bus station. If you can get hold of a 4WD vehicle, you could drive along the beach at low tide from Miri all the way to Hawaii Beach.

You could also try the RIHGA Royal Hotel's pool which has a public day on Sunday, entry RM2. Use of the pool at the Miri Port Club is RM7 for a full day, but beers are a reasonable RM6; to get there take a No 7 bus from the local bus station

Diving

The coast off Miri is about the only place in Sarawak where it's possible to dive. Within a short boat trip of Miri there's a number of shoals and reefs, and one wreck. However, the seas west of Sarawak are shallow and muddy, and the diving is nowhere near as good as Sabah's. Scuba Sarawak can organise trips, equipment and training – see the following Organised Tours entry and the Diving & Snorkelling section in the Terengganu chapter for advice about safe and responsible diving.

Organised Tours

Miri has plenty of travel agents for booking flights and confirming tickets. Numerous tour operators organise trips to Mulu, Niah and other places – the Visitors' Information Centre has plenty of brochures. Visiting the caves in Mulu is easy and cheaper as an independent traveller, but if you want to trek to the Pinnacles or take the Headhunters' Trail, you should compare tour company prices.

City tours of Miri are about RM85 per person (a ridiculous price) and a full day tour to Niah costs about RM180. Prices quoted for Mulu trekking are hundreds of ringgit, but often include accommodation at Royal Mulu Resort; you don't have to stay at the resort but you'll have to negotiate a price with the tour company. A list of some established tour operators follows.

Borneo Adventure
(☎ 085-414935) Pacific Orient Hotel, 49 Jalan Brooke. A long-established and reliable operator; also has a desk in the lobby of the Royal Mulu Resort.

Borneo Jungle Safari
(☎ 085-436566) Level 3, 2 Jalan Brooke

Borneo Overland Services
(☎ 085-430255) 1st floor, 1089 Jalan Merpati

Scuba Sarawak
(☎ 085-421121) Ground floor, RIHGA Royal Hotel. Dive trips to sites near Miri and in Sabah, including Sipadan, Labuan Wrecks and Layang Layang.

Transworld Travel Services
(☎ 085-422277) 2nd floor, Wisma Pelita Tunku. City tours, as well as further afield.

Tropical Adventure Tours
(☎ 085-419337) Ground floor, Mega Hotel. One of the largest agencies, with an interesting range of tours, including professionally run Mulu trekking; also has an office at Mulu park HQ.

Places to Stay – Budget

Miri has little in the way of budget accommodation. The cheaper places to stay are all near the markets at the south end of town. They are handy if you are heading on to Niah Caves the next day, but most are noisy and seedy. If you can afford one, the mid-range hotels offer much better value for money.

The cheapest option is the dorm in the Chinese *Tai Tong Lodging House* (☎ 085-411072), at 26 Jalan Cina, although there's little privacy and no security. Dorm beds in the lobby cost RM9 (there's no extra charge for the bedside spittoons), although it's noisy and smoky. Other basic but clean singles/doubles go for RM28/32 with fan and shared bathroom, or RM45 for a double with bathroom and air-con. The walls are thin and the dorm is not secure – this place is probably not suitable for solo female travellers.

Slightly better, but dilapidated, choices include the *Mulu Inn* on Jalan Melayu, where fan-cooled rooms with shared bathroom are RM25 and air-con rooms with bathroom cost RM37/42; and the *South East Asia Lodging House* (☎ 085-415488), on the square behind the Cathay Cinema, where all rooms have a shared bathroom, and cost RM28 with fan or RM40 with air-con.

The *Fairland Inn* (☎ 085-413898), on the same square, is quieter than the preceding and probably the best choice. Small, clean singles/doubles with windows, air-con, bathroom and TV cost RM35.

Places to Stay – Mid-Range

There are lots of places to choose from in this category, and some are very good value. All have attached bathrooms, air-con and carpet, and most provide a TV and IDD phone. Many offer discounts on their published rates; discounted rates are listed here. In dry spells the cheaper hotels can sometimes run out of water – check before booking in.

The best value is offered by the *Brooke Inn* (☎ 085-412881), 14 Jalan Brooke. Simple but clean air-con rooms with bathroom, TV and in-house video cost RM40/ 45/50 a single/double/triple.

Across Jalan Brooke, the *Miri Hotel* (☎ 085-421212), at No 47, has clean, spacious rooms starting at RM55/67 for a single/double. For the extra ringgit this hotel is very good value and includes cable TV. The *Pacific Orient Hotel* (☎ 085-413333), next door at 49 Jalan Brooke, is a step up in price at RM73/77 a single/double, though the rooms are no better.

There's a cluster of mid-range hotels near the Imperial Mall at the top end of town. The *Classy Inn* (☎ 085-425793), down a pedestrian mall off Jalan Yu Seng Utara, is good value for RM50/60 a single/double. The *Kingwood Inn* (☎ 085-415888), 826 Jalan Yu Seng Utara, is quiet, and singles/doubles with fridge go for RM75/80. The *Metro Inn* (☎ 085-411663), Jalan Merpati, has bright, airy rooms starting at RM55/58.

Across Jalan Yu Seng Utara, *De Central Inn* (☎ 085-424168) is starting to look a bit tatty, but it is popular with expat oil workers and rooms start at RM50/60. Avoid the rooms next to the lively bar/coffee shop at the back.

There's not much difference between three mid-range places further down Jalan Yu Seng Selatan. All have smallish singles/doubles, but are well positioned. Rooms at the *Cosy Inn* (☎ 085-415522) cost RM50/55;

the *Genial Inn* (☎ 085-410966), 381 Jalan Yu Seng Selatan, is cheaper and OK value for RM40/46; and the *Million Inn* (☎ 085-415077), 6 Jalan Yu Seng Selatan, has poky rooms optimistically priced at RM63/68. All these choices are central, but there are plenty of others nearby.

Places to Stay – Top End

Big, modern hotels with all mod cons get thrown up with incredible speed in Miri, and by the time you read this there may be even more to choose from. What this means is that there's a glut at the top end and even the best will probably offer a 'promotional price' as a matter of course. Remember to add the 10% service charge and 5% tax to all prices.

Miri's best – and priciest – hotel is the *RIHGA Royal* (☎ 085-413877), on the beach about 4km south of the town centre. There's a beautiful swimming pool, gym, business centre, restaurants and coffee shops. Singles/doubles range from RM235/265 to RM360/390, although discounts of up to 40% may be available.

Next to the RIHGA, the *Holiday Inn Miri* (☎ 085-418888) looks decidedly tired, but has an international-standard fitness centre and a Jacuzzi with swim-up bar. Rates start at RM300, or RM320 with a sea view. The Holiday Inn has a free shuttle service into town.

Back in town, the newest and pinkest of the posh establishments is the four star *Grand Palace Hotel* (☎ 085-428888) at Km 2 Jalan Miri-Pujut. Singles/doubles range from RM170/190 to RM220/240; suites are also available. There's no pool and the views leave something to be desired.

Two faded top-end hotels that were probably once the flower of Miri may now offer big discounts, though the mid-range places are almost as good for a few dollars less. At 27 Jalan Brooke there's the *Gloria Hotel* (☎ 085-416699), which has windowless economy rooms for RM96/111, and better rooms for RM107 to RM130. The *Park Hotel* (☎ 085-414555) is on Jalan Melayu, near the Visitors' Information Centre, but its top-end pretensions are laughable unless you're a fan of 60s vinyl furniture. Published rates start at RM120/135, but big discounts are usually available and can push an ordinary room as low as RM58. The *Kingwood Inn* (☎ 085-415888), 579 Jalan Yu Seng Utara, is a smaller place where rooms start at RM120.

The *Mega Hotel* (☎ 085-432432) dominates the Miri skyline and is right in the centre of town. Rates for standard rooms start at RM240/280 and suites are RM460 to RM3000. The once-grand *Dynasty Hotel* (☎ 085-421111), Jalan Miri Pujut, sits next to the abandoned Oil Town shopping mall and will probably offer a good discount if you ask. Standard singles/doubles cost from RM190/210 and deluxe rooms are RM230/250.

Places to Eat

There are plenty of good places to eat in Miri, especially in the blocks between Jalan Brooke and the waterfront, and something to suit every budget.

Cheap choices include a small *food centre* near the Chinese temple, where you'll find the usual Malay and Chinese hawker stalls. There's also a small fruit and vegetable market. Inside this market, the *Aseanika Restoran* does excellent rotis and also serves Indonesian food. The *Tamu Muhibbah* has food stalls open during the day.

The *Taman Selera* food centre has the best outdoor setting – on the beach, 3km south of town. It cranks up in the evening and is popular with locals. On Jalan Brooke, the *Taman Seroja* is another pleasant open-air food stall centre, although it's on a noisy street corner. Here you can try good satays and more expensive seafood.

Bilal Restaurant is one of the better Indian restaurants you'll find in Sarawak and is very good value. It is on Jalan Persiaran Kabor, a pedestrian mall, and in the evenings tables are set up on the pavement. The curries, tandoori dishes and excellent rotis can all be recommended. There's a good Chinese *kedai kopi* downstairs at the Miri Hotel.

On Jalan Yu Seng Selatan there are quite a few more upmarket and fast food places. One of the best restaurants in Miri is the open-air *Apollo Seafood*, which serves superb Chinese food, steamboat and of course seafood. Prices are reasonable, but it can get packed with locals and expats. Another good seafood place on this street is *Sin Mui Pin*, near the Cosy Inn; it's a big coffee shop that serves delicious fish grilled in banana leaves. A few doors away is the *New Thomson*, a good place for greasy steaks, grills and fish and chips at moderate prices.

Western breakfasts can be enjoyed from 6 till 10 am at the *Chatterbox Coffee House*, on the ground floor of the Mega Hotel. There's a good buffet for RM18, and the à la carte choice includes delicious blueberry pancakes for RM6. The *Base Camp Cafe* near the Bintang Plaza has cheaper western breakfasts, plus steaks and the usual noodles and rice, at very reasonable prices.

The best seafood in Miri is probably at *Maxim Delicious Seafood*, on Jalan Miri-Pujut, 100m north of Bintang Plaza, though it's not cheap. Fresh fish in a banana leaf is one of the specialities. *Tam Nak Thai* is an excellent – though pricey – Thai restaurant nearby. More good seafood can be enjoyed at *Yi Hah Hai Seafood Restaurant*, near the river in the north of the centre. *Everyday Vegetarian Food* on Jalan Calliandra caters to vegetarian tastes.

The big shopping plazas, such as the Bintang or Imperial, are fast-food paradise, with branches of *Pizza Hut*, *KFC* and *Sugar-Bun*. These chains are well represented around town, and there's a *McDonald's* in the plaza next to the Mega Hotel.

Entertainment

Miri's large expat population and its proximity to deadly dull Brunei has endowed it with the liveliest nightlife scene in Sarawak. There are pubs with bands and clubs packed with people even in the middle of the week, but things don't get going until around 11 pm. There are no cover charges and, like elsewhere in Sabah and Sarawak, beers usually cost around RM9.

A good place to start the evening is *The Pub*, on Jalan Yu Seng Utara, which is just a friendly watering hole until 11.30 pm, when the deejay turns up. Near Bintang Plaza, *Chaplin's* has an English soccer theme; *Benny's*, nearby, is a cocktail lounge where you can relax to golden oldies like Echo & The Bunnymen.

The *Ranch* has live music from around 10.30 pm. It gets packed by about 1 am some nights and features Filipino cover bands. *Clippers* is an English-style pub out at the Holiday Inn where techno music is played; it attracts many Miri locals on the weekends. *Rigs*, next door at the RIHGA Royal, is also a trendy spot, but drinks are very expensive. Also at the RIHGA, *Flags Bar* has a happy hour between 5 and 9 pm, when drinks are two for the price of one. Both are inconveniently located. Back in town, *Workshop* is a lively club and popular with transvestites. There are lots more.

Shopping

Miri has a few arts and crafts stores, but the range is pretty junky and nowhere near as good as in Kuching. The Imperial and Bintang shopping plazas have the best selection of handicraft shops. Longhouse Handicraft Centre is on the 3rd floor of the Imperial Plaza and Kong Hong Enterprise is on the 3rd floor of the Bintang Plaza; Kong Hong also has a small branch at the Wisma Pelita Tunku shopping centre.

The new shopping malls have a wide range of stores selling every imaginable type of consumer goods. There's a branch of the Japanese Ngiuku chain in the Bintang Plaza.

Getting There & Away

Air The Malaysia Airlines office (☎ 085-411444) opposite the Mega Hotel, is on Jalan Yu Seng Selatan. It is open Monday to Friday from 8.30 am to 4.30 pm, and Saturday from 8.30 am to 4 pm. Malaysia Airlines has Twin Otter services to Bario (daily, RM70), Labuan (twice daily, RM57), Lawas (four daily, RM59), Limbang (seven daily, RM45), Long Lellang (twice weekly, RM66), Long Seridan (weekly, RM57), Marudi (three daily, RM29) and Gunung Mulu National Park (three daily, RM69).

Bigger aircraft fly to Bintulu (four daily, RM69), Kota Kinabalu (six daily, RM104), Kuching (at least seven daily, RM164) and Sibu (eight daily, RM112).

Bus The long-distance bus station is about 4km north of town along Jalan Miri Pujut, although local buses also go to Lambir Hills and Niah Caves national parks. Major companies operating from Miri include Biaramas Express (☎ 085-434319), Borneo Express Bus (☎ 085-430420), Borneo Highway Express (☎ 085-434053), Sarawak Transport Co (☎ 085-432272), Suria Express (☎ 085-430416) and Syarikat Bas Suria (☎ 085-434317).

For buses to Kuala Baram and the crossing to Brunei go to the local bus station at the southern end of the town centre.

Bintulu, Batu Niah & Lambir Hills There are express bus services daily to Bintulu roughly every hour between 6 am and 8.30 pm; the trip takes about 4½ hours and the fare is RM16.80 or RM18 (air-con).

Syarikat Bas Suria has buses from Miri direct to Batu Niah, departing at 6.40, 7.30, 8.30, 9.30 and 10.30 am, and at noon, 1, 2, 2.15, 3 and 4 pm. The trip costs RM9 and takes about two hours. Buses to Batu Niah and Lambir Hills can be caught from the bus stop over the road from the Visitors' Information Centre.

All buses to Batu Niah and Bintulu pass Lambir Hills National Park on the highway; the fare to park HQ is RM2.40.

Sibu The trip to Sibu takes about eight hours and costs RM34 (air-con). Companies making the daily run include Suria Express, which does the trip at 7 and 9 am, and at 1 and 5.30 pm; and Lanang Express, which runs buses at 6.30, 8.30 and 11.30 am.

Brunei To get to Brunei take a bus over the border to Kuala Belait, then another bus to Seria, then another bus to Bandar Seri Begawan, Brunei's capital.

The Miri Belait Transport Company (☎ 085-419129) plies this route and has its office at the local bus station. Five services daily run to Kuala Belait, at 7, 9 and 10.30 am, and at 1 and 3.30 pm (2½ hours, RM12.50). It's worth avoiding this trip on Sunday, when hordes of expats and Bruneians return to their peaceful homes after living it up at the pleasure domes of Miri.

A river crossing is made at Kuala Baram, where vehicles often have to queue before reaching the ferry – most passengers get out and wait by the edge of the river. You can leave your bags on the bus.

The Malaysian immigration checkpoint is just across the river and after clearing it you reboard the same bus for the two minute ride to the Brunei immigration checkpoint. Here you must take all your belongings when you go through passport control and customs.

Once through customs you board a Brunei bus, which takes you to the Sungai Belait for another ferry crossing. The queues here are often horrendous – and can last for hours – but the bus driver and passengers leave the bus on one side, cross on the ferry (free), then board another bus on the other side. Your ticket from Miri takes you all the way to Kuala Belait.

At Kuala Belait you are dropped at the bus station, from where you can take another bus to Seria. Start early to avoid having to spend the night in Kuala Belait because all accommodation is expensive here.

If you need to change money there's a branch of the Hongkong Bank opposite the bus station in Kuala Belait. You can also change ringgit into Brunei dollars (and vice versa) with the ferry hands on the ferry across the Sungai Belait. It's a good idea to know the exchange rates if you do this.

From Seria, you must take another bus to Bandar Seri Begawan. See the Seria section in the Brunei chapter for details.

Marudi Miri Belait Transport Company has buses to Kuala Baram every half-hour or so between 6 and 11 am, then roughly every hour until 9 pm (45 minutes, RM2.50). From Kuala Baram, express boats to Marudi cost RM18 and leave at 7.15, 7.40, 8.15, 9 and 11 am, noon, 1, 2 and 3 pm.

Getting Around

Bus For the long-distance bus station, bus No A1 (they're antiquated things – jalopies, really) leaves regularly from the local bus station next to the Visitors' Information Centre; the fare is 50 sen. Bus No 7 plies between Miri and the airport from 6.15 am to 8 pm; it costs RM1. For Taman Selera, take bus No 1, 5 or 11 from the local bus station; the cost is 50 sen.

Car GSC Motor (☎ 085-411557), 925A Lorong 3, Jalan Jee Foh, Krokop, hires reliable air-con vehicles from RM140 per day with unlimited kilometres.

Taxi Taxis to and from the airport cost RM12. A taxi to the long-distance bus station costs RM8. Long-distance taxis operate from the bus station, but you'll probably have a long wait for other passengers to share a ride.

LOAGAN BUNUT NATIONAL PARK

This little-visited park in the Miri hinterland covers 10.7 sq km and protects the largest natural freshwater lake in Sarawak, although at 650 hectares it's not exactly huge. The surrounding forest hosts breeding colonies of water birds such as darters, herons and egrets. Local Berawans practise a unique form of fishing which has enabled them to keep the lake stocked with fish even during times of drought.

For keen wildlife watchers or those trying to get off the tourist trail Loagan Bunut could be an interesting trip. Access is difficult and there are no visitors' facilities in the park, although there is a hostel with basic fan-cooled rooms nearby. The hostel has cooking facilities and fresh water, but you must bring your own supplies.

Getting There & Away

Most travellers visit the park as a day trip with a tour. If you try to get there yourself you'd be better off in a group since expensive river travel is involved. First take a local bus to Tinjar or Lapok from the local bus station in Miri (2½ hours, RM8.50). From there you will have to charter a car or Land Cruiser to Logan Pengkalan, where you charter a boat to the park. Charter costs are RM120 for one person and less for each person in a group. Telephone ☎ 011-292164 to arrange transport and accommodation.

MARUDI

Marudi's only attraction is yet another of the Brooke outposts, Fort Hose, although this one doubles as a fine local museum. You could find yourself passing through the town on your way to or from the interior, and unless you fly from Miri to Bario, you'll need to stop here for a permit to head further up the Batang Baram.

Marudi sits on the north bank of the Batang Baram and the main street, Jalan Cinema, is aligned roughly east-west. It's a small town and most places to stay and eat are within a block or two of the main street; a square runs from Jalan Cinema down to the river and all boats moor at the adjacent jetty. Fort Hose is on a low hill at the east end of town and the airport is about 1km (10 minutes walk) east of the centre.

There are two banks in town, Maybank and Bank Simpanan Nasional, where you can change foreign currency.

Things to See & Do

A few hundred metres east of the town square, **Fort Hose** sits on a hilltop. Built in 1901, it's now an interesting museum with tribal artefacts and photos of local tribespeople taken by Charles Hose, an administrator under the Brooke governorship. The museum is open every day (except Friday and public holidays) from 9 am to 6 pm; admission is free. There are good views over the river from the hilltop.

There is a road network around Marudi and you can visit **longhouses** at Long Selaban and Long Moh, although the only way to get there is by hitching or taxi.

Places to Stay & Eat

The *New Alisan Hotel* (☎ 085-755971), 81 Jalan Kapitan Lim Ching Kiat, has grubby fan-cooled rooms for RM20 and bigger air-con rooms for RM30. The *Hotel Zola*

(☎ 085-755311), on Jalan Cinema, is a notch better and has air-con rooms with TV from RM31 to RM58. The *Mayland* (☎ 085-755106), at the western end of the main street, has shabby but acceptable air-con rooms starting at RM26/37 with TV (double only) and bathroom.

The *Victoria Hotel* (☎ 085-756067), on Maidan Queen near the waterfront at the foot of the hill, has doubles with no window for RM36, or windowed singles/doubles from RM40/45 to RM55. Under the same management, the *Grand Hotel* (☎ 085-755711), Marudi Bazaar, is two blocks north of Jalan Cinema and is Marudi's most up-market accommodation. Spacious air-con rooms have TV and in-house video; cheaper singles/doubles are RM38/42 and bigger ones with bathroom cost RM63.

There are plenty of Chinese *kedai kopi* around the square and along the main street. The *Koperselera,* an Indian Muslim restaurant at the west end of Jalan Cinema, has good rotis. For Chinese food the *Rose Garden* has been recommended and there's more expensive fare at the *Grand Hotel* restaurant.

Getting There & Away

Air The Malaysia Airlines agent is Tan Yong Sing (☎ 085-755240), next to the Grand Hotel. The airline operates Twin Otter flights to Miri (daily, RM29), Bario (daily, RM55), Sibu (three weekly, RM100), Long Lellang (twice weekly, RM46), Long Seridan (weekly, RM42) and Gunung Mulu (Monday and Thursday, RM40).

Flights are often full and it's advisable to book ahead. However, Malaysia Airlines doesn't impose any penalty for cancellations and space often becomes available at the last minute. This is particularly so on runs to Bario and other parts of the interior. It's worth rolling up to the airport just in case. The airstrip is within walking distance of town.

Boat The ekspres boats from Marudi to Kuala Baram operate roughly every hour between 8.30 am and 3 pm (2½ hours, RM18). There's no extra charge for the kungfu or wrestling videos.

Heading up the Baram, ekspres boats to Kuala Apoh or Long Terawan (depending on the water level) leave when they have enough passengers (3½ hours, RM20). Express boats to Long Lama cost RM18 and leave at 7.30 and 10 am, noon and 2.30 pm.

Time and frequency of travel beyond Long Lama depends on the water level.

BATANG BARAM

The mighty Batang Baram is north-east Sarawak's main artery. From Marudi it runs deep into the interior through Kayan and Kenyah territory, and even continues, via its tributary the Dapur, right up into the Kelabit Highlands around Bario. Its upper reaches are also home to the Penan, the semi-nomadic hunter-gatherers who have become symbolic of a disappearing way of life for the indigenous Dayak tribespeople of Sarawak. The Baram region is also one of the remaining major areas of primary forest in Borneo, and one of the most heavily logged. The north-east is the centre of disputes between the government, logging companies and local tribes.

Logging roads in the Baram catchment have been blockaded many times in the past, and activists, including tribespeople, have been arrested. The Sarawak government is very wary of individual travellers venturing too far up the Baram and permits for individual travel must be obtained in Marudi. First, report to the police station on the other side of the airport from town. You will be interviewed and asked why you want to visit the region; keep it simple, stick to your story – you're a tourist – and be prepared to show onward tickets and passport. If you get through this process you will be referred to the District Office, where a permit will be issued – probably for no more than a week – and you can then proceed. Travel agents in Miri can arrange tours along the Baram.

If you have plenty of time and money, and particularly want to experience a remote longhouse, then exploring this region would be worthwhile. But be warned, much of the forest has been devastated and it's not a pleasant sight.

Getting There & Away

Doing it alone is not easy, or cheap, assuming you can get a permit. From Marudi, express boats go as far as Long Lama, and from there it is possible to go by regular boat to Long Miri. From Long Miri travel is by smaller longboat, which must be chartered (at least RM150 per day plus fuel). It is a full day's travel by boat to Long Akah, and then a day or more to Long Matoh.

The alternative is by road, which involves expensive 4WD hire. From the main highway south of Miri it is possible to go by a good logging road to Long Miri and all the way to Long Akah. This road is being pushed further into the jungle towards Long Lellang and beyond.

GUNUNG MULU NATIONAL PARK

Gunung Mulu is undoubtedly the greatest of Sarawak's national parks and one of the most popular destinations in the state. Heavily promoted by travel agents, it is justifiably famous for rugged rainforest-clad mountains, a huge network of beautiful caves, superb trekking and great wildlife.

Gunung Mulu is Sarawak's largest national park and covers 529 sq km. Among its remarkable features is the fact that two mountain ranges, one of sandstone and one of limestone, abut within its boundaries. The sandstone peaks climb to 2377m Gunung Mulu, and limestone Gunung Api reaches 1750m. In between are more rugged mountains, deep gorges with clear rivers, and a unique mosaic of habitats supporting fascinating and diverse wildlife; underneath is a network of underground passages, stretching some 51km, which includes the largest cave chamber in the world. Perhaps Mulu's most famous attraction is the Pinnacles – a forest of razor-sharp limestone peaks towering 45m above the rainforest. Cave explorers recently discovered the largest cave chamber in the world, the Sarawak Chamber.

The park is an unspoilt wilderness with caving, trekking and wildlife that can be enjoyed simply for its beauty or as a challenge that even experienced outdoors enthusiasts will relish. Access to the park is simple for independent travellers. Unfortunately, smoke haze can disrupt flights to Mulu and you should try to get information in advance from the Visitors' Information Centre in Miri or the park office at Gunung Mulu. Smoke isn't usually a problem at the park itself and in any case, you probably won't regret getting stuck in Mulu for an extra day or two. See the Trekking in Sarawak section later in this chapter for details on the three trails in the park.

Permits & Bookings

All necessary paperwork – permits and accommodation bookings – should be made at the Visitors' Information Centre in Miri. You can simply turn up at the park office and book, but it's a popular spot and you run the risk of finding all the places to stay booked out. There is accommodation outside the park, but it's either expensive or run by tour companies, and also may be full.

When you get to the park office present your booking slip and you'll be allocated a room or bed. See Places to Stay & Eat for more information. Here you must also pay the RM3 park entry fee and a RM5 camera fee.

Hiring Guides

A visit to Mulu can be expensive if you go trekking or visit some of the more remote parts by boat, but the only compulsory fee is for the guides to see the Show Caves. It's charity really, since you can't get lost in these caves and some guides speak little English, but they will carry your bag for you while you take photos or walk around.

The park office handles all bookings and fees for guides, and can also arrange transport. On arrival, some boat operators will offer to arrange a cave tour for you on the spot. Avoid them if you are looking for a group to join – transport and a guide can be arranged at any time at the park office.

Guides should be waiting for visitors at the entrances to the caves. For the Show Caves guides cost RM20 per group – separate guides are needed for Clearwater and Wind caves, and for Deer and Lang's caves.

If there's only one of you it will cost the same, so round up as many people as you can. Permits are checked at a booth at the start of the trail to the caves.

The cost for trekking guides depends on the distance covered – the park office has a schedule of fees according to the number of people. For example, guide fees for a group of five trekking to the Pinnacles over three days and two nights costs RM110; and to the summit of Gunung Mulu costs RM264. There's an additional fee of RM8 per night at Camps 3, 4 and 5. Bigger groups mean less expense per person, but if a group is too large you'll see less wildlife along the way.

Boat hire is by negotiation, but costs range from RM85 for a visit to Clearwater Cave to RM250 for the Pinnacles trek. If you want to visit all the caves and do a lot of trekking, then an organised tour starts to look cost-effective. Most travel agents charge around RM350 for four days/three nights and RM500 for six days/five nights. This includes a visit to all the caves, a trek, all transfers and accommodation. Packages which include accommodation at Royal Mulu Resort cost a whole lot more.

Some boat operators and guides have been known to line up individual travellers for a cave tour, put them all in one boat and then try to charge each of them for the hire of a complete boat and an individual guide. Pay only the group rates, and complain to the ranger if this happens.

Caves

The Deer, Lang, Clearwater and Wind caves are all known as the Show Caves, and are easily accessible to visitors. The other caves are closed to the public because they are inaccessible or considered dangerous, while some contain fragile formations that park authorities want to preserve and protect from further deterioration. Adventure caving trips can be arranged by negotiation with park staff or tour operators.

Deer Cave & Lang's Cave The Deer Cave and adjoining Lang's Cave are the two caves closest to park HQ. At 2160m long and 220m deep, they have the world's largest cave passage. Both are very safe, with walkways and wooden steps where necessary.

Lang's Cave has lights until 4 pm – though a strong torch (flashlight) is useful for the darker areas. There are pretty stalagmites and stalactites and some strange formations. Water cascades from openings in the roof after heavy rain. You enter the cave on one side of the mountain, exit from the other and it takes about 30 minutes to walk the entire length. A guide is compulsory, though hardly necessary, and will stay until about 6 pm.

Deer Cave is a gaping cavern in the mountainside, huge beyond comprehension. It doesn't have the attractive formations of Lang's Cave, but you will wander through with mouth agape until the stink of ammonia assaults you from piles of guano on the floor. Look up and you will see the cause – some two million free-tailed bats clinging to the roof so distant that they appear as a seething black mass. The bats emerge from the cave entrance between 5 and 6 pm each night in a vast chittering stream that can last for half an hour. It's a sight not to be missed and one of the wildlife highlights of Mulu.

A bat 'observatory' was under construction outside the cave entrance at the time of writing. There are toilets and picnic tables where you can get a great view of the bat spectacle in the evenings – it's very popular so get there early for a good position. You don't need a guide to walk to the entrance of the cave and watch the bats.

The Lang's and Deer caves are a nice 3km walk from park HQ along a plankwalk.

Clearwater Cave & Wind Cave Wind Cave is part of the Clearwater Cave system and the starting point for some of the longest tunnels. It opens out in a cliff above the Sungai Melinau and has a plankwalk right through. The Wind Cave has some impressive caverns and limestone formations, although the main Clearwater Cave which has a river running through it, is more interesting. Parts of the plankwalk are rotten, and a good torch and caution are advised.

continued on page 437

TREKKING IN SARAWAK

Sarawak offers a range of jungle trekking options for the fit and adventurous as well as more gentle ambles for those who don't aspire to super-human status. Remember, this is hiking through rainforest in hot, humid and sometimes wet conditions, so it's exhausting and you'll probably have leeches for company. But the rewards are valuable if you persist – you'll see superb rainforest and alpine plateaus in the Kelabit Highlands, stone forests and jagged peaks in Gunung Mulu National Park, and have the opportunity to visit fascinating longhouses.

PLANNING

When to Go

Although the wettest months in Sarawak are from October to March, the timing of monsoon seasons has been less consistent in recent years. Sarawak has high rainfall year-round and you should be prepared for heavy rain on one or more days of your stay. Flights into Gunung Mulu and Bario will be cancelled if the weather is poor, so be prepared to be stranded for a couple of days on the return trip.

What to Bring

There are no special equipment requirements to enjoy walking in the region, but it can get cold at night and rain for days on end – take a poncho or waterproof jacket. Good running shoes are preferable to heavy walking boots; a pair of thongs is useful for going in and out of longhouses. Wear light cotton clothing and carry a light jumper and trousers for the evenings. If camping or staying in a longhouse, you will need a sleeping bag or blankets.

Most of your load's weight will be water. Remember to drink a lot to replace the fluids you lose sweating. It's also generally safe to drink water from streams (upstream from the longhouse, of course); ask your guide for advice. A torch (flashlight), insect repellent and sunscreen lotion would also be useful.

Gunung Mulu National Park

Gunung Mulu National Park offers excellent jungle trekking for the fit and determined. There are three main treks in Mulu – the Gunung Mulu Summit, the Pinnacles and the Headhunters' Trail. An attempt at any of them will involve some expense and it's best to go with a group to reduce the cost of transport and guide. Ask around when you get to park HQ to see if anyone's interested in sharing costs.

You should not attempt any of the following trails without a guide – and you won't be permitted to anyway. Expect rain, leeches, slippery and treacherous conditions, and a very hot workout – carry lots of water. Your guide should let you go at your own pace. Many who attempt the Pinnacles or Gunung Mulu don't make it to the top. Guides can be arranged at the park HQ – see Hiring Guides in the Gunung Mulu National Park section of the Sarawak chapter.

THE TREKS

The Pinnacles

The Pinnacles is an incredible stone forest towering 45m high, halfway up the side of Gunung Api. Getting to the Pinnacles involves travel by boat and a tough three day trek.

The trek to the Pinnacles starts with a two or three hour boat trip (depending on the level of the river) from park HQ to Long Berar. From here it is an 8km trek to Camp 5 by the Sungai Melinau. Camp 5 is hostel-style accommodation with running water, cold showers, a cooking area, 'American' toilet and covered sleeping quarters. Sleep overnight at this picturesque spot before climbing Gunung Api.

Unfortunately you must climb virtually the whole distance to see the Pinnacles – there's no easy way out. The three to four hour ascent is very steep and slippery in parts. It's best to start early in the morning, when it's a lot cooler and you're more likely to see wildlife. The ultimate destination is a small viewing point looking out over the Pinnacles. It is possible to camp here, but the Pinnacles trip is usually done in one day and most trekkers return to Camp 5. If you start at sunrise it's possible to continue back to park HQ.

From Camp 5 you can walk north to Lubang Cina on the Sungai Terikan. From this river it is possible to continue right down to Limbang on the coast via the Sungai Medalam, though this journey is usually done in reverse.

Guides' fees are RM110 for a three day/two night trek; each extra day costs RM20 plus RM10 allowance per night. The park rate for boat hire to Long Berar from park HQ is RM350 return for one to four people, or RM85 per person for five or more. One way costs RM200 for up to four people, or RM45 per person for five or more.

Gunung Mulu Trail

The climb to the summit is normally done as a four day trek and is the highlight of many a traveller's visit to Mulu. You must carry enough food for the entire trip, as well as your own cooking utensils and a sleeping bag (it gets quite cold at night). It's not unusual for it to rain every day, in which case you could find yourself wallowing in mud along the way. Wear good walking shoes, leech-proof socks if you have them and carry a poncho to keep off the rain.

There are several camps (basic wooden huts) along the trail; Camps 1, 3 and 4 are the ones usually used for overnight stops. The most common schedule involves an easy first day (about three or four hours walking) and overnight at Camp 1 beside a beautiful river. On day two you're faced with a long (four or five hours) hard and extremely steep climb to Camp 4. If it hasn't rained there won't be any water at Camp 4, so carry some up from Camp 3.

On day three leave your pack at Camp 4 and climb to the summit of Gunung Mulu. You can either sleep at Camp 3 another night and return to the park HQ on day four, or descend the mountain in one day. The latter is quite tough on the legs, but you can cool down in the river along the way.

TOURISM MALAYSIA

View of the Pinnacles from Pinnacle lookout on Gunung Api.

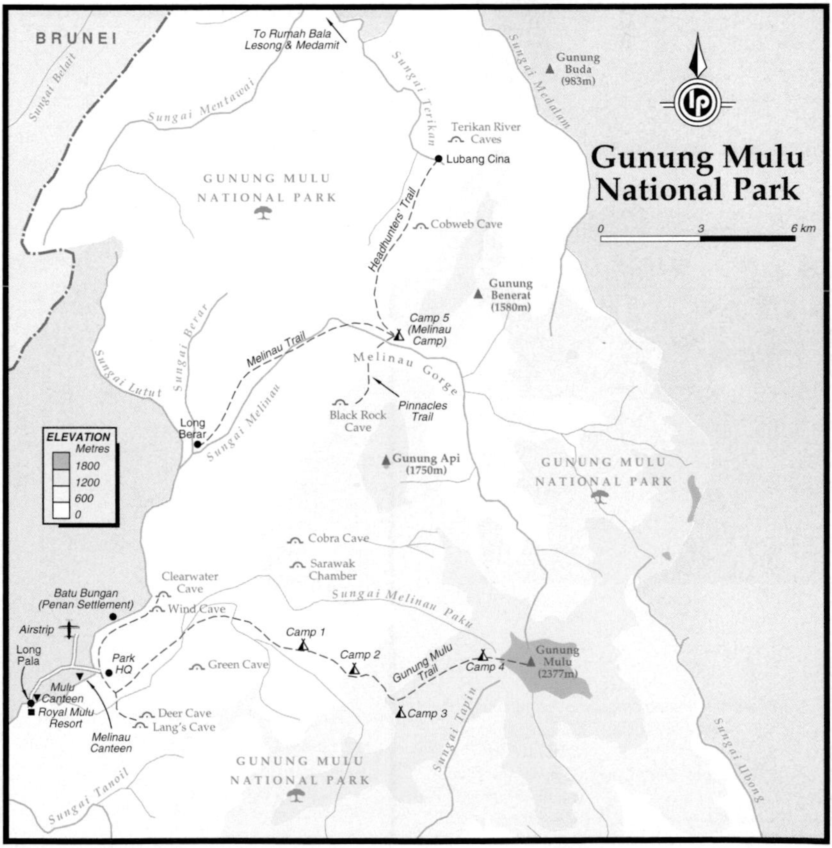
Gunung Mulu National Park
0
3
6 km
BRUNEI
To Rumah Bala Lesong & Medamit
Sungai Belait
Sungai Mentawai
Sungai Terikan
Sungai Medalam
Gunung Buda (983m)
Terikan River Caves
Lubang Cina
GUNUNG MULU NATIONAL PARK
Headhunters' Trail
Cobweb Cave
Gunung Benerat (1580m)
Sungai Berar
Camp 5 (Melinau Camp)
Melinau Trail
Melinau Gorge
Sungai Lutut
Sungai Melinau
Pinnacles Trail
Black Rock Cave
Long Berar
ELEVATION
Metres
1800
1200
600
0
Gunung Api (1750m)
GUNUNG MULU NATIONAL PARK
Cobra Cave
Sarawak Chamber
Clearwater Cave
Batu Bungan (Penan Settlement)
Wind Cave
Sungai Melinau Paku
Airstrip
Long Pala
Park HQ
Camp 1
Camp 2
Gunung Mulu Trail
Camp 4
Gunung Mulu (2377m)
Green Cave
Mulu Canteen
Royal Mulu Resort
Deer Cave
Lang's Cave
Camp 3
Melinau Canteen
Sungai Tapin
Sungai Ubong
GUNUNG MULU NATIONAL PARK
Sungai Tanoil

TOURISM MALAYSIA

TOURISM MALAYSIA

TOURISM MALAYSIA

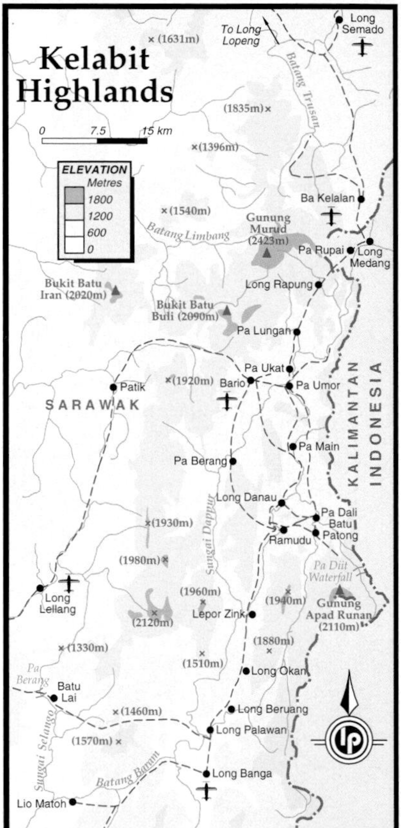

Top Left: Illuminated limestone formations inside Wind Cave, Gunung Mulu National Park.
Top Right: Deer Cave, Gunung Mulu National Park.
Bottom: Walkway into Lang's Cave, Gunung Mulu National Park.

If you are reasonably fit and healthy the return trip to Gunung Mulu can be done in three days, which evens out the exertion. If you leave park HQ at dawn or before, you can reach Camp 3 in one long day and sleep there. See the Gunung Mulu National Park section in the Sarawak chapter for details on how to arrange accommodation.

Headhunters' Trail
The Headhunters' Trail is a backdoor route from Gunung Mulu to Limbang and can be done in either direction, although most organised trips start in the national park. This trail is named after the Kayan war parties that used to make their way up the Sungai Melinau from the Baram area to the Melinau Gorge, then drag their canoes overland to the Sungai Terikan to raid the peoples of the Limbang region. A 3m-wide road lined with poles was used to move the canoes, and a canal was dug around Batu Rikan.

To do the Headhunters' Trail independently you should gather a group together to share costs, and ask around for a guide at park HQ. The usual procedure is to take a boat to Long Berar (RM250), walk to Camp 5 (about four hours) and overnight there (RM8 per person) on the first day. Day two involves an 11km walk to the Sungai Terikan (four or five hours), where you could spend the night at the rangers' station (Mentawai) or proceed to a longhouse, Rumah Bala Lesong, another three or four hours away. After overnighting in the longhouse, the boat trip continues downriver to Medamit, from where it is possible to travel by minibus to Limbang. The boat from the Sungai Terikan to Medamit should cost about RM500; the guide's fee would come to about RM230; a suitable payment for food and lodging at the longhouse could be about RM20; and the minibus from Medamit to Limbang costs RM5. Extra costs would include food for the stay at Camp 5, gifts for the longhouse and a tip for your guide if you feel it is warranted.

You could do the Pinnacles trek, return to Camp 5 then set off on the Headhunters' Trail the following day. This trip is equally possible in the opposite direction – take a bus to Medamit, where a boat can be arranged to the longhouse or the national parks office at Mentawai.

Bario & the Kelabit Highlands

Bario is ringed by forested hills, and a network of basic roads and tracks offer some great trekking options. Those more inclined to amble can take easy half-day or day walks; there's plenty to see and the elevation means it's a pleasant temperature.

Of the longhouses close to town, you can walk east to Pa Umor (about one hour) and nearby Pa Ukat. The trail then continues on to Pa Lungan. A Kelabit burial ground is close to town on the way to Pa Ramapuh, about a 1½ hour walk. There is a waterfall about an hour beyond Pa Ramapuh. Another day walk is to Pa Berang, a Penan settlement three hours from Bario.

Longer, more strenuous walks can take you through superb rainforest and on to alpine plateaus, staying overnight at longhouses en route, or across the Indonesian border where you can catch a plane back to Bario or elsewhere. For certain sectors you are strongly advised to hire a guide – trails are sometimes indistinct, terrain can be rugged, and it may be wet and slippery. Visitors occasionally get lost up here and you should seek local information before setting out – Tarawe's can advise you on conditions, costs and etiquette (see Places to Stay & Eat under Bario in the Sarawak chapter).

The most popular walk is the two day walk to Ba Kelalan and then a flight out, but it's also possible to walk to Long Lellang from where there's also a flight. The trip to Long Lellang is a four to six day trek via the Penan settlement of Pa Tik. Expect rain, mud, leeches and some regrets, because jungle walking is no Sunday stroll. But if you're prepared the experience is unforgettable. Guides are recommended, and essential for longer walks away from inhabited areas.

The guest books in the longhouses are full of good information. Lots of the Kelabits are Christians and don't smoke, so bring sugar, seeds, tea, kerosene or anything imaginative for the chief.

THE TREKS

Bario-Pa Lungan-Gunung Murud

A four hour walk on a wide trail takes you to Pa Lungan, a friendly longhouse with a pleasant river to swim in. The chief has a room for visitors with mats, blankets, pillows and mosquito net.

From there you can hire guides and bearers to climb the 2423m Gunung Murud, the highest peak in Sarawak, over a two day walk.

Bario-Ba Kelalan-Long Semado

Another possibility is to walk to Ba Kelalan, a day's walk beyond Pa Lungan, and then fly to Lawas (daily flights; RM46), or continue walking to Long Semado, which is also connected to Lawas by Twin Otter flights (twice weekly; RM40). Walks in this area are not a picnic – you need to be self-sufficient in food and shelter, and be prepared for some hard walking. It's a very good idea to hire a local guide. This costs around RM40 per day and the guide will usually carry some of your gear. As well as a guide, in theory you also need a Border Permit from the army in Bario, as the route takes you into Kalimantan via Pa Rupai. Ask Tarawe's in Bario how to get this permit.

Bario-Lio Matoh

You can also walk to Lio Matoh in seven to nine days, depending on your speed. It's a great trek, staying in longhouses most nights (and basic jungle huts other nights), but you must take a guide.

The nightly stops and walking times on a nine day walk are:

Day 1	Long Danau	9 hours
Day 2	Ramudu	5 hours
Days 3, 4, 5	Jungle Huts	15 hours total
Day 6	Long Palawan	7 hours
Day 7	Long Banga	3 hours
Day 8	Jungle hut	6 hours
Day 9	Lio Matoh	7 hours

Considerations for Responsible Trekking

The popularity of trekking is placing great pressure on the natural environment. Please consider the following tips when trekking and help preserve the ecology and beauty of Sarawak.

RUBBISH

- Carry out all your rubbish. Don't overlook those easily forgotten items, such as silver paper, orange peel, cigarette butts and plastic wrappers. Make an effort to carry out rubbish left by others.
- Never bury your rubbish: digging disturbs soil and ground cover, and encourages erosion. Buried rubbish will more than likely be dug up by animals, who may be injured or poisoned by it.
- Minimise the waste you must carry out by taking minimal packaging and taking no more food than you will need. If you can't buy in bulk, unpack small-portion packages and combine their contents in one container before your trip.
- Don't rely on bought water in plastic bottles. Disposal of these bottles is creating a major problem, particularly in developing countries. Use iodine drops or purification tablets instead of contributing to the problem.
- Sanitary napkins, tampons and condoms should also be carried out despite the inconvenience. They burn and decompose poorly.

HUMAN WASTE DISPOSAL

- Contamination of water sources by human faeces can lead to the transmission of hepatitis, typhoid and intestinal parasites, such as giardia, amoebas and roundworms. It can cause severe health risks to you, local residents and wildlife.
- Where there is a toilet, please use it.
- Where there is none, bury your waste. Dig a small hole 15cm deep and at least 100m from any watercourse. Consider carrying a lightweight trowel for this purpose. Cover the waste with soil and a rock. Use toilet paper sparingly and bury it as well.
- If the area is inhabited, ask locals if they have any concerns about your chosen toilet site.
- Ensure that these guidelines are applied to a portable toilet tent if one is being used by a large trekking party. Encourage all party members, including porters, to use the site.

WASHING

- Don't use detergents or toothpaste in or near watercourses, even if they are biodegradable.
- For personal washing, use biodegradable soap and a water container (or even a lightweight, portable basin) at least 50m from the watercourse. Disperse the waste water widely to allow the soil to filter it before it finally makes it way back to the watercourse.
- Wash cooking utensils 50m from watercourses using a scourer or sand instead of detergent.

EROSION

- Hillsides and mountain slopes, especially at high altitudes, are prone to erosion. Stick to existing tracks and avoid short cuts that bypass a switchback. If you blaze a new trail straight down a slope, it will turn into a watercourse with the next heavy rainfall and eventually cause soil loss and deep scarring.
- If a well-used track passes through a mud patch, walk through the mud: walking around the edge will increase the patch's size.
- Avoid removing the plant life that keeps topsoil in place.

FIRES & LOW IMPACT COOKING

- Don't depend on open fires for cooking. Cutting wood for fires in popular trekking areas can cause rapid deforestation. Cook on a light-weight kerosene, alcohol or Shellite (white gas) stove and avoid those powered by disposable butane gas canisters.
- If you are trekking with a guide and porters, supply stoves for the whole team. Ensure that all members are outfitted with enough clothing so that fires are not a necessity for warmth.
- If you patronise local accommodation, select those places that do not use wood fires to heat water or cook food.
- Fires may be acceptable below the tree line in areas that get very few visitors. If you light a fire, use an existing fireplace. Don't surround fires with rocks as this creates a visual scar. Use only dead, fallen wood. Remember the adage 'the bigger the fool, the bigger the fire'. Use minimal wood, just what you need for cooking. In huts leave wood for the next person.
- Ensure that you fully extinguish a fire after use. Spread the embers and douse them with water. A fire is only truly safe to leave when you can comfortably place your hand in it.

WILDLIFE CONSERVATION

- Do not engage in or encourage hunting. It is illegal in all parks and reserves. However the indigenous Penan people are allowed to hunt in Gunung Mulu with traditional weapons.
- Don't buy items made from endangered species.
- Don't assume animals in huts to be non-indigenous vermin and attempt to exterminate them. In wild places they are likely to be protected native animals.
- Don't feed the wildlife as this can lead to animals becoming dependent on hand-outs, unbalanced populations and diseases.

PARK REGULATIONS

- Take note of and observe any rules and regulations particular to the national or state reserve that you are visiting.

TREKKING IN POPULATED AREAS

- Follow the social and cultural considerations when interacting with the local community and staying in longhouses. See the Longhouse Etiquette entry in the Up the Batang Rejang section of the Sarawak chapter for more details on appropriate behaviour.

continued from page 430

The Clearwater Cave is 51km long (the longest cave passage in South-East Asia) and 355m deep. It takes its name from an underground river that spills through a natural grate to form a crystal clear swimming pool near the cave entrance. The cave is lit, though it is a good idea to take a strong torch to see the finer details of its various features and limestone formations. Access is via steep concrete steps up a hillside then along a walkway which can be slippery in places. A bridge across the underground river had been washed away at the time of writing, but was due for replacement.

There's a trail from the park HQ to the Wind and Clearwater caves which takes about an hour; it's a pleasant walk that follows the Sungai Melinau for part of the way. The walk from the Wind Cave to Clearwater Cave takes about 10 minutes.

Boat hire from park HQ costs about RM85, including a visit to the Wind Cave and time for a swim outside Clearwater Cave. You could walk one way and hitch a ride back, which shouldn't cost more than RM10 – negotiate with the boatman.

You could include a visit to the Batu Bungan Penan settlement on the way to the caves.

Adventure Caving There are plenty of other caves in the park; more are discovered regularly and the number of those that are known is extended by subsequent expeditions. It is estimated that the number of caves already explored represents only about 40% of the total number present in Gunung Mulu.

It is possible to explore the nooks and crannies of the Show Caves away from the pedestrian plankwalks. Adventure caving expeditions allow you to crawl, climb and swim your way through the many passages of the caves.

The most frequently visited is the Sarawak Chamber, the largest known cave in the world and reputed to be the size of 16 football fields. To explore the chamber and two side caves a guide costs RM88, which can be shared between up to five people. Equipment is provided, although park staff are used to dealing with tour groups and you may have to be persistent to organise a trip.

Wildlife

Gunung Mulu National Park features eight types of forest, including peat swamp, tall dipterocarp and, at the summits of the higher peaks, stunted moss forest. Thousands of species of plants have been recorded, and every scientific expedition finds new ones. Among the prizes are over 170 species of orchids and 10 species of pitcher plants.

Mulu is part of traditional Penan hunting grounds and the tribe is still allowed to hunt in the park using traditional weapons. As a consequence, many of the larger birds and mammals are scarce, or at best shy. Nevertheless, a staggering 275 species of birds have been recorded (the highest number so far in Sarawak), as well as 75 species of mammals, 74 of frogs, 281 species of butterflies and – while we're counting – 458 species of ants.

Around the park HQ you'll see a few common species of birds, such as bulbuls and sunbirds, but look out for the white-fronted falconet – the world's smallest bird of prey and only slightly larger than a sparrow. Either of the walks to the Show Caves can be very good for spotting birds, particularly in the early morning. At the caves themselves you'll see plenty of swiftlets nesting on the cave walls, as well as a selection of birds of prey that pick off bats as they come pouring out. Along the rivers you could see the stork-billed kingfisher, with its massive red bill, and the amazing black and red broadbill – a clownish-looking bird with a fat blue bill.

With the exception of bats, most of Mulu's mammals are shy and difficult to see, although you'll probably encounter squirrels along the trails – look out for the pygmy squirrel along the plankwalks, and the striking Prevost's squirrel in the trees.

As long as it's not raining you'll see an incredible variety of butterflies along the trails. When it is raining you can expect lots of leeches (but not many different species), and they'll be very glad to see you.

Batu Bungan Penan Settlement

The Gunung Mulu region is home to the Berawan people, but the government has settled a Penan group on the banks of the Sungai Melinau as part of their campaign to 'civilise' these nomads.

If you get tired of looking at the beautiful forest and wildlife, you can always spend a few minutes gaping at this poor settlement. However, the village is used to tourism, and the Penan are very friendly and hospitable people. The women make cane bangles and basketwork which they will offer for sale.

Batu Bungan is about halfway between the park HQ and Clearwater Cave. A visit can be combined with a trip to the caves. It is also possible to walk there from the airport. You may also run into Penan hunters along the trails in the park.

Eight different types of hornbill can be found in Gunung Mulu National Park.

Places to Stay & Eat

Given the preference for tour groups and Mulu's popularity, it can sometimes be difficult to get a booking for accommodation, but private accommodation is available outside the park.

The standard of accommodation at the park is very good. There's a 15-bed *hostel* where a bed costs RM10, and an *annexe* where five-bed rooms with bathroom and fan are RM15 per bed. There are two classes of *chalet* where rooms have a ceiling fan and bathroom: rooms in the Class 3 chalets have four beds and cost RM60, and rooms in a Class 2 chalet have three beds and cost RM90 per night. There's also a *VIP chalet resthouse* with a three-bed room for RM200.

There's a *cafeteria* at park HQ where you can buy good meals, soft drinks and beer, although you may have to go to the cafe over the river to get bottled water. It's open from 8 am to 9.30 pm and there's also a pool table and TV.

If you're *self-catering* there are gas stoves and fridges at the chalets and hostel, but you'll have to ask at the park office for cutlery, crockery, pots and pans. You must bring all your food requirements from Miri.

Outside the park, the place to head for is the *Melinau Canteen* (☎ 011-291641 or ☎ 085-657884 in Miri). It is just a few hundred metres downriver from the jetty at the park HQ, around the bend on the other side of the river. A bed at this Berawan-owned place costs RM6 per person in bunk rooms. Tour groups occasionally fill the place up, but usually you will have no problem getting a room to yourself. Meals are available, and a provisions shop sells tinned goods, snacks, beer etc.

Further downriver at Long Pala there are more *guesthouses* owned by the tour companies, such as Tropical Adventure, Seridan Mulu and Alo Doda. It is possible to stay here for around RM15 upwards per night if they are not full, though they are a long way from the park HQ.

The *Royal Mulu Resort* (☎ 085-790100) is an enormous luxury hotel about 3km from the park entrance. It's tastefully built around limestone bluffs overlooking the river, with nicely appointed rooms and a garden full of flowers, butterflies and birds. There's also a swimming pool and satellite TV, although the staff are not very helpful. Rooms cost from RM210 to RM250, and suites are RM500 to RM2000 – plus the usual luxury tax and service charge. These prices usually include breakfast and discounts are often available. The resort's *coffee shop/restaurant* has a surprisingly limited menu and average food for the price; it's certainly not worth a special trip from the park unless you're dying for fish and chips.

Across the river from the park office there's a *cafe* where you might have to go for bottled water (and get stung for RM5 per bottle!). It has a deck over the river and is a pleasant place for a meal. The cafe's open until late if you want a nightcap. The *Mulu Canteen* is directly across the river from the Royal Mulu Resort and is a good place to buy basic noodle and rice dishes and soft drinks, if you're not at the resort on a package deal. Even if you are, it's the place to head if you want a beer in the evening since the short walk will save you lots of money.

Getting There & Away

Air Malaysia Airlines has flights to Gunung Mulu from Miri (three daily, RM69), Marudi (two weekly, RM40) and Limbang (two daily, RM40). The pilot will, upon request, fly in low between the peaks before circling back to land – a breathtaking experience. Royal Brunei also has regular flights to Mulu from BSB.

Bus/Boat It is possible – but difficult, time consuming and ultimately no cheaper – to travel to Mulu by a combination of bus and boat. From Miri take a local bus to Kuala Baram for RM2.20. Buses depart Miri regularly, but if you want to get to the national park in one day, take the 6 am bus. Alternatively, you can stay in Marudi for the night.

From Kuala Baram there are express boats to Marudi for RM18; the first departure is at 7.15 am and they leave at least hourly until 3 pm. The trip takes about three hours. From Marudi, the next stage is Long Terawan. Launches make the journey when they have enough passengers, and if the water is high enough they go all the way through. If not, you will have to change boats at Long Apoh. The trip from Marudi to Long Terawan costs RM20.

Travel onwards to the national park from Long Terawan is via charter boat. The official rate is RM150 or RM35 per person if there are more than five of you. In practice, however, few local boat owners are willing to do the trip for RM150 and you may end up paying more, or waiting until more people turn up. The journey takes around two hours.

For the return trip from the park you need to be up at 5 am to get the boat to Long Terawan (or Kuala Apoh/Long Panai) in time to get the connecting boat to Marudi. You could fly to the park and take a boat back to experience river travel.

Getting Around

The airport is over the river from the park HQ. There are minibuses running between the airport and park HQ, but there's no regular service. You may be able to cadge a lift from the resort bus (about RM2) but drivers are unhelpful. Be persistent because they go right past the park turn-off and it's only 200m or so to walk from there. Otherwise it's a 10 to 15 minute walk along this road to the park office. A boat to the park or Melinau Canteen costs about RM5 and boats to Long Pala cost about RM10.

BARIO

Bario is a tiny settlement in a beautiful valley 1500m up in the Kelabit Highlands, close to the Indonesian border. Part of Bario's appeal lies in its clear mountain air and isolation, but the region also features friendly Kenyah and Kelabit longhouses, and great highland treks to suit all levels of fitness and motivation. The nearby hills are covered in largely untouched forest with abundant wildlife, and in the kerangas there are pitcher plants, rhododendrons and orchids. Although the hills surrounding Bario are not officially protected, there are moves afoot to have them declared a national park.

Unlikely as it seems, sleepy Bario played a pivotal role in Borneo's modern history: it was here that Major Tom Harrisson and a British commando unit parachuted during WWII to organise resistance against the Japanese occupation. Some of the tribespeople involved still live in nearby longhouses.

Tour companies visit the region, but it is easy to organise your own trekking with or without a guide. Officially you need a permit to visit Bario, although the chances are nobody will ask to see it unless you walk into Indonesia. It's advisable to get one just in case, and they can be obtained painlessly from the Resident's Office in Miri – see the Miri section for details. On arrival it's generally not a problem to go straight to one of the nearby Kenyah or Kelabit longhouses.

The only access is by air and there's no telephone or fax in Bario. Travellers are urged to bring enough cash for accommodation, food and guides; small denominations, such as RM10, RM5 and RM1, will be useful and take extra in case you are stranded; there are no credit card facilities in the Kelabit Highlands. Bario and Ba Kelalan have shops where you can stock up on supplies and gifts to take to the longhouses.

See the Trekking in Sarawak section earlier in this chapter for descriptions of short ambles and long treks in the area.

Places to Stay & Eat

There is excellent backpackers/trekkers accommodation at *Tarawe's*, run by a local and his English wife. You can't book ahead, but someone from Tarawe's should be waiting to meet the flight. If not, ask around – Bario is a small, friendly place where locals will soon put you on the right track. The cost is RM15 per person in three-bed rooms; breakfast costs RM3 or more, depending on what you have, and delicious, home-cooked meals are also available on request. A chalet with self-catering facilities was being built at the time of writing and will accommodate a small group or family. Tarawe's welcomes travellers and is a fund of information on trekking, local history and customs, and travel in general.

Getting There & Away

The Malaysia Airlines agent is the Bario Cooperative Society. The only way in to Bario is by the daily Malaysia Airlines Twin Otter flight from Miri (RM70), usually via Marudi (RM55). There are also flights to Long Banga (RM35). The flights are dependent on the weather and cancellations are not uncommon, so make sure your schedule isn't too tight. These flights are often booked out in advance, especially during the busy school holidays, but because the airline doesn't impose a penalty for cancellations, it's possible that a seat will become available at the last minute – it may pay to wait at the airport in Miri or Marudi.

LIMBANG

This small, prosperous riverside town is sandwiched between the two parts of Brunei. It's a tidy, picturesque place straddling the banks of the Batang Limbang, but there's not much to do here. You may find yourself coming through on the way to or from Brunei or Gunung Mulu – Limbang is the starting or ending point for the Headhunters' Trail (see the Trekking in Sarawak section earlier in this chapter).

Orientation

The main part of Limbang sits along the east bank of the Batang Limbang, which throws its loops across a forested plain before emptying into Brunei Bay. A range of low hills further east marks the border with Brunei's Temburong district.

The older – and more interesting – part of town is only a couple of hundred metres square, and bordered on the riverbank by a huge two storey, blue-roofed market. A massive new hotel and shopping complex, in glorious peach and aqua, was being built at the time of writing and will dominate the skyline north of the centre. Beyond it and downstream about 200m from the old town, there are blocks of newer, white shophouses with cafes, karaoke bars and snooker halls; here you'll find more upmarket accommodation. Across the river, brightly painted houses and mosques sit on stilts.

Boats to Brunei and Labuan leave from the wharf below the blue-roofed new market and taxis park just outside. Boats to Lawas tie up at the jetty a few hundred metres downstream. The airport is about 4km south of town.

Things to See & Do

A tamu is held on Friday in the car park in front of the new market and is attended by villagers from the surrounding district. Limbang's small **Muzium Wilayah** is upstairs in another of Charles Brooke's forts and well worth the five minute walk along the river. The collection is well presented and features archaeology, culture and crafts of the region. The museum is open every day except Monday and public holidays from 9 am to 6 pm; admission is free. To get there, just follow the riverbank south past the police station.

Just down the road from the museum and up a steep drive opposite the Limbang Recreation Club there's a pretty **park** with an artificial lake backed by forest. It's a pleasant place to kill time if you're waiting for a flight.

Places to Stay

Like Miri, Limbang has been turned into a sin centre by Brunei's religious police, and some of the cheap-looking places on and around the main street opposite the wharf are decidedly sleazy. The decent places are mostly mid-range air-con hotels and you can pay by credit card at some.

The *Muhibbah Inn* (☎ 085-212488) is a maze of corridors where air-con rooms start at RM52, but there are windowless economy rooms with air-con, shower and toilet for RM38 which are perfectly adequate. Rooms at the *Metro* (☎ 085-211133), near the market, start at RM53 with air-con, shower, TV and minibar. This is a popular hotel and often full.

The three mid-range hotels facing the river in the newer blocks north of town all offer similar quality and facilities, but the rooms are somewhat less grand than their spacious, marble-faced foyers promise. Rooms at the *Royal Park* (☎ 085-213345) start at RM60; the *National Inn* (☎ 085-212922) has better rooms for RM68 and up; and the somewhat tatty *Centre Point Hotel* (☎ 085-213699) has standard rooms starting at RM50, but you'll have to pay in cash for this one.

Places to Eat

There are *food stalls* on the 1st floor of the market, at the bus station and at the bottom of the old town near the police station. Cheap Malaysian food, rotis and murtabaks can be had in the *Muslim cafes* in the same building as the Muhibbah Inn.

Limbang has plenty of coffee shops, including *Maggie's,* next to the National Inn on the riverside, where excellent grilled fish and cold beer is served at tables overlooking the river. On the other side of the block, the *Tong Lok* is a smart, air-con Chinese restaurant. The *Limbang Recreation Club*, near the museum, has a covered deck over the river and has good seafood at outdoor tables.

Getting There & Away

Air Malaysia Airlines has Twin Otter flights to Miri (seven daily, RM45), Gunung Mulu (two weekly, RM40), Lawas (two daily, RM25) and Kota Kinabalu (three weekly, RM60). The airport is 4km south of the town centre and a share taxi costs RM5 per person. A taxi to the airport costs RM5 per person if there's a full load; it's hard to get a taxi to take you on your own for less than RM10.

Willing Travel (☎ 085-211323), on the main street opposite the wharf, can book flights.

Road There is a local road network that crosses the border into Brunei. It is possible to travel by car between the two halves of Brunei via Limbang, but there are no buses. It is difficult and expensive to go from Limbang to the western half of Brunei, but taxis regularly make the trip for RM20 to the eastern Brunei border, and all the way to Bangar by negotiation. Make sure you call at the Brunei immigration checkpoint on the road into Bangar; it is open every day from 6 am to 10 pm. From Bangar it is possible to go overland to Lawas and on to Sabah, but it involves an expensive taxi ride (see the Lawas section for details).

Regular buses to other parts of the Limbang district leave from the bus station at the north-east corner of the old town. There are services to Pandaruan, Buagsiol, Batu

Danau, Kubong, Ukong, and Tedungan. If you are planning to do the Head- hunters' Trail into Gunung Mulu National Park, the bus for Medamit leaves roughly every hour between 5.30 am and 4.30 pm and costs RM4 (see the Gunung Mulu section for more details).

Boat There are plenty of boats daily to Bandar Seri Begawan, the capital of Brunei. The trip takes about 30 minutes and costs RM18 from Limbang, B$10 from Brunei. Boats go when they have a full load of 12 passengers, but this route has a lot of traffic and you shouldn't have to wait long. The last boat leaves at around 4.30 pm.

An express boat goes to Lawas every morning at 8 am for RM20. The express boat to Labuan in Sabah leaves at 7.30 am, costs RM20 and takes 1½ hours. From Labuan to Limbang the boat leaves at 12.30 pm. Buy your ticket at the wharf.

LAWAS

Lawas is a busy little town on the banks of the Batang Lawas. Like Limbang, it is a transit point where you may find yourself en route to or from Brunei and Sabah, or to take the short flight to Miri. Logging is a big industry in this part of Sarawak and a logging road runs from Lawas to Long Semado. It is impossible to get lost here: the bus station is in the middle of town and all places to stay and eat are in the shophouses surrounding it.

EAST MALAYSIA

Places to Stay & Eat

There's no decent budget accommodation in Lawas. The *Soon Seng* (☎ 085-285871), on Jalan Punang, has clean and comfortable fan-cooled doubles for RM35 and air-con rooms starting at RM45; it is a good choice. Other air-con options include *Hotel Muhibbah* (☎ 085-285509), on the river side of the main road, which has singles/doubles for RM35/40; and the *Million Hotel* (☎ 085-285088), Jalan Muhibbah, which has better rooms with TV for RM40/45, although the cheaper ones are very small.

The best place in town is the flash *Gaya Inn* (☎ 085-285855), 18 Jalan Punang (in the same block as the Soon Seng), where well-appointed 'semi-standard' air-con rooms with bathroom are RM70 and more luxury comes for up to RM155. If it's not full you may be able to get a good discount.

Lawas has *food stalls* on the top floor of the riverside market and clustered around the tiny town Padang. There are numerous good *kedai kopi* around town. The best ones are in the block between the Gaya Inn and the Soon Seng; the one under the Soon Seng is a popular hang-out and serves good food.

Getting There & Away

Air The Malaysia Airlines agent is the Eng Huat Travel Agency (☎ 085-855570), near the bus station. Lawas is well served by Malaysia Airlines Twin Otters. There are flights to Kota Kinabalu (weekly, RM47), iri (six daily, RM59), Limbang (two most days, RM25), Ba Kelalan (daily, RM47), Long Semado (weekly, RM40), Labuan (weekly, RM31); and Long Pasia (weekly, RM30).

Bus There are two buses daily to Kota Kinabalu and towns en route, leaving at 7.30 am and 1.30 pm. It's a long boring trip over a nightmarish road in places. The fare to KK is RM22.

If you miss the express service, catch a minibus to Merapok (RM5), on the Sarawak/Sabah border, from where you can catch another one to Sipitang and on to Beaufort.

If you miss the boat to Brunei, you could travel by taxi to Bangar in Temburong, then take a boat to Bandar Seri Begawan (BSB). Clear Malaysian immigration in Lawas at the ferry wharf, and ask the driver to take you to the Brunei immigration office, a few kilometres the other side of Bangar, then bring you back to the Bangar wharf. All up this procedure takes about 40 minutes and the taxi should cost RM100. Boats leave regularly for BSB from Bangar until about 4.30 pm; the fare is B$7.

Boat All boats leave from the riverside wharf east of the town centre.

For Brunei, the only boat goes at 7 am daily and costs RM20. It returns at 12.30 pm.

One boat a day goes to Labuan at 7.30 am for RM20 – book at the Bee Hiong Restaurant (☎ 085-285137) underneath the Hotel Million. The boat to Limbang goes at 9 am and costs RM20. The trip takes 30 minutes.

MERAPOK

Merapok is a one-street hamlet in the middle of nowhere, but it does have a pool hall where you can pot a few balls while you wait for a bus. The Sabah/Sarawak border and police checkpoint is a few hundred metres out of town. There are immigration posts on both sides of the border and you must report to both. They close at 6 pm, but the police checkpoint will handle immigration formalities outside office hours.

Getting There & Away

Minibuses go to Lawas and Sipitang, though you may be in for a wait. You can also catch the Kota Kinabalu-Lawas bus on the highway. If you want to try hitching, traffic is regular but light.

Sabah

Sabah is Malaysia's second biggest state and northernmost province, and together with Sarawak makes up East Malaysia. But despite its closeness to Sarawak it shares little of its southern neighbour's tribal diversity and the two states probably have as many differences as similarities. Sabah's natural riches have drawn traders and raiders for centuries. Among its past masters have been Sulu sultans and foreign invaders, and it has seen its share of bloody conflict; Sabah's closeness to Indonesia and the Philippines ensures both nations claim parts of the state as their own. And with some justification it would seem, for Sabah and the Philippines have many cultural similarities; and unlike Sarawak it shares a strong Islamic tradition with Peninsular Malaysia.

Sabah's natural features attract travellers in search of a different sort of South-East Asian experience, and those with a taste for adventure will find that Sabah has just about got it all. There are beaches to lie on and fine coral reefs, but most visitors head straight for Mt Kinabalu, one of the highest mountain in South-East Asia and, as mountains go, pretty easy to climb. Among nature-lovers Sabah is legendary and the lush tropical forests have more than their fair share of unique wildlife. Easily accessible national parks and reserves ensure that some animals, such as the rare orang-utan, can be seen in their natural environment.

Budget travellers will generally find Sabah more expensive than Peninsular Malaysia, but if you stick to the beaten path it is possible to keep costs to a minimum. Most of the major attractions have inexpensive accommodation and cheap eats. On the other hand, mid-range travellers will generally find Sabah offers good value for money.

But if you're blasé or optimistic about the future of the world's natural resources, Sabah may be a sobering lesson. The dense rainforests that cloaked the land from coast to coast only a generation ago have largely

HIGHLIGHTS

- **Mt Kinabalu** – an improbably high granite peak that just begs to be climbed, surrounded by beautiful rainforest with gentle walking trails
- **Sepilok Orang-Utan Rehabilitation Centre** – one of only four in the world; the antics of these apes are not to be missed
- **Sungai Kinabatangan** – possibly the best wildlife-watching in South-East Asia: a great range of birds and mammals, including the proboscis monkey
- **Tunku Abdul Rahman National Park** – white-sand beaches, crystal-clear water and good snorkelling, all a short boat ride from Sabah's capital
- **Beaufort-Tenom Railway** – Sabah's only railway follows a narrow-gauge track that winds up a scenic mountain range; great views and lots of fun
- **Poring Hot Springs** – natural thermal pools turned into an outdoor spa; nature's remedy for weary bones after the conquest of Mt Kinabalu
- **Kota Belud Market** – traders, local farmers and horse-riding tribesmen wake up this quiet town every Sunday when they gather to haggle and barter
- **Turtle Islands National Park** – prehistoric sea turtles lumber ashore to lay their eggs on a remote tropical island
- **Pulau Sipadan** – superb diving and abundant sealife down the face of a 600m drop at this isolated coral-fringed island

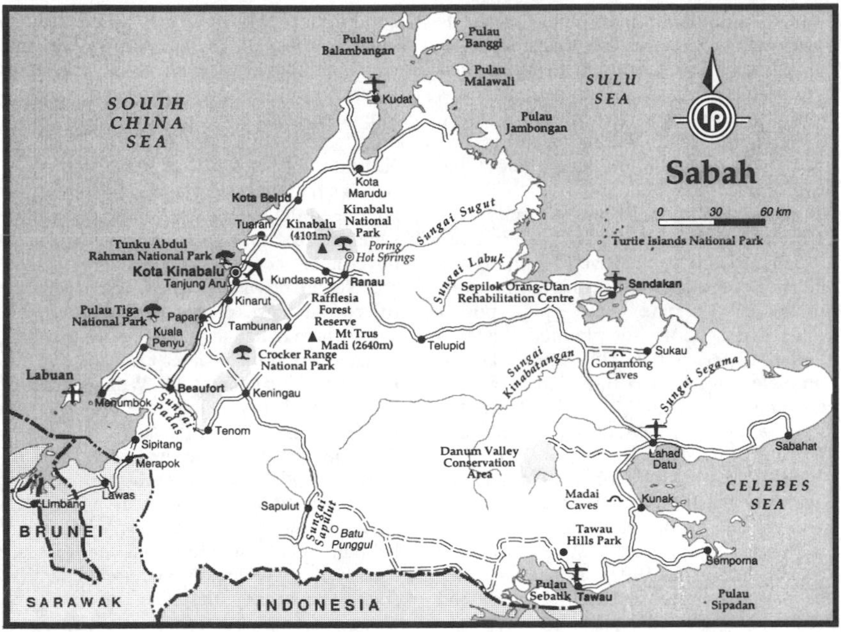

gone, felled for timber and thousands of square kilometres of plantations. See it now, because it's going fast.

History

Before Malaysia's independence Sabah was known as North Borneo and administered by the British North Borneo Company. After WWII both Sabah and Sarawak were handed over to the British government, and both decided to merge with the peninsular states to form the new nation of Malaysia in 1963.

But Sabah's natural wealth attracted other prospectors and its existence was disputed by two powerful neighbours – Indonesia and the Philippines. There are close cultural ties between the people of Sabah and the Filipinos of the nearby Sulu Archipelago and Mindanao. Several small islands to the north of Sabah are disputed by the Philippines and a busy smuggling trade operates from Sabah into Mindanao. Mindanao's Muslim rebels often retreat down towards Sabah when pursued by government forces and pirates based in the Sulu Sea continue to raid parts of Sabah's coast.

After independence, Sabah was governed for a time by Tun Mustapha, who ran the state almost as a private fiefdom and was often at odds with the central government in Kuala Lumpur. In 1967 he even threatened secession. He disappeared from view in 1975. In 1985 the Kadazan-controlled Sabah United Party (Parti Bersatu Sabah – PBS) came into power and joined the National Front Alliance.

However, tensions with the federal government were rife. In 1990 the PBS pulled out of the alliance with the National Front just days before general elections. The PBS claimed that the federal government was not equitably returning the wealth that the state generated and in 1993 it banned the export of logs from Sabah, largely to reinforce this point. The federal government used its powers to overturn the state decision.

Partly as a result of the state's bad relations with the federal government, Sabah is currently the poorest of Malaysia's states. Although it is rich in natural resources, one third of the population lives below the poverty line.

Today the National Front is back at the helm in Sabah. No sooner had it been elected into power than RM185 million was allocated for social and economic redevelopment of the state. New roads, power plants and schools are planned. Sabah's chief minister, Salleh Tun Said, plans to eliminate poverty and turn Sabah into an economic hub by 2000. A tall order, but if there's anywhere in Malaysia that needs a kick-start it's Sabah.

Poverty is still all too obvious in many of Sabah's towns and a recent economic downturn in the region has exacerbated the problem. To add to the state's woes, a drought during the 1997 wet season and a pall of smoke haze, caused by widespread burning, has affected local economies.

Visas & Permits

Sabah is semi-autonomous and, like Sarawak, has its own immigration controls. On arrival most nationalities are likely to be given a visa for two months' stay and it is rare to be asked to show money or onward tickets. Most visitors arrive at the capital, Kota Kinabalu, but it is possible to travel into Sabah overland from Sarawak; from Kalimantan (Indonesia) into Tawau in the state's south-east; by ferry from the Philippine city of Zamboanga to Sandakan; and even from Brunei. See the relevant sections for more details of these routes.

Visas can be renewed at immigration offices at or near most points of arrival, even at small places like Merapok near Beaufort. If you miss them it's not a problem – just report to another immigration office, even if it's several days later, and explain your situation to the officials.

Apart from entry to national parks and other reserves (see relevant sections for conditions), permits are required only to visit Danum Valley Conservation Area and two commercially sensitive cave systems where birds' nests are harvested, Gomantong and Madai.

National Parks & Other Reserves

Sabah's national parks and their inhabitants are one of the main reasons tourists visit the state. But the reserve system is not wholly government-controlled and many of the best reserves are privately owned. The experience offered at these places is first class, but everywhere in Sabah you'll feel the grasping tentacles of private enterprise and for this reason a visit can be costly. With a couple of exceptions, it is possible to travel independently so budget travellers can reduce costs. Accommodation in national parks was recently privatised so expect more price rises.

Sabah's national parks preserve some outstanding examples of scenery, wildlife and habitat. Accommodation and facilities are usually very good and if you are prepared to spend the money they can be excellent. Budget accommodation is available in or near the major reserves and if the weather is kind camping is possible in some.

A lot of effort goes into park maintenance and access, and you will be captivated by the astonishing variety of plant and animal life that in general is easy to see. Sabah's major parks include:

Crocker Range National Park (139 sq km)
Preserves a huge swathe of forested escarpment overlooking the east coast; no facilities yet.

Kinabalu National Park (754 sq km)
Easily accessible from Kota Kinabalu, this is the state's largest and most popular national park. It offers straightforward climbing at Mt Kinabalu and there's a thermal pool system at Poring Hot Springs. The park has very good facilities and accommodation.

Pulau Tiga National Park (15 sq km)
The park comprises three islands 50km southwest of Kota Kinabalu: one was formed by volcanic mud eruptions; one is famous for breeding sea snakes; and the third has been virtually washed away by wave action. The islands are difficult to get to but accommodation is available.

Tawau Hills Park (29 sq km)
Near Tawau in the state's south-east, this park has forested volcanic hills, waterfalls and hot springs. There's basic accommodation and facilities, but access is difficult.

Tunku Abdul Rahman National Park (4929 hectares)
A group of five islands, one quite large, a few kilometres west of the capital. Features include beaches, snorkelling, diving and hiking. There's good accommodation on one island.

Turtle Islands National Park (1740 hectares)
This national park comprises three tiny islands 40km north of Sandakan that protect the nesting ground of green and hawksbill sea turtles. There's accommodation on one of the islands.

Two cave systems – Gomantong and Madai – are administered by the Wildlife Department and can be visited; non-government reserves include Danum Valley Conservation Area and Sepilok Orang-Utan Rehabilitation Centre; and huge nature reserves have been set up (with no visitors' facilities) for the preservation of rare animals such as the Sumatran rhino. Negotiations were under way at the time of writing to preserve a large tract of orang-utan habitat near Sandakan.

General Costs

Compared to most of the region, Sabah is an expensive place to travel around. Only at a few places, such as Kota Kinabalu (KK), Sepilok, Mt Kinabalu and Poring Hot Springs, will you find accommodation that could be classed as 'budget'. Be prepared to fork out at least RM20 per night – and often much more – for a place to sleep.

Many of the cheaper places to stay are used for prostitution – which doesn't mean you can't stay there, only that they tend to be seedy and probably aren't secure. This inevitably pushes the budget traveller up the price scale to mid-range accommodation. Top-end accommodation attracts a 10% service charge and 5% government tax. At some places, such as Danum Valley and Pulau Sipadan, you'll have no choice but to pay through the nose for accommodation.

Sabah also has a number of government resthouses, which are normally reserved for government officials and their families. However, if one is not full, travellers are *sometimes* permitted to stay. At RM40 per person per night, they are a reasonable mid-range option. Bookings are made through the district officer of the appropriate town and there are listings in the government pages of the telephone directory. There are resthouses in Keningau, Kota Belud, Kota Marudu, Kuala Penyu, Kudat, Kunak, Lahad Datu, Papar, Ranau, Semporna, Sipitang, Tambunan and Tenom.

Getting Around

Road Sabah has an excellent road system and almost all the major roads are sealed, including the highway from KK to Sandakan and Tawau. Notable exceptions are the 47km stretch between Beaufort and Sipitang in the south – a real kidney-bruiser – and between Kota Belud and Ranau in the north. However, subsidence and washouts frequently put stretches of highway under repair and can slow down a trip considerably. And although it's sometimes marked on maps, the route from Tawau to Keningau is an unsealed logging road and little used by travellers.

Air-conditioned express buses run between KK and most major centres, including Mt Kinabalu. These are relatively punctual and usually cost only a few ringgit more than minibuses. Minibuses are quick and efficient but don't have air-con, so unless you particularly enjoy being squashed into a minibus, express buses are the best way to get around Sabah.

There are frequent departures of express buses and minibuses from most centres until around noon; afternoon departures can be scarce on the longer runs. See individual sections for more information.

Hitchhiking is possible in Sabah, although traffic is usually light. In this chapter we've indicated where hitching is feasible. However, hitching is never entirely safe and travellers who decide to hitch should understand that they are taking a small but potentially serious risk. People who do choose to hitch will be safer if they travel in pairs and let someone know where they are planning to go.

Train There is a railway between KK and Tenom. For details, see the Tenom-Beaufort Railway section and Getting There & Away in the Kota Kinabalu, Tenom and Beaufort sections.

Kota Kinabalu

Sabah's capital, Kota Kinabalu, sits on the edge of the South China Sea overlooking a cluster of coral-fringed islands. With the towering Crocker Range as a backdrop and the granite peaks of mighty Mt Kinabalu in the far distance, it's a shame the town planners didn't take advantage of the city's natural attributes: KK, as everyone calls it, is a functional sort of place with wide avenues flanked by office blocks, hotels and charmless shopping malls.

Part of the blame for this goes back to WWII when Jesselton, as it was then known, was razed by the retreating British in order to prevent the Japanese using it as a base for operations.

Just three years later Jesselton was again flattened, this time by Allied bombing as the Japanese were pushed out of Borneo. The city was rebuilt from scratch and renamed Kota Kinabalu in 1963.

One of Asia's fastest growing cities, with a population of around 200,000, KK is an interesting blend of European, Malay and Chinese culture. A recent influx of Filipino migrants has added another flavour to the cultural gumbo. It has little of the laid-back atmosphere of Sarawak's big towns and poverty is all too obvious in places, but despite appearances it's safe to walk around.

It's worth spending a few days in KK to sample the excellent restaurants – something which is sadly lacking elsewhere in Sabah – and to visit the islands offshore, where there are beaches and good snorkelling. In any case, you'll have to go to KK to book accommodation for the trip to Mt Kinabalu, Sabah's number one attraction.

EAST MALAYSIA

Orientation

KK sprawls for many kilometres along the coast from the international airport at Tanjung Aru north to the bayside suburb of Likas. Most places to stay and eat, banks, tourist offices, travel agents, the main post office and transport centres lie in a built-up grid of just a few blocks between the waterfront and a range of low forested hills to the east. The booking office for Mt Kinabalu, major airline offices and a few other administrative offices are just south of the centre.

There is no single bus station in town, although one has been on the drawing board for some time. Rather, there are three areas in central KK where you can find the bus you want – see Getting There & Away. Taxis can be found all over town, but seem to congregate in the area between the main post office and the council offices. Ferries leave for Tunku Abdul Rahman National Park, Labuan and Brunei from the waterfront behind the Hyatt Kinabalu.

The main road changes name four times between the south end of town and the north, which is confusing when you're trying to find an address. At the southern end it's called Jalan Lebuh Raya Pantai Baru, then Jalan Pasar Baru, Jalan Tun Razak and Jalan Haji Saman. KK's main shopping complexes line the main drag. On the west side of Jalan Tun Razak are two sprawling, grid-like blocks of dilapidated two or three-storey shophouses – Kompleks Segama and Kompleks Sinsuran. Between Jalan Haji Saman and the waterfront there's the newer Wisma Merdeka and at the opposite end, on the way to the airport, you'll find the huge Centre Point and Api-Api Centres. Opposite Api-Api Centre there's Asia City, a concrete maze with some fine restaurants.

Luxury hotels and shopping complexes are being thrown up at an astonishing rate. There's an undeveloped landfill on the north edge of the city, and between town and the airport a massive reclamation project will become Sutera Harbour, a luxury development with marina, resorts and golf course so modern and beautiful it will leave you breathless. So the ads say, anyway.

DAVID ANDREW

SIMON ROWE

GLENN BEANLAND

TOURISM MALAYSIA

SIMON ROWE

SIMON ROWE

Sarawak
Top: Stilt village, Santubong Peninsula (left); palm frond, Bako National Park (right).
Centre Left: A plank walk through the jungle leads to Niah Caves.
Centre Right: Traditional Iban culture lives on in Sarawak.
Bottom Left & Right: The coastal cliffs and furrowed sand of Bako National Park.

TOURISM MALAYSIA

SIMON ROWE

GLENN BEANLAND

SIMON ROWE

MICHAEL AW

Sabah
Top: Borneo's 'man of the jungle', the orang-utan (left); arrivals in Kota Kinabalu (right).
Centre Right: Tunku Abdul Rahman National Park.
Bottom Left: Sharks' fins are sought after by restaurateurs for the famous sharks' fin soup.
Bottom Right: Close encounter with a hawksbill turtle at Turtle Islands National Park.

Information

Tourist Offices Kota Kinabalu has two excellent tourist offices. Tourism Malaysia (☎ 088-211732) is on the ground floor of the Wing Onn Life building on the corner of Jalan Gaya and Jalan Dua, at the northern end of the city centre. The staff here are knowledgeable and helpful, and it is open from Monday to Friday from 8 am to 12.45 pm and 2 to 4.15 pm, and on Saturday from 8 am to 12.45 pm.

The Sabah Tourism Promotion Corporation (STPC; ☎ 088-218620), 51 Jalan Gaya, is housed in the historic post office building and is open Monday to Friday from 8 am to 4.15 pm, and on Saturday from 8 am to 12.45 pm. Staff can answer most queries and hand out informative brochures on Sabah's tourist attractions. There's also a shop selling a few handicrafts, maps and books. The STPC also has an office on Level 1 of the airport building.

National Park & Conservation Area Bookings Accommodation in Mt Kinabalu (including Poring Hot Springs) and Tunku Abdul Rahman national parks was recently privatised. Bookings are now handled by Kinabalu Gold Resorts (☎ 088-243629), 3rd floor, Block C, Kompleks Karamunsing. Opening hours are Monday to Friday from 8 am to 5 pm and Saturday from 8 am to 2 pm.

Kompleks Karamunsing is south of the city centre, about five minutes walk along Jalan Tunku Abdul Rahman past the Hotel Shangri-La then off to the left.

Mt Kinabalu is a very popular place with both overseas visitors and locals, and accommodation at the park HQ is often booked up a week in advance. The further ahead you make reservations, the better chance you have of being able to go when you want to.

The Sabah Parks office (☎ 088-211585) is at Block K, Kompleks Sinsuran, Jalan Tun Fuad Stephens. This office now handles reservations for accommodation only at Pulau Tiga National Park. Opening hours are Monday to Thursday from 8.30 am to 4 pm, Friday from 8.30 to 11.30 am and 2 to 4 pm, and Saturday from 8.30 am to noon.

Bookings for the Borneo Rainforest Lodge at Danum Valley can be made at the Innoprise Jungle Lodge office (☎ 088-243245), in the Kompleks Sadong Jaya, opposite the KWSP building. Bookings can also be made at the office in Lahad Datu.

Foreign Consulates The Indonesian consulate (☎ 088-219110) is south of the city centre off Jalan Kemajuan. Visas can be issued here without fuss on the day of application. There is also a consulate in Tawau (☎ 089-772052) if you are heading to Kalimantan via Tarakan. In Wisma Yakim there is a Japanese consulate (☎ 088-254695) on the 5th floor and an Australian consulate (☎ 088-236569) on the 10th floor.

Immigration The immigration office (☎ 088-280772) is on the 4th floor of Wisma Dana Bandang, the tall building near Jalan Tunku Abdul Rahman. It's open Monday to Friday from 8 am to 12.45 pm and 2 to 4.15 pm (closing at 11.30 for lunch on Friday); and Saturday from 8 am to 12.45 pm.

Money Most major banks have branches at the north end of town, where you'll find Hongkong Bank and Standard Chartered. Standard Chartered offers the best exchange rates, but takes a hefty commission of RM20 per transaction. Sabah Bank is next to the Sabah Parks office if you're staying in the Sinsuran Kompleks, and there are plenty of other banks around the town centre. You'll find moneychangers on the ground floor of Centre Point and Wisma Merdeka.

Post The main post office is in the centre of town and has an efficient poste restante counter. Opening hours are 8 am to 5 pm Monday to Saturday. Parcels are weighed and sent from the open-air offices to the left of the main entrance.

Telephone For international calls, most public phone booths are Uniphone but if you have a Telekom card you can use the Telekom booths near the post office and at the Telekom office on Jalan Tunku Abdul

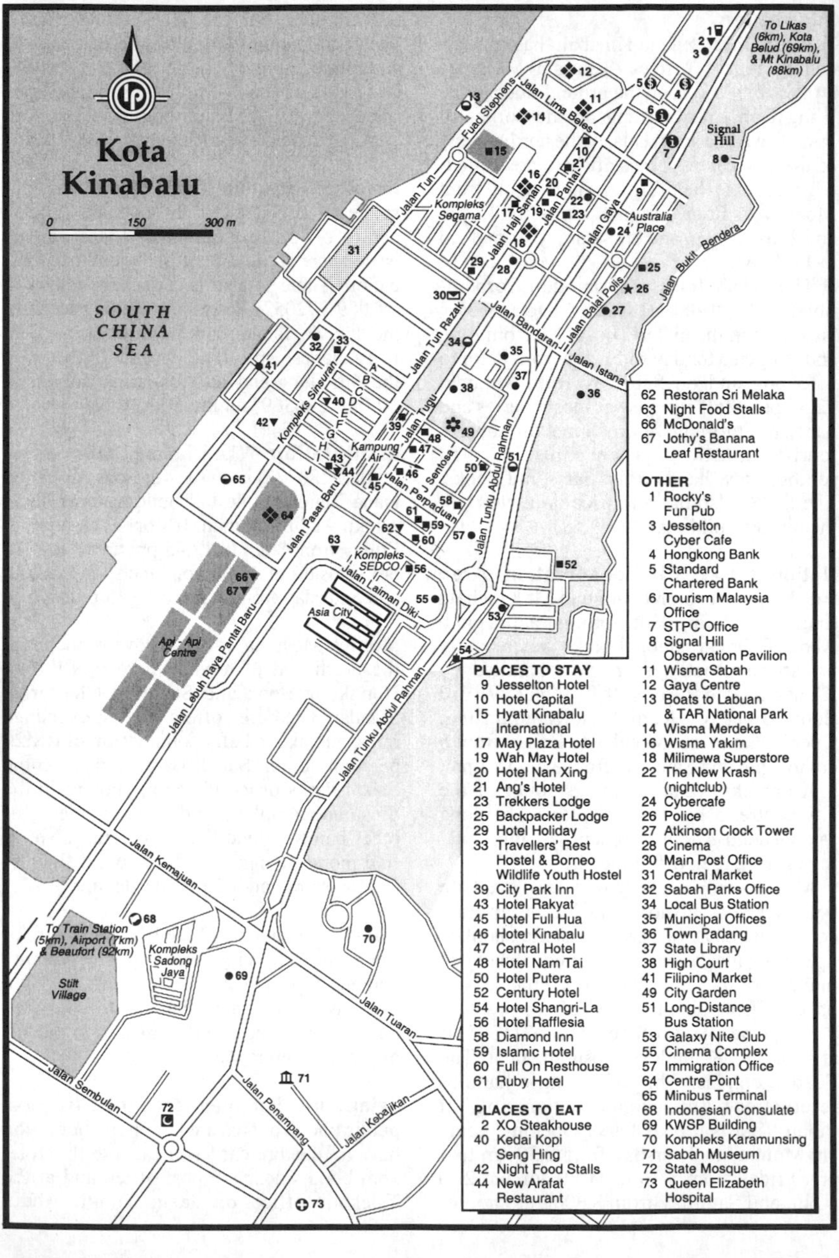

Kota Kinabalu
0
150
300 m
SOUTH CHINA SEA
To Likas (6km), Kota Belud (69km), & Mt Kinabalu (88km)
Signal Hill
To Train Station (5km), Airport (7km) & Beaufort (92km)
Jalan Tun Fuad Stephens
Jalan Lima Belas
Jalan Haji Saman
Jalan Pantai
Jalan Gaya
Australia Place
Jalan Bukit Bendera
Jalan Balai Polis
Jalan Bandaran
Jalan Istana
Jalan Tun Razak
Kompleks Segama
Kompleks Sinsuran
Jalan Tugu
Kampung Air
J Sentosa
Jalan Perpaduan
Jalan Pasar Baru
Jalan Tunku Abdul Rahman
Kompleks SEDCO
Jalan Laiman Diki
Asia City
Api - Api Centre
Jalan Lebuh Raya Pantai Baru
Jalan Kemajuan
Kompleks Sadong Jaya
Stilt Village
Jalan Tuaran
Jalan Sembulan
Jalan Penampang
Jalan Kebajikan
PLACES TO STAY
9 Jesselton Hotel
10 Hotel Capital
15 Hyatt Kinabalu International
17 May Plaza Hotel
19 Wah May Hotel
20 Hotel Nan Xing
21 Ang's Hotel
23 Trekkers Lodge
25 Backpacker Lodge
29 Hotel Holiday
33 Travellers' Rest Hostel & Borneo Wildlife Youth Hostel
39 City Park Inn
43 Hotel Rakyat
45 Hotel Full Hua
46 Hotel Kinabalu
47 Central Hotel
48 Hotel Nam Tai
50 Hotel Putera
52 Century Hotel
54 Hotel Shangri-La
56 Hotel Rafflesia
58 Diamond Inn
59 Islamic Hotel
60 Full On Resthouse
61 Ruby Hotel
PLACES TO EAT
2 XO Steakhouse
40 Kedai Kopi Seng Hing
42 Night Food Stalls
44 New Arafat Restaurant
62 Restoran Sri Melaka
63 Night Food Stalls
66 McDonald's
67 Jothy's Banana Leaf Restaurant
OTHER
1 Rocky's Fun Pub
3 Jesselton Cyber Cafe
4 Hongkong Bank
5 Standard Chartered Bank
6 Tourism Malaysia Office
7 STPC Office
8 Signal Hill Observation Pavilion
11 Wisma Sabah
12 Gaya Centre
13 Boats to Labuan & TAR National Park
14 Wisma Merdeka
16 Wisma Yakim
18 Milimewa Superstore
22 The New Krash (nightclub)
24 Cybercafe
26 Police
27 Atkinson Clock Tower
28 Cinema
30 Main Post Office
31 Central Market
32 Sabah Parks Office
34 Local Bus Station
35 Municipal Offices
36 Town Padang
37 State Library
38 High Court
41 Filipino Market
49 City Garden
51 Long-Distance Bus Station
53 Galaxy Nite Club
55 Cinema Complex
57 Immigration Office
64 Centre Point
65 Minibus Terminal
68 Indonesian Consulate
69 KWSP Building
70 Kompleks Karamunsing
71 Sabah Museum
72 State Mosque
73 Queen Elizabeth Hospital

EAST MALAYSIA

Rahman, a 10 minute walk south of the town centre, where there are also international telephone booths.

Email & Internet Access There are two cyber cafes in central KK and Net Card booths at the airport.

Cybercafe
(netgate@pop3.jaring.my/www.sabahnet.om.my/cybercafe), 95 Jalan Gaya; open Monday to Friday from 1.30 pm to midnight, and Saturday and Sunday from 9.30 am to midnight. Basic rates are RM15 per hour, but they have special deals for members and gimmicks such as ladies' nights.

Jesselton Cyber Cafe
(cybercafe@mail.sabahnet.com.my), 1st floor, 52 Jalan Gaya; open Monday to Saturday from 11 am to 11 pm, and Sunday from 2 to 11 pm. Costs are RM10/12 for students/workers, less if you become a member.

Travel Agencies There are dozens of travel agencies scattered around KK that can help with airline bookings, ticketing and confirmations. Cometra Travel (☎ 088-225368), ground floor, Wisma Yakim, is in a handy location on the main street.

There's a host of tour operators offering expensive trips to Mt Kinabalu, Kota Belud, Sepilok and other places that are easy to get to, but you might consider using one for scuba diving or an upmarket tour to the Sungai Kinabatangan or Danum Valley. Ask about tours at budget places to stay – they can often put you onto a cheap operator.

Api Tours
(☎ 088-221233) Wisma Sabah; organises white-water rafting on the Sungai Padas and trekking

Borneo Divers & Sea Sports
(☎ 088-222226) 4th floor, Wisma Sabah; the longest-established Borneo dive outfit, it can arrange courses and dives just about anywhere and has accommodation on Pulau Sipadan

Borneo Eco Tours
(☎ 088-234005) 6J Sadong Jaya; offers 'adventure' tours and jungle trekking

Borneo Sea Adventures
(☎ 088-218216) 1st floor, 8A Karamunsing Warehouse; another dive company that has accommodation on Sipadan

Borneo Wildlife Adventure
(☎ 088-213668) Lot 4, Block L, Kompleks Sinsuran; arranges tailor-made adventure and educational tours; also runs Borneo Wildlife Youth Hostel (see Places to Stay)

Discovery Tours
(☎ 088-221244) Ground floor, Wisma Sabah; offers rafting trips on the Kiulu and Padas rivers, and day tours around KK

Popeye Tours & Travel
(☎ 088-218669) 2nd floor, Block N, Kompleks Sinsuran; can organise trips to Pulau Tiga

Seaventures Tours & Travel
(☎ 088-251669) 4th floor, Wisma Sabah; offers diving instruction and trips around KK, and big game fishing further afield. Seaventures also has a dive shop on the ground floor of Wisma Sabah.

Travellers' Rest Hostel
(☎ 088-224720) 3rd floor, Block L, Kompleks Sinsuran; offers white-water rafting trips at competitive prices. A day trip, which involves taking the Tenom train part of the way and then rafting back along the river, costs around RM180; with travel and preparation time normally this leaves two to three hours of rafting.

Wildlife Expeditions
(☎ 088-246000) ground floor, Tanjung Aru Resort; arranges trips to the Sungai Kinabatangan and Danum Valley

See the Pulau Sipadan section for a list of operators with accommodation on the island.

Bookshops & Libraries The best selections of books on Sabah and Borneo are at Iwase Bookshop and Borneo Craft, both on the ground floor of Wisma Merdeka. Other reasonable shops worth a look are the Arena Book Centre, in Block L of the Kompleks Sinsuran, and the Penguins Bookstore in the Api-Api Centre, which stocks general fiction and non-fiction books, as well as the *Borneo* magazine.

The State Library, on Jalan Tunku Abdul Rahman, is open to the public from 9 am daily, closing at 9 pm from Monday to Friday, 5 pm on Saturday and at 1 pm on Sunday.

The British Council Library (☎ 088-248055) is on the 2nd floor of the Wing Onn Life building at the northern end of the city, above the Tourism Malaysia office.

Film & Photography There are photo processing labs all over the town centre and in the shopping malls. Fuji is the most popular brand of film on sale, followed by Konica, but only print film is widely available – if you have particular film requirements you should buy them before you get to KK.

Laundry There are branches of Laundry Mart on the ground floor of Block A, Kompleks Segama, and in Centre Point.

Medical Services The Queen Elizabeth Hospital (☎ 088-218166) is on Jalan Penampang, past the Sabah Museum. Dial ☎ 999 in emergencies.

Klinik Dr Suzain (☎ 088-223185), ground floor, Wisma Yakim, is a women's clinic open every day except public holidays. Hours are Monday to Friday from 8.30 am to 12.30 pm and 2 to 9 pm (closing an hour earlier for lunch on Friday); Saturday from 8.30 am to noon and 2 to 4.30 pm; and Sunday from 9 am to noon.

Sabah Museum & Science Centre

The Sabah Museum is a modern four storey structure inspired by the longhouses of the Rungus and Murut tribes. It's a little south of the town centre, on a hill at the corner of Jalan Tunku Abdul Rahman and Jalan Penampang. The museum and gardens are definitely worth a visit, the adjoining science centre and art gallery less so.

Inside are good collections of tribal and historical artefacts, including ceramics; nicely presented exhibits of flora and fauna with a display of Sabah's spectacular butterflies and other insects; and the 'time tunnel', an absorbing walk which traces the history of KK with artefacts, old photos, costumes and weaponry. The top floor is devoted to Muslim culture and history, but it's pretty dull stuff compared to the excellent Muslim displays in Kuching and Brunei. From here you can get onto the roof for good views across to the state mosque.

The Science Centre & Art Gallery is next to the main building. Displays change periodically, but include demonstrations and exhibitions of the latest in computer technology and telecommunications. On the 1st floor there's an art gallery where the work of local artists is displayed. It's not terribly well organised and there's next to no biographical information, but some of the paintings and sculptures are quite good.

The museum building is surrounded by historic cars and locomotives, boats and ordnance. It's worth strolling around the grounds, where there are fern and orchid gardens; the **Sabah Plant Heritage Centre**, which has interesting exhibits on the medicinal value of native flora; an **Ethnobotanic Garden**, with cheesy replicas of tribal longhouses and other dwellings around an artificial lake; and caged animals being terrified by school children.

There's a restaurant with views over the gardens and out to Mt Kinabalu on a clear day and the museum has a good souvenir shop on the ground floor.

The museum, science centre and art gallery are all open Monday to Thursday from 10 am to 4.30 pm (closed Friday); and weekends and public holidays from 9.30 am to 5 pm. Entry is free.

To get there, catch a bus along Jalan Tunku Abdul Rahman for 50 sen and get off just before the mosque.

State Mosque

This fine example of contemporary Islamic architecture makes a tranquil sanctuary from the heat and noise of downtown KK and is well worth a visit. It's south of the town centre past Kampung Air (see Other Attractions) and you'll see it on your way to or from the airport.

The mosque can accommodate 5000 male worshippers and has a balcony where there's room for 500 women to pray. Non-Muslim visitors are allowed inside, but must remove shoes before entering and dress appropriately, ie bare legs and shoulders are forbidden. Never walk in front of someone praying and non-Muslims are not allowed to touch the Koran.

To reach the mosque take a bus along Jalan Tunku Abdul Rahman.

Atkinson Clock Tower

This minor attraction has the dubious distinction of being one of the only structures to survive the Allied bombing of Jesselton in 1945. It's a square, 15.7m-high wooden clock tower that was completed in 1905 and named after the first district officer of the town, FG Atkinson, a high achiever who died of malaria aged 28.

The clock tower stands on a low hill near the main police station on Jalan Balai Polis, close to the city centre.

Markets

The market is in two sections – the waterfront area for fish and an area in front of the harbour for fruit and vegetables. The area next to the main market on the waterfront is known as the Filipino Market; not surprisingly, all the stalls are owned by Filipinos and they sell a wide variety of handicrafts made in the Philippines.

A night market fills up Jalan Sentosa and adjoining streets on some nights, although it's geared mainly to locals and most stalls sell clothing. On Sunday morning a street market sets up along Jalan Gaya and spills onto side streets.

Other Attractions

Kota Kinabalu has its own **stilt village** just south of the city centre. Once an extensive settlement stretching south along the shore, all that remains is a small collection of rickety dwellings cut off from the sea by a massive land reclamation scheme. It's a picturesque sight in the evening and can be visited on the way to the state mosque.

To get to Kampung Air walk down Jalan Pasar Baru for about 1km past Centre Point; the village is on your left.

Take a stroll to the observation pavilion on **Signal Hill**, at the eastern edge of the city centre, to escape the noise and traffic. The view is best as the sun sets over the islands of Tunku Abdul Rahman National Park. To get there, take the path off Jalan Tunku Abdul Rahman to the clock tower then follow the gentle slope left along Jalan Bukit Bendera.

Places to Stay – Budget

Along with the Sepilok Orang-Utan Rehabilitation Centre near Sandakan, KK has the best range of backpackers' accommodation in Sabah – if not the whole of Borneo.

The super clean and friendly *Backpacker Lodge* (☎ 088-261495) at Australia Place has beds in segregated dorms for RM18 including breakfast; there's also a double room if you want privacy. There are laundry facilities and tour information, and it's well positioned for places to eat and transport.

Another bright and spotless place is the *Trekkers Lodge* (☎ 088-213888), at 46 Jalan Pantai (enter from the lane at the back). Air-con dorm beds are RM20 and there's a double room for RM45; prices include breakfast. This friendly, helpful place has laundry facilities, a small library and travel information.

City Park Inn (☎ 088-260607), 2 Jalan Pasar Baru, is a combined backpackers' dorm and mid-range hotel. It's very clean and centrally located. Dorm beds are RM20 including linen and pillows, and air-con singles/doubles are RM52/60.

There are two cheap options in the Kompleks Sinsuran, near the Filipino Market. The *Travellers' Rest Hostel* (☎ 088-224720), on the 3rd floor in Block L, is a long-standing budget travellers' hang-out, but it has seen better days. Still, at RM13 including breakfast the dorm beds are good value. Also available are rooms with fan for RM20/25 a single/double, and air-con rooms for RM36/40 for singles/doubles, or RM45 with bathroom. The hostel also has laundry facilities and a travel service that provides inexpensive tours to destinations around Sabah.

Next door, the *Borneo Wildlife Youth Hostel* (☎ 088-213668) has basic but clean dorm rooms at RM15 per bed for HI members and RM20 for others. Other than toilet and shower, the only facilities are a TV, kettle and fridge.

Farida's Bed & Breakfast (☎ 088-428733), 413 Jalan Saga, Likas, is a delightful place set in quiet suburbia 6km north of town. Although it's a long way from the centre, it knows just what backpackers want and can arrange transport and tours to sights around KK. Dorm beds are RM16 per person and double fan or air-con rooms cost RM25 (RM18 for a bed only if you don't want to sleep in the dorm). To get there, take any minibus that goes along Jalan Tuaran and get off at the Likas Baptist church. Walk 100m down Jalan Likas and then turn right into Jalan Saga – Farida's is 200m on the left.

The travellers' hostels provide better value for money than KK's budget hotels, many of which tend to be noisy and a bit seedy. Some mid-range hotels have cheaper fan-cooled rooms on the higher floors – it's worth asking.

Two options near the long-distance bus station are the *Islamic Hotel*, 8 Jalan Perpaduan (above the restaurant of the same name), where fan-cooled rooms with shared bathroom cost RM27; and *Hotel Putera* (☎ 088-252814), on Jalan Merdeka near the corner of Jalan Tunku Abdul Rahman, a basic Chinese hotel with large single/double rooms for RM20/25 with fan, or RM35 to RM45 for a double with air-con.

For a little more money, the *Hotel Rakyat* (☎ 088-222715), in Block I of the Kompleks Sinsuran, is very good value. Rooms in this clean, friendly, Muslim-run hotel cost RM37 with fan and bathroom, and from RM40 to RM55 with air-con and bathroom. It's central and handy for cheap eating.

If the above are full, the *Central Hotel* (☎ 088-513522), 5 Jalan Tugu, has air-con rooms with attached bathroom for RM40/48. Nearby on Jalan Merdeka, you'll find the *Hotel Nam Tai* (☎ 088-514803). It's fairly clean and has double rooms from RM35 to RM45.

Places to Stay – Mid-Range

Kota Kinabalu has dozens of mid-range hotels, though a room that would cost RM40 elsewhere in Malaysia costs RM60 and upwards in KK. All are carpeted with air-con, IDD phones and TV; extras may include a minibar and a bath.

The *Full On Resthouse* (☎ 088-219321), 10 Jalan Perpaduan (down the alley adjacent to the Islamic Hotel), has reasonable air-con rooms for RM42 with shared bathroom; rooms with private bathrooms are RM48/54 with no window and RM54/58 with a window. It's a clean but tatty option.

The well organised *Hotel Kinabalu* (☎ 088-245599), 21 Jalan Tugu, has pleasant singles/doubles starting at RM60/67. The *Hotel Full Hua* (☎ 088-234950), 14 Jalan Tugu, is a friendly place with big rooms that cost RM68 and up to RM88 for a king-sized room. These two places offer some of the best mid-range value in this part of town.

The *Diamond Inn* (☎ 088-261222), Jalan Haji Yakub, has big but worn rooms at RM60 for a standard single or comfortable doubles for RM65 to RM75. The *Ruby Hotel* (☎ 088-213222), Jalan Laiman Diki, is part of the same chain and has spacious rooms with a fridge ranging from RM70 for a standard to RM80/95 for singles/doubles.

Hotel Rafflesia (☎ 088-239635), Block B, SEDCO Complex, is a big musty dump where singles/doubles cost RM60/70. There is plenty of choice nearby.

Heading up Jalan Tun Razak, the *Hotel Holiday* (☎ 088-213116) is upstairs in Block F of the Kompleks Segama. It's in a very central location next to the main post office, but the rooms are nothing special at RM66 to RM105; those on the upper floors are more expensive but probably quieter.

Further north again, the *May Plaza Hotel* (☎ 088-215418), Block A, Kompleks Segama, sits above a shop selling a great range of chinoiserie. Spacious but faded rooms are quite good value at RM60/75, but those overlooking the street are a bit noisy.

There are three good mid-range places almost side by side at the top end of Jalan Haji Saman. The *Wah May Hotel* (☎ 088-266118), at No 36, is a well run and popular hotel with single rooms from RM71 to singles/doubles at RM76/85 and upwards for bigger rooms. If it's full, the *Hotel Nan Xing* (☎ 088-239388) next door has slightly cheaper rooms starting at RM69/75. Nearby, *Ang's Hotel* (☎ 088-234999) is cheaper still and better value at RM49/57 up to RM65/74, although its rooms are starting to look a bit worn.

Places to Stay – Top End

Among the seemingly endless redevelopment of KK are some massive new luxury hotels offering all the trappings of the leading hotels in Singapore and Kuala Lumpur. Competition is fierce, and promotional discounts are often to be had for the asking. Remember to add 10% service charge and 5% tax to all top-end prices.

The *Century Hotel* (☎ 088-242222), 12 Jalan Masjid Lama, has good singles/doubles for RM115/138, but it's in a grotty part of town. Nearby, the three star *Hotel Shangri-La* (☎ 088-212800), 75 Bandaran Berjaya, is a notch up in quality, with rooms from RM185/215. You'll recognise this one by the Rolls-Royces parked out the front.

The *Hotel Capital* (☎ 088-231999), 23 Jalan Haji Saman, is a more upmarket option at the north end of town. Rooms start at RM160/170 for standard singles/doubles and the nicer ones look out over the bay.

The four star *Jesselton Hotel* (☎ 088-223333), 69 Jalan Gaya, is the oldest of KK's many hotels and probably the most pleasant. Its 33 rooms are tastefully fitted in mock colonial wood and marble, and the doorman wears a pith helmet. Rates start at RM280 for a standard, RM340 for a superior and RM750 for a suite. There's a good restaurant, coffee shop and piano bar.

Under pressure from the new luxury hotels in town, the *Hyatt Kinabalu International* (☎ 088-221234), Jalan Datuk Salleh Sulong, was undergoing a facelift at the time of writing. It's in a perfect location opposite the waterfront and has a swimming pool, restaurants and business facilities. Standard rooms are RM340, although discounts on rooms without a sea view are possible.

If you have no reason to stay in the town centre, it's worth considering the *Shangri-La Tanjung Aru Resort* (☎ 088-225800), on the beach at Tanjung Aru near the airport. It has an impressive array of facilities, and rates from RM360/395 for singles/doubles.

Places to Eat

For the variety of restaurants and quality of food, KK ranks with Kuching as the best city in Borneo. There are Chinese *kedai kopi* and Malaysian *Muslim restorans* scattered everywhere, but particularly in the Segama and Sinsuran complexes, Asia City and opposite the long-distance bus station. Other choices include fine seafood, Indian, Japanese and western restaurants in the centre of town.

Food Stalls The best night market in town is at the *SEDCO Complex*. The speciality is seafood, but other dishes are also available. The stall owners have an uncanny instinct for the arrival of rain and can have the whole area covered in minutes. Hawkers set up around the *Filipino Market* at night and in the vacant lot near Asia City on Jalan Pasar Baru. The top floor of the *central market* also has good food stalls.

KK's shopping malls are good foraging grounds for cheap fare. The basement of *Centre Point* has a collection of moderately priced eating places serving Malay and Chinese food. On the 2nd floor of the *Yaohan department store* there are some slightly more expensive food stalls in squeaky-clean air-con surroundings; and *Wisma Merdeka* has a small but good food centre on the 2nd floor overlooking the sea.

Chinese The *kedai kopi* under Ang's Hotel is a popular spot, as is the one opposite the Jesselton on Jalan Gaya. *Kedai Kopi Seng Hing*, in Block E of the Kompleks Sinsuran, is an unremarkable Chinese cafe which serves remarkable prawn mee soup at lunchtime – recommended. Dim-sum breakfasts can be enjoyed on weekends at the air-con restaurant downstairs at the *Hotel Nan Xing*.

Indian For cheap Indian food, try the *New Arafat Restaurant* in Block I of the Kompleks Sinsuran. This 24-hour place is run by very friendly Indians and serves good curries, rotis and murtabaks. This and other Indian places in Sinsuran get crowded with people watching loud videos in the evenings.

For fine Indian cooking look no further than *Restoran Ranasahib*, in Block G of Asia City. There is a large range of vindaloos, masalas and tandoori, and if you have a favourite that's not on the menu, just ask and they might be able to whip it up. The mango lassi is a classic – leave room for one or two.

Jothy's Banana Leaf Restaurant, Api-Api Centre, is a cheap, air-con restaurant with a good range, including curries and rotis, served on a banana leaf.

Malay Cheap 24 hour *Muslim restaurants* opposite the long-distance bus station on Jalan Tunku Abdul Rahman serve rotis and murtabaks that make ideal snacks before you hop on a bus. Tell the bus touts where you are and they'll come and get you when it's time to leave.

Don't be put off by the smoked glass windows and credit-card signs at the *Restoran Sri Melaka*, 9 Jalan Laiman Diki. It has excellent local dishes for around RM6 to RM8.

Air-con restaurants in upmarket hotels serve more expensive (but good), Malay fare as well as western favourites. The *Tivoli Restaurant* in the Hotel Shangri-La has a good evening Malay buffet.

International For something a little upmarket, the *XO Steakhouse*, at 54 Jalan Gaya, serves 'air-chilled' steaks flown in from Australia and the USA, and the three course set lunch is good value at RM16.50.

The best – and probably the most expensive – western food in town is at the *Gardenia* in the Jesselton Hotel. The diverse menu includes good beef cuts and fresh fish; if this place has a fault it's that the dessert list is a bit short.

Bistretto is a clean, bright place on the ground floor of the Kompleks Karamunsing with an Italian theme. The selection includes delicious toasted sandwiches, soups, pastas and savoury pancakes, which can be followed by excellent milk shakes, ice cream and sundaes.

Among the good hotel restaurants that serve fish and chips, burgers and other favourites are the *Wishbone Cafe & Restaurant* in the Jesselton, and the *Sri Kapitol Coffee House* in the Hotel Capital.

Fast Food If you need to 'access American food' KK offers a huge choice of all the favourites: there's a *McDonald's* at the Api-Api Centre, which also has a *Jollibee* and a *Singapore Chicken Rice*; Centre Point's basement has *SugarBun* and *Pizza Hut*; there's another SugarBun and Pizza Hut near the Milimewa Superstore; the Kompleks Karamunsing has a *Kenny Rogers Roasters*; and as for *KFC*, well you'll see the Colonel's smiling face mos' everywhere.

Other Food The restaurants and coffee shops at the Jesselton, Capital and Hyatt hotels do the best western-style breakfasts. The Hyatt starts earliest, at 6 am.

Tam Nak Thai is a good if pricey Thai restaurant with all the classic dishes. It's at the southern end of the Api-Api Centre and is open for lunch and dinner.

For expensive but good Japanese food, try the *Nagisa* in the Hyatt Kinabalu or the *Nishiki* opposite the Tourism Malaysia office.

Season Cake House has a branch in the Milimewa Superstore and one in Wisma Merdeka that does delicious waffles – turn right as you go in the main entrance on Jalan Haji Saman then follow your nose. There's another good bakery under the Hotel Holiday.

If you need a pep-up, there's an outlet of *Gomantong Swiftlets* in Wisma Merdeka that sells bird's-nest soup; a bowl of this panacea will set you back RM33.

Entertainment

KK's nightlife doesn't really start happening until very late; don't arrange any morning activities for the day after if you are planning a night out. *Shenanigan's* at the Kinabalu Hyatt is probably the most popular place in town. Live music is provided by Filipino cover bands some nights, and the place gets packed at weekends. Entry is free, but drinks are very expensive – RM13 per beer – and dress standards may be enforced.

Rocky's Fun Pub is a bar until 10.30 pm and then transforms into a disco. *The New Krash*, a club on the ground floor of the Sabah Inn, plays good western and eastern dance music; again, the place is usually deserted before 10.30 pm.

The *Galaxy Nite Club* overlooks the roundabout at the south end of Jalan Tunku Abdul Rahman; it's open from 8 pm till the wee hours.

One entertainment option that you'll see advertised in lights along the streets of KK is *MTV parlours*, where you can rent and watch laser-disc movies in private rooms. There's no limit to how many can share the fun and you can drink, smoke and eat in the rooms. Costs range from RM20 to RM30 per movie and most places stay open till 1 or 2 am.

Shopping

Although a major centre, KK isn't a great place for handicrafts. Much of what is on offer is mass-produced for the tourist trade, such as scorpions mounted as paperweights, fridge magnets and key rings. If you're travelling on to Kuching in Sarawak, save your money till you get there.

There are several souvenir and handicraft shops on the ground floor of Wisma Merdeka, including Sabah Craft and Batik, Rafflesia and The Crafts; Borneo Craft has a good range of postcards.

There's a small range in the shop at the Sabah Tourism Promotion Corporation building, and on the ground floor of Centre Point there's Borneo Handicraft & Ceramic Shop and two branches of Classic Batik & Craft. A small shop in the Shangri-La Tanjung Aru Resort sells reasonably pricey handicrafts and souvenirs.

You can buy Filipino crafts in the market on the waterfront and for folk medicines, cheap clothes, watches, sunglasses and virtually anything else, the markets around town are fun to browse through.

For a souvenir with a difference, Gomantong Swiftlets, on the ground floor of Wisma Merdeka, sells dried birds' nests in 37.5g packages ranging from RM250 to RM562, depending on quality.

Getting There & Away

Air The Malaysia Airlines office (☎ 088-213555) is in the Kompleks Karamunsing, south of the centre. It is open Monday to Friday from 9 am to 5.30 pm and Saturday from 9 am to 1 pm. There's another Malaysia Airlines office at the airport (☎ 088-240632) which is open from 5 am to 7 pm daily, although it only handles direct ticketing.

The KWSP building, over the other side of Jalan Tunku Abdul Rahman, has offices for a number of other airlines, including Dragonair (also Cathay Pacific Airways) (☎ 088-254733), Royal Brunei Airlines (☎ 088-242193), Singapore Airlines (☎ 088-255444) and Thai International Airways (☎ 088-232896).

Travel agents closer to town all book Malaysia Airlines flights for the same price.

Around Sabah & Sarawak KK is the hub of the Malaysia Airlines network in Sabah and there are regular flights to Bintulu (daily, RM127), Brunei (up to three times daily, RM99), Kuching (up to nine daily, RM228), Labuan (seven daily, RM52), Lahad Datu (at least three daily, RM106), Miri (six daily, RM104), Sandakan (usually seven daily, RM83), Sibu (usually three daily, RM180) and Tawau (usually nine daily, RM96).

There are also 12-seater Twin Otter flights from KK to Limbang (twice weekly, RM60), Lawas (weekly, RM47), Kudat (twice weekly, RM50) and Semporna (RM100).

Peninsular Malaysia & Singapore The cheapest way of getting from Peninsular Malaysia to KK is by purchasing a 14 day advance-purchase ticket from Johor Bahru for RM295; the regular fare is RM347. There are also economy night flights from Kuala Lumpur for RM306, advance-purchase fares for RM372, or the regular fare of RM437.

The KK-Singapore fare is RM584 (S$391 from Singapore), so it is cheaper to take the flights to or from Johor Bahru and cross the Causeway on the Malaysia Airlines bus, which takes you right into Singapore.

Hong Kong Malaysia Airlines flies twice daily to Hong Kong; direct flights take a little under three hours. Cathay Pacific has three flights weekly between Hong Kong and KK.

Direct flights are often fully booked, making a change in Singapore necessary, though this costs around RM100 extra.

The Philippines Malaysia Airlines flies from KK to Manila three times a week. Other Philippine destinations served by Malaysia Airlines are Cebu and Davao.

Bus There is no main bus station in KK; long-distance air-con express buses, long-distance minibuses and local buses depart from three places around the town centre.

Long-Distance Bus Air-con express buses are the best way to reach Mt Kinabalu and major towns on the east coast. Buses leave from the open area south-east of the municipal offices on Jalan Tunku Abdul Rahman; long-distance buses leave in the morning from about 7.30 am. Buses to the KK suburb of Lidas and the coastal town of Tuaran also depart from here.

Touts will accost you well before you reach the bus station; they're a bit 'in your face' but don't get flustered – most are helpful and will guide you to the right bus. A myriad of companies service the main routes; some (but not all) have wooden shacks where you can make advance bookings. It's probably better to book ahead on weekends for Sandakan, but generally you can just turn up before the scheduled departure time and hop on. In any case, the bus may wait for an hour or so for more passengers to turn up. Buses leave the long-distance station daily for:

Kampung Likas: Buses leave every 30 minutes between 6 am and 8 pm; the journey takes 30 minutes (70 sen)

Lahad Datu (for Danum Valley): All buses to Tawau pass through Lahad Datu; about seven hours (RM40)

Lawas (Sarawak): Departures at 7.30 am and 1 pm; buses pass through Papar, Beaufort and Sipitang; four hours (RM25)

Mt Kinabalu: Buses leave for the national park at 7.30 am every day. The fare is RM15 and the trip takes about three hours. You could also take any bus going to Ranau or Sandakan and ask to be dropped off at the entrance road, from where the park HQ is 100m.

Ranau (for Poring Hot Springs): Departures at 8.30 am and 12.30 pm; 3½ hours, RM10. All Ranau buses pass through Kundassang (RM8).

Sandakan: Several departures daily between 7 and 9 am; six hours. Fares hover between RM20 and RM25, and it's advisable to book ahead.

Tawau: HWA Lean First Express and Atour Enterprise buses leave at 7.30 am daily; the nine hour trip costs RM50. Buses to Tawau can drop passengers at Lahad Datu and at the turn-off for Kunak (RM45).

Tuaran: Buses leave approximately every 15 minutes between 6 am and 9 pm; 45 minutes (RM2)

Air-con Land Cruisers leave when full for Sandakan; this is a faster, more comfortable way to travel, but it's also more expensive. They leave at approximately 7 am daily and the fare is RM30.

Minibus The large vacant lot behind Centre Point is a busy minibus park that services the market. Most buses from here are local, but also go to centres around KK, such as Penampang, Papar and Tuaran, and further north to Kota Belud and Kudat. Minibuses are not air-conditioned and can get crowded. On long trips you'll be far more comfortable if you pay a few ringgit more for an air-con express.

Minibuses leave when they're full. You'll be pressured by touts to take a certain minibus, but don't commit yourself until you see how many people are on board. There'll often be more than one leaving and if yours is empty there could be a long wait until it fills up. If you get to the bus stand and there isn't a minibus with even one passenger going your way, hang back for a few minutes; chances are there's one nearly full doing a lap of the town trying to fill the last couple of seats.

Departures are frequent in the early morning, fewer later in the day, and can't be counted on for long-haul destinations in the afternoon. The general rule is make sure you travel early, and the further you travel the earlier you should leave.

Some examples of minibus services from KK are:

Beaufort: regular departures until about 5 pm; two hours (RM5)
Keningau: regular departures to about 1 pm; about 2½ hours (RM13)
Kota Belud: departures until 5 pm; two hours (RM6)
Kudat: departures until about 5 pm; three hours, (RM15)
Papar: departures until 4 pm; one hour (RM3)
Ranau: mainly early-morning departures, but may leave as late as 6 pm (all buses pass Kinabalu National Park); 3½ hours (RM15)
Sandakan: departures early morning only; six to seven hours (RM25) (express buses are a more comfortable way of doing this run)
Tenom: regular departures; three to four hours, RM20 by minibus or RM25 by share-taxi.
Tuaran: departures throughout the day; 45 minutes (RM2.50)

As with express buses, if you're heading for Kinabalu National Park from KK, you can take a minibus for Ranau or Sandakan and get off at the park entrance (about three hours, RM10); ask the driver to drop you off.

Train Sabah's only railway runs between Tanjung Aru, south of KK, Beaufort and Tenom. See the boxed text 'Beaufort-Tenom Railway' later in this chapter for details.

Only one train leaves daily for Beaufort and Tenom – a cargo train on Monday to Saturday and a passenger train on Sunday. Departures from KK are at 10 am Monday to Saturday, arriving at Beaufort at 12.56 pm, and at 8 am on Sunday, arriving Beaufort at 10.37 am. Should you wish to take this service all the way to Tenom you would arrive there at 3.55 pm on Monday through Saturday and at 1 pm on Sunday. The fare from KK to Beaufort is RM4.80 and to Tenom costs RM7.50.

Bookings can be made by contacting the Tanjung Aru station (☎ 088-254611), or the stations at Beaufort (☎ 087-211518) or Tenom (☎ 087-735514). Bookings can be made by phone, but try to get to the station at least an hour in advance to pay for your ticket. There may be cancellations at the last minute, but don't bank on it, especially at weekends. Although the stretch between Beaufort and Tenom is spectacular and well worth the ride, it is easier and quicker to get to Beaufort or Tenom from KK by road.

The railway station is 5km south of the city centre, close to the airport.

Taxi There are share-taxis to most minibus destinations. They also leave when full, but the fares are at least 25% higher than the minibuses. Their big advantage is that they are much quicker and more comfortable.

Boat Fast passenger boats leave daily for Labuan from the jetties behind the Hyatt Kinabalu; there are connecting services to Muara in Brunei. The trip to Labuan generally takes about three hours and the fare is RM28/33 for economy/1st class by fast ferry or RM28 on the *Sanergy Rafflesia* catamaran.

The earliest – and most comfortable – service is provided by the *Sanergy Rafflesia*, a flash new catamaran that leaves at 7.30 am daily.

Labuan Express Dua and *Express Ming Hai* leave at 8 am; *Express Kinabalu* leaves at 10 am; and *Duta Muhibbah No 3* leaves at 1.30 pm.

Boarding time is 15 minutes before departure and because Labuan is a Federal Territory you will need to take your passport.

There's usually no need to book in advance, but if you want to you can contact Rezeki Murni (☎ 088-236834), Lot 3, 1st floor, Block D, Kompleks Segama. Tickets for *Sanergy Rafflesia* can be bought at the Sabah Parks jetty, where you also catch boats to Tunku Abdul Rahman National Park.

The South China Sea is generally calmest in the early morning, but can get quite rough later in the day. Services may be disrupted and even cancelled when smoke haze is bad. See the Labuan Getting There & Away section for return times.

Getting Around

To/From the Airport Kota Kinabalu's modern international airport is at Tanjung Aru, 7km south-west of the centre. To get there, take any minibus marked Petagas or Jalan Kepayan from behind Centre Point and ask to be dropped off at the airport. The fare is 80 sen. Minibuses leave when full between about 8 am and 7 pm, although services are less frequent in the afternoon.

Buses marked Putatan from the local bus station also pass the airport turn-off. Departures are irregular, but there is usually at least one an hour during the day; the fare is 80 sen. This bus stops opposite the access road, from where it's a 10 minute walk to the terminal. Heading into town, there's a bus stop to the right as you leave the airport, 10 minutes walk from the terminal.

The airport is new and modern, with an efficient Malaysia Airlines office, a post office, hotel and hire car booking desks, a Telekom office, exchange bureaus (open only for international flights), a good (but expensive) bookshop, a fish shop and junk food outlets.

The 15 minute taxi ride to the airport normally costs RM12.50, but you may be charged more late at night. Leaving the terminal, there's a taxi desk on the ground floor where you can buy a fixed-price coupon for RM12.50 into town.

Bus Local buses leave from the stand between the municipal offices and Jalan Tun Razak. The only time you'll need one is to get to the airport (80 sen) or to Tanjung Aru train station (50 sen). Minibuses that pass the airport also pass the railway station. If you don't feel like walking to the Kompleks Karamunsing south of the city centre – jump on a bus going along Jalan Tunku Abdul Rahman (50 sen).

Taxi KK's taxis are plentiful. They are not metered, so negotiate the fare before you set off. Taxi stands are all over town, but most can be found in the area between the municipal offices and the main post office. Most trips around town cost RM5.

Car There's a number of car rental operators, including:

Adaras Rent a Car
(☎ 088-216671) Ground floor, Wisma Sabah
Ais (no, not Avis)
(☎ 088-238954) 1st floor, Lot 5, Block A, Asia City
Kinabalu Rent a Car
(☎ 088-248333) Hyatt Kinabalu International
Padas Jaya Rent a Car
(☎ 088-233239) 1st floor, Block B, Kompleks Karamunsing

Car hire is expensive but competition is brisk and you should be able to get a better deal for longer rental. The going rate for a Proton Saga is RM180 per day with unlimited kilometres, while a Toyota Land Cruiser costs around RM400 per day.

AROUND KOTA KINABALU

Tunku Abdul Rahman National Park

Five almost unspoilt islands a short distance west of KK – Pulau Manukan, Gaya, Sapi, Mamutik and Sulug – and the reefs in between make up Tunku Abdul Rahman National Park, which protects a total area of 4929 hectares. Only a short boat ride from the city centre, they offer some of the best beaches in Borneo, crystal-clear waters and a wealth of corals and tropical marine life.

There is accommodation on Manukan and it is possible to camp on some islands, but it is easy enough to get to any of them to enjoy a day snorkelling, hiking, lazing on a beach – or all three.

There's a park entrance fee of RM2 per person, which is valid for all the islands.

Pulau Manukan Manukan is the most popular destination for KK residents and has well developed facilities. It is the second-largest island in the group and its 20 hectares are largely covered in dense vegetation. There's a good beach with coral reefs off the southern and eastern shores, and a walking trail around the perimeter. There's quite a good range of tropical fish – and many can be seen simply by looking down from the jetty.

Other wildlife includes the Tabon scrubfowl, a primitive bird that lays its eggs in piles of rotting vegetation. The birds are shy, but can be seen by walking quietly along the island's jogging path early or late in the day. In the gardens around the chalets you could see sunbirds and fruit-pigeons.

Equipment for hire includes mask, fins and snorkel (RM15), surf mat (RM5) and rubber tubes (RM5); a security deposit is also payable. There's also a shop selling postcards, T-shirts, sun hats, ice creams and souvenirs.

Pulau Gaya With an area of about 1465 hectares and rising in places to 300m, Pulau Gaya is by far the largest island in the park. It's also the closest to KK and, apart from the stilt village which can easily be seen from the city waterfront, Gaya is virtually covered in undisturbed tropical forest. There are about 20km of marked hiking trails and a good stretch of sand – Police Beach – at Bulijong Bay. If you're lucky, you may see monkeys, pangolins or even a bearded pig.

The stilt villages, inhabited by about 500 Malaysians and 4700 Filipino refugees, are actually outside the park boundaries.

Pulau Sapi Pulau Sapi (Cow Island) lies just off the south-western tip of Pulau Gaya and is the most visited island in the park. With an area of just 10 hectares, the island has good beaches, a nature trail and some of the best snorkelling in the park. Monkeys live in the forest and sometimes go down to the beach to look for crabs.

There is no accommodation, but there are shelters, changing rooms, toilets and barbecue pits. Snorkelling equipment can be hired at RM15 for a snorkel and mask.

Pulau Mamutik This is the smallest island in the park, with an area of just six hectares.

There are good beaches right around the island and some good coral reefs, particularly on the eastern side.

Pulau Sulug This island, covering eight hectares, is the least visited of the group, probably because it's the furthest away from KK. It has only one beach, on the eastern shore, but the snorkelling is quite good and this would make a quiet day trip.

Places to Stay & Eat Manukan is the only island with chalets, and also has a restaurant, swimming pool and squash courts. The chalets sleep up to four people and have air-conditioning; all are fully furnished with a desalinated shower and kitchen/dining facilities. Chalet rental costs RM200 per night for weekends, public holidays and school holidays, and RM140 during the week.

It is possible to camp on Gaya, Sulug, Mamutik and Sapi for RM5 per person, if you bring your own tent and apply for permission in writing from the Sabah Parks office (see Information under Kota Kinabalu). Officially, you must do this 'well in advance'.

The *Coral Garden Seafood Restaurant* on Manukan is open from 7 am to 9 pm, and serves a wide range of western and Malay dishes. There's a good range of seafood, though price depends on availability; a whole fish is RM25, tiger prawns are RM25 to RM30, cheaper fish dishes are RM10 to RM15, and grilled chicken is RM15. There are also sandwiches, salads and set menus.

Getting There & Away Koktas runs boats regularly every day from the national parks jetty behind Wisma Merdeka, despite what the touts from other boat operators may tell you. Scheduled departures are at 8, 9, 10 and 11 am, and noon, 2 and 4.30 pm. The fare is RM5/10 for children/adults, and the trip to Manukan takes about 40 minutes. Boats leave Manukan at 7.30, 9.30, 10.30 and 11.30 am, and 1, 3 and 4 pm. Depending on demand, most call at Pulau Sapi as well.

Coral Island Tours (☎ 088-266015), in an office behind the Hyatt Kinabalu Hotel, organises tours. It's best to get a group together to charter a boat but they can take you to any or all of the islands. Apart from the charter costs, you'll also have to pay the RM2 park fee, which covers all the islands.

If you just want to go across to Pulau Gaya's water village, boats shuttle back and forth from the Filipino Market and from near the Hyatt. Private boats and operators can also be hired from the area next to the Hyatt. The charge is very much open to negotiation, but a boat to any of the islands should cost about RM40 to RM50 return with enough time to explore.

Likas Bay Wetland Reserve

Just 4km north of the town centre, a series of freshwater lagoons separated from the beach lining Likas Bay has been reserved for wildlife. The lily-covered swamps are thick with birds and the best time to go is late afternoon, when the setting sun gives perfect viewing conditions. You're unlikely to see any edible species such as ducks, but among the birds present are graceful egrets and herons, bitterns skulking in the long grass, migratory waders and, in the evening, skeins of night herons leaving their roosts.

The best part of the reserve is south of the new mosque. Take any local bus going along Jalan Tun Fuad Stephens, get off at the roundabout next to the new mosque then walk south along the side of the lagoon towards the city centre. A taxi will cost about RM6 each way, and you could arrange to be picked up. Food stalls set up in the car park beside the beach.

Sabah Foundation Building

You'll probably see tourist literature adorned with photographs of this cylindrical, mirrored, 31 storey tower at the north end of Likas Bay. This opulent tribute to the profitability of the Sabah Foundation, Sabah state's huge commercial and social development corporation, houses ministerial suites and has a revolving restaurant. The literature gushes about this landmark and insists that you include it in your programme. It really isn't worth the effort. It can be seen from a distance, en route to Kinabalu National Park. A taxi to the building costs RM8 and there's a revolving restaurant with a good view.

Beaches

There are a few shallow paddling beaches near the highway south of KK. The nearest is at the plush Shangri-La Tanjung Aru Resort (see Places to Stay in the KK section), but other accommodation is available along the coast between the airport and Papar. The beaches won't win any awards, but you could pleasantly laze away a day or two before catching a plane. Female travellers who aren't covered from head to toe while sunbathing can expect to be gawked at by local men on any beach.

Places to Stay The *Seaside Travellers Inn* (☎ 088-750555), H30 Gaya Park, Jalan Penampang, is 20km south of KK and makes a cheap alternative to the resorts. A bed in a fan-cooled dorm with shared bathroom costs RM20; economy rooms with shared facilities are RM33 to RM55. More expensive rooms and bungalows range from RM66 to RM99 with hot water, air-con and TV. All prices include a continental breakfast.

Further down the coast, *Beringgis Resort* (☎ 088-752333), Km 26, Jalan Papar, is a more upmarket resort on the beach near Kinarut. Air-con rooms cost RM85, including breakfast, plus tax.

Getting There & Away To get to the beaches south of KK take a Papar minibus from behind Centre Point. For the Seaside Travellers Inn get off near the Km 20 mark and the inn is a short walk past the school. Beringgis Resort is right next to the highway – just ask the driver to stop.

PULAU LAYANG LAYANG

Some 300km north-west of Kota Kinabalu, Layang Layang is a tiny oceanic island surrounded by a coral atoll. It's an exclusive dive location and part of the famous (among divers at least) Borneo Banks. Layang Layang is also one of the disputed Spratlys, a collection of about 600 islands, reefs and atolls strategically located in the South China Sea. With the prospect of undersea oil reserves and rich fishing, parts of the Spratlys are claimed by China, Vietnam, Taiwan, the Philippines, Malaysia and even plucky Brunei. China and Vietnam have already clashed over Chinese occupation of several islands and Malaysia has a small naval base on Layang Layang.

Layang Layang covers only six hectares, but is surrounded by an atoll over 7km long and 2km wide. The diving is excellent, particularly down the wall, where pelagic species such as tuna and barracuda are encountered, and reef sharks and hammerheads are seen regularly (see the Diving & Snorkelling section in the Terengganu chapter for information about dive sites and safe and responsible diving). Soft corals are a feature and in shallower water manta rays are seen. The island is also a breeding ground for sea birds such as boobies and terns.

Getting There & Away

Layang Layang can only be visited as part of an expensive tour. There is only one resort on the island and live-aboard vessels depart from Kota Kinabalu between April and September.

Bookings for the *M-Ocean Resort* can be made direct through Layang Layang Island Resort (☎ 03-243-3166), 3rd floor, Sungei Wang Plaza, Jalan Ismail, Kuala Lumpur.

Borneo Divers & Sea Sports (☎ 088-222226), 4th floor, Wisma Sabah, KK, can organise trips to the island. A 10 day/nine night trip combined with a visit to Sipadan costs about US$2200, including all transfers, meals, accommodation and dives. Scuba hire is extra.

The MV *Coral Topaz* is a fully equipped live-aboard dive vessel that runs regular trips to Layang Layang and other islands in the South China Sea. Bookings can be made through Coral Island Cruises (☎ 088-223490), ground floor, Wisma Sabah, Kota Kinabalu.

South of Kota Kinabalu

The Crocker Range is the backbone of western Sabah, rising from near Tenom in the south and culminating in the north at massive Mt Kinabalu and its outlier, Mt Trus Madi. Nearly 1500m below the range is the fertile coastal plain on which KK and other large settlements developed. Logging has taken a devastating toll on most of Sabah, but the Crocker still has good stands of intact forest and much of it is now preserved as the Crocker Range National Park. Unfortunately, the park has no facilities, trails or accommodation.

A highway climbs steeply from KK over Gunung Alab to Tambunan then veers south to the central valley towns of Keningau and Tenom. From here you can travel by river to visit Murut longhouses and Batu Punggul.

Heading south from KK, another road follows a coastal plain past Papar before reaching Beaufort, Sipitang and the Sarawak border. A popular and scenic way of closing the loop is to take the railway from Beaufort to Tenom, and there's a rough overland route between the coast road and Keningau.

RAFFLESIA FOREST RESERVE

Near the top of the range next to the highway is the Rafflesia Forest Reserve, devoted to the world's largest flower. The rafflesia is a parasitic plant that grows hidden within its host, the stems of jungle vines, until it bursts into bloom. The large bulbous flowers can be up to 1m in diameter. The 12 or so species of rafflesias are found only in Borneo and Sumatra; several species are unique to Sabah, but their blooming is unpredictable.

The Rafflesia Information Centre (☎ 087-774691), on the highway 59km from KK, has interesting displays and information devoted to the rafflesia. It is open Monday to Friday from 8 am to 12.45 pm and from 2 to 5 pm, and on weekends from 8 am to 5 pm. From the centre, trails lead into the forest where the rafflesias can be found. Whether you will find one in bloom is very much a matter of luck, though the staff at the centre can tell you of the latest sightings. The flowers may be close to the information centre or involve a walk deep into the forest. In theory, guides are available to take you to the flowers at fixed times, but in fact staff are rarely available.

Even if there are no rafflesias, there are pleasant walks at the reserve. There is also a good walk to Air Terjun Sensuron, a waterfall just off the highway, 4km from the information centre towards KK. It is a 45 minute walk down to the falls from the highway, and near the starting point on the other side of the road is a lookout point and picnic tables.

Places to Stay & Eat

There is no accommodation at the reserve. *Gunung Emas Highlands Resort* (☎ 088-256955), Km 52, KK-Tambunan Rd, is perched on the side of the mountain 7km back towards KK from the Rafflesia Information Centre. The views are superb and the climate refreshing, if not downright cold. This resort has a variety of accommodation, but apart from the dormitories, it's very expensive. A dormitory bed costs RM21, or RM31.50 with breakfast; simple but comfortable rooms in the main building annexe start at RM126 per double and soar up to RM210 for the VIP suite, which is popular with honeymooners. On the other side of the highway and a steep climb up the mountain there are hilltop cabins built around tree trunks. They're a great novelty, but small and very rustic for RM63 a double. It is an almost vertical walk up to the shower blocks near the cabins and down to the restaurant on the highway.

The *restaurant* at the resort serves good Chinese dishes. On weekends it is overrun with day-trippers, and cars and noise from video games destroy the tranquil atmosphere.

The resort also owns the *Goldenhill Motel*, 100m back down the road to KK, which has a restaurant and singles/doubles for RM40/70.

Further on towards Tambunan, the *Gunung Alab Resort* (☎ 088-302279) is a similar but newer hotel with a *Muslim restaurant* and superb views over the Crocker Range. Spotless but characterless rooms cost RM60 with shared bathroom or RM80 with attached bathroom.

Gunung Alab Resort also has an **insect museum**, which is worth the 15 minute diversion to look at some beautiful and spectacular specimens from around the world. The museum is open Monday to Saturday from 10 am to 5 pm, and Sunday and public holidays from 9 am to 5 pm; entry costs RM3. If it's locked just ask for the key at the hotel reception.

Getting There & Away

Take a Tambunan or Keningau minibus from Kota Kinabalu to the reserve or the resort for RM8. From Tambunan the cost is RM4 and the journey takes 30 minutes.

TAMBUNAN

Tambunan, a small agricultural service town about 81km from KK, is the first settlement across the Crocker Range. The region was the last stronghold of Mat Salleh, who became a folk hero for rebelling against the British late in the 19th century. He eventually negotiated a truce with the British, which so outraged his own people that he fled to the Tambunan plain where he was eventually besieged and killed. His gravestone is in a cemetery just off the main road, 750m out of town towards Ranau.

There's nothing of interest in the town, but if you have your own 4WD, or are well equipped for trekking, some interesting side trips can be done from Tambunan. **Air Terjun Mawar** is a pretty waterfall in the Crocker Range, though getting to it is an expedition. From Tambunan head towards Ranau; 7.5km past the turn-off to KK there is a small shop and a very difficult-to-see sign to 'Air Terjun Mawar'. Turn left and keep going past rural areas and new Murut settlements, high up into the mountains. It is beautiful countryside, though the road is long and tortuous and fords a small river.

Places to Stay

If you get stuck in Tambunan, the *Tambunan Village Resort Centre* (☎ 087-774076), Jalan TVRC, is off the main road about 1km north of the shopping centre. It's not cheap, but there are modern facilities including tennis courts and pool tables. Comfortable chalets cost RM70, two-bedroom chalets are RM80 and basic rooms in three-bedroom chalets cost RM50. If you have equipment a campground site costs RM3/6 for students/adults.

Getting There & Away

Regular minibuses ply the roads between Tambunan and KK (RM10), Ranau (RM6), Keningau (RM7) and Tenom (RM8).

MT TRUS MADI

On the opposite side of the highway from Tambunan's shopping area, a road leads to Sabah's second highest peak – 2642m-high Mt Trus Madi. Though Trus Madi is surrounded by logging concessions the upper slopes and peak are wild and jungle-clad, and there are plans to turn the mountain into a wilderness reserve.

There are a couple of muddy trails to the summit that are treacherous in parts – just the thing for those who find Mt Kinabalu a bit pedestrian. Independent trekkers must be well equipped and take all food and water up the mountain. Before setting off you are strongly advised to hire a guide or at least get maps and assistance from the Forestry Department (Jabatan Perhutanan; ☎ 087-774691) at the District Office in Tambunan. They might also be able to arrange transport for the 1½ hour trip up to the trails. Some tour operators from KK have treks to Trus Madi – see the list in the KK section.

To get to the mountain from Tambunan, take the road towards Kaingaran. Past Kampung Batu Lapan take the road to the right which leads to a network of logging roads. With good maps or a guide, it is possible to go by 4WD up to about 1500m, from where it is a five to seven hour climb to the top of Trus Madi. From Tambunan it's a 28km walk to the peak along the pleasant valley road then up through logging roads.

KENINGAU

The only reason to stop in Keningau is to see the large *tamu* (weekly market) that takes place every Thursday. Otherwise, this lumber and agricultural boomtown has little to offer the traveller. Although it's deep in the heart of Murut country, it's most unlikely you'll see anyone dressed in traditional tribal wear. Attracted by the prospects of well paid employment, people have flocked here from neighbouring districts, and the town's population has more than doubled since the 1960s.

Places to Stay & Eat

In the unlikely event you are forced to overnight in Keningau, there are plenty of hotels. The cheaper places are very seedy, but at the time of writing Keningau was feeling hard times and top-end accommodation was a bargain.

The *Hotel Tai Wah* (☎ 087-332092), on the Tambunan-Tenom road, is close to the central square where buses and taxis congregate. It's pretty musty, but air-con singles/doubles with bathroom and TV are OK value at RM30/45. Down the main road opposite the police station, the *Aily Hotel* (☎ 087-332143) is better, with clean air-con singles/doubles for RM29/40.

Keningau's poshest hotel, and tallest building, is the *Hotel Juta* (☎ 087-337888), at the southern end of the main centre. It is sparkling, with marble fittings and spacious rooms, and will probably be empty. The prices reflect the high standard of this immaculate hotel – standard single and double rooms range from RM160 to RM220 plus taxes – but discounts of more than 50% may be available.

Dominating the skyline about 1km from the town centre towards Tambunan is the *Hotel Perkasa Keningau* (☎ 087-331045). It is not as luxurious as the Juta and big quiet rooms with all mod cons start at RM92/115. Nearby there's a sports complex which has a good swimming pool.

Across the road is the *Rumah Annex Keningau*, Keningau's government resthouse, but there are only three rooms and you'll have to do some fancy talking at the District Office (☎ 087-331535) to get in.

Keningau has a good selection of *kedai kopi* and *Muslim cafes*, and there's a *KFC* along the Tambunan-Tenom road opposite the market.

Getting There & Away

Share-taxis and minibuses are the only transport available and can be found around the central square by the market. The cheapest way to travel from Keningau to KK is by minibus for RM13; the journey takes about 2½ hours. Share-taxis do the same trip for RM20.

Keningau to Tenom costs RM5 by taxi or minibus and takes about one hour along a good bitumen road. There are also taxis and minibuses to Tambunan (RM7) and Ranau. From Ranau you can go to either Sandakan or Kinabalu National Park.

A logging road runs down the rugged and spectacular Crocker Range from Keningau towards the coast then links up with the Papar-Beaufort road. It is only recommended for 4WD vehicles – and remember that logging trucks always have right of way.

TENOM

Tenom is the home of the friendly Murut people, most of whom are farmers. Soya beans, maize and vegetables are grown in this fertile area, and there are several cocoa plantations. It's a very pleasant rural town and is also the end of the railway line from Tanjung Aru (KK).

Despite the peaceful setting, there's absolutely nothing to do in the town – except play snooker or get assaulted by the cacophony in one of the video-game parlours. The Tenom Agricultural Research Station outside town (see the Around Tenom section) makes an interesting diversion and the train trip to Beaufort is highly recommended.

Tenom is a compact little place and it's very easy to find your way around. Minibuses park near the *Padang* (town square) and cruise up and down the main street, while taxis are in front of the Yun Lee Restaurant.

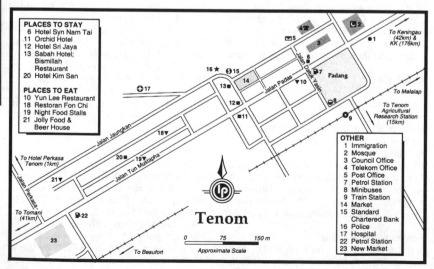

Places to Stay

The *Hotel Syn Nam Tai* on Jalan Padas is a basic Chinese hotel with fan-cooled rooms for RM18/24 with shared bathroom. A little bargaining may be required.

The Indian-run *Sabah Hotel* (087-735534) is entered through the Bismillah Restaurant. Simple but clean fan rooms cost RM20 and air-con rooms are RM37. The *Hotel Kim San* (☎ 087-735485), set back from the main road, has run-down air-con doubles for RM28.

For something slightly more upmarket, the *Hotel Sri Jaya* (☎ 087-735669), on Jalan Padas, is a newer hotel and a good mid-range place. Singles/doubles with air-con, TV and bathroom cost from RM33/35. Opposite, the *Orchid Hotel* (☎ 087-737600) is newer, and has doubles for RM60 and twins for RM72.

The *Hotel Perkasa Tenom* (☎ 087-735811) perches high on a hill above the town like a

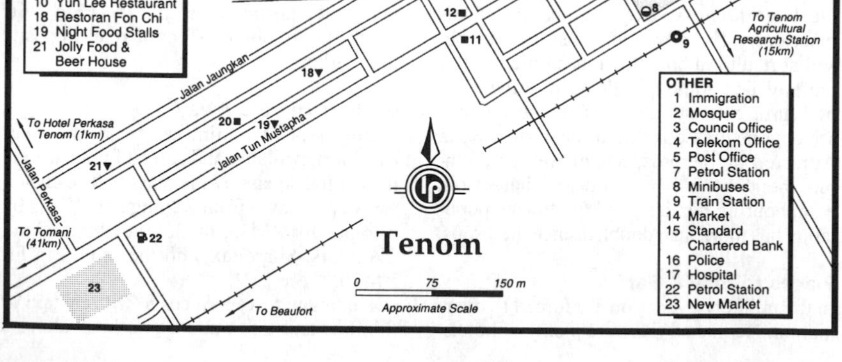

Transylvanian castle. Its 70-odd fully air-con rooms, restaurant and minibars seem totally over the top for sleepy Tenom, and in fact it has a very low occupancy rate. Rooms cost RM75/86 for a single/double, though discounts may be available. It's a very steep walk, so if you want to check in phone from the town and someone will come down to collect you; otherwise take a taxi for RM2.

Places to Eat

Food stalls set up in the evening in the car park down the main road from the Padang. There are plenty of Chinese *kedai kopi* in town selling basic Chinese food. The *Yun Lee Restaurant* on Jalan Padas is popular with the locals, but it closes in the early evening; the *Restoran Fon Chi*, not far from the Hotel Kim San, stays open a bit later.

For good Indian food, rotis and murtabak, try the *Bismillah Restaurant* in the Sabah Hotel. The more upmarket *Jolly Food & Beer House* also offers alfresco dining in the evenings, or you can try the air-con bar section inside. The *Hotel Perkasa Tenom* has a *malam kampung* (village night) on Saturday night until midnight. Hawker-style stalls sell local favourites on the lawns overlooking the town; the prices are moderate and the setting is the best in town.

Getting There & Away

Bus Dozens of minibuses cruise up and down the main street trying to drum up business. Most are going to Keningau (RM5, one hour), but some also go to KK (RM20, three to four hours). If you want to explore the Murut longhouse country, there are a few minibuses heading south to Tomani (RM4).

Train Although the railway line goes as far as Melalap, further up the valley, Tenom is the railhead as far as passenger trains are concerned. The 46km journey to Beaufort is the most spectacular part of the trip and is recommended if you've come from Tambunan or Keningau and are on your way to Sarawak, Brunei or back to KK. For more information on this service, see the boxed text 'Beaufort-Tenom Railway' under Beaufort.

Taxi Share-taxis also make the run to Keningau (RM5) and on to KK (RM25), usually with a wait in Keningau for passengers. Early morning is the best time to catch one.

AROUND TENOM

Murut Longhouses

There are some interesting longhouses around Tenom, but they can be a bit difficult to reach. The best examples are along the Sungai Padas towards Sarawak, as far as Tomani and beyond.

Buses from Tenom to Tomani cost around RM4, or you may be able to get a boat there. Ask around at the hotels or petrol station for a contact, but be prepared to wait a couple of days before anything starts to happen.

Agricultural Research Station

This research station run by the Department of Agriculture is at Lagud Sebrang, about 15km south-east of Tenom. There are ongoing research programmes into cocoa, food crops, coffee, fruit trees and apiculture (bee-keeping).

The main point of interest for the casual visitor is the Orchid Centre, which has been established over a period of years by a British man, Anthony Lamb, who has spent many years in Borneo.

Visits are by appointment only (☎ 087-735661) and possible Monday to Thursday from 8 am to 2 pm, Friday and Saturday from 8 to 11 am.

To reach the centre, take a Lagud Sebrang minibus from beside the sports field in Tenom. They run about every hour or so throughout the morning (RM2), but services dry up in the early afternoon. Taxis do the return trip for RM20; negotiate how long you want them to wait.

BATU PUNGGUL

Not far from the Kalimantan border, Batu Punggul is a jungle-topped limestone outcrop towering nearly 300m above the Sungai Sapulut. This is deep in Murut country and Batu Punggul was one of several sites sacred to these people. It is difficult and expensive to get there; the trip involves a long ride by motorised canoe along the jungle-clad Sungai Sapulut, but it is a part of Sabah that few tourists visit and affords a chance to rub shoulders with the Muruts.

The only place to stay is the Batu Punggul Lodge. There are forest trails and it's possible to climb the outcrop and explore caves. The resort centres on a traditionally styled Murut longhouse, and offers jungle walks, canoeing and visits to nearby caves. It's a popular place with youth groups and can get crowded, but mostly it's nearly empty.

Places to Stay & Eat

Accommodation at *Batu Punggul Lodge* must be booked through the Rural Development Corporation (☎ 088-426051), Km 9, Tuaran Rd, Kota Kinabalu. The choice consists of a comfortable resthouse with modern amenities, a replica longhouse or camping. A space on the longhouse floor costs RM6 (mattress and linen can be hired for RM5 per night) and a bed in shared rooms costs RM32. For a bit more comfort, the resthouse has a four bed 'master bedroom' (with attached bathroom) for RM150, and basic doubles for RM20. Camping costs RM2 per day, and tent hire starts at RM6 for two people. Kitchen facilities must be hired and food must be bought at the villages of Sapulut, Labang or Batu Punggul.

Getting There & Away

Getting to the lodge by yourself is possible but very expensive, and it is probably as well to arrange a boat through the Rural Development Corporation. Guests at the lodge usually go by road from Keningau to Sapulut and then take a longboat up the river to the lodge. Minibuses go from Keningau to Sapulut in the morning (RM5, three hours). A boat from Sapulut to Batu Punggul and back costs RM200 and can take up to six people. The trip takes 2½ hours.

The logging road from Keningau continues all the way to Tawau. There is no regular transport, but it is used by private vehicles and logging trucks that hurtle along in the centre of the road, so you may be able to hitch a lift through to Tawau.

BEAUFORT

Beaufort is a quiet provincial town on the Sungai Padas about 90km south of KK. Its

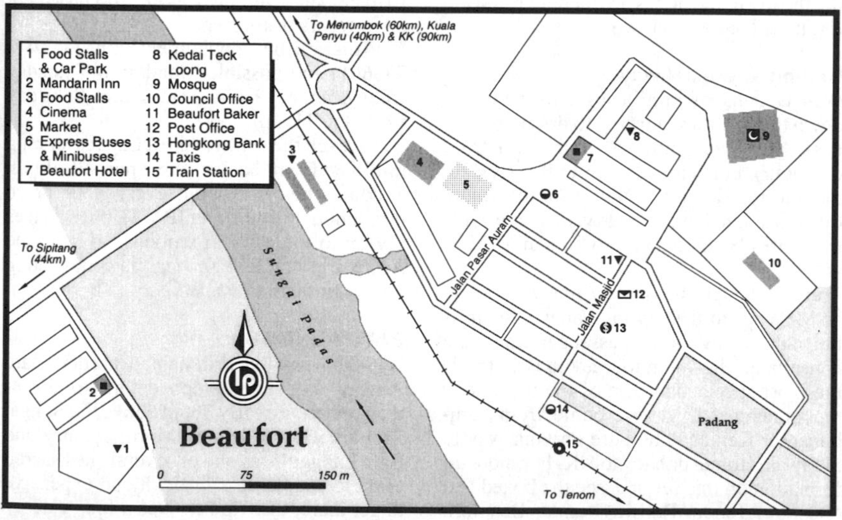

blue-painted, two-storey wooden shophouses have a certain dilapidated charm, and the people make you feel welcome, but the only reason to stop is to catch the train to Tenom.

There's a branch of the Hongkong Bank which will change travellers cheques. There is no bank at Sipitang, further south-west.

Places to Stay
If you miss the train to Tenom, you'll have to spend a night in Beaufort. The two hotels in town are the same standard and have air-con rooms with TV and bathrooms. Both charge RM36/42 for singles/doubles. The *Beaufort Hotel* (☎ 087-211911) is near the mosque and the *Mandarin Inn* (☎ 087-212800) is across the river. The Beaufort Hotel wins by a nose for position.

Places to Eat
Beaufort has numerous *kedai kopi* offering the standard rice and mee dishes. There are

Beaufort-Tenom Railway
The only rail system in East Malaysia runs from KK south to Beaufort then climbs the escarpment of the steep Crocker Range to Tenom, a total distance of 154km. The best part of the trip is between Beaufort and Tenom, where the narrow track follows the Sungai Padas, past spectacular gorges and over wooden bridges through steaming jungle that in places forms a bower overhead. Some travellers enjoy it so much they do the return trip in one day.

There are two types of passenger trains. The railcars are the best for comfort, speed and views. The ordinary diesel trains are the ones to take if you want a slower, more colourful journey, packed with the local people and their produce. Trains run more frequently on Sunday, Tenom's tamu day.

The railcar is basically an overgrown minibus with just 13 seats. Make a booking as soon as you arrive in Beaufort (☎ 087-211518), Tenom (☎ 087-735514) or at the Tanjung Aru station in KK (☎ 088-254611). It is sometimes fully booked, but it's worth going to the station at departure time because last minute cancellations are frequent.

Try to sit in the front seat on the right going from Beaufort, on the left from Tenom, to get the best views of the river and a clear view of the narrow track unravelling in front of you. The car has been designated '1st class' and therefore gets a 1st class price; it completes the whole journey in about 1½ hours.

The diesel trains are cheaper and slower than the railcars, and take about two hours. A goods train diesel also does the run and is the slowest of all, taking 2¾ hours. Details of the schedule are listed in the accompanying table – but check with the station just in case because the service has been reduced recently.

The railcar costs RM8.35 (plus a 50 sen booking fee) and the diesel train RM2.75; on Sunday a return ticket can be bought for RM4.50.

Train Departure Times

Beaufort-Tenom

Mon-Sat	8.15 am (D)	1.30 pm (G),	3.10 pm (D)	
Sun	6.45 am (D)	10.50 am (D)	2.30 pm (D)	4.05 pm (R)

Tenom-Beaufort

Mon-Sat	7.30 am (D)	10.30 am (D)	3.00 pm (D)
Sun	7.20 am (R)	7.55 am (D)	

R = Railcar, D = Diesel, G = Goods Train

a few in the blue godowns across from the station. The *Restoran Kim Wah*, underneath the Hotel Beaufort, does good Chinese food and has an air-conditioned section around the corner. The nearby *Kedai Teck Loong* has a wide range of fresh fruit juices. For cakes, buns and other pastries the *Beaufort Baker* near the market has a good selection – if you're just passing through, you'll have time to duck in when the bus stops.

Getting There & Away

Bus Express buses and minibuses gather in the square near the market. Express buses leave daily for KK at 10.30 am and 4 pm; the fare is RM14 and the trip takes 1½ hours. The express bus from KK to Lawas passes through Beaufort at around 9.30 am;.the fare from Beaufort to Lawas is RM15.

Minibuses cruise around town honking hopefully at pedestrians when they're nearly full. There are frequent departures for Papar (RM6) and KK (two hours, RM7), and less frequent departures for Sipitang (1½ hours, RM6), Lawas (RM15) and Kuala Penyu (RM5). The road to Kuala Penyu is a disaster so start out early to make sure you get back on the same day – there's nowhere to stay there.

To Menumbok (for Labuan) there are plenty of minibuses until early afternoon. The trip, along a gravel road, takes one hour and costs RM6.

Train It is possible to take the Sabah State Railway from KK to Beaufort, but it's a slow, rather dull stretch and a bus or minibus is quicker.

The route between KK and Beaufort is covered only by diesel trains, which take about three hours, leaving KK at 10 am from Monday to Saturday and 8 am on Sunday. Going in the other direction trains leave Beaufort at 1.05 pm from Monday to Saturday and 10.40 am on Sunday. The Beaufort-KK run costs RM4.80. See the boxed text 'Beaufort-Tenom Railway' for details of services between Beaufort and Tenom.

KUALA PENYU

Kuala Penyu is at the northern end of a flat swampy peninsula dotted with water buffalo. This is the place to get to Pulau Tiga National Park. The town is unremarkable, but there are some good beaches nearby. The best is around the headland from the estuary, 8km out of town; there are picnic tables and toilets but no other facilities.

There's nowhere to stay in Kuala Penyu, but if you book ahead (through Sabah Parks – see the KK section) you can stay on Pulau Tiga National Park.

Getting There & Away

Take a minibus from behind Centre Point in KK for RM10; the journey takes about two hours. From Beaufort take a Menumbok minibus and get off at the Kuala Penyu turn-off (just before Membakut, a 20 minute ride) where minibuses or taxis are usually waiting. It is a long, dusty road that ends at a river on the other side of the town – a car ferry shuttles across between 6 am and 6 pm. A minibus from Kuala Penyu to Menumbok is RM5.

PULAU TIGA NATIONAL PARK

The name Pulau Tiga means simply 'Three Islands', but only two of the original three remain in this 15 sq km park north of Kuala Penyu. Pulau Tiga is the largest island; about 1km to the north-east lies tiny Pulau Kalampunian Damit; and in between are the remains of the third island, now only a sandbar eroded by wave action.

The main island was formed by the eruption of mud volcanoes. It is covered by dense vegetation, but volcanic activity in the form of bubbling mud and escaping methane gas can still be seen at the summit of the island. There are walking trails, fine sandy beaches and good snorkelling around the island.

Tiny Pulau Kalampunian Damit is little more than a large rock covered in dense vegetation, but it is famous for the sea snakes that come ashore in their hundreds to mate. On any one day up to 150 snakes can be present, curled up under boulders, among roots and in tree hollows. It's a fascinating phenomenon made enigmatic by the fact that the snakes are never seen on nearby Pulau Tiga. Not surprisingly, the local name for this islet is Pulau Ular – Snake Island. Negotiate transport to this island with your boatman. Beware of the snakes – all sea snakes are poisonous.

There is accommodation on the main island, but Pulau Tiga is very difficult and expensive to reach. Accommodation can be booked through the Sabah Parks office in KK, but staff cannot arrange transport to the islands. Beds in basic four-bed dorms cost RM10 each, while more comfortable doubles (there are only two) cost RM60. Take all supplies with you, including water.

To get to Pulau Tiga, take a minibus from KK to Kuala Penyu, then ask around for a boatman – a boat should cost around RM120 for the return trip. Arrange a time for his return, but don't leave it too late so you can get a minibus from Kuala Penyu.

PAPAR

This is a coastal Kadazan town 38km south of KK. Local produce includes coconut wine and there's a weekly tamu on Sunday. There's a beach out of town where you can swim, and you could take a boat ride along the Sungai Papar.

Minibuses leave throughout the day from KK; the fare is RM3. Express buses pass through and can drop you in the town.

SIPITANG

Sipitang is 44km south of Beaufort, 144km from KK and the closest town in Sabah to the Sarawak border.

Located on a wide, shallow bay, Sipitang is pleasant enough, though the only reason to stop here is to organise bus connections. If you are heading to Lawas for a boat to Brunei or Limbang, you should spend the night in Lawas or you'll miss the early-morning departures.

The Sarawak border is 18km south and buses stop at Merapok, where passports and visas are checked at both Sabah and Sarawak immigration offices. The offices are open every day from 6 am until 10 pm; see the Sarawak chapter for more details.

Places to Stay & Eat

Sipitang has some reasonable hotels if you have to stay the night. The *Hotel Asinol* is the cheapest in town. Small singles/doubles with fan cost RM20/25, and air-con rooms go for RM35. The *Hotel Lian Hin* (☎ 087-821506), near the waterfront, has air-con singles/doubles with bathroom for RM30/35. Top of the range, but only just, is the *Shangsan Hotel* (☎ 087-821809), also near the waterfront. It has air-con rooms with bathroom and TV for RM40/45, and triples for RM65.

Sipitang has a number of *kedai kopi* and *food stalls* on the main street. *Restoran Anda* has basic Malay fare, but at the back of the restaurant you can sit over the ocean and enjoy the sea breezes.

Getting There & Away

Minibuses ply between Beaufort and Sipitang throughout the day and cost RM6, and buses go to Merapok in Sarawak for RM3. From Beaufort there are buses, taxis and trains to KK or Tenom. The 47km road to Beaufort is a dusty bone-cruncher. In contrast, the good road south to Merapok and Lawas is paved and very scenic in parts as it runs parallel to jungle-clad mountains.

A boat to Labuan leaves at 7.30 am; the trip takes an hour and costs RM20.

PULAU LABUAN

Labuan is an island about 8km off the coast of Sabah at the mouth of Brunei Bay. It has an interesting history, but the only reason for travellers to come here is to catch a ferry to Sarawak or Brunei.

Just to confuse regional politics, Labuan is a Federal Territory governed directly from Kuala Lumpur. The government is pouring money into the island and pushing it as a major off-shore banking haven. Labuan is also a duty-free centre that attracts alcohol-starved hordes from nearby Brunei.

The Sultan of Brunei ceded Labuan to the British in 1846 and, apart from three years under Japanese occupation, it remained British for 115 years until Malaysia's independence. Labuan's modern anonymity belies the fact that it was the cockpit of Borneo during WWII: the Japanese landed here and the Allies counter-invaded; the Japanese forces in North Borneo surrendered here at the end of the war; and the Japanese officers responsible for the 'death marches' from Sandakan were tried by an Australian War Crimes Court on Labuan. There's a war cemetery and peace park to mark these horrific events. Labuan was once a coal-mining centre and now has major petroleum gas installations.

Bandar Labuan is the main town and the transit point for ferries between Brunei and Sabah. WWII veterans sometimes make a pilgrimage to see the memorials, but the only compelling reason to come here is to enjoy some of the best wreck diving in Asia.

Information

Labuan has a small helpful Tourism Malaysia information office (☎ 087-423445) on the corner of Jalan Dewan and Jalan Berjaya.

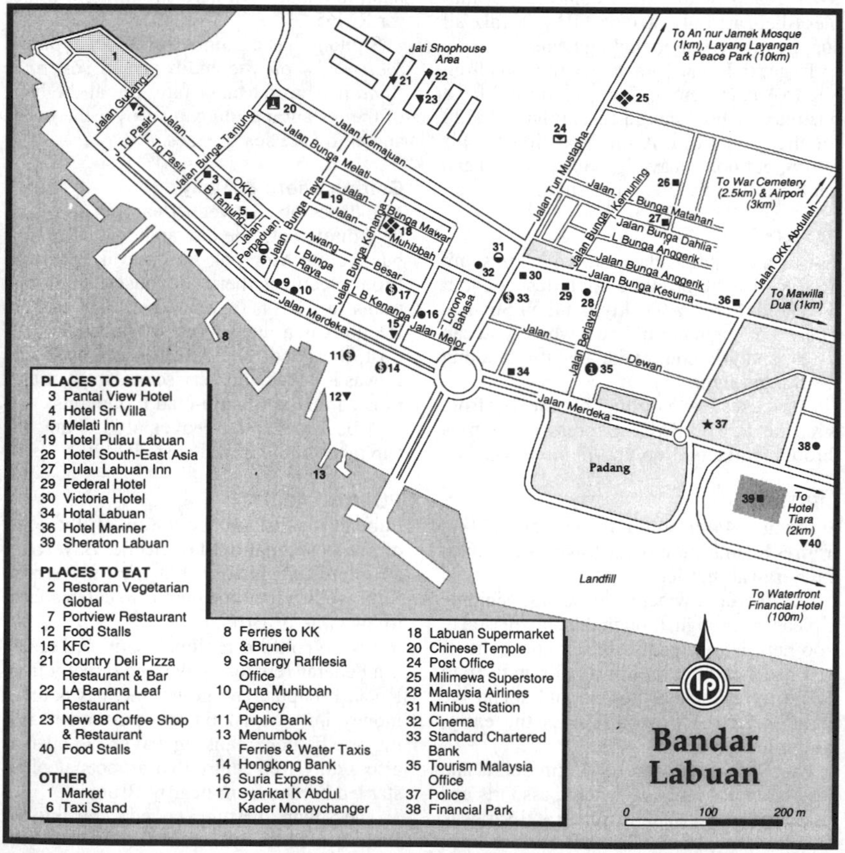

There are numerous banks around town – the Hongkong Bank is the best for changing travellers cheques. Moneychangers around town will change cash and travellers cheques at good rates; try Syarikat K Abdul Kader at 90 Jalan OKK Awang Besar.

Syarikat Aifas is a book and gift store in the lobby of the Hotel Labuan with a reasonable selection of books on Borneo and general books in English.

Things to See

Bandar Labuan has a small covered **market**, and water-taxis carry passengers to the **stilt villages**, Kampung Patau-Patau Satu and Kampung Patau-Patau Dua, that fringe the bay west of town. A 15 minute walk from the jetty there's the **An'nur Jamek Mosque**, an impressive piece of Star Wars-meets-Arabia architecture.

The **Labuan War Cemetery** has row upon row of headstones dedicated to the nearly 4000 Commonwealth servicemen, mostly Australian and British, who lost their lives in Borneo during WWII. The cemetery is near the golf course, 2km east of town along Jalan OKK Abdullah.

A **Peace Park** on the west of the island at Layang Layangan commemorates the place of Japanese surrender and has a Japanese war memorial.

The island has some good **beaches** at Pohon Batu and south from Layang Layangan along the west coast, but ask locals whether there are jellyfish and stingrays before swimming here. A chimney is all that remains of an old factory at the north of the island; it's a minor attraction from where there are good views along the coast.

Pulau Kuraman, Pulau Rusukan Kecil and Pulau Rusukan Besar are uninhabited **islands** lying south-west of Labuan that are to be gazetted as a marine park. These beaches are pristine, but unfortunately dynamite fishing has destroyed much of the coral. **Pulau Papan** is another island, 5km south-east of Bandar Labuan, that's being developed as a tourist attraction. See Getting There & Away for information on how to get there.

Wreck Diving

Four shipwrecks have been discovered off Labuan. Two were sunk during WWII and two were commercial vessels that sank in the 1980s.

The **American Wreck** is the USS *Salute*, a minesweeper built in late 1943 and sunk – by a mine – in 1945. This wreck sits on a sandy bottom at 33m.

The identity of the **Australian Wreck** is still uncertain. It was a freighter built in Rotterdam in 1900, captured by the Japanese in 1942 and sunk by the Royal Australian Air Force (hence the name) in 1945.

The **Cement Wreck** is the MV *Tung Hwang*, a freighter which hit a sandbank in 1980 while carrying cement for the Sultan of Brunei's new palace. It sits upright in 30m of water and its masts are 8m below the surface.

The **Blue Water Wreck** is the MV *Mabini Padre*, a Philippine trawler that sank in November 1981. Being further offshore, this wreck usually has the best visibility.

Of all the wrecks, the Cement Wreck is the easiest to dive and is used for wreck-dive training. The American Wreck and the Blue Water Wreck are for experienced wreck divers only.

Borneo Divers (☎ 087-415867) has an office at the Waterfront Financial Hotel and can organise reef and wreck diving off Labuan. Wreck dives cost RM100 to RM160 (US$40 to US$60) per dive or RM185 to RM235 (US$75 to US$95) for two dives. (See the Diving & Snorkelling section in the Terengganu chapter for details on safe and responsible diving.)

Places to Stay – Budget

Budget accommodation in Bandar Labuan is very limited. On weekdays there is some latitude for bargaining, but on weekends and public holidays you'll probably have to take whatever is going.

The *Pantai View Hotel* (☎ 087-411339), Jalan Bunga Tanjung, has fan-cooled rooms with shared bathroom that are comparatively cheap at RM30; there are also air-con rooms with bathroom and TV for RM45. If you can afford it, you're better off elsewhere.

Around the corner on Jalan OKK Awang Besar, *Hotel Sri Villa* (☎ 087-416369) has large fan-cooled rooms for RM35; air-con rooms start at RM40.

The nearby *Melati Inn* (☎ 087-416307) has small air-con rooms with shared bathroom for RM45; rooms with an attached bathroom cost virtually the same at RM45/48 for singles/doubles.

Places to Stay – Mid-Range

The *Hotel South East Asia* (☎ 087-415140) on Jalan Bunga Seroja has air-con rooms for RM50 and twins for RM60.

The other mid-range hotels are a noticeable jump up in quality and price. The two star *Victoria Hotel* (☎ 087-412411), Jalan Tun Mustapha, charges RM70/92 for airy and spacious singles/doubles or RM81/103 for larger rooms with a minibar. Close by on Jalan Bunga Kesuma, the *Federal Hotel* (☎ 087-411711) is slightly cheaper at RM66/88, and offers a 25% discount for cash payment.

The *Hotel Pulau Labuan* (☎ 087-416288) on Jalan Bunga Raya is better, with discounted rooms for RM69/83; rooms are big and clean, with bathroom and minibar. The same people also run the smaller, new *Pulau Labuan Inn* (☎ 087-416833), which is in a less salubrious part of town and offers smaller rooms for the same price.

If you don't want to stay in town, chalets on Pulau Papan cost RM90 with air-con and RM70 without. For bookings phone ☎ 087-249222.

Places to Stay – Top End

These hotels add a 10% service charge, but in tax-free Labuan hotels do not charge the usual 5% government tax. Promotional discounts and weekend rates are sometimes available.

The *Hotel Labuan* (☎ 087-412502) is in a central location and costs RM130 for superior rooms and RM150 for deluxe rooms. The two star *Hotel Mariner* (☎ 087-418822), on the corner of Jalan Bunga Kesuma and Jalan OKK Abdullah, has smaller, so-so singles/doubles starting at RM149/193. Unless you can get a discount here this is an outrageous rate.

Labuan's best hotels are east of the town centre. The spanking new *Sheraton Labuan* (☎ 087-422000), 462 Jalan Merdeka, has rooms starting at RM350 and suites from RM850 to RM3500. This fine hotel has a pool, good restaurants and safes in the rooms.

Nearby, the four star *Waterfront Financial Hotel* (☎ 087-418111), Jalan Wawasan, is a sprawling place which is popular with businesspeople. Rates range from RM330 to RM530.

The five star *Hotel Tiara* (☎ 087-414300), Jalan Tanjung Batu, is a little out of town towards the Labuan War Cemetery, but it's nicely positioned near a beach. Large suites start at RM260 and it's a quiet, exclusive spot.

Places to Eat

Bandar Labuan has plenty of cafes and restaurants. Prices in air-con places often reflect their Bruneian patronage, but in duty-free Labuan alcohol is cheap and a big bottle of beer can cost as little as RM3.

Food stalls can be found on Jalan Muhibbah between the Labuan Supermarket and the cinema, and there's a small *food centre* behind the Hongkong Bank. There's another food stall centre between the Sheraton Labuan and the Waterfront Financial Hotel. The *Sri Villa*, underneath the hotel of the same name, is a good Indian restaurant with cheap fare and roti canai for breakfast.

The area of shophouses north of the Hotel Pulau Labuan – known as the Jati Shophouse Area – is a good area for restaurants; among the choices are the *Country Deli Pizza Restaurant & Bar*, *LA Banana Leaf Restaurant* and *New 88 Coffee Shop & Restaurant*.

Despite its name, the air-con *Restoran Vegetarian Global* serves mainly expensive (RM12 to RM16) seafood; more good seafood can be enjoyed at the *Portview Restaurant*, right next to the jetty where you catch the boat for KK or Brunei.

Opposite the Hotel Tiara, the *Labuan Beach Restaurant* has outdoor dining on a veranda overlooking the beach. The choice includes seafood and western food, but the staff can be a bit surly.

Getting There & Away

Air The Malaysia Airlines office is in the same building as the Federal Hotel; opening hours are from 8.30 am to 5 pm Monday to Friday and 8.30 am to 1 pm on Saturday.

Labuan is well served by the Malaysia Airlines domestic network. There are regular flights to Kota Kinabalu (eight daily, RM52), Kuala Lumpur (six daily, RM372), Kuching (daily, RM199) and Miri (at least twice daily, RM66). There is also a daily flight to BSB in Brunei (RM63). There are also weekly Twin Otter flights between Labuan and Lawas (RM31) and Long Pasia (RM54) in Sarawak.

Boat Boat services from Bandar Labuan include the following:

Brunei Four or five express passenger boats depart for Muara in Brunei daily. Normal departure times are listed below, but the schedule changes and extra services may be available on weekends and public holidays.

The *Sanergy Rafflesia* is a fast catamaran with a cafeteria and is probably the most comfortable option. Aim to arrive at the wharf at least half an hour before departure. The journey to Muara takes 1½ to two hours.

Tickets can be bought at the small kiosk at the ferry terminal building before departure, but it is best to book in advance for weekend services. Ticket agents in town include Duta Muhibbah Agency (☎ 087-413827), Sinmatu (☎ 087-412261), Sanergy Rafflesia (☎ 087-410826) and Borneo Leisure Travel (☎ 087-410255) – all on Jalan Merdeka. Schedules and costs at the time of writing include:

Suria Express: 8.30 am departure; RM24
Sanergy Rafflesia: 11 am departure; RM24 (one class only)
Sri Labuan Tiga: noon departure; RM22
Mutiara Laut: departure at either 2 or 3 pm (alternates with *Ratu Samudra*); RM24
Ratu Samudra: departure at either 2 or 3 pm (alternates with *Mutiara Laut*); RM24

Sabah Fast motorised passenger ferries – including *Sanergy Rafflesia* – connect Labuan to KK. The trip takes about three hours. Tickets can be bought just before departure, or you can book in advance; ticket offices are the same as for the Brunei ferries. The fare to KK is RM28/33 for economy/1st class, except for *Sanergy Rafflesia*, which is RM28 (one class only).

Duta Muhibbah No 3: 8.30 am departure
Labuan Express Dua: 1 pm departure
Express Ming Hai: 1 pm departure
Express Kinabalu: 3.30 pm departure
Sanergy Rafflesia: 3.30 pm departure

The cheapest option to Sabah is the slow car ferry to Menumbok, which leaves at 8 am, 1 and 4 pm, costs RM5 for passengers and takes around 1½ hours. Buy tickets at the wharf where it departs from behind the Hongkong Bank.

There are also small launches which shuttle back and forth frequently. The crossing takes about 30 minutes and costs RM10. Boats leave when full (you shouldn't have to wait more than half an hour) from the main ferry terminal between 7.30 am and 5 pm. From Menumbok there are frequent minibuses to Beaufort (one hour, RM8) and KK (two hours, RM15).

Small launches also connect Bandar Labuan and Sipitang. They operate from 10 am to noon and go when full (about one hour, RM20) from the main ferry terminal.

Sarawak There is one service daily to Limbang (departs 12.30 pm, one hour, RM20) and Lawas (departs 1 pm, one hour, RM20). Buy your ticket at the ferry terminal on the morning of departure.

Getting Around

Bus Labuan has a good minibus network. Buses leave regularly from outside the cinema on Jalan Mustapha. Their numbers are clearly painted on the front and fares range from 50 sen for a short trip to RM2 for a trip to the top of the island. Destinations and fares are as follows:

No 1: war cemetery (RM1) and airport (RM1.50)
No 2: mosque and Patau-Patau (RM1.20)
No 3: Bebuloh (RM1.50)
No 4: mosque, Peace Park & Layang Layangan (RM1.20)
No 6: mosque, chimney (RM1.50)

Car Daily car hire rates start from RM180. Adaras Rent A Car (☎ 087-421590) has a desk at the airport; and E & C Limousine Services (☎ 087-422098) has an office at the Waterfront Financial Hotel.

Taxi Taxis – mostly unmetered private cars – are plentiful. There's a taxi rank in the town centre. The standard fare for a journey of up to a few kilometres is RM5; a taxi to the airport should not cost more than RM8.

Boat Boats for Pulau Papan leave from the jetty at Mawilla Dua 1km east of town and cost RM8 for a return trip. There is no scheduled timetable; negotiate when you book.

North of Kota Kinabalu

The road north from the capital leads to small coastal towns and stilt villages, then over low hills to the market town of Kota Belud. The route to Kota Belud is well travelled and almost de rigueur on the itineraries of tour groups. However, apart from Kota Belud town, most travellers probably won't find much of interest.

Beyond Kota Belud the highway traverses fertile plains planted with rice, coconut, oil palm and bananas. A scenic peninsula with some nice beaches leads into the country of the Rungus people and on to the town of Kudat.

Kudat doesn't see many tourists and is the end of the line to all but the boldest: ownership of the islands to the north and east is disputed by the Philippines and out of bounds to most foreigners.

TUARAN

Tuaran, 33km from KK, is a bustling little town with tree-lined streets. Tamu day is Sunday and on the road into town there's a nine storey Chinese pagoda which is probably the tallest building between KK and the Philippines.

Telipok is a village on the highway 10km south of Tuaran. Much of the pottery sold in souvenir shops in KK comes from here. There are three main outlets along the highway coming north from KK: Soon Yi Song, at Km 8, fires pots in traditional kilns; Grace Dynamic at Km 11, and Sinar Pottery at the Km 12 mark, both have big shops selling all manner of earthenware.

There's a turn-off 2km before Tuaran that leads to two luxury resorts and **Mengkabong Water Village**, a Bajau stilt village built over an estuary. It was once a very picturesque spot, though it's hardly the 'Venice of the East', as it's described in some tourist brochures. Unfortunately, it has become modernised and incredibly garbage-strewn in recent years, and is now of little interest to travellers.

There's a much better stilt village at **Penimbawan**. To get there, take a minibus to Susarup (RM1) then charter a motorboat at the jetty for about RM30 (there and back). The trip takes about 20 minutes and the boat will wait while you look around.

Places to Stay

Tuaran is best done as a day trip, but if you get stuck here the *Orchid Motel* (☎ 088-793789) in the main street has very basic fan-cooled bunk rooms for RM30, or RM40 with air-con; and air-con singles/doubles for RM60/80.

The alternative is a choice of two luxury resorts on the road to Mengkabong Water Village; both are set on nice beaches. The *Sabandar Bay Resort* (☎ 088-251622) is a sprawling place with a swimming pool, water slides, a conference centre and disco. Rooms start at RM160, semidetached chalets cost RM300 and detached chalets RM400.

The *Rasa Ria Resort* (☎ 088-792888) is a massive place adjoining the Dalit Bay Golf

& Country Club with its own forest and tame wildlife. Rooms are the last word in luxury and there's a couple of good restaurants. Standard singles/doubles are RM360/390, or RM410/440 for rooms facing the sea; suites are RM700 to RM900.

Getting There & Away

Minibuses go regularly between KK and Tuaran (45 minutes, RM2). Minibuses from Tuaran to Tamparuli are RM1; to Mengkabong they are less frequent and cost 60 sen. Regular minibuses go from Tuaran to Kota Belud (one hour, RM4).

The resorts have regular shuttle services to KK – phone for times. Hitching from Tuaran is a good bet on weekends.

KOTA BELUD

Every Sunday Kota Belud hosts one of Sabah's largest and most interesting tamus. It's a colourful melee of vendors and hagglers, spruikers and quacks, Bajaus arguing with Chinese and Indian traders; travelling salesmen knocking down plastic toys with all the skill of a Sotheby's auctioneer; medicine men backing up their claims with dramatic photos; and, wandering through it all, brightly dressed children and itinerant cows.

Tamus are not simply open-air markets where villagers gather to sell their farm produce and to buy manufactured goods from traders; they are also social occasions where news and stories are exchanged. Farmers haggle all morning over the price of a buffalo calf and the Bajau sell their horses, although they don't put on their traditional dress unless there's a tour bus in town.

The action starts at first light and it's a popular destination for camera-clicking tour groups – get there as early as possible. Unfortunately, you'll be disappointed if you're looking for tribal handicrafts. You may have more luck at the Sunday tamu at Sikuati, 23km from Kudat, which is attended by the Rungus people who live in nearby longhouses.

Kota Belud is just a small, sleepy rural town. The biggest building is the new *pasar*

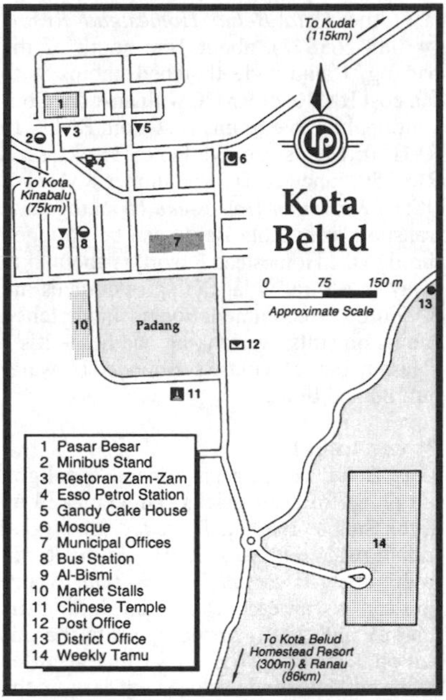

besar, the meat and vegetable market. Everything closes down early and the only nightlife is that enjoyed by the cows, horses and dogs that roam the streets foraging through the garbage.

About 14km north of Kota Belud on the way to Kudat the road passes an area of marsh and coastal scrub that is home to water birds. It's not signposted, but it's an unofficial sanctuary that in the wet season can be jumping with birdlife – look out for the beautiful blue-throated bee-eater perched on wires.

It's difficult to explore the area without your own transport. A reedy lake west of the highway marks the start of the sanctuary; turn off at the sign for Rampayan Laut and look in the marsh and padis along the road.

Places to Stay

Most people visit Kota Belud as a day trip from KK. The only accommodation in town is at the *Kota Belud Homestead Resort* (☎ 088-265842), about 1km south of the padang, Bajau-style thatched cabins with fan cost RM40, or RM70 with air-con. Conventional double rooms cost from RM90 to RM130. Meals are available: breakfast is RM7.50, lunch RM13 and dinner RM15.

The *Kulambai Homestead* (bookings and transport from Kota Belud can be arranged through the Homestead Resort) is about 8km away in a rural village; singles/doubles are RM60/80. Accommodation is in thatched cabins on stilts overlooking paddies – it's a pleasant, peaceful place surrounded by water buffalo and birds.

Places to Eat

Kota Belud is not a gastronome's delight, but plenty of tasty snacks can be picked up at the Sunday market. There are some good Indian restaurants around the old market in town, such as *Restoran Zam-Zam*, where you can get an early roti before hitting the market, and the *Al-Bismi,* opposite the bus station. Kota Belud has a few Chinese coffee shops but they tend to close very early in the evening. *Gandy Cake House* is a good bakery for cakes and pastries.

Getting There & Away

The main area for minibuses and share-taxis is at the bus station in front of the old market. Most of these serve the Kota Belud-KK route, which costs RM6 and takes about two hours. A new freeway covers most of the route from KK to Kota Belud. On Sunday, tamu day, the number of minibuses and taxis has to be seen to be believed. On other days it's much quieter.

Minibuses north to Kudat cost RM8 and take about two hours.

To get to Kinabalu National Park, take any minibus going to KK and get off at Tamparuli, about half way there. The trip takes about half an hour and costs RM5. From Tamparuli there are several minibuses to Ranau every day until about 2 pm. All of them pass the park entrance – tell the driver to drop you off there. The ride to the park is RM7 and to go all the way to Ranau costs RM10. The journey to the national park HQ takes about an hour from Tamparuli along a good sealed road; the direct road from Kota Belud to Ranau is very rough and not used by minibuses. A minibus to KK from Tamparuli is RM3.

KUDAT

Kudat is a fairly large but quiet port town in the very north of Sabah, 190km from Kota Kinabalu. Kudat has a noticeable Filipino influence, as much of the trade here is with the Philippines, and the surrounding countryside is the home of the friendly Rungus people, tribal cousins of the Kadazans.

Kudat has little of interest and few travellers make it this far north. It is difficult to get around without your own transport, but there are fine beaches west of town and it is possible to visit Rungus longhouses near the highway.

The commercial centre of Kudat is near the harbour and divided into two parts by a new two storey market building. The older section next to the harbour is a picturesque but dilapidated collection of godowns; you'll find most of the shops and cheaper places to stay here. The new part of town comprises a couple of blocks of offices, hotels and shops about 200m across a park west of the old town.

Places to Stay & Eat

In the old part of town, the *Hotel Oriental* has worn but OK fan-cooled rooms for RM20 and air-con rooms for RM35. All the other hotels are mid-range air-con places.

Hotel Kian Dai (☎ 088-614934) has air-con doubles with TV for RM46. The *Hotel Sunrise* (☎ 088-611517) is of a reasonable standard; fan-cooled/air-con rooms with shared bathroom cost RM20/28; single/double air-con rooms with bathroom and TV are RM40/48.

The *Hotel Kinabalu* (☎ 088-613888), in the new section of town, is a good option. Singles/doubles with air-con, TV and bathroom cost RM42/56, though some of the singles are windowless. *Hotel Greenland* (☎ 088-613211), in the same street as the

Kinabalu, is similar but not such good value. Rooms without bathroom cost RM35, most with bathroom cost RM49/56.

There are some good Chinese and Muslim *cafes* in the newer blocks west of the market. *Big Bites Cafe* is one of the only air-con options in the old part of town; it's a clean, friendly place which serves sandwiches, burgers and pasta as well as Malay dishes. It's down the end of the main street at the opposite end to the waterfront.

Getting There & Away

Air There are Malaysia Airlines Twin Otter flights from Kudat to Kota Kinabalu (three weekly, RM50) and Sandakan (five weekly, RM54).

Bus Several minibuses a day make the three to four hour trip from KK for RM15. The two hour journey from Kota Belud costs RM8. Buses stop in the old part of town.

AROUND KUDAT

You'll find some of the best beaches in Sabah around Kudat where the water is shallow and safe for paddling. **Bak Bak**, about 11km from Kudat, is the town beach. It has clear water, picnic and toilet facilities and food stalls on weekends, though the beach itself is only a narrow strip of sand against a retaining wall. The fishing villages further north of Bak Bak have some even better white-sand beaches, but there is no accommodation and they are difficult to get to.

More and more Rungus people are building their own houses in preference to living in traditional longhouses, but there are still some interesting longhouses around Kudat. If you visit one, it's polite to take a few small gifts of food or cigarettes. The best known of these longhouses is **Matunggung**, on the highway south of Kudat. It is well frequented by tour groups, but other longhouses can be found further inland from the highway. This is a traditional thatched-roof longhouse with enclosed bamboo-slatted sides. Inside, each family's living quarters, called a *valai*, is composed of sleeping, dining and living areas and an attic.

The traditional dress for Rungus women is a black sarung and colourful, beaded necklaces. On festive occasions, heavy brass bracelets are worn as well. The Rungus tribes produce some elaborate beadwork and you can sometimes buy their handicrafts at the Sunday tamu held at **Sikuati**, 23km south of Kudat. Sikuati is on the highway, 1km from the coast, where there is a good beach. Teluk Sikuati has a long, sweeping white-sand beach, though the water can be choppy and it is not as clear as that around Bak Bak.

Getting There & Away

Bak Bak is difficult to get to without your own transport – count on RM10 for a taxi out there, RM12 to be picked up. Sikuati and Matunggung are both on the highway and minibuses can drop you off.

RANAU

Ranau is a small provincial town on the route between KK and Sandakan. There's a colourful and busy tamu on Saturday at the bridge a few hundred metres south of town, but few travellers stay overnight since the big attraction is Poring Hot Springs, about 19km to the north. It is primarily a place to get a bus connection to or from Poring or Mt Kinabalu.

Ranau is only a few hundred metres square. Express buses park at the top end of town behind the Esso station. In the blocks of shophouses across the road there are cafes and hotels, and minibuses line up in droves down the main street to the west of the bus stand.

Places to Stay & Eat

If you get stuck, Ranau has a couple of pricey mid-range hotels to choose from. *Hotel Ranau* (☎ 088-875661) is the first place you see when entering the town and is opposite the Shell petrol station. The choice ranges from simple fan-cooled rooms for RM30/45, up to RM70 with air-con, TV and bathroom.

Hotel Kinabalu (☎ 088-876028), west of the main street, has similar rooms and even similar décor – all garish plastic and frills –

for the same price and suites for RM80. Both are of a good standard, but the Hotel Kinabalu is a tad better.

Ranau has plenty of coffee shops, mostly Chinese. *Kedai Makan Mien Mien* has a variety of dishes, including an excellent chicken curry in thick coconut gravy. Rice, vegetables and a meat dish will cost around RM3. *Restoran Seri Malaysia*, opposite the long-distance bus station, has excellent rice and noodle dishes.

Getting There & Away

Bus Bus services operate regularly from Ranau.

Kota Kinabalu Express buses depart Ranau until about 1.30 pm. The fare is RM15 and the trip takes about 3½ hours. HWA Lean 1st Express (☎ 088-875460) has a ticket office where the buses pull in.

Minibuses and share-taxis depart daily until about 4 pm; the fare to KK is RM15. It is best to catch them in the morning because afternoon runs are less frequent.

All services to KK pass the entrance to Mt Kinabalu National Park (RM5).

Sandakan All buses to Sandakan pass the Sepilok Orang-Utan Rehabilitation Centre; ask to be dropped off. Air-con express buses are the best way to travel, and these leave Ranau for Sandakan between 7.30 am and noon; the fare is RM20 and the journey takes about 3½ hours. Minibuses go throughout the day but can take a while to fill up, especially in the afternoon.

Poring Hot Springs On weekends it's easy and cheap to get to the hot springs from Ranau. Drivers cruise around the blocks, shouting 'Poring, Poring!'. The price is RM4 per person and the transport leaves when it's full (which doesn't take long because many locals go there for an afternoon trip).

On weekdays it isn't quite so easy, especially if you arrive in Ranau during the afternoon. If this happens you'll have to ask around the cafes and shops to see if anyone wants to share the cost.

Taxi Share-taxis are available, but drivers will probably try to convince you to charter the whole taxi. Charter costs RM20, which is fine between three or four people, but painful if you're on your own. Bargain hard, but paying RM20 is better than staying in Ranau.

PORING HOT SPRINGS

The Poring Hot Springs were developed by the Japanese during WWII and since the war have become a popular weekend retreat for local people. The complex is actually part of the Kinabalu National Park, but the park HQ is 43km away via Ranau.

Steaming, sulphurous water is channelled into pools and tubs in which visitors can relax their tired muscles after the trek to the summit of Mt Kinabalu. The pools are in a pretty garden setting with hibiscus and other flowers which attract hordes of butterflies. Poring is also famous among birdwatchers, and a good selection of birds can be seen around the gardens and along walking trails.

There's a souvenir shop at the park office, and planned developments include a rafflesia centre, orchid garden and butterfly farm.

Baths

The outdoor tubs are of varying sizes and can easily fit a couple of people. They have hot and cold water taps, so you can regulate your ideal temperature. The water from the springs is very hot – you can boil eggs for breakfast in it, but, as the sign indicates, only inside a plastic bag. The baths are open from 7 am to 6 pm daily, although locals flaunt this rule. Western women will probably be ogled in the tubs.

Private spa cabins are also available. A standard cabin has a tub and shower, and costs RM15 for the first hour or part thereof, then RM25 for every additional hour. Larger spa cabins can accommodate up to eight people. The deluxe cabins have a lounge area, Jaccuzzis, shower and toilet, and cost RM20 for the first hour, then RM30 for each additional hour.

After a hot bath you can take a cooling dip in the rock pool.

continued on page 495

CLIMBING KINABALU

Title Page: Spectacular view from the summit of Mt Kinabalu. (photograph by Simon Rowe)

GLENN BEANLAND

GLENN BEANLAND

SIMON ROWE

Changing Scenery

Top: View to the peak from beyond the power station.
Middle: Tropical rainforest and jungle streams en route.
Bottom: The final arduous climb to the summit.

Climbing Kinabalu

Towering above the coastal plain and what's left of the lush tropical forests of North Borneo, Mt Kinabalu is the biggest tourist attraction in Sabah and the centrepiece of the vast 754 sq km Kinabalu National Park. At 4101m, it is the highest mountain between the mighty Himalaya and New Guinea. And it's still growing: researchers have found it increases in height by about 5mm a year. It is 50km inland, but on a clear day you can see the Philippines from the summit; and before smoke haze became a serious problem, Kinabalu's bare granite peaks were visible most mornings from many places along the west coast.

Despite these awesome facts, Mt Kinabalu is one of the easiest mountains in the world to climb, and thousands of people of all ages and fitness levels scale the summit every year. No special skills or equipment are required; all you need is some stamina, determination and weatherproof clothing – it can get very cold and wet up there.

Those who persevere will be rewarded with a memorable experience. The views are magnificent, even before you get to the top, and the sunsets incredible.

While the climb is the main reason most foreigners come to the park, only about 10% of its 170,000 annual visitors actually climb the peak. The park itself is a beautiful spot, and many visitors come just to escape the heat and humidity of the coast. There are walking trails in the superb rainforest at the base of the mountain, the climate is agreeably cool – even cold at night – and the accommodation is very good.

HISTORY

The first recorded ascent of the mountain was made in 1851 by Sir Hugh Low, the British colonial secretary on the island of Labuan. Kinabalu's highest peak is named after him, as is the mile-deep 'gully' on the other side of the mountain.

In those days the difficulty of climbing Mt Kinabalu lay not in the ascent itself, but in getting to its base through the trackless jungles – and finding local porters willing to go there. The Dusun (now called Kadazan) tribesmen who accompanied Low believed the mountain to be inhabited by the spirits of their dead. Low was therefore obliged to protect the party, and a guide carried a large basket of quartz crystals and teeth, as was the custom. The ceremonies performed by the guides to appease the spirits on reaching the summit became more elaborate as time went on, so that by the 1920s they had come to include loud prayers, gunshots and the sacrifice of seven eggs and seven white chickens; however, in recent times the custom appears to have died out.

These days there's a sealed road all the way from Kota Kinabalu to the foot of the mountain, but Low's Gully – the abyss on the other side of the summit – didn't give up its secrets as easily as Low's Peak. The first expedition to abseil into the gully got lost for several

The Legend of Mt Kinabalu

A colourful local Kadazan legend tells how Mt Kinabalu got its name. Many years ago, the emperor of China heard that on this mountain there was a fabulous pearl guarded by a dragon. He told his three sons that whichever of them could bring him the pearl would be the next emperor.

Two sons tried and failed; the third son managed to snatch the pearl, but just as he was sneaking away the dragon woke and gave chase. The prince hid in the jungle with the pearl while the rest of his party went on, with the dragon in hot pursuit. They jumped back into their boat and hightailed it for China, but still the dragon followed. In desperation they fired their cannons at it. Thinking the cannonballs were the pearl, the dragon devoured them and eventually drowned.

Meanwhile, back in the jungle, the prince took a local wife and raised a family, but after some years decided it was time to return to China to claim the throne. He promised his wife he would come back to fetch her, but of course he never showed up. In despair she climbed to the top of the mountain to pray for his return and died in the process. Hence *Kina*, meaning China, and *balu*, widow.

days, and it was only as recently as February 1998 that a joint British-Malaysian expedition explored the bottom, returning with several new species of plants and insects.

GEOLOGY

From its immense size you might think Mt Kinabalu is the ancient core of Borneo, but in fact the mountain was formed relatively recently. Its origins go back a mere nine million years, to when a solidified core of volcanic rock began swelling up from the depths below and pushed its way through the overlying rock. This upward movement is apparently still continuing.

In geological terms Mt Kinabalu is still very young. Little erosion has occurred on the exposed granite rock-faces around the summit, though the effects of glaciers which used to cover much of the mountain can be detected by the trained eye. The glaciers have disappeared, but at times ice forms in the rock pools near the summit.

FLORA

Exhilarating though it is, the climb to the top isn't the only rewarding experience that awaits you. Mt Kinabalu is a botanical paradise in which over half the species growing above 900m are unique to the area; many more are no doubt blooming unnamed in unexplored gullies and ridges. Among the more spectacular flowers are more than 1000 species of orchids and many rhododendrons; many species grow in profusion along the summit trail.

The park's most famous plant inhabitants are the insectivorous *Nepenthes*, or pitcher plants. The only place where they rival Mt Kinabalu for profusion is Bako National Park in Sarawak. Pitcher plants come in many shapes, sizes and colours, although you probably won't be as lucky as the 19th century botanist Spencer St John, who reported finding a specimen of *Nepenthes rajah* with a pitcher 30cm in diameter – it contained 2½ litres of watery fluid and a drowned rat!

Most pitcher plants are only large enough to trap unwary insects attracted to nectar which the plants secrete. On your way to the summit, try exploring a few metres in the undergrowth on either side of the trail – you're bound to come across one sooner or later.

Park HQ is surrounded by tall dipterocarp forest, better known as rainforest and characterised by huge trees with buttress roots. The canopy is dense and festooned with creepers, ferns and orchids. Some spectacular fungi grow on the forest floor.

Between 900m and 1800m the forest is comprised chiefly of oaks, laurels and chestnuts, and this type of forest occupies half the park's area. In this vegetation zone trees are smaller and more light passes through the canopy, allowing the growth of a dense ground cover and an abundance of orchids and mosses.

Above 1800m, where annual rainfall can reach over 450cm, there is a distinct transition to dense, stunted rhododendron forest, whose trunks and branches are often covered with mosses and orchids.

On the windswept slopes above Laban Rata the vegetation is stunted and clings to niches in the granite; sayat-sayat is a common woody shrub at this height. The uppermost slopes of the mountain are bare of plant life.

FAUNA

Nearly all of Borneo's mammal species have been recorded in Mt Kinabalu National Park, though more are seen in the lowland rainforest surrounding Poring Hot Springs than at higher altitudes around park HQ. The park is surrounded by cultivation and villages, and poaching is common along the borders: edible species such as deer and monkeys are not as common as they once were.

Still, the overall variety is staggering and among the park's more commonly seen mammals are many species of squirrels. Prevost's squirrel, with grey, orange and black fur, is a particularly handsome species, and the mountain ground squirrel is frequently seen along the summit trail. Around park HQ, tree-shrews can sometimes be seen raiding rubbish bins.

Birdwatchers will be that bit closer to heaven: more than 280 species of birds have been recorded, including nearly all of Borneo's endemic species. The action starts around park HQ, where common birds among the noisy feeding flocks include the Bornean treepie (a noisy relative of the magpie), fantails, bulbuls, sunbirds and laughing-thrushes. The veranda at Kinabalu Balsam restaurant is a good place to sit and watch the birds, and there are excellent birdwatching opportunities on the walking trails in the early morning – especially the Liwagu and Silau-Silau trails.

If you're climbing to the summit, look out for a number of birds seen only at higher altitudes. These include the Kinabalu friendly warbler, which is found only on these slopes, the dainty mountain black-eye and the mountain blackbird.

Other wildlife includes colourful butterflies and the moon moth – a huge green moth with long trailing wing streamers.

FURTHER READING

You might like to check out a little about what's in store for you on the mountain by reading the national parks publication *A Guide to Kinabalu National Park* by Susan Kay Jacobson; it is on sale at the gift shop at the park. Hugh Low's experiences on the mountain were recounted by his friend Spencer St John in *Experiences in the Forests of East Asia*. It was originally published in London in 1864, but a paperback reprint is available locally.

There are many books on the natural history – particularly the botany – of the area. Even if you aren't a botanist, *Nepenthes of Mount Kinabalu* by Shigeo Kurata is a complete guide to the diverse pitcher plants found on the mountain that's worth browsing through. The soft cover *Photographic Guide to the Birds of Mt Kinabalu* by Hitoshi Nakayasu will help you identify most of the common birds around park HQ and on the trails, plus give some handy hints on looking for them.

The last word on the park is the *Mt Kinabalu Handbook*, an encyclopaedic reference that goes into detail on the history, geology, flora, fauna and folklore of the area. It's a superb book with great photos and available at good bookshops in KK or Kuching.

ORIENTATION & INFORMATION

Kinabalu park HQ is 88km from KK and set in beautiful gardens with a magnificent view of the mountain. At 1588m it is an agreeably cool climate – average temperatures range from 20°C during the day to 13°C at night.

Accommodation at park HQ can be tight and even tighter on the mountain. Reservations must be made in advance (see Information in the KK section). On arrival check in at the park office and, if staying overnight, present your reservation slip from KK and you'll be allocated your bed or room. Valuables can be deposited in safety boxes at the office and excess baggage can be stored there until you return from the mountain (there's no charge for these services).

All the hostels and resthouses are within walking distance of the park office. In the old administration building there's a small museum, and a slide and video show presented here from Friday to Monday at 7.30 pm gives an excellent introduction to the mountain.

Next to the park office there's a souvenir shop selling T-shirts, film, ice creams and every type of souvenir imaginable. If you don't have a rain coat you can buy one here for RM15. There's also a reasonable range of books on the park and other places in Sabah, and a 30 minute photo-processing service. The shop is open from 7 am to 7 pm.

A climbing permit and Climber's Personal Accident Insurance are compulsory for any ascent of Mt Kinabalu. The permit costs RM50 for foreigners and RM25 for Malaysians; insurance costs RM3.50 per person per journey. All this is payable at the park HQ before you climb.

A guide is only compulsory if you intend to venture beyond Laban Rata, ie to the summit. Guide fees are RM25 per day for one to three persons, RM28 per day for four to six people and RM30 per day for seven to eight climbers (the maximum per guide).

There are conflicting opinions about the use of guides and it's

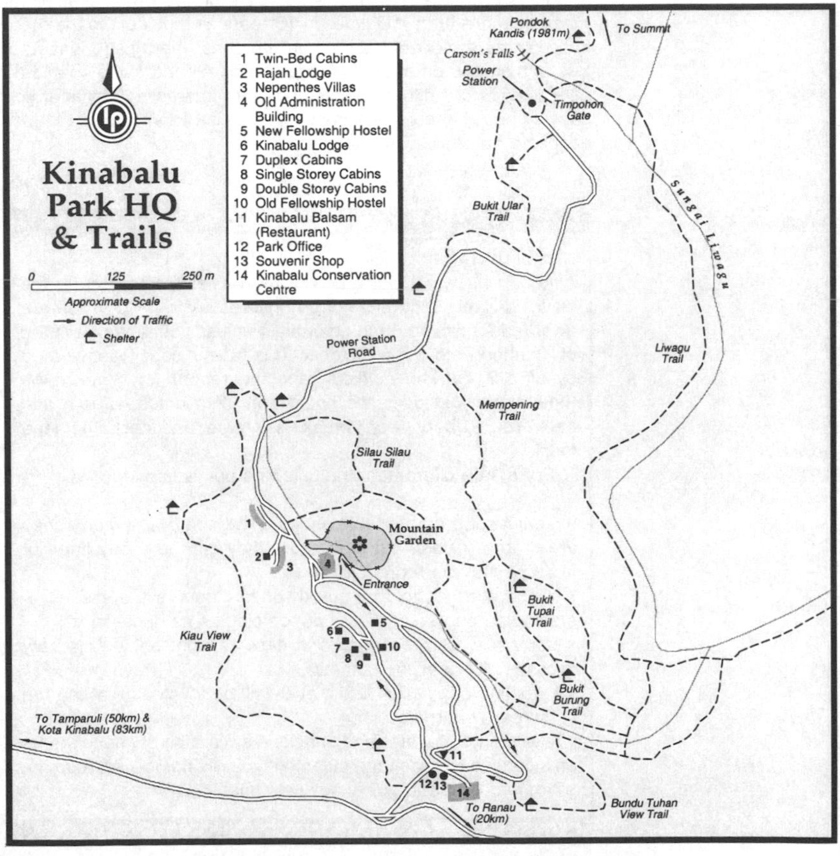

expensive if you can't share the cost with other people. Sabah Parks says guides are compulsory because climbers can 'easily lose their way on the rock surface when the fog and mist start covering the upper part of the mountain'. Another theory is that with compulsory guides the chances of people stealing pitcher plants and smuggling them out of the country are greatly reduced.

On arrival at the park HQ, you will be told to come to the park office on the morning of your climb and a guide will be assigned to you. On most mornings, there is a throng of people waiting for a guide – the earlier you start, the better. The park staff will try to attach individual travellers to a group so that guide fees can be shared – but ask, just in case. Couples can expect to be given their own guide.

The guides and porters are usually Kadazans from local villages, and not employees of the national park. Some of these professional guides are amazing: one is 55 years old and has climbed Mt Kinabalu more than 700 times in 16 years as a guide! On the other hand, some travellers have complained that their guide was useless and sloped off at the first opportunity. A good guide should be able to point out pitcher plants and other interesting sights; if you have a special interest ask the park office if it can find you a knowledgeable guide.

Climbing Safely

Although Mt Kinabalu is one of the easiest mountains in the world to climb, it should not be underestimated. No prizes are awarded for racing up the mountain unless you take part in the climbathon held every October. This race is usually dominated by ultra-fit Gurkha soldiers, and the record for climbing Mt Kinabalu is just over two hours and 42 minutes – there and back! You probably won't break this record, and there's no need to try.

For a safe climb bear the following points in mind:

- Wear strong comfortable shoes with good grip – gym shoes are probably best, but make sure they can be easily dried or frostbite may be a problem.
- Temperatures can drop quickly on the mountain; dress in layers so you can take off and put on clothes as necessary.
- Carry a waterproof jacket in case of rain; snow falls very occasionally near the summit.
- A woollen cap, scarf and gloves will be invaluable at the top in the early morning.
- Take plenty of water and snacks – save a bit of chocolate as an incentive to reach the summit if you're finding it hard going.
- Wear sunblock to guard against sunburn.

Porters are optional. A porter's fee is RM25 per day for a maximum load of 11kg up to the Panar Laban huts and RM1 for every extra 500g. For the second segment, up to the Sayat-Sayat hut, it's RM28 per day and RM1.20 for every 500g over 11kg.

WALKING TRAILS

It's well worth spending a day exploring the marked trails around park HQ; if you have time, it may be better to do it before you climb the mountain – you may not feel like it afterwards. All the trails and lookouts are shown on the Kinabalu Park HQ & Trails map.

All the trails link up with others at some stage, so you can spend the whole day, or indeed days, walking at a leisurely pace through the beautiful forest. Some interesting plants, plenty of birds and, if you're lucky, the occasional mammal can be seen along the Liwagu Trail, which follows the river of the same name. When it rains, watch out for slippery paths and armies of leeches.

At 11.15 am each day a guided walk starts from the park office and lasts for one to two hours. It's well worth taking and follows an easy path. The knowledgeable guide points out flowers, plants, birds and insects along the way. If you set out from KK early it's possible to arrive at the park in time for the guided walk.

Many of the plants found on the mountain are cultivated in the Mountain Garden behind the administration building; it is also well worth a look.

The Climb

The climb is normally done over two days. Most people climb as far as Laban Rata or the nearby huts the first day, then climb to the summit at dawn and return to park HQ that day. It is wise to stay overnight at the park HQ at least the night before the climb. This will allow you to make an early start and to acclimatise a bit – Mt Kinabalu is high enough for altitude sickness to occur.

The climb is uphill 99% of the way; it is unrelenting, steep in places and there are seemingly endless steps – actually there are 2500 – as far as Laban Rata. Then it gets a whole lot tougher. The trail becomes even steeper as you approach the summit, then disappears altogether on vast, near-vertical fields of slippery granite. Every step can be a struggle as you gasp for breath in the thin air. Still keen?

The secret to climbing Mt Kinabalu is stamina. Take it slowly – very slowly if you are tired and out of breath. Many people start off briskly then have to take frequent and increasingly longer rest breaks, while the old hands just keep trudging along. Take it easy and walk at a comfortable pace.

Signboards showing your progress are spaced along the trail and there's a marker every 500m. There are rest shelters *(pondoks)* at regular intervals with clean squat-style toilets and tanks of cool, fresh drinking water. The walking times that follow are conservative estimates published by the Sabah Parks office.

SIMON ROWE

Follow the signposts to the summit.

CLIMBING KINABALU

Leeches

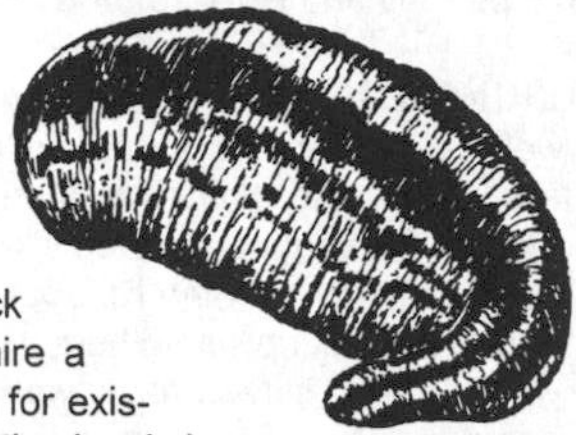

You are bound to meet some leeches in Borneo's rainforests, and if it's raining you will probably encounter hordes. Two species are common: the brown and the tiger leech (recognisable by its cream and black stripes). It is difficult to admire a creature whose main reason for existence is to suck blood, but the leech is remarkably adapted to its – admittedly repulsive – lifestyle.

These small relatives of earthworms are armed with a sucker at both ends, and on the front sucker there are three sets of minute teeth. When a leech senses the approach of a warm-blooded animal – in this case you, but more often a deer or pig – it makes for a prominent twig or leaf and rotates its body while anchored by the rear sucker. As its victim brushes past, the leech attaches itself and, once aboard, wastes no time in getting a meal. Supple and able to squeeze through clothing, it finds a bare patch of skin, bites painlessly then gorges itself on blood. Its saliva is armed with substances that anaesthetise the wound, dilate the blood vessels and stop a clot forming to ensure a constant flow.

When it has finished, the leech – now bloated and many times its original size – drops off into the leaf litter once more. Unless you catch it in the act, your first knowledge of its handiwork will be a trickle of blood.

Leeches are harmless, but a bite could become infected. Prevention is better than cure, but once they sense blood, these clinging parasites are persistent. To deter leeches, apply insect repellent and/or salt to your feet and ankles before putting on socks and shoes; also cover shoes and socks with insecticide on the outside. Salt is a leech's deadliest enemy and a powerful deterrent. Leech-proof socks are made of calico too dense for leeches to get through and could be a shrewd purchase.

Safe and effective ways to dislodge them include flicking them off sideways – any attempt to pull a leech off by the tail will only make it dig in harder – and burning them with a cigarette or match.

Not surprisingly, very few people have a kind word for the leech. But the forest hunters of Borneo regarded it as good luck to be bitten by one, and leeches are found only in primary forest – a small price to pay for enjoying the rainforest.

EQUIPMENT

As long as it's not raining you can walk as far as Laban Rata in normal hiking gear. It's only at the summit that you'll need warm clothes – and then you'll really need them. You'll appreciate gloves and a woollen hat, and a raincoat should be carried at all times. A torch (flashlight) is required if you're getting up before dawn. Bring snacks for the climb and food if you intend to do your own cooking. Water bottles can be filled along the trail, except between Laban Rata and the summit. Don't be fooled by the clouds – the sun is fierce at that altitude and to avoid sunburn it is very important to carry sunblock. Bedding is provided in the huts en route, but if you're staying beyond Laban Rata, pick it up from there on the way through.

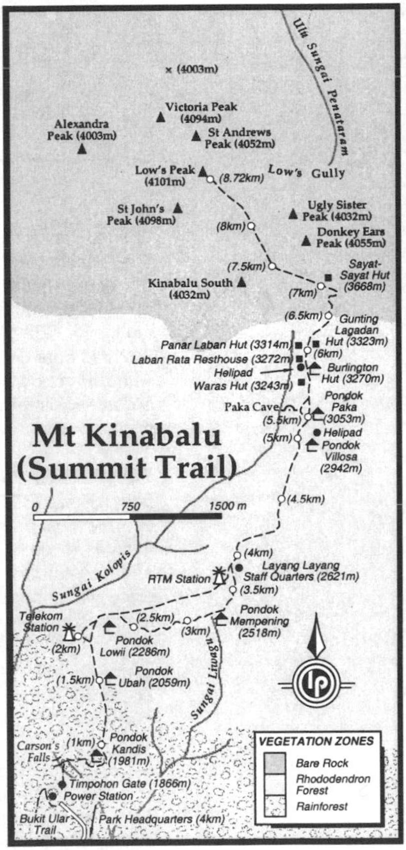

PARK HQ – POWER STATION

The trail officially starts at the Timpohon Gates (1866m), from where it's an 8.72km walk to the summit. Unfortunately it's nearly an hour's uphill walk from park HQ to the gate – or power station as it's commonly called. A minibus shuttles back and forth from the park HQ to the power station between 7 am and about 5 pm; it takes only 15 minutes, costs RM2 and will considerably shorten your day's walking. An earlier start can be negotiated with the park office.

It is not much fun walking along the road, though the Liwagu Trail to the power station is a scenic alternative for those who can afford to add an extra three hours or so to the climb.

POWER STATION – LAYANG LAYANG

After a short, deceptive *descent*, the trail leads up steep stairs through magnificent tall forest. There's a small waterfall – Carson's Falls – beside the track shortly after the start and the forest can be alive with birds and squirrels in the morning. Five pondoks are spaced at intervals of 15 to 35 minutes and it's about three hours to Layang Layang (2621m), where there's a small staff quarters. At Pondok Kandis (1981m) the tall forest gives way to dense, stunted rhododendron forest. Near Pondok Lowii (2286m) the trail follows an open ridge giving great views over the valleys and up to the peaks.

LAYANG LAYANG – PONDOK PAKA

It's about 1¾ hours on to Pondok Paka (3052m), the seventh shelter on the trail and 5.5km from the start. The trail passes through increasingly stunted rhododendron forest, leaving the walker more

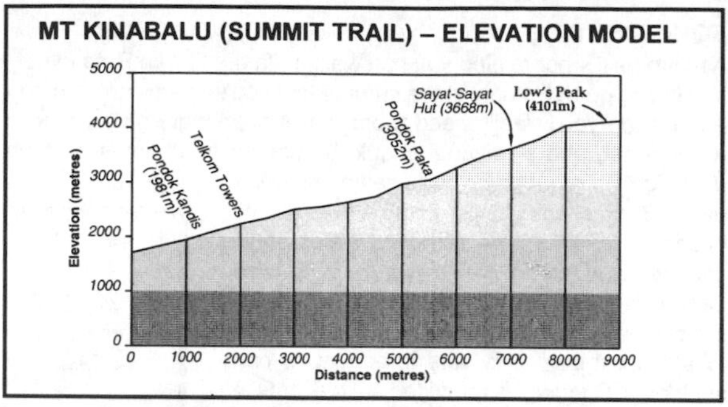

open to the elements. Occasional flat sections come as a relief after the endless steps. Cloud often closes in by late morning, refreshing the beard moss and orchids growing on the trees. This stretch is good for pitcher plants, although you probably won't see any growing by the side of the track – look among the dense vegetation.

A half hour detour can be made to Paka Cave – a rock overhang with a bamboo platform where the early explorers spent the night before tackling the summit. It is not that interesting and can be left for the descent when the lungs are less taxed.

PONDOK PAKA – LABAN RATA

Laban Rata (3272m) marks the treeline and is the night's resting spot for most people attempting the summit. This leg takes about 45 minutes to walk. The hut has heating, hot water, comfortable beds and a restaurant with fine views. This is the place to rest, commiserate with or boast to your fellow climbers, and settle in for the night, though some press on to the spartan Sayat-Sayat hut after a meal.

LABAN RATA – SAYAT-SAYAT

The one hour climb to Sayat-Sayat hut (3668m) involves crossing the sheer Panar Laban rock-face. Vegetation is no more than waist high, except where overhangs provide some respite from the wind. It is one of the toughest parts of the climb and doesn't get any easier in the dark and cold at 4 am, when the early risers from Laban Rata are urged onwards to see the dawn.

Thick ropes are used to haul yourself up the granite sheets; it's hard work, hauling and juggling a torch, but in a way it's good to be using arm muscles instead of legs! Narrow wooden steps and hand rails help in places, but often you'll use the smooth, gnarled branches of bushes for support as you gasp for breath.

SAYAT-SAYAT – SUMMIT

The steepest and hardest part of the climb is saved till last. Past Sayat-Sayat, more desolate rock-faces and ropes await the string of climbers stretched out in the dark, trying to keep warm while holding ropes and torches. In the daylight thick veins of quartz can be seen stretching as straight as painted lines on the rock-face.

The summit looks deceptively close and, although it's just over a kilometre, the last burst can take up to two hours from Sayat-Sayat. Many are reduced to crawling on hands and knees up the last few boulders to the small area that is the top of Borneo. Climbers crowd together and huddle against the cold, priming their cameras for a shot of the sunrise, the nearby Donkey Ears and St John's Peak, and the mysterious abyss of Low's Gully. When the sun has risen and the photos are taken, there is a quick exodus down the mountain to Laban Rata, while the late risers, perhaps the wisest of all, make their way to the less crowded summit.

The climb down to the Power Station takes about five hours – don't underestimate the descent and leave plenty of time to get back before night. Allow another hour to walk from the power station to your accommodation. While it is easier than the climb up, it can be a lot more damaging on under-used muscles. Aim to leave the summit by about noon and to be well under way by 1 pm. The weather can close in very quickly and, although you probably won't get lost, the granite is slippery even when it's dry – and it can get very wet at the top.

First-class certificates are issued for RM1 to those who complete the climb, but certificates are also issued for making it to Laban Rata. They can be collected at the park HQ.

Places to Stay & Eat

Overnight accommodation is available around park HQ, on the Ranau road between the park turn-off and Kundassang, at Poring Hot Springs (see the Poring Hot Springs section in the Sabah chapter), in the resthouse on the mountain and in mountain huts on the summit trail.

Accommodation in the park is booked at Kinabalu Gold Resorts (☎ 088-243629), 3rd floor, Block C, Kompleks Karamunsing, KK (see Information in the KK section in the Sabah chapter). Book as far in advance as possible (at least several days to a week), and note that on weekends, school holidays and public holidays all the accommodation may be taken. Mountain huts also need to be booked.

Reservations can be made by post or phone, but they will not be confirmed until fully paid for.

PARK HQ

There's a variety of very good accommodation at the park HQ to suit all budgets. The cheapest places are the 46-bed *Old Fellowship Hostel* and the 52-bed *New Fellowship Hostel*, which cost RM10 per person, or RM5 for anyone under 18 years. Both hostels are clean and comfortable, have cooking facilities and a dining area with an open fireplace. The Old Fellowship Hostel tends to be less cramped.

The rest of the accommodation at park HQ is good but expensive;

rates jump considerably on weekends and public holidays. The rates listed in this section are for the whole room or chalet.

Twin-bed cabins are RM50/80 on weekdays/weekends. The *annexe suites* are in the old administration building and sleep up to four people for RM100/160. Two-bedroom *duplex cabins,* which can sleep up to six people, cost RM150/200 per night. Then there are the *single storey deluxe cabins*, for five people, and *double storey deluxe cabins*, for seven people, costing RM150/200 and RM180/250 respectively.

Going up in quality and price, the two-bedroom *Nepenthes Villa*, which sleeps four people, costs RM180/250 on weekdays/weekends. At the four-bedroom *Kinabalu Lodge* eight people can share the cost – RM270/350 per night. Finally, at the top of the range, *Rajah Lodge* sleeps 10 people and costs RM800/1000.

There are two restaurants at park HQ. The cheaper and more popular of the two is *Kinabalu Balsam*, directly below the park office, which offers Malaysian, Chinese and western dishes at reasonable prices. It also has a small but well stocked shop selling tinned and dried foods, chocolate, beer, spirits, cigarettes, T-shirts, bread, eggs and margarine.

It's is open Monday to Friday from 6 am to 10 pm, and on weekends and public holidays until 11 pm. You can sit and admire the mountain from a covered balcony.

The *Mt Kinabalu Restaurant* is in the old administration building, just past the hostels. It's more expensive than the Balsam, but there's a huge range of dishes, including set breakfasts (RM8 to RM12); standard Malaysian and Chinese noodle and rice dishes; packed morning or afternoon teas (RM6); and steamboats for three or more people for RM20 per person. A packed lunch (chicken, sandwiches, fruit and soft drink) for your climb costs RM12. It opens every day at 6 am, closing at 10 pm on weekdays, and 11 pm on weekends and public holidays.

ON THE MOUNTAIN

On your way up to the summit you will have to stay overnight at one of the mountain huts at 3300m or at the 54-bed *Laban Rata Resthouse*, which costs RM25 per person in four-bed rooms. It has heating, hot water and a restaurant, and is by far the most comfortable overnight stop on the mountain. It also has one double room with bathroom for RM100 and a four-bed suite with bathroom for RM200.

At Laban Rata there's a *restaurant* selling hot noodle and rice meals for about RM5.50 to RM6.50; the restaurant is open for regular meals, and also from 2 to 3 am so you can grab some breakfast before attempting the summit climb.

There's also a shop selling film, cold drinks (RM3), headache tablets and other basic medicines, chocolates (RM3 to RM5) and – don't laugh – walking sticks for RM12; you may find this a shrewd purchase for the descent.

It's only RM10 to stay in the mountain huts (RM5 for those under

18) near Laban Rata. There's the 12-bed *Waras* and *Panar Laban* huts and the 44-bed *Gunting Lagadan* hut, which has a basic kitchen. These places are more spartan and aren't heated, but a sleeping bag is provided and they're close to the restaurant.

If you're one of those people who likes a cold shower and a 10km hike before breakfast, then you'll love the *Sayat-Sayat* hut. This eight bunk tin shed is about 1.5km from the summit and is the most primitive of the lot. There's no electricity, and water has to be carried up (or you can boil muddy water from a nearby stream). It also costs RM10, or RM5 for those under 18.

For most climbers the huts around Laban Rata are far enough to walk in one day, but if you stay overnight in the Sayat-Sayat hut you don't have to get up in the middle of the night in order to reach the summit by dawn. Collect sleeping bags at Laban Rata on the way through if you intend staying there.

It may not matter where you overnight because the air is rather thin and you may sleep quite fitfully. It's *very* cold in the early morning (around 0°C!), so take warm clothing with you.

OUTSIDE THE PARK

It is preferable to stay in the park, but if the park accommodation is full a number of places to stay are spread out along the road between park HQ and Kundassang. Some have great mountain views, though most look out over the cultivated valley south of the park.

A few hundred metres back along the road to KK, the *Kinabalu Resort Hotel* (☎ 088-889781) is a grim-looking place overlooking the valley. Rooms cost RM50 with bathroom and TV, or RM90 for family rooms. Breakfast is included and there's a *Cantonese restaurant* with a limited menu.

A few hundred metres towards Ranau from the park turn-off, *Rina Ria Lodge* (☎ 088-889282) is much better. There's a variety of accommodation, including a dorm for RM15; bedrooms sleeping two for RM60 (RM100 on weekends); and a two or three bedroom house with full amenities for RM150/200. All rooms have balconies overlooking the valley, and there's a shop with a good range of tinned and dried goods.

Molly Wong (☎ 088-889291), about 1km past the park turn-off towards Ranau, has simple rooms with bathroom from RM40 to RM50/60 for doubles/triples. There's a good *kedai kopi* here.

About 500m further on, *Fairy Garden Resort* (☎ 088-889688) looks like a Tibetan lamasery dangling over the drop. Rooms are from RM50 to RM70, and there's a cavernous air-con *restaurant*. *Kinabalu Rose Cabin* (☎ 088-889233) is 2km from the park entrance and has modern, air-con rooms for RM70 (RM100 on weekends) to RM100, and suites sleeping four for RM126 (RM180). Opposite is the new *Merlin Resort* (☎ 088-889085) with similar rates.

Just before Kundassang, about 5km from the park turn-off, the *Mountain View Motel* (☎ 088-889819) has triple share rooms for RM18 per person including breakfast; otherwise, there are basic singles/doubles for RM29/49 with bathroom.

Kundassang is at the bottom of the mountain, halfway to Ranau, and has a grotty market that straggles the roadside. Perched high on a hill above town is the three star *Hotel Perkasa Mt Kinabalu* (☎ 088-214142), the most luxurious accommodation near the park. Singles/doubles cost RM135/165 and suites start at RM250. It has *restaurants*, a tennis court and 360° views, but it's a soulless place. The hotel shuttle bus charges RM15 for the 7km trip to park HQ and RM25 to Poring Hot Springs.

On the other side of town towards Ranau, *Kinabalu Pine Resort* (☎ 088-889388) is a tasteful and comfortable upmarket hotel with great views of the mountain. The midweek rates are RM121, including 'American breakfast', rising to RM145 at weekends.

Getting There & Away

All express and minibuses between KK and Ranau or Sandakan pass the park turn-off, from where it's 100m to park HQ. From Kota Belud, north of KK, change at Tamparuli for Ranau and the park.

KOTA KINABALU

Air-con express buses leave from the long-distance bus station in KK for the national park at 7.30 am every day; the fare is RM15 and the trip takes about three hours. For Sandakan, most buses leave between 7 and 9 am; there are departures to Ranau as late as 12.30 pm from the long-distance bus station, but in the afternoon you'd be safer taking a minibus from behind Centre Point. The trip to the turn-off takes about three hours.

If you're heading back towards KK, minibuses pass the park entrance until mid-afternoon, but the best time to catch one is between 8 am and noon. Stand by the side of the main road to wave one down. If you can't be bothered waiting, hitching is quite easy.

KOTA BELUD & TAMPARULI

Tamparuli is where the road up the coast to Kudat branches for Kota Belud and Ranau. If you've been visiting Mengkabong Water Village or Kota Belud and then plan to head for Kinabalu National Park, first go to Tamparuli.

From Tamparuli there are several minibuses and share-taxis daily to Ranau (until about 2 pm) which will drop you at the park entrance (two hours, RM7). A taxi will cost you at least double the price. It's about 2½ hours travelling time to the park from Kota Belud.

RANAU & SANDAKAN

To travel east from the park HQ wait at the side of the main road for a minibus going to Ranau or Sandakan, or hitch. Air-con express buses to Sandakan pass park HQ until about noon. There may be no free seats on a weekend. The trip to Sandakan takes at least four hours and costs RM20.

Minibuses pass the park entrance en route to Ranau until about 2 pm. The 22km journey to Ranau takes about half an hour (RM5).

continued from page 480

Canopy Walkway

This unusual attraction consists of a series of walkways suspended from trees up to 30m above the jungle floor. It offers a monkey's-eye view of the surrounding forest, but the springy walkways are not for the faint-hearted. It's quite safe and great fun, but get there early if you want to see birds or other wildlife.

The canopy walkway is open between 6.30 am and 5.30 pm. Admission is RM1/2 for children/adults and there's a camera/video fee of RM5/30. Entry can be arranged at special times – such as night or early morning – on request, although it's a bit pricey at RM60 for one to three people.

Walks

There are several kilometres of forest trails around the springs. The **Air Terjun Kipungit** are only about 15 minutes walk away; it's a beautiful spot in a cool glade where you can swim at the base of the falls.

Over the stream the trail gets steeper, and after another 15 minutes you reach what are known as the **Bat Caves**, which are just a jumble of huge boulders between which bats and swiftlets roost. There's not much to see but the surrounding forest is very pretty.

Air Terjun Langanan is a steep walk and a further 1¼ hours away on the same trail via Kipungit and the bat caves. It's best to set out early and take plenty of water. This walk is legendary among birdwatchers as a haunt of the rarely seen blue-banded pitta.

Places to Stay & Eat

Poring is a popular place (there were nearly 167,000 visitors in 1997) and especially so on weekends. If you intend to stay overnight you must reserve and pay for accommodation at the Kinabalu Gold Resorts office in KK; see Information in the KK section.

The *Poring Hostel* has two units – one with 48 beds and one with 80 beds. It costs RM10 per person (RM5 if you are under 18 years of age), and blankets and pillows are provided free of charge. There is a clean, spacious kitchen with gas cookers.

Cabins with cooking facilities and air-conditioned chalets with all facilities are also available. A cabin sleeping six people costs RM75/100 on weekdays/weekends; a cabin sleeping four costs RM60/80; and a chalet sleeping six costs RM180/250.

The mosquitoes at Poring can be vicious, so take coils and insect repellent.

A campground is also available for RM5 per tent. Tents can be hired through the park office. Pillows and blankets can be hired for 50 sen each.

There's a good *restaurant* overlooking the swimming pool between the public baths and the river. There are also three inexpensive eating places right opposite the park entrance. If you're self-catering, you can buy food for cooking here as well, though it is cheaper if you bring your own from KK.

Getting There & Away

Poring is 19km north of Ranau along a bitumen road and can be reached by minibus, taxi or hitching – see the Ranau Getting There & Away section.

Leaving Poring can be tricky. Minibuses leave for Ranau from outside the park office at 6.30 am, and then at roughly 10 am and 2 pm, depending on demand; the fare is RM5. On weekends there are nearly always share-taxis parked near the office; the fare is by negotiation but if it's a full load it should only cost RM5 per person. Four people could charter a taxi for RM20 to Poring.

The park staff can probably help arrange a lift. Otherwise wait for a minibus that is dropping off passengers from Ranau.

Eastern Sabah

After enjoying Sabah's major attraction, Mt Kinabalu, many travellers head for the world-famous Sepilok Orang-Utan Rehabilitation Centre near Sandakan. Apart from Sepilok, which is indeed a 'must-see' attraction, the state's less-travelled eastern side has much to offer, especially to those interested in wildlife. Admittedly, travel is more difficult and costs are much higher – and one or two sights are pretty well the exclusive preserve of tour groups – but an enthusiast's route could take in Sepilok, Turtle Islands National Park, a half day at the Gomantong Caves then a trip to the Sungai Kinabatangan, and finish with some diving at world-famous Pulau Sipadan. And if your budget allows it, you could indulge in a few days at the magnificent Danum Valley for an upmarket rainforest experience.

SEPILOK ORANG-UTAN REHABILITATION CENTRE

One of only four orang-utan sanctuaries in the world, Sepilok is about 25km from Sandakan in the state's north-east. The Centre was established in 1964; it now covers 4000 hectares and has become one of Sabah's top tourist attractions. Some visitors feel it is too commercial, but most remember the sight of semi-wild orang-utans looping through the trees as a highlight of their trip.

Orang-utans are the only species of great ape found outside Africa and a mature male is an impressive, not to mention hairy, creature with an armspan of 2.4m weighing up to 100kg. It was once said that an orang-utan could swing from tree to tree from one side of Borneo to the other without touching the ground. Sadly this is no longer the case and hunting and habitat destruction have taken their toll.

Orphaned and injured orang-utans are brought to Sepilok to be rehabilitated to return to forest life, and so far the centre has handled about 80, although only about 20 still return regularly to be fed. It's unlikely you'll see anywhere near this number at feeding time – three or four is more likely.

Females which have returned to the wild often come back to the feeding platforms when they're pregnant and stay near the sanctuary centre until they've given birth, after which they go back to the forest.

The orang-utans are fed fruit, such as bananas, twice daily from a platform in the forest, about 10 minutes walk from the centre. There's no guarantee they'll show up, as this feeding is just to supplement what they can find for themselves in the jungle.

Young orang-utans are endlessly appealing, with ginger fur and intelligent eyes. The daily feeding routine can be a hilarious spectacle. If you can take your eyes off the main event, look down to the forest floor, where tree shrews and squirrels dart out of the undergrowth to feed on scraps dropped by the apes above. Macaques also join the feast. It's quite dark under the forest canopy and if you're taking photographs you'll need ASA 400 film.

As one of Sabah's prime tourist attractions, Sepilok is very well organised and professionally managed. It can resemble a zoo at feeding time, when crowds of people jostle to take photos, but don't let this put you off. A lot of good work is done here and the reserve is well worth a visit.

Orientation & Information

The feeding schedule can change, and the daily programmes (morning and afternoon) are posted at the Visitor Reception Centre, where there is a souvenir shop and a cafeteria. There's also a Nature Education Centre with interesting displays about the wildlife in the reserve. Rangers leave for the daily feedings from outside the Nature Education Centre at 10.30 am and 2.30 pm.

Admission to the Centre is RM10 (RM1 for Malaysians). Visiting hours at the centre are from 9.10 to 11 am and 2.10 to 3.30 pm every day. A 25 minute video, *Orphans of Borneo,* is shown at the park office at 9.15 and 10.40 am and 2.15 pm. To see all the programme you should arrive early because it can get crowded. Feeding time is at 10 am and 3 pm; get there at least half an hour early to enjoy the show.

There are lockers for your valuables – orang-utans have been known to relieve tourists of hats, sunglasses, cameras and even clothing.

Walking Trails

Walking trails lead further into the forest, but you'll have to get special permission to use them. Note that you wander through the forest at your own risk. Although orang-utans are not usually aggressive animals, on no account should you provoke or pester any wild animal. If you are carrying any food, the macaques will scent it and try to relieve you of it – don't argue with them because they'll probably win.

Two walking trails branch off from the Nature Education Centre. The waterfall trail takes about an hour. The main mangrove trail is a 1½ to two hour walk and leads right down to the estuaries behind the reserve. This is a favourite trail for birdwatchers and many bird species can be spotted at Sepilok, including the rarely seen Bornean bristlehead. Make sure you wear hiking boots, take water and expect to find leeches and plenty of mosquitoes.

Places to Stay & Eat

After KK, Sepilok has the best selection of backpackers' accommodation in Sabah, and there's no need to stay in Sandakan unless Sepilok is full. Two can be found along the turn-off to the centre – Jalan Sepilok – and virtually adjoin it; two more are a short drive back along the road to KK.

Sepilok B&B (☎ 089-532288) is a professionally run place set in peaceful gardens 100m off Jalan Sepilok, about 500m short of the centre entrance. This friendly, establishment has four dorms sleeping 10 for RM15 each and there are fan-cooled twin share rooms for RM40. All rates include breakfast and free tea and coffee.

Sepilok Jungle Resort I (☎ 089-533031) is in the opposite direction off Jalan Sepilok. It has a range of accommodation, including

Don't Monkey with the Orang-Utans

The term *orang* crops up in Borneo often – *orang-putih* (white people), *orang-blander* (Dutch people – used in reference to proboscis monkeys), *orang-ulu* (river people) and so on. *Orang-utan* means people of the forest and is a term intended to connote respect. Most visitors see semi-wild orang-utans at Sepilok, but these rare animals can be difficult to see in the wild. An encounter with a wild orang-utan can be a memorable experience, as one traveller recounted:

> I was birdwatching when I saw a large male orang-utan making a nest for the night. I marked the spot and told some photographers back at camp where to find it so they could stake it out at first light. Next day they duly went to the spot, hoping to catch this rare beast on celluloid. I caught up with them at about 8 am at the site, but no orang-utan had appeared. I wandered off again and came back at about 11 am to find still nothing had happened. We all began to think it had moved off before dawn.
>
> Suddenly, the branches in the treetop nest began to rustle and out poked the dishevelled head of the male I had seen the evening before. He stretched and looked around, then, to our astonishment, stood up and pissed over the side of his nest before settling back down for another kip!
>
> Truly a 'man of the forest!'

Tom Smith, Australia

At Sepilok there used to be a large semi-wild male called Rajah who in one well-publicised case stripped a tourist naked. Whether this was for pleasure or to get at some tasty morsel hidden in a pocket is not clear, but Rajah has since been moved elsewhere.

Some of the orang-utans at Sepilok have been maltreated by their captors or traumatised by accidents. Although they look harmless and very cute, they are immensely strong and may act unpredictably. And like their human relatives they are not above mischief or pilfering. Orang-utans have been known to snatch things from tourists, so store your valuables in lockers at the park office.

fan-cooled dormitories at RM20 a bed; fan-cooled doubles/twins for RM50/60; and air-con rooms from RM75 to RM150 including TV and minibar. A second stage of this resort, closer to the centre, was under construction at the time of writing.

Labuk B&B (☎ 089-533190), Mile 15, Jalan Labuk, is a couple of kilometres back along the KK road. This delightful family-run concern sleeps 14 guests in fan-cooled bunk or double rooms with shared facilities; rates are RM20 per person. Dinner is also available for RM10. Labuk often acts as an informal host to visiting wildlife researchers and you'll probably find yourself in stimulating company here.

Uncle Tan (☎ 089-531917), Mile 16, Jalan Labuk, is a long-established tour operator based about 3.5km from the Sepilok turn-off towards KK. A bed in simple dorms costs RM20 including breakfast. There have been mixed reports about this place; it's basic accommodation and it's a little inconvenient for Sepilok. Mountain bikes are available for RM2 per day – a good way to visit Sepilok.

More expensive accommodation is available at the *Orang-Utan Rehabilitation Centre Rest House* (☎ 089-531180), just outside the park centre. Fan-cooled rooms cost RM45 and air-con rooms are RM65.

The *cafeteria* at the rehabilitation centre is open from 7 am to 4 pm, and serves breakfast, sandwiches, noodle and rice dishes, and drinks. At busy times it may run out of all but the basics.

Getting There & Away

All express buses from KK can drop you at the turn-off to the centre – Jalan Sepilok, 1.5km from the centre – or at Labuk B & B or Uncle Tan's. Just ask the driver and remind him as you get closer.

You can hail long-distance buses on the highway to get back to KK, but it can be difficult finding one with a free seat. Your best chance is early in the morning, otherwise you may have to take a bus into Sandakan and then out again from the bus station. The fare from KK is RM20 to RM25.

To get to the centre from Sandakan take the blue Labuk bus marked 'Sepilok Batu 14' from the local bus stand next to the central market on the waterfront. The fare is RM1.40 and the journey takes about 45 minutes. There are departures at 9.20 and 11.20 am, and 1 and 3 pm. There are also minibuses which make the trip every hour or so. A Labuk Road bus going to Batu 19 or beyond can drop you at Labuk B&B or Uncle Tan's for RM1.50.

Most of the backpackers' hostels can organise transport to and from bus stations and the airport for a nominal fee. A taxi from Sepilok to the airport costs about RM15.

SANDAKAN

Sandakan is a thriving commercial centre at the entrance to a beautiful island-studded bay. Most activity centres around the busy docks and wharves that sprawl along the waterfront for many kilometres. Barges, ferries and motorboats of every description buzz around, unloading fish and other produce, and taking away rattan, timber, rubber, copra, palm oil and even birds' nests. West of town passenger ferries shuttle back and forth to Zamboanga in the Philippines. In the bay, container vessels ride at anchor awaiting their turn to unload.

Sandakan is an anonymous, functional sort of place, but it doesn't deserve the bad press it gets from some travellers. The real attractions lie outside town, but if you're stranded for a day or so there are some good beaches nearby, excellent seafood to enjoy, and mesmerising views from the hills at sunset.

Forty kilometres offshore there's Turtle Islands National Park, one of the world's few turtle sanctuaries, and further afield there's the Gomantong Caves and superb wildlife watching at the Sungai Kinabatangan.

History

At the height of the timber boom Sandakan was said to have the world's greatest concentration of millionaires. It was perhaps an extravagant claim, but the region has always been renowned for luxury goods such as pearls, sea cucumbers and birds' nests, and attracted trade from the nearby Philippines and as far away as China.

In the 18th century Sandakan came under the suzerainty of the Sultan of Sulu, who ruled the southern islands of the present-day Philippines. British traders came to the region in the 19th century, but the first foreign settlement was mainly by Germans who settled on Pulau Timbang, in Teluk Sandakan, in the 1870s.

In 1878 Baron von Overbeck, an Austrian, acquired a lease from the Sultan of Sulu for much of eastern Sabah, and this was later sold to Alfred Dent, a Hong Kong-based publisher. Sandakan was established by the Resident, William Pryer, and it boomed. In 1884 Sandakan became the capital of British North Borneo, and it remained the capital until the Japanese invasion and subsequent Allied bombing in 1945 virtually destroyed the town. In 1946 the capital was moved to Jesselton, now called Kota Kinabalu.

Orientation

The centre of Sandakan consists of only a few blocks squashed between the waterfront and a steep escarpment from where you can look out over the bay. In the centre you'll find most of the hotels and restaurants, banks, Malaysia Airlines office, and the local and long-distance bus stands. The main road west along the bay, Jalan Leila, passes the commercial centres of Bandar Ramai-Ramai and Bandar Leila, where there are more hotels, places to eat and backpackers' accommodation.

Finding a specific address in the centre gets confusing because the streets are numbered Jalan Dua, Jalan Tiga etc, and 'Jalan' and 'Lebuh' seem to be used interchangeably. Fortunately, the centre is very small and it's hard to get lost.

The local bus station (for the Leila and Labuk bus companies) is right by the markets along the waterfront. Local and long-distance

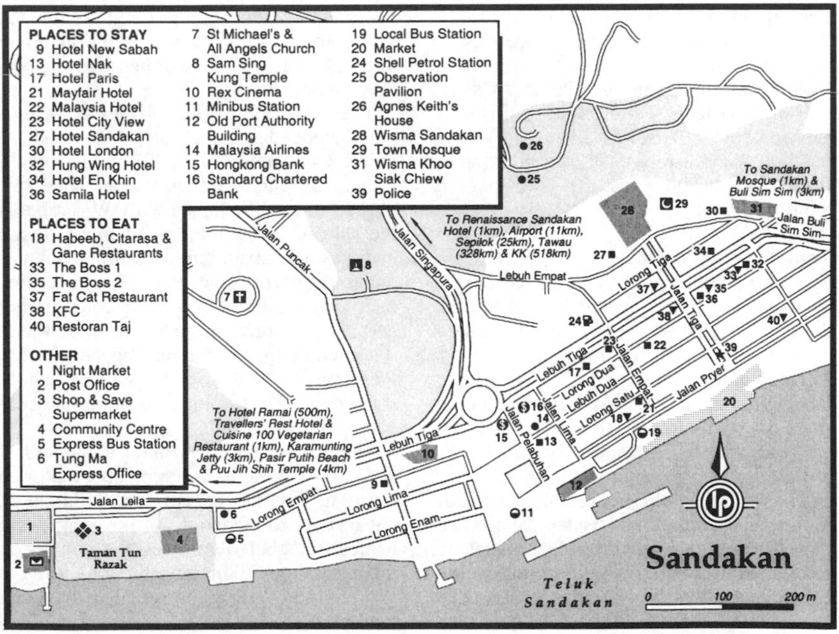

minibuses leave from the open area just past the old Port Authority building. Air-con express buses to Kota Kinabalu leave from the bus stand next to the Sandakan Community Centre, at the west end of the centre.

Information

Sandakan has no tourist information office, although the SI Tours office on the 1st floor of the airport building may be able to help with inquiries. The post office is on Jalan Leila at the western end of town, just past the Shop & Save Supermarket.

The immigration office is in the Secretariat building, just past the roundabout at Batu 7 on the Ranau road, 11km from the centre of town. To get there take any Batu 7 or higher bus (Batu 8, 12, 19, 30 etc). If you're going to the Philippines you can clear immigration at the Karamunting Jetty before boarding.

Bookings & Permits Bookings and transport for Turtle Islands National Park (Pulau Penya National Park) are now handled by Crystal Quest (☎ 089-212711), 12th floor, Wisma Khoo Siak Chiew; it is open usual business hours.

For a permit for the Gomantong Caves, you must visit the Ministry of Tourism & Environment's Wildlife office (☎ 089-666550), housed in a flash new building at Batu 7, about 500m past the 11km peg on the Ranau road.

Things to See & Do

The town doesn't have any 'must see' attractions, but it's pleasant enough to walk around the busy **waterfront** and watch the fishing boats, barges and ferries around the wharves.

The **market** is always a hive of activity, though it can get a bit fetid in the heat of the day. Locals will warn you about pickpockets; we have had no complaints from travellers, but guard your valuables just in case.

The **Puu Jih Shih Temple**, 4km west of the centre, is a large Buddhist temple perched on a steep hill overlooking Teluk Sandakan. Take a bus to Tanah Merah and ask for the temple. Near the temple on the coast road is **Pasir Putih Beach**, a dull patch of grey sand overlooked by a good seafood restaurant. Closer to town, the **Sam Sing Kung Temple** dates from 1887 and fronts the Padang.

For some religious extravagance and fine views over the stilt villages which line Teluk Sandakan, visit **Sandakan Mosque,** 1km east of town. Another building of note is **St Michael's & All Angels Church**, built in the 19th century and one of the few stone buildings in East Malaysia. **Buli Sim Sim** is a picturesque stilt village, 3km east of the centre, where you can wander around between the houses.

For a fine view over the town and bay, head up the hill towards the Renaissance Sandakan Hotel and turn right at Jalan Istana near the roundabout. An **observation pavilion** a few hundred metres along offers panoramic views. Just behind is **Agnes Keith's House**, an old two storey wooden villa. Keith was an American who came to Sandakan in the 1930s with her husband, who was the Conservator of Forests. She wrote about her experiences in three books, the most famous being *Land Below the Wind*. She was imprisoned by the Japanese during WWII – just one of her many adventures in Sabah.

The **Australian War Memorial** is in a quiet, wooded park just past the government buildings at Batu 8 (Km 12) on the road to Ranau. Despite its tranquil appearance, this was the site of the Japanese POW camp and the starting point for the infamous 'death marches' to Ranau. Large, rusting machines under the trees have plaques telling how many men died during their construction and how prisoners tried to sabotage them. It's fascinating but grim reading, and despite the tropical heat the place has a melancholy if not eerie air. It is not surprising that local ghost stories abound.

To get there, take any Batu 8 or higher bus and get off at the Esso station about 1km on the right past the government buildings at the airport roundabout. Walk along Jalan Rimba for about 10 minutes; the camp is on the right about 100m after the road turns to gravel. It is well signposted on the main road.

The Sandakan Death Marches

Sandakan was the site of a Japanese prisoner of war camp during WWII, and in September 1944 there were 1800 Australian and 600 British troops interned here. What is probably not widely known is that more Australians died here than during the building of the infamous Burma Railway.

Early in the war, food and conditions were bearable, and the death rate was around three per month. But as the Allies closed in near the end of the war, it became clear to the officers in command that they didn't have enough staff to guard against a rebellion in the camps. They decided to cut the prisoners' rations to weaken them; disease spread and the death rate began to rise.

It was also decided to move the prisoners inland – 250km through the jungle to Ranau. On 28 January 1945, 470 prisoners set off; 313 made it to Ranau. On the second march, 570 started from Sandakan; just 118 reached Ranau. The third march consisted of the last men in the camp and numbered 537. Conditions on the marches were deplorable: many men had no boots, rations were less than minimal and many men fell by the wayside; the Japanese disposed of any prisoners who couldn't walk. Once in Ranau, the surviving prisoners were put to work carrying 20kg sacks of rice over hilly country to Paginatan, 40km away. Disease and starvation took a horrendous toll, and by the end of July 1945 there were no prisoners left in Ranau. The only survivors from the 2400 at Sandakan were six Australians who had escaped, either from Ranau or during the marches.

Organised Tours

It's easy to visit Sepilok Orang-Utan Rehabilitation Centre independently and you could also get to Gomantong Caves if you were determined, but the Sungai Kinabatangan is virtually impossible to reach without taking a tour.

The cheapest tours are operated by Uncle Tan (see Places to Stay in the Sepilok Orang-Utan Rehabilitation Centre section), and the Travellers' Rest Hostel (see Places to Stay). Both operate jungle camps on the Sungai Kinabatangan, and Uncle Tan can arrange budget tours to Tanjung Aru, a fishing village on an island in Teluk Sandakan.

Sandakan has plenty of tour operators offering trips to these places and further afield. Among them are:

Api Tours
(☎ 089-219958) Ground floor, C1, Block 50, Jalan Leila

Discovery Tours
(☎ 089-274106) 10th floor, Wisma Khoo Siak Chiew

SI Tours
(☎ 089-673503) 1st floor, Sandakan airport terminal building

Wildlife Expeditions
(☎ 088-219616) 9th floor, Wisma Khoo Siak Chiew; also at the Sandakan Renaissance Hotel (☎ 089-273093)

A city tour costs around RM40, to Sepilok is RM95 and longer trips taking in Sepilok, Gomantong Caves and the Sungai Kinabatangan cost from RM310 to RM550 including accommodation.

Places to Stay – Budget

If you are only visiting Sandakan to see the Orang-Utan Rehabilitation Centre at Sepilok, it's better to stay out there since it's about 25km from the town centre (see the Sepilok section for information on budget accommodation).

In Sandakan, most budget travellers head for the *Travellers' Rest Hostel* (☎ 089-216454), 2nd floor, Block E, Bandar Leila, about 1km west of town. It's a friendly place with fan-cooled dorm beds at RM20 and a couple of simple doubles for RM25. The Travellers' Rest also runs a jungle lodge on the Sungai Kinabatangan (see that section for more information), and can organise tours to other attractions around the city.

The *Hotel Paris* (☎ 089-218488), Lorong Dua, has clean rooms from RM25/35 with fan and bathroom, or RM48 for an air-con double with bathroom.

Places to Stay – Mid-Range

Most hotel accommodation in Sandakan is pricey; the mid-range hotels are all similar in standard and their cheaper rooms go quickly.

The *Hotel London* (☎ 089-216371) on Lebuh Empat is probably the best in this price range. It is clean and well run, and staff can help with local information and maps. Air-con singles/doubles cost RM40/50 with bathroom.

The *Hotel En Khin* (☎ 089-217377), 50 Lebuh Tiga, is a good, cheap Chinese place and reasonable value for RM40/50. *Mayfair Hotel* (☎ 089-219855), 24 Jalan Empat, is a good value hotel close to the waterfront and bus stations; air-con rooms with bathroom cost RM36/45.

The *Hotel New Sabah* (☎ 089-218711) on Jalan Singapura has good rooms with air-con, TV and bathroom for RM54/61. *Hung Wing Hotel* (☎ 089-218034) – the entrance is round the back, but you can enter through the Tay Travel Agency on Lebuh Tiga – is no bargain at RM69 for air-con rooms with TV and bathroom. Rooms on the higher floors are cheaper at RM63 but there's no lift.

Samila Hotel (☎ 089-271555), opposite KFC on Jalan Tiga, has pretty good rooms with shower, air-con and TV for RM58/68 up to RM78. It's better value than the Hung Wing. *Hotel Ramai* (☎ 089-273222), Jalan Leila about 500m west of the post office, has spacious rooms starting at RM68/78, although those overlooking the main road are a bit noisy.

Places to Stay – Top End

The *Hotel Nak* (☎ 089-272988), Jalan Pelabuhan, was once Sandakan's best but it's now looking very much the worse for wear. Poorly lit rooms cost from RM57 to RM110, although the more expensive ones are huge and face the harbour.

Advertised rates at the *Hotel City View* (☎ 089-271122), Lebuh Tiga, are from RM140/170 to RM190/210 for well appointed rooms with minibar and TV, although discounts of up to 60% may be available.

The shiny new *Hotel Sandakan* (☎ 089-221122), next to Wisma Sandakan, is a centrally located two star hotel with cafes, bars and a business centre. Published rates range from RM100 to RM160/180 for rooms and RM200 to RM270 for suites. Discounts may be available.

The only international-standard hotel, and a favourite of the Sepilok tour groups, is the four star *Renaissance Sandakan Hotel* (☎ 089-213299), about 1.5km up the hill from the main roundabout in town. It has a swimming pool, sporting facilities and restaurants set in quiet gardens. Room prices range from RM310 to RM340, and suites are from RM500 to RM1700.

Places to Eat

Despite its size, Sandakan has nowhere near KK's variety of restaurants. For no-frills food, try one of the *stalls* upstairs in the central market. A couple of ringgit will get you a decent meal, but choose carefully as hygiene might not be 1st class. There's more market food at the *night market* which sets up outside the post office each evening.

Sandakan has many cheap *Chinese restaurants* and *coffee houses* particularly near the waterfront, serving standard rice or noodle dishes. For good Malay food try the *Habeeb Restoran* on Jalan Pryer near the market. It does excellent murtabak, and also has an air-con room upstairs. There are a couple of similar places close by, including the *Citarasa* and *Restoran Gane*.

The Boss and *The Boss 2* are near each other on Lebuh Tiga, and serve good, cheap Malay dishes. The Boss 2 is air-conditioned and has freshly squeezed vegetable and fruit juices from RM2 to RM3.50.

For vegetarian food with a difference, try *Cuisine 100 Vegetarian Restaurant*, Block C, Bandar Leila, where a sign on the wall proclaims 'No Smoking, No Meat, No Beer, No Spit'. The incredibly diverse menu features vegetarian food made to look and taste like every dish imaginable, including fish, pork and chicken.

For western meals, *Hawaii Restaurant*, in the Hotel City View, has a good a la carte range and does a three course set lunch/dinner for RM13/19, plus taxes.

For fast food, there is a *KFC* and a *Fat Cat Restaurant* on Lebuh Tiga, and a branch of *SugarBun* on the ground floor of the Hotel Nak.

Upmarket restaurants offer more expensive western and Asian dining possibilities. Pick of the bunch is probably the *Ming Restaurant* in the Renaissance Sandakan Hotel, which offers excellent Cantonese and Sichuan food, and a dim sum breakfast and lunch.

Bandar Hsiang Garden, along Jalan Leila just past the Hotel Ramai, is a newer shopping and industrial area with a number of more expensive restaurants. Here you'll find the Korean *Seoul Garden*, the *Regent Garden* in the Hotel Hsiang Garden, and the *XO Steakhouse*, which does western-style fish and lobster dishes as well as steaks and chops.

The *Pasir Putih Seafood Centre* is a few kilometres west of town along the waterfront past Bandar Ramai-Ramai. Friendly staff will help you choose your own seafood from tanks behind the restaurant; the beachside setting is very pleasant and it's open late if you want to down a few beers.

Getting There & Away

Air The Malaysia Airlines office (☎ 089-273966) is at Wisma Sabah, opposite the Hotel Nak; office hours are Monday to Friday from 8.30 am to 5 pm, and Saturday from 8.30 to 1 pm.

Sandakan is well served by the Malaysia Airlines domestic network and there are direct flights to Kota Kinabalu (seven daily, RM83), Kudat (five weekly, RM54) and Tawau (two daily, RM74).

Bus The long-distance bus station is next to the community centre, out towards the post office. All the long-distance minibuses, Land Cruisers and air-con expresses to KK congregate here. Most go early in the morning, though a few minibuses and Land Cruisers leave in the afternoon.

Most express buses to KK leave at 6.30 or 7 am (the last one is at noon); the trip takes about six hours and costs from RM20 to RM25. Mizume Enterprise (☎ 011-887787) has a ticket booth at the station and Tung Ma Express (☎ 089-614162) has a desk in the Sandakan Milk Bar around the corner.

The same buses pass the turn-off to Kinabalu National Park headquarters (RM25). Minibuses to Ranau cost RM20 and the journey takes about four hours.

Buses depart daily for Lahad Datu between 6.30 am and 5 pm (about three hours, RM15), and for Tawau between 6.30 and 8 am (about 5½ hours, RM20).

There's also a bus to Semporna at 8 am costing RM20 and taking about 5½ hours. If you miss the bus to Semporna you can take one to Lahad Datu, from where there are more frequent minibuses to Semporna.

Minibuses depart frequently throughout the morning for Lahad Datu, some going on to Tawau. A Land Cruiser departs Sandakan for Tawau at 3 pm and costs RM25.

Boat Passenger ferries now operate between Sandakan and Zamboanga in the Philippines. The trip takes 18 hours and costs from RM60.

The MV *Sampaguita* leaves Sandakan on Saturday at 1 pm, arriving in Zamboanga at 8 am the following day. It leaves the Philippines for Sandakan on Thursday at 1 pm, arriving on Friday at 8 am.

The *Lady Mary Joy* departs Sandakan on Thursday at 3 pm, arriving Friday at 9 am; the return trip is on Tuesday at 3 pm, arriving Sandakan on Wednesday at 9 am.

Tickets can be bought in advance from the Karamunting Jetty, about 4km west of town, where you also clear immigration when boarding. Take a Pasir Putih bus for 90 sen.

Getting Around

To/From the Airport The airport is about 11km from the city. The Batu 7 Airport bus runs by the airport but stops on the main road about 500m from the terminal. The fare to/from the city centre is 70 sen. A taxi to the airport will cost RM15.

Car Inno Travel & Tour Services (☎ 089-671718) operates Sandakan's only car rental business. You'll find the office is at the airport terminal.

A Proton Saga costs RM180 per day including insurance and unlimited kilometres; a 4WD Nissan Safari costs about RM425.

Taxi Taxis are plentiful – clustered near the markets and main hotels, and easy to hail along main roads. Most are unmetered rattletraps, but most drivers seem honest and can sometimes help with tourist information. Trips around the town centre cost RM5; to Puu Jih Shih Temple it's RM6.

TURTLE ISLANDS NATIONAL PARK

Also known as the Pulau Penyu National Park, this park comprises three small islands – Pulau Selingan, Pulau Bakungan Kecil and Pulau Gulisan – which lie 40km north of Sandakan, within swimming distance of nearby islands of the Philippines. The islands are famous because two species of marine turtles – green and hawksbill – come ashore to lay their eggs at certain times of the year. Since their laying seasons are virtually complementary, there's a good chance of seeing one or the other at almost any time of year.

Sea turtles are harmless vegetarians that spend most of their lives at sea. They are strong, graceful swimmers that grow to a great age and size. Adult sea turtles have few natural enemies, but females must return to land to lay their eggs. After dark, the female turtles haul themselves laboriously up the beach to a site above the high water mark, where they dig a nest hole with their flippers. In it they lay between 40 and 190 white, rubbery eggs about the size of a ping pong ball, and cover them with sand to allow the sun's heat to incubate them. The whole laying process takes about an hour, after which the fond parent lumbers back down the beach never to see her progeny again.

The green turtle commonly lays on Pulau Selingan and Pulau Bakungan Kecil between July and October; and the smaller hawksbill turtle lays its eggs on Pulau Gulisan from February to April.

The eggs are collected by permanent staff based on Pulau Selingan and transferred to fenced hatcheries, where they are safe from illegal collection by fishermen who eat them. With luck, your visit could coincide with a hatching and you may get the opportunity to usher a cute baby turtle into the sea.

Pulau Selingan has an information centre, accommodation and a turtle hatchery. As well as offering a good chance of seeing the turtles, the islands have beautiful white-sand beaches and clear water with good opportunities for snorkelling.

Places to Stay & Eat

It is no longer possible to visit Turtle Islands on a day trip, and thanks to the recent privatisation of several national parks in Sabah, any excursion must be arranged through Crystal Quest (☎ 089-212711), 12th floor, Wisma Khoo Siak Chiew, Sandakan.

The only accommodation is in *chalets* on Pulau Selingan, and meals and transfers are now included in the tour packages. Currently these cost RM150 per person per night, including dinner and breakfast, or RM170 including three meals a day. These prices are on a twin share basis, so if you're travelling alone try to team up with someone or you're in for even more expense. Extra meals are available for a set RM20 per person.

Try to book ahead because facilities are limited and tour companies often take bulk bookings.

Getting There & Away

Transport to the islands is included as part of a tour, and Crystal Quest will try to put individuals in with a group.

GOMANTONG CAVES

These limestone caves are Sabah's most famous source of the swiftlets' nests used for that Chinese panacea, bird's-nest soup. The caves are on the opposite side of the bay from Sandakan, about 20km inland, and are difficult to reach as an independent traveller. In theory, a permit is required and should be obtained in advance from the Wildlife office in Sandakan (see the Information entry in the Sandakan section), but if you just front up you should be able to talk your way in.

The most accessible of the caves is a 10 minute walk along the trail near the information centre and office. A boardwalk leading off to the right doubles back to the entrance road – it's a pleasant walk but it won't get you to the caves. Continue past the living quarters of the nest collectors to get to the main cave, **Simud Hitam** (Black Cave). You can venture in, though it involves wading through ankle-deep guano alive with insects. In the season, you can watch the nests being collected from the cave's roof, as they are at Niah Caves in Sarawak, by men climbing long, precarious bamboo poles.

The left-hand trail from the office leads to the top of the mountain. After a few metres the trail forks again. To the right a 15 minute walk reaches a top entrance of the cave, while the left-hand trail continues for 30 minutes and leads high up the mountain to **Simud Putih** (White Cave). This cave contains the more valuable white nests. Both trails are steep and involve some sweaty rock climbing.

The area around the caves is covered in forest and dense vegetation. There's plenty of wildlife, especially birds, and the walks are worthwhile, but the caves are difficult to reach. The great caves of Gunung Mulu and Niah national parks in Sarawak are more spectacular and easier to visit, and the Madai Caves near Lahad Datu are quite interesting and more accessible.

Getting There & Away

It is possible to visit the caves using public transport, but it takes at least two hours from Sandakan and may involve a lot of walking. First, take any Lahad Datu minibus and ask to be dropped at the Sukau turn-off. The turn-off is in the middle of nowhere, but there's a small shop from where infrequent buses pass the turn-off to the caves, 20km along the road to Sukau. The chances of a lift are quite good because there's an almost constant stream of traffic to the oil-palm plantations. From the turn-off it is 4.5km to the park HQ. Be prepared to walk. There's a security gate 4km from the caves. If you don't have a booking, tell them the Wildlife office was shut; you'll have to sign a visitors' book and give your passport number.

All things considered, if you're desperate to see the caves you're probably just as well to take a tour; most operators include it as part of a package to the Sungai Kinabatangan (see the Sandakan section for a list of tour operators).

SUNGAI KINABATANGAN

The Sungai Kinabatangan is Sabah's longest river and measures 560km from its headwaters in the south-west side of the state to where it empties into the Sulu Sea east of Sandakan. Logging and clearing for plantations have devastated the upper reaches of the river, but by a strange irony the riverine forest near the coast is so hemmed in by oil-palm plantations that an astonishing variety of wildlife is both common and easy to see. This is one of the best places in Borneo – indeed, in all of South-East Asia – to observe wildlife, and the Kinabatangan will be a highlight of any nature lover's trip to Sabah. The river will be interesting at any time of year. The wet season will have most bird activity, but conditions will be uncomfortable and mammals can be seen at any time of year. However during the dry, oxbow lakes may not have water in them.

A narrow corridor of rainforest, only a few hundred metres wide in places, cloaks the riverbanks from the Sandakan-Lahad Datu road downstream to the mangrove-fringed estuary. Sightings of the unique proboscis monkeys are virtually guaranteed in the late afternoon; two macaque species – long-tailed and pig-tailed – are common; and orang-utans are also seen, particularly downstream, where negotiations are under way to preserve a large slice of habitat as an orang-utan sanctuary. Among the felines there's a chance of seeing marbled cat in the forest, and flat-headed cat is seen regularly at night along the Menungal (a tributary of the Kinabatangan); other mammals include elephant (very shy), deer and giant squirrel.

Birdwatchers will find it incredible: all eight of Borneo's hornbill species are seen regularly; two species of the gorgeous pittas are reasonably common; and rarities include Storm's stork and the bizarre Oriental darter or snake-bird.

There are trails around the Uncle Tan's and Travellers' Rest jungle camps, but the best way to see animals is to cruise up and down the river or its tributaries in a small boat. You can ask to be landed at certain spots, such as oxbow lakes, and walk through the forest, but the best viewing is from boats. Spotlighting trips can also be arranged – you'll almost certainly see the large buffy fish-owl.

Places to Stay & Eat

Independent travel to the Kinabatangan is virtually impossible, but if wildlife is your passion then make room in your budget to visit this incredible place. Backpackers and budget travellers are catered for in jungle camps, and there's a cluster of more expensive lodges near the riverside village of Sukau.

Travellers' Rest Jungle Camp is run by the backpackers' place of the same name in Sandakan; bookings and transport can be arranged through the hostel. This place gets good reports and wild orang-utans are occasionally seen around the sleeping huts. Accommodation and meals cost RM15 per day.

Uncle Tan's Wildlife Camp is a longstanding budget option. It's ultra-basic accommodation, but among diehards it's a legend; the food is very good and many return for a second visit. Tan also charges RM15 per person per day for accommodation and meals.

Sukau is the main village on the lower Kinabatangan, 25km along the road past the Gomantong Caves. Lodges operated by tour companies near Sukau offer the same wildlife experience as the jungle camps, but in upmarket comfort. There's not much difference between them; all have comfortable, mosquito-proof rooms with fan and bathroom, fully catered meals and bar, and trained guides who will try to maximise your wildlife viewing. On a twin share basis, expect to pay about RM250 per night at a lodge, including transfers; most tours include Gomantong Caves as a part of the package, but you can opt out of this if you wish. See the Sandakan Organised Tours section for a list of companies that use the lodges.

Getting There & Away

Transport to the jungle camps is by bus from Sandakan to where the highway crosses the river, and then by boat for the hour-long trip to the camp. Both Travellers' Rest and Uncle Tan's charge RM130 per person for the return trip, so obviously it's better if you stay a few days.

All camp and lodge operators will arrange transport to and from the river, and can help with forward transport further south if you need it.

If you're heading further south ask to be dropped at the highway, from where you can catch a minibus to Lahad Datu – it'll save you repeating the long drive from Sandakan.

LAHAD DATU

Lahad Datu is a plantation and timber service town of 20,000 people, including a high percentage of Filipino and Indonesian migrants or refugees. There are very few tourists and the only reason for visiting is if you are en route to or from Danum Valley, 85km to the west. Since most people visit Danum on an expensive tour, Lahad Datu will probably fall off the travellers' map entirely.

The town has an isolated feel about it and women sit on corners trying to eke out a living by selling cigarettes. This area of eastern Sabah around the Celebes Sea is also known for its pirates, equipped with the essentials of modern piracy – machine guns and speed boats. Don't even think about trying to catch a boat from here. Pirate raids on ships and coastal villages are common, and raids on buses have also been reported on the back roads.

Information

Bookings for Danum Valley Borneo Rainforest Lodge can be made at Innoprise Corporation (☎ 089-881092), Block 3, Ground floor, Fajar Centre. You can also book in KK (see the Information entry in the KK section). The office in Lahad Datu is open usual office hours. If you're travelling by minibus from Sandakan ask to be dropped off at the BRL office – it's about 2km north of town.

The Malaysia Airlines office (☎ 089-81707) is on the ground floor of the Hotel Mido on the main street, Jalan Terati.

To change money, try the Standard Chartered Bank opposite the Hotel Mido or the Sabah Bank around the corner, which has good rates and low fees for travellers cheques.

Places to Stay

Lahad Datu has nothing to offer visitors, but if you are marooned here most of the places to stay are along Jalan Terati and down a side street opposite the Esso station.

The *Rumah Tumbangan Malaysia* (☎ 089-883358), on the side street just around the corner from the Ocean Hotel, has the cheapest rooms – from RM15 to RM28 with fan and shared bathroom. The rooms on the upper floors are cheapest; all are quite acceptable and the management is friendly and helpful.

The *Hotel Venus* (☎ 089-886816), on the opposite side of the same street, offers far less value at RM25 for fan-cooled rooms and RM35 for air-con rooms. The *Hotel Ocean* (☎ 089-881700), on Jalan Terati opposite the post office, is a more upmarket option with air-con and bathroom for RM40/48. Opposite the Hotel Venus, the *Hotel Perdana* (☎ 089-881400) has similar rooms with air-con, TV and bathroom for RM42/48.

The *Hotel Mido* (☎ 089-881800), at the harbour end of Jalan Terati, is the tallest building in town. Economy singles/doubles are RM50/60 and prices increase to RM80/90 for a deluxe room. The cheaper rooms are quite good value.

Places to Eat

The *food stalls* next to the Chinese temple, behind the cheap hotels, are good and specialise in Filipino food. In the evenings hawkers set up stalls in the area behind the Hotel Mido. Three or four ringgit will get you a decent feed.

There are Chinese *kedai kopi* and Muslim Malay *restorans* serving good rotis and murtabaks in the shophouses near the minibus station and along the waterfront. *Azura Restoran*, near the minibus station, has good curries, rotis and murtabak.

The *Sentosa Coffee House* in the Hotel Mido has western breakfasts and cheap meals in its air-con restaurant. Most mains cost RM4 to RM6, or the three course set lunch is good value at RM10. This place makes excellent milk shakes.

Getting There & Away

Air Malaysia Airlines operates services between Lahad Datu and Kota Kinabalu (three daily, RM106). The airport is 2km north of town on the highway. A taxi to town costs RM3.

Bus The long-distance minibuses leave from a vacant lot near the waterfront; turn left at the roundabout as you enter the main street from the highway.

There are frequent departures for Sandakan (three hours, RM15), Semporna (two hours, RM10) and Tawau (two hours, RM10). There are plenty of departures to all places until around 3 pm; buses to Semporna and Tawau pass the Kunak turn-off for Madai Caves; the fare is RM7. The road south to Semporna and Tawau is disintegrating and long stretches may be under repair, making for an uncomfortable ride.

DANUM VALLEY CONSERVATION AREA

Danum Valley is part of a vast logging concession owned by the Sabah Foundation, who in its wisdom set aside the Conservation Area to preserve 43 sq km of pristine wilderness on the Sungai Segama, some 85km west of Lahad Datu. For some years research into rainforest ecology was carried out at a Field Studies Centre, and until recently the region was the almost exclusive preserve of scientists and birdwatchers, among whom Danum Valley is legendary.

Perhaps alone among Sabah's forests, it has stood unlogged or otherwise exploited since Europeans arrived, and it still supports an incredible diversity of wildlife: botanical riches include 200 species of trees per hectare; 275 bird species have been recorded, including many endemic to Borneo; and 110 species of mammals have been seen, including great rarities such as the Sumatran rhino and the beautiful clouded leopard.

It's a rare privilege to stand under the towering canopy of ancient trees and see some of Borneo's superb wildlife. But access to non-scientists is only possible by staying at the Borneo Rainforest Lodge (BRL), and it's a privilege for which you'll pay through the nose. The Lodge is marketed internationally in conjunction with Tiger Tops in Nepal; among its guests have been film stars and crowned heads of Europe (who'll hardly notice the cost). The search for wildlife in rainforest can be difficult and to get the most out of Danum Valley it's best to spend a few days here; unfortunately this puts it beyond the range of most travellers.

Borneo Rainforest Lodge will try to give you a rainforest experience with an emphasis on education. On arrival you will be given an introductory slide show on Danum Valley and allotted a guide who will try to arrange activities to suit you. If you have a particular interest insist on a specialist – some travellers have complained that their guides didn't seem to know much.

Jungle Walks

A number of trails have been cleared around the BRL, although you won't be allowed on most without your guide. To be fair there is a chance of running into potentially dangerous animals, such as elephants or sun bears, but it would be hard to get lost on the trails.

There's a short nature trail near the lodge which points out interesting facts about the surrounding forest, but you'll probably be so overwhelmed by the colours and sounds that you'll just want to absorb it as you walk along.

Longer trails follow the Sungai Segama, but one of the best climbs up a bluff where there's an ancient hardwood coffin and the remains of bodies buried in a cliff face. On the return you can swim at refreshing waterholes – a natural Jacuzzi.

Night walks are organised most nights and led by guides. There's a chance of seeing snakes, frogs and mammals such as flying squirrels and bearded pigs.

Leeches are common when it's wet. Jungle boots and leech-proof socks are recommended; the latter are usually available at the BRL and cost RM15. See the 'Leeches' boxed text in the special Climbing Kinabalu section earlier in this chapter for details on how to deal with these creatures.

Canopy Walk

One of the highlights of BRL is a walkway suspended 25m above the rainforest floor. It's an ideal spot to look for birdlife and saves craning your neck to look into the tree tops. At the time of writing the canopy walkway had been damaged by a storm – check that it's open before booking so you don't miss out.

Night Drives

Not to be missed! This is the best way to see some of the valley's mammals. Successful wildlife viewing depends on many factors, but on a good night this is as close as you'll get to an African safari in South-East Asia. Expect to see one or two species of giant flying squirrels, sambar deer, civets, porcupines and possibly leopard cats; lucky sightings could include elephants, slow loris and clouded leopards.

Night drives leave the BRL most nights; the best trips are the extended night drives, which depart at about 8.30 pm and return at 1 or 2 am. Cost is about RM50 per person. Take a light waterproof jacket, camera with flash, binoculars and powerful torch (flashlight).

Birdwatching

Although there is a high diversity of bird species, rainforest birding can oscillate between spectacular and niggardly; you have to put in the hours. The best vantage points are along the access road to the BRL – ask the staff to drive you up to the entrance in the late afternoon then walk the 4km back to the lodge. You'll hear much more than you see, but hornbills are relatively common and argus pheasants are often heard.

Field Studies Centre

The field centre was set up by the Sabah Foundation, the Royal Society and a number of private companies to provide facilities for research and education in the rainforest. Many of the sponsors are involved in logging and one of the main areas of study is forest regeneration. It is not possible to stay at the field centre, but if you want to see scientists in their natural habitat it can be visited as a day trip.

Places to Stay & Eat

Access to Danum Valley is tightly controlled and only possible as part of a tour or by booking direct.

Accommodation is in the *Borneo Rainforest Lodge*, a 1st class resort with vast, comfortable rooms, good dining and a bar. Costs, on a twin share basis in standard chalets with full board, are RM350 a night per person! If you can't team up with someone, you'd better come prepared with extra money, because it'll cost a whole lot more. Activities such as day and night walks are included in the price, but extended night drives are extra. There's also an entry fee of RM30 per person and transport costs.

There's also a 'tented camp', 5km walk from the lodge, where you can stay for RM250 per person. Although it's a wilderness experience, staff will cook and attend to your whims so you won't be too uncomfortable.

Bookings and permits can be arranged through Innoprise Jungle Lodge (☎ 088-243245), 3rd floor, Block D, Sadong Jaya Kompleks, KK, or at the Lahad Datu booking office (see the Lahad Datu section).

Getting There & Away

Borneo Rainforest Lodge is 97km by road from Lahad Datu. Access to Danum Valley is only by the Lodge's transport or by private vehicle. There is a checkpoint at the start of the logging concession and you will not be allowed entry without a permit. Entry permits for foreign visitors cost RM10 for day visitors.

Guests of BRL are met at Lahad Datu airport and shuttled out to Danum Valley in air-conditioned comfort. The fee for this is RM100 per person.

MADAI CAVES

Like the better-known Gomantong Caves to the north, these limestone caves are famed for their birds' nests. At the entrance to the cave system there's a sprawling *kampung* (village) of empty wooden shanties. When the swiftlets start nesting these become the temporary dwellings of the nest collectors. So highly prized are these little cups of bird saliva that the collectors risk life and limb by climbing to the roof of the caves on precarious bamboo poles to gather the nests. The most valuable – and rarest – nests are the white ones, which can fetch RM750 or more for a kilogram.

A small river runs through the caves and emerges at the entrance. A torch (flashlight) is necessary to explore properly and a guide is needed to go any distance inside. It is possible to walk right through the main cave but you must wade through the river, which is thigh-deep in places, and then through ankle-deep guano seething with beetles. The exit is reached by clambering over slippery rocks – it is easier to take the trail outside round to the top entrance of the caves. A guide and torch can be hired in the village for around RM5.

The caves are near the Lahad Datu-Tawau Highway. The turn-off is 69km from Lahad Datu, and then it is 3.5km to the caves. Make yourself known at the village, but foreign visitors are unlikely to be poachers and it's unlikely you'll be challenged if you're just looking around.

The Madai area is rarely visited by tourists, and it is difficult to explore without your own transport, but it does have a few points of interest. The large **Air Terjun Madai** (Madai Falls) is next to the highway, 58km from Lahad Datu. The small **Hutan Rekreasi**

Madai is a forest reserve around the falls with picnic facilities and food stalls. The office has a good map of the area and can provide information on the forests and walks nearby. Just opposite the falls is the **Kletus Muyuk Trail**, a 45km walking trail which leads back to the caves and further inland to the Madai-Baturong Forest Reserve.

Places to Stay

The only accommodation is at Kunak, an unremarkable town off the main highway, 18km from the caves. The *Dreamland Hotel* (☎ 089-851322) is an expensive, unimpressive mid-range place where air-con rooms with bathroom and TV start at RM52/62 for singles/doubles. If you were self-sufficient you could probably camp near the caves or stay in one of the huts – ask at the village for information.

Getting There & Away

All buses between Lahad Datu and Semporna or Tawau pass the turn-off to the caves; you should be able to get a minibus to take you all the way to the caves, but you may have to walk back out to the highway. Buses run to the caves from Kunak for RM2, but you could be in for a long wait. Traffic on the road to the caves is light.

SEMPORNA

Semporna is just about the end of the road in south-eastern Sabah. The town really comes alive at the end of March when a colourful regatta takes place, but normally it's a quiet little spot. It's on a pretty bay fringed with stilt villages and there are islands with good beaches not far offshore. However its proximity to Indonesia ensures a hefty police presence. For most travellers Semporna is only a transit stop en route to Pulau Sipadan, the famous dive island 36km to the south-east of the town.

The Semporna Ocean Tourism Centre is a large tourist development on stilts over the harbour. It has a hotel, restaurant, souvenir shops and a pathetic aquarium at the end of the pier. The complex is connected to the shore by a causeway.

Places to Stay & Eat

The main hotel in Semporna is the expensive *Dragon Inn* (☎ 089-781088), built on stilts over the water. The bamboo and thatch air-con rooms cost an outrageous RM165, including double bed, bathroom and TV. Family rooms are cheaper at RM110, but these are usually full. It looks nice but this place gets our vote for the biggest rip-off in expensive Sabah.

The only alternative is the friendly but run-down *Hotel Semporna* (☎ 089-781378), on the main street in town. Air-con rooms are poor value at RM40 with shared bathroom, or RM60 with attached bathroom.

The *Pearl City Chinese Restoran* is a vast seafood restaurant that forms most of the Semporna Ocean Tourism Centre. The food is good but expensive: prawn and crab dishes are RM10 to RM15, vegetable and bean curd dishes are about RM8, and fresh fish and lobster can be bought by the gram or kilogram. Travellers have complained about some staff asking for money here.

The *Floating Restoran & Bar* is a cheaper seafood option halfway along the short causeway which connects the town to the Ocean Tourism Centre. The food is uninspiring and this place looks like it's about to fall in the drink.

There's a clean and friendly *cafe* at the end of the causeway past the Sipadan Dive offices. In town there are numerous Chinese *kedai kopi* and a branch of *Singapore Chicken Rice*.

Getting There & Away

Minibuses leave from the town centre for Lahad Datu (2½ hours, RM8) and Tawau (1½ hours, RM4). There are also share-taxis to Tawau for RM10. Private car owners with nothing better to do may offer to take you to Tawau; it's a quicker, air-con way to travel, but bargain hard and don't pay more than RM30.

PULAU SIPADAN

This small island 36km off the south-east coast of Sabah attracts experienced and novice divers from all over Asia and further afield. Sipadan's five hectares is the tip of a limestone pinnacle that rises 600m from the seabed. Within 25m of the eastern side of the island you can float over a near-vertical 'wall' and gaze into the inky depths. It's rather awe-inspiring; myriads of colourful tropical fish swim in the warm water near the surface, but deep down huge groupers and wrasse nose about, and the water gets so dark you don't know what may be lurking there.

The best way to find out is to scuba dive down the wall, and a number of outfits run dive/accommodation packages to Sipadan. The sea is teeming with marine life and the island is billed as one of the world's great diving destinations. There are plans to make Sipadan part of a marine park, but Indonesia has also laid claim to the island and the issue has not been resolved.

Sipadan is fringed by a beautiful white-sand beach, but it takes only half an hour to walk around the island and the real fun is under the water. To get the most out of a visit you should dive; it's an expensive place and if you're only snorkelling there's better value to be had elsewhere (such as Tunku Abdul Rahman National Park off KK).

Diving

Dives are held from early morning until after dark by all operators, and qualified personnel accompany each trip. All visitors are briefed on local conditions when they arrive, and equipment can be hired on the island or is included in the price of a package.

Diving off the wall can be exhilarating and frightening. The deeper water offshore is home to schools of barracuda and tuna, occasional whale sharks and friendly hammerheads which sometimes investigate a dive team. Sea turtles are common, and experienced divers can explore an undersea cavern in which turtles periodically lose their way and perish.

The best snorkelling is near the jetty, where you can float over the dropoff and watch a good variety of common wrasse, parrotfish, batfish and others. In the shallow water around the island you won't have to go far to see turtles and you can also snorkel around the dive boats in deeper water. The current over the reef can be quite strong.

Borneo Divers has installed a hyperbaric (decompression) chamber on the island. Make sure your travel insurance covers diving accidents, because at US$1000 an hour the decompression chamber is no tanning salon. See the Diving & Snorkelling section in the Terengganu chapter for advice on safe and responsible diving.

Places to Stay & Eat

Five companies operate dive resorts on Sipadan. Visitors are limited to 160 people per night, and it is advisable to book ahead.

Accommodation is in comfortable, rather than luxurious, fan-cooled chalets with bathrooms and desalinated showers. All meals are included in packages and the food is generally good; alcoholic drinks are extra.

All the Sipadan dive centres have offices on the causeway in Semporna. They offer better deals than in KK, but it may be difficult to get accommodation on Sipadan at the last moment.

All operators offer a small discount for snorkellers. For two days/one night of snorkelling expect to pay about RM300 per person plus equipment hire. Hire of mask and snorkel costs RM5, and fins RM5, per day. Current operators include:

Abdillah Sipadan Paradise
(☎ 088-258105) 2nd floor, Block A, Taman Fortuna Shoplots, Jalan Penampang, KK; has a lodge on Sipadan

Borneo Divers
(☎ 089-761214) 1st floor, 46 Jalan Dunlop, Tawau; the original Sipadan operators; offers all-inclusive trips costing US$675 per person for two days/one night ex-KK, up to US$1065 for a five day trip. Borneo Divers also has trips from Tawau.

Borneo Sea Adventures
(☎ 088-218216) 1st floor, 8A Karamunsing Warehouse, KK; Borneo Adventures runs Sipadan Lodge; prices start at RM600 for two-day/one-night dive packages from Semporna, up to RM2100 for seven days/six nights

Pulau Sipadan Resort
(☎ 089-765200) 1st floor, 484 Bandar Sabindo, Tawau; divers' packages start at RM1250 for three days/two nights from Tawau

Seaventures
(☎ 088-251669) 4th floor, Wisma Sabah, KK; Seaventures offers a two day/one night package ex-KK for RM815

Sipadan Dive Centre
(☎ 088-240584) 11th floor, Wisma Merdeka, KK; prices start at RM1275 (RM965 for non-divers) for two-day trips ex-KK, up to RM1900 (RM1520 for non-divers) for five-day trips. Packages from Semporna cost RM400 for two days/one night.

Getting There & Away

The 45 minute boat ride from Semporna is usually included in the dive package. Getting to Sipadan under your own steam is expensive. Hiring a fishing boat for a day trip from Semporna costs around RM250, but a group could share the fee. Dive centres ask about RM400 for their speedboats.

TAWAU

A mini-boomtown way down south near the Indonesian border, Tawau is a provincial capital and a centre for the shipping of timber, rubber, Manilla hemp, cocoa, copra and tobacco. It's a tough town, where groups of idle men hang around street corners and immigrants from the Philippines and Indonesia live in squalor near the waterfront. Single women may feel distinctly uncomfortable walking around after dark.

There's nothing to do or see in town, although the nearby Tawau Hills Park has hot springs, waterfalls and fine rainforest. For most travellers Tawau is a transit point for diving packages to Sipadan, and the embarkation point for Tarakan in Kalimantan.

Orientation & Information

All places to stay and eat, banks and bus stations are in or near the centre. The only time you're likely to need public transport is to get to the airport, which is 1km north-west of town, or to the Indonesian consulate, about 3km east of the centre.

There's no tourist office, although the reception desk at the Belmont Marco Polo Hotel may be able to help with inquiries.

The Malaysia Airlines office (☎ 089-765522) is in Wisma SASCO on the eastern edge of the town centre. It is open Monday to Friday from 8.30 am to 5 pm, and Saturday from 8 am to 1 pm.

Bouraq is an Indonesian feeder airline that flies to Tarakan and other destinations in Kalimantan. The agent is Merdeka Travel (☎ 089-772531) at 41 Jalan Dunlop.

The Indonesian consulate (☎ 089-772052) is on Jalan Apas, 3km from the centre on the main road coming into town.

Bookings for Pulau Sipadan can be made at the Borneo Divers office (☎ 089-761214), upstairs at 46 Jalan Dunlop. The office for Pulau Sipadan Resort (☎ 089-765200) is at 1st floor, Bandar Sabindo.

Places to Stay – Budget

The so-called budget hotels in Tawau are poor value for money. There's a couple of basic lodging houses that aren't brothels, but they are not recommended for women travellers.

The cheapest is the *Penginapan Kinabalu Lodging House*, Jalan Chester, where basic rooms can be bargained down to RM15/20 for a single/double. Much better is the *Hotel Soon Yee* (☎ 089-772447), 1362 Jalan Stephen Tan, where a simple fan-cooled room costs RM18, and air-con rooms with bathroom start at RM28. This is a clean, well run place – a sign at reception says 'No Prostitutes'.

Places to Stay – Mid-Range

The *Tawau Hotel* (☎ 089-771100), 73 Jalan Chester, has basic, musty and tatty fan-cooled rooms for RM27.50 or air-con rooms with bathroom for RM38.50. The *Loong Hotel* (☎ 089-765308), on Jalan Abaca, is probably the best option in this price range. Clean air-con rooms with bathroom and TV start at RM38/48 for singles/twin share, while a room with a double bed will cost you RM53.

The *North Borneo Hotel* (☎ 089-763060), 52 Jalan Dunlop, and the *North City Hotel* (☎ 089-773100), near the Empire Cinema, are run by the same company and offer decent rooms with TV, clean bathroom and hot water for RM50/60.

RICHARD I'ANSON

RAFFLES HOTEL

ARASU RAMASAMY

RICHARD I'ANSON

RAFFLES HOTEL

Singapore
Top: Jurong Bird Park (left); Raffles Hotel, built in 1887, is a landmark as well as a hotel (right).
Bottom Left: The modern skyline of Singapore by night.
Centre Right: Murals at Haw Par Villa retell Chinese myths.
Bottom Right: The plush lobby of the refurbished Raffles Hotel.

ALL PHOTOGRAPHS BY MARY ANN HEMPHILL

Brunei

Top Left: A worshipper enters Omar Ali Saifuddien Mosque for prayer, Bandar Seri Begawan.
Top Right: The stilt villages of Kampung Ayer house 30,000 Bruneians.
Centre Right: The Omar Ali Saifuddien Mosque dominates Bandar Seri Begawan's skyline.
Bottom: Children at Kampung Ayer.

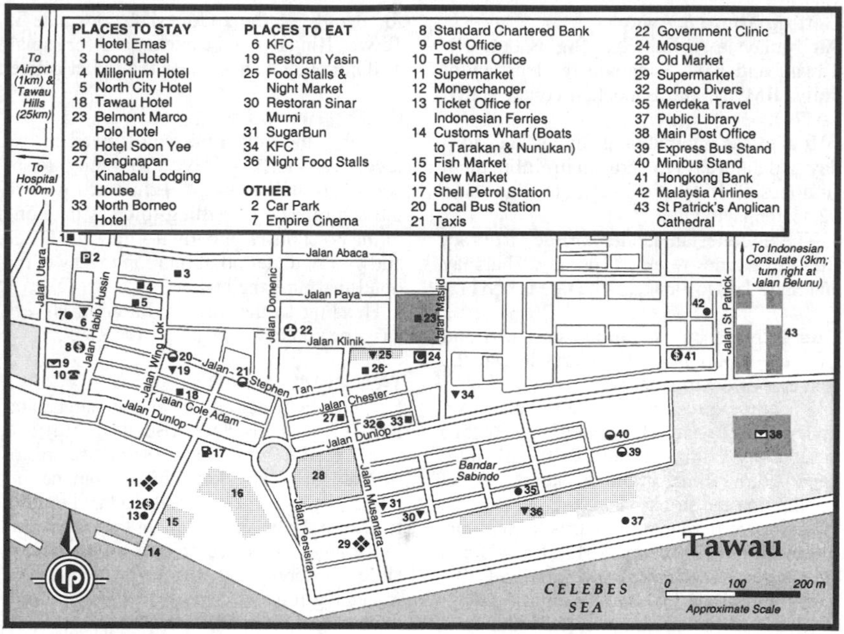

Places to Stay – Top End

Tawau's top hotel is the *Belmont Marco Polo* (☎ 089-777988), where rooms cost RM145/155, or RM180/210 on the executive floor; suites range from RM410 to RM1000 – plus the usual tax. There's a business centre and restaurants, and the front desk can arrange airport transfer and car hire.

The new *Millenium Hotel* (☎ 089-771155), 561 Jalan Bakau, is a friendly place with airy, bright double/twin share/suites for RM90/100/135. Ask about promotional rates.

Recent renovations pushed the *Hotel Emas* (☎ 089-762000), Jalan Utara, into the top price bracket. Comfortable rooms with TV and minibar cost from RM80 to RM200; the cheaper rooms are good value.

Places to Eat

There's plenty of choice in Tawau. *Hawkers' stalls* seem to spring up wherever there's a vacant lot and you won't have to go far for a cheap feed. Indonesian and Malay favourites can be picked up at the old and new markets, along the waterfront near the public library, and next to the mosque on Jalan Klinik.

For good Malay food try the *Restoran Sinar Murni* near the waterfront and there's a good Chinese *kedai kopi* downstairs at the Loong Hotel. The central *Restoran Yasin* does good murtabaks and curries.

There are also a couple of branches of *SugarBun* and *KFC* around town.

For a bit of a splurge, the restaurant in the *Hotel Emas* has good food; a western breakfast is about RM10, a three course lunch RM14 and there's sometimes a steamboat buffet in the evening. The *Venice Coffee House* in the Belmont Marco Polo offers good set price meals: the breakfast buffet is RM14, and lunch or dinner is RM16.50 (plus tax). The *Kublai Restaurant* in the same hotel offers fine Chinese dining – at a price.

Getting There & Away

Air Malaysia Airlines has flights between Tawau and Kota Kinabalu (at least eight daily, RM96), and Sandakan (twice daily, RM74).

It also has international flights (on Monday and Saturday) to Tarakan in Kalimantan (Indonesia). It's just a 35 minute flight on a 12 seater Twin Otter.

The Indonesian feeder airline, Bouraq, flies three times weekly (Tuesday, Thursday and Saturday) to Tarakan. The fare is RM175.

Bus Express buses, minibuses and Land Cruisers depart from the vacant lots at the east end of the town centre.

Air-con express buses to Sandakan (5½ hours, RM20) and KK (nine hours, RM50) leave daily from 5.30 until 8.30 am. Book ahead if travelling on the weekend – ticket booths line the street where the buses park.

There are frequent minibuses to Semporna and Kunak (1½ hours, RM5), Lahad Datu (2½ hours, RM12) and Sandakan (RM20).

Land Cruisers leave from about 7.30 am until mid-morning for KK (RM60), Sandakan (RM25) and Lahad Datu (RM10). One also leaves at about 8 am and takes the logging road all the way to Keningau; it costs RM80.

Boat Boats for Indonesia leave from the customs wharf at the back of the large supermarket. The *CB88 Express* usually departs daily for Tarakan in Kalimantan, though Sunday departures are less reliable and the schedule is haphazard. The KM *Saturiah II* operates between Tawau and Nunukan at approximately 8 am daily, returning from Nunukan at noon (be there by 11 am).

Purchase tickets at the office near the customs wharf opposite the fish market. A sign displays the next sailing times. The trip to Tarakan takes three hours and costs RM65; Nunukan is an hour away and costs RM25 (or 11,000 rp plus 1000 rp departure tax from Nunukan).

Indonesian visas cannot be issued on arrival and must be procured before you make the crossing; see the Information entry for details of the Indonesian consulate in Tawau. Ringgit can be exchanged for rupiah at the moneychanger near the ticket office.

Getting Around

Probably the only time you'll need to use local transport is if you're going to or coming from the airport, 1km north-west of the centre. The best thing to do is take one of the hotel buses into town – they're all free and you're under no obligation to stay at the hotel that runs the bus.

Heading to the airport, hitching is very easy, or you can take a taxi for RM5.

TAWAU HILLS PARK

Hemmed in by agriculture and human habitation, Tawau Hills Park, (Bukit Tawau) is a small reserve that protects 28,000 hectares of forested hills rising dramatically from the surrounding plain. The park was declared in 1979 to protect the water catchment for settlements in the area, but not before most of the accessible rainforest was logged. Much of the remaining forest clings to steep-sided ridges that rise to 1310m Gunung Magdalena.

On a clear day the park's peaks make a fine sight and Tawau Hills is a popular weekend destination for day-trippers from town. A trail leads to hot springs and a waterfall three hours walk north of the park HQ, and there's a 30 minute walk to 530m Bombalai Hill to the south. Old forestry trails crisscross the forest north of park HQ, but they aren't signposted and you could get lost.

The only accommodation at the park is in a 76 bed hostel where a bed costs RM20 per night (RM10 if you're under 18). There's also a campground which costs RM5 per adult and RM2 for those under 18; campers must be self-sufficient. Bookings can be made at the park (☎ 089-753564) or by writing to the Ranger in Charge, Tawau Hills Park, WDT No 118, 91009 Tawau. There's also a park entrance fee of RM2 if you're not staying the night.

Tawau Hills is about 25km north-west of Tawau. To get there you'll have to take a taxi from town or hitch; a taxi should cost RM25 and the trip takes about an hour.

SINGAPORE

PAUL HELLANDER

Facts about Singapore

HISTORY

Malay legend has it that long ago a Sumatran prince visiting the island of Temasek saw a strange animal, which was identified to him as a lion. The good omen prompted the prince to found a city on the spot of the sighting which he named Singapura, or 'Lion City' in Sanskrit.

This may be a legend, but it is no less plausible than much of Singapore's official history. From the arrival in 1819 of Sir Thomas Stamford Raffles – officially declared Singapore's founder in the 1970s in order to 'neutrally' settle rival claims by local Malays and Chinese – to the present, Singapore's past has been moulded to fit political and economic demands. Nonetheless, beneath the serene surface of gentrified colonial buildings lies an intriguing tale of the rise and fall of local empires, European colonial 'great games' and the enduring legacy of 19th century British rule.

Early Empires

Chinese traders en route to India had plied the waters around what is now Singapore from at least the 5th century AD. Some sources claim that Marco Polo visited a flourishing city in 1292 where Singapore now stands.

It is certain, however, that Singapore was not the first of the great entrepôt cities in the region. By the 7th century Sriwijaya, a seafaring Buddhist kingdom centred on Palembang in Sumatra, held sway over the Straits of Malacca (now Melaka); by the 10th century it dominated the Malay Peninsula as well. At the height of Sriwijaya's power, Singapore was at most a small trading outpost.

Raids by rival kingdoms and the arrival of Islam spelled the eclipse of Sriwijaya by the 13th century. Based mainly on the thriving pirate trade, the sultanate of Melaka quickly acquired the commercial power once wielded by Sriwijaya. It was a cosmopolitan, free port emporium at which traders were spared the complex procedures found elsewhere for dealing with 'polluting' foreigners – money spoke first in Melaka.

Colonial Great Games

Armed with the cross and cannon, the Portuguese took Melaka in 1511, hoping to drive Islam and its trading hegemony out of the region. Once the city had fallen to the mercantile Christians, however, Melaka's Muslim traders moved on. The equally ardent Dutch founded Batavia (now Jakarta) to further undermine Melaka's position, finally wresting the city from their European competitors in 1641.

In the late 18th century the British began looking for a harbour in the Straits of Melaka to secure lines of trade between China, the Malay world and their interests in India. Renewed war in Europe led, in 1875, to annexation of The Netherlands by the French,

In 1819 Sir Thomas Stamford Raffles established a British base in Singapore, which later became part of the British Straits Settlements.

prompting the British to seize Dutch possessions in South-East Asia, including Melaka.

When, after the end of the Napoleonic Wars, the British agreed to restore Dutch possessions in 1818, there were those who were bitterly disappointed at the failure of the dream of British imperial expansion in South-East Asia. One such figure was Stamford Raffles, Lieutenant-Governor of Java. Raffles soon procured permission to found a station to secure British trade routes in the region. The Dutch beat him to his choice of Riau, an island near modern Singapore, and Raffles was instructed to negotiate with the sultan of nearby Johor for land.

Raffles' City Emerges

When Raffles landed at Singapore in early 1819, the Empire of Johor was divided. When the old sultan had died in 1812, his younger son's accession to power had been engineered while an elder son, Hussein, was away. The Dutch had a treaty with the young sultan, but Raffles threw his support behind Hussein, proclaiming him sultan and installing him in residence on Singapore. In Raffles' plans the sultan wielded no actual power but he did serve to legitimise British claims on the island. Raffles also signed a treaty with the more eminent *temenggong* (senior judge) of Johor and set him up with an estate on the Singapore River. Thus, Raffles had acquired the use of Singapore in exchange for modest annual allowances to Sultan Hussein and the temenggong, which ended with a cash buyout of the pair in 1824 and transfer of Singapore's ownership to Britain's East India Company. In 1826 Singapore, Penang and Melaka became part of the Straits Settlements, controlled by the East India Company in Calcutta but administered from Singapore.

Raffles' first and second visits to Singapore in 1819 were brief, and he left instructions and operational authority with Colonel William Farquhar, formerly the Resident (chief British representative) at Melaka, now Resident of Singapore. Three years later, Raffles returned to run the now thriving colony for a year, with a vision to make Singapore the lasting successor to the great entrepôts of the Sriwijayan Kingdom, but under the rule of British law and empire. While Raffles was a firm believer in Britain's right to rule, he also preached the virtues of making Singapore a free port and opposed slavery. He also proclaimed limitations on indentured labour. Raffles was also a keen and sympathetic student of the peoples of the region, though in typically colonial fashion he romanticised the distant Malay past while regarding Malays of the present as degraded and lacking the Protestant work ethic – a view that ironically still prevails.

Raffles initiated a town plan which included levelling one hill to form a new commercial district (now Raffles Place), and erecting government buildings around another, Forbidden Hill (now Fort Canning Hill). The plan also embraced the colonial practice, still operative in Singapore today, of administering the population according to neat racial categories, with the Europeans. Indians, Chinese and Malays each living and working in their own separate and distinct quarters.

How the East was Won

Recognising the need for cooperation with Chinese communities, Raffles also sought registration of the *kongsi* (clan organisations for mutual assistance known variously as ritual brotherhoods, heaven-man-earth societies, triads and secret societies). Labour and dialect-based kongsi would become increasingly important to Singapore's success in the 19th century as overseas demand for Chinese-harvested products grew enormously. Singapore's access to kongsi-based economies in the region, however, depended largely on revenues from an East India Company product from India bound for China – opium.

Farquhar had established Singapore's first opium farm for domestic consumption, and by the 1830s excise and sales revenues of opium accounted for nearly half the administration's income, a situation that continued for a century after Raffles' arrival. But the British Empire produced more than Chinese

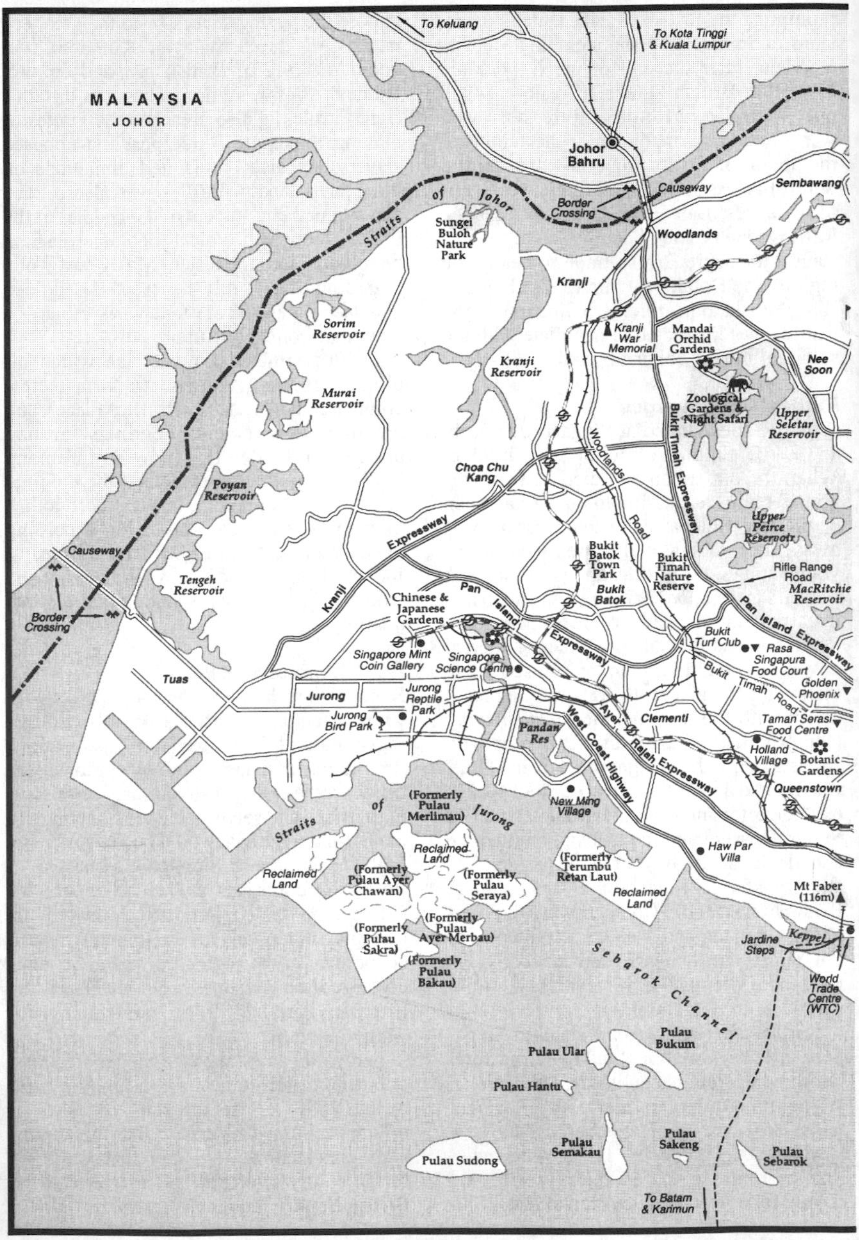
To Keluang
To Kota Tinggi & Kuala Lumpur
MALAYSIA
JOHOR
Johor Bahru
Straits of Johor
Causeway
Sembawang
Border Crossing
Sungei Buloh Nature Park
Woodlands
Kranji
Sorim Reservoir
Kranji War Memorial
Mandai Orchid Gardens
Kranji Reservoir
Nee Soon
Murai Reservoir
Zoological Gardens & Night Safari
Upper Seletar Reservoir
Woodlands Road
Bukit Timah Expressway
Choa Chu Kang
Poyan Reservoir
Upper Peirce Reservoir
Expressway
Bukit Batok Town Park
Causeway
Bukit Timah Nature Reserve
Rifle Range Road
Tengeh Reservoir
Kranji
MacRitchie Reservoir
Bukit Batok
Pan Island Expressway
Chinese & Japanese Gardens
Border Crossing
Bukit Turf Club
Rasa Singapura Food Court
Singapore Mint Coin Gallery
Singapore Science Centre
Pan Island Expressway
Tuas
Bukit Timah Road
Golden Phoenix
Jurong
Jurong Reptile Park
Jurong Bird Park
Clementi
Taman Serasi Food Centre
Pandan Res
Ayer Rajah Expressway
West Coast Highway
Holland Village
Botanic Gardens
Queenstown
New Ming Village
Straits of Jurong
(Formerly Pulau Merlimau)
Reclaimed Land
(Formerly Terumbu Retan Laut)
Haw Par Villa
Reclaimed Land
(Formerly Pulau Ayer Chawan)
(Formerly Pulau Seraya)
Reclaimed Land
Mt Faber (116m)
(Formerly Pulau Ayer Merbau)
(Formerly Pulau Sakra)
(Formerly Pulau Bakau)
Keppel
Jardine Steps
Sebarok Channel
World Trade Centre (WTC)
Pulau Ular
Pulau Bukum
Pulau Hantu
Pulau Semakau
Pulau Sakeng
Pulau Sudong
Pulau Sebarok
To Batam & Karimun

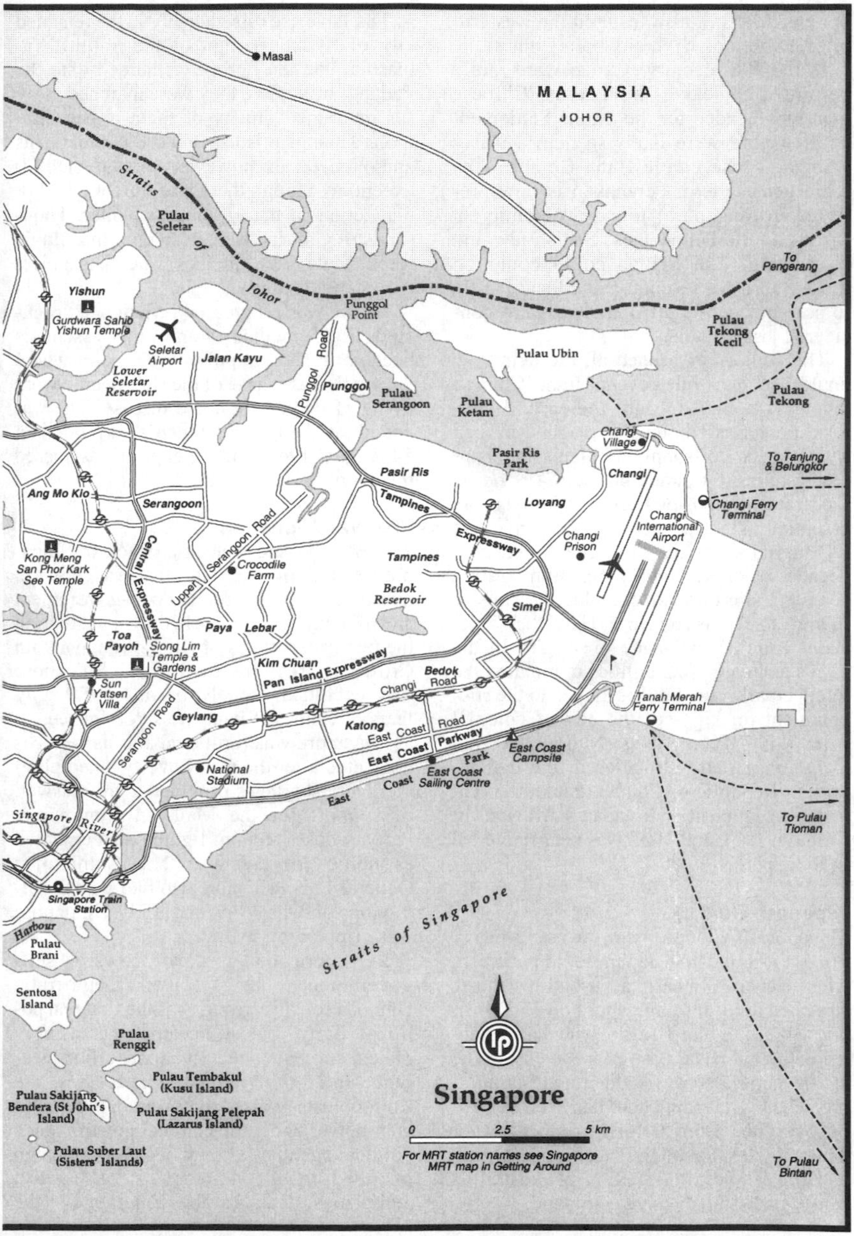
Masai
MALAYSIA
JOHOR
Straits of Johor
Pulau Seletar
Yishun
Gurdwara Sahib Yishun Temple
Seletar Airport
Lower Seletar Reservoir
Jalan Kayu
Punggol Point
Punggol Road
Punggol
Pulau Serangoon
Pulau Ketam
Pulau Ubin
To Pengerang
Pulau Tekong Kecil
Pulau Tekong
Changi Village
Pasir Ris Park
Pasir Ris
Changi
To Tanjung & Belungkor
Changi Ferry Terminal
Loyang
Tampines Expressway
Changi International Airport
Changi Prison
Ang Mo Kio
Serangoon
Upper Serangoon Road
Crocodile Farm
Kong Meng San Phor Kark See Temple
Central Expressway
Tampines
Bedok Reservoir
Simei
Toa Payoh
Paya Lebar
Siong Lim Temple & Gardens
Kim Chuan
Pan Island Expressway
Bedok Road
Changi Road
Sun Yatsen Villa
Serangoon Road
Geylang
Katong
East Coast Road
East Coast Parkway
Tanah Merah Ferry Terminal
East Coast Campsite
East Coast Park
East Coast Sailing Centre
National Stadium
To Pulau Tioman
Singapore River
Singapore Train Station
Harbour
Pulau Brani
Straits of Singapore
Sentosa Island
Pulau Renggit
Pulau Tembakul (Kusu Island)
Pulau Sakijang Bendera (St John's Island)
Pulau Sakijang Pelepah (Lazarus Island)
Pulau Suber Laut (Sisters' Islands)
Singapore
0 2.5 5 km
For MRT station names see Singapore MRT map in Getting Around
To Pulau Bintan

SINGAPORE

opium addicts; it also fostered the western-oriented outlook of Straits-born Chinese.

In the 19th century women were rarely permitted to leave China; thus, Chinese men who headed for the Straits Settlement of Singapore were likely to marry Malay women. These creole Baba Chinese (the more general term Peranakan is now preferred in Singapore) found an identity in loyalty to the Union Jack, British law and citizenship. The British could count on those Babas with capital and a local family to stay put, while other traders were considered less reliable.

The authorities needed all the help they could get, for while revenues and Chinese labourers poured in until the early 1930s, Singapore was continually plagued by bad sanitation, water-supply problems and man-eating tigers, by piracy on the seas, and by the strain of imposing European ideals on an essentially Chinese city. Despite a massive fall in rubber prices in 1920, the ensuing decade saw more boom times. Immigration soared, and millionaires, including Chinese migrants such as Aw Boon Haw, the 'Tiger Balm King', were made overnight. In the 1930s and early 40s, politics dominated the intellectual scene. Indians looked to the subcontinent for signs of the end of colonial rule, while Kuomintang (Nationalist) and Communist party struggles in the disintegrating Republic of China attracted fervent attention. Opposition to Japan's invasions of China in 1931 and 1937 was near universal in Singapore.

Japanese Rule

Singaporean Chinese were to pay a heavy price for opposing Japanese imperialism when General Yamashita pushed his thinly stretched army into Singapore on 15 February 1942. For the British, who had established a vital naval base near the city in the 1920s, surrender was sudden and humiliating. The loss of Singapore has been blamed on everyone from British prime minister Churchill to squabbling British commanders and the wholesale desertion of Australian troops under the divisive command.

The Japanese ruled harshly in the renamed city of Syonan (Light of the South). Yamashita had the Europeans herded onto the Padang; from there they were marched away for internment, many of them at the infamous Changi prison. Chinese Communists and intellectuals, however, were targeted for execution, though there was little method or distinction in the ensuing slaughter. Thousands of Chinese were murdered in a single week. Malays and Indians were also subject to systematic abuse.

As the war progressed inflation skyrocketed. Food, medicines and other essentials became in short supply, to the point where during the last phase of the war, people were dying of malnutrition and disease. The war ended suddenly with Japan's surrender on 14 August 1945, and Singapore was spared the agony of recapture.

Postwar Alienation

The British were welcomed back to Singapore but their right to rule was now in question. Plans for limited self-government and a Malayan Union were drawn up, uniting the peninsular states of British Malaya with Crown possessions in Borneo. Singapore was excluded, largely because of Malay fears of Chinese Singapore's dominance.

Singapore was run-down and its services neglected after the war. Poverty, unemployment and shortages provided a groundswell of support for the Malayan Communist Party, whose freedom fighters had emerged as heroes of the war. The Communist General Labour Union also had a huge following, and in 1946 and 1947 Singapore was crippled by strikes.

Singapore moved slowly towards self-government. The Malayan Democratic Union, a socialist group, was the first real political party, but it became increasingly radical and boycotted Singapore's first elections in 1947. After early successes, the Communists realised they were not going to gain power under the colonial government's political agenda and they began a campaign of armed struggle in Malaya. In 1948 British authorities declared the Emergency: the

Communists were outlawed and a bitter guerrilla war was waged on the peninsula for 12 years. There was no fighting in Singapore, but left-wing politics languished under the repression of Emergency regulations.

Lee Kuan Yew's Singapore

By the early 1950s, the Communist threat had waned and left-wing activity was again on the upswing, with student and union movements to the fore of political activity.

One of the rising stars of this era was Lee Kuan Yew, a third generation Straits-born Chinese who had studied law at Cambridge University. The socialist People's Action Party (PAP) was founded in 1954 with Lee as secretary-general. A shrewd politician, Lee appealed for support to both the emerging British-educated elite and to radicalist passions – the party included a Communist faction and an ambitious post-Raffles plan of its own: strong state intervention to industrialise Singapore's emporium economy.

Under the arrangements for internal self-government, the PAP won a majority of seats in the new Legislative Assembly in 1959, and Lee Kuan Yew became the first Singaporean to hold the title of prime minister.

By the early 1960s Britain had found a way to exit colonial rule in the region. A new state of Malaysia, uniting Malaya with Sabah, Sarawak and Singapore, would balance ethnic numbers and politically unify long-standing economic ties. The arrangement lasted only two years – in 1965 Singapore was booted out of the federation, mainly because Malay fears of Chinese control remained unassuaged. The island was left to

Singapore Malaysia Relations

Ever since the untidy divorce in 1965 when Singapore was unceremoniously kicked out of the short-lived Federation of Malay, relations between the two countries have been warm(ish) at best, to pretty chilly at worst. Senior minister and former prime minister of Singapore Lee Kuan Yew didn't foment much good will when in early 1997 he suggested that the city of Johor Bahru on the Malaysian side of the Causeway was 'a place of gangsters and car-jackers'. It took a goodwill visit the following year by current Prime Minister Goh Chok Tong to Malaysian Prime Minister Dr Mahathir Mohamad to smooth over the ruffled feathers.

It's not hard to see why things have not always been smooth between the two nations. Singapore, the upstart sibling, was dismissed at the time of the separation by Malaysia for refusing to afford the same rights to its own Malay citizens as in Malaysia. Singapore ultimately came out on top with a well-ordered society and a well-run economy while Malaysia, the big brother, still wrestles with economic woes, unemployment and other social ills that Singapore seems to have largely eliminated.

There are certainly niggling unresolved issues like dual territorial claims over a small island in the Singapore Straits, and Malaysian Railways land-holdings on Singapore. There are also petty restrictions on citizens operating freely within the commercial sector of the other country and an unspoken grudge held by the Chinese over positive discrimination in Malaysia in favour of the Bumiputra or native-born Malays.

Notwithstanding this, the two nations are more united by common interests than divided by dissimilarities and talk of reunification resurfaces regularly in the press on both sides of the Straits. There has even been a serious proposal by some keen advocates of union to fill in the Singapore Straits, using Singapore's technical expertise in landfilling operations, and physically join the two nations. The two countries will only survive and thrive by tolerance, trade and exchanges of technology and ideas. The prevailing thinking is that they must engage in a mutually profitable symbiosis in a region that recently has had more than its fair share of discontent.

fend for itself as the Republic of Singapore. Despite Lee Kuan Yew's public tears and real fears at the messy divorce, both peninsular Malays and Singapore's Chinese were mostly relieved that the marriage of convenience was over.

Making the most of one-party rule in independent Singapore, under Lee's paternal control the PAP set to work moulding its multiracial citizens and fragile state into a viable entity. Industrialisation paid off, and ambitious infrastructure, defence, health, education, pension and housing schemes were rigorously pursued. Housing and urban renovation, in particular, despite their controversial impact on Singapore's physical environment, have been keys to the PAP's success.

Ostensibly following the basic tenets of Confucianism, Singapore's leaders also sought order and progress in the strict regulation of social behaviour and identity: banning chewing gum and smoking in public, installing cameras and automatic locks in lifts to catch public urination in the act, setting up state-sponsored matchmaking venues and offering financial incentives to well-educated Chinese women to have more children.

Under Lee, high economic growth rates supported political stability, which was further ensured by exiling or jailing dissidents, banning critical publications and controlling public speech. In prime minister Goh Chok Tong's more relaxed, liberalised regime of the 1990s, politicians who raise touchy issues tend to find themselves suddenly accused of defamation.

Life after Lee

In 1990 Lee Kuan Yew resigned as prime minister (though he still holds the conspicuous position of Special Minister), the same year the Mass Rapid Transit (MRT) subway system – an impressive testament to Singapore's ultra-modernisation and technological capabilities – was completed.

As the century ends, Lee, the 'father of modern Singapore', and Goh's PAP face the situation of all parents. Having reared a population of mobile technophiles for a globalised economy, the children have grown up. Many, especially Indian and Chinese professionals, find better prospects elsewhere; those who remain, like Malay and Chinese youths, are chided for chafing at old expectations. The Lion City has been given plenty of courage and brains; many Singaporeans seem to feel what it needs now is a heart.

GEOGRAPHY

Singapore consists of the main, low-lying Singapore Island and 58 much smaller islands within its territorial waters. It is situated just above 1°N in latitude, a mere 137km north of the equator. Singapore Island is 42km long and 23km wide, and together with the other islands, the republic has a total landmass of 646 sq km (and growing through land reclamation). The other main islands are Pulau Tekong (24.4 sq km), which is gazetted as a military area but planned to be semi-residential eventually; Pulau Ubin (10.2 sq km), which is a rural haven from downtown Singapore; and Sentosa Island (3.3 sq km), Singapore's fun park. Built-up urban areas comprise around 50% of the land area, while parkland, reservoirs, plantations and open military areas occupy 40%. Remaining forest accounts for only 4%.

Bukit Timah (Hill of Tin), in the central hills, is the highest point on Singapore Island at an altitude of 162m. The central area of the island is an igneous outcrop, containing most of Singapore's remaining forest and open areas. The western part of the island is a sedimentary area of low-lying hills and valleys, while the south-east is mostly flat and sandy.

Singapore is connected with Peninsular Malaysia by a main 1km-long causeway and a newer bridge-cum-causeway in the west of the island. Under current plans, further land reclamation and housing developments will dramatically change Singapore's geography. Land reclamation has already changed the physical geography around the city centre and also in the Tanah Merah and Changi airport area to the east of the island. The small islands south of the Jurong industrial park are steadily being expanded to make room for more oil storage facilities.

CLIMATE

Singapore has a typically tropical climate. It's hot and humid all year, and can be very uncomfortable initially. But once you're used to the tropics it never seems too uncomfortable. The temperature almost never drops below 20°C (68°F), even at night, and usually climbs to 30°C (86°F) or more during the day. Humidity hovers around 75%.

Rain, when it comes, tends to be short and sharp. You may be unlucky and strike rain on every day of your visit, but don't believe local legend about it raining every day for months on end. Only about half the days of the year receive rain. Singapore is wettest from November to January and driest from May to July, but the difference between these two periods is not dramatic and the country gets an abundance of rainfall every month.

Because it is almost on the equator, Singapore receives a steady supply of 12 hours daylight every day. The sun shines for about half of the day on average (less from November to January). Much of the sunshine is filtered through thin cloud but can be intense.

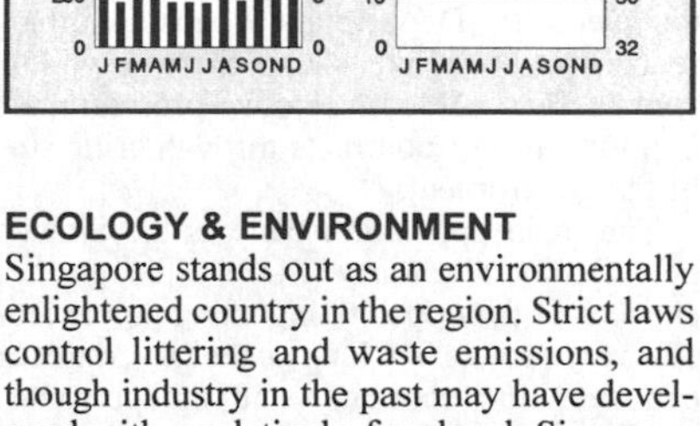

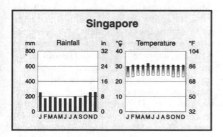

ECOLOGY & ENVIRONMENT

Singapore stands out as an environmentally enlightened country in the region. Strict laws control littering and waste emissions, and though industry in the past may have developed with a relatively free hand, Singapore is now much more environmentally aware.

The island, always spotless and well organised, is becoming even cleaner and greener. Though little is left of Singapore's wilderness, growing interest in the ecology has seen new bird sanctuaries and parkland areas gazetted by the government. In such a built-up urban environment, the government has always been aware of the need for sound planning, and ordinary Singaporeans, who perhaps crave wide-open spaces, are increasingly focusing on the environment.

The most significant contribution to a healthy environment has been the government's commitment to public transport and control of the motor car. It has an ambitious S$20 billion 'World-Class Land Transport System' vision for the 21st century. The MRT network is to more than double in size, while computer-directed buses and light transit trains are planned to increase public transport use from 51% to 75%.

Heavy import duties, registration fees and licensing quotas put a lid on the Singaporean desire to own cars. As a result, the country is remarkably pollution free compared to other cities in Asia, which are beset by choking traffic and exhaust emissions.

Unfortunately the forest fires in Kalimantan and Sumatra in Indonesia in 1997 caused havoc with Singapore's hitherto pristine environment. A heavy smoke haze hung over the island for several weeks providing a gloomy reminder of its precarious geographical position in the region.

FLORA & FAUNA

Singapore was once covered in tropical rainforest, with mangrove and beach forest in the coastal areas. Today only around 300 hectares of primary rainforest and 1800 hectares of secondary forest remain in the centre of the island, in and around the Bukit Timah Nature Reserve. The undeveloped northern coast and the offshore islands are still home to some mangrove forest.

Although they are now believed to be extinct from the island, tiger, clouded leopard, slow loris, Malayan porcupine and mouse deer all once inhabited Singapore. The animal that you are most likely to see is the long-tailed macaque, known locally as the kera – the grey-brown monkeys that form troupes in forest areas. Squirrels are common and Singapore has several species of flying squirrel, and the tree shrew, which looks like a squirrel but is classified as a primate. The flying lemur is occasionally sighted, as are civet cats (musang) and the distinctive pangolin (also known as the scaly anteater), but these are all nocturnal.

Reptiles, frogs and toads are frequently encountered. The reticulated python, which grows to up to 10m, is one of Singapore's most common snakes, while other island species include the poisonous pit viper and black spitting cobra.

Singapore has over 300 bird species and migrant species are observed in the migratory season from September to May. In urban areas common birds include the myna, Eurasian tree sparrow, black-naped oriole, yellow-vented bulbul and spotted dove.

Abundant insect life includes numerous species of butterfly and moth, of which the atlas moth is one of the world's largest. Scorpions include the wood scorpion and the large scorpion. Bites are painful but not fatal.

Visitors who want to sample some of Singapore's natural flora and fauna should visit Pulau Ubin (see the Northern Islands section under Things to See & Do in the Singapore chapter), an island off the north-east corner of Singapore. Alternatively, take a hike in the Bukit Timah Nature Reserve (see under Things to See & Do in the Singapore chapter for full details).

GOVERNMENT & POLITICS

Singapore's government is based on the Westminster system. The unicameral parliament has 81 elected members representing 52 electoral divisions. Voting in elections is compulsory. Governments are elected for five years, but a ruling government can dissolve parliament and call an election at any time.

As well as elected members the government has instituted a system that allows it to appoint an opposition. Nonconstituency Members of Parliament (NCMPs) are members who have failed to win enough votes, but are appointed to parliament as runners-up if less than four opposition members are elected. Six prominent citizens are appointed as Nominated MPs (NMPs) to give nonpartisan views. NCMPs and NMPs are not allowed to vote on financial and constitutional bills, although they can be involved in parliamentary debate.

Singapore also has a president who is elected to the position by popular election. The position is largely ceremonial however, and real power lies with the prime minister and his government. The current president is Ong Teng Cheong.

The legal system is also based on the British system. The Supreme Court is the ultimate arbitrator and consists of the High Court, the Court of Appeal and the Court of Criminal Appeal. Most cases are heard by the District Courts and Magistrates Courts, except for the most serious criminal or civil hearings.

Theoretically Singapore has a democratically elected government and a political system similar to many western democracies. However, the political practice is somewhat different.

The judiciary's independence is enshrined in the constitution, but many judges are appointed on short tenure and their renewal is subject to party approval. Rulings that have gone against the government have seen new laws quickly enacted by parliament to ensure government victory. The old Communist bogey is used to justify Singapore's Internal Security Act, which is still there to detain outspoken critics. Singapore's Internal Security Department keeps detailed records of its citizens and there is widespread fear of losing jobs, promotional opportunities or contracts through criticism of the government.

The main opposition party is the Singapore Democratic Party (SDP), although the chances of the opposition gaining power are still very remote. As long as the government can keep the economy and the personal wealth of its citizens growing, the opposition is unlikely to gain many converts.

ECONOMY

Singapore has traditionally been seen as one of Asia's four 'dragons' – the Asian economic boom countries of Taiwan, Korea, Hong Kong and Singapore. For over 20 years it has recorded phenomenal growth rates averaging at around 9% (although the crisis in South-East Asia reduced that to -2% for 1998). Nonetheless, Singapore has a large current account surplus, it is a net creditor and inflation remains low.

Singapore's economy is based on trade, shipping, banking and tourism, with a growing programme of light industrialisation. It also has a major oil-refining business producing much of the petroleum for the South-East Asian region. Singapore's port vies with Hong Kong to be the busiest in the world.

For many western countries with mounting foreign debt, declining exports and increasing imports, Singapore is seen as a model free-market economy. But while it may be a model economy, its approach is not free market.

Singapore is very definitely a managed economy in the Japanese mould. The government provides direction by targeting certain industries for development and offering tax incentives, or by simply telling them what to do.

While the government promotes free trade, it always reserves the right to intervene, as it did in 1985 when it closed the stock exchange for three days after a major Singaporean company, Pan Electric Industries, went into receivership.

The Monetary Authority of Singapore (MAS) is a major example of government involvement in the economy. It acts as a central bank and powerful financial market regulator to promote sustained economic growth and provide stability in the financial services sector. Singapore's finance market is one of the largest in Asia and provides 25% of the country's income.

Singapore does have its share of free marketeers though, and many in the business community want less government involvement in the economy. Singapore wants to assume the role of Asia's finance centre, especially with Hong Kong's handover to mainland China, but investors in freewheeling Hong Kong are wary of the more regulated Singaporean markets.

Singapore guarantees its citizens decent housing, health care, high standards of education and superannuation, making it a welfare state in comparison with its Asian neighbours. There are no unemployment payments or programmes, but unemployment is low and the government insists that anyone who wants work can find it. In fact, Singapore has to import workers from neighbouring countries, particularly to do the hard, dirty work which Singaporeans no longer want any part of.

During the 1997/98 currency crisis that almost floored neighbouring countries, the Singapore dollar (singdollar) remained reasonably stable and essentially unaffected. However, the longer-term effect of the ensuing reduced trade and tourism with the larger South-East Asian countries has yet to be felt.

Singaporeans are no longer feeling quite so complacent about their future wellbeing in a region where shared prosperity is essential for continued growth and stability.

POPULATION

Singapore's polyglot population numbers 3.04 million. It's made up of 77.3% Chinese, 14.1% Malay, 7.3% Indian and 1.3% from a variety of races.

Singapore's population density is high but the government waged a particularly successful birth control campaign in the 1970s and early 1980s. In fact, it was so successful that the birth rate dropped alarmingly, especially in the Chinese community. To reverse the trend and further the government's genetic-engineering programme, tax incentives were introduced for university-educated women who had children, although at the same time rewards of S$10,000 were offered to those willing to be sterilised.

Later policies offered tax rebates of up to S$20,000 for couples who had a third and fourth child. In another move, government sponsored marriage brokers taught social skills to hard-working Singaporeans so dedicated to their work that they don't know how to woo the opposite sex. Government sponsored 'love boats' cruised the harbour with potential breeding stock.

PEOPLE

Singapore's character, and the main interest for the visitor, lies in the diversity of its population. Chinatown still has some of the sights, sounds and rituals of a Chinese city, Little India is a microcosm of the subcontinent, and in Arab St the *muezzin's* call from the mosque still dominates the lives of its inhabitants. But modern Singapore is essentially a Chinese city with strong western influences.

The principal language of education is English, and growing prosperity sees Singaporeans consuming western values along with western goods. For the government, this divergence from traditional values threatens to undermine the spirit – the work-oriented Chinese spirit – that built Singapore. In an attempt to reverse the new ways of the young, the government runs campaigns to develop awareness of traditional culture and values. It's compulsory for pupils to study their mother tongue in schools.

Government policy has always been to promote Singapore as a multicultural nation where the three main racial groups can live in equality and harmony while still maintaining their own cultural identities. The government strives hard to unite Singaporeans and promote equality, though there are imbalances in the distribution of wealth and power among the racial groups. For the most part, the government is successful in promoting racial harmony, a not-always-easy task in multiracial Singapore.

Chinese

The Chinese first settled in the Nanyang, as South-East Asia is known in China, as far back as the 14th century. In the 19th and 20th centuries waves of Chinese migrants in search of a better life poured into Singapore and provided the labour that ran the colony.

The migrants came mostly from the southern provinces: Hokkien Chinese from the vicinity of Amoy in Fujian Province; the Teochew from Swatow in eastern Guangdong Province; Hakka from Guangdong and Fujian; and Cantonese from Canton. Hokkiens and Teochews enjoyed an affinity in dialect and customs, but the Cantonese and Hakkas may as well have come from opposite ends of the earth. The Chinese settlers soon established their own areas in Singapore, and the divisions along dialect lines still exist to some extent in the older areas.

Settlement for the immigrants was made easier by Chinese organisations based on clan, dialect and occupation. Upon arrival, immigrants were taken in by the various communities and given work and housing. The secret societies were particularly prevalent in Singapore in the 19th century; they provided many useful social functions and were more powerful than the colonial government in the life of the Chinese. However, they eventually declined and became nothing more than criminal gangs.

Nowadays, most Chinese are born in Singapore. The campaign to speak Mandarin has given the Chinese a common dialect (see the boxed text 'Speak Mandarin – Please!' later in this chapter), but English is also a unifying tongue. Increasing westernisation and English education have for the most part not undermined traditional customs and beliefs.

Malays

The Malays are the original inhabitants of Singapore. They are the main racial group throughout the region stretching from the Malay peninsula across Indonesia to the Philippines. Many Malays migrated to Singapore from the peninsula, and significant numbers of Javanese and Bugis (from Riau and Sulawesi) also settled in Singapore.

Malays in Singapore are Muslim. Islam provides the major influence in everyday life and is the rallying point of Malay society. The month of Ramadan, when Muslims fast from sunrise to sunset, is the most important month of the Islamic year. Hari Raya Puasa, the end of the fast, is the major Malay celebration.

The Peranakans

PAUL HELLANDER

Upper storey of a beautifully restored terraced rown on Peranakan Place.

The Peranakans are the descendants of early Chinese immigrants who settled in Melaka and married Malay women. With the formation of the Straits Settlements, many moved to Penang and Singapore. The Peranakans' culture and language are fascinating hybrids of Chinese and Malay traditions: the Peranakans (the Malay word for half-caste) took the names and religion of their Chinese fathers, but the customs, language and dress of their Malay mothers. Nyonya cooking is perhaps the best metaphor for describing Peranakan culture – Chinese dishes with Malay ingredients and flavours.

Baba is the term for a Peranakan man and Nyonya is a woman, so the term Baba-Nyonyas is used. However, Peranakans also used the terms 'Straits-born' or 'Straits Chinese' to distinguish themselves from later arrivals from China, whom they looked down upon.

Peranakans were often wealthy traders, allowing them to indulge in their passion for sumptuous furnishings, jewellery and brocades. Peranakan terrace houses were gaily painted, with patterned tiles embedded in the walls for extra decoration, while heavily carved and inlaid baroque-style furniture was favoured. Nyonyas wore fabulously embroidered *kasot manek* (slippers) and *kebaya* (blouses over sarongs) tied with beautiful *kerasong* brooches, usually of fine filigree gold or silver. Babas assumed western dress in the 19th century, reflecting their wealth and contacts with the British, and their finery was saved for important occasions such as the wedding ceremony, a highly stylised and intricate ritual exhibiting Malay *adat* (traditional custom).

The Peranakan patois is a Malay dialect but contains many Hokkien words, making it largely unintelligible to Malay speakers. It is a dying language, and it is estimated that fewer than 5000 people speak it in Singapore. Western culture is supplanting Peranakan tradition among the young, and the language policies of the government are also helping in its decline. The Peranakans are ethnically Chinese, and Mandarin, which they are required to study at school, is increasingly used as the main language at home, along with English. Many Peranakans marry within the broader Chinese community, resulting in the further decline of Peranakan patois. *Mas Sepuloh* by William Gwee is a widely available book on the Peranakan language.

Peranakan societies such as the Peranakan Association and the Gunong Sayang Association report growing interest in Peranakan traditions as Singaporeans discover their roots, but when the older generation passes it is likely that Peranakan culture and language will be consigned to history books.

For visitors to Singapore, the Peranakan Place Museum offers a look inside a Nyonya and Baba house as it was at the turn of the 20th century. The Katong district has a number of Peranakan restaurants and the Katong Antique House on East Coast Rd is a repository of Peranakan artefacts. See the Things to See & Do section in the Singapore chapter for information about these attractions.

You can also see Peranakan architecture and eat Peranakan food in Penang and Melaka states in Malaysia, also home to the Baba-Nyonya people.

Islam was brought to the region by Arab and Indian traders and adopted in the 15th century, but traditional Malay culture still shows influences of pre-Islamic Hindu and animist beliefs. For example, *wayang kulit*, the Malay shadow puppet play, portrays tales from the Hindu epics of the *Ramayana* and *Mahabharata*.

Malays have a strong sense of community and hospitality, and the *kampung*, or village, is at the centre of Malay life. The majority of Malays live in high-rise districts such as Geylang, but in fast-diminishing rural Singapore and the islands to the north, a few Malay kampungs still exist.

Indians

Indian migration dates mostly from the middle of the 19th century when the British recruited labour for the plantations of Malaya. While many Indians arrived in Singapore, most passed through and eventually settled in Malaya.

In Singapore, approximately 60% of the Indian population are Tamil and a further 20% are Malayalis from the southern Indian state of Kerala. The rest come from all over India and include Bengalis, Punjabis and Kashmiris. The majority of Indians are Hindu, but a large number are Muslim and there are also Sikhs, Parsis, Christians and Buddhists.

Major Indian celebrations are Thaipusam and Deepavali.

ARTS

Singapore is a country that is normally associated with business and technology, and the arts have tended to take a back seat to economic development. In the liberalised environment under Goh Chok Tong, contemporary arts are starting to flourish, and the more traditional forms of music and dance can still be seen.

The Substation (see the Entertainment section in the Singapore chapter) an avant-garde, alternative arts venue, has been particularly active in the promotion of arts in the city with an all-encompassing programme of events showcasing such diverse activities as Chinese calligraphy and batik painting as well as live jazz and blues concerts.

Chinese Opera

Chinese drama is a mixture of dialogue, music, song and dance. It is an ancient form of theatre but reached its peak during the Ming Dynasty from the 14th to 17th centuries. It went through a decline in the 19th century but its highest form survived in the Beijing opera, which has enjoyed a comeback in China after the Cultural Revolution. Chinese opera, or *wayang*, in Singapore and Malaysia has come from the Cantonese variety, which is seen as a more music hall, gaudy style.

What it lacks in literary nuance is made up for by the glaring costumes and crashing music that follows the action. Performances can go for an entire evening, and it is usually easy enough for the uninitiated to follow the gist of the action. The acting is heavy and stylised, and the music can be searing to western ears, but a performance is well worthwhile if you should chance upon one. Street performances are held during important festivals such as Chinese New Year, Festival of the Hungry Ghosts or the Festival of the Nine Emperor Gods.

The band that accompanies the action is usually composed of fiddles, reed pipes and lutes, drums, bells and cymbals. There is little scenery and props rarely consist of more than a table and chairs – it is the action that is important.

Lion Dance

This dance is accompanied by musicians who bash cymbals and drums to invoke the spirits. The intricate papier-mâché lion's head is worn by the lead performer while another dancer takes the part of the body. At its best it is a spectacular, acrobatic dance with the 'head' jumping on the shoulders of the 'body', climbing poles and performing acrobatic tumbling. The lion may also be attended by two clowns.

The dance is usually performed during Chinese festivals to gain the blessings of the gods, and traditionally a dance troupe would

TONY WHEELER

The spectacular Lion Dance is a feature of Chinese festivals in Singapore.

be paid with *ang pow* (red packets of money) held up high to be retrieved with acrobatics. The dragon dance is a variation on the theme.

Other Performing Arts

Malay and Indian dances sometimes can be seen. *Bangsawan*, or 'Malay opera', was introduced from Persia and is a popular drama form still performed in Singapore.

Singapore's theatre scene is becoming more active and more local plays are being produced. The Substation is an alternative venue, while the Drama Centre, the Victoria Theatre and Kallang Theatre stage local and overseas productions.

The Victoria Concert Hall is the home of the Singapore Symphony Orchestra. Classical Chinese music concerts are performed here by the Singapore Broadcasting Corporation's Chinese Orchestra.

The Singapore Festival of Arts, which features many drama performances, is held every second year around June. Music, art and dance are also represented at the festival and it also includes a Fringe Festival featuring plenty of street performances. (See Public Holidays & Special Events in the Singapore Facts for the Visitor chapter for more information.)

Film

Singapore's film industry is definitely still nascent, but the government is keen to develop the film business and attract movie studios to Singapore. Singapore was producing Malay movies back in the 1960s and 70s, but the long drought of local production was broken in 1991 with *Medium Rare*, based on a true story about an occult murderer. It was followed by the local box office success, *Bugis Street*, about Singapore's transvestites, and was notable for getting its nudity and sex scenes past the censors.

At the time of writing, the latest home-grown offering is Glen Goei's *Forever Fever*, a Singaporean remake of the popular 1970s *Saturday Night Fever*. Asked why the movie was likely to be a winner leading actor Adrian Tang replied: 'It's got the nipples and naughtiness of *The Full Monty*, the sweet-and-sour sauciness of *As Good as it Gets*, the touchy-feely-good factor of *Good Will Hunting*, the wham-bam action of *LA Confidential* and the dancing is a helluva lot more exciting than *Saturday Night Fever*'.

Literature

Singapore has recently experienced a literary boom and many young novelists are hard at work writing in English about Singapore. Of the old guard, Goh Sin Tub is a respected writer who has written many books. *Goh's 12 Best Singapore Stories* is widely available. *Juniper Loa* by Lin Yutang is set mostly in the 1920s and is typical of earlier literature looking back at the motherland and the immigrant experience. It is about a young man who leaves China for Singapore and Juniper Loa is the woman he leaves behind.

Of the recent novelists, Philip Jeyaretnem is one of the leading lights and his *Raffles Place Ragtime* is a Singaporean bestseller. *A Candle or the Sun* by Gopal Baratham was published in 1991, after years of rejection by skittish Singaporean publishers. It is about a Christian group that runs foul of the authorities by questioning the government's authoritarianism. Suchen Christine Lim's *Fistful of Colours*, a winner of the Singapore Literature Prize, contrasts the difference and tensions between the modern and traditional, the old and the young in Singapore's ethnic communities. Catherine Lim is another highly regarded woman writer. Her books, such as *Little Ironies – Stories of Singapore*, are mostly about relationships, with Singapore as a backdrop.

SOCIETY & CONDUCT

Singapore is a society in transition. The change of leadership in 1991 has had some effect, though the real dynamic is the younger generation. The society is moving away from its immigrant-Chinese outlook as Singaporeans keenly examine and redefine their own unique identity.

Singapore is often portrayed by outsiders as a soulless money-making machine, an unkind assessment but not without some basis. Cultural pursuits have taken a back seat to technology and economic progress, but as the population becomes wealthier, more educated and broad-minded, the restrictive focus on economic development alone is fading.

The government is keen to define the Singaporean identity, especially in its promotion of 'Asian Values'. Its 'neo-Confucian' ideals are based on traditional subservience to family and society, hard work and the desire to succeed. This dovetails neatly with its authoritarian notions of 'Asian democracy', arguing that western pluralism and democracy are decadent luxuries that Singapore cannot afford. Traditional Chinese culture is stressed, yet Singapore enjoys diverse and growing cultural expression, despite political restrictions.

The widespread use of English and the inheritance of British institutions has meant that Singapore has always been much more western-oriented than other South-East Asian nations. This western orientation, though, has largely been confined to an English-educated elite, while the large Chinese-educated working class has traditionally defined Singaporean society. This is changing with a growing middle class and the increasing use of English.

Young Singaporeans have eagerly embraced Levis, Walkmans and western popular culture. But, as in Japan, it is wrong to assume that Singapore is simply aping the west and development will turn it into a European society. Traditional values and customs remain, adapting and blending with the

Kiasu or What?

One of the buzz words of the 1990s in Singapore has been *kiasu*.

The Hokkien word meaning 'afraid to lose' is best summed up by Mr Kiasu, a Singaporean cartoon hero, whose philosophy from A to Z includes: Always must win; Everything also must grab; Jump queue; Keep coming back for more; Look for discounts; Never mind what they think; Rushing and pushing wins the race; and Winner takes it all! all! all!

And are Singaporeans kiasu? At the risk of generalising, it's true that Singaporeans are competitive and that a bargain will never pass a Singaporean by, but would Singapore's economy be so dynamic if Singaporeans were otherwise? It can sometimes be frustrating trying to get out of a lift or MRT train as fellow passengers push to get off while boarding passengers rush to get in, but it is better than trying to board the subway in New York or Tokyo. Singaporeans haven't inherited the British love of queues and, as in most Asian countries, they don't have much time for deferential excesses such as continually saying 'please', 'thank you' and 'sorry', but in a world of plastic smiles and 'have a nice day' the no-nonsense Singaporean approach has something going for it.

Singaporeans have taken the kiasu tag in good humour, as shown by the popularity of Mr Kiasu, and fast-food outlets even offer kiasu burgers. So, when in Singapore, hunt out those bargains, don't pay unless you have to, overindulge at buffets and have a kiasu good time.

trappings of development. Singaporeans have a confident vision of themselves as a dynamic Asian nation, even if what it means to be Singaporean is still being defined.

The great icons of Singaporean culture still tend to be food, but chicken-rice, or *roti prata*, do not a culture make. Yet the nascent but growing interest in the arts has seen a rush of publications examining Singaporean society and traditions, while in other areas, such as theatre and music, Singaporeans examine their identity as never before. Much of it is retrospective – reminiscences of street hawkers or ponderings on the loss of the kampung life – but modern life is also explored despite discouragement to question the structure of Singaporean society.

Though the dominant Chinese culture and growing westernisation are the most obvious facets of Singaporean society, of course Malay and Indian traditions have also shaped Singapore. Traditional customs and beliefs among the various ethnic groups are given less importance or have been streamlined by the pace of modern life, but the strength of traditional religious values and the practice of time-honoured ways remains.

For details on Chinese, Malay and Indian customs, see the Society & Conduct section in the Facts about Malaysia chapter.

RELIGION

The variety of religions found in Singapore is a direct reflection of the diversity of races living here. The Chinese are predominantly followers of Buddhism and Shenism (or deity worship), though some are Christians. Malays are overwhelmingly Muslim, and most of Singapore's Indians are Hindus from South India, though a sizeable proportion are Muslim and some are Sikhs.

Despite increasing westernisation and secularism, traditional religious beliefs are still observed by the large majority of Singaporeans. They overwhelmingly celebrate the major festivals associated with their own religions, though religious worship has declined among the young and the more highly educated, particularly the English-educated. In the Chinese community, for example, almost everyone will celebrate Chinese New Year, while the figure for those who profess Chinese religion is around 70%. An interesting reversal of the trend away from religion is the increase in Christianity, primarily among the English-educated Chinese elite, and the charismatic movements in particular are finding converts.

The government is wary of religion and has abolished religious instruction in schools with the stated aim of avoiding religious intolerance and hatred – but interestingly, religious groups have been at the forefront of political opposition. The government's stated philosophy is Confucian, which is not a religion but a moral and social model. Its ideal society is based on the Confucian values of devotion to parents and family, loyalty to friends, and the emphasis is on education, justice and good government.

For an explanation of the major religions of the region, see the Religion section in the Facts about Malaysia chapter.

LANGUAGE

The four official languages of Singapore are Mandarin, Malay, Tamil and English. Malay is the national language. It was adopted when Singapore was part of Malaysia, but its use is mostly restricted to the Malay community. Tamil is the main Indian language; others include Malayalam and Hindi.

Chinese is still widely spoken, especially among the older Chinese. The most common dialects are Hokkien, Teochew, Cantonese, Hainanese and Hakka. The government's long-running campaign to promote Mandarin has been very successful and increasing numbers of Chinese now speak it at home.

All children are taught their mother tongue (which in the case of the Chinese is Mandarin) at school. This policy is largely designed to unite the various Chinese groups and to make sure Chinese Singaporeans don't lose contact with their traditions.

English is becoming even more widespread. Singapore has developed its own brand of English, humorously referred to as Singlish. While irate Singaporeans write to

Speak Mandarin – Please!

Singapore is a country with many languages and people, but it is the Chinese who ultimately predominate. When their forbears came from China they brought with them a number of Chinese languages and dialects – including Hokkien, Teochew, Hakka, Cantonese and Mandarin – most of which are as dissimilar as foreign languages. The British colonialists temporarily solved the problem by making English the *lingua franca* of the tropical colony and to a large degree that still remains the case today.

However, the Singapore government, in an effort to unite its disparate Chinese peoples to speak one language, has been encouraging minority language speakers to use the language of administration used by Beijing – Mandarin. It is hoped this step will help eliminate disunity and differences and the concept of a better Singaporean nation can be realised.

The campaign initially targeted monolingual Chinese speakers, but over the years it has spread to encompass English-educated Chinese who have begun to show an increasing willingness to use Mandarin as their main vehicle for communication in business and pleasure. The government is so intent on its 'Speak Mandarin Campaign' that it has a Web site where would-be converts can be motivated. It's at www.gov.sg/spkmandarin.

the *Straits Times* and complain about the decline in the use of the Queen's English, many Singaporeans revel in their own unique patois. It contains borrowed words from Hokkien and Malay, such as *shiok* (delicious) and *kasar* (rough), and is often a clipped form of English, dropping unnecessary prepositions and pronouns. The ever-present 'lah' is an all-purpose word that can be added to the end of sentences for emphasis.

Should you wish to try your hand at Malay, you'll find a guide to the language and a list of useful words and phrases in the Language chapter towards the end of this book.

Facts for the Visitor

PLANNING

When to Go

Any time. Climate is not a major consideration, as Singapore gets a fairly steady annual rainfall. Your visit may coincide with various festivals – Singapore has something happening every month (see the Public Holidays & Special Events entry later in this chapter). Thaipusam, occurring around February, is one of the most spectacular festivals, or if shopping and eating are your major concerns, the Singapore Food Festival and Great Singapore Sale are held in July.

Maps

Various good free maps, many in Japanese as well as English, are available at tourist offices, at Changi airport, at most mid-range and top-end hotels and at some shopping centres.

Of the commercial maps, *Nelles* and *Periplus* are the best. The best reference if you plan on spending any length of time in Singapore or want to rent a car is the *Singapore Street Directory*, a bargain at S$10 plus GST, available at most bookshops.

TOURIST OFFICES

Local Tourist Offices

The Singapore Tourism Board (STB) has two Tourist Information Centres. The first is on the ground floor at its head office at 1 Orchard Spring Rd (☎ 1-800-738 3778), off Cuscaden Rd in the Orchard Rd area. The other is conveniently located at 02-34 Raffles Hotel Arcade (☎ 1-800-334 1335) on North Bridge Rd. Both can answer most queries and have a good selection of hand-outs. The big hotels and Changi airport also stock a range of tourist leaflets and free tourist maps.

Pick up a copy of the *Singapore Official Guide*, which is updated monthly and has the latest opening hours, prices and bus routes. The STB also produces other excellent publications, such as food, hotel, shopping and nightlife guides.

If you have access to the Internet and want to get the latest on Singapore before you go, the STB's official site, www.newasia-singapore.com, is excellent.

STB Offices Abroad

The STB offices overseas include:

Australia
(☎ 02-9290 2888; fax 02-9290 2555) Level 11, AWA Bldg, 47 York St, Sydney, NSW 2000; (☎ 08-9325 8578; fax 08-9221 3864) 8th floor, St Georges Ct, 16 St Georges Tce, Perth, WA 6000

Canada
(☎ 416-363 8898; fax 416-363 5752) The Standard Life Centre, 121 King St West, Suite 1000, Toronto, Ontario M5H 3T9

China
(☎ 021-6248 8145; fax 021-6248 3150) 202A, Main Bldg, Hotel Equatorial, 65 Yanan Rd West, Shanghai 200040; (☎ 0852-2598 9290; fax 0852-2598 1040) Room 2003, Central Plaza, 18 Harbor Rd, Wanchai, Hong Kong

France
(☎ 01-42 97 16 16; fax 01-42 97 16 17) Centre d'Affaires Le Louvre, 2 Place du Palais-Royal, 75044 Paris Cedex 01

Germany
(☎ 069-920 7700; fax 069-920 8922) Hochstrasse 35-37, 60313 Frankfurt am Main

Japan
(☎ 03-3593 3388; fax 03-3591 1480) 1st floor, Yamoto Seimei Bldg 1-Chome, 1-7 Uchisaiwai-cho Chiyoda-ku, Tokyo 100

Switzerland
(☎ 01-211 7474; fax 01-211 7422) Löwen strasse 51, CH 8001 Zürich

UK
(☎ 0171-437 0033; fax 0171-734 2191) 1st floor Carrington House, 26-130 Regent St, London W1R 5FE

USA
(☎ 213-852 1901; fax 213-852 0129) 8484 Wilshire Blvd, Suite 510, Beverly Hills, CA 90211; (☎ 212-302 4861; fax 212-302 4801) 590 Fifth Ave, 12th floor, New York, NY 10036; (☎ 312-938 1888; fax 312-938 0086) Two Presidential Plaza, 180N Stetson Ave, Suite 1450, Chicago Ill 60601

VISAS & DOCUMENTS

Citizens of British Commonwealth countries (except India) and citizens of the Republic of Ireland, Liechtenstein, Monaco, the Netherlands, San Marino, Switzerland and the USA do not require visas for any number of visits. Citizens of Austria, Belgium, Denmark, Finland, France, Germany, Iceland, Italy, Japan, Korea, Luxembourg, Norway, Spain and Sweden do not require visas for social purposes for stays of up to 90 days.

Upon arrival a 14 day or 30 day permit is usually issued depending on your stated length of stay. You can easily extend a 14 day permit for another two weeks but you may be asked to show an air ticket out of Singapore and/or sufficient funds to stay. Further extensions are more difficult but in theory most nationalities can extend for up to 90 days. The Immigration Department (☎ 1-800 391 6400) is at 10 Kallang Rd, one block southwest of the Lavender MRT station.

If you're planning to drive in Singapore, bring your current home driver's licence as well as an International Driving Permit issued by a motoring association in your country.

Students should bring their international student card – it's not of much use, as student discounts are almost invariably for Singaporeans only, but you might be able to bluff a discount at some attractions. A Hostelling International (HI) card is not worth acquiring because Singapore has no HI hostels but, again, bring it if you already have one as flashing it like a student card might bring discounts.

Travel insurance is always a wise investment and should be purchased before you leave home.

EMBASSIES

Singaporean Embassies Abroad

Some Singaporean embassies and high commissions overseas include:

Australia
(☎ 02-6273 3944; fax 02-6273 3260) 17 Forster Crescent, Yarralumla, Canberra ACT 2600

China
(☎ 0106-532 3926; fax 0106-532 2215) No 1 Xiu Shui Bei Jie, Jianguomenwai, Beijing 100600

France
(☎ 01-45 00 33 61; fax 01-45 00 58 75) 12 Square de l'Avenue Foch, 75116 Paris

Germany
(☎ 228-951 0314; fax 228-310 527) Südstrasse 133, 53175 Bonn

India
(☎ 011-688 6506; fax 011-688 6798) E6 Chandragupta Marg, Chanakyapuri, New Delhi 110 021

Indonesia
(☎ 021-520 1489; fax 021-520 1486) Jalan HR Rasuna Said, Block X/4, KAV No 2, Kuningan, Jakarta 12950

Japan
(☎ 03-3586 9111; fax 03-3582 1085) 5-12-3 Roppongi, Minato-ku, Tokyo 1060032

Malaysia
(☎ 03-261 6277; fax 03-264 1013) 209 Jalan Tun Razak, 50400 Kuala Lumpur

New Zealand
(☎ 04-479 2076; fax 04-479 2315) 17 Kabul St, Khandallah, Wellington

Philippines
(☎ 02-816 1764; fax 02-818 4687) 6th floor, ODC International Plaza Bldg, 219 Salcedo St, Legaspi Village, Makati, Metro Manila

Thailand
(☎ 02-286 2111; fax 02-287 2578) 129 South Sathorn Rd, Bangkok 10120

UK
(☎ 0171-235 8315; fax 0171-245 6583) 9 Wilton Crescent, London SW1X 8RW

USA
(☎ 202-537 3100; fax 202-537 7086) 3501 International Place NW, Washington, DC 20008

Foreign Embassies in Singapore

Many foreign consulates and embassies are conveniently located around Orchard Rd. Addresses for some of them include:

Australia
(☎ 737 9311; fax 735 1242) 25 Napier Rd, 258507

Brunei
(☎ 733 9055) 325 Tanglin Rd, 247955

Canada
(☎ 325 3200; fax 325 3297) 80 Anson Rd, 14-00 IBM Towers, 079907

China
(☎ 734 3478; fax 734 9639) 11-01/03, 1 Tanglin Rd, 247905
France
(☎ 466 4866; fax 466 1072) 5 Gallop Rd, 258960
Germany
(☎ 737 1355; fax 737 2653) 545 Orchard Rd, 14-01 Far East Shopping Centre, 238882
India
(☎ 737 6777; fax 732 6909) 31 Grange Rd, 239002
Indonesia
(☎ 737 7422; fax 737 5037) 7 Chatsworth Rd, 249761
Ireland
(☎ 339 3533; fax 339 2334) 177 River Valley Rd 04-18, 179730
Japan
(☎ 235 8855; fax 324 2616), 16 Nassim Rd, 079907
Malaysia
(☎ 235 0111; fax 835 1267) 02-06, 268 Orchard Rd, 238856
Myanmar (Burma)
(☎ 735 0209; fax 735 6236) 15 St Martin's Drive, 257996
Netherlands
(☎ 737 1155; fax 737 1940) 541 Orchard Rd, Ngee Tower A 13-00, 238881
New Zealand
(☎ 235 9966; fax 733 9924) 391A Orchard Rd, 15-00 Ngee Ann City Tower A, 238873
Philippines
(☎ 737 3977; fax 733 9544) 20 Nassim Rd, 258395
South Korea
(☎ 256 1188; fax 356 1805) 101 Thomson Rd, 13-05 United Square, 307591
Thailand
(☎ 737 2644; fax 732 0778) 370 Orchard Rd, 238870
UK
(☎ 473 9333; fax 475 9706) 100 Tanglin Rd, 247919
USA
(☎ 476 9100; fax 476 9340) 27 Napier Rd, 258508
Vietnam
(☎ 462 5938) 10 Leeden Park, 267887

CUSTOMS

Visitors to Singapore are allowed to bring in 1L of wine, beer or spirits duty-free. Electronic goods, cosmetics, watches, cameras, jewellery (but not imitation jewellery), footwear, toys, arts and crafts are not dutiable, and for other items such as clothes the usual duty-free concession for personal effects applies. Singapore does not allow duty-free concessions for cigarettes and tobacco. The importation of chewing gum is banned and possessing it is considered an offence.

Duty-free concessions are not available if you come from Malaysia or if you leave Singapore for less than 48 hours (so you can no longer stock up on duty-free goods on a day trip to Batam in Indonesia).

Drugs, fire crackers, toy coins and currency, obscene or seditious material, gun-shaped cigarette lighters, endangered species of wildlife or their by-products and pirated recordings and publications are prohibited. The importation or exportation of illegal drugs carries the death penalty for more than 15g of heroin, 30g of morphine, 500g of cannabis or 200g of cannabis resin, or 1.2kg of opium. Trafficking in lesser amounts ranges from a minimum of two years in jail and two strokes of the *rotan* to 30 years and 15 strokes. If you bring in prescription drugs you should have a doctor's letter or prescription confirming they are necessary.

There is no restriction on the importation of currency.

MONEY

Currency

The unit of currency is the Singapore dollar. Singapore uses 1c, 5c, 10c, 20c, 50c and S$1 coins, while notes are in denominations of S$2, S$5, S$10, S$50, S$100, S$500 and S$1000; Singapore also has a S$10,000 note – not that you'll see too many.

Exchange Rates

The following table show approximate exchange rates at the time of publication:

Australia	A$1	=	S$0.98
Brunei	B$1	=	S$0.96
Canada	C$1	=	S$1.00
European Union	€1	=	S$1.88
France	FF10	=	S$2.85
Germany	DM1	=	S$0.96
Indonesia	1000rp	=	S$0.19

Japan	¥100	=	S$1.35
Malaysia	RM1	=	S$0.41
New Zealand	NZ$1	=	S$0.90
Thailand	100B	=	S$4.08
UK	UK£1	=	S$2.64
USA	US$1	=	S$1.55

Exchanging Money

Most of the major banks are in Singapore's Central Business District, although there are also a number of banks along Orchard Rd and local banks are located all over the city. Exchange rates tend to vary from bank to bank and some even have a service charge on each exchange transactions – this fee is usually S$2 to S$3, so make sure you check first. Banks are open from 9.30 am to 3 pm during the week and from 9.30 to 11.30 am on Saturday.

Cash Cash is always useful and usually necessary for the payment of small items like meals in hawker centres, food courts and bars and for buying items from street vendors. However, Singapore is moving more and more towards becoming a cashless society and in some cases – like hiring cars or paying for hotel bills – cash is considered almost suspect.

Travellers Cheques This time-honoured method of safe money transport is still popular and is always a fail-safe fall-back should the ATMs, credit card dial-up links and cashcard systems of Singapore fail. It is a good idea to always have some travellers cheques as they can often be used instead of direct cash payments in shops and restaurants. Travellers cheques can be bought at post offices in Singapore.

ATMs Most ATMs will accept your credit card from home. It is a good idea to credit your account with cash before you go to avoid any unpleasant surprises when you get back. It also reduces the risk of running out of credit when you most need it. It's a good idea to use only ATMs outside banks for easier retrieval of your card should it be inadvertently swallowed up.

Credit Cards All major credit cards are widely accepted, although you're not going to make yourself too popular after a hard bargaining session for a new camera if you then try to pay for it with plastic. The tourism authorities suggest that if shops insist on adding a credit card surcharge you contact the relevant credit company in Singapore. Most hotels and car-hire companies will insist on a credit card and will probably demand full payment upfront if you cannot produce one.

Moneychangers Moneychangers do not charge fees, so you will often get a better overall exchange rate for cash and travellers cheques than at the banks. You will find moneychangers in just about every shopping centre in Singapore. Indeed, most of the shops will accept foreign cash and travellers cheques at a slightly lower rate than you'd get from a moneychanger.

Apart from changing other currencies to Singapore dollars, moneychangers also sell a range of other currencies and will do amazing multiple-currency transactions in the blink of an eye. You can even get good rates for some restricted currencies.

Costs

Singapore is much more expensive than other South-East Asian countries and the strength of the Singapore dollar against most currencies has seen a substantial rise in costs for most visitors.

If you are travelling on a shoestring budget, prices will come as a shock but you can still stay in Singapore without spending too much money. The great temptation is to run amok in the shops and blow your budget on electrical goods or indulge in all the luxuries you may have craved while travelling in less-developed Asian countries.

Expect to pay S$9 per night or more for a dorm bed and from S$22 to S$45 for a double room in a cheap hotel or guesthouse. You can eat well in Singapore for a reasonable price. A good meal at a food centre can cost less than S$5. Transport is cheap in Singapore and many of the island's attractions

The 'Fine' Country

'Singapore is a fine country', said the taxi driver. 'In Singapore we have fines for everything.'

In Singapore a number of activities are frowned upon, and the sometimes Draconian methods of dealing with minor transgressions have caused both mirth and dread among visitors. The famous campaign against long hair is a thing of the past, but it wasn't that long ago that immigration inspections included looking at hair length, and long-haired men were turned away on arrival or given a short-back-and-sides on the spot.

Singapore remains tough on a number of other minor issues, however, and the standard way of stamping out un-Singaporean activities is to slap a S$1000 fine on any offender. Actually, it is very rare that anybody does get fined that much, but the severity of the fines is enough to ensure compliance.

Smoking in public places – buses, lifts, cinemas, restaurants, air-conditioned shopping centres and government offices – is hit with a S$500 fine. You can smoke at food stalls and on the street (as long as you dispose of your butt, of course). The move to ban smoking in private cars was eventually quashed because of the difficulty of enforcing it. A few years ago it was fashionable among Singapore subversives to urinate in elevators, but a successful campaign of heavy fines and security cameras has stamped that one out.

Jaywalking is a relatively minor crime – walk across the road within 50m of a designated crossing and it could cost you S$50. The successful anti-littering campaign continues, with fines of up to S$1000 for dropping even a cigarette butt on the street. Not surprisingly, Singapore is amazingly clean.

The MRT, Singapore's pride and joy, attracts some particularly heavy fines. Eating, drinking and smoking are forbidden, and watch out if you use the MRT toilet and don't flush it. In fact, the 'flush or fine' campaign applies all over Singapore and has prompted apocryphal reports of flush sensors in the toilets to detect offenders.

The latest frowned-upon activity in Singapore is gum chewing. Antisocial elements were leaving gum deposits on the doors of the MRT, causing disruptions to underground rail services. The sale, importation and possession of chewing gum is now banned and subject to heavy fines.

are free. So it is possible to stay in Singapore for under S$25 per day, though S$50 is a more realistic minimum. You should be prepared to spend a lot more if you want to eat in some restaurants, check out the nightlife or visit a lot of the attractions.

If you have more to spend, then most of your cash will be absorbed in hotel bills and restaurants. Mid-range, second-string hotels cost from S$60 to S$100, though hotels at the top of this range are of a pretty good standard. International-standard hotels cost from S$300 and go way up. Depending on discounts available, top-end hotels may offer good value for the facilities on offer. A good meal in an old-style coffee shop, restaurant or fast food restaurant will cost S$15. For S$20 to S$30 you can eat at a fancier restaurant, and you can dine in top restaurants in this range if set meals, buffets or cheaper lunch menus are on offer. Above S$30 should get you high standards of food and service, though you will generally have to spend S$50 or much more to dine at Singapore's best restaurants.

Taxis are quite cheap in Singapore, as are many other nonessentials.

Tipping & Bargaining

Tipping is not usual in Singapore. The most expensive hotels and restaurants have a 10% service charge, in which case tipping is discouraged. Don't tip at hawker stalls, though the more expensive coffee shops and restaurants that do not add a service charge may expect a tip. Taxi drivers do not expect a tip and may actually round a fare down if it is S$0.10 or S$0.20 above an even dollar, though they may also expect you to round it up. Staff in the international hotels, such as the room staff or the doorman who hails your taxi, may expect a tip if they have provided good service.

Bargaining is falling by the wayside in Singapore, but tourists should still expect to haggle for luxury items and souvenirs in some stores. It is unnecessary to bargain for everyday goods or transport, as happens in many Asian countries, though it doesn't hurt to ask about discounts at the more expensive hotels.

Many shops and department stores have fixed prices for clothes and luxury items. A fair number of small shops in the tourist areas, especially electronic shops, don't display prices. In this case bargaining is almost always required, and a request for prices is usually greeted with talk of special offers and the production of a calculator. For antiques, handicrafts and other popular tourist purchases, a price tag doesn't mean you can't bargain, and you usually should.

Some smaller traders put only a small mark-up on goods, while others are very greedy. You need to know prices. With so many large discount stores and fixed-price shops, it hardly seems worth bargaining in Singapore anymore.

Taxes & Service Charges

Singapore has a 3% Goods & Services Tax (GST) applied to all goods and services. Visitors purchasing goods worth S$300 or more through a shop participating in the GST Tourist Refund Scheme can apply for a refund of GST. Shops participating in the scheme display a 'tax refund' sticker, and you must fill in a claim form and show your passport at the shop. The claim form and the goods must then be presented to the relevant counter at Changi or Seletar airports on departure. You then mail the customs-stamped form back to the shop, which will post a cheque for the refund.

In addition to the 3% GST, a 10% service charge and 1% 'cess' (government entertainment tax) is added to the more expensive hotel and restaurant bills, as well as at most nightspots and bars. This is the 'plus-plus-plus' that follows quoted prices, for example, S$120+++. Some of the cheaper establishments don't add taxes but absorb them into the quoted price. This is the 'nett' price.

POST & COMMUNICATIONS

Post

The main post office on Fullerton Rd, near Raffles Place, is currently closed for renovations and letters addressed to post restante c/-GPO are being held at the Robinson Rd post office near Sheraton House. The Comcentre, 31 Exeter Rd, near the Somerset MRT station on Orchard Rd, is open from 8 am to 6 pm from Monday to Friday and from 8 am to 2 pm on Saturday. The Changi airport post offices in the departure lounge of both terminals are open from 8 am to 9.30 pm daily.

An air mail letter to most Asia-Pacific countries costs S$0.60 or S$0.70 for the first 20g, and S$0.25 or S$0.30 for each extra 10g; to Europe and the Americas the cost is S$1 for the first 20g and 35c for each additional 10g. It costs S$0.50 to send a postcard.

Parcel rates by surface mail to countries outside the region cost around S$14 to S$19 for up to 1kg, around S$25 to S$30 for up to 5kg. For up to 10kg the cost is around S$35 to S$40, the main exception being the USA, where heavier parcels are about double the rate to any other destination. For full details call the Postage Rate Helpline ☎ 165.

Postal Codes There is now a six digit postal code system which should be used when addressing mail to and within Singapore. Ask for the *Postal Code Directory* at any post office or call the Postal Code HelpLine (☎ 1-800 240 7678) to find a particular code. Alternatively, visit the Web site www.singpost.com.sg for full details.

Telephone

From telephone booths, the cost of a call is S$0.10 for three minutes. Local calls from inside the terminal at Changi airport are free. A few hotels have free local calls, though most charge around S$0.50 per call and some charge by the minute. Local and overseas calls can be made from public phone booths. The surcharge on international calls is 25%.

As well as at public phones and hotels, you can make international phone calls at a Telecom centre, such as the ones at 15 Hill St (near Fort Canning Park) or 71 Robinson Rd (near Raffles Quay), or at selected post offices, such as the main post office.

For directory information call ☎ 100; the police emergency number is ☎ 999.

The country code for calling Singapore is 65. The international access code is 001.

Phone Cards The easiest way to make a phone call (local or international) is to dial it yourself from a public pay phone, but you'll need a phone card and a phone which accepts these cards (many pay phones will now operate only with phone cards, not coins). Phone cards, which come in denominations of S$2, S$5, S$10, S$20 and S$50, are available at Telecom centres, post offices and a number of retail outlets such as newsagents and some supermarkets.

Credit-Card Phones Credit-card phones are also available (just swipe your Amex, Diners, MasterCard or Visa card through the slot). At the phone centres, there are also Home Country Direct phones – press a country button to contact the operator, reverse the charges or have the call charged to your international telephone card. The Home Country Direct service is available from any phone by dialling the appropriate code, listed in the front pages of the phone book.

Mobile Phones Mobile phone users will find that your phone will automatically tune in to one of Singapore's two GSM digital providers, as long as you have requested the global roaming facility from your home provider.

Fax

Faxes can be sent from all post offices, Telecom centres and hotels but the service tends to be a costly business. Hotels will also normally charge you to receive faxes. Travellers can use a free service via the Internet that covers a large range of countries. The Internet Fax Company (known commonly as TPC) has a Web site with details (www.usa.tpc.int/pc_home.html).

Email & Internet Access

Email is widely available to Singaporeans and its use is strongly encouraged by the government. The problem for travellers can be getting access. The simplest way is to buy time at an Internet cafe. This typically costs anywhere from S$8 to S$11 per hour.

The addresses of some of Singapore's Internet cafes are:

Cyberheart Cafe
(☎ 734 3877) 442 Orchard Rd
email: cyheart@pacific.net.sg
It has 12 terminals charged at S$10 an hour. It's open daily from 11 am to 11 pm.

CyberNet Cafe
(☎ 324 4361) 57 Tanjong Pagar Rd
email: admin@cybertrek.com.sg
Internet: www.cybertrek.com.sg
Plenty of terminals with access time charged at S$8 per hour. A tutorial session for beginners costs S$15 an hour. It's open from 11 am to 10 pm Monday to Saturday, 2 to 7 pm Sunday.

PI@Boat Quay
(☎ 538 1380), The Coffee Bean, 52 Boat Quay
email: info@pacific.net.sg
Internet: www.pacific.net.sg
Computer time is charged at S$10 an hour or S$6 for 30 minutes. It's open daily except Sunday from 11 am to 9 pm. There are further Pacific Internet (PI) cafes at Parco Bugis Junction (☎ 334 3379) and Parkway Parade (☎ 346 3379) on the east coast.

The National Library on Stamford Rd next to the National Museum has a wonderful multimedia centre on the 2nd level where you can access the Internet (Web only) for only S$2 per hour, but you'll need a cashcard attached to a bank account in Singapore.

Be aware that the government is trying to control access to undesirable information on the Net through a regulatory board. This board requires users and Internet Service

Providers who notice antisocial activities on the Net to report them. In other words, there's the makings of a voluntary Net police.

INTERNET RESOURCES

There is a bewildering amount of information on all aspects of Singapore on the Internet. Look via the usual search engines. Most of the sites given here also provide useful cross links.

Please note that Web site addresses, though correct at the time of going to press, are particularly prone to change.

www.travel.com.sg
: The home site of the Singapore Tourism Board; the text suffers from a surfeit of PRese but there's plenty of good material on shopping, eating, festivals etc.

www.happening.com.sg
: An offbeat, online listings magazine with articles, reviews and what's on information; it's updated daily.

www.asia1.com.sg
: The Web site of Asia One, the company that owns all the papers. The site has links to the *Straits Times*, the *New Paper* and the *Business Times*, among others.

www.sintercom.org
: A great, general link to Singapore's burgeoning Internet community.

www.changi.airport.com.sg
: A detailed guide to Singapore's world-beating airport.

BOOKS

Lonely Planet

Lonely Planet publishes the *Singapore city guide*, a *Malay phrasebook* and a *Mandarin phrasebook*. LP's *South-East Asia on a shoestring* is our overall guidebook to the region. There are also individual guidebooks to all South-East and North-East Asian countries.

Guidebooks

A recent publication *Handbook for Expatriates* by Goh Kheng Chuan is probably the best practical guide for everyday living tips for foreigners. *Living in Singapore* by the American Association of Singapore is handy for westerners planning to set up house in Singapore. Both books are useful introductions to life in the tropical city-state.

History & Politics

Several books deal with various events in Singapore's history.

A History of Singapore by CM Turnball is the best choice for a detailed overview of Singapore's history from prehistory to the present. It is an excellent scholarly work which is also very readable and a mine of interesting information. The author has also written *A Short History of Malaysia, Singapore & Brunei*.

Raffles by Maurice Collins is the straightforward story of the man who founded Singapore.

Lee Kuan Yew – The Struggle for Singapore by Alex Josey covers all the twists and turns of Lee Kuan Yew's rise to power and the successful path along which his PAP has piloted Singapore.

No Man is an Island by James Minchin is hard to find in Singapore. For an insight into both sides of the PAP story, this warts-and-all portrait of Lee Kuan Yew is one of the best.

Chee Soon Juan, the leader of the Singapore Democratic Party, is a thorn in the side of the government. After standing in the 1992 elections against Goh Chok Tong, he was sacked from his academic post for allegedly misusing postage funds and then sued for S$1 million for claiming that his dismissal was politically motivated. His book *Dare to Change: an Alternative Vision for Singapore* roundly criticises the government and offers social-democratic alternatives. It was such a local success that it has been followed by *Singapore: My Home Too*.

Another thorn in the side of the government, and also a former academic at the National University of Singapore, is Christopher Lingle. His article in the *International Herald Tribune*, questioning the judiciary's independence, resulted in yet another defamation suit in the government's favour. Dr Lingle fled the country and continues the battle in *Singapore's Authoritarian Capitalism*, a damning study of political repression and the government's 'Asian Values'.

Nick Leeson's *Rogue Trader* makes fascinating reading from the man who brought down Barings Bank single-handedly through a series of ill-conceived futures speculations. According to Leeson, everyone other than himself is to blame for the fiasco.

People & Society

Tales of Chinatown by Sit Yin Fong is a readable and informative piece on Chinese life. Fong was a journalist in Singapore for many years and writes anecdotal short stories about Chinese customs and beliefs.

Son of Singapore by Tan Kok Seng is the fascinating autobiography of a labourer who grew up in Singapore in the 1950s. *The Babas Revisited* by Felix Chia is a classic study of the history, culture and language of the Straits Chinese.

Fiction

Singapore and Malaysia have always provided a fertile setting for novelists, and Joseph Conrad's *The Shadow Line* and *Lord Jim* both use the region as a backdrop. Somerset Maugham spent time in Singapore writing his classic short stories, many of which were set in Malaya – look for the *Borneo Stories*.

See under Literature in the Arts section of the Facts about Singapore chapter for more information on home-grown literature.

General

Portraits of Places by Brenda SA Yeoh & Luly Kong is an interesting sociological study of changing Singapore, examining selected areas from Orchard Rd to Kampung Wak Selat, the 'last village in Singapore', near Kranji.

David Brazil's *Street Smart Singapore* is a lively look at the Lion City stacked with interesting titbits on its history and culture. *Culture Shock: Singapore* by Jo Ann Craig, one of a popular series, explains the customs, cultures and lifestyles of Singapore's polyglot population primarily to expatriates working there.

The *Mr Kiasu* comic books portray the 'kiasu' (selfish, pushy, always-on-the-lookout-for-a-bargain) Singaporean. The Singlish-speaking, nonconformist, 'everything also must grab' Mr Kiasu has reached celebrity status in Singapore. These original and distinctly Singaporean cartoons are proof that Singaporeans can laugh at themselves.

Birds – An Illustrated Field Guide to the Birds of Singapore is written by Lim Kim Seng, a local birdwatcher. Some 350 species from resident to migrant birds are covered in this excellent guide.

Bookshops

Singapore's main bookshop chains are MPH and Times, with a huge range of books in English. The Orchard Rd area, Centrepoint and Plaza Singapura shopping centres have a good selection of bookshops.

MPH's main shop at 71-77 Stamford Rd in the colonial district has been extensively renovated and is probably the best general bookshop in the region. It is also the most salubrious, and has a coffee shop and a record store. MPH also has other stores on the 4th floor of Centrepoint on Orchard Rd, on Robinson Rd and at Changi airport.

Times also has a large bookstore on the 4th floor of Centrepoint on Orchard Rd, and at Lucky Plaza and Plaza Singapura on Orchard Rd, Holland Village, Changi airport, Marina Square and a large store at Raffles City.

The newer Borders Bookshop in the Liat Towers on Orchard Rd has a huge selection of books and strategically placed armchairs for the comfort of the browsers and buyers.

NEWSPAPERS & MAGAZINES

Singapore has three Chinese daily newspapers with a combined daily circulation of over 450,000 and three English newspapers with a slightly higher circulation. There is also a Malay daily and a Tamil daily. The major newspapers come under the umbrella of the gigantic Singapore Press Holdings.

The English daily newspapers are the establishment *Straits Times*, the *Business Times* and the *New Paper*, an evening tabloid. The *Straits Times* has good regional and foreign news and some good feature articles. The best independent views on Singaporean politics are found in the readers' letters.

The *New Paper* is a long way behind the *Straits Times* in circulation and is seen as the fun alternative. It is a more staid version of an English tabloid and comes up with some amazingly trite, attention-grabbing headlines, but little news. *Time*, *Newsweek* and other foreign magazines are available.

The press in Singapore knows its limits and there is very little criticism of the government. The foreign media sometimes doesn't know its limits, and the government has restricted the circulation of foreign publications that do not report to its liking, as the *Far Eastern Economic Review* and others have found out.

Racy magazines with sexy covers are nonexistent and magazine displays will appear bland and tame at first.

RADIO & TV

The state-run Singapore Broadcasting Corporation (SBC) was corporatised in 1994. Government controls on broadcasting were slightly relaxed, although TV censorship is still fairly strict.

The Radio Corporation of Singapore controls most of the radio stations, with 10 stations transmitting in four languages – Malay, Mandarin, Tamil and English – on the AM, FM and short-wave bands. The BBC transmits in Singapore on 88.9 FM.

Singapore has three TV channels: 5, 8 and 12, which broadcast in English, Mandarin, Malay and Tamil. Cable TV is becoming more popular and Singaporeans can also pick up Malaysian TV – TV1 and TV2.

Channel 8 carries mostly local productions, a booming area. Singapore has been making local news shows, game shows and fairly amateurish dramatic productions for years, but local production is looking healthy and starting to out-rate the many American imports. *Under One Roof* is an enormously popular Singaporean sitcom that has already inspired two offshoots.

PHOTOGRAPHY & VIDEO

Film & Equipment

Film is cheap and readily available. A Kodak 24 exposure roll costs S$4.50, while a roll of Fuji Sensia slide film costs S$8.50. Processing is also reasonably priced: printing and developing a 24 exposure print film will cost around S$11.40, or S$15.60 for 36 exposures. Slide processing costs S$15 for a 36 exposure film.

Restrictions

It is polite to ask permission before photographing people or taking pictures in places of worship, especially mosques. There is usually no objection to taking photographs in Chinese temples. See Photography & Video in the Malaysia Facts for the Visitor chapter for tips on good photography.

TIME

Singapore is eight hours ahead of GMT/UTC (London), 16 hours ahead of US Pacific Standard Time (San Francisco and Los Angeles), 13 hours ahead of US Eastern Standard Time (New York) and two hours behind Australian Eastern Standard Time (Sydney and Melbourne). So, when it is noon in Singapore, it is 8 pm in Los Angeles and 11 pm in New York (the previous day), 4 am in London, and 2 pm in Sydney and Melbourne.

ELECTRICITY

Electricity supplies are reliable and run at 220-240V and 50 cycles. Plugs are of the three-pronged, square-pin type used in the UK.

WEIGHTS & MEASURES

Singapore uses the metric system, though you may occasionally come across references to odd measurements such as the *thola*, an Indian weight, or *batu*, the Malay word for mile (literally meaning stone).

LAUNDRY

Singapore has plenty of laundries, such as the Laundryland chain. There is a Laundryland at 01-06 Orchard Towers, at the western end of Orchard Rd. Check the telephone directory for other addresses. A large load, including drying and folding, costs around S$10. All major hotels offer a laundry service, which can set you back a small fortune, and even most cheap hotels do laundry at more moderate rates.

HEALTH

In Singapore you can eat virtually anywhere and not worry, and the tap water is safe to drink. If you are coming from a yellow fever infected area, you will need to have a yellow fever vaccination certificate. There is no risk of malaria. The main health concern is the heat; it is important to avoid dehydration by drinking plenty of fluids. For more information on this and other health problems, see the Health section in the Malaysia Facts for the Visitor chapter.

Medical facilities are of a high standard and readily available. A visit to a general practitioner costs around S$30. Singapore's public hospitals will accept self-referred patients. Singapore General Hospital (☎ 222 3322) is on Outram Rd, near Chinatown and the Outram Park MRT station.

WOMEN TRAVELLERS

Singapore is probably the safest Asian country to travel in and sexual harassment is rare. Women are not cloistered in Singaporean society and enjoy much more freedom and equality than in the rest of Asia. Government policy favours sexual equality, and abortion is available on request, but not for 'foreign' pregnancies (non-Singaporean women).

GAY & LESBIAN TRAVELLERS

Homosexuality is illegal in Singapore and you can be sentenced to between 10 years and life for engaging in homosexual activities. Singapore isn't completely straight, however, and there is a local gay and lesbian scene. People Like Us (PLU), PO Box 0299, Raffles City post office, Singapore 911710, is the city's grass-roots gay organisation for men and women. It has monthly meetings and many young professionals attend. For more details email plu-singapore@geocities.com or follow the links from the site at www.utopia-asia.com.

See also under Bars, Bands & Discos in the Entertainment section in the Singapore chapter for gay venues or mixed bars with gay nights.

DISABLED TRAVELLERS

Access Singapore is a guidebook for the disabled produced by the Singapore Council of Social Services. It is available from STB offices (see under Tourist Offices at the start of this chapter for addresses) or contact the National Council of Social Services (☎ 336 1544; fax 336 7732), 11 Penang Rd.

SENIOR TRAVELLERS

Singapore is an ideal destination for senior travellers who want a taste of Asia without the hassles of less-developed countries. The health care system is on a par with any western country, access facilities to hotels and restaurants are excellent and there is a wide range of ready-made tours to cater for all tastes.

The Singapore Tourism Board puts out a booklet called *Mature Travellers*, though in practice the information it contains is almost equally relevant to younger travellers.

SINGAPORE FOR CHILDREN

Singapore is a safe and healthy country for children, and it is easy and cheap to get around. The food is nutritious, and noisy, easy-going hawker centres are an ideal place for wayward young children to commit crimes that would bar them from restaurants. Except perhaps for the heat, Singapore is an ideal family destination.

Family attractions include Sentosa, Haw Par Villa, Tang Dynasty City, the Science Centre, Singapore Zoo, Jurong Bird Park and Jurong Reptile Park and Clarke Quay.

For more information on all these places see the Things to See & Do section in the Singapore chapter.

DANGERS & ANNOYANCES

Singapore is a very safe country with low crime rates. Pickpockets are not unknown, but in general crime is not a problem. This is not surprising given the harsh penalties meted out to offenders and the fact that hundreds of suspected criminals are held in jail without trial because the government doesn't have enough evidence to ensure conviction.

The importation of drugs carries the death penalty and, quite simply, drugs in Singapore should be avoided at all costs, not that you are likely to come across them. In case you think the government is bluffing, the tally of executions for drug convictions stands at over 50 so far, an astonishing number given the size of Singapore's population.

BUSINESS HOURS

In Singapore, government offices are usually open from Monday to Friday and Saturday morning. Hours vary, starting at around 7.30 to 9.30 am and closing between 4 and 6 pm. On Saturday, closing time is between 11.30 am and 1 pm.

Shop hours are also variable. Small shops are generally open Monday to Saturday from 10 am to 6 pm, while department stores and large shopping centres are open from 10 am to 9 or 9.30 pm, seven days a week. Most small shops in Chinatown and Arab St close on Sunday, though Sunday is the big day in Little India.

PUBLIC HOLIDAYS & SPECIAL EVENTS

The following days are public holidays in Singapore. For those days not based on the western calendar, the months they are likely to fall in are given:

New Year's Day
1 January

Hari Raya Puasa
19 January 1999, 9 January 2000

Chinese New Year
Two days, 16 February 1999, 5 February 2000, 24 January 2001, 12 February 2002, 1 February 2003

Hari Raya Haji
28 March 1999, 16 March 2000

Good Friday
April (April 2 1999)

Labour Day
1 May

Wesak Day
April or May

National Day
9 August

Deepavali
November

Christmas Day
25 December

With so many cultures and religions, there are an amazing number of celebrations in Singapore. Many of the religious events are the same as those celebrated in Malaysia. The tourist office puts out a *Festivals & Events* brochure each year, and the *Singapore Official Guide* has more specific and detailed listings for each month.

Chinese New Year is the major holiday and the streets come to life. The dramatic Thaipusam Hindu festival is also celebrated in Singapore with masochistic feats. See the Thaipusam entry in the Places of Worship

Sugarcane Deliverance

If you are in Singapore around Chinese New Year and chance upon people wandering around with large sugarcanes in their hands, do not be surprised. You are witnessing a cultural manifestation of the Hokkien Chinese people.

The ninth day of the Chinese New Year has special significance for the Hokkiens, who each year celebrate the birthday of Tian Gong (Tee Kong in Hokkien), who is the God of Heaven. The main celebration takes place at midnight on the day before, with offerings of food such as chicken, duck and fruit.

It is also customary to place a pair of sugarcanes at the altar or entrance of the home as a symbol of deliverance, because of an incident during the Song Dynasty (960-1279). The Hokkiens had provoked the emperor's wrath by pledging allegiance to a rebel group. They hid in sugarcane farms for eight days, until they were finally pardoned by the emperor because it was a festive season.

Today sellers of sugarcanes make a quick dollar by selling around the streets of Singapore – and yet another Chinese tradition lives on.

section under the Malaysia Facts for the Visitor chapter for a description of this event.

The Singapore Festival of Arts is a biennial event held every even year, featuring a programme of art, dance, drama and music. The innovative Fringe Festival includes free performances. It alternates with a Festival of Asian Performing Arts held every odd year.

In July, the Singapore Food Festival celebrates the national passion, with special offerings at everything from hawker centres to gourmet restaurants.

During the Great Singapore Sale, Orchard Rd is decked out with banners and merchants are encouraged by the government to drop prices in an effort to boost Singapore's image as a shopping destination. It is held for one month around July and usually overlaps with the Food Festival for a couple of weeks.

Singapore National Day is held on 9 August, when a series of military and civilian processions and fireworks display celebrate Singapore's independence in 1965.

The Pilgrimage to Kusu Island, held around November, honours Tua Pek Kong, the Taoist God of Prosperity.

Singapore 'light-ups', when the streets are decked with lights, are a speciality. During Deepavali, Little India is ablaze with lights for a month to celebrate the most important Hindu festival. At Christmas, Orchard Rd celebrates with shopfront displays and the Christmas light-up.

FOOD & DRINKS

Eating is a national pastime in Singapore, and the variety of places to enjoy it is simply astonishing. Hawker centres are everywhere, and Singapore's restaurants serve every type of cuisine imaginable.

The traditional Chinese, Indian and Malay dishes found in Malaysia are mostly the same as those found in Singapore – see also the Tastes of Malaysia, Singapore & Brunei section in the Malaysia Facts for the Visitor chapter and the Food section in the Glossary at the end of this book. If Singapore has a national dish it is *Hokkien fried mee*, which Singaporeans have adopted as their own and call 'Singapore fried noodles'.

Singapore has the same favourite drinks as Malaysia, and there are no dry areas here!

Getting There & Away

AIR

Singapore is a major travel hub in Asia and a good place to buy air tickets. The overwhelming bulk of international air traffic goes through Changi airport (see the Singapore Getting Around chapter), while the small Seletar airport services only a handful of short regional flights.

Travel Agents in Singapore

Singapore is a good place to look for cheap plane tickets, and it competes with Bangkok and Penang to be the discount flight centre of the region.

For good travel agents, STA Travel (☎ 734 5681) in the Orchard Parade Hotel, 1 Tanglin Rd, is part of the international budget travel chain and it also has an office (more a booth) at 127 Bencoolen St under the Why Not Homestay in the colonial district. Also on Bencoolen St at 171C in the same building as Hawaii Hostel is Harharah Travel (☎ 337 2633). All these travel agents sell air, bus and train tickets. Airpower Travel (☎ 294 5664; fax 293 1215) at 2A Pahang St near Arab St and on Bencoolen St is recommended by many travellers.

Fares Singapore has hundreds of travel agents all over town where you can check prices on flights. There's a good selection of large travel agents upstairs at Chinatown Point on New Bridge Rd in Chinatown. Try here for one-stop shopping for tickets and tours.

Fares vary according to when you want to fly and the airline you choose. The cheapest fares are likely to be with the least-loved airlines, via inconvenient routes with forced stopovers at awkward times.

Some typical rock-bottom discount fares being quoted in Singapore include South-East Asian destinations such as Bangkok from S$200 one way, Denpasar from S$220 one way or S$370 excursion return and Jakarta S$120 one way or S$200 return. To the subcontinent, you can fly to Delhi or Kathmandu for S$450 one way or Madras for S$400.

Fares to Australia include Sydney or Melbourne for S$500 one way or S$650 excursion return and Perth from $420 one way or S$500 return. London, or other European destinations, cost from S$550 one way with the Eastern European airlines and from S$620 one way with better airlines.

One-way fares to the west coast of the USA are around S$650 direct or with a stop in Manila.

Airline Offices Below are some of the major airline offices in Singapore. Check the Business Yellow Pages for any that are not listed here.

Aeroflot
(☎ 336 1757) 01-02/02-00, Tan Chong Tower, 15 Queen St

Air Canada
(☎ 256 1198) 01-10, 101 Thomson Rd

Air India
(☎ 225 9411) 17-01, UIC Bldg S, Shenton Way

Air New Zealand
(☎ 535 8266) 24-08 Ocean Bldg, 10 Collyer Quay

American Airlines
(☎ 339 0001) 04-01, 108 Middle Rd

British Airways
(☎ 839 7788) 04-02 The Promenade, 300 Orchard Rd

Cathay Pacific Airways
(☎ 533 1333) 16-01 Ocean Bldg, 10 Collyer Quay

Garuda Indonesia
(☎ 250 2888) 01-02, 442 Orchard Rd

KLM-Royal Dutch Airlines
(☎ 737 7622) 12-06 Ngee Ann City Tower, 391A Orchard Rd

Lufthansa Airlines
(☎ 737 9222) 05-01 Palais Renaissance, 390 Orchard Rd

Malaysia Airlines
(☎ 336 6777) 02-09 Singapore Shopping Centre, 190 Clemenceau Ave

Pelangi Air
(☎ 481 6302) Bldg 24, 960 Seletar Airport, West Camp
Qantas Airways
(☎ 839 7788) 04-02 The Promenade, 300 Orchard Rd
Royal Brunei Airlines
(☎ 235 4672) 04-08, 25 Scotts Rd
Royal Nepal Airlines Corporation
(☎ 339 5535) 03-07, 3 Coleman St
Silk Air
(☎ 542 8111) 03-00 SATS Bldg
Singapore Airlines
(☎ 223 8888) 77 Robinson Rd
Thai Airways International
(☎ 1-800 224 9977) 02-00 The Globe, 100 Cecil St
United Airlines
(☎ 220 0711) 01-03 Hong Leong Bldg, 16 Raffles Quay

The USA

Tickets to Singapore in the low season start from as little as US$705 return from the US west coast, US$1075 return from the east coast. High-season prices from June to August can jump to US$1100 from the west coast, US$1290 from New York.

Singapore Airlines (SIA) and others have direct flights but it is usually cheaper to fly via another port, such as with China Airlines via Taipei or Cathay Pacific via Hong Kong.

It is also worth looking into Circle Pacific flights. From Los Angeles or San Francisco you can fly Honolulu-Denpasar-Singapore, then overland to Bangkok, flying on to Hong Kong, and then return to the USA for around US$1359/1469 (low/high season). For US$1399/1759, you can go via Fiji and Sydney or Auckland. Add another US$200 to include both Sydney and Auckland.

The *New York Times*, the *LA Times*, the *Chicago Tribune* and the *San Francisco Examiner* all produce weekly travel sections in which you'll find many travel agents' ads. Council Travel and STA Travel have offices in major cities nationwide.

The magazine *Travel Unlimited* (PO Box 1058, Allston, MA 02134) publishes details of the cheapest air fares and courier possibilities for destinations all over the world from the USA.

Australia

Advance purchase return fares from the east coast to Singapore vary from around A$700 to A$1100, depending on the season of travel and the length of stay. From Perth, fares are around A$600 to A$940. The 30 day or 45 day excursion fares are cheapest, while the most expensive is a return ticket valid for over 60 days in the high season, generally from 15 November to 31 January.

Many of the airlines that fly from Australia to Asia, the Middle East and Europe stopover in Singapore. Two of the cheapest are Gulf Air and Lauda Air. Gulf Air flights for around A$780 return are the cheapest and bookings should be made well in advance. Singapore Airlines and Qantas are the main carriers. Both have cheap package tours and good stopover accommodation deals, as does Malaysia Airlines. Malaysia Airlines sometimes has cheap flights to Singapore via Kuala Lumpur.

For cheap tickets, STA Travel has competitive prices for air fares to Asia, as does the Flight Centre, another Australia-wide chain which can also offer good accommodation discounts, but shop around.

New Zealand

A number of airlines fly from Auckland to Singapore. Return tickets range from around NZ$1399 in the low season to NZ$1460 in the high season. The high season is generally December and January. British Airways, Air New Zealand, Singapore Airlines, Qantas and Garuda all fly direct to Singapore, or stopovers are possible in Indonesia and Australia.

Flight Centre and STA Travel are large discount travel agents with offices throughout the country.

The UK

London has the best deals for flights to Singapore and is serviced by a host of airlines. Singapore Airlines, British Airways and Qantas are major carriers, but cheaper tickets are usually available with less loved airlines such as Aeroflot (via Moscow) or Pakistan International Airlines (via Karachi) for as little as UK£220 one way, UK£399 return. Finnair (via Helsinki) and some of the Arab airlines such as Royal Jordanian and Emirates, are other discounters.

Prices for direct flights with Singapore Airlines or Qantas start at around UK £699 for a return fare.

For information on travel agents and special deals, check the Sunday papers and weekly listings magazines such as *Time Out*. London's 'bucket' shops can offer some great deals, but some of these places are fly-by-night operations. Most British agents are registered with the Association of British Travel Agents (ABTA), which guarantees tickets booked with member agents.

Popular and reliable British agents are Campus Travel (☎ 0171-730 8111), with 41 branches nationwide; STA Travel (☎ 0171-361 6262); Trailfinders (☎ 0171-938 3366), with branches in London, Birmingham, Bristol, Glasgow and Manchester; and Crusader Travel (☎ 0181-744 0474).

Continental Europe

Special round-trip fares to Singapore from Amsterdam have recently ranged from f2409 to f7486 and from Paris from FF 9270 to FF 14,440. From Frankfurt to Singapore the return fares are DM1430/1700 in low/high season.

Malaysia

The shuttle service operated by Malaysia Airlines and Singapore Airlines has frequent flights between Kuala Lumpur and Singapore for RM166 (S$129 from Singapore); seats are available on a first-come, first-served basis. Booked seats cost RM222 (S$170). Malaysia Airlines also connects Singapore to Kuantan (RM204, S$158), Langkawi (RM305, S$237) and Penang (RM255, S$197) in Peninsular Malaysia, and Kuching (RM286, S$224) and Kota Kinabalu (RM584, S$454) in East Malaysia. First class fares are around 40% extra.

Pelangi Air (☎ 481 6302; fax 481 3112) has two daily direct 40 minute flights from Seletar airport to Pulau Tioman (RM197, S$125) at 12.20 and 1.15 pm. Silk Air has daily flights to/from Kuantan (RM204, S$158) and Langkawi (RM252, S$197).

Return fares are double the single fares quoted here. Fares from Singapore to Malaysia are almost the same price as Malaysia to Singapore, but with the considerable difference in the exchange rate it is much cheaper to buy tickets in Malaysia So rather than buying a return fare to Kuala Lumpur from Singapore, buy a one way ticket and the return leg in Kuala Lumpur.

Going to Malaysia, you can save quite a few dollars if you fly from Johor Bahru rather than Singapore. For example, to Kota Kinabalu the fares are RM418 from Johor Bahru but S$391 from Singapore. To persuade travellers to take advantage of these lower fares, the SPS (☎ 250 3333) bus service operated by Malaysia Airlines runs directly from the Novotel Orchid, 214 Dunearn Rd, to the Johor Bahru airport. It costs S$12 and takes about two hours. In Singapore, tickets for internal flights starting in Malaysia are only sold by Malaysia Airlines (☎ 336 6777; fax 334 1891), 02-09 Singapore Shopping Centre, 190 Clemenceau Ave, near Fort Canning Park.

Indonesia

A number of airlines fly from Singapore to Jakarta for as low as S$120 one way and around S$200 return. The fare to Bali is from S$220 one way. Garuda is the main carrier, though Air France has been offering the lowest prices. Garuda also has direct flights between Singapore and Medan, Padang, Palembang, Pekanbaru, Pontianak and Surabaya.

Internal flights are cheaper if tickets are bought in Indonesia. For Pontianak in Kalimantan and some destinations in Sumatra, such as Pekanbaru, it is cheaper to take the ferry to Batam and then an internal flight. Garuda offers an internal air pass costing US$300 for three flights, but this is only economical for very long distances.

From Jakarta to Singapore, flights cost from as little as US$65 (Air India is currently one of the cheapest). For international flights, the travel agencies on Jalan Jaksa, the budget accommodation area, are convenient places to start looking.

LAND

Malaysia

Bus For Johor Bahru, the air-con express bus operated by Singapore-Johor Express Ltd (☎ 292 8149) departs every 15 minutes between 6.30 am and midnight from the Queen St bus station on the corner of Queen and Arab Sts. It costs S$1.80. Alternatively, the public SBS bus No 170 also leaves from the Queen St station and costs S$1.10; the Bugis MRT station is within walking distance. Bus No 170 can be hailed anywhere along the way, such as on Rochor, Rochor Canal or Bukit Timah Rds.

The bus stops at the Singapore checkpoint, but don't worry if it leaves while you clear immigration – keep your ticket and hop on the next one that comes along. The bus then stops at Malaysian immigration and customs at the other end of the Causeway, 1km away. After clearing the Malaysian checkpoint, you can then catch the same bus (your ticket is still valid) to the Johor Bahru bus terminus on the outskirts of town, or you can walk to town from the Causeway. Moneychangers, whose first offer will usually be less than the going rate, will approach you, but there are plenty of banks and official moneychangers in Johor Bahru.

If you are travelling beyond Johor Bahru, it is easier to catch a long-distance bus from Singapore, but there is a greater variety of bus services from Johor Bahru and the fares are cheaper.

In Singapore, long-distance buses to Melaka and the east coast of Malaysia operate from the Lavender St bus station on the corner of Lavender St and Kallang Bahru, opposite the large Kallang Bahru complex. It is to the north-east of Bencoolen St, near the top end of Jalan Besar. Take the MRT to the Lavender station, then bus No 5 or 61; otherwise it's a 500m walk.

Pan Malaysia Express (☎ 294 7034) has express buses to Kuala Lumpur (S$30) at 9 am and 4.30 pm, and non-express buses (S$25) at 11 am and 10 pm; Mersing (S$13.10) at 8, 9 and 10 am, and 10 pm; Kuantan (S$16.50) at 9 and 10 am and 10 pm; and Kota Bharu (S$35.10) at 7.30 pm. Also at the bus station, Hasry (☎ 294 9306) has standard buses to Kuala Lumpur (S$17) at 8 am, 2 and 9.30 pm and Super VIP coaches (S$25) at 8.30, 9.30, 10 and 10.30 am and at noon, 2.30 and 8.30 pm; and to Melaka (S$11) at 8.30 am and 2.30 pm. The journey to Kuala Lumpur takes between five and six hours depending on the type of bus; it's about three hours to Mersing, four hours to Kuantan and 3½ hours to Melaka.

Melaka-Singapore Express (☎ 293 5915) has buses to Melaka at 8, 9, 10 and 11 am and 2, 3 and 5 pm. The fare is S$11 for an air-con bus and the trip takes 4½ hours. It is preferable to buy your tickets the day before departure. Many travel agents also sell bus tickets to Malaysia.

For destinations north of Kuala Lumpur, most buses leave from the Golden Mile Complex, 5001 Beach Rd, at the north-east end near Arab St. The Lavender MRT station is about 500m away. This terminal handles all the buses to Thailand and other northern destinations on the way including Ipoh, Butterworth, Penang and Alor Setar. It costs around S$33 to Penang and most buses leave in the afternoon and evening. Bus agents line the road outside the building. Kwang Chow Travel (☎ 293 8977) and Gunung Raya (☎ 294 7711) are two of the bigger agents handling Malaysia's west coast destinations.

Morning Star Travel (☎ 292 9009), at the Lavender MRT station, has buses to Kuala Lumpur (S$25) at 8 am and 9 pm, Penang (S$38) at 8.30 pm, Alor Setar (S$40) at 9 pm (only in June) and Melaka (S$15) at 8.30 am on weekends only. All buses leave from next to the MRT station.

You can also catch buses to Kuala Lumpur from the Queen St bus station on the corner of Queen and Arab Sts. Kuala Lumpur-Singapore Express (☎ 292 8254) has buses to Kuala Lumpur at 9 am, and 1 and 10 pm for S$17.30 or S$22 VIP.

Most of the buses are new and in immaculate condition with modcons such as radio, TV, toilet and freezing air-conditioning.

Seating on the VIP coaches is three (instead of four) across and there is ample room to spread out. There's also a lunch and a snack break on the way.

Hitchhikers to Malaysia should go to Johor Bahru before starting, but remember the usual cautions apply. See the Malaysia Getting Around chapter for information and warnings on hitching.

Train Singapore is the southern termination point for the Malaysian train system (Keretapi Tanah Malayu or KTM). Malaysia has two main rail lines: the primary line from Singapore to Kuala Lumpur, Butterworth, Alor Setar and then Thailand; and a second line branching off at Gemas and going through the centre of the country to Tumpat, near Kota Bharu on the east coast.

The Singapore train station (☎ 222 5165 for fare and schedule information) is on Keppel Rd, south-west of Chinatown, about 1km from the Tanjong Pagar MRT station. The booking office is open from 8.30 am to 2 pm and from 3 to 7 pm.

Three trains depart every day to Kuala Lumpur. The *Ekspres Rakyat* leaves at 8.15 am (arrives 2.11 pm), the *Ekspres Sinaran* departs at 2.25 pm (arrives 8.15 pm), and the *Senandung Malam* leaves at 10.30 pm (arrives 6.20 am).

There are three ordinary trains to Keluang, Gemas and Gua Musang (on the east coast line to Tumpat) that depart daily at 11.20 am, 6.05 pm and 8.45 am respectively. There is a daily mail train to KL leaving at 8.15 pm. It takes 10 hours.

All trains are efficient, well maintained and comfortable, but ordinary and mail trains stop at all stations and are slow. The express trains are well worth the extra money, and the *Ekspres Rakyat* continues to Butterworth, arriving at 9.25 pm. There is also an express train to Tumpat (in the far north-east of Malaysia). The *Express Timuran* leaves at 9.15 pm and reaches Jerantut at 3.29 am for access to Taman Negara National Park.

For further details check out the KTM Web site (www.ktmb.com.my) or email KTM (passenger@ktmb.com.my).

Nonexpress and express train fares (S$) from Singapore to Malaysia include:

Destination	***Fare***		
Nonexpress:			
	1st	***2nd***	***3rd***
Butterworth	118.50	51.40	29.20
Ipoh	91.50	39.70	22.60
Jerantut	60.00	26.00	14.80
Johor Bahru	4.20	1.90	1.10
Kuala Lumpur	60.00	26.00	14.80
Tumpat	112.50	48.80	27.70
Express:			
Butterworth	127	60	34
Ipoh	100	48	27
Jerantut	68	34	19
Johor Bahru	13	10	6
Kuala Lumpur	68	34	19
Tumpat	121	57	32

While there is a noticeable jump in comfort from 3rd to 2nd class, 1st class is not much better than 2nd class but is considerably more expensive.

You can buy a 30 day rail pass allowing unlimited travel in Malaysia for US$120, or a 10 day pass for US$55. The pass entitles you to travel on any class of train, but does not include sleeping berth charges. Rail passes are only available to foreign tourists and can be purchased at a number of main train stations. See the Malaysia Getting There & Away chapter for more information.

From Singapore, there is also a *relbas* service to Kulai, just past Johor Bahru. This train is a different way to get to Johor Bahru, but you should allow up to an hour to buy your ticket and clear customs. The buses are much quicker and more convenient. Trains leave at 8.45 and 11.20 am, and 6.05 pm. From JB to Singapore, however, there are seven daily departures.

Taxi Malaysia has a cheap, well-developed, long-distance taxi system that makes Malaysian travel a real breeze. A long-distance taxi plies between set destinations, and as soon as a full complement of four passengers turns up, off you go. From Singapore, the best bet is to go to Johor Bahru and then take a taxi from there – it's cheaper and there are many more services – but Singapore also has such taxis to destinations in Malaysia.

For Johor Bahru, taxis leave from the Queen St bus station on the corner of Queen and Arab Sts. They cost S$7 per person, and an extra S$1 if there are long delays at the Causeway. Foreigners are likely to have to pay more or hire a whole taxi for S$28 since they take longer to clear the border than Singaporeans or Malaysians.

Crossing the Causeway The Causeway is that 1km link between Singapore and the mainland. An impressive piece of engineering in its day, it has difficulty coping with the amount of traffic on weekends, especially on long weekends and public holidays. If you're travelling by private vehicle or taxi, try to avoid these times. Take a bus, as buses sail past in the express lane while the cars are stuck in the interminable queues.

A new bridge-cum-causeway has been built on the western side of Singapore linking the suburb of Tuas with Geylang Patah in Malaysia. This new crossing will undoubtedly alleviate some of the bottleneck problems at the main Causeway, but is unlikely to be of immediate help to travellers without their own transport.

Thailand

If you want to go direct from Singapore to Thailand overland, the quickest and cheapest way is by bus.

Bus The main station for buses to and from Thailand is at the Golden Mile Complex, 5001 Beach Rd. It's at the north-eastern end of Beach Rd, where it meets Crawford St; the Lavender MRT station is within walking distance. A number of travel agents specialising in buses and tours to Thailand operate from here. Grassland Express (☎ 292 1166) has buses at 7 and 8.30 pm to Hat Yai. Phya Travel (☎ 293 6692) has buses to Hat Yai and Bangkok at 3.30 and 7 pm, with connections to Phuket and Suratthani from Hat Yai. Kwang Chow Travel (☎ 293 8977) has a bus to Hat Yai and Bangkok at 7.30 pm, or there are many other agents. Most leave in the afternoon and travel overnight.

Fares cost around S$35 to S$45, reflecting the difference in the buses, though all buses are air-con. The S$45 VIP coaches have videos and include a free meal. Most of these buses also stop in Butterworth.

Train The rail route into Thailand is on the Butterworth-Alor Setar-Hat Yai route, which crosses into Thailand at Padang Besar. From Butterworth, trains go to and from Singapore. You can take the *International Express* from Butterworth in Malaysia all the way to Bangkok after a connection from Singapore. The *International Express* leaves Butterworth at 2.35 pm, arrives in Hat Yai at 4.35 pm and in Bangkok at 8.30 am the following morning. The fare from Singapore to Bangkok is S$91.70 (2nd class).

A variation on the *International Express* is the *Eastern & Oriental Express*, which departs on alternate Fridays, Wednesdays, and Sundays. The train caters to the well heeled and is done out in antique opulence – South-East Asia's answer to the *Orient Express*. It takes 42 hours to do the 1943km journey from Singapore to Bangkok. Don your linen suit, sip a gin and tonic and dig deep for the fare: S$2140 per person in a double compartment, up to S$5510 in the presidential suite. You can also take the train just to Kuala Lumpur or Butterworth for less. For details call (☎ 323 4390; fax 224 9265) and see the reference in the Malaysia Getting There and Away chapter.

SEA

Singapore has a number of ferry connections to Malaysia and the Indonesian islands of the Riau Archipelago. Cruise trips in the region have also become very popular with Singaporeans.

The big cruise centre at the World Trade Centre (WTC) south-west of the train station, is the main departure point for ferries and cruises. The WTC is a mini Changi airport with duty-free and other shops. A host of agents handle bookings for the ferries, cruises and resorts. To get to the WTC, take the MRT to Tanjong Pagar, then bus No 10, 97, 100 or 131. Buses Nos 65 and 143 go from Orchard Rd to the WTC. From the colonial district buses Nos 97 and 167 go from Bencoolen St or No 100 goes from Beach Rd.

The new Tanah Merah ferry terminal to the east near Changi airport also handles ferries to the Indonesian island of Bintan, the Malaysian island of Tioman and Johor Bahru. Changi, at the far eastern tip of the island, also has ferries to Malaysia.

Malaysia

Tanjung Belungkor A ferry operates from Changi Village to Tanjung Belungkor, east of Johor Bahru. It is primarily a service for Singaporeans going to Desaru in Malaysia. The 11km journey takes 45 minutes and costs S$18/28 one way/return. Ferries leave Singapore at 8.15 and 11.15 am and 2.15 and 5.15 pm; from Tanjung Belungkor departures are at 9.45 am and 12.45, 3.45 and 6.45 pm. From the Tanjung Belungkor jetty buses operate to Desaru and Kota Tinggi.

To get to the Changi terminal, take bus No 2 to Changi Village and then a taxi. The ferry terminal is behind Changi airport just off Changi Coast Rd.

Pengerang From Changi Village, ferries also go to Pengerang across the strait in Malaysia. This is an interesting back-door route into Malaysia. Ferries don't have a fixed schedule, which is most unlike Singapore, and leave throughout the day when a full quota of 12 people is reached. The cost is S$5 per person or S$60 for the whole boat. There's more ferry traffic early in the morning so the best time to catch one is before 8 am. Clear Singapore immigration at the small post on the Changi River dock.

Pulau Tioman Auto Batam (☎ 271 4866), 02-40 World Trade Centre, is the agent for the high-speed catamaran that does the trip to Pulau Tioman in four hours. Departures are at 8.30 am from the Tanah Merah ferry terminal, and the fare is S$85/160 one way/return. There are no services during the monsoon season from 31 October to 1 March.

Indonesia

Curiously, there are no direct shipping services between the main ports in Indonesia and Singapore, but it is possible to travel between the two nations via the islands of the Riau Archipelago.

The Riau Archipelago is the cluster of Indonesian islands immediately south of Singapore. The two most visited islands are Batam and Bintan, both of which can be reached by ferry from Singapore. Most nationalities are issued a tourist pass for Indonesia, valid for 60 days, upon arrival and do not require a visa. See the Indonesian visas entry in the Malaysia Facts for the Visitor chapter for more information. The ferries are modern, fast and air-conditioned, and show movies. From Batam, boats go to Sumatra, a popular way to enter Indonesia.

Batam Pulau Batam is a resort and industrial park. From Singapore it only takes 30 minutes to reach Sekupang or 45 minutes to Batu Ampar, both on this island.

Departures are from the WTC. The main agents to Batam are Auto Batam (☎ 271 4866) and Dino Shipping (☎ 270 2228) which have offices on the 2nd floor of the WTC. Between them they have dozens of daily departures to Batam – at least every half hour from 7.30 am to 8.15 pm. Tickets cost S$17/30 one way/return. Ferries dock at Sekupang, where there are boats to Tanjung Buton on the Sumatran mainland, then it's a three hour bus ride to Palembang. This is a popular travellers' route to Sumatra.

Ferries also go to Batu Ampar on Batam, which is close to the main town of Nagoya, roughly every hour from 7.50 am to 8.15 pm. Dino Shipping also has two ferries a day at 9.35 am and 4.45 pm to Nongsapura, in the north of the island.

Bintan The companies operating ferries to Batam also have services to Bintan from the Tanah Merah ferry terminal (☎ 542 7102), off the East Coast Parkway just before Changi airport. From here ferries go to Tanjung Pinang, the main city on the island, at 9.20 and 11.10 am and 1.20 and 3.25 pm. Tickets cost S$39/46 one way/return for the 1½ hour journey. There are also boats to Lobam on the west side of Bintan at 8.40 am and 1.25 pm (8.40 am only on Saturday). Lobam is connected to Batan by regular local ferries.

There are also ferries to JB in Malaysia once a day and twice on weekends. This could be a good way to avoid the weekend crush at the Causeway. The ferry departs from the Tanah Merah ferry terminal and the trip takes 65 minutes. To get to the Tanah Merah ferry terminal, take the MRT to Bedok or Tanah Merah and then bus No 35. A taxi fare from the city is around S$12 to S$15.

Karimun From the WTC, Kalpin Tours and Dino Shipping have three ferries daily to Tanjung Balai, the main port of Pulau Karimun, another Riau resort island of minor note. The cost is S$28/49 one way/return.

Cruises

There is no shortage of cruises operating from Singapore or including Singapore in their itineraries. Plenty of cruises around Asia depart from Singapore (especially to Indonesia, Malaysia and Thailand), Australia, India, Kenya, Europe and other destinations. International companies such as P&O, Seven Seas, CTC and Winstar operate services, but the best deals are with the Singaporean operators that offer cheap cruises departing from the WTC. These have become very popular with Singaporeans.

Cruises range from a two-day/one-night ocean cruise for S$90 twin share, to longer cruises to Phuket or Manila. Three-day/two-night cruises to Penang are very popular and start from S$492 for two people. The best deals are advertised in the newspaper travel sections, but check for 'administration fees' and 'holiday surcharges'. A S$30 seaport tax is usually payable in addition. Contact Channel Holidays (☎ 270 2228; fax 276 9700) for details of the Penang and other cruises.

The main operator is Star Cruise (☎ 733 6988; fax 733 8622), 13-01 Ngee Ann City Tower B, 391 Orchard Rd, which operates a number of liners. Vessels range from the large and somewhat crowded *Star Aquarius* to the more luxurious Megastar ships. Morning Star Travel (☎ 292 9009; fax 292 4340) is a major agent with offices all over Singapore.

New Century Tours (☎ 732 6765; fax 296 8226) operates the *Leisure World* liner, which has an emphasis on youth and Chinese pop music.

Getting Around

Singapore is undoubtedly the easiest city in Asia to get around and has an excellent public transport system. While other cities like Bangkok, Jakarta and Kuala Lumpur are choked by massive traffic jams and attempt to solve their problems with stop-gap, privately funded public transport systems, Singapore has bitten the bullet and invested huge amounts in transport infrastructure.

With a typical mixture of far-sighted social planning and authoritarianism, the government has built a magnificent rail system and controls private cars by a restrictive licensing system and prohibitive import duties that make owning a car primarily a preserve for the rich. The island has excellent roads and an efficient expressway system, and cars entering the Central Business District (CBD) have to buy special licences.

Singapore also has an extensive bus network and cheap taxis, making getting around Singapore a breeze.

The *TransitLink Guide*, S$1.50 from bookshops, is a good investment if you will be using a lot of public transport. The guide lists all bus routes and the Mass Rapid Transit (MRT) rail network in a convenient pocket-size format. Maps show the surrounding areas for all MRT stations, including bus stops. The *TransitLink Map* (S$5) maps the whole island with numbered bus routes and MRT stations, but while it's good for outlying districts, it doesn't show bus stops in the central city area. The *Singapore Official Guide*, a free hand-out from the tourist office, lists Singapore's major attractions and how to reach them by bus and MRT.

THE AIRPORTS

Changi International Airport

Singapore's ultramodern Changi international airport is another of those miracles that Singapore specialises in. It's vast, efficient and organised and was built in record time. It has banking and money-changing facilities, a post office (open 24 hours), credit-card phones and free phones for local calls, Internet facilities, free hotel reservation counters open from 8 am to 11 pm, left-luggage facilities (S$3 per bag for the first day and S$4 per day thereafter), nearly 100 shops, restaurants, day rooms, fitness centres, saunas and business centres. There are free films, audio/visual shows, bars with entertainment, hairdressers, medical facilities, a swimming pool, a mini Science Discovery Museum (in Terminal 2) etc. In fact, Changi has just about everything, so you can book into a hotel room in the terminal, pig out on Singapore's food, take a free city tour and you've done Singapore!

Changi is not really one airport but two – Terminal 1 and the newer, even more impressive, Terminal 2 – each in themselves international airports to match the world's best. They are connected by the Changi Skytrain, a monorail that shuttles between the two. Terminal 2 is expected to handle Singapore's increasing air traffic well into the 21st century, but Terminal 1 still handles most of the airlines. The following airlines use Terminal 2: Air France, Delta, Finnair, Malaysia Airlines, Myanmar Airways, Philippine Airlines, Royal Brunei Airlines, Silk Air, Singapore Airlines and Swiss Air. All other airlines use Terminal 1.

On your way through the arrivals concourse at Changi, pick up the free booklets, maps and other guides available from stands. They give you a lot of useful information and good colour maps of Singapore Island and the city centre. There are even guides to the airport and the glossy monthly travel rag *Changi*.

Changi airport continues to poll in the various travel-trade magazines as the best airport in the world. You'll understand why when you arrive and are whisked through immigration to find your bags waiting on the other side.

Well-appointed day rooms at the airport cost S$66.65 per six hours in both Terminal

1 and Terminal 2. The Transit Hotel in Terminal 1 has a rooftop swimming pool and jacuzzi, which non-guests can use for S$15. The hotels are on the departure side of immigration and you must stay at the terminal you depart from. Or, if you just need a shower, you can have one for S$10, including towel and soap.

If you are one of the millions of air travellers fed up with overpriced and terrible food at airports, then Changi airport has a variety of restaurants serving a whole range of cuisines at normal prices. Terminal 2 just pips Terminal 1 for the silver fork award in dining excellence. To find even cheaper food, go to the hawker food centre in the upstairs level of the car park just outside Terminal 2. The elevator beside McDonald's on the arrival level in Terminal 1 will take you to the Basement 1 Food Centre. It's actually the staff cafeteria but the public can eat here.

To/From the Airport

Singapore's Changi international airport is at the extreme eastern end of the island, about 20km from the city centre. Airport buses and public buses (catch them in the basement), taxis and the more expensive limousine services run along the expressway into the city centre.

The most convenient bus is the Airbus (☎ 542 1721), running every 20 minutes or so from 6 am to midnight. Three routes service all the main hotels in the colonial district (it also drops off on Bencoolen St), as well as the hotels along Orchard, Tanglin and Scotts Rds. The cost is S$5 (children S$3).

Public bus No 16 operates every eight to 12 minutes from 6 am to 8 pm and takes about half an hour to reach the city. The 16E (Express) also operates from 6 to 9 am and from 5 to 8 pm. The cost is S$1.50, but bus drivers don't give change so make sure you get some coins when you change money. As this bus approaches the city, it comes off the flyover into Raffles Blvd and then Stamford Rd. For Beach Rd, get off when you see the round towers of the Raffles City skyscraper on your right, just past the open playing fields of the Padang on your left. Just 500m further along is the National Museum and the stop for Bencoolen St. The bus then continues up Penang Rd, Somerset Rd and Orchard Blvd (which all run parallel to Orchard Rd). When heading out to the airport, catch these buses on Orchard or Bras Basah Rds.

An alternative is to take the No 27 bus (S$1.20, 20 minutes) from the basement or terminals 1 or 2 to the Tampines Interchange, then hop on the MRT. From Tampines to City Hall costs $1.40 and takes 25 minutes.

Taxis from the airport are subject to a S$3 supplementary charge on top of the meter fare, which is around S$12 to most places in the city centre. This supplementary charge only applies to taxis from the airport, not from the city.

Seletar Airport

Singapore does have another 'international' airport – forgotten Seletar, which handles a few services for the smaller regional airlines, such as Pelangi flights to Pulau Tioman in Malaysia.

Seletar is in the north of the island, and the easiest way to get there is by taxi for around S$11; otherwise bus 103 will take you from outside the National Library to the gates of the Seletar Air Force base where you'll have to change to a local base bus to get to the airport terminal. Also from the base gates, bus 59 will take you to the nearest MRT station, Yio Chu Kang. You will be questioned by gate guards before you will be allowed to enter the Seletar base area.

Departure Tax

From Singapore, the airport departure tax is S$15 and is now usually included in the airline ticket price.

MASS RAPID TRANSIT

Singapore's ultramodern Mass Rapid Transit (MRT) subway system is the easiest, quickest and most comfortable way of getting around Singapore, and it can transport you across town in air-conditioned comfort in minutes.

The MRT was primarily designed to provide a cheap, reliable rail service from the

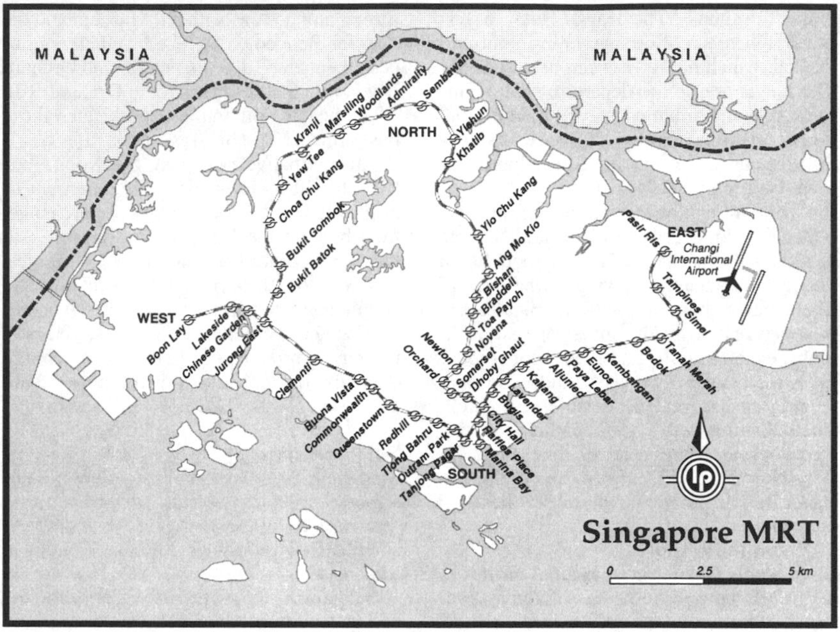

Singapore MRT

housing estates to the city and industrial estates. Most of the 44km of underground track is in the inner-city area, but out towards the housing estates the MRT runs above ground. Not content with this impressive system, the government is constructing new lines from the World Trade Centre to Punggol in the north-east (to be completed in 2002) and to Changi airport. The Changi extension is due to be finished in 2001 and train services to the airport will operate from Outram park station.

The Orchard Rd area is well serviced by the Somerset, Orchard and Newton MRT stations. In the colonial district, the Dhoby Ghaut station is close to Bencoolen St, while the Beach Rd accommodation area is between the City Hall and Bugis stations. The Raffles Place MRT station is right in the heart of the CBD and the Outram Park and Tanjong Pagar stations are on the edge of Chinatown.

Using the subway system is extremely simple. Check the map showing fares from your station, put money in the slot and press the button for the fare you want. You can get a single-trip ticket or a stored-value card that is valid until you've used up the value of the ticket. Insert the ticket into the entry gate to enter and on departure the ticket is retained by the exit gate unless it still has 'stored value', in which case retrieve your card from the return slot before proceeding. Note the remaining stored value indicated on the entry/exit gate read-out.

Single-trip tickets cost from S$0.60 to S$1.50. Ticket machines take 10c, 20c, 50c and S$1 coins; they also give change. Note-changing machines change S$2 notes. The stored-value cards called Farecards which can be used on buses as well as the MRT are available in values from S$10 to S$50 (plus S$2 deposit). They can be purchased from the TransitLink sales offices at MRT stations and the main bus interchanges. Farecards work out 15% cheaper than cash fares, so they are worthwhile if you plan to use the MRT and bus network for any length of time.

The trains run from around 6 am to midnight. At peak times, trains run every three to four minutes, and at off-peak periods every six to eight minutes.

You can also purchase special edition souvenir tourist tickets which give you all the benefits of the Farecard for only S$7 (with a stored value of S$6), but they are only valid for the MRT and cannot be topped up. Keep the ticket as a souvenir.

BUS

Singapore has an extremely frequent and comprehensive bus network. While the MRT is easy and convenient to use, for door-to-door public transport it is hard to beat the buses. You rarely have to wait more than a few minutes and a bus will get you almost anywhere you want to go. If you intend to do a lot of travelling by public transport, a copy of the *TransitLink Guide*, S$1.50 from bookshops, lists all bus and MRT services and is a good investment.

Bus fares start from S$0.60 (S$0.70 for air-con buses) for the first 3.2km and go up in S$0.10 increments for every 2.4km to a maximum of S$1.20 (S$1.50 air-con). There are also a few flat-rate fare buses. When you board the bus drop the exact fare into the change box. No change is given.

The TransitLink Farecard is a stored-value card that can be used on the MRT and on buses that have validator ticket machines. Put the card in the validator, select the correct fare and then retrieve your Farecard and bus ticket from the slot below. Farecards can be bought at MRT stations and bus interchanges in values from S$10 (S$2 deposit) to S$50, and are valid for six months.

There are often queues at the ticket offices so be prepared to wait. Farecards are also available at over 80 7-Eleven stores, if queuing isn't your cup of tea.

Singapore Explorer tickets cost S$5 for one day and S$12 for three days of unlimited travel on buses. A map of the major tourist attractions is included. These maps are also available from many hotels, including the YMCAs and travel agents, or phone ☎ 1-800-287 2727 for more details.

Tourist Bus

The Singapore Trolley is a grotesque bus made to look like an old-fashioned tram. It runs from the Botanic Gardens to the Orchard Rd area, the colonial district, CBD, Chinatown and the World Trade Centre, stopping at the major hotels and points of interest. It's a handy route and the bus is distinctive and easy to find. All-day (from 9 am to 4.30 pm) tickets cost S$9 for adults and S$7 for children.

TAXI

Singapore has a good supply of taxis – over 10,000 of them – and it's usually not too difficult to find one. The exceptions may include rush hours or meal times (Singaporean cabbies are not at all enthusiastic about missing a meal). It should be noted that drivers are very reluctant to pick up in the central area at places other than designated taxi stands.

It is easy to recognise Singapore taxis, although they come in several varieties – most are black with a yellow roof, or pale blue. All taxis are metered and the meters are used – unlike in some Asian countries where the meters always seem to be 'broken'. The fare is S$2.40 for the first 1.5km, then S$0.10 for each additional 240m.

From midnight to 6 am, there is a 50% surcharge on the meter fare. From the airport, there is a surcharge of S$3 for each journey – but not to the airport. Radio bookings cost an additional S$2.20, or S$3.20 if booked 30 minutes or more in advance. There is also a S$1 surcharge on all trips from the CBD between 4 and 7 pm on weekdays and from noon to 3 pm on Saturday. You may also have to pay a surcharge (see Restricted Zone & Car Parking in the section below) if you take the taxi into the CBD during restricted hours.

Singapore taxi drivers are generally refreshingly courteous and efficient, plus the cars are super-clean since drivers can be fined for driving a dirty cab. Some taxis also accept Visa cards. There are many taxi companies; for radio bookings 24 hours, NTUC (☎ 452 5555) is one of the biggest companies.

TRISHAW

Singapore's bicycle rickshaws are fast disappearing, although you'll find a few still operating in Chinatown, on Bugis St and off Serangoon Rd. Trishaws had their peak just after WWII when motorised transport was almost nonexistent and trishaw riders could make a healthy income. Today, they are mainly used for local shopping trips or to transport articles too heavy to carry. They rarely venture on to Singapore's heavily trafficked main streets.

There are, however, trishaws at many tourist centres in case you want to try one. Always agree on the fare first. On the street, a very short ride is S$2 and the price goes up from there.

Trishaw tours of Chinatown and Little India are operated from many of the larger hotels.

CAR

Singaporeans drive on the left-hand side of the road and the wearing of seat belts is compulsory. Unlike in most Asian countries, traffic is orderly, but the profusion of one-way streets and streets that change names can make driving difficult for the uninitiated. The *Singapore Street Directory* is essential for negotiating Singapore's streets and can be bought at good bookshops.

Rental

Singapore has branches of the three major regional rent-a-car operators – Sintat, Hertz and Avis. There is also a large number of small, local operators. If you want a car for local driving, many of the smaller operators quote rental rates that are slightly cheaper than the major companies. Rental rates are higher than in Malaysia and there are high surcharges to take a Singapore rent-a-car into Malaysia. If you intend renting a car to drive in Malaysia for any length of time, it is much better to rent a car in Johor Bahru or elsewhere in Malaysia.

Rates for driving in Singapore start from S$100 a day, while a collision damage waiver will cost about S$20 per day for a small car such as a Toyota Corolla or Mitsubishi Lancer. Ask about special deals, especially for longer-term rental, which may be available. There are hire booths at the Changi international airport and in the city; phone numbers and addresses of some of the main operators are:

Avis
(☎ 737 1668) Boulevard Hotel, Cuscaden Rd
Budget
(☎ 532 4442) 26-01A Clifford Centre, 24 Raffles Place
Hertz Rent-a-Car
(☎ 734 4646) 125 Tanglin Rd
Ken-Air Rent-a-Car
(☎ 737 8282) 01-41 Specialists Centre, 227 Orchard Rd
Sintat
(☎ 295 2211) 60 Bendemeer Rd

Restricted Zone & Car Parking

From 7.30 am to 6.30 pm Monday to Friday, and from 10.15 am to 2 pm on Saturday, the area encompassing the CBD, Chinatown and Orchard Rd is a restricted zone where cars may enter as long as they pay a surcharge via a special in-vehicle cashcard unit. Cars passing into the CBD are automatically tracked by means of sensors on over-hanging gantries. Under this system drivers are asked to insert their cashcard into the in-vehicle unit which will extract the appropriate toll. This also applies on certain major island highways.

Anyone who doesn't pay the entry toll is automatically photographed by cameras on the gantries and a fine will soon arrive at the car owner's address.

Parking in many places in Singapore is operated by a coupon system. Booklets of coupons are for sale at parking kiosks and post offices. You must display a coupon in your car window with holes punched out to indicate the time, day and date your car was parked.

BICYCLE

Singapore's fast-moving traffic and good public transport system do not make bicycling an attractive proposition. Bicycles can be hired at a number of places on the East Coast Parkway, but they are intended mostly for weekend jaunts along the foreshore. Mountain bikes, racers and tandems are available for around S$3 to S$6 per hour. See the East Coast & Changi section under Things to See & Do in the main Singapore chapter for details. Bikes can also be rented at Sentosa Island and on Pulau Ubin.

WALKING

Getting around the old areas of Singapore on foot has one small problem – apart from the heat and humidity – 'five-foot ways' (instead of footpaths). A five-foot way, which takes its name from the width, is a walkway at the front of the traditional Chinese shophouses, but enclosed, veranda-like, in the front of the building.

The difficulty is that every shop's walkway is individual. It may well be higher or lower than the shop next door or closer to or further from the street. Walking becomes a constant up and down and side to side movement, further complicated by the fact that half the shops seem to overflow across the walkway or motorcycles and bikes are parked across them, forcing you to venture into the street.

Even newer areas like Orchard Rd suffer from the five-foot way syndrome where there are shopping centres on different levels. The hazards are complicated by the flash, but very slippery, tiles out the front that are an essential part of shopping centre architecture. You can count the tourists falling after a rainstorm on Orchard Rd.

BOAT

You can charter a bumboat (motorised sampan, originally used for transporting goods up the river) to take a tour up the Singapore River or to go to the islands around Singapore. There are regular ferry services from the World Trade Centre to Sentosa and the other southern islands, and from Changi Village to Pulau Ubin. Or you can take river tours or boat tours around the harbour – see under Organised Tours for details.

It is also possible to charter boats – the Singapore Tourism Board (☎ 339 6622) can put you in touch with charter-boat operators.

ORGANISED TOURS

A wide variety of tours are available in Singapore. They can be booked at the desks of the big hotels or through the operators. The *Singapore Official Guide* lists tours and the operators. Any of Singapore's travel agents can also book tours for you, or you could contact the tourist office.

Tours include morning or afternoon trips around the city or to Jurong Bird Park, the east coast or the various parks and gardens in Singapore. Most tours go for around 3½ hours, though full-day tours are offered. Tours vary in price, depending on their length and the cost of admission to the attractions covered, but most half-day tours cost between S$20 and S$40, while full-day tours can cost up to S$70.

The city tours vary, but generally take in the colonial district and the CBD, Chinatown, Orchard Rd, Mt Faber, Little India or the Botanic Gardens and possibly a handicraft shop (take the 'very good discounts' with a grain of salt).

Historical tours cover some of the same areas as city tours but focus on the founding of Singapore. War tours cover the battlefields, Changi prison, war memorials, armed services bases etc. There are tours of Chinatown, Little India and Arab St, and some involve touring by bicycle rickshaw.

Jurong Bird Park is covered by many operators and extended tours of Jurong also include Crocodile Paradise, Chinese Garden, Ming Village or a visit to the Tiger Brewery.

Other tours include the zoo, Tang Dynasty City, Sentosa, the east coast, horse racing and the Singapore Science Centre. Nature tours including Bukit Timah, Pulau Ubin and other similar sights are currently very popular. In fact, tours cover almost all of Singapore, so it is just a matter of finding one that covers your particular interests.

The Singapore Trolley (see the Bus section earlier in this chapter) allows you to put together your own tour of central Singapore. It plies a set route and you can get on and off where you like. Helicopter tours are also available for a view of the city that even the heights of Westin Stamford (the tallest hotel in the world, in the colonial district) can't match. A half-hour trip from Seletar airport costs S$150 for adults and S$75 for children.

Don't forget the free city tour for transit passengers from Changi airport who have four hours to spare. Two hour tours go at 10 am, and then on the hour from 1 to 7 pm. You can tour the city in sealed no-man's land, at least in theory. You don't clear customs and the interior of the bus could be classed as international territory.

Cruises

River Cruises One of the best ways to get a feel for central Singapore and its history is to take a river cruise. Singapore River Boat (☎ 227 0802) operates a half-hour river tour for S$9 per adult and S$3 per child. It leaves from the Clarke Quay jetty, just south-west of Fort Canning Park. You can buy tickets at the booth there, and tours leave on the hour from 9 am to 11 pm. The tour goes down-river to the harbour and Clifford Pier and then returns. A taped commentary, complete with weak jokes, gives a good rundown on the history of the buildings along the river.

Harbour Cruises A whole host of operators have harbour cruises departing from Clifford Pier, just east of Raffles Place. There is no shortage of touts trying to sell you tickets, or you can buy them at the Clifford Pier booking offices. Companies offer *tongkang* (Chinese junk) cruises as well as a number of lunch and dinner cruises. Most of them do the rounds of the harbour, which involves a lot of time passing oil refineries, then take a look at Sentosa and the southern islands of St John's, Lazarus and Kusu. The short stop at Kusu is worthwhile and you will get some good views of the city and harbour.

Fairwind (☎ 533 3432) has 2½ hour tours at 10.30 am and 3 pm that cost S$20 for adults and S$10 for children. Its 1½ hour tour at 4 pm costs the same but doesn't stop at Kusu. Watertours (☎ 533 9811) operates tours at the same times for S$24 (morning) and S$29 (afternoon, including tea). Its gaudy Chinese junks look like refugees from Haw Par Villa, but it is a comfortable option.

J&N Cruise (☎ 223 8217) covers much the same route in a catamaran from the World Trade Centre. The 1½ hour luncheon cruise at 12.30 pm costs S$35 for adults and S$20 for children, and the two hour cruise at 3 pm costs S$30 for adults and S$17 for children. All prices exclude 3% GST.

These companies and Resort Cruises (☎ 278 4677) operate dinner and/or evening cruises. Dinner cruises cost S$34 to S$80.

Singapore

ORIENTATION

Singapore is a city, an island and a country. While there are built-up, high-density areas all around the island, the main city area is in the south.

The City

Raffles founded Singapore on the Singapore River, and this waterway is still very much at the heart of the city. Just south of the river mouth is the CBD (City Centre; Map 4), centred around Raffles Place, and along the river banks are the popular renovated districts of Boat Quay and Clarke Quay.

To the south-west, Chinatown (Map 4) adjoins the CBD, further inland from Robinson Rd. South Bridge Rd runs through the centre of Chinatown, while New Bridge Rd further west is the main shopping area.

To the north of the river is the colonial district (Maps 3 & 4), with many reminders of British rule, as well as a number of top-end hotels and shopping centres. The Raffles Hotel is on the corner of Bras Basah and Beach roads. Between Rochor and Bras Basah roads is the main budget accommodation area, centred on Beach Rd and Bencoolen St. Further north are Little India (Map 3), centred on Serangoon Rd, and Arab St. Both are interesting, more traditional areas.

From the colonial district, Bras Basah Rd heads north-west to become Orchard Rd (Map 2), Singapore's main tourist area, with dozens of luxury hotels, shopping complexes, restaurants and bars. South of Orchard Rd and west of Chinatown, Havelock Rd is a quieter and much smaller hotel enclave.

Singapore Island

On the western side of the island, Jurong is an industrial area, but it also contains a number of tourist attractions. The east coast has some older suburbs and a major beach park, and at the far east of the island is Changi international airport. The eastern and north-eastern parts of the island are

HIGHLIGHTS

- **Chinatown, Little India and Arab St** – fascinating ethnic areas to wander around, although they're quickly becoming dining and drinking venues rather than repositories of traditional culture
- **Singapore River** – one of Singapore's most successful redevelopment projects really comes alive in the evening when the restaurants and bars are packed; a river boat tour is an excellent way to view this historic artery
- **Boat Quay & Clarke Quay** – Boat Quay is now Singapore's premier nightspot, while Clarke Quay has retained more family oriented
- **Sentosa Island** – Singapore's answer to Disneyland, with plenty of rides, family attractions and even beaches; Fort Siloso, Images of Singapore and Underwater World provide more educational entertainment
- **Singapore Zoo** – the spacious and well-designed enclosures make it seem like an animal resort compared with most zoos
- **Night Safari** – allows you to view nocturnal Asian wildlife along jungle paths at night
- **Jurong Bird Park** – beautifully landscaped gardens with a huge variety of birdlife and well-tended enclosures
- **Botanic Gardens** – an enormous number of plant species, in both a manicured garden setting and in primary jungle, these gardens also house a herbarium and an orchid enclosure with more than 12,000 orchids
- **Bukit Timah Nature Reserve** – walk in the jungle to get about as far away from the city as possible
- **Orchard Rd** – a dazzling strip of modern delights, with shopping centres, luxury hotels, hundreds of restaurants and a profusion of nightspots

home to some huge housing developments. The central north of the island has much of Singapore's undeveloped land and most of the remaining forest. Points of interest include the zoo and a number of parks. The north-west is less developed, especially along the coast, which is a live firing area containing many reservoirs.

Addresses

Unlike many Asian cities, Singapore is well laid out with signposted streets and logically numbered buildings. As many of the shops, businesses and residences are in high-rise buildings, addresses are often preceded by the number of the floor and then the shop or apartment number. Addresses do not quote the district or suburb. For example, 03-12 Far East Plaza, Scotts Rd is shop No 12 on the 3rd floor of the Far East Plaza.

Things to See & Do

Singapore's greatest attraction is its ability to offer a taste of Asian culture in a small, accessible package, as well as the opportunity to pursue a range of activities.

COLONIAL SINGAPORE (Maps 3 & 4)

The mark of Stamford Raffles is indelibly stamped on central Singapore. His early city plans moved the business district south of the river and made the area north of the river the administrative area. This early framework remained the plan for central Singapore through generations of colonial rule and the republican years of independence. While Singapore is now a modern city, many reminders of old Singapore remain.

North of the river is colonial Singapore, where you'll still find the imposing monuments of British rule – the stone grey edifices of the town hall, parliament and museum, the churches and Victorian architecture. Many of these buildings still serve their original purpose. The Central Business District is the commercial heart of Singapore, though its monuments are now the skyscrapers of modern finance. Dividing these two areas is the Singapore River, which has always been the centre of Singapore. It was the site of the first British arrivals and for a long time the main artery of Singapore's trade.

The colonial district is easily reached by Mass Rapid Transit (MRT); get off at either the City Hall or Raffles Place stations. The quickest option is to walk the short distance from the Raffles Place MRT station to Cavenagh Bridge and the Singapore River, a good starting point for a tour of the area.

Singapore River

The river was once the thriving heart of Singapore but is now a quiet pedestrian precinct – an escape for lunchtime office workers, the spot to cast a line for fish, a weekend haunt for wedding photography sessions, or the place to dine in one of the renovated terraces or godowns next to the river. The bustling activity of sampans, bumboats, cranes and yelling, sweating labourers have all gone, and the new river front is a recreational stretch of photo opportunities and colonial restoration.

At the mouth of the river stands Singapore's symbol of tourism, the **Merlion**, a much photographed water-spouting, half-lion/half-fish statue. The small park around it is open from 7 am to 10 pm daily. Heading upstream, **Anderson Bridge** is the first of the old bridges spanning the river. The next along is **Cavenagh Bridge**, built in 1869, now for pedestrians only. It provides good access to **Empress Place**. Named in honour of Queen Victoria, Empress Place is the city's oldest pedestrian area, and is surrounded by many reminders of British rule. The **Empress Place building**, built in 1865, is an imposing Georgian structure that was once a court house and later housed a number of government offices. Most recently used as a museum, it was undergoing further refurbishment at the time of writing.

Nearby, next to the river at Raffles Landing Site, is **Raffles' Statue**, standing imperiously by the water. It's approximately in the place where Stamford Raffles first set foot on the island of Singapore.

The half-lion, half fish Merlion stands guard at the mouth of the Singapore River.

Naturally, there are plenty of places to eat along the river, the most popular strip is on the south bank, where **Boat Quay** is a picturesque area of restored shops with soaring office buildings behind. The stretch of renovated terraces along to South Bridge Rd and Elgin Bridge is one of Singapore's most popular restaurant and nightlife strips and is abuzz until the early hours of the morning.

Crossing the river, North Boat Quay leads upriver to **Clarke Quay**. From the landing at the eastern end of Boat Quay take the Clarke Quay River Taxi, a cheap bumboat tour to Clarke Quay, for S$1 (S$2 in the evening).

The old Clarke Quay godowns on this bend of the river have been completely rebuilt in the name of restoration, and the new development is a more varied complex of shops and children's amusements. It is also a popular dining spot, well stocked with eating possibilities from satay stalls to wine bars and floating restaurants on the river. It is fairly family oriented with amusement arcades, toy and children's wear shops, and a playground upstairs. The central square regularly has music and other diversions. Also in this area, **Clarke Quay Adventure** is a fairly corny river-boat ride which takes you past alcoves with wax dummies portraying a dubious, raucous history of Singapore. It is open daily from 11 am to 11 pm; admission is S$5 (children S$3). On Sunday afternoon a market is held on the pedestrian footbridge which crosses the river.

At Clarke Quay is the jetty for the **river boat tours**, one of the best ways to explore the river. Singapore River Boat (☎ 227 0802) operates a half-hour river tour for S$9 per adult and S$4 per child. Tours leave on the hour from 9 am to 11 pm daily, and tickets can be bought at the jetty. Tours are in old bumboats that used to clog the river, shuttling goods to and fro when the river was the centre of Singapore's commerce, only a few years ago. The tour goes down river to the harbour and Clifford Pier, and then returns.

The Padang

There is no more quizzical a symbol of British colonialism than the open field of the Padang. It is here that flannelled fools played cricket in the tropical heat, cheered on by members in the Singapore Cricket Club pavilion at one end of the Padang. At the other end is the Singapore Recreation Club, set aside for the Eurasian community. Cricket is still played at weekends, but segregation is, officially, no longer practised.

The Padang was a centre for colonial life and a place to promenade in the evenings. The Esplanade Park opposite the Padang on the foreshore is still the place for an evening stroll, give or take the odd crane and new foreshore developments. The Padang also witnessed the beginning of the end of colonial rule; it was here that the invading Japanese herded the European community, before marching them off to Changi Prison.

The Padang is ringed by imposing colonial buildings. The **Victoria Concert Hall & Theatre**, (☎ 338 1230; fax 336 6382) built in 1862, was once the town hall. It is now used for many cultural events and is the home of the Singapore Symphony Orchestra.

continued on page 572

Central Singapore
SINGAPORE - MAP 1
MAP 2
MAP 4
Novotel Orchid Hotel
Singapore Botanic Gardens
Singapore Botanic Gardens
Farrer Road
Duneam Road
Bukit Timah Road
Newton Road
Balmoral Road
Stevens Road
Newton
Anderson Road
Orange Grove Road
Scotts Road
Cairnhill Road
Napier Road
Napier Road
Tanglin Road
Orchard Road
Orchard
Orchard Boulevard
Cairnhill Circle
Orchard Road
Central Expressway
Cavanagh Road
Orchard Road
Somerset
Grange Road
Exeter Road
Hoot Kiam Road
Alexandra Canal
Tanglin Road
Kim Seng Road
Alexandra Road
Tiong Bahru Road
Redhill
Alexandra Road
Zion Road
Havelock Rd
Singapore River
Henderson Road
Tiong Bahru
Tiong Bahru Road
Jalan Bukit Merah
Pearl's Hill City Park
Ayer Rajah Expressway
Central Expressway
Outram Road
Outram Park
Lower Delta Road
Jalan Bukit Merah
Alkaff Mansions
Neil Road
Cantonment Road
Mt Faber Park
Singapore Train Station
0
0.5
1 km
Ayer Rajah Expressway
Mt Faber (116m)
To World Trade Centre (1km)

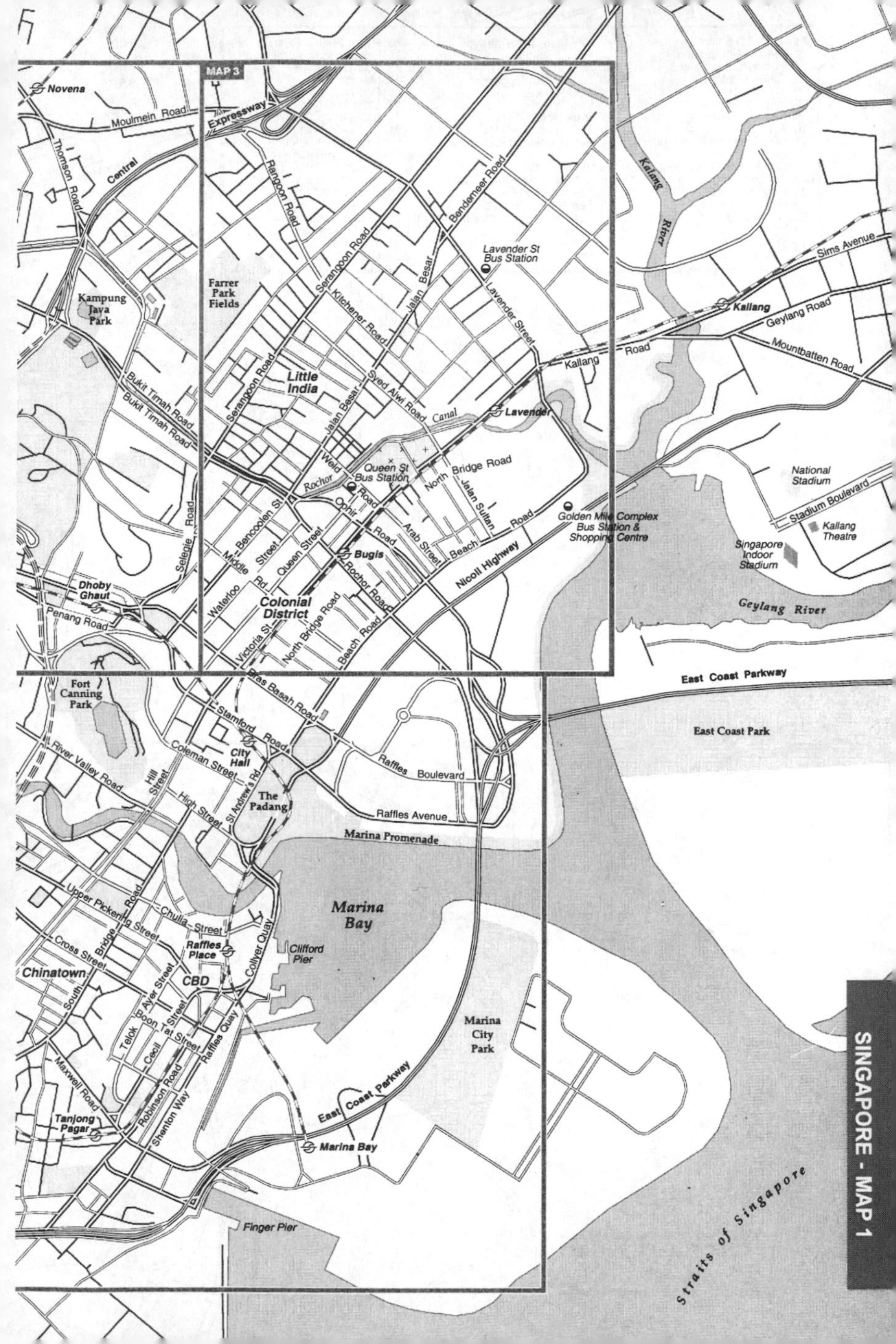
MAP 3
Novena
Moulmein Road
Expressway
Central
Thomson Road
Rangoon Road
Bendemeer Road
Kallang River
Sims Avenue
Lavender St Bus Station
Serangoon Road
Jalan Besar
Farrer Park Fields
Kampung Java Park
Kitchener Road
Lavender Street
Kallang
Geylang Road
Kallang Road
Mountbatten Road
Little India
Serangoon Road
Syed Alwi Road
Canal
Lavender
Bukit Timah Road
Bukit Timah Road
Jalan Besar
Weld Road
Queen St Bus Station
North Bridge Road
Jalan Sultan
National Stadium
Stadium Boulevard
Rochor
Ophir Road
Arab Street
Beach Road
Golden Mile Complex Bus Station & Shopping Centre
Kallang Theatre
Singapore Indoor Stadium
Bencoolen St
Middle Rd
Queen Street
Bugis
Nicoll Highway
Selegie Road
Dhoby Ghaut
Penang Road
Waterloo St
Colonial District
Rochor Road
Geylang River
Victoria St
North Bridge Road
Beach Road
Bras Basah Road
East Coast Parkway
Fort Canning Park
Stamford Road
City Hall
East Coast Park
Coleman Street
River Valley Road
Hill Street
St Andrew's Rd
The Padang
Raffles Boulevard
High Street
Raffles Avenue
Marina Promenade
Marina Bay
Upper Pickering Street
Bridge Road
Chulia Street
Cross Street
Raffles Place
Collyer Quay
Clifford Pier
Chinatown
CBD
South Bridge Road
Ayer Street
Telok Ayer Street
Boon Tat Street
Cecil Street
Raffles Quay
Marina City Park
Maxwell Road
Robinson Road
Shenton Way
East Coast Parkway
Tanjong Pagar
Marina Bay
Finger Pier
Straits of Singapore

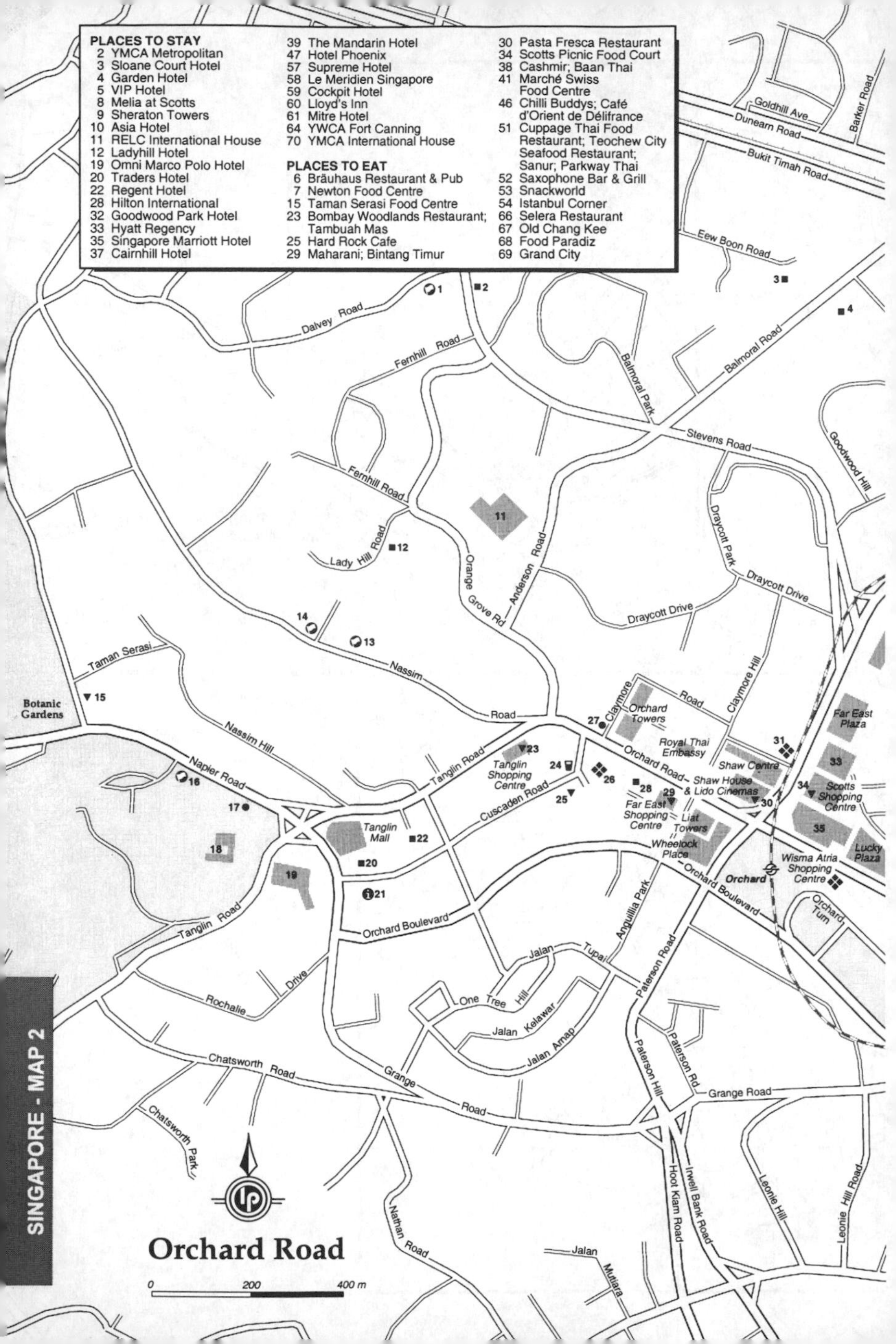

PLACES TO STAY
2 YMCA Metropolitan
3 Sloane Court Hotel
4 Garden Hotel
5 VIP Hotel
8 Melia at Scotts
9 Sheraton Towers
10 Asia Hotel
11 RELC International House
12 Ladyhill Hotel
19 Omni Marco Polo Hotel
20 Traders Hotel
22 Regent Hotel
28 Hilton International
32 Goodwood Park Hotel
33 Hyatt Regency
35 Singapore Marriott Hotel
37 Cairnhill Hotel
39 The Mandarin Hotel
47 Hotel Phoenix
57 Supreme Hotel
58 Le Meridien Singapore
59 Cockpit Hotel
60 Lloyd's Inn
61 Mitre Hotel
64 YWCA Fort Canning
70 YMCA International House
PLACES TO EAT
6 Bräuhaus Restaurant & Pub
7 Newton Food Centre
15 Taman Serasi Food Centre
23 Bombay Woodlands Restaurant; Tambuah Mas
25 Hard Rock Cafe
29 Maharani; Bintang Timur
30 Pasta Fresca Restaurant
34 Scotts Picnic Food Court
38 Cashmir; Baan Thai
41 Marché Swiss Food Centre
46 Chilli Buddys; Café d'Orient de Délifrance
51 Cuppage Thai Food Restaurant; Teochew City Seafood Restaurant; Sanur; Parkway Thai
52 Saxophone Bar & Grill
53 Snackworld
54 Istanbul Corner
66 Selera Restaurant
67 Old Chang Kee
68 Food Paradiz
69 Grand City
Goldhill Ave
Dunearn Road
Barker Road
Bukit Timah Road
Eew Boon Road
Dalvey Road
Fernhill Road
Balmoral Park
Balmoral Road
Stevens Road
Goodwood Hill
Draycott Park
Draycott Drive
Lady Hill Road
Orange Grove Rd
Anderson Road
Taman Serasi
Nassim Road
Botanic Gardens
Claymore Road
Claymore Hill
Orchard Towers
Royal Thai Embassy
Far East Plaza
Nassim Hill
Napier Road
Tanglin Road
Tanglin Shopping Centre
Orchard Road
Shaw Centre
Shaw House & Lido Cinemas
Scotts Shopping Centre
Cuscaden Road
Far East Shopping Centre
Liat Towers
Wheelock Place
Tanglin Mall
Wisma Atria Shopping Centre
Lucky Plaza
Orchard
Orchard Boulevard
Orchard Turn
Anguillia Park
Jalan Tupai
Paterson Road
Rochalie Drive
One Tree Hill
Jalan Kelawar
Jalan Arnap
Chatsworth Road
Grange Road
Paterson Hill
Paterson Rd
Chatsworth Park
Nathan Road
Hoot Kiam Road
Irwell Bank Road
Leonie Hill
Leonie Hill Road
Jalan Mutiara
Orchard Road
0 200 400 m

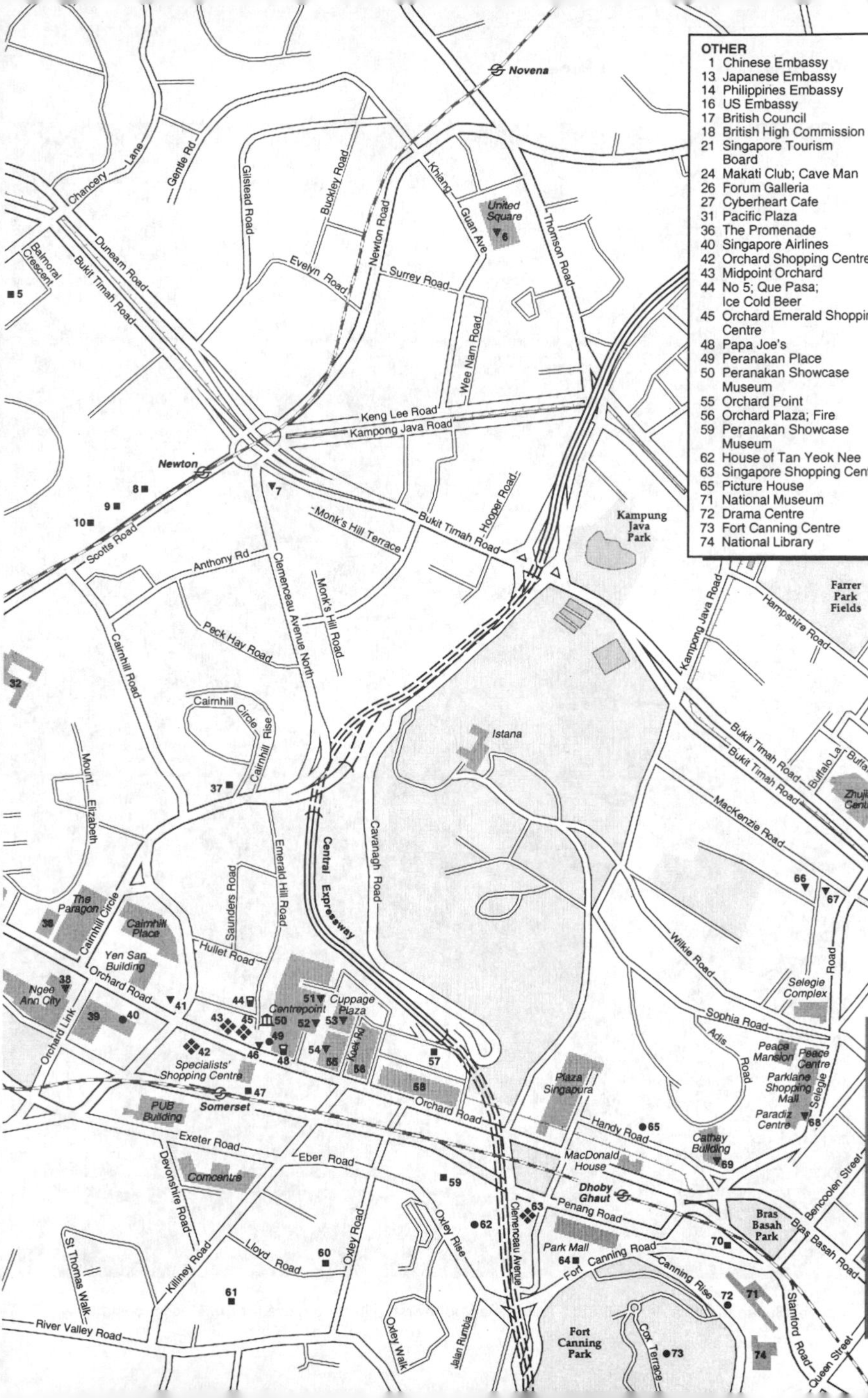
OTHER
1 Chinese Embassy
13 Japanese Embassy
14 Philippines Embassy
16 US Embassy
17 British Council
18 British High Commission
21 Singapore Tourism Board
24 Makati Club; Cave Man
26 Forum Galleria
27 Cyberheart Cafe
31 Pacific Plaza
36 The Promenade
40 Singapore Airlines
42 Orchard Shopping Centre
43 Midpoint Orchard
44 No 5; Que Pasa; Ice Cold Beer
45 Orchard Emerald Shopping Centre
48 Papa Joe's
49 Peranakan Place
50 Peranakan Showcase Museum
55 Orchard Point
56 Orchard Plaza; Fire
59 Peranakan Showcase Museum
62 House of Tan Yeok Nee
63 Singapore Shopping Centre
65 Picture House
71 National Museum
72 Drama Centre
73 Fort Canning Centre
74 National Library
Novena
Newton
Somerset
Dhoby Ghaut
Chancery Lane
Gentle Rd
Gilstead Road
Buckley Road
Newton Road
Khiang Guan Ave
United Square
Thomson Road
Balmoral Crescent
Dunearn Road
Bukit Timah Road
Evelyn Road
Surrey Road
Wee Nam Road
Keng Lee Road
Kampong Java Road
Scotts Road
Monk's Hill Terrace
Hooper Road
Kampung Java Park
Anthony Rd
Clemenceau Avenue North
Monk's Hill Road
Peck Hay Road
Cairnhill Road
Cairnhill Circle
Cairnhill Rise
Farrer Park Fields
Hampshire Road
Istana
Buffalo La
Buffalo Road
Zhujiao Centre
MacKenzie Road
Mount Elizabeth
Emerald Hill Road
Saunders Road
Cavanagh Road
Central Expressway
The Paragon
Cairnhill Circle
Cairnhill Place
Yen San Building
Hullet Road
Orchard Road
Ngee Ann City
Orchard Link
Centrepoint
Cuppage Plaza
Koek Rd
Specialists' Shopping Centre
Wilkie Road
Selegie Complex
Sophia Road
Adis Road
Peace Mansion
Peace Centre
Parklane Shopping Mall
Selegie Road
Paradiz Centre
Plaza Singapura
PUB Building
Handy Road
Cathay Building
Exeter Road
Eber Road
MacDonald House
Devonshire Road
Comcentre
Penang Road
Bencoolen Street
Bras Basah Park
Bras Basah Road
Oxley Road
Oxley Rise
Clemenceau Avenue
Park Mall
Fort Canning Road
Canning Rise
St Thomas Walk
Killiney Road
Lloyd Road
River Valley Road
Oxley Walk
Jalan Rumbia
Fort Canning Park
Cox Terrace
Stamford Road
Queen Street

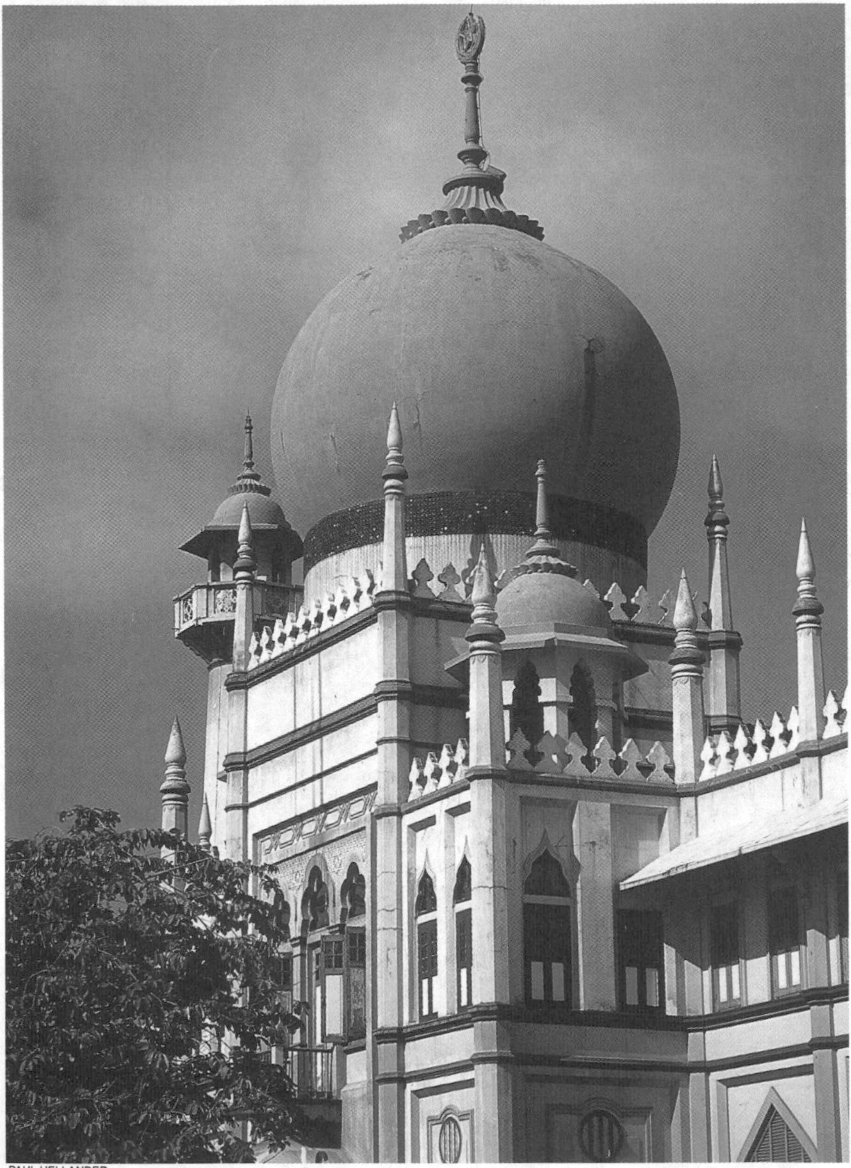

PAUL HELLANDER

Above: Sultan Mosque, largest and liveliest place of worship in Singapore for the Muslim community.

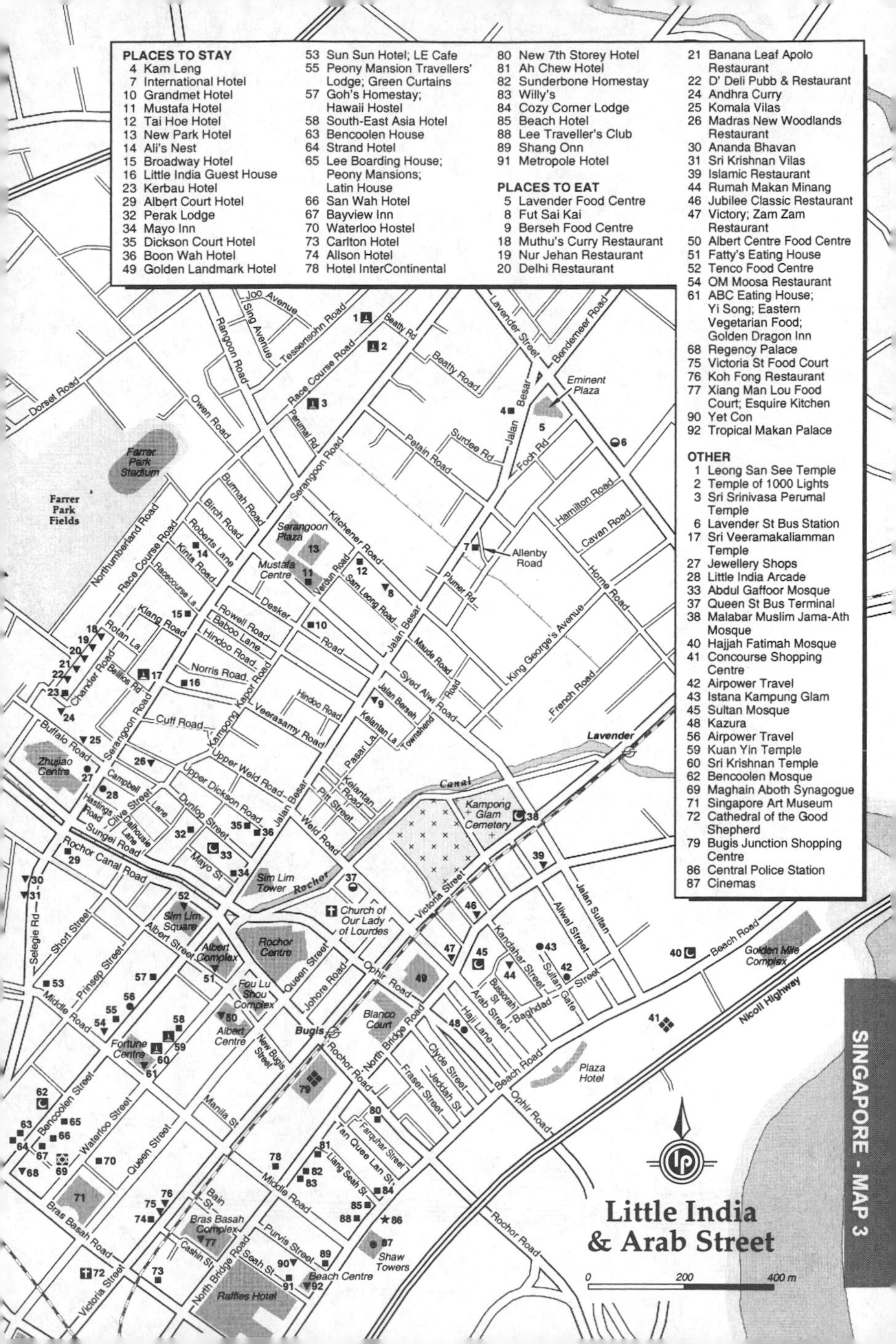
PLACES TO STAY
4 Kam Leng
7 International Hotel
10 Grandmet Hotel
11 Mustafa Hotel
12 Tai Hoe Hotel
13 New Park Hotel
14 Ali's Nest
15 Broadway Hotel
16 Little India Guest House
23 Kerbau Hotel
29 Albert Court Hotel
32 Perak Lodge
34 Mayo Inn
35 Dickson Court Hotel
36 Boon Wah Hotel
49 Golden Landmark Hotel
53 Sun Sun Hotel; LE Cafe
55 Peony Mansion Travellers' Lodge; Green Curtains
57 Goh's Homestay; Hawaii Hostel
58 South-East Asia Hotel
63 Bencoolen House
64 Strand Hotel
65 Lee Boarding House; Peony Mansions; Latin House
66 San Wah Hotel
67 Bayview Inn
70 Waterloo Hostel
73 Carlton Hotel
74 Allson Hotel
78 Hotel InterContinental
80 New 7th Storey Hotel
81 Ah Chew Hotel
82 Sunderbone Homestay
83 Willy's
84 Cozy Corner Lodge
85 Beach Hotel
88 Lee Traveller's Club
89 Shang Onn
91 Metropole Hotel
PLACES TO EAT
5 Lavender Food Centre
8 Fut Sai Kai
9 Berseh Food Centre
18 Muthu's Curry Restaurant
19 Nur Jehan Restaurant
20 Delhi Restaurant
21 Banana Leaf Apolo Restaurant
22 D' Deli Pubb & Restaurant
24 Andhra Curry
25 Komala Vilas
26 Madras New Woodlands Restaurant
30 Ananda Bhavan
31 Sri Krishnan Vilas
39 Islamic Restaurant
44 Rumah Makan Minang
46 Jubilee Classic Restaurant
47 Victory; Zam Zam Restaurant
50 Albert Centre Food Centre
51 Fatty's Eating House
52 Tenco Food Centre
54 OM Moosa Restaurant
61 ABC Eating House; Yi Song; Eastern Vegetarian Food; Golden Dragon Inn
68 Regency Palace
75 Victoria St Food Court
76 Koh Fong Restaurant
77 Xiang Man Lou Food Court; Esquire Kitchen
90 Yet Con
92 Tropical Makan Palace
OTHER
1 Leong San See Temple
2 Temple of 1000 Lights
3 Sri Srinivasa Perumal Temple
6 Lavender St Bus Station
17 Sri Veeramakaliamman Temple
27 Jewellery Shops
28 Little India Arcade
33 Abdul Gaffoor Mosque
37 Queen St Bus Terminal
38 Malabar Muslim Jama-Ath Mosque
40 Hajjah Fatimah Mosque
41 Concourse Shopping Centre
42 Airpower Travel
43 Istana Kampung Glam
45 Sultan Mosque
48 Kazura
56 Airpower Travel
59 Kuan Yin Temple
60 Sri Krishnan Temple
62 Bencoolen Mosque
69 Maghain Aboth Synagogue
71 Singapore Art Museum
72 Cathedral of the Good Shepherd
79 Bugis Junction Shopping Centre
86 Central Police Station
87 Cinemas
Farrer Park Stadium
Farrer Park Fields
Serangoon Plaza
Mustafa Centre
Eminent Plaza
Allenby Road
Kampong Glam Cemetery
Canal
Rochor
Lavender
Sim Lim Tower
Sim Lim Square
Zhujiao Centre
Church of Our Lady of Lourdes
Rochor Centre
Albert Complex
Fou Lu Shou Complex
Albert Centre
Fortune Centre
Blanco Court
Bugis
Golden Mile Complex
Plaza Hotel
Bras Basah Complex
Shaw Towers
Beach Centre
Raffles Hotel
Little India & Arab Street
0 200 400 m
SINGAPORE - MAP 3

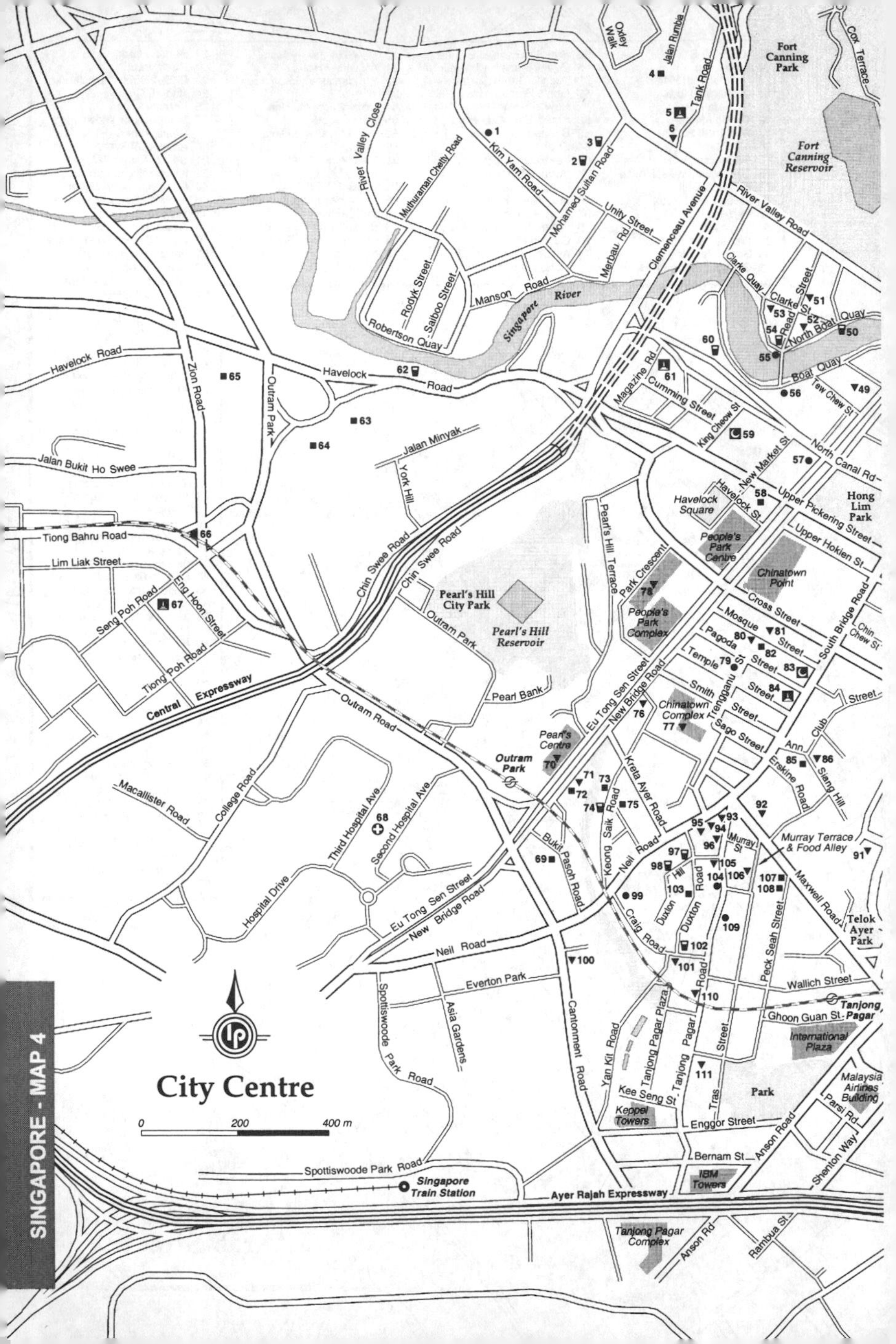
City Centre
0
200
400 m
Fort Canning Park
Fort Canning Reservoir
Cox Terrace
Oxley Walk
Jalan Rumbia
Tank Road
River Valley Close
Muthuraman Chetty Road
Kim Yam Road
Mohamed Sultan Road
Unity Street
Merbau Rd
Clemenceau Avenue
River Valley Road
Rodyk Street
Saiboo Street
Manson Road
Singapore River
Robertson Quay
Clarke Quay
Clarke St
Read Street
North Boat Quay
Boat Quay
Tew Chew St
Havelock Road
Havelock Road
Zion Road
Outram Park
Magazine Rd
Cumming Street
King Cheow St
New Market St
North Canal Rd
Jalan Minyak
York Hill
Jalan Bukit Ho Swee
Havelock Square
Havelock St
Upper Pickering Street
Hong Lim Park
Upper Hokien St
People's Park Centre
Chinatown Point
Pearl's Hill Terrace
Tiong Bahru Road
Lim Liak Street
Seng Poh Road
Eng Hoon Street
Tiong Poh Road
Chin Swee Road
Chin Swee Road
Pearl's Hill City Park
Pearl's Hill Reservoir
Outram Park
Park Crescent
People's Park Complex
Cross Street
Mosque Street
Pagoda Street
Temple Street
Smith Street
Sago Street
South Bridge Road
Chin Chew St
Central Expressway
Pearl Bank
Eu Tong Sen Street
New Bridge Road
Chinatown Complex
Trengganu St
Club Street
Ann Siang Hill
Erskine Road
Outram Road
Pearl's Centre
Outram Park
Kreta Ayer Road
Keong Saik Road
Macallister Road
College Road
Third Hospital Ave
Second Hospital Ave
Bukit Pasoh Road
Neil Road
Murray St
Murray Terrace & Food Alley
Duxton Hill
Duxton Road
Maxwell Road
Telok Ayer Park
Hospital Drive
Eu Tong Sen Street
New Bridge Road
Craig Road
Neil Road
Peck Seah Street
Everton Park
Wallich Street
Tanjong Pagar
Ghoon Guan St
International Plaza
Spottiswoode Park Road
Asia Gardens
Cantonment Road
Yan Kit Road
Tanjong Pagar Plaza
Tanjong Pagar
Tras Street
Park
Malaysia Airlines Building
Parsi Rd
Kee Seng St
Keppel Towers
Enggor Street
Anson Road
Shenton Way
Bernam St
IBM Towers
Spottiswoode Park Road
Singapore Train Station
Ayer Rajah Expressway
Tanjong Pagar Complex
Anson Rd
Rambua St
1
2
3
4
5
6
49
50
51
52
53
54
55
56
57
58
59
60
61
62
63
64
65
66
67
68
69
70
71
72
73
74
75
76
77
78
79
80
81
82
83
84
85
86
91
92
93
94
95
96
97
98
99
100
101
102
103
104
105
106
107
108
109
110
111

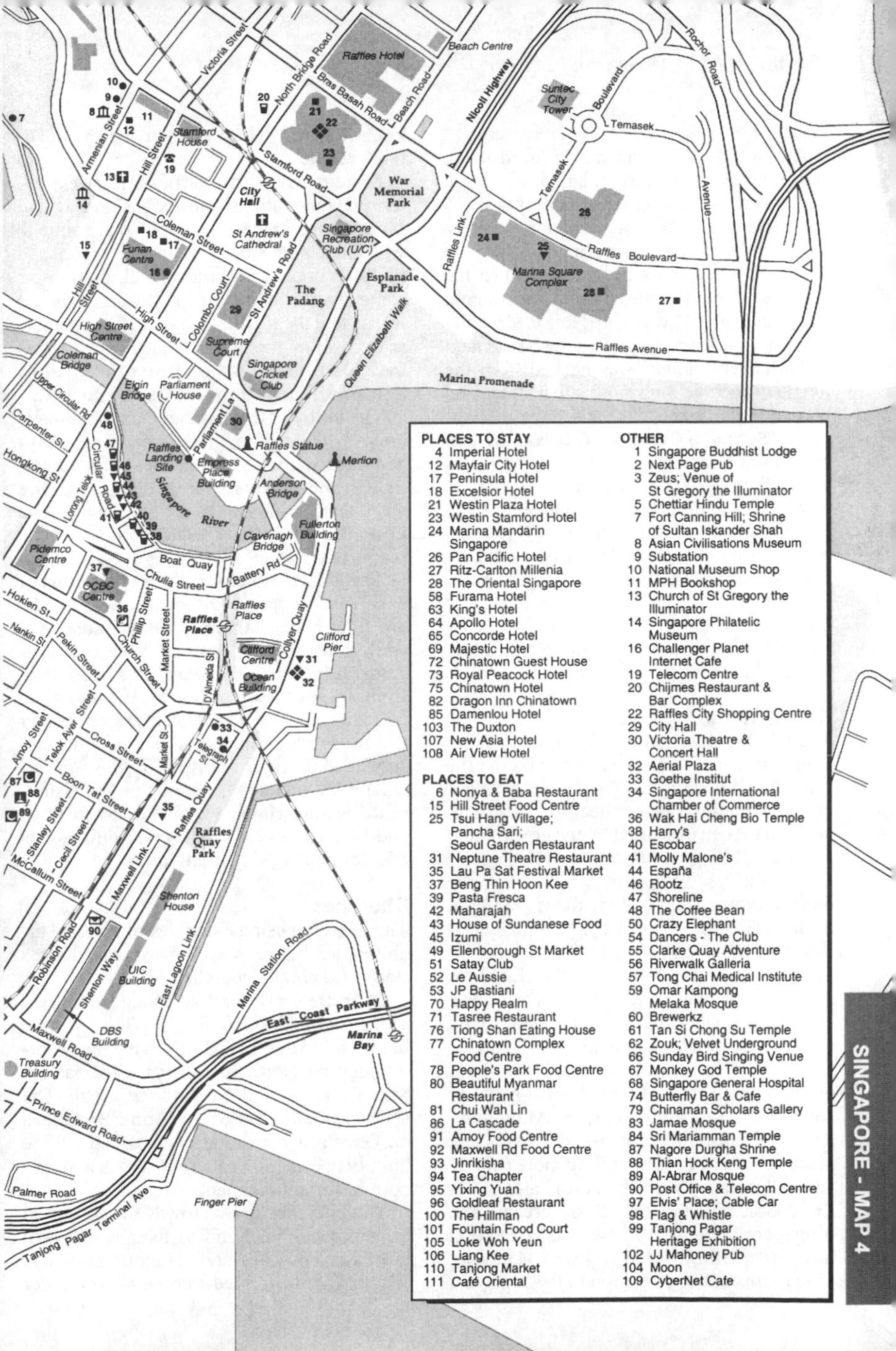

PLACES TO STAY

4 Imperial Hotel
12 Mayfair City Hotel
17 Peninsula Hotel
18 Excelsior Hotel
21 Westin Plaza Hotel
23 Westin Stamford Hotel
24 Marina Mandarin Singapore
26 Pan Pacific Hotel
27 Ritz-Carlton Millenia
28 The Oriental Singapore
58 Furama Hotel
63 King's Hotel
64 Apollo Hotel
65 Concorde Hotel
69 Majestic Hotel
72 Chinatown Guest House
73 Royal Peacock Hotel
75 Chinatown Hotel
82 Dragon Inn Chinatown
85 Damenlou Hotel
103 The Duxton
107 New Asia Hotel
108 Air View Hotel

PLACES TO EAT

6 Nonya & Baba Restaurant
15 Hill Street Food Centre
25 Tsui Hang Village; Pancha Sari; Seoul Garden Restaurant
31 Neptune Theatre Restaurant
35 Lau Pa Sat Festival Market
37 Beng Thin Hoon Kee
39 Pasta Fresca
42 Maharajah
43 House of Sundanese Food
45 Izumi
49 Ellenborough St Market
51 Satay Club
52 Le Aussie
53 JP Bastiani
70 Happy Realm
71 Tasree Restaurant
76 Tiong Shan Eating House
77 Chinatown Complex Food Centre
78 People's Park Food Centre
80 Beautiful Myanmar Restaurant
81 Chui Wah Lin
86 La Cascade
91 Amoy Food Centre
92 Maxwell Rd Food Centre
93 Jinrikisha
94 Tea Chapter
95 Yixing Yuan
96 Goldleaf Restaurant
100 The Hillman
101 Fountain Food Court
105 Loke Woh Yeun
106 Liang Kee
110 Tanjong Market
111 Café Oriental

OTHER

1 Singapore Buddhist Lodge
2 Next Page Pub
3 Zeus; Venue of St Gregory the Illuminator
5 Chettiar Hindu Temple
7 Fort Canning Hill; Shrine of Sultan Iskander Shah
8 Asian Civilisations Museum
9 Substation
10 National Museum Shop
11 MPH Bookshop
13 Church of St Gregory the Illuminator
14 Singapore Philatelic Museum
16 Challenger Planet Internet Cafe
19 Telecom Centre
20 Chijmes Restaurant & Bar Complex
22 Raffles City Shopping Centre
29 City Hall
30 Victoria Theatre & Concert Hall
32 Aerial Plaza
33 Goethe Institut
34 Singapore International Chamber of Commerce
36 Wak Hai Cheng Bio Temple
38 Harry's
40 Escobar
41 Molly Malone's
44 España
46 Rootz
47 Shoreline
48 The Coffee Bean
50 Crazy Elephant
54 Dancers - The Club
55 Clarke Quay Adventure
56 Riverwalk Galleria
57 Tong Chai Medical Institute
59 Omar Kampong Melaka Mosque
60 Brewerkz
61 Tan Si Chong Su Temple
62 Zouk; Velvet Underground
66 Sunday Bird Singing Venue
67 Monkey God Temple
68 Singapore General Hospital
74 Butterfly Bar & Cafe
79 Chinaman Scholars Gallery
83 Jamae Mosque
84 Sri Mariamman Temple
87 Nagore Durgha Shrine
88 Thian Hock Keng Temple
89 Al-Abrar Mosque
90 Post Office & Telecom Centre
97 Elvis' Place; Cable Car
98 Flag & Whistle
99 Tanjong Pagar Heritage Exhibition
102 JJ Mahoney Pub
104 Moon
109 CyberNet Cafe

continued from page 563

A new refurbishment has spruced it up, and a merchandising shop has been added. Tickets are often very reasonably priced.

Parliament House is Singapore's oldest government building. Originally a private mansion, it became a court house, then the Assembly House of the colonial government and finally the Parliament House for independent Singapore. High St, which runs next to Parliament House, was hacked from the jungle to become Singapore's first street, and was an Indian area in its early days.

The **Supreme Court** and **City Hall** are two other stoic colonial buildings on St Andrew's Rd. Built in 1939, the Supreme Court is a relatively new addition, and is notable for what it replaced – the Grand Hotel de L'Europe, which once outshone Raffles as Singapore's premier hotel. This fine building features Corinthian column murals by Italian artist Cavaliere Rodolfo Nolli. Next door, City Hall was where Lord Louis Mountbatten surrendered to the Japanese in 1945.

Raffles Hotel

The Raffles Hotel on Beach Rd is far more than just an expensive place to stay or the best known hotel in Singapore. It's a Singapore institution, an architectural landmark which has been classified by the government as a part of Singapore's 'cultural heritage'.

The Raffles was opened in 1887 by the Sarkies brothers, three Armenians who built a string of hotels which become famous throughout the east. They include the Strand in Yangon (Rangoon) and the E&O in Penang, as well as the Raffles. It started as a 10 room bungalow, but its heyday began with the opening of the main building in 1899.

The Raffles soon became a byword for oriental luxury and featured in novels by Joseph Conrad and Somerset Maugham. Rudyard Kipling recommended it as the place to 'feed at' when in Singapore (but he advised against staying there), and in its Long Bar, Ngiam Tong Boon created the Singapore Sling in 1915 (see the boxed text 'Singapore Sling' in the Tastes of Malaysia, Singapore & Brunei section in the Malaysia Facts for the Visitor chapter for the cocktail's recipe.

More recently, the Raffles underwent extensive renovations and extensions; it had fallen from grace and could not compete with Singapore's modern hotels. It reopened in 1991, once again a top hotel, though for some it wasn't the same old Raffles. While it is true that the Raffles is now a slick exercise in tourism marketing, for many it still oozes the old-fashioned atmosphere of the east as Somerset Maugham would have known it.

The **lobby** of the restored main building is open to the public (dress standards apply) and high tea is served in the Tiffin Room, though the Writers' Bar next door is little more than an alcove. In the other wings, the **Long Bar** or the **Bar & Billiard Room** are the places to sip a Singapore Sling at S$17 a pop.

The Raffles Hotel Arcade is a collection of expensive shops, and hidden away on the 3rd floor is the **Raffles Hotel Museum**. It is well worth a look, especially the old postcards. Admission is free and it is open daily from 10 am to 9 pm. Raffles memorabilia, including the hotel crockery, are on sale at the museum shop. Next to the museum, Jubilee Hall theatre puts on *Raffles Revisited*, a multimedia presentation on the history of the Raffles Hotel. Viewing times are at 10 and 11 am and 12.30 and 1 pm. Admission is S$5 for adults, S$3 for children.

Churches

The most imposing examples of colonial architecture between Coleman St and Bras Basah Rd are the churches.

St Andrew's Cathedral is Singapore's Anglican cathedral, built in Gothic style between 1856 and 1863. It's in the block surrounded by North Bridge Rd, Coleman St, Stamford Rd and St Andrew's Rd. The Catholic **Cathedral of the Good Shepherd** on Queen St is a stolid neoclassical edifice built between 1843 and 1846 and is a Singapore historic monument.

The churches draw crowds of well-to-do Singaporeans on Sunday, though many of the other churches and religious buildings are being transformed into new uses under the auspices of the Urban Redevelopment Authority. The magnificent St Joseph's Institution, a former Catholic boy's school, is now the Singapore Art Museum (see the following entry). On the corner of Bras Basah Rd and Victoria St, the equally impressive **Convent of the Holy Infant Jesus** is now part of the Chijmes restaurant and bar complex. See the Bars, Bands & Discos entry in the Entertainment section later in the chapter.

The Armenian **Church of St Gregory the Illuminator** is the oldest church in Singapore. It's on Hill St but is no longer used for services.

Singapore Art Museum

One of Singapore's finest colonial buildings, St Joseph's Institution, near the corner of Bras Basah Rd and Queen St, has been restored and converted into this fine arts museum.

Rotating exhibits showcase modern art from Singapore and South-East Asia. Even if the art is not your cup of tea, the building is worth a look and the museum has a good cafe facing Queen St.

The museum is open from 9 am to 5.30 pm daily, closed Monday. Entry costs S$3 (children S$1.50).

Fort Canning

If you continue north-west up Coleman St from the Padang, you pass the Armenian Church of St Gregory the Illuminator and come to Fort Canning Hill, a good viewpoint over Singapore. Once known as Forbidden Hill, it contains the shrine of Sultan Iskander Shah, the last ruler of the ancient kingdom of Singapura. Archaeological digs in the park have uncovered Javanese artefacts from the 14th century Majapahit Empire.

When Stamford Raffles arrived, the only reminder of any greatness that the island may once have claimed was an earthen wall that stretched from the sea to the top of Fort Canning Hill. Raffles built his house on the top of the hill, and it became Government House until the military built Fort Canning in 1860. There is little left of the historic buildings that were once on the hill, but it is a pleasant park and you can wander around the old Christian cemetery and see the many gravestones with their poignant tales of hopeful settlers who died young. On the top of the hill is the Fort Canning Centre, previously a barracks which now houses the Singapore Dance Theatre.

National Museum

The National Museum on Stamford Rd traces its ancestry back to Raffles himself, who first suggested the idea of a museum for Singapore in 1823. The original museum opened in 1849, then moved to another location in 1862 before being re-housed in the present building in 1887.

The museum is not extensive but has substantial collections focusing on regional cultures, history, crafts etc. Exhibits include archaeological finds from the Asian region, articles relating to Chinese settlement and trade in the region, Malaysian and Indonesian arts and crafts, Peranakan artefacts and a wide collection of items relating to Stamford Raffles. The museum also has a superb jade collection donated by the Aw brothers, of Tiger Balm fame. The family amassed not only this priceless collection of jade pieces, but also a variety of other valuable pieces of art.

The trouble with the National Museum has always been that only a fraction of its collection is on show, and as the exhibits are rotating, it is potluck as to what you see. However, the collections are being dispersed into the many new museums popping up around the city, such as the Singapore Art Museum and the Asian Civilisations Museum, just around the corner on Armenian St.

The National Museum is open Tuesday to Saturday from 9 am to 5.30 pm. Admission is S$3. Tours of the museum for groups of 10 to 12 are available; call ☎ 1-800 336 1460 for details. The National Museum Shop, a short walk away on Armenian St, has publications and an attractive array of gifts.

Singapore Philatelic Museum

This philatelic museum is housed in a colonial building dating from 1908. Stamp collectors will find it interesting as it is well presented with rare and not-so-rare stamps from Singapore and around the world, and the stamp-making process is traced from artwork through to printing. An audio-visual theatre and interactive games provide a high-tech touch.

The museum is open daily from 9 am to 4.30 pm; closed Monday and public holidays. Entry is S$2 (children S$1). Free guided tours start at 11 am and 2 pm.

New Bugis St

For years Bugis St was famous as Singapore's raucous transvestite playground. In a country that banned jukeboxes and long hair, Bugis St was proof that Singapore dared to be daring. Bugis St was never, officially, more than another food-stall centre but, in practice, at the witching hour certain young men turned into something more exotic than pumpkins. It was the place to be until the early hours of the morning, to join the crowds and watch the goings on – that is until Bugis St was totally demolished during the building of the MRT. As is the case with so many of Singapore's attractions, the answer was to rebuild it, to make it newer and better than ever.

So now Singapore has a New Bugis St, just south-west of the MRT station, complete with new terrace look-alikes and new lock-up wooden stalls with new canvas awnings. Transvestites are not allowed and, of course, New Bugis St is a pale shadow of its former self. Nonetheless it is a pleasant, even if much quieter, place to hang out in the evening. Some of the open-air restaurants and bars stay open until 3 am, or until the last customers go home. There are fruit and food stalls, and you can pick up an imitation of an expensive watch or a T-shirt. The Bugis MRT station is right across the way, and the large and very popular Bugis Junction shopping centre continues on with the theme of neocolonial architecture.

Kuan Yin Temple

This temple on Waterloo St is one of the most popular Chinese temples – after all, Kuan Yin is one of the most popular goddesses. This temple was rebuilt in 1982, but the flower sellers and fortune tellers out the front make it one of the liveliest temples in Singapore. A few doors away is **Sri Krishnan Temple**, which also attracts wor- shippers from the Kuan Yin Temple, who show a great deal of religious pragmatism by also burning joss sticks and offering prayers at this Hindu temple.

Central Business District

Once the vibrant heart of Singapore, **Raffles Place** is now a rather barren patch of grass above the MRT station surrounded by the giant high-rise buildings of the central business district. There are a few shopping possibilities nearby, including **Aerial Plaza**, a collection of small shops and aggressive Indian tailors, from where you can cross Collyer Quay to **Clifford Pier**, the place to hire a boat or catch a harbour tour (see Organised Tours in the Singapore Getting Around chapter). Singapore's harbour is one of the busiest in the world; there are always boats anchored offshore, with one arriving or departing at least every 15 minutes.

Further south along the waterfront, you'll find large office blocks, airline offices, more shops and the **Lau Pa Sat Festival Centre** housed in the Telok Ayer Centre, a fine piece of cast-iron Victoriana that was once a market. It was pulled down during the construction of the MRT, but has been restored and now stands on its original site. It has a wide selection of eating places and craft stalls, and cultural performances are occasionally held here. It is lively in the evening, when adjoining Boon Tat St is closed off and hawker carts are set up. Singapore's disappearing Chinatown is inland from this modern city centre.

CHINATOWN (Map 4)

Singapore's cultural heart is Chinatown, providing a glimpse of the old ways – the ways of the Chinese immigrants that shaped and built modern Singapore.

Many buildings in this area have been demolished and redeveloped over the last 30 years, though the greatest changes have occurred since around 1990. Many of the old colonial shop fronts, synonymous with the Chinese on the Malay peninsula, have been restored, or rather ripped down and rebuilt in the same style, under the direction of the Urban Redevelopment Authority.

The redevelopments are faithful to the original, and it is wonderful to see the spirit of the old buildings winning out over the concrete high-rises, but the re-creations are now desirable properties commanding high rents for businesses, shops and restaurants. Many of the traditional businesses have moved out and a new gentrified Chinatown has taken its place. Much of the old Chinatown is now fashionable restaurants and expensive shops.

Chinatown is still a good place to wander around. Though many of the traditional crafts and businesses have gone, it contains some of Singapore's most notable temples and there are plenty of eating and shopping possibilities. Chinatown is roughly bounded by the Singapore River to the north, New Bridge Rd to the west, Maxwell and Kreta Ayer roads to the south, and Cecil St to the east.

Walking Tour

You can start a Chinatown walking tour from the Raffles Place MRT station in the central business district. From the station, wander west along Chulia St and south down Philip St to the **Wak Hai Cheng Bio Temple**. This Teochew Taoist temple is quite run-down, but has some interesting scenes depicted under, and on top of, the roof of the main temple.

Continue down Philip St and over Church St to Telok Ayer St. Up until only a couple of years ago, this was a clamouring district of traditional business, but the blocks around Pekin and Cross streets are now being redeveloped and construction is progressing fairly briskly.

At the junction with Boon Tat St, you'll find the **Nagore Durgha Shrine**, an old mosque built by Muslims from south India during 1829 and 1830. It's not that interesting, but just a little south-west down the street is the Chinese **Thian Hock Keng Temple**, or Temple of Heavenly Happiness, one of the most interesting temples in Singapore (see the following entry).

Continue walking along Telok Ayer St and you'll soon come to the **Al-Abrar Mosque**, which was originally built in 1827 and rebuilt in its present form from 1850 to 1855. A right turn and then another right turn will bring you into **Amoy St**, a Hokkien area that once catered to sailors and the sea trade. This street has been almost totally modernised, and represents the first look at the new Chinatown.

The Old Trades of Chinatown

When wandering around Chinatown, you may come across some disappearing trades which have been part of the area since it came into being.

The letter writer will set up a streetside table and pen letters for the old residents of Chinatown who have never learned to read or write. Traditionally the letter writer would deftly pen the Chinese characters in letters destined to relatives back in China, though these days he is more often than not a sign writer, producing the lucky scrolls with messages of prosperity that will be hung outside houses during the Chinese New Year.

The *chop* is a Chinese stamp that serves as a signature for documents, and a chop maker will carve them for his customers. Traditionally they were made of bamboo or ivory, though these days plastic is often used. It has a unique imprint, bearing both a unique design and the style of its maker, and cannot be replicated.

Rickshaw drivers have been a part of Chinatown ever since the *jinriksha*, or man-pulled rickshaw, arrived from Shanghai. They were later replaced by bicycle rickshaws, which still ply the streets of Chinatown. Drivers take passengers for the short trips from the shopping centres to the nearby housing estates. The goods rickshaw has a platform at the front and is still a convenient way to transport freight around the backstreets.

Continue north-east up Amoy St and turn left (north-west) up Cross St to Club St. The quiet area around Club St, Ann Siang Rd and Ann Siang Hill was a clove and nutmeg plantation until it became a prime residential area for Hokkien merchants. This area was noted for its highly decorated terraces, a number of which housed the old Chinese guilds, though only a few remain now. **Ann Siang Hill** in particular has some fine terrace houses, both restored and untouched.

Further south, South Bridge Rd becomes Neil Rd. Wedged between here and Tanjong Pagar Rd is the **Tanjong Pagar** conservation area, the first major restoration project in Chinatown. The beautifully restored terraces accommodate a variety of restaurants and bars. The old Jinrikisha station on the corner of Neil and Tanjong Pagar roads, now a restaurant, is an interesting triangular building that was once the depot for the hand-pulled rickshaws. The **Tanjong Pagar Heritage Exhibition** in the 51 Neil Rd complex is a small, interesting exhibition with old photographs showing what Chinatown used to be like. It is open daily from 11am to 9 pm. Admission is free.

Near Tanjong Pagar, the **Bukit Pasoh area** is a traditional part of Chinatown. Bukit Pasoh Rd, where you'll find the Majestic Hotel, is known as the street of the clans because of the many clan association houses here. Keong Saik Rd is a curving street of old terraces with coffee shops, clan houses and clubs. Many buildings in this street have been renovated with hotels and bars replacing the traditional businesses.

Heading back to the centre of Chinatown, north-east up to South Bridge Rd, you enter the **Kreta Ayer district**, the real heart of Chinatown. The street hawkers and many of the traditional businesses have gone, but some of the old atmosphere of Chinatown remains. The Chinatown Complex, on the corner of Trengganu and Smith streets, is a lively local shopping centre and a popular meeting place outside in the cool of the evening. Along with Smith St, Temple, Pagoda and Mosque streets are traditionally the heart of old Chinatown, but new developments have destroyed a lot of the atmosphere and most of Pagoda St has been renovated. Smith St has gold, jade, souvenir and traditional medicine shops. Mosque St has a good row of old-fashioned coffee shops. The whole area has plenty of old and new souvenir and trinket shops selling masks, reproduction bronzes, bamboo ware, carvings and silk dressing gowns. Bargain hard.

The **Chinaman Scholars Gallery** is upstairs at 14B Trengganu St. This living museum is styled as a Cantonese house of the 1930s and includes furniture, clothing, artefacts, photographs and musical instruments from the period. It is open daily from 9 am to 4 pm; admission is S$6 for adults, S$4 for children.

Also in this area is the **Sri Mariamman Temple**, Singapore's oldest Hindu temple (see the entry in this section). The **Jamae (or Chulia) Mosque** on South Bridge Rd is only a short distance from the Sri Mariamman Temple. It was built by Indian Muslims from the Coromandel Coast of Tamil Nadu between 1830 and 1855.

Across New Bridge Rd from Pagoda St is the huge **People's Park Complex**, a modern shopping centre, but with much more local appeal than the general run of Orchard Rd centres.

Further north-east along Eu Tong Sen St is the **Tong Chai Medical Institute**. This architecturally interesting building in the style of a Chinese godown is classified as a national monument. To finish off the walk, and perhaps quench your thirst with a beer (well-deserved of course), head east along North Canal Rd until you hit Boat Quay's bars and restaurants, a 10 minute walk from here.

Thian Hock Keng Temple

The Temple of Heavenly Happiness on Telok Ayer St in Chinatown is the oldest and one of the most colourful temples in Singapore. The temple was originally built in 1840 and dedicated to Ma-Cho-Po, the queen of heaven and protector of sailors.

At that time it was on the waterfront and, since many Chinese settlers were arriving by sea, it was inevitable that a joss house be built where they could offer thanks for a safe voyage. As you wander through the courtyards of the temple, look for the rooftop dragons, the intricately decorated beams, the burning joss sticks, the gold-leafed panels and, best of all, the beautifully painted doors.

Sri Mariamman Temple

The Sri Mariamman Temple on South Bridge Rd, right in the heart of Chinatown, is the oldest Hindu temple in Singapore. It was built in 1827 but rebuilt in 1862. With its colourful *gopuram*, or tower, over the entrance gate, this is clearly a temple in the South Indian Dravidian style. A superb collection of colourfully painted Hindu figures decorate the gopuram.

Around October each year, the temple is the scene for the Thimithi festival, during which devotees walk barefoot over burning coals – supposedly feeling no pain, although spectators report that quite a few hotfoot it over the final few steps.

LITTLE INDIA (Map 3)

Although Singapore is a predominantly Chinese city, it does have its minority groups and the Indians are probably the most visible, particularly in the colourful streets of Little India along Serangoon Rd. This is another area, like Chinatown, in which you can simply wander around and take in the flavours. Indeed, around Serangoon Rd it can be very much a case of following your nose because the heady aroma of Indian spices and cooking seems to be everywhere.

If you want a new sari, a pair of Indian sandals, a recent issue of *India Today* or the *Indian Movie News*, a tape of Indian music or a framed portrait of your favourite Hindu god, then Little India is the place to go.

It's also, not surprisingly, a good place to eat. Since many of Singapore's Indians are Hindu Tamils from the south of India, Little India has many vegetarian restaurants, and there are some superb places to eat vegetarian food.

Walking Tour

Little India is not very extensive, and you can sample its sights, scents and sounds in an hour or two. Little India is roughly the area bounded by Sungei Rd to the south, Lavender St to the north, Race Course Rd to the west and Jalan Besar to the east. The real centre of Little India is at the southern end of Serangoon Rd and the small streets that run off it. Here, the shops are wall-to-wall Indian, but only a hundred metres or so away the Chinese influence reappears.

Unfortunately, much of the western side of Serangoon Rd has been flattened and consists of open fields, but there are interesting temples further north. Race Course Rd has a few shops and some good restaurants at its southern end, but the housing estates have made an unmistakable contribution to its atmosphere. Sunday is the big day in Little India, when the temples are buzzing and hundreds of Indian men and Bangladeshi immigrant workers come out to socialise, milling around the streets arm-in-arm or squatting by the side of the road to chat.

The **Zhujiao Centre** on Serangoon Rd near Buffalo Rd is Little India's market. It was known as the KK market (Kandang Kerbau, meaning 'cattle pens', as this was once a cattle-holding area) before it was re-housed in this modern building. Downstairs is a 'wet market', the Singaporean term for a produce market, and it is one of the liveliest local markets in Singapore, selling all types of fruit and vegetables as well as meat and fish. The hawker centre here has plenty of Indian food stalls. Upstairs, stalls sell a variety of clothes and everyday goods, and you can also buy brassware and Indian textiles.

Across Serangoon Rd is the **Little India Arcade**, presenting the new face of Little India. This block of renovated shophouses has its fair share of tourist-oriented souvenir shops, but manages to maintain the traditional atmosphere of Little India, with Indian textile, grocery and flower shops, making it a more successful project than many parts of Chinatown. From here wander around the backstreets with the names of imperial India, such as Clive, Hastings and Campbell. This is the heart of Little India, with a variety of shops selling spices, Indian music cassettes, saris, religious artefacts and everyday goods for the Indian household. Dunlop St in particular maintains much of its old-fashioned charm. This is also a **restaurant area** and the best place to sample south Indian vegetarian food. At 12-14 Buffalo Rd is the famous relocated Komala Vilas restaurant, and around the corner in Upper Dickson Rd is the equally good Madras New Woodlands restaurant.

Apart from the ubiquitous gold shops, there are a few interesting **jewellers** on Serangoon and Buffalo roads which make jewellery crafted with traditional designs.

The southern end of Race Course Rd has the best collection of non-vegetarian restaurants in Singapore, from the tandoori food of north India to Singapore's famous fish-head curry, which sounds and looks terrible, but tastes delicious.

On the corner of Belilios and Serangoon roads is the **Sri Veeramakaliamman Temple**, a Shivaite temple dedicated to Kali. It is always popular with worshippers, especially at dusk.

Further north-east along Serangoon Rd is the **Serangoon Plaza**. Architecturally, historically and culturally it's a write-off, but the department stores here are good places for bargains. The range may not be extensive, but the fixed prices for electrical goods and other household items are usually as good as you'll find anywhere in Singapore. The Mustafa Centre around the corner is a new, larger offshoot, crammed with places for bargain hunters.

Also in this area, in the alleyways behind Desker Rd, are the infamous brothels. Rows of blockhouse rooms line the alley with women standing in doorways while a constant stream of men wander past. Outside, hawkers sell condoms and potency pills, and makeshift tables are set up with card games to gamble on.

It is fairly seedy but very lively, and the coffee shops with outdoor tables here do a roaring trade. This area is the successor to old Bugis St, without the tourists and carnival atmosphere, and later in the evenings the transvestites strut their stuff. It doesn't have the atmosphere of old Bugis St, but it is lively and the coffee shops, such as the Choon Huat at 2 Desker Rd and the Hong Fa nearby, are interesting places to sit out on the pavement for noodles or a beer.

In complete contrast, the **Sri Srinivasa Perumal Temple** is a large temple dedicated to Vishnu. The temple dates from 1855 but the impressive gopuram is a relatively recent addition, built in 1966. Inside the temple, you will find a statue of Perumal, or Vishnu, and his consorts Lakshmi and Andal, as well as his bird-mount Garuda. This temple is the starting point for devotees who make the walk to the Chettiar Hindu Temple during the Thaipusam festival (see the Chettiar Hindu Temple entry later in this chapter).

Not far from the Sri Srinivasa Perumal Temple is the Sakaya Muni Buddha Gaya Temple, better known as the **Temple of 1000 Lights** (see the entry following this section). It's a glitzy, slightly tacky Thai-influenced temple, but one of Singapore's best known, and it welcomes visitors. A more beautiful temple is the **Leong San See Temple** over the road. This Buddhist and Taoist temple has some fine ceramic carvings inside.

From Little India, you can wander across to **Jalan Besar**. The Indian influence is not so noticeable here; the fine old pastel-coloured terraces with intricate stucco and tiles are Peranakan in style. Of particular note are the terraces on Petain Rd, and those on the corner of Plumer Rd and Jalan Besar.

A number of traditional businesses are on and around Jalan Besar, and the area around Kelantan and Pasar lanes is a place to look for antiques. On Sunday a flea market operates, selling everything from old shoes and computer chips to motorcycle parts, and if you rummage around you can find old coins, porcelain and brassware.

Just off Jalan Besar on Dunlop St, down towards Rochor Canal Rd, is the **Abdul Gaffoor Mosque**. It's an intriguing fairytale blend of Arab and Victorian architecture.

Temple of 1000 Lights

Towards the north-eastern end of Race Course Rd at No 366, close to the corner of Serangoon and Beatty roads, is the Sakaya Muni Buddha Gaya Temple, or the Temple of

1000 Lights. This Buddhist temple is dominated by a brightly painted 15m-tall seated figure of Buddha. The temple was inspired by a Thai monk named Vutthisasara. Although it is a Thai-style temple, it's actually very Chinese in its technicolour decoration.

Apart from the Buddha image, the temple includes oddities like a wax model of Gandhi and a figure of Ganesh, the elephant-headed Hindu god. A huge mother-of-pearl footprint, complete with the 108 auspicious marks which distinguish a Buddha foot from any other 2m-long foot, is said to be a replica of the footprint on top of Adam's Peak in Sri Lanka.

Behind and inside the giant statue is a smaller image of the reclining Buddha in the act of entering nirvana. Around the base, models tell the story of Buddha's life, and, of course, there are the 1000 electric lights which give the temple its name.

Any bus going north-east along Serangoon Rd will take you to the temple.

ARAB ST (Map 3)

While Chinatown provides Singapore with a Chinese flavour and Serangoon Rd is where you head to for the tastes and smells of India, Arab St is the Muslim centre. Along this street, and especially along North Bridge Rd and side streets with Malay names like Pahang St, Aliwal St, Jalan Pisang and Jalan Sultan, you'll find batiks from Indonesia and sarungs, hookahs (water-pipes), rosaries, flower essences, *hajj* caps, *songkok* hats, basketware and rattan goods.

Walking Tour

The easiest way to begin a tour of the Arab St area is to take the MRT to the Bugis station and walk up Victoria St to Arab St.

Arab St is traditionally a textile district, and while the big merchants inhabit the textile centre on Jalan Sultan, Arab St is still alive with textile shops selling batiks, silks and more mundane cloth for a sarung or shirt. A number of craft shops sell leather bags and souvenirs, and up towards the end of Arab St near Beach Rd are the caneware shops.

Sultan Mosque (see the following entry), the focus for Singapore's Muslim community, is on the corner of Arab St and North Bridge Rd. It is the largest mosque in Singapore and the most lively. You'll also find good Indian Muslim food at restaurants across the street on North Bridge Rd. One street back towards the city is **Haji Lane**, a narrow picturesque lane lined with two storey shophouses that contain a number of textile and other local businesses. Kazura, at No 51, is a traditional perfume business with rows of decanters containing perfumes such as 'Ramadan' and 'Aidal Fitri' for the faithful. At the end of Haji Lane turn left into Beach Rd.

If you have time for a detour north-east along Beach Rd, the **Hajjah Fatimah Mosque** is interesting. It's a monument built around 1845 by a Melakan-born Malay woman Hajjah Fatimah, on the site of her home. The architecture shows colonial influences.

Otherwise, turn back up Arab St. Heading north-east up Baghdad St from Arab St, you find more batik and craft shops, and then you cross **Bussorah St**. During the month of Ramadan, when Muslims fast from sunrise to sunset, the area is alive with food stalls, especially in Bussorah St, where the faithful come to buy food at dusk. Bussorah St has become the new yuppie Arab St. The old terraces have been renovated and palm trees have been planted to give that Middle Eastern 'oasis look'.

At 43A Baghdad St you may find **stone carvers** crafting the small headstones for Muslim graves, and further along between Sultan Gate and Aliwal St are other stone carvers, who also produce carvings for Chinese temples and graves.

If you turn left into Sultan Gate you come to the historic gates that lead to the **Istana Kampong Glam**. The *istana* (palace) was the residence of Sultan Ali Iskander Shah and was built around 1840. The Kampong Glam area is the historic seat of the Malay royalty, resident here before the arrival of Stamford Raffles. In the early days of Singapore, it was allocated not only to the original Malays but also to Javanese, Bugis and Arab merchants and residents.

The palace isn't open to visitors, but if you walk through the gateway and around to the left, a doorway in the palace wall leads to Kandahar St, behind the Sultan Mosque. Muscat St winds behind the mosque back to Arab St, or you can continue up Kandahar St to North Bridge Rd. Cross over North Bridge Rd and you'll find a number of venerable Indian Muslim restaurants selling roti prata and biryani.

On the corner of Jalan Sultan and Victoria St is **Malabar Muslim Jama-Ath Mosque**, a beautiful little mosque covered in blue tiles, which is at its fairy-tale best when lit up in the evenings during Ramadan. Behind it is the old **Kampong Glam cemetery**, where it's said that the Malay royalty is buried among the frangipani trees and coconut palms. Many of the graves have fallen into ruin, but more recent graves are tended, evidenced by cloths placed over the headstones.

Sultan Mosque

The Sultan Mosque on North Bridge Rd near Arab St is the biggest mosque in Singapore. It was originally built in 1825 with the aid of a grant from Stamford Raffles and the East India Company as a result of Raffles' treaty with the sultan of Johor. A hundred years later, the original mosque was replaced by a magnificent gold-domed building. The mosque is open to visitors from 5 am to 8.30 pm daily; if you can manage it, the best time to visit is during a religious ceremony.

ORCHARD RD (Map 2)

Singapore's international tourists and its wealthy residents also have whole areas of Singapore to themselves. Orchard Rd is where the high-class hotels predominate, and north-west of this busy thoroughfare you enter the area of the Singapore elite. Prior to independence, the mansions of the colonial rulers were built here, and today the wealthy of Singapore, as well as many expatriates, live in these fine old houses.

Orchard Rd itself is mostly a place to shop, eat and stay. Its rows of modern shopping centres hold a variety of shops selling everything from the latest in Japanese gadgetry to the antiques of the east. Here you'll also find most of Singapore's international hotels, many nightspots, and a host of restaurants, bars and lounges. It's is a showcase for modern Singapore and the delights of capitalism, but it also has a few points of cultural interest where you don't need a credit card.

Peranakan Place

Among the glass and chrome is Peranakan Place, a complex of old Baba-Nyonya shophouses on the corner of Orchard and Emerald Hill roads.

Peranakan culture is that of the Straits-born Chinese who spoke a Malay dialect and developed their own customs which are a fascinating hybrid of Chinese and Malay. 'Nyonya' is the word for an adult Peranakan woman, 'Baba' her male counterpart. The **Peranakan Showhouse Museum** is one shophouse decorated with Peranakan artefacts, furniture and clothing. If traditional Straits Chinese culture interests you, don't miss this one. The museum is in a terrace house a few doors back from Orchard Rd. Interesting tours are available on demand and cost S$4 for adults and S$2 for children. The museum is open Monday to Friday from 10.30 am to 12.30 pm and 2 to 3.30 pm.

From Peranakan Place wander north up Emerald Hill Rd, where some fine terrace houses remain. This whole area was once a nutmeg plantation owned by William Cuppage, an early Singapore settler. Around 1900, much of it was subdivided, and it became a fashionable residential area for Peranakan and Straits-born Chinese merchants. Today it is a fashionable drinking spot with some good bars.

Peranakan Place is just north of the Somerset MRT station. See the boxed text 'The Peranakans' in the Singapore Facts for the Visitor chapter for details of these people.

Istana

The Istana is the home of Singapore's president and is also used by the prime minister for ceremonial occasions. Formerly Government House, the Istana is set about 750m back from the road in large grounds. The closest you are likely to get to it are the well-guarded gates on Orchard Rd, but the Istana is open to the public on selected public holidays, such as New Year's Day. If you are lucky enough to be in Singapore on one of these days, take your passport for identification and join the queues to get in.

House of Tan Yeok Nee

On the corner of Clemenceau Ave and Penang Rd, near Orchard Rd, the House of Tan Yeok Nee was built in 1885 as a townhouse for a prosperous merchant in a style then common in the south of China. This national monument was the Salvation Army headquarters for many years, but has recently changed hands and is now closed to the public.

Chettiar Hindu Temple

On Tank Rd at the intersection of River Valley Rd, not far from Orchard Rd, this temple was completed in 1984 and replaces a much earlier temple built by Indian *chettiars*, or money lenders. It is a Shivaite temple dedicated to the six headed Lord Subramaniam, and is at its most active during the Thaipusam festival, when the procession ends here. Worshippers make offerings of coconuts, which are smashed on the ground to crack them open.

JURONG

Jurong Town, west of the city centre, is more than just a new housing area. A huge industrial complex has been built on land that was still a swamp at the end of WWII. Today, it is the powerhouse of Singapore's economic success story. The Jurong area also has a number of tourist attractions, in Jurong Town itself and on the way to Jurong from the city centre.

Haw Par Villa

About 10km west of the city centre on Pasir Panjang Rd, this is a Chinese mythological theme park which features theatre performances, boat rides, and an exotic collection of concrete and plaster figures that made the original Tiger Balm Gardens so famous. The hillside park, previously known as Tiger Balm Gardens, was built with the fortune the Aw brothers made from their miracle cure-all Tiger Balm, and featured a gaudy grotesquerie of statues illustrating scenes from Chinese legends and the pleasures and punishments of this life and the next.

Renovations and high-tech additions have changed the face of this long-popular monument to bad taste, but the surviving statuary remains its major attraction. Favourite displays include the Ten Courts of Hell, where sinners get their gory comeuppance in the afterlife, and the 'moral lessons' aisle, where sloth, indulgence, gambling, and even wine, women and song lead to their inevitable unhappy endings.

New additions include a heart-in-the-mouth roller-coaster boat ride and theatres where the inevitable 'multimedia' displays narrate Chinese myths and legends. The large, covered amphitheatre has live performances which are popular with children, and new schedules advertise daily performances, such as lion dances and performers on stilts.

Haw Par Villa is popular with local families – it's fun for the kids, teaches them Chinese mythology and the moral tales scare the heck out of them if they misbehave. Entry costs S$5 for adults and S$2.50 for children.

Haw Par Villa is open from 9 am to 6 pm daily. To get there, take the MRT to the Buona Vista station, from where bus No 200 goes to Haw Par Villa; or from the Clementi station take bus No 10.

Jurong Bird Park

This beautifully landscaped 20 hectare park has over 8000 birds representing 600 species and includes a two hectare walk-in aviary with an artificial waterfall at one end. Exhibits include everything from cassowaries, birds of paradise, eagles and cockatoos to parrots, macaws and even penguins in an air-conditioned underwater viewing gallery. The nocturnal house includes owls, kiwis and frogmouths. The South-East Asian Birds Aviary is a major attraction and features a simulated rainforest thunderstorm every day at noon. The park also has one of the world's largest collections of hornbills, as well as a new walk-through parrot aviary.

A number of other shows are held throughout the day, including the World of Hawks at 10 am, Hornbill Chit Chat at 11.45 am, the Wonderful World of Birds at noon, 1 and 2 pm, and King of the Skies at 4 pm. Breakfast with the Birds is the park's answer to bird-singing contests, and the S$12.50 buffet breakfast from 9 to 11 am is a pleasant way to start the day.

You can walk around the park or take the Panorail service – an air-con monorail that tours the park, stopping at the Waterfall Aviary. The Panorail costs S$2.50 for adults, S$1 for children.

Admission to the park is S$10.30 for adults and S$4.12 for children. The park is open from 9 am to 6 pm Monday to Friday, and from 8 am to 6 pm on weekends and public holidays. To get there, take the MRT to the Boon Lay station and then special loop bus No 194 or the more frequent No 251. The bird park is on Jalan Ahmad Ibrahim. You can climb Jurong Hill, beside the park, from where there is a good view over Jurong.

Jurong Reptile Park

Formerly known as Jurong Crocodile Paradise, this theme park has been re-created and now boasts a scaly collection of other reptiles and amphibians such as Komodo Dragons and giant tortoises.

Right next to Jurong Bird Park, this is the largest of the crocodile parks with the best set-up for tourists. Although the emphasis is less on crocs than before, there are still plenty of these fierce creatures to be seen. Crocodile wrestling and feeding are two of the supposed highlights. It is open from 9 am to 6 pm daily, and costs S$7 for adults and S$3.50 for children. It is easily combined with a trip to Jurong Bird Park.

Chinese & Japanese Gardens

Off Yuan Ching Rd, the Chinese and Japanese gardens adjoining Jurong Bird Park each cover 13.5 hectares. The Chinese Garden, which occupies an island on Jurong Lake, is colourful and has a number of Chinese-style pavilions. The main attraction is the large *penjing* (Chinese bonsai) display. Linked by a bridge, the less interesting Japanese Garden has large grassed areas and a few buildings. Garden lovers will find Singapore's Botanic Gardens of more interest, but the Chinese Garden is very pleasant and a must for bonsai enthusiasts.

The gardens are open from 9 am to 7 pm Monday to Saturday and from 8.30 am to 7 pm on Sunday and public holidays. Admission to both gardens is S$4.50 for adults and S$2 for children. The Chinese Garden MRT station is right by Jurong Lake and a five minute walk away from the Chinese Garden.

Singapore Science Centre

On Science Centre Rd, off Jurong Town Hall Rd, the Science Centre is great fun. It attempts to make science come alive by providing countless opportunities to try things out for yourself. There are handles to crank, buttons to push, levers to pull, microscopes to look through and films to watch. The centre is primarily designed to encourage an interest in science among Singapore's school children, but it is amazing how many adults compete with the kids to have a go on the hands-on exhibits. The centre is open from 10 am to 6 pm Tuesday to Sunday, and admission is S$3 (children S$1.50).

One of the main attractions is the Omni Theatre, next to the main science centre building, with 3D whiz-bang IMAX format movies covering topics from space flights to journeys inside the atom. Entry is S$10. There's also a planetarium here.

The easiest way to get there is to take the MRT to the Jurong East station and then walk 500m west or take bus No 66 or 335 from the station.

Changi airport also has a free mini science centre in Terminal 2.

Tang Dynasty City

This multimillion-dollar theme park is a recreation of old Chang'an (modern-day Xian), the Tang Dynasty capital, which was the centre of China's golden age from the 6th to

8th centuries AD. Behind the massive 10m-high walls, Tang Dynasty City's main street features a courthouse, geisha house and shops, and there are temples, restaurants and theatres, all built in Chinese style and attempting to re-create the period. 'Silk Road' camel rides, craft demonstrations, performances and antique displays, such as a jade suit and the reproduction of the life-size Xian terracotta army, are all part of the experience.

Like most theme parks it is just a little artificial, but the size and style of the buildings are impressive and Tang Dynasty City makes an interesting diversion. The park also has shops selling tea, wine and antiques, a wax museum with a talking Mao and other notables from Chinese history, and kungfu and other street performers.

Tang Dynasty City is open daily from 9.30 am to 6.30 pm. Admission is S$15.45 (S$10.30 for children). Buffet lunch shows, featuring acrobatic troupes from China, are also held.

Tang Dynasty City is on the corner of Yuan Ching Rd and Jalan Ahmad Ibrahim, near the Chinese and Japanese gardens. Take the MRT to the Lakeside station and then bus No 154 or 240, or it is a 2km taxi ride from the station.

New Ming Village & Pewter Museum

This pottery workshop at 32 Pandan Rd produces reproduction porcelain from the Ming and Qing dynasties. You can see the artisans create their pottery and, of course, you can buy their works. It is open daily from 8.30 am to 5.30 pm. Admission is free. The complete production process is done on the premises and guided tours are available on demand for groups.

Ming Village is owned by Royal Selangor Pewter. Consequently the village also has a small pewter museum with some interesting pieces, and the showroom sells an extensive selection of pewter as well as pottery. Although the pewter is made in Malaysia, the polishing and hand-beaten designs are demonstrated at the village.

To get there, take the MRT to Clementi and then bus No 78 to Pandan Rd.

Singapore Mint Coin Gallery

This gallery, at Singapore's mint on Jalan Boon Lay just east of the Boon Lay MRT station, exhibits coins and medals from Singapore and a few coins from around the world. This place is essentially an outlet for the gold medallions that the mint sells, but a few mint sets of Singapore coins are also for sale. Only dedicated coin enthusiasts would want to make the trip out here. It is open Monday to Friday from 9 am to 4.30 pm. Admission is free.

EAST COAST & CHANGI

East Coast Park is a popular recreational haunt for Singaporeans. It is the place to swim, windsurf, lie on the sand, rent a bike or, of course, eat. The stretch of beach along the east coast, south of the East Coast Parkway expressway, was born of reclaimed land and won't win any awards as a tropical paradise, but it is by far Singapore's most popular beach and has good recreational facilities.

Further inland are the interesting areas of Geylang and Katong, largely Malay districts, which are rarely visited by foreign tourists. Geylang is as close to a 'Little Malaysia' as you'll find; and Katong, centred on East Coast Rd, has Peranakan influences and interesting dining possibilities.

Changi is known for its renowned airport and infamous prison, both attractions in their own right, while further out is Changi Village and its nearby beach.

Geylang

If you want to experience Malaysia, the real thing is just across the Causeway. However, there are Malay areas in Singapore, though Malay culture is not so obvious nor easily marketed as a tourist attraction.

Geylang Serai is a Malay residential area, though you are not going to see traditional *atap* (thatch-roofed) houses and sarung-clad cottage industry workers. The area has plenty of newer high-rise buildings, though there are some older buildings around, especially in the *lorong* (alleys) that run off Geylang Rd. The lorongs house one of Singapore's most active red-light districts.

Geylang Serai is easily reached by taking the MRT to the Paya Lebar station. From here it is a short walk down Tanjong Katong Rd to Geylang Rd, the main shopping street.

A short walk east along Geylang Rd will bring you to the **Malay Cultural Village**. This complex of traditional Malay-style houses was built as a showpiece of Malay culture, though it hasn't really taken off as a tourist attraction. On weekends it attracts Singaporean families desperately seeking *kampung* (village) nostalgia, but is very quiet during the week. Admission is free to wander around the craft shops and bird market or to eat at the satay stalls and restaurants. For S$10 (children S$7), you can visit the Kampung Days museum and the Legenda Fantasi show. The museum has kampung buildings with waxworks figures, a few artefacts, and interesting videos on Malay weddings, games and kampung life. The Legenda Fantasi is a good, whiz-bang show for the kids with laser effects and a booming sound system telling Ali Baba stories with a Singaporean slant. The best time to go is on the weekend when free dance performances are held from 7 to 9 pm.

Just next door to the cultural centre is the **Geylang Serai Market**. It's hidden behind some older-style housing blocks on Geylang Rd, and entrance is through a small laneway that leads to a crowded, traditional Asian market that hasn't yet been rebuilt as a concrete box. It is a good place to browse and much more interesting than most of Singapore's new markets. It reaches its peak of activity during Ramadan, when the whole area is alive with market stalls that set up in the evenings to cater for the faithful after their long day of fasting.

SINGAPORE

Katong

From the Geylang Serai Market you can head down Joo Chiat Rd to the East Coast Rd and explore the Katong district. **Joo Chiat Rd** has a host of local businesses operating during the day, and at night the restaurants and music lounges are popular. Despite some restoration, the streetscape has largely escaped the developer; some fine Peranakan-style terraces and some of the atmosphere of old Singapore remain.

Stop in at Amoy Tea at 331 Joo Chiat Rd, a traditional shop selling a variety of Chinese tea and some superbly crafted tea sets. Nearby are some antique shops, such as Dragon Arts & Crafts at No 341. Guan Hoe Soon at No 214 has Peranakan/Chinese food and Casa Bom Vento at No 467 is an interesting Eurasian restaurant.

On Koon Seng Rd, just west around the corner from Joo Chiat Rd, are some of the finest **terrace houses** in Singapore. They exhibit the typical Peranakan love of ornate design and are decorated with plaster stucco dragons, birds, crabs and brilliantly glazed tiles. *Pintu pagar* (saloon doors) at the front of the house are another typical feature which let in the breeze while retaining privacy.

Further south, Joo Chiat Rd runs into **East Coast Rd**, a well-to-do, 'village' shopping stretch that is the centre of Katong. Before land reclamation moved the beach, Katong was a quiet village by the sea. Now East Coast Rd bustles with city traffic and Singapore's modern developments have engulfed the east coast. Despite this, Katong still retains its delightful village atmosphere. East Coast Rd is noted for its Peranakan influence, mostly because of the opportunity to sample Peranakan food and view the fascinating collection of Peranakan antiques at the Katong Antique House at No 208. The intricately hand-embroidered Nyonya slippers are hard to resist, though opening hours are haphazard. Also on the itinerary is a visit to Katong Bakery & Confectionery, at No 75. Nyonya cakes and pastries are served in this relic from pre-war Singapore.

It is also worth wandering the back-streets of Katong around Joo Chiat and East Coast roads where you'll find more terraces, coffee shops and temples. Just off East Coast Rd in Ceylon Rd is the **Hindu Senpaga Vinayagar Temple**, and about a kilometre away in Wilkinson St is a Sikh temple, **Sri Guru Nanak Sat Sangh Sabha**.

East Coast Rd changes its name to Mountbatten Rd as it heads into the city and crosses Tanjong Katong Rd, which leads back to

Geylang and the Paya Lebar MRT station. This area contains a number of grand old villas, such as the **Villa Dolce** at 164 Tanjong Katong Rd. Mountbatten Rd also has some fine old houses.

Parkway Parade is a huge shopping centre on Marine Parade near the end of Joo Chiat Rd. The East Coast Park and seaside is just behind it, but you have to cross the East Coast Parkway expressway – take a taxi.

From East Coast Rd, bus Nos 12 and 32 head into the city along North Bridge Rd in the colonial district, while bus No 14 goes down Stamford Rd and then Orchard Rd. Coming from the city, bus No 16 can be boarded in Orchard and Bras Basah roads, and goes along Joo Chiat Rd, crossing East Coast Rd.

East Coast Park

Stretching along Singapore's east coast on reclaimed land, East Coast Park comes alive on the weekends with Singaporeans relaxing by the beach, eating at seafood outlets or indulging in more strenuous sporting activities. The foreshore parkland has a track running right along the coast for bicycling, jogging or rollerblading, and you can hire bicycles, canoes and sailboards. The beach is reasonable, with a continuous sandy stretch and calm waters, though like all of Singapore's beaches the water is hardly crystal clear.

The **Singapore Crocodilarium** is at 730 East Coast Parkway and has a large number of crocodiles crammed into concrete tanks. It's open daily from 9 am to 5 pm, and admission costs S$2 for adults and $1 for children.

Big Splash, 902 East Coast Parkway, is a water fun park with swimming pools and a huge water slide. It has been superseded by Fantasy Island at Sentosa and is currently closed undergoing works.

The **East Coast Recreation Centre** is the big place in East Coast Park, with bowling, squash, mini golf, fun rides, a selection of restaurants and food stalls, and canoe and bicycle hire. Racers (S$3 per hour), mountain bikes (S$4 per hour) and tandems (S$6 per hour) can be hired.

A kilometre further away from the city is the **East Coast Lagoon**, noted for its seafood. The UDMC Seafood Centre has a number of restaurants. Also here is the East Coast Sailing Centre (☎ 449 5118), a private club which rents sailboards to the public for S$20 for the first two hours and S$10 for each subsequent hour. Bicycles and canoes can also be hired at the kiosk near the food centre.

The only bus to East Coast Park is No 401, operating from the Bedok MRT station along the service road in the park on Sunday and public holidays. All other buses whiz by on the East Coast Parkway expressway, so you'll have to catch a taxi (S$8 to S$10 depending on where you are coming from in central Singapore).

Changi Prison Museum

Changi is still used as a prison, but next to the main gate is a museum with a bookshop and a poignant replica of the simple thatched prison chapel built and used by Allied prisoners of war during their horrific internment at the hands of the Japanese during WWII. Pinned to the chapel are notes from those who lost loved ones in Changi. The small museum features drawings made by the prisoners depicting life in Changi, as well as photographs and other exhibits providing an overview of the war in Asia. The museum is open Monday to Saturday from 9.30 am to 4.30 pm, though you can visit the chapel outside these hours. A service is held at the chapel on Sunday from 5.30 to 6.30 pm.

Changi Prison is on Upper Changi Rd near the airport and can be reached by bus No 2 from Victoria St in the colonial district.

Changi Village

The village of Changi, on the east coast of Singapore, is an escape from the hubbub of central Singapore. Don't expect to find traditional kampung houses – the buildings are modern – but Changi does have a village atmosphere. Changi's beach is not exactly a tropical paradise, but it has a good stretch of sand and offers safe swimming. It's popular on weekends but almost deserted during the week. The food in Changi is an attraction, and there are some good seafood restaurants and food stalls near the beach.

From Changi, you can catch ferries to Pulau Ubin (see the Other Islands section later in this chapter). Ferries also go to Pengerang across the strait in Malaysia (see the Singapore Getting There & Away chapter).

You can reach Changi on bus No 2 from Victoria St in the colonial district; it also passes Changi Prison.

SENTOSA ISLAND

Sentosa Island, just off the south coast of Singapore, is the grand-daddy of all Singapore's fun parks. It is Singapore's most popular attraction, especially popular with locals who flock here on weekends. A host of activities are spread around this landscaped island, and while, like its beaches of imported sand, it is a synthetic attraction, Sentosa is a good place for children and there is enough to keep adults occupied. Sentosa has museums, aquariums, beaches, sporting facilities, walks, rides and food centres. It is easy to spend a day at Sentosa but if that isn't enough there's a campground, a hostel and two luxury hotels.

Sentosa is open daily from 7.30 am until around 11 pm, an hour or so later on weekends. Many of the attractions close at 7 pm but cultural shows, plays and bands are sometimes held in the evening – check with the tourist office (☎ 1-800-738 3778) or the Sentosa Information Office (☎ 275 0388).

Basic admission to Sentosa is S$5 for adults (S$3 after 6.30 pm) and S$3 for children under 12. This covers entry and transport on the monorail and buses around Sentosa. Most attractions cost extra, and can really add up if you want to see them all.

The free bus service runs around the island roads with departures every 10 minutes. The free monorail loop service is the most scenic but slowest way to get around the island. You can get around Sentosa by bicycle – rent a bike from the hire kiosk by the ferry terminal, and it's very easy to find your way around.

Underwater World

This spectacular aquarium is one of Sentosa's most popular attractions. Displays include the turtle pool, moray eel enclosure, reef enclosures with live coral, a theatre showing continuous films, and a touch pool where visitors are invited to dip their digits into the pool and fondle the sealife. These exhibits are just mere entrées to Underwater World's 'travellator', an acrylic tunnel that takes spectators through the main tanks while all manner of fish swim around you in all their natural technicolour glory. There is nothing quite like the sight of a huge manta ray, 60kg grouper, or shark swimming up to you and then passing overhead.

The latest addition to this nautical menagerie, in the words of the aquarium's own publicity blurb, is the 'gigantic, ugly and slimy' exhibit of creatures of the deep featuring a giant octopus, the 'ugly' wolf eel and the giant spider crab.

Underwater World is open daily from 9 am to 9 pm, and costs S$12 for adults and S$6 for children.

Images of Singapore

The Pioneers of Singapore waxwork museum relives history and re-creates life as it was in old Singapore. It gives an excellent account of Singapore's past and focuses on the traditional cultures of the country's main communities. The adjoining Surrender Chamber exhibit traces the history of Singapore's occupation during WWII up to the formal surrender by the Japanese forces in 1945. These days it is surprisingly popular with Japanese tour groups.

A new addition is Festivals of Singapore, which has wax dummy exhibits and explanations of Singapore's many festivals.

Admission is S$5 for adults and S$3 for children. It is open daily from 9 am to 9 pm.

Fort Siloso

Once used as a military base, the gun emplacements and underground tunnels of Fort Siloso, which date from the late 19th century, can be explored. The guns were all pointing in the wrong direction when the Japanese invaded in WWII and the island was then used by the victorious Japanese as a prisoner of war camp.

From 1989 until 1993, Fort Siloso housed Sentosa's most unusual attraction, political prisoner Chia Thye Poh. Chia, arrested in 1966 under the Internal Security Act for allegedly being a Communist, served 23 years in jail before being banished to complete his bizarre sentence among the holiday delights of Sentosa Island.

A guided walk leads around the gun emplacements, tunnels and buildings, with waxwork recreations of life in a colonial barracks. A mini sound-and-light show relives the period immediately before the Japanese invasion, and a 'Behind Bars' exhibit focuses on prison life for the POWs under the Japanese. It is a pleasant walk with good views and, though not wildly exciting, it is one of Sentosa's more interesting attractions for the money.

Fort Siloso is open daily from 9 am to 7 pm, and costs S$3 for adults and S$2 for children.

Fantasy Island

This is a huge water theme park with swimming pools, 13 different water rides and 32 slides. Rides range from 'river rafting' to the more terrifying Gang of Four, Blackhole and Kyag slides. The park also has an Entertainment Mall with electronic games at the entrance.

It's great for the kids, and bad for the wallet. Entrance costs S$12 (children S$6), lockers are S$1, and floats are S$3 and S$4. Fantasy Island is open Monday to Friday from 10 am to 7 pm, from 10 am on weekends and public holidays.

Volcanoland

Based on a Mayan city and dominated by a giant, concrete volcano, Volcanoland is Sentosa's tackiest attraction. Singaporean 'Mayan' Indians put on dances and drape snakes around tourist necks for photos. The show inside the volcano is held every half hour and takes you through an explorer's tunnel and mock mine-elevator trip to a theatre, where even the booming sound effects cannot enliven the dull movie on the evolution of life. The eruption finale is a fizzer and when the exit doors open to reveal the gift shop it is almost a relief. Save your S$10. The volcano 'erupts' every half hour with a bang and a puff of smoke which you can see from outside.

Butterfly Park & Insect Kingdom Museum

At the Butterfly Park, you can walk among live butterflies of over 50 species. In the museum there are thousands of mounted butterfly specimens, rhino beetles, *Dynastes hercules* (the world's largest beetles) and scorpions, among other insects. The walk through the butterfly house is the highlight.

It is open from 9 am to 6 pm Monday to Friday, and until 6.30 pm weekends and public holidays. Entry costs S$5 for adults and S$3 for children.

Asian Village

This collection of craft shops and food outlets reflects Asia's various cultures: Japan, China, India, Thailand, Philippines, Malaysia and Indonesia. The crafts range from cheap kitsch to reasonably good, and the food is pretty reasonable. The theme park buildings are vaguely styled after traditional houses, and the entertainment park rides are popular. Entry is free, though the rides cost extra. It is open daily from 10 am to 9 pm.

Other Attractions

The **Maritime Museum** (open from 10 am to 7 pm; adults S$2, children $S0.50) has exhibits recording the history of Singapore's port and shipping, as well as fishing tools and primitive crafts. **Sentosa Orchid Gardens** (open from 9.30 am to 6.30 pm; adults S$2, children S$1) is an orchid garden with a Japanese theme.

Of the free attractions on Sentosa Island, the **Nature Walk** is in a relatively natural environment, except for the Dragon Trail section, which has dragons and fossils to liven it up. Long-tailed macaques are common, but be sure to hide your food from these aggressive monkeys. You can also wander around the impressive ferry terminal, Fountain Gardens and Flower Terrace.

At night, the **Musical Fountain** spurts water to music and flashing, coloured lights, while the **Pasar Malam** (Night Market) stalls sell souvenirs. Nearby is the **Rasa Sentosa Food Centre** – naturally Sentosa has a hawker centre – and the ferry terminal also has some dining possibilities.

Other attractions are an adventure golf theme park and the Merlion Tower, a huge Merlion with good views from the top.

Beaches & Recreational Facilities

Sentosa's southern coastline is devoted to beaches: **Siloso Beach** at the western end, **Central Beach** and **Tanjong Beach** at the eastern end. As a tropical paradise, Sentosa has a long way to go to match the islands of Malaysia or Indonesia, but in a case of 'if Mohammed won't come to the mountain' Singapore has imported its beaches from Indonesia and planted coconut palms to give it a tropical ambience. The imported sand does make for a good beach, probably Singapore's best.

The beaches have shelters and four rest stations, with kiosks, changing facilities, deck chairs and umbrellas. Pedal cats, aquabikes, fun bugs, canoes and surf boards are all available for hire.

Sentosa has a 5.7km bicycle track that loops the island and takes in most of the attractions. Bicycles can be hired at bicycle stations on the track, such as the kiosk at Siloso Beach or at the ferry terminal, and cost from S$2 to S$5 per hour.

There is also a roller-skating rink, which costs S$2 entry. There are two 18 hole golf courses: Serapong, for members only; and Tanjong, which is open to the public and costs S$80 for a round on Monday to Friday or S$120 on weekends.

Getting There & Away

Take Sentosa Bus Service (SBS) bus No 65 or 143 from Orchard Rd, or No 61, 84, 143, 145 or 166 from Chinatown to the World Trade Centre (WTC). Tourist buses, such as the Singapore Trolley, also run to the WTC. From the bus station across from the WTC, take Sentosa Bus Service A. Alternatively, take the MRT to the Tiong Bahru station and then Sentosa Bus Service C or M. Services A and C run from around 7 am to 11.30 pm; service M from 4 to 11 pm, and on weekends and holidays from 8 am to 11 pm. The cost for any of these buses is S$6 (children S$4), including admission to Sentosa.

From Orchard and Bras Basah roads, Service E runs all the way to Sentosa every 10 or 15 minutes from 10 am to 11.15 pm. The last bus returns from Sentosa at 8.30 pm. The bus costs S$7 (children S$5), including admission.

The other alternatives are to take the ferry from the WTC or the cable car.

The ferry used to be the main access to the island before the bridge was built. It is still one of the most pleasant ways to reach Sentosa and costs S$0.80 one way, S$1.30 return. Ferries operate from 9.30 am to 9 pm.

The cable car leaves from the top of Mt Faber from 8.30 am to 9 pm, or you can board it at the WTC. The fare is S$5.50 (children S$3), and you can buy tickets for separate stages. The cable-car ride, with its spectacular views, is one of the best parts of a visit to Sentosa. Take the ferry across and then the cable car back to Mt Faber – it is easier walking down Mt Faber than up.

OTHER ISLANDS

Singapore's other islands include Kusu and St John's, Pulau Sakeng, the Sisters' Islands (all south of Singapore), and islands that accommodate the refineries that provide much of Singapore's export income. Others, such as Salu, Senang, Rawai and Sudong, are live firing ranges. However, there are a few off-the-beaten-track islands where you can find a quiet beach. Pulau Sakeng has a village and many inhabitants work at nearby Pulau Bukum, where the Shell refinery is located. Further south are many more islands, such as the scattered Indonesian islands of the Riau Archipelago. There are also other islands to the north-east between Singapore and Malaysia.

You don't have to leave the island of Singapore to find beaches and indulge in water sports. Although the construction of Changi international airport destroyed one of Singapore's favourite stretches of beach, there is still the East Coast Park on the East Coast Parkway.

Scuba diving enthusiasts will find coral reefs at Sisters' Islands and Pulau Semakau. Pulau Hantu is also popular. Other islands include Pulau Sakijang Pelepah (Lazarus Island), Buran Darat, Terumbu Retan Laut and Pulau Renggit.

To reach these islands, you must rent a motorised bumboat from Clifford Pier or Jardine Steps at the WTC. Expect to pay around S$50 per hour. The boats will take six to 12 people. You can ask individual boat owners or contact the Singapore Motor Launch Owners' Association on the 2nd floor at Clifford Pier, just east of the Raffles Place MRT station.

St John's & Kusu Islands

Although Sentosa is Singapore's best known island, there are two others which are also popular with locals as a city escape. On weekends, they can become rather crowded, but during the week you'll find St John's and Kusu fairly quiet and good places for a peaceful swim. Both islands have changing rooms, toilet facilities, grassy picnic spots and swimming areas.

St John's is much bigger than Kusu and has better beaches for swimming, though Kusu is the more interesting. Kusu has a Chinese temple, the Tua Pek Kong Temple near the ferry jetty, and a Malay shrine *(kramat)* up a steep flight of steps to the top of a hill at the south-eastern end of the island. Kramat Kusu is dedicated to Sahed Abdul Rahman, his mother Nanek Ghalib and his sister Puteri Fatimah. Though kramat worship is frowned upon by the Islamic clergy, this is Singapore's most popular shrine, especially for childless couples who pray for children, as evidenced by the pieces of cloth tied around trees on the way up to the shrine. Kusu is the site of an important annual pilgrimage, honoured by Taoists.

Ferry Schedule to Kusu & St John's Island

Monday to Saturday

Depart from

WTC	*Kusu*	*St John's*	*Kusu*
10.00 am	10.45 am	11.15 am	11.45 am
1.30 pm	2.15 pm	2.45 pm	3.15 pm
	(Last ferry)		(Last ferry)

Sunday & Public Holiday

Depart from

WTC	*Kusu*	*St John's*
9.45 am	10.20 am	10.35 am
11.15 am	11.50 am	12.05 pm
12.45 pm	1.20 pm	1.35 pm
2.15 pm	2.50 pm	3.05 pm
3.45 pm	4.20 pm	4.35 pm
5.15 pm	5.50 pm	6.05 pm
(Last ferry)	(Last ferry)	(Last ferry)

Most of the harbour tours pass St John's and stop at Kusu for 20 minutes or so (see Organised Tours in the Getting Around chapter). You can walk around Kusu in 20 minutes.

To get to these islands, take a ferry from the WTC. It costs S$6.20 (children S$3.10) for the round trip and takes 30 minutes to reach Kusu. The ferry then continues on to St John's.

Northern Islands

The easiest northern island to visit is Pulau Ubin, which makes a pleasant day trip and is reached by boat from Changi Village. Pulau Tekong, Singapore's largest island, tends to be forgotten because it is often cut off the eastern edge of Singapore maps (including the one in this book). It's now off limits since the military took it over in the early 1990s.

Pulau Ubin From Changi Village, you can wander down to the ferry jetty and wait for a bumboat to take you across to Pulau Ubin. You can tell that this is a different side of Singapore where everything is scheduled to the nano-second; here you wait for the ferry to fill up – they go when a quota of 12 people is reached and there is no fixed schedule. Pulau Ubin has quiet beaches, a kampung atmosphere and popular seafood restaurants. This rural island is as unlike 'Singapore' as you will find. It is also a natural haven for many species of birds that inhabit the mangroves and forest areas.

The best way to explore the island is by bicycle, which can be hired for S$8 to S$15 per day near the jetty. If you ask the bicycle hire operator you may get a hand drawn map, though the island is small enough to explore without getting lost, and there are map boards dotted at strategic locations. Not all of the island is open to the public, so watch where you go.

You can visit a spectacular disused quarry with granite walls. There are also a number of temples, including a Thai Buddhist temple and another reached via the beach only at low tide. It is a peaceful rural scene of fish farms, coconut palms and a few houses. The island's most popular seafood restaurant is the Ubin First Stop Restaurant.

The old bumboat ferries to Pulau Ubin cost S$1.50 one way and run daily between 6 am and 10 pm, but you may be in for a wait if there are no other passengers – often the case during the week.

NORTHERN & CENTRAL SINGAPORE

Singapore has been dubbed the 'Garden City' and with good reason; it's green and lush, with parks and gardens scattered everywhere. In part, this fertility is a factor of the climate; you only have to stick a twig in the ground for it to become a tree in weeks. The government has backed up this natural advantage with a concentrated programme that has even turned the dividing strip on highways into flourishing gardens – you'll notice it as you drive into Singapore from Malaysia on the Causeway.

Despite the never-ending construction, land reclamation and burgeoning Housing & Development Board (HDB) estates, Singapore has large areas of parkland and even natural forest. These areas are mostly found to the north of the city in the centre of Singapore Island.

Botanic Gardens

Singapore's 127-year-old Botanic Gardens are on the corner of Cluny and Holland roads, not far from Orchard Rd. They are a popular and peaceful retreat for Singaporeans.

The Botanic Gardens contain an enormous number of plant species, in both a manicured garden setting and in four hectares of primary jungle. The gardens also house the **herbarium**, where much work has been done on breeding the orchids for which Singapore is famous. The **orchid enclosure** contains over 12,000 orchids representing 2000 species and hybrids in total. In an earlier era, Henry Ridley, director of the gardens, successfully propagated rubber tree seeds sent from Kew Gardens in 1877, after they were smuggled out of Brazil. Consequently, the Singapore Botanic Gardens pioneered the Malayan rubber boom.

The 54 hectare gardens are open daily from 5 am to midnight; admission is free. Early in the morning, you'll see hundreds of Singaporeans jogging here.

Within the Botanic Gardens is the **National Orchid Garden**, with the world's largest display of orchids featuring over 60,000 orchid plants. It will cost you S$2 to get in and it is open from 8.30 am to 6 pm.

The gardens can be reached on bus No 7 or 174, which run along Stamford Rd and Orchard Blvd. Bus No 106 runs along Bencoolen St and Orchard Blvd to the gardens.

Sunday Morning Bird Singing

One of the nicest things to do on a Sunday morning in Singapore is to go and hear the birds sing. The Chinese love caged birds, as their beautifully ornate birdcages indicate. The birds – thrushes, *merboks*, *sharmas* and *mata putehs* – are treasured for their singing ability. To ensure the quality of their song, the doting owner will feed the bird a carefully prepared diet, and once a week crowds of bird fanciers get together for a bird song session.

The birdcages are hung up on wires strung between trees or under verandas. They're not mixed indiscriminately – sharmas sing with sharmas, merboks with merboks – and each type of bird has its own design of cage. Tall and pointy ones for tall pointy birds, short and squat ones for short squat birds.

Having assembled the birds, the proud owners then congregate around tables, sip coffee and listen to their birds go through their paces. It's a delightful scene both musically and visually.

The main bird-concert venue is at the junction of Tiong Bahru and Seng Poh roads, only a few hundred metres from the Havelock Rd hotel enclave, on Sunday morning from around 8 to 11 am. Its coffee shop is always well patronised on concert days.

To get there take the MRT to the Tiong Bahru station, then walk east 500m. By bus, take No 123 from Orchard Rd.

Zoological Gardens

In the north of the island at 80 Mandai Lake Rd, Singapore's world class zoo has over 2000 animals, representing 240 species, on display in almost natural conditions. Wherever possible, moats replace bars, and the zoo is spread out over 90 hectares of lush greenery. Exhibits of particular interest are the pygmy hippos, Primate Kingdom, Wild Africa and Children's World. As well as providing a play area, Children's World includes a domesticated animals section where children can touch the animals, see Friesian cow milking demonstrations and sheep dogs in action at the sheep roundup show.

There is a breakfast programme at 9 am and high tea at 4 pm, where you are joined by one of the orang-utans. However, you will be hit for an extra S$13 (S$10.30 for children) for the privilege.

There are also elephant rides and work performances. At most times of the day, you have a good chance of seeing one of the animal performances or a practice session in the zoo's outdoor theatre. Primates & Reptiles shows are held at 10.30 am and 2.30 pm; Elephants & Sealions at 11.30 am and 3.30 pm.

The Komodo dragons are another popular attraction and you can see their feeding frenzy on Sunday afternoon, though in fact they are not all that ferocious.

The zoo is open daily from 8.30 am to 6 pm. Admission is S$10.30 (children S$4.60). There is a zoo tram which runs from the main gate and costs S$2.50 for adults and S$1.50 for children.

To get to the zoo, take the MRT to the Ang Mo Kio station, and then bus No 138.

Night Safari Not content with having an excellent zoo, Singapore also opened the impressive Night Safari, on a 40 hectare site next to the zoo in secondary forest. Open nightly from 7.30 pm to midnight, walking trails criss-cross the park and allow a unique opportunity to view nocturnal animals. The park is divided into a number of habitats, focusing mostly on Asian wildlife, and special lighting picks out the animals. With 1000 animals representing 100 species, the Night Safari is not as diverse as the zoo, but wandering the trails at night is a recommended experience.

There is also a tram, including a commentary, which loops through the park and stops near the East Lodge restaurant at the far side of the park. Noisy, camera flashing passengers can spoil the ride, despite being exhorted to keep quiet and avoid flash photography. The western side of the park is only accessible by tram. To explore all of the park, it is best to do a complete loop and then walk around the trails. The complete East Loop walking trail is 2.8km in length and will take you about an hour.

The Night Safari costs S$15.45 or S$10.30 for children under 12 years. The tram ride costs an extra S$4 (children S$3). The entrance is directly opposite the zoo entrance, a few hundred metres away. Transport details for the Night Safari are the same as for the zoo.

Mandai Orchid Gardens

Singapore has a major business in cultivating orchids and the Mandai Orchid Gardens, beside the zoo on Mandai Lake Rd, is the best place to see them – four solid hectares of orchids! The gardens are open daily from 8.30 am to 5.30 pm, and admission is S$2 for adults, S$0.50 for children.

Bukit Timah Nature Reserve

Singapore is not normally associated with nature walks and jungle treks, but they can be enjoyed at this 81 hectare nature reserve. It is the only large area of primary forest left in Singapore and is a haven for Singapore's wildlife. On Upper Bukit Timah Rd, 12km from the city, the reserve also boasts the highest point in Singapore, 162m Bukit Timah.

The reserve is run by the National Parks Board, and at the entrance to the reserve is an exhibition hall with interesting displays on Singapore's natural history. Adjoining the hall are changing rooms and showers. The other national parks run by the board are the much more urban Fort Canning Park and Singapore Botanic Gardens.

Of the walks in the park, the most popular is the summit walk along a paved road to the top of Bukit Timah. Even during the week it attracts a number of walkers, though few venture off the footpath to explore the side trails. The road cuts a swathe through dense forest, and near the top there are panoramic views across Upper Pierce Reservoir.

The best trails to explore the forest and see the wildlife run off the summit road. Try the North View, South View or Fern Valley paths, where it is hard to believe that you are in Singapore. These paths involve some scrambling over rocks in parts, but are easily negotiated.

The park has over 800 species of native plants, including giant trees, ferns and native flowers. Wildlife is difficult to see, though long-tailed macaques and squirrels are in abundance. Flying lemurs, reticulated pythons and birds such as the racquet-tailed drongo and white-bellied sea eagle inhabit the reserve. Try to pick up either one of the two editions of *A Guide to the Bukit Timah Nature Reserve* explaining the reserve's flora and fauna (available at Mobil and BP petrol stations and some bookshops).

The exhibition hall is open from 8.30 am to 6 pm. Entry is free. It is a good idea to bring a water bottle if you intend going on some extended walks. A towel and even a change of clothes are also worth bringing, as the walks are strenuous in parts and the conditions are hot and very humid.

To get to Bukit Timah, take bus No 171 or 182, which both run along Orchard and Stamford roads in the colonial district and pass the Newton MRT station. Get off just past the 12km mark at the large, yellow Courts Mammoth Super Store on Upper Bukit Timah Rd. The entrance to the park is on the other side, about a kilometre along Hindhede Drive.

Sungei Buloh Nature Park

This 87 hectare wetland nature reserve is home to 140 species of birds, most of them migratory. From the visitor centre with its well-presented displays, trails lead around ponds and mangrove swamps to hides for observing the birds. The birdlife, rather than the walks, is the main reason to visit as the area is mostly former orchard and fish ponds.

Sungei Buloh is open from 7.30 am to 7 pm on Monday to Friday, and from 7 am to 7 pm on weekends and holidays. Admission is S$1 for adults (children S$0.50). Audiovisual shows on the park's flora and fauna are held at 9 and 11 am, and 1 and 3 pm. Guided walks are also held at 9.30 am and 4 pm, weather permitting. Allow yourself three hours to do the park justice.

The park is in the north-west of the island, overlooking the Straits of Johor. Take the MRT to the Choa Chu Kang station, then bus No SS7 to Woodlands Interchange, then bus No 925.

Other Parks

Despite Singapore's dense population, there are many small parks and gardens.

MacRitchie Reservoir has a 12 hectare park area with a jogging track, exercise area, playground and tea kiosk. It is a pleasant retreat from the city, and popular with joggers. A band often plays on Sunday (check the newspapers). To the north of MacRitchie Reservoir is **Upper Seletar Reservoir**, where paddle boating is possible, and further east is **Lower Seletar Reservoir**, where you can go fishing. For MacRitchie Reservoir take bus No 167 from Stamford

Rd, No 132 from Orchard Rd or No 156 from the Bishan MRT station. For Upper Seletar take bus No 138 from the Ang Mo Kio MRT station. For Lower Seletar, take the MRT to Yishun, then bus No 851, 852, 853, 854 or 855.

Off Kampong Bahru Rd, the 116m **Mt Faber** is a pleasant park with fine views over the harbour and the city. To get there, take the cable car up from the WTC. Mt Faber can be conveniently visited in conjunction with a trip to Sentosa Island.

Pasir Ris Park on the north-east coast is for the most part a manicured park with a narrow stretch of beach. The park also has a wooden walkway that goes through a mangrove swamp area which is good for birdwatching. The park is often empty during the week, but comes alive on holidays and weekends, when the nearby trade-union-run NTUC Pasir Ris Resort fills up. To get there take the MRT to the Pasir Ris station and then bus No 350 to the resort, only a short walk from the beach.

Bukit Batok, also known as Little Guilin, was a quarry and is now a park. It's often compared to the spectacular limestone formations and lakes of Guilin in southern China, hence the name. This pleasant park is built around a hilly outcrop and lake, but it is a poor imitation of Guilin. It is near the Bukit Gombok MRT station, 14km north-west of the city.

Bukit Turf Club

The horse-racing calendar is part of the Malaysian circuit and races are held in Singapore once a month at the Bukit Turf Club on Bukit Timah Rd. At other times, races are broadcast on the huge video screen. The racecourse is to be redeveloped for housing and is slated to move to Woodlands in the future.

The races are usually held on weekends, and admission is S$5.15 or S$10.30 under the fans in the stand. If you are going to blow your dough at the races then you might as well spend S$20.60 for a seat in the air-conditioned members' stand – it gets very hot in the ordinary section on a crowded race day. Show your passport and buy a ticket to the members at the tourist information booth outside. The only drawback is that you cannot get down to view the horses from the sealed-off members' stand.

The Bukit Turf Club produces a racing calendar, which is available at the Singapore Tourism Board (STB) offices; or ring ☎ 469 3611 for information. All betting is government controlled, and the minimum win or place bet is S$5. A lot of money passes through the windows on race days, which regularly attract about 30,000 punters. Despite government crackdowns, race fixing is growing with the popularity of the sport.

Be sure to dress properly – no shorts, sandals or T-shirts are allowed. The turf club also has a good hawker centre.

Holland Village

If you're wondering what the life of an expatriate is like, head for Holland Village. It's on Holland Rd, a westerly continuation of Orchard Rd, and services the garden belt suburbs of the well-to-do.

Holland Village is, in fact, just a suburban shopping centre where foreigners can shop, sip coffee and feel at home, but it has a definite village community atmosphere. It is best known for its host of fashionable restaurants and watering holes, concentrated on Lorong Mambong, just back from the main road. The Holland shopping centre, a modern complex, is a good place to shop for antiques, furnishings and crafts, including porcelain ware, batik, wood carvings etc.

The nearest MRT station is Buona Vista, about a 15 minute walk along Buona Vista Rd from Holland Village. Or take bus No 7, 105 or 106 from Penang Rd/Orchard Blvd.

Temples

The central city areas of Singapore provide plenty of opportunities to experience Singapore's colourful temples, but a couple of temples of note are found in the outer areas.

Siong Lim Temple This is one of the largest temples in Singapore and includes a Chinese rock garden. It was built in 1908 but includes more recent additions. It features

Thai Buddha statues and 2000kg incense burners. There is a monastery next to the main temple, and next to the monastery is another temple featuring a gigantic Buddha statue. It's at 184E Jalan Toa Payoh, north of the city centre, about 1km east from the Toa Payoh MRT station.

Kong Meng San Phor Kark See Temple

This is the largest temple in Singapore and covers 12 hectares. A modern temple, it is impressive in its size and design, though its main function is as a crematorium: funerals, complete with paper effigies, are frequent. The attached old people's home is reminiscent of the old 'death houses' that used to exist in Chinatown's Sago St. Old folk were once packed off to death houses towards the end of their lives, thus avoiding the possible bad luck of a death in the home. The temple is on Bright Hill Drive, about 1.5km west of the Bishan MRT station.

Kranji War Memorial

Near the Causeway off Woodlands Rd, the Kranji War Memorial includes the graves of thousands of Allied troops who died in the region during WWII. The walls are inscribed with the names of those who died, and a register is available for inspection. It can be reached by bus No 182 from Somerset Rd.

Housing Estates

Still another side of Singapore is found in the modern HDB satellite cities like Toa Payoh, Pasir Ris, Tampines and Bukit Panjang. Nearly 90% of Singaporeans live in these government housing blocks, and once again it's a programme that Singapore manages to make work.

While high-rise housing has become a dirty word in many countries, in Singapore it's almost universally popular. Many of the residents own their own flats, with subsidised interest rates provided by the HDB.

The MRT makes it simple to visit HDB areas. Just jump on a train and pop up somewhere like Toa Payoh, or Tampines, where you'll find the big new Century Park shopping mall. True, you won't see stunning architecture and breathtaking landscapes, you won't be spellbound by exotic ritual, but you will get a glimpse of what life is like for the overwhelming majority of Singapore's residents. The estates are often good places to shop – straightforward, cheap and without the inflated prices and haggling that often go with the more popular tourist areas – and, of course, they have plenty of places to eat. You may find the best *ah balling* or the cheapest chicken-rice in Singapore.

Kampungs

There are still a few kampungs in Singapore, though they may have iron roofs, electricity and a car parked next to the house. The government has met strong resistance in the past from the Malay community when villages have been torn down to make way for HDB estates.

In the north-east of the island, for example near the coast between Sembawang and Punggol, you can still come across rural scenes, and can still find kampungs. Some of the islands such as Pulau Ubin are also rural and very Malay in character, and they have kampungs that have so far escaped the ravages of development.

Sun Yatsen Villa

This old villa was Sun Yatsen's residence in Singapore before the overthrow of the Qing (or Manchu) Dynasty, which saw an end to imperial China, and Dr San Yatsen's promotion to president of the new republic in 1912. His time in Singapore was largely spent organising secret societies and fund-raising for the overthrow of the Qing Dynasty. The house is a fine example of an old villa and inside are personal items and photographs of the Chinese revolutionary, while upstairs is a Chinese library.

The villa is on Ah Hood Rd, about 500m south of the Toa Payoh MRT station. Bus No 145 goes from Balestier Rd – get off at Ah Hood Rd.

SPORTS

Singapore's private clubs and country clubs have excellent sporting facilities, but there are also fine public facilities, such as those at Farrer Park near Little India, and a host of commercial ventures.

Archery

Contact the Archery Club of Singapore (☎ 258 1140) at 5 Bintang Walk.

Badminton

Badminton is popular in South-East Asia and the region has produced world champions in this sport. Courts at the Singapore Badminton Hall (☎ 344 1773), 102 Guillemard Rd, are open daily from 8 am to 11 pm; bookings are essential.

Bicycling

Recreational cycling ranges from a leisurely peddle along the foreshore of the east coast to mountain biking at Ulu Pandan.

The easiest riding possibilities are the east coast, Sentosa and Pulau Ubin. Bikes can also be hired at these places.

Bukit Timah has two mountain bike trails, 7km in all, running around the edge of the nature reserve between Chestnut Ave and Rifle Range Rd. The trails cut though jungle and abandoned quarry sites and, though hilly in parts, are well surfaced.

The Ulu Pandan Boy's Brigade Mountain Bike Track is a more challenging, unpaved 4km trail. It's opposite the Singapore Polytechnic on Dover Rd.

Bowling

Tenpin bowling is very popular in Singapore. The cost per game is around S$3 to S$3.80; shoe hire is around S$0.50. Some alleys are:

Singapore Tenpin Bowling Congress
(☎ 355 0136) 01-01 Balestier Plaza, 400 Balestier Rd
Superbowl
(☎ 221 1010) 15 Marina Grove, Marina South

Cricket

The Singapore Cricket Club holds matches every weekend on the Padang from March to October. The club is for members only, but spectators are welcome.

Golf

Singapore has plenty of golf courses, though some are for members only, or do not allow visitors to play on weekends. A game of golf costs around S$90 on Monday to Friday, and from S$100 to S$220 on weekends. Club hire is expensive. The following courses have 18 holes, except for Changi, Seletar and Warren, which are nine hole courses:

Changi Golf Club
(☎ 545 5133) Netheravon Rd
Jurong Country Club
(☎ 560 5655) 9 Science Centre Rd
Keppel Club
(☎ 273 5522) Bukit Chermin
Marina Bay Golf & Country Club
(☎ 221 2811) 6 Marina Green
Raffles Country Club
(☎ 861 7655) 450 Jalan Ahmad Ibrahim
Seletar Country Club
(☎ 481 4745) Seletar Airbase
Sembawang Country Club
(☎ 257 0642) Sembawang Rd
Sentosa Golf Course
(☎ 275 0022) Sentosa Island
Singapore Island Country Club
(☎ 459 2222) Upper Thomson Rd
Warren Golf Course
(☎ 777 6533) Folkestone Rd

Singapore has driving ranges at the Parkland Golf Driving Range (☎ 440 6726), 920 East Coast Parkway, and Green Fairways (☎ 468 8409), Bukit Turf Club, Fairways Drive. Cost here starts from S$3 for 48 balls.

Squash

Most of the country clubs listed in the previous Golf entry have squash courts. Some of the public courts are:

East Coast Recreation Centre
(☎ 449 0541) East Coast Parkway
National Stadium
(☎ 440 6839) Kallang

Swimming

Singapore has a number of beaches for swimming – try East Coast Park, Changi Village, Sentosa or the other islands. Singapore also has plenty of public swimming pools; admission is S$1. The Farrer Park Swimming Complex in Dorset Rd is the closest to the Bencoolen St and Orchard Rd areas.

Tennis

Tennis courts cost from S$3 to S$6 per hour. Courts available for hire include:

Farrer Park Tennis Courts
(☎ 299 4166) Rutland Rd
Singapore Tennis Centre
(☎ 442 5966) 1020 East Coast Parkway

Water Sports

The East Coast Sailing Centre (☎ 449 5118), 1210 East Coast Parkway, is the place to go for windsurfing and sailing. Sailboards for hire cost S$20 for two hours; lessons are available. It also rents laser-class boats for $20 per hour. Sailboards and aquabikes are also available for hire on Sentosa Island.

For water-skiing, William Water Sports (☎ 282 6879) at Ponggol Point, north of the island, rents boats, a driver and gear for S$65 per hour. Cowabunga Ski Centre (☎ 344 8813), 10 Stadium Walk, Kallang, is the home of the Singapore Water Ski Federation and offers lessons and equipment.

Places to Stay

Singapore has a wide variety of accommodation in all price categories – you can get a dormitory bed in a guesthouse for S$8, a room in a cheap Chinese hotel for around S$30, pay over S$300 for a room in an 'international standard' hotel or over S$6000 for the best suite at the Raffles. Hotel standards are usually high but so are prices, making Singapore the most expensive city in South-East Asia for hotels and an equal contender with other expensive cities around the world.

In the major hotels, a 3% GST, 1% government tax and 10% service charge are added to your bill. This is what's called the dreaded 'plus-plus-plus' which follows the quoted price (eg S$140+++), while 'nett' means the price includes tax and service charge. The hotels stipulate that you should not tip when a service charge applies. The 4% taxes (ie GST and government taxes) also apply to the cheaper hotels but they are usually included in the quoted price.

PLACES TO STAY – BUDGET

Budget accommodation is found in guesthouses and the ever-shrinking number of cheap Chinese hotels.

Singapore's guesthouses are just residential flats or office space broken up into dormitories and cubicle-like rooms. The trouble with them is that overcrowding tends to stretch the limited facilities, and the rooms really are small. In addition, everybody else staying there will be a traveller, just like yourself. On the other hand, they're good sources of information, good places to meet people and you won't find any cheaper accommodation in Singapore.

New guesthouses are constantly opening, and the services they provide are improving. Dormitory beds cost from S$8 and rooms from S$20, though most rooms go for around S$25 to S$30 and range up to S$50 for hotel-standard rooms with air-con, bathroom and TV. Cheap rooms are often small spartan boxes with a fan. Free tea and coffee are standard offerings, and a basic breakfast is usually thrown in. Singapore does not have an official youth hostel.

Guesthouses do move around, usually in search of cheaper rents or under eviction notices initiated by other tenants in the building. The guesthouses listed in this chapter are the more accessible and well-established ones. Others tend to come and go, so keep your eyes open, or just wander around Bencoolen St or Beach Rd with a backpack and you're sure to get plenty of offers. Touts at the airport and train station will also offer accommodation. Some places don't advertise and are merely residential flats that rent out rooms on an adhoc basis. They can offer some of the best accommodation and are good options for long-term stayers.

The other main budget accommodation option is the cheap Chinese hotels. Most of these have seen better days, but they do have more character than the guesthouses. They appear to be resigned to redevelopment and are, sadly, deteriorating each year. Rooms range from around S$30 to S$65. This will get you a fairly spartan room with a bare floor, a few pieces of furniture, a sink and a fan. Toilets are usually shared but you often get hot water in the showers. Couples should always ask for a single room – a single usually means just one double bed, whereas a double has two. Singapore also has three YMCAs, though these are more mid-range options, and two inconveniently located campgrounds.

The main area for budget accommodation is in the colonial district bounded by Bras Basah, Rochor, Beach and Selegie roads. Bencoolen St has traditionally been the backpackers' centre in Singapore, and while it still has a number of guesthouses, most of the old buildings and Chinese hotels have fallen to the wrecker's ball. Many backpackers' places have relocated to the Beach Rd area. Other cheap possibilities are found in Chinatown, and further north in Little India and nearby Jalan Besar. A number of cheap hotels can also be found out in the lorongs of Geylang, east of the city, but most travellers find them far too inconvenient.

Bencoolen St Area (Map 3)

Bencoolen St has traditionally been the budget accommodation centre, and at almost any time of the night or day you can see travellers with backpacks seeking out a cheap hotel or guesthouse. Bencoolen St itself has very little character left, but it's within walking distance of the city centre, Orchard Rd and Little India.

From Changi airport, public bus No 16 or 16E will drop you on Stamford Rd. Get off near the National Museum, cross Stamford Rd and walk north through the small park to Bras Basah Rd and Bencoolen St. From the Singapore train station, bus No 97 also stops on Stamford Rd. From the Lavender St bus station, almost all buses that run along Jalan Besar also go down Bencoolen St. The nearest MRT station is Dhoby Ghaut, about 10 minutes walk from Bencoolen St.

Guesthouses Singapore's original backpackers' centre is at 46-52 Bencoolen St. There's no sign at all; go around the back and take the lift. Almost the entire building is devoted to guesthouses, some of which have been running for almost 20 years. The place looks like it – filthy stairwells and graffiti-adorned lift – though some of the places offer reasonable rooms.

At the top, at least in elevation, *Lee Boarding House* (☎ 338 3149; fax 333 1997) has its reception at No 52 on the 7th floor, but it has rooms on other floors. It's a large place with dorms for S$9, or less crowded air-con dorms for S$10. Standard singles/doubles with fan start at S$22/28, and air-con rooms range from S$30/45 right up to some good hotel-style rooms with air-con and bathroom for S$45 to S$60. *Peony Mansions* (☎ 338 5638; fax 339 1471), one of the original guesthouses, is on the 4th floor. Dormitory beds cost S$8 or S$9 with air-con, a single room with fan costs S$18 and a double with fan S$22. Doubles with air-con cost S$30 to S$45. The dorms aren't great but the rooms are reasonable, and many have been upgraded. There are other guesthouses in the block, like *Latin House* (☎ 339 6308) on the 3rd floor at No 46, which is an anonymous place with run-down rooms.

On the other side of Bencoolen St, between the Strand and Bencoolen hotels, is *Bencoolen House* (☎ 338 1206) at No 27. The reception area is on the 7th floor. Dorm beds cost S$7, a few singles cost S$20, but most rooms cost from S$25 to S$45 for air-con. It's a bit rundown but OK.

In the thick of things, the *Peony Mansion Travellers' Lodge* (☎ 334 8697; fax 334 7014), 131A Bencoolen St, is a popular place with an excellent 24 hour Indian restaurant downstairs. It has a variety of reasonable rooms from S$25 for a fan room with two bunk beds to S$50 for rooms with air-con and shower. *Green Curtains* (☎ 334 8697) next door at No 131A is an offshoot of Peony

Mansions, with well-maintained rooms. The S$25 fan rooms are fairly small and dark but better rooms range to S$45.

Another centre for guesthouses is at 171 Bencoolen St. *Goh's Homestay* (☎ 339 6561; fax 339 8606), up a long flight of stairs to the 3rd floor at No 169D, has an eating/meeting area where you can get breakfast, snacks and drinks. The rooms are clean but small, without windows and fairly pricey at S$36/46 for singles/doubles; dorm beds cost S$14. There is Internet access at S$6 per hour. *Hawaii Hostel* (☎ 338 4187) on the 2nd floor at No 171B is an impersonal place, with 10-bed dorms for S$10, pokey singles for S$25 and better air-con doubles for S$35. Basic breakfast is included.

Hotels Redevelopment in the area has seen the demise of most of the old hotels. The *San Wah* (☎ 336 2428; fax 334 4146) at 36 Bencoolen St is a little better than the cheapest Chinese hotels. Many of the rooms have air-con and it has a pleasant courtyard area set back from the street. Fan/air-con doubles cost S$50/55.

At 260-262 Middle Rd, near the corner of Selegie Rd, is the good, spotlessly clean *Sun Sun Hotel* (☎ 338 4911). It's a cut above the other traditional Chinese hotels; some rooms have their own balconies and there's a handy confectionery shop downstairs. Singles/doubles cost S$40/45, or air-con doubles cost S$50. There is a discount for stays over three days.

Beach Rd Area (Map 3)

Beach Rd, a few blocks from Bencoolen St towards the (ever-receding) waterfront, is another centre for cheap hotels. If you aspire to the Raffles but can't afford it, at least you can stay nearby. From Changi airport, bus No 16 or 16E can drop you near the towering Raffles City complex, opposite the Padang, from where it's a short walk to Beach Rd. From the train station and the WTC take bus No 100. Bus Nos 82 and 107 run down Beach Rd from the Lavender St bus station, and pass the Golden Mile Complex bus station on Beach Rd only a 10 minute walk from the cheap hotels. The Beach Rd area is about halfway between the City Hall and Bugis MRT stations.

Guesthouses *Lee Traveller's Club* (☎ 339 5490) is on the 6th floor of the Fu Yeun building at 75 Beach Rd, with more rooms on the other floors. It is a large place and popular, and not as cramped as some others. It costs S$8 in an eight bed, air-con dorm; singles start at S$15, though most rooms are air-con doubles for S$35 and S$40. It is one of the better guesthouses, with a small kitchen for guests' use.

Willy's (☎ 332 1585) at 494 North Bridge Rd is a reasonable if cramped place, with open dorms for S$8, air-con dorms for S$12, or better air-con doubles for S$30 and S$38. *Waffles Home Stay* (☎ 334 1608), 490 North Bridge Rd, is on the top floor of an Indian restaurant and two doors down from Willy's. It is a friendly place, with dorms for S$8 and S$12, and a few basic doubles for S$26. In between Willy's and Waffles is the *Sunderbone Homestay* (☎ 333 9335), where you might get a room, though they are mostly taken by long-term guests. Prices are the same and facilities are similar to the two previous places since they are all run by the same management. Enter all three places via the front restaurants or via the back lane, after hours.

Liang Seah St, which runs into Beach Rd, has a couple of guesthouses which are holding on in the face of all the redevelopment along this street. The popular *New Backpackers Lodge* (☎ 338 7460) at No 18A is in an old terrace with Chinese hotel-style rooms, but chopped in half and without any furniture. It has lost a bit of its shine and can be crowded. A dorm bed with air-con costs S$8 though most rooms go for S$25. Breakfast is included. The *Cozy Corner Lodge* (☎ 333 4656), at No 2A nearer to Beach Rd, is a good, new place that tries harder and offers a slightly better standard of rooms. Dorms cost S$9, doubles cost S$25 with fan.

Hotels The hotels here are all of a similar basic standard: traditional Chinese hotels with wire-topped walls, shuttered windows, a few pieces of furniture and a basin with running water. They are rundown but good for the price.

The *Shang Onn* (☎ 338 4153), at 37 Beach Rd on the corner of Purvis St, is a little more expensive than the other places. Singles/doubles will cost you S$30/34. The rooms are very clean and have character but not much else.

On the corner of Liang Seah St and North Bridge Rd is the *Ah Chew Hotel* (☎ 336 3563), a very traditional old Chinese hotel. The S$30 non-air-con rooms are basic, but at least the eyeball-sized holes in some of the rooms have been taped over. The old guys who run the place are very friendly, and the shared bathrooms are spotless.

Chinatown (Map 4)

Chinatown, an interesting area to stay, has a few cheap hotels, most of which are within walking distance of the train station and the Outram Park and Tanjong Pagar MRT stations.

Guesthouses The friendly *Chinatown Guest House* (☎ 220 0671), 5th floor, 325D New Bridge Rd, opposite Pearl's Centre, has dorm beds for S$10, and reasonable rooms for S$30 and up to S$50 with air-con. It's about the cheapest option in Chinatown and handy to the Outram Park MRT station.

Hotels On Peck Seah St are a couple of carpeted, air-con hotels. The *New Asia Hotel* (☎ 221 1861; fax 223 9002) is on the corner of Maxwell Rd and Peck Seah St. Most rooms are small but reasonable value for S$40/58 for singles/doubles or S$5 extra with TV. A couple of doors down at No 10, the *Air View Hotel* (☎ 225 7788; fax 225 6688) is a bit better than the New Asia, and costs S$60 for doubles or S$75 with two double beds. All rooms have a shower cubicle and TV.

Little India & Jalan Besar (Map 3)

Little India and Jalan Besar, near the Lavender St bus station (where most buses to Malaysia leave from), also have a number of cheap hotels. It is not as convenient as the other areas, but its proximity to the Lavender St bus station is handy if you arrive by long-distance bus from Malaysia, and it is close to Little India and Arab St.

See the Little India map (Map 3) for the location of places to stay in this area.

Guesthouses At least one decent guesthouse has managed to survive in Little India. The popular *Ali's Nest* (☎ 291 2938) at 23 Roberts Lane is run by the friendly Ali, who lived in the Netherlands and speaks Dutch. Beds in dorms containing four to eight beds are S$9. A few small singles go for S$20, or better doubles cost S$30.

Hotels The *Little India Guest House* (☎ 294 2866) is just off Serangoon Rd in the heart of Little India at 3 Veerasamy Rd. It is more a small hotel than a guesthouse. Small, well-appointed rooms with shared bathrooms cost S$38/50 for singles/doubles.

Jalan Besar has a few cheap hotels, but this is not a convenient location unless you arrive at the Lavender St bus station and can't be bothered looking further. The nearest is just down Jalan Besar at No 383, the *Kam Leng* (☎ 298 2289), a rather rundown old hotel with rooms at S$30 with fan and S$36 with air-con. At No 290A, the architecturally interesting *International Hotel* (☎ 293 9238) has singles without bathroom for S$35 or large doubles for S$40 or S$50 with bathroom, most have balconies.

Other Areas

Hotels The *Mayfair City Hotel* (☎ 337 4542) is at 40-44 Armenian St near Orchard Rd, opposite the Asian Civilisations Museum, in the colonial district. It's in one of Singapore's oldest streets and within walking distance of many attractions. Good rooms with air-con, shower and TV cost S$60/70 for singles/doubles.

The *Mitre Hotel* (☎ 737 3811), 145 Killiney Rd, is the cheapest hotel anywhere near Orchard Rd (which is 500m to the north). It would have to be the most dilapidated fleapit in Singapore, but it does have a good deal of character. It is in an old villa with large grounds set back off the street. The dingy bar on the ground floor is popular with the oil-rig workers who stay here. Rooms range from S$24 for a rough single with fan to S$36 for a passable double with air-con and bathroom.

The Ys Singapore has three YMCAs, which take men, women and couples. They provide good mid-range accommodation and, though not the bargain they used to be, are still popular. Advance bookings in writing with one night's deposit are usually essential. Book at least six weeks in advance for the YMCA International House and around three weeks in advance for the others. Non-YMCA members must pay a small charge for temporary membership.

The *YMCA International House* (☎ 336 6000; fax 337 3140) is at 1 Orchard Rd in a handy position, with good facilities, including a fitness centre, roof-top swimming pool, squash and badminton courts, and a billiards room. There's also a restaurant, which offers a cheap daily set meal, and a McDonald's. All rooms have air-con, TV, telephone and bathroom, but are of a fairly average mid-range standard and becoming expensive at S$80 single, S$90 double, S$105 family and S$115 superior room, plus 13% tax and service charge. A bed in a four bed dorm costs S$25.

The *YWCA Fort Canning* (☎ 338 4222; fax 337 4222) at 6 Fort Canning Rd re-opened in April 1997 offering good accommodation, though pricey for a 'Y'. Dorm beds are from S$35 to S$45 whereas a standard single room is a whopping S$110.

The *Metropolitan YMCA* (☎ 737 7755; fax 235 5528), 60 Stevens Rd, also has well appointed rooms, a pool and a cafe. It is a good 15 minute walk north of Orchard and Tanglin roads and less conveniently located than the YMCA in Orchard Rd. Singles/doubles with bathroom, TV and air-con range from S$64 to S$98 for a 'pool view' room.

Camping The best place for camping is at *Sentosa Island*, where pre-erected four-person tents cost S$12 per night plus 3% tax. Camp beds cost an extra S$0.50 each. It caters primarily for groups, but individuals can stay by booking in advance through the Sentosa Information Centre (☎ 270 7888). The nearby youth hostel is only open to organised groups and an air-con bunk room for up to 12 people costs S$120.

There's also the good *East Coast Campsite* on East Coast Parkway, at the 5km marker, but officially you must book three months in advance and obtain a permit from the People's Association (☎ 340 5113) on Stadium Link, opposite the National Stadium.

PLACES TO STAY – MID-RANGE

Singapore is experiencing a mini boom in mid-range accommodation. New hotels are springing up in Chinatown, Little India and the colonial district to cater for independent visitors who want a little luxury but not the price tag of the five star hotels. Most of the new hotels have well appointed rooms with bathroom, hot water, air-con, phone and TV but forego the trimmings of the big hotels.

The cheaper hotels listed here are mostly second-string, older places which have comfortable rooms but could do with a face-lift.

Colonial District (Maps 3 & 4)

The *New 7th Storey Hotel* (☎ 337 0251) at 229 Rochor Rd, at the northern end of the colonial district, is an older, upmarket cheapie. Reasonable budget rooms with air-con, TV, telephone and carpets go for S$65, or S$80 with bathroom. It is close to the MRT but the immediate area around the hotel is rather barren.

The *South-East Asia Hotel* (☎ 338 2394; fax 338 3480) at 190 Waterloo St is quiet and good value. All rooms have air-con, bathroom, TV and phone. Doubles cost S$70, or S$86.50 with two double beds.

Waterloo Hostel (☎ 336 6555), 55 Waterloo St, is not your average hostel and offers very good air-con rooms with TV, phone and fridge. Part of the Catholic Centre, it is quiet and well run with singles/doubles for S$63/68, or S$73/83 with bathroom. The tariff includes breakfast.

A modern hotel with air-con and bathrooms is the *Strand Hotel* (☎ 338 1866; fax 336 3149) at 25 Bencoolen St, diagonally opposite the backpacker centre. Excellent, upgraded rooms are a good alternative to the top-end hotels and cost S$95 for a double. The hotel has a coffee shop and bar.

The *Metropole Hotel* (☎ 336 3611; fax 339 3610), on Seah St behind the Raffles, is an older three star hotel that has lost its shine, but it has a good coffee shop and restaurant called The Barn. The rooms have had a minor face-lift and start at S$100/115 plus 14% for singles/doubles.

The *Beach Hotel* (☎ 336 7712; fax 336 7713), 95 Beach Rd, is a new hotel, with doubles for S$95, S$105 and S$120. The rooms are well appointed and many of the attached bathrooms have bath tubs, but the hotel has no coffee shop or other facilities.

Orchard Rd Area (Map 2)

You can find a few reasonably priced hotels around Orchard Rd. At Kramat Rd, one block north of Orchard Rd, the *Supreme Hotel* (☎ 737 8333) is central and a good buy for the position. It is a good mid-range hotel and costs S$85 a double.

Lloyd's Inn (☎ 737 7309; fax 737 7309), 2 Lloyd Rd, is a small but modern hotel less than a 10 minute walk from Orchard Rd. It is in a quiet street among the old villas of Singapore and the rooms are spread out, motel style, around the reception building. The well appointed rooms for S$85 a double or S$95 a double with fridge are good value. Bookings are advisable.

In the quiet residential area to the north of Orchard and Tanglin roads are some good hotels, but they are a little out of the way. The *Sloane Court Hotel* (☎ 235 3311), 17 Balmoral Rd, is a pleasant Tudor-style hotel in a garden setting with an English pub. The rooms are comfortable but nothing special and cost S$80/90, plus 14%, for singles/doubles. A few hundred metres away is the *VIP Hotel* (☎ 235 4277; fax 235 2824) at 5 Balmoral Crescent. The rooms are a little run-down, but the hotel has a swimming pool and rooms are reasonable value at S$99.

Next to the Shangri-La Hotel, the *RELC International House* (☎ 737 9044; fax 733 9976) at 30 Orange Grove Rd has large well appointed doubles with balcony and fridge from S$110, after discount, making them good value. RELC stands for Regional English Language Centre, and the bottom floors are devoted to conference rooms and teaching facilities, while the top floors are occupied by a good standard hotel.

Chinatown (Map 4)

Chinatown's renovated terraces are also home to a number of mid-range hotels offering rooms with character, but because of the terrace design the cheaper rooms are often windowless. Prices are high in these small hotels and, given that some are charging close to top-end hotel rates but have limited facilities, expect discounts.

The *Dragon Inn Chinatown* (☎ 222 7227; fax 255 6033), 18 Mosque St, is in a row of renovated shophouses. Its rooms are well appointed with air-con, bathroom and TV. Small singles for S$65 are dark and many are located around the noisy air-con shaft. Doubles are much better at S$98 or S$118 for larger rooms with bar fridge.

The cute *Damenlou Hotel* (☎ 221 1900; fax 225 8500), 12 Ann Siang Rd, has more character and a good cafe. Well appointed rooms cost S$100 to S$120, but some are better than others so it pays to look at a few.

At the southern edge of Chinatown near the Outram Park MRT station is the *Chinatown Hotel* (☎ 225 5166), 12-16 Teck Lim Rd. It is a good small guesthouse-style hotel. After discount, singles/doubles are S$88/98, including breakfast in the lobby dining area. The larger *Royal Peacock Hotel* (☎ 223 3522; fax 221 1770), 55 Keong Saik Rd, is more luxurious and has a stylish bar/cafe. All rooms have minibars and cost from S$130/140 to S$175/185 for singles/doubles, but the cheapest rooms are dark.

Little India (Map 3)

Little India is experiencing a boom in mid-range accommodation, as new hotels spring up because of the renovations in the area.

Though Little India is a less convenient area for visiting Singapore's attractions, the hotels in this area are currently the best buys in this range.

The *Boon Wah Hotel* (☎ 299 1466), at 43A Jalan Besar on the corner of Dickson Rd, has reasonable rooms with air-con, TV and bathroom for S$52/63 for a single/double.

Close to Serangoon Rd, the *Tai Hoe Hotel* (☎ 293 9122) at 163 Kitchener Rd is a modern, bustling hotel offering excellent rooms with bathroom, TV, phone and bar fridge. Opening rates of S$68/78 for singles/doubles make it one of the best mid-range buys in Singapore, but prices may rise.

The small *Kerbau Hotel* (☎ 297 6668) at 54-62 Kerbau Rd is another new hotel. Spotless rooms with bathroom, phone and TV cost S$70/80 for singles/doubles. Rooms are on the small side, and those on the ground floor are windowless, but the more expensive upstairs rooms are better.

The multistorey *Broadway Hotel* (☎ 292 4661), 195 Serangoon Rd, is one of the oldest hotels in Little India, but is well maintained. Its singles/doubles have air-con, TV and bathrooms and cost S$80/90, or S$90/100 for deluxe rooms, plus 4% tax. The hotel has a good Indian restaurant.

The *Mustafa Hotel* (☎ 295 5855), 145 Syed Alwi Rd, is the hotel for shoppers. It is upstairs above the Mustafa Centre, a large department store bustling with bargain hunters. New, quite luxurious rooms are good value. Singles/doubles go for S$90/105.

Slap-bang in the heart of Little India is the newish and very attractive *Grandmet Hotel* (☎ 297 8797; fax 297 8171) at 65A-75A Desker Rd. Air-con singles/doubles start at S$58/68. There's also a convenient restaurant of the same in this building.

Other new hotels include the delightfully tasteful *Perak Lodge* (☎ 296 9072; fax 392 0919) at 12 Perak Rd. It's a small, private guesthouse in a renovated, Peranakan-style building. Its wood-floored, air-con rooms start at S$70/80 for singles/doubles. Breakfast is included. About 150m south-east of the Perak Lodge is the handy *Mayo Inn* (☎ 295 6631; fax 295 8218) at 9A Jalan Besar. Rooms are reasonably sized and very clean, but try to avoid those overlooking the noisy Jalan Besar. Singles/doubles cost S$80/90.

Also at the top of this range, over near Jalan Besar, the *Dickson Court Hotel* (☎ 297 7811), 3 Dickson Rd, is a new boutique hotel with 51 well appointed rooms from S$105 to S$155 plus 14%. Designed around new shophouses, it's stylish, but some rooms are small and dark. It has a restaurant and bar.

PLACES TO STAY – TOP END

The rates for Singapore's international standard hotels constantly change as they ride the roller coaster of supply and demand. Discounts are not usually available if you walk in off the street, but it is always worth asking. Travel agents overseas should be able to secure good deals on accommodation.

The Singapore Hotel Association (☎ 339 9918; fax 339 3795) operates an outlet at Changi international airport and keeps an up-to-the-minute list of available rooms. You don't pay extra for the service, and you will be quoted the current discount rates.

All these hotels will be air-conditioned, all rooms will have bathrooms, TV and minibar, and in almost all cases there will be a swimming pool and a variety of restaurants, coffee shops and bars. They are all of international standard and often there is little to distinguish one from the other – the choice boils down to price and location.

The hotels in the budget category of this range are of a good standard but are either getting a little old or lack the extensive facilities of the larger hotels.

The following rundown contains details of most top-end hotels. Unless otherwise stated, all prices are '+++', that is plus the 10% service charge, 3% GST and 1% government tax. The rate quoted is the published rate for a standard single/double room. These prices should be used as a guide only, as Singapore's hotel rates are subject to large variations. Discounts of 20% or more (sometimes much more) on the published rates are often available.

Orchard Rd Area (Map 2)

Orchard Rd is where everyone wants to stay, and consequently hotels tend to be a little more expensive here than elsewhere. However, Orchard Rd has some moderately priced hotels of a high standard.

The *Cockpit Hotel* (☎ 737 9111; fax 737 3105) has a good location just off Orchard Rd at the city end. It's looking a little weary and the facilities are limited but it is comparatively moderately priced at S$190 for a single room.

Some cheaper, smaller hotels can be found to the north and west of Orchard Rd – an easy walk to the action.

The *Ladyhill Hotel* (☎ 737 2111; fax 737 4696) on Lady Hill Rd is a moderately priced low-rise place with an attractive garden setting. The best rooms with private balconies overlooking the pool are in the chalet block. Singles cost from S$170 to S$210.

The *Garden Hotel* (☎ 235 3344; fax 235 9730; email garden@pacific.net.sg) at 14 Balmoral Rd has a pleasant covered courtyard/atrium area and a courtyard pool. Single rooms cost from S$160 to S$180.

The *Cairnhill Hotel* (☎ 734 6622; fax 235 5598) at 19 Cairnhill Circle is a short walk from Orchard Rd. It's a notch below the quality of most of its peers, but it is reasonably priced at S$210 for a single.

The *Hotel Phoenix* (☎ 737 8666; fax 732 2024; email rsvp@phoenix.com.sg), 277 Orchard Rd across from Le Meridien Singapore (which itself is a very good hotel but only worth considering if you can get a large discount), is at the lower end of the price range for the Orchard Rd area and lacks a lot of facilities; the big plus is that it sits over Somerset MRT station. There's another entrance off Penang Rd. Singles go for S$250.

Most of the top hotels are at the western end of Orchard Rd around Scotts and Tanglin roads.

The impressive *Regent* (☎ 733 8888; fax 732 8838), 1 Cuscaden Rd, is edging into the super luxury category with singles starting at S$350.

The new *Traders' Hotel* (☎ 738 2222; fax 831 4314; email thsbc@singnet.com.sg), between the Imperial and Marco Polo, has well appointed rooms with a reasonable single room rate from S$235.

On the corner of Scotts and Orchard roads, the *Singapore Marriott Hotel* (☎ 735 5800; fax 735 9800) has had a complete recent makeover. It's exceedingly opulent but expect to fork out S$380 and upwards for a bed here.

The *Mandarin Singapore* (☎ 737 4411; fax 737 2361) at 100 Orchard Rd is one of Singapore's best. Single room rates are S$300 and upwards.

Sheraton Towers (☎ 737 6888; fax 737 1072; email anssh2@po.pacific.net.sg), 39 Scotts Rd, is a big favourite with business types. Singles cost from S$370.

The *Melia at Scotts* (☎ 732 5885; fax 732 1332; email meliasct@pacific.net.sg), next to Sheraton Towers and near Newton MRT station, is popular with tour groups. Published singles start at S$260 but travel agents can usually get better discounts.

The *Goodwood Park Hotel* (☎ 737 7411; fax 732 8558), 22 Scotts Rd, was designed by the architect responsible for Raffles. If anything, it is more ornate and more delightful even than its more famous sibling. Set on six hectares, it is one of Singapore's most expensive hotels with singles starting at S$385.

Colonial District (Maps 3 & 4)

The colonial district's real estate may not be as prestigious as Orchard Rd but most of the hotels in this area are more convenient for most of Singapore's attractions.

The *Bayview Inn* (☎ 337 2882; fax 338 2880), 30 Bencoolen St, is a good, three star hotel among the backpackers' guesthouses. Published single room rates start at S$150, but regular discounts make it a good buy.

The *Hotel InterContinental* (☎ 338 7600; fax 338 7366) is a new hotel in the Bugis Junction complex. Shophouse rooms out the front re-create the style of the complex, and high-rise rooms are also decorated in period style. It has plenty of class and all the trimmings of a top hotel. Singles start at S$325.

The *Peninsula Hotel* (☎ 337 2200; fax 339 3847) and its sister hotel, the *Excelsior*

(☎ 338 7733; fax 339 3847), are moderately priced with published room rates starting at around S$215. Both are on Coleman St, over towards the business centre of Singapore.

The *Carlton Hotel* (☎ 338 8333; fax 339 6866; email carltsin@singnet.com.sg), 76 Bras Basah Rd, has excellent facilities and offers discounts on its rather pricey advertised rates, which are currently upwards of S$300 for a single.

The *Allson Hotel* (☎ 336 0811; fax 339 7019), 101 Victoria St, is another very good tourist hotel, and regular discounts make it reasonable value. The opening price for a single is S$230. Both the Allson and the Carlton hotels are close to the City Hall MRT station.

The twin, 73 storey *Westin Stamford Hotel* (☎ 339 6633; fax 336 5117; email westin1@singnet.com.sg) and *Westin Plaza Hotel* (☎ 339 6633; fax 336 5117; email westin1@singnet.com.sg), built over the Raffles City shopping centre and City Hall MRT station, are the tallest hotels in the world. With countless restaurants and lounges, and two roof-top swimming pools, they are also among the best hotels in Singapore. A single at either hotel will set you back anywhere between S$325 and S$400.

Nearby, on the edge of the colonial district, the massive Marina Square complex holds a cluster of super luxury hotels. The group includes the *Marina Mandarin* (☎ 338 3388; fax 339 4977), the *Oriental* (☎ 338 0066; fax 339 9537) and the *Pan Pacific* (☎ 336 8111; fax 339 1861; email panpac@pacific.net.sg), all with lobbies that owe their inspiration to Hollywood special effects movies. The *Ritz-Carlton Millenia* (☎ 337 8888; fax 338 0001) next door is even more plush and more expensive: starting rates for singles are S$320 at the Marina Mandarin but reach as high as S$550 at the Ritz-Carlton.

The venerable *Raffles* (☎ 337 1886; fax 339 7650; email raffles@pacific.net.sg), at the junction of Bras Basah and Beach roads, is as much a tourist attraction as it is a hotel. In recent times it has undergone massive renovations to restore its grandeur and it's now ringed by new extensions. To the purist it ain't the old Raffles but the restorations are faithful to the original spirit. What other hotel can claim that a tiger was once shot in the billiard room? The limited number of beautiful antique-decorated rooms are only for those with money to burn, at S$6000 per night. Alternatively, you can slum it in a regular suite for S$650.

Chinatown (Map 4)

If you want to experience the atmosphere of Chinatown, the futuristic *Furama Singapore Hotel* (☎ 533 3888; fax 534 1489; email fhs60@singnet.com.sg), 60 Eu Tong Sen St, is right in the centre of things. Singles cost from S$200 to S$220.

The *Duxton* (☎ 227 7678; fax 227 1232; email duxton@singnet.com.sg) in the Tanjong Pagar area is a boutique hotel in a renovated terrace. Rooms are furnished in an opulent, antique style and the suites have an attractive mezzanine bedroom. Singles start at S$280.

Other Areas

In Little India and the Arab St area there are a few good, reasonably priced hotels.

The *New Park Hotel* (☎ 291 5533; fax 297 2827; email newpark@singnet.com.sg) on Kitchener Rd in Little India is popular with tour groups and close to good shopping opportunities. Published single room rates are S$230.

The *Albert Court Hotel* (☎ 339 3939; fax 339 3252), on Albert St at the southern edge of Little India, is a boutique hotel in a new shophouse redevelopment. It's a bit on the small side and lacks many of the extras found in the bigger hotels, but the dining court centre next to the hotel is a convenient bonus if you're staying here. Starting rates for singles are S$180.

The *Golden Landmark Hotel* (☎ 297 2828; fax 298 2038), in the block bounded by Victoria and Arab streets and North Bridge and Ophir roads near the Bugis MRT station, has Middle Eastern inspired architecture. Its rates are very competitive, with singles starting at S$180.

Places to Eat

Singapore is the food capital of Asia. When it comes to superb Chinese food, Hong Kong may be a step ahead but Singapore's variety and low prices make it hard to beat. Equally important, Singapore's food is accessible – you don't have to search out obscure places, you don't face communication problems and you don't need a lot of money.

Alternatively, if you want to make gastronomic discoveries, there are lots of little out-of-the-way little places where you'll find marvellous food that few visitors know about. The Singaporean enthusiasm for food (and economical food at that) is amply illustrated by newspaper and magazine articles on the best hawker stalls in the city. Everyone has their favourite chicken-rice (roti prata) stall tucked away in one of the hundreds of hawker centres that dot the city.

To get to grips with food in Singapore, you need to know the types of food available and where to find them. The STB's *Singapore Official Guide* and the *Eating Out in Singapore* booklets are good introductions to Singaporean food, with restaurant recommendations. The annual *Singapore's Best Restaurants* is a selection of fine restaurants, chosen by a survey of *Singapore Tattler* magazine subscribers, a decidedly well-to-do bunch. Moderately priced restaurants are increasingly included so it's worth buying a copy of one of these publications at a bookshop or newsagent. Other publications come and go, but every newspaper and magazine has a food section listing the latest gastronomic discoveries and promotional offers.

Dining possibilities range from streetside hawker stalls to fancy five star hotel restaurants, with a whole gamut of possibilities in between. In a hawker centre you can eat excellent food for under S$5. This is the real Singaporean dining experience, not to be missed.

Next up the scale are the coffee shops, or *kopi tiam* (kopi is Malay for 'coffee' and tiam is Hokkien for 'shop'). These spartan, open-fronted restaurants with marble-topped tables often have similar food to the hawker centres, and within each coffee shop you may find two or three different stalls serving their own specialities. Other coffee shops are more restaurant-like with more extensive menus; the food may be as good as a top restaurant and cost a fraction of the price. The old coffee shops, typically housed in a terrace or under an old hotel, are a dying breed.

Restaurants run the full range, from glorified coffee shops to luxury restaurants. The price increases with the quality of the decor and the efficiency of the service. Unlike most Asian cities, where western chain food is a luxury item, Singapore's Asian and western chain restaurants are reasonably priced.

All the luxury hotels have a selection of restaurants, and they house most of Singapore's fine dining establishments, though they are facing increasing competition from new restaurants springing up all over town. It may be sacrilegious to say so, but Singapore has too many restaurants and many will not survive the current boom. In the meantime, stiff competition will keep the already high prices down; many restaurants currently offer good buffet and special promotional deals.

Mid-range and expensive restaurants will normally add a 10% service charge and 4% tax. Many restaurants offer good value set lunches and more expensive set dinners. Keep an eye out for buffets, which allow you to try a number of dishes as you stuff yourself to the eyeballs at very reasonable prices. Many restaurants have lunch and dinner buffets, but the big hotels are the traditional buffet specialists.

See the illustrated section Tastes of Singapore, Malaysia & Brunei in the Malaysia Facts for the Visitor chapter and the Glossary at the end of the book for other details.

HAWKER FOOD

Traditionally, hawkers had mobile food stalls (pushcarts), set up their tables and stools around them, and sold their food right on the streets. Real, mobile, street hawkers have now been replaced by hawker centres, where a large number of stationary hawkers can be found under the one roof. These centres are the baseline for Singapore food, where the prices are lowest and the eating is the most interesting.

Scattered among the hawkers are tables and stools, and you can sit and eat in any area you choose – none of them belong to a specific stall. A group of you can sit at one table and all eat and drink from different stalls.

One of the wonders of food-centre eating is how the various operators keep track of their plates and utensils, and how they manage to chase you up with the bill. The real joy of these food centres is the sheer variety; while you're having Chinese food, your companion can be eating a biryani and across the table somebody else can be trying the satay. As a rough guide, most single-dish meals cost from S$3 to S$4, but the price is higher for more elaborate dishes.

There are hundreds of hawker centres all over Singapore, and many new shopping complexes and housing blocks set aside areas for the hawkers. Even Changi international airport has good food centres. A variation on the hawker centres are the food courts, essentially the same thing but air-conditioned and more like cafeterias with slightly higher prices. All centres are licensed by the government and are subject to health department regulations.

City Centre (Map 4)

Near the waterfront towards Chinatown is *Lau Pa Sat Festival Centre*, on Raffles Quay near the Raffles Place MRT station. Housed in the renovated Telok Ayer market building, it's a wonderful example of intricate Victorian cast-iron architecture in the mould of railway stations of the time. It has some souvenir stalls and occasionally stages cultural exhibits, but the main emphasis is on the favourite Singaporean pastime – food. Hawkers inside serve Nyonya, Korean and western food, as well as the more usual fare; and the famous Zam Zam restaurant has also opened a very popular *Indian Muslim stall.* Restaurants with bars are also found here. Lau Pa Sat is more sanitised and expensive than the usual hawker centres, but as part of the re-creation of old Singapore, *quasi-mobile hawkers* set up in the evenings on Boon Tat St, where the dining is cheaper and cooler than inside.

Orchard Rd (Map 2)

Newton Food Centre is at the north-eastern end of Scotts Rd, near the Newton MRT station. It is very popular with tourists and therefore tends to be a little more expensive, but it is lively and open 24 hours.

The *Kopitiam* food centre in the basement of Le Meridien Singapore is new on the scene and offers local, Japanese and western foods. It's also open 24 hours.

The *Scotts Picnic Food Court* in the Scotts Shopping Centre on Scotts Rd, just off Orchard Rd by the Hyatt Regency Hotel, is a glossy food court, with stalls offering a variety of international Asian cuisine, including Thai and Japanese.

Orchard Rd has a number of other food courts. *Orchard Emerald Food Court* in the basement of the Orchard Emerald shopping centre, on the corner of Emerald Hill Rd, has a range of Asian food. In the same vein are the food stalls downstairs in *Orchard Towers*, on the corner of Orchard and Claymore roads, at the west end of Orchard Rd, and the *Food Life Food Court* on the 4th floor of the Wisma Atria. The latter is small but has a good selection of local dishes and 'moderne' decor from the 1950s.

The *Asian Food Mall* in the basement of Lucky Plaza has a good range of local hawker favourites and is as cheap as you'll find anywhere.

Colonial District (Maps 3 & 4)

The *Albert Centre* on Albert Rd, between Waterloo and Queen streets, is an extremely good, busy and very popular centre, which has all types of food at low prices. On the corner of Bencoolen and Albert streets, in the basement of the Sim Lim Square complex, is the *Tenco Food Centre*, a very clean establishment.

Victoria St has a good selection of hawker centres. *Victoria St Food Court*, near the

Allson Hotel, is a notch up from most food centres. It has an air-con section at the back and a bar with draught beer. The food is cheap and good, and you can get western-style breakfasts. A few doors away, the *Koh Fong Restaurant* is not a restaurant, but a grouping of food stalls around open-air tables. Across the road in the Bras Basah Complex, the *Xiang Man Lou Food Court* is a small, new, air-con food court with Malay and Indian tandoori stalls, which also offer some Chinese favourites. It is open 24 hours.

The new *Bugis Junction* shopping centre on North Bridge Rd has an excellent food court in the basement, right near the entrance to the Bugis MRT station. It is more expensive than most, but has a good range and is great for Japanese food.

Food Paradiz, in the basement of the Paradiz Centre on Selegie Rd, is another good air-con food court.

The *Tropical Makan Palace* in the basement of the Beach Centre, 15 Beach Rd, is close to the Raffles and the budget accommodation area. It has food stalls in the air-conditioned section, or you can eat outside.

Just north of the river on Hill St, the large *Hill St Food Centre* is popular, and across the road the *Funan Centre* has a very good air-con food court on the 7th floor.

Little India (Map 3)

On Serangoon Rd at the start of Little India, the large *Zhujiao Centre* is a market with a number of food stalls. As you would expect, Indian food dominates. Opposite the market, the new, air-con *Hastings Food Court* in the Little India Arcade has vegetarian and non-vegetarian food, Kerala specialities and north Indian tandoori dishes.

On Jalan Besar there are two food centres, the *Berseh Food Centre* halfway down on the corner of Jalan Berseh and the lively *Lavender Food Centre* at the end of Jalan Besar near Lavender St, which is good for seafood and stays open until early morning.

Chinatown (Map 4)

Chinatown has a number of excellent food centres. The *People's Park Complex* on Eu Tong Sen St has a good, large food centre, and the *Maxwell Rd Food Centre* is an old-fashioned centre on the corner of South Bridge and Maxwell roads. The pig's trotters in black bean sauce is a speciality.

Some of the best Chinese food stalls in town are on the 2nd floor at the *Chinatown Complex* on the corner of Sago and Trengganu streets, where there is also a market. Try the *Fu Ji Crayfish*, stall No 02-221, where crayfish hor fun costs only S$3, or a superb crayfish (actually scampi) or prawn claypot with vegetables and rice costs around S$5.

The *Fountain Food Court* at 51 Craig Rd is a different type of food centre in keeping with the new Chinatown. You can dine in air-conditioned comfort, and the *nouveau decor* includes sand-blasted and bag-painted walls. The food is good, but some dishes are at restaurant prices. They have satay and other Malay food, popiah and kueh, and good (and cheap) congee.

Other hawker centres can be found alongside the *Tanjong Market*, not far from the train station, and at the *Amoy St Food Centre*, where Amoy St meets Telok Ayer St.

The famous *Satay Club* has finally fallen into the hand of the redevelopers, but many of the vendors have relocated from opposite the Padang to Clarke Quay, where over a dozen vendors fan their charcoal grills. The satay here is still the best in Singapore; just make sure you specify how many sticks (S$0.40 a time) you want, or vendors will assume your appetite is much larger than it actually is. It is at its liveliest in the evening. Clarke Quay also has an air-con *food court*.

Other Areas

The *Taman Serasi Food Centre* has one of the best settings – it is next to the Botanical Gardens north-west of the city centre on Cluny Rd, just off Napier Rd. The stalls are predominantly Malay. Try the 'roti John', a type of fried sandwich with chilli, washed down with the fabulous soursop fruit juice.

The *Rasa Singapura Food Court* is a collection of hawkers selected in a special competition to find the best stalls for each dish. It used to be on Tanglin Rd, but most of the hawkers have moved to the Bukit Turf Club on Turf Club Rd and they have taken the name with them. During the week, it's open for lunch and dinner until 11 pm. On weekends, it's open all day until midnight but you have to pay entry to the races until 6 pm.

CHINESE FOOD

Singapore has plenty of restaurants serving everything from a South Indian rice plate to an all-American hamburger, but naturally Chinese restaurants predominate. Many Chinese restaurants cater for family and work groups, offering banquets for eight or more people. For groups, they offer a wonderful opportunity to try a whole range of dishes at a reasonable price. Even at the à la carte restaurants, dishes are meant to be shared, and restaurants offer small, medium and large servings to cater for different size groups. The prices of dishes quoted here are for small servings.

Cantonese

The famous *Fatty's Eating House* (☎ 338 1087), at 01-33 Albert Complex on Albert St, near the corner of Bencoolen St, has been popular with westerners ever since Fatty became a favourite with British troops based in Singapore during the Emergency. The food is consistently good and moderately priced. Most dishes cost around S$5 to S$8, but can go up to S$20 or more for crab. The restaurant is always crowded, but the ever-busy staff turn the tables around quickly so you shouldn't have to wait long.

The *Hillman Restaurant* (☎ 221 5073) at 159 Cantonment Rd, near the Outram Park MRT station at the edge of Chinatown, is an open-fronted restaurant with a good reputation. You can have a good meal for under S$15 per person and pot-cooked dishes are the speciality: try the pot beef. The picture of Paul Bocuse, signed with a glowing recommendation from the master chef, is now faded, but the food is fresh and still good.

The *Esquire Kitchen* (☎ 336 1802), 02-01 Bras Basah Complex in the colonial district, is a moderately priced air-con place with typical red Chinese decor and good food. It does excellent value set lunches and dinners – three dishes and dessert costs S$18 for two people. More expensive banquets are also available.

Grand City (☎ 338 3622), 07-04 Cathay building, on the corner of Handy and Selegie roads, is a more expensive restaurant, and has a varied menu with good seafood and chicken dishes. Set menus start at around S$40 for two. It is near the Dhoby Ghaut MRT station, right at the start of Orchard Rd.

Tsui Hang Village (☎ 338 6668), 02-142 Marina Square, 6 Raffles Blvd, south-east of Raffles Hotel, is a popular Hong Kong-style restaurant. You can fill yourself on a good set lunch for around S$40 for two, or the set dinners start at S$60; à la carte meals are available. It also has a branch at the Asia Hotel, 37 Scotts Rd, near Orchard Rd

For dim sum a good bet is the *Tiong Shan Eating House*, an old-fashioned coffee shop on the corner of New Bridge and Keong Saik roads in Chinatown. A plate of dim sum is around S$1.50, and as good as you'll find anywhere. It has other dishes as well.

More expensive dim sum can be had in more luxurious air-con surroundings at the *Regency Palace* (☎ 338 3281) in the Plaza by the Park, 51 Bras Basah Rd, in the colonial district. The prices are reasonable and most plates cost about S$2 to S$4. Many of the big restaurants offer dim sum, but remember that dim sum is a lunchtime or Sunday breakfast dish – in the evening these restaurants change to other menus.

Just off Orchard Rd, Cuppage Plaza is a good little restaurant strip for cheap eats. A variety of restaurants are scattered around here, but the eastern side is lined with various *Chinese coffee shops*, with tables on the pavement. Steamboats from S$15 are a speciality, though most dishes cost S$4 to S$8.

Hainanese

Chicken-rice is a common and popular dish all over town. Originating in Hainan Island, off southern China, it's is a dish of elegant simplicity, and in Singapore you can find it at most hawker centres and food courts.

Yet Con (☎ 337 6819) at 25 Purvis St, just north of Raffles Hotel, is reputed to be the best of all Singapore's chicken-rice eateries. A similarly popular, but more expensive location, is the *Mandarin Hotel* on Orchard Road. The area west of Beach Rd is something of a Hainanese stronghold.

Hokkien

The *Beng Thin Hoon Kee* (☎ 553 7708) is on the 5th floor of the OCBC Centre on Chulia St; it is a short walk from the Raffles Place MRT station and has moderately priced dishes, including Hokkien seafood.

Szechuan

Spicy Szechuan, or Sichuan, food is popular with Singaporeans and restaurants are fairly common, though usually expensive.

The cheapest is the *Magic of Chongqing Hot Pot* (☎ 734 8135) on the 4th floor of the Tanglin shopping centre, offering a simple rustic eating ambience. Hot pot or steamboat features prominently and the 'eight treasure tonic tea' is perfect for cleansing the palate. A set dinner costs S$23.80, while a set lunch goes for a reasonable S$17.90. Both prices incur +++ taxes.

Next in line price-wise is the *Dragon City Sichuan* (☎ 254 7070) in the Novotel Orchid Hotel on Dunearn Rd. Its decor is fairly old-fashioned Chinese, but the food is excellent. Try the chef's favourite fried prawns with dried chilli. Dinner will cost two people about S$60. Smoking is not allowed.

Further along in price is the *Min Jiang* (☎ 730 1704) in the Goodwood Park Hotel on Scotts Rd. Szechuan hot and sour soup should be sampled, as well as the steamed dumplings. A romantic meal for two costs an impressive S$160.

Teochew

Teochew food is widely available in Singapore. It originated in south-eastern China near Guangzhou. Teochew invented the steamboat and is famed for the braised duck with soy sauce and chillies.

Among the many coffee shops in Chinatown's Mosque St you'll find a good range of Teochew food. These traditional restaurants are good places to sample simple Teochew food in the atmosphere of old Chinatown. Menus are hard to come by but a request for suggestions and prices will be readily answered, and the prices are low.

The *Chui Wah Lin* (☎ 221 3305) at 49 Mosque St has very good porridge – try the duck porridge for S$3. *Liang Kee* (☎ 225 5415) at 16 Murray Terrace is another good Teochew eatery. A tasty crayfish sambal goes for S$16.

The *Ellenborough St market*, near Boat Quay in Chinatown, is also noted for its Teochew food stalls.

For moderately priced Teochew food in more luxurious surroundings, try the *Teochow City Seafood Restaurant* (☎ 733 3338), 05-16 Centrepoint, 176 Orchard Rd.

Seafood

Singapore has another variation on Chinese food – seafood. In Singapore it is simply superb, whether it's prawns or abalone, fish-head curry or chilli crabs. Most of the specialists are some distance out from the city centre but the trip is worthwhile. Seafood isn't cheap, and a whole fish, crab or prawns start at just under S$20 per dish. Many places don't have set prices, but base them on 'market price' and the size of the fish. Make sure you check the price first.

The *UDMC Seafood Centre*, at the beach on East Coast Parkway, has a number of seafood restaurants and is very popular in the evenings. The food and the setting are good, but they tend to hustle a bit at some of these places, so definitely check the prices first.

Punggol Seafood is one of the better known restaurants here, having had a loyal following for years at its rural location at Ponggol on the north-east coast, before housing developments forced it to move. The food is still excellent, though slightly more expensive at around S$35 a head.

Long Beach Seafood Restaurant (☎ 445 8833), 1018 East Coast Parkway, is one of Singapore's best known seafood restaurants. It is famous for its black pepper crabs and 'live drunken prawns' (soaked in brandy). It is a casual, huge restaurant next to the Singapore Tennis Centre, and it also has a branch at UDMC.

The Bugis St area in the colonial district also has a couple of hustling seafood places; it is a pleasant place to dine under the stars and people-watch. There are also other, cheaper dishes at fixed prices available from the menus.

Something Different

Tanjong Pagar, to the south of Chinatown, has a number of Chinese tea houses, where the emphasis is on the art and presentation of tea drinking. Take your shoes off at the door, and as you sit on cushions on the floor the waitress will bring you a tea set (complete with burner and kettle of boiling water) and demonstrate the art of tea preparation.

Tea Chapter (☎ 226 1175), 9A Neil Rd, boasts Queen Elizabeth and Prince Philip among the clientele. Dim sum snacks are served for around S$2 per plate, and the extensive range of Chinese teas costs from S$6 to S$15. It's open from 11 am to 11 pm. A few doors away at No 23, *Yixing Yuan* offers a small dim sum lunch for around S$7, or you can have dim sum for around S$2 to S$3 per plate, washed down with the tea of your choice. Both these tea houses also have shops selling tea and tea paraphernalia – for a price.

Snackworld (☎ 732 6921), 01-12, 13 Cuppage Plaza, including the annexe outside on Cuppage Terrace off Orchard Rd, has crocodile on the menu, starting at S$25 a plate. If you can stomach the thought of eating the wildlife (actually it is farmed and, of course, it is supposed to taste like chicken), it has a wide range of dishes at some of the best prices in town.

Not far away, and right in the middle of Peranakan Place, is *Chilli Buddys* (☎ 732 9108) at 180 Orchard Rd. Home to the 'hottest in and outdoor restaurant', Chilli Buddys specialises in, well, chillies. The menu features a good selection of chilli-style dishes and describes fascinating stories about chillies. A mean, chilli-laced nasi goreng will cost you about S$13.50.

The *Imperial Herbal Restaurant* (☎ 337 0491) in the Metropole Hotel, 41 Seah St, near the Raffles Hotel in the colonial district, is an unusual restaurant with an extensive range of dishes cooked with medicinal herbs. You can order dishes recommended by the resident herbalist and sample weird and wonderful things like scorpions and deer penis. Expect to pay about S$40 per person.

Vegetarian

On Bencoolen St in the colonial district, the Fortune Centre is a good place for cheap vegetarian food. On the ground floor you'll find the *ABC Eating House* and *Yi Song* food stalls, which have cheap vegetarian food in air-con surroundings. Upstairs on the 4th floor is the *Eastern Vegetarian Food* coffee shop, offering rice or noodles with three selections of dishes from S$2. It is open on Sunday and public holidays.

At 143, 147 and 153 Kitchener Rd in Little India, the *Fut Sai Kai* (☎ 298 0336), which translates as 'monk's world', is a spartan old coffee shop and has an air-con restaurant next door. Most main dishes cost around S$8 to S$10. Similarly priced is the *Kwan Yim* (☎ 338 2394), another traditional, long-running vegetarian restaurant. It's at 190 Waterloo St in the South-East Asia Hotel, in the colonial district.

Chinatown has some moderately priced vegetarian restaurants, including the *Happy Realm* (☎ 222 6141) on the 3rd floor of Pearl's Centre on Eu Tong Sen St, one of the best around. Main dishes cost around S$5 to S$6 and it has good claypot dishes. *Loke Woh Yeun* (☎ 221 2912), 20 Tanjong Pagar Rd, is another in Chinatown where you can have a meal for under S$15. While it is mostly vegetarian, it also has chicken and prawn dishes.

INDIAN FOOD

There are three types of Indian food in Singapore: South Indian, Indian Muslim and north Indian.

South Indian food is mostly vegetarian and Little India is the main centre for it. You can get a thali, an all-you-can-eat rice plate with a mixture of vegetable curries, for less than S$5.

Indian Muslim food is something of a hybrid. It is the simpler South Indian version of what is basically north Indian food. Typical dishes are biryani, served with chicken or mutton curry, roti and murtabak. It can be found all over Singapore but the main centre is in North Bridge Rd opposite the Sultan Mosque. Indian Muslim food is also well represented in the hawker centres; you can have a superb chicken biryani from just S$2.50 to S$3.50.

For the rich north Indian curries and tandoori food, you have to go to more expensive restaurants. They can be found all around Singapore, but Little India has a concentrated selection of very good restaurants on Race Course Rd where you'll pay considerably less than Indian restaurants in the more fashionable areas.

To sample eat-with-your-fingers south Indian vegetarian food, the place to go is the Little India district off Serangoon Rd. The famous and very popular *Komala Vilas* (☎ 293 6980) at 12-14 Buffalo Rd was established soon after WWII, and has an open downstairs area where you can have masala dosa (S$1.50) and other snacks. The upstairs section is air-conditioned and you can have a thali for S$5. Remember to wash your hands before you start, use your right hand and ask for eating utensils only if you really have to. On your way out, try an Indian sweet from the showcase downstairs.

Two other thali specialists are *Sri Krishna Vilas* at 229 Selegie Rd and *Ananda Bhavan* at 219-221 Selegie Rd (the southern extension of Serangoon Rd).

There are several other Indian eateries on and off Serangoon Rd, and a main contender in the local competition for the best south Indian food is the *Madras New Woodlands Restaurant* (☎ 297 1594) at 14 Upper Dickson Rd, off Serangoon Rd. A branch of the well known Woodlands chain in India, New Woodlands serves freshly prepared vegetarian food in very clean air-conditioned rooms. The yoghurt is particularly good. Prices are about the same as at Komala Vilas.

Race Course Rd, a block north-west from Serangoon Rd, is the best area in Singapore for non-vegetarian curry. Try the *Banana Leaf Apolo Restaurant* (☎ 293 8682) at 56 Race Course Rd for superb Indian food, including Singapore's classic fish-head curry. Although luxurious with gleaming granite and air-con, prices are still reasonable with set meals at S$5.50 for vegetarian, S$6.50 for non-vegetarian and S$17 for fish-head curry. The very popular *Muthu's Curry Restaurant* (☎ 293 2389) at 78 Race Course Rd also specialises in fish-head curry and other seafood dishes. Thali varies from S$4 to S$6 depending on what you choose, or fish-head curry starts at S$16 for a serve to share.

In the same block on Race Course Rd are good north Indian restaurants with typically dark decor. They serve the cheapest, and some of the best, Indian tandoori food in Singapore. *Delhi Restaurant* (☎ 296 4585) at No 60 has Mughlai and Kashmiri food, with curries from S$5 to S$12. Expect to pay around $20 per person for a substantial meal with bread and side dishes. The food is excellent and this restaurant is always popular. If it is full, the sister restaurant a few doors down at No 48, *D'Deli Pubb & Restaurant* (☎ 294 5276), has the same fare with a bar at the front. *Nur Jehan* (☎ 292 8033) at No 66 is slightly cheaper, and has good tandoori and other north Indian food. *Maharajah's Tandoor* (☎ 293 0865) at No 70 offers a similar range of food and prices.

Just around the corner is *Andhra Curry* (☎ 293 3935) at 41 Kerbau Rd, with tasteful decor in a renovated Peranakan terrace. Cheap vegetarian and non-vegetarian set meals are offered for lunch and dinner, but the most popular part of the restaurant is the food-stall area, in a beer garden setting out the front.

Another cheap north Indian restaurant in Little India is the small *Delhi Restaurant*, in the Broadway Hotel at 195 Serangoon Rd. It has curries and kormas for around S$4.50 and breads such as naan.

For Indian Muslim food (chicken biryani for S$3.50, as well as murtabak and fish-head curry), there are a couple of cheap, venerable establishments on North Bridge Rd in the Arab St area, opposite the Sultan Mosque. Each of them has the year of founding proudly displayed on their signs out front. The *Victory* (established 1910) is at 701 North Bridge Rd, the *Zam Zam* (established 1908) is at No 699. Newly renovated and further along at No 791-797 is the *Islamic*. Slightly more upmarket, in renovated and air-conditioned surrounds, the *Jubilee Classic Restaurant*, at No 749, has the same Muslim dishes and a few more at very reasonable prices.

There's a small, basic Indian Muslim place called *OM Moosa Restaurant* under the backpackers' guesthouses at 129 Bencoolen St near Middle Rd, across from the Fortune Centre, in the colonial district. It has very good food and specialises in fish dishes, including fish-head curry, but has chicken and vegetable dishes too. Meals are around S$4 and it is open 24 hours. In Chinatown, a similarly lively and cheap 24 hour restaurant is the *Tasree Restaurant*, at 323 New Bridge Rd opposite the Pearl's Centre.

In the Orchard Rd area, *Maharani* (☎ 235 8840) is on the 5th floor of the Far East Shopping Centre, 14 Scotts Rd. The north Indian food and the service are good in this casual restaurant. You can eat well for S$20 per person and lunch buffets are offered on weekends.

There's also a vegetarian Woodlands restaurant in this area; the *Bombay Woodlands Restaurant* (☎ 235 2712), B1-01 Tanglin shopping centre, 19 Tanglin Rd. The decor is very Orchard Rd and the prices are about three times what you pay in Little India, but the buffet lunches for S$10 are still reasonable value.

Boat Quay near Chinatown has a good selection of more expensive north Indian restaurants for dining inside, or overlooking the river. *Maharajah* (☎ 535 0122) at No 41 is one of the cheaper options with curries for around S$8 to S$14. A good meal costs S$25 or less per person. The fashionable *Royal Bengal* at No 72 is lavishly decorated in colonial style, as are the staff. The food is not just Bengali, and a meal will cost around S$35. The marginally cheaper *Hazara* is a small 'north Indian frontier' restaurant at No 57, with Indian antiques and efficient service. The food is very good, though the serves are small.

Possibly the best Indian restaurant in town is the *Cashmir* (☎ 735 5506) on the 4th floor of Ngee Ann City at 391 Orchard Rd. Its subtly elegant dining area is enough to win points before you even order your food, while the dishes are touted as 'fine food fit for moghuls'. Biryani rice with mutton is the speciality but prawn masala vies competitively for the title of top dish. A meal for two should not exceed a reasonable S$70.

MALAY & INDONESIAN FOOD

Though Malay food is scattered throughout Singapore, Malay restaurants are not abundant. The occasional stall or two at some of the food centres serve Malay food, and satay is easily found. Indonesian food shares many similarities with Malay cuisine, though some dishes, such as gado gado, are uniquely Indonesian.

The Orchard Rd area has a number of good restaurants. *Bintang Timur* (☎ 235 4539), 02-13 Far East Plaza, 14 Scotts Rd, has excellent Malay food at excellent prices. You can try a good range of dishes and eat your fill for S$20 or less. *Tambuah Mas* (☎ 733 3333), 04-10/13 Tanglin shopping centre, 19 Tanglin Rd, is a cheap Indonesian restaurant with a good selection of seafood dishes and Indonesian favourites such as rendang, gado gado and cendol. Another good Indonesian restaurant is *Sanur* (☎ 734 2192), 04-17/18 Centrepoint, 176 Orchard Rd. Most mains are S$7 to S$10 and range up to S$20 for whole fish.

Pancha Sari (☎ 338 1032), 03-239 Marina Square, is a reasonably priced Indonesian restaurant in the colonial district. Most mains cost S$6 to S$10 and you can eat well for under S$20. The small lunch set menu is S$6.50.

If you like the fiery food of north Sumatra, there are a few nasi padang specialists, the best known being *Rendezvous*, 02-19 in the Raffles City shopping centre on Bras Basah

Rd, in the colonial district. The good and cheap *Rumah Makan Minang* is in a renovated shophouse on the corner of Muscat and Kandahar streets, behind the Sultan Mosque on Arab St.

House of Sundanese Food (☎ 345 5020), 218 East Coast Rd, east of the city towards Katong, specialises in the cuisine from West Java. There are a number of dishes, nasi padang style, many of which cost around S$4. The chicken dishes are particularly good, or try the charcoal-grilled whole fish for around S$20. It also has a branch at 55 Boat Quay, but it is not as good as the one at East Coast Rd.

The Geylang district in the east coast area has plenty of Malay eateries. For Malay food stalls during the day, go to the *Geylang Serai Market* on Changi Rd. This is the predominantly Malay area in Singapore, and it's worth a visit just t o see the market, which is more traditional than the new complexes. To get there, take the MRT to the Paya Lebar station and walk east along Sims Ave to Geylang Serai.

About 1km from Geylang Serai Market, *Casa Bom Vento*, 467 Joo Chiat Rd, is an interesting restaurant serving Eurasian food, which is a mixed cuisine, basically Malay in origin with a Portuguese bent. Try the beef smor (pepper steak) or the debal (devil curry), a traditional post-Christmas dish of leftover meats and vegetables cooked up in a fiery curry. mains cost around S$6 to S$10.

NYONYA FOOD

Nonya & Baba Restaurant (☎ 734 1382) at 262-264 River Valley Rd is one of the best restaurants to try Nyonya food at reasonable prices. Most mains cost around S$6 for small claypots, or up to S$15 for large serves. A variety of snacks and sweets are also available. It is near the corner of Tank Rd and directly behind the Imperial Hotel, west of Fort Canning Park. The Dhoby Ghaut MRT station at the start of Orchard Rd is a 15 minute walk away.

There are Nyonya buffets at the *King's* and *Apollo* hotels in Havelock Rd (north-west of Pearl's Hill City Park), and the *Bayview Inn* in Bencoolen St in the colonial district has a good lunchtime buffet for S$13.80 on Wednesday and weekends. In Holland Village, west of the city, the *Baba Cafe* (☎ 468 9859) at 25B Lorong Liput offers good value food in an attractive setting.

One of the best places to go for Nyonya food is east of the city in the Geylang and Katong districts. Along (and just off) Joo Chiat Rd, between East Coast and Geylang roads in particular, is a good hunting ground for all kinds of Asian foods. *Guan Hoe Soon* (☎ 344 2761), 214 Joo Chiat Rd, is a long-running, moderately priced restaurant, noted for its Nyonya dishes. Although it has air-conditioning, it's just a glorified coffee shop.

East Coast Rd in Katong is a great place to try Nyonya food. The *Peranakan Inn* (☎ 440 6194), 210 East Coast Rd, is one of the cheapest places in Singapore to eat Nyonya food in an air-con setting. Most dishes cost S$4 to S$6, and more expensive seafood dishes are around S$15. On the corner of East Coast and Ceylon roads, the *Hok Tong Hin Restaurant* is a hawker-style coffee shop where you can get superb *laksa* for only S$2.50. The *Carlton Restaurant*, on the corner of East Coast Rd and Lorong Stangee, is similar. During the day, try the Nyonya kueh and curry puffs at the *Katong Bakery & Confectionary* (☎ 344 8948), 75 East Coast Rd. This wonderful, old-fashioned cake shop is a throwback to the Singapore of yesteryear. But if you prefer more sanitised surroundings, East Coast Rd also has plenty of new cake shops for take-aways. The best bus for East Coast Rd is No 14, which goes along Orchard and Bras Basah roads in the colonial district. Bus Nos 10, 12 and 40 will also get you there from the colonial district.

OTHER ASIAN FOOD

Thai

The Golden Mile Complex at 5001 Beach Rd, just north-east of Arab St, is a modern shopping centre catering to Singapore's Thai community. Here you'll find a number of small coffee shops serving Thai food and Singha beer. Prices are cheap – you can get a good meal for S$4 or S$5. You'll also find the *Pornping Thai Seafood Restaurant* (☎ 298 5016), which is a notch up in quality, and has a bar and an extensive Thai menu.

Parkway Thai (☎ 737 8080) in Centrepoint, 176 Orchard Rd, has an extensive menu – small mains range from S$8 up $15 for seafood. *Cuppage Thai Food Restaurant* (☎ 734 1116), 49 Cuppage Rd, is not the greatest Thai restaurant but it has set dinners for two at S$28 and S$38, and a pleasant alfresco setting just off Orchard Rd.

Baan Thai (☎ 735 5562), 04-23 Ngee Ann City, Orchard Rd, is one of the best Thai restaurants in Singapore, with good sized mains for around S$14 to S$20.

Japanese

Singapore has experienced a Japanese restaurant boom, which reflects the Japanese tourist boom. While you can spend a small fortune at a Japanese restaurant, you can also find food at moderate prices.

The Cold Storage supermarket in the *Takashimaya department store* at Ngee Ann City, Orchard Rd, has a great take-away bar for sushi (raw fish) and sashimi (raw fish accompanied by horseradish, pickled ginger and soy sauce) at very low prices. Also at Takashimaya, *Nogawa* (☎ 735 9918) on the 4th floor is a reasonably priced Japanese restaurant with sushi from S$4 and mains for around S$15 to S$18.

A few food courts also have teppanyaki (chicken, beef and seafood grilled on a hot plate) with a dining bar. There's one in the basement at *Bugis Junction shopping centre* on North Bridge Rd in the colonial district, with grills for around S$6 to S$10, and S$15 for set meals. *Teppanyaki Place* in the Tanglin Mall Food Court on Tanglin Rd, at the northern end of Orchard Rd, has grills at S$16 for two.

Small Japanese restaurants displaying plastic-glazed meals in the window can be found all around Singapore. *Restaurant Hoshigaoka* is a chain of Japanese restaurants, with branches at 03-45 Centrepoint and 01-18 Wisma Atria on Orchard Rd, and 03-237 Marina Square, east of the Padang. Small set meals, such as tempura (seafood and vegetables deep-fried in light batter) and sushi, are around S$20.

Izumi (☎ 534 3390) at 48 Boat Quay is more expensive but worth it. Cheaper set dinners for S$30 are available. *Sumos* in the Bugis Junction shopping complex basement is a great place for a quick and inexpensive meal. A teppanyaki set with beer will be no more than S$12.

For top-of-the-range Japanese food, try the *Keyaki* (☎ 336 8111), in the Pan Pacific Hotel on Raffles Blvd, east of the Padang.

Korean

Seoul Garden is a Korean chain which has branches at 05-01 Shaw Centre, 1 Scotts Rd in the Orchard Rd area, and 03-119 Marina Square, 6 Raffles Blvd, among others. The Korean BBQ set lunches for around S$12 and the slightly more expensive set dinners are excellent value. Tanjong Pagar Rd in Chinatown also has a number of Korean restaurants, and Clarke Quay has riverside Korean BBQ stalls. The Clarke Quay *towkangs*, refurbished Chinese junks moored on the Singapore River, also have Korean and other BBQs. A good feed with beer will cost around S$20.

Burmese

There are not too many places where you can eat good Burmese food around town, but one you should not miss, if you fancy something different, is the *Beautiful Myanmar Restaurant* at 11 Mosque St in Chinatown. This small, friendly and modern establishment stills caters for mainly Burmese clients, and its house speciality is Yangon dun bouk (golden rice with a choice of meats). Try the spicy and supposedly very healthy mjin khwa thoke salad full of green chillies, vegetables and crunchies. You can eat well for well under S$20, including beer.

Taiwanese

Try the reasonably priced *Goldleaf* at 24-24A Tanjong Pagar Rd in Chinatown. A speciality is chicken covered in whole fried chillies. You can eat very well for less than S$20.

In Katong at 199 East Coast Rd is the *Lung Yee Family Restaurant*, which specialises in Taiwanese food and gets good write-ups in the local press for its home-style Taiwanese fare. Porridge is only S$3, and other dishes you could try are fairy duck, imperial chicken and drunken prawns all at reasonable prices.

INTERNATIONAL FOOD

Fast Food

Yes, you can get western food in Singapore too. There are over 50 *McDonald's*, found all over town. It's good to see that the corporate smile and 'have a nice day' haven't really caught on in Singapore – you can be served with the same brusque efficiency as you would find in any Singaporean coffee shop.

There are also *A&W*, *KFC*, *Burger King*, *Dunkin' Donuts*, *Denny's*, *Pizza Hut*, *Baskin Robbins* and *Swensen's Ice Cream* outlets – obviously there's no shortage of western fast food.

French

A number of restaurants do a pretty good job of convincing you that you're in France, even though you're almost on the equator.

La Cascade, 7 Ann Siang Hill Rd in Chinatown, is one of the cheaper French restaurants with set meals for around S$48.

Le Restaurant de France (☎ 733 8855) in the Le Meridien Hotel, 100 Orchard Rd, is one of the better French restaurants in Singapore. Or you may like to take a credit card or two to *Maxim's de Paris* in the Regent Hotel, 1 Cuscaden Rd, in the Orchard Rd area. The best value is the dinner buffet for S$95.

Italian

Gone are the days when Italian food was only available at a few super expensive restaurants or chain stores serving soggy pizza and insipid pasta. Italian is 'in' and Italian restaurants are sprouting up everywhere.

Boat Quay near Chinatown has its fair share of Italian restaurants. One of the best for the money is *Pasta Fresca* (☎ 469 4920) at 30 Boat Quay; it has a huge range of very authentic pastas from S$10, and small pizzas from S$12 to S$15. Round off a meal with tiramisu, the most fashionable Italian dessert in Singapore. It is open 24 hours. This restaurant is part of chain and it also has an outlet on the 4th floor of Shaw House, 350 Orchard Rd on the corner of Scotts Rd.

At 31 Boat Quay, *Luna Luna* (☎ 538 2030) specialises in seafood. It is enormously popular, as much due to the Boat Quay location as the good food. A meal will set you back at least S$35, but cheaper set lunches and dinners are available. *Al Dente Trattoria* (☎ 536 5366) at 70 Boat Quay is another restaurant serving primarily pasta and pizza.

Sketches (☎ 339 8386) in the Bugis Junction shopping centre at 200 Victoria St is an unusual kind of 'design-your-own' Italian pasta restaurant, in which you create your own dish from a tick-off menu. Meals are tasty and priced in the mid-range. It's very close to the Bugis MRT station.

Ristorante Bologna (☎ 338 3388) in the Marina Mandarin Hotel in the Marina Square complex, on the edge of the colonial district, is one of the best and most expensive Italian restaurants in town.

Other International Food

Hard Rock Cafe (☎ 235 5232), 50 Cuscaden Rd, near the corner of Orchard and Tanglin roads, is popular for American-style steaks, BBQ grills and ribs. Main meals cost around S$20, and snacks such as burgers cost around S$8. The restaurant finishes serving meals at around 10.30 pm when the bands start, but there is a small snack bar that stays open.

Bob's Tavern (☎ 467 2419), 17A Lorong Liput, Holland Village, to the west of the city, is an English-style pub popular with expats who, for some reason, miss English food. It does good steaks, fish and chips etc. Main meals cost around S$20. You can drink at the bar, or dine outside on the veranda.

Singapore steak houses are mostly run by chains such as *Ponderosa*, which has three locations: 68 Orchard Rd; 02-232 Marina Square; and 02-20 Raffles City shopping centre in the colonial district. A steak and a serving from the salad bar costs around S$20. The *Sizzler* chain is also moving into Singapore, but the biggest chain is *Jack's Place* with restaurants all over town, including 03-18, 19 Wisma Atria, 435 Orchard Rd and 01-01 Bras Basah Complex in the colonial district. Grills cost from S$16 to S$22, while pasta and chicken dishes cost around S$12.

Many other cuisines are represented in Singapore. For German food, there is the *Bräuhaus Restaurant & Pub* (☎ 250 3116), United Square, 101 Thomson Rd, to the north of the city centre. The *Treffpunkt Cafe*, B2-09 Tanglin shopping centre in the Orchard Rd area, is a small deli serving German sausages and the like.

Istanbul Corner, 01-11 Cuppage Plaza, right near the corner of Orchard Rd, is one of the few Middle Eastern restaurants and is pretty cheap. Greek food can be had at *Olea* near Holland Park at 833 Bukit Timah Rd. The menu is comprehensive, but prices are a bit on the high side.

El Felipes Cantina (☎ 468 1520), 34 Lorong Mambong in Holland Village, is an old favourite that has large serves and moderate prices. Tex-Mex dishes cost around S$12 to S$15, and innovative mains with a Spanish touch are slightly more expensive. Next door, the similar *Cha Cha Cha* (☎ 462 1650), 32 Lorong Mambong, is the most popular Mexican restaurant in town, as much for the margaritas as the good food. *Chili's Bar & Grill*, 75 Boat Quay near Chinatown, has American grills with overtones of Tex-Mex and is moderately priced.

Saxophone Bar & Grill (☎ 235 8385), 23 Cuppage Terrace just off Orchard Rd, is a pleasant place to dine al fresco and listen to the music coming from inside. The food is French/continental and expensive.

JP Bastiani Wine Bar (☎ 339 0392), 01-13 Clarke Quay, is a wine merchant with a very chic wine bar where high fliers like to be seen. Its wine buffet on Thursday and Friday nights for S$45 has cheese, antipasto, meats and a number of varieties of wine included in the price.

Alkaff Mansions (☎ 278 6979), west of the city at 10 Telok Blangah Green, has ambience plus-plus-plus. This restored mansion offers Dutch rijsttafel (buffet 'rice table') with an endless parade of dishes served with a touch of colonial theatre for a whopping S$65 – this is popular with tour groups. Much cheaper, but still allowing you to take in the serene surroundings and the gracious mansion, are the western and Asian buffets for S$28 for lunch and S$35 for dinner.

BREAKFAST, SNACKS & DELIS

The big international hotels offer large international breakfast buffets of course (around S$20 to S$25), but there are still a few old coffee shops which do cheap Chinese and Indian breakfasts – take your pick of dosa and curry or yu tiao and hot soy milk.

Roti canai with a mild curry dip is a delicious and economical breakfast available at *OM Moosa Restaurant*, 129 Bencoolen St, in the cheap hotel area. Most of the old coffee shops will rustle you up toast and kaya (egg and coconut jam).

There are many places which do a fixed-price breakfast – continental or American. Try the *Silver Spoon Coffee House* at B1-05 Park Mall, 9 Penang Rd, off Orchard Rd. *McDonald's* and *A&W* do fast-food breakfasts: you can have a McDonald's 'big breakfast' for S$3.90. In Bencoolen St, the *Golden Dragon Inn* is a Chinese coffee shop on the 2nd floor of the Fortune Centre that does a reasonable job of western grills. If you crave cholesterol for breakfast, ham and eggs costs only S$3, and later in the day steak or prawns with chips and eggs served on a sizzler costs S$6.

The buffet breakfasts at *Coleman's Cafe* (S$13.50) in the Peninsula Hotel and *Cafe Victoria* (S$18) in the Carlton Hotel in the colonial district are good.

One of the nicest breakfasts is undoubtedly *Breakfast with the Birds* (☎ 265 0022) at Jurong Bird Park. Although closed at the time of writing it was due to reopen soon after this book's publication.

For western-style pastries, head for the *Café d'Orient de Delifrance* at Peranakan

Place on Orchard Rd – the croissants and coffee are hard to beat. This is the original branch with the best setting, but you can find others everywhere in Singapore.

Old Chang Kee is a chain that specialises in that old favourite – curry puffs. There is a branch at Lau Pa Sat, on Raffles Quay, and another on the corner of McKenzie and Niven roads, near Selegie Rd in the colonial district. On the opposite corner, the *Selera Restaurant*, 15 McKenzie Rd, is the best place in town for curry puffs. Try its range, washed down with coffee in an old-style *kopi tiam*. The small *L E Cafe* at 264 Middle Rd, under the Sun Sun Hotel almost at Selegie Rd, is an old-fashioned place with European and oriental cakes and pastries to take away.

Singapore has plenty of delis catering to lunching office workers and snacking shoppers. In the Orchard Rd area, *Aroma's Deli*, 01-05 Tanglin shopping centre on Tanglin Rd, has good coffee and a changing menu. *Seah Street Deli* in the Raffles Hotel is slightly misnamed. Singapore's answer to a New York deli, it has pastrami, bagels and rye at higher than average prices but still excellent.

HIGH TEA

Most of the coffee shops in the big hotels do 'high tea', featuring local cakes and snacks, and all the tea or coffee you can drink. They are usually buffet affairs held in the afternoon, around 4 pm, and are good value and delightful eating experiences. Add 14% taxes to all the following prices.

Cafe Oriental in the Amara Hotel near Chinatown has a Nyonya buffet, one of the most popular cuisines for high tea, for S$10 from 3 to 6 pm on weekdays.

The *Coffee Lounge* at the exclusive Goodwood Park Hotel in the Orchard Rd area has a good Nyonya kueh buffet from 3 to 5.30 pm for S$13.80. The *Cafe Espresso* at the Goodwood Park Hotel has an English high tea for S$18.50.

The *Bar & Billiard Room* at the Raffles Hotel has high tea from 3.30 to 5 pm featuring Asian and continental food. Though expensive at S$25++, it is one of the most affordable things you can do at the Raffles.

Coleman's Cafe in the Peninsula Hotel, just west of the Padang, is particularly good value at S$7.50 for a range of savoury hawker favourites, but only on Saturday from 3.15 to 6 pm.

The *Kaspia Bar* at the Hilton does a good English high tea from 3 to 6 pm on weekdays. Buttered crumpets, scones with jam and cream, sandwiches and cheeses are featured. It costs S$16.50.

The *Melting Pot Cafe* at the Concorde Hotel, west of Chinatown, has the longest high tea in town – from noon to 5 pm on weekends – for S$13.80.

CYBERCAFES

High-tech Singapore is jumping on the Internet bandwagon as the government exhorts the nation to surf the Net and look for new business opportunities. Cybercafes seem to be springing up everywhere, though food definitely takes a back seat to the information superhighway.

The *CyberNet Cafe* (☎ 324 4361), 57 Tanjong Pagar Rd in Chinatown, has a bank of terminals for S$8 per hour. Coffee, soft drinks and a very limited selection of snacks are available. It is open from 11 am to 10 pm Monday to Saturday, 2 to 7 pm on Sunday. There is also a branch in Terminal 2 at Changi airport

The *Coffee Bean* (☎ 438 1037), 52 Boat Quay at the North Bridge Rd end, is a geek escape in the liveliest restaurant and bar strip in Singapore. It is open daily from 8 am to midnight. A wide variety of coffees, teas, sandwiches, pastries, desserts and drinks, including beer, are served. A small area with computer terminals run independently by Pacific Net allows you to Netsurf or check your email for S$10 an hour or S$6 for 30 minutes.

On the top floor of the Funan Centre at 109 North Bridge Rd is the handy *Challenger Planet Cafe* (☎ 336 7747). There are only two terminals, but you can easily and quickly check your email and surf, while enjoying a cup of coffee and a snack.

The *Cyberheart Cafe* (☎ 734 3877) at 442 Orchard Rd, in the basement of the Orchard

Hotel shopping centre, offers pizzas and other snacks, and about a dozen terminals for you to surf and munch.

SUPERMARKETS

Singapore has plenty of supermarkets with everything from French wine and Australian beer to yoghurt, muesli, cheese and ice cream. *Cold Storage* is one of the largest chains and it has well-stocked supermarkets in the basements of Takashi-maya at Ngee Ann City and Centrepoint, both on Orchard Rd. Another is at Bugis Junction on Victoria St in the colonial district.

For late night groceries, *Smart*, on the northern side of the Marina Square complex, just west of the Padang, is open 24 hours. 7-Eleven stores are found all over town. In the colonial district you'll find a branch at 75 Victoria St, and in the Centrepoint Complex on Orchard Rd.

Entertainment

Singapore's nightlife is burgeoning, as the young middle class spends its increasing wealth on entertainment. It's not of the Bangkok sex and sin variety, nor does a wild club scene exist, but the huge number of bars and discos are becoming increasingly sophisticated. Pool, wine and cigars are cool, and that's what you'll find the young things indulging in at all the groovy hang-outs.

Many of the casual, smaller bars springing up everywhere have live music. Boat Quay is packed nightly until the early hours of the morning, but Orchard Rd and Chinatown also have their fair share of good bars. Smoking is permitted in bars, though if food is also served smoking is restricted until after meal hours. For better bands, you have to go to the clubs and discos, where a cover charge normally applies. Dress is smart casual, drinks are expensive and the bands mostly play covers. Almost every four star hotel has a Filipino band playing in the lobby, every five star hotel has a jazz band in the lobby, while even many three star hotels can muster up a piano bar.

Highbrow entertainment in the form of classical music, ballet and theatre can be enjoyed in Singapore, as well as Chinese opera and tourist-oriented cultural shows.

The free tourist magazines and the local newspapers have limited entertainment sections. The *Straits Times* is good for cultural and special events. *Eight Days*, the weekly TV and entertainment magazine, has the best listings. For nightlife look out for the free *I-S Magazine* at tourist locations.

BARS, BANDS & DISCOS

The time to drink is during the happy hours, usually around 5 to 8 pm, when drinks are as cheap as half price. Though most of the bars also serve food, the serious drinking is done outside meal times – you can grab a stool at the bar anytime.

Many bars feature bands. Imports still dominate – mostly Filipino bands and occasionally western musicians – playing jazz, pop covers, old favourites or even something more risqué like the blues. Singapore has hardcore bands like Stompin' Ground, but they won't be playing in Orchard Rd. It is difficult to see original Singaporean performers singing about life in the HDB estates, or dissatisfaction with the oppressive nature of Singaporean society, but they do exist and Singaporean music is developing its own identity. *Substation* in Armenian St in the colonial district occasionally puts on concerts of original local performers. Popular artists such as Dick Lee and Kopi Kat Klan laid the foundation for local performers singing songs with Asian themes and a Singaporean voice. The local recording scene is expanding, but still nascent.

Singapore has no shortage of discos. They tend to be big on decor and are yuppie hangouts with strict dress codes. A few dance party clubs exist but they are fairly tame. A cover charge of around S$15 to S$20 applies on Monday to Friday and S$25 to S$35 on weekends, but this usually includes the first drink. Women often pay less.

Some venues don't have a cover charge, but drinks are expensive and you can expect to pay around S$10 for a glass of beer. Those that do have a cover charge usually provide the first drink free. For most venues, a 10% service charge and 4% government tax are added to the drinks and the cover charge. Most have happy hours until around 8 pm, when the beers are up to half price, but the music doesn't start until later.

Orchard Rd Area (Map 2)

The Orchard Rd area is still the main centre for nightlife, with a host of bars and pubs mainly in the hotels and shopping centres.

One of the biggest discos, *Fire*, 04-19 Orchard Plaza, 150 Orchard Rd, is teenage techno heaven. The cover charge is S$12 for girls (S$21 on weekends), S$15 for boys (S$24 on weekends). Under the same management, and the favourite in Singapore at the moment, is *Sparks*, Level 7, Ngee Ann City. The dance floor jumps to the biggest music system in town, and everything stops for the dazzling laser show. For something quieter in the same complex, try the *Jazz Evergreen*. *Fabrice's World Music Bar* at the Marriott Hotel, 320 Orchard Rd, is home to some interesting bands, with music ranging from reggae and African to Latin American. Cover charges range from S$15 on Monday to Friday to S$25 on weekends.

Orchard Towers at 400 Orchard Rd has a concentration of venues. It has been tagged the 'Four Floors of Whores', which, though there are a few bar girls, makes it sound more risqué than it is. *Top Ten* on the 4th floor is a large barn of a place with Manhattan-skyline decor and an affluent clientele. It is primarily a disco, but a band alternates brackets. Entry costs S$22 for the first drink on Friday, S$28 on Saturday and S$17 for the rest of the week. *Ginivy*, on the 2nd floor of Orchard Towers, has two types of music – country and western. It's a casual place with middle-aged cowboys and a smattering of bar girls. In a similar vein but smaller and quieter is *FB's* on the 3rd floor, featuring football and Fosters.

Anywhere, 04-08 Tanglin shopping centre, 19 Tanglin Rd, is a long-running rock 'n' roll venue. The band Tania has been playing here since 1981 and features a cross-dressing lead singer. The band has a regular following of mostly expats and can belt out a song when they try. This place has a casual, convivial atmosphere and no cover charge.

Hard Rock Cafe, 50 Cuscaden Rd, has the usual rock memorabilia and good atmosphere. It has better bands than most venues, and occasionally imports some big names from overseas. The music and cover charge starts, and the ash trays come out, after 10.30 pm when the dining stops. Entry is S$15, except Sunday – otherwise get there early. It stays open until around 2 or 3 am.

Opposite the Hard Rock Cafe in the basement of the Ming Arcade, *Cave Man* is a cool little bar with graffiti everywhere and modern music on the jukebox. Not a lot happens, but it's a casual bar for conversation. The *Makati Club* on the 7th floor is a large, smoky Filipino disco with no cover charge.

Brannigan's in the Hyatt Regency is a popular, casual pick-up spot, with a mixed clientele and its fair share of bar girls. Good bands play until 1 or 2 am, and happy hours are from 5 to 8 pm. It is packed on weekends.

Emerald Hill Rd has a collection of bars in the renovated terraces just up from Orchard Rd. *No 5* at, you guessed it, 5 Emerald Hill Rd, is very popular with a largely tourist clientele and its chilli vodka has a mean reputation. The bar is usually crowded, or you can drink at the tables outside, while acoustic music plays upstairs. Next door at No 7, *Que Pasa* is a popular tapas bar with a Spanish theme and smokers will enjoy the snazzy upstairs smoking room. Next along at No 9, *Ice Cold Beer* has the coldest beer in town and lots of different brands. You can even watch movies for free upstairs.

Upstairs at Peranakan Place on the corner of Emerald Hill and Orchard roads, *Papa Joe's* is another popular place with a covers band on the weekend and a first drink cover charge.

Nearby, the *Saxophone Bar & Grill* at 23 Cuppage Terrace, near the corner of Orchard Rd, is a small place with some good blues, jazz and funk music. It's so small that the musician O'Donel Levy and his R&B band have to play on a platform behind the bar, but you can sit outside and listen after the dining finishes. There's no cover charge.

The *Tapas Bar* at the Omni Marco Polo Hotel, 247 Tanglin Rd, is another very popular bar with a Latin theme and a lively dance floor. The band has salsa and flamenco rhythms, and the tapas buffet for S$5 is good, though not exactly Spanish.

Vincent's Lounge, 6/F Lucky Plaza, is a small gay pub that is popular any night of the week.

The River (Map 4)

The renovated banks of the Singapore River in the centre of town are the happening place in Singapore, especially Boat Quay. Further along the river, Clarke Quay is less frenetic but also has its fair share of watering holes which are popular on the weekend.

Boat Quay Is there life after Boat Quay? This place has become so incredibly popular that the rest of Singapore seems dead in comparison. The crowds start coming around 6 pm for a quiet drink or a meal, and keep growing through the night. Weekends are very busy until 2 or 3 am, while weekdays are marginally quieter and most bars close by 1 am. Boat Quay attracts everyone from the rich and famous to young Singaporean kids vomiting into the gutter after a night of overindulgence.

Boat Quay has so many bars that you can just wander along until one takes your fancy.

Rogue Trader – Nick Leeson

When the beer is flowing at Harry's, on Boat Quay, the talk among the expat regulars still frequently returns to the subject of one of the bar's most infamous patrons. On 23 February 1995 Nicholas William Leeson, general manager at Barings Futures Singapore, a shade short of his 28th birthday, disappeared from his office having single-handedly wrought a disaster of catastrophic financial dimensions.

He had totally wiped out the 233-year-old Barings Investment Bank in a cumulative series of ill-conceived investment gambles on the derivatives market – a game that few in financial circles knew much about, nor cared to master. He bet heavily on the future direction of the Nikkei Index, which he hoped would rise at the beginning of 1995. With the Japanese economy on a gradual slide, and coupled with the Kobe earthquake, Leeson's financial gambles on the Nikkei went from bad to ruinous.

All this time Leeson had managed to persuade his superiors that he was making money for Barings when, in fact, he was losing money by the barrow-load. Since he acted as both front-office trader and back-office settlements manager he was able to disguise his manoeuvrings, while at the same time pulling in an enormous salary of his own. By December 1994, the cumulative debt in the ultimately inauspiciously numbered account, No 88888, had topped $512 million. By the end of his gambling spree he had cost Barings $1.3 billion.

Nick Leeson was a working class Londoner with a thirst for the good life and a brash ability to persuade others that he was doing fine in what is generally viewed as a high-risk financial activity. When the chips were down he finally skipped Singapore. He was arrested in March 1995, while on a stopover in Germany, and extradited back to Singapore, where he was sentenced to six and a half years. In 1999, he was released after three and a half years, for good behaviour.

Nick Leeson, the man who was once expelled from Harry's Bar for baring his backside, now has a lot of time to remember, and rue, his high-flying life in Singapore's adrenaline-driven financial markets. A movie documenting the events is in production at the time of writing. It promises to be a fascinating insight into one of Singapore's juiciest scandals.

At the eastern end, *Harry's* at No 28 gets going early in the evening as city workers flock for happy hour until 8 pm. Corporate high fliers and wannabes, mostly expat, meet over beers and are joined later in the evening by a mixed, upmarket crowd who come for the jazz bands. Singapore cocktail barmen haven't yet invented the Nick Leeson Slammer, but if they did it would be at Harry's or *Escobar*, a few doors down at No 37. These places finish up around midnight.

Just around the corner, *Molly Malone's*, 42 Circular Rd, is an Irish pub and a good place for a change of pace. It has a real pub atmosphere, with Guinness on tap and traditional Irish bands upstairs. It closes at midnight, and on Sundays.

Back on Boat Quay, *Culture Club* at No 38 sometimes has decent bands, as does the newer *España* at No 45. *Exclusiv 56* at No 56 is a quieter bar with an older clientele and jazz on the jukebox.

Rootz at No 60 is popular with young Malays, and has reggae and hip-hop music. Further along are the *Riverbank* at No 68 and *Shoreline*, very popular with young Singaporeans. They stay open until 2 am from Monday to Friday and 3 am on weekends when everything else is closed.

Right at the end of Boat Quay near the bridge, *The Coffee Bean* at No 52 is a hip coffee shop with computer terminals for surfing the Net. It closes at midnight.

Clarke Quay Though the quieter cousin of Boat Quay, Clarke Quay has a good selection of places for a beer. The bars are not so overwhelmed by crowds and they tend to be more convivial.

The *Crazy Elephant*, right next to the river at Trader's Market, is the most happening bar at Clarke Quay. It has some decent rock bands and plenty of room on the footpath outside for chatting. The *Wild West Tavern* up some stairs from the street nearby is decked out like a saloon and is popular for country music of sorts, though the band seems more intent to play old pop covers. The 'Dream Team' appears nightly at *Dancers-The Club*, and is open from 8 pm on weekends, and *JP Bastiani* is a chic wine bar nearby, as is the newer *Le Aussie* with a wide selection of good Australian wines. *Brewerkz* across the river from Clarke Quay, at the Riverside Point Centre, is the best place for designer beers. Try the India Pale Ale.

The towkangs moored on the river at Boat Quay house moderately priced restaurants with bars which sometimes have acoustic music. Music also plays at the central square near the Satay Club.

Chinatown (Map 4)

The Tanjong Pagar area in Chinatown has a number of pubs in the renovated terraces, though they have dropped in popularity as Boat Quay has grabbed much of the clientele. Tanjong Pagar Rd, Duxton Rd and Duxton Hill all have a number of bars, and the beers are a little cheaper than elsewhere.

Duxton Hill has a string of bars that are pleasant, if relatively quiet places to have a drink. *Elvis' Place*, 1A Duxton Hill, is lined with Elvis memorabilia, though it has foregone the 50s music and it is much like any other bar. The *Cable Car* at No 2 is done out like a San Francisco cable car, while further along at No 10 the *Flag & Whistle* is an English-style pub which is great for conversation – you could hear a pin drop.

The pick of the pubs in this area is the *JJ Mahoney Pub* at 58 Duxton Rd. It has a big range of beers, including Murpheys on tap, a band on the ground floor, a games room bar on the 2nd floor and karaoke on the 3rd.

The liveliest nightspot in Tanjong Pagar is *Moon*, 62 Tanjong Pagar Rd, a small but happening place with a lively dance floor and a club atmosphere. It is open until 2 am Monday to Thursday, and until 3 am on Friday and Saturday when a S$23 cover charge will buy you entry and two drinks.

Closer to the Outram Park MRT station, the *Butterfly Bar & Cafe*, 55 Keong Saik Rd, is a funky little place with postmodern decor and happy hours until 8 pm.

Colonial District (Maps 3 & 4)

Of course you can have a drink at the *Raffles*, at the Long Bar or the Bar & Billiard Room, where that infamous tiger was supposedly shot. One of the favourite pastimes in the elegant Long Bar is throwing peanut shells on the floor – swinging stuff. The billiard room is laid back, and you can recline in the wicker chairs, tickle the ivories or chug-a-lug outside on the patio. In the evenings both bars have light jazz from 7.30 pm, and serve food. Sip your expensive drinks, there are no happy hours. Avoid the expensive Sling, it now comes from a barrel!

The in-scene to *be* seen these days is at *Chijmes,* a bar and restaurant complex on Bras Basah Rd just round the corner from the stuffy Raffles Hotel. This is a converted church and convent complex, built between 1855 and 1910, which now boasts some quite classy European-style bars and restaurants. The Fountain Court, with gurgling water, stone walls and greenery all dominated by a rather imposing Gothic chapel is a very atmospheric spot for a pre-dinner cocktail, while *Father Flanagan's,* yet another Irish pub, serves a mean but pricey pint of Guinness stout for S$13. Next to Father Flanagan's, *Jump* is a hot bar where things really happen after 10 pm. Smart dress code applies.

The *Compass Rose* on the 70th floor of the Westin Stamford Hotel, 2 Stamford Rd, has stunning views and prices to match. After 8.30 pm a minimum charge of S$15 applies. This is not the place to wear jeans. *Somerset's*, in the Westin Plaza next door, is a jazz venue.

The bar in the *Marina Mandarin's* lobby has evening jazz played in salubrious surroundings. Nearby, the new Millenia Walk complex at the Ritz Carlton Hotel is planning to house a branch of the *Planet Hollywood* chain.

A less pretentious and much cheaper place to drink is at New Bugis St. You can have a beer at the food stalls under the stars in the evening until 3 am, or whenever everyone goes home. If you want to pay more, there are a couple of places that have karaoke and bad Filipino bands. For something different, the *Boom Boom Room* (☎ 339 8187), 3 New Bugis St, is a supper club with a cabaret and Singapore's only regular stand-up comic. The cover charge is S$17.

Other Areas

Zouk, 17-21 Jiak Kim St, near the Havelock Rd hotels, is a legendary dance club. Housed in an old godown by the Singapore River, it has the dubious honour of being busted and closed for drugs, but has reopened and is as popular as ever. A cover charge of around S$25 applies on weekends, S$15 Monday to Friday.

Just off River Valley Rd, about 800m west of Clark Quay is Mohamed Sultan Rd, home to a sprinkling of popular late-night bars. Of these the *Next Page Pub* is the rowdiest and most popular, with a gregarious expat crowd which is renowned for getting up onto the bar to boogie after a few frozen margaritas. Here you can rave, play pool or just chill out until 3 am. *Zeus* and the *Venue* in the same street offer retro and house music to a mainly younger clientele on the weekends. Don't bother checking in to these places until way after 9 pm.

Not far from Arab St on Beach Rd, The Concourse shopping centre is home to a couple of retrospective theme pubs on the basement level – the 50s *Elvis at The Concourse* and the *Pyschedelic Cafe Pub*, decked out with 60s memorabilia.

Wala Wala Bar & Grill, on Lorong Mambong, out in Holland Village to the west of the city, has one of those sin machines that were banned for many years in Singapore – a jukebox. It is an American-style restaurant and bar popular with expats. Happy hours are from 4 to 9 pm.

Chaplin's is another on Lorong Liput, the continuation of Lorong Mambong, if you are looking to kick on after a meal at one of the many restaurants here, though the restaurants themselves, such as *Cha Cha Cha* are popular watering holes. For a quiet drink in English pub ambience, try *Bob's Tavern*, 17A Lorong Liput.

CINEMAS

There are plenty of cinemas in Singapore, with the main fare being Hollywood hits.

Chinese kungfu films and all-singing, all-dancing Indian movies are also popular. Recently, alternative cinema has found an outlet in Singapore: the Cathay Cinema's *Picture House*, 6 Handy Rd, at the city end of Orchard Rd, regularly shows art house movies, as does *Jade Classics* in Shaw Towers, 100 Beach Rd. Multi-theatre cineplexes are at Shaw Towers on Beach Rd, and at the Shaw Centre on Scotts Rd, near the corner of Orchard Rd. *United Artists Theatre* is a four theatre cineplex at Bugis Junction on Victoria St.

Singapore has an annual film festival, and the various expatriate clubs also show movies. The *Alliance Française* often has movies open to the public, some with English subtitles.

THEATRE

Singapore's nascent theatre scene is starting to come of age as Singaporeans become more interested in expressing, and discovering, their identity. More local plays are being produced, and alternative theatre venues such as the *Substation* (☎ 337 7800), 45 Armenian St in the colonial district, are helping to foster an interest in theatre. Plays, workshops, poetry readings and visual art exhibits are held here, and at the back the Garden has craft and art works for sale.

The main venues for theatre are the *Drama Centre* (☎ 336 0005) on Canning Rise (north-west of Fort Canning Park), the *Victoria Theatre* (☎ 336 2151), Empress Place (opposite Boat Quay) and *Kallang Theatre* (☎ 345 8488), opposite the National Stadium on Stadium Rd. Performances range from local and overseas plays performed by a variety of local theatre companies, to the blockbusters such as *Phantom of the Opera* and *Les Misérables*. Some of the hotels, such as the Hilton and Raffles, also stage theatre shows from time to time.

The Singapore Festival of Arts, which features many drama performances, is held every second year (in even years) around June. There's also music, art and dance at the festival, which includes a Fringe Festival featuring plenty of street performances.

CHINESE OPERA

In Chinatown or in the older streets of Serangoon Rd and Jalan Besar, you may chance upon a *wayang* – a brilliantly costumed Chinese street opera. In these noisy and colourful extravaganzas, overacting is very important; there's nothing subtle about it at all. The best time of year to see one is around September during the Festival of Hungry Ghosts. They are often listed in the 'What's On' section of the *Straits Times*.

CLASSICAL MUSIC

Highbrow entertainment of the western kind can be found at the *Victoria Concert Hall* (☎ 338 1230), the home of the Singapore Symphony Orchestra opposite the Padang. Tickets are reasonably priced starting at S$5, or more depending on the visiting musicians. Enter the building from the south side.

CULTURAL SHOWS

At the *Mandarin Hotel* on Orchard Rd there is an ASEAN night every night at 8 pm. It features dancing and music from all over the region. The show costs S$24 for adults and S$15 for children; including dinner it is S$48 for adults and S$26 for children.

OTHER ENTERTAINMENT

The big hotels have cocktail lounges and there are some Chinese nightclubs around the city. The *Neptune Theatre Restaurant*, Collyer Quay in the city centre, has a Chinese cabaret, Cantonese food and hostesses. It is glitzy but just this side of seedy, and the shows are as risqué as Singapore allows. The *Red Lantern Beer Garden* downstairs is definitely seedy and has a band in the evening, and cheap meals, good prices for beer and a band at lunchtime. *Lido Palace* in the Concorde Hotel on Outram Rd has a Chinese cabaret and dance hostesses. In the same vein is *Golden Million Nite-Club* in the Peninsula Hotel on Coleman St, just north of the river.

If you're worried that Singapore is simply too squeaky clean for belief, you may be relieved to hear that there's a real locals-only, low-class, red-light district stretching along the laneway behind Desker Rd, between

Jalan Besar and Serangoon Rd in Little India. For more information about this area, see the Walking Tour entry in the Little India section earlier in this chapter.

The predominantly Malay district of Geylang, east of the city, is full of houses and bars operated by organised Chinese gangs who 'employ' women of all nationalities, including Indonesians, Indians and the occasional Caucasian. They are found in the lorongs off Sims Ave. Of course, Singapore caters to business needs, and there is no shortage of 'health centres' and escort services.

Shopping

One of Singapore's major attractions is shopping. Although the sheer range is impressive and prices for many goods are still competitive with other discount centres, these days, with tariffs dropping around the world, Singapore is not the bargain centre it once was. 'Duty free' and 'free port' are somewhat throwaway terms. Remember that not everything is loaded down with import duty in your own country, and Singapore also protects some local industries.

Before you leap on any item as a great bargain, it pays to know prices at home. Depending on your country of residence, Singapore may have few bargains to offer. Americans, for example, will find lower prices at home for many goods.

Shop around to find out what the 'real' price is. In Singapore, fixed price shops are increasingly becoming the norm, but bargaining is still often required, especially in the tourist areas. Many of the small shops, such as electronic and souvenir shops, don't display prices and you should bargain at these outlets. Even when prices are displayed it doesn't always mean that prices are fixed. If you are unsure, ask if the price is the 'best price'. Try the big fixed-price department stores where the price is unlikely to be rock bottom, but most likely in the ball park.

Given the existence of larger discount stores offering fixed prices, if you're not practised at bargaining and don't know prices it's better to frequent them. Except for antiques, handicrafts and souvenirs, where bargaining is almost always required, you can find good deals without haggling.

Singapore has consumer laws and the government wants to promote the island as a good place to shop; but you should be wary when buying. Make sure you get exactly what you want before leaving the store.

Guarantees are an important consideration if you're buying electronic gear, watches, cameras or the like. Make sure the guarantee is international and that it is filled out correctly with the shop's name and the serial number of the item written down.

Check for the right voltage and cycle when you buy electrical goods. Singapore, Australia, New Zealand, Hong Kong and the UK use 220V to 240V at 50 cycles, while the USA, Canada and Japan use 110V to 120V at 60 cycles. Check the plug – most shops will fit the correct plug for your country.

If you have any problems take your purchases back to the store, though many shops, particularly the small ones, are not noted for after-sales service. Otherwise contact the Consumers' Association of Singapore (☎ 270 5433) or the STB. The STB's *Singapore Official Guide,* available at Changi airport and at most hotels, lists 'errant traders' that have been found guilty of tourist rip-offs. Traders in Lucky Plaza on Orchard Rd and Sim Lim Tower in the colonial district seem to figure regularly.

WHERE TO SHOP

Singapore is almost wall-to-wall with shops, and while there are certain places worth going to for certain items, shopping centres usually have a mixture of shops selling electronics, clothes, sporting goods etc.

Orchard Rd Area (Map 2)

The major shopping complexes on and around Orchard Rd have a mind-boggling array of department stores and shops selling whatever you want. The prices here aren't necessarily the best, but the range of goods is superb, and this is certainly a good place for high quality, brand-name items.

Orchard Point, Orchard Plaza and Cuppage Plaza have a variety of shops and food outlets. Centrepoint is one of the liveliest shopping centres, with good bookshops on the 4th floor, and Marks & Spencer and Robinson's department stores.

On the corner of Orchard Rd and Orchard Link is the Ngee Ann City, which houses the large Takashimaya department store. The basement is great for food, especially Japanese cuisine, while the individual shops are dominated by exclusive outlets. The Paragon and the Promenade are upmarket shopping centres with many designer boutiques.

Further along and much more downmarket is Lucky Plaza. It is a bustling place with dozens of shops crammed together. It's good for cheap clothes, bags and shoes, but bargain hard and shake off the touts and pesky tailors. Opposite Lucky Plaza, Wisma Atria has an Isetan department store and boutiques. On the corner of Scotts and Orchard roads is Tang's, one of Singapore's oldest, establishment department stores.

Scotts Rd is another good place to shop. The Shaw Centre has the large Isetan department shore. Also on Scotts Rd, the Scotts shopping centre has plenty of boutiques and an excellent food court in the basement. The Far East Plaza is a big centre with electronics and a bit of everything.

At the top of Orchard Rd, the Far East shopping centre has sporting shops good for golfing needs and bicycles. The Forum Galleria is good for toys and children's gear.

Tanglin Rd is quieter, and the main shopping centre is the Tanglin shopping centre, which has a good selection of expensive Asian arts and antiques. It's well worth a browse, but bargain if you want to buy.

Colonial District (Maps 3 & 4)

In the colonial district, Raffles City is architecturally one of the most impressive shopping centres, and has some interesting small shops. Sogo department store is here. Nearby, Marina Square has a huge array of shops in a massive complex which includes three hotels and plenty of restaurants.

Bugis Junction, a new shopping centre on Victoria St, has added life to the area. Built on the old Bugis St, above the Bugis MRT station, it comprises shophouse re-creations covered by an atrium, the Seiyu department store and the Hotel InterContinental.

On Bencoolen St in the Little India area, Sim Lim Square is renown for computers and electronic goods. Sim Lim Tower across Rochor Canal Rd is a big electronic centre with everything from capacitors to audio and video gear. These places are popular with tourists looking for bargains so the first asking price is often higher than elsewhere.

Chinatown (Map 4)

Chinatown is a popular shopping area with more local flavour. The People's Park Complex and the People's Park Centre are good places to shop. They are large complexes with plenty of electronics, clothing and department stores. The electronics are only as cheap as you make them. The Chinatown Complex has an interesting market for everyday goods and cheap shops.

Chinatown Point specialises in craft shops, and the quiet Riverwalk Galleria has some more arts and craft shops. Smith St has some craft and souvenir shops.

Other Areas

Little India has lots of oddities, and the Serangoon Plaza department stores have electrical and everyday goods at honest prices. They have proved so popular for cheap electronics, clothes and household goods that the large Mustafa Centre department store has opened around the corner on Syed Alwi Rd.

Arab St is good for textiles, basketware and South-East Asian crafts.

Housing estate areas have plenty of shopping for cheaper clothes and household items, and bargaining is the exception rather than the rule. Try Ang Mo Kio, Bedok, Clementi, Toa Payoh, Geylang – all easily reached by the MRT. Tampines has the big Century Park shopping mall.

WHAT TO BUY

Arts, Crafts & Antiques

There's no shortage of arts and antiques, mostly Chinese but also from all over Asia.

Tanglin shopping centre on Tanglin Rd in the Orchard Rd area is good for quality but expensive arts and antiques. The Singapore Handicraft Centre in Chinatown Point has dozens of shops selling Chinese lacquerware, pottery, jewellery etc, but also sells some Indonesian and other Asian crafts as well.

Arab St is a good place for South-East Asian crafts, such as caneware, batik and leather goods. In Chinatown around Smith St, small shops sell goods ranging from trinkets and souvenirs, basketware, fans and silk dressing gowns, to more expensive curios and antique pottery.

Cameras & Film

Cameras are available throughout the city. Camera equipment is not such a bargain these days, as camera prices are often as heavily discounted in the west as in Singapore or Hong Kong. When buying film, bargain for lower prices if you're buying in bulk.

Clothes & Shoes

Clothes and shoes – imported, locally made and made to measure – are widely available. Singapore is not as cheap as most other Asian countries, but the range is excellent, especially for brand-name items.

Many of the department stores have reasonably priced clothes. Nison in the People's Park Complex in Chinatown has cheap clothes. Lucky Plaza on Orchard Rd is a good centre for cheap clothes and shoes, but bargain hard for everything. The Peninsula shopping centre is good for men's shoes.

Wisma Atria, Orchard C&E and OG department store are good places on Orchard Rd for clothes.

Computers

Singapore is enforcing international copyright laws, so cheap software and software manuals are not as openly displayed as in other Asian countries. The Funan Centre on North Bridge Rd, just east of Fort Canning Park, is the main computer centre, with dozens of computer shops on the top floors, as well as a large Challenger Superstore. The top floors of Sim Lim Square, on the corner of Bencoolen St and Rochor Canal Rd, are good for cheap computers and peripherals.

Electronic Goods

You can buy electronic goods everywhere in Singapore. Sim Lim Square, on the corner of Bencoolen St and Rochor Canal Rd, has a concentrated range of electronics shops. Sim Lim Tower, nearby on Jalan Besar, has everything from cassette players to capacitors, but be wary and be prepared to bargain hard to get a reasonable deal.

Other Items

Guitars, keyboards, flutes, drums, electronic instruments, recording equipment etc are all good buys in Singapore, though not necessarily as cheap as the country of origin. A good shop to try is City Music, 02-12 Peace Centre, 1 Sophia Rd, on the corner of Selegie Rd. Yamaha has a number of showrooms in Singapore.

Cheap pirated tapes are things of the past but legitimate tapes and CDs are reasonably priced. Tower Records on the 4th floor of the Pacific Plaza, 9 Scotts Rd, near the corner of Orchard Rd, has the biggest and best selection at higher prices. MPH bookstore at 71-77 Stamford Rd in the colonial district has a good CD section upstairs, and the newer Borders bookshop in the Liat Towers on Orchard Rd has an enormous selection of all kinds of CDs.

For sporting goods, most department stores have well-stocked sports sections. For general sports shops, try the Far East shopping centre on Orchard Rd. Lucky Plaza on Orchard Rd also has sports shops, including diving shops. For brand-name bicycles and components, try Soon Watt & Co, 482 Changi Rd.

BRUNEI

MARY ANN HEMPHILL

Brunei Darussalam

Wedged between the north-eastern corner of Sarawak and the South China Sea, Brunei is one of the smallest countries in the world; it's also one of the wealthiest. And this tiny Islamic sultanate is all that remains of an empire that in the 16th century controlled all of Borneo.

The country's full name is Negara Brunei Darussalam, which is usually translated as 'Brunei – the Abode of Peace'. And with alcohol virtually unobtainable, no nightlife to speak of, a political culture of quiet acquiescence to the edicts of the sultan and Islamic laws (that, among other things, forbid boys and girls to hold hands), it certainly is peaceful.

Presiding over it all is His Majesty Paduka Seri Beginda Sultan Haji Hassanal Bolkiah Mu'izzaddin Waddaulah, the 29th of his line and better known as the Sultan of Brunei. The sultan is among the richest men in the world; in 1993 *Fortune* magazine estimated his personal fortune at a shade over US$37 billion. He has two wives, and his possessions include a reported 153 cars, private aircraft, the Dorchester Hotel in London and the Beverly Hills Hotel in Los Angeles. He lives in a US$350 million palace and indulges his passion for polo by keeping 200 Argentine ponies at a private park in air-conditioned stalls.

Although the sultan's exploits occasionally make it into the world's scandal rags, most Bruneians seem to regard him as a benevolent despot, intolerant of political dissent perhaps, but generous with his largesse and happy as long as he has the means to lavishly indulge his interests.

Brunei's economy is awash with oil, which comes mainly from offshore wells at Seria and Muara. And to be fair, *everyone* in Brunei benefits from oil money. There are no taxes, there are pensions for all, free medical care, free schooling, free sport and leisure centres, cheap loans, subsidies for many purchases (including cars) and the highest minimum wages in the region. In short, the 'Abode of Peace' is a little slice of contrived heaven – an Islamic Disneyland. Just to prove the point, the sultan had a huge fun park built for his subjects to enjoy for free – just as long as they don't hold hands.

Most visitors are scratching around for something to do after a couple of days, but Brunei is a strangely fascinating anomaly in South-East Asia that draws its share of sightseers. And Bruneians are some of the friendliest people you'll meet.

HIGHLIGHTS

- **Omar Ali Saifuddien Mosque** – a massive tribute to Brunei's wealth and devotion to Islam
- **Kampung Ayer** – a reminder of the days before Brunei struck it rich: a photogenic collection of stilt villages on Sungai Brunei
- **Brunei Museum & the Malay Technology Museum** – exhibits on Brunei and traditional Malay culture
- **Jerudong Playground** – an enormous free amusement park worth enjoying for an evening
- **Temburong** – the eastern part of Brunei makes a good day trip from Bandar Seri Begawan for jungle walks and a visit to an Iban longhouse

Facts about Brunei

HISTORY

In the 15th and 16th centuries Brunei Darussalam, as this country is formally known, was a considerable power in the region with its rule extending throughout Borneo and into the Philippines.

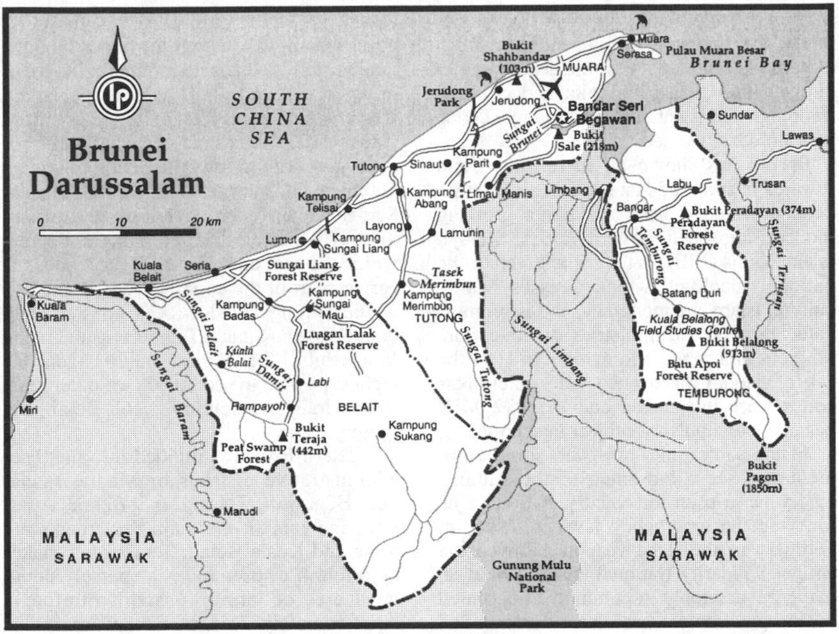

The Spanish and the Portuguese were the first European visitors, arriving in the 16th century. The Spanish actually made a bid to take over, but were soon ousted.

The arrival of the British in the guise of James Brooke, the first white raja of Sarawak, in the early 19th century, spelt the end of Brunei's power. A series of 'treaties' was forced onto the sultan as James Brooke consolidated his hold over Kuching with the aim of developing commercial relationships and suppressing piracy, a favourite Bruneian and Dayak occupation (piracy was a common excuse for justifying European land grabs). Brunei became a British protectorate in 1888 and was gradually whittled away until, with a final dash of absurdity, Limbang was ceded to Sarawak in 1890, thus dividing Brunei into two parts.

In 1929, just as Brunei was about to be swallowed up entirely, oil was discovered. The present sultan's father, who abdicated in 1967, kept Brunei out of the Malayan confederacy, preferring that the country remain a British protectorate.

In 1962, in the lead up to amalgamation with Malaysia, the British pressured Sultan Omar Saifuddien to hold elections. The opposition Ra'ayat Party, led by AM Azahari, which wanted to keep Brunei independent and make the sultan a constitutional monarch within a democracy, won an overwhelming victory. As the sultan's plans to take Brunei into union with Malaysia became clear, Azahari fled to the Philippines, from where he directed an armed rebellion with the support of Indonesia. The rebellion was quickly crushed with British military backing and the sultan later opted for independence from Malaysia. The 'Abode of Peace' has been under emergency laws ever since though you'll see little evidence of this.

Early in 1984 the popular young sultan and *yang di-pertuan* (king) reluctantly led his tightly ruled country somewhat reluctantly into complete independence from Britain. The then 37-year-old leader rather enjoyed the British umbrella and colonial trappings that it entailed, and independence was almost unwanted.

Brunei has shown an increasing trend towards Islamic fundamentalism since independence, and is keen to counter growing modernisation and western values. Melayu Islam Beraja (MIB) is the name given to the national ideology, which stresses Malay culture, Islam and monarchy, and is promulgated through the ministries of education, religious affairs and information. In 1991 the sale of alcohol was banned and stricter dress codes were introduced and in 1992 MIB became a compulsory subject in schools.

At the same time, however, some commentators see a loosening of the sultan's autocratic grip on the country. Although he renewed the emergency laws in 1995, in February of the same year he allowed the Brunei Solidarity National Party to hold an inaugural assembly. A committee appointed by the government has also recommended constitutional changes to allow for an elected parliament. This hardly amounts to a gathering tide of democratic reform, but it does indicate that the sultan may be aware that, as an absolute Islamic monarchy, Brunei is out of step with its ASEAN neighbours and in the long run, some reform is necessary.

In recent years the government of Brunei has recognised a growing unemployment problem and disaffected youths have been blamed for isolated incidents of crime. Brunei has also been badly affected by smoke haze from uncontrolled fires across the region; at the height of the problem schools closed and many expats took their families out of the country. The royal family has also had its own problems, see the boxed text 'The Prince Formerly Known as Minister'.

GEOGRAPHY

Present-day Brunei is one of the smallest countries in the world: the entire sultanate covers an area of only 5765 sq km. On the map, it looks like two wedges driven between the South China Sea and the north coast of Sarawak, which surrounds it on the landward side. It has no mountain ranges or great rivers, and at its widest the larger, western part measures only 120km from side to side. White sandy beaches along the coast give way to low hills rising to around 300m in the interior. The capital, Bandar Seri Begawan (BSB), overlooks the estuary of the mangrove-fringed Sungai Brunei, which opens onto Brunei Bay and the eastern part of the country, Temburong.

Temburong consists of a coastal plain drained by the Sungai Temburong and rising to a height of 1841m at Bukit Pagon, the highest peak in the country. Two other main rivers drain the country – the Belait and Tutong.

Western Brunei is divided into the three administrative districts of Muara-Bandar Seri Begawan, Tutong and Belait. Apart from the capital, the main settlements are Seria and Kuala Belait. Temburong makes up a fourth district and is a sparsely populated area of largely unspoilt rainforest. Approximately 75% of Brunei retains its original forest cover.

CLIMATE

Being only a slice of Borneo, Brunei is subject to that great island's prevailing climatic conditions. Thus, it is out of the typhoon belt and enjoys high average temperatures, humidity and rainfall.

Temperatures are consistently around 24°C minimum and 31°C maximum, with an average humidity of 79%. Average annual rainfall is about 3295mm, though Brunei

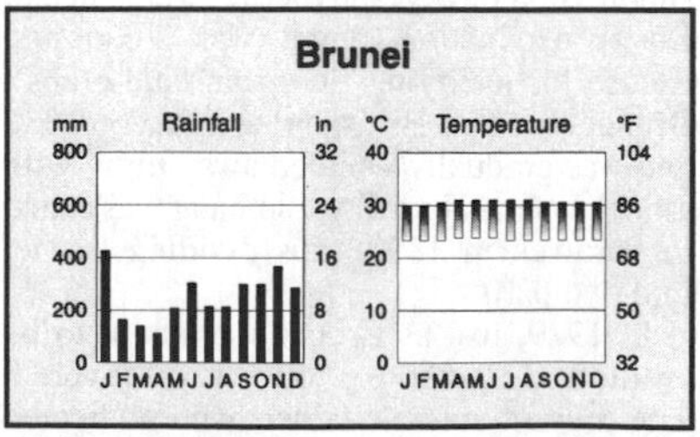

The Prince Formerly Known as Minister

Picture this: you're the youngest brother of the richest man in the world, finance minister of your country, head of a major conglomerate and born into the royal family – you'd be set for a gilded carriage ride through life, right? Wrong! The extraordinary saga of Prince Jefri of Brunei shows how spectacular incompetence can overwhelm even the greatest good fortune.

At 43, Jefri's star was already on the wane by 1997, due to alleged financial impropriety and to his dubious personal life, of the kind which tends to be described as 'flamboyant'. In early 1997, Jefri was suddenly sacked from his post as finance minister, a position he had held for 10 years, by his oldest brother, the Sultan of Brunei (who promptly took over the portfolio himself). Rumours started swirling about Amedeo Development Corporation, a classic Asian family conglomerate headed by Jefri with diversified interests including golf courses, five star hotels, fisheries and telecommunications. The rumours of alleged misuse of Amedeo's funds were temporarily overwhelmed in early 1998, however, by the two sensational court cases against Jefri. One, brought by an American model, centred on allegations that Jefri (and Sultan Hassanal Bolkiah himself) had lured women from around the world with promises of employment, only to keep them as sex slaves once they entered Brunei. (Jefri also allegedly kept a harem in London's Dorchester Hotel, owned by older bro', and apparently had two luxury yachts in Brunei, named 'Tit One' and 'Tit Two', for partying purposes.) The second case involved alleged contractual breaches regarding land deals. Both were settled out of court, but lurid speculation continued.

The party came to a crashing end in July 1998, when Amedeo collapsed owing a mere US$16 billion to its creditors after the Sultan cut off all government funding to the company, and relieved Jefri of his control of the Brunei Investment Agency. In addition, the law minister and two senior public servants in the Law Ministry were booted out, presumably for failing to notice the scale of the Amedeo disaster. Prince Jefri's son, Hakim, was also sacked as chairman of government-owned Datastream Technology, a lucrative telecom company. In a clear sign of his continuing displeasure, the following month the Sultan formally named his eldest son, Al-Muhtadee Billah, as heir to the throne. Obviously, it was bad enough for the Sultan that Jefri had jeopardised Brunei's international reputation as a tightly controlled but morally upright Muslim nation; but displaying such remarkable financial incompetence, if not actual corruption, was evidently the last straw.

Jefri's few remaining supporters insisted that he was the victim of a 'conspiracy' against his supposed democratic and liberal tendencies, a conspiracy possibly headed by mysterious foreigners (well, consultants Arthur Andersen were hired to trawl through the wreckage of Amedeo), assisted by Jefri's more conservative older brother, Mohamed, the foreign minister, who controls a rival conglomerate, QAF. Strangely, though, Jefri's democratic ideals had not been much in evidence previously (unless one included his 'liberal' selection of women from around the world for wild parties). After the music stopped for Jefri, he fled to New York. According to an *Asiaweek* report, a spokesman for the prince said Jefri would go 'anywhere but Brunei. He won't go near the place'.

It's a measure of Brunei's staggering wealth that the government was able to subsequently announce that the Amedeo fiasco and the loss of US$16 billion would have little or no effect on Brunei's economy. Nevertheless, with the price of oil dropping severely during 1998, and the general economic turmoil in Asia leading to thousands of contract workers being sent home, it was clear that not even Brunei was immune to the 'Asian flu'. And in a truly shocking sign o' the times, *Forbes* magazine's annual list of the world's richest people had Sultan Hassanal, the perennial No 1, dropping down to No 3, with only US$36 billion in personal wealth.

If there's a moral to this sordid story, it's probably this: no amount of money and influence can buy simple common sense and intelligence.

(Sources: *Asiaweek* 17 July 1998, *Far Eastern Economic Review* July 1998 and August 1998, the *Age* July 1998)

Greg Alford

doesn't really have marked wet and dry seasons. The wettest months are from September to January, during the north-east monsoon, and the driest period is February to April.

Changes in climatic patterns, which have been popularly attributed to the El Niño effect, have contributed to a recurring smoke haze problem in Brunei. During dry months, when there is no wind, open burning in Brunei can cause dense smoke to linger over parts of the country, reducing visibility and endangering the health of old people and children.

GOVERNMENT & POLITICS

Brunei is a monarchy, and the sultan appoints ministers to assist him in governing the country. The sultan is the self-appointed prime minister and defence minister. Two of the sultan's brothers are also ministers. Democracy is not on the government's agenda, and the only democratic elections ever held were in 1962.

Judicial power is vested in the Supreme Court (comprising the Court of Appeal and the High Court) and the Magistrate's Court. Islamic, or *syariah*, courts deal with offences against Islam committed by Muslims. The judicial system is loosely based on the British system, but the philosophy of MIB is being applied to the law.

Brunei is a member of ASEAN and enjoys close relations with near neighbours Malaysia and Singapore.

ECONOMY

Oil! The country is virtually dependent on the stuff and the pumps are not expected to run dry until 2020. In anticipation of that dark day the government has instituted some economic diversification plans. These include more rice-farming, some forestry and eventual self-sufficiency in beef production. To this latter end, the government bought a cattle station in Australia's Northern Territory which is larger than Brunei itself! Fresh beef is flown into BSB daily.

The prospect of an oil-less Brunei is still a long way off. Oil production was increased during the 1990s and new fields have been discovered. Brunei exports a small amount of rubber and is also one of the world's largest exporters of liquefied natural gas.

The government, with Brunei Shell Petroleum (the only oil company with a major stake in Brunei), is by far the country's largest employer. All government workers get subsidised holidays and trips to Mecca – which probably wouldn't be too bad if you could organise a stopover in Bangkok.

Traditional agriculture in Brunei consists of shifting cultivation, which continues in remote areas. Farming is largely a part-time occupation and there are no large estates. About 80% of the country's food must be imported.

The recent formation of a trading bloc with nearby countries resulted in the unlikely acronym BIMP-EAGA, which stands for Brunei, Indonesia, Malaysia and Philippines-East ASEAN Growth Area.

POPULATION & PEOPLE

The latest estimate of Brunei's population was about 305,100, of whom 201,100 lived in the BSB-Muara district and only 8700 lived in Temburong. Malays, including indigenes of the Kedaya, Tutong, Belait, Bisaya, Dusan and Murut tribes, constitute 67% of the population; Chinese make up 15%; Indians, people of smaller tribes, and some 20,000 expatriate workers from Europe and Asia make up the remainder.

ARTS

During the height of the Brunei sultanates, brass and silver artisans produced work of fine design and great beauty. Brass gongs, cannons and household vessels, such as kettles and betel containers, were prized throughout Borneo and beyond. They were often embossed with designs of serpents and animals or verses from the Koran, and prized pieces were believed to have special powers. Cannons, in particular, were used not only for war, but for paying dowries and for ceremonial purposes. Today they are family heirlooms and can be found in Malay homes or remote Dayak villages, where they have been given spiritual significance. There's a good collection of cannons in the Brunei Museum.

Artisans used the wax technique to cast brass, a method believed to have been introduced during the reign of Sultan Bolkiah at the end of the 15th century. The art declined with the fortunes of the Brunei sultanate, and the great brassware of Brunei is now a lost tradition.

Silverwork was probably introduced from Java about the same time as brass casting, and the Portuguese explorer Pigafetta noted the silver and gold vessels he found in Brunei in 1521. Silversmithing, like brass casting, was an art passed down through families and guilds in Kampung Ayer. The exponents of silverwork these days are to be found at the Handicraft Centre, which was set up to preserve Brunei's dying crafts.

The weaving art of *jong sarat* has survived, and jong sarat sarungs are still prized for ceremonial occasions. Jong sarat uses gold thread and coloured cotton woven on a loom in stylised floral designs known as *sukma-indera*. Bright colours are used sparingly, and the designs are restrained.

SOCIETY & CONDUCT

Bruneians are mostly Malay, and their customs, beliefs and pastimes are very similar, if not identical, to those of the Malays of Peninsular Malaysia. *Adat*, or customary law, governs many of the ceremonies in Brunei, particularly on royal and state occasions. There is even a government department of *adat istiadat*, which is responsible for preserving ceremony and advising on protocol, dress and heraldry. See the Facts about Malaysia chapter for more detailed information and explanations of Malay customs.

The usual Asian customs apply: only the right hand should be used for offering or passing something; pointing with the forefinger is rude and should be done with the thumb; beckoning someone is done with an open hand with the fingers waving downwards. Bruneians shake hands by only lightly touching then bringing the hands to the chest; and it is not customary to shake hands with the opposite sex.

In consideration of Islamic beliefs, the following guidelines should also be observed:

- Offering pork or alcohol to Muslims could not only cause offence – it is tempting them to break the law.
- It would be inconsiderate to eat in front of Muslims during the fasting month, Ramadan.
- Smoking tobacco and eating shellfish are tolerated but not considered the done thing.
- When entering a mosque or a house, remove your shoes first.

In addition, women are expected to dress 'respectably', so dresses above the knee and sleeveless tops are not permitted (and they mean it – you won't be allowed on rides at Jerudong Playground and certainly won't be allowed inside a mosque).

RELIGION

Brunei is a reasonably strict Muslim country, and a Ministry of Religious Affairs has been set up to foster and promote Islam. The ministry also has special officers who investigate

Correct Behaviour in a Mosque

Correct attire is essential before you will be permitted to enter any of BSB's magnificent mosques. To avoid offence, please observe the following guidelines:

- Always remove your footwear before entering the mosque.
- Neither men nor women are allowed inside with bare legs, although most mosques can lend you a robe to wear while you are in the building.
- Shoulders must be covered, and women should cover their head.
- Do not walk in front of any praying person.
- Non-Muslims must not touch the Koran.

And don't fret about doing the wrong thing – someone will soon let you know.

breaches of Islamic law by Muslims, and apparently government men prowl the streets after dark looking for unmarried couples standing or sitting too close to each other. Getting nailed for this crime, known as *khalwat*, can mean imprisonment and a fine. The sale of alcohol is banned and non-Islamic restaurants (such as Chinese places) display signs stating that they are not suitable for Muslims (don't get excited – it's because they serve pork, not alcohol).

The constitution permits other religions to be practised in peace and harmony, and non-Muslim visitors needn't worry about being spat upon and abused for being infidels. Bruneians are very friendly and hospitable, and not all are as zealous as the government.

LANGUAGE

The official language of Brunei is Malay but English is also widely spoken. Jawi (Malay written in Arabic script) is taught in schools, and most signs in the country are written in both Jawi and Roman script. See the Language chapter at the end of this book for a guide to Malay and a list of useful words and phrases. For a more comprehensive guide to the language get a copy of Lonely Planet's *Malay phrasebook*.

Facts for the Visitor

TOURIST OFFICES

There is no tourist information centre in Brunei, but there is an information desk at the airport where you should pick up some useful leaflets and the excellent *Explore Brunei* booklet. *Explore Brunei* has a recent map of BSB and useful information on sights and accommodation.

VISAS

For visits of up to 14 days, visas are not necessary for citizens of Belgium, Canada, France, Germany, Indonesia, Japan, Luxembourg, the Netherlands, New Zealand, Norway, the Philippines, South Korea, Sweden, Switzerland, Thailand and the Republic of the Maldives. British, Malaysian and Singaporean citizens do not require a visa for visits of 30 days or less. US citizens do not need a visa for visits of up to 90 days.

If entering from Sarawak or Sabah, there's no fuss on arrival – no money-showing, no requirement for an onward ticket, and it's unlikely your bags will even be looked at. A one week visa is more or less automatically granted and if you ask you can usually get two weeks – it might be useful, you never know.

People of all other nationalities, including British overseas citizens and citizens of British dependent territories, must have a visa to visit Brunei. Brunei embassies overseas have been known to give incorrect advice, so you should double-check if your nationality is not listed above and you are told that you do not require a visa to enter the country.

Transit passengers are issued a 72 hour visa at Brunei international airport and if you intend to make a short trip to Brunei, it would be worth taking advantage of this visa. Three days is enough to see most of the sights, but this visa does tie you to travelling by air.

EMBASSIES & CONSULATES

Brunei Embassies

Brunei has diplomatic offices in the following countries:

Australia
(☎ 02-6290 1801) 16 Bulwarra Close, O'Malley, ACT 2606

Canada
(☎ 613-234 5656) No 395, Laurier Ave East, Ottawa, Ontario K1N 6R4

France
(☎ 01-53 64 67 60) No 4, Rue de Presparg, Paris 75017

Germany
(☎ 0228-672044) No 18, Kaiser Karl Rinc, 53111 Bonn 1

Indonesia
(☎ 021-574 1437) Wisma GKBI, Suite 1194, Jalan Sudirman No 28, Jakarta 10210

Japan
(☎ 03-3447 7997) 5-2 Kita-Shinagawa 6-Chome, Shinagawa-Ku, Tokyo 141

Malaysia
(☎ 03-261 2828) 8th and 9th floors, Wisma SHL, Jalan Tun Razak, 50400 Kuala Lumpur
Philippines
(☎ 02-816 2836) 11th floor, BPI Bldg, Ayala Ave, Makati City, Metro Manila
Singapore
(☎ 065-733 9055) 325 Tanglin Rd, Singapore 247955
Thailand
(☎ 02-391 6017) No 154, Soi Ekamai 14, 63 Sukhumvit Rd, Bangkok 10110
UK
(☎ 0171-581 0521) 20 Belgrave Square, London SW1X 8PG
USA
(☎ 202-342 0159) Watergate Suite 300, 2600 Virginia Ave NW, Washington, DC 20037

Brunei also has diplomatic representation in Belgium, Cambodia, China, Egypt, India, Iran, Jordan, South Korea, Laos, Myanmar (Burma), Oman, Pakistan, Saudi Arabia, Switzerland, UAE and Vietnam.

Foreign Embassies in Brunei

Countries with diplomatic representation in Bandar Seri Begawan include:

Australia
(☎ 02-229435) 4th floor, Teck Guan Plaza, Jalan Sultan
Canada
(☎ 02-220043) Suite 51/52, Britannia House, Jalan Cator
France
(☎ 02-220960) 301-306, 3rd floor, Jalan Kompleks, Jalan Sultan
Germany
(☎ 02-225547) 6th floor, Wisma Raya Bldg, Lot 39-50 Jalan Sultan
Indonesia
(☎ 02-330180) Simpang 528, Lot 4498, Sungai Hanching Baru, Jalan Muara
Japan
(☎ 02-229265) 1 and 3 Jalan Jawatan Dalam, Kampong Mabohai
Malaysia
(☎ 02-345652) Lot 27 and 29, Simpang 396-39, Kampong Sungai Akar, Mukim Berakas B, Jalan Kebangsaan
New Zealand
(☎ 02-331612) 36A Seri Lambak Complex, Jalan Berakas
Philippines
(☎ 02-241465) 4th and 5th floors, Badiah Bldg, Mile 1, Jalan Tutong
Singapore
(☎ 02-227583) 5th floor, RBA Plaza, Jalan Sultan
UK
(☎ 02-222231) Unit 2.01, Block D, 2nd floor, Complex Yayasan Sultan Haji Hassanal Bolkiah
USA
(☎ 02-229670) 3rd floor, Teck Guan Plaza, Jalan Sultan

Austria, Bangladesh, Belgium, China, Denmark, Finland, India, Iran, Korea, Myanmar (Burma), the Netherlands, Norway, Oman, Pakistan, Saudi Arabia, Sweden, Thailand and Vietnam also have diplomatic representation in Brunei.

CUSTOMS

Duty-free allowances for persons over 17 years of age are 200 cigarettes or 250g of tobacco, 60ml of perfume and 250ml of toilet water. Non-Muslims may import two bottles of liquor and 12 cans of beer, which must be declared upon arrival.

The importation of drugs carries the death penalty.

MONEY

Currency

The official currency is the Brunei dollar (B$), but Singapore dollars are equally exchanged and can be used (nobody's wants Malaysian ringgit – there's about a 40% difference between the B$ and the RM). Banks give around 10% less for cash than they do for travellers cheques.

Brunei uses 1c, 5c, 20c and 50c coins, and B$1, B$5, B$10, B$50, B$100, B$500, B$1000 and B$10,000 notes.

Exchange Rates

The following table shows the exchange rates:

Australia	A$1	=	B$0.98
Canada	C$1	=	B$1.00
European Union	€1	=	B$1.88
France	FF10	=	B$2.80

Germany	DM1	=	B$0.95
Hong Kong	HK$10	=	B$2.00
Indonesia	1000rp	=	B$0.19
Japan	¥100	=	B$1.35
Malaysia	RM1	=	B$0.41
New Zealand	NZ$1	=	B$0.83
Singapore	S$1	=	B$0.96
Thailand	100B	=	B$4.07
UK	UK£1	=	B$2.63
USA	US$1	=	B$1.55

Exchanging Money

Travellers cheques can be exchanged readily in major banks in BSB and Kuala Belait, although a hefty commission is charged for the privilege. American dollars and pounds sterling are the safest currencies to travel with, but you shouldn't encounter any problems with other western currencies. If you're travelling to expensive Brunei from Malaysia remember that nobody will want your ringgit; if you're coming from Labuan or Lawas there are moneychangers at Muara, and if travelling by boat from Limbang you can change ringgit on Jalan Macarthur in BSB to tide you over until you can get to a bank.

International credit cards such as Visa, Diners' Club and American Express are readily accepted at most hotels; in fact it's usually the expected method of payment. Likewise, if you're dining at hotel restaurants credit card payments are fine. There are ATMs outside major banks and in the YSHHB Complex in BSB. If you're flying to BSB you can change money at the airport (moneychangers open for all flights), but if you take a free shuttle bus to one of the major hotels you'll probably get a better rate at the banks in the city centre.

Costs

Brunei has held its own during the recent economic upheavals in the region. If you're travelling from a neighbouring country you'll find the cost of living much higher; accommodation in particular is very expensive by South-East Asian standards. There is only one budget option in the country and it cannot always be relied upon for a bed, though some top-end hotels are not that much more expensive than the equivalent in Malaysia. Transport is comparable to prices in Sabah and Sarawak in Malaysia, and you won't have to use it much anyway. Food is reasonably priced unless you eat at western restaurants, but since you can't obtain alcohol anywhere you could even save money on dining out.

POST & COMMUNICATIONS

Post offices are open from 7.45 am to 4.30 pm Monday to Thursday and Saturday; opening hours on Friday are from 8 to 11 am and 2 to 4 pm. All post offices are closed on Sunday. The cost of an air mail postcard to Malaysia and Singapore is B$0.20; to most other places in South-East Asia it's B$0.35; to Europe, Africa, Australia and the Pacific it's B$0.50; and to the Americas it's B$0.60.

Phone cards – Hallo Kad and JTB are the most common – are available from Telecom offices and retail stores in denominations of B$10, B$20, B$50 and B$100. They can be used in public booths to make international calls. Most hotels have IDD phones, and faxes can be sent from the Telecom office or from major hotels.

To call Brunei from outside the country, the country code is 673.

Major hotels have a business centre; rates vary but expect to pay around B$30 per hour to use facilities.

Brunet is a Web site set up by the Ministry of Communications. It's at www.brunet.bn. There's a Cyber Cafe (☎ 02-453306) on the 1st floor, Block A, of the Kiarong Complex, outside the city centre on the road to Gadong.

BOOKS & MAPS

Books on Brunei are few and far between, but there are a few useful titles for travellers and glossy publications which make good permanent mementos.

Explore Brunei is the free government tourist guide and contains much useful information for visitors. It is available at major hotels, travel agents and at the airport information desk.

Brunei Darussalam, A Guide is an informative, glossy book with beautiful photos. It outlines a host of day trips and sights around the country, although it is a bit out of date. If you will be spending more than a few days in Brunei, this is your guide. Very few bookshops stock it, but it can be bought at the publications office of Brunei Shell in BSB, opposite the Hongkong Bank.

By God's Will – A Portrait of the Sultan of Brunei by Lord Chalfont is a measured look at the sultan and Brunei.

For an exhaustive analysis of everything to do with Brunei, including statistics, the glossy government publication entitled *Brunei Darussalam in Profile* is available on request from Brunei diplomatic missions. Those entering business or employment in Brunei will probably find the *Brunei Yearbook*, published by the Borneo Bulletin, very useful. *Brunei Darussalam in Brief* and *Selamat Datang* are other useful publications.

If you're thinking of exploring the hinterland with a hire car, the *Road Map and Street Index of Brunei Darussalam*, published by Shell, is an excellent publication. Apart from detailed maps of all built-up areas, it has information on where to go and what to see. Shell also publishes a folding road map of Brunei but it is not as useful.

NEWSPAPERS & MAGAZINES

The *Borneo Bulletin* is the country's only English-language daily. Malaysian and Singaporean newspapers are available, as are foreign magazines, including *Time*, *Newsweek* and *Asiaweek*. The government prints two newspapers in Malay: *Media Pertama* and the weekly *Pelita Brunei*. *Brunei Darussalam Newsletter* is a fortnightly newsletter in English which is mainly concerned with the sultan's latest official engagements or public utterances.

Regal is a glossy lifestyle magazine advising Bruneians how to emulate western yuppies. Among reviews of the latest products from Rolex, Porsche and Givenchy, there are interesting articles on Brunei's history, culture and wildlife. It is available at hotels or by subscription. *Muhibah* is the inflight magazine of Royal Brunei Airlines and *Your Future* is a 'youth interest' mag.

RADIO & TV

Brunei has two radio channels transmitting on both the medium wave and FM bands: one in Malay, called the National Network, and the other in English, Chinese and Gurkhali (for the Gurkha soldiers who guard Brunei's oilfields), the Pilihan Network. English transmission times are from 6.30 to 8.30 am, 11 am to 2 pm and 8 to 10 pm. A third network, Pelangi Network, is bilingual (Malay and English) and operates on the FM band. Five times a day, during Muslim prayer times, the radio and TV transmit the muezzin's call nationally. London's Capital Radio and Capital Gold can be picked up on the FM band.

Brunei is proud of the fact that it was the first country in the region to introduce colour TV in 1975, although you'll probably be underwhelmed by the quality of local content. Radio & Television Brunei (RTB) transmits local and overseas programmes for about eight hours on weekdays, 12 hours on Friday and 15 hours on weekends. TV is broadcast on channel 5 for most of the country; Malaysian TV can also be received. Major hotels usually provide free access to cable networks, such as CNN, BBC or Star TV.

TIME

Brunei is in the same time zone as Malaysia and Singapore; 16 hours ahead of US Pacific Standard Time (San Francisco and Los Angeles), 13 hours ahead of US Eastern Standard Time (New York), eight hours ahead of GMT/UTC (London) and two hours behind Australian Eastern Standard Time (Sydney and Melbourne). Thus, when it is noon in Brunei, it is 8 pm in Los Angeles and 11 pm in New York the previous day, 4 am in London, and 2 pm in Sydney and Melbourne.

ELECTRICITY

Electricity supplies are reliable and run at 220-240V AC, 50 cycles. Plugs are of three square-pins, as in Malaysia and Singapore.

WEIGHTS & MEASURES

Like almost everywhere in the world, Brunei uses the metric system.

HEALTH

Generally speaking, Brunei has high standards of hygiene. Tap water is considered safe to drink and there is no risk of malaria.

Smoke haze is a problem, however, and at its worst, face masks are de rigueur in central BSB. At times the smoke is dangerous enough to force the closure of schools, but it is hard to predict how this will be in future. Seek information before you arrive (word of mouth and flight cancellations are the best guide), especially if taking young children; it's probably best to avoid Brunei altogether if the situation is bad.

Remember this is a tropical climate, so take the usual health precautions against heat exhaustion and dehydration – see the Health section in the Malaysia Facts for the Visitor chapter.

The Hart Medical Clinic (☎ 02-225531), 1st floor, Wisma Setia, is a clinic in the centre of Bandar Seri Begawan. The RIPAS hospital just north of Jalan Tutong is a fully equipped, modern hospital.

WOMEN TRAVELLERS

Brunei is a very safe country to travel in. Muslim women are required to cover up from head to toe, with only the face and hands exposed. However because of the large expatriate population many Bruneians are used to western ways.

Bruneian men are generally very polite, and seem less inclined to leer openly than their Malaysian counterparts. Bare shoulders and short dresses are considered inappropriate, although Chinese women often ignore these conventions.

To avoid offence and possible unwelcome attention, dress should be conservative and not revealing. There's no need to cover elbows and knees, or to wear a scarf, unless you really want to impress a pious host. There are strict dress and behaviour rules for visiting mosques (see the boxed text 'Correct Behaviour in a Mosque' under Religion). The usual western swimwear is fine at hotel pools and a one-piece suit or T-shirt and shorts will attract less attention elsewhere. Topless bathing is not accepted.

BUSINESS HOURS

Government offices are open daily from 7.45 am to 12.15 pm and 1.30 to 4.30 pm, except on Friday and Sunday, when they are closed. Private offices are generally open from 9 am to 5 pm Monday to Friday and from 9 am to noon on Saturday; banks are open from 9 am to 3 pm Monday to Friday and from 9 to 11 am on Saturday. Most shops in the central area open around 9 am and are closed by 6 pm. Shopping malls generally open an hour or so later and close at 9.30 or 10 pm. In major shopping precincts, such as Jalan Tutong and Gadong, shops stay open until 9 or 9.30 pm. Hours may be shorter during Ramadan.

PUBLIC HOLIDAYS

Holidays and festivals in Brunei are mostly religious celebrations or festivities which mark the anniversaries of important events in the history of the country.

As in Malaysia and Singapore, the dates of most religious festivals are not fixed because they are based on the Islamic calendar.

Fixed holidays are:

New Year's Day
1 January

National Day
23 February

First Day of Hijrah 1419
28 April

Anniversary of the Royal Brunei Armed Forces
31 May

Prophet Mohammad's Birthday
6 July

Sultan's Birthday
15 July

Christmas Day
25 December

Variable holidays include:

Chinese New Year
January or February

Nuzul Al-Quran
January or February

Hari Raya Aidilfitri
January or February

Isra Dan Mi'Raj
February
Awal Ramadan (1st day of Ramadan)
March
Anniversary of the Revelation of the Koran
April
Hari Raya Aidilfitri (end of Ramadan)
April
Hari Raya Haji
June
First Day of Hijrah
July
Hari Moulud (Prophet's Birthday)
July or August
Israk Mikraj
November
1st Day of Ramadan
December

Getting There & Away

AIR

Royal Brunei Airlines has direct flights from BSB to 27 destinations, including regional capitals such as Singapore, Kuala Lumpur, Manila, Taipei and Hong Kong; major centres in Borneo, such as Kuching, Gunung Mulu National Park and Kota Kinabalu; Darwin, Perth and Brisbane in Australia; Bali and Jakarta in Indonesia; and further afield to Abu Dhabi, London and Frankfurt. Malaysia Airlines, Singapore Airlines, Thai Airways International also covers the routes to their home countries.

Although published rates for flights with Royal Brunei Airlines may seem extortionate, good discounts are usually available if you buy your ticket in the country of your departure. Being a Muslim airline, Royal Brunei does not serve alcohol on its flights.

For airline office contacts in Brunei, see the Getting There & Away entry under BSB.

Departure Tax

There is a departure tax of B$5 when flying to Malaysia and Singapore and B$12 to all other destinations.

Malaysia & Singapore

To Kuching the economy fare is B$243 (RM309 from Kuching), Kota Kinabalu B$81 (RM103 from KK), Kuala Lumpur B$411 (RM544 from KL), Labuan B$37 (RM66), Miri B$59 (RM91), Gunung Mulu National Park B$59 (RM91) and Bintulu B$91 (RM145). Because of the difference in exchange rates it is around 40% cheaper to fly to Brunei from Malaysia than vice versa. The standard economy fare to Singapore is B$389 one way (S$389 from Singapore) or 30 day excursion fares are available for B$530 (S$530) return. Discounts are not usually available on these flights.

Other Asian Destinations

Published one way fares to other Asian destinations include Bali and Jakarta B$471 (US$450 return from Bali), Manila B$458 (US$468 return from Manila), Taipei B$763, Hong Kong B$686 and Yangon B$749. On flights where Royal Brunei Airlines has competition, discounting of up to 20% is available if tickets are bought through a travel agent. To Bangkok the discounted fare is around B$520 and to Manila B$458. Some of the cheapest flights from Bangkok to Perth or Darwin go via Brunei.

Australia

The cheapest one way/return flights to BSB are from Darwin and cost A$382/764. From Perth or Brisbane the respective fares are around A$438/876 or A$413/826. Royal Brunei is the only carrier that has direct flights – at least two weekly – from each city. From the east coast of Australia, it is usually cheaper to fly via Singapore or Kuala Lumpur.

UK, Europe & North America

Royal Brunei Airline's published fares from Frankfurt and London are B$3094 and B$3255, respectively, but discount fares from all countries are usually available; check with the Royal Brunei office or your travel agent – and shop around. For example, take any airline flying to Bangkok or Kuala Lumpur then take a Royal Brunei flight from there. For travellers from North America, Royal Brunei doesn't fly direct, so the best option is to shop around for a good fare to Bangkok or KL and then make your connection to Brunei.

LAND

The main overland route is via bus from Miri in Sarawak. See the Kuala Belait Getting There & Away section in this chapter for details. It is easy to travel overland between Limbang or Lawas in Sarawak and Bangar in the eastern part of Brunei, although a boat to BSB is the usual method. Overland travel between Lawas and Bangar is expensive. See the Bangar section and the Limbang and Lawas sections in the Sarawak chapter for details on these border crossings.

SEA

Boats connect Brunei to Lawas and Limbang in Sarawak, and to Pulau Labuan, from where boats go to Sabah. With the exception of boats to Limbang, all international boats now leave from Muara, 25km north-east of BSB, where Brunei immigration formalities are also handled.

Normally the South China Sea is glassy smooth, but during the wet season it can get choppy. Services may be disrupted or cancelled when smoke haze is bad.

Pulau Labuan

Labuan is a duty-free island between Brunei and Sabah from where you can take a ferry direct to Kota Kinabalu or Menumbok (or a bus to Kota Kinabalu or Lawas in Sarawak); and flights to Sabah, Sarawak or Peninsular Malaysia. For more details, see the Pulau Labuan Getting There & Away section in the Sabah chapter.

Buy your ticket the day before if you are catching an early boat, especially on weekends and public holidays, and aim to check in 45 minutes before departure time to clear immigration. You'll need to catch the first express bus to Muara from BSB to get the first ferry.

From Brunei there are four or five daily services to Labuan. New Island Shipping and Trading (☎ 02-234605), 2nd floor, Gock Tee building, Jalan McArthur, handles the bookings for *Mutiara Laut* and *Ratu Samudra*. Departures are at 8 am daily with an additional departure at 9 am on Friday and Sunday; returning from Labuan the boat leaves at 2 pm daily with an extra service at 4 pm on Friday and Sunday. The economy/1st class fare is B$15/20; economy class is perfectly adequate. These tickets are valid for three months from date of purchase, although a B$5 fee is payable if they are not used on the allocated date.

Other Labuan services are:

Suria Ekspres leaves at 8.30 am, returning at 3 pm (B$15 each way). Book at the Zaza Ayu Boutique (☎ 02-235614) on the 1st floor of the Teck Guan Plaza.

Sanergy Rafflesia leaves Muara at 1 pm daily ($B15/RM24 from Labuan). Bookings can be made in BSB at Churiah Travel Service, 63 Jalan McArthur, or at the Muara ferry terminal.

Sri Labuan Tiga departs at 3.30 pm. Book at Halim Tours (☎ 02-226688), 61 Jalan McArthur; the office is in the laneway opposite the Limbang ticket stall.

Sarawak

Lawas One express boat daily goes from Muara to Lawas at 11.30 am. It costs B$15 and takes about two hours. You can make bookings at Halim Tours (☎ 02-226688).

See under Lawas in the Sarawak chapter for details of transport to Sabah and Labuan, and flights in Sarawak.

Limbang Boats to Limbang leave from the customs wharf at the end of Jalan Roberts in BSB, where there is also an immigration office. Private ekspres boats do this run between 7 am and 4 pm, and depart when full. Buy your ticket at the stall on Jalan McArthur near the customs wharf. The fare is B$10 (RM15 coming from Limbang) and the trip takes about 30 minutes.

There isn't much to see or do in Limbang, but from there you can fly to Gunung Mulu National Park, Miri, Lawas or Kota Kinabalu. See Limbang in the Sarawak chapter for further details.

Getting Around

Transport around Brunei is by bus, hire car or taxi. The public bus system is cheap and reliable, but only in and around BSB. Buses run between 6 am and 6 pm. Buses on the main highway between BSB and Kuala Belait are regular.

If you want to get off the main road to explore the hinterland, a hire car is the least expensive option. Organised tours are also pricey and metered taxis are prohibitively so. See Getting Around in the BSB section for more information.

Hitchhiking is another option. In Brunei, hitchhikers are such a novelty that the chances of getting a lift are good, although cars hurtle along the main highway and are less inclined to stop on long stretches. While Brunei is generally a safe place to travel, hitching is never entirely safe anywhere, and we don't recommend it. Travellers who decide to hitch should understand that they are taking a small, but potentially serious risk. People who choose to hitch will be safer if they travel in pairs and let someone know where they are planning to go.

Regular boats connect Bangar in the Temburong district with BSB. Taxis are the only transport around Temburong.

Bandar Seri Begawan

The capital, Bandar Seri Begawan (usually called BSB or Bandar for short), is the largest town in Brunei and one of the few places worth visiting in the country. It's a neat, very clean and modern city with wide roads to accommodate the air-conditioned cars that are the preferred mode of transport. You won't see any bicycles, trishaws or even motorcycles, and by Asian standards even taxis are thin on the ground. What this means, unlikely as it seems, is that the usually empty streets get congested at peak times.

Islam and oil money are BSB's defining characteristics. Arabic script graces the street signs, and domes and minarets dot the skyline. The sprawling public buildings, mosques and stadiums, culminating conspicuously in the splendour of the sultan's palace, belie the fact that this is a city of just 60,000 people. But then Brunei can afford it.

In contrast to the opulent symbols of Allah's omnipresence, traditional water villages on stilts fringe the Sungai Brunei. BSB has some worthwhile museums, but its nightlife makes it odds-on favourite for the title of 'most boring city in the world': the streets are almost deserted by 9 pm. On the plus side, a relatively stable and large expat community has fostered a very high standard of dining and if you're tired of endless mee and nasi dishes you'll enjoy tucking into some fine Italian and Indian food in BSB.

Orientation

Central BSB is a compact grid aligned roughly north-south and bounded on three sides by water: the Brunei and Kedayan rivers on the south and west, respectively, and a tidal canal on the east. In the centre you'll find most hotels and places to eat, banks, the bus station, airline offices and shops. The Omar Ali Saifuddien Mosque on the western edge of the centre dominates the skyline; next to it on the riverside is an ultramodern shopping mall, the Yayasan Sultan Haji Hassanal Bolkiah (usually written as the YSHHB Complex). Most sights are within walking distance or a short bus ride of the centre. Boats to Limbang leave from the Customs wharf below Jalan McArthur.

Information

Tourist Offices There's no tourist information centre in BSB. Try to get a copy of *Explore Brunei*, a glossy free guide with a good map to Brunei's attractions; it's available at travel agents and most hotels.

Money All banks in BSB charge a commission to change travellers cheques. Least expensive is the Hongkong Bank, which charges B$10.50; the Standard Chartered usually offers higher exchange rates but charges B$15 commission per transaction! There are moneychangers along Jalan McArthur if you're arriving by boat from Limbang, and at the airport.

Post & Communications The main post office is on the corner of Jalan Sultan and Jalan Elizabeth Dua. It is best avoided at lunchtimes, when it is understaffed.

Adjoining the post office on Jalan Sultan is a JTB office, open daily from 8 am to midnight, which sells Hello Kads and JTB cards. You can also send telegrams or faxes, make international calls or use the videophone booth. International calls can also be made from public phones (they only accept phone cards): the telephone office has one, but there are more across Jalan Elizabeth Dua and a couple opposite Wisma Jaya.

Travel Agencies There's a host of travel agents in the city centre where you can book flights and local tours. Some also operate as exclusive booking agencies for ferries to Labuan in Malaysia. Prices for tours depend on the number of paying customers, and are far cheaper if there are two or more people. Half-day tours of BSB start at B$45 per person; and a range of expensive trips into the countryside start at B$55 (B$25 for children). Operators include:

Freme Travel Service
: (☎ 02-335025) 4th floor, Wisma Jaya, Jalan Pemancha. Offers general tours including BSB sights.

Jasra Harrisons
: (☎ 02-243911) Cnr Jalan McArthur and Jalan Kianggeh. Organises trips to Temburong; also the British Airways agent.

Ken Travel
: (☎ 02-223127) 1st floor, Teck Guan Plaza. Sells general tours; also the American Express agent.

Sunshine Borneo
: (☎ 02-446812) 2nd floor, Block C, Abdul Razak Complex, Batu 3½, Jalan Gadong. Runs tours to Temburong.

Bookshops The best range of books and magazines can be found at Best Eastern on the ground floor of the Teck Guan Plaza, on the corner of Jalan Sultan and Jalan McArthur. It also has branches in Plaza Athirah, near the Yaohan department store, and at Centrepoint in Gadong. STP Distributors has a book and stationery store on Jalan Sultan, down from the Hongkong Bank. Wordzone Bookshop, in the basement of the YSHHB Complex, has a range of periodicals and newspapers. Magazines and a limited range of books are available at the airport.

Cultural Centres The British Council is a long way out of town at 45 Simpang 100, Jalan Tungku Link. It's open Monday to Thursday from 8 am to 12.15 pm and 1.45 to 4.30 pm, on Friday and Saturday from 8 am to 12.30 pm.

Omar Ali Saifuddien Mosque

Named after the 28th sultan of Brunei, this golden-domed structure stands next to the Sungai Kedayan in its own artificial lagoon. It is one of the tallest buildings in BSB and one of the most impressive structures in South-East Asia.

This grand mosque dominates the skyline and makes an impressive sight at any time: lit up at night, or silhouetted as the sun sinks through the smoke haze. You'll probably hear the call to prayer echo throughout the city centre, starting from before dawn.

The interior is simple but tasteful, although no match for the stunning exterior. The floor and walls are made from the finest Italian marble; the stained-glass windows were crafted in England; and the luxurious carpets were flown in from Saudi Arabia and Belgium. A Venetian mosaic of 3.5 million pieces decorates the inside of the main dome, and pools and quadrants surrounding the building throw beautiful reflections. The ceremonial stone boat sitting in the lagoon is used for special occasions.

You may be allowed to take the elevator to the top of the 44m minaret or walk up the winding staircase without charge. The view over the city and Kampung Ayer is excellent.

The mosque is open to non-Muslims from Saturday to Wednesday between 8 am and noon, 1 and 3 pm and 4.30 and 5.30 pm (ie outside prayer times). It is closed to non-Muslims on Thursday, and on Friday it is open only from 4.30 to 5 pm. The compound is open between 8 am and 8.30 pm. Remember to dress appropriately and to remove your shoes before entering. Muslim travellers can enter the mosque to pray at any time.

Kampung Ayer

For centuries the people and rulers of Brunei have lived in this collection of rickety-looking houses on stilts along the Brunei and Kedayan rivers. It's a strange mixture of ancient and modern that hasn't changed much since 1521, when Magellan's chronicler Pigafetta first described it to the west.

A visit to one of the villages is probably the most interesting experience you'll have in Brunei. It's a maze of wooden planks connecting brightly painted shacks to shops, villages to schools, clinics to workshops. It's fascinating to wander at random – even if you do end up in someone's kitchen. Bougainvilleas festoon the eaves as they surely did in Pigafetta's time, but the Princess Diana T-shirts drying in the breeze are a more recent addition. And underneath it all, egrets poke about for mudskippers among the piles of garbage.

There are 28 *kampungs* (villages) in all, housing about 30,000 people; when BSB was being modernised many elected to stay in these traditional dwellings, although today they have modern plumbing, electricity and colour TVs. The kampungs are serviced by schools and clinics – of cement rather than wood – shops, mosques and even a water-borne fire brigade (it's been shown that the average dwelling takes all of seven minutes to burn to the waterline). City workers leave their cars parked along the riverbank and commute to their kampung by water taxi after work.

The quickest way to get to Kampung Ayer is to select a path behind the Omar Ali Saifuddien Mosque and start wandering. To get to those along the Sungai Brunei, a water taxi can take you across for a negotiable fee – it should be B$0.50, but expect to pay B$1 or more. A boat trip right around Kampung Ayer takes at least 30 minutes, and the boat operators will probably ask B$30 for their efforts. Bargain hard – B$10 is more like the 'real' price. Water taxis shuttle people back and forth between early morning and late evening, and congregate at the area next to the Customs wharf.

There are all sorts of shops and businesses among the houses in Kampung Ayer. You might stumble across a handicraft shop selling silverwork, brass, woven cloth and baskets. If not, ask a boat operator to take you to one.

Brunei Museum

This fine museum is at Kota Batu, 4.5km east of the centre of BSB, and overlooks the Sungai Brunei. Combined with a visit to the Malay Technology Museum on the riverbank below, it's well worth the short trip out of town.

The museum has displays of artefacts representing the cultural heritage of Brunei, and a natural history section with exhibits of mounted mammals, birds and insects. But perhaps the most interesting display is the Islamic gallery, which has an astonishing collection of beautiful ceramics, jewellery, silverwork and weaponry from across the Islamic world. Look out for the illuminated Korans, jade sword handles inlaid with gems, and begging bowls carved from coconut husks.

There is a section about oil, where an amusing vignette shows local life with and without the benefits that oil brings. A good ethnography section has examples of musical instruments, baskets and brassware, and there is a large collection of Chinese ceramics dating from 1000 AD.

The museum is open Tuesday to Thursday from 9.30 am to 5 pm; Friday from 9.30 to 11.30 am and 2.30 to 5 pm; Saturday and Sunday from 9 am to 5 pm; closed on Monday. Bags must be left at the door and can be stored in lockers. Admission is free.

Purple bus Nos 11 and 39 pass the museum; the fare is B$1. It's a bit of a walk from town but you could probably hitchhike

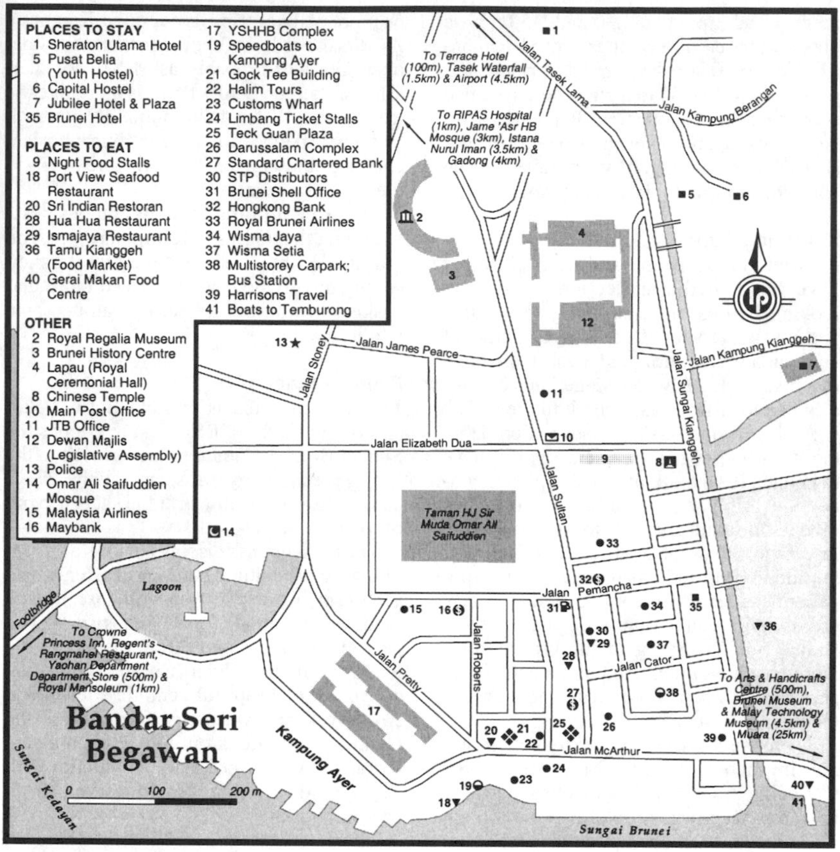

easily. After visiting the museum, you can walk down the steep bank to the Malay Technology Museum.

Malay Technology Museum

This impressive museum, built on the edge of the river below the Brunei Museum, has three galleries devoted to traditional lifestyles and artisans.

Gallery 1 features water villages and has reconstructions of how kampung architecture has evolved over the last 150 years or so. Gallery 2 has exhibits of handicrafts and fishing techniques practised by the people of the water villages. These include silversmithing, brass casting and weaving, and there are some fine examples on display. Gallery 3 shows the tools and techniques used by the indigenous tribes of the interior for food gathering, agriculture and hunting, although the mannequins in striped pyjamas look more like convicts than indigenous Bruneians. Brunei's first gunboat is on display in front of the museum.

The museum is open every day from 9 am to 5 pm, except Friday, when it is open from

9 to 11.30 am and 2.30 to 5 pm, and Tuesday, when it is closed. Admission is free.

Royal Regalia Museum

This museum was gutted by fire early in 1998 and was under repair at the time of writing. It is devoted to the Sultan of Brunei – no surprises there – and exhibited photographs of HM and other members of the royal family. Among the priceless artefacts were his report from Sandhurst Royal Military Academy, and coronation hardware such as the throne, crowns, ceremonial sceptres, krises and costumes. Before the fire, the enormous royal carriage was in the foyer, and a re-enactment of the coronation procession, complete with the costumes of the attendants, was displayed in an ante-room. Check in *Around Brunei* to see if the museum has reopened.

Brunei History Centre

The Brunei History Centre is devoted to researching Brunei's history and recording the sultan's family history. At the entrance to the centre is a small museum devoted to the lineage of the sultan. It has replicas of all the royal tombs and shows their locations around BSB. It is open from Monday to Thursday and on Saturday from 7.45 am to 12.15 pm and 1.30 to 4.30 pm; it is closed on Friday. Admission is free.

Arts & Handicraft Centre

This grandiose handicraft centre was built to help develop local craftwork. It's on the waterfront towards the Brunei Museum, visible from town and within easy walking distance. However, if you're interested in traditional crafts it is disappointing; only new silverwork and weaving produced by the students are available, and some items are very expensive. A traditional umbrella costs about B$20; model water taxis start at B$230; a kris and scabbard will set you back B$550; and silverwork starts at B$10 and goes up to thousands of Brunei bucks for intricate pieces. Workshops are open to visitors.

The centre is open daily from 8 am to 12.15 pm and 1.30 to 4.30 pm, except on Friday and Sunday, when the hours are 8.30 am to noon and 2 to 4.15 pm. Entry is free.

Taman Peranginan Tasek

This park is a pleasant retreat from the city. It has picnic areas and peaceful walks to a small waterfall and reservoir.

The park is a short distance from town. Walk along Jalan Tasek Lama north from the town centre past the Terrace Hotel, and after two sets of traffic lights turn right. From the entrance gates by the parking lot it is about 1km to the falls – continue past the flowerbeds and picnic tables, then follow the stream to the falls. They are best in the wet season, when the water is deeper – you can swim here but women should remember the usual rules of modesty apply; T-shirt and shorts are safe. Another road by the gate leads to a 15 minute walk uphill to a view over the reservoir.

The Sheraton Utama Hotel hands out a map for joggers which shows the walks.

Chinese Temple

There is a Chinese temple on the corner of Jalan Elizabeth Dua and Jalan Sungai Kianggeh decorated with colourful, pictorial tiles and carved, gilded wood. It's a busy place on Saturday evening, and *wayang* (Chinese opera) is sometimes held here.

Jame'Asr Hassanil Bolkiah Mosque

This is the latest minaretted and domed addition to the Bruneian skyline. It is the largest mosque in the country, constructed at great expense, and as the local tourist literature trumpets, 'a symbol of Islam's firm hold in the country'. It's a fabulous sight. It's a few kilometres from the town centre; take bus No 1 or 22 to get there.

Istana Nurul Iman

The sultan's palace, Istana Nurul Iman, is a magnificent sight, especially when lit up at night. It is larger than the Vatican Palace and no expense was spared: it cost US$350 million and, among other features, has 1788 rooms, 200 toilets and a banquet hall with seating for 4000. Unfortunately, the istana is only open to the public during Hari Raya Aidilfitri, the end of the fasting month of Ramadan, when the sultan often deigns to meet his people.

The istana is 4km out of town on the Tutong road and the grounds back on to the Sungai Brunei. You could spend a leisurely hour walking there or charter a water taxi then walk to the front of the palace. The Tutong and Seria buses pass the istana, but they are infrequent. On the hill opposite the istana are homes belonging to other members of the royal family.

Other Attractions

Overlooking the river about 500m from the Yaohan department store is the **Royal Mausoleum** (Makam Di-Raja), the burial place of the last four sultans; other members of the royal family are buried in the grounds.

On the other side of town on the way to the Brunei Museum is the **Tomb of Sultan Bolkiah** and mausoleum of the fifth sultan of Brunei, who lived from 1473 to 1521, during a period when Brunei was the dominant power in the region. Apart from the view across the river, it's hardly worth getting off the bus for this one.

All over town you'll notice uniquely designed, oversized state buildings that seem to serve no other purpose than to attest to Brunei's wealth and glorify the reign of HM. The **Lapau** (Royal Ceremonial Hall) and **Dewan Majlis** (Legislative Assembly) complex are opposite the youth centre in the centre of town. The former was the coronation hall for the sultan in 1968. Royal ceremonies are occasionally held here, but it lies empty most of the time. None of these buildings can be visited.

The food market, **Tamu Kianggeh**, is on the canal at the east side of the centre. It's not very extensive but has plenty of local colour. Water taxis hurtle up and down the canal transporting passengers to and fro. There's another market behind the Customs building on Jalan McArthur.

In the middle of the river across from the Istana Nurul Iman, **Pulau Ranggu** is home to a large colony of proboscis monkeys – Brunei is one of the strongholds of these amazing primates. Macaques also inhabit the island. If you take a water taxi along the river around sunset you may glimpse a monkey; the bargaining price will probably start at B$60. Nearby on the riverbank, the **Persiaran Damuan** is a landscaped park from where you can get good views of the istana. Access is from Jalan Tutong.

Activities

The **Hassanal Bolkiah National Stadium** is of Olympic proportions and includes a track and field complex, tennis centre, squash courts and swimming pool. It is open to the public from 8 am to noon and 1.30 to 4.30 pm, and the pool is often nearly deserted. The stadium is 5km north of town; to get there take purple bus No 1 or 34.

Golfers can enjoy an international standard course at Mentiri Golf Club near BSB, and there's a driving range at the Royal Brunei Sports Complex near the airport.

The Utama Bowling Alley is near the Yaohan Megamart on Jalan Tutong.

Some tour operators run dive trips, but you're probably better off going to one of the centres in Sabah, such as Labuan or Sipadan.

Places to Stay – Budget

The only budget option in Brunei is *Pusat Belia* (☎ 02-229423), a youth hostel on Jalan Sungai Kianggeh, a short walk from the town centre. A bed in an air-conditioned four-bed dorm costs B$10 for one to three nights and B$5 for each subsequent night (no bathroom). It is often empty but can sometimes fill up with sports groups. Officially you need a youth hostel or student card to stay. Entry without a card is at the discretion of the manager, who may make things difficult if he doesn't like the look of you. Some males with long hair have been turned away.

The youth centre, which the hostel is part of, has a swimming pool (entry B$1) and a cafe with a very limited menu.

If you draw a blank here and can't afford the mid-range places you're in trouble. Some travellers have resorted to sleeping out in the parks or on a beach when the youth centre has been full, but this is not appreciated by the authorities and you run the risk of having your slumber disturbed by the police. Showers are available in the changing rooms of the youth centre pool for B$1.

Places to Stay – Mid-Range

If you are on a tight budget, the jump in price from budget to mid-range accommodation will probably give you hysterics. All rooms include air-con, TV, hot water and IDD phones. A 10% service charge applies to all prices quoted here. On the positive side, many hotels will give a 'promotional discount' if you ask politely.

The *Capital Hostel* (☎ 02-223561), off Jalan Tasek Lama just behind the Pusat Belia, has faded singles/doubles from B$80/95 to B$118/138. The restaurant downstairs serves reasonably priced meals and western breakfasts.

The *Crowne Princess Inn* (☎ 02-241128), Km 2.5 Jalan Tutong, is across the Sungai Kedayan near the Yaohan department store; take the footbridge behind the Omar Ali Saiffudien Mosque. It is inconveniently located, but reasonably priced at B$110 for a room, and a discount can make this very good value by Brunei standards.

Places to Stay – Top End

BSB has a good selection of top-end hotels, although the mid-range accommodation is perfectly adequate. For the extra money you can take advantage of trappings such as a pool, business centre and minibar full of soft drinks. A 10% service charge applies in all these hotels but most offer discounts.

Most centrally located is the *Brunei Hotel* (☎ 02-242372), on the corner of Jalan Sungai Kianggeh and Jalan Pemancha. Singles/doubles start at B$160/180 and suites range from B$220 to B$400. Discounts of around 20% are sometimes offered.

The *Jubilee Hotel* (☎ 02-228070) is in the Jubilee Plaza on Jalan Kampung Kianggeh. Small singles/doubles with spacious bathrooms start at B$100/120 and suites range from B$160/180 to B$380. Other hotels are probably better value, although there is a restaurant, supermarket and an excellent coffee shop in the plaza.

The *Sheraton Utama Hotel* (☎ 02-244272) is Brunei's top hotel and close to the centre on Jalan Tasek Lama. Singles/doubles range from B$245/265 to B$265/285 and suites range from B$520 up to B$1555. The Sheraton has a pool and a business centre.

The *Terrace Hotel* (☎ 02-243554), on Jalan Tasek Lama, is a little way from the centre of town and poor value unless you get a discount. This is frequently available, but posted rates range from B$148/158 for singles/doubles to B$328 for a suite. The hotel restaurant is quite good and there's a swimming pool.

The *Riverview Hotel* (☎ 02-238238), Km 1 Jalan Gadong, is one of Brunei's best. It is north of town on the way to the airport. Singles/doubles cost B$175/195 and suites range from B$230 to B$880.

The Centrepoint (☎ 02-430430), in the Gadong shopping precinct, has serviced apartments starting at B$235, climbing up to B$1650 for the Presidential Suite. There's an impressive range of marble-clad facilities including an expensive Chinese restaurant, business centre, swimming pool, sports centre and private dining rooms – what more could you want, besides a stiff drink? There's a branch of the Yaohan Megamart downstairs.

Places to Eat

All the hotels and the youth centre have their own restaurants. The *canteen* in the youth centre is cheap but the choice is very limited. The meals at the *Capital Hostel* are pretty good and quite cheap; tasty Hokkien noodles and other dishes cost around B$5.

There are food stalls and street cafes in the centre of BSB, and cheap outdoor eating can be enjoyed at several spots around the centre. The *Gerai Makan* food centre is on the riverfront just over the canal from the customs wharf, although not much happens in the evening.

The food stalls at the *Tamu Kianggeh* are across the canal, near the intersection of Jalan Sungai Kianggeh and Jalan Pemancha.

In the evening only, another group of stalls springs up in the car park behind the Chinese temple, opposite the post office. You can get good cheap food here including satay, barbecued fish, chicken wings and kueh melayu (sweet pancakes filled with peanuts, raisins and sugar). The only drawback is that neither of these places has seating.

There are clean, air-conditioned *food courts* on the 2nd floor of Wisma Setia, in Jalan Pemancha, and at YSHHB Complex.

The main street, Jalan Sultan, has the cheapest restaurants in the town centre. *Ismajaya Restaurant* has rice and curry meals for around B$3, and a few doors down the *Sin Tai Pong* has chicken-rice for B$2.50. The *Hua Hua Restaurant* nearby is more expensive – about B$6 to B$8 for most dishes – but the food is very good and it has a wide range including seafood, noodle and claypot dishes. The Hua Hua and the Ismajaya stay open until 9 pm. On Jalan McArthur the *Sri Indah Restoran* has decent roti and murtabak.

BSB has some good bakeries. Decent French pastries can be enjoyed at *Delifrance*, on the ground floor of the YSHHB Complex; good almond croissants cost B$2.50 and in the Wisma Jaya next to the Brunei Hotel there's a *McBrumby Bake House*. The *shopping centres* in the central part of town also have cheap air-con restaurants serving Malay and Chinese food.

You'll find a good range of western fast food around the town centre, but it's not particularly cheap. In the modern YSHHB Complex there's a *SugarBun*, *Jollibee*, *KFC* and *Pizza Hut*. Another branch of Pizza Hut on the corner of Jalan Sultan and Jalan McArthur does take away slices for B$1.90. In the Gadong shopping precinct, 5km out of the city, you'll find branches of all these chains plus *McDonald's* and *Swensen's*.

For real pizza and superb pasta dishes go to *Fratini*, on the ground floor of the YSHHB Complex. Pizzas are B$11 to B$15, pasta ranges from B$12 to B$14 and fixed-price three-course lunches and dinners are available.

If you're self-catering, *Hua Ho* supermarket in the basement of the YSHHB Complex stocks every type of food product imaginable.

The restaurant at the *Crowne Princess Hotel* offers Sunday dim sum breakfast from 7.30 till 11 am costing B$12. For fresh seafood the *Port View Seafood Restaurant*, overlooking the river, is very good. A fixed price lunch and dinner is B$29 and B$37, respectively, including all drinks.

Excellent coffee and muffins can be found at *Deli-Bites*, on the 1st floor of the Jubilee Plaza.

The shopping area on Jalan Tutong around the Yaohan department store has a number of restaurants, mostly moderately priced Chinese *kedai kopi*, some of which stay open until 10 pm or later.

Regent's Rang Mahel, near the Crowne Princess Inn, is an air-con Indian restaurant with a wide selection of excellent vegetarian and meat dishes, including dosa and tandoori breads. Most curries cost around B$3 and you could stuff yourself for B$10 and still have change; good buffet lunches are B$6 and buffet dinners cost B$10 on Thursday and Saturday. The upstairs section is a bit more refined (and costly), and does a superb chicken masala.

Shopping

Most of the quality shopping is in the air-conditioned plazas. If you are wondering where Bruneians spend their excess oil-soaked dollars, take a look round the shiny YSHHB Complex. It stays open till late and has a dazzling selection of shops selling watches, sunglasses, Iranian chandeliers and other essentials. Across the bridge through Kampung Ayer there's a huge Yaohan department store which sells imported clothes, electrical goods and books; the supermarket in the basement is stocked with imported foodstuffs from around the world.

Nearby are a number of shopping plazas, such as Plaza Athirah, Mohamad Yossof and Badiah. It's about 20 minutes walk to the Yaohan department store from the centre via the stilt villages of Kampung Ayer, starting from the back of Omar Ali Saifuddien Mosque.

The other big shopping centre is at Gadong, about 5km north-west of the city centre. There's no reason to make a special trip here, but there are plenty of supermarkets and department stores, a couple of decent bookshops, a number of restaurants and the Yaohan Megamart all collected together in the massive air-con Centrepoint shopping centre.

There are numerous photo-processing, camera and film shops in the shopping malls in the town centre and at Gadong, although if you have any special film requirements you should get them before you come to Brunei. There is no advantage to buying duty-free in Brunei, since the exchange rate in Malaysia will get you far more for your money.

Getting There & Away

Air Airlines which fly into Brunei include Royal Brunei Airlines, Malaysia Airlines, Singapore Airlines and Thai Airways International. Tickets to Malaysia and Singapore are at a fixed rate, but other international tickets are up to 20% cheaper if bought through travel agents rather than the airlines. Royal Brunei Airlines' travel shop sells discounted fares; it's in the same building as its office.

Airline offices or general sales agents in BSB include:

British Airways
(☎ 02-243911) Harrisons (GSA), Cnr Jalan Kianggeh and Jalan McArthur

Garuda Indonesia
(☎ 02-235870) 49-50, 3rd floor, Wisma Raya, Jalan Sultan

Malaysia Airlines
(☎ 02-224141) 144 Jalan Pemancha

Royal Brunei Airlines
(☎ 02-242222) RBA Plaza, Jalan Sultan

Singapore Airlines
(☎ 02-244901) 1st floor, 49-50 Jalan Sultan

Thai Airways International
(☎ 02-242991) 401-403, 4th floor, Kompleks Jalan Sultan, 51-55 Jalan Sultan

Bus The main highway in Brunei links BSB to Seria, Kuala Belait and the Sarawak border near Kuala Baram. See the Kuala Belait Getting There & Away section later in this chapter for details.

It is possible, though difficult, to reach Limbang by road through Bangar from BSB; from there you could travel overland to Lawas, although boat is a cheaper and quicker option. It has been said that the government deliberately keeps the roads out of Brunei in a miserable condition to make any invasion by land difficult!

The bus station for both local and long-distance buses in BSB is on Jalan Cator (beneath the multistorey car park).

For Miri in Sarawak, take a bus to Seria, where you change for Kuala Belait and then change again to get to Miri. Set out early from BSB if you want to reach Miri in one day. See the Kuala Belait section for more information.

There are many buses every day to Seria between 7.30 am and about 3 pm. The fare is B$4 and the journey takes 1½ to two hours.

Car Hire car is the only feasible way to explore the hinterland of Brunei. You could comfortably see most sights in two days, but it's impossible to get a car across to Temburong unless you drive the long way round through Limbang in Sarawak.

Hire rates start at about B$90 per day, including free mileage and insurance, although surcharges apply if the car is taken into Sarawak. Discounts may be available depending on demand and season – don't be afraid to ask. Most rental agencies will bring the car to your hotel and arrange to pick it up when you've finished. Petrol is cheap and the main roads are in good condition, but the back roads can be appalling. There are a dozen or so hire car companies, including:

Avis Rent A Car
(☎ 02-426345) Ground floor, Hj Daud Complex, Jalan Gadong

Budget U-Drive
(☎ 02-445846) E17, 1st floor, Bangunan GP, Jalan Gadong

National Car Systems
(☎ 02-424921) 1st floor, Bangunan Hasbullah 4, Jalan Gadong

Boat Apart from flying, the only way to get to Sabah or the Sarawak outposts of Limbang and Lawas is to use a launch or launch/taxi combination. See the Bangar Getting There & Away section for details.

Bangar Regular launches ply between BSB and Bangar in Temburong. The first departure is around 6.30 am and the last at 4.30 pm. Launches leave when full from the jetty near the Gerai Makan food centre, and the trip costs B$7.

Getting Around

To/From the Airport Purple bus Nos 11, 23, 24, 36, 38 and 57 will get you to and from the airport for B$1. As you leave the terminal, walk diagonally right across the car park to get to the bus stop.

Some major hotels have courtesy phones at the arrivals hall where you can request a free pick-up. You could always take the ride, say the rooms don't meet your standard then walk to the youth hostel.

If you don't have too much baggage you could take a purple taxi to the airport for B$3; it will drop you about 100m from the terminal. A metered taxi costs around B$20. But you can't rely on catching a taxi from the airport because they're not allowed to queue here. The big, modern airport is 8km north-west of the city.

Bus The government bus network reaches most sights in and around the city, and also serves the international ferry terminal at Muara. The bus station is beneath the multistorey car park on Jalan Cator and route numbers are emblazoned on the front of each bus. A route map is displayed at the terminal, and reproduced in colour in tourist leaflets. Apart from the Muara express service, all fares are B$1 and useful routes are:

Airport – Route Nos 11, 23, 24, 36, 38 and 57
Brunei Museum & Malay Technology Museum – Route Nos 11 and 39
Gadong Shopping Precinct – Route No 1
Hassanal Bolkiah National Stadium & Immigration Department – Route Nos 1 and 34
Jame'Asr Hassanil Bolkiah Mosque – Route Nos 1 and 22
Jerudong Playground – Route Nos 55 and 57
Muara & Serasa beaches – Route Nos 33

For the ferry terminal at Muara, express buses leave every half hour between 6.50 am and 4.50 pm; the trip takes 40 minutes and the fare is B$2. The last bus back is at 5 pm.

Taxi There are two options for taxis around BSB. The City Transport Service (CTS) taxis (better known as purple taxis) can take you anywhere within the city limits for a fixed B$3 (plus B$1 if you book by phone). Unfortunately, purple taxis are not allowed to drop you at the airport terminal, but will take you to within a short walk. Purple taxis operate from 6 am to 10 pm and can be found at the multistorey car park or booked on the CTS hotline (☎ 02-343434).

The other option is an expensive metered taxi. You shouldn't need one for transport around town, but if you have a lot of luggage and can't take a hotel shuttle bus you'll have to get one to the airport. A metered taxi to the ferry terminal at Muara will cost about B$75! Flagfall is B$3, a surcharge of B$5 applies for trips to/from the airport and the meters tick over very quickly. Between 9 pm and 6 am a surcharge of 50% of the metered fare is effective. There is also a B$1 charge for each item of luggage put in the boot. The best places to look for a taxi are at the bus station on Jalan Cator and the Sheraton Utama; or you can book one on (☎ 02-222214) and pay a booking charge of B$3.

Water Taxi Water taxis, popularly known as flying coffins, are longboats with powerful outboard motors that hurtle up and down the Sungai Brunei transporting passengers to and from the villages of Kampung Ayer. They are most easily caught near the Customs wharf or the Tamu Kianggeh food market. Fares start at 50c and range up to B$2, although you'll have to bargain a bit. To charter a boat for a tour of Kampung Ayer and the river shouldn't cost more than B$20 per hour – less if you bargain hard.

Around Bandar Seri Begawan

None of Brunei's sights is more than a few hours from the capital, but a car is essential to reach most of them. There's not a great deal to see – some good beaches and forest reserves make pleasant day trips, and with some extra effort and expense you can take river trips and visit a longhouse. For trekking and wildlife viewing in pristine rainforest, head for Temburong. Other than camping, the only accommodation outside BSB is at Kuala Belait, which is just a transit point for travel to and from Miri in Sarawak, and at the Rainforest Studies Centre at Batang Apoi.

BEACHES

Muara is a small container port at the top of the peninsula north of BSB.

Pantai Muara (Muara Beach), 2km from town, is a popular weekend retreat. The white sand is clean, but like many beaches in Borneo it is littered with driftwood and the debris of logging. It is quiet during the week and has food stalls, picnic tables and a children's playground. Other beaches around Muara include **Serasa** and **Meragang**.

Purple bus No 33 will take you to Muara or Serasa beaches; the fare is $1. You'll have to get to Meragang under your own steam or hitch a ride; the beach is about 4km west of Muara along the Muara-Tutong Highway.

BUKIT SHAHBANDAR FOREST RECREATION PARK

This 70 hectare park is a popular picnic spot on the Muara-Tutong Highway, 15km from BSB. Roads run through much of the park, and walking trails lead off through secondary forest and plantations of pine and acacia. The main trail leads to Triangle Point, a hill with views across the sea and coastline. An information booth at the park entrance has pamphlets showing the trails. It's a pleasant spot, and there is a small artificial lake, toilets and picnic shelters, but if you are after jungle walks Temburong is a better bet.

It is possible to camp in the park, but permission must be obtained in advance from the Forestry Department (☎ 02-222687) in BSB.

JERUDONG PLAYGROUND

The sultan presented this sprawling amusement park to his adoring subjects to mark his 48th birthday. Jerudong Playground is near the coast north of BSB and claimed to be the biggest amusement park in the world (although the Disney Corporation may dispute this). It certainly is huge, but although an estimated 2000 people go there every evening it hardly seems crowded. All rides are free and you rarely have to queue for any. They lack the daredevil feel that some of their counterparts have in other countries, but it would be a great place to take children. However, just to remind you that this is Brunei, women wearing sleeveless tops are not allowed on the rides.

The playground is open Monday to Wednesday from 5 pm to midnight, Thursday and Saturday from 5 pm till 2 am, and Friday, Sunday and public holidays from 2 pm until midnight. There are food and drink stalls at the car park.

Getting There & Away

It's easy to get to the playground – just take purple bus No 55 or 57 from the multistorey car park – but the last bus leaves at 5.30 pm and getting back can be a problem. Major hotels have shuttle services with prearranged pick-up times; for B$20 per person it's hardly cheap, but unless you cadge a ride from a friendly local or expat, it's that or take a metered taxi. Some companies run expensive tours to the playground.

JERUDONG PARK

Jerudong is where the sultan indulges in his favourite pastime, polo. **Jerudong Park** is a huge complex with a polo stadium and luxurious stables housing polo ponies flown in from around the world, including many from

Argentina. A golf course and trapshooting and croquet facilities are also at the park. It's very grand and impressive, but uninvited visitors won't be allowed in. If you have your own car, you can avoid the guard post and drive around the back of the stables for a look. On the other side of the highway are stud farms with more expensive horseflesh. The **Istana Nurul Izzah**, home of the sultan's second wife, is nearby on a hill.

Behind Jerudong Park is **Jerudong Beach**, where stalls sell fresh fish delivered each day by local fishing boats. There are cliffs to the north of the beach and at the southern end is yet another istana. The istana is an impressive piece of modern architecture, but the Gurkha guards are unlikely to allow you inside.

Buses to Seria pass the park, but it is a long walk to the beach and you won't be able to see much of the area unless you have a car.

LIMAU MANIS

Limau Manis is a kampung 35km south-west of BSB; a few kilometres further on is the Sarawak border. Brunei has an immigration post here but the Malaysian equivalent is at Limbang. It is possible to go by road from Limau Manis through Sarawak's Limbang district to Temburong, the eastern half of Brunei, but public transport stops at the border. To get to Limau Manis take bus No 42, 44 or 48.

WASAI KANDAL

Wasai Kandal, 12km from BSB, is a forest area with waterfalls and pools. A path leads past picnic ponds and pools to Air Terjun Tinggi, the most impressive falls, and then a rough track proceeds to another waterfall, Air Terjun Rendah, which has another picnic area. It is about a half hour walk each way. The trail starts at Kampung Kilanas, which is just off Jalan Tutong before the turn-off to Limau Manis. You'll have to hire a taxi to get here.

TUTONG

Tutong is the main town in Tutong district and about halfway between Seria and BSB. Buses to Seria pass by on the main highway, but if you want to see the attractions around Tutong you really need a hire car – getting anywhere by taxi will cost a small fortune.

Pantai Seri Kenangan (often simply referred to as Pantai Tutong) is a popular beach with picnic tables and a simple restaurant. It is on a spit of land with the ocean on one side and the Sungai Tutong on the other. The white-sand, casuarina-lined beach is probably the best in Brunei. The royal family has a surprisingly modest **istana** at Pantai Seri Kenangan, which is a couple of kilometres off the highway just outside Tutong town. The turn-off is near the Tamu Tutong, where a **market** is held daily in the morning. The road to the beach continues for another 5km to Kuala Tutong; the beach at the end of the road is quiet and ideal for camping.

TASIK MERIMBUN

Tasik Merimbun, 27km inland from Tutong, is Brunei's largest lake. It is a pretty, tranquil spot surrounded by forest where you might see monkeys and birdlife. Wooden walkways lead around the shore to picnic pavilions and this picturesque, swampy lake has an island in the middle. There's a restaurant overlooking the lake near the car park.

Unfortunately the only way to get here is by car. Access is via an appalling road; the lake is poorly signposted and you could easily get lost – ask for Tasik Merimbun.

LABI

Before Seria, a road branches inland to Labi. About halfway to Labi is **Luagan Lalak Forest Reserve** where there are good views over a lake that fills up in the rainy season. From Labi several modern **Iban longhouses** can be visited, including Rumah Panjang Mendaram Besar and Rumah Panjang Teraja. There are fine views over the forest from the road, but there's very little traffic so if you don't have transport, you'll have to walk. Take a few small gifts, such as sweets for the children, and cigarettes. Where the sealed road ends a trail leads to **Rampayoh**, a waterfall about two hours walk away. At the end of the road, past Rumah Panjang

Teraja, there's the Sungai Teraja and a trail to another waterfall and **Bukit Teraja**. Bukit Teraja is the highest hill in the area and affords fine views across Brunei and Sarawak. The main trail to the summit is signposted and starts about 6km beyond Rampayoh. The walk through primary forest takes about two hours to the top.

It is also possible to visit Dusun and Punan villages, but this involves hiring a boat (expect to pay around B$300 per day) to take you deep into the interior along the Sungai Belait. The best place to hire a boat is at Kampung Sungai Mau, on the Labi road where it meets the Sungai Belait before Luagan Lalak.

SERIA

Seria is an ugly company town sprawling along the coast between Tutong and Kuala Belait. It consists of some big Shell Brunei installations, the Gurkha battalions that protect them, and hundreds of prefab dwellings where expatriate workers live.

The coastal plain between here and Kuala Belait is the main centre for oil production in Brunei and at a beach just outside of town the **Billionth Barrel Monument** commemorates the billionth barrel of oil produced at the Seria field. It's hardly worth stopping for.

There are a few modern blocks of shops and a market, bounded at the eastern end by a mosque in BP colours, but the nearest accommodation is in Kuala Belait. If you're travelling by bus to Miri you must change at Seria.

Getting There & Away

The road from BSB is excellent and about 10 buses daily make the two hour trip; the fare is B$4. The first bus leaves BSB at 7.30 am and the last one leaves Seria at 2.30 pm. Buses to Kuala Belait leave approximately every 20 minutes between 6.20 am and 7.30 pm, and cost B$1.

KUALA BELAIT

The last town before Malaysia, Kuala Belait is the main town in Belait district and the place to get buses to Miri. 'KB' (not to be confused with Kuala Baram on the Sarawak side of the border) has colonial shophouses in the centre and a reasonable beach, though you won't miss much if you just pass through. The best place to change money is at the Hongkong Bank, diagonally opposite the bus station on Jalan McKerron.

You can hire a motor launch by the market for trips up the river to **Kuala Balai**, a small river village that was once the largest settlement in the district. It is now almost deserted because the residents have left to find work in the oil industry on the coast. The 45 minute trip (one way) goes by good jungle at the river's edge. Along the way ask the boatman to stop at the wooden case of skulls mounted on stilts. Price is by negotiation, but expect to pay about B$150 each way for the river trip.

Places to Stay & Eat

At the cheaper end of the scale there's a *Government Rest House* (☎ 03-334288). Rooms are generally reserved for government officials, but if they're not full you may be allowed to stay. A room including breakfast should cost about B$30. It is on the beach, a 10 minute walk along Jalan McKerron from the bus station, and then 200m to the right.

In town there's the *Hotel Sentosa* (☎ 03-334341), at 92 Jalan McKerron near the bus station. Comfortable but ordinary rooms with air-con, TV and phone cost B$135, although discounts may be available.

The *Seaview Hotel* (☎ 03-332651), Jalan Maulana, is the best hotel outside BSB and better value than the Sentosa. Singles/doubles cost B$100/110 including breakfast, but the hotel was being renovated at the time of writing and price increases were expected. There's a swimming pool, hire car office and a well-stocked supermarket frequented by expats. It is 4km from town on the beach road to Seria.

Kuala Belait has plenty of *kedai kopi*, but for western-style dishes try the *Buccaneer Steakhouse* which is next door to the Hotel Sentosa. For fast food there's a *Jollibee* nearby.

Getting There & Away

See the Seria section for details of buses to Kuala Belait. Buses for Malaysia leave KB at 7.30, 9.30 and 11 am, and at 1.30 and 3.30 pm; the fare is B$10.20 for the 2½ hour trip to Miri.

From Kuala Belait it's a five minute bus ride (20 minute walk) to the Sungai Belait, where a car ferry plies back and forth to the other side. Although the queue of cars can be incredibly long, especially on weekends, bus passengers cross the river on the ferry and pick up another bus on the other side, thus avoiding the queues.

Once you cross the river it's a short ride to the Brunei immigration checkpoint. After going through Brunei customs board a Malaysian bus to get to the Malaysian immigration checkpoint. From here it's a short ride to the queue at the Sungai Baram, which usually takes 15 to 30 minutes to cross. From here the road to Miri is good.

Temburong

Temburong district is the eastern slice of Brunei, surrounded by Sarawak and cut off from the sultanate when Raja Brooke grabbed what is now the Limbang district. It is a quiet backwater reached by boat from BSB and rarely visited by travellers. The boat trip in itself is worthwhile: the boats go down the Sungai Brunei and into the open sea, then weave through the maze of dense mangroves fringing Brunei Bay into the mouth of the Sungai Temburong. Police boats wait in hiding, checking for illegal immigrants – take your passport just in case. Temburong has little industry or development and much of the district is unspoilt forest.

Bangar can be visited in a day trip from BSB if you catch an early boat. The Peradayan Forest Reserve makes a good outing for a jungle walk, or the Iban longhouse at Batang Duri can be visited. For a longer jungle experience, the Kuala Belalong Field Studies Centre receives visitors.

BANGAR

Bangar is a sleepy, pleasant little town on the banks of the Sungai Temburong. It is the district centre and has a row of shops, a mosque and government offices, but there is no accommodation. There are two Chinese coffee shops and the *Hasinah Indian Restaurant*, which is a helpful place if you want to organise transport.

Boats pull up and leave from a wharf on the west bank of the Sungai Temburong.

The immigration office is a few kilometres west of Bangar on the way to Limbang; opening hours are 6 am to 10 pm daily.

Getting There & Away

Road Temburong has two main roads; both are tarred but traffic is light. One leads south to Batang Duri and the other runs between the east and west borders with Sarawak.

Taxis are the only form of transport in the district and congregate near the wharf. They are unmetered and prices must be negotiated.

Taxis go to Limbang in Sarawak for about B$10. There is no border post so make sure you stop at the immigration office in Bangar before leaving Brunei. Report to immigration in Limbang.

It is possible, but expensive, to cross the eastern border to Lawas in Sarawak. This is an alternative route into Sabah, but it's cheaper to take a boat from Muara. A taxi to Lawas costs about B$75, including a trip to the immigration office near Bangar. In Lawas, clear immigration at the jetty where the Brunei ferries tie up.

Hitching is possible, though you may be in for a wait, especially on the way back from Batang Duri. The chances of a lift to the Peradayan Forest Reserve are better, but allow plenty of time for the return to Bangar if you want to catch the boat back to BSB. The road to the reserve – and Lawas – is across the bridge from Bangar wharf.

Boat Boats leave BSB regularly from the wharf near the Gerai Makan food centre and cost B$7. For the return journey, buy your ticket at Bangar wharf. Boats leave approximately every 30 minutes between 6.30 am and 4.30 pm, and the journey takes about 45 minutes.

BATANG DURI

Batang Duri is an Iban longhouse on the Sungai Temburong, 17km south of Bangar. Boats to the Kuala Belalong Field Studies Centre leave from the village jetty. If you visit the longhouse, introduce yourself first, preferably to the *penghulu* (chief). Take your shoes off when you enter and don't wander up and down the veranda; this is like walking unannounced into someone's lounge room.

Taman Batang Duri is a park and small zoo about 2km north of Batang Duri. There are forlorn-looking civets, monkeys, otters and birds, and a stall selling snacks and drinks. It is open every day until 6 pm; admission is free.

A private taxi to Batang Duri from Bangar should cost around B$20 for the return journey, including the wait while you look around the longhouse and/or zoo.

KUALA BELALONG FIELD STUDIES CENTRE

This scientific research centre is in the **Batu Apoi Forest Reserve**, a large area of primary rainforest that covers most of southern Temburong. The centre was developed by Brunei Shell and the Universiti Brunei Darussalam to provide facilities for research into tropical rainforest. It is primarily for scientists and school groups, though interested overseas visitors can stay at the centre.

The forest is rich in flora and fauna, and the jungle can be explored along walking trails. The main trail is a rugged two day walk to Bukit Belalong and there's a canopy walkway which is among the largest in the world.

Tour companies in BSB (see the BSB section) can arrange accommodation at the Field Studies Centre, guides and transport. A visit to the park is not cheap: with a minimum of two people, prices start at B$135 per person for a day trip and B$220 for an overnight trip; longer trips can also be arranged.

Access is by longboat from Batang Duri; a longboat would cost about B$200 so you probably won't save anything by doing the trip yourself, unless you're in a group.

PERADAYAN FOREST RESERVE

This forest reserve is about 15km from Bangar along the road to Lawas and protects the forested peaks of Bukit Patoi and Bukit Peradayan. Walking trails lead to the summits and this is the most accessible rainforest for visitors to Brunei. You'll have to start early to maximise your chances of seeing the mainly nocturnal mammals, but the park also contains many bird species, including hornbills.

The most popular walk is to **Bukit Patoi**, which starts at the entrance to the park. The trail is steep in parts but well marked, with rest huts along the way. It is about a half hour walk to Batu Berdinding, a sandstone outcrop, and then another 15 minutes to the summit. All up, the walk shouldn't take more than an hour with plenty of rests on the way. At the summit there are fine views to the east across the South China Sea and the Lawas area of Sarawak – if there's no smoke haze.

Most walkers descend back along the trail, but it is possible to continue over the other side of the summit and around to Bukit Peradayan. This trail is harder and indistinct in parts, though trees along the trail are marked to show the way. The trail eventually rejoins the road, 12km from Bangar near the Labu Km 5 marker. Three hours should be allowed for the walk from Bukit Patoi to Bukit Peradayan and back to the road.

There are picnic tables and a toilet block at the start of the trail, but bring water and food for the walk. The return taxi trip from Bangar should be only B$20. The driver will wait for you to do the summit walk, or if you want to spend more time in the reserve arrange a time for him to return.

Language

The languages of Bahasa Malaysia (known officially as Bahasa Melayu or simply Malay) and Bahasa Indonesia are virtually the same – only a few differences in the vocabulary distinguish them. Many of these differences are in the loan words – English-based for Malay and Dutch-based for Indonesian. If you're coming from Indo-nesia and have developed some profi-ciency in the language, you may initially be confused by Malay pronunciation. Bahasa Indonesia is a second language for most Indonesians – pronunciation is learnt in schools and, as a result, tends to remain fairly standard. Bahasa Malaysia, however, is subject to greater regional variation in pronunciation and slang – so much so that a Malaysian from Negeri Sembilan may have difficulty understanding someone from Kelantan.

In its most basic form, Malay is very simple. Verbs aren't conjugated for tense; the notion of time is indicated by the use of adverbs such as 'yesterday' or 'tomorrow'. For example, you can change any sentence into the past tense by simply adding *sudah* (already). Many nouns are pluralised by simply saying them twice – thus *buku* is 'book', *buku-buku* is 'books', *anak* is 'child', *anak-anak* is 'children'. There are no articles (a, an, the). Thus 'a good book' or 'the good book' is simply *buku baik*. There is no verb 'to be', so again it would be *buku baik* rather than 'the book is good'. Malay is also a very poetic and evocative language – 'the sun', for example, is *mata-hari*, or 'the eye of the day'.

Many Malay terms have found their way into the everyday English of Malaysia. You'll often see the word *bumiputra* (literally 'sons of the soil') in English-language newspapers, usually in ads for positions vacant; it's a term used to indicate that the job is open only to 'native' Malays, not Indian Malaysians or Chinese Malaysians. Similarly, you may see English-language articles about *jaga keretas*, the people who operate car-parking rackets – pay them to 'protect' your car while it's parked or you'll wish you had. Another expression is *khalwat* (literally 'close proximity') – unmarried Muslim couples definitely do not wish to find themselves suspected of *khalwat*!

For a more comprehensive guide to Bahasa Malaysia, get hold of Lonely Planet's *Malay phrasebook*. It's a handy pocket-sized introduction to the language.

New Spelling

The new spelling system of Bahasa Malaysia brings it into line with Indonesian. However, many of the old spellings are still in use for places and people's names. The main changes are that the letter 'c' replaces the combination 'ch' (as in 'church'), and the letter 'u' often replaces 'o' when it occurs in a word-final syllable, eg *kampung* not *kampong*, *teluk* not *telok*.

Pronunciation

Most letters are pronounced the same as their English counterparts, although a few vowels and consonants differ.

Vowels

a as the 'u' in 'hut'
e a neutral vowel such as the 'e' in 'paper' when unstressed, eg *besar* (big); sometimes hardly pronounced at all, eg in the greeting *selamat*, (when said quickly, pronounced more like 'sla-mat'). When the stress falls on **e** it's more like the 'a' in 'may', eg *meja* (table). There's no single rule which determines whether **e** is stressed or unstressed.
i as in 'hit'
o as the 'oa' in 'boat'
u as in 'flute'
ai as the 'i' in 'line'
au as a drawn out 'ow', as in 'cow'
ua each vowel is pronounced, as 'oo-a'

Consonants
Consonants are pronounced much the same way as they are in English, with these few exceptions:

c	as the 'ch' in 'chair'
g	always hard, as in 'go'
ng	as the 'ng' in 'singer'
ngg	as 'ng + g', as in 'anger'
j	as in 'join'
r	pronounced clearly and distinctly
h	as the English 'h' but slightly stronger like a sigh); at the end of a word it's almost silent
k	as the English 'k', except at the end of the word, when it's more like a silent closing of the throat
ny	as the 'ni' in 'onion'

Word Stress
In Malay words, most syllables carry equal emphasis; as a general rule stress falls on the second-last syllable. The main exception is the unstressed **e** in words such as *besar* (big), pronounced be-SAR.

Greetings & Farewells

Good morning.	*Selamat pagi.*
Good day. (around midday)	*Selamat tengah hari.*
Good afternoon.	*Selamat petang.*
Good night.	*Selamat malam.*
Goodbye. (said by person staying)	*Selamat tinggal.*
Goodbye. (said by person leaving)	*Selamat jalan.*

Basics

Yes/No.	*Ya/Tidak*
Thank you (very much).	*Terima kasih (banyak).*
You're welcome.	*Sama-sama.*
Please.	*Tolong/Silakan.*
Sorry/Pardon?	*Maaf.*
Excuse me.	*Maafkan saya.*

Small Talk

How are you?	*Apa khabar?*
Fine thanks.	*Khabar baik.*
What's your name?	*Siapa nama kamu?*
My name is ...	*Nama saya ...*
Where are you from?	*Dari mana asal saudara?*
I'm from ...	*Saya dari ...*
How old are you?	*Berapa umur saudara?*
I'm (20 years old).	*Umur saya (duapuluh tahun).*
Good/Very nice.	*Bagus.*
No good.	*Tidak baik.*
Good/Fine.	*Baik.*

Language Difficulties

Do you speak English?	*Bolehkah anda berbicara bahasa Inggeris?*
I understand.	*Saya faham.*
I don't understand.	*Saya tidak faham.*
Please write that word down.	*Tolong tuliskan perkataan.*
Please repeat it.	*Tolong ulangi.*

Getting Around

How can I get to ...?	*Bagaimana saya pergi ke ...?*
How many km?	*Berapa kilometre?*
Where is ...?	*Di mana ...?*
What time does the ... leave?	*Pukul berapakah ... berangkat?*
bus	*bas*
train	*keretapi*
ship	*kapal*
boat	*bot*
rickshaw/trishaw	*beca*
Where can I hire a bicycle?	*Di mana tempat sewa basikal?*
Where can I rent a car?	*Di manakah saya boleh menyewa kereta?*
Please give me two tickets.	*Tolong berikan saya dua tiket.*
ticket window	*tempat tikit, kaunter*
1st/economy class	*kelas satu/ekonomi*

Directions

Which way?	*Ke mana?*
Go straight ahead.	*Jalan terus.*

Turn left.	*Belok kiri.*
Turn right.	*Belok kanan.*

at the T-junction	*di pertigaan*
at the traffic lights	*di lampu lalu lintas*
in front of	*di hadapan*
next to	*di samping/di sebelah*
behind	*di belakang*
opposite	*berhadapan dengan*
here/there	*di sini/di sana*
north/south	*utara/selatan*
east/west	*timur/barat*

Around Town

Where is a/the ...?	*Di mana ada ...?*
bank	*bank*
embassy	*kedutaan besar*
hospital	*hospital*
hotel	*hotel*
museum	*muzium*
police station	*stesen polis*
post office	*pejabat pos*
public telephone	*telepon umum*
public toilet	*tandas awam*
tourist office	*pejabat pelancong*
town square	*dewan perbandaran*

When does it open?	*Bila buka?*
When does it close?	*Bila tutup?*
I want to call ...	*Saya mahu menelefon ...*
I want to change a travellers cheque.	*Saya mau menukar cek pengembaraan.*

SIGNS

Masuk	Entrance
Keluar	Exit
Panas/Sejuk	Hot/Cold
Di Larang Merokok	No Smoking
Buka	Open
Tutup	Closed
Telepon	Telephone
Tandas	Toilets
Lelaki	Men
Perempuan	Women

Accommodation

hotel	*hotel*
cheap hotel	*hotel yang murah*
nice hotel	*hotel yang bagus*
inexpensive hotel	*hotel yang murah*

I'd like a room ...	*Saya perlu bilik ...*
for one person	*untuk satu orang*
for two people	*untuk dua orang*
with a bathroom	*dengan bilik mandi*
with air-con	*dengan alat penyejuk*

Is there a room available?	*Ada bilik kosong?*
How much per night/person?	*Berapa harga satu malam/orang?*
Can I see the room?	*Boleh saya lihat biliknya?*
I don't like this room.	*Saya tidak suka bilik ini.*

bed	*tempat tidur*
dirty	*kotor*
expensive	*mahal*
room	*bilik*
sleep	*tidur*
soap	*sabun*

Food

I don't want fish, chicken or meat.	*Saya tidak mau ikan, ayam atau daging.*

beef	*daging lembu*
chicken	*ayam*
crab	*ketam*
egg	*telur*
fish	*ikan*
frog	*kodok*
pork	*babi*
potatoes	*kentang*
prawns	*udang*
vegetables	*sayur-sayuran*

fried rice	*nasi goreng*
boiled rice	*nasi putih*
rice with odds & ends	*nasi campur*
fried noodles	*mee goreng*
soup	*sup*

noodle soup	*mee kuah*
fried vegetables & crispy noodles	*cap cai tami*
sweet & sour omelette	*fu yung hai*

sweet	*manis*
steaming hot	*panas*
spicy hot	*pedas*
cold	*sejuk*
delicious	*enak*
special	*istimewa*

Drinks

coconut milk	*air kelapa*
coffee	*kopi*
drinking water	*air minum*
drinks	*minum-minum*
milk	*susu*
orange juice	*air jeruk/air oren*
sugar	*gula*
tea (without sugar)	*teh (tanpa gula)*

Shopping

How much?	*Berapa?*
Can you lower the price?	*Boleh kurang?*

barber	*tukang cukur*
bookshop	*kedai buku*
chemist	*farmasi*
grocery	*kedai makanan*
market	*pasar*
night market	*pasar malam*
shop	*kedai*
shopping centre	*pusat membeli-belah*
this/that	*ini/itu*
big/small	*besar/kecil*

Health

Where is a ...	*Di mana ada ...*
dentist	*doktor gigi*
doctor	*doktor*
hospital	*hospital*
medicine	*ubat*
pharmacy	*apotik/farmasi*

I'm allergic to ...	*Saya alergik kepada ...*
penicillin	*penisilin*
antibiotics	*antibiotik*

I'm pregnant.	*Saya hamil.*

antibiotics	*antibiotik*
antiseptic	*antiseptik*
aspirin	*aspirin*
penicillin	*penisilin*
quinine	*kina*
sleeping pills	*pil tidur*
tablet/pill	*pil*

Time, Days & Numbers

When?	*Bila?*
How long?	*Berapa lama?*
What time is it?	*Pukul berapa?*
7 o'clock	*pukul tujuh*
hour	*jam*
week	*minggu*
year	*tahun*
tomorrow	*besok*
yesterday	*kelmarin*

Monday	*hari Isnin*
Tuesday	*hari Selasa*
Wednesday	*hari Rabu*
Thursday	*hari Kamis*
Friday	*hari Jumaat*
Saturday	*hari Sabtu*
Sunday	*hari Minggu*

½	*setengah*	10	*sepuluh*
1	*satu*	11	*sebelas*
2	*dua*	12	*dua belas*
3	*tiga*	20	*dua puluh*
4	*empat*	21	*dua puluh satu*
5	*lima*	22	*dua puluh dua*
6	*enam*	30	*tiga puluh*
7	*tujuh*	53	*lima puluh tiga*
8	*delapan/lapan*	100	*seratus*
9	*sembilan*	1000	*seribu*

Emergencies

Help!	*Tolong!*
There's been an accident!	*Ada kemalangan!*
Call a doctor!	*Panggil doktor!*
Call an ambulance!	*Panggil ambulans!*
Stop!	*Berhenti!*
Go away!	*Pergi!*
I've been robbed!	*Saya dirompak!*
I'm lost.	*Saya sesat.*

Glossary

The following is a list of words and phrases which you may come across:

adat – Malay customary law
adat temenggong – Malay law with Indian modifications. Adat temenggong is the law governing the customs and ceremonies of the sultans.
air – water
air terjun – waterfall
alor – groove, furrow, main channel of river
ampang – dam
ang pow – red packets of money, traditional payment for a dance troupe
arrack – distilled fire-water
ASEAN – Association of South-East Asian Nations
atap – roof thatching

Baba-Nyonyas – Straits Chinese; original Chinese settlers in the Straits Settlements of Melaka, Singapore and Penang, who intermarried with Malays and adopted many Malay customs. Sometimes spelt Nonya.
bajang – evil spirit (takes the form of a cat)
bandar – a port
Bangsawan – Malay opera
batang – stem, tree-trunk, the main branch of a river
batas – boundary wall of a padi field
batu – stone, rock, milepost
belukar – secondary forest
bendahara – chief minister
bendang – irrigated land
bomoh – Islamic spiritual healer
bukit – hill
bumiputra – indigenous Malaysians (literally 'sons of the soil')
bunga raya – hibiscus flower (national flower of Malaysia)

dada – drugs
dato, datuk – literally 'grandfather', but general male non-royal title of distinction
dipterocarp – family of trees native to Malaysia which have two-winged fruits
dusun – small town

genting – mountain pass
godown – river warehouse
gua – cave
gunung – mountain

hilir – lower reaches of a river
hutan – jungle, forest

imam – keeper of Islamic knowledge and leader of prayer
istana – palace

jalan – road

kain songket – traditional Malay handwoven fabric with gold threads
kali – river
kampung – village (sometimes kampong)
kangkar – Chinese village
kedai kopi – coffee shop
kerangas – distinctive vegetation zone of Borneo, usually found on sandstone containing pitcher plants and other unusual plants
khalwat – 'close proximity', or exhibition of public affection between the sexes
kopi tiam – coffee shop
kota – fort or city
kramat – Malay shrine
KTM – Keretapi Tanah Malayu (Malaysian Railways System)
kuala – river mouth, or place where a tributary joins a larger river

labuan – port
laksamana – admiral
langur – small, mostly tree-dwelling monkey
laut – sea
Lebuh Raya – expressway or freeway, usually refers to the North-South Highway that runs from Johor Bahru to Bukit Kaya Hitam at the Thai border.
lorong – narrow street, alley
lubuk – deep pool

macaque – any of several small species of monkey
mandi – South-East Asian wash basin

masjid – mosque
Melayu Islam Beraja (MIB) – Brunei's national ideology
merdeka – independence
Merlion – half-lion, half-fish animal and symbol of Singapore
MRT – Mass Rapid Transport railway system
muara – river mouth
muezzin – the official of a mosque, who calls the faithful to prayer

negara – country
negeri – state
nyonya – see *Baba-Nyonyas*

orang asing – foreigner
Orang Asli – Malaysian aborigines (literally 'original people')
orang laut – indigenous coastal people
Orang Ulu – upriver people

padang – grassy area, usually the city square
pantai – beach
parang – long jungle knife
parit – ditch
pasar – market
pasar malam – night market
pekan – market place or town
penghulu – chief or village head
pengkalan – quay
Peranakan – literally 'half-caste', refers to the Baba-Nyonyas or Straits Chinese
PIE – Pan-Island Expressway, one of Singapore's main road arteries
pua kumbu – traditional finely woven cloth
pulau – island
puteri – princess

raja – prince, ruler
rakyat – common people
rantau – straight coastline
rattan – stems from climbing palms used for wickerwork and canes
rimba – jungle
rotan – cane used to punish miscreants
roti – bread (as in roti canai, flaky Indian bread normally served with a curry sauce)

sampan – bumboat
sebrang – far bank of a river
selat – strait
semenanjung – peninsula
simpang – junction of more than two roads
songkok – traditional Malay male headdress
sungai – river
syariah – Islamic system of law

tambang – river ferry (Kuching)
tamu – weekly market
tanah – land
tanjung – headland
tasik – lake
teluk – bay
temenggong – Malay administrator
towkang – Chinese junk
tuai rumah – longhouse chief (Sarawak)
tunku – royal prince

ujung – cape
UMNO – United Malays National Organisation

warung – small eating stalls
wayang – Chinese opera
wisma – office block or shopping centre

yang di-pertuan – 'he who is lord'
yang di-pertuan agong – Malaysia's head of state, or 'king'
yang di-pertuan besar – head of state in Negeri Sembilan
yang di-pertuan muda – underking
yang di-pertuan negeri – governor

Food

This glossary of Asian culinary terms will be helpful when you're selecting dishes at a restaurant or shopping at the market.

achar – Indian vegetable pickle
ais kacang – similar to *cendol* but made with evaporated milk; also spelt ice kacang (Malay/Indonesian)
aloo gobi – Indian potato and cauliflower dish

attap seeds – sugar plam seeds used in *cendol* and *ais kacang*
ayam goreng – Malay fried chicken

bak chang – Chinese rice dumpling filled with savoury or sweet meat and wrapped in leaves
bak choy – variety of Chinese cabbage that grows like celery, with long white stalks and dark green leaves
bak kutteh – Chinese pork-rib soup which has hints of garlic and Chinese five spices
beef rendang – beef stewed with spices and coconut milk (Malay/Indonesian)
belacan – fermented prawn paste used as a condiment in Chinese, Malay and Indonesian cuisine
belacan kankung – green vegetables stir-fried in prawn paste
bhindi – okra or lady's finger (Indian)
bird's nest – edible nest of the swiftlet, made chiefly of glutinous secretions from their salivary glands (Chinese)
biryani – a North Indian dish of basmati rice and meat, seafood or vegetables
brinjal – aubergine or eggplant (Indian)
buah keras – see *candle-nut*

candle-nut – called *kemiri* in Indonesian and *buah keras* in Malay, it is a smallish white-fleshed nut, shaped like a hazelnut
cardamom – seed pods of a member of the ginger family and a fragrant spice often used in north Indian and Mogul dishes
carrot cake – omelette-like dish made from radishes, egg, garlic and chilli (Nyonya)
cendol – Malay dessert; a cone of ice shavings topped with coloured syrups, brown sugar syrup and coconut milk filled with red beans, attap seeds and jelly
chapati – griddle-fried wholewheat bread (Indian)
char kway teow – broad noodles, clams and eggs fried in chilli and black bean sauce (Chinese)
char siew – sweet roasted pork fillet (Chinese)
cheng ting – dessert consisting of a bowl of sugar syrup with pieces of herbal jelly, barley and dates (Chinese)
chicken-rice – dish where the rice is cooked in a clay casserole with pieces of chicken, Chinese mushroom, Chinese sausage and soy sauce (Chinese; see also *claypot rice*)
chilli padi – extremely hot small chilli
choi sum – popular Chinese green vegetable, served steamed with oyster sauce
chye tow kway – see carrot cake
claypot rice – see *chicken-rice*
congee – Chinese porridge
coriander – fragrant herb with pungent-smelling leaves and stems; also known as Chinese parsley

daun kunyit – turmeric leaf (Malay)
daun pisang – banana leaf, used as a plate in Malaysia
dhal – a dish of pureed lentils (Indian)
dian xin – called *dim sum* in Cantonese; refers to Chinese sweet and savoury buns, dumplings and mini-dishes served at breakfast and lunch
dim sum – see *dian xin*
dosa – large, light, crispy pancake brimming with potatoes, onions and spices (Indian)
dow see – fermented, salted black beans (Chinese)

es avocado – chilled avocado vegetable shake (Malay/Indonesian)
es delima – dessert of water chestnut in sago and coconut milk (Malay/Indonesian)

fish-head curry – red snapper in curry sauce; a famous Singapore Indian dish
fish sauce – liquid made from fermented anchovies and salt; used widely in South-East Asian cooking

gado gado – cold dish of bean sprouts, potatoes, long beans, tempeh, bean curd, rice cakes and prawn crackers, topped with a spicy peanut sauce (Malay/Indonesian)
galangal – ginger-like root used to flavour various dishes
garam masala – sweet, mild mixture of freshly ground spices, usually black peppercorns, coriander seeds, cumin seeds, cloves and black cardamom (Indian)
garoupa – white fish popular in South-East Asia
gathat – large pan (Indian)
ghee – clarified butter (Indian)
gingko nut – meaty nut used in soups and desserts or roasted and chopped for sauces, salads and meat dishes
gula jawa – brown palm sugar sold in thin blocks (Malay)

gulab jumun – fried milk balls in sugar syrup (Indian)

Hainanese chicken rice – Singaporean speciality: chicken dish served with spring onions and ginger dressing, soup and rice boiled in chicken or coconut oil (Hainan)
halal – food that has been prepared according to Muslim dietary laws
hoisin sauce – thick seasoning sauce made from soya beans, red beans, sugar, flour, vinegar, salt, garlic, sesame, chillies and spices; sweet-spicy and tangy (Chinese)
Hokkien mee – yellow noodles fried with sliced meat, boiled squid, prawns and garnished with strips of fried egg (Chinese)

idli – steamed rice cake (Indian)
ikan asam – fried fish in sour tamarind curry (Malay)
ikan bilis – small deep-fried sardines (Malay/Indonesian)

kaen cud – soup (Thai)
kaen paad – curry (Thai)
kaen phet kai – hot chicken curry (Thai)
kai tom kha – lemon grass chicken soup with coconut milk (Thai)
kang kung – water convolvulus, thick-stemmed type of spinach (Chinese)
kari ayam – curried chicken (Malay/Indonesian)
kecap – soy sauce (Indonesian/Malay)
keema – spicy minced meat (Indian)
kemiri – see *candle-nut*
kepala ikan – fish-head, usually in a curry or grilled (Malay/Indonesian)
khao – rice (Thai)
kofta – minced meat or vegetable ball (Indian)
korma – mild Indian curry with yoghurt sauce
kueh melayu – sweet pancakes filled with peanuts, raisins and sugar
kueh mueh – Malay cakes
kway teow – broad rice noodles (Chinese)

laksa – spicy coconut soup of thin white noodles garnished with bean sprouts, quail eggs, prawns, shredded chicken and dried bean curd; also called Nyonya laksa to differentiate it from Penang laksa, which has no coconut milk and a prawn paste-based gravy (Malay/Singaporean)
laksa balik pulau – rice-noodles with a thick fish broth, mint leaves, pineapple, onions and fresh chillies (Nyonya)
laos – see *galangal*
larb – minced chicken or pork flavoured with spices, herbs and lime (Thai)
lassi – yoghurt-based drink (Indian)
lemon grass – called *takari* in Thai and *sereh* in Indonesian, it has long, spear-shaped, grass-like leaves; the stalk has a strong lemon-citrus taste
lombok – type of hot chilli (Malay)
lontong – rice cakes in a spicy coconut-milk gravy topped with grated coconut and sometimes bean curd and egg (Malay/Indonesian)
lor mee – noodles served with slices of meat, eggs and a dash of vinegar in a dark brown sauce (Chinese)

masala – spices (Indian)
masala dosa – thin pancake rolled around the masala (spicy) vegetables with *rasam* on the side (Indian)
mee pok – flat noodles made with egg and wheat (Chinese)
mee rebus – yellow noodles served in a thick sweetish sauce made from sweet potatoes, garnished with sliced hard-boiled eggs and green chillies (Malay)
mee siam – white thin noodles in a sourish and sweet gravy, made with tamarind (Malay)
mee soto – noodle soup with shredded chicken (Malay)
mi krob – crisp, thin noodles with shrimp, egg and sweet and sour sauce (Thai)
morel – mushroom of genus *Morcella*
mulligatawny – spicy beef soup (Indian)
murgh – chicken (Indian)
murtabak – *roti prata* filled with pieces of mutton, chicken or vegetables (Indian)

naan – tear-shaped leavened bread baked inside a clay oven (Indian)
nasi biryani – saffron rice flavoured with spices and garnished with cashew nuts, almonds and raisins (Malay/Indonesian)
nasi goreng – fried rice (Indonesian)
nasi lemak – rice boiled in coconut milk (Malay)
nasi padang – Malay rice and the accompanying meat and vegetable dishes (Malay)
pak krasan – leafy cabbage-like legume unique to Thailand

pakora – vegetable fritter (Indian)
pappadam – Indian cracker
phrik – chillies (Thai)
pilau – rice fried in ghee and mixed with nuts, then cooked in stock (north Indian)
pla thot sam rot – fried *garoupa* with sweet and sour sauce (Thai)
poo paad gari – curried crab (Thai)
popiah – vegetarian rice cakes (Malay)
pudina – mint sauce (Indian)

raita – side dish of cucumber, yoghurt and mint used to cool the palate (Indian)
rasam – spicy soup (Indian)
rendang – spicy Indonesian coconut curry with beef or chicken
rijstaffel – literally 'rice table'; a buffet of Indonesian dishes (Dutch)
rogan gosh – stewed mutton in a rich sauce (Indian)
roti canai – breakfast meal made from *murtabak* dough dipped in dhal or curry
roti prata – flat pancake-like bread (Indian)

saag – spicy chopped spinach dish (Indian)
salam – plant the leaves of which are used much like bay leaves in cooking (Malay)
sambal – sauce of chilli, onions and prawn paste which has been fried (Malay)
sambal udang – hot curried prawns (Malay)
sambar – fiery mixture of vegetables, lentils and split peas (Indian)
samosa – Indian pastry filled with vegetables or meat
santen – coconut milk (Malay)
satay – pieces of chicken, beef or mutton which are skewered onto wooden sticks and grilled (Malay/Indonesian)
sereh – see lemon grass
shiitake – brown-black mushrooms with pale cream gills, also called black or winter mushrooms; firm with intense flavour and fragrant when cooked (Japanese/Chinese)
som sa – citrus fruit unique to Thailand
soto ayam – spicy chicken soup with vegetables and potatoes (Malay)
steamboat – style of cooking in which meats, seafood and vegetables are dipped into a pot of boiling clear stocks and cooked at the table (Teochew Chinese)
straw mushroom – tall thin, leafy mushroom, also called grass or paddy straw mushroom
Szechuan – region in south central China famous for its spicy cuisine, also Sichuan

tahu goreng – fried soya bean curd and bean sprouts in peanut sauce (Malay)
takari – see lemon grass
tamarind – large bean from the tamarind tree, it has a brittle shell and inside a dark brown, sticky pulp used for its sweet-sour taste
tandoori – Indian style of cooking in which marinated meat is baked in a clay oven
taro – vegetable with leaves like spinach, stalks like asparagus and a starchy root similar in size and taste to the potato
tau hui – by-product of soya bean, served as a local dessert with sugar syrup
teh tarek – tea made with evaporated milk, which is literally 'pulled' or 'stretched' from one glass to another (Indian)
tempeh – preserved soybeans which have been deep-fried (Malay)
thali – rice, curried vegetables, soup, curries and bread often served on a banana leaf (Indian)
tikka – small pieces of meat and fish served off the bone and marinated in yoghurt before baking (Indian)
tom yum kung – hot and sour, spicy seafood soup (Thai)

umai – raw fish marinated and served with onions (Melanau, Sarawak)

vindaloo – fiery Indian vinegar-based curry

won ton mee – soup dish with shredded chicken or braised beef (Chinese)

yam – Thai word for 'salad'; yam nua is the popular Thai beef salad
yong tau foo – bean curd stuffed with mince meat (Hakka)
yu char kway – deep-fried Chinese bread sticks
yu tiao – deep-fried pastry eaten for breakfast or as a dessert (Chinese)

Index

ABBREVIATIONS

B – Brunei
M – Malaysia
S – Singapore

MAPS

TEXT

Map references are in **bold** type.

A

B

N

Boxed Text

LONELY PLANET

Phrasebooks

Lonely Planet phrasebooks are packed with essential words and phrases to help travellers communicate with the locals. With colour tabs for quick reference, an extensive vocabulary and use of script, these handy pocket-sized language guides cover day-to-day travel situations.

- handy pocket-sized books
- easy to understand Pronunciation chapter
- clear & comprehensive Grammar chapter
- romanisation alongside script to allow ease of pronunciation
- script throughout so users can point to phrases for every situation
- full of cultural information and tips for the traveller

'... vital for a real DIY spirit and attitude in language learning'
– Backpacker

'the phrasebooks have good cultural backgrounders and offer solid advice for challenging situations in remote locations'
– San Francisco Examiner

Arabic (Egyptian) • Arabic (Moroccan) • Australian *(Australian English, Aboriginal and Torres Strait languages)* • Baltic States *(Estonian, Latvian, Lithuanian)* • Bengali • Brazilian • British • Burmese • Cantonese • Central Asia (Uyghur, Uzbek, Kyrghiz, Kazak, Pashto, Tadjik • Central Europe *(Czech, French, German, Hungarian, Italian, Slovak)* • Eastern Europe *(Bulgarian, Czech, Hungarian, Polish, Romanian, Slovak)* • Ethiopian (Amharic) • Fijian • French • German • Greek • Hebrew • Hill Tribes • Hindi & Urdu • Indonesian • Italian • Japanese • Korean • Lao • Latin American Spanish • Malay • Mandarin • Mediterranean Europe *(Albanian, Croatian, Greek, Italian, Macedonian, Maltese, Serbian, Slovene)* • Mongolian • Nepali • Pidgin • Pilipino (Tagalog) • Portugese • Quechua • Russian • Scandinavian Europe *(Danish, Finnish, Icelandic, Norwegian, Swedish)* • South-East Asia *(Burmese, Indonesian, Khmer, Lao, Malay, Tagalog Pilipino, Thai, Vietnamese)* • South Pacific Languages • Spanish (Castilian) *(also includes Catalan, Galician and Basque)* • Sri Lanka • Swahili • Thai • Tibetan • Turkish • Ukrainian • USA *(US English, Vernacular, Native American languages, Hawaiian)* • Vietnamese • Western Europe *(Basque, Catalan, Dutch, French, German, Greek, Irish, Italian, Portuguese, Scottish Gaelic, Spanish (Castilian), Welsh)*

LONELY PLANET

Lonely Planet Journeys

JOURNEYS is a unique collection of travel writing – published by the company that understands travel better than anyone else. It is a series for anyone who has ever experienced – or dreamed of – the magical moment when they encountered a strange culture or saw a place for the first time. They are tales to read while you're planning a trip, while you're on the road or while you're in an armchair in front of a fire.

These outstanding titles explore our planet through the eyes of a diverse group of international writers. JOURNEYS books catch the spirit of a place, illuminate a culture, recount a crazy adventure or introduce a fascinating way of life. They always entertain, and always enrich the experience of travel.

ISLANDS IN THE CLOUDS
Travels in the Highlands of New Guinea
Isabella Tree

This is the fascinating account of a journey to the remote and beautiful Highlands of Papua New Guinea and Irian Jaya: one of the most extraordinary and dangerous regions on the planet. Tree travels with a PNG Highlander who introduces her to his intriguing and complex world, changing rapidly as it collides with twentieth-century technology. *Islands in the Clouds* is a thoughtful, moving book.

SEAN & DAVID'S LONG DRIVE
Sean Condon

Sean and David are young townies who have rarely strayed beyond city limits. One day, for no good reason, they set out to discover their homeland, and what follows is a wildly entertaining adventure that covers half of Australia.

'a hilariously detailed log of two burned out friends' – *Rolling Stone*

DRIVE THRU AMERICA
Sean Condon

If you've ever wanted to drive across the USA but couldn't find the time (or afford the gas), *Drive Thru America* is perfect for you. In his search for American myths and realities – along with comfort, cable TV and good, reasonably priced coffee – Sean Condon paints a hilarious road-portrait of the USA.

'entertaining and laugh-out-loud funny' – *Alex Wilber, Travel editor, Amazon.com*

BRIEF ENCOUNTERS
Stories of Love, Sex & Travel
edited by Michelle de Kretser

Love affairs on the road, passionate holiday flings, disastrous pick-ups, erotic encounters . . . In this seductive collection of stories, 22 authors from around the world write about travel romances. Combining fiction and reportage, *Brief Encounters* is must-have reading – for everyone who has dreamt of escape with that perfect stranger.

Includes stories by Pico Iyer, Mary Morris, Emily Perkins, Mona Simpson, Lisa St Aubin de Terán, Paul Theroux and Sara Wheeler.

LONELY PLANET

Lonely Planet Travel Atlases

Lonely Planet has long been famous for the number and quality of its guidebook maps. Now we've gone one step further and produced a handy companion series: Lonely Planet travel atlases – maps of a country produced in book form.

Unlike other maps, which look good but lead travellers astray, our travel atlases have been researched on the road by Lonely Planet's experienced team of writers. All details are carefully checked to ensure the atlas corresponds with the equivalent Lonely Planet guidebook.

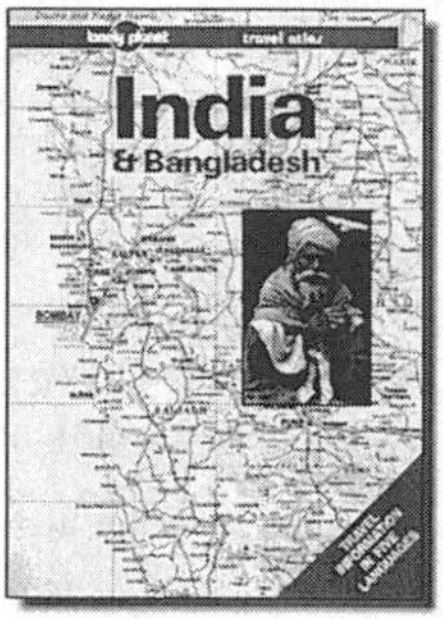

- full-colour throughout
- maps researched and checked by Lonely Planet authors
- place names correspond with Lonely Planet guidebooks
- no confusing spelling differences
- legend and travelling information in English, French, German, Japanese and Spanish
- size: 230 x 160 mm

Available now: Chile & Easter Island • Egypt • India & Bangladesh • Israel & the Palestinian Territories • Jordan, Syria & Lebanon • Kenya • Laos • Portugal • South Africa, Lesotho & Swaziland • Thailand • Turkey • Vietnam • Zimbabwe, Botswana & Namibia

---

Lonely Planet TV Series & Videos

Lonely Planet travel guides have been brought to life on television screens around the world. Like our guides, the programs are based on the joy of independent travel, and look honestly at some of the most exciting, picturesque and frustrating places in the world. Each show is presented by one of three travellers from Australia, England or the USA and combines an innovative mixture of video, Super-8 film, atmospheric soundscapes and original music.

Videos of each episode – containing additional footage not shown on television – are available from good book and video shops, but the availability of individual videos varies with regional screening schedules.

Video destinations include: Alaska • American Rockies • Australia – The South-East • Baja California & the Copper Canyon • Brazil • Central Asia • Chile & Easter Island • Corsica, Sicily & Sardinia – The Mediterranean Islands • East Africa (Tanzania & Zanzibar) • Ecuador & the Galapagos Islands • Greenland & Iceland • Indonesia • Israel & the Sinai Desert • Jamaica • Japan • La Ruta Maya • Morocco • New York • North India • Pacific Islands (Fiji, Solomon Islands & Vanuatu) • South India • South West China • Turkey • Vietnam • West Africa • Zimbabwe, Botswana & Namibia

The Lonely Planet TV series is produced by: Pilot Productions
The Old Studio
18 Middle Row
London W10 5AT, UK

LONELY PLANET

FREE Lonely Planet Newsletters

We love hearing from you and think you'd like to hear from us.

Planet Talk

Our FREE quarterly printed newsletter is full of tips from travellers and anecdotes from Lonely Planet guidebook authors. Every issue is packed with up-to-date travel news and advice, and includes:

- a postcard from Lonely Planet co-founder Tony Wheeler
- a swag of mail from travellers
- a look at life on the road through the eyes of a Lonely Planet author
- topical health advice
- prizes for the best travel yarn
- news about forthcoming Lonely Planet events
- a complete list of Lonely Planet books and other titles

To join our mailing list, residents of the UK, Europe and Africa can email us at go@lonelyplanet.co.uk; residents of North and South America can email us at info@lonelyplanet.com; the rest of the world can email us at talk2us@lonelyplanet.com.au, or contact any Lonely Planet office.

Comet

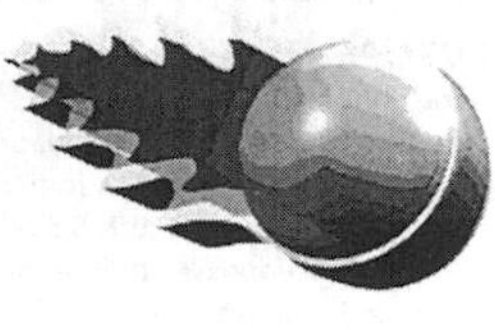

Our FREE monthly email newsletter brings you all the latest travel news, features, interviews, competitions, destination ideas, travellers' tips & tales, Q&As, raging debates and related links. Find out what's new on the Lonely Planet Web site and which books are about to hit the shelves.

Subscribe from your desktop: www.lonelyplanet.com/comet

LONELY PLANET

Guides by Region

Lonely Planet is known worldwide for publishing practical, reliable and no-nonsense travel information in our guides and on our Web site. The Lonely Planet list covers just about every accessible part of the world. Currently there are 16 series: Travel guides, Shoestring guides, Condensed guides, Phrasebooks, Read This First, Healthy Travel, Walking guides, Cycling guides, Watching Wildlife guides, Pisces Diving & Snorkeling guides, City Maps, Road Atlases, Out to Eat, World Food, Journeys travel literature and Pictorials.

AFRICA Africa on a shoestring • Cairo • Cape Town • Cape Town City Map • East Africa • Egypt • Egyptian Arabic phrasebook • Ethiopia, Eritrea & Djibouti • Ethiopian (Amharic) phrasebook • The Gambia & Senegal • Healthy Travel Africa • Kenya • Malawi • Morocco • Moroccan Arabic phrasebook • Mozambique • Read This First: Africa • South Africa, Lesotho & Swaziland • Southern Africa • Southern Africa Road Atlas • Swahili phrasebook • Tanzania, Zanzibar & Pemba • Trekking in East Africa • Tunisia • Watching Wildlife East Africa • Watching Wildlife Southern Africa • West Africa • World Food Morocco • Zimbabwe, Botswana & Namibia
Travel Literature: Mali Blues: Traveling to an African Beat • The Rainbird: A Central African Journey • Songs to an African Sunset: A Zimbabwean Story

AUSTRALIA & THE PACIFIC Auckland • Australia • Australian phrasebook • Australia Road Atlas • Bushwalking in Australia •Cycling New Zealand • Fiji • Fijian phrasebook • Healthy Travel Australia, NZ and the Pacific • Islands of Australia's Great Barrier Reef • Melbourne • Melbourne City Map • Micronesia • New Caledonia • New South Wales & the ACT • New Zealand • Northern Territory • Outback Australia • Out to Eat – Melbourne • Out to Eat – Sydney • Papua New Guinea • Pidgin phrasebook • Queensland • Rarotonga & the Cook Islands • Samoa • Solomon Islands • South Australia • South Pacific • South Pacific phrasebook • Sydney • Sydney City Map • Sydney Condensed • Tahiti & French Polynesia • Tasmania • Tonga • Tramping in New Zealand • Vanuatu • Victoria • Watching Wildlife Australia • Western Australia
Travel Literature: Islands in the Clouds: Travels in the Highlands of New Guinea • Kiwi Tracks: A New Zealand Journey • Sean & David's Long Drive

CENTRAL AMERICA & THE CARIBBEAN Bahamas, Turks & Caicos • Baja California • Bermuda • Central America on a shoestring • Costa Rica • Costa Rica Spanish phrasebook • Cuba • Dominican Republic & Haiti • Eastern Caribbean • Guatemala • Guatemala, Belize & Yucatán: La Ruta Maya • Healthy Travel Central & South America • Jamaica • Mexico • Mexico City • Panama • Puerto Rico • Read This First: Central & South America • World Food Mexico • Yucatán
Travel Literature: Green Dreams: Travels in Central America

EUROPE Amsterdam • Amsterdam City Map • Amsterdam Condensed • Andalucía • Austria • Baltic States phrasebook • Barcelona • Barcelona City Map • Berlin • Berlin City Map • Britain • British phrasebook • Brussels, Bruges & Antwerp • Budapest • Budapest City Map • Canary Islands • Central Europe • Central Europe phrasebook • Corfu & the Ionians • Corsica • Crete • Crete Condensed • Croatia • Cycling Britain • Cycling France • Cyprus • Czech & Slovak Republics • Denmark • Dublin • Dublin City Map • Eastern Europe • Eastern Europe phrasebook • Edinburgh • Estonia, Latvia & Lithuania • Europe on a shoestring • Finland • Florence • France • Frankfurt Condensed • French phrasebook • Georgia, Armenia & Azerbaijan • Germany • German phrasebook • Greece • Greek Islands • Greek phrasebook • Hungary • Iceland, Greenland & the Faroe Islands • Ireland • Istanbul • Italian phrasebook • Italy • Krakow • Lisbon • The Loire • London • London City Map • London Condensed • Madrid • Malta • Mediterranean Europe • Mediterranean Europe phrasebook • Moscow • Mozambique • Munich • Norway • Out to Eat – London • Paris • Paris City Map • Paris Condensed • Poland • Portugal • Portuguese phrasebook • Prague • Prague City Map • Provence & the Côte d'Azur • Read This First: Europe • Romania & Moldova • Rome • Russia, Ukraine & Belarus • Russian phrasebook • Scandinavian & Baltic Europe • Scandinavian Europe phrasebook • Scotland • Sicily • Slovenia • South-West France • Spain • Spanish phrasebook • St Petersburg • St Petersburg City Map • Sweden • Switzerland • Trekking in Spain • Tuscany • Ukrainian phrasebook • Venice • Vienna • Walking in Britain • Walking in France • Walking in Ireland • Walking in Italy • Walking in Spain • Walking in Switzerland • Western Europe • Western Europe phrasebook • World Food France • World Food Ireland • World Food Italy • World Food Spain
Travel Literature: Love and War in the Apennines • The Olive Grove: Travels in Greece • On the Shores of the Mediterranean • Round Ireland in Low Gear • A Small Place in Italy

INDIAN SUBCONTINENT Bangladesh • Bengali phrasebook • Bhutan • Delhi • Goa • Healthy Travel Asia & India • Hindi & Urdu phrasebook • India • Indian Himalaya • Karakoram Highway • Kerala • Mumbai

LONELY PLANET

Mail Order

Lonely Planet products are distributed worldwide. They are also available by mail order from Lonely Planet, so if you have difficulty finding a title please write to us. North and South American residents should write to 150 Linden St, Oakland, CA 94607, USA; European and African residents should write to 10a Spring Place, London NW5 3BH, UK; and residents of other countries to Locked Bag 1, Footscray, Victoria 3011, Australia.

(Bombay) • Nepal • Nepali phrasebook • Pakistan • Rajasthan • Read This First: Asia & India • South India • Sri Lanka • Sri Lanka phrasebook • Tibet • Tibetan phrasebook • Trekking in the Indian Himalaya • Trekking in the Karakoram & Hindukush • Trekking in the Nepal Himalaya
Travel Literature: The Age of Kali: Indian Travels and Encounters • Hello Goodnight: A Life of Goa • In Rajasthan • A Season in Heaven: True Tales from the Road to Kathmandu • Shopping for Buddhas • A Short Walk in the Hindu Kush • Slowly Down the Ganges

ISLANDS OF THE INDIAN OCEAN Madagascar & Comoros • Maldives • Mauritius, Réunion & Seychelles

MIDDLE EAST & CENTRAL ASIA Bahrain, Kuwait & Qatar • Central Asia • Central Asia phrasebook • Dubai • Hebrew phrasebook • Iran • Israel & the Palestinian Territories • Istanbul • Istanbul City Map • Istanbul to Cairo on a shoestring • Jerusalem • Jerusalem City Map • Jordan • Lebanon • Middle East • Oman & the United Arab Emirates • Syria • Turkey • Turkish phrasebook • World Food Turkey • Yemen
Travel Literature: Black on Black: Iran Revisited • The Gates of Damascus • Kingdom of the Film Stars: Journey into Jordan

NORTH AMERICA Alaska • Boston • Boston City Map • California & Nevada • California Condensed • Canada • Chicago • Chicago City Map • Deep South • Florida • Hawaii • Hiking in Alaska • Hiking in the USA • Honolulu • Las Vegas • Los Angeles • Miami • Miami City Map • New England • New Orleans • New York City • New York City City Map • New York City Condensed • New York, New Jersey & Pennsylvania • Oahu • Out to Eat – San Francisco • Pacific Northwest • Puerto Rico • Rocky Mountains • San Francisco • San Francisco City Map • Seattle • Southwest • Texas • USA • USA phrasebook • Vancouver • Virginia & the Capital Region • Washington, DC City Map • World Food Deep South, USA
Travel Literature: Caught Inside: A Surfer's Year on the California Coast • Drive Thru America

NORTH-EAST ASIA Beijing • Cantonese phrasebook • China • Hiking in Japan • Hong Kong • Hong Kong City Map • Hong Kong Condensed • Hong Kong, Macau & Guangzhou • Japan • Japanese phrasebook • Korea • Korean phrasebook • Kyoto • Mandarin phrasebook • Mongolia • Mongolian phrasebook • Seoul • South-West China • Taiwan • Tokyo
Travel Literature: In Xanadu: A Quest • Lost Japan

SOUTH AMERICA Argentina, Uruguay & Paraguay • Bolivia • Brazil • Brazilian phrasebook • Buenos Aires • Chile & Easter Island • Colombia • Ecuador & the Galapagos Islands • Healthy Travel Central & South America • Latin American Spanish phrasebook • Peru • Quechua phrasebook • Read This First: Central & South America • Rio de Janeiro • Rio de Janeiro City Map • Santiago • South America on a shoestring • Santiago • Trekking in the Patagonian Andes • Venezuela
Travel Literature: Full Circle: A South American Journey

SOUTH-EAST ASIA Bali & Lombok • Bangkok • Bangkok City Map • Burmese phrasebook • Cambodia • Hanoi • Healthy Travel Asia & India • Hill Tribes phrasebook • Ho Chi Minh City • Indonesia • Indonesian phrasebook • Indonesia's Eastern Islands • Jakarta • Java • Lao phrasebook • Laos • Malay phrasebook • Malaysia, Singapore & Brunei • Myanmar (Burma) • Philippines • Pilipino (Tagalog) phrasebook • Read This First: Asia & India • Singapore • Singapore City Map • South-East Asia on a shoestring • South-East Asia phrasebook • Thailand • Thailand's Islands & Beaches • Thailand, Vietnam, Laos & Cambodia Road Atlas • Thai phrasebook • Vietnam • Vietnamese phrasebook • World Food Thailand • World Food Vietnam

ALSO AVAILABLE: Antarctica • The Arctic • The Blue Man: Tales of Travel, Love and Coffee • Brief Encounters: Stories of Love, Sex & Travel • Chasing Rickshaws • The Last Grain Race • Lonely Planet Unpacked • Not the Only Planet: Science Fiction Travel Stories • Lonely Planet On the Edge • Sacred India • Travel with Children • Travel Photography: A Guide to Taking Better Pictures

The Lonely Planet Story

Lonely Planet published its first book in 1973 in response to the numerous 'How did you do it?' questions Maureen and Tony Wheeler were asked after driving, bussing, hitching, sailing and railing their way from England to Australia.

Written at a kitchen table and hand collated, trimmed and stapled, *Across Asia on the Cheap* became an instant local bestseller, inspiring thoughts of another book.

Eighteen months in South-East Asia resulted in their second guide, *South-East Asia on a shoestring*, which they put together in a backstreet Chinese hotel in Singapore in 1975. The 'yellow bible', as it quickly became known to backpackers around the world, soon became *the* guide to the region. It has sold well over half a million copies and is now in its 9th edition, still retaining its familiar yellow cover.

Today there are over 350 titles, including travel guides, walking guides, language kits & phrasebooks, travel atlases, diving guides and travel literature. The company is the largest independent travel publisher in the world. Although Lonely Planet initially specialised in guides to Asia, today there are few corners of the globe that have not been covered.

The emphasis continues to be on travel for independent travellers. Tony and Maureen still travel for several months of each year and play an active part in the writing, updating and quality control of Lonely Planet's guides.

They have been joined by over 120 authors and 280 staff at our offices in Melbourne (Australia), Oakland (USA), London (UK) and Paris (France). Travellers themselves also make a valuable contribution to the guides through the feedback we receive in thousands of letters each year and on our web site.

The people at Lonely Planet strongly believe that travellers can make a positive contribution to the countries they visit, both through their appreciation of the countries' culture, wildlife and natural features, and through the money they spend. In addition, the company makes a direct contribution to the countries and regions it covers. Since 1986 a percentage of the income from each book has been donated to ventures such as famine relief in Africa; aid projects in India; agricultural projects in Central America; Greenpeace's efforts to halt French nuclear testing in the Pacific; and Amnesty International.

LONELY PLANET OFFICES

Australia
PO Box 617, Hawthorn, Victoria 3122
☎ 03 9819 1877 fax 03 9819 6459
email: talk2us@lonelyplanet.com.au

USA
150 Linden St, Oakland, CA 94607
☎ 510 893 8555 TOLL FREE: 800 275 8555
fax 510 893 8572
email: info@lonelyplanet.com

UK
10a Spring Place, London NW5 3BH
☎ 020 7428 4800 fax 020 7428 4828
email: go@lonelyplanet.co.uk

France
1 rue du Dahomey, 75011 Paris
☎ 01 55 25 33 00 fax 01 55 25 33 01
email: bip@lonelyplanet.fr
www.lonelyplanet.fr

World Wide Web: www.lonelyplanet.com *or* AOL keyword: lp
Lonely Planet Images: lpi@lonelyplanet.com.au